Child and Adolescent Development

Child and Adolescent Development

FOURTH EDITION

Kelvin L. Seifert

THE UNIVERSITY OF MANITOBA

Robert J. Hoffnung

UNIVERSITY OF NEW HAVEN

HOUGHTON MIFFLIN COMPANY   BOSTON   NEW YORK

For my students, whether currently children or formerly children K.L.S.

For my sister Michele and brother Dan R.J.H.

Sponsoring editor David Lee
Senior associate editor Jane Knetzger
Senior project editor Rosemary Winfield
Senior production/design coordinator Jill Haber
Senior manufacturing coordinator Marie Barnes
Marketing manager David Lenehan

Cover design: Harold Burch, Harold Burch Design, New York City; photo collage: David McGlynn, New York City

Anatomical and biological illustrations by Nancy Kaplan: Figures 4.2, 4.4, 5.2, 5.3, 8.3, 12.1

Illustrations by Patrice Rossi: Figures 2.2, 12.3, 13.1

Illustrations by Elizabeth Seifert: Figure 8.4

All other credits appear on page A-1, which constitutes an extension of the copyright page.

Printed in the U.S.A.

ISBN: 0-395-79613-X

123456789-VH-99 98 97 96

Brief Contents

Contents   vi
Special Features   xiv
Preface   xvi

Part I   Studying Development   1

1. Introduction: Studying
    Development   2
2. Theories of Development   28

Part II   Beginnings   57

3. Genetics   58
4. Prenatal Development and Birth   90

Part III   The First Two Years   131

5. The First Two Years: Physical
    Development   132
6. The First Two Years: Cognitive
    Development   162
7. The First Two Years: Psychosocial
    Development   198

Part IV   Early Childhood   235

8. Early Childhood: Physical
    Development   236
9. Early Childhood: Cognitive
    Development   262
10. Early Childhood: Psychosocial
    Development   296

Part V   Middle Childhood   336

11. Middle Childhood: Physical
    Development   338
12. Middle Childhood: Cognitive
    Development   360
13. Middle Childhood: Psychosocial
    Development   394

Part VI   Adolescence   435

14. Adolescence: Physical Development   436
15. Adolescence: Cognitive Development   468
16. Adolescence: Psychosocial
    Development   500

Glossary   G-1
References   R-1
Acknowledgments   A-1
Author/Name Index   I-1
Subject Index   I-7

Contents

Special Features   xiv

Preface   xvi

Studying Development   1

PART ONE

Chapter 1   Introduction: Studying Development   2

The Nature of Developmental Change   3

Three Domains of Development   4
An Example of Development: Jodi   6

Why Study Development?   8

■ *Perspectives: Wanted—A Child and Family Policy*   9

The History of Developmental Study   10

Early Precursors to Developmental Study   10
The Emergence of Modern Developmental Study   10

■ *Working with Pamela Mitchell, Primary School Teacher: The Many Purposes of Play*   11

Basic Issues in Developmental Study   12

Nature and Nurture   13
Continuity and Discontinuity   13

■ *A Multicultural View: Growing Up in India*   14

Universal and Context-Specific Development   14
Deficit and Difference   15

Methods of Studying Children and Adolescents   16

The Scientific Method   16
Variations in Time Frame   17
Variations in Control: Naturalistic and Experimental Studies   19
Sampling Strategies   22

Ethical Constraints on Studying Development   24

Strengths and Limitations of Developmental Knowledge   26

Chapter 2   Theories of Development   28

The Nature of Developmental Theories   29

What Is a Developmental Theory?   30
How Developmental Theories Differ: Four Developmental Themes   30

Psychodynamic Developmental Theories   32

Freudian Theory   32
Erikson's Psychosocial Theory   34

■ *Perspectives: Erik Erikson's Identity Crisis—An Autobiographical Perspective*   34

Other Psychodynamic Approaches   37
Evaluation of Developmental Themes in Psychodynamic Approaches   39

Behavioral and Social Cognitive Learning Developmental Theories   39

Behavioral Learning Theories   40
Social Cognitive Learning Theory   41
Evaluation of Developmental Themes in Behavioral
and Social Cognitive Learning Approaches   42

Cognitive Developmental Theories   43

Piaget's Cognitive Theory   43
Neo-Piagetian Approaches   45
Information-Processing Theory   46
Evaluation of Developmental Themes in Cognitive
Approaches   47

■ *A Multicultural View: Cultural Context and Cognitive
Development*   48

Contextual Developmental Theories   48

Ethological Theory   50
Evaluation of Developmental Themes in Contextual
Approaches   50

Developmental Theories Compared: Implications
for the Student   51

■ *Working with John Daviau, Residential Treatment
Program Director: Understanding Multiproblem
Adolescents*   52

Beginnings   57

Chapter 3   Genetics   58

Mechanisms of Genetic Transmission   59

The Role of DNA   59
Meiosis and Mitosis   61

Individual Genetic Expression   63

Genotype and Phenotype   63
Dominant and Recessive Genes   64
Transmission of Multiple Variations   65
Polygenic Transmission   66
The Determination of Sex   66

Genetic Abnormalities   68

Disorders Due to Abnormal Chromosomes   68
Abnormal Genes   70

Genetic Counseling   73

■ *A Multicultural View: Cultural Differences and
Genetic Counseling*   74

Prenatal Diagnosis   75

■ *Working with Gail Stewart, Genetic Counselor:
Advising Parents about Genetic Problems*   78

Early Medical Treatments   79

Relative Influence of Heredity and Environment   80

Key Concepts of Behavior Genetics   80
Animal Studies   83
Adoption and Twin Studies   83

■ *Perspectives: The Race and Intelligence
Controversy—Social Policy Implications*   84

Cautions and Conclusions about the Influence of
Heredity and Environment   86

Genetics and Developmental Psychology   87

Chapter 4   Prenatal Development
and Birth   90

Stages of Prenatal Development   91

Conception   91
The Germinal Stage (First Two Weeks)   92
The Embryonic Stage (Third Through Eighth
Weeks)   93
The Fetal Stage (Ninth Week to Birth)   95
Infertility   97
The Experience of Pregnancy   98

■ *Perspectives: Technological Alternatives to Normal
Conception*   98

■ *A Multicultural View: Reasons for Having a Child
in the United States and Eight Other Countries*   100

Prenatal Influences on the Child   101

Key Concepts   101
Maternal Age and Physical Characteristics   103

Diseases   104
Drugs   107
Environmental Hazards   110
Domestic Violence   111
Teenage Pregnancy   111
Diet and Nutrition   111
Prenatal Health Care   112
Stress   114

Birth   114

Stages of Labor   115
Childbirth Settings and Methods   117

■ *Working with Katie Glover, OB-GYN Nurse Practitioner: Preparing for Childbirth*   118

Problems During Labor and Delivery   123
Low-Birth-Weight Infants   125
Birth and the Family   126

From Biological to Psychological Development   127

The First Two Years   131

PART THREE

Chapter 5   The First Two Years: Physical Development   132

Appearance of the Young Infant   133

The First Few Hours   133
Is the Baby All Right? The Apgar Scale   134
Newborn Weight   135
Size and Bodily Proportions   136

Development of the Nervous System   137

Growth of the Brain   138
States of Sleep and Wakefulness   139

■ *Perspectives: Sudden Infant Death Syndrome*   141

Sensory Development   143

Visual Acuity   143
Auditory Acuity   143

■ *Working with Helen Turman, Pediatric Nurse: Continuity and Change in Infants' Behavior*   144

Taste, Smell, and Touch   144

Motor Development   146

Early Reflexes   146
The First Motor Skills   147
Variations in Motor Skill Development   149

Variations in Infant Growth   151

Low-Birth-Weight Infants   151
Helping Low-Birth-Weight Infants   153

Nutrition During the First Two Years   154

Breast Milk Versus Formula   154

■ *A Multicultural View: Breast Feeding among the Gusii*   156

Nutrition in Later Infancy   156
Infant Mortality   159

Infancy: The Real End of Birth   160

Chapter 6   The First Two Years: Cognitive Development   162

Ways of Studying Perception and Cognition in Infants   164

Arousal and Infants' Heart Rates   164
Recognition, Memory, and Infant Habituation   164

Infant Perception   166

Visual Perception   166
Auditory Perception   169

Infant Cognition   171

Piaget's Theory of Sensorimotor Intelligence   171
Baby Jill's Intelligence: An Example   177
Assessment of Piaget's Theory of Infant Cognition   179

Behavioral Learning in Infancy   181

Classical Conditioning   182
Operant Conditioning   183

■ *Working with Gillian Luppiwiski, Infant Care Provider: Fostering Infants' Thinking*   184

Imitation   185

Perspectives: Extremes in Language Acquisition—What Do They Mean?   186

Language Acquisition   187

Phonology   188
Semantics and First Words   190
Influencing Language Acquisition   191

■ *A Multicultural View: Cognitive Effects of Talking to Infants—A Cross-Cultural Perspective*   192

The End of Infancy   196

Chapter 7   The First Two Years: Psychosocial Development   198

Emotions and Temperament in Infancy   200

Emotions in Infancy   201
Temperament   202

■ *A Talk with Jennifer, Age Eight Months, and Her Parents: Infant Temperament*   203

Early Social Relationships   206

Transition to Parenthood   206

■ *Working with Rachelle Turner, Infant Day Care Coordinator: Understanding Infant Social Development:*   208

Caregiver-Infant Synchrony   208
Social Interactions with Fathers and Siblings   210
Interactions with Nonparental Caregivers   212
Interactions with Peers   214

Attachment Formation   215

Phases of Attachment Formation   217

■ *A Multicultural View: Cross-Cultural Variations in Attachment*   218

Assessing Attachment: The "Strange Situation"   218
Consequences of Different Attachment Patterns   219
Influences on Attachment Formation   220

■ *Perspectives: Family-Leave Policies in the United States and Europe*   222

Limitations of Attachment Theory   224

Toddlerhood and the Emergence of Autonomy   225

Sources of Autonomy   226
Development of Self-knowledge and Self-awareness   227
Development of Competence and Self-esteem   229

The Competent Toddler   231

Early Childhood   235

Chapter 8   Early Childhood: Physical Development   236

Influences on Normal Physical Development   237

Genetic Background   239
Disease   240
Nutritional Needs During the Preschool Years   241
Social Influences on Growth   242

■ *A Multicultural View: Cultural Influences on Children's Sleep*   242

The Connection Between Health and Poverty   244

Poverty as a Health Problem   244
Responding to Child Poverty   245

Brain Development   246

■ *Perspectives: Reforming Children's Health Care*   246

Organization of the Brain   247
Hemispheric Lateralization   248
Lateralized Behaviors   248

Other Bodily Changes   249

Preschool Sensory Development   249
Bladder and Bowel Control   250

Motor Skill Development   250

P A R T   F O U R

Fundamental Motor Skills   251

■ *Working with Audrey Reimer, Speech-Language Pathologist: The Psychological Impact of Motor Skill Development*   252

Can Motor Skills Be Taught?   253
Fine Motor Coordination: The Case of Drawing Skills   254
Sex and Gender Differences in Physical Development   256

Effects of Children's Physical Growth   257

Effects on Adults   257
Effects on the Child   260

Chapter 9   Early Childhood: Cognitive Development   262

Thinking in Preschoolers   263

Piaget's Preoperational Stage   264
Symbolic Thought   265
Children's Theories of Mind   266
The Appearance-Reality Distinction   267
Other Aspects of Children's Conceptual Development   267
Distinguishing Natural Kinds and Artifacts   270
How Cognitive Development Occurs   271
Neostructuralist Theories of Cognitive Development   272

Language Acquisition in Early Childhood   273

The Nature of Syntax   274
Beyond First Words: Semantic and Syntactic Relations   275
Mechanisms of Language Acquisition   277

■ *A Talk with Audrey, Age Four: Cognitive Development in the Preschool Years*   279

Innate Predisposition to Acquire Language: LAD   280
Parent-Child Interactions   281

Language Variations   282

Gender Differences in Language   282
Socioeconomic Differences in Language   283
Language of Deaf and Hearing-Impaired Children   283

■ *Working with Carolyn Eaton, Preschool Teacher: Introducing Sign Language to Young Children*   284

Relationships Between Language and Thought   286

Piaget: Action as the Basis for Both Language and Thought   286

■ *Perspectives: Christopher, the Multilingual Savant—Speaking Without Understanding*   287

Vygotsky: The Gradual Integration of Language and Thought   288

Early Childhood Education   289

Early Education and Cognitive Theories of Development   290
Effectiveness of Early Childhood Education   290
Cultural Diversity and Best Practice in Early Education   291

■ *A Multicultural View: Parents' Beliefs about Intelligence—A Cross-cultural Perspective*   292

Chapter 10   Early Childhood: Psychosocial Development   296

Play in Early Childhood   298

The Nature of Play   297
Theories of Play   298
Cognitive Levels of Play: Developmental Trends   300
Social Levels of Play   303
Other Influences on Play   304

Relationships with Others   306

Relationships with Parents   306

■ *Perspectives: Extended Family Supports for Childrearing*   308

Relationships with Siblings   311
Friendships in Early Childhood   312

■ *A Talk with Larry, Age Four: Friendship and Play in Early Childhood*   313

Empathy and Prosocial Behavior   315
Conflict and Aggression   317
The Effects of Television   323

Gender Development   325

Developmental Trends During Early Childhood   325
Influences on Gender Development   326
Androgyny   328

Child Abuse and Neglect   329

Causes   329

■ *A Multicultural View: The Cultural Context of Child Abuse and Neglect*   330

Consequences   331

■ *Working with Javier Hernandez, Preschool Program Coordinator: Play and Friendships Among Preschoolers*   332

Treatment and Prevention   332

The End of Early Childhood   333

Middle Childhood   336

AIDS and the School-age Child   353
Attention Deficit Hyperactivity Disorder   355

Effects of Growth on Thinking and Feeling   357

Chapter 12   Middle Childhood: Cognitive Development   360

Piaget's Theory: Concrete Operational Skills   361

Conservation in Middle Childhood   363
Conservation Training   364
Other Concrete Operational Skills   365
Piaget's Influence on Education   365

Information-Processing Skills   367

Memory Capacity   367
Influences on Memory Development   369

   A Multicultural View: Cultural Differences in Learning Mathematics   372

Metacognition and Learning Strategies   372
Difficulties with Information Processing: Learning Disabilities   376

   Working with Terry Wharton, Special Education Teacher: Giving Children a Second Chance to Learn   377

Language Development in Middle Childhood   379

Understanding Metaphor   379
Bilingualism and Its Effects   380
Black English   382

Defining and Measuring Intelligence   383

Issues Regarding Intelligence   383
Psychometric Approaches to Intelligence   384
Information-Processing Approaches to Intelligence   386
Sociocultural Approaches to Intelligence   389

   Perspectives: Gifted Students: Victims or Elite?   390

Cognition and Social Development   392

Chapter 11   Middle Childhood: Physical Development   338

Trends and Variations in Height and Weight   339

Height Variations Due to Puberty   340

   A Multicultural View: Dieting in Cross-Cultural Perspective   342

Excess Weight and Obesity   342

Motor Development and Athletics in Middle Childhood   344

   Working with Katherine Paterson, Pediatric Occupational Therapist: Diagnosing Children's Coordination Difficulties   344

Physical Effects of Early Athletics   345
Psychological Effects of Early Athletics   346

   A Talk with John, Age Eleven: Growing Older   347

Gender and Early Athletics   348

Health and Illness in Middle Childhood   349

   Perspectives: How Children Understand Death   350

Death Rates and Accidents Among Schoolchildren   350
Illnesses   352

Chapter 13   Middle Childhood: Psychosocial Development   394

Psychosocial Challenges of Middle Childhood   395

The Sense of Self   397

The Development of Self in Childhood   398
Processes in Constructing a Self   399

The Age of Industry and Achievement   399

Latency and the Crisis of Industry   400
Achievement Motivation   401

■ *A Multicultural View: Parental Expectations and Academic Achievement* 404

Peer Relationships 405

What Theorists Say about Peer Relationships 405
The Functions of Peers 407
Influences on Peer Group Membership 407

■ *Perspectives: The Psychological Functions of Preadolescent Peer Activities* 408

■ *Working with Lisa Truong, Fourth-Grade Teacher: Reducing Gender Role Stereotyping in Play* 410

Popularity, Social Acceptance, and Rejection 414
Conformity to Peers 417

Family Relationships 418

The Quality of Parent-Child Relationships in Middle Childhood 418
The Changing Nature of Modern Families 419
Divorce and Its Effects on Children 420
The Effects of Work on Families 425
Other Sources of Social Support 428

School Influences 429

School Culture 429
The Informal Curriculum 430
Teacher Influences 430
The Student's Experience 431

Beyond Childhood 432

Adolescence 435

Chapter 14 Adolescence: Physical Development 436

The Concept of Adolescence 438

Adolescence: From Idea to Social Fact 438
Theoretical Views of Adolescence 439

Growth in Height and Weight 440

The Secular Trend 442

■ *A Talk with Jason, Age Fourteen: Physical Development at Age Fourteen* 443

Puberty 444
Primary Sexual Maturation 444
Maturation of Secondary Sex Characteristics 445
Hormonal Changes and Their Physical Consequences 446
The Extent of Physical Sex Differences 447

Psychological Effects of Physical Growth in Adolescence 448

Body Image and Self-esteem 448

■ *Working with Barbara Donohue, Nutritionist: Treating Nutritional Problems and Eating Disorders During Adolescence* 449

Early- Versus Late-Maturing Adolescents 451

■ *A Multicultural View: How Do Ethnic Differences in Physical Appearance Affect Social Development During Adolescence?* 452

Health in Adolescence 455

Continuity with Health in Childhood 455
Causes of Death Among Adolescents 456
Adolescent Health Problems 457

■ *Perspectives: Two Serious Eating Disorders: Anorexia Nervosa and Bulimia* 464

Finally Young Adults? 465

Chapter 15 Adolescence: Cognitive Development 468

General Features of Adolescent Thought 470

The Cognitive Developmental Viewpoint: Formal Thought 471

Possibilities Versus Realities 471
Scientific Reasoning 471
Logical Combination of Ideas 472
Concrete Versus Formal Thought: Reasoning about Bending Rods 472
Cognitive Development Beyond Formal Thought 474
Implications of the Cognitive Developmental Viewpoint 474

Information-Processing Features of Adolescent Thought   475

Improved Capacity to Process Information   476

■ *A Talk with Joan, Age Fifteen: Thinking in Adolescence*   477

Expertise in Specific Domains of Knowledge   478
Implications of the Information-Processing Viewpoint   479

■ *Working with Carole Castleton, Psychiatric Group Worker: Cognitive Strategies for Social Problems*   480

Supporting Adolescents' Cognitive Development   480

The Nature of Critical Thinking   480
Programs to Foster Critical Thinking   482

The Development of Social Cognition   483

Egocentrism During Adolescence   484
The Development of Political Ideas   485
Religious Beliefs and Orientation   487

Moral Development: Beliefs About Justice and Care   489

■ *A Multicultural View: Cross-Cultural Misunderstandings in the Classroom*   490

Kohlberg's Six Stages of Moral Judgment   490

■ *Perspectives: What Creates a Life of Moral Commitment?*   492

Enduring Issues About the Development of Moral Judgment   491
Gilligan's Ethics of Care   495
The Ethics of Care During Adolescence   496

Chapter 16   Adolescence: Psychosocial Development   500

Individuation and Identity Development   501

Theories of Identity Development   504

■ *A Talk with Don, Age Eighteen: Social Relationships Among Adolescents*   507

Social Relationships During Adolescence   507

Relationships with Parents   508
Divorce, Remarriage, and Single Parenthood   513
Friendship   514
Peer Groups   516
The Influence of School and Work   519

■ *Perspectives: Can Parents Influence Their Adolescent's Choice of Peer Group?*   520

■ *A Multicultural View: Adaptive Strategies of Families of Minority Youth*   522

Sexuality During Adolescence   526

Sexual Fantasies and Masturbation   526
Heterosexuality   527
Nonheterosexual Orientations   530
Sex and Everyday Life   531

Special Problems of Adolescence   531

Adolescent Pregnancy and Parenthood   531

■ *Working with Janet Whalen, Nurse Practitioner: Helping Pregnant Teenagers*   532

Teenage Depression and Suicide   535
Juvenile Delinquency   536

The Emerging Adult   537

Glossary   G-1

References   R-1

Acknowledgments   A-1

Author/Name Index   I-1

Subject Index   I-7

Special Features

Multicultural Views

Growing Up in India   14

Cultural Context and Cognitive Development   48

Cultural Differences and Genetic Counseling   74

Reasons for Having a Child in the United States and Eight Other Countries   100

Breast Feeding Among the Gusii   156

Cognitive Effects of Talking to Infants: A Cross-Cultural Perspective   192

Cross-Cultural Variations in Attachment   218

Cultural Influences on Children's Sleep   242

Parents' Beliefs about Intelligence: A Cross-Cultural Perspective   292

The Cultural Context of Child Abuse and Neglect   330

Dieting in Cross-Cultural Perspective   342

Cultural Differences in Learning Mathematics   372

Parental Expectations and Academic Achievement   404

How Do Ethnic Differences in Physical Appearance Affect Social Development During Adolescence?   452

Cross-Cultural Misunderstandings in the Classroom   490

Adaptive Strategies of Families of Minority Youth   522

Perspectives

Wanted: A Child and Family Policy   9

Erik Erikson's Identity Crisis: An Autobiographical Perspective   34

The Race and Intelligence Controversy: Social Policy Implications   84

Technological Alternatives to Normal Conception   98

Sudden Infant Death Syndrome   141

Extremes in Language Acquisition: What Do They Mean?   186

Family Leave Policies in the United States and Europe   222

Reforming Children's Health Care   246

Christopher, the Multilingual Savant: Speaking Without Understanding   287

Extended Family Supports for Childrearing   308

How Children Understand Death   350

Gifted Students: Victims or Elite?   390

The Psychological Functions of Preadolescent Peer Activities   408

Two Serious Eating Disorders: Anorexia and Bulimia   464

What Creates a Life of Moral Commitment?   492

Can Parents Influence Their Adolescent's Choice of Peer Group?   520

"Working with . . ." Interviews

Pamela Mitchell, Primary School Teacher: The Many Purposes of Play 11

John Daviau, Residential Treatment Program Director: Understanding Multiproblem Adolescents 52

Gail Stewart, Genetic Counselor: Advising Parents About Genetic Problems 78

Katie Glover, OB-GYN Nurse Practitioner: Preparing for Childbirth 118

Helen Turman, Pediatric Nurse: Continuity and Change in Infants' Behavior 144

Gillian Luppiwiski, Infant Care Provider: Fostering Infants' Thinking 184

Rachelle Turner, Infant Day Care Coordinator: Understanding Infant Social Development 208

Audrey Reimer, Speech Language Pathologist: The Psychological Impact of Motor Skill Development 252

Carolyn Eaton, Preschool Teacher: Introducing Sign Language to Young Children 284

Javier Hernandez, Preschool Program Coordinator: Play and Friendships Among Preschoolers 333

Katherine Paterson, Pediatric Occupational Therapist: Diagnosing Children's Coordination Difficulties 344

Terry Wharton, Special Education Teacher: Giving Children a Second Chance to Learn 377

Lisa Truong, Fourth-Grade Teacher: Reducing Gender Role Stereotyping in Play 410

Barbara Donohue, Nutritionist: Treating Nutrition and Eating Disorders During Adolescence 449

Carole Castleton: Psychiatric Group Worker: Cognitive Strategies for Social Problems 480

Janet Whalen, Nurse Practitioner: Helping Pregnant Teenagers 532

"A Talk with . . ." Interviews

A Talk with Jennifer, Age Eight Months, and Her Parents: Infant Temperament 203

A Talk with Audrey, Age Four: Cognitive Development in the Preschool Years 279

A Talk with Larry, Age Four: Friendship and Play in Early Childhood 313

A Talk with John, Age Eleven: Growing Older 347

A Talk with Jason, Age Fourteen, Physical Development at Age Fourteen 443

A Talk with Joan, Age Fifteen: Thinking in Adolescence 477

A Talk with Don, Age Eighteen: Social Relationships Among Adolescents 507

Preface

We are delighted that again we have had the opportunity to refine, enhance, and update *Child and Adolescent Development*. The book remains a comprehensive introduction to the field, of course, but it is more than that: it is a tool for kindling students' enthusiasm about children and youth, for helping them to become more thoughtful about developmental processes, for assisting them in thinking about the relevance of developmental processes, and for assisting them in thinking about the relevance of developmental psychology to current careers and social issues. We hope, as you get to know the book, that you will see these values in it as well.

As a text, *Child and Adolescent Development* is appropriate for all undergraduates taking a first course in development, regardless of the department in which the course is taught. The Fourth Edition incorporates two major changes that make the book better than ever for such students: a much more explicit focus on applications of developmental knowledge and a substantially stronger focus on multicultural research about children, youth, and families.

Important Continuities with Previous Editions

These new directions for the Fourth Edition grow out of our previous commitments in earlier editions. As always, we seek the following:

- To communicate to students the freshness and vitality of real, fully dimensional children and the idea that development, above all, is a human process.

- To convey that the developmental psychologist's understanding of children and adolescents is based on information derived scientifically and, further, that good science involves a synthesis of classic and recent findings.

- To keep our writing clear, low-key, and nontechnical and to weave abundant concrete details about children and youth into our discussions.

- To explore the influence of cultural and social factors on development: the impact of ethnicity, for example, of language background, of gender, and of socioeconomic status.

- To help students appreciate the connections among the key developmental domains: physical, cognitive, and psychosocial.

- To explore, for both scientific and practical reasons, the roles of the adults who nurture, care for, and educate children.

These goals were foremost in our thoughts as we developed and revised the content and features of the Fourth Edition. They are expressed most obviously in some of the specially marked features of the text, but they are also woven into the body of the text itself.

A Renewed Applications Emphasis

More than in previous editions, we have added material related to occupations and vocations that use knowledge from developmental psychology. In every chapter of the Fourth Edition, there is no missing the relevance and importance of developmental processes in daily life! Students who read this book—and especially those who also have an interested instructor and classmates with whom to discuss ideas—will find their practical interests respected, encouraged, and stimulated. These benefits will happen, of course, in the context of learning sound information from developmental research. Here is a sampling of some of that applied, but research-based information:

- Prenatal counseling: who should seek it (Chapter 3).

- Birth and the family: preparing children for the new arrival (Chapter 4).

- Breast feeding: the most recent information for parents (Chapter 5).

- Low birth weight infants: ways that nurses and parents can assist with their development (Chapter 5).

- Language development: ways that parents and caregivers can foster it (Chapter 6).

- Transition to parenthood: how having a new baby affects couples (Chapter 7).

- Characteristics of good child care (Chapter 7).

- Impact of poverty on children's health (Chapter 8).

- Early childhood education: the best, developmentally appropriate practice from a multicultural perspective (Chapter 9).

- Language development in children who are deaf or hard of hearing (Chapter 9).

- Helping aggressive children and their parents (Chapter 10).

- How parents can influence their children's TV viewing (Chapter 10).

- Impact of athletics on the physical development of school-age children (Chapter 11).

- Attention deficit hyperactivity disorder (ADHD): what to look for and how to help children who have it (Chapter 11).

- Learning disabilities in school and ways of assisting students with them (Chapter 12).

- Suggestions for divorcing parents (Chapter 13).

- The impact of neighborhood and community violence (Chapter 13).

- The timing of puberty and adolescent adjustment (Chapter 14).

- Body image and adolescent self-esteem (Chapter 14).

- Critical thinking in adolescents and ways of fostering this skill (Chapter 15).

- The impact of work on the lives of adolescents (Chapter 16).

- The transition to middle school: recommendations for improving middle school education (Chapter 16).

In addition to this new and updated coverage, each chapter contains an interview (called "Working With . . .") with a professional who works with children or youth and whose work depends on applying knowledge of developmental psychology. The careers selected are ones that students of developmental psychology are likely to consider, and the interviews offer glimpses of where students might eventually go with their working lives and why developmental psychology might help them once they get there. This feature is described in greater detail below.

Strong Multicultural Coverage

In the Fourth Edition, we have strengthened the multicultural coverage of the book well beyond what it contained in the last edition. This change reflects our commitment to inclusivity, both in the field of developmental psychology and in society itself. We are convinced that all children are worthy of study, throughout both society and the world, and that knowledge of and respect for human diversity is indeed a fundamental purpose of developmental psychology as a field.

To this end we have retained a specially designated multicultural topic in each chapter, presented in a box called "A Multicultural View," which has proven to be popular with users of the text. The most successful, relevant, and current multicultural boxes have been retained from the previous edition, but a significant number of new boxes have been written for the Fourth Edition. These reflect changes in the field of developmental psychology as well as our increased commitment to the principle of inclusivity.

More important, but less immediately visible, multicultural findings such as those listed here have been added generously throughout the text. In Chapter 1, the discussion of research methods uses about equal parts of multicultural and "local" (that is, North American) examples as illustrations, and the North American examples include studies of nonwhite as well as white children or families. In Chapter 2, psychosocial and contextual theoretical approaches highlight the developmental importance of culture and historical change. Ethnicity and risk of genetic disorder are explored in Chapter 3, and cultural differences in perceptions of pain related to childbirth are discussed in Chapter 4. In Chapter 5, the discussion of children's sleep is enriched with a comparison of differences between Dutch and American children's sleep patterns, and the reasons for the differences. Cultural differences in infant temperament and in nonparental care giving are considered in Chapter 7. In Chapter 8 and 11, the discussion of physical growth includes comparisons across cultures, with comments on possible reasons for the differences. Chapter 10 looks at the role of cultural differences in childrearing and prosocial behavior. In Chapter 12, discussion of language development includes substantial comment on bilingualism and its effects on development. The developmental influence of SES and culture on peer relations, adolescent health care, and parenting styles and school dropouts are explored in Chapters 13, 14, and 16, respectively.

Enhanced Illustration Program

Because we are aware that a picture is worth a thousand words, we have enhanced the illustration program in the Fourth Edition. Numerous new graphs, figures, and tables have been added to make key explanations, ideas, and concepts more clear. All students, and especially those who prefer or need to learn in visual, as well as verbal ways, will find these additions helpful.

Responses to the Third Edition photo program were so positive that we have retained the same approach to illustrating key ideas by choosing photographs that emphasize the multicultural, contemporary, and human aspects of child and adolescent development.

Special Features

The Fourth Edition of *Child and Adolescent Development* includes a number of unique features designed to enhance students' understanding of developmental psychology. Some of these have been mentioned already but deserve fuller explanation:

A Multicultural View   A Multicultural View is a series of boxed inserts that focus on important multicultural topics related to child and adolescent development. Appearing in each chapter, they cover such topics as breastfeeding practices in contrasting societies, cultural variations in parent-child language interactions, beliefs about the nature of "intelligence" in diverse societies, social stereotypes about physical attractiveness in different cultures, cross-cultural differences in attachment, and adaptive strategies of families of minority youth. We hope that these boxes will increase readers' awareness of the importance of cultural context in the development of children and adolescents and of the importance of an inclusive perspective about human problems. A complete list of topics appears on page xiv.

Working With . . .   Working With . . . is a new set of interviews with experienced professionals who work with children or adolescents in some way and whose work depends on knowledge of developmental psychology. The interviews offer examples of how developmental psychology can be used to improve the lives of children and youth and of some of the careers that students might consider if they are interested in developmental psychology. One professional is interviewed for each chapter, and each individual has been selected because his or her work relates to a theme or domain of the chapter. Because Chapter 5 is about physical development in infancy, for example, we interview a pediatric nurse about her experiences on a maternity ward. Because Chapter 15 is about cognitive development in adolescence, we interview a psychiatric group worker about her use of a cognitive or educational approach to emotionally disturbed teenagers. Among other occupations represented are a genetic counselor, an infant day care coordinator, and a nutritionist. For a complete list of careers and topics featured, see p. xv.

A Talk With . . .   A Talk With . . . are interviews with children and adolescents that reinforce and bring to life the text's coverage of concepts and theories. The interviews convey some of the experience of childhood and adolescence (and the delight that is possible from close observation of them!). They are based on an extensive collection of tape-recorded interviews conducted especially for this text by one of the authors (Robert Hoffnung). A full list appears on p. xv.

Perspectives   Perspectives are boxed inserts that extend the text discussions by highlighting significant research on human development or by identifying issues of social policy related to the welfare of children. The Perspectives boxes emphasize the connectedness of developmental psychology with all aspects of the human condition, both intellectual and practical. In Chapter 3, for example, the race and intelligence controversy and its social policy implications are explored, while the Perspectives box in Chapter 8 documents the close relationship between SES and children's health and suggests ways of making health care more equitable for children and youth. In Chapter 16, the question of how parents can influence their adolescent's choice of peer group is considered. See p. xiv for a complete list of Perspectives topics.

What Do You Think?   What Do You Think?, a feature given greater prominence in the Fourth Edition, are sets of questions designed to stimulate reflection on issues and concepts of developmental psychology. The questions recognize the importance of dialogue in constructing knowledge about children and youth and invite students to enter that dialogue. What Do You Think? sections are located periodically throughout every chapter and can be used as a basis for classroom discussions and activities. Many are designed to encourage collaboration among classmates.

Special Learning Aids   Other pedagogical features include opening chapter outlines, initial focusing questions, summaries of key points, lists of key terms, and suggested further readings for each chapter. By organizing important information from the text, these features help students significantly to understand important themes, ideas, and concepts. Indirectly, by assisting in the mastery of content, they free students to develop their personal perspectives about the field of developmental psychology and about its practical uses.

Ancillaries

The Fourth Edition of *Child and Adolescent Development* is accompanied by an extensive package of teaching and learning aids. Heading the list are a test bank, an instructor's resource manual, and a study guide that are unified by a shared set of learning objectives.

Test Bank   The Test Bank, carefully revised by Robert Rycek of the University of Nebraska, Kearney, includes one hundred multiple-choice and four essay questions per chapter. Each multiple-choice question is keyed to a text page number and a learning objective, and each is identified as requiring factual, applied, or conceptual knowledge. The Fourth Edition Test Bank features far more applied and conceptual questions than previous editions have. The essay questions include sample response guides.

Instructor's Resource Manual The Instructor's Resource Manual has been almost completely revised by Gregory Cutler of Bay de Noc Community College. It offers numerous resources to facilitate course preparation and student assessment. Each chapter begins with a chapter map that keys all activities and test questions to specific points in each text chapter. Also included are a chapter overview and outline, learning objectives, sections on students' anticipated trouble spots and examples for use in class, lecture topics, news stories of relevance to developmental psychology, journal writing topics, in-class activities, out-of-class projects, and recommended Internet sites, videos, transparencies, and further readings.

Study Guide For each chapter, the Study Guide, prepared by both Robert Rycek and Gregory Cutler, contains learning objectives, a chapter overview and outline, a fill-in review of key terms and concepts, and an expanded set of multiple-choice practice questions, divided into two parts that test factual and applied knowledge, respectively. The special multiple-choice answer key explains why each option is correct *or incorrect*, a feature particularly appreciated by students.

Computerized Test Bank The test items are available on disk, providing maximum flexibility for instructors who wish to generate tests electronically, as well as edit test items or add their own.

Videos A wide range of video programs on child development is available to qualified adopters. Your Houghton Mifflin representative has details.

Video Rental Policy Qualified adopters can also borrow films or videos free of charge through a consortium of university film libraries.

Transparencies The accompanying set of overhead transparencies contains images from both within and outside the text.

Acknowledgments

A number of reviewers made constructive suggestions and provided thoughtful reactions at various stages in the development of the Fourth Edition, and we are very appreciative of the help we received from them. In particular, we would like to thank

Ann M. Berghout Austin, Utah State University
Edward Brady, Belleville Area College
James P. Buchanan, University of Scranton
Linda A. Carson, Des Moines Area Community College
Gary Creasey, Illinois State University–Normal
Lorraine DeJong, Furman University
Susanne Denham, George Mason University
Alice Sterling Honig, Syracuse University
Carollee Howes, University of California at Los Angeles
John R. Hranitz, Bloomsburg University
Patricia Anne Jarvis, Illinois State University–Normal
Laverne K. Jordan, Olivet Nazarene University
Paul E. Jose, Loyola University-Chicago
Joel King, University of Maine at Farmington
Robert Kovacs, Camden County College
Joan A. Lovensheimer, Butler County Community College
Richard E. Miller, Navarro College
Ardis L. Peterson, Contra Costa Community College
Lisa M. Reboy, Emporia State University
Robert Siegler, Carnegie Mellon University
Beverly Uhlenberg, University of North Dakota
Jerina Wainwright, Anne Arundel Community College
M. Gawain Wells, Brigham Young University
Mary Virginia Wyly, Buffalo State College

We would like to thank the many people who have made this book possible: there are so many after four editions, in fact, that it is now difficult to list them all. For the Fourth Edition, special thanks go to Jane Knetzger and Karla Paschkis for their insightful comments in developing the manuscript, as well as commendably dogged awareness of deadlines and their implications. As always, families and close personal relationships have had made room for us to work on the Fourth Edition; those people, along with our students, are in some indirect sense the creators of this book

Kelvin L. Seifert   Robert J. Hoffnung

Child and Adolescent Development

PART ONE

Studying

Development

As infants grow into children and children grow into adolescents, a great many changes occur. Some of these changes are small and fleeting, and many are relatively profound and long-lasting. These developmental changes are the subject of this book and of the field of study known as *developmental psychology*.

The study of development offers much insight into human nature—why we are what we are and how we became that way. Because describing development is a complex task, this book begins with two chapters that orient you to what lies ahead. They explain just what development is and describe some of the most important tools of developmental psychology, namely the theories and methods that guide our understanding of child and adolescent development. After completing these two chapters, you will be ready to begin looking at the focus of developmental psychology: the children themselves.

1

INTRODUCTION

Studying Development

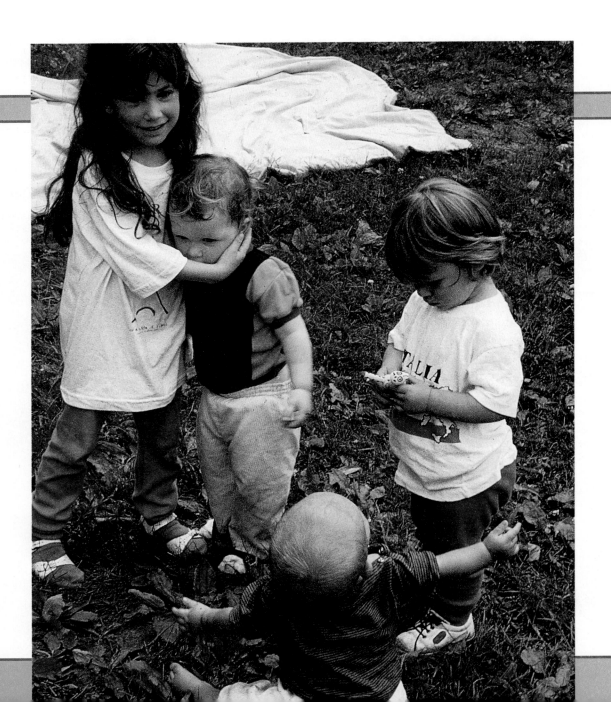

The Nature of Developmental
Change

Three Domains of Development
An Example of Development: Jodi

Why Study Development?

The History of Developmental Study

Early Precursors to Developmental Study
The Emergence of Modern Developmental
Study

Basic Issues in Developmental
Study

Nature and Nurture
Continuity and Discontinuity
Universal and Context-Specific
Development
Deficit and Difference

Methods of Studying Children and
Adolescents

The Scientific Method
Variations in Time Frame
Variations in Control: Naturalistic and
Experimental Studies
Sampling Strategies

Ethical Constraints on Studying
Development

Strengths and Limitations of
Developmental Knowledge

Focusing Questions

- What in general is human development?

- Why is it important to know about development?

- What general themes or issues are important in developmental psychology?

- How do developmental psychologists go about studying children and adolescents?

- What ethical considerations should guide the study of children?

D o you remember your childhood? In important ways you were probably a different person then. When you were two, you probably could not tie a shoelace, button your coat, or turn a doorknob reliably. When you were six, you may have struggled to read even one line of print. When you were twelve, you may have wondered whether you would ever be truly liked and respected by your friends.

Changes like these—and many others—mark every human life. Some are obvious, such as the transformation of a speechless infant into a talkative preschooler or the increasing sophistication with which children handle academic tasks as they get older. Other changes are subtle and may go unnoticed: alterations in hormones circulating in the blood as children approach adolescence or an increasing reliance on peers from one year to the next. But whether obvious or subtle, changes make us human, and many changes alter our lives profoundly.

THE NATURE OF DEVELOPMENTAL CHANGE

This book is about change. In particular, it is about human **development**—changes in a person's long-term growth, feelings, and patterns of thinking. Some developmental changes are relatively specific, such as when an infant takes her first unassisted step. Others are more general, such as when a schoolchild becomes increasingly able to co-operate with peers in work projects or in play. But on the whole, developmental changes tend to unfold gradually, even though once they appear they may seem quite unlike any behaviors a child showed previously. A ten-year-old boy, for example, may not believe that he will likely go on a date with a girl sometime during the next five years; indeed, his own parents may find this hard to believe!

Not every change is truly developmental, however. Cold weather in the winter causes changes in behavior, such as putting on warmer clothing and selecting indoor activities more frequently. But when the weather warms up again, these behavioral changes tend to disappear. Such changes *can* result in human development (for example, when a preschooler is able to put on a winter coat and boots with no help from anyone else), but most of the time they do not. On the other hand, not every human development involves change. Some developments are characterized primarily by continuity; once a child's basic sense of self develops, it remains fairly constant as the child grows older.

3

Three Domains of Development

As these examples suggest, human development can take many forms. For convenience, this book distinguishes among three major types, or **domains,** of development: physical, cognitive, and psychosocial. The first domain deals with **physical development,** or biological growth. It includes changes in the body (in the brain, sense organs, muscles, bones, and so forth) and in the ways a person uses his or her body (motor skills and sexual development, for example). It also includes the effects of aging, such as changes in eyesight or in muscular strength. But it usually does not include physical changes that result from accidents, illnesses, or other special events. Like other forms of development, physical growth or maturation often spans very long periods.

physical changes

Changes happen in all domains at once—physical, cognitive, and psychosocial. As this baby refines her motor and thinking skills and develops a capacity for empathy and caring, she (hopefully) will grab the cat less and pet it more. In time, she may display toward it the same degree of affection and loyalty shown by this school-age boy toward his horse.

Cognitive development involves changes in reasoning and thinking, language acquisition, and the ways individuals gain, store, and remember or recall knowledge of their environments. It includes what we commonly call "learning," but a great deal more. *Learning* refers to comparatively permanent changes in thinking, feeling, and behavior, but it tends to be limited to changes that result from relatively specific experiences or events. Often, too, learned changes occur over a short time—sometimes just hours or even minutes—but, as later chapters show, some important cognitive developments take much longer to occur.

changes in thinking

Psychosocial development concerns changes in feelings or emotions as well as changes in how individuals relate to other people. It includes relationships with family, peers, and teachers as well as an individual's personal identity, or sense of self. Because identity and social relationships tend to evolve simultaneously, we discuss them together throughout this book. But both aspects of development also depend on other kinds of change. How a person looks physically can affect how she feels about herself and influence her relationships with her friends. Her powers of reasoning can influence her ability to understand the needs of others and, in this way, affect the quality of her relationships with others. Each form of development appears to influence all of the others.

changes in emotions

The three domains interconnect in many ways (see Figure 1.1 for examples). For instance, physical growth makes the cognitive process of language acquisition possible, and language facilitates early social relationships. In turn, social relationships provide settings for further cognitive learning and for nurturing further physical growth. Later chapters point out connections such as these wherever appropriate.

FIGURE 1.1
Selected Landmarks of Development
Development is a continual unfolding and integration of changes in all domains, beginning at birth. Changes in one domain often affect those in another domain.

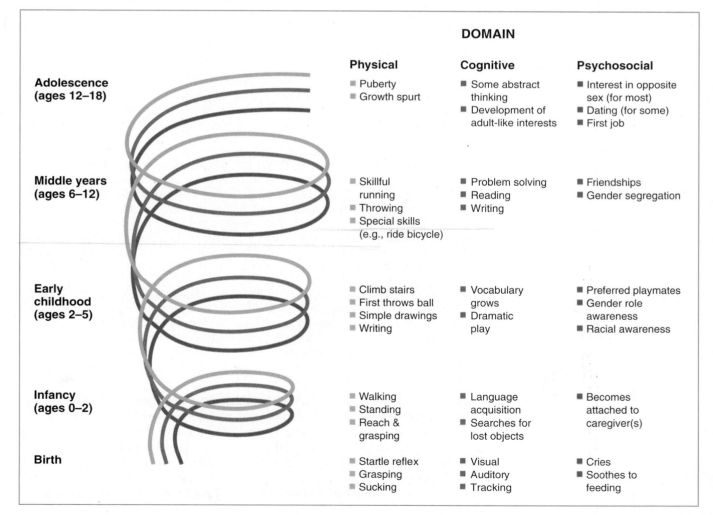

DOMAIN

	Physical	Cognitive	Psychosocial
Adolescence (ages 12–18)	■ Puberty ■ Growth spurt	■ Some abstract thinking ■ Development of adult-like interests	■ Interest in opposite sex (for most) ■ Dating (for some) ■ First job
Middle years (ages 6–12)	■ Skillful running ■ Throwing ■ Special skills (e.g., ride bicycle)	■ Problem solving ■ Reading ■ Writing	■ Friendships ■ Gender segregation
Early childhood (ages 2–5)	■ Climb stairs ■ First throws ball ■ Simple drawings ■ Writing	■ Vocabulary grows ■ Dramatic play	■ Preferred playmates ■ Gender role awareness ■ Racial awareness
Infancy (ages 0–2)	■ Walking ■ Standing ■ Reach & grasping	■ Language acquisition ■ Searches for lost objects	■ Becomes attached to caregiver(s)
Birth	■ Startle reflex ■ Grasping ■ Sucking	■ Visual ■ Auditory ■ Tracking	■ Cries ■ Soothes to feeding

Sometimes human behavior can be pretty puzzling! The field of human development can help in understanding apparent contradictions and inconsistencies—like when this child first does, and then does not, want to take a bath.

An Example of Development: Jodi

You may have noticed that these opening comments are rather general; we seem to be speaking of changes that happen to *every* child. But what about changes that happen to just one individual child? Can developmental psychology say anything about these? We believe it can, though it does so by framing specific experiences in relatively general terms. Specific changes—such as when a four-year-old "reads" his name or completes a somersault—can be understood both as examples and as creators of larger, more universal human changes. For this reason, among others, developmental psychology can be a very practical and useful field of study. To see what we mean, consider a child whom one of the authors knows personally: Jodi.

> When Jodi was four, one of her brothers died. Roger had been 2½ years older, a friendly kid and a decent sibling. Jodi played with him more than with her sister and other brother, who were both older than Roger. He died suddenly one winter from complications of chicken pox. The doctors said he may have reacted to the aspirin he had taken for his fever. They said you weren't supposed to give aspirin to children, but Jodi didn't know that, and apparently her parents didn't know it either.
>
> For a few years after that, they were a three-child family "with a hole in the middle," said Jodi to her best friend, where Roger was supposed to be. It was not ideal for Jodi, but it was tolerable: she didn't have the playmate she used to have, but she did have her family ("What's left of it!") and her friends from school. Life got back to normal—sort of.
>
> When Jodi was nine, her parents adopted another child, a boy of twelve, about the same age Roger would have been had he lived. Frank had lived in numerous foster care homes, some of which had not been happy experiences for him. In two homes the discipline had been extremely strict, but it was hard for Jodi to know this, because Frank did not tell her as much as he told the social workers or his new adopted parents, and her parents did not say much about Frank's past. In fact, Frank said little to Jodi about anything; he seemed distinctly cool toward all three of his new siblings.
>
> Except for his periodic visits to Jodi's room at night. The first time it happened, Jodi was startled out of her sleep: Frank was standing by her bed and demanded that she take off her nightgown. That was all for that time. But he came back every few weeks, each time asking for more than the time before and threatening to hurt her badly if she revealed "our secret."
>
> So Jodi learned not to sleep deeply. She also learned to avoid being alone in the house with Frank. In school she learned to avoid talking to boys very much, except in a joking way and in the presence of lots of other kids. In class she learned to look interested in what the teacher said even on the morning after a visit from Frank. And she learned to keep awake during the day, even when, as she later put it, "I was sleeping inside." Jodi learned a lot from Frank, though not things she wanted to learn and not things most of her classmates were learning.

Jodi's story shows several things about human development. It shows, for example, that the domains of development all unfold together. Jodi's thoughts and feelings about Frank occurred in the context of physical changes happening to herself. Being physically older or younger may not have protected her from abuse, but it probably would have altered the experience, either in impact or in quality.

Jodi's story also suggests the importance of unique, personal experiences when exploring developmental psychology in general. Some things about Jodi may always be unique because of her encounters with Frank; she may always be a bit mistrustful of boys and men, for example. But other things about Jodi can be understood as examples of human changes that are universal or nearly universal. In experiencing abuse, for example, Jodi responds to gender role differences that pervade nearly all societies; in most societies, women experience less power than men.

Urie Bronfenbrenner, a developmental psychologist, has originated a widely used framework for thinking about the multiple influences on children like Jodi (Bronfenbrenner, 1989; Garbarino, 1992). He describes the contexts of development as *ecological systems,* which are sets of people, settings, and recurring events that are related to one another, have stability, and influence the child over time. (See Figure 1.2 and Table 1.1.)

1. The *microsystem* refers to situations in which the child has face-to-face contact with influential others. For Jodi, the microsystem consists of her immediate family (though note that the membership of this family changed over time) as well as her teachers and peers at school.   *[handwritten margin note: face-to-face contact]*

2. The *mesosystem* refers to the connections and relationships that exist between two or more microsystems and influence the child because of their relationships. An example would be the contacts between Jodi's parents and the social workers responsible for Frank's adoption: their contacts led them (perhaps wrongly) to withhold information about Frank from Jodi.   *[handwritten margin note: connections between 2 face-to-face contacts (middlemen)]*

3. The *exosystem* consists of settings in which the child does not participate but still experiences decisions and events that affect him or her indirectly. An example in Jodi's case might be the medical system, which either lacked the knowledge needed to save Roger at the time of his death or had been organized in a way that interfered with communicating needed medical knowledge to Jodi's parents.   *[handwritten margin note: settings child does not participate but affects child]*

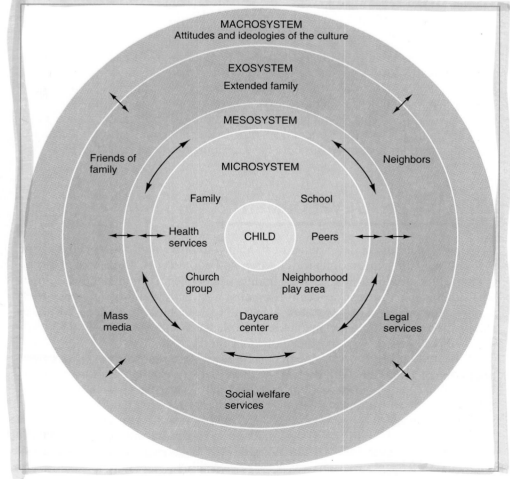

FIGURE 1.2
Bronfenbrenner's Four Ecological Settings for Developmental Change
Bronfenbrenner describes human development as a set of overlapping ecological systems, as shown. All of them operate together to influence what a child becomes as he or she grows into an adult. In this sense development is not exclusively "in" the person, but is also "in" the person's environment.
Source: Garbarino (1982).

TABLE 1.1 *Ecological System Levels*

Ecological Level	Definition	Examples	Issues Affecting Children
Microsystem	Situations in which the child has face-to-face contact with influential others	Family, school, peer group, church	Is the child regarded positively? Is the child accepted? Is the child reinforced for competent behavior? Is the child exposed to enough diversity in roles and relationships? Is the child given an active role in reciprocal relationships?
Mesosystem	Relationships between micro-systems; the connections between situations	Home–school, home–church, school–neighborhood	Do settings respect each other? Do settings present basic consistency in values?
Exosystem	Settings in which the child does not participate but in which significant decisions are made affecting the child or adults who do interact directly with the child	Parents' place of employment, school board, local government, parents' peer group	Are decisions made with the interests of parents and children in mind? How well do supports for families balance stresses for parents?
Macrosystem	"Blueprints" for defining and organizing the institutional life of the society	Ideology, social policy, shared assumptions about human nature, the "social contract"	Are some groups valued at the expense of others (e.g., sexism, racism)? Is there an individualistic or a collectivistic orientation? Is violence a norm?

Source: Garbarino (1982).

4. The *macrosystem* is the overarching institutions, practices, and patterns of belief that characterize society as a whole and take the smaller micro-, meso-, and exosystems into account. An example that affected Jodi was gender role: a widespread belief that men should dominate women may have contributed to Frank's coercive actions against Jodi, though of course it was probably not the only reason for them.

In the pages ahead we will try to keep in mind these multiple systems, such as those implied by Jodi's story, as well as distinctions among the major domains of development. Only in this way will we be able to convince you that developmental psychology has something to say about the particulars of human change: about how you, I, or a specific friend change and grow and what those changes may signify. We therefore encourage you to return to Jodi from time to time to remind yourself that in real life, the particulars and universals both have meaning for human development.

WHY STUDY DEVELOPMENT?

Knowing about human development can help you in five major ways. First, it can give you realistic expectations for children and adolescents. Developmental psychology tells you, for example, when infants usually begin talking, and it suggests when schoolchildren tend to begin reasoning abstractly. Admittedly, it generally tells you only averages for children: when a "typical" child acquires a particular skill, behavior, or emotion. Nonetheless, knowledge of these averages can help you know what to expect from specific, individual children.

Second, knowledge of development can help you respond appropriately to children's actual behavior. If a preschool boy tells his mother that he wants to marry her, should she ignore his remark or make a point of correcting his misconception? If a third-grade child seems more interested in her friends than in her schoolwork, should her teacher discourage contact with friends or try to figure out ways to use the friends to support the child's school studies? Developmental psychology can help answer such questions by indicating the sources and significance of many of the thoughts, feelings, and behavior patterns of children.

Third, knowledge of development can help you recognize when departures (3) from normal are truly significant. If a child talks very little by age two, should her parents and doctors be concerned? What if she still does not talk much by age three or four? If a teenager admits to having had sexual intercourse "once or twice" by age fifteen, should his parents worry that he is becoming promiscuous? How about if he is only thirteen or even eleven? We can answer these questions more easily if we know what *usually* happens to children and adolescents. And knowing what usually happens—being aware of the universal trends—makes up a great deal of the content of developmental psychology.

Fourth, studying development can help you understand yourself. Developmental psychology makes explicit the processes of psychological growth, processes that each of us may overlook in our personal, everyday lives. Even more important, it can help you make sense out of your own experiences, such as whether it really mattered that you reached puberty earlier (or later) than your friends did. (4)

Finally, studying development can make you a better advocate for the needs and (5) rights of children. By knowing in detail the capacities and potential of youngsters, you will be in a good position to persuade others of the importance and value of children. The "others" are diverse: they include parents, professionals who work with children, and political and business leaders. These groups, which include most of us reading this book, have a common interest in the future of society and therefore in the future of children. Yet, as the accompanying Perspectives box indicates, we as a society can do a better job of supporting child development than we in fact have done.

Perspectives

Wanted: A Child and Family Policy

Parents generally do value their children, want the best for them, and make sacrifices on their behalf. In spite of this support, though, the lives of children are often difficult:

□ In the early 1990s, more than 20 percent of all children in the United States under age six lived in families that were officially poor (Huston, 1994). This is more than twice the rate of poverty in Canada and about ten times the rate of poverty in Sweden.

□ A similar proportion of children have failed to receive routine immunizations against polio, measles, and other childhood diseases. Here too the United States ranks much lower than many other developed countries.

□ About a third of all children living today will eventually experience the divorce of their parents, with all of the stress it brings (Hetherington, 1995). One of the stresses will be poverty, because the parent who usually has major custody, the mother, tends to earn much less than the father.

□ In the United States, on average, an infant is born into poverty every thirty-five seconds, a child is physically punished in school every four seconds, and a preschooler is murdered every fourteen hours (Children's Defense Fund, 1995).

A major reason these problems exist is that the United States lacks a comprehensive, integrated set of policies for caring for its children. Programs to remedy social problems have tended to focus on problems selectively rather than recognizing the impact of one problem on another. School programs to assist with learning difficulties, for example, tend to work with children individually, even though health, nutrition, illness, and family disruptions contribute to learning difficulties in major ways. More effective is to provide a set of related and coordinated services to support families: pediatric care, combined with special help at school and a supportive social worker or nurse to visit parents at home to provide encouragement and information. When Victoria Seitz and Nancy Apfel tried this approach with some low-income families, they found improvements in cognitive abilities not only for the children originally at risk but also for their siblings who had not even been a focus of the intervention (Seitz & Apfel, 1994)!

Such combined approaches to children's welfare may look expensive and difficult when organized as special demonstration projects, but experience in other developed countries suggests that costs decrease markedly when implemented universally and that organizational problems can in fact be solved (Chafel, 1993; United States General Accounting Office, 1993). The real challenge, it seems, may be political: enlisting the support of leaders in government and business to develop comprehensive policies for children, and thereby ensuring the future of society.

What Do You Think?

What do *you* hope to gain by studying developmental psychology (besides a university credit, of course!)? Take a minute to think about this question—maybe even jot down some notes about it. Then share your ideas with two or three classmates. How do they differ?

THE HISTORY OF DEVELOPMENTAL STUDY

Until just a few hundred years ago, children in Western society were not perceived as full-fledged members of society or even as genuine human beings (Ariès, 1962). During medieval times, infants tended to be regarded rather like talented pets: at best interesting and even able to talk, but not creatures worth caring about deeply. Children graduated to adult status early in life, around age seven or eight, by taking on major, adultlike tasks for the community. At that time, children who today would be attending second or third grade might have been caring for younger siblings, working in the fields, or apprenticed to a family to learn a trade.

Because children took on adult responsibilities so soon, the period we call *adolescence* was also unknown. Teenagers assumed adult roles. Although these roles often included marriage and childrearing, most people in their teens lived with their original families, helping with household work and with caring for others' children until well into their twenties.

All this may seem harsh by modern, middle-class standards, but perhaps it was simply realistic. Relatively large numbers of children died early in life, especially in infancy. Some historians suggest that this made it unrealistic for parents to care too deeply about infants when they were first born. Others have argued that parents did care, but the economic circumstances of the community required early participation by children in community life (Hareven, 1986; Sommerville, 1990). There was little time left for play and fun, but children also enjoyed higher economic status than do most modern children.

Early Precursors to Developmental Study

Why did awareness of childhood eventually emerge? Society was becoming less rural and more industrialized. During the eighteenth century, factory towns began attracting large numbers of workers, who often brought their children with them. "Atrocity stories" became increasingly common: reports of young children in England becoming caught and disabled in factory machinery and of children being abandoned to the streets. Partly because of these changes, many people became more conscious of childhood and adolescence as unique periods of life, periods that influence later development. At the same time, they became concerned with arranging appropriate, helpful experiences for children.

The Emergence of Modern Developmental Study

During the nineteenth and twentieth centuries, the growing recognition of childhood led to new ways of studying children's behavior. One of these was the *baby biography,* a detailed diary of a particular child, usually the author's own. One of the most famous English biographies was written and published by Charles Darwin (1877) and contained lengthy accounts of his son Doddy's activities and accomplishments. The tradition of rich description continued in the twentieth century with Arnold Gesell, who observed children at precise ages doing specific things, such as building with

Pamela Mitchell, PRIMARY SCHOOL TEACHER

The Many Purposes of Play

Pamela Mitchell taught kindergarten for many years. Most recently she has been responsible for an innovative program that deliberately integrates first-, second-, and third-grade children into one class. She spoke eloquently about her students and the changes she sees in them as a result of activities that engage them in class. As she talked, it became clear that Pamela deeply cares about giving children *choices,* so I asked her to talk more about that.

Kelvin: How do you provide for choice in the classroom?

Pamela: One thing I do is put aside an hour every morning for "Choice Time." I set up materials around the room that relate to the current theme—things like cooking, science experiments, new activities on the computer, building blocks, games, or new art activities. If the kids don't want to choose one of them, that's OK too. There are so many possibilities!

Kelvin: Isn't Choice Time what most of us would call "play"? Why not just call it that?

Pamela: You're right, it really *is* play. If you walked into my room, you would see kids "playing" every morning for an hour. I always call it Choice Time, though, because I think *choice* highlights what play accomplishes, both for me and for the kids.

Kelvin: Which is . . . ?

Pamela [*smiling broadly*]: You know what? Choice Time is probably the most valuable time of the day. It gives me a chance to see each child holistically—to see how each one sets priorities, combines what they're learning and seeing. Choice Time lets the kids "put it all together"; it's when they organize their knowledge.

Kelvin: It sounds pretty "cognitive" in its benefits.

Pamela: Yes, Choice Time—play—definitely has cognitive benefits, but it has social and emotional benefits too. It also helps with motor skills!

In the cognitive area, play helps children with their language. They have to listen and talk with others. Of course, talking is also a social activity—the kids have to negotiate how to share or how to work their way into an activity. They're figuring out *what* to say and *when* to talk and when to keep silent.

Playing with others can be pretty emotional, too! I've had children shed tears when someone else was using a book or an activity they wanted. Children learn to deal with those things through play.

Kelvin: What about motor skills? Your classroom seems pretty small, which might limit your options.

Pamela: You'd be surprised. Building with blocks takes motor skills; so does drawing. When the kids go out in the hallway to measure just how long a twenty-six-foot dinosaur would be, it takes motor skills to lay out the tape measure, along with cooperation and strategizing about how to measure such a big distance. But you're right—we don't do running-around, gym-type games in here.

Kelvin: I should think that some people might consider Choice Time a poor use of class time. Some parents or even some other teachers might say, "it's *just* play," belittling its value.

Pamela: But it isn't just play—it's the element of *choice* that makes it so valuable. The kids choose an activity that interests them, and that makes them feel empowered to learn. If a parent seems unsure about Choice Time, I might say, "Think about how you learn something new. Say you recently learned to use a computer. You

didn't just read a book about using it; you *played* with it!" That's how we all learn.

Kelvin: For all the good things about Choice Time, do you see any pitfalls?

Pamela: You have to be really involved during Choice Time; it's probably the busiest time of my day. I'm talking to individual kids, following up on their initiatives and maybe suggesting other materials or activities to support them further. I try to check in with as many of the children as possible during that time. It's critical to connect what the kids choose to do, what I've done with them earlier, and what I'll be doing later.

Kelvin: So involvement is a key to success with children's play?

Pamela: You could say that. The key is to believe in your heart that children learn by choosing and by constructing knowledge on their own initiative. When you do, it changes your whole attitude about teaching and learning.

What Do You Think?

1. Do you agree with Pamela's ideas about play? If you were teaching a primary-grade class, would you feel comfortable organizing it the way she has?

2. Think back to an activity or a skill that you do well, and ponder *how* you learned it. Did your mastery involve periods of play and/or free exploration? Compare your experience with those of two or three classmates. Does everyone seem to have needed playful exploration, or only some people?

3. If play is so closely intertwined with cognitive learning, social development, and motor development, why is it not more common in school programs? What factors do you think might limit its use? After you formulate your own answer, you might find it helpful to get the opinion of an experienced teacher about this question as well.

The concept of childhood as a distinct period in a person's life is a relatively new invention, at least as judged by how children have been portrayed in paintings over the centuries. Until the nineteenth century, painters generally depicted children as miniature adults, with adultlike clothing, facial expressions, and bodily proportions. By the nineteenth century, though, childhood had come to be seen—and valued—as a unique time, one quite different from adulthood. Children were expected to wear special types of clothing and hairstyles and engage in their own kind of activities and pastimes.

blocks, jumping, and hopping (Gesell, 1926). After studying more than five hundred children, Gesell generalized standards of normal development, or **norms**—behaviors typical of children at certain ages. Although the norms applied primarily to white, middle-class children and to specific situations and abilities, they gave a wider-ranging picture of child development than was possible from baby biographies alone.

The method of descriptive observation in child development research has persisted into the present. An influential observer in this century has been Jean Piaget, who described many details of his own three children's behavior as infants (Piaget, 1963). He did not observe all of the children's possible behaviors but focused on those that illustrated their cognitive skills, or ability to think. Piaget has influenced modern developmental psychology to such an extent that we discuss his work at length later in this book.

What Do You Think?

What are the merits and problems of descriptive study of children? One way to find out is for you and two or three classmates to make separate written observations of the "same" events. Visit a place with people in it (even your developmental psychology classroom), and separately write about what you see one particular person doing. Afterward, compare notes. How well do they agree, and when and how do they differ?

BASIC ISSUES IN DEVELOPMENTAL STUDY

As child development has evolved as a discipline, four basic issues about the nature of human development have emerged: nature and nurture, continuity and discontinuity, context and universality, and deficit and difference in development. These issues influence how developmental psychology is organized, and therefore also influence what you can expect when you study it. They are summarized in Table 1.2.

TABLE 1.2   ***Basic Issues In Developmental Psychology***

Issue	Crucial Question
Nature and nurture	How much are qualities, behaviors, and skills inborn, and how much are they acquired through experience?
Continuity and discontinuity	How much does development simply continue earlier acquisitions, and how much does it lead to qualitatively new behaviors and skills?
Universal and context-specific development	How much can developmental psychology identify developmental changes that happen to everyone throughout the world, and how much should it take specific human and cultural contexts into account?
Deficit and difference	Are certain developmental changes and milestones inherently more desirable than others?

Nature and Nurture

How much are you the result of genetic, inborn qualities, and how much the result of learning and experience? The first alternative (genetics and inborn qualities) is your **nature,** and the second (learning and experience) is your **nurture**. It seems sensible to expect that each of us combines nature and nurture in a lot of ways. Your height depends on how tall your parents are (nature), but it also depends on the nutrition and exercise you get as you grow up (nurture).

Developmental psychologists have many questions about exactly how nature and nurture interact and whether one is sometimes more important than the other. Robert Plomin and his associates, for example, studied the temperaments (or emotional styles) of two groups of infants: one a group of identical twins, and therefore completely the same genetically, and the other fraternal twins, and therefore only as similar genetically as ordinary siblings (Plomin et al., 1993). The identical twins were somewhat more similar to each other in their emotional reactions than were the fraternal twins—they responded to strangers with similar degrees of shyness, for example—suggesting that genetics influenced their reactions and styles. But the tendency to be more similar was only modest, suggesting that experiences since birth also affected the babies' emotional temperaments.

Continuity and Discontinuity

Developmental psychologists also note, as perhaps you have too, that some long-term changes seem like obvious continuations of earlier qualities and skills, whereas others seem new and unprecedented. Take memory, for example: older children usually can recall and define more words than younger children, as if this developmental change were simply a matter of accumulating more verbal memories. But is that all there is to it? In recalling and using terms, is an older child really just doing "more" of what a younger child does or doing something altogether different? Michelene Chi wondered about this question and, through some ingenious memory tests (Chi, 1985), concluded that later memory is not necessarily more of earlier memory but something altogether different in quality. She asked a first-grade girl to recall the names of as many of her classmates as possible. The girl performed this task quite well, but by using a strategy different than that used by most older children and adults: instead of recalling classmates' names alphabetically, as older children and adults probably would have done, the girl recalled them according to the children's seating arrangement in the classroom. When asked to recall a list of unfamiliar names in alphabetical order, on the other hand, she performed poorly compared to older persons. It appeared, therefore, that her memory was limited, or "undeveloped," when expected to perform the task in an adultlike way. She did not lack knowledge of classmates' names; rather, she organized her knowledge differently than older persons do.

A Multicultural View

Growing Up in India

In many parts of the world today, childhood means something different than it does in the West, because most cultures emphasize interdependence among family members more than in the West (Greenfield, 1994). India is a good case in point. In the traditional Hindu sects of this society, infants and young children receive a good deal more protection and intimate nurturance than their counterparts in Western families do (Kakar, 1982; Kurtz, 1992). Typically, infants are breast-fed well into toddlerhood, far beyond what is usual in the West. During the first four or five years of life, children are rarely separated from their mothers; they come along on virtually all errands and visits, even when the excursions do not concern them. During this period, mothers take child nurturing very seriously and are expected to do so by Hindu society. Guidance, discipline, and spoiling—major concerns among Western parents—are not serious issues for traditional Hindu mothers, who see their primary task as helping children develop a deeply trustful attitude toward the world.

But eventually the protection and nurturance come to an end. For a boy, the end comes suddenly at about age five, when parents and other relatives expect him to begin conforming to adult standards of behavior, give up playing with younger children, and spend most of his time in the company of other boys and men. The boy must even give up eating meals with his mother and other females and take his meals exclusively with males.

For a girl, protection and nurturance persist a few years longer than for a boy. But she too faces a drastic change: sometime between ages eleven and thirteen she gets married, not to someone she chooses but to a young man selected by her parents and the man's parents. At this point, she is likely to leave home permanently to live with her husband's family. Many of her in-laws will be virtual strangers to her, sometimes including her new husband.

Because the changes occur so suddenly for each sex, they often create stress for young Hindus, as well as sadness and nostalgia for times past. Yet in most cases the changes are manageable, thanks to the emotional and practical supports provided by Hindu families. A major form of support is the extended family, which consists of adult relatives living together (usually brothers) who have brought their spouses to live with them after they marry. This arrangement helps reduce the loneliness children experience after they leave the intense early care of their mothers. A Hindu boy may miss his mother when he stops eating meals with her, but his new companions—his father and other males—have had similar experiences and respond to his feelings tactfully, albeit with reserve. A Hindu girl also may miss her mother when she marries, but she may become a mother herself by her late teens. In the context of an extended family, her pregnancy is not considered the burden that a teenage pregnancy is in the West. On the contrary, early pregnancy confers status on the mother-to-be, and in any case the girl's extended family is likely to contain other, more experienced women to assist her with child care.

Universal and Context-Specific Development

An important issue in developmental psychology has to do with the universality of human development. Are there principles of growth and maturation that hold true for all people, regardless of circumstances? What, for example, do the minds and feelings of these boys and girls have in common?

As a practical matter, most of us (including developmental psychologists) recognize that who we are and become depends in various ways on the settings and situations in which we grow up. If I grow up among English-speaking adults, I will learn to speak English, not some other language. If I grow up in a Hindu family in India, as described in the accompanying Multicultural View box, my entire personality will

Compared to Western children, then, Hindu children experience longer and more intense nurturance from a larger number of relatives, but at the price of a relatively sudden transition away from intimacy with their mothers. Western children avoid such a sudden transition, but encounter more mixed responses about intimacy even from birth. Western parents admire and love their children, of course, but they are also likely to worry incessantly about fostering independence and self-reliance (Elkind, 1994). These are reasonable concerns given the unique conditions of Western family life, where parents can count on much less help in raising children than in the majority of societies.

In the Hindu parts of India, mothers give their young children a good deal more physical care and emotional nurturance than commonly occurs in North America. Observing the effects of these differences can give insight into the impact and significance of child rearing techniques in general.

develop differently than if I grow up in a Christian family in the midwestern United States. What makes developmental psychologists curious is the extent and importance of such influences: when are they superficial and limited (such as wearing one color of clothing instead of another), and when are they profound, far-reaching, and part of our human essence?

Patricia Greenfield studied routine parent-teacher conferences between Anglo teachers and Hispanic mothers in terms of differences in personal and family values between the two groups (Greenfield, 1995). During the conferences, the Anglo teachers uniformly sought to highlight the individual achievements of the child ("Carmen is doing well with her spelling"). But many of the Hispanic mothers preferred to direct the conversation toward how the child fit into the family and into the classroom group ("Carmen is such a help to me, and so friendly"). The parents' remarks reflected differences in general cultural values—the Anglo parents valuing independence somewhat more, but the Hispanic parents (sometimes) valuing *inter*-dependence more. The result was frustration with the conference on the part of both teachers and parents and less effective support for the children in their efforts to succeed socially and academically.

Deficit and Difference

When children develop in different ways, are some children deficient or lacking in some way, or are they merely different from others? Are certain developmental milestones inherently more desirable than others? To the extent that developmental psychologists (as well as the rest of the world) can agree on which changes are truly desirable, they (and other professionals) can actively work to encourage them and to discourage unwanted or undesirable directions of growth and change in children.

At some general level, some changes must surely be more desirable than others. Nearly everyone would agree, for example, that acquiring some sort of language is better than acquiring no language at all, because language gives a child a way to communicate with others. But as often as not, one developmental change is not clearly "better" than another. Although acquiring language in general may be good for a child, it may not matter *which* particular language is acquired: Spanish, Chinese, American Sign Language, and all dialects (or "accents") of English are equally capable of expressing the full range of human thoughts and feelings. Speaking (or signing) these various languages makes children different, but does not make some children deficient compared to others.

The effort to identify general developmental trends sometimes makes developmental psychologists prone to equate differences in children with deficiencies. Recently a number of psychologists have explored an example of this tendency in studying how children and adults develop morality: a sense of ethics, or of right and wrong. Until the early 1980s, the psychological study of moral development focused on children's general sense of justice or fairness (Colby et al., 1983). Is it always right, for example, to pay a person in proportion to his or her productivity? Is it always wrong to steal? More mature (and therefore "better") development seemed to be associated with the ability to reason abstractly about principles of fairness. An implication was that people who cannot or do not reason as abstractly as others are not just different but deficient in their moral reasoning.

More recent research has suggested that this view of moral development is unfair to many people's ethical ideas. Carol Gilligan interviewed adolescent girls and young women who were considering having abortions and found that their sense of right and wrong focused much less on general principles of fairness ("Is abortion always/sometimes/never right?") and more on the welfare of the particular people affected (the baby, the father, the woman herself, her family). This approach, an "ethics of care" rather than of justice, becomes well developed in many women (and some men) and is used by them to resolve a variety of ethical dilemmas (Brown & Gilligan, 1992; Colby & Damon, 1993). Its existence suggests a new way of thinking about moral reasoning: perhaps children develop not toward a common endpoint but toward multiple possible endpoints. Some may develop moral reasoning oriented toward general principles of justice, whereas others develop an ethics of care. One orientation would be different from the other, but not necessarily deficient.

What Do You Think?

A psychologist once said that "every parent believes in nurture until they have their *second* child." What do you think she was getting at with this comment? If you happen to be a parent of at least two children, share your opinion of the comment with a classmate who is not a parent or with one who is a first-time parent. And vice versa: if you've raised no children, or only one, compare your opinions to those of a second- or third-time parent.

METHODS OF STUDYING CHILDREN AND ADOLESCENTS

The Scientific Method

All research studies of human development follow the **scientific method,** systematic procedures to ensure objective observations and interpretations of observations.

Even though it is not always possible to follow these methods perfectly, they form an ideal to which psychological research tends to aspire (Cherry, 1995; Levine & Parkinson, 1994). Here they are:

1. *Formulating research questions* Research begins with questions. Sometimes these questions refer to previous studies, such as when a developmental psychologist asks, "Are Professor Deepthought's studies of thinking consistent with studies of thinking from less developed countries?" Other times they refer to issues important to society, such as "Does preschool education make children more socially skilled later in childhood?"

2. *Stating questions as hypotheses* A **hypothesis** is a statement that expresses a research question precisely. In making a hypothesis out of the preschool education question above, a psychologist needs to be more specific about the terms *preschool education* and *socially skilled*. Does *preschool education* mean a part-time nursery or a full-time child care center? Does *socially skilled* refer to a child who initiates activities or only to a child who smiles frequently and cooperates?

3. *Testing the hypothesis* Having phrased a research question as a hypothesis, researchers can conduct an actual study about it. As the next section describes further, they can do this in a number of ways. The choice of method usually depends on convenience, ethics, and scientific appropriateness.

4. *Interpreting and publicizing the results* After conducting the study itself, psychologists have a responsibility to report their results to others by presenting them at conferences and publishing them in journal articles. Their reports should include reasonable interpretations or conclusions based on the results and enough details to allow other psychologists to replicate (or repeat) a study themselves to test the conclusions. In practice, the limits of time (at a conference presentation) or space (in a journal) sometimes compromise this ideal.

There is a wide range of ways to carry out these steps, each with its own strengths and limitations. Viewed broadly, studies can vary in time frame, the extent of intervention and control, and the sampling strategies used. These dimensions often get combined in various ways, depending on the questions the studies are investigating. Table 1.3 summarizes the various possible methods, and the next sections explain them more fully.

Variations in Time Frame

In general, developmental psychologists can either compare people of different ages at one point in time (called a cross-sectional study) or compare the same people at

TABLE 1.3 *Methods of Studying Children and Adolescents*

Method	Purpose
Cross-sectional study	Observes children of different ages at one point in time
Longitudinal study	Observes same group(s) of children at different points in time
Naturalistic study	Observes children in naturally occurring situations or circumstances
Experimental study	Observes children where circumstances are carefully controlled
Correlational study	Observes tendency of two behaviors or qualities of a child to occur or vary together; measures this tendency statistically
Survey	Brief, structured interview or questionnaire about specific beliefs or behaviors of large numbers of persons or children
Interview	Face-to-face conversation used to gather complex information from children or adults
Case study	Investigation of just one individual or a small number of individuals using a variety of sources of information

different times as they get older (called a longitudinal study). Each method has its advantages and problems.

Cross-sectional Study   A cross-sectional study compares children of different ages at a single point in time. One such study compared preschool children (age four) and early-school-age children (age six) on their ability to distinguish between real and apparent emotions (Joshi & MacLean, 1994). Half of the children lived in India, and the other half lived in Great Britain. All of the children listened to stories in which a character sometimes had to conceal his or her true feelings (such as when an uncle gives a child a toy that the child did not really want) and described both how the character really felt as well as how the character seemed to feel. The results shed light on how children distinguish sincerity from tactfulness. The older children were more sensitive to this distinction than the younger ones, but the Indian children (especially girls) also were more sensitive to it than the British children.

Longitudinal Study   A longitudinal study observes the same subjects periodically over a relatively long period, often years. A recent example is the twenty-three-year follow-up of the effects of a demonstration preschool program for low-income children that originally took place in 1967. The four-year-old "graduates" of the program were assessed (and continue to be) every few years following the program; at the latest report, they were all twenty-seven years old (Schweinhart et al., 1993). Researchers gathered interviews, school achievement test results, and reports from teachers and (later) employers and compared them to results from an equivalent group of four-year-olds who had been identified at the time of the program but did not participate in it. The results are gratifying: the graduates have succeeded in school and employment better than the nongraduates and cost taxpayers less by needing less public aid and fewer medical and police services.

Cross-sectional and longitudinal studies both have their advantages and limitations. Cross-sectional studies can be completed more quickly, but they do not guarantee to show actual change *within* individuals. In the study of children's knowledge of emotions, for example, the fact that older children were more knowledgeable does not ensure that each *individual* child becomes more knowledgeable. It shows only an average trend for the group; in certain individuals knowledge of emotions may improve little as they get older, or even decrease, whereas other individuals may experience a huge leap in knowledge! Why these differences in individ-

Longitudinal studies are especially well suited to studying long-term constancy and change in particular individuals or groups. These brothers keep the same smiles from childhood to adolescence, but a longitudinal study might also reveal other continuities—and eventually some significant changes as well.

In much naturalistic research, psychologists observe children's behavior as it normally occurs in everyday settings. These girls' ordinary play at the park, for example, can suggest many ideas about their physical development, such as their current state of motor skill development. And it can suggest many ideas about their social development, such as whom they like to be friendly with, and who leads her peers in deciding on activities.

ual change occur remains a question—and an urgent one if you work with children as a teacher, a nurse, or a counselor.

Longitudinal studies may therefore be more truly "developmental" because they show the steps by which individuals actually change. But they too pose a practical problem: by definition, they take months or even years to complete. Over this much time, some of the original children move away; investigators may become hopelessly bogged down with other work and fail to complete the original study; or government funding to support the work may disappear prematurely. Given these problems, psychologists have organized cross-sectional studies much more often than longitudinal studies, despite the latter's special value.

Variations in Control: Naturalistic and Experimental Studies

Developmental studies also vary in how much they attempt to control the circumstances in which children are observed. When children are observed in naturally occurring settings, the studies are naturalistic; when circumstances are controlled tightly, the studies are experimental.

Naturalistic Studies   At one extreme, **naturalistic studies** purposely observe behavior as it normally occurs in natural settings, such as at home, on a playground, or in a classroom. Reed Larson and Maryse Richards (1994) used this strategy to explore the daily emotional lives of parents and their adolescent children. For several weeks, each member of the family carried an electronic pager that beeped at random intervals to remind the person to report on his or her current moods and activities by telephoning a prearranged number. In every other respect, however, the family members engaged in their normal daily activities—school, job, homemaking, or whatever. The researchers discovered many interesting facts about individuals' responses to family

Experimental studies control conditions carefully, so that only key variables are allowed to vary. In this experiment, for example, an infant sits in a quiet room and observes colorful images on TV, while psychologists observe—and later interpret—her responses to them.

life. Being at home *relieved* stress for fathers ("Then I can relax"), for example, but often *created* it for mothers ("Home is my 'second job'"). Figure 1.3 illustrates this trend. Teenage children felt far more hassled by small daily chores than their parents realized ("They don't notice it when they overdo the reminders about chores").

Experimental Studies   In contrast to naturalistic studies, experimental studies arrange circumstances so that just one or two factors or influences vary at a time. For example, Henry Wellman and Anne Hickling (1994) investigated how children understand the human mind: do they think of "the mind" as the center of a person, as adults do, or more as an impersonal switchboard, perhaps like a computer or the motor of a car? To study this question, the investigators designed an experiment in which children had to explain the meanings of metaphorical statements about the mind ("My mind wandered" or "His mind played tricks on him"). Many conditions

FIGURE 1.3

Mothers' and Fathers' Self-Rated Emotions During Various Activities
The idea of "his" marriage and "her" job contains some truth. In this naturalistic study, in which family members reported their emotions at random intervals, mothers and fathers rated a number of activities (though not all) differently.
Larson & Richards (1994).

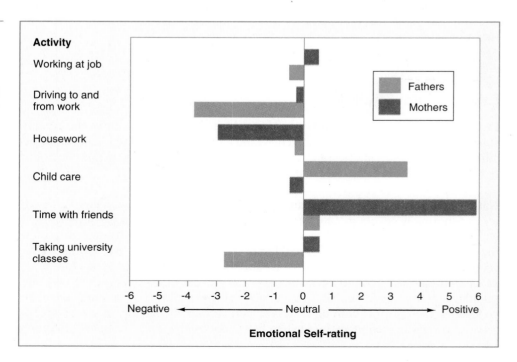

of the experiment were held constant: all children were interviewed in the same room, by the same person, and asked exactly the same questions. Children were selected from specific ages between 2½ and 10 to allow investigators to infer when the children began believing in a personified view of the mind. (The result? At 2½ children had only hazy notions of the mind as human or personified, but by age 8 most children did. Figure 1.4 depicts part of this trend.)

Because this study was an experiment, Wellman and Hickling held constant all the factors that might influence children's responses to metaphorical notions *except* age, the one they were studying. This deliberately varied factor is often called the **independent variable**. The factor that varied as a result of the independent variable—in this case, the children's success at interpreting metaphorical statements about the mind—is often called the **dependent variable**.

The experimental method also requires making decisions about the population, or group, to which the study refers. When every member of the population has an equal chance of being chosen for the study, the people selected comprise a **random sample**. If not everyone in a population has an equal chance of being chosen, the sample is said to be *biased*. Investigators can never be completely sure that they have avoided systematic bias in selecting children to study, but they can improve their chances by defining the population they are studying as carefully as possible and then selecting subjects (in this case, children) only from that population. When Wellman and Hickling studied children's beliefs about the human mind, for example, the population to which they limited their observations consisted only of children of a certain age range—2½ to 10 years—and they sampled children within this range at random. Interpretations of their results therefore apply only to this population of children. In later studies, they (or other investigators) could sample other populations, such as children of other ages or specific ethnic backgrounds.

Experimental studies incorporate a number of precautions to ensure that their findings have **validity,** meaning they measure or observe what they intend to measure. One way to improve validity is to observe not one but two sample groups, one an experimental, or treatment, group and the other a control group. The **experimental group** receives the treatment or intervention related to the purposes of the experiment. The **control group** experiences conditions that are as similar as possible to the conditions of the experimental group, but without experiencing the crucial experimental treatment. Comparing the results for the two groups helps to explicitly establish the effects of the experimental treatment.

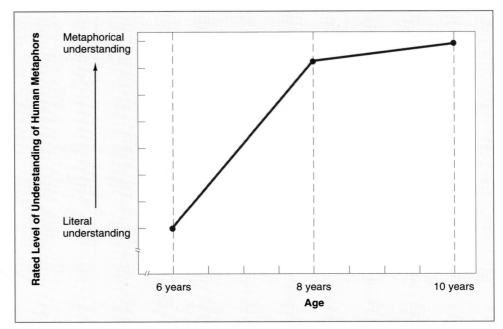

FIGURE 1.4
Children's Understanding of Human Metaphors of Mind
In this experimental study, children were asked to explain statements that contained metaphorical expressions for the human mind (e.g., "my mind fell asleep"). Results suggested that children begin understanding these expressions as metaphors sometime after their sixth birthday, but do not achieve full understanding until age ten.
Adapted from Wellman & Hickling (1994).

Comparisons of experimental and control groups are widespread in developmental research, but especially for problems involving interventions to improve the welfare of infants or children. One team of investigators used the strategy to study the impact of a program to develop literacy skills in low-income preschoolers (Whitehurst et al., 1994). The investigators used classrooms from Head Start, a nationwide early intervention program. They randomly assigned certain classrooms to an experimental group, which received the special literacy program. Other classrooms were randomly assigned to the control group, which received the usual Head Start program.

At the end of one year, they tested all classrooms in both groups for improvements in literacy skills. As you might expect, the experimental group improved more than the control group; children in the literacy program could identify more letters and their own names, for example. What is especially important is that the control group *also* improved somewhat, just by growing older; so the investigators were able to make allowances for this fact in evaluating the impact of the literacy program.

Because of its logical organization, the experimental method often gives clearer results than naturalistic studies do. But because people sometimes do not behave naturally in experimental situations, one criticism of the experimental method is that its results can be artificial. Naturalistic research does not face this particular problem, but it does run a greater risk of ambiguity in its results.

Correlations Whether naturalistic or experimental, most research studies look for correlations among variables. A **correlation** is a systematic relationship, or association, between two behaviors, responses, or human characteristics. When the behaviors, responses, or characteristics tend to change in the same direction, the relationship is called a *positive correlation;* when they tend to change in opposite directions, it is called a *negative correlation.* The ages of married spouses are a positive correlation: older husbands tend to have older wives (though not strictly so). The age of a child and the frequency of bed wetting is a negative correlation: the older the child, the less frequent the bed wetting (though again, not strictly so).

When correlated factors can be expressed numerically, psychologists use a particular statistic, the *correlation coefficient* (abbreviated *r*), to indicate the degree of relationship between two behaviors or characteristics. The correlation coefficient is calculated in such a way that its value always falls between +1.00 and −1.00. The closer to +1.00 the value, the more positive the correlation; the closer to −1.00 the value, the more negative the correlation. Correlations near 0.00 indicate no systematic relationship between behaviors or characteristics, or an essentially random relationship. For various reasons, psychologists tend to consider correlations above +0.70 or below −0.70 as strong ones and those between +0.20 and −0.20 as weak ones.

When you read or talk about correlations, it is important to remember that correlations by themselves do not indicate whether one behavior or characteristic *causes* another; they indicate only that some sort of association exists between the two. The age of one spouse, for example, does not cause the age of the other spouse to be similar; the ages are associated only numerically. Additional information is needed to determine what causes the relationship to exist. In the case of spouses' ages, the correlation may be caused by society's beliefs about appropriate ages for spouses, or by the way modern schooling is age-segregated and therefore facilitates meeting people of roughly your own age. A correlation only challenges us to consider these possible explanations; further research would be needed to determine their truth or importance.

Sampling Strategies

In addition to all the variations described so far, developmental studies vary in how many people they observe or collect information about.

Surveys   At one extreme are large-scale **surveys,** specific, focused interviews of large numbers of people. Grace Kao (1995) used this method to examine patterns of school achievement among Asian-American youth. She was particularly interested in a common stereotype of Asian youth as "model students:" the belief that they always excel academically. Using interviews with about fifteen hundred Asian-American students, parents, and teachers, as well as with about twenty-five thousand Anglo-American counterparts, Kao compared family incomes, educational levels, and ethnic backgrounds with academic achievement. She found that the stereotype of the "model student" is rather misleading. Academic success varies substantially among particular Asian ethnic groups. It also depends more heavily on how much time and money particular parents invest in education for their particular children than on the educational, financial, or ethnic backgrounds of the family as such. In these ways, the Asian-American youth were no different from their Anglo-American counterparts.

These conclusions seem especially persuasive because of the rather large sample of families on which they are based—an advantage of the survey method. But the method also has limitations. Survey questions tend to be "cut and dried" to ensure that responses can be compared among large numbers of respondents. They tend not to explore subtleties of thinking or the reasons people have for taking certain actions or holding certain beliefs. Did some of Kao's Asian-American families invest more in education because their culture encourages them to do so or because they correctly sensed the danger of discrimination due to their ethnic background and regarded education as insurance against such discrimination? To answer questions such as these, researchers need methods that invite respondents to comment more fully, such as interviews and case studies.

Interviews   A research study that seeks complex or in-depth information may use **interviews,** or face-to-face directed conversations. Because they take time, interview studies usually focus on a smaller number of individuals than surveys do, perhaps several dozen or so. Regina Campos and her colleagues (1994) used interviews to assess how well low-income children in Brazil coped with daily life on the streets. Several dozen children were interviewed both individually and in groups about their experiences, both stressful and satisfying. Some of the children spent their days on the street either working at a low-paying job or begging, and came home only at night to sleep. Others were truly homeless and slept on the streets. As you might guess, the truly homeless children generally engaged in more illegal activities and experienced more stresses (such as illness). The interview format allowed insight into the reasons for the difference: an impoverished home offered rest and refuge, provided adults who offered protection, occasional nurturance, and information useful for survival. By providing children with social ties, furthermore, a home offered children a reason to find work. Childhood employment was therefore perceived as less burdensome to the home-based street children than it was to the homeless.

Case Studies   When a study uses just one or a few individuals, it is called a **case study**. In general, a case study tries to pull together a wide variety of information and observations about the individual case and then present the information as a unified whole, emphasizing relationships among specific behaviors, thoughts, and attitudes in the individual. An example is a study by Jimenez, Garcia, and Pearson (1995) comparing the language skills and knowledge about reading of just three school-age children: one proficiently bilingual Hispanic student, one proficiently monolingual Anglo student, and one modestly bilingual Hispanic student. Each child was interviewed at length about her perceptions of her own skills with each language. Each was also invited to "think aloud" while reading samples of text in each language (that is, the child told about her thoughts as she read along). Because of the time taken with each individual, the investigators were able to discover important subtleties about how each student read. The proficient bilingual reader, for example, thought of *each* language as an aid to understanding the other language, whereas the less fluent bilingual reader believed simply that her Spanish assisted her English.

By its nature a case study can explore an aspect of child development, looking for new or unexpected connections among the child's behaviors, needs, or social relationships. This is the most common use of case studies. Second, it can confirm whether connections previously found in experimental studies actually occur in everyday, non-experimental situations, even when conditions are not carefully controlled. The second use resembles the naturalistic studies described earlier in this section.

What Do You Think?

Are some methods of child study inherently more effective than others? Try answering this question by organizing a multisided debate. Pick a successful developmental study (you can use any of the ones described in this chapter, for example), and assign each of three or four debating teams to design and argue the merits of some *alternative* method of studying the same question. In a second round of the debate, each team can try to refute the arguments of any of the other teams. Remember: there will be more than two sides to this discussion!

ETHICAL CONSTRAINTS ON STUDYING DEVELOPMENT

Sometimes ethical concerns influence the methods that can be used to study a particular question about development. Take the question of punishment: what kinds of punishment work best with children, and for what reasons? For ethical reasons, we may be unable to study certain aspects of this problem directly. Observing parents actually scolding and reprimanding their children would require delicacy at best. At worst, if the punishment became severe or physical, ethics might require our active intervention simply to protect the child from abuse.

For ethically sensitive questions, we may instead have to satisfy ourselves with less direct but more acceptable methods of study. We can interview a variety of parents about the methods of punishment they use, or we can ask experts who work directly with families what methods they think parents typically use. A few courageous families might allow us to observe their daily activities, with the understanding that we are interested in observing how they punish their children. But by being volunteers, these few families may not represent other families very well.

Generally, research about human beings faces at least three ethical issues: confidentiality, full disclosure of purposes, and respect for the individual's freedom to participate (American Psychological Association, 1992). In developmental psychology, all of these issues are complicated by the youthfulness of the subjects and by their parents' responsibilities for them.

1. *Confidentiality* If researchers collect information that might damage individuals' reputations or self-esteem, they should take care to protect the identities of the participants. Observing parents' methods of punishment might require this sort of confidentiality. Parents may not want just anyone knowing how much and how often they experience conflicts with their children. Chances are that the children would not want this information made public either. In such cases, investigators should not divulge the identities of participating families without their consent, either during the conduct of the study or afterward when the results are published.

2. *Full disclosure of purposes* Parents (and their children) are entitled to know the true purposes of any research study in which they participate. Most of the time, investigators understand and follow this principle carefully. But at times it can be tempting to mislead participants. In studying parents' punishment techniques, researchers might suspect that stating this purpose honestly will cause certain families to avoid participation, especially those with the most discipline

problems. Or investigators might suspect that telling families the truth about the study will make them distort their behavior, perhaps making them self-consciously hide their worst conflicts. According to this argument, therefore, intentional misleading of parents would produce more complete observations of conflicts and parental punishment techniques. In this sense, dishonesty might make the research more "scientific." But investigators would purchase this benefit at the cost of their long-run reputations with the participants. Purposeful deception may sometimes be permissible, but only when no other method is possible and when participants are fully informed after the study of the deception and its reasons.

3. *Respect for individual's freedom to participate* As much as possible, research studies should avoid pressuring parents or children to participate. This may not be as simple as it first appears. Because psychologists have a relatively high status in society, some parents may be reluctant to decline an invitation from them to participate in "scientific research." Investigators therefore may have to bend over backward to assure parents that participation is indeed voluntary. They cannot simply assume parents or children will automatically feel free to decline if approached. After all, what parent wants to interfere with the progress of science?

When all three principles are closely followed, they allow for what psychologists call **informed consent:** the people or groups being studied understand the nature of the research, believe their rights are being protected, and feel free to either volunteer or refuse to participate. Informed consent therefore forms a standard, or ideal, for research to aim for and one that most studies do in fact approximate.

As the preceding discussion indicates, however, a completely informed consent may prove difficult to achieve in some cases. This is especially so for research about children, who tend to be dependent on the goodwill and wisdom of parents and other adults, including researchers. In studying children, investigators may sometimes wonder whether their participants can fully understand the purposes of a study, even when those purposes are explained. How well can children really understand why investigators want to observe conflicts between them and their parents? Even if such a goal makes sense to children, can they really feel free to participate or to decline? Or will children usually think they must cooperate with whatever adult investigators request? If the children are very young, perhaps parents can decide on their behalf, but when do children become mature enough to be consulted directly?

As these questions imply, the developmental level of the child should influence the way investigators resolve ethical issues in studying children (Thompson, 1990). As a rule, younger children understand the purposes of a research project less well than do older children, making it less crucial that the younger ones themselves be thoroughly informed but more important that the parents be informed. Younger children also are more vulnerable to stressful research procedures, such as experimentation with the effects of personal criticism on the child. Older children, on the other hand, are more prone to self-consciousness and are more likely to detect implied personal criticisms. Thus, investigators need to be more careful in studying problems that might shame a child publicly (such as by asking, "How often do you cry?" or "What problems have you had because your parents are divorced?").

Wherever possible, the right to decide about whether to participate in a research study rests with the child, provided the child understands the nature of the study and feels truly free to decline participation. When these conditions hold only partially, such as with young children, parents share the ultimate right to decide with the child. When the conditions do not hold at all, such as with infants, parents essentially take over the right to decide about participation.

However, these guidelines do not relieve research investigators of responsibility for the child's decision to participate, particularly when the child is young. Investigators must still follow a principle called **in loco parentis,** a Latin phrase meaning "in place of parents." The principle of in loco parentis requires investigators to act at all times in the best interests of the children being studied, much as the children's parents do in everyday affairs (Steininger et al., 1984). This means not only respecting parents' and children's decisions about participating but also looking after the children's welfare once a study is under way. If a study of children's games led (accidentally) to aggression or hurt feelings, in loco parentis would require the investigator to do whatever the parents might do to remedy the problem, including stopping the games.

What Do You Think?

Why do you think ethics has become a bigger concern for developmental research in the past two decades? Brainstorm as many ideas about this as you can: have children changed, or research projects, or the conditions of modern life, or . . . ?

STRENGTHS AND LIMITATIONS OF DEVELOPMENTAL KNOWLEDGE

As this chapter has demonstrated, human development has to be studied in particular ways and with certain limitations in mind. Because time is a major dimension of development, its impact must be approached thoughtfully. Yet the very nature of time poses real problems for studying at least some major questions. Sometimes people "take too long" to develop within the time frame available to study them. Also, because developmental psychologists deal with people, they must treat their subjects with respect and abide by the usual standards of decency and consideration for human needs. Finally, because they deal with especially young people, developmental psychologists sometimes must take extra care to determine the true best interests of their subjects, even when those subjects do not know what they are being asked to do or do not feel free to refuse even when they do know.

Lest these limitations sound overly discouraging, be assured that in spite of them, developmental psychologists have accumulated considerable knowledge of children and adolescents in recent decades and continue to do so. The remaining chapters of this book should make that point amply clear. Developmental psychology does not have definitive answers for some important questions about human nature, but it *does* have the answers for a good many others.

SUMMARY OF MAJOR IDEAS

The Nature of Developmental Change

1. Developmental psychology concerns how thoughts, feelings, personality, social relationships, and motor skills evolve as individuals get older.

2. Development occurs in three major domains: physical, cognitive, and psychosocial.

3. The domains of development interact in many ways, and individuals always develop as whole persons rather than in separate parts.

Why Study Development?

4. Studying development can help give you appropriate expectations about the behavior of children and adolescents.

5. A knowledge of development can help you respond appropriately to children's actual behavior.

6. A knowledge of development can help you recognize when unusual behaviors are cause for concern.

7. Studying development can give you self-knowledge and understanding of your past.

The History of Developmental Study

8. Until just a few hundred years ago, childhood and adolescence were not regarded as distinct periods of life.

9. Societal changes in the eighteenth century led to awareness of children's unique needs.

10. In the nineteenth and twentieth centuries, the first research studies of children consisted of baby biographies and structured observations of children at specific ages.

Basic Issues in Developmental Study

11. In general, developmental psychology focuses on four major issues: the impact of nature and nurture, the extent of continuity and discontinuity in development, the universality of development, and the problem of deficit and difference in development.

Methods of Studying Children and Adolescents

12. Research about developmental psychology tries to follow the scientific method: formulating research questions, stating them as hypotheses, testing the hypotheses, and interpreting and publicizing the results.

13. Studies vary in the time frame (cross-sectional or longitudinal), in control of the context (naturalistic or experimental), and in sampling strategies used (surveys, interviews, or case studies).

14. Cross-sectional studies compare individuals of different ages at one point in time.

15. Longitudinal studies observe human change directly by following the same children over relatively long periods of time.

16. Naturalistic methods observe children in natural contexts as much as possible.

17. Experimental methods try to control or hold constant extraneous conditions while varying only one or two specified variables.

18. Surveys, interviews, and case studies each sample different numbers of people, and each has unique advantages and problems.

Ethical Constraints on Studying Development

19. Ethical considerations guide how development can be studied and sometimes rule out certain studies altogether.

20. Generally, developmental studies should be guided by the principles of confidentiality, full disclosure of purposes, and respect for the individual's freedom to participate.

21. Research about children should strive for informed consent from children and their parents.

22. The specific ethical concerns in studying development depend on the age or developmental level of the children being studied as well as on the content of the study itself.

23. Even after a study has begun, researchers should follow the principle of in loco parentis, acting according to the best interests of the child.

KEY TERMS

development *(3)*	nature *(13)*
domain *(4)*	nurture *(13)*
physical development *(4)*	scientific method *(16)*
cognitive development *(5)*	hypothesis *(17)*
	cross-sectional study *(17)*
psychosocial development *(5)*	longitudinal study *(18)*
	naturalistic study *(19)*
norms *(12)*	experimental study *(20)*
independent variable *(21)*	correlation *(22)*
dependent variable *(21)*	survey *(23)*
random sample *(21)*	interview *(23)*
validity *(21)*	case study *(23)*
experimental group *(21)*	informed consent *(25)*
control group *(21)*	in loco parentis *(25)*

FOR FURTHER READING

Ariès, P. *Centuries of Childhood: A Social History of Family Life,* trans. Robert Baldick. New York: Vintage Books, 1962.

Somerville, J. *The Rise and Fall of Childhood.* 2nd ed. New York: Vintage Books, 1990.

A fascinating body of literature exists about the history of childhood as a concept and an institution; here are two prominent ones. The book by Ariès argues that until the Industrial Revolution, children were regarded as miniature adults and parents therefore felt little special attachment to them. The more recent book by Somerville qualifies this idea somewhat, showing evidence that parents often did care about their own children and that modern parents in any case often think of their children as economic assets, much as they did in the Middle Ages.

Bronfenbrenner, U. *The Ecology of Human Development: Experiments by Nature and by Design.* Cambridge, Mass.: Harvard University Press, 1979.

This book presents one of the clearest and most thorough arguments for the importance of social context in human development. The author describes many psychological studies that can make sense only if the circumstances surrounding the studies are taken fully into account. He also argues that psychological research can progress only if it uses *both* naturalistic and experimental methods.

Elkind, D. *Ties That Stress: The New Family Imbalance.* Cambridge, Mass.: Harvard University Press, 1994.

Larson, Reed, and Maryse Richards. *Divergent Realities: The Emotional Lives of Fathers, Mothers, and Adolescents.* New York: Free Press, 1994.

Each of these books describes the current realities faced by parents and professionals who care about the welfare of children in today's society. Life is not always easy for parents or their children, but it can also be satisfying at unexpected times and places.

Grodin, M., and L. Glantz, eds. *Children as Research Subjects: Science, Ethics and Law.* New York: Oxford University Press, 1994.

Society for Research on Child Development. "Ethical Guidelines for Working with Children." In *Newsletter of the Society for Research on Child Development,* 1990, pp. 3–7.

The ethics of doing research on children, including your own projects for courses, has become a major concern in developmental psychology. The book by Grodin and Glantz discusses the dilemmas of research on children in detail, though with some bias toward medically related studies. The guidelines published by the Society for Research on Child Development provide the most authoritative statement for developmental psychology, but without the thoroughness of the Glodin and Glantz book.

2

Theories of Development

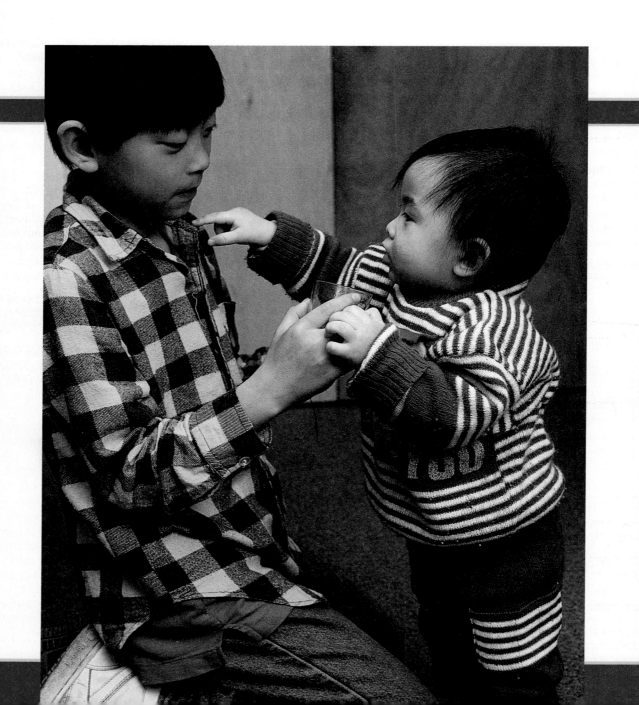

The Nature of Developmental Theories

What Is a Developmental Theory?
How Developmental Theories Differ:
    Four Developmental Themes

Psychodynamic Developmental Theories

Freudian Theory
Erikson's Psychosocial Theory
Other Psychodynamic Approaches
Evaluation of Developmental Themes in
    Psychodynamic Approaches

Behavioral Learning and Social Cognitive Learning Developmental Theories

Behavioral Learning Theories
Social Cognitive Learning Theory
Evaluation of Developmental Themes in
    Behavioral and Social Cognitive Learning
    Approaches

Cognitive Developmental Theories

Piaget's Cognitive Theory
Neo-Piagetian Approaches
Information-Processing Theory
Evaluation of Developmental Themes in
    Cognitive Approaches

Contextual Developmental Theories

Ethological Theory
Evaluation of Developmental Themes in
    Contextual Approaches

Developmental Theories Compared: Implications for the Student

Focusing Questions

- What are developmental theories? How are they useful?

- How have psychodynamic theories such as Freud's and Erikson's influenced thinking about development?

- How have developmental theories based on learning principles contributed to our understanding of developmental change?

- How does Piaget's theory of cognitive development help us understand changes in our capacity to think and solve problems from childhood through adolescence?

- How have contextual approaches to development broadened our view of developmental change?

- Given the variety of developmental theories, how do you decide which theory or combination of theories is best for you?

 hen Elizabeth, age three, began nursery school, she cried and screamed every day when her mother left her. "Home!" and "Mama!" were the only words she seemed able to produce between sobs, which continued for much of each morning. *Her* concerned teachers met to discuss what to do about Elizabeth.

"It's best to ignore the crying," said one teacher. "If you give her lots of special attention because of it, you will reinforce the crying, and she'll just keep going longer."

"But we can't just ignore a crying child," said another. "This is a new and strange situation, and her crying shows that she's feeling insecure and abandoned. Look at her! She needs comfort and emotional support so that she can feel safer and more secure. At least give her a hug!"

"I think she's unsure whether her mother really will come back for her," said a third teacher. "Maybe we can find ways to help her understand and remember our daily routine here."

The teachers decided to follow all of this advice. They agreed not to fuss too much over Elizabeth's tears and to give her lots of comfort and support when she was not crying. They also helped Elizabeth draw a picture chart of the daily schedule and tape it to her cubbyhole. Finally, they talked with her mother about what they had observed and the solutions they were trying.

How well did it work? Elizabeth stopped crying—more quickly, in fact, than any of the teachers had expected. Although all three teachers agreed that Elizabeth clearly was happier and more at ease, no one was sure exactly how or why the change had come about.

THE NATURE OF DEVELOPMENTAL THEORIES

Each of Elizabeth's teachers' approaches reflects a different set of ideas and beliefs about children and their development. Whether they know it or not, most people—teachers, parents, students, and even children themselves—are guided by "informal theories" of human development.

What Do You Think?

In reading about Elizabeth, did you find yourself agreeing in particular with one of the teacher's comments? If so, you probably share that teacher's informal theoretical orientation. It might be interesting to compare your informal theory with those of several classmates.

What Is a Developmental Theory?

As we point out in Chapter 1, *human development* refers to long-term changes that occur during a person's lifetime and the patterns of those changes. Theories are useful because they help us organize and make sense of large amounts of sometimes conflicting information about children's development, a task that at times can be complicated and confusing. For example, how do we decide whether day care is good for children and, if so, what type of day care is developmentally best? For that matter, how do we make developmental sense of different approaches to parenting and family life or education? In contrast to informal theories, the more formal developmental theories we are about to discuss attempt to provide clear, logical, and systematic frameworks for describing and understanding the events and experiences that make up developmental change and discovering the principles and mechanisms that underlie the process of change.

What qualities should a good theory ideally have? First, a theory should be *internally consistent,* meaning its different parts fit together in a logical way. Second, a theory should *provide meaningful explanations* of the actual developmental changes we are interested in, be they changes in children's thinking with age or the long-range effects of divorce on their social adjustment. Third, a theory should be *open to scientific evaluation* so that it can be revised or discarded if new or conflicting evidence appears or if a better theory is proposed. Fourth, a theory should *stimulate new thinking and research.* Finally, a theory should *provide guidance* to parents and professionals in their day-to-day work with children and adolescents.

Many motor skills, such as jumping rope or riding a bike, develop in predictable sequences or stages.

How Developmental Theories Differ: Four Developmental Themes

Developmental theories differ in some important ways. In this chapter, we will look at how each theory deals with the following four themes: (1) *the role of maturation versus experience,* (2) *children's active versus passive participation in their development,* (3) *the role of developmental stages,* and (4) *breadth of focus.*

Role of Maturation versus Experience   Theories differ in the importance they assign to maturation and experience as causes of developmental change. *Maturation* refers to developmental changes that seem to be biologically determined because they occur in all infants and children relatively independently of their particular experiences. Examples of changes due to maturation include growth in height and weight and increases in the muscle coordination involved in sitting up, walking, and running. Examples of changes due to experience include increasing skill in playing baseball, basketball, or tennis, which clearly seems to be due mostly to formal and informal learning.

But for many developmental changes, the relative contributions of maturation and experience are less clear. Talking is a good example. To what degree do all children learn to talk regardless of their particular learning experiences? How much does their talking depend on their particular experiences in the family, community, and culture in which they grow up?

The Active Versus Passive Role of the Child   Developmental theories also differ in their view of how actively children contribute to their own development. For instance, behavioral learning theorists believe developmental change is caused by events in the environment that stimulate individuals to respond, resulting in the learned changes in behavior that make up development. Theorists who are interested in how thinking and problem-solving abilities develop, such as Jean Piaget, propose that such changes depend on the child's active efforts to master new intellectual problems of increasing difficulty. Likewise, Erik Erikson's theory of identity development proposes that a child's personality and sense of identity are strongly influenced by his or her active efforts to master the psychological and social conflicts of everyday life (Hall & Lindzey, 1978; Miller, 1993).

The Role of Stages   Developmental theories also differ in whether they propose that development is made up of a series of small, continuous changes or distinct, stagelike steps. Theorists such as Erik Erikson and Jean Piaget assume that developmental change occurs in distinct stages. All individuals follow the same sequence, or order. Each successive stage is qualitatively unique from all other stages, is increasingly complex, and integrates the developmental changes and accomplishments of earlier stages.

Erikson's theory, for example, assumes that an infant must first master the crisis of *trust versus mistrust;* that is, she must come to trust her caregiver's ability to meet her needs. Only then can she move on to tackle the crisis that defines the next stage: *autonomy versus shame and doubt. Autonomy* refers to a child's capacity to be independent and self-directed in her activities. These and other stages of development proposed by Erikson are discussed later in the chapter.

Learning theories, on the other hand, see development as a relatively smooth and continuous process. The development of trust and autonomy, or of more sophisticated thinking and problem-solving skills, is thought to occur through the many, many small changes that unfold as a child interacts with his environment.

Still other theories, such as that of Robbie Case, take a more balanced view. They see developmental change as a sequence of more rounded, overlapping slopes rather than as one continuous incline or a series of sharply defined stages. Figure 2.1 illustrates these three views about the shape of developmental change.

Breadth of Focus   Finally, developmental theories differ in how broadly (or narrowly) they define the range of factors and circumstances that may influence development, in how many areas of developmental change they seek to explain, and in the number of specific developmental processes and mechanisms they propose. For example, Uri Bronfenbrenner's *ecological systems theory* emphasizes the broad range of situations and contexts in which development occurs. These include the child's direct and indirect experiences with family, school, work, and culture, all of

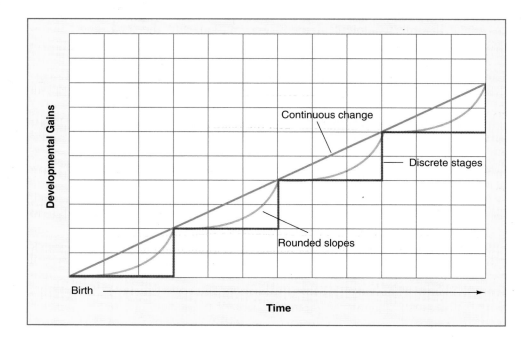

FIGURE 2.1
The Shape of Developmental Change

which act together to create developmental change. However, these theories say little about the specific processes or mechanisms involved. On the other hand, *social learning theories* explain just a few specific issues, such as the development of gender roles and aggression, but describe several mechanisms—in this case, types of learning—that are involved.

What Do You Think?

Does developmental change occur in stages, or is it a continuous process? How might different answers to this question affect how parents raise their children? How might they affect how teachers educate their students?

PSYCHODYNAMIC DEVELOPMENTAL THEORIES

Psychodynamic theorists believe development is an active, dynamic process that is influenced by both a person's inborn, biological drives and his or her conscious and unconscious social and emotional experiences. According to Sigmund Freud, a child's development is thought to occur in a series of stages. At each stage, the child experiences unconscious conflicts that he must resolve to some degree before going on to the next stage. Other influential psychodynamic approaches, such as those of Erik Erikson and object relations theorists, place less emphasis on biological drives and unconscious conflict. These theorists focus more on the development of a sense of identity as a result of important social, emotional, and cultural experiences.

Freudian Theory

Sigmund Freud and his daughter Anna, who became a psychoanalyst herself and whose work with young children has been influential.

Sigmund Freud (1856–1939) was the creator of *psychoanalysis,* the approach to understanding and treating psychological problems on which psychodynamic theory is based. Much of Freud's formal theory is outdated. However, his ideas continue to influence our understanding of personality development, including such areas as early infant-caregiver attachment, diagnosis and treatment of childhood emotional disorders, adolescent identity formation, and the long-range consequences of divorce.

The Three-Part Structure of Personality   Freud described each individual's personality as consisting of three hypothetical, or imaginary, mental structures: the id, the ego, and the superego.

The **id,** which is present at birth, is unconscious. It impulsively tries to satisfy a person's inborn biological needs and desires by motivating behaviors that maximize pleasure and avoid discomfort with no regard for the realities involved. In this view, the newborn infant is all id, crying for food and comfort but having no idea of how to get them because he cannot distinguish between wishful fantasy and reality.

The **ego** is the largely rational, conscious, problem-solving part of the personality. It is closely related to a person's sense of self. The ego functions according to the *reality principle,* a process by which the infant learns to delay her desire for instant satisfaction and redirect it into more realistic and appropriate ways of meeting her needs. This involves a shift of psychological energy from fantasy to the real parents and other caregivers who can in fact meet the infant's needs. Thus, a hungry infant shifts from imagining that the wish for food will satisfy her hunger to a more realistic focus on anticipating the appearance of her parent or other caregiver, who will feed her. An infant's developing ego, or sense of self, is based on her internalized mental images of her relationships with these caregivers.

③ The **superego** is the moral and ethical component of the personality. It develops at the end of early childhood. The superego includes the child's emerging sense of *conscience,* or right and wrong, as well as the *ego-ideal,* an idealized sense of how he should behave. The superego acts as an internalized, all-knowing parent. It punishes the child for unacceptable sexual or aggressive thoughts, feelings, and actions with guilt and rewards him for fulfillment of parental standards with heightened self-esteem. The superego can sometimes be overly moralistic and unreasonable, but it provides the child with standards by which to regulate his moral conduct and take pride in his accomplishments.

Stages of Psychosexual Development   Freud believed development occurs through a series of *psychosexual* stages. Each stage focuses on a different area of the body that is a source of excitation and pleasure. At each stage, developmental changes result from conflicts among the id, ego, and superego. These conflicts can threaten the child's ego, or sense of self. Pressures from the id push the child to act impulsively to achieve immediate pleasure; pressures from the ego encourage her to act more realistically by delaying satisfaction until it can be attained; and pressures from the superego push her to meet standards of moral behavior and achievement that may be overly strict or unrealistically high. Freud's psychosexual stages and the developmental processes that occur are summarized in Table 2.1.

The ego uses defense mechanisms to protect itself from such conflicts. *Defense mechanisms* are unconscious distortions of reality that keep conflicts from the ego's (self's) conscious awareness. One such defense mechanism is *repression,* in which unacceptable feelings and impulses are forced from memory and forgotten. Another is *projection,* in which a person's conflict-producing feelings, such as feelings of aggression, are mistakenly attributed to another person.

According to Freud, unresolved id-ego and superego-ego conflicts can lead to a *fixation,* or a blockage in development. Fixation can also result from parenting that is not appropriately responsive to a child's needs. For example, overindulgence during the oral stage (see Table 2.1) may result in excessive dependence on others later in life. On the other hand, infants who experience severe deprivation and frustration of their needs may later feel they have to exploit or manipulate others to meet their needs. In this view, an individual's personality traits reflect the patterns typical of the stage at which a fixation occurred.

TABLE 2.1   *Freud's Psychosexual Stages and Developmental Processes*

Psychosexual Stage	Approximate Age	Description
Oral	Birth–1 year	The mouth is the focus of stimulation and interaction; feeding and weaning are central.
Anal	1–3 years	The anus is the focus of stimulation and interaction; elimination and toilet training are central.
Phallic	3–6 years	The genitals (penis, clitoris, and vagina) are the focus of stimulation; gender role and moral development are central.
Latency	6–12 years	A period of suspended sexual activity; energies shift to physical and intellectual activities.
Genital	12–adulthood	The genitals are the focus of stimulation with the onset of puberty; mature sexual relationships develop.

Developmental Processes

Development occurs through a series of psychosexual stages. In each stage the child focuses on a different area of her body, and how she invests her libido (sexual energy) in relationships with people and things reflects the concerns of the stage she is in. New areas of unconscious conflict among the id, ego, and superego, the three structures of personality, also occur. Conflicting pressures from the id to impulsively achieve pleasure, from the ego to act realistically by delaying gratification, and from the superego to fulfill moralistic obligations and to achieve idealistic standards all threaten the ego. The ego protects itself by means of unconscious defense mechanisms, which keep these conflicts from awareness by distorting reality.

Erikson's Psychosocial Theory

Erik Erikson (1902–1994) grew up in Europe. He studied psychoanalysis with Freud's daughter, Anna, who strongly influenced his ideas about personality development. The accompanying Perspectives box describes the relationship between Erikson's life and his theory.

In Erikson's view, personality development is a *psychosocial* process, meaning internal psychological factors and external social factors are both very important. Developmental changes occur throughout a person's lifetime and are influenced by three interrelated forces: (1) the individual's biological and physical strengths and limitations; (2) the person's unique life circumstances and developmental history, including early family experiences and degree of success in resolving earlier developmental crises; and (3) the particular social, cultural, and historical forces at work during the individual's lifetime (for example, racial prejudice, poverty, rapid technological change, or war).

Psychosocial Stages of Development   Erikson proposed that development occurs in a series of eight stages, beginning with infancy and ending with old age. Each stage is named for the particular *psychosocial crisis,* or challenge, that every child must resolve to be able to move on to the next. Successful mastery of the psychosocial crisis at a particular stage results in a personality strength, or *virtue,* that will help the individual meet future developmental challenges (Miller, 1993). Table 2.2 summarizes Erikson's stages and developmental processes.

Perspectives

Erik Erikson's Identity Crisis: An Autobiographical Perspective

How do theorists' own life experiences influence their theories of development? Here is what Erik Erikson has written about his own identity crises and how they influenced his developmental theory.

Erik Erikson was born in 1902 and died in 1994. He grew up in southern Germany with his mother, who was Danish, and her husband, a German pediatrician. Erikson recalls that "all through my earlier childhood, they kept secret from me the fact that my mother had been married previously; and that I was the son of a Dane who had abandoned her before my birth" (E. Erikson, 1975, p. 27).

As Erikson entered puberty and adolescence, identity conflicts intensified. "My stepfather was the only professional man in an intensely Jewish small bourgeois family, while I . . . was blond and blue-eyed, and grew flagrantly tall. Before long, then, I was referred to as a 'goy' [outsider] in my stepfather's temple, while to my schoolmates I was a 'Jew.' . . . Although during World War I, I tried desperately to be a good German chauvinist, [I] soon became a 'Dane' when Denmark remained neutral" (pp. 27, 28).

During this period, Erikson decided he would be an artist and a writer, rejecting his family's more middle-class values and expectations. He spent most of his time traveling, painting, writing, occasionally taking art classes, and teaching art. In looking back at these years,

Erikson said that he now considered them to be an important part of his training (pp. 25, 26).

In fact, it was not until Erikson was almost thirty and moved to Austria that his career as a psychoanalyst and developmental theorist really began. His training in psychoanalysis was conducted by Anna Freud, who accepted him as a student after observing his work with children as a teacher in a small private school. After studying and practicing psychoanalysis in Vienna, Erikson was forced to leave Austria by the rise of Hitler. He emigrated to the United States, where he lived and worked the rest of his life.

Erikson achieved his outstanding accomplishments as a teacher, scholar, and therapist without the benefit of even a college degree, much less any other professional credentials. In the 1930s, Erikson worked as a psychoanalyst with children and debated whether to return to school for a professional degree. Instead, he accepted a research appointment at Yale Medical School and the Yale Institute of Human Relations, where he worked with an interdisciplinary team of psychologists, psychiatrists, and anthropologists and conducted field studies of the Sioux Indians in South Dakota.

In the 1940s, Erikson moved to California to study the life histories of children living in Berkeley and then the lives of the Yurok Indians. He joined the faculty of the University of California at Berkeley in the early 1950s,

TABLE 2.2 Erikson's Psychosocial Stages and Develolpmental Processes

Psychosocial Stage	Approximate Age	Description
Trust versus mistrust	Birth–1 year	Focus on oral-sensory activity; development of trusting relationships with caregivers and of self-trust (hope)
Autonomy versus shame and doubt	1–3 years	Focus on muscular-anal activity; development of control over bodily functions and activities (will)
Initiative versus guilt	3–6 years	Focus on locomotor-genital activity; testing limits of self-assertion and purposefulness (purpose)
Industry versus inferiority	6–12 years (latency period)	Focus on mastery, competence, and productivity (competence)
Identity versus role confusion	12–19 years (adolescence)	Focus on formation of identity and coherent self-concept (fidelity)
Intimacy versus isolation	19–25 years (early adulthood)	Focus on achievement of an intimate relationship and career direction (love)
Generativity versus stagnation	25–50 years (adulthood)	Focus on fulfillment through creative, productive activity that contributes to future generations (care)
Ego integrity versus despair	50 and older	Focus on belief in integrity of life, including successes and failures (wisdom)

Developmental Processes

Development of the ego, or sense of identity, occurs through a series of stages, each building on the preceding stages and focused on successfully resolving a new psychosocial crisis between two opposing ego qualities. No stage is fully resolved, and more favorable resolution at an earlier stage facilitates achievement of later stages.

but was soon fired because he refused to sign a "loyalty oath," part of the fanatical anticommunist crusade of Senator Joe McCarthy. Erikson was reinstated as politically dependable, but resigned in support of others who were not rehired. Erikson says of this experience, "As I think back on that controversy now, it was a test of our American identity; for when the papers told us foreign-born among the nonsigners to 'go back where we came from,' we suddenly felt quite certain that our apparent disloyalty to the soldiers in Korea was, in fact, quite in line with what they were said to be fighting for. The United States Supreme Court has since confirmed our point of view" (pp. 42–43).

Erikson continues, "It would seem almost self-evident now how the concepts of 'identity' and 'identity crisis' emerged from my personal, clinical, and anthropological observations in the thirties and forties. I do not remember when I started to use these terms; they seemed naturally grounded in the experience of emigration, immigration, and Americanization. . . . I will not describe the pathological side of my identity confusion, which included disturbances for which psychoanalysis seemed, indeed, the treatment of choice. . . . No doubt, my best friends will insist that I needed to name this crisis and to see it in everybody else in order to really come to terms with it in myself" (pp. 26, 43).

Using Freud's theory as a starting point, Erik Erikson expanded it to cover the life span and modified the stages to place more emphasis on social encounters.

Psychodynamic theories focus on the early emotional experiences of the child. Babies certainly show emotion, but critics question Freud's theory of early emotional development.

Stage 1: trust versus mistrust. The earliest basic trust is indicated by the infant's capacity to sleep, eat, and excrete in a comfortable and relaxed way. Parents who reliably ensure daily routines and are responsive to their infant's needs provide the basis for a trusting view of the world. The proper ratio, or balance, between trust and mistrust leads to the development of hope. *Hope* is the enduring belief that one's wishes are attainable despite the many irrational impulses an infant experiences at birth. Failure to develop such trust may seriously interfere with a child's sense of security and compromise her ability to successfully master the challenges of the stages that follow.

Stage 2: autonomy versus shame and doubt. As mentioned earlier, *autonomy* refers to a child's capacity to be independent and self-directed in his activities. It also reflects his ability to balance his own demands for self-control with demands for control from his parents and others (Hall & Lindzey, 1978). *Shame* involves a loss of self-respect due to a failure to meet one's own standards (Lewis, 1992). During toilet training, for example, a child will sometimes have accidents. A child who is treated with firmness, reassurance, and respect for her failures as well as for her successes eventually will achieve autonomy (independence and self-direction) in this area. A child who is consistently shamed may have difficulty developing confidence in his ability to express himself freely and to self-regulate his thoughts, feelings, and behaviors. A successful outcome for this stage is the virtue of will. *Will* refers to the capacity to freely make choices based on realistic knowledge of what is expected and what is possible.

Stage 3: initiative versus guilt. During this stage, the child focuses on her genitals as a source of pleasure and on achieving greater mastery and responsibility. *Initiative* combines autonomy with the ability to explore new activities and ideas and to purposefully pursue and achieve tasks and goals. *Guilt* involves self-criticism due to failure to fulfill parental expectations. This crisis often involves situations in which the child takes on more than he can physically or emotionally handle, including the powerful sexual and aggressive feelings children often act out in their play.

If a child's conflicting feelings of love and hate and conflicting impulses to be independent and dependent are ignored, belittled, or ridiculed, destructive feelings of guilt can result. If a child is treated respectfully and helped to formulate and pursue her goals without feeling guilty, she will develop the virtue of *purpose* in her life.

Stage 4: industry versus inferiority. This stage runs roughly from ages six to twelve. As a child leaves the protection of his family and enters the world of school, he must come to believe in his ability to learn the basic intellectual and social skills required to be a full and productive member of society and to start and complete tasks successfully. The virtue of *competence* is the result. A failure to feel competent can lead to a sense of inferiority. The child who consistently fails in school is in danger of feeling alienated from society or of thoughtlessly conforming to gain acceptance from others.

Stage 5: identity versus role confusion. This stage coincides with the physical changes of *puberty* and the psychosocial changes of adolescence. A successful resolution of this crisis is the development of the virtue of *fidelity,* the ability to sustain loyalties to certain values despite inevitable conflicts and inconsistencies. *Identity* involves a reliable, integrated sense of who one is based on the many different roles one plays. *Role confusion* refers to a failure to achieve this integration of roles. During this stage, teenagers undergo reevaluation of who they are in many areas of identity development, including the physical, sexual, intellectual, religious, and career areas. Frequently conflicts from earlier stages resurface.

As we will see in Chapter 16, modern industrial society makes it difficult for teenagers to establish identities that meet both their own needs for independence and individuality and society's expectations. Children who lack the family support and adult role models they need may fail to successfully resolve this crisis. Three potentially destructive outcomes of this crisis are premature choice of identity, prolonged identity and role confusion, and choice of a permanently "negative" identity that may be associated with delinquent and antisocial behavior.

Erikson's final three stages occur after adolescence.

Stage 6: intimacy versus isolation. Successful resolution of this stage results in the virtue of being able to experience *love.* The young adult must develop the ability to establish close, committed relationships with others and cope with the fear of losing her own identity and separate sense of self that such intense intimacy raises.

Stage 7: generativity versus stagnation. This stage occurs during adulthood and midlife. Successful resolution brings the virtue of *care,* or concern for others. *Generativity* is the feeling that one's work, family life, and other activities are both personally satisfying and socially meaningful in ways that contribute to future generations. *Stagnation* results when life no longer seems purposeful.

Stage 8: ego integrity versus despair. This stage occurs during later adulthood and old age. Successful resolution brings the virtue of *wisdom. Ego integrity* refers to the ability to look back on the strengths and weaknesses of one's life with a sense of dignity, optimism, and wisdom. It is in conflict with the despair resulting from health problems, economic difficulties, social isolation, and lack of meaningful work experienced by many elderly persons in our society.

According to Erikson, psychosocial conflicts are never fully resolved. Depending on his or her life experiences, each individual achieves a more or less favorable ratio of trust to mistrust, industry to inferiority, ego integrity to despair, and so on. Therefore, conflicts from earlier stages may continue to affect later development.

Other Psychodynamic Approaches

A number of psychodynamic theorists have sought to extend Freud's basic insights about the importance of a child's object relations. **Object relations** refer to the child's relationships with the important people (called *objects*) in his environment and the process by which their qualities become part of his personality and mental life. Object relations theorists such as Margaret Mahler, Daniel Stern, and Heinz Kohut study how children internalize the images, memories, and values of people who are important to them and with whom they have strong emotional attachments (Barlow & Durand, 1995).

Object relations theorists have largely rejected Freud's idea that all developmental change is based on the satisfaction of primary inborn, biological drives such

According to Erikson, during the school years youngsters devote a great deal of time and energy to achieving new physical and social skills and to mastering the developmental crisis of industry versus inferiority.

TABLE 2.3   Mahler's Phases of Development

Phase	Approximate Age	Description
Autistic phase	0–2 months	Safe, sleeplike transition into the world
Symbiotic phase	2–6 months	Development of an emotionally charged mental image of the primary caregiver
Separation-individuation phase	6–24 months	Functions as a separate individual
Hatching subphase	6–10 months	Responds differently to primary caregivers versus others
Practicing subphase	10–16 months	Safe separation and disengagement
Rapprochement subphase	16–24 months	Experiments more fully with leaving and returning to the safe home base of the caregiver
Object constancy phase	24–36 + months	Maintains stable and reliable mental images of the primary caregivers

as hunger and sex. Instead, they cite research evidence with humans and other animals supporting the view that human infants possess an inborn tendency to develop close physical and emotional attachments with their caregivers that are *independent* of the basic drives of hunger, sex, and aggression (Eagle, 1984; Hamilton, 1989). (See Chapter 7 for a discussion of attachment.)

Margaret Mahler, for example, proposes that during the first three years of life, children go through four phases in developing a psychological sense of self. A newborn infant begins life in an *autistic phase,* meaning she is self-absorbed and has little psychological awareness of the world around her. Next, during the *symbiotic phase,* the infant experiences herself as being completely connected with and dependent on her primary caregiver rather than as a psychologically separate person. During the *separation-individuation phase,* she begins to develop a separate sense of self. Finally, during the *object constancy phase,* the infant achieves a more stable sense of self based on her increasing ability to form reliable mental representations of her primary caregivers (called *objects*) and their responses to her (Mahler et al., 1975). (See Table 2.3.)

An alternative description of the development of the psychological self is offered by Daniel Stern, who studied infant-parent interactions both in the laboratory and in naturalistic settings. According to Stern, a *core self,* based on an infant's awareness of being physically separate from others, emerges between two and six months. A *subjective self,* based on an organized mental representation of relationships with others, appears between seven and nine months. Finally, a sense of *verbal self* emerges between fifteen and eighteen months with the development of language and symbolic thought (Stern, 1985a; Cushman, 1991). (See Table 2.4.)

A third theorist, Heinz Kohut, suggests that a newborn infant's sense of self is at first fragmented and incomplete. Through a process called *empathic mirroring,* a caregiver responds to her infant in ways that accurately and sensitively reflect, or *mirror,* her awareness and appreciation of her baby's feelings, needs, and experiences. This empathic mirroring allows an infant to form a progressively more complete and well-organized set of mental representations of himself and his caregivers. From these mental portraits, an infant eventually constructs a reliable and independent sense of self (Eagle, 1984).

TABLE 2.4   Stern's Stages of Development

Stage	Approximate Age	Description
Emergent self	0–2 months	Active seeking of stimulation; more mature regulation of sleeping, eating, responsiveness, and emotional state
Core self	2–6 months	Development of sense of integrated self based on mental representations of past interactions that have been generalized (RIGs)
Subjective self	6–12 months	Organized perspective about relationships with others
Sense of verbal self	12 months +	Development of language and symbolic thinking skills

Evaluation of Developmental Themes in Psychodynamic Approaches

This section evaluates psychodynamic approaches with regard to the four developmental themes discussed at the beginning of the chapter.

The Roles of Maturation and Experience   While Freud and, to a lesser extent, Erikson believed biologically determined maturational processes play a significant role in developmental change, they also emphasized the importance of experience. For example, in Freud's theory inadequate parenting at any stage can contribute to weak or overly rigid defenses and to later personality problems in the child. Erikson emphasized not only the child's unique life circumstances and experiences but also the broader social, cultural, and historical forces that influence development and shape the identity crises each individual confronts. Object relations theorists generally place even less emphasis on maturation and propose that a child's social and emotional experiences with caregivers play a very central role in development.

The Active Role of the Child   All of the psychodynamic theories discussed view the child as a participant in his or her own development. However, Freud puts the least emphasis on the child's active role, whereas Erikson and object relations theorists emphasize it more.

The Role of Stages   Both Freud's and Erikson's theories strongly support a stage view of developmental change. Mahler, Stern, and Kohut view stages as a way to organize observations of children rather than as a central mechanism of change.

Breadth of Focus   Freud's theory is broad in that it attempts to explain the development of adult personality through childhood experiences. It is also narrow in its focus on the psychosexual domain of experience to the exclusion of physical, cognitive, and broader social, cultural, and historical factors. While Erikson covers the entire lifespan, including social, cultural, and historical forces, in his theory, he too says little about physical or cognitive development. Mahler, Stern, and Kohut emphasize important social, emotional, and, to some extent, cognitive aspects of development, but limit their explanations to infancy and early childhood.

What Do You Think?

Erikson proposed that cultural and social forces play a major role in developmental change. With this in mind, how might growing up as a member of an ethnic minority, growing up in poverty, or growing up female influence how an adolescent deals with the crisis of identity versus role confusion?

BEHAVIORAL LEARNING AND SOCIAL COGNITIVE LEARNING DEVELOPMENTAL THEORIES

Learning is generally defined as relatively permanent changes in observable behavior that result from experience. According to the learning theories, the learning experiences that occur over a person's lifetime are the source of developmental change. Thus, changes in existing learning opportunities or the creation of new ones can modify the course of an individual's development.

We first discuss the work of two founders of the behavioral learning approach, Ivan Pavlov and B. F. Skinner. Next, we briefly review the social cognitive learning approach of Albert Bandura. Although few developmental theorists today are strict behaviorists, the ideas of Pavlov and Skinner continue to play an influential role.

Behavioral Learning Theories

Classical Conditioning
CS, CR, US, UR

Pavlov: Classical Conditioning   Ivan Pavlov (1849–1936) was a Russian scientist who first developed his behavioral theory while studying digestion in dogs. In his well-known experiments, Pavlov rang a bell just before feeding a dog. Eventually the dog salivated whenever it heard the bell, even if it received no food. Pavlov called this process **classical conditioning.** He named the salivation itself the *conditioned response,* the food stimulus the *unconditioned stimulus,* and the dog's salivatory response the *unconditioned response.* The last was so named because the connection between the food stimulus and the dog's response was an inborn, *unconditioned reflex,* that is, an involuntary reaction similar to the eyeblink and knee-jerk reflexes.

Through the processes involved in classical conditioning, reflexes that are present at birth may help infants to learn about and participate in the world around them. For example, conditioning of the sucking reflex, which allows newborn infants to suck reflexively in response to a touch on the lips, has been reported using a tone as the conditioned stimulus (Lipsitt & Kaye, 1964). Other stimuli, such as the sight of the bottle and the mother's face, smile, and voice, may also become conditioned stimuli for sucking and may elicit sucking responses even before the bottle touches the baby's lips. Although even newborns' behavior may be classically conditioned, it cannot be reliably observed over a wide range of reflexes until about six months of age (Lipsitt, 1990). Figure 2.2 illustrates the process of classical conditioning.

Skinner: Operant Conditioning   B. F. Skinner (1904–1991) is best known for his learning theory, which is also known as **operant conditioning.** This theory is based on a simple concept called **reinforcement,** the process by which the likelihood that a particular response will occur again increases when that response is followed by a certain stimulus. *Positive reinforcement* occurs when, following a particular response (a baby saying "da-da"), a rewarding stimulus (his father smiling and saying "good boy!") is given that strengthens the response and increases the likelihood that it will recur under similar circumstances. *Negative reinforcement* also strengthens a response and increases the chance of its recurrence, but does so by removing an undesirable or unpleasant stimulus following the occurrence of that response. Consider Sarah, a four-year-old who has been crying and misbehaving at the dinner table. By quieting down once she gets her parents' attention, she may actually be negatively reinforcing (increasing) her parents' attention-giving responses by removing the unpleasant stimulus of crying and misbehaving.

Punishment weakens or suppresses a behavioral response by either adding an unpleasant stimulus or removing a pleasurable one following the response's occurrence. Taking away television privileges or adding an extra chore following a child's misbehavior are both forms of punishment. *Extinction* refers to the disappearance of a response when a reinforcer that was maintaining it is removed. Frequently the best way to extinguish an undesirable response is to ignore it and reinforce an alternative, more desirable response.

Shaping occurs when a child learns to perform new responses not already in her repertoire, or "collection." This is achieved by starting with an existing response and then modifying, or shaping, it by reinforcing small changes that bring it closer and closer to the desired behavior. Consider a dad who wishes to teach his seven-year-old daughter to hit a ball with a bat. Since she already can swing a bat, careful encouragement (a good reinforcer) for better and better swings and eventually for actually making contact with the ball (which is itself a good reinforcer) will transform, or shape, his daughter's bat-swinging behavior into ball-hitting behavior, a far more enjoyable and useful one.

B.F. Skinner developed one of the most well-known forms of behaviorism—operant conditioning. Its success may stem from its many practical applications to child and adolescent development.

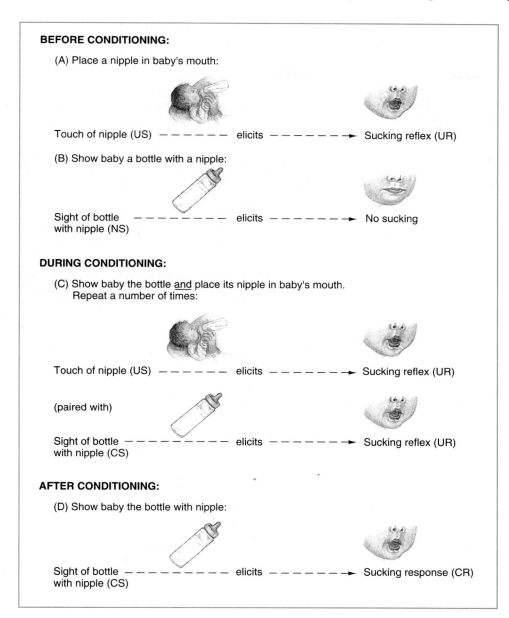

BEFORE CONDITIONING:

(A) Place a nipple in baby's mouth:

Touch of nipple (US) — — — — — elicits — — — — — → Sucking reflex (UR)

(B) Show baby a bottle with a nipple:

Sight of bottle — — — — — — — elicits — — — — — → No sucking
with nipple (NS)

DURING CONDITIONING:

(C) Show baby the bottle <u>and</u> place its nipple in baby's mouth.
Repeat a number of times:

Touch of nipple (US) — — — — — elicits — — — — — → Sucking reflex (UR)

(paired with)

Sight of bottle — — — — — — — elicits — — — — — → Sucking reflex (UR)
with nipple (CS)

AFTER CONDITIONING:

(D) Show baby the bottle with nipple:

Sight of bottle — — — — — — — elicits — — — — — → Sucking response (CR)
with nipple (CS)

FIGURE 2.2
***Illustration of Classical
Conditioning***
*In this example, the nipple in the
baby's mouth is an unconditioned
stimulus (US), which with no prior conditioning brings about, or elicits, the
sucking reflex, an unconditioned
response (UR). (A) The nipple in the
mouth elicits a sucking reflex; (B) the
sight of a bottle is a neutral stimulus
(NS) and has no effect; (C) once the
sight of the bottle (neutral stimulus) is
repeatedly paired with the nipple in the
mouth (UCS), the sight of the bottle
becomes a conditioned (learned) stimulus (CS), which now elicits sucking,
the conditioned response (CR).*

Social Cognitive Learning Theory

Albert Bandura believes that developmental change occurs largely through **observational learning,** or learning by observing others. Learning is *reciprocally determined,*
meaning it results from interactions between the child (including behaviors, cognitive processes, and physical capacities) and his physical and social environment.

Observational learning takes two forms: imitation and modeling. In *imitation,* a
child is directly reinforced for repeating or copying the actions of others. In *modeling,* the child learns the behaviors and personality traits of a parent or other model
through vicarious (indirect) reinforcement. A child learns to behave in ways similar
to those of a parent or other model by merely observing the model receiving reinforcement for his or her actions. How influential the model will be depends on a
variety of factors, including the model's relationship to the child, his or her personal
characteristics, and how the child perceives them (Bandura, 1989; Miller, 1993).
Children's levels of cognitive development strongly influence their ability to observe,
remember, and later perform in ways similar to the models they have watched.

It is likely that observational learning plays an important role as these girls learn to prepare bread dough.

The social cognitive learning approach has been useful in explaining gender development, the development of aggression, and the developmental impact of television and other media. It has also been useful to counselors and therapists who work with problems in the parent-child relationship and with children with a variety of behavioral and adjustment difficulties in both outpatient and residential treatment settings. Now let's look at how these theories view the four developmental themes.

Evaluation of Developmental Themes in Behavioral and Social Cognitive Learning Approaches

The Roles of Maturation and Experience   The learning theories of Pavlov and Skinner are striking in their exclusive emphasis on experience as the sole source of developmental change. Although Bandura's social cognitive approach notes that cognitive maturation plays a developmental role, it too focuses mainly on learning as the source of developmental change.

The Active Role of the Child   Both Pavlov and Skinner assume the child is a passive reactor rather than an active participant in the learning process and exclude the cognitive processes required for a more active role. Bandura views the child as a highly active participant in the social and cognitive learning interactions responsible for developmental change.

The Role of Stages   Pavlov, Skinner, and learning theorists in general view development as continuous rather than stagelike. While Bandura's most recent revision of his theory makes some mention of stages, stages play a relatively minor role in his view.

Breadth of Focus   Although learning approaches have proposed to explain all of developmental change using relatively few principles and processes focused on how learning occurs, until fairly recently they have maintained a relatively narrow focus on observable social behavior. More current cognitive learning approaches have expanded their views to include cognitive development and certain emotional processes. Nevertheless, they are still limited in these areas.

What Do You Think?

Think of some examples of developmental changes in a young child's behavior that might be accurately explained using behavioral learning theories. Then think of an example of a developmental change that doesn't seem to fit the behavioral model.

COGNITIVE DEVELOPMENTAL THEORIES

In this section, we discuss three theoretical approaches to cognitive development: Piaget's cognitive theory, neo-Piagetian theories, and information-processing theory. All of these theories share a strong focus on how children's thinking and problem solving develop and how such cognitive activities contribute to the overall process of child and adolescent development.

Piaget's Cognitive Theory

Jean Piaget (1896–1980) was one of the most influential figures in developmental psychology. Just as Freud's ideas radically changed thinking about human emotional development, Piaget's ideas have changed our understanding of the development of human thinking and problem solving, or *cognition.*

Key Principles of Piaget's Theory   Piaget believed that children's thinking develops in a series of increasingly complex stages, or periods, each of which incorporates and revises those that precede it. Piaget's cognitive stages and developmental processes are summarized in Table 2.5. His theory is discussed in greater detail in the chapters on cognitive development.

What exactly makes a child develop from one stage of thinking and problem solving to the next? Piaget believed that three processes are involved: (1) direct learning, (2) social transmission, and (3) maturation.

Direct learning results when a child actively responds to and interprets new problems and experiences based on patterns of thought and action he already knows. Piaget called these existing patterns of thought and actions schemes. A scheme is a systematic pattern of thoughts, actions, and problem-solving strategies that helps the child deal with a particular intellectual challenge or situation.

According to Piaget, an infant's first understanding of the world is based on a limited number of *innate schemes* made up of simple patterns of unlearned reflexes that are inherited at birth, such as sucking, grasping, and looking. These schemes

TABLE 2.5   ***Piaget's Cognitive Stages and Developmental Processes***

Cognitive Stage	Approximate Age	Description
Sensorimotor	Birth–2 years	Coordination of sensory and motor activity; achievement of object permanence
Preoperational	2–7 years	Use of language and symbolic representation; egocentric view of the world
Concrete operational	7–11 years	Solution of concrete problems through logical operations
Formal operational	11–adulthood	Systematic solution of actual and hypothetical problems using abstract symbols

Developmental Processes

The earliest and most primitive patterns, or schemes, of thinking, problem solving, and constructing reality are inborn. As a result of both maturation and experience, thinking develops through a series of increasingly sophisticated stages, each incorporating the achievements in preceding stages. These changes occur through the processes of assimilation, in which new problems are solved using existing schemes; accommodation, in which existing schemes are altered or adapted to meet new challenges. Together, these processes create a state of cognitive balance or *equilibrium,* in which the child's thinking becomes increasingly stable, general, and harmoniously adjusted to the environment.

According to Piaget, children think in qualitatively different ways as they develop. Very young children usually think about objects and experiences by looking and touching. Many adolescents, on the other hand, can plan and reason abstractly, as illustrated in the two photos.

rapidly change as the infant encounters new experiences through the complementary processes of *assimilation* and *accommodation*.

Assimilation is the process by which an infant interprets and responds to a new experience or situation in terms of an existing scheme. For example, a two-month-old baby who is presented with a bottle for the first time understands what is needed to suck from the bottle based on her existing sucking scheme for her mother's breast. The infant has assimilated a new situation, sucking from a bottle, into her existing scheme for sucking.

As children grow older, schemes involve increasingly complex mental processes. For example, a preschooler sees a truck but calls it a "car" because the concept of *car* is already well established in his thinking. But this same child correctly uses the concept of *bird* to refer to several very different winged creatures, say, a chicken, a pigeon, and a parakeet.

In **accommodation,** a child changes existing schemes, or ways of thinking, when faced with new ideas or situations in which the old schemes no longer work. Instead of calling a truck by the wrong name, the preschooler searches for a new name and begins to realize that some four-wheeled objects are not cars.

According to Piaget, development results from the interplay of assimilation and accommodation, a process called *adaptation.* **Adaptation** results when schemes are deepened or broadened by assimilation and stretched or modified by accommodation.

Social transmission, Piaget's second explanation for development, is the process through which one's thinking is influenced by learning from social contact with and observation of others rather than through direct experience. *Physical maturation,* Piaget's third explanation for developmental change, refers to the biologically determined changes in physical and neurological development that occur relatively independently of specific experiences. For example, a child must reach a certain minimal level of biological development to be able to name an object.

According to Piaget, a central goal of intellectual activity is to establish *equilibrium,* a stable and harmonious balance between one's thought processes and one's experiences with the environment. If an earlier way of thinking or acting does not work in a new situation, cognitive change is stimulated. Such changes increase the sophistication and maturity of a child's thinking and allow the child to move into a new phase of development—a new cognitive stage.

While research at least partially supports many of Piaget's ideas, it has found a number of shortcomings. One problem is how to explain why, in many instances, tasks that are logically equivalent are mastered at very different points in children's development. It is also hard to explain why a child's cognitive performance on two logically similar tasks is often very different. Finally, Piaget's exclusive emphasis on the predetermined "logical" aspects of children's functioning often does not match the actual thought processes children appear to use and largely ignores the social, emotional, and cultural factors that influence children's thinking (Case, 1992;

Rogoff & Chavajay, 1995). Some of these issues are discussed in the Multicultural View box that appears later in this chapter.

Neo-Piagetian Approaches

Neo-Piagetian theories are new or revised models of Piaget's basic approach that attempt to go beyond Piaget's thinking. While these theories generally agree with Piaget's general ideas about overall stages of cognitive development, they disagree about some of the details of how these broad changes work.

Robbie Case, for example, proposes that cognitive development results from increases in the child's mental space. *Mental space* refers to the maximum number of schemes the child can apply simultaneously at any given time (Case, 1991b, 1991c, 1991d). During early childhood most cognitive structures are rather specific and concrete, such as drawing with a pencil, throwing a ball, or counting a set of objects. As the structures guiding these actions become coordinated with one another, they form new, more efficient, higher-level cognitive structures, which in turn begin to be coordinated with other, similar structures. Thus, a child's ability to use increasingly general cognitive structures enables him to think more abstractly. Different forms of the same logical problem may require different processing skills and capacities. As a result, a child's performance on two logically similar tasks may differ significantly, and mastery of each task may occur at very different points in her development.

Kurt Fischer, another neo-Piagetian theorist, also accepts Piaget's basic idea of stages. However, Fischer uses specific *skills* instead of *schemes* to describe the cognitive structures children use in particular problem-solving tasks or sets of tasks. The breadth of a skill is determined by both the level of maturation a child's central nervous system has reached and the range of specific learning environments to which a child has been exposed (Fischer, 1980; Fischer & Pipp, 1984). Thus, support from parents, teachers, and others in the environment is important for skill acquisition. Also, at any given point in each child's development, there is an optimal level of skill performance that cannot be exceeded without further central nervous system development.

Case's "breadth of skill" idea has much in common with Lev Vygotsky's "zone of proximal development," which you will read about later in this chapter.

The chess-playing abilities of these youngsters are closely tied to increases in their knowledge of chess and to their awareness and understanding of their own thought processes and problem-solving strategies.

Information-Processing Theory

Another alternative to Piaget's cognitive theory is **information-processing theory,** which focuses on the precise, detailed features or steps involved in mental activities (Klahr, 1989; Seifert, 1993). Like a computer, the mind is viewed as having distinct parts that make unique contributions to thinking in a specific order.

Key Principles of Information-Processing Theory   Figure 2.3 shows one information-processing model of human thinking. According to this model, when a person tries to solve a problem, she first takes in information from her environment through her senses. The information gained in this way is held briefly in the *sensory register,* the first memory store. The sensory register records information exactly as it originally receives it, but the information fades or disappears within a fraction of a second unless the person processes it further.

Information to which a person pays special attention is transferred to *short-term memory (STM),* the second memory store. The short-term memory corresponds roughly to "momentary awareness," or whatever the person is thinking about at a particular instant. The short-term memory can hold only limited amounts of information—in fact, only about seven pieces of it at any one time. After about twenty seconds, information in short-term memory is either forgotten or processed further. At this point, it moves into *long-term memory (LTM),* the third memory store.

Information can be saved permanently in long-term memory. But doing so requires various cognitive strategies, such as rehearsing information repeatedly or organizing it into familiar categories. Unlike short-term memory, long-term memory probably has unlimited capacity for storage of new information. The problem comes in retrieving information. As odd as it sounds, a person cannot always remember how to recall something. Most of us experience this problem when an old acquaintance's name is on the tip of our tongue or when we remember only that the person's name "begins with the letter *w,* I think." But most of us can remember certain events that occurred long ago better than many more recent events.

The information-processing model provides a useful way to understand thinking. As the following discussion shows, certain processing functions change as children grow older.

Developmental Changes in Information Processing   As children grow older, they experience several cognitive changes that allow them to process information more efficiently and comprehensively. Changes occur in cognitive control processes, in metacognition (knowledge about knowledge), and in the amount of knowledge itself.

FIGURE 2.3
An Information-Processing Model of Learning

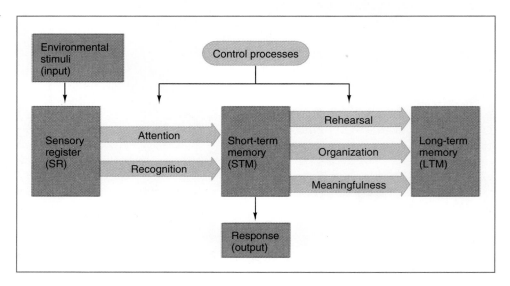

Control Processes   The most important developmental change in information processing is the acquisition of control processes. *Control processes* direct an individual's attention toward particular input from the sensory register and guide the response to new information once it enters short-term memory. Usually control processes organize information in short-term memory, such as when a student reads an arithmetic problem, ponders it in his head, and immediately announces the answer. Sometimes control processes also relate information in STM to previously learned knowledge from LTM, such as when a youth hears a song on the radio and notes its similarity to another song heard previously. And sometimes control processes consist of strategies for learning information effectively, such as strategies for remembering a person's telephone number.

Metacognition   As children grow older, they develop metacognition. **Metacognition** is an awareness and understanding of how thinking and learning work, and it assists learning in a number of ways. It allows a person to assess how difficult a problem or learning task will be and therefore to plan appropriate ways to approach it. More specifically, metacognition involves knowledge of self, knowledge of task variables, and knowledge of which information-processing strategies are effective in which situations (Forrest-Pressley et al., 1985).

Knowledge Base   In addition to metacognition, children acquire many other kinds of knowledge. Some children gradually become comparative experts in particular areas, such as math, sports, or getting along with peers. *Knowledge base* refers to children's current fund of knowledge and skills in various areas. A child's knowledge base in one area makes acquiring further knowledge and skills in the same area easier because the child can relate new information to prior information more meaningfully.

According to many information-processing theorists, changes in the knowledge base are not general, stagelike transformations such as those proposed by Piaget (Chi et al., 1989). Instead, they are specialized developments of expertise based on the gradual accumulation of specific information and skills about a field, including information and skills about *how* knowledge in the field is organized and learned efficiently. A very good chess player is an expert in chess but is not necessarily advanced in other activities or areas of knowledge. Her skill probably reflects long hours spent in one major activity: playing chess games. Each hour of play enables her to build a larger knowledge base about chess: memories of board patterns, moves, and game strategies that worked in the past.

Now let's see how the cognitive developmental theories stand in regard to the four major developmental themes.

Evaluation of Developmental Themes in Cognitive Approaches

The Roles of Maturation and Experience   Piaget's theory assigns important roles to both maturation and experience. While maturational factors are necessary to the unique structural qualities of the stages and to the progression from lower to higher stages, without experience cognitive development would not occur. Neo-Piagetian theories also accept the importance of maturation, but emphasize the child's specific experiences in interacting with the environment as the source of cognitive development. The information-processing approach assumes the processes and structures involved in cognitive development are primarily a product of the child's experiences.

The Active Role of the Child   Piaget believes children play a relatively active role in their own development. Neo-Piagetian theorists and information-processing approaches stress the child's active participation even more strongly.

A Multicultural View

Cultural Context and Cognitive Development

According to Lev Vygotsky's theory, cognitive development is largely "context specific," meaning it must be understood in terms of the particular social, cultural, and historical processes of people's everyday experiences (Vygotsky, 1978; Wertsch, 1985). Individuals growing up in different societies, cultures, and historical periods are likely to display differences in how they think and solve problems and in how cognitive development occurs. This view is very different from that of Jean Piaget, who believed cognitive development is largely "universal," meaning all children progress through the same developmental stages at approximately the same ages relatively independently of their particular situations and experiences.

Research based primarily on observations of children from Western industrialized societies, where formal schooling is heavily stressed, has generally supported Piaget's ideas. Studies of children growing up in other societies and cultures, however, have been more consistent with Vygotsky's views. Children growing up in cultures with little formal schooling have been found to take much longer to achieve the *concrete operational stage* of think-

ing and appear unable to achieve the *formal operational stage* of thinking, Piaget's final stage (Rogoff & Chavajay, 1995). Michael Cole, a pioneer in studying culture and cognitive development, concluded that the superior performance of children who had formal schooling was due to the common structure and activities of schooling and tests of cognitive development rather than to the effects of schooling on children's thinking (Cole, 1990).

Performance on tasks that require subjects to classify test items into categories is one good example. Whereas individuals from Western countries typically classify test items based on their type (for example, putting animals in one group, food items in another, and tools in a third), individuals in many other nations sort the same items based on their function (for example, putting a hoe with a potato because a hoe is used to dig up a potato) (Rogoff & Chavajay, 1995).

Logical tasks that require a person to draw conclusions based on abstract, hypothetical reasoning rather than on direct personal experience are another example. Nonliterate individuals who are able to make excellent

The particular cultural context in which communion and other important events occur can significantly influence a child's development.

The Role of Stages   Piaget's theory places major emphasis on developmental stages that are closely tied to maturation of the capacity to perform certain predetermined logical operations. The stages neo-Piagetian theorists propose are similar to Piaget's but are more closely tied to the increases in processing efficiency and skill level that result from specific experiences than to predetermined operations. Information-processing theory views developmental change as a continuous rather than stagelike process.

Breadth of Focus   Both Piaget's theory and the neo-Piagetian revisions limit their focus to the domain of cognitive change. They say little about the role of social, emotional, and physical factors in cognitive development or the ways cognitive development may influence these domains. The information-processing approach limits its focus to developing and testing models to explain the role of memory and information processing in cognitive change.

What Do You Think?

How might the cognitive approach be useful to an elementary school math teacher who is preparing lesson plans? Would this theoretical approach be of any use in a health education class?

CONTEXTUAL DEVELOPMENTAL THEORIES

Contextual approaches view development as a process of reciprocal, patterned interactions between the developing child and his physical and social environment. A logical judgments when dealing with the immediate, practical problems of their everyday life experiences may, for cultural reasons, be unwilling to demonstrate similar reasoning abilities in situations that are not culturally familiar. The following example, taken from an interview with a nonliterate Central Asian peasant, illustrates this point:

Interviewer: In the Far North, where there is snow, all bears are white. Novaya Zemlya is in the Far North and there is always snow there. What color are the bears there?

Peasant: . . . We always speak of only what we see; we don't talk about what we haven't seen.

Interviewer: But what do my words imply?

Peasant: Well, it's like this: our tsar isn't like yours, and yours isn't like ours. Your words can be answered only by someone who was there, and if a person wasn't there he can't say anything on the basis of your words.

Interviewer: But on the basis of my words—in the North, where there is always snow, the bears are white—can you gather what kind of bears there are in Novaya Zemlya?

Peasant: If a man was sixty or eighty and had seen a white bear and had told me about it, he could be believed, but I've never seen one and hence I can't say. (Luria, 1976, pp. 108–109, quoted in Rogoff & Chavajay, 1995, p. 861)

Differences in performance of common cognitive tasks may also reflect cultural differences in how a problem is defined and how it should be solved (Goodnow, 1976). European Americans, for example, believe that intelligence involves technical rather than social skills. Kipsigis (Kenyan) parents include responsible participation in family and social life in their definition. For the Ifaluk of the western Pacific, intelligence means not only having knowledge of good social behavior but also performing it. Ugandan villagers associate intelligence with being slow, careful, and active, whereas westernized groups associate it with speed (Rogoff & Chavajay, 1995).

Future research will provide additional evidence regarding the social and cultural contexts of cognitive development.

leading example of this approach is the ecological systems theory of Urie Bronfenbrenner. *Ecological systems theory* proposes that a child's development is influenced by four interactive and overlapping contextual levels: (1) the *microsystem*—the face-to-face physical and social situations that directly affect the child (family, peer group, classroom); (2) the *mesosystem*—connections and relationships among the child's microsystems; (3) the *exosystem*—the settings or situations that indirectly influence the child (parent's place of employment, the school board, the local government); and (4) the *macrosystem*—the values, beliefs, and policies of society and culture that provide frameworks, or "blueprints," for organizing our lives and indirectly influence the child through their affects on the exosystem, mesosystem, and microsystem. (See Chapter 1 for a discussion of Bronfenbrenner's theory.)

Another interesting example of contextual theory was developed by the Russian psychologist Lev Vygotsky (1896–1934). Vygotsky was interested in how changing historical and cultural contexts within which children's activities occur influence their cognitive development. According to Vygotsky, higher mental functions grow out of the social interactions and dialogues that take place between a child and parents, teachers, and other representatives of the culture. Through these interactions, children internalize increasingly mature and effective ways of thinking and problem solving. Some of these changes occur through discoveries that the child initiates on her own.

Many developmental tasks, however, occur in what Vygotsky called the *zone of proximal development*. The **zone of proximal development** refers to the range of tasks that a child cannot yet accomplish without active assistance from parents and others with greater knowledge (Blanck, 1990; Rogoff, 1990; Wertsch, 1989). Vygotsky's ideas are useful in helping teachers and parents to provide children with the right amounts of structure and guidance and in understanding how children's private speech (talking to themselves) may help them to regulate their own behavior when adult guidance is not available (Berk, 1994). (See the accompanying Multicultural View box for a discussion of culture and cognitive development.)

Ethological Theory

The ethological approach attempts to apply the principles of evolutionary biology and ethology to behavioral and psychological characteristics (Hinde, 1989; Miller, 1989). This approach has its roots in *ethology,* the study of various animal species in their natural environments. Ethology emphasizes the ways widely shared species behaviors evolved through the process of natural selection to ensure species survival. Developmental ethologists are interested in how certain behavioral and psychological traits or predispositions that appear to be widely shared among human beings may have developed to help ensure the evolutionary survival of the human species.

An underlying assumption is that just as human evolution has imposed certain constraints on our physical development, it may have influenced the range and nature of our behavioral development. Developmental ethologists also attempt to understand how individual differences in traits such as aggressiveness, shyness, competitiveness, and altruism reciprocally interact with the social environment to mutually influence development.

One area of ethological interest has been the study of infant emotions and *temperament*—relatively enduring individual differences in infant responsiveness and self-regulation that appear to be present at birth. (See Chapters 3 and 7.)

A second important application of the ethological approach is the study of infant-caregiver *attachment*—the mutually reinforcing system of physical, social, and emotional stimulation and support between infant and caregiver. This pattern of attachment behaviors has been observed in other species, and ethologists presume it has survival value for humans as well (see Chapter 7).

Evaluation of Developmental Themes in Contextual Approaches

The Roles of Maturation and Experience   With the exception of ethological theory, contextual approaches focus almost exclusively on the child's experiences in multiple contexts as the moving force in developmental change. Bronfenbrenner and Vygotsky propose that developmental change occurs primarily through patterns of reciprocal interaction rather than through maturational influences. Ethological theorists, on the other hand, strongly believe that certain inborn physical and behavioral tendencies and characteristics predispose children to develop in certain ways. However, ethological theory also emphasizes that developmental change reflects how behavioral tendencies interact with the environmental and cultural contexts in which the child lives.

The Active Role of the Child   All of the contextual theories view the child as a highly active participant in his own development and see development as the product of highly reciprocal, mutually determined interactions between the child and the multiple contexts in which he exists.

The Role of Stages   Stages are not a feature of contextual theories. Development is seen as a continuous process.

Breadth of Focus   Contextual approaches include a broad range of social, cultural, and historical developmental influences. On the other hand, they tend to focus on social development and less on emotional, cognitive, and physical development. Similarly, they tend to emphasize a limited range of developmental issues rather than a comprehensive and balanced view of developmental change.

What Do You Think?

To what degree does your informal theory of development include the different developmental contexts proposed by these theorists? Are there any you would add? Any you would delete?

DEVELOPMENTAL THEORIES COMPARED: IMPLICATIONS FOR THE STUDENT

We have reached the end of our review of several of the most important theories in developmental psychology. What conclusions might we draw? In what ways are these theories useful as we investigate children's development in the remainder of this book?

As we suggested at the beginning of this chapter, theories are useful because they help us systematically organize and make sense of large amounts of sometimes inconsistent information about children's development. Theories also stimulate new thinking and research and guide parents and professionals in their day-to-day work with children.

Psychodynamic theories such as Erikson's help us anticipate and better understand the crises we encounter in our own development. For example, knowledge about the crisis of autonomy versus shame and doubt can help parents and day care teachers who work with toddlers to respond to children with the right mixture of structure, control, and freedom. Erikson's ideas have also helped parents, teachers, and researchers to better understand normal and problematic identity development during adolescence and young adulthood (Glasser, 1967; Redl & Wineman, 1951; Selman, 1980). (See the Working With interview on pages 52–53.)

Psychodynamic and object relations theories help us appreciate the considerable capabilities, needs, and vulnerabilities of infants and young children. They have increased our awareness of the importance of the quality of infant-caregiver relationships and have helped parents, teachers, pediatric nurses, and child therapists understand what constitutes quality parenting and caregiving both inside and outside the home.

Behavioral and social cognitive learning theories and the principles and techniques of classical and operant conditioning and social learning have helped parents and educators to concretely achieve some of the more abstract goals associated with good caregiving. For example, appropriate and respectful use of reinforcement and modeling have been helpful to nurse-midwives and school nurses working with sexually active or pregnant teens, probation officers and drug counselors working with troubled youths, and mental health professionals working with youngsters who have eating disorders.

Piaget's theory of cognitive development has helped parents and teachers to develop realistic expectations of children at different stages of thinking and to remember that readiness to solve certain types of intellectual problems depends not only on a suitable learning environment but also on a child's maturational readiness.

Finally, concepts from contextual theories such as Lev Vygotsky's zone of proximal development have been useful in designing home- and school-based learning environments that provide the optimal amount of guidance for children. By focusing our attention on the multiple and overlapping situations in which development occurs, contextual theories also help us to understand the numerous factors involved in problems such as "at-risk" families, child abuse, school failure, drug use, and juvenile delinquency (for example, see Garbarino, 1992; Ramey et al., 1988).

Although each theory has significantly expanded knowledge in its particular area of focus, none should be thought to provide a complete explanation of development. Taken together, the theories are complementary and can be used in conjunction with one another to provide a fairly comprehensive view of child and adolescent development. Table 2.6 summarizes the main features, key concepts, and four developmental themes for each theoretical approach discussed.

Last, but not least, theories help us understand and actively participate in our own development. Theories can also broaden and deepen our understanding of ourselves, the factors influencing our development, and the choices we have. They can

Developmental theories help us to better understand children's play and its contribution to the development of sex roles and gender.

TABLE 2.6   *Developmental Theories Compared*

	Psychodynamic				Behavioral Learning
	Freud	*Erikson*	*Mahler*	*Stern*	*Pavlov; Skinner*
Main Focus	Personality (social, emotional)	Personality (social, behavior, identity)	Personality (social, emotional, self)	Personality (interpersonal, cognitive, emotional, self)	Learning specific observable responses
Key Concepts	Id, ego, superego; psychosexual conflict; defense mechanisms	Lifespan development; psychosocial crises	Birth of psychological self; separation-individuation	Interpersonal sense of self; RIGs	Classical and operant conditioning, extinction, reinforcement, punishment
Four Developmental Themes					
Role of maturation	Moderate	Weak	Strong	Moderate	Weak
Role of experience	Strong	Strong	Moderate	Strong	Strong
Active role of child	Moderate	Moderate	Moderate	Strong	Weak
Stages	Yes	Yes	Yes	Yes	No
Breadth of focus	Wide	Wide	Narrow	Moderate	Narrow

Working with   John Daviau, RESIDENTIAL TREATMENT PROGRAM DIRECTOR

Understanding Multiproblem Adolescents

John Daviau was interviewed in a classroom at the University of New Haven, where he is currently enrolled as a part-time graduate student in the Community-Clinical Psychology Program. John has worked in residential treatment for the past ten years and was interested in discussing how developmental theory helps guide his day-to-day work.

Rob: Could you tell me a little about your work?

John: I'm a program director for an adolescent group home. Basically it's a long-term residential setting for abused, neglected, and emotionally disturbed adolescents.

Rob: How did you become involved in this type of work?

John: It's interesting. Years ago I was a landscape foreman and was looking for a career change, so I enrolled in a certificate program in counseling and

human relations. When I finished the program, I got an entry-level position as a child care worker in a group home, where I eventually became director. After moving to Connecticut, I worked as a program director in a community criminal justice program for two years before beginning my present job.

Rob: Do you find that developmental theory influences how you work with these youngsters?

John: Actually, it influences me all the time. I think developmental theory is very important because disturbed adolescents can be very demanding, egocentric, frustrating people to work with. If you're not a parent and you haven't experienced adolescents as a parent or adult caregiver, it helps to know what to expect—what's normal or atypical behavior for a fourteen-year-old, for instance.

Rob: And theory can tell you this? Can you give some examples of how theory may be helpful?

John: Psychodynamic theories give us some useful guidelines for what is developmentally normal and age appropriate. They help us understand the adolescent's inappropriate behavior in terms of developmental delays and unresolved conflicts and crises. They also give us tools to better understand our own feelings as caregivers—and, hopefully, to see the difficulties that come up between these youngsters and staff as opportunities for positive change.

Rob: How might you apply developmental theory to your work?

John: Swearing is a good example. When teens get angry—and this population of adolescents is very angry—it often comes out as swearing. A lot

Social-Cognitive Learning	Cognitive			Contextual Approaches		
Bandura	Piaget	Case; Fischer	Information Processing	Bronfenbrenner	Vygotsky	Ethological
Learning behavior, cognitive response patterns, social roles	Cognitive (thinking, problem solving)	Cognitive; problem-solving skills and capacities	Cognitive; steps and processes involved in problem solving and other mental activities	Contextual; interactive contextual influences	Contextual; cultural/ historical influences	Contextual; biological and ethological influences
Imitation, social learning, modeling, cognitive learning, reciprocal determinism; skill capabilities	Schemes, assimilation, accommodation, equilibrium; mental space, routinization of schemes	Skill acquisition, optimal level of performance, higher-level skills	Sensory register, short-term memory (STM), long-term memory (LTM), meta-cognition, knowledge base, control processes	Developmentally instigative characteristics; ecological contexts	Dialogues; zone of proximal development	Behaviorial predispositions, ethological context
No	Yes	No	No	No	No	No
Weak	Strong	Moderate	Strong	Weak	Weak	Moderate
Strong	Moderate	Moderate	Moderate	Strong	Strong	Moderate
Moderate	Moderate	Moderate	Narrow	Broad	Moderate	Moderate
Strong	Moderate	Strong	Strong	Strong	Strong	Moderate

of times it will be directed at you to see what kind of reaction they can get from the authority figures. If you realize where they're coming from and what kind of anger and issues they have, you're going to react differently. You're better able to respond in a more constructive way that's respectful and empathic to their feelings, and not start yelling back at them.

Rob: Not always easy to accomplish.

John: No, it isn't.

Rob: What other ideas influence the work you do at the center?

John: Fritz Redl's ideas have been very useful. He established Pioneer House, a psychoanalytically oriented residential treatment program for antisocial adolescents in the 1940s. Redl believed that conscience and behavior controls break down in children who have been raised in disorganized and abusive environments. Since these environments have no adequate caregiving or role models, the children use hatred to defend themselves against the adults in their lives. This framework has certainly influenced how we structure our program and how we make individual treatment decisions.

Rob: Earlier you mentioned social cognitive learning approaches.

John: I was thinking of William Glasser's reality therapy approach, which helps children learn more effective problem-solving strategies and take responsibility for the consequences of their actions.

Rob: Can you give an example?

John: Yes. Sometimes it really helps to go through problem solving. It gets kids to realize consequences and to think about making changes. Simple things like "So when you get angry, what do you do?" "Well, I get angry and I punch the wall." "How does that make you feel?" "Well, I hurt my hand and I'm p---d off, and . . . " "Do you like that way of expressing anger? Does it help you? What does it do for you?" "Well, no, I guess I don't really like it, it doesn't really solve the problem." "Then maybe you could think about doing something differently."

What Do You Think?

1. How might unresolved crises related to Erikson's stages help explain the behaviors exhibited by these teenagers?

2. If you were a worker on John's staff, how might you respond to a teenager who swore at you?

3. What theoretical ideas would help you respond constructively?

help us better understand how our family dynamics and relationships may have influenced our current personalities and our struggles with issues such as identity, intimacy, gender role, and sexuality.

However, uncritical reliance on theories has several pitfalls. Because theories guide and direct our perceptions of and thinking about children, reliance on a given theory may lead us to focus on certain aspects of development, make certain assumptions, and draw conclusions about development that are consistent with the theory but not necessarily accurate. For example, overreliance on Piaget's cognitive approach may lead a teacher to underestimate the contributions of social and emotional factors to a child's academic difficulties. Similarly, parents who tend to interpret their child's irresponsible behavior in terms of psychological conflict may overlook the fact that the same behavior is frequently modeled and reinforced by the child's older sibling.

As you read the chapters that follow, notice that the theories are applied selectively based on the ages and developmental issues being discussed. We encourage you to refer back to this chapter whenever you have questions about the material and to make your own judgments about which theory (or theories) fits best. Finally, keep an eye on how your own theories of development change as you read the book and talk with your instructor and classmates. By the end of the course, if not sooner, you are likely to have a much clearer idea of your preferred theoretical orientation(s), as well as a much clearer perspective of what development is all about.

What Do You Think?

Remember three-year-old Elizabeth at the beginning of this chapter? Now that you have learned more about theories of development, which theory (or theories) do you think is most useful in understanding her situation and helping her adjust to her first days of nursery school? Why?

SUMMARY OF MAJOR IDEAS

The Nature of Developmental Theories

1. Theories are useful in organizing and explaining the process of development and in stimulating and guiding developmental research, theory, and practice.

2. Developmental theories differ in the degree to which they emphasize maturation versus experience, active versus passive participation, continuous versus stagelike development, and breadth of theoretical focus.

Psychodynamic Developmental Theories

3. In the theories of Freud and Erikson, development is a dynamic process that occurs in a series of stages, each involving psychological conflicts that the developing person must resolve.

4. According to Freud, personality development is energized by three conflicting functions: the unconscious, irrational, pleasure-seeking id; the largely conscious, rational, realistic ego; and the superego, which is the voice of conscience and morality.

5. The Freudian approach describes five stages of psychosexual development: oral, anal, phallic, latency, and genital.

6. Erikson's psychosocial theory outlines eight developmental stages encompassing the lifespan, each defined by a unique psychological crisis that is never completely resolved.

7. During infancy, a basic sense of trust (versus mistrust) results in *hope*. During toddlerhood and the preschool years, a child achieves a sense of autonomy (versus shame and doubt) and initiative (versus guilt), resulting in *will* and *purpose*.

8. During the school years a child must resolve the crisis of industry (versus inferiority), and during adolescence the crisis of identity (versus role confusion), resulting in *competence* and *fidelity*.

9. Erikson's final three stages occur after adolescence. They include young adulthood and the crisis of intimacy (versus isolation), adulthood and the crisis of generativity (versus stagnation), and old age and the crisis of ego integrity (versus despair). Successful resolution brings *love, care,* and *wisdom*.

10. Object relations approaches emphasize development as resulting from a child's internalized mental representations of early social and emotional relationships with parents and important others.

11. According to Mahler, the infant goes through autistic, symbiotic, separation-individuation, and object constancy phases in developing a sense of psychological self. For Stern, the process involves a core self, a subjective self, and a verbal self. For Kohut, empathic mirroring by caregivers helps the infant to develop a cohesive and reliable set of mental representations out of which a sense of self emerges.

Behavioral Learning and Social Cognitive Learning Developmental Theories

12. Pavlov's theory emphasizes learning through classical conditioning as the main process by which developmental changes occur.
13. Skinner's operant conditioning theory emphasizes the influence of reinforcement, punishment, and extinction on developmental change.
14. Bandura's social cognitive theory emphasizes reciprocal and interactional processes involving both direct, observational learning and vicarious reinforcement.

Cognitive Developmental Theories

15. Piaget's theory explains the underlying structures and processes involved in the development of children's thinking and problem solving.
16. According to Piaget, thinking develops in a series of increasingly complex and sophisticated stages, or periods, each of which incorporates the achievements of those preceding it.
17. New ways of thinking and problem solving are achieved through the joint processes of assimilation (fitting a new scheme of thinking or action into an existing one) and accommodation (changing an existing scheme to meet the challenges of a new situation).
18. The neo-Piagetian theories emphasize the roles of mental space, skill acquisition, and information-processing capacity in cognitive development.
19. Information-processing theory focuses on the steps involved in thought processes. Information is first stored in the sensory register, then in short-term memory, and finally in long-term memory. As children grow older, they experience cognitive changes in control processes, metacognition, and their knowledge bases.

Contextual Developmental Theories

20. Bronfenbrenner's ecological systems theory proposes that the microsystem, mesosystem, exosystem, and macrosystem form interactive and overlapping contexts for development. Vygotsky emphasizes the contributions of history and culture to development that take place within a child's zone of proximal development.
21. Ethological theory focuses on the developmental roles of behavioral dispositions and traits, such as temperament and attachment, that are thought to have evolutionary survival value for the human species.

Developmental Theories Compared: Implications for the Student

22. Although developmental theories differ in both focus and explanatory concepts, together they provide a fairly comprehensive view of the process of developmental change.
23. By systematically organizing what we already know about development and proposing explanations that can be tested through formal and informal observations, developmental theories are so useful for experts and nonexperts alike that they are well worth the effort required to understand them.

KEY TERMS

id (32)
ego (32)
superego (33)
trust versus mistrust (36)

autonomy versus shame and doubt (36)
initiative versus guilt (36)
industry versus inferiority (36)
identity versus role confusion (37)
intimacy versus isolation (37)
generativity versus stagnation (37)
ego integrity versus despair (37)
object relations (37)
classical conditioning (40)
operant conditioning (40)
reinforcement (40)
punishment (40)
observational learning (41)
scheme (43)
assimilation (44)
accommodation (44)
adaptation (44)
information-processing theory (46)
metacognition (47)
zone of proximal development (49)

FOR FURTHER READING

Eagle, M. *Recent Developments in Psychoanalysis: A Critical Evaluation.* New York: McGraw-Hill, 1984.

This book provides intensive coverage of the most recent developments in psychoanalysis and critically examines the underlying assumptions, theoretical arguments, and conclusions of each.

Erikson, E. *Identity, Youth and Crisis.* New York: Norton, 1968.

Erikson presents his developmental theory with an emphasis on identity development during adolescence and young adulthood. Chapter 3, "The Life Cycle: Epigenesis of Identity," is most relevant for the student who wants to sample Erikson's work firsthand.

Garbarino, J. *Children and Families in the Social Environment.* 2nd ed. New York: Aldine De Gruyter, 1992.

This book presents several excellent applications of Bronfenbrenner's ecological systems approach to a wide variety of developmental issues, including sociocultural risks and opportunities for children, family influences, childbearing and childrearing, cultural diversity and identity formation, and the developmental roles of formal and informal social supports.

Miller, P. *Theories of Developmental Psychology.* 3rd ed. New York: W. H. Freeman, 1993.

This book gives an excellent overview of developmental theories and their role in developmental psychology.

Phillips, J. *The Origins of Intellect: Piaget's Theory.* San Francisco: Freeman, 1969.

Phillips presents a clear and concise review of Piaget's cognitive theory.

Skinner, B. F. *Walden Two.* New York: Macmillan, 1948.

This novel describes a fictional utopian community that is guided by the assumptions of behavioral learning theory and the principles of operant conditioning.

Stern, D. N. *The Interpersonal World of the Infant: A View from Psychoanalysis and Developmental Psychology.* New York: Basic Books, 1985.

This book presents a comprehensive review of Stern's approach to development, including how it may be practically applied to clinical situations.

PART TWO

Beginnings

Although you may think human development starts in infancy, it actually begins at the moment of conception. We become individuals partly because of our genetic endowments, which are determined the moment sperm meets egg; partly because of events we experience while still in our mothers' wombs; and partly because of events that occur in the wider environment.

The next two chapters look at these influences. They show some of the ways heredity and environment affect who a child becomes, not only physically but cognitively and socially. They describe what actually happens during the thirty-eight weeks or so before birth, as well as the events surrounding birth itself. By childbirth—a time of wonder, anxiety, and joy—the baby already has undergone many changes. But there is plenty of room to learn from experience, and the child will undergo many more changes throughout his or her life.

3

Genetics

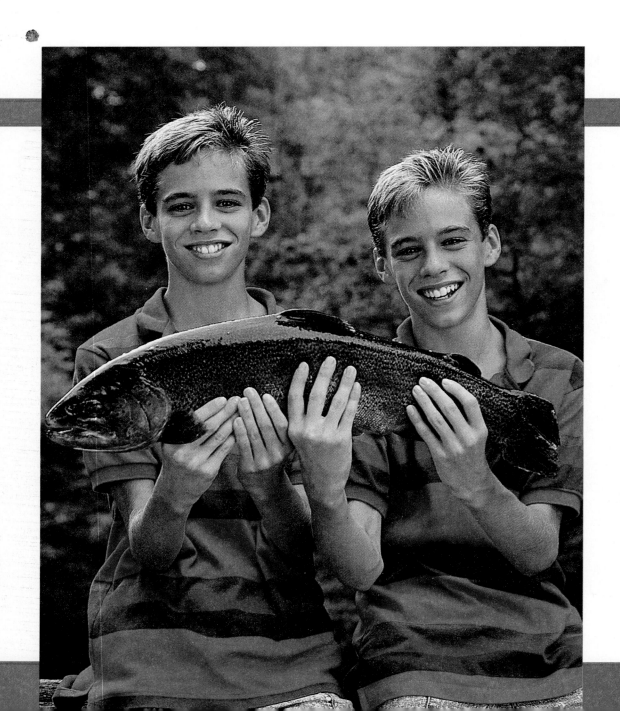

Mechanisms of Genetic Transmission

The Role of DNA
Meiosis and Mitosis

Individual Genetic Expression

Genotype and Phenotype
Dominant and Recessive Genes
Transmission of Multiple Variations
Polygenic Transmission
The Determination of Gender

Genetic Abnormalities

Disorders Due to Abnormal Chromosomes
Abnormal Genes

Genetic Counseling

Prenatal Diagnosis
Early Medical Treatments

Relative Influence of Heredity and Environment

Key Concepts of Behavior Genetics
Animal Studies
Adoption and Twin Studies
Cautions and Conclusions about the
    Influence of Heredity and Environment

Genetics and Developmental Psychology

Focusing Questions

- How does inheritance work, and how are genetic differences usually transmitted from one generation to the next?

- How do genes work to make a person a distinct individual?

- What is our current state of knowledge about common genetic abnormalities and their causes?

- How can experts in genetics help parents diagnose and respond to potential genetic problems?

- How do we sort out the unique contributions heredity and environment make to the development of individual children?

I nheritance affects a vast number of human qualities, from the color of our eyes and how tall we are to more complex characteristics such as athletic ability, intelligence, and temperament. What makes these things "run in families?" How is genetic information passed on from one generation to the next?

In this chapter, we explore answers to these questions. First, we describe the basic biological processes involved in human reproduction. Then we explain how genetic information from two individuals is combined and conveyed from parents to children. Genetic abnormalities receive special attention, not because they outnumber normal genetic processes but because they shed considerable light on those processes. Then we address an issue that psychologists have found especially important: the relationship between heredity and environment. Experts generally agree that both factors influence human development, but the exact nature of these influences is often complex and ambiguous. Finally, we describe ways to use knowledge of these relationships to benefit parents and children.

MECHANISMS OF GENETIC TRANSMISSION

Although we still lack many details about how genetic information is combined and transmitted, we do know that it begins with **gametes,** the reproductive cells of a child's parents. In the father the gametes are produced in the testicles, and each is called a **sperm** cell. In the mother they develop in the ovaries, and each is called an **ovum,** or *egg cell.* The sperm and egg cells contain genetic information in molecular structures called **genes,** which form threads called **chromosomes.** Chromosomes thus contain the genetic material that the child will inherit from the parent.

Each human sperm or egg cell contains twenty-three chromosomes. All other cells of the body contain forty-six chromosomes and approximately one hundred thousand genes. A single chromosome may contain as many as twenty thousand genes. Figure 3.1 shows a picture, or *karyotype,* of the chromosomes for a normal human male.

The Role of DNA

The genes themselves are made of **DNA (deoxyribonucleic acid).** All DNA molecules have a particular chemical structure—a double helix, or spiral—that allows them to divide easily and create new, duplicate DNA molecules reliably. DNA

FIGURE 3.1

Chromosomes for the Normal Human Male

This karotype depicts the twenty-two pairs of chromosomes and the two sex chromosomes for the normal human male. In females, the twenty-third pair of chromosomes consists of an XX instead of an XY pair.

contains the complex protein code of genetic information that directs the form and function of each body cell as it develops (see Figure 3.2).

DNA shares this information at conception. *Conception* occurs when, following sexual intercourse, a sperm from the father successfully attaches itself to the surface of an ovum, or egg, from the mother. Once it becomes attached, the sperm gradually penetrates the egg. Within a few hours, the walls of the sperm cell and the *nucleus,* or center, of the egg cell both begin to disintegrate, allowing each one to

FIGURE 3.2

Genetic Structures

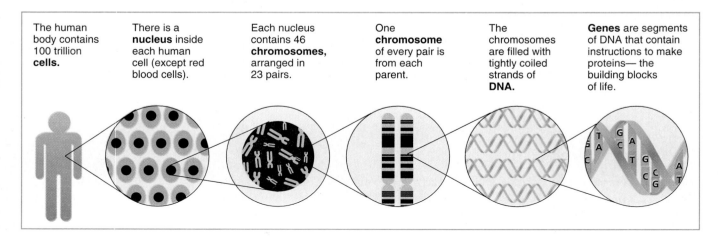

| The human body contains 100 trillion **cells.** | There is a **nucleus** inside each human cell (except red blood cells). | Each nucleus contains 46 **chromosomes,** arranged in 23 pairs. | One **chromosome** of every pair is from each parent. | The chromosomes are filled with tightly coiled strands of **DNA.** | **Genes** are segments of DNA that contain instructions to make proteins— the building blocks of life. |

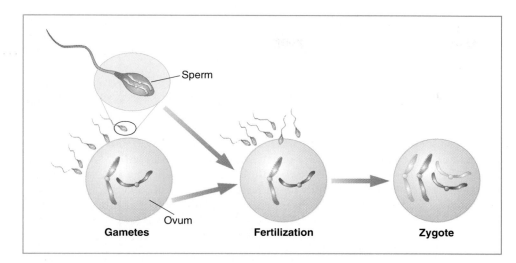

FIGURE 3.3
Gametes and Zygote
*Each gamete, whether sperm or ovum,
contains twenty-three single chromosomes. (Two chromosomes are shown
in each gamete here.) At fertilization,
sperm and ovum combine to form a
zygote with forty-six chromosomes in
twenty-three pairs. (Two pairs are
shown here.) In each pair, one chromosome is from the mother and one is
from the father.*

release its chromosomes, which join to form a new cell. The new cell formed by the
egg and sperm is called a **zygote** (see Figure 3.3). At this point, the zygote is still so
small that hundreds of them could fit on the head of a pin. Yet it contains all of the
necessary genetic information in its DNA molecules to develop into a unique human being. A fuller discussion of the process of conception appears at the beginning of Chapter 4.

Meiosis and Mitosis

All of the cells that make up a human being develop from this original zygote
through a process of cell division. As mentioned earlier, the sperm and ova contain
only twenty-three chromosomes, making them unique from other body cells. This

*This color enhanced photo shows a
human sperm fertilizing an egg.
Conception occurs when a sperm cell
penetrates an egg cell, forming a
zygote. Almost immediately, the wall
of the new zygote changes so that no
other sperm can enter.*

ensures that when an egg and sperm cell join to form a new zygote during conception, the zygote will contain the complete set of forty-six chromosomes (twenty-three pairs). This is important, because the zygote contains the genetic material from which all of an individual's cells are formed.

Therefore, two kinds of cell division occur. Reproductive cells divide through a process called *meiosis.* All other body cells divide through a process known as *mitosis.*

Meiosis involves the following steps. First, the twenty-three chromosomes of the egg (or sperm) cell duplicate themselves. Then they break up into smaller pieces and randomly exchange segments of genetic material with each other. Next, the new chromosome pairs divide to form two different cells. Finally, the two new cells divide again. Each new cell now ends up with only *one-half* the usual number of chromosomes carried by all other cells—just twenty-three chromosomes instead of forty-six. This means that the single-cell zygote formed during conception will contain the normal forty-six chromosomes: twenty-three chromosomes from the egg and twenty-three from the sperm. (See Figure 3.4.)

Once the zygote forms, it and all of its descendants divide through the process called *mitosis.* **Mitosis** involves the following steps. First, the twenty-three pairs of chromosomes of a cell duplicate themselves and divide into two identical sets. Next, the two sets of chromosomes move to opposite sides of the cell. Finally, a new wall forms between them, resulting in two new, identical cells instead of the one that existed before. Each cell of a developing child therefore acquires exact copies of the same forty-six chromosomes, and each cell thus contains the same set of genes, the same DNA molecules, and the same code, or genetic instructions, to guide its de-

---

FIGURE 3.4
The Process of Meiosis for Sperm Cells
As meiosis begins, (a) DNA replicates as in mitosis. However, before the replicated arms split apart, one member of each pair of chromosomes moves to become part of each first-generation daughter cell (b). Once the first generation of daughter cells is established, DNA copies then split as part of the second meiotic division (c). Thus, one copy of one member of the pair of chromosomes is contributed to each second-generation daughter cell (d). These two successive divisions produce four cells, each with twenty-three chromosomes.

Cell with 46 chromosomes (only one pair of homologous chromosomes is shown here). Each member of the pair has begun to replicate similar to mitotic cell division.

First meiotic cell division begins. One member of each homologous pair becomes a part of the first-generation daughter cell.

The second meiotic division proceeds after the first is completed; now the replicated chromosome acquired in the first-generation daughter cell splits apart.

Each of the four gametes produced by the two-step process now has acquired one member of the pair of homologous chromosomes.

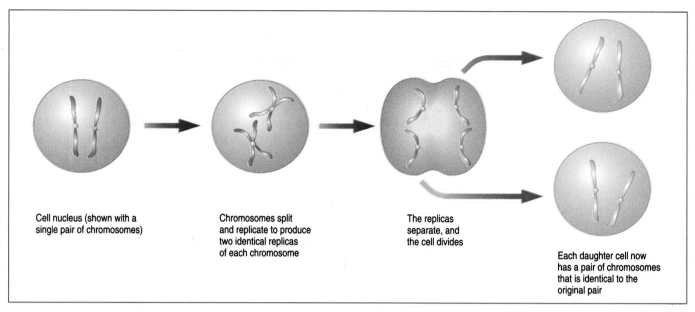

FIGURE 3.5
The Process of Mitosis
Mitotic cell division produces nearly all the cells of the body except the gametes. During mitosis, each chromosome replicates to form two chromosomes with identical genetic blueprints. As the cell divides, one member of each identical pair becomes a member of each daughter cell. In this manner, complete genetic endowment is replicated in nearly every cell of the body.

velopment. (See Figure 3.5.) This process goes on continually in all tissues of all human beings throughout their lifetimes.

What Do You Think?

Sometimes a good way to check your understanding of rather complex material is to explain it to another person. Team up with a classmate and explain the roles of mitosis and meiosis to him or her in your own words. Then ask your classmate to explain it back to you. What unanswered questions do you still have?

INDIVIDUAL GENETIC EXPRESSION

How does the genetic information contained in our cells influence the development of our unique physical, intellectual, social, and emotional characteristics? In this section, we explore some of the ways genetic information is (and sometimes is not) translated into developmental change.

Genotype and Phenotype

Behavioral geneticists and others interested in understanding the relationship between genetics and behavior generally find it useful to distinguish between genotype and phenotype. **Genotype** refers to the genes a person inherits, that is, to the specific genetic information that may influence a particular trait such as eye color, height, intelligence, or shyness. **Phenotype** refers to the physical and behavioral characteristics an individual actually exhibits at a particular point in his or her development, such as blue eyes, a height of five feet, ten inches, a certain intelligence test score, or a certain level of shyness. A person's phenotype is never just the result of his or her genotype. Rather, phenotype results from all of the interactions of that person's genotype with the environmental influences that occur from the formation of the first cell at conception onward.

In some cases, there is a close match between a person's original genotype and the phenotype that results. For example, having genes for blue eyes generally results in having blue eyes. In other cases, phenotype does not coincide so closely with genotype. For example, two newborn infants may have inherited the identical genotype for weight at the time of conception, but one may end up heavier than the other because of differences in prenatal nutrition and differences in diet and exercise during infancy and childhood. On the other hand, children who are of the same weight (have the same phenotype) may have different genotypes. One may have reached that weight by dieting and the other simply by eating whatever she wanted.

Dominant and Recessive Genes

Genes are inherited in pairs, one from each parent. Some genes are dominant and others are recessive. A **dominant gene** will influence a child's phenotype even if it is paired with a recessive gene. A **recessive gene,** however, must be paired with another recessive gene to be able to influence the phenotype. If it is paired with a dominant gene, its influence will be controlled or blocked. More than one thousand human characteristics appear to follow the dominant-recessive pattern of inheritance (McKussick, 1988). Table 3.1 lists a number of common dominant and recessive traits.

Eye color is a good example. Suppose human eyes came in only two colors, blue and brown. Most Caucasian children are born with blue eyes, but from about six months of age, a child's eyes remain blue only under certain conditions. Because blue eyes are a recessive trait and brown eyes are a dominant trait, a child's eyes will remain blue only if he has received the appropriate blue-producing gene from both parents. If he has received it from only one parent or from neither, he will end up with brown eyes.

Even for simple traits such as eye color, however, the dominant-recessive distinction does not explain phenotype fully. Very few physical traits have a completely

TABLE 3.1   *Some Common Dominant and Recessive Traits*

Dominant Trait	Recessive Trait	Dominant Trait	Recessive Trait
Brown eyes	Gray, green, hazel, or blue eyes	Short fingers	Fingers of normal length
Hazel or green eyes	Blue eyes	Double-fingers	Normally jointed fingers
Normal vision	Nearsightedness	Double-jointedness	Normal joints
Farsightedness	Normal vision	Type A blood	Type O blood
Normal color vision	Red-green color blindness	Type B blood	Type O blood
Brown or black hair	Blond hair	Rh positive blood	Rh negative blood
Nonred hair	Red hair	Normal blood clotting	Hemophilia
Curly or wavy hair	Straight hair	Normal red blood cells	Sickle-cell disease
Full head of hair	Baldheadedness	Normal protein metabolism	Phenylketonuria (PKU)
Normal hearing	Some forms of congenital deafness	Normal physiology	Tay-Sachs disease
Normally pigmented skin	Albino (completely white) skin	Huntington disease	Normal central nervous system functioning in adulthood
Facial dimples	No dimples	Immunity to poison ivy	Susceptibility to poison ivy
Thick lips	Thin lips		

Note: Many common traits show dominant or recessive patterns. Sometimes too, a pattern may be dominant with respect to one trait but recessive with respect to another.

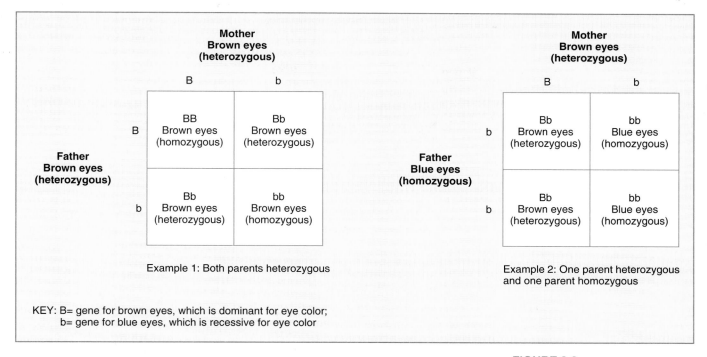

Example 1: Both parents heterozygous

Example 2: One parent heterozygous and one parent homozygous

KEY: B= gene for brown eyes, which is dominant for eye color;
b= gene for blue eyes, which is recessive for eye color

either-or quality—not even eye color, for that matter. If you look carefully at all of your friends, you will probably see that a few have hazel or greenish eyes and some have darker brown eyes than others. How can we account for variations such as these?

Transmission of Multiple Variations

The genes responsible for eye color—and, in fact, for any other trait—often take on two or more alternative forms called **alleles.** Earlier we assumed that the gene responsible for eye color can take only two allele forms, blue and brown. In reality, the gene for eye color occasionally takes on a third allele, which often leads to hazel eyes. A person who inherits two identical alleles for a particular trait is **homozygous** for that trait. A person who inherits two different alleles for the trait is **heterozygous** for that trait. In the case of eye color, a heterozygous person (one brown and one blue/hazel allele) will therefore show the phenotype of the dominant allele and thus have brown eyes. Only a person who is homozygous will display the phenotype of one of the recessive alleles and have blue or hazel eyes. From a genetic standpoint, there are three times as many ways to have brown eyes as there are to have blue ones. Figure 3.6 illustrates this example.

Many genes have more than two alleles. As a result, the traits they govern can vary in more complex ways. The four major human blood types, for example, are based on three alleles of the same gene. Two of these alleles, type A and type B, are dominant forms, and the O allele is recessive. Figure 3.7 illustrates how these three alleles for blood type can combine in six possible ways but produce only four blood types, A, B, O, and AB. The AB blood type is an example of *codominance,* a situation in which the characteristics of both alleles are independently expressed in a new phenotype rather than one or the other being dominant, or as a mixture of the two. Because each blood type has a unique chemistry that allows it to mix only with certain other blood types, determining the compatible blood genotype is very important for people who receive blood transfusions.

Not all alleles occur with equal frequency. One of the three alleles of blood type does not occur nearly as often as the other two do, and different parts of the world's

FIGURE 3.6
Genetic Transmission of Eye Color
Example 1: Three out of four offspring will have brown eyes, and one out of four will have blue eyes. Example 2: Two out of four offspring will have brown eyes, and two out of four will have blue eyes.

FIGURE 3.7
Inheritance of Blood Type
In blood type inheritance, both A and B alleles are dominant and the O allele is recessive. Therefore, the following proportions of blood types are likely to occur in the general population:
Type A (AA or AO): 3/9
Type B (BB or BO): 3/9
Type AB: 2/9
Type O (OO): 1/9

	Possible Alleles from Mother		
	A	B	o
A	AA	AB	Ao
B	AB	BB	Bo
o	Ao	Bo	Oo

Possible Alleles from Father

population inherit the blood-typing alleles with different frequencies. In fact, population geneticists have used blood samples from two thousand communities and tribes to map the worldwide geographic distribution of allele frequencies for such traits as blood type, eye and skin color, and body shape. Perhaps their most important finding is that although some group differences in alleles for such surface traits exist, there is little genetic evidence to support the idea of different "races." In fact, groups previously thought to be racially different are remarkably alike in their genetic makeup, whereas genetic diversity among individuals within these groups is enormous (Subramanian, 1995).

Polygenic Transmission

Unlike eye color and blood type, which can vary only in a limited number of qualitatively distinct ways, many other traits, such as height and weight, seem to vary along a continuum of degree. For example, while two tall parents usually have tall children and two very short parents usually have short children, more often than not a tall or a short parent will have children who are of medium height. This is because height differs from eye color in the way it is genetically transmitted.

Traits such as height and weight appear to result from the combined influence of many genes, each of which contributes a small part to the trait. Such traits are called *polygenic,* meaning they come from many genes. Most traits appear to be polygenic. In addition to height and weight, hair color and skin color have this quality. So do intelligence and shyness. In all these cases, children show a marked tendency to have a phenotype that is intermediate between those of their parents (Plomin, 1989, 1990).

Because polygenic phenotypes vary by small degrees, environment can influence them in relatively important ways. An overweight person can become more slender through a change in diet, for example, and a shy person can learn to be more outgoing. Such experiences matter less for traits that are simply transmitted by a single gene; there is no way to change eye color, even though you can cover your irises with tinted contact lenses.

The Determination of Sex

One pair of chromosomes among the usual twenty-three pairs is largely responsible for determining whether a child develops as a male or a female. In women, this pair

Most physical traits result from the combined influences of gene pairs inherited from both parents. The degree of resemblance between a child and a given parent depends on the particular pattern of gene variations involved.

looks pretty much like any other pair of matched chromosomes. In men, one member of the pair is noticeably shorter than the other. The longer reproductive or sex chromosome in either gender is called *X*, and the shorter one in men is called *Y*. Genetically normal men therefore always have a mixed combination, XY, whereas normal women always have an XX combination.

Whether a child becomes male or female depends on events at conception. All ova, or egg cells, contain a single X chromosome, whereas a sperm cell may contain either an X or a Y. If a Y-bearing sperm happens to fertilize the egg, a male (XY) zygote develops; if the sperm is X-bearing, a female (XX) zygote develops.

How does this work? During the first several weeks following conception, the developing male or female embryos possess a set of bisexual gonadal, or sex, tissues, meaning they can develop into either male or female sex structures. Between the fourth and eighth weeks of the embryo's development, the gonadal tissue develops into testes or ovaries depending on the presence or absence of a small section of the Y chromosome, referred to as *TDF*, or *testis-determining factor*. Fertilized ova that lack the Y chromosome (and TDF) develop into embryos that are female. For ova fertilized by a Y-bearing sperm, TDF is present, and male embryos result (Page et al., 1987).

Oddly enough, more Y sperm than X sperm succeed in fertilizing the ovum, even though the Ys have no advantage in numbers. This may be due to their smaller size and faster speed. The Y success rate produces perhaps as much as 30 percent more male zygotes. The advantage decreases during prenatal development. By birth, on the average, boy babies outnumber girl babies by only about 6 percent, although the ratio varies among different societies and racial groups. Later in life, the tables turn: by about age thirty-five, women begin to outnumber men. This trend suggests that males may be more vulnerable than females, at least genetically.

Much of this vulnerability is related to *sex-linked transmission*. Recall that unlike women, who carry XX chromosomes, males carry XY chromosome pairs. Because the Y chromosome carried by all males is much shorter than its matching X chromosome and therefore may lack many of the gene locations of its matching X chromosome, many genes from the mother may not be matched or counteracted with equivalent genetic material from the father. As a result, genetic abnormalities on the single complete X chromosome are more likely to result in phenotypic abnormalities in males than in females. Table 3.2 lists a number of **sex-linked recessive traits,** abnormalities that are transmitted on the single complete X chromosome.

TABLE 3.2   *Sex-Linked Recessive Traits*

Condition	Description
Colorblindness	Inability to distinguish certain colors, usually reds and greens
Hemophilia	Deficiency in substances that allow the blood to clot; also known as *bleeder's disease*
Muscular dystrophy (Duchenne's form)	Weakening and wasting away of muscles, beginning in childhood
Diabetes (two forms)	Inability to metabolize sugars properly because the body does not produce enough insulin
Anhidrotic ectodermal dysplasia	Lack of sweat glands and teeth
Night blindness (certain forms)	Inability to see in dark or very dim conditions
Deafness (certain forms)	Impaired hearing or total hearing loss
Atrophy of optic nerve	Gradual deterioration of vision and eventual blindness

Note: All of the above traits are carried by the X chromosome, and all are recessive. As a result, they occur less often in females than in males.

	Carrier Mother	
	X	X
Normal Father X	XX Normal Daughter (25%)	XX Carrier Daughter (25%)
Y	XY Normal Son (25%)	XY Hemophilic Son (25%)

FIGURE 3.8
Inheritance of Hemophilia, a Sex-Linked Disorder
In this example of the inheritance of hemophilia, the mother is a carrier of the disease. Each daughter has a 25 percent chance of inheriting a pair of normal chromosomes (XX) and a 25 percent chance of being a carrier (XX) like her mother. However, she herself will not be affected by the disorder because her second X chromosome protects her. Each son has a 25 percent chance of being normal (XY) and a 25 percent chance of inheriting the abnormal chromosome and being hemophilic. This is because as a male, his second chromosome is a Y, which does not protect him from the disorder.

One such trait is **hemophilia,** an inability of the blood to clot and therefore to stop itself from flowing. Since clotting is so slow, internal bleeding can at times be life threatening, as can the risk of encountering AIDS from transfusions with blood that hasn't been carefully screened (American College of Obstetricians and Gynecologists [ACOG], 1990). Because the gene for hemophilia is located on the X chromosome, a female carrier is protected by having a normal gene on her second X chromosome. Each of her children will have a fifty-fifty chance of inheriting the abnormal gene. Daughters who get the gene will be carriers, like their mother, while sons will develop hemophilia because they lack a second X chromosome to counteract the gene's effects. (See Figure 3.8.)

What Do You Think?

Now that you know how eye color and blood type are inherited, see if you can figure out how you inherited *your* eye color. How about your blood type?

GENETIC ABNORMALITIES

Once in awhile, genetic reproduction goes wrong. Sometimes too many or too few chromosomes transfer to a newly forming zygote. Sometimes the chromosomes transfer properly but carry particular defective genes that affect a child physically, mentally, or both. The changes almost always create significant disabilities for the child, if they do not prove fatal.

A large-scale international research effort called the *human genome project* is currently under way. Its goal is to map the locations and describe the biochemical composition of all of the approximately one hundred thousand genes that comprise the twenty-three pairs of human chromosomes. Approximately 40 percent of the human X chromosomes have been mapped so far. Genes associated with twenty-six inherited diseases have been reproduced and genes associated with fifty others identified. Most of these abnormalities are either fatal to a fetus or put it at serious medical risk (Garver & Garver, 1994; Mandel et al., 1992).

Disorders Due to Abnormal Chromosomes

Most of the time, inheriting one too many or one too few chromosomes proves fatal. After all, one extra chromosome forces several thousand "wrong" genes on the developing fetus, and it certainly cannot cope easily with so much genetic misinformation. In a few cases, however, children with an extra or a missing chromosome survive past birth and even live fairly normal lives. Three such cases are mentioned here; each is named after the doctor who first published a description of it.

Down Syndrome   People with *Down syndrome* have almond-shaped eyes, round heads, and stubby hands and feet. Many also have abnormalities of the heart and intestinal tract, and facial deformities. They also show greater than usual vulnerability to a number of serious diseases, such as leukemia. Most children with Down syndrome live until middle adulthood, but about 14 percent die by age one and 21 percent die by age ten.

Children with Down syndrome achieve many of the same developmental milestones normal children do, but at a much slower pace. Many children with Down syndrome learn to manage a good deal of their own lives and are able to hold routine jobs. Because their intellectual and psychosocial limitations prevent them from being fully independent, self-supporting adults, children with Down syndrome generally require extensive, ongoing support from their families and community service programs (Sloper et al., 1990; Stratford, 1994).

Children with Down syndrome, like this girl, learn academic material very slowly. But with special educational help and proper social support, they can lead satisfying lives.

Down syndrome is much more frequent in babies of mothers over age thirty-five and among older fathers. This is because as men and women grow older, they experience longer exposure to environmental hazards, such as chemicals and radiation, that may affect their ovaries and sperm. In addition, since a woman's ova are formed before she is born, they are likely to undergo progressive deterioration with age (Arehart-Treichel, 1981; Baird & Sadovnick, 1987; Feinbloom & Forman, 1987). Figure 3.9 summarizes the risk of having a Down syndrome baby for women of different ages.

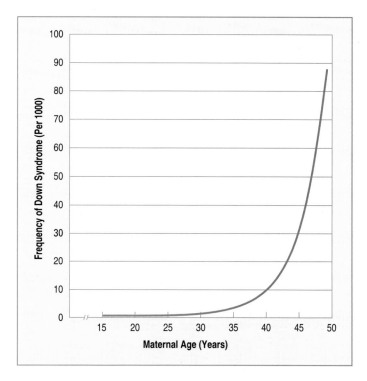

FIGURE 3.9
Relationship Between Maternal Age and the Incidence of Down Syndrome
As women get older, their chances of giving birth to a baby with Down syndrome increase. At age twenty-one, 1 in every 1,500 babies is born with Down syndrome. At age thirty-nine, 1 in 150 babies is born with the disorder. At age forty-nine, 1 in 10 babies is born with Down.

Klinefelter Syndrome   *Klinefelter syndrome (XXY)* results from inheriting at least one extra chromosome, usually an extra X chromosome, creating an XXY pattern. A person with this syndrome is phenotypically male but tends to have small testes even after puberty and to remain sterile throughout his lifetime. Klinefelter affects about one in eight hundred newborn males (ACOG, 1990).

Turner Syndrome   *Turner syndrome (XO)* affects only females, those who are born with only a single X in the sex chromosome instead of the normal XX. Females with Turner syndrome grow to be very short as adults (four and five feet) and have short, "webbed" necks and ears that are set lower than usual. During puberty, they generally fail to develop secondary sexual characteristics such as breasts and pubic hair. They show basically normal verbal intelligence, but may have serious difficulties with spacial judgment, memory, and reasoning ability (McCauley et al., 1987; Rovet, 1993).

Abnormal Genes

Even when a zygote has the proper number of chromosomes, it may inherit specific genes that can create serious medical problems for the child after birth. In many cases, these problems prove lethal. In others, genetic diseases are at least manageable, if not fully curable.

There are three main types of genetic disorders: *dominant gene disorders, recessive gene disorders,* and *multifactorial gene disorders.* Table 3.3 lists some common examples of each and the risk of their presence at birth.

Dominant Gene Disorders   Dominant gene disorders require only one abnormal gene from either parent to affect a child. Figure 3.10 illustrates the inheritance of a dominant gene disorder.

TABLE 3.3 **Risk of Selected Genetic Disorders**

Disorder	Risk of Having a Fetus with the Disorder	
	Overall	With One Affected Child
Dominant gene		
Huntington disease	1/15,000–1/5,000	50%
Recessive gene		
Cystic fibrosis	1/2,500[2]	25%
Sickle-cell disease	1/625[1]	25%
Tay-Sachs disease	1/3,600[3]	25%
PKU	5/100,000–10/100,000	25%
X-linked		
Hemophilia	1/2,500 males	50% for boy, 0% for girl
Colorblindness (red and green)	1/15 males	
Chromosomal		
Down syndrome	1/800[4]	1–2%
Klinefelter syndrome	1/800 males	N/S[5]
Turner syndrome	1/3,000 females	N/S[5]
Multifactorial		
Congenital heart disease	1/125	2–4%
Neutral tube defects	1–2/1,000	2–5%
Cleft lip/cleft palate	1/1,000–1/500	2–4%

[1]African American persons.
[2]White persons.
[3]Ashkenazi Jews.
[4]Average risk increases with mother's age.
[5]No significant increase.
Source: American College of Obstetricians and Gynecologists (1992, p. 71)

Huntington Disease   Huntington disease is a dominant gene disorder that results in a gradual deterioration of the central nervous system, causing uncontrollable movements and mental deterioration. Typically it does not appear until affected people are in their thirties or forties, and it always proves fatal. Before that age, people usually have no way of knowing whether they will get the disease (ACOG, 1990).

Researchers have recently identified specific sections of human genome that are exclusively linked to Huntington disease. The gene for the disorder appears to be located somewhere on chromosome four. Although it may now be possible to develop a genetic blood test for Huntington, an understanding of how the gene actually causes the disease and treatments are likely to be many years away (Horgan, 1993).

Recessive Gene Disorders   Recessive gene disorders can occur when the fetus inherits a pair of recessive genes, one from each parent. Figure 3.11 illustrates the inheritance of a recessive gene disorder.

Cystic Fibrosis   Cystic fibrosis is the most common genetic disease among people of northern European descent. This disability involves the production of abnormally thick mucus, clogging the lungs and causing serious difficulties in breathing and digestion, delayed growth and sexual maturation, high vulnerability to infections, and shortened life expectancy (ACOG, 1990).

Sickle-Cell Disease   By now you may be wondering why so many harmful genetic abnormalities evolved or why they do not disappear as the generations pass, given the serious health problems they cause. **Sickle-cell disease** suggests one possible answer to this question. Sometimes a genetic condition may benefit people in general even though it hurts individuals in particular. About 1 in 635 African Americans are affected with sickle-cell disease, and about 1 in 10 are carriers of it. Sickle-cell disease is especially common in tropical climates such as Africa, the Mediterranean, India, and the Middle East.

A clue to the survival ability of this disorder is that the same gene that causes it also causes increased resistance to malaria, an especially troublesome disease in tropical areas. However, the gene confers this resistance only among people with a particular genotype: individuals who are *heterozygous,* meaning they carry just one abnormal sickle-cell allele along with one dominant, non-sickle-cell allele (ACOG, 1990).

In this disease, the oxygen-carrying protein of the red blood cells takes on a rigid *sickle* shape inside the cells rather than the normal round, *doughnut* shape. These abnormal red blood cells get caught in the blood vessels, cutting off circulation, reducing the oxygen supply, and causing pain. Other symptoms include increased bacterial infections and degeneration of organs that need a great deal of oxygen, including the brain, kidneys, liver, heart, spleen, and muscles. Infants with this illness must be given daily doses of oral penicillin beginning at two months of age to reduce the chance of infection. Even with careful care, however, the majority of victims die before age twenty and few live past age forty (Diamond, 1989; Selekman, 1993).

As mentioned earlier, individuals having only one abnormal allele show a few signs of sickle-cell disease but also a strong immunity to malaria. There is some physical cost, however. Most live normal lives, but when deprived of sufficient oxygen, such as during intense physical exercise or at high altitudes, the *sickling* of their red blood cells can be triggered, causing pain. Individuals with two dominant or two recessive genes either avoid sickle-cell disease completely by having two dominant genes or suffer badly from it because they have two recessive genes. Either way, they contract malaria at very high rates. As it turns out, very large percentages of individuals in tropical areas are heterozygous. The troublesome allele

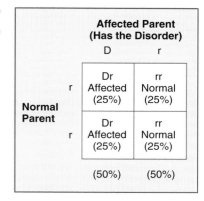

FIGURE 3.10

Inheritance of a Dominant Gene Disorder

When one parent has a dominant gene disorder, each child has a 50 percent chance of inheriting the dominant abnormal gene for the disorder (D) and a 50 percent chance of inheriting a pair of recessive genes (rr) and being unaffected.

FIGURE 3.11

Inheritance of a Recessive Gene Disorder

When both parents are carriers of a recessive gene disorder, each child faces the following possibilities: (1) a 25 percent chance of inheriting the pair of recessive genes (rr) required to inherit the disorder; (2) a 25 percent chance of inheriting a pair of dominant genes (DD) and being unaffected; or (3) a 50 percent chance of inheriting one dominant and one recessive gene (Dr) and being a carrier like both parents.

	Carrier Mother	
	D	r
Carrier Father D	DD (25%)	Dr (25%)
r	Dr (25%)	rr (25%)

seems to have evolved for their benefit and at the expense of people who contract sickle-cell disease.

Although no cure exists yet for this disease, a new drug called *hydroxyurea* appears to reduce the production of sickle cells by switching on a gene that triggers the production of fetal hemoglobin, a type produced by babies before and shortly after birth that does not sickle (Leary, 1995).

Tay-Sachs Disease   *Tay-Sachs disease* is a disorder of the nervous system that occurs most frequently among people of German or Eastern European Jewish origin (ACOG, 1990; B. Muir, 1983). Tay-Sachs disease disturbs the chemical balance in an infant's nerve cells. At birth the baby may seem fairly normal, but by about six months of age she or he may show poor tolerance for sudden loud noises and seem weak and slow to develop. Motor skills initially acquired may later be "forgotten" or lost, and the baby becomes progressively apathetic and irritable. Eventually, deterioration of the nervous system may cause convulsive seizures and lead to deafness and blindness. Most Tay-Sachs babies die by their third birthday, most frequently from a common illness such as pneumonia, because of their reduced resistance to disease.

Phenylketonuria   *Phenylketonuria (PKU),* which occurs in five to ten out of every one hundred thousand births, is a disorder that severely diminishes a child's ability to utilize an amino acid called *phenylalanine,* which is found in protein-based foods, such as milk and meat, that are essential to normal nutrition and growth.

The disorder is caused by a single recessive allele carried by a relatively small percentage of people. But because PKU is recessive, many people are carriers without realizing it. Left untreated, PKU causes phenylalanine to build up to dangerous levels in the child's blood and spinal fluid. This appears to damage the *prefrontal cortex* of the brain, causing deterioration in cognitive functioning and mental retardation. Because very small increases in phenylalanine can affect the brain, prenatal detection, early diagnosis, and a carefully planned diet from birth onward may be required to prevent the symptoms from occurring.

Long-term continuation of an extremely restrictive diet is very difficult for children and their families. In addition, pregnant women must maintain a restrictive diet to avoid passing on high levels of phenylalanine to their fetuses. These strategies help individual children and their families, but do not remove the gene that causes the problem in the first place (Diamond, 1993; Mazzocco et al., 1994).

PKU illustrates clearly the difference between genotype and phenotype. Depending on the nutrition their environment provides, infants with one particular genotype, the PKU deficiency, can either grow into a healthy phenotype or get sick enough to die. Infants with two different genotypes, one normal and one abnormally sensitive to PKU, can end up with similar, healthy phenotypes when conditions are right.

Multifactorial Disorders   **Multifactorial disorders** result from a combination of genetic and environmental factors. The incidence of these disorders varies widely in different parts of the world, largely because of the great differences in existing environmental conditions.

Neural tube defects result when the tube enclosing the spinal cord fails to close completely or normally. In some instances, the upper part of the brain is absent or underdeveloped; in others, the lower part of the neural tube fails to close properly, leaving the spinal cord and nerve bundles exposed. Both conditions are generally fatal or result in severe retardation or other serious long-term problems for children who do survive (ACOG, 1990).

Cleft palate/lip is a condition in which the upper lip and/or roof of the mouth (palate) fail to grow together, resulting in a "cleft," or split. The two conditions may occur separately or together. Depending on severity, they may lead to difficulties in breathing, speech, hearing, and eating. Corrective surgery at birth can repair most clefts (Blatt, 1988).

Congenital heart disease refers to structural and/or electrical abnormalities in the formation of the heart. Depending on the type of defect, medication may be prescribed or corrective surgery performed after birth (Blatt, 1988).

Genetic Screening   The rapid advances made in new technologies to screen for genetic disorders raise important ethical and social policy concerns about who should control these technologies and how they should be used. One danger is that people who are carriers of genetic disorders will be denied health care coverage on the basis that they have a *preexisting condition.* In one recent survey of the country's main types of health care insurers, approximately 75 percent of health maintenance organizations (HMOs), 40 percent of commercial insurers, and 35 percent of Blue Cross/Blue Shield plans agreed that the carrier of a genetic disease trait has a preexisting condition. In an increasing number of cases, employers, HMOs, and adoption agencies have used genetic information to discriminate against individuals with genetic abnormalities, even when they were carriers who were healthy or had extremely mild symptoms (Rennie, 1994).

Privacy is another important issue. If someone is a carrier of a defective gene or has a genetic disease, does someone else have the right to know? When asked this question in a recent survey, 57 percent of the respondents answered yes, 41 percent said no, and 2 percent were uncertain. Furthermore, if someone else deserves to know, who should it be? When those who believe someone else does deserve to know were asked this question, 100 percent said that a spouse or fiancé should know, 70 percent said family members, approximately 59 percent said the insurer, and about 32 percent said the employer (Rennie, 1994).

A third issue concerns how such tests should be regulated or controlled. Should private companies whose goal of maximizing investor profits may conflict with insuring high-quality and affordable health care for all be allowed to control the development, costs, and use of such tests? Or should technology that is so central to people's well-being be regulated by our democratically elected government representatives?

What Do You Think?

Woody Guthrie, the famous folk singer and father of Arlo Guthrie (also a famous folk singer), died of Huntington disease. Based on your new knowledge about this disorder, what questions might you ask Arlo about how his genetic inheritance has affected his life decisions, such as whether or not to have children?

GENETIC COUNSELING

Some genetic problems can be reduced or avoided by sensitive counseling for couples who may carry genetic disorders. Couples in need of such counseling may know of relatives who have suffered from genetic diseases. Or they may belong to an ethnic group at risk for a particular disorder, such as African-Americans, who are at risk for sickle-cell disease. More immediate signs of genetic risk include the birth of an infant with some genetic disorder or the spontaneous abortion of earlier

A Multicultural View

Cultural Difference and Genetic Counseling

The growing Asian-American population in the United States tends to use genetic counseling infrequently. Reasons for this include lack of information and misperceptions about such services and cultural attitudes that strongly discourage seeking outside help for family problems.

In traditional Asian cultures, the family is the most important social unit. It is a source of material, social, and emotional support for its members and is responsible for maintaining the cultural and religious traditions that connect the present generation with past and future ones. The personal decisions and actions of an individual regarding pregnancy and genetic counseling reflect not only on herself but on her *nuclear family* (spouse and children), her *extended family* (parents, siblings, and other relatives), and *past and future generations* of her family (Chan, 1991; Wang & Marsh, 1992). John Roland, a psychologist who has studied personality development in India and Japan, believes that in addition to an *individual* and *spiritual* sense of self, individuals growing up in such traditional societies develop a powerful *familial* self. Within this sense of self, a person experiences himself as an inseparable part of the family unit and one whose actions will be largely determined by family needs and expectations (Roland, 1988).

Three other areas of cultural difference are important for genetic counselors to understand: (1) *collective versus personal autonomy,* (2) *shame and stigma,* and (3) *directive versus nondirective authority* (Wang & Marsh, 1992).

Collective Versus Personal Autonomy

A belief in *personal autonomy* is a cornerstone of Western genetic counseling, which views the patient as a self-determining individual who is largely free from the external control of family and other outside influences. The counselor's goal is to help the patient make an informed, autonomous decision about what is best by providing information in a nondirective and value-free way. This approach, however, frequently conflicts with cultural expectations of Asian patients, who hold a *collective* view of autonomy.

Collective autonomy presumes that a patient is an inseparable part of the traditional family unit and one whose actions will be largely determined by family interests. Family roles and responsibilities are rigidly and hierarchically defined based on generation, age, and gender, with the father occupying a position of unquestioned leadership and authority. This pattern serves to minimize family conflict by allowing little room for individuality and independence on the part of its members and to maintain family harmony and further the family's welfare and reputation (Wang & Marsh, 1992; Roland, 1988).

pregnancies. Table 3.4 presents guidelines for determining who should seek prenatal genetic counseling.

Genetic counselors should be thoroughly trained in genetics, in counseling, and in working with other professionals, because they must have complete access to potential parents' medical and genetic histories to help couples estimate their chances of having a healthy baby. Making such estimates may be harder than it first appears,

---

TABLE 3.4   *Who Should Seek Prenatal Counseling?*

1. Couples who already have a child with some serious defect such as Down syndrome, spina bifida, congenital heart disease, limb malformation, or mental retardation
2. Couples with a family history of a genetic disease or mental retardation
3. Couples who are blood relatives (first or second cousins)
4. African Americans, Ashkenazi Jews, Italians, Greeks, and other high-risk ethnic groups
5. Women who have had a serious infection early in pregnancy (rubella or toxoplasmosis) or who have been infected with AIDS
6. Women who have taken potentially harmful medications early in pregnancy or who habitually use drugs or alcohol
7. Women who have had X rays taken early in pregnancy
8. Women with two or more of the following: stillbirth, death of newborn baby, miscarriage
9. Any woman thirty-five years or older

Source: Adapted from Feinbloom & Forman (1987, p. 129).

Shame and Stigma

In traditional Asian culture, which places tremendous importance on successfully marrying off a daughter, infertility is viewed as a handicapping stigma that will make a young woman unmarriageable and bring shame to herself and her family. Such problems are therefore

As in the case of this multigenerational Asian-American family, effective genetic counseling must be responsive to cultural differences.

managed within the family. To seek outside help from a genetic counselor would be a public admission of failure (Sue & Zane, 1987; Wang & Marsh, 1992).

Directive Versus Nondirective Authority

A *nondirective approach to authority* is a second cornerstone of genetic counseling that directly conflicts with the cultural expectations of Asian patients. This approach assumes the patient is responsible for making her own decisions and should not be influenced by the counselor's own views and values. In contrast, the *directive approach* assumes that as an expert authority, the counselor should provide the patient with clear and highly structured guidance about what he should do.

The directive approach is much more consistent with the authority relations and role expectations in Asian families. It therefore is more likely to relieve high levels of anxiety, shame, and doubt by providing practical and immediate solutions to problems (Wang & Marsh, 1992). Stanley Sue, who has written extensively about these issues, suggests that families from Asian and other traditional cultures will seek help from professionals who earn credibility and trust by responding to their need for directive, immediate assistance while also working with them to achieve more self-directed, long-term solutions (Sue & Zane, 1987).

because couples (and their doctors) do not always know all the genetically relevant information, such as what diseases various relatives experienced in past generations. Of course, estimates of risk may be even harder for couples to live with than for counselors to make because the parents must face considerable uncertainty about the fate of their future child. Nonetheless, it probably is better to decide whether to risk conception on the basis of knowledge rather than of ignorance.

Once the actual genetic risk is clarified, counselors can discuss alternatives from which a couple can choose. The two most obvious alternatives are to (1) avoid conception completely or (2) take the chance of conceiving a healthy baby. Modern medical techniques sometimes offer two further options: (3) prenatal diagnosis and possible abortion and (4) medical treatments early in infancy. The usefulness of these techniques, however, depends on the specific genetic problem, and all four alternatives have certain drawbacks.

Differences in cultural beliefs and expectations can affect who receives genetic counseling and the forms it takes. The accompanying Multicultural View box discusses this issue.

Prenatal Diagnosis

Sometimes genetic disorders can be detected after conception but before birth using various diagnostic techniques. This section discusses current diagnostic techniques to screen for genetic disorders. (See Table 3.5.)

TABLE 3.5   *Conditions That Prenatal Diagnosis Can Detect*

Procedure	Timing	Conditions Detected
Ultrasound	Throughout pregnancy	Pregnancy; multiple pregnancies; fetal growth and abnormalities such as limb defects; tubal (ectopic) pregnancy; multiple pregnancies; atypical fetal position; fetal abnormalities (e.g., limb defects).
Amniocentesis	14–18 weeks	Chromosomal disorders such as Down syndrome; neurological disorders; gender of the baby
Chorionic villus sampling (CVS)	9–13 weeks	Tests for most of the same genetic disorders as amniocentesis, but is less sensitive to more subtle abnormalities
Fetoscopy	15–18 weeks	Used to confirm results from a prior prenatal test or to assess the severity of a disability already identified
Maternal serum alpha-fetoprotein (MSAFP)	15–18 weeks	Various problems, including neural tube defects and Down syndrome; positive first test is followed by additional testing, such as ultrasound and amniocentesis
Percutaneous umbilical blood sampling (PUBS)	18–36 weeks	Down syndrome, neural tube defects, Tay-Sachs disease, cystic fibrosis, sickle-cell disease; gender of the fetus; fetal infections such as rubella, toxoplasmosis, or AIDS

Sources: Feinbloom & Forman (1987); Blatt (1988); D'Alton & DeCherney (1993); ACOG (1990).

Ultrasound   With **ultrasound,** high-frequency sound waves are projected through the mother's womb. When they bounce off the fetus, they create a television image of the size, shape, and position of the fetus. Ultrasound can be used throughout a pregnancy to assess the age of the fetus, multiple pregnancies, and gross physical defects in external and internal organs. It now can also be used to detect Down syndrome, which is identified by a characteristic extra skin fold on the back of the neck. Ultrasound is also used to guide instruments during prenatal procedures such as amniocentesis, chorionic villus sampling, fetoscopy, and PUBS (discussed shortly). So far, any potential negative effects of ultrasound have not been discovered (Blatt, 1988; D'Alton & DeCherney, 1993).

Amniocentesis   **Amniocentesis,** which is performed at weeks fourteen through eighteen of pregnancy, can detect abnormalities in the fetus's chromosomes well before birth. In amniocentesis, with the aid of ultrasound, a slender needle is carefully inserted through the mother's abdomen into the uterus and the amniotic sac, and a tiny sample of the amniotic fluid is withdrawn. This fluid contains cells that have the fetus's genetic makeup rather than the mother's, so it can be used to determine whether the fetus has abnormal chromosomes, as children with Down syndrome or neurological disorders do. It can also be tested for alpha-fetoprotein, a protein produced by the fetus that is present in the amniotic fluid and in the mother's blood. Then fetal cells are cultured in the laboratory over a two-to-four-week period and prepared so that their chromosomes can be studied under a microscope. The test reveals the presence of chromosomal disorders such as Down syndrome (an extra chromosome), as well as the gender of the baby.

Minor complications, such as uterine cramping, vaginal bleeding from the uterus, and leaking of amniotic fluid through the vagina, occur in about one out of one hundred procedures. A small increase in the rates of miscarriage, maternal bleeding at birth, or injury to the fetus is associated with this procedure (ACOG, 1990; Feinbloom & Forman, 1987).

Chorionic Villus Sampling   **Chorionic villus sampling (CVS)** tests for most of the same genetic disorders that amniocentesis does. Because it can be performed between the eighth and tenth weeks of pregnancy and results obtained within about ten days, it allows for earlier detection than does amniocentesis. CVS involves col-

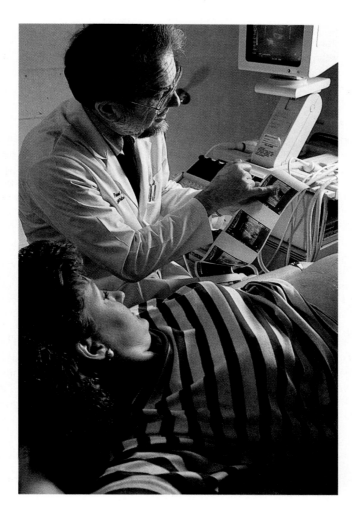

In this photo, ultrasound helps a mother to "see" a picture of her unborn child.

lecting and analyzing tissue by inserting a thin, hollow tube (catheter) through the vagina into the uterus between the uterine lining and the chorion. The *chorion* is a tissue layer that surrounds the embryo for the first two months of its development and later develops into the placenta. A syringe attached to the tube sucks up several of the *chorionic villi,* projections of tissue that transfer oxygen, food, and waste between the mother's and embryo's circulatory systems and are genetically identical with the embryo.

This technique allows parents to know in the very early weeks of pregnancy whether the fetus has inherited a serious defect and gives them time to decide whether to have a therapeutic abortion. However, CVS cannot detect more subtle chromosomal abnormalities; therefore, amniocentesis sometimes is also required. A second limitation is that CVS currently is available only in a small number of major teaching hospitals. The primary risk of CVS is abortion, which at present occurs in about 0.2 percent of the cases studied (ACOG, 1990; D'Alton & DeCherney, 1993).

Fetoscopy   *Fetoscopy* involves inserting a fetoscope—a thin, telescopelike instrument with a fiber-optic lens—through the mother's abdomen into the uterus to observe the amniotic fluid, placenta, and fetus. Usually performed fifteen to eighteen weeks after conception, fetoscopy is used to confirm results from a prior prenatal test or to assess the severity of a disability already identified, such as a cleft lip or a missing limb seen on ultrasound. It can also help determine the prospects for performing fetal surgery in utero (Blatt, 1988).

Working with   Gail Gardner, GENETIC COUNSELOR

Advising Parents about Potential Problems

Gail Gardner has worked as a genetic counselor at a university medical center for the last three years. Gail developed an interest in genetics as an undergraduate biology major and went on for a master's degree in the field. The interview took place in her office next to the genetics laboratories.

Rob: What does a genetic counselor do?

Gail: My basic work involves meeting families and helping them understand what their risks are, or might be in the future, for having children with genetic problems. Some families don't yet have children and aren't expecting a child, but want to know from their family medical history, and maybe occupational exposure history, what risks they face if they have children. I also see couples who are cur-rently expecting and want to know their risk for having a child with a genetic problem. Then there are families with either a child or an adult member with a known genetic condition. I also counsel individuals about chances for developing problems themselves in the future.

Rob: What do you do when you meet with a family?

Gail: Based on their family medical history and life circumstances, I help them to assess their risks of having children with genetically related problems. I explain the condition and recommend tests where appropriate. I try to help the family or individual reach the best decision for them given their particular religious, cultural, and emotional situation. I also try to help them cope with the decision they do make, and remain available to help them live with those decisions.

Rob: This sounds like a potentially sensitive discussion.

Gail: Oh, it is. I don't just deal with gathering information and passing it along; the issues are very personal and have a lot of psychological implications for each parent and for their relationship with each other. For example, if one parent is found to be a carrier, meaning the parent passes a condition to a child but doesn't actually cause it, there may be a lot of guilt. A lot of blaming could occur.

Rob: Do you ever need to refer families to a psychologist or psychiatrist for additional professional help?

Maternal Serum Alpha-fetoprotein   *Maternal serum alpha-fetoprotein (MSAFP)* is a test that measures the amount of alpha-fetoprotein (AFP) in the mother's blood and is performed between weeks fifteen and eighteen of pregnancy. Alpha-fetoprotein is produced by the fetus and passes from the amniotic fluid through the placenta into the mother's blood stream. Abnormally high levels of AFP are associated with various problems. The test will identify 90 percent of fetuses with anencephaly (lacking a brain), 75 percent of fetuses with spina bifida (having an opening in the back that exposes the spinal cord), and about 25 percent of fetuses with Down syndrome in women under age thirty-five. Because only a small percentage of women who test positive actually have problems, a positive first test is followed by additional testing that may include ultrasound and amniocentesis (ACOG, 1990).

Percutaneous Umbilical Blood Sampling   *Percutaneous umbilical blood sampling (PUBS)* is an experimental method of sampling fetal blood by guiding a needle through the mother's abdomen and uterus into the umbilical vein. PUBS can be performed between weeks eighteen and thirty-six of pregnancy. It is used to help identify a number of conditions associated with genetic abnormalities that were discussed earlier in this chapter. These include Down syndrome, neural tube defects, Tay-Sachs disease, cystic fibrosis, and sickle-cell disease. PUBS is also used to determine the gender of the fetus and to test for the presence of certain antibodies to fetal infections such as rubella, toxoplasmosis, and AIDS. This method provides a direct connection to the fetus, so it can also be used for intrauterine blood transfusions, to administer medications, and, perhaps in the future, to replace missing enzymes or proteins (Blatt, 1988; D'Alton & DeCherney, 1993).

Preimplantation Genetic Testing   *Preimplantation genetic testing* is one of the new technologies that has emerged with our rapidly increasing knowledge about

Gail: Sometimes I do. And if it looks as if there's a really difficult moral dilemma, I might refer to clergy, if that's appropriate.

Rob: Can you give an example of how you work with a particular genetic disorder?

Gail: Tay-Sachs disease is a good example. Jewish people of Ashkenazi or Western European background have a one in thirty chance of carrying a gene for Tay-Sachs disease compared to only one in three hundred in the general population. It's inherited in a recessive fashion—both parents must carry the gene for their children to get it. A simple blood test will identify whether parents are carriers or not.

Rob: What can a couple do if both carry the Tay-Sachs gene?

Gail: Well, one option is to go ahead and take their chances and have their own children. They have a 25 percent, or one in four, chance of having a child who inherits double recessive genes for the disease. Two out of four times a child will inherit only one recessive gene and become a carrier, and one out of four times no Tay-Sachs gene will be inherited.

Rob: What are the other options?

Gail: Other options include artificial insemination, in vitro fertilization, and, of course, adoption. Preimplantation genetic testing is also a possibility now, but is very expensive. This involves taking ova and sperm selected from the mother and father and fertilizing and growing them in the laboratory. We then analyze the DNA of the pre-embryos, and if successful, we select those that don't have the Tay-Sachs trait and implant them in the mother, where one of them will hopefully survive to term.

What Do You Think?

1. What are the most challenging aspects of the job for a genetic counselor? Why?

2. Given what you've learned about dominant/recessive traits in the chapter, what kinds of questions about family history do you think a genetic counselor would ask?

3. What other questions might you ask Gail about her work?

human genetics. In this experimental procedure, ova and sperm from parents who are carriers of a genetic disorder such as cystic fibrosis are collected, fertilized, and grown in the laboratory. Then a number of developing pre-embryonic cells are subjected to DNA analysis. Finally, a healthy pre-embryo is selected and implanted into the mother, where it can complete its prenatal development (Rennie, 1994).

Early Medical Treatments

Fortunately, approximately 95 percent of fetuses examined through prenatal diagnosis are normal. If a problem is detected and a couple decides to continue an abnormal pregnancy to term, medical treatments sometimes can alleviate or even eliminate certain genetic disorders. As we already discussed, the effects of PKU can be avoided by careful planning of an infant's diet to avoid the particular amino acids that PKU babies cannot utilize. Rh disease, which produces an incompatibility between the baby's and mother's blood, can be treated even after it affects a pregnancy through blood transfusions to the fetus or newborn infant.

More often than not, however, genetic disorders cannot be cured or controlled effectively. Couples at genetic risk need to face this fact and decide what they want to do about it. Genetic counselors cannot make these choices for couples. They can only lay out the facts and alternatives and offer support for whatever choices couples make in the end.

As we have seen, genetic inheritance has a profound impact on an individual's development. The environment in which a person grows up also plays an important role. In the next section, we examine how genetics and environment interact to influence the course of developmental change.

What Do You Think?

Do modern medical techniques unwittingly maintain several hereditary disorders by keeping alive many abnormal children who in the past might have died? If so, does this pose an ethical problem?

RELATIVE INFLUENCE OF HEREDITY AND ENVIRONMENT

The importance of hereditary (genetic) influences on individual differences in development has gained wide acceptance. Interestingly, the very same data from behavior-genetic research that support the significance of heredity also provide the best available evidence for the importance of environmental influence. This is because most complex behaviors of interest to psychologists and society, such as temperament, intelligence, and personality, are influenced at least as heavily by environmental factors as by genetic ones (Plomin, 1989).

Key Concepts of Behavior Genetics

Untangling the effects of heredity from those of environment has become the special focus of behavior genetics. **Behavior genetics** is the scientific study of how genetic inheritance (*genotype*) and environmental experience *jointly* influence physical and behavioral development (*phenotype*). In fact, every characteristic of an

How much of the resemblance between this family is due to heredity and how much due to environment? Note the similarities in their facial features and perhaps even in their smiles and temperaments.

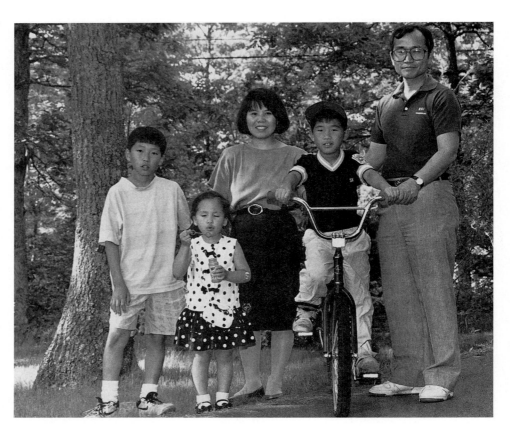

organism is the result of the unique interaction between the organism's genetic inheritance and the sequence of environments through which it has passed during its development. For some traits, the variations in environment have minimal effect. Thus, once the genotype is known, the eventual form or phenotype of the organism is pretty much specified. For other traits, knowing the genetic makeup may be a poor predictor of the eventual phenotype. Only by specifying both the genotype and the environmental sequence can the character, or phenotype, of the organism be predicted.

Range of Reaction   **Range of reaction** refers to the range of possible phenotypes that an individual with a particular genotype might exhibit in response to the specific sequence of environmental influences he or she experiences (Gottesman, 1963; Turkheimer & Gottsman, 1991). For example, if three infants start life with different genetic inheritances (genotypes) for intelligence—one low, one middle, and one high—the different levels of intelligence they actually develop (phenotypes), as measured by IQ tests, will depend on how well each child's intellectual development is nurtured and supported by his or her experiences from conception onward, including the conditions created by the child's family, school, and community. Thus, in an enriched environment, the child with low genetic endowment may achieve an IQ that is actually equal to (or even higher than) that of the child with a middle-range endowment who grows up in a restricted or below-average environment. Nevertheless, the first child cannot be expected to achieve an IQ score equal to that of children with high genetic endowment, because this is beyond the upper limit of that child's range of reaction: the highest level of intellectual functioning possible for that child. Range of reaction for intelligence is illustrated in Figure 3.12.

Canalization   **Canalization** refers to the tendency of genes to narrowly direct or restrict the development of certain phenotypic characteristics to a single or relatively limited number of outcomes in spite of environmental pressures toward other outcomes. The more deeply canalized a genetic predisposition is, the more resistant it will be to environmental influence (Waddington, 1966). For example, the stages of a normal infant's perceptual-motor development (sucking, turning over, sitting up, crawling, and walking) are strongly canalized and will predictably occur for all infants within a wide range of family and cultural childrearing environments.

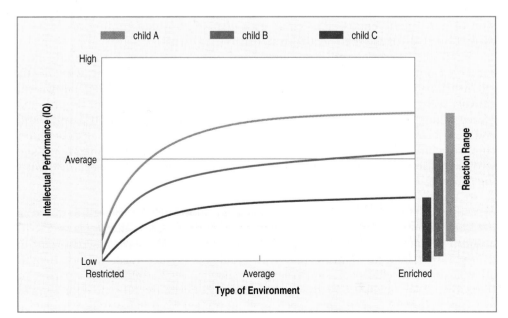

FIGURE 3.12
The Concept of Range of Reaction for Intellectual Performance
Range of reaction *refers to the range of possible phenotypes as a result of different environments interacting with a specific genotype. As this figure shows, while intellectual performance will be retarded or facilitated for all children depending on whether the environment is restricted, average, or enriched, the range of potential intellectual performance in reaction to different environments will be limited by the child's genetic inheritance for intelligence.*
Source: Gottesman (1963); Turkheimer & Gottesman (1991).

Recently, however, Esther Thelan (1995) has challenged this view. She has suggested that even the stepping reflex, which has always been presumed to be genetically preprogrammed (highly canalized), may in fact be the product of a mutual and active process of gene-environment interaction. A *stepping reflex* is exhibited by newborn infants who perform a well-coordinated, alternating-step-like pattern of movements when held upright with their feet resting on a supporting surface. However, it mysteriously disappears within a few months, reappearing later when children begin to stand and walk. Thelan suggests that the disappearance is due not to some canalized genetic program but to the rapid gain in body fat (but not muscle or strength) that babies of this age experience. Although the stepping reflex is still there, this weight gain temporarily makes the infant's chubby legs too heavy to lift from an upright, stepping position. Infants are able to perform the stepping reflex when submerged in waist-deep warm water (which makes their legs lighter). They can also lift their chubby legs when lying down, a movement that involves exactly the same actions the stepping reflex does but is made easier by gravity as the leg is raised from this position. Clearly, sorting out the sources of developmental change is not a simple task!

Many other important developmental characteristics, such as personality, temperament, and intellectual functioning, appear to be minimally canalized and are strongly influenced by environmental factors that include family, school, and culture.

The Gene-Environment Relationship   The **gene-environment relationship** refers to the patterns of interaction between a newborn infant and his or her caregiving environment and the extent to which that pattern supports the expression and development of the child's inborn traits. Parents directly influence their children's traits, such as athletic ability or shyness, through the genes their children inherit. They may also exert this influence indirectly by displaying their own genetically influenced behavioral traits (athletic ability or shyness) that support the development of similar traits in their children.

A *passive gene-environment relationship* exists if support for the development of certain traits comes mainly from others (parents and other family members), with the infant or child having little or no influence over this development. For example, parents who are themselves genotypically inclined to be good athletes or to be shy will probably expose their children to environments that support athletic activities or shy behavior in addition to having already given them a similar genetic endowment for these traits at birth.

An *evocative gene-environment relationship* exists when a child's early expression of her genetic endowment (such as a display of athletic ability or shyness) evokes support for these behaviors from others.

Finally, as children grow older and broaden their experiences to include environments outside the family, a third relationship often occurs. An *active gene-environment relationship* exists when a child with a particular genetic endowment actively seeks out and creates environmental situations, or *niches,* that support and increase his tendencies. A child who is athletic may sign up for Little League and choose friends who like sports, whereas a child who is shy may join the computer club and choose friends who are also shy. This tendency for children to choose environments that support their traits has been humorously referred to as *niche picking* (Scarr & McCartney, 1983).

Measures of Hereditary Influence   Two statistical measures are used to describe the influence of heredity on various complex human characteristics or traits. **Heritability estimates** measure the *degree* of genetic influence for traits that vary in degree rather than in an all-or-none way. Examples of such traits include height, athletic ability, intelligence, and shyness. To calculate the heritability of a particular trait, such as intelligence, the average correlation between the IQ scores for pairs of *fraternal twins* (50 percent shared genes) is subtracted from the average correlation for IQ scores for *identical twins* (100 percent shared genes) and then doubled.

Heritability scores range from 0.00 (no genetic influence) to 1.00 (complete genetic determination). For example, the heritability estimate for height is .90, meaning 90 percent of the variation in height is accounted for by genetic variation, while .10, or 10 percent, is due to diet and other environmental factors. Heritability estimates of intelligence are around .50, meaning about half of the variation we observe in children's intelligence appears to be due to differences in their genes (Horgan, 1993; Plomin, 1989).

Concordance rates are used to quantify the influence of heredity on traits that are thought to occur in an all-or-none way. These include certain physical disorders, such as cystic fibrosis, and mental disorders, such as schizophrenia and major depressive disorders. The concordance rate is stated as the percentage of instances in which both members of a pair of genetically similar individuals (such as identical twins) display a given trait, such as cystic fibrosis or schizophrenia.

Animal Studies

Animal studies use selective breeding for certain traits, such as endurance, speed, intelligence, and aggressiveness, *and* control of environmental conditions to better understand the relative contributions of heredity and environment. Because genetic partners can be selected based on their observable traits and environmental influences can be carefully controlled, the effects of genes can be systematically studied. The breeding of racehorses is a very successful example of this approach.

Newly developed *targeted gene replacement* techniques have been used to study the genome, or genetic makeup, of mice. In this method, a healthy gene on a chromosome of a mouse embryo is replaced with a gene that has been mutated with a DNA-damaging chemical that is chemically marked so that its effects on the embryo's development can be studied. Next, mice that now carry the targeted mutation are bred with normal mice, producing offspring that are heterozygous, meaning they have one mutated copy and one normal copy of the gene. Finally, when heterozygous mice are mated, 25 percent of the offspring will display abnormalities that will reveal the normal functions of the target gene in all of their tissues (Cepecchi, 1994).

If you are wondering what mice and people have in common, you may be surprised to learn that an estimated 99 percent or more of the genes in mice and humans are the same and serve similar purposes. As a result, behavioral genetic studies of rats may eventually help us better understand the more than five thousand human genetic defects. However, a note of caution is in order. Although this approach has already helped us to better understand the inheritance of the gene for cystic fibrosis, most genetic disorders are not tied to a single gene. Rather, they are the result of the complex series of interactions of many genes and many environmental factors that emerge from conception onward (Cepecchi, 1994).

Since neither selective breeding, environmental manipulation, nor target gene replacement are likely to be ethically acceptable choices for research with human beings, methods based on "naturally occurring" opportunities must be relied on to sort out the relative contributions of heredity and environment to human development.

Adoption and Twin Studies

Adoption Studies   **Adoption studies** compare the degree of physical or behavioral similarity between adoptive children and members of their adoptive families (with whom they have little in common genetically) with the degree of physical or behavioral similarity between these same children and members of their biological families (with whom they share half of their genes). If adoptive children share similar environments but not genes with their adoptive family members, differences in trait similarity with their adoptive versus biological relatives should tell something about the influence of their genetic differences. For example, if the IQ scores of adopted

The Race and Intelligence Controversy: Social Policy Implications

The practical importance of understanding how genes and environment influence development is vividly demonstrated by recent claims that group differences between blacks and whites in average IQ test scores are due to genetic rather than environmental differences (Hernstein & Murray, 1994; Jensen, 1969a, 1969b). Most twin adoption studies report average heritability scores of about .50 for *within-group* differences in IQ among pairs of individuals who have a *known degree* of genetic similarity but have been raised in unequal environments. This, however, tells us nothing about average IQ differences *between groups*. This is because even though a trait such as IQ may be equally heritable for pairs of individuals *within* two different groups (say, blacks and whites), the two groups are very likely to differ in their average IQ scores if, on the average, their members grow up in environments that provide unequal support and opportunities.

Unfortunately, this appears to be the case for whites and blacks in our society. Large differences in pre- and postnatal health care, income, education, and general living conditions continue to exist despite a variety of ef-

forts to reduce them (Holmes, 1995). Until we have convincing evidence that these between-group differences in environment have been eliminated, such environmental inequalities will remain the most likely explanation for differences in average group IQ scores. Additional support for this explanation comes from studies showing that when black and white children are raised in environments that are equally supportive of their intellectual development, average between-group differences disappear (Gordon, 1995; Lane, 1994).

On what basis, then, do people such as Hernstein and Murray conclude that group differences in intelligence are genetically based? Part of the answer appears to lie in confusion about race. While a great deal of evidence exists that race serves as a *social and cultural* category that influences attitudes, perceptions, and behaviors, existing scientific evidence lends little support for a *genetics*-based concept of race. Population geneticists working with the Human Genome Diversity Project, for example, recently completed a worldwide mapping of human genetic characteristics. They found that with very minor

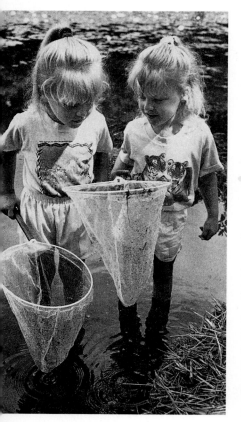

Because these twins are identical, they share entirely the same genotype, and differences between them reflect differences in their environments.

children correlated more highly with the IQ scores of their biological families versus their adoptive families, we might conclude that heredity made a strong contribution to intelligence. However, if the IQ scores of these adoptive children were significantly higher (or lower) than those of their biological parents, this might also indicate the influence of family circumstances and other environmental factors.

One major limitation of family comparisons is that because many different *mini* environments exist within the same family, two children raised in the same family may have very different developmental experiences based on the unique set of expectations and interactions that develop.

Twin Studies   **Twin studies** compare pairs of *identical twins* raised in the same family with pairs of *fraternal twins* (50 percent shared genes) raised in the same family. Since identical twins have the exact same genetic makeup, greater similarity between identical twins than between fraternal twins on a trait such as intelligence or shyness would probably reflect the influence of heredity.

Twin Adoption Studies   Studies of identical twins reared apart since birth provide the strongest method for understanding the gene-environment relationship in humans. Identical twins inherit exactly the same genes. Therefore, if we could compare pairs of identical twins raised in truly different family environments, we would be able to separate out the relative contributions of heredity and environment. The catch is to find twins who are growing up in adoptive families. An additional problem is that adoptive families are most frequently chosen with the goal of offering twins similar socioeconomic, cultural, and religious conditions and experiences, raising the question of how different their adoptive family environments really are. Despite these limitations, studies of twins reared apart and of adopted children have shed a great deal of light on the relative contributions of heredity and environment to human development (Horgan, 1993).

variations, all humans share a single genetic makeup and therefore belong to a single genetic or racial group. What appear to be racial differences based on readily observable physical differences are mainly allelic adaptations to climate that evolved as people migrated from their common African origin to their current locations around the world. For example, although Australian aborigines and Africans share such superficial traits as skin color and body shape, Australians are in fact genetically most different from Africans and genetically most similar to Southeast Asians, their geographic neighbors (Garver & Garver, 1994; Montagu, 1975).

Another reason group genetic differences are unlikely to underlie group differences in IQ has to do with the concept of intelligence itself. Ideas of what intelligence is and how it is demonstrated vary so widely across different cultures and have changed so much over time that it is highly unlikely that the genes that have evolved for "intelligence" are related to any culturally specific definition of that trait, such as IQ. Since the very trait we are predicting is influenced by differing and changing cultural assumptions and behaviors, it is likely that the genetic contribution to intelligence will turn out to be quite general and flexible rather than specific to a particular cultural or ethnic group. In fact, human evolution has been *biosocial* rather than strictly biogenetic. This means our social and cultural evolution, including language, problem solving, and sophisticated use of tools, occurred simultaneously with our genetic evolution, raising the question of whether genetic and cultural contributions to intelligence can ever be separated (Kamin, 1995; Montagu, 1975).

Some critics have suggested that supporters of a racial-genetic view of group differences in IQ may be politically motivated. They point out that the conclusion that racial differences in intelligence are genetic is based on insufficient evidence and misleading applications of the principles of behavior genetics. They assert that proponents of this view use it to attack social programs designed to reduce economic and social inequality, claiming that group differences in IQ are inherited and therefore unchangeable (Gordon, 1995; Kamin, 1995; Lane, 1994; Montagu, 1975).

Linkage and Association Studies Linkage and association studies allow researchers to identify *polymorphisms*—certain segments of human DNA that are inherited together in a predictable pattern—as genetic markers for the genes near which they are located. *Linkage studies* seek to discover polymorphisms that are coinherited, or "linked," with a particular trait in families unusually prone to that

Separated at birth, the Mallifert twins meet accidentally.

Shared genes or shared experiences? Studies of genetically identical twins who are reared in different environments from birth attempt to evaluate the degree to which shared behavioral characteristics are determined by shared genes versus shared experiences.

trait. This was the case in the discovery of a genetic marker for Huntington disease, which was described earlier in this chapter. *Association studies* compare the relative frequency of polymorphisms in two populations, one with the trait and one without it (Horgan, 1993).

Intelligence   General intelligence—as measured by standardized IQ tests, for example—shows both hereditary and environmental components. While considerable controversy revolves around how much genetic inheritance contributes to intelligence, most researchers agree that genotype makes some contribution. Close relatives tend to have more similar IQ scores than distant relatives do, and relatives in general have more similar scores if they live together than if they live apart. Studies have generally found that about 50 percent of the difference among individuals *within* a given group is genetic. Longitudinal studies have found that genetic influence on IQ increases substantially during childhood and that these differences continue into adulthood (Plomin et al., 1988).

Critics of twin studies caution us that in some studies, identical twins supposedly raised apart were sometimes in fact raised by members of their families or unrelated families in the same neighborhood and that some have had extensive contact with each other while growing up. The media coverage and publicity associated with such studies motivate subjects to downplay previous contacts and exaggerate their similarities (Horgan, 1993).

Our understanding of how genes and environment influence intelligence has major social policy implications as well. The accompanying Perspectives box discusses this issue.

Cautions and Conclusions about the Influence of Heredity and Environment

While substantial evidence exists that genetic inheritance plays at least a moderate role in differences in physical, intellectual, and personality traits, it is likely that such differences are due to *both* heredity and environmental experience, even for strongly canalized characteristics such as height and certain physical abilities. Our understanding of the mechanisms of behavioral genetics has increased substantially, but the degree and manner in which genes and environment influence development still remain unclear.

Even for children who grow up in the same family, environmental influences tend to operate on an individual-by-individual rather than a family-by-family basis. Thus, they tend to make children in the same family different from one another rather than making the same family different from other families. Siblings in the same family appear to experience considerably different environments in terms of parental treatment and their interactions with one another and their peers (Plomin, 1989). The pattern by which genes and environment interact to influence the long-term development of any individual can be understood only on a case-by-case basis that reflects that person's particular developmental contexts and experiences. The contribution of heredity tends to remain most stable where there is a passive relationship between heredity and environment and most subject to change when an active relationship between heredity and environment exists. Thus, an infant who is irritable at birth will be more likely to continue to exhibit that trait if her family and other experiences support it and less likely to do so if they do not. Even with our greatly increased knowledge of the biochemistry of genetics, successful prediction of long-term intellectual and personality characteristics may never be possible given that we can neither predict nor control the continuing changes they will undergo over the individual's course of development.

Currently there is a growing trend toward minimizing environmental contributions in favor of a genetic determinism: a belief that most, if not all, human characteristics, from intellectual functioning to gender roles and career choice, are determined primarily by genes. The belief that complex human thoughts and actions and their development can be fully understood at the biogenetic level is a form of *reductionism.* This tendency toward genetic reductionism may be partly a reaction to environmental reductionism, an equally simplistic view that sees experience as the central or sole cause of developmental change and dismisses the possibility that genes may also make a significant contribution.

A *nonreductionist view* holds that explanation of complex human thoughts, feelings, and actions cannot be meaningfully explained at the genetic level. Existing scientific evidence suggests that it is highly unlikely that either biogenetic reductionism or environmental reductionism can ever provide an adequate understanding of human characteristics. Rather, human development is always the product of multiple levels of influence of *both* genes and environment, be the influences molecular, biochemical, physical, social, or psychological. More important, *any* approach that reduces developmental change to predetermined processes, whether genetic or environmental, denies the uniquely human capacity for self-determination and free choice and for holding ourselves and others morally accountable for the choices we make.

What Do You Think?

Based on what you have just read, how do you view the relationship between genes and environment? To what degree do you believe that most or all of human development will someday be explainable in terms of genetics? What unanswered questions do you have about these issues?

GENETICS AND DEVELOPMENTAL PSYCHOLOGY

Despite its limitations, knowledge of human genetics contributes to human welfare in two ways. First, it clarifies the origins of many behaviors. According to conventional wisdom, behaviors are either "learned" or "inborn;" human genetics suggests instead that many behaviors are actually both. Second, knowledge of genetics can suggest realistic limits as to how much to expect from many ordinary life experiences. How much can education really make people "more intelligent?" How much can parents expect a child with an active temperament to learn to be quieter? After learning the complex answers genetics usually gives to questions such as these, professionals can—and should—shift attention to individuals: How can we know whether *this* child will develop normally or whether *that* one will experience a chronic disorder? For these more personal questions, we need more knowledge of individual development, such as that genetic counseling offers. Such an orientation is also provided by other branches of developmental psychology, which we describe in the following chapters.

SUMMARY OF MAJOR IDEAS

Mechanisms of Genetic Transmission

1. Genetic information is contained in a complex molecule called deoxyribonucleic acid *(DNA).*

2. Most body cells produce tissue by simple division of their genes, chromosomes, and other cellular parts by means of a process called *mitosis.*

3. Reproductive cells, or gametes, divide by a process called meiosis and recombine into a zygote at conception.

4. The process of meiosis gives each gamete one-half of its normal number of chromosomes; conception brings the number of chromosomes up to normal again and gives the new zygote equal numbers of chromosomes from each parent.

Individual Genetic Expression

5. A person's phenotype is the pattern of traits the person actually shows during his or her life.

6. A person's genotype is the set of inherited genetic traits; it depends on the pattern of chromosomes and genes inherited at conception.

7. Although most genes exist in duplicate, some—called dominant genes—may actually influence the phenotype if only one member of the pair occurs.

8. Recessive genes do not influence the phenotype unless both members of the pair occur in a particular form.

9. Many genetic traits are transmitted by the combined actions of several genes.

10. Gender is determined by one particular pair of chromosomes, called the X and Y chromosomes, and a testis-determining factor (TDF) located on a small section of the Y chromosome.

Genetic Abnormalities

11. Some genetic abnormalities occur when an individual inherits too many or too few chromosomes.

12. The most common abnormalities of this type are Down syndrome, Klinefelter syndrome, and Turner syndrome.

13. Other genetic abnormalities occur because particular genes are defective or abnormal even though their chromosomes are normal. Examples are Huntington disease, cystic fibrosis, sickle-cell disease, Tay-Sachs disease, and phenylketonuria (PKU).

Genetic Counseling

14. Experts on genetics can provide parents with information about how genetics influences the development of children and about the risks of transmitting genetic abnormalities from one generation to the next.

15. Several methods now exist for diagnosing genetic problems before a baby is born, including amniocentesis, CVS, ultrasound, and various blood tests.

16. Given the permanence and importance of genetic problems when they occur, genetic counselors should help couples reach informed decisions about pregnancy that take personal circumstances as well as scientific information into account.

17. Cultural differences in beliefs and expectations significantly affect the counseling situation.

Relative Influence of Heredity and Environment

18. According to behavioral geneticists, every characteristic of an organism is the result of the unique interaction between the genetic inheritance of that organism and the sequence of environments through which it has passed during its development.

19. Behavioral geneticists use the concepts of range of reaction, canalization, heritability, and concordance to describe the strength and directness of genetic predisposition.

20. The gene-environment relationship can be passive, active, or evocative.

21. Studies of identical twins and of adopted children suggest that heredity and environment operate jointly to influence developmental change.

22. Linkage and association studies use repeated DNA segments called polymorphisms as genetic markers to locate abnormal genes.

23. Certain personality traits, such as shyness, may be inherited to a certain extent, but they are also substantially influenced by environmental experiences.

24. When environmental factors are significant, they operate on an individual rather than a family basis.

25. The controversy over the reasons for between-group differences in IQ demonstrates the practical social policy implications of the concepts of behavioral genetics.

KEY TERMS

gamete (59)
sperm (59)
ovum (59)
gene (59)
chromosome (59)
deoxyribonucleic acid (DNA) (59)
zygote (61)
meiosis (62)
mitosis (62)
genotype (63)
phenotype (63)
dominant gene (64)
recessive gene (64)
alleles (65)
homozygous (65)
heterozygous (65)

sex-linked recessive traits (67)
hemophilia (68)
sickle-cell disease (71)
ultrasound (76)
amniocentesis (76)
chorionic villus sampling (CVS) (76)
behavior genetics (80)
range of reaction (81)
canalization (81)
gene-environment relationship (82)
heritability estimate (82)
concordance rate (83)
adoption study (83)
twin study (84)

FOR FURTHER READING

Blatt, R. J. R. *Prenatal Tests: What They Are, Their Benefits and Risks, and How to Decide Whether to Have Them or Not.* New York: Vintage Books, 1988.

This book describes in nontechnical language the current range of prenatal tests, their advantages and disadvantages, the nature of the results, and implications for the family.

Lerner, R. M. *Final Solutions: Biology, Prejudice, and Genocide.* University Park, Pa.: Pennsylvania State University Press, 1992.

This book discusses the role of values and the place of science in current political struggles regarding the practical social policy consequences of bio-behavioral theory and research.

McKie, R. *The Genetic Jigsaw: The Study of the New Genetics.* New York: Oxford University Press, 1988.

This book covers recent developments in genetics and genetic engineering in an informative and interesting way and is a good introduction to the topic.

Plomin, R. *Nature and Nurture: An Introduction to Human Behavioral Genetics.* Pacific Grove, Cal.: Brooks/Cole, 1990.

This paperback provides an interesting and readable review of recent genetic research for the lay reader.

Suzuki, D., and P. Knudtson. *Genethics: The Clash Between the New Genetics and Human Values.* Cambridge, Mass.: Harvard University Press, 1989.

This book offers well-organized coverage in nontechnical language of state-of-the-art developments in genetics. It provides a balanced presentation of the ethical questions involved in such issues as genetic screening in the workplace, gene therapy, biogenetic weapons, and the patenting of genetic material.

4

Prenatal Development and Birth

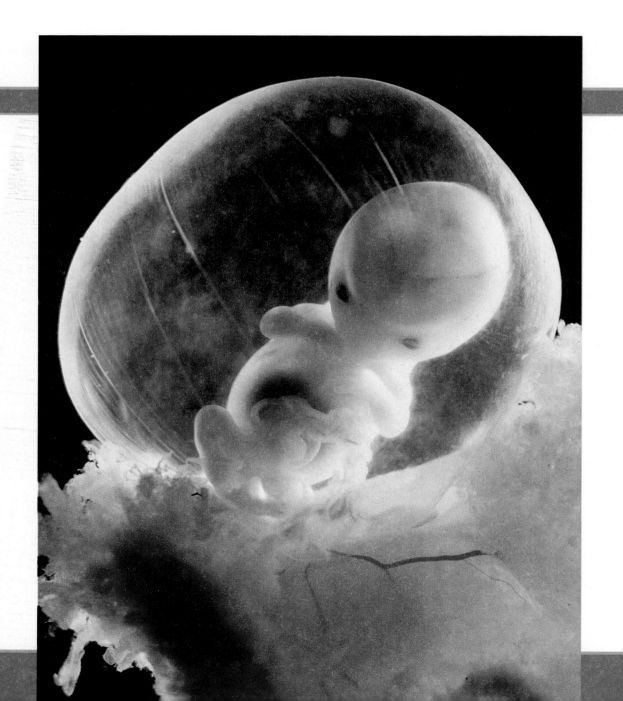

Stages of Prenatal Development

Conception
The Germinal Stage (First Two Weeks)
The Embryonic Stage (Third Through
  Eighth Weeks)
The Fetal Stage (Ninth Week to Birth)
Infertility
The Experience of Pregnancy

Prenatal Influences on the Child

Key Concepts
Maternal Age and Physical Characteristics
Diseases
Drugs
Environmental Hazards
Domestic Violence
Teenage Pregnancy
Diet and Nutrition
Prenatal Health Care
Stress

Birth

Stages of Labor
Childbirth Settings and Methods
Problems During Labor and Delivery
Low-Birth-Weight Infants
Birth and the Family

From Biological to Psychological Development

F rom the moment of conception a child becomes a biological entity, even if the one-celled zygote's status as a human being is questionable. Early during its nine months inside the womb, a fetus acquires all the essential human physical features and some rudimentary human behaviors. It is influenced by changes in its environment, by its own rapid physical growth, and by the well-being of its mother and the stresses and supports that affect her. Together these internal and external influences create a truly unique person.

How do microscopic cells become people? In this chapter, we describe the events and processes of development before birth and point out how these developments affect the child after birth. We also look at some risks and problems of prenatal development and of birth and their long-term impact on the child.

Focusing Questions

- What must happen for normal conception to occur? What alternatives are currently available for couples who have problems conceiving a child?

- What happens to the developing embryo during the three stages of prenatal development that occur between conception and birth?

- What risks do a mother and baby normally face during pregnancy, and how can they best be minimized?

- What methods are currently available to help parents prepare for the birth process?

- What happens during the three stages of the birth process? What are the possible difficulties, and how are they handled?

STAGES OF PRENATAL DEVELOPMENT

In this section, we see that prenatal development begins with conception and continues through discrete periods, or stages. The first is the **germinal stage,** or period of the ovum, which occurs during the first two weeks of pregnancy; the **embryonic stage** lasts from the third week to the eighth week; and the **fetal stage** lasts from the eighth week until birth.

Conception

Let us look first at the microscopic actors of prenatal development, the gametes we described in Chapter 3. One gamete is the *ovum,* or *egg cell.* The egg cells develop in two small, almond-shaped organs, the ovaries, which normally release one egg cell during each menstrual cycle. The egg travels down one of the fallopian tubes toward the uterus, where the baby will develop. The opening of the uterus, the cervix, connects to the woman's vagina, which receives the male's penis during intercourse and, upon ejaculation, the male's reproductive cells.

Egg cells start to develop well before a girl begins having menstrual cycles or is otherwise ready for intercourse. In fact, at birth a girl's ovaries contain several hundred thousand ova, which are already partially developed. Many of these ova degenerate or die during the dozen or so years before the girl begins menstruating, and many more fail to mature fully after that. So a woman ends up with approximately four hundred ova, a fixed supply that must last her entire reproductive life (Silber, 1991). In this respect, she differs markedly from a man.

Male reproductive cells are called *spermatozoa,* or *sperm cells.* They develop in the testes, which are located in the bag of skin called the *scrotum* that is underneath and behind the penis. The sperm get a late start compared to ova; the testes do not begin producing sperm in quantity until puberty, or about age twelve to fourteen years. They soon make up for lost time, however, by producing millions of sperm, and production continues relatively undiminished well into a man's old age. Each sperm cell has a head and a long tail, rather like a tadpole, that helps it swim through the female reproductive organ.

To create a *zygote*, a fertilized egg cell, at least one sperm cell from the man has to find and penetrate one egg cell from the woman. **Conception** occurs the moment a sperm cell penetrates and fertilizes an egg cell. Potential parents may consider conception all too easy to accomplish, but from the gametes' point of view the job is extremely challenging. For a couple to conceive successfully, each of the following conditions must be met:

1. The ovaries must release one healthy egg cell.
2. The egg cell must migrate most of the way down the fallopian tube.
3. Millions of sperm cells must be deposited as far as possible up the vagina, preferably at or near the cervix.
4. At least some of the sperm must swim in the right direction: up through the uterus to the fallopian tubes.
5. At least some of these sperm must survive the journey; the woman's uterus is slightly acidic and therefore toxic to sperm.
6. A few sperm must reach the ovum.
7. One sperm must penetrate the ovum to form a zygote.

Timing is crucial in this process. The ovum normally lives only about twenty-four hours after it is released and the sperm only about forty-eight hours (Silber, 1991). These limits give a couple about three days, or seventy-two hours, each month when intercourse is likely to result in conception and pregnancy. The period lasts from about two days before the egg is released (the sperm can survive that long) until about one day afterward (when the egg dies). This fertile period usually occurs about halfway through a woman's menstrual cycle, but it may occur at some other time.

Other, less direct factors also affect whether conception occurs. For example, some men produce much denser concentrations of sperm than others do, although even a relatively low concentration usually contains more than enough gametes to ensure conception if the sperm can reach the ovum. Also, the number of sperm is reduced considerably if intercourse already occurred recently—say, within the previous twenty-four hours. And conception becomes less likely if either partner is more than forty years old (Silber, 1991). Apparently age diminishes the man's concentration of sperm somewhat; more important, it may lead to an increased number of defective gametes in either the man or the woman. Stress also can reduce the chances of conception. Stress can interfere directly by discouraging lovemaking or indirectly by somehow preventing ovulation or implantation of the zygote.

All of these influences can amount to either obstacles or preventatives, of course, depending on whether a woman wants to become pregnant. Either way, they can be frustrating because of the indirectness with which they operate. And either way, getting pregnant can prove as difficult for some couples as it is easy for others. A significant number of individuals have difficulty conceiving normally.

The Germinal Stage (First Two Weeks)

Once a sperm and an ovum join successfully, the resulting zygote begins to divide and redivide. The original cells form a tiny sphere called a *blastocyst,* which looks something like a miniature mulberry. After about three days, the blastocyst contains about sixty cells, but these become smaller as the cells increase in number, so the blastocyst is still scarcely larger than the original zygote. While these divisions occur, the blastocyst floats down the remainder of the fallopian tube, helped in part by gentle squeezing motions similar to the digestive motions of the intestines.

The blastocyst, which is filled with fluid, rapidly undergoes a number of important changes. The cells along one of its sides thicken to form the embryonic disk, out of which the baby will eventually develop. The blastocyst also differentiates into three layers. The *ectoderm,* or upper layer, later develops into the epidermis, or outer layer of skin, nails, teeth, and hair, as well as the sensory organs and nervous system. The *endoderm* (lower layer) becomes the digestive system, liver, pancreas, salivary glands, and respiratory system. The *mesoderm,* or middle layer, develops somewhat later and becomes the dermis (inner layer of skin), muscles, skeleton, and circulatory and excretory systems. In a short time the *placenta, umbilical cord,* and *amniotic sac* (to be discussed shortly) also will form from blastocyst cells.

After a few more days—about one week after conception—the blastocyst attaches to the wall of the uterus. The attachment process is called **implantation,** because the blastocyst buries itself like a seed in the wall of the uterus. The fully implanted blastocyst is now referred to as the **embryo.** Implantation takes about another week to complete, so it ends about the time the woman might expect another menstrual period. It also signifies the end of the germinal stage and the beginning of the next phase of prenatal growth, during which the developing child begins to grow differentiated cells. Figure 4.1 illustrates the changes that occur during the germinal stage of prenatal development.

The Embryonic Stage (Third Through Eighth Weeks)

Growth during the embryonic stage (and the fetal stage that follows) occurs in two patterns: a *cephalocaudal* (head-to-tail) pattern and a *proximodistal* (near-to-far, from the center of the body outward) pattern. Thus, the head, blood vessels, and heart—the most vital body parts and organs—begin to develop earlier than the arms, legs, hands, and feet. Figure 4.2 (upper portion) on page 103 illustrates these changes.

FIGURE 4.1
The Germinal Stage of Prenatal Development
The sperm and ovum join to form a single-celled zygote, *which then divides and redivides and becomes a multicelled* blastocyst. *The blastocyst buries, or* implants, *itself in the uterine wall. The fully implanted blastocyst is now called an* embryo.

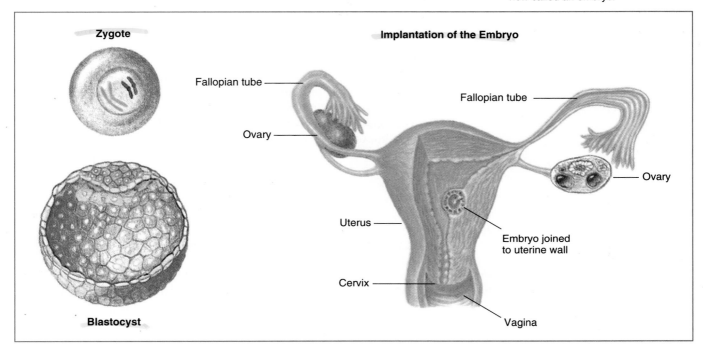

Zygote

Blastocyst

Implantation of the Embryo

Fallopian tube

Ovary

Fallopian tube

Ovary

Uterus

Embryo joined to uterine wall

Cervix

Vagina

The environment and anatomy of an embryo change dramatically during the first two months of pregnancy. By the end of the third week, the embryo is surrounded by a thin sac of fluid, which cushions it from bumps and provides a more uniform temperature. The embryo shown here is at the end of the fifth week after conception. Note its leg buds and eyes.

At *three weeks,* the head, tail, and brain regions begin to develop. The circulatory system has also begun to develop, and the heart has begun beating. At *four weeks,* the embryo is not much more than an inch long. The beginnings of a spinal cord, arms, and legs are evident, a small digestive system and a nervous system have developed, and the brain has become more differentiated. The embryo's parts do not have the fully adult shapes, but nonetheless they are unmistakable (P. Harris, 1983). During *week five,* hands and lungs begin to form. During *week six,* the head grows larger, the brain becomes more fully developed, and hands, legs, and feet become more fully formed. During *weeks seven and eight,* muscles form, and the cerebral cortex begins to develop.

While these developments are taking place, a placenta forms between the mother and the embryo. The **placenta** is an area on the uterine wall through which the mother supplies oxygen and nutrients to the embryo and the embryo returns waste products from her bloodstream. In the placenta, thousands of tiny blood vessels from the two circulatory systems intermingle. Although only minute quantities of blood can cross the separating membranes, nutrients pass easily from one bloodstream to the other. Some of them are pushed actively from one to the other as though by a pump, and others float freely through the vessel walls by a process called *osmosis.* Although many toxic chemicals and drugs in the mother's system do not spread easily by osmosis, others do. As we discuss later, seemingly harmless chemicals sometimes prove devastating to the child.

The **umbilical cord** connects the embryo to the placenta. It consists of three large blood vessels, one to provide nutrients and two to carry waste products into the mother's body. The cord enters the embryo at a place that becomes the baby's belly button, or navel, after the cord is cut following birth. The cord contains no nerves, so cutting it hurts neither the mother nor the child. For the same reason, mother and child can exchange no neural signals or messages through the cord before birth, even though they certainly communicate in other ways.

By the end of the eighth week, an amniotic sac has developed. The **amniotic sac** is a tough, spongy bag filled with salty fluid that completely surrounds the embryo and serves to protect it from sudden jolts and maintain a fairly stable temperature. The baby floats gently in this environment until birth, protected even if its mother goes jogging, sits down suddenly, or shovels heavy snow.

The Fetal Stage (Ninth Week to Birth)

At about *eight weeks* of gestation, the embryo develops its first bone cells, which marks the end of differentiation into the major structures. At this point the embryo acquires a new name, the **fetus,** and begins the long process of developing relatively small features, such as fingers and fingernails and eyelids and eyebrows. Their smallness belies their importance, however. For example, the eyes undergo their greatest growth during this stage of development. The fetus's newly developing eyelids fuse shut at about ten weeks and do not reopen until the eyes themselves are essentially complete, at around twenty-six weeks.

Not only the eyes but most other physical features become more adult looking during this period and more truly human in proportion (P. Harris, 1983). The head becomes smaller relative to the rest of the body (even though it remains large by adult standards), partly because the fetus's long bones, the ones supporting its limbs, begin growing significantly. Thus, its arms and legs look increasingly substantial.

By *twelve weeks,* the fetus is about three inches long and able to respond reflexively to touch. By *sixteen weeks,* it has grown to about 4½ inches in length. If its palm is touched, it exhibits a grasp reflex by closing its fist; if the sole of its foot is touched, its toes spread (Babinski reflex); and if its lips are touched, it will respond with a sucking reflex. In addition, the fetal heartbeat can now be heard through the wall of the uterus.

Between the *fourth* and *fifth months* (sixteen to twenty weeks), hands and feet become fully developed, eyes can open and close, hearing is present, lungs become capable of breathing in and out, and nails, hair, and sweat glands develop. Around the sixteenth week, most pregnant women feel *quickening,* the movement of the fetus inside the womb. Actually these movements have been going on for many weeks by the time most mothers notice them, but as the womb becomes more

By the twelfth week, arms, hands, fingers, toes, and feet are clearly visible. The fetus begins exercising its limbs almost as soon as they develop, but it is not until sometime around the fourth or fifth month that the mother begins feeling these movements. The umbilical cord connecting the fetus to the placenta remains taut—and therefore untangled—because it is constantly filled with blood. Vessels and arteries proliferate throughout the fetus's body and are easily visible because the skin is still rather transparent.

During the middle trimester of pregnancy, the fetus grows rapidly, as you can see by comparing this sixteen-week-old fetus with the eleven-week-old fetus in the previous photograph. By sixteen weeks, the fetus looks quite human, but it still cannot survive outside the womb.

crowded, the fetus inevitably hits its walls more often. In fact, studies of fetal movement cycles observe "jerky,' or "sporadic," head and neck movements as early as the seventh gestational week and fetal respiratory movement at ten weeks. Fetal movements appear to grow progressively stronger and more frequent from eighteen weeks on, reaching a maximum between twenty-eight and twenty-nine weeks, after which they diminish somewhat until delivery. Fetal movements are an indicator of central nervous system integrity and function and can be studied through maternal perceptions as well as with ultrasound, fetal heart rate monitors, and other electromechanical devices (Primeau, 1993).

Although the fetus's weight increases throughout pregnancy, large gains do not occur until near the end of pregnancy. By twenty weeks, or about halfway to birth, the fetus typically measures about 50 percent of its final prenatal length but only about 10 percent of its final weight (Hamilton, 1984). That makes the fetus about twelve inches long and only about ten ounces in weight; it is still a very tiny baby. But this slow weight gain seems slow only relative to the development lying ahead; compared with what has already happened, the fetus has made impressive gains. At four weeks, for example, the fetus measured only about one-eighth of an inch long and weighed only about one-hundredth of an ounce!

By the beginning of the *seventh month,* the fetus is about sixteen inches long and weighs approximately three to five pounds. It is able to cry, breathe, swallow, digest, excrete, move about, and suck its thumb. The reflexes mentioned earlier are fully developed. Because of these capacities, the fetus is said to have attained *age of viability,* meaning it could survive if born at this point.

By the *eighth month,* the fetus weighs between five and seven pounds and has begun to develop a layer of body fat that will help it to regulate its body temperature after birth, and by *nine months* it has achieved its full birth weight. Toward the end of nine months, the average baby is about 7.5 pounds and almost 20 inches long. Growth in size stops, although fat continues to be stored, heart rate increases, and internal organ systems become more efficient in preparation for birth and independent life outside the womb.

The developing fetus is also responsive to stimuli in the external environment. One study recorded changes in fetal heart rate in response to sound and vibration (Kisilevsky et al., 1992). This raises the question of the effects of prenatal stimulation on behavior after birth. In an intriguing study designed to help answer this question, pregnant mothers were asked to read a children's story, Dr. Seuss's *The Cat in the Hat,* out loud to their unborn babies twice a day for the final six weeks of pregnancy. A few days after birth, the infants were exposed to the same story or to one they had not heard before. To test which story they preferred, the infants were given a special pacifier that allowed them to turn each recording on and off by increasing or decreasing the interval of time between sucks. The infants increased their rate of sucking each time they heard *The Cat in the Hat,* but did not do so with the new story. They showed an obvious preference based on their prenatal experience with the Dr. Seuss story. A more recent study using a short children's rhyme found similar results (DeCasper et al., 1994).

Infertility

> Letisha and Alvin had always wanted children, but put off conceiving until both were in their early thirties and had established successful careers. After almost two frustrating years of unsuccessful attempts at conception, they finally decided to go to a fertility clinic to get help in finding out what might be causing the problem and what could be done about it.

Alvin and Letisha's situation is not uncommon. Approximately 15 percent of American couples experience *infertility,* meaning they are unable to conceive or carry a pregnancy to term after one year of unprotected intercourse. In about 80 to 90 percent of couples receiving medical treatment, it is possible to discover a clear medical reason for their infertility (American College of Obstetricians and Gynecologists [ACOG], 1990; Greil, 1993a). The social and emotional consequences of infertility can be considerable. In America, parenthood remains an important part of the transition, or "rite of passage," to adulthood. Although the number of couples choosing not to have children has risen, studies still find that 90 to 95 percent of American women view childlessness as an undesirable state for themselves and for others. Given the continuing importance attached to childbearing and parenting, infertility can become a symbol of significant role failure and a cause of personal and marital conflict and unhappiness (Greil, 1993a).

A problem during any part of the complex process of conception can make a couple infertile. If the problem is in the male's reproductive system, it usually is related to the quantity or strength of the sperm produced. If the problem is due to the female's reproductive system, it is likely the result of structural abnormalities in the fallopian tubes or uterus or of failure to ovulate and release mature eggs from the ovaries. An estimated 1 million American women a year develop *pelvic inflammatory disease* when sexually transmitted infections such as *chlamydia* spread into the uterus and fallopian tubes, and one in four women with the disease lose their ability to conceive. Indeed, sexually transmitted diseases account for one-fifth of infertility cases. Other causes include genetic or chromosomal abnormalities; exposure to harmful chemicals or radiation; excessive exercise, weight loss or gain, or drug or alcohol use; and infections other than sexually transmitted diseases (Liebmann-Smith, 1993; McTigue, 1993).

If infertility has been diagnosed and structural problems ruled out, the first course of treatment is fertility drugs that increase ovulation and chances of pregnancy even in cases where a woman's ovulation is normal but sperm quality or production is a problem. A growing number of new reproductive technologies are now available as alternatives to normal conception for couples who are infertile. These alternatives are discussed in the accompanying Perspectives box.

The Experience of Pregnancy

Pregnancy involves many physical changes for the expectant mother. In this section, we discuss these changes and how they are experienced.

The support she receives from her partner make the experiences of pregnancy much easier for this expectant mother.

> Sudah is nearing the end of her pregnancy—just eight weeks to go! She has been careful to eat a good, balanced diet and has gained about twenty-four pounds, which her doctor says is fine for her size and weight. Lately her belly feels like a basketball, and she sometimes worries whether Dan, her husband, still finds her attractive and whether she will ever get her normal figure back. During the first two months of pregnancy, Sudah felt nauseous a lot of the time and found it hard to keep food down. She found that eating small amounts of food (especially plain crackers) throughout the day helped, as did resting more frequently—which was hard to do, since she was still working full time.
>
> Until recently, aside from getting tired more easily, Sudah has felt pretty good. During the last few weeks, however, she has had some swelling in her legs and some back pain, and has had to go to the bathroom much more frequently because of the pressure of the baby on her bladder. Although she and Dan both can't wait for the baby to arrive, they are somewhat apprehensive about whether they are grown up enough to be parents and take on the responsibilities of parenthood.

Sudah's complaints are fairly typical of those associated with the hormonal and physiological changes of pregnancy. More than 50 percent of pregnant women experience some degree of nausea during the first trimester, but this usually disappears by the twelfth week. Strategies for relieving nausea include eating small amounts of food frequently, increasing protein intake, eating dry crackers or plain yogurt, and resting more often during the day. Frequent urination is another symp-

Perspectives

Technological Alternatives to Normal Conception

Earlier in this century, the only alternative for couples who were infertile was to adopt a child or to remain childless. But today's medical techniques offer a growing number of alternative options. These alternatives vary in practicality and popularity, but from a strictly medical standpoint they all work fairly reliably.

Artificial (donor) insemination (DI) is used in cases where infertility is caused by problems in sperm quality or production. In this procedure, fresh or previously frozen sperm from a donor are inserted into the woman's vagina and held in place for a few hours. While in most cases the donor is anonymous, he can also be a friend or a relative. Artificial insemination is safe and easy to carry out and induces pregnancy as effectively as does normal intercourse between fertile partners—a 20 percent success rate in any one month (Liebmann-Smith, 1993; Silber, 1991). A controversial application of artificial insemination is *surrogate mothering,* in which sperm from the future father are inserted into the womb of a woman who agrees (usually for a fee) to give up the baby once it is born.

In vitro fertilization (IVF) is used if both eggs and sperm are normal and infertility is caused by blocked fallopian tubes that cannot be surgically repaired. With IVF, ovulation is induced with medications that cause multiple eggs to be produced. With the aid of a laparoscope or ultrasound, one or more eggs are then removed through the woman's vagina under local anesthesia. They are mixed in a laboratory dish with sperm from the male and allowed to fertilize in an incubator. Two days later, the fertilized egg or embryo is transferred back into the woman's uterus through her vagina. Additional embryos can be frozen (cryopreserved) for future use. Although fertilization rates are high, getting the embryos to implant is much harder to achieve. Pregnancy rates with IVF are about 15 percent (Liebmann-Smith, 1993; Silber, 1991).

Gamete intrafallopian tube transfer (GIFT), a variation of IVF, solves the implantation problem and can be used by women with healthy fallopian tubes. The GIFT procedure is exactly the same as IVF, except that the sperm and eggs are both surgically placed directly into the woman's fallopian tube, where they are naturally tom of early pregnancy and is due to hormonally induced softening of the pelvic muscles, which allows the enlarged uterus to press on the bladder. Other symptoms include fatigue, headaches, dizziness and fainting, constipation, leg cramps, heartburn, shortness of breath, swelling of legs, hands, or face, varicose veins, and backache (Davis, 1993).

In addition to the influence of hormonal changes, some of these symptoms are due to weight gain during pregnancy. Both a woman's weight before pregnancy and her weight gain during pregnancy influence the baby's birth weight. Current recommendations are that women of normal weight before pregnancy gain about thirty pounds, women who are overweight about twenty pounds, and women who are underweight about thirty-four pounds, with the exact amount reflecting the woman's height and prepregnancy weight.

Where does the weight gain go? The increased size of the uterus, breast tissue, blood volume, body fluid, and extra fat to prepare the woman to produce milk for breast feeding all contribute to the additional pounds (ACOG, 1990). Table 4.1 summarizes how the average weight gain during pregnancy is distributed.

TABLE 4.1   *Average Weight Gain During Pregnancy*

Maternal stores (fat, protein, and other nutrients)	7.0 pounds
Increased fluid volume	4.0 pounds
Increased blood volume	4.0 pounds
Breast enlargement	2.0 pounds
Uterus	2.0 pounds
Baby	7.5 pounds
Amniotic fluid	2.0 pounds
Placenta	1.5 pounds
Total weight gain	30.0 pounds

Source: ACOG (1990).

fertilized, and then moved to the uterus at the appropriate time. Pregnancy rates with GIFT are approximately three times higher than with IVF. With GIFT, it is also possible to use donor eggs when a woman no longer ovulates or has a genetic condition she wants to avoid passing on to her offspring (Silber, 1991).

Zygote intrafallopian transfer (ZIFT) is a modification of GIFT and IVF. After the egg and sperm are fertilized in the laboratory, the resulting embryo, or zygote, is placed in the fallopian tube rather than the uterus (with IVF, the "test-tube" embryo is placed in the uterus; with GIFT, the unfertilized sperm and eggs are placed in the fallopian tube). ZIFT is used when the sperm's ability to fertilize the woman's eggs is questionable. It also allows the surgeon to select and transfer only eggs that have been fertilized, thus increasing the chances of a pregnancy (Silber, 1991). GIFT and ZIFT produce identical pregnancy rates. However, whereas GIFT requires only a short (forty-five-minute) operation, ZIFT involves egg retrieval (aspiration) and in vitro fertilization, followed two days later by a procedure to transfer the embryo into the fallopian tube.

Finally, *micromanipulation (microfertilization)* is an experimental procedure in which a few sperm are microsurgically placed directly into the outside layer (zona) of the egg, making it possible for a man with very few viable sperm to fertilize his partner's egg.

What are the experiences of families with children conceived by the new reproductive technologies? In a recent British study that compared families with a child conceived by in vitro fertilization or donor insemination with families whose children were conceived naturally or adopted, Susan Golombok and her associates found no group differences in the quality of children's emotions, behavior, or overall relationships with their parents (Golombok et al., 1995). Mothers of IVF and DI children, in fact, showed greater warmth toward and deeper emotional involvement with their children, and both mother- and father-child interactions were more positive. At least for the families studied, genetic ties appeared to be less important for family functioning than a strong desire to become a parent.

A Multicultural View

Reasons for Having a Child in the United States and Eight Other Countries

Attitudes of Parents in the United States

Pregnancy is a beginning, and expectant parents prepare for the birth of their baby and parenthood by creating, often unconsciously, a set of images of what being parents will be like (Galinsky, 1987). These images of parenthood are based partly on memories of the couple's own actual and wished-for childhood experiences, as well as on their own firsthand (or secondhand) experiences with parenthood and wishes for the future. Images are also influenced by life circumstances, one of the most important being the reasons for wanting (or not wanting) the child.

When researchers asked prospective parents, "Why do you want to have a child?", the following reasons were most frequently given:

1. Validation of adult status and social identity
2. Expansion of self, including ties to the future and a sense of immortality
3. Achievement of moral values in the sense that one is doing something "good" by having and raising a child
4. The need to obtain primary-group ties and affection by creating a family larger than just husband and wife
5. Stimulation, novelty, and fun
6. Achievement, competence, and creativity (people take pride in producing a baby)
7. Power and influence through directing and controlling the baby's life

8. Economic utility, based on the expectation that when grown, the baby will help provide economic and emotional support for the family (Hoffman, 1988; Hoffman & Hoffman, 1973).

For parents who already have a child, the desire to provide a sibling for the first child is a major reason for having a second one. Another common reason for wanting a child, particularly for teenagers, is to have someone to love and be loved by. A person's reasons for wanting a child and whether a pregnancy is planned or unplanned also can influence feelings about pregnancy. For example, women who planned their pregnancies and who wanted children for self-growth reasons have been found to be more positive about having children than women who did not. These women see parenthood as an opportunity to expand their sense of self and to intensify and enrich their marriages. Women who are more negative about becoming a parent either have unplanned pregnancies, see having a child as a way to escape current life circumstances, or consider a child to be a source of status or security (Leifer, 1977).

A Cross-Cultural Comparison

Do reasons for having children differ across cultures? A cross-cultural study of the advantages of having children as reported by mothers in the United States and eight other countries suggests that they do (Hoffman, 1988). As the accompanying table shows, the three most com-

---

The physical changes of pregnancy, of course, make a woman's body dramatically different than the one she started out with, and most women have mixed feelings about their changed appearance. A big concern is whether their bodies will ever return to their normal size and shape. The answer is generally yes, although typically it takes some time and a reasonable approach to eating and exercise for this to occur. Women who are conscious of diet and exercise before and during pregnancy are likely to have an easier time returning to their prepregnancy appearance than women who are not.

Pregnancy is a powerful experience that can significantly affect how both the mother and the father feel about themselves and each other. For most prospective parents, it raises the question "Am I ready to be emotionally and economically responsible for this baby?" Couples who are experiencing pregnancy together may wonder, "How will having a baby affect our relationship with each other?" The feelings and expectations associated with pregnancy are related to reasons for having a baby, which are discussed in the accompanying Multicultural View box.

What Do You Think?

If you are a woman, what do you imagine it would be like to be pregnant? How has what you have read about pregnancy influenced your views about the experience? If you are a man,

Reasons for Having Children, as Reported by Mothers, by Country (Percentage)

	United States	Turkey	Indonesia (Japanese)	Indonesia (Sudanese)	Philippines	Thailand	Korea	Taiwan	Singapore
Economic-utility	6.0	54.0	94.1	79.6	71.3	74.6	35.7	44.4	46.8
Primary ties and affection	66.1	34.3	14.0	34.7	46.1	12.9	36.8	44.8	58.6
Stimulation and fun	60.0	21.7	12.8	38.2	58.2	9.2	46.8	68.6	70.9
Expansion of self	35.3	10.4	28.6	41.5	8.9	4.7	23.7	38.1	21.2
Adult status and social identity	21.9	13.8	2.1	4.7	5.9	2.0	5.8	8.3	9.1
Achievement	11.1	4.6	7.8	7.7	3.4	1.8	30.1	2.8	3.0
Morality	6.8	6.7	0.5	0.4	1.9	1.9	2.3	0.4	0.2
Power	2.2	1.8	0.1	0.2	2.0	0.1	1.2	0.1	0.2
n	1,259	1,539	984	965	1,567	2,288	1,433	2,103	904

mon needs children satisfy are economic utility; the need for primary-group (family) ties, love, and affection; and the need for fun and stimulation.

Considerable variation exists, however. In Turkey, Indonesia, the Philippines, and Thailand, the most common value of children mentioned is economic utility. Primary ties and affection are the most common reason in the United States, whereas stimulation and fun are the reason most frequently given in Korea, Taiwan, and Singapore. Because the number of responses given and coded differed somewhat from country to country, it is more meaningful to compare the relative importance of the reasons for having a child in each country than the actual percentages of any particular response.

These cross-cultural differences likely reflect societal differences in how intensely each need is felt, the extent to which children are seen as a way to satisfy the need, and what sources other than children exist for satisfying the particular need.

what do you imagine pregnancy would be like? In what ways might your thoughts and feelings be similar to those of the mother?

Prenatal Influences on the Child

Key Concepts

Despite the individuality sometimes attributed to unborn children, biologically they develop in ways that are far more alike than different. As we have noted, physical structures develop in a particular sequence and at fairly precise times. Psychologists and biologists sometimes call such regularity canalization. **Canalization** refers to the tendency of genes to narrowly direct or restrict growth and development of particular physical and behavioral characteristics to a single (or very few) phenotypic outcomes and to resist environmental factors that push development in other directions (McCall, 1981). However, early exposure to certain drugs and other harmful environmental influences can also canalize, or restrict, the direction of future development, almost always in negative ways (Gottlieb, 1991). Under normal, "good enough" conditions, however, specific events or influences tend to have little long-term effect on highly canalized maturation, even if they affect development temporarily. Whether a pregnant mother drinks four glasses of milk every day or drinks no milk at all may not change the course of her pregnancy noticeably, as long as she includes calcium in her diet and her fetus gets enough nutrients. By nature, ordinary differences such as this make no difference to maturation, as long as they *are* "ordinary."

Typically prenatal development is a highly reliable process, so prospective parents generally worry much more than they need to about whether their baby will be "all right." In fact, 97.5 percent of human infants are perfect at birth, and of the 2.5 percent who are not, half have only minor defects such as hammertoes, extra fingers or toes, or birthmarks (Guttmacher & Kaiser, 1984).

But certain conditions can interfere with even the highly canalized processes of fetal development. These conditions are sometimes called *risk factors* because they increase the chance that the future baby will have medical problems but do not guarantee that these problems will actually appear. One set of risk factors are the mother's biological characteristics, including age and physical condition, as well as biological factors that are influenced by psychological and social stresses. Other risks include exposure to diseases, drugs, chemicals, and other environmental hazards during pregnancy.

As the complex sequence of prenatal growth proceeds, the timing of the development of each new organ or body part is particularly important. **Critical period** (also called *sensitive period*) refers to a time-limited period during which certain developmental changes are particularly sensitive to disruption. This "window of opportunity" is dictated by complex genetic codes in each cell *and* by the particular set of prenatal conditions that must be in place for each change to occur. If development is disturbed or blocked during a critical period, the changes that were scheduled to occur may be disrupted or prevented from occurring at all.

Especially during the early weeks of its life, development of the embryo is particularly vulnerable to disruption if the embryo is exposed (through the mother) to certain harmful substances called teratogens. A **teratogen** is any substance or other environmental influence that can interfere with or permanently damage an embryo's growth. Named after an ancient Greek word meaning "monster-creating," teratogens can result in serious physical malformations and even the death of the embryo. Teratogens are most harmful if exposure occurs during the critical or sensitive period for the particular physical change to occur. Teratogens include many *medicinal and nonmedicinal drugs; other chemicals; diseases* (viruses and bacteria); and certain *other harmful environmental influences,* such as radiation. A substance is classified as a teratogen based on its ability to disrupt prenatal development.

A teratogen's effects are influenced by several factors. The first is the *timing of exposure.* The nine months of pregnancy generally are divided into three *trimesters,* each lasting three months. Development is most vulnerable during the first trimester, so disruption during this period may lead to spontaneous abortion or serious birth defects. For example, disruption during the third week, when the basic structures of the heart and central nervous system are just beginning to form, is likely to threaten further development. Similarly, interference in the fourth and fifth weeks, which are within the critical period for the first stage of arm and leg development, may lead to underdeveloped and malformed limbs. Because the critical periods for embryonic and fetal development are in the first trimester, disruptions in the second and third trimesters generally are less likely to have severe consequences. Figure 4.2 describes the effects teratogens at different stages of prenatal development.

A second factor that determines the impact of a teratogen is the *intensity and duration of exposure.* For example, the higher the dose and the longer the use of a harmful drug such as alcohol or cocaine, the greater the chances that the baby will be harmed and that the harm will be more severe than if dose and duration are less. A third factor is the *number of other harmful influences* that are also present. The greater the number, the greater the risk. A fourth factor is the *biogenetic vulnera-*

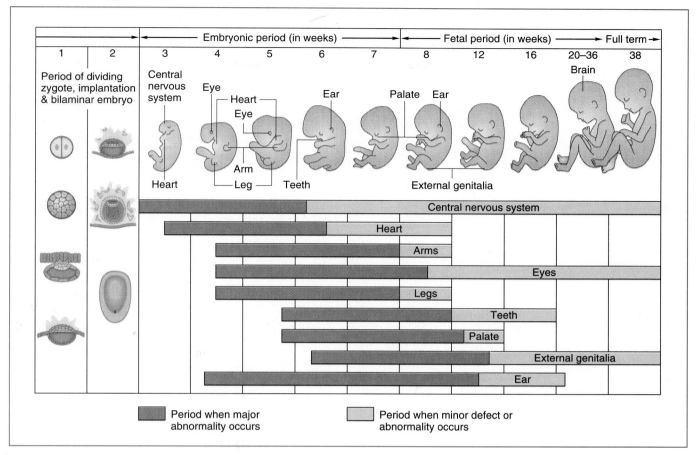

FIGURE 4.2
Timing and Effects of Teratogens During Sensitive or Critical Periods
This figure illustrates the sensitive or critical periods in human development. The dark band indicates highly sensitive or critical periods; the light band indicates stages that are less sensitive to disruption caused by teratogens. Note that each structure has a critical period during which its development may be disrupted. Note also that development proceeds from head to tail (cephalocaudal) and from the center of the body outward (proximodistal).
Source: Reprinted from Before We Are Born: Basic Embryology and Birth Defects, *2nd ed., by K.L. Moore, p. 111, with permission of W.B. Saunders Company, ©1983.*

bility of the mother and the infant. Individual mothers and their infants will differ in the degree to which they will be affected by exposure to a particular type and level of teratogen. For example, whereas heavy and prolonged drinking is likely to affect almost all babies, very moderate drinking may cause considerable harm for one infant but no measurable harm for another. For alcohol and certain other teratogens, however, there is no minimal dose that is known to be "safe."

Maternal Age and Physical Characteristics

The biological risks associated with childbearing increase with age. Complications of pregnancy and prenatal development are somewhat more likely for women who are older than thirty-five and having a first child. Compared with women in their twenties, they are more likely to be ill during pregnancy, have longer and more difficult labors, and deliver infants who are small, premature, or stillborn or have congenital defects such as Down syndrome (Browne & Dixon, 1978). (See Chapter 3.) But when pregnant women older than thirty-five with major medical problems are eliminated from study, healthy older women are not at significantly greater risk for any of these complications (with the exception of Down syndrome) than younger women (ACOG, 1990; Grimes & Gross, 1981; A. Stein, 1983).

On the other hand, very young mothers, especially those in their early teens, are at significantly greater risk of having low-birth-weight infants, stillbirths, or problems during delivery. This is partly because teenage mothers have not completed their own growth, so their bodies are unable to meet the extra nutritional demands of a developing fetus. Teenage mothers are more likely to be poor and less likely to get adequate prenatal care and have the maturity of judgment to adapt their lifestyles to the demands of pregnancy (Furstenberg et al., 1989; Fraser et al., 1995).

Several other physical characteristics of the mother during pregnancy can increase the chance of spontaneous abortion or miscarriage (McKenzie, 1983):

1. Having had several previous pregnancies (at least four or five), especially if some of them involved medical problems
2. Being very overweight or underweight, that is, more than about 25 percent over or under the average weight for the mother's height and frame (being only a little overweight or underweight does not create risk)
3. Being very short (under five feet tall, to be specific) and small in size of frame

But many women who live with risks such as these have no problems at all with their pregnancies. This is especially true of women who have only one risk factor, but it is even true of women with more than one. Being "at risk" means only that there is a higher than usual chance of having problems; it does *not* mean a certainty. The distinction is important for all risks to pregnancy, including those we discuss in the following sections.

Diseases

Exposure of a pregnant woman to certain viral, bacteriological, and parasitic diseases can adversely affect her baby's development. Table 4.2 summarizes the teratogenic effects of exposure to selected diseases (and drugs) during pregnancy.

Rubella   Also called *German measles,* the rubella virus apparently can infect the embryo or fetus by passing through the placenta into the fetal bloodstream. During the first two months of pregnancy, it is likely to cause blindness, deafness, heart defects, damage to the central nervous system, and mental retardation. During the second trimester, after the fetus is fully formed, rubella's effects are less severe but may include hearing, vision, and language problems. Because of the successful public health efforts to inoculate schoolchildren and women at risk, on the average only twenty new cases of rubella are reported per year in the United States (Blackman, 1990).

Syphilis and Gonorrhea   A pregnant woman with untreated syphilis can transmit the disease to her fetus. In 25 percent of cases, death of the fetus results, usually during the second trimester. An additional 25 percent of infected fetuses die soon after birth. Of those who survive, about 25 percent show symptoms such as jaundice, anemia, pneumonia, skin rash, and bone inflammation. If the syphilis is untreated, the child may develop dental deformities, hearing difficulties, and many of the problems associated with adult syphilis that are discussed in Chapter 14 (Blackman, 1990).

Fetuses that contract gonorrhea in the birth canal may later develop eye infections or become blind. It is now standard practice to put drops of silver nitrate or penicillin in newborns' eyes to protect them against these conditions, because gonorrhea may be present in the mother without obvious symptoms.

TABLE 4.2 **Teratogens and Their Effects**

Teratogen	Effects
Maternal Diseases	
Rubella	*First trimester:* blindness, deafness, heart defects, damage to central nervous system, mental retardation; *second trimester:* problems with hearing, vision, and language
Syphilis and gonorrhea	Fetal death, jaundice, anemia, pneumonia, skin rash, bone inflammation, dental deformities, hearing difficulties, blindness
Genital herpes	Disease of skin and mucous membranes, blindness, brain damage, seizures, and developmental delay
Cytomegalovirus	Jaundice, microcephaly (very small head), deafness, eye problems, increased risk for severe illness and infant death
AIDS	Abnormally small skull; facial deformities; immune system damage; enlarged lymph glands, liver, spleen; recurrent infections; poor growth; fever; brain disease; developmental delay; deteriorated motor skills
Toxoplasmosis	Spontaneous abortion, prematurity, low birth weight, enlarged liver and spleen, jaundice, anemia, congenital defects, mental retardation, seizures, cerebral palsy, retinal disease, blindness
Drugs	
Medicinal Drugs	
Thalidomide	Birth defects such as missing, shortened, or misshapen arms and legs, deafness; severe facial deformities; seizure disorders; dwarfism; brain damage; fetal/infant death
Diethylstilbestrol (DES)	*Grown daughters:* vaginal and cervical cancer; spontaneous abortions and stillbirth; autoimmune disorders such as pernicious anemia, myasthenia gravis (a nerve-muscle disorder), intestinal disorder, multiple sclerosis; *grown sons:* abnormalities in reproductive organs, testicular cancer
Nonmedicinal Drugs	
Heroin	Withdrawal symptoms, including vomiting, trembling, irritability, fever, disturbed sleep, an abnormally high-pitched cry; delayed social and motor development
Cocaine	Miscarriage or premature delivery, low birth weight, irritability, respiratory problems, genital and urinary tract deformities, heart defects, central nervous system problems
Alcohol	*Fetal alcohol effects (FAEs):* lower birth weight, lack of responsiveness and arousability, heart rate and respiratory abnormalities; delayed cognitive development; learning disabilities; *fetal alcohol syndrome (FAS):* central nervous system damage, heart defects, small head, distortions of joints, abnormal facial features; mental retardation; behavioral disorders such as hyperactivity and poor impulse control; impaired growth and/or failure to thrive
Tobacco	Spontaneous abortion, prematurity, fetal/infant death, reduced birth weight, poorer postnatal adjustment

Genital Herpes   Genital herpes causes blisters on the genitalia of both men and women. It is most frequently transmitted to the baby at birth as the newborn comes through the birth canal and in contact with herpes sores on the mother's genitals (Feinbloom & Forman, 1987; Hanshaw, 1985). The incidence of neonatal herpes infection ranges from 0.03 to 0.3 per 1,000 live births.

There are two types of neonatal herpes infection. In the first type, the infant develops a mild disease of the skin and mucous membranes of the mouth and eyes. In the second, more severe type, about 33 percent of infected newborns die and another 25 to 35 percent suffer disabilities such as blindness, permanent brain damage, seizures, and developmental delay. Transmission of herpes by mothers with active herpes infections can be prevented by caesarean delivery, a procedure in which the baby is surgically delivered through the mother's abdomen. Herpes infection in newborns is now treated with antiviral drugs (Blackman, 1990).

Cytomegalovirus   Cytomegalovirus (CMV) is a viral infection that is difficult to detect because people who have it rarely show symptoms. When symptoms occur, they are similar to those of mononucleosis and include fever, fatigue, swollen lymph glands, and sore throat. CMV can be passed to the baby through the placenta, the vagina, or breast milk. Although the risk of a primary infection in a woman is only 2 percent, about 50 percent of fetuses are infected, with 10 percent developing symptoms at birth. Infants who have symptoms are at higher risk for severe illness, death, or disabilities and are more likely to have problems such as jaundice, microcephaly (a very small head and mental retardation), deafness, and eye problems (ACOG, 1990). Infected newborns can harbor and excrete CMV for months, so pregnant women and child care workers should practice careful handwashing techniques after handling the babies or their diapers (Feinbloom & Forman, 1987).

AIDS   In 1989, children with *acquired immunodeficiency syndrome (AIDS)* accounted for almost 2 percent of the total reported cases of AIDS in the United States, and the rate of pediatric AIDS is increasing by an estimated 200 percent a year. Of the approximately 4 million babies born in the United States each year, it is estimated that between one thousand and two thousand will have HIV (Lee, 1995; Task Force on Pediatric AIDS, 1989). *HIV,* or *human immunodeficiency virus,* is the virus that causes the symptoms of AIDS.

Seventy-eight percent of AIDS cases in children involve perinatal (at the time of birth) transmission from an infected mother to her child, either through the placenta or through contact with HIV-contaminated blood at the time of delivery (American Academy of Pediatrics, 1991). In the majority of these cases, the mother's infection can be linked to her own intravenous (IV) drug use or that of her sexual partner. African-American and Hispanic children make up three-quarters of all pediatrics AIDS cases in the United States, although they account for only one-fourth of all American children. Because AIDS has an incubation period of up to five years in adults, pregnant women may be unaware that they have the virus or that it can be transmitted to their offspring.

Although most children infected *perinatally* show symptoms before age one, some may live for years without symptoms. Because newborns retain the protective antibodies they receive from their mothers for several months after birth, testing a newborn for HIV antibodies can give accurate information only about the mother (Lee, 1995; Richter, 1993).

AIDS may also cause serious malformations in the developing embryo and fetus. Prenatal AIDS infection can lead to an abnormally small skull and facial deformities that include a prominent, boxlike forehead, eyes that are widely spaced and off center, and thickened lips. These abnormalities are more severe and appear in the first year of life when the virus was transferred to the fetus early in the fetus's development. Other symptoms of AIDS relate to a damaged immune system and include enlargement of lymph glands, liver, and spleen, recurrent infections, poor growth, and fever. There may also be disease of the brain resulting in developmental delay, deterioration of motor skills and intellectual abilities, and behavioral abnormalities. Seventy-five percent of babies born with AIDS die before their second year (American Academy of Pediatrics, 1991; Blackman, 1990).

Treatment of HIV-infected mothers and their children with antiviral drugs is still in its early stages. Recent studies suggest that women who take the drug AZT during pregnancy and labor can reduce the risk of having an HIV-infected baby from 15 to 30 percent to about 8 percent (Lee, 1995). Treatment of the secondary infections that result from the immunodeficiency has improved, but it is unlikely that a cure for this terminal illness will be found in the near future. Although children with AIDS appear to survive longer than AIDS-afflicted adults, the typical life expectancy of a child born with AIDS is not yet known.

The psychological as well as the medical consequences of AIDS/HIV are devastating. A multidisciplinary team approach that works with the medical, psychological, social, and economic problems and stresses caused by AIDS has been found to be most effective in caring for afflicted infants and children (Task Force on Pediatric AIDS, 1989).

Toxoplasmosis   At some point in their lives, about 25 percent of the U.S. population contracts and develops antibodies to *toxoplasmosis,* a disease caused by a parasite present in uncooked meat and in the feces of infected cats. The approximate incidence of toxoplasmosis is about one or two per one thousand live births. Toxoplasmosis may result in spontaneous abortion or premature delivery. Affected infants are characterized by low birth weight, an enlarged liver and spleen, jaundice, and anemia. Congenital defects include hydrocephalus, microcephaly, and calcifications in the brain. Later problems include mental retardation, seizures, cerebral palsy, and diseases of the retina that result in blindness. It is strongly recommended that women avoid all contact with cat litter boxes during pregnancy (Blackman, 1990).

Drugs

Almost all drugs may affect the developing embryo or fetus, depending on their particular characteristics, dosage, frequency, timing of use, and so on. This has led many doctors to stress to pregnant women the dangers of drugs and to prescribe medication only in extreme cases. It is wise for pregnant women to take no drugs (including nonprescription drugs) without their doctors' permission.

Medicinal Drugs   Although a growing number of medications are being developed to help cure illness and relieve pain, many of these same medications may negatively affect a child's development if taken during pregnancy. A drug called *thalidomide* illustrates dramatically how such damage can occur. It also illustrates the political, economic, and social policy implications of new medical and scientific discoveries that affect human growth and development.

Thalidomide is a seemingly harmless sedative that during the late 1950s and early 1960s was widely prescribed for calming the nerves, promoting sleep, and reducing morning sickness and other forms of nausea during the early weeks of pregnancy. Although it was advertised as being completely safe, between 1958 and 1962

Crack addicted babies such as the ones in the picture often require intensive medical care at birth and ongoing special attention thereafter to minimize negative long term effects.

thousands of babies were born with birth defects that included missing, shortened, or misshapen arms and legs, deafness, severe facial deformities, seizure disorders, dwarfism, and brain damage. It took until 1961 for the drug to be banned, in part because the effects of teratogens were less understood then and because the federal Food and Drug Administration (FDA) was under political pressure from the drug industry to keep thalidomide on the market.

It is estimated that there are currently about eight thousand thalidomide-affected adults and that twice that many babies were stillborn (dead at birth) or died shortly afterward because of defects caused by thalidomide (Stout, 1993). Teratogenic drugs pose an even greater developmental risk in developing countries in South America, Africa, and Asia, where drugs are less strictly regulated than in the United States. In Brazil, one of the world's largest producers of thalidomide, the drug is used to help treat the symptoms of leprosy, which afflicts almost 300,000 people in that country. This has led to a growing number of birth defects in babies born to mothers with leprosy who have taken the drug because they are not aware of its effects (Gorman, 1993).

Unfortunately, the damage done by toxic drugs or chemicals does not always show itself as obviously or as soon as in the case of thalidomide. For about twenty-five years following World War II, another drug, *diethylstilbestrol (DES),* was taken by 3 million to 6 million pregnant women with histories of spontaneous abortions to prevent miscarriages. The drug was especially useful during the early months, when miscarriages occur most often. At birth the babies of women who took DES seemed perfectly normal, and they remained so throughout childhood. As they became young adults, however, abnormal development of vaginal cells and structural abnormalities of the uterus were found in all female babies who had been exposed, and about one in one thousand eventually developed cancer of the vagina or of the cervix. The sons of DES mothers developed abnormalities in the structure of their reproductive organs and have a higher rate of testicular cancer. Even the daughters who did not get cancer had significantly more problems than usual with their own pregnancies, including higher rates of spontaneous abortion and stillbirth as well as more minor problems, and they had them whether or not their families had histories of difficult births. More recently, as most of the people exposed to DES before birth are now reaching midlife, there is growing evidence of increased risk for autoimmune disorders such as pernicious anemia, myasthenia gravis (a nerve-muscle disorder), serious intestinal disorders, and multiple sclerosis as a result of DES damage to the immune system (Brody, 1993). DES support networks and social action groups for affected individuals and families have been formed in both Canada and the United States (Linn et al., 1988; Sato, 1993).

Other medications that can harm the fetus include *isotreitinoin (accutane),* a treatment for acne; *streptomycin,* an antibiotic used to treat tuberculosis; and *tetracycline,* an antibiotic used to treat a wide variety of infections.

Nonmedicinal Drugs   Not surprisingly, drugs such as *heroin, cocaine,* and *alcohol* also affect the fetus.

Heroin   At birth, the child of a woman who uses heroin immediately begins to have withdrawal symptoms, including vomiting, trembling, irritability, fever, disturbed sleep, and an abnormally high-pitched cry. Unfortunately, the symptoms may not become noticeably serious until several days after birth, when the baby has left the hospital. Even when the infant has recovered from withdrawal, she or he often develops slowly during the first year, exhibiting less attentiveness to the environment and poor motor skill performance. Some infants display longer-term attention deficits in their childhood years, but others do not (de Cubas & Field, 1995; East & Steele, 1987; Vorhees & Mollnow, 1987).

Cocaine   Mothers who use cocaine and cocaine derivatives such as *crack* generally have a greater than normal risk of miscarriage or premature delivery. Their babies are more likely to have lower than normal birth weight, be more irritable, and be more susceptible to serious respiratory problems. There is growing evidence that cocaine is also associated with genital and urinary tract deformities, heart defects, and central nervous system problems (Bartol, 1986; Chasnoff et al., 1989; MacGregor et al., 1987; R. Weiss & Mirin, 1987).

Alcohol   Even in biblical times, people suspected that alcohol harms an unborn child: "Behold, thou shalt conceive and bear a son; and now drink no wine nor strong drink, neither eat any unclean thing" (*Judges 13:7*). Both then and now, many babies born to mothers who consume alcohol during pregnancy display fetal alcohol effects (FAEs), and the most severely affected babies exhibit a cluster of defects known as *fetal alcohol syndrome (FAS)*. *Fetal alcohol effects* refer to a set of symptoms that include lower birth weight, lack of responsiveness and arousability, and increased occurrences of heart rate and respiratory abnormalities in infants. These infants achieve lower mental development scores at eight months and at four years and have higher rates of learning disabilities (Barr et al., 1990; Streissguth et al., 1989).

Symptoms of **fetal alcohol syndrome (FAS)** include central nervous system damage and physical abnormalities such as heart defects, small head, distortion of joints, and abnormal facial features, including a flattened mid-face region and a thin upper lip; mental retardation and/or behavioral disorders such as hyperactivity and poor impulse control; and impaired growth and/or failure to thrive (discussed in Chapter 5). Babies of heavy drinkers, particularly in the last three months of pregnancy, are at much greater risk for these problems. It is estimated that 50 to 75 percent of infants born to chronically alcoholic women may be affected.

You may be wondering what level of alcohol consumption is safe for a pregnant woman. At present, the only completely safe answer is *none*. Even moderate daily drinking during pregnancy (two ounces of hard liquor, nine ounces of wine, or two beers) is associated with an increase in these disorders. The chance of fetal alcohol effects in the infant of a mother who consumes more than four drinks daily is estimated to be about 33 percent and about 10 percent for a woman who consumes between two and four drinks per day. However, no completely proven safe dosage of alcohol for a pregnant woman has yet been determined (Feinbloom & Forman, 1987).

Despite our knowledge of the risks of drinking, the national Centers for Disease Control (CDC) report that the rate of FAS increased almost sevenfold over a fifteen-year period from 1 per 10,000 births in 1979 to 6.7 per 10,000 births in 1993 (*New York Times*, 1995a). FAS could be prevented if alcohol were not consumed during pregnancy, but this goal has not been easy to achieve. As with a number of other problem drugs, alcohol use is deeply embedded in many aspects of people's lives, including their individual histories; family, neighborhood, and work situations; social and economic conditions; and ethnicity and culture. Drug use can be seen as an attempt to self-medicate to relieve the pain and unhappiness of a difficult life, a pattern that is difficult to break without significant societal changes. In the case of alcohol (and tobacco, which is discussed shortly), widespread use has been strongly encouraged and financed by powerful economic interests. Sales of alcohol play a major role in our economy in terms of jobs, profits, and tax revenues, and for many people alcohol use is supported by long-standing cultural practice.

Programs to help pregnant mothers curb their drinking have had best results for the children when they emphasize the importance of not drinking at all, even if only for the last few months of pregnancy. Mothers who cut back throughout pregnancy give birth to healthy, alert babies more often than do mothers who only cut back early and resume drinking later in their pregnancies (Rosett et al., 1980).

Tobacco   Cigarette smoking also can harm the fetus, but the effects are more general than those for alcohol. Two key elements of cigarette smoke, nicotine and carbon monoxide, appear to interfere with the supply of oxygen to the fetus and to contribute to increased fetal heart rate. Smoking during pregnancy has been associated with reduced birth weight, increased risk of spontaneous abortion, prematurity, higher infant mortality during the birth process, and poorer postnatal adjustment. Even exposure to smoke from others (passive smoke) can adversely affect pregnant women and their fetuses (Armstrong, 1992; McDonald et al., 1992a, 1992b). It is estimated that smoking during pregnancy causes the deaths of about 5,600 babies and 115,000 miscarriages every year, contributes to 53,000 low-birth-weight babies and 22,000 babies who require intensive care at birth, and is implicated in 1,900 annual cases of sudden infant death syndrome (discussed in Chapter 5) (*New York Times,* 1995b).

Women who stop smoking before becoming pregnant or during the first trimester are likely to have infants of normal birth weight. Women who stop smoking before their thirtieth week will, on average, have higher-birth-weight infants than women who continue to smoke throughout pregnancy. Despite growing awareness of the dangers of smoking, however, between 24 and 30 percent of pregnant smokers continue to smoke during pregnancy (U.S. Department of Health and Human Services, 1990).

It is estimated that elimination of smoking during pregnancy could prevent 5 percent of fetal/infant deaths, 20 percent of low-birth-weight deliveries, and 8 percent of premature deliveries each year in the United States. For young, unmarried, and/or uneducated mothers—groups with a high prevalence of smoking (and other pregnancy risk factors)—elimination of smoking could prevent 10 percent of fetal/infant deaths, 35 percent of low-birth-weight deliveries, and 15 percent of premature births (Miller, 1993). As in the case of other teratogens, reducing the incidence of smoking during pregnancy is not easy. Smoking is difficult to give up because of its addictive and habit-forming qualities, particularly for women whose lives are high in stress and low in social support. While better education and cessation programs, that offer adequate social support for women who smoke, can help, reducing the promotion and sale of cigarettes may prove to be more effective. Heavy tobacco industry advertising in popular magazines and at sporting events that targets teenagers and young adults is a big part of the problem. Among people age twenty-four or younger, the percentage of female smokers is now higher than that for male smokers. Furthermore, it is expected that female smokers of all ages will soon outnumber male smokers because more girls than boys start smoking and women quit less often than men do (Miller, 1993).

Environmental Hazards

A broad range of environmental hazards can be destructive to prenatal development. These include exposure to radiation from nuclear explosions, nuclear plant accidents, industrial materials, and medical X-rays; to industrial chemical pollutants such as carbon monoxide, "passive" cigarette smoke, lead, mercury, and PCBs in the air or water; to fertilizers, herbicides, and pesticides in the food supply; to food additives; and even to excessive heat and humidity. Although the careful parent may take steps to avoid some of these hazards, many are beyond individual control and require efforts on a national or even international scale.

Currently the majority of women are employed outside the home, and most women who are employed when they become pregnant continue working throughout their pregnancies. Many of the environmental hazards to pregnant women and their babies are encountered in the workplace. These include (1) physical hazards such as noise, radiation, vibration, stressful physical activity, and materials handling; (2) biological hazards such as viruses, fungi, spores, and bacteria; and (3) chemical hazards such as anesthetic gases, pesticides, lead, mercury, and organic solvents. As yet, there is no consistent overall finding regarding the effects of such workplace hazards on prenatal development (Bernhardt, 1990).

Domestic Violence

Domestic violence presents another serious hazard to pregnant women and their babies. Studies of prenatal clinic patients report that between 7 and 8 percent of pregnant women are beaten by their partners, and that women who are battered have twice as many miscarriages as women who are not. While 87.5 percent of pregnant women who are battered had been abused before, it is estimated that 1 percent of all pregnant women with no history of being battered will be abused during pregnancy (Helton et al., 1987). These rates probably are actually higher, since poor and teenage mothers, who are at greatest risk for abuse, are less likely to receive prenatal care or to be included in such studies. Abuse during pregnancy is correlated with unemployment, substance abuse, poverty, and family dysfunction, making it difficult to determine the relative contribution of each of these risks (Moran, 1993).

Teenage Pregnancy

The United States has the highest rate of teenage pregnancy of all industrialized countries (Lawson & Rhode, 1993). Because teenage parents are still completing their own physical, cognitive, and social development, meeting their babies' prenatal and postnatal developmental needs frequently conflicts with meeting their own. This is especially true because a high proportion of teenage pregnancies occur among adolescents whose life circumstances are lacking in economic, educational, and social support and opportunities. In addition, most pregnant teenagers do not have the support of the father during their pregnancies and become single parents after their babies are born.

Pregnant teenagers are much less likely than pregnant adults to maintain nutritious diets and get adequate prenatal care during pregnancy, and more likely to suffer complications such as anemia and toxemia and to experience more prolonged and difficult labor. Babies born to teenagers are more likely to be premature and suffer from low birth weight and its associated problems (see Chapter 5). They also have higher rates of neurological defects and are more likely to die during their first year. They are also more likely to encounter developmental problems during their preschool and school years.

The direct cause of teenage pregnancy is the failure to use effective and consistent methods of birth control. For many teens who become pregnant, the prospect of having a baby of their own represents one of the few routes available to feel needed and loved and to achieve adult status. In contrast, their families, schools, and neighborhoods may provide little opportunity to achieve these things.

Teenage pregnancy and its prevention are discussed more fully in Chapter 16.

Diet and Nutrition

Several types of indirect evidence suggest that serious undernutrition can hurt unborn children. Studies of children born during World War II to families living in combat areas where severe famine pevailed found these children were smaller than usual and that an unusually large number of stillbirths occurred (Stein et al., 1975). Other studies indicate that for mothers with poor diets, rates of prematurity and infant mortality are higher, birth weights are lower, and the risk of congenital malformations increases. Nutritionally deprived infants are less responsive to environmental stimulation and irritable when aroused. Malnourished infants are found to have a significantly reduced number of brain cells, especially when the malnutrition occurred during the last trimester or during the first three months following birth (Lozoff, 1989).

Although the effects of moderate undernutrition are likely to be less severe, it is still very important that a pregnant woman maintain a diet that provides adequate nutrition for both her baby and herself. Every diet should include proteins, carbohydrates (sugars and starches), fats, vitamins, and minerals selected from the four major food groups: (1) fruits and vegetables; (2) whole-grain or enriched breads and cereals; (3) milk and milk products; and (4) meat, poultry, fish, eggs, nuts, and beans (ACOG, 1990).

Nutritionists also agree that a pregnant woman should eat between two hundred and one thousand calories more per day than she ate before pregnancy, as long as the extra calories consist mainly of carbohydrates and protein. As noted earlier in this chapter, experts now recommend that women of normal weight before pregnancy gain about thirty pounds, women who are obese around twenty pounds, and women who are underweight about thirty-four pounds, with the exact amount reflecting their height and prepregnancy weight.

Pregnant women are also advised to get extra calcium (usually by drinking milk) to provide for the growing bones of the fetus and sometimes for breast feeding, and also to use multiple vitamin and mineral supplements. Currently folic acid is commercially added to foods such as flours to reduce birth defects such as *spina bifida,* which may result from a dietary shortage of that nutrient. It is especially important that low-income women who have had a poor prepregnancy diet obtain at least adequate amounts of nutrients during prenatal development. Each year in the United States, between 80,000 and 120,000 infants are born who are seriously malnourished. The federally sponsored *Special Supplemental Food Program for Women, Infants, and Children (WIC)* provides foods such as milk and cheese to about 60 percent of poor and low-income women; however, due to inadequate funding, only 60 percent of those eligible receive this help (ACOG, 1990; Children's Defense Fund, 1990).

Prenatal Health Care

Adequate early prenatal care is critical to infant and maternal health, and mothers who begin prenatal care early in pregnancy have improved pregnancy and newborn outcomes, including decreased risk of low birth weight and preterm delivery. The quality of prenatal care is strongly influenced by the woman's life circumstances, with race and economics playing a major role. In 1988, only 79 percent of white mothers and 61 percent of African American mothers began care in the first trimester. Five percent of white mothers and 11 percent of African American mothers delayed care until the last trimester or received no care at all. These mothers were most likely to be teenage, be unmarried, have less than twelve years of education, and already have three or more children. Although the risk of problems increases the later prenatal care is begun, by far the worst outcomes occur for mothers receiving no care at all. Figure 4.3 illustrates racial differences in adequacy of parental care, based on both the number of prenatal visits made and the gestational age of the baby. Table 4.3 summarizes the relationship among timing of prenatal care, mother's education and race of baby, and the percentage of low-birth-weight deliveries.

How can the prenatal care of high-risk mothers be improved? The *Prenatal/Early Infancy Project* conducted by David Olds and his colleagues is one promising answer to this question (Olds, 1988). The program was designed to improve low-income women's prenatal health habits, infant caregiving skills, use of informal social support and community services, and educational and occupational achievement. Beginning in the second trimester of pregnancy, nurses established helping relationships with the women through regular home visits. They provided education about diet and weight gain; the effects of cigarettes, alcohol, and drugs; signs of pregnancy complication; the importance of regular rest, exercise, and personal hygiene; preparation for labor and delivery and early care of the newborn; effective use of the health care system; planning for subsequent pregnancies; returning to

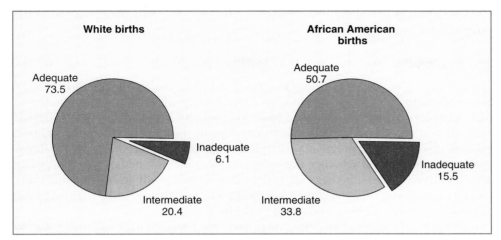

FIGURE 4.3
Racial Differences in the Adequacy of Prenatal Care
Adequacy of care is based on both the number of prenatal visits made and the baby's gestational age (number of months since conception). Note that almost three-quarters (73.5 percent) of white babies received adequate care compared to approximately half (50.7 percent) of African American babies and that 6.1 percent of white babies versus 15.5 percent of African-American babies received inadequate care.
Source: Lewis (1993), p. 340.

school; and finding employment. Nurses also educated mothers about early infant temperament and how to promote infants' social, emotional, and cognitive development. Finally, nurses helped mothers expand their informal support network to include husbands, boyfriends, and other family and friends and to develop reliable, ongoing relationships with their pediatricians and other health and human service providers. Participation in the program lasted for two years, and a follow-up study was conducted when the children were four years old.

Pregnant women who participated in the program made more use of formal services, experienced greater informal social support, improved their diets more, and reduced the number of cigarettes smoked compared to similar women not in the program. Very young teenagers in the program showed a significant improvement (395 grams) in their babies' birth weights, and smokers showed a 75 percent reduction in preterm deliveries. After delivery, these women displayed higher levels of infant and child care and made better use of health and social services. There was also a 75 percent reduction in verified cases of child abuse and neglect and a 42

TABLE 4.3   *Percentage of Full-Term Births of Low Birth Weight by Trimester of Pregnancy Prenatal Care Began, Educational Attainment of Mother, and Race of Child: 1988*
The percentage of low-birth-weight babies decreases the earlier prenatal care begins and the more years of education the mother has. Percentages of low-birth-weight infants are higher for African-Americans (versus whites) among mothers who began prenatal care at the same time and had similar levels of education.

Educational Attainment and Race	Trimester of Pregnancy Prenatal Care Began			
	1st	2nd	3rd	No Care
White				
0–11	4.0%	4.3%	4.5%	8.7%
12	2.4	3.4	3.8	7.5
13–15	1.8	2.5	2.9	6.2
16+	1.5	1.8	2.1	*
African-American				
0–11	6.6	7.1	7.5	14.6
12	5.3	5.9	6.3	12.8
13–15	4.3	5.6	5.5	14.5
16+	3.6	4.7	3.5	*

*Figure does not meet standard of reliability.
Source: Adapted from Lewis (1993, p. 340).

percent decrease in subsequent pregnancies among poor, unmarried women in the program (Olds, 1988).

Stress

Stress refers to chronic feelings of worry and anxiety. Most mothers (and fathers) feel significant stress simply about having a baby, which is something of a crisis even in the most well-adjusted families. Parents often feel surprised or even shocked at the news of pregnancy, even if they have planned to have a child. Later they may worry about whether the baby will be normal, whether they really can afford to have it, and whether they are psychologically ready to be parents. These feelings are all stressful, but when kept within reasonable bounds, they are quite normal and cause no long-run damage to the baby.

Women who experience severe and prolonged anxiety just before or during pregnancy, however, are more likely to have medical complications and to give birth to infants with abnormalities than women who do not. Emotional stress has been associated with greater incidence of spontaneous abortion, difficult labor, premature birth and low birth weight, newborn respiratory difficulties, and physical deformities (Norbeck & Tilden, 1983; Omer & Everly, 1988). Maternal stress and anxiety during late pregnancy have been associated with newborns who are hyperactive, irritable, and irregular in their feeding, sleeping, and elimination, but this is probably due to continuing anxiety in the mothers after childbirth (Sameroff & Chandler, 1975; B. Vaughn et al., 1987). Although these findings suggest that maternal stress is associated with certain difficulties, no causal relationship between maternal stress and infant problems has yet been established.

What Do You Think?

If good prenatal diet and health care are so closely related to healthy prenatal and postnatal development, why don't all expectant mothers follow nutritious diets and receive good health care? How can adequate health care be made available to all pregnant women?

BIRTH

After thirty-eight weeks in the womb, the fetus is considered to be "full term," or ready for birth. At this point it will weigh around 7½ pounds, but it can weigh as little as 5 or as much as 10 pounds and still be physically normal. The fetus measures about twenty inches or so at this stage, almost one-third of its final height as an adult.

During the last weeks, the womb becomes so crowded that the fetus assumes one position more or less permanently. This orientation is sometimes called *fetal presentation*. **Fetal presentation** (or *orientation*) refers to the body part of the fetus that is closest to the mother's cervix. The most common fetal presentation, and the most desirable one medically, is head pointing downward (called a *cephalic presentation*). Two other presentations also occur: feet and rump first (*breech presentation*) or shoulders first (*transverse presentation*). These two orientations used to jeopardize an infant's survival, but modern obstetric techniques have greatly reduced their risk.

Although parents and doctors often dearly wish they could predict the exact moment of the onset of labor, so far no one has been able to do so. However, several theories have been suggested to explain why labor begins when it does. It may be that the uterus becomes stretched beyond some natural limit and as a result evacuates itself, rather as an overly full intestine does. Or perhaps certain hormones in the fetus combine with hormones in the mother (in particular, *oxytocin*) to initiate the process; the combination may reach some crucial concentration or balance. If so, then to some extent the fetus tells the mother when it is ready.

Most fetuses develop normally for the usual thirty-eight to forty weeks and face their birth relatively well prepared. When the labor process begins, it too usually proceeds normally. The uterus contracts rhythmically and automatically to force the baby downward through the vaginal canal (see Figure 4.4). The contractions occur in a relatively predictable sequence of stages, and as long as the baby and mother are healthy and the mother's pelvis is large enough, the baby usually is out within a matter of hours.

Stages of Labor

It is common for the mother to experience "false labor," or *Braxton-Hicks contractions*, in the last weeks of pregnancy as the uterus "practices" contracting and relaxing in preparation for actual labor. These contractions do not open the cervix as real labor contractions do.

FIGURE 4.4
The Process of Delivery
(A) Before labor begins; (B) labor; (C) crowning; (D) emergence of the head

A

B

C

D

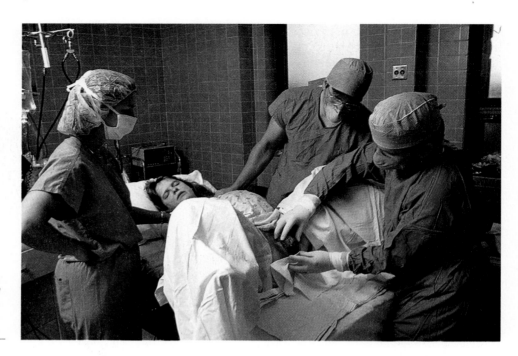

Crowning—when the baby's head can first be seen at the opening of the vagina—marks the beginning of the second stage of labor.

Labor consists of three stages. The **first stage of labor,** which lasts from the first true contraction until the cervix (the opening of the uterus) is completely open, or *dilated* to 10 centimeters (4.5 inches), is the longest stage. It usually begins with relatively mild and irregular contractions of the uterus. As contractions become stronger, more regular, and more frequent, *dilation,* or widening, of the cervix increases until there is enough room for the baby's head to fit through. As it stretches and dilates, the cervix also becomes thinner, a process referred to as *effacement.*

Toward the end of this first stage of labor, which may take from eight to twenty-four hours for a first-time mother, a **period of transition** begins. The cervix approaches full dilation, contractions become more rapid, and the baby's head begins to move into the birth canal. Although this period generally lasts for only a few minutes, it can be the most intense and challenging one because contractions become

After a few additional pushes by the mother, the head emerges, followed shortly thereafter by the newborn's shoulders, chest, legs, and feet.

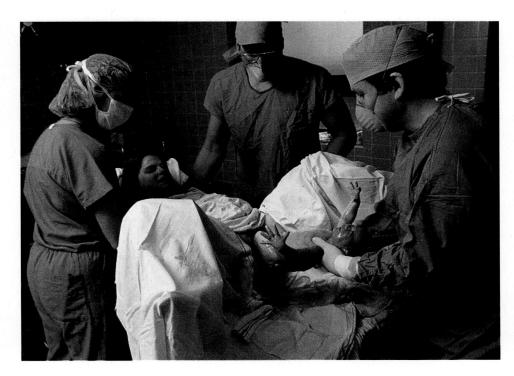

After all the hard work of labor, a baby! No matter how exhausted she may feel a mother is usually glad to see her new child, especially once reassured that it is healthy.

stronger and more deeply felt, lasting from forty-five to ninety seconds each. Managing each contraction involves a great deal of concentration and energy; women typically use the period between contractions to catch their breath and prepare for the next contraction. During transition, a woman often experiences a variety of physical changes, including trembling, shaking, leg cramps, nausea, back and hip pain, burping, and perspiring, and tends to be preoccupied with feelings of pain, pressure, and hoped-for relief (McKay, 1993).

The **second stage of labor** ranges from complete dilation of the cervix to birth. Contractions continue, but may be somewhat shorter, lasting forty-five to sixty seconds. Although the baby now has only a few more inches to move down the vagina to be born, the process can be slow, usually lasting between one and two hours for a first baby and less than a half-hour for women who have previously given birth. Although dilation is complete, for most women the reflexive urge to push the baby out by bearing down full strength usually develops toward the end of this stage, and often becomes irresistible. When a woman first begins to push, she may be uncoordinated and need to learn to push "with" the contraction and rest in between. How hard she pushes will depend on the strength of the contractions, which varies throughout labor. If a woman doesn't feel the urge to push, guidance from a partner can help, particularly if she had an epidural block or other local anesthetic that interferes with her bearing-down reflex.

During the **third stage of labor,** which lasts between five and twenty minutes, the afterbirth, which consists of placenta and umbilical cord, is expelled. Contractions still occur but are much weaker, and the woman may have to push several times to deliver the placenta. The medication oxytocin is frequently given to help the placenta to detach from the side of the uterus. Putting the baby to the mother's breast also can help, because stimulation of the nipple naturally releases oxytocin (McKay, 1993).

Childbirth Settings and Methods

Until the 1800s, births in the United States generally took place in the woman's home. Usually it was attended by midwives, friends, neighbors, and family members,

Working with   Katie Glover, OB-GYN NURSE PRACTITIONER

Preparing for Childbirth

Katie Glover was interviewed in her office at the primary health care clinic where she works. Despite her hectic schedule, Katie has a relaxed and unhurried manner. She has a three-year-old son and is currently seven months pregnant. Our interview focused on preparation for childbirth.

Rob: What advice do you give pregnant women about their nutrition?

Katie: Pregnant women need three to four glasses of milk a day and should increase consumption of fruits and vegetables, which many people don't eat regularly. As a bottom line, we recommend a balanced diet plus a few extra calories and vitamin supplements. We also recommend a twenty-five-to-thirty-pound weight gain over the course of a pregnancy, depending on the woman's size, build, and weight.

Rob: Why do you recommend weight gain?

Katie: If you figure the average baby weighs roughly 6½ to 7½ pounds and the average placenta weighs maybe 3 to 5 pounds, and add the extra fluid a woman retains and extra subcutaneous fat her body stores as added protection, that's about twenty to twenty-five pounds right there.

Rob: How do weight gain and other changes of pregnancy affect women?

Katie: They certainly change their body image. How a woman feels about that directly relates to how she feels about being pregnant. Someone who's thrilled about pregnancy will be happy to see her belly getting bigger. Someone who resents the pregnancy is likely to have a harder time with her body's changes. It's not just that her breasts are getting larger or her stomach is getting bigger. She can't run up and down the stairs as easily, and she can't find a comfortable position to sleep in. Pregnancy gets in the

way of your life. You have to alter how you move and how you eat and how often you go to the bathroom—day and night. When all you really want is a good eight hours of sleep, you may start wondering if it's all worth it!

Rob: Pregnancy can be stressful, then.

Katie: Yes. In a way, pregnancy is a crisis. How a person copes with that crisis has a lot to do with her feelings about being pregnant as well as what her social and emotional support system is like. If her partner, parents, or friends provide good, solid support and appreciation for what she's experiencing, pregnancy is likely to be a more positive experience than if she doesn't have such support.

Rob: What preparation for childbirth do you offer your patients?

Katie: Most medical practices encourage some kind of childbirth classes.

and was viewed as a natural process rather than as a medical procedure. The **midwife** was a woman experienced in pregnancy and childbirth who traditionally served as the primary caregiver during pregnancy, childbirth, and the month or so following birth. During the 1800s, political and social factors and the emergence of medicine as a scientifically based and politically powerful profession led to the replacement of midwives by physicians as the chief birth attendants. In the 1900s, delivery was moved to the hospital, where it was increasingly treated as a medical rather than a naturally occurring community event (Bogdon, 1993; Steiger, 1993).

These changes brought the benefits of modern medical technology to the birth process and resulted in decreased mortality rates for mothers and their babies, particularly in the case of high-risk pregnancies. However, they also shifted the birth process from being a natural event controlled by the pregnant woman, her family, her friends, and the community to a medical event controlled by physicians. As a result, all babies and their mothers were exposed to the risks associated with hospital-based medical procedures, including overreliance on medication and on procedures such as episiotomies and caesarian sections (discussed a bit later).

Hospital Births   Currently more than 90 percent of all births in the United States occur in hospitals under the supervision of a physician. Until recently, a typical hospital birth called for a sterilized, clinical delivery room full of bright lights and imposing equipment and attended mostly by comparative strangers, the doctors and nurses. In recent years, the maternity wards of many hospitals have modified their environments to be more comfortable and supportive of pregnant women and their families. A growing number of hospitals now have *birthing rooms* with more com-

Classes typically cover the various stages of pregnancy, physiological and psychological changes a woman might experience, changes in the couple's relationship. We talk about labor and what the hospital will be like. We talk about the different kinds of pain medications that might be offered, their effects, and the risks and benefits. Most classes also teach basic relaxation and breathing techniques, which are very important. Knowing what to expect and how to deal with the anxiety and pain can really help make labor a more positive experience.

Rob: How do you feel about birth clinics and home deliveries?

Katie: For many people who don't want to give birth in a hospital, a birth center is ideal, whether it's freestanding or directly attached to a hospital. It offers a little more freedom of movement, a little more comfort, a different atmosphere, and reassurance that medical backup is available if needed, including quick transfer to a fully equipped hospital. Of course, parents who come to a birth center should be carefully screened beforehand for any potential medical complications.

Rob: What about home birth?

Katie: I think it's a good option for the very small percentage of people who are truly suited for it.

Rob: Why is that?

Katie: It takes a very high level of commitment to arrange a home birth. Real problems can arise if it's not something both partners agree on and believe in deeply. If both partners are always there for each other, if the home situation is a nice, clean, supportive place, and if a pediatrician and a well-trained, experienced obstetrician or midwife and good emergency medical backup are available, then go for it!

What Do You Think?

1. Katie suggests that pregnancy is a type of crisis and that how a woman copes with it will depend on her attitudes toward pregnancy and the social support she receives. How might this knowledge be used to design programs to help pregnant teenagers cope better with the "crisis" of pregnancy?

2. How might a woman's pregnancy affect the father and other family members?

3. Katie discusses alternatives to hospital birth. What additional information might you need to consider these alternatives for yourself?

fortable furniture, muted colors and lighting, and soft music, and facilities for *rooming in* that allow mother and baby to stay together until both are ready to leave the hospital. Most hospitals now allow a partner to be present during the delivery, a practice that was rarely allowed just two decades ago. Nurse-midwives currently assist in only 5 percent of all births. This is due primarily to political and legal obstacles to practicing, which include issues of licensing, third-party reimbursement, malpractice insurance, and resistance from obstetrician-gynecologists who currently control access to medically supervised births, rather than to lack of adequate training (Steiger, 1993).

Nonhospital Settings   **Freestanding birth centers (FBCs)** are nonhospital facilities organized to provide family-centered maternity care for women who are judged to be at low risk for obstetrical complications (Rooks et al., 1989). Approximately 240 centers currently operate in both urban and rural areas as for-profit and nonprofit medical centers and office practices run by nurse-midwives, physicians, investors, and other individuals. Equipped and staffed to handle all but the most serious medical emergencies and designed like simple but comfortable hotels, birth centers encourage the active involvement of the mother, her family, and her friends in a birth process that minimizes technical intervention deemed to be medically unnecessary and physiologically and psychologically stressful in low-risk deliveries (Eakins, 1993).

Recent large-scale studies concluded that low-risk women delivering at freestanding birth centers are no more likely to have poor birth outcomes than are low-risk women delivering in hospitals. Birth centers were much less likely to employ *caesarean section* (surgical delivery) than were hospitals with patients of similar risk, and had very low neonatal and maternal mortality rates. Almost all major health insurance companies now cover birth center delivery, which is about one-third the cost of a normal hospital birth due to the type of facility used, the use of nurse-midwives rather than obstetrician-gynecologists, and the reduced need for certain costly medical equipment (Eakins, 1993; Rooks et al., 1989; Eakins, 1989).

Home birth is another alternative to hospital birth available for low-risk pregnancies. In a typical home birth, normal daily activities continue through the first stage of labor. When contractions increase, the nurse-midwife or physician is called to monitor the labor. Backup arrangements with a doctor or hospital are generally in place should they be needed, and women planning on home birth are carefully screened to minimize last-minute complications requiring hospital equipment or procedures. In addition to the widely held view that hospitals are the place of choice for birth, difficulty in obtaining malpractice insurance and resistance by the medical profession are major barriers to widespread acceptance of home birth.

Prepared Childbirth   In the past two decades or so, the majority of hospitals and nonhospital birth settings have offered programs to help women and their partners prepare for the physical and psychological experience of birth. These include preparatory visits to the hospital or birth facility, where pregnant women and their partners can become familiar with the physical setting and procedures. Various methods of **prepared childbirth** have been devised to help parents rehearse, or simulate, the actual sensations of labor well before the projected delivery date. Although the various prepared childbirth programs now available in most hospitals and communities differ from one another in certain details, all generally emphasize educational, physical, and emotional preparation for the birth process and active involvement of the mother and father (or other partner). Typically, they encourage the mother to find a coach (often her spouse or a relative) to give her personal support during labor (Lamaze, 1970).

One well-known preparation program, the Lamaze method, strongly advocates participation of *both* mother and father during the weeks preceding delivery and during the delivery itself. Women are taught techniques for managing the discomfort of labor that include relaxation techniques and breathing methods for each

Pregnant women and their "birth coaches" attend a Lamaze birth class to help them prepare for the experience of childbirth.

stage of labor. Labor either without drugs or with minimal drugs is encouraged, and the importance of birth as a shared emotional experience is stressed. Women giving birth using Lamaze techniques report less discomfort, more positive attitudes regarding the birth process, and less reliance on medication to manage the discomfort (Cogan, 1980).

Women who have participated in prepared childbirth also report more favorable attitudes toward labor and delivery, decreased stress during the birth process, and more sensitive interaction with the newborn baby (Lindell, 1988). Not only the mother benefits from the Lamaze or similar methods. A father's involvement in preparing for delivery and in the delivery process itself has been found to positively influence his experience of birth, his behavior toward mother and baby during delivery, and his relationship to his new infant (Markman & Kadushin, 1986; Peterson et al., 1979).

What about the experience of the infant? Frederick Leboyer, a French obstetrician, believed that conventional hospital deliveries in which the infant is suddenly thrust from the warm, dark, quiet, and protective environment of the mother's womb into the bright, noisy, cold, and overstimulating world of the delivery room are disruptive and upsetting to the newborn. He developed a "gentle birth" experience in which both parents actively participate. The delivery room is warm, quiet, and dimly lit. Immediately after birth, the infant is placed on the mother's abdomen and remains there for several minutes before the umbilical cord is cut. The baby is then placed in a warm bath by the father and gently bathed and massaged by both parents (Leboyer, 1975).

Are Leboyer's claims of lasting benefits for children born using his method supported by research? Studies that compared deliveries using the Leboyer method with deliveries in which lighting was not dimmed, the cord was cut within sixty seconds, and no bath was given (but mothers and fathers actively participated in the birth and gently handled their newborn infants) failed to discover any significant behavioral or developmental differences between gentle-birth and conventional-birth babies during their first year of life (Maziade et al., 1986; N. Nelson et al., 1980).

Medicinal Methods During Delivery   Despite adequate psychological preparation, most mothers feel some pain during labor contractions. Under good conditions, many mothers can endure this pain until the baby is delivered. But conditions are not always good: sometimes labor takes an unusually long time, and sometimes a mother finds herself less prepared than she thought. In such cases, pain-reducing drugs such as narcotics or other sedatives can make the experience bearable. But such medications must be used cautiously. Most pain relievers cross the placenta and therefore can seriously depress the fetus if they are given at the wrong time or in improper amounts.

During the final stages of delivery, two other forms of pain relief are available. Doctors may inject a sedative into the base of the woman's spine. The two most common of these procedures are called an *epidural* and a *spinal.* They allow the mother to remain awake and alert during the final stages of labor, but they also prevent her from controlling her contractions, which can be quite helpful when the baby is finally expelled. Nitrous oxide, which dentists commonly use, also has been used to take the edge off the pain of the peak contractions while allowing the mother to remain conscious.

Giving a mother either a general or a local anesthetic before delivery removes all pain, of course, but both mother and child may take a long time to recover from it. Mothers who receive general anesthetics for delivery stay in the hospital for more days after delivery, on the average, than do mothers who receive other kinds of medication. This is partly because it takes several days for them to recover from the medication (Hamilton, 1984). In addition, the bonding between mother and child

TABLE 4.4   ***Major Medications During Childbirth and Their Effects on the Baby***

Type	Administration	Positive Effects for Mother	Negative Effects for Baby
Analgesics	By injection (in controlled doses) during the first stage of labor to reduce pain	Reduces pain, causes some drowsiness and euphoria (sense of well-being and tranquility); women participate in labor and delivery	May cause drowsiness and decreased responsiveness for first few hours after birth or longer; naloxone hydrochloride (Narcon) can be used to reverse these effects
Local anesthesia			
Spinal	By injection into spinal canal in controlled doses when cervix is fully dilated (beginning of second stage of labor); numbs sensory and motor nerves so that mother's pelvic area and legs cannot move voluntarily	Mother can remain awake and aware during labor and delivery; can be used for either vaginal or caesarean birth; is highly effective in eliminating pain	No negative effects reported
Epidural	By injection during active phase of first stage of labor to numb sensory nerves after their exit from spinal canal	Pain and sensations are generally eliminated; mother is awake; some voluntary movement is preserved, although it is less effective because a woman's sense of position and tension are blocked by the medication	No negative effects reported
General Anesthesia	A mixture of nitrous oxide and oxygen is inhaled; is less commonly used than blocking agents	Easily administered, rapid onset of effect; anesthetic of choice in emergencies in which time is critical and baby must be delivered quickly	Decreased alertness and responsiveness following birth

Source: Feinbloom & Forman (1987).

is delayed while both are recovering from the effect of anesthesia. Table 4.4 lists the major types of medications used during labor and delivery, their administration, and their effects (Feinbloom & Forman, 1987).

Perceptions of Pain During Childbirth   An important issue in modern childbirth involves decisions about whether and when medication should be used to manage the discomfort and pain often associated with the birth process. Professionals who assist women in deliveries find it difficult to determine how much discomfort or distress a laboring woman is in and how to respond appropriately. Cultural differences in how pain or discomfort is experienced and expressed also complicate such assessments.

To better understand cultural differences in perceptions of pain related to childbirth, Janice Morse and Caroline Park studied expectant parents from four cultural groups living in western Canada: English-speaking Canadians, Ukrainians, Hutterites, and East Indians (Morse & Park, 1988). These parents, who were about to have hospital deliveries, were asked to compare the pain of childbirth with eight other painful events: heart attack, kidney stone, severe burn, toothache, gallstones, eye injury, broken bone, and migraine. Figure 4.5 shows the mean pain ratings of women and men from each cultural group.

The Canadian parents expected the most pain. Like most middle-class Americans, they planned to use a variety of nonmedicinal methods to prepare for it. However, they also knew that if labor became too uncomfortable, they would be offered medications to relieve the pain. The East Indian parents were next highest in expected pain. The emphasis on purity and innocence in East Indian culture means females are not taught directly about the process of birth. During labor, East Indian women frequently expressed their discomfort by vocalizing (crying, yelling, or complaining) continually.

The Hutterite parents anticipated considerably less pain. Hutterites live in a collection of religious and agricultural communities that reject technology and

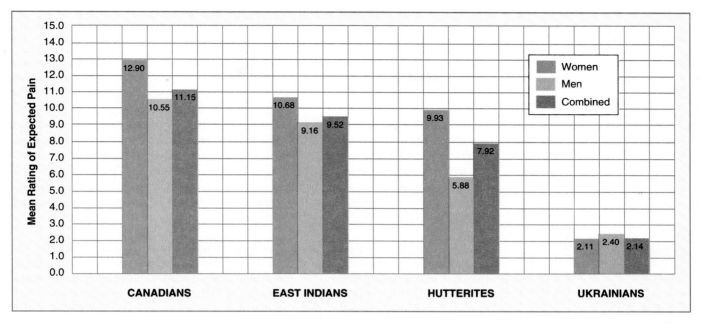

maintain strict traditional and patriarchal customs and values that rigidly restrict women to the maternal role. Contraception is not allowed unless maternal health is threatened, and family size averages 10.4 children. During pregnancy there is no change in a woman's work role or diet, and the discomfort of childbirth is viewed as God's will. The Ukrainian parents reported the lowest overall ratings of discomfort during childbirth. Ukrainians are also an agricultural community with strong religious values, but are more flexible regarding the use of contraception and the roles of women. Deliveries for both the Hutterite and Ukrainian parents were relatively calm and unemotional, with the women dealing with their discomfort in a quiet and uncomplaining manner.

Morse and Park note that the two cultures that rate childbirth discomfort the highest (Canadians and East Indians) do not consider childbirth to be a natural event, as reflected in the medicalization of childbirth in Canadian culture and the withholding of information about birth in East Indian culture. On the other hand, the Hutterite and Ukrainian cultures consider childbirth to be a natural event that need not be extensively managed or purposefully ignored. Whatever their causes, such differences in cultural expectations may affect the amount of distress actually experienced during labor and delivery. It is important that they be considered by professionals and others involved in the labor and delivery process.

FIGURE 4.5
Differences in Mean Ratings of Expected Pain During Childbirth among Four Cultural Groups
As the bar graphs show, Canadian parents expected the most pain, followed by East Indian parents and Hutterite parents. Ukrainian parents anticipated the least pain, with ratings much lower than those for the three other groups.
Source: Morse & Park (1988).

Problems During Labor and Delivery

Interference with labor and delivery can occur in three ways: through *faulty power* in the uterus, a *faulty passageway* (the birth canal), or a *faulty passenger* (the baby itself). These problems actually interconnect in various ways, but it is convenient to distinguish among them (Buckley & Kulb, 1983).

Faulty Power   Sometimes the uterus does not contract strongly enough to make labor progress to a delivery. The problem can occur at the beginning of labor or develop midway through a labor that began quite normally, especially if the mother becomes worn out and discouraged after hours of powerful contractions. In many cases, the doctor can strengthen the contractions by giving the mother an injection of the hormone oxytocin. But the resulting artificial contractions must be watched carefully, because often they do not match the needs of the baby or the mother as well as natural contractions do. Such *induced labor* can harm both baby and mother by forcing the baby through the canal before the canal is ready or wasting the mother's scarce energy just when she needs it most.

In about one in two thousand deliveries, the uterus ruptures because of the power of its contractions (Hamilton, 1984). This condition is quite serious; the mother may bleed to death in just a few moments if she is unattended, and in the process the baby almost always dies. Because uterine rupture occurs somewhat more often among mothers who have previously delivered babies surgically, hospitals used to require such mothers to plan on delivering all future babies by caesarean section (discussed shortly). Recent improvements in surgical techniques, however, have left these mothers with stronger uterine walls. As a result, many doctors now permit mothers to attempt natural labor as long as the hospital staff watches carefully for any signs of rupture. If problems develop, a caesarean section can still be arranged and performed quickly and safely.

Faulty Passageway   Problems can also occur with the placenta. Sometimes the placenta develops too close to the cervix and blocks the baby from moving down the birth canal during labor. This condition is called *placenta previa,* from the Latin meaning "placenta in front of the passageway." Placenta previa usually makes itself known by causing bleeding from the vagina late in pregnancy, but because this bleeding is painless, mothers (and doctors) tend to underestimate its significance. If left untreated, placenta previa can leave the fetus somewhat undernourished, because it prevents sufficient blood from reaching it. Sometimes it blocks a normal delivery entirely so that the baby must be delivered by caesarean section.

Even if the placenta implants far enough away from the cervix, it occasionally partly separates from its base against the wall of the womb, a condition called *abruptio placenta.* This condition also causes vaginal bleeding, but unlike with placenta previa, the bleeding can be quite painful. Partly as a result, doctors are more likely to detect the problem relatively soon after it occurs. No sure remedy exists except for the mother to live sensibly and relatively quietly. Sometimes doctors advise complete bed rest if they believe substantial portions of the placenta have separated, but this degree of enforced inactivity can cause mothers almost as much worry as the condition itself (Hamilton, 1984).

Faulty Passenger   Usually a baby enters the birth canal head first, but occasionally one turns in the wrong direction during contractions. A breech presentation—with the bottom leading—is risky for the baby, for its spine can be broken if a contraction presses it too hard against the mother's pelvis. Or the baby may not get enough oxygen because it cannot begin breathing on its own until after its nose comes out. In some cases a skilled midwife or doctor can deliver a breech baby with no problem, but if the baby gets stuck partway out of the vagina, medical staff may use *forceps* to pull it the rest of the way out. In most cases, breech babies are either turned to the right position during delivery or delivered surgically by caesarean section.

A small but significant proportion of babies are simply too big to pass through the mother's pelvis and vaginal canal, a problem sometimes called *cephalopelvic disproportion (CPD)*—literally, a disproportion of the head and pelvis. Extra hours of labor do not help push such babies through; their heads are too big to fit, although often by only a fraction of an inch. Unfortunately, the problem usually is not revealed until well into labor. Such a mismatch of size can result from genetic influence, but ironically it also results from an especially healthy, well-nourished pregnancy, which creates an exceptionally large baby. In any case, if the mismatch is too severe, it can threaten the life of the mother or the child. Thus, the doctor may interrupt the labor and deliver the baby surgically.

Caesarean Section   **Caesarean section,** or *C-section,* is a procedure used in cases where the baby cannot be safely delivered through the vagina and therefore has to be removed surgically. Techniques for this surgery have improved substantially over the past decades. The operation now takes only about half an hour, most of which is devoted to sewing the mother up after getting the baby out. Also, the incision is smaller than it used to be (just a few inches), generally oriented horizontally, and located rather low on the mother's abdomen.

Partly because of these improvements, the number of C-sections for live births rose from 205,000 in 1970 to 966,000 in 1988, although the total number of births increased by only 5 percent. Much of this increase was due to a sharp rise in C-section rates for teenagers and women in their twenties, which almost quadrupled between 1970 and 1988. Currently the C-section rate appears to have leveled off at about one in four births, but many experts and parent advocates are concerned that the rates are still too high and that they reflect medical practices that are not in the best interests of mothers and their babies (Taffel, 1989, 1993).

Both supporters and critics of caesarean birth agree that there are a number of good reasons to select a C-section as the safest way to deliver a baby. These include some of the problems of placenta previa, placenta abruptio, and cephalopelvic disproportion already noted, as well as prolapsed cord, where the umbilical cord cuts off the baby's oxygen; an unusual position of the baby that makes vaginal delivery impossible; severe fetal distress that cannot be corrected; and active herpes, which the baby may contract through vaginal birth.

Selection of a caesarean delivery purely for the convenience of the physician, a previous caesarean delivery (currently the most common reason for doing the procedure), inactive herpes, and suspected cephalopelvic disproportion not confirmed by a period of strong, frequent contractions are all no longer accepted as valid reasons for a caesarean delivery. Reasons for considering a vaginal birth after a previous C-section include less risk of surgical complications, shorter recovery time, and the opportunity for greater involvement of the mother in the delivery process (ACOG, 1990).

Fetal Monitoring   Most hospitals use *electronic fetal monitoring* to record uterine contractions and the fetal heart rate. Uterine contractions are externally measured by a pressure gauge strapped to the mother's abdomen that electronically represents changes in the shape of the uterus on graph paper. Fetal heart rate can be picked up by an *external* ultrasound monitor placed on the abdomen over the uterus or *internally* by a wire, leading through the vagina and screwed into the fetus's scalp, that records more subtle electrical changes in the fetus's heart.

Although internal fetal monitoring is extremely helpful in high-risk and emergency situations, experts have questioned its routine use for low-risk deliveries. Because the amniotic membranes must be ruptured to permit attachment of the electrode to the baby's scalp, the very procedure designed to identify the fetus at risk of distress may itself contribute to fetal distress. In addition, the mother must lie in bed for as long as the wires are attached (Feinbloom & Forman, 1987). Experts have also noted that "high-tech" birth imposes psychological burdens as well by shifting the center of focus from the experience of mother and baby to readouts from the equipment. This makes birth a less "human" experience (Davis-Floyd, 1986).

Low-Birth-Weight Infants

The average weight of a full-term newborn infant is about 7.5 pounds (3,400 grams). **Low-birth-weight** infants, in contrast, weigh 5.5 pounds or less at birth. These babies account for between 6 and 7 percent of all births in the United States. The incidence of low birth weight varies widely among developed and underdeveloped countries, due largely to differences in rates of poverty, famine, and malnutrition. Percentages of low-birth-weight infants range from 50 percent in Bangladesh;

20 percent in the Philippines; less than 5 percent in France, Japan, New Zealand, and Australia; and less than 4 percent in Sweden, Finland, Netherlands, and Norway (Grant, 1986; Sen, 1993).

The majority of low-birth-weight infants are also preterm. *Preterm* (commonly called *premature*) refers to babies who are born three or more weeks early and therefore are immature in their prenatal development compared to babies who have the full thirty-nine weeks to prepare for birth. Preterm babies account for approximately 10 percent of live births in the United States. Some low-birth-weight infants are *small for date,* which refers to infants who are born on time (close to their due dates) but weigh less than the average for babies of the same gestational age.

Low-birth-weight infants generally are at risk for a wide range of developmental, neurological, and health problems, with the risks increasing as birth weight and maturity decrease. If they are *preterm,* they are likely to suffer from *respiratory distress syndrome (RDS),* a leading cause of death in newborns, and to have more abnormalities in physical growth, motor behavior, neurological functioning, and intellectual development than full-term babies (Kopp & Parmalee, 1979; Taub et al., 1977). Small-for-date infants are at somewhat greater risk than other low-birth-weight infants, having higher rates of death, susceptibility to illness, and neurological problems during their first year and greater developmental difficulties than preterm infants as they get older (Teberg et al., 1988). One promising program to prevent low-birth-weight pregnancies was discussed earlier in the chapter, and additional coverage of this topic appears in Chapter 5.

Birth and the Family

The arrival of a new baby can be particularly difficult for parents who lack the economic resources and social and emotional support that are so important in adjusting to the complicated demands of caring for a new baby. While it is unwise to generalize too broadly, adolescent parents, single parents, and parents who are educationally and economically disadvantaged are more likely to find parenthood difficult. As you might imagine, having a baby that is low birth weight can be even more traumatic. Here again, home visiting programs that provide various forms of physical, educational, social, and emotional assistance to new parents can be particularly helpful (Ramey & Ramey, 1993).

Despite the various problems just mentioned, the great majority of births in this country occur without significant problems and to families whose economic, social, and psychological resources enable them to become effective parents. For women (and their partners) who receive good preparation and training for the birth process and obtain adequate social and emotional support from family, friends, and culture, birth is likely to be a very positive and welcome event. For most families, the arrival of a new baby brings many changes that take some time to adjust to. For first-time parents, learning to care for a new baby and rearranging family schedules to be able to provide the almost constant attention a newborn requires are very big challenges, to say the least.

For parents who already have children, a newcomer to the family also creates stresses. Children naturally worry that they will lose their special place in the family and the exclusive attention they enjoy once the newcomer arrives. Involving the child in the preparation for birth, for the period when the mother is in the hospital, and for the changes that will occur with the new arrival are all important ways to help a child adjust to the changes. Talking to the child about these things and listening carefully to his or her questions and concerns are particularly important. Especially with preschoolers, providing concrete information about birth, newborn babies and what they are like, and the specific changes that will occur in the family before and after the baby's birth can help allay their fears. In recent years, a number of good books and related materials designed for young children have become available to assist parents in this process.

Birth is a family event. Involving children in the preparation for birth can play a very important role in helping them adjust to the changes.

After the new baby arrives home, parents can do a number of things to assist the adjustment process. Giving the older child lots of verbal reassurance helps, but concrete actions speak louder than words. One strategy is to give the child an important role in the event by providing special activities, asking friends and family members to bring a gift for the child as well as for the new baby, and including the child in daily activities with the new infant. High priority should also be placed on continuing routine activities with the older child and ensuring that each parent spends lots of special time just with him or her.

What Do You Think?

How might the process of birth vary depending on a family's circumstances such as age, marital status, income, race, and culture? To explore this question, have yourself and several classmates play the roles of expectant parents from different life circumstances. What did you discover?

FROM BIOLOGICAL TO PSYCHOLOGICAL DEVELOPMENT

The process of prenatal development presents a contradictory picture. On the one hand, it seems highly predictable and insensitive to the influences that might change its course. Starting from a single cell, the process rapidly unfolds and develops in an increasingly complex sequence of interrelated patterns of change, all of which have become highly canalized over the thousands of years of human evolution. It is as though from the moment of conception, the emergence of the newborn baby nine months later were never in doubt. Although deviations from these normal developmental pathways occur, they are not genuine departures from normal prenatal development; rather, they seem to further emphasize the predictability of most embryos and fetuses.

On the other hand, although birth marks the end of prenatal development, it is only the beginning of the incredible range of developmental changes that follow—changes that are much less canalized or predictable. The fact that biology seems to lose its hold on the child once she or he emerges from the womb and the environment and experience take over may be overwhelming to a new parent. Nevertheless, as we discover in the chapters that follow, biology and experience remain too closely intertwined to be sharply distinguishable from each other. The path a child's development takes will be only partly determined by the child's experiences, including the efforts of the parents.

SUMMARY OF MAJOR IDEAS

Stages of Prenatal Development

1. Prenatal development begins with conception, in which a zygote is created by the union of a sperm cell from the father and an egg cell, or ovum, from the mother.

2. Prenatal development consists of discrete periods, or stages.

3. The germinal stage occurs during the first two weeks following conception; the zygote forms a blastocyst, which differentiates into three distinct cell layers and then implants itself in the uterine wall to form the embryo.

4. During the embryonic stage, which lasts from the third through eighth weeks of pregnancy, the placenta and umbilical cord form and the basic organs and biological systems begin to develop.

5. During the fetal stage, which lasts from the ninth week until the end of pregnancy, all physical features complete their development.

6. Infertility, the inability to conceive or carry a pregnancy to term after one year of unprotected intercourse, affects approximately 15 percent of all married couples of childbearing age.

7. The experience of pregnancy includes dramatic changes in a woman's physical functioning and appearance, as well as significant psychological changes, as prospective mothers and fathers anticipate the birth of a baby.

Prenatal Influences on the Child

8. Although prenatal development is highly canalized, or directed, there are critical periods (particularly during the first trimester) when embryonic development is highly vulnerable or at risk to disruption from teratogens.

9. Teratogens are substances or other environmental influences that can permanently disrupt and damage an embryo's growth. Their effects depend on the timing, intensity, and duration of exposure, the presence of other risks, and the biological vulnerability of baby and mother.

10. Certain biological risks to prenatal development are associated with the physical and biological characteristics of the mother, including her age, physical size, and state of health.

11. Diseases such as rubella, syphilis, genital herpes, and AIDS are also teratogens that can irreversibly harm the embryo or fetus, particularly during critical periods of development.

12. Certain medicinal drugs such as thalidomide and DES and nonmedicinal drugs such as heroin, cocaine, alcohol, and tobacco also can have teratogenic effects on prenatal development.

13. Environmental hazards such as radiation or industrial pollution can harm the developing embryo or fetus.

14. The risk of domestic violence increases during pregnancy and is highest for women who are teenagers and living in impoverished and dysfunctional families and communities.

15. Teenage pregnancy increases risks to healthy prenatal and postnatal development, as well as developmental risks to the mother.

16. Adequacy of maternal diet and prenatal care, as well as levels of stress, can all influence prenatal development.

17. Adequate prenatal nutrition and health care for the mother and her developing baby is associated with a successful pregnancy, a normal birth, and healthy neonatal development.

Birth

18. Toward the end of the third trimester, the mother may experience "false labor," including contractions of the uterus; she may also have a bloody vaginal discharge shortly before true labor begins.

19. Labor occurs in three distinct but overlapping stages. During the first stage of labor, which may last from eight to twenty-four hours for a first-time mother, uterine contractions increase in strength and regularity, and the cervix

dilates sufficiently to accommodate the baby's head. The second stage of labor lasts from the complete dilation of the cervix until birth and takes from sixty to ninety minutes. During the third stage of labor, which lasts only a few minutes, the afterbirth is expelled.

20. Nonhospital birth centers and home birth are two alternatives to hospital-based birth.

21. Prepared childbirth is now widely used in both hospital and nonhospital birth settings to help women actively and comfortably meet the challenges of giving birth.

22. Pain-reducing medications can make the experience of childbirth more comfortable, but in recent years they have been used more cautiously because of their potentially adverse effects on the recovery of both infant and mother.

23. One problem that may arise during labor and delivery is insufficient uterine contractions, or faulty power. A faulty passageway caused by blockage of the birth canal by the placenta (placenta previa) is another potential problem. A faulty passenger may occur if the baby's physical position or large head size prevents completion of the journey through the birth canal.

24. Most hospitals use electronic fetal monitors to keep track of fetal heart rate and uterine contractions.

25. Low-birth-weight babies may experience significant complications after birth; however, the bigger and more mature they are at birth, the greater are their chances for survival and healthy development.

26. While learning to care for a new baby is a welcome challenge for most new parents, it may be especially difficult for adolescent parents, single parents, and parents who are educationally and economically disadvantaged.

KEY TERMS

germinal stage *(91)*
embryonic stage *(91)*
fetal stage *(91)*
conception *(92)*
implantation *(93)*
embryo *(93)*
placenta *(94)*
umbilical cord *(94)*
amniotic sac *(95)*
fetus *(95)*

canalization *(101)*
critical period *(102)*
teratogen *(102)*
fetal alcohol syndrome (FAS) *(109)*
fetal presentation *(114)*
first stage of labor *(116)*
period of transition *(116)*
second stage of labor *(117)*
third stage of labor *(117)*

midwife *(118)*
freestanding birth center (FBC) *(119)*
prepared childbirth *(120)*
caesarean section *(124)*
low birth weight *(125)*

FOR FURTHER READING

Bean, C. A. *Methods of Childbirth.* New York: Morrow, 1990.
This book provides thorough and readable coverage of the later stages of pregnancy, delivery, and postnatal care.

The Boston Women's Health Collective. *The New Our Bodies, Ourselves: A Book by and for Women.* New York: Simon and Schuster, 1984.
This revised and updated edition discusses many aspects of women's bodies, health care, and well-being from the personal perspectives of women. The section on pregnancy is an excellent source of information about what the events and experiences are really like.

Kitzinger, S. *Your Baby, Your Way: Making Pregnancy Decisions and Birth Plans.* New York: Pantheon, 1987.
This guide for expectant mothers and fathers discusses the physical and psychological factors involved in pregnancy and childbirth and the decision-making options available.

Nilsson, L. *A Child Is Born.* New York: Delacorte, 1990.
This book provides up-to-date coverage of the physical and psychological aspects of prenatal development and birth, with exceptional full-color photographs and illustrations.

Rothman, B. K., ed. *The Encyclopedia of Childbearing.* New York: Henry Holt, 1993.
This rich, well-researched, and highly readable resource book contains brief essays by more than two hundred experts on a wide range of current childbearing and child-rearing topics, including multicultural, legal, historical, and social policy issues.

Sears, W., and M. Sears. *The Birth Book: Everything You Need to Know to Have a Safe and Satisfying Birth.* Boston: Little, Brown, 1994.
This is a clear, well-illustrated, practical guide for expectant parents and people who want to know what childbirth in the United States involves.

Silber, S. J. *How To Get Pregnant with the New Technology.* New York: Warner Books, 1991.
This book provides comprehensive coverage of recent developments in reproductive technology.

PART THREE

The First
Two Years

s parents and other proud relatives continually discover, infants grow and change more rapidly than the rest of us. Parents who take snapshots of their children find they must do so every few months, or even weeks, to keep up with all these changes. In a matter of months, infants are able to smile, sit, and babble. In just a few more months, they acquire language and the earliest symbolic skills and take their first tentative steps. And during their first year of life, they also acquire close attachments to particular caregivers.

These changes are crucial in many ways. They make infants seem much more "human" than they appeared as newborns. They also lay important foundations for all future development. The next three chapters describe these critical changes.

5

THE FIRST TWO YEARS

Physical Development

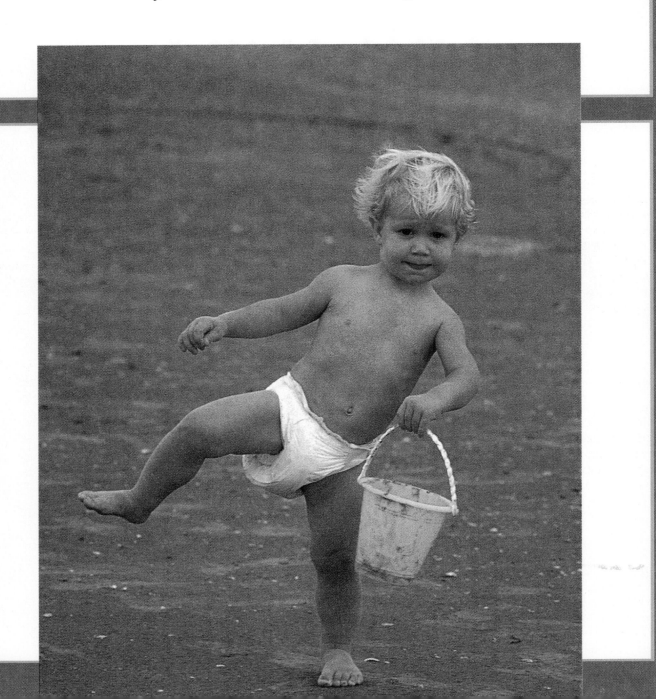

Appearance of the Young Infant

The First Few Hours
Is the Baby All Right? The Apgar Scale
Newborn Weight
Size and Bodily Proportions

Development of the Nervous System

Growth of the Brain
States of Sleep and Wakefulness

Sensory Development

Visual Acuity
Auditory Acuity
Taste, Smell, and Touch

Motor Development

Early Reflexes
The First Motor Skills
Variations in Motor Skill Development

Variations in Infant Growth

Low-Birth-Weight Infants
Helping Low-Birth-Weight Infants

Nutrition During the First Two Years

Breast Milk Versus Formula
Nutrition in Later Infancy
Infant Mortality

Infancy: The Real End of Birth

nne was looking at the journal she had kept about her daughter since Michelle was seven months old.

■ February 7: This week Michelle began pushing herself backward on her stomach to get around—not very efficient, but it works!

■ April 9: For two weeks she has been *creeping,* not crawling. She raises up her tummy, pushes her body forward (like a seal!), and plops down. Jim and I can't help laughing—she looks so ridiculous.

■ June 10: Crawling all over the place—mostly after the dog. Gets mad when King walks away; then she cries and "forgets" how to locomote.

■ August 10: Michelle's really working at walking. Three to five steps at a time, mostly when one of us is encouraging her. She really looks different, especially now that she's vertical.

As Anne can attest, during the first months of life a baby's behaviors evolve rapidly. In this chapter, we trace some of these physical developments through the first two years of life. We begin by discussing what young infants look like. Then we investigate babies' nervous systems, including the growth of their brains and how they are affected by sleep patterns. We go on to discuss the development of the senses. Then we turn to how infants develop motor skills, sampling both early, inborn reflexes and major early voluntary skills, such as walking. Next, we discuss infants' nutritional needs: what food they need immediately at birth, how these needs change as they get older, and how diet can affect their physical development or even their very survival.

Focusing Questions

• What do infants look like, and how do they act during the first two years of life?

• How do infants' sleep and wakefulness patterns change as they get older? Can parents influence these patterns?

• How do infants' senses operate at birth?

• What are some motor skills that evolve during infancy?

• What are the risks of low birth weight on infant development?

• What do infants need nutritionally?

• What nutritional deficiencies are common in North America and around the world?

• What are the relative advantages of breast milk and formula?

APPEARANCE OF THE YOUNG INFANT

As we saw in the last chapter, birth continues rather than initiates physical development. Most organs have already been working for several weeks, or even months, prior to this event. The baby's heart has been beating regularly, his muscles have been contracting sporadically, and his liver has been making its major product, bile, which is necessary for normal digestion after birth. Even some behaviors, such as sucking and arm stretching, have already developed. Two physical functions, however, do begin at birth: breathing and ingestion (the taking in of foods).

The First Few Hours

When it first emerges from the birth canal, a newborn baby (also called a **neonate**) definitely does not resemble most people's stereotypes of a beautiful baby. No matter what its race, its skin often looks rather red—redder than parents usually expect, especially if they have never paid close attention to young babies before. The infant may be covered with various substances, such as fluid from the amniotic sac, blood from the placenta, and bits of brownish fluid from its own bowels. If they are born a bit

In the first few minutes after birth, healthy newborn babies are quite alert and responsive to sights and sounds. Soon, however, they begin spending most of their time asleep—perhaps just as well for mothers who may be tired after labor.

early, many neonates also have a white, waxy substance called *vernix* on their skin, and their bodies may be covered with fine, downy hair called *lanugo.* If the baby was born vaginally rather then delivered surgically, its head may be somewhat elongated or have a noticeable point on it; the shape comes from the pressure of the birth canal, which squeezes the baby's skull for several hours during labor. Within a few days or weeks, the head fills out again to a more rounded shape, leaving gaps in the bones. The gaps are sometimes called *fontanelles,* or "soft spots," although they are actually covered by a tough membrane that can withstand normal contact and pressure. The gaps eventually grow over, but not until the infant is about eighteen months old.

Healthy newborns react vigorously to their surroundings during the first fifteen or thirty minutes of life. They may cry, look around, or suck, using the inborn reflexes described later in this chapter. Before long, though, they fall asleep (labor can wear them out, too!) and do not wake for a few hours.

Is the Baby All Right? The Apgar Scale

Because hospitals cannot always afford to have a pediatrician (a doctor with special expertise in children and infants) attend every birth, doctors and nurses need a way to decide quickly which newborns need immediate medical attention and which are healthy enough to wait a bit longer. The **Apgar Scale** (named after its originator, Dr. Virginia Apgar) helps to meet this need (Apgar, 1953). The scale consists of ratings that are simple enough for nonspecialists to make, even amid the distractions surrounding the moment of delivery. To use it, someone present at the delivery calculates the baby's heart rate, breathing effort, muscle tone, skin color, and reflex irritability and assigns a score of 0 to 2 to each of these five characteristics. Babies are rated one minute after they emerge from the womb and again at five minutes. For each rating they can earn a maximum score of 10, as shown in Table 5.1. Most babies in fact earn nine or ten points, at least by five minutes after delivery. A baby who scores between four and seven points at one minute is given immediate special medical attention (Apgar & Beck, 1973), which usually includes examination by a pediatrician, and is then carefully observed during the next few hours and days for any problems that may develop.

Newborns who score less than 4 on the Apgar Scale face serious medical risk. Their heart rates are slow, their breathing is irregular and labored, and their muscle tone is weak. Instead of having the healthy reddish-pink color that results from an

TABLE 5.1   **The Apgar Scale**

Characteristic	Score		
	0	**1**	**2**
Heart rate	Absent	Less than 100 beats per minute	More than 100 beats per minute
Efforts to breathe	Absent	Slow, irregular	Good; baby is crying
Muscle tone	Flaccid, limp	Weak, inactive	Strong, active motion
Skin color	Body pale or blue	Body pink, extremities blue	Body and extremities pink
Reflex irritability	No response	Frown, grimace	Vigorous crying, coughing, sneezing

Source: Apgar (1953)

ample supply of oxygen in their blood, babies with low Apgar ratings may look blue in their extremities or even all over their bodies. Also, they do not respond strongly when stimulated; a sudden noise, for example, produces no startle reaction. Such babies need intensive care immediately if they are to survive. Their most immediate problem usually concerns breathing: often they need extra oxygen and special apparatus to facilitate breathing. If intensive care is available, however, most low-Apgar babies do survive.

Newborn Weight

At birth a typical baby weighs about 7½ pounds, or 3,400 grams, about as much as an average cat or a small dog. Because they are small, neonates have a rather large surface area relative to their weight. As a result, they lose heat more rapidly than adults do, and they have to consume more calories just to keep warm. But neonates also need to gain weight during the earliest months; by four or five months of age, they typically have doubled their birth weight. (See Figure 5.1.) How, then, can they keep themselves warm and gain quite a lot of weight at the same time?

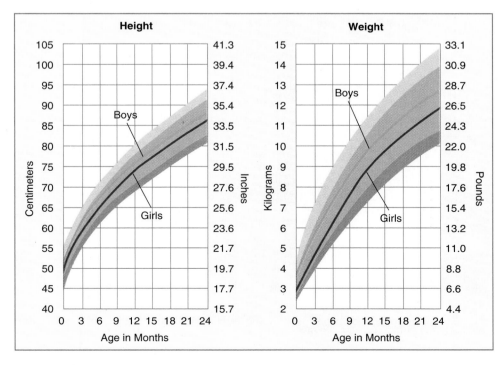

FIGURE 5.1

Height and Weight Growth During the First Two Years

Girls and boys gain rapidly in height and weight during infancy. The colored bands show the range of sizes possible for all but the tallest and shortest 5 percent of children and for all but the most and least heavy 5 percent. The line in the middle of each band indicates average height and weight for each age. Note that although girls are slightly shorter and lighter than boys, the genders overlap more than they differ.

The answer is, they eat. Because they still have no teeth, they have to drink all their calories. A newborn usually consumes about one quart of breast milk or infant formula in twenty-four hours. As a proportion of body weight, this is the same as an adult drinking ten to twenty quarts per day. And, of course, the baby must excrete after capturing the valuable nutrients from these huge amounts. No wonder, then, that diapers and feedings form the center of a newborn's life.

Size and Bodily Proportions

Lying down, a newborn baby measures about twenty inches, or fifty centimeters. Her length matches her adult size more closely than her weight does: her twenty inches represent more than one-quarter of her final height, whereas her 7½ pounds represent only a small percentage of her adult weight.

This fact suggests that newborns should look skinny, but actually they usually look chubby or even overweight. Babies' heads take up almost one-quarter of their length, and their limbs are disproportionately short. (See Figure 5.2.) Their chests seem small compared to their stomachs, which often stick out like a middle-aged person's pot belly. Bones contribute much less to overall weight than they do for adults; they are small and thin in proportion to the baby's size. For all these reasons, babies tend to look rather fat and cute.

Babies' proportions and general physical appearance may have psychological consequences by fostering **attachments,** or bonds, between infants and the people who care for them. Such bonds promote feelings of security. The cuteness of infants' faces in particular seems to help. No matter what their racial or ethnic background, most babies have unusually large foreheads, features that are concentrated in the lower part of the face, eyes that are large and round, and cheeks that

The normal facial features of infants— large forehead and eyes, high cheekbones, small mouth—may help stimulate attachment in adults. Similar facial proportions also exist in the young of many other animals; puppies, for example, have larger eyes and cheekbones than adult dogs.

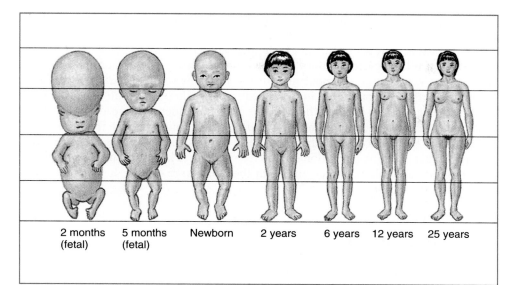

FIGURE 5.2
Body Proportions, Fetal Period Through Adulthood
In addition to increases in size, growth involves major changes in the proportions of various body parts. From conception to adulthood, the head steadily becomes proportionately smaller than the body and the limbs become proportionately larger. The chest and abdomen remain in relatively constant proportion.

| 2 months (fetal) | 5 months (fetal) | Newborn | 2 years | 6 years | 12 years | 25 years |

are high and prominent. Dolls and cartoon characters have these facial features too, although often in exaggerated form, and so do a variety of animal species. The pattern of babyish features occurs so widely among animals, in fact, that biologists who study animal behavior suspect it has a universal and genetically based power to elicit parental or nurturing responses among adult animals (Lorenz, 1970). Mothers in some species of ducks, for example, take care of baby ducks even when the babies are not their own.

Cuteness apparently affects humans in comparable ways, although not as automatically as among other animals. The mere sight of a babyish face creates interest in most people and in a wide variety of situations. This interest is both conscious and unconscious. Not only do people say they find babies attractive; their bodies respond to babies with enlarged pupils and a faster heartbeat. Unlike many other animal species, humans are interested in infants even if they are not parents or other adults; babies, for example, seem very interested in other babies and even in their own images in a mirror (Priel & Zeidman, 1990).

What Do You Think?

What do you think attracts parents to their newborn children? Explore this question with the parents of a physically handicapped infant. How did they feel about their child (and about themselves) when the child was first born?

DEVELOPMENT OF THE NERVOUS SYSTEM

The **central nervous system** consists of the brain and nerve cells of the spinal cord, which together coordinate and control the perception of stimuli as well as motor responses of all kinds. The more complex aspects of this work are accomplished by the brain, which develops rapidly from just before birth until well beyond a child's second birthday. At seven months past conception, the baby's brain weighs about 10 percent of its final adult weight, but by birth it has more than doubled to about

25 percent of final adult weight. By the child's second birthday, it has tripled to about 75 percent of its final adult weight (Parkins, 1990, pp. 51–78).

Most of this increase results not from increasing numbers of nerve cells, or **neurons,** but from the development of a denser, or more fully packed, brain. This happens in two ways. First, the neurons put out many new fibers that connect them with one another. Second, certain brain cells called **glia** put out fatty sheathing, or **myelin,** that gradually encases the neurons and their fibers. Because impulses can travel relatively easily through myelin sheaths, myelin allows nerve fibers to transmit impulses much more quickly (more than ten times!) as well as more reliably. The myelin acts like the insulation on an electric cord: it keeps impulses from short-circuiting on other fibers and ensures that they discharge only at designated places along the nerve fibers.

Growth of the Brain

At birth and for about the first six months thereafter, neural activity is dominated by the relatively primitive, or "lower," areas of the brain called the **brainstem** and the **midbrain,** which regulate relatively automatic functions such as breathing, digestion, and general alertness or consciousness. Another part, the **cerebellum,** regulates balance and coordination. Figure 5.3 shows where these parts are located in the brain. As babies approach their first birthday, the "higher" part of the brain,

FIGURE 5.3
The Brain
Different parts of the brain regulate different human functions. The midbrain regulates automatic activities such as breathing and digestion; the cerebellum regulates physical coordination; and the cerebral cortex regulates "higher" functions such as thinking and speaking.

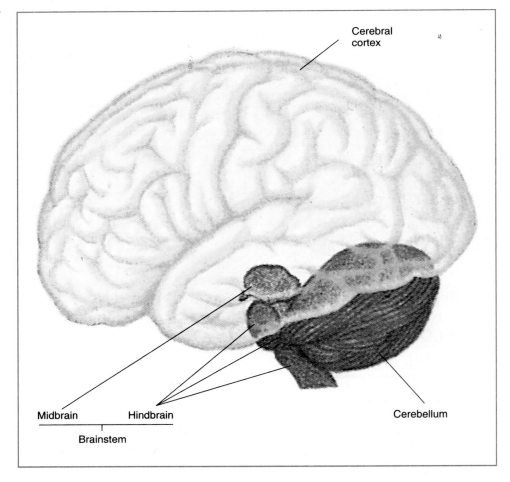

Cerebral cortex

Midbrain   Hindbrain   Cerebellum

Brainstem

Infants spend more time sleeping than doing anything else. Even by age two, most babies still need to sleep twelve hours a day. But like adults, they vary in how deeply they sleep and in how long they sleep at one time.

called the **cerebral cortex,** becomes more active. Although even newborns respond to sights and sounds, it is not until age one that their responses seem conscious and they can perform at will coordinated motor actions such as reaching and grasping with their fingers.

By the end of infancy, the overall anatomical features of the brain are reasonably well established, but its various parts continue to develop specialized functions. The left hemisphere, for example, appears to specialize in language. As a result, most three-year-olds understand language more accurately and easily if it is fed into the left hemisphere (compared to the right) of their brains with special earphones (Hellige, 1993). Despite such specialization, however, other facts suggest that children's brains retain flexibility for many years. Children whose normal brain language centers are damaged, for example, usually recover most of their language ability as long as the damage occurred before adolescence. Apparently they recover because their brains find new areas of the brain to devote to language processing.

States of Sleep and Wakefulness

One important function of the brain is to control infants' states of sleep and wakefulness. Thus, the brain regulates the amount of stimulation infants experience, both externally and internally. Periodic sleep helps infants to shut out external stimulation and thereby allows them to obtain general physical rest.

Sleep Very young infants move from deep sleep to wakefulness, with much more of the former than the latter. In the days immediately after birth, newborns sleep an average of sixteen hours per day, although some sleep as little as eleven hours a day and others as much as twenty-one (Michelsson et al., 1990). For most infants, the amount of sleep decreases steadily with each passing month. By age six months babies average just thirteen or fourteen hours of sleep per day, and by twenty-four months only eleven or twelve. But these hours still represent considerably more sleeping time than is typical for adults.

Newborns divide their sleeping time about equally between relatively active and quiet periods of sleep (see Figure 5.4). The more active kind is named **REM sleep,** after the "*rapid eye movements,*" or twitchings, that usually accompany it. REM sleep generally seems restless: sometimes infants' limbs or facial muscles twitch, and their breathing seems faster and more irregular. In the quieter kind of sleep, **non-REM sleep,** infants breathe regularly and more slowly, and their muscles become much limper. During the night, infants experience cycles of REM and non-REM sleep. For young infants, the night begins with REM sleep, and each cycle lasts about one hour.

Unfortunately for parents, a baby's extra sleep time does not usually include long, uninterrupted rest periods, even at night. In the first few months, it is more common for the baby to waken frequently—often every two or three hours—but somewhat unpredictably. Studies of brain development suggest that much of the unpredictability may result from the physical immaturity of the baby's nervous system: his brain may have frequent, accidental "storms" of impulses because it is not yet fully formed (Sheldon et al., 1992). In a very small percentage of infants, irregularities in neural activity may be related to "crib death," or sudden infant death syndrome (see the accompanying Perspectives box).

The unpredictability of infants' sleep can create chronic sleep deprivation in some parents; obviously somebody has to wake up during the night to calm or feed a crying baby! Some of the cure for fussiness depends on physical maturation, but parents can also influence their infant's sleep patterns by developing regular

FIGURE 5.4
Developmental Changes in Sleep Requirements
Sleep changes in nature as children grow from infancy to adulthood. Overall they sleep less (shown by the top line decreasing to the right), and the proportion of REM (rapid-eye-movement) sleep decreases sharply during infancy and childhood (shown by the space decreasing between the two lines).
Source: Reprinted with permission from Roffwary, Muzio & Dement, 1966 (revised 1969), "Ontogenetic Development of the Human Sleep-Dream Cycle," Science, 152, 604–619. Copyright 1966, 1969 American Association for the Advancement of Science.

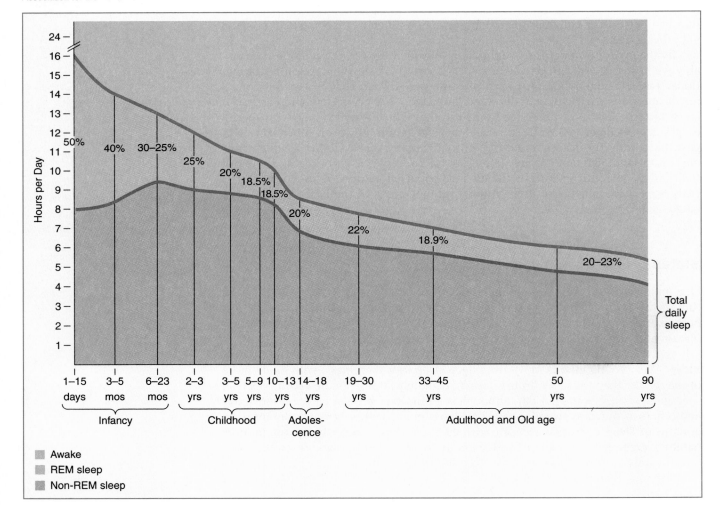

Perspectives

Sudden Infant Death Syndrome

Each year about two out of every one thousand young infants die in their sleep for no apparent reason. Doctors call this phenomenon **sudden infant death syndrome (SIDS),** or "crib death." The problem is most frequent among infants between ages two months and four months, although SIDS can affect babies as young as one month and as old as one year. It is the leading cause of death among infants who survive the first few weeks after delivery.

SIDS is disturbing because it is so mysterious. Typically parents put a seemingly healthy baby down to sleep as usual, but when they come in to get her up again, they discover she is dead. Sadly, because the baby had exhibited no health problems, the parents often blame themselves for the death, suspecting that somehow they neglected their child or hurt him in some way (Kaplan, 1995). Even more unfortunately, friends and relatives often concur in blaming the parents, simply because they can think of no other way to explain SIDS. Other obvious causes simply do not happen. The baby does not choke, vomit, or suffocate; she just stops breathing.

What causes SIDS? One theory is that SIDS is an exaggerated form of normal *sleep apnea,* temporary cessations of breathing during sleep (Hunt, 1992). Another theory suggests that SIDS occurs primarily at a special transition in development, just when inborn reflexive control of breathing begins to fade in importance but before infants have firmly established voluntary control of breathing. For most infants, this transition occurs at about two to four months of age, just when SIDS strikes most often. A third theory suggests that SIDS infants suffer from heart problems: their nervous systems may fail to prompt regular, strong heartbeats and in essence cause them to suffer a heart attack (Levy & Schwartz, 1994). Unfortunately, no clear evidence points to any of these alternative explanations.

If medical researchers could identify a basic cause, they would help future infants at risk for SIDS. Those babies could wear monitors that would indicate interruptions in breathing (if lungs are the problem) or heart rate (if that is it) and prompt parents or medical personnel to give the baby immediate, appropriate help. But so far the use of monitors has not been practical on a widespread scale because they can be cumbersome, cause a lot of unnecessary alarm, and occasionally fail to function properly.

Medical research has identified several factors that make a particular family or infant more likely to experience SIDS (Byard & Cole, 1994). Very young mothers and fathers (less than twenty years) stand a greater chance of having a SIDS infant; so do mothers who smoke cigarettes or have serious illnesses during pregnancy. Mothers who are poorly nourished during pregnancy also carry more risk than mothers who keep reasonably well nourished. But certain babies also are at greater risk for SIDS independently of their parents' qualities or behaviors. Boys die of SIDS more often than girls, for example, and infants born small (less than seven pounds) die more often than bigger infants. These relationships do not mean, however, that being a boy or being small actually *causes* SIDS; they imply only that for reasons still not understood, SIDS seems to strike boys and small infants more frequently.

Even taken together, these factors do not predict SIDS very accurately. The vast majority of high-risk infants never die, whereas some infants with few risk factors die of SIDS anyway. This circumstance creates problems in translating the studies of risk factors into concrete recommendations for medical personnel and parents, because taking the risk indications too literally can arouse fears in parents unnecessarily. The most useful recommendations tend to be valid for all families, whether or not they are at risk for SIDS (United States Department of Health and Human Services, 1994). For example, it is a good idea to recommend that parents not smoke and that an infant's room be humidified, if possible, whenever the baby catches a cold. Recent research also has found that SIDS is less likely to occur if infants sleep on their backs rather than on their stomachs. These are good pieces of advice for everyone, but unfortunately they do not guarantee complete protection from SIDS. For parents whose babies do die, many hospitals and communities have created support groups in which couples can share their grief and come to terms with it.

(though not rigid) times for and methods of waking, feeding, and sleeping that involve the infant. One study found that infants change toward more adultlike levels of wakefulness and sleep within six weeks after arriving home, provided routines are (relatively) regular (Bamford et al., 1990). Another study found that regularity offers dividends later in childhood: comparisons of Dutch and American families found fewer sleep problems among the young children of Dutch families, whose culture encourages regularity of daily routines more strongly than North American society does (Harkness & Keefer, 1995).

The advice to strive for (relatively) regular routines is widely supported among parent advice experts, but it makes crucial assumptions that not all families can meet. In some families, routines cannot be made regular because of competing pressures from other children, because of exhaustion from work or from earlier ill-timed wakings or feedings, or because the family has only one parent to begin with. Under these conditions, parents need additional support from friends, extended family, or social service workers. They cannot do it all themselves.

States of Arousal   Although infants show various states of arousal from the day they are born, as they get older their patterns of arousal begin to resemble those of older children (Berg & Berg, 1987). Table 5.2 summarizes the various states. The largest share of time, even among older infants, goes to the most completely relaxed and deepest form of sleep.

Variations in arousal make a practical difference to parents, other caregivers, and babies themselves. During the alert times, the baby is most likely to look at her surroundings and begin forming initial impressions of them. She begins noticing human faces almost immediately after birth, but increasingly so throughout the first year. Sometime before her six-month birthday, she begins to show a special preference for the faces of the people who care for her the most. She also begins to notice that various sounds and sights usually occur together—that a mouth opening and shutting, for example, usually occurs when a human voice comes her way. These experiences may stimulate perceptual abilities and early attachments, provided the child is awake to have them!

A fully alert state may not be the only condition under which young babies learn. Infants fail to *habituate,* or get used to, sounds and other stimuli that occur during more active REM sleep. Heart rates speed up in reaction to such stimulation, suggesting that infants may do some sort of mental processing of the stimulation even while asleep. On the other hand, it may also show neural *disorganization.* Babies who are born prematurely or who are extremely small for their age show more variablity in heart rate when they hear sounds in their sleep (Spassov et al., 1994).

What Do You Think?

How do parents deal with differences in children's sleep patterns? Ask a classmate or friend who is a parent of more than one child, or ask your own parent(s), how he or she responded to sleep differences in the children as infants. Combine your information with several other classmates'. Do you see any trends?

TABLE 5.2   *States of Arousal in Infants*

State	Behavior of Infants
Non-REM sleep	Complete rest; muscles relaxed; eyes closed and still; breathing regular and relatively slow
REM sleep	Occasional twitches, jerks, facial grimaces; irregular and intermittent eye movements; breathing irregular and relatively rapid
Drowsiness	Occasional movements, but fewer than in REM sleep; eyes open and close; glazed look; breathing regular, but faster than in non-REM sleep
Alert inactivity	Eyes open and scanning; body relatively still; rate of breathing similar to drowsiness, but more irregular
Alert activity	Eyes open, but not attending or scanning; frequent, diffuse bodily movements; vocalizations; irregular breathing; skin flushed
Distress	Whimpering or crying; vigorous or agitated movements; facial grimaces pronounced; skin very flushed

Source: Wolff (1966).

SENSORY DEVELOPMENT

All of the human senses operate at birth. This conclusion is supported by a variety of observations and experiments with neonates. For example, newborn infants sometimes prefer slight changes in brightness, as shown by their staring longer at a light that changes slightly in intensity than at one that does not. Behaviors and responses such as these show that newborns have the use of their senses. But observations also reveal that they have certain sensory limitations as well.

Visual Acuity

Infants can see at birth, but without the clarity of focus or *acuity* (keenness) characteristic of adults with good vision. They can track a bright light even before they leave the hospital delivery room, as long as the light lies near their line of vision and moves fairly slowly. For a newborn to see a single line, the line must be about ten times as wide as necessary for adults, and if the line lies off to one side of the infant's line of vision, it must be even wider (Aslin, 1987). When looking at stationary contours and objects, newborns see more clearly at short distances, especially at about eight to ten inches—about the distance, incidentally, between a mother's breast and her face. Their vision is better when tracking moving objects, but even so their overall vision is rather poor until about one month of age (Banks & Danemiller, 1987).

Visual acuity improves a lot during infancy, but it does not reach adult levels until the end of the preschool years. An older infant (ages one to two) often has 20/30 or 20/40 vision, meaning he can see fine details at twenty feet that adults can see at thirty or forty feet. This quality of vision is quite satisfactory for everyday, familiar activities; in fact, many adults can see no better than this, without even realizing it. But this level of visual acuity does interfere with seeing distant objects.

Auditory Acuity

Auditory acuity refers to sensitivity to sounds. Infants can hear at birth, but not as well as adults. Any sudden loud noise, such as that caused by dropping a large book on the floor, demonstrates they can hear. The sound produces a dramatic startle reaction, called a *Moro reflex:* the neonate withdraws her limbs suddenly, sometimes shakes all over, and may also cry (see also the discussion later in this chapter). Not all noises produce this reaction; pure tones, such as the sound of a flute, cause relatively little response. Complex noises containing many different sounds usually produce a stronger reaction; a bag of nails spilling on the floor, for example, tends to startle infants reliably.

Even when they do not startle overtly, however, newborn infants respond internally to sounds. Electrodes attached to their heads register minor electrical responses to most ordinary noises that are moderately loud, suggesting that newborns can even discriminate between certain common consonant sounds, such as *b* and *p* (Molfese et al., 1991). Quiet sounds or noises do not evoke electrical responses, even when they are loud enough to do so in adults. Judged in this way, infants seem a bit hard of hearing compared to adults, although of course they are far from deaf. These differences persist through much of the second year of life.

Children begin to sense very soft sounds sometime toward the end of infancy, judging both by the electrical brain waves just described and by their increasingly overt responses to sounds, language, and music as observed by parents. Frequency (or pitch) discrimination shows comparable improvements. By about five months,

Working with   Helen Turman, PEDIATRIC NURSE

Continuity and Change in Infants' Behavior

Helen Turman has been a public health nurse for nearly twenty years. She has worked with infants and their mothers and other relatives in the postpartum nursery of a hospital, looking after newborns and helping mothers and babies get used to each other, as a public health nurse, visiting mothers and babies who had recently been discharged from the hospital, and at "well baby" clinics run by public health nurses. Helen talked about her experiences in the postpartum nursery.

Kelvin: What are some of the differences that you see among babies? Surely they differ among themselves . . .

Helen: Well, they do and they don't; it depends on how you look at it. It seems to me that *all* babies need certain things: cuddling, the warmth of a human body, feeding at the right times. And bundling—wrapping them up snugly—usually quiets them right down. All babies respond to these things from day one, but they keep needing them for quite awhile too.

Kelvin: What about the differences?

Helen: One of the earliest differences is in feeding patterns. Some babies nurse often but take in smaller amounts; others eat less frequently but stay on the breast longer and take more. You see variety in sucking patterns. Some babies seem businesslike: they lock on to the mother's breast and won't let go for anything until they're done! The mother can talk, eat her dinner with one hand, even walk around, and the baby will keep nursing.

Other babies get distracted. They won't start feeding right away, even when the mother offers the breast and even if the baby has been fussing like she's hungry. Then they get distracted at the least thing, like if someone is talking across the room. Feeding takes forever.

Kelvin: Do these differences in "style" seem to last beyond infancy?

Helen: Oh, for sure. Some babies don't seem very hungry when they're first born; maybe mucus is filling their stomachs or something. That can be disturbing. Mothers worry when their baby won't eat! And their breasts become engorged—it's uncomfortable.

Kelvin: Can you see the differences while you work in the postpartum nursery? It seems like your time with individual babies would be pretty short.

Helen: Yes, it is indeed short. These days, if a birth is uncomplicated and mother and child are both healthy, the two of them might go home twenty-four hours after delivery! But you actually see them longer than that

infants respond to small differences in high pitches—those at the upper third of a piano keyboard—as well as adults do, although it takes them longer than this to learn to discriminate among low pitches (Olsho et al., 1988).

Taste, Smell, and Touch

Even at birth, infants clearly prefer sweet tastes; they suck faster when an artificial nipple delivers sugar water than when it delivers plain water. When assessed by their sucking, however, other taste preferences seem much less clear-cut than they are among children and adults (Mistretta & Bradley, 1985). Newborn infants will suck *less* for saltwater, for example, but only if the saltwater is delivered automatically between bursts of sucking. If saltwater comes as a result of each suck, they show no significant decrease from their normal rates of sucking. Other tastes (bitterness and sourness) have even less effect on newborns' sucking behavior.

Newborns also react to a variety of smells, both good and bad. A faint odor of ammonia or vinegar, for example, makes one-week-old infants grimace and avert their heads. On the other hand, they can also recognize the odor of their mothers' breasts (Cernoch & Porter, 1985). If two breast pads, only one of which has previously been worn by a nursing mother, are hung in front of one-month-old infants, the babies spend more time facing or looking at the pad that has come from the nursing mother, presumably because of its aroma. Even non-breast-fed infants, who have not had the opportunity to learn the smell of mother's milk, show this preference. Infants also prefer the odor of mother's milk even if it did not originate with because of our hospital's new system of "family-oriented care." That's where labor, delivery, and recovery all happen in the same room, even if the mother needs a surgical delivery! In that case, though, mother and child would stay longer.

Kelvin: What kinds of differences do you see among the mothers?

Helen: Well, pretty quickly you sense which mothers are apprehensive, which have a lot of questions, and which seem receptive to "teaching" from me or the other nurses.

Kelvin: "Teaching" about what?

Helen: About getting started with breast feeding, and nutrition for themselves, and help with diaper changes. Mothers vary dramatically in how much they involve us, the nurses, during the time after delivery and in how much they care for their own infants. Some act like they already know how much

work the baby is going to be, so they want *me,* the nurse, to do as much as possible now so they can get some rest. Others want to do it all themselves; then I don't get to know the mother or the baby as well.

Kelvin: Does age make a difference? Are older mothers different with their babies than younger mothers?

Helen: Yes, but not always the way you might expect. Some teenage mothers I've seen actually don't worry as much as the older mothers, the thirty-five-year-olds. A teenager can be very giving and nurturant with her baby. Maybe she just doesn't know yet what there is to worry about, so she relaxes and enjoys the baby. Trouble might come later, when she has to juggle the responsibilities of school, child care, maintaining relationships with the baby's father or with her own parents, and so on.

What Do You Think?

1. Given differences such as those Helen points out, how helpful is it to speak of "typical" infant development? Take another look at the chapter's discussion of breast feeding and sleep patterns, for example, and think about how you might rewrite the material to better account for individual differences.

2. What factors do you think might influence a mother's level of involvement with her newborn infant in the postpartum nursery? Previous childrearing experience? Extent and nature of family relationships at home? Amount of career and work involvement? Compare your opinions about these possibilities with those of a classmate.

3. Ask a classmate about his or her own preferred times and ways of eating. Are they more or less regular than yours? Speculate about how eating patterns get established and whether they are connected to a person's personality.

their own mothers, though they do show a preference for their own mothers' aroma when given a choice (Makin & Porter, 1989).

What about touch? Newborns exhibit many reflexes that imply sensitivity to touch. A light stroke on the cheek, for example, normally causes a baby to turn his head in the direction of the stroke, and placing a finger on the baby's lips typically causes him to make sucking motions. Parents in many cultures have discovered that wrapping newborn infants in a cloth or blanket, or even just holding them firmly, tends to reduce crying and fussing. In part such quieting implies sensitivity to touch, although it may also result from the interesting sights and sounds that accompany being swaddled or held.

In newborns, in fact, touch may assist development in many ways. Much of the benefit occurs by way of the central nervous system. The closeness brought on by touching, holding, and carrying relaxes both the baby and the caregiver (Shair et al., 1991). Thus, tactual behaviors seem to encourage healthy physical development in the baby on the one hand and stimulate the caregiver to be more alert and attentive to the baby on the other.

At birth, one particular tactile sensation, pain, seems less developed than among slightly older infants or children. It is possible to evoke a response of pain or other negative reaction to a pinprick, such as that a baby might receive for a blood test, in one-day-old infants. But most infants this young seem somewhat less sensitive to painful stimuli than they do even a few days later (McGrath, 1990). The insensitivity may help newborn infants to endure the highly stressful experience of birth itself; or, alternatively, the stress of birth itself may release hormones that reduce the baby's sensitivity to pain for a short time after birth.

What Do You Think?

Do parenting books agree with our comments that young infants have the use of their senses? Check the comments made in two or three books about the capabilities of newborn babies. Do they seem consistent, or at least not *in*consistent?

MOTOR DEVELOPMENT

The infant's very first movements or motions appear to be inborn and automatic and are called **reflexes.** During the first months of life, most reflexes disappear or become incorporated into relatively purposeful or voluntary movements. When they have these qualities, they are called **skills.** Both reflexes and skills are also called **motor abilities** (the term *motor* refers to movement or motion).

Early Reflexes

Pediatricians have identified more than two dozen inborn reflexes. A few of these reflexes, such as sucking, clearly help the baby to adapt to the new life outside the womb. Others look more like evolutionary vestiges of behaviors that may have helped earlier versions of *Homo sapiens* to cope, for example, by clinging to their mothers at the sound of danger. A few reflexes, such as blinking, breathing, and swallowing, persist throughout a person's life, but most reflexes disappear from the infant's repertoire of skills during the first few months. Their disappearance, in fact, helps doctors to judge whether a baby is developing normally. Newborn reflexes that persist over many months may suggest damage to the nervous system or generally retarded development (Menkes, 1994).

Mouthing is one of the first reflexes infants exhibit. As they get older, they begin mouthing objects voluntarily to "get the feel" of them. Still later, mouthing is replaced with intentional handling of objects, as a way of learning about the environment.

Rooting and Sucking   If you gently stroke the cheek of a newborn, he will turn his head to the side you are stroking. This searching behavior is called **rooting.** Under normal circumstances, rooting helps the baby to locate his mother's breast, because he will nose around for it if it brushes the side of his face just prior to nursing. If the baby then finds the nipple, he will begin **sucking** powerfully and rhythmically— and without having been taught. Actually, any object will elicit sucking if it intrudes far enough into his mouth; a finger, for example, makes a good pacifier. Later in the infant's first year, the sucking reflex comes under more voluntary control and broadens to become *mouthing,* a mixture of gnawing and chewing. The baby begins using his mouth as a primary way to learn about new objects; for a time, it seems, he puts just about everything in his mouth!

Moro Reflex   A newborn will startle dramatically in response to a sudden loss of support, even if the loss does not really threaten to hurt her. The startle response is called the **Moro reflex.** Normally the infant will thrust her arms outward, shake, make horrible faces, and possibly cry. Gradually she will bring her arms together again, as though to grab at something. The response looks much like the startle of children and adults and may in fact be a precursor to it.

At some time earlier in human evolution, the Moro reflex may have helped infants who were being carried to grab more tightly when they experienced a sudden loss of support. At present, however, it is significant mostly because it helps doctors to diagnose normal development of the nervous system. Healthy infants show the response when they are born, but lose much of it as they approach their sixth month. Well before their second birthday, their startle responses come to resemble those of normal adults: they startle less often, and their responses become more abbreviated and less dramatic.

Grasping   If you place something firm, such as a finger, in a neonate's palm, he will grasp it. Like some other reflexes, the early grasping may facilitate later, more intentional versions of the same behavior, such as the grasping needed to explore toys and hang on to a railing for balance.

Table 5.3 summarizes these and other reflexes of newborn babies. Some, such as breathing, serve obvious physical needs; in Table 5.3, they are called **survival reflexes.** Others, such as the tonic neck reflex, serve no obvious physical purpose, although they may be vestiges of important reflex behaviors at earlier stages of human evolution; these are called **primitive reflexes.** Among both survival and primitive reflexes, some may set the stage for developing more refined versions of the behavior later in childhood. Even if they do facilitate later learning, though, infants must also have appropriate later experiences. For example, the grasping reflex may develop into mature grasping only if a child has chances to grasp actual objects as she grows toward toddlerhood.

The First Motor Skills

Motor skills are voluntary movements of the body or parts of the body. They can be grouped conveniently according to the size of the muscles and body parts involved. **Gross motor skills** involve the large muscles of the arms, legs, and torso. **Fine motor skills** involve the small muscles located throughout the body. Walking and jumping are examples of gross motor skills, and reaching and grasping are examples of fine motor skills.

TABLE 5.3 **Major Reflexes in Newborn Infants**

Reflex	Description	Development	Significance
Survival Reflexes			
Breathing reflex	Repetitive inhalation and expiration	Permanent, although becomes partly voluntary	Provides oxygen and expels carbon dioxide
Rooting reflex	Turning of cheek in direction of touch	Weakens and disappears by six months	Orients child to breast or bottle
Sucking reflex	Strong sucking motions with throat, mouth, and tongue	Gradually comes under voluntary control	Allows child to drink
Swallowing reflex	Swallowing motions in throat	Permanent, although becomes partly voluntary	Allows child to take in food and to avoid choking
Eyeblink reflex	Closing eyes for an instant ("blinking")	Permanent, although gradually becomes voluntary	Protects eyes from objects and bright light
Pupillary reflex	Changing size of pupils: smaller in bright light and bigger in dim light	Permanent	Protects against bright light and allows better vision in dim light
Primitive Reflexes			
Moro reflex	In response to a loud noise, child throws arms outward, arches back, then brings arms together as if to hold something	Arm movements and arching disappear by six months, but startle reaction persists for life	Indicates normal development of nervous system
Grasping reflex	Curling fingers around any small object put in the child's palm	Disappears by three months; voluntary grasping appears by about six months	Indicates normal development of nervous system
Tonic neck reflex	When laid on back, head turns to side, arm and leg extend to same side, limbs on opposite side flex	Disappears by two or three months	Indicates normal development of nervous system
Babinski reflex	When bottom of foot stroked, toes fan and then curl	Disappears eight to twelve months	Indicates normal development of nervous system
Stepping reflex	If held upright, infant lifts leg as if to step	Disappears by eight weeks, but later if practiced	Indicates normal development of nervous system
Swimming	If put in water, infant moves arms and legs and holds breath	Disappears by four to six months	Indicates normal development of nervous system

Before learning to walk, infants use a variety of methods for moving about; creeping is one of the first. New locomotion allows investigation of objects, like the baby on the right, and stimulates grasping reflexes, which develop into voluntary grasping skills suitable for a variety of objects and situations.

Viewed broadly, the sequence in which skills develop follows two general trends. The **cephalocaudal principle** ("head to tail") refers to the fact that upper parts of the body become usable and skillful before lower parts do. Babies learn to turn their heads before learning to move their feet intentionally, and they learn to move their arms before they learn to move their legs. The **proximodistal principle** ("near to far") refers to the fact that central parts of the body become skillful before peripheral, or outlying, parts do. Babies learn to wave their entire arms before learning to wiggle their wrists and fingers. The former movement occurs at the shoulder joint, near the center of the body, and the latter occurs at the periphery. Stated differently, the shoulder movement is relatively proximal, whereas the finger movement is relatively distal.

Gross Motor Development in the First Year   Almost from birth, and before reflex behaviors disappear, babies begin doing some things on purpose. By the age of four weeks or so, most babies can lift their heads up when lying on their stomachs. At six or seven months, many babies have become quite adept at using their limbs; they can stick their feet up in the air and "bicycle" with them while a parent struggles valiantly to fit a diaper on the moving target. At ten months the average baby can stand erect, but only if an adult helps. By their first birthday, one-half of all babies can dispense with this assistance and stand by themselves without toppling over immediately (Savelsbergh, 1993). By age seven months, on the average, babies become able to locomote, or move around, on their own. At first, their methods are crude and slow; a baby might simply pivot on her stomach, for example, to get a better view of something interesting. Consistent movement in one direction develops soon after this time, although the movement does not always occur in the direction the baby intends!

Crawling and creeping offer new opportunities and make new demands on parents. On the one hand, locomotion lets babies entertain themselves better than before. They can relieve boredom on their own initiative simply by traveling to a new location or reaching and grasping a toy for themselves. On the other hand, parents discover that babies who move can get into everything, including poisons hidden in a low cupboard and electrical outlets. "Childproofing" becomes a major concern for many parents at this point as they continually scrutinize their living quarters for hazards to mobile infants.

Reaching and Grasping   As pointed out earlier in this chapter, even newborn infants will reach for and grasp objects they can see immediately in front of them. They often fail to grasp objects successfully; they may make contact with an object but fail to enclose it in their fingers. This early, crude reaching disappears fairly soon after birth, only to reappear at about four or five months of age as two separate skills, reaching and grasping (Pownall & Kingerlee, 1993). These skills soon serve infants in many ways. For example, by their second birthday most babies can turn the pages in large picture books one at a time, at least if the paper is relatively indestructible. But they can also point at the pages without grasping for them.

Walking   A reasonably predictable series of events leads to true walking in most children; Figure 5.5 describes some of these milestones. By about twelve to thirteen months, most children take their first independent steps. Well before two years, they often can walk not only forward but backward or even sideways. Some two-year-olds can even walk upstairs on two feet instead of on all fours. Usually they use the wall or a railing to do so. Usually, too, coming downstairs proves more difficult than going up; one solution is to creep down backward, using all four limbs.

How do these changes develop? To some extent, the earlier skills may stimulate and give practice in the later ones. Sitting, for example, may give practice in balance, which helps in standing next to furniture; standing by furniture, in turn, improves balance and muscle development so that standing alone becomes possible; and so on. Each step in such a sequence rewards the child simply by giving her new opportunities to explore her body and see her world from new perspectives. The practice and sense of accomplishment may be their own rewards.

As reasonable as this explanation sounds, however, it has certain flaws. Not all children learn movement skills according to a predictable sequence; some, for example, creep only after they have mastered walking. And individual children who are normal in all respects learn motor skills at rather different ages: full-fledged walking, for example, may occur as early as nine months or as late as eighteen months. Yet all these children presumably have access to the crucial learning tool, namely their own legs and feet. Do some infants therefore practice harder or simply have an inborn ability to learn faster?

Variations in Motor Skill Development

Nature and Nurture   The question about the origins of walking illustrates the important issue of *nature* (genetic endowment) versus *nurture* (life experience) in children's growth. A reasonable position on this issue is that most changes, including walking, depend on both genetics and experience. But the *way* in which each factor contributes often seems unclear. The problem is illustrated by a classic study

FIGURE 5.5
Milestones of Motor Development
Walking alone is one of the major physical achievements of the first year of life. Quite a few other physical skills usually develop prior to walking, as the figure shows. Note, though, that skills appear at different times for different individuals. As a result, some skills may even appear "out of sequence" in some children.

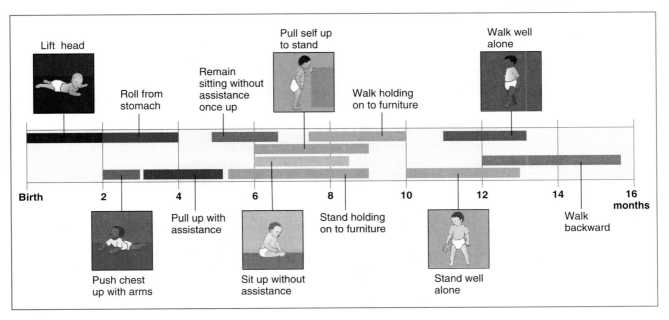

that "taught" infants basic motor skills (Gesell & Thompson, 1929). One member of a pair of identical twins was taught to climb stairs beginning at age forty-six weeks. Her training began with assistance from an adult at moving from one step to the next, often at first simply by being lifted. Her twin received no training and in fact was prohibited from all encounters with stairs until she was fifty-three weeks old. At this point, the trained twin could climb stairs much better than her inexperienced sister. Yet even on her very first attempt, at fifty-three weeks, the untrained sister managed to climb the stairs! After just three weeks more, both girls performed equally well despite their prior differences in training.

Although the study suggested that maturation (or effects due to the aging process) matters more than learning (acquired knowledge and skill), it may really show only how children can learn a skill indirectly. The untrained twin encountered no stairs during her waiting period, but she was free to crawl every day and to practice any other motor techniques she chose. Such crawling may have given her preparation relevant for climbing stairs, even if the preparation was indirect; so experience and maturation may both account for the results.

Cultural Differences in Motor Development   Similar ambiguities exist if we compare motor development across cultures or societies. Differences do sometimes occur, but sometimes also do not last, and sometimes no differences occur even where we might expect them. Certain African cultures, for example, give their infants unusually frequent chances to sit upright and to practice their "walking" reflex when held at a standing position by adults and older children (Munroe et al., 1981). These opportunities seem to stimulate toddlers in these societies to learn to walk earlier and better than North American toddlers. Early walking, in turn, may prove especially valuable in these societies, which do not rely heavily on cars, bicycles, or other vehicles that make walking less important. Yet early walking may also be a genetic trait (at least partially) for these groups; without comparable training in reflex walking for North American infants, there is no way to be sure.

Yet differences in motor skills do not always appear where they might be expected. Take the Navaho Indians, whose infants spend nearly all of their first year

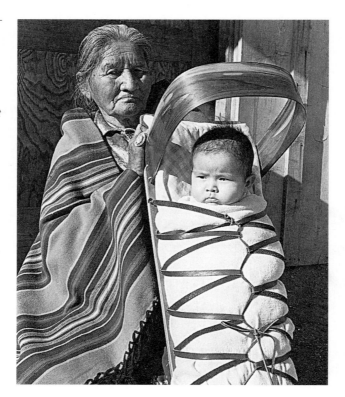

Swaddling infants, as is done with this Navajo infant, is practiced in many cultures. Swaddling tends to slow motor development at first, but not permanently. It may also allow caregivers to carry infants with them during daily activities—a circumstance that could make vocalizing by infants a less urgent skill to develop.

bound and swaddled tightly to a flat board, with their arms and legs extending straight down along their bodies (J. Whiting, 1981). Apparently as a result, Navaho toddlers do tend to acquire walking a little later than Anglo-American children. But they do not show delays in other skills inhibited by swaddling, notably reaching and grasping, and the deficit in walking disappears by the end of the preschool years in most cases (Kagan, 1984).

Sex Differences   Do boys and girls differ, on the average, in motor development? The answer depends on distinguishing what infants *can* do from what they typically *do* do. What they can do—their competence—has relatively little relationship to sex. Boy and girl babies sit upright at about the same age, for example, and stand and walk at about the same time. Similar equality exists for all of the motor milestones of infancy.

How infants use their time is another matter. Almost as soon as they can move, boys show more activity than girls. The trend begins even before birth, when male fetuses move about in their mothers' wombs more than female fetuses do (Ames, 1983). After birth, the trend continues: infant boys remain more active than infant girls, using what locomotor skills they have developed thus far, whereas girls spend more of their time using their emerging fine motor skills. Of course, the differences in use of time may stem partly from parents' encouragement (praise) for "gender-appropriate" behaviors. Given the young age of the children, though, and the fact that activity actually precedes birth, part of the difference must come from genetic endowment: an inborn tendency to be more (or less) active.

By their second birthday (and onward throughout childhood), boys and girls tend to differ in motor skills even in optimal, testlike situations; what they *can* do motorically begins to differ, on the average. Girls excel more often at fine motor skills, such as building a tower of blocks with fewer mistakes; boys excel more often at gross motor skills, such as running or throwing. But the origins of the gender differences—nature or nurture—remain obscure (Fausto-Sterling, 1985). Practice must surely contribute, with each gender accumulating more time with its "favorite" sorts of skills. But emerging awareness of gender roles may also contribute, with each sex beginning to know the skills in which society expects it to excel. With these influences operating on all children, it is noteworthy that boys and girls grow up more alike than different: many boys have good balance, and many girls pound their play dough (and occasionally another child) very hard indeed.

What Do You Think?

If motor skills develop partly through learning, why not just deliberately teach infants to walk? What do you think would be the result of doing so? Do similar considerations apply for certain other important developments in infancy?

VARIATIONS IN INFANT GROWTH

Of course, infants vary in how they grow and develop. Some grow faster than others do, and not all acquire motor skills in the same order. Two otherwise similar children may learn to walk at different times, one when only ten months old and the other when nearly sixteen months old. Yet both may fall within the normal range of motor development.

Low-Birth-Weight Infants

For medical purposes, newborns are considered **low-birth-weight** infants if they are born weighing less than 2,500 grams, or about 5½ pounds. Such low weight can

Low-birth-weight infants, like this one being held by its mother, are at risk for breathing problems for the first few weeks or months after birth. Modern medical techniques, however, have increased survival rates substantially, and also shown the value of handling and cuddling a low-birth-weight infant just as any other.

occur for either of two reasons. First, some babies do not develop as quickly as is normal, even though they are carried for about the usual term of forty weeks. These babies are called **small-for-date** infants. Second, some babies develop at about normal rates but are born significantly earlier than usual. If they are born sooner than about thirty-seven weeks from conception, they are called **preterm,** or short-gestation, infants. Until recently, medical research did not distinguish clearly between small-for-date and preterm infants; both were simply regarded as "premature" infants (Phelan, 1992).

Preterm infants face many more medical risks than do small-for-date infants. The extent of the risks depends on the infant's physical maturity. Physically immature infants look different from normal full-term infants: they tend to be redder and darker than normal, whatever their race, and their skin is often transparent enough to see blood vessels through it. Often they are covered with a downy hair called *lanugo* and a white, waxy substance called *vernix*. And, of course, immature newborns are smaller than usual; an infant will weigh only about two pounds if born two months early.

Causes of Low Birth Weight   Low birth weight, whether the infant is preterm or small for date, can result from several factors. As we saw in Chapter 4, one of the most common causes is malnourishment of the mother during pregnancy. But other harmful practices, such as smoking cigarettes, drinking alcohol, or taking drugs, also can depress birth weight. Mothers from certain segments of the population, such as teenagers and the very poor, are especially likely to give birth to preterm babies, most likely because of their own poor nourishment or their lack of access to good prenatal care. But even mothers who are well nourished and well cared for sometimes have infants who are smaller than is medically desirable. Multiple births (e.g., twins, triplets) usually result in small-for-date babies; so do some illnesses or mishaps, such as a serious traffic accident that causes damage to the placenta.

Consequences of Preterm Birth   Despite recent advances in helping preterm infants survive and develop, their neurological abilities are initially impaired by early birth (Brooten, 1992). In general, the reflexes of preterm infants tend to be sluggish, weak, and poorly organized. Preterm infants do not startle as reliably or grasp as automatically and strongly at objects. Their muscles often seem flabby or overly relaxed, which is a sign not only of immature muscle development but also of nerve impulses insufficient to stimulate good muscle tone. Preterm infants tend to lie fully extended instead of with their arms and legs slightly flexed or bent. If someone pulls gently on their arms to extend them, their arms do not recoil as completely or smoothly as those of a full-term infant; jerky, random movements dominate instead, and sometimes there is no recoiling movement at all. At comparable points in their gestation, full-term infants presumably have these limitations too, but they are still inside their mothers' wombs at the time.

Outside that protected environment, preterm infants must cope with many tasks for which they are inadequately prepared. These tasks include the obvious vital processes, such as breathing and digesting food. But they also include some less obvious ones. Preterm infants suddenly must regulate the amount of sensory stimulation they receive. Just as full-term babies do, they need to see things and hear things to stimulate the development of their senses. But they also need to avoid overloading their senses with too many sights and sounds. One way to avoid over-stimulation is to sleep periodically and deeply; yet even though preterm infants sleep more than full-term infants do, they have more trouble keeping their sleep peaceful and smooth. For example, they experience **sleep apnea,** periods when breathing stops for perhaps fifteen or twenty seconds, more frequently.

In some preterm infants, neurological limitations persist for the first two or three years of life, causing the babies to develop specific motor skills a bit later than full-term infants. Some of the delay is more apparent than real. A four-month-old born two months preterm, for example, in many ways resembles a two-month-old born at full term; both infants have lived eleven months from conception. Other de-lays may reflect stresses associated with preterm birth (such as parents' overprotec-tiveness) rather than the physical effects of early birth as such.

For the most part, however, preterm infants develop into normal children. Only infants with *very* low birth weight (less than 1,000 grams, or 2.2 pounds) show a significant risk of permanent impairment of motor or cognitive skills (Goldson, 1992), and even among these tiny babies only about 10 to 20 percent are affected by the time they reach school age. For newborns in the range of 1,000 to 2,500 grams, research suggests that toddlers and preschoolers who were preterm develop normal attachments to their parents despite their initial unresponsiveness as new-born infants (Easterbrooks, 1989). By school age, the "big" preterm children show slightly more risk of encountering learning disabilities, but their overall cognitive ability seems indistinguishable from that of full-term children.

Helping Low-Birth-Weight Infants

Because conventional hospital routines often fail to help preterm infants to regulate their sensory needs, health care providers have begun experimenting with ways to do so. For example, some hospitals can provide such babies with miniature water-beds, which rock gently and slowly at about the same speed as a mother's normal breathing (Institute of Medicine, 1985; Korner, 1987). In theory, the arrangement simulates a normal experience in the womb. Other programs have tried stimulating preterm infants with extra handling despite their initial unresponsiveness (Luding-ton et al., 1990). Both approaches have shown very encouraging results. Infants raised in waterbeds were healthier and physically larger after several months than preterm infants raised in conventional, stationary hospital cribs. Infants who re-ceived extra handling were more responsive to sounds and displayed more normal motor behaviors. All in all, these techniques seem promising.

Even after low-birth-weight babies go home, their parents may continue to worry about their health and face challenges in forming close relationships with them. Low-birth-weight infants tend to respond to their parents less intensely than normal babies do, such as by smiling, at least at first. Under good conditions, however, these initial differences need not become lasting problems, and the parents and children eventually develop relationships that are healthy and gratifying. But if the parents face other stresses, such as insufficient economic resources, they may lack the time or energy to overcome the initial difficulties in making contact with their baby. To avoid forming a permanently poor relationship, such parents may need help from a social worker or a nurse to understand their infant's development so that they can enjoy that development as it unfolds.

What Do You Think?

Imagine that you are writing a brief (two-paragraph) article for expectant mothers in the local newspaper about "What to do if your baby is born two months early." What would you say, and where would you find further information for your article? Sketch out your answers, but also consult with a few classmates about how to construct this article.

NUTRITION DURING THE FIRST TWO YEARS

Of course, the physical developments described in this chapter depend on good nutrition during the first two years. Like adults, babies need diets with appropriate amounts of protein, calories, and specific vitamins and minerals. For various reasons, however, infants do not always get all the nutrients they need. Often poverty accounts for malnutrition: parents with good intentions may be unable to afford the right foods. In other cases, conventional eating practices interfere: despite relatively expensive eating habits, such as going to fast-food restaurants, some families may fail to provide their children with a balanced diet.

Compared with older children, infants eat less in overall or absolute amounts. A well-nourished young baby in North America might drink somewhat less than one liter (about .95 quarts) of liquid nourishment per day. This amount definitely would not keep an older child or a young adult well nourished, although it might prevent starving. In proportion to their body weight, however, infants need to consume much more than older children or adults do. For example, every day a three-month-old baby ideally should take in more than two ounces of liquid per pound of body weight, whereas an eighteen-year-old needs only about one-third of this amount (Queen & Lang, 1993).

Breast Milk Versus Formula

Someone (usually parents) must provide for an infant's comparatively large appetite. Whenever breast feeding is possible, health experts generally recommend human milk as the sole source of nutrition for at least the first six months or so of most infants' lives and as a major source for at least the next six months. In some cases, of course, this recommendation proves difficult or impractical to follow. Babies who need intensive medical care immediately after birth cannot be breast fed without special arrangements. Also, for one reason or another, some women may choose not to breast feed, and certain babies and mothers may not succeed in this activity even after trying it. For these infants, formulas can be prepared and fed in bottles.

Why do pediatricians recommend breast feeding? Studies of infants and mothers suggest four major reasons. First, human milk seems to give young infants more protection from diseases and other ailments. Breast-fed infants catch fewer colds and

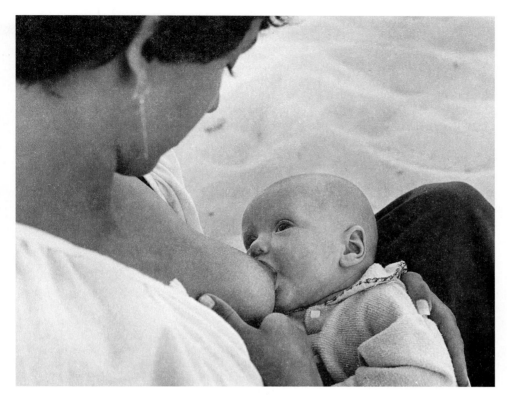

In recent decades, increasing numbers of mothers in our society have chosen to breast-feed their babies as recommended by most pediatricians. For a significant number of infants, however, partial or complete bottle-feeding remains a better option—for example, if fathers wish to be involved in feedings.

viruses of all types, experience fewer allergies, and suffer fewer serious illnesses. The ways in which human milk confers this benefit are not understood completely, but one reason is that human milk is always sterile, even at comfortable, lukewarm temperatures at which bottle milk may begin to grow bacteria. In addition, the protein in human milk contains substances that may bind or attach themselves to viruses and bacteria in the infant's intestine, thereby rendering them harmless. In any case, the disease resistance benefit of milk is so important that many hospitals now try to offer human milk in bottles to infants needing intensive care.

The second reason concerns the nutritional composition of human milk. Overall, such milk matches the nutritional needs of human infants more closely than formula preparations do. Human milk contains more iron (an important nutrient for infants) but less casein (a protein prominent in cow's milk that many infants have trouble digesting). Human milk also contains helpful amounts of cholesterol, a form of fat that contributes to heart problems in later life but seems to protect against this possibility when digested in early infancy.

A third reason for preferring breast feeding is physical. Breast feeding better develops the infant's jaw and mouth muscles because it requires stronger sucking motions than bottle feeding does. For much the same reason, the breast also tends to satisfy infants' intrinsic needs for sucking better than a bottle does. This fact makes pacifiers less necessary, and it makes excessive sucking, and therefore overeating, less likely to occur.

A fourth reason for preferring breast feeding is more speculative: advocates of breast feeding argue that it benefits mother-infant relationships (La Leche League, 1991). Breast-fed infants spend more time snuggling close to their mothers, and vice versa. A breast-feeding mother and child undeniably spend a lot of time gazing into each other's eyes, like two people in love, and the mother appears to offer feeding sessions in closer response to the infant's true hunger demands. These behaviors may promote strong, secure attachments between mother and child, which enhance the infant's social and cognitive development later in childhood. (However,

A Multicultural View

Breast Feeding among the Gusii

The Gusii are an agricultural and sheep-herding people living in the hills of Kenya, a country in eastern Africa, and have been observed and interviewed extensively by Robert Levine and his associates (1994). Gusii mothers might find the discussion of breast feeding in this chapter strange: why, they might ask, are the authors trying so hard to show its merits? Among the Gusii, mothers universally breast-feed their infants for at least the first eighteen months of life, eventually interrupting the process only to care for their next baby.

This routine may sound grueling by North American standards, but consider the context. Throughout Africa (and including among the Gusii), parents widely regard infancy as the most life-threatening period of life—and with good reason, since the majority of deaths do in fact occur during that developmental period. Therefore, the best defense against the dangers of infancy is close, continuous contact between mother and infant. A mother will carry her young baby everywhere, often strapped in swaddling clothes to her back, soothe it at the least sign of discontent, and breast-feed it frequently and on demand. These practices pay dividends in the form of healthier and more contented babies toward the end of infancy. Observations of Gusii infants in the waiting room of a community health clinic in Kenya, for example, found almost no crying among the babies, a situation unheard of for comparable groups of sick infants in the United States (Levine et al., 1994).

Anthropologists who have observed the Gusiis' approach call it the "pediatric model" of infant care and contrast it to the "pedagogical model" of care that prevails in North America. The pediatric model of care centers on protecting the child from life-threatening illness, whereas the pedagogical model of care emphasizes promoting active exchange between parent and child. A North American mother sees herself as her child's first teacher (among other things). So she talks with her child long before the child is able to understand language; she procures interesting toys for the child to play with even before the youngster's motor skills have developed very much; and she generally arranges for "quality" (meaning "highly interactive") time with her infant (Harkness & Super, 1992). These non-Gusii priorities are possible, of course, because she takes the health of

mothers in societies other than ours might find these comments odd; see the accompanying Multicultural View box.)

Nutrition in Later Infancy

After about six months, infants can be introduced gradually to solid foods such as strained cereals and strained fruits. As babies become tolerant of these new foods, parents can introduce others that sometimes require a more mature digestive system, such as strained meats and cooked eggs. Overall, the shift to solid foods often takes many months to complete (see Table 5.4 for guidelines about how to do this). As it occurs, parents must begin paying more attention to their baby's overall nutritional needs, since many solid foods lack the broad range of nutrients that breast milk and formula provide.

Malnutrition in North America   Often North American diets fail to provide enough of three specific nutrients: vitamin A, vitamin C, and iron. Prolonged deficiencies of vitamins A and C seem to create deficits in motor ability (Pollitt et al., 1984), and deficiency of iron appears to create deficits in cognitive performance (Pollitt, 1987). For about 4 to 5 percent of infants, these nutritional deficiencies are serious and require immediate remedy. For another group about the same size, the nutritional deficiencies are less severe but are still a cause for concern.

Even when undernourished infants appear healthy and "bright," they may be at risk for later problems in development because poorly nourished families often experience other serious deprivations, such as poor sanitation, inadequate health care, and lack of educational opportunities. Under these conditions, it may not take much to turn mild undernourishment into severe malnutrition and thus reduce cognitive and motor performance to below satisfactory levels.

her baby for granted and feels little fear that the baby will die unexpectedly.

But there is more to this story than just mothers' fear of their infants' death. As an agricultural and sheep-herding people, the Gusii need able-bodied persons to work in the fields and pastures and to ensure that their large and widely scattered homesteads run smoothly. Families (and therefore mothers) who bear more children can accomplish these goals more successfully; children, in effect, are an economic asset. Gusii mothers therefore rarely practice birth control, even though government officials have made information and birth control materials widely available in the area. From the time a Gusii mother gets married (around age fifteen or sixteen) until menopause, she is usually either pregnant or nursing a young infant.

Again, this may sound grueling by North American standards, but consider again the context. A typical Gusii homestead is an extended family, or a grouping of one or two dozen relatives. Therefore, as the youngest infant moves into toddlerhood, many people are readily available to take partial responsibility for the newest member of the family. Typically the mother will assign primary responsibility to an older sibling (age six to eight), but these children will in turn be the responsibility of still older siblings or other relatives. It is this larger group, rather than the mother (or father) alone, that introduces the child to the ways of the (Gusii) world. Under these conditions, Gusii children become genuine contributors to their homesteads' wealth at very early ages. Anthropologists have observed children as young as eight years planting and successfully harvesting a large field of flaxseed.

Eventually, of course, these patterns will have to change. If all Gusii mothers continue to bear numerous children, the Gusii people will overpopulate themselves in time. If they respond by limiting the number of births, however, they will give up the economic benefits of bearing large numbers of children. Once those benefits decrease, further changes may occur that at this point are hard to foresee. What, for example, will happen to the extended family and to the child care that it makes possible?

Obesity and Overnutrition   In calorie-loving societies such as our own, eating too much can pose a serious problem for some individuals. The most obvious result of eating too much is to become extremely overweight, or **obese.** The nature and extent of obesity depend partly on how much an infant overeats and when during development the overeating occurs.

In the short run, what infants eat affects how much they weigh. Big, heavy infants tend to have diets high in calories. They tend to drink more milk than usual and to be started early on solid foods, which often are relatively high in calories. Contrary to what some parents fear, however, weight in infancy correlates little with weight in childhood and even less with weight in adulthood (Williams & Kimm,

TABLE 5.4 *Changing Nutritional Needs During Infancy*

Age in Months	Parents May Begin
Birth–4	Complete diet of breast milk or baby formula
4–6	Introduce puréed single-grain cereal, preferably iron-fortified. Begin with 1–2 teaspoons, work up to 1/2 cup, twice per day.
5	100% fruit juices, could be diluted, 1/2 cup serving per day.
6–8	Introduce puréed vegetables or fruit, one at a time. Begin with 1–2 teaspoons, work up to 1/4–1/2 cup per serving, twice per day. Introduce "finger" foods (e.g., chopped banana, bits of dry cereal).
10–12	Introduce puréed meats or poultry, beginning with 1–2 teaspoons, working up to 1/4–1/2 cup per serving, 3–4 times per day. Introduce soft but chopped foods (e.g., lumpy potatoes). Introduce whole milk, 1/2 cup per serving, 4–5 times per day.
24	Introduce low-fat milk, 1/2 cup per serving, 4–5 times per day.

Source: Adapted from International Food Information Council, 1993.

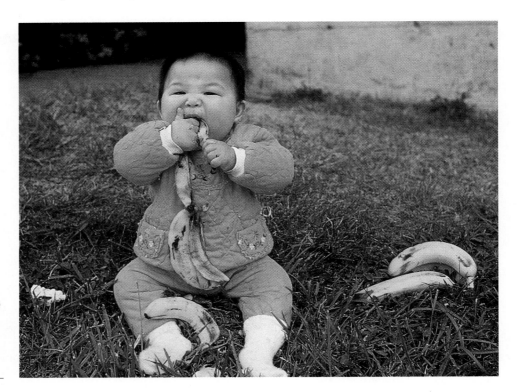

Parents should introduce solid foods slowly to ensure that their infants have developed enough to digest the food comfortably. The sensory experience of food remains a primary motive for eating throughout infancy—as indeed it does throughout life.

1993). Heavy babies stand only a slightly greater chance than lighter ones of becoming heavy children, and then only if they are very heavy indeed to begin with.

Infants seem to develop somewhat differently if they are extremely overweight (say, more than 30 percent above average). In addition to developing enlarged fat cells, these infants also grow completely new fat cells. Once formed, these new fat cells do not disappear; they remain as storage places for any future extra calories. Extremely overweight infants therefore may live with some added risk of remaining overweight throughout childhood and adulthood. Nevertheless, the risk does not guarantee obesity later on. As long as such children follow a moderately healthy diet and get reasonable amounts of exercise, they tend to develop quite normally.

Failure to Thrive   An infant or a preschool child who fails to grow at normal rates for no apparent medical reason suffers from a condition called **failure to thrive.** About 6 percent of North American children show this condition at one time or another, although not necessarily continuously (Woolston, 1993). In some ways the condition resembles malnutrition, especially as it occurs in developing nations. Failure-to-thrive and malnourished children both develop motor and cognitive skills more slowly than usual; both experience higher rates of school failure and learning disabilities; and both are more likely to live in disadvantaged circumstances and to have parents who are enduring physical or emotional stress.

At one time, professionals tended to attribute failure to thrive to lack of nurturing and love between parent and child. A more complex picture may be closer to the truth: failure to thrive may have many sources, both physical and psychological, and depend on both the child and the environment. Consider this pattern. An infant has a genetically quiet, slow-to-respond temperament, making it more difficult for her mother to establish emotional contact. If the mother also is experiencing a number of other stresses (low income, illness, or disapproval of the new baby from others), the relationship between mother and infant is put at risk. A vicious cycle may develop of poorly timed feedings and ineffective efforts to nurture the infant, who persistently resists the mother's love—and even her food. However, the cycle may not develop at all, and even when it does, it does *not* develop because the mother does not care about her infant or because the infant does not want food or affection. Intentions are usually good. Partly for this reason, parents and children eventually can get out of such awkward, frustrating relationships if professionals help the parents understand how the situation developed.

Infant Mortality

In the past several decades, health care systems in North America and around the world have substantially improved their ability to keep infants alive. The **infant mortality rate,** the proportion of babies who die during the first year of life, has declined steadily during this century. In 1950 in the United States, about twenty-nine out of every one thousand infants died; four decades later, this number was fewer than ten out of every one thousand infants (United States National Center for Health Statistics, 1991). The averages conceal wide differences within society, some of which are listed in Table 5.5. Families with very low incomes are about twice as likely to lose an infant as are families with middle-level incomes (about eighteen to twenty babies per one thousand versus nine per one thousand). Likewise, African-American families are twice as likely as Caucasian families to lose an infant, perhaps because of the historical correlation of race with income level and access to health care in American society (Pritchett, 1993). As a result, mortality rates in some nonwhite, low-income areas of major cities rival the rates found in less developed countries around the world.

On average, the infant mortality rate in the United States and Canada is two or three times lower than that in many less developed countries. Even so, infant mortality in the United States actually is *higher* than in nineteen other developed nations, including Canada, Japan, Sweden, France, and Great Britain (United Nations International Children's Emergency Fund, 1995). The high mortality rate comes as a surprise, because the United States generally is more affluent than many of these other nations, and the American medical system originated many of the life-saving techniques that have lowered infant mortality rates around the world. Distribution of infant health care, it seems, is far from ideal in the United States.

Cross-cultural investigations of infant mortality rates in European countries have given further clues about the reasons for the relatively high U.S. rate and have suggested ways to improve it. The research overwhelmingly indicates that parents need social supports as much as they need access to basic medical services and knowledge. In Europe, this support takes several forms. Most European countries provide pregnant mothers with free prenatal care. Frequently this care is provided by medically trained (and usually female) midwives, who are better able to give the time needed to establish a supportive relationship with pregnant women.

Most European countries also protect working mothers by law. Pregnant women get special, generous sick leave, get at least four months of maternity leave with pay, and are protected from doing dangerous or exhausting work (such as night shifts). Every European country also begins a regular cash payment to parents when their child is born, the amount and duration depending on the condition of the child and the number of children already in the family. Altogether, these policies and practices communicate emotional support to pregnant mothers and their spouses in ways not currently available in the United States.

What Do You Think?

If you (or your spouse) were expecting a child, would you prefer that the baby be breast fed or bottle fed? Discuss this question with a classmate of the *same* sex, and see if you can develop a consensus. Then compare your joint position with that of a group of the *opposite* sex. Are there any gender differences?

TABLE 5.5 *Infant Mortality in Selected Nations*

Nation	Infant Mortality (per 1,000 live births)
Finland	5.5
Japan	6.3
Sweden	6.7
Switzerland	6.9
Hong Kong	7.5
Canada	7.9
Denmark	7.9
Netherlands	7.9
France	8.0
United States, white	**8.5**
Norway	8.5
Germany	8.9
Ireland	8.9
Singapore	9.3
United Kingdom	9.3
Belgium	9.4
Australia	10.0
Spain	10.5
United States, average	**10.6**
New Zealand	10.8
Italy	10.9
Austria	11.0
Israel	12.3
Greece	14.0
Czechoslovakia	14.0
United States, nonwhite	**17.5**

Sources: UNICEF (1993); U.S. Bureau of the Census (1992).

INFANCY: THE REAL END OF BIRTH

During the first two years of infants' lives, several changes make them seem much more like individuals, or "real" people, than they did on the day they were born. As children approach their second birthday, for example, many of their basic physical needs and skills have stabilized. Now they can swallow and even chew a variety of foods, even if they still lack a lot of teeth and make a mess out of eating. And now they can (sometimes!) sleep through the night.

Complementing this new stability are new behaviors. Two-year-olds can move around, even if they are sometimes still clumsy. Most important, a lot of their movement is voluntary; a toddler may wander away in a department store, for example, because he wants to. Such movements are facilitated by infants' physical growth during the first two years. By their second birthday, they can use their hands and feet to help them implement choices, however crudely at first. As the next chapters show, the first two years also make infants seem more human in two other major ways: by preparing them to think in symbols and by helping them to form definite attachments to parents and peers.

SUMMARY OF MAJOR IDEAS

Appearance of the Young Infant

1. The average newborn infant born at full term weighs about 7½ pounds. Newborns' bodily proportions, such as their large heads, make them look appealing. These proportions may foster the formation of attachments with adult care-givers.

2. The health of newborns born in hospitals is assessed quickly after delivery with the Apgar Scale.

Development of the Nervous System

3. A child's brain grows rapidly during infancy, and at the same time parts of it begin to develop special functions.

4. Infants sleep almost twice as much as adults do, but the amount gradually decreases as they get older. They also experience distinct states of arousal from deep sleep to full alertness.

Sensory Development

5. At birth infants already can see and hear, but with less accuracy or acuity than adults can.

6. All of the senses develop rapidly and reach adult levels of acuity and sensitivity by the end of infancy.

Motor Development

7. Infants are born with a number of physically useful reflexes, such as rooting and sucking.

8. Infants are also born with several reflexes, such as the Moro reflex, whose primary significance is to indicate normal development of the nervous system.

9. Motor skills appear during the first year of infancy and include reaching, crawling, walking, and grasping.

10. Motor skills develop differently depending on special learning experiences, cultural background, and sex, though the precise nature of these influences is ambiguous.

Variations in Infant Growth

11. One of the most important influences on early motor development is low birth weight, caused by either slow prenatal development or a short gestational period.

12. Preterm infants often show many abnormalities: they may have trouble breathing and digesting, and their reflexes may be poorly developed.

Nutrition During the First Two Years

13. Infants need more protein and calories per pound of body weight than older children do.

14. Compared with formula and bottle feeding, breast feeding has several advantages. Breast milk confers immunity to illnesses; breast milk is more nutritionally complete; breast feeding helps develop an infant's jaw and mouth muscles; and breast feeding may benefit the mother-infant relationship.

15. After weaning from breast or bottle, infants need a diet rich in protein and calories. Although most North American families can satisfy these requirements, many fail to provide specific nutrients children need, which in extreme cases can lead to deficits in development.

16. A common problem in North American diets is overnutrition, which can make infants seriously overweight, or obese. Mild amounts of extra fat in an infant, however, usually do not influence how much the infant weighs as a child or an adult.

17. For a variety of reasons, infants sometimes fail to grow normally, a condition called *failure to thrive.*

18. The rate of infant mortality has decreased in the recent past, but in the United States it is still higher than it should be.

KEY TERMS

neonate *(133)*	rooting *(146)*
Apgar Scale *(134)*	sucking *(146)*
attachment *(136)*	Moro reflex *(146)*
central nervous system *(137)*	survival reflexes *(147)*
	primitive reflexes *(147)*
neuron *(138)*	motor skills *(147)*
glia *(138)*	gross motor skills *(147)*
myelin *(138)*	fine motor skills *(147)*
brainstem *(138)*	cephalocaudal principle *(148)*
midbrain *(138)*	
cerebellum *(138)*	proximodistal principle *(148)*
cerebral cortex *(139)*	
REM sleep *(140)*	low birth weight *(151)*
non-REM sleep *(140)*	small for date *(152)*
sudden infant death syndrome (SIDS) *(141)*	preterm *(152)*
	sleep apnea *(153)*
reflex *(146)*	obesity *(157)*
skills *(146)*	failure to thrive *(158)*
motor abilities *(146)*	infant mortality rate *(159)*

FOR FURTHER READING

Brazelton, T. B. *What Every Baby Knows.* New York: Ballantine Books, 1988.

Brazelton has a gift for colorful and readable descriptions of infants, children, and their families and the everyday problems and challenges they encounter. This book, like others by Brazelton, intersperses real-life descriptions and interviews with family members with commentary that helps put the concrete accounts into perspective. Because the children and families are all "real," the book does not confine itself to physical developments; it also includes cognitive and social developments.

La Leche League International. *The Womanly Art of Breast-feeding.* 35th annual edition. New York: Plume Books, 1991.

This book focuses on the merits of breast feeding. It supports breast feeding unabashedly and enthusiastically and has relatively little tolerance for bottle feeding.

Leach, Penelope. *Children First: What Our Society Must Do— and Is Not Doing—for Our Children Today.* New York: Alfred Knopf, 1994.

Penelope Leach is a well-known author of childrearing advice books for parents. In this book, she comments in a readable, accessible way on what modern society must do to support the needs of children. If you think your interest in children has nothing to do with the larger social changes occurring in society, read this book and think again.

Stern, Daniel. *Diary of a Baby: What Your Child Sees, Feels, and Experiences.* New York: Basic Books, 1990.

Here is another book that conveys what it feels like to be an infant. It is written with parents and prospective parents in mind. The author presents passages written from the baby's point of view, as if he or she could write, think, and talk. Then he interprets and analyzes the baby's comments from an adult's point of view.

6

THE FIRST TWO YEARS

Cognitive Development

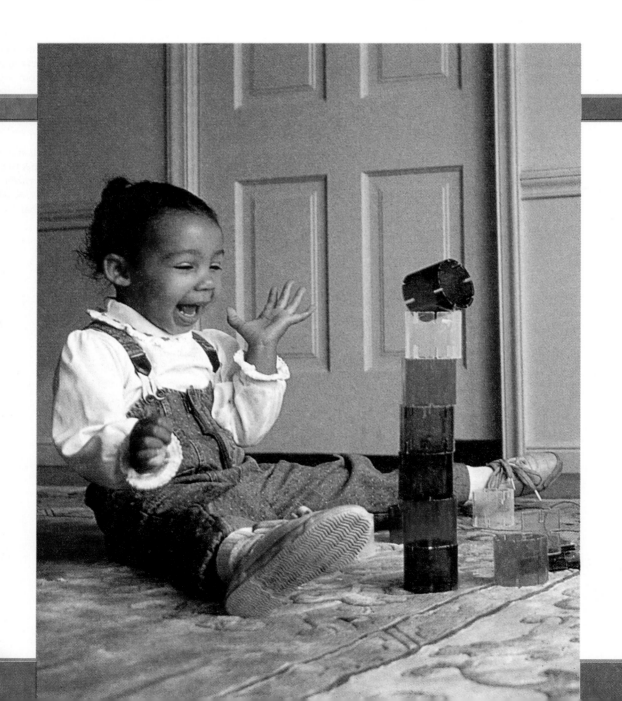

Ways of Studying Perception and Cognition in Infants

Arousal and Infants' Heart Rates
Recognition, Memory, and Infant Habituation

Infant Perception

Visual Perception
Auditory Perception
Culture and Infant Perception

Infant Cognition

Piaget's Theory of Sensorimotor Intelligence
Baby Jill's Intelligence: An Example
Assessment of Piaget's Theory of Infant
  Cognition

Behavioral Learning in Infancy

Classical Conditioning
Operant Conditioning
Imitation

Language Acquisition

Phonology
Semantics and First Words
Influencing Language Acquisition

The End of Infancy

Focusing Questions

- What clues do infants give about their cognitive processes? How can we learn about infants' thinking?

- Do infants see and hear in the same way adults do?

- What does "thinking," or cognition, consist of at different periods of infancy?

- What are the three types of learning, and how do infants demonstrate them?

- What steps do infants and toddlers go through in acquiring language, and how do adults affect this language acquisition?

From birth, infants begin acquiring knowledge about their environment. Consider William and Greta.

William, nine months old, laughs when his father puts on a Halloween mask. But two days later, when a family friend tries on the same mask, William cries in distress. Six months later he laughs when the friend tries on the mask again, but he shies away from trying it on himself. The same mask seems to have changed meaning for him more than once.

One day Greta, eighteen months old, cannot find a favorite toy, a stuffed cat. For a time she forgets everything else to look for her cat—under her bed, on the shelves, in the closet. She is so engrossed that her mother cannot get her to stop until the cat is found.

These examples illustrate two psychological processes: perception and cognition. **Perception** refers to the processes involved in the brain's immediate or direct organization and interpretation of sensations. Perceptual processes occur when an infant notices that a toy car is the same car no matter which way he orients it. As the infant turns the car upside down in his hands, his visual image of it changes; yet he still perceives the changing patterns as one unchanging car. He is not fooled into thinking that the car has acquired a different identity when he turns it upside down. Perception has an automatic, involuntary quality as well, such as when William cannot help noticing that different people wearing the same mask look similar but also just a bit different.

Cognition refers to all the processes involved in thinking and other mental activities. It includes reasoning, attention, memory, problem solving, and the ability to represent objects and experiences. Greta uses cognitive skills when she searches for her favorite stuffed cat. William, on the other hand, is so young that his reaction to the mask may be based more on perception than on conceptual thinking; the mask has violated the constancy and stability that his brain automatically provides for the objects he encounters. Preschool children and adults almost surely would feel less distress than William does, because they would do more than perceive the mask. They might also consciously wonder who was behind the mask each time, why the person had put it on, and the like. They would *conceptualize* the experience and, in doing so, perhaps alter their perceptions of it as well.

Whatever your age or maturity, most of your activities include both perception and cognition. When you hear a university professor lecture, you may perceive the sounds she or he makes as language, but you probably also apply cognitive skills to make sense of them; otherwise, the lecture is only so much linguistic noise. Research on infancy suggests that infants may be more influenced by perception than older individuals are, but the difference is only a matter of degree. The fact that babies can imitate behaviors and search for a favorite toy suggests that they also experience deliberate conceptual thought (Mandler, 1988).

In this chapter, we look at how infants develop conceptual and perceptual abilities. We begin by examining how such abilities can be discovered and studied, even at remarkably early ages and well before infants are able to express themselves with language. Then we describe the major cognitive achievements of infancy. Among these milestones are the beginnings of language, a topic so important that we discuss it further in Chapter 9, with reference to language developments in the preschool years.

WAYS OF STUDYING PERCEPTION AND COGNITION IN INFANTS

How can we know whether a very young infant, who mostly just sleeps, is actually noticing an interesting sight or sound, much less thinking about it? Consider Elizabeth, who is only two months old.

> For two hours Elizabeth had slept. Now she lay in her mother's arms with eyes barely open, while her mother talked affectionately to her. The mother nodded her head while she talked, exaggerated her voice to a singsong, and even dangled a key chain in front of Elizabeth's eyes for a moment. Elizabeth stared more or less in the direction of all these events. She did not respond in an obvious way, but she did not avert her eyes from it all or go back to sleep.

Maybe Elizabeth noticed her mother's efforts, but then again maybe she did not. Either way, we could not find out by simple observation; a more complex investigation would be required. Infant psychologists have developed several interrelated techniques for inferring the perceptions and "thoughts" of babies. One measures changes in infants' states of arousal; another assesses how they respond to especially familiar sights and sounds; and still another measures their readiness to habitually perform those behaviors they find rewarding.

Arousal and Infants' Heart Rates

One way to understand an infant's cognition is to measure his heart rate (HR) with a small electronic stethoscope attached to his chest. The changes in HR are taken to signify variations in the baby's arousal, alertness, and general contentment.

Psychologists who study infants make this assumption because among adults, HR varies reliably with attention and arousal. Typically HR slows down, or decelerates, when adults notice or attend to something interesting but not overly exciting, such as reading the newspaper. If adults attend to something *very* stimulating, their HRs speed up, or accelerate. Watching a lab technician draw blood from your own arm, for example, often causes your HR to speed up. On the whole, novel or attractive stimuli produce curiosity and a slower HR, whereas potentially dangerous or aversive stimuli produce defensiveness, discomfort, and a faster HR, at least among adults.

Very young infants, from one day to a few months old, show similar changes, but we need to take several precautions when we study their HRs. For one thing, observations of infants' attention should be made when infants are awake and alert, and, as we already pointed out, newborn babies often spend a lot of time being drowsy or asleep. For another, newborn and very young infants are much more likely to respond to relatively gentle and persistent stimuli, such as a quiet, continuous sound or a soft light that moves slowly or blinks repeatedly (Slater & Morrison, 1991). Many stimuli that lead to deceleration in adults or older children lead to acceleration in infants. Many one-month-olds show a faster HR at familiar sights, such as their mothers, even though the infants may look like they are just staring calmly into space. Despite these problems, however, studies of HR have provided a useful way to measure infants' attention, perception, and memory.

Recognition, Memory, and Infant Habituation

Although infants cannot describe what they remember, they often indicate recognition of particular objects, people, and activities. Familiar people, such as mothers, bring forth a special response in one-year-olds, who may coo suddenly at the sight of them, stretch out their arms to them, and even crawl or walk to them if they

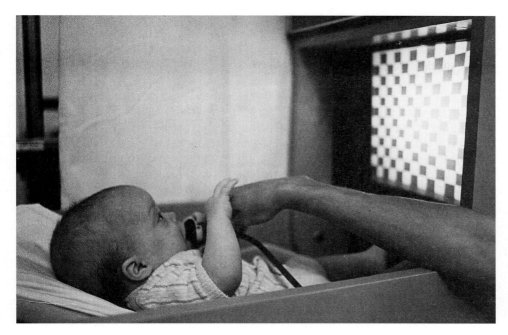

Babies often show preferences for novel stimuli. By sucking on a special nipple, the baby in the experiment pictured here brings a visual pattern into or out of focus. Typically a new pattern prompts intense and rapid sucking at first, but as the baby habituates or gets used to the pattern, the baby sucks less frequently.

know how. Less familiar people, such as neighbors or the family doctor, tend not to produce responses like these and in fact may even produce active distress, depending on the age of the infant.

Babies' responses to the familiar and the unfamiliar offer infant psychologists a second way to understand infant perception and conceptual thought. Psychologists study infants' tendency to get used to and therefore ignore stimuli as they experience them repeatedly; this tendency is called **habituation** (Bornstein, 1989). One habituation strategy repeatedly offers a baby a standard, or "study," stimulus—a simple picture to look at or a simple melody to hear. Like most adults, the baby attends to the study stimulus carefully at first, but on subsequent occasions gradually pays less attention to it. As this happens, the baby is said to be *habituating* to the stimulus. After the baby has become habituated, the investigators present the original study stimulus along with a few other stimuli. If the baby really recognizes the original, she probably will attend to the others *more* because they are comparatively novel. Her HR will slow down as well.

This method has shown that young babies recognize quite a lot of past experiences. One classic habituation study found that four-month-old girls recognized a familiar visual pattern among three others that differed from the original (McCall & Kagan, 1967). Another showed that HR slowed down when five-month-olds heard a familiar melody replayed in a different rhythmic pattern (Chang & Trehub, 1977b). Still another found habituation even in newborns: they "noticed" when a light brush on their cheeks changed location, as revealed by changes in their HRs (Kisilevsky & Muir, 1984). Sometimes, too, recognition persists for very long periods. Three-month-olds, it seems, can still recognize a picture or toy two weeks after they first see it, as long as the objects are presented in a familiar context the second time—a performance that matches adults' recognition memory (Hayne et al., 1991).

What Do You Think?

Given the research described in this section, when is it fair to say that a young infant first begins to "recognize" his or her parents? Talk to one or two recent mothers of infants about when they felt they were first recognized. Then compare what you learn from them with similar interviews conducted by two or three of your classmates.

INFANT PERCEPTION

As mentioned earlier, *perception* refers to how the brain organizes and interprets sensations. Perception operates relatively automatically: when your best friend walks up to you, your brain almost instantly converts an oval-shaped pattern of colors and lines from an unorganized batch of sensations into an organized whole called your friend's face. The automatic quality of perception has made many psychologists suspect that it is either genetically programmed or learned very early in infancy. Either way, it would be a primary feature of infant cognition.

Children indeed acquire a number of important perceptual skills during infancy. Each skill corresponds to one or another of the five human senses: vision, hearing, touch, taste, and smell. The first sense, vision, has been studied more than any of the others, and vision and hearing together account for the large majority of research about infants' perception. This emphasis reflects society's widespread (but probably unjustified) belief that touch, taste, and smell are "minor" senses, ones we can live without more easily than vision and hearing.

Visual Perception

Given that children can see at least to some extent during infancy, what do they perceive? Some of the earliest research on this question stirred up a lot of interest because it seemed to show that infants, even those just two days old, could discriminate between human faces and abstract patterns and that they looked at faces longer than at either patterned disks or plain, unpatterned disks (Fantz, 1963). The researchers presented infants with various combinations of these stimuli side by side and carefully observed which object the babies spent the most time looking at. At all ages studied (birth to six months), the infants showed a clear preference: they stared at a picture of a human face almost twice as long as at any other stimulus picture. Young infants, it seemed, were inherently interested in people.

Young infants concentrate longer on certain shapes and contours, even when these are not part of a human face. Newborns are especially attracted to contours and to patches of light and dark. A few months later, they prefer complex patterns over simpler ones, and curved lines over straight ones. Such changes are one reason (among many) why a baby's interest in crib toys waxes and wanes over time.

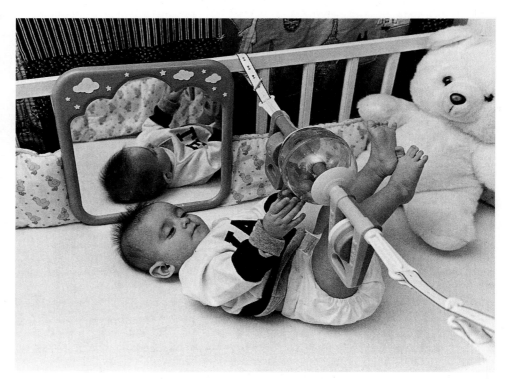

More recent studies of visual preferences, however, have qualified this conclusion substantially (Yonas, 1988). It is not the humanness of faces that infants enjoy looking at but their interesting contours, complexity, and curvature. Newborns are particularly attracted to contours, or the edges of areas of light and dark. But such edges can be provided either by the hairline of a parent's head or by a properly constructed abstract drawing. When infants get to age two or three months, their perceptual interest shifts to complexity and curvature. At this age, infants prefer looking at a pattern of many small squares rather than one of just a few large squares. They also prefer looking at curved lines to looking at straight ones. These qualities too are conveniently provided to most babies by human faces, but not by faces alone.

Also by age two or three months, infants can distinguish at least some of the colors that adults normally perceive (Teller & Lindsey, 1993). They even show a preference for red and blue over green and yellow, as judged by how long they choose to look at sample patches of each of these colors. The color preferences parallel those of adults, suggesting that they are at least partly inborn and not entirely the result of cultural learning. What infants conceptualize about colors at such a young age, however, remains ambiguous; it would seem they have much learning and experience to undergo before they can associate *red* with *fire*.

Object Perception   *Object constancy* refers to the perception that an object remains the same in some way despite constant changes in the sensations it sends to the eye. A baby's favorite toy duck never casts exactly the same image on her retina from one second to the next. The image continually varies depending on its distance and its orientation, or angle of viewing. Somehow the baby must learn that this kaleidoscope of images really refers to only one constant duck—that the duck always *is* the same but keeps *looking* different. Several studies show that infants begin acquiring this knowledge very early indeed.

Consider the development of *size constancy,* the perception that an object stays the same size even when viewed from different distances. In a typical study, newborn babies are conditioned to suck on pacifiers (see Chapter 2 for an explanation of this process) at the sight of a cube of some specified size and placed at some precise distance. During conditioning training, sucking at the sight of cubes of other sizes or distances is deliberately not reinforced so that the sucking provides an indicator of the baby's recognition of an object of a particular size and at a given distance.

Later the conditioned infants are shown several cubes of different sizes and placed at different distances. The test cubes include one that casts an image exactly the size of the original but is in fact larger and farther away (see Figure 6.1). Typically, the babies are not fooled by this apparent identity of retinal images. They prefer to look at the original cube regardless of its distance; that is, they suck on their pacifiers more vigorously while looking at the original cube than while looking at

FIGURE 6.1
Size Constancy in Infancy
Even babies just a few weeks old show size constancy; that is, they distinguish between an object that is larger but farther away and one that is smaller but closer. In general, they prefer looking at objects that are relatively close in distance, whatever their size.

any substitute. Apparently they know when an object really is the same size and when it only looks the same size.

But size constancy is imperfect. Regardless of an object's size or shape, infants prefer objects at certain distances, especially nearby ones, objects with contrasting hues and brightnesses and objects near their center line of vision (Banks & Sharman, 1993). Anything that meets these conditions attracts a newborn's attention especially well and therefore can create the impression of attentiveness just described. When all these factors are controlled, infants still show some size constancy, but not as much as in everyday life when hue, brightness, and distance tend to work together to confirm the size constancy of most objects.

Do babies perceive an object as being the same even when its shape changes because the angle from which it is viewed changes? This particular perception, sometimes called *shape constancy,* depends on the ability to recognize apparent but unreal changes in shape. A rubber doll held upright casts a different image on the eye than the same doll lying down. But this change in shape is only apparent; compare it with the real change caused by squeezing the rubber doll hard with both hands.

In general, research on this skill suggests that infants acquire shape constancy gradually, beginning at around three months of age. Typically they demonstrate this skill, as they do many others, by habituating—in this case, to shapes viewed at various angles or orientations, or undergoing various motions or rotations (Columbo, 1993). A variety of experiments have shown that during their first year, infants prefer to watch the same object under different orientations and movements rather than some other object undergoing comparable changes.

Infants begin their first year showing shape constancy only for simple shapes, such as spheres or cubes. As the year goes on, they develop constancy for increasingly complex forms, such as faces or abstract drawings presented at sidelong or tilted angles (Aslin, 1993). For the most complex figures, gentle movement or rotation seems to help infants identify shapes. In these cases, older infants react somewhat like adults who are viewing a piece of sculpture: they must see all sides of it to be able to perceive its full identity.

All of these qualifications make it hard to name a precise age at which babies acquire either shape or size constancy. A young infant's daily expression of various object constancies is likely to seem tentative and ambiguous to a parent or other adult. One day the child responds as though an object were the "same" at different distances or orientations, yet the next day the child conveys ignorance of constancy. The variability occurs because object constancy depends partly on the child's attentiveness and partly on the child's prior memories of the object, both of which are somewhat fragile in early infancy.

Whatever the timing of their appearance, shape and size constancies serve important functions in babies' long-term development. These skills help infants to distinguish familiar objects from novel ones and to begin seeing the world as predictable and secure. Gradually mother is mother and father is father, whether viewed from the side or from the front and whether viewed from ten feet or two feet. Shape and size constancies also help infants learn about new, inanimate objects more efficiently. Familiar objects are recognized more often and more quickly, allowing the baby to concentrate on newer, unexplored objects.

Depth Perception   Even if the infant perceives the sizes and shapes of objects fairly accurately, he or she still must navigate successfully from one place to another. Consider Joel, who recently learned to crawl around his house. Joel must realize that the rooms in his house stay put when he crawls or walks, even though they look like they move. And he must notice that stairs differ from floors. Such realizations require Joel to orient his actions to the world or space outside his own body and to understand its layout accurately. In other words, he must perceive depth and spatial orientation accurately. Each of these perceptions appears and then changes during the course of infancy.

Infants' behavior on a visual cliff reflects both their knowledge and their feelings about depth. Even babies too young to crawl or creep find the deep side of the cliff more interesting than the shallow side. But only babies who have begun crawling or creeping show fear or wariness of the deep side.

Depth perception refers to a sense of how far away objects are or appear to be. Infants begin acquiring this kind of perceptual skill about as soon as they can focus on objects at different distances, at around two or three months of age. This conclusion is suggested by research that has developed out of the now classic experiment with the visual cliff (E. Gibson & Walk, 1960). In its basic form, the **visual cliff** consists of a table covered with strong glass under which is a textured surface with colored squares, such as that shown in the photograph on this page. Part of the textured surface contacts the glass directly, and another part is separated from it by several feet. Visually, then, the setup resembles the edge of a table, but the glass provides ample support for an infant, even in the dropped-off area. A baby who is placed onto it will seem to float in midair.

On this apparatus, even babies just two months old discriminate between the two sides of the visual cliff. They find the deep side more interesting, as suggested by the extra time they take to study it. Young babies show little fear of the deep side, judging either by their overt behavior or by their heart rates, which tend to decrease during their investigations of the cliff. This finding implies they are primarily curious about the cliff rather than fearful of it.

Babies old enough to crawl, however, show significant fear of the visual cliff. Their heart rates increase markedly, and they will not crawl onto the deep side despite coaxing from a parent and the solid support they feel from the glass. Why the change? Perhaps infants' crawling skills allow them to perceive distances more accurately than before, since the motion of crawling causes faraway objects (including the deep side of the cliff) to move less than nearby objects (such as the shallow side). Perhaps, too, infants old enough to crawl are also old enough to focus their eyes more accurately for each side of the cliff, a physical skill that provides further perceptual information about the difference in distance of the two sides (Kermoian & Campos, 1988).

Auditory Perception

Infants respond to sounds even as newborns. But what do they perceive from sounds? What sense do they make of the sounds they hear? These questions are important, because infants' ability to discriminate among sounds makes a crucial difference in their acquisition of language, as discussed later in this chapter.

Gaining skill at discriminating among sounds takes many months. Consider LaVonne and Daniel.

At about five o'clock each day LaVonne, two months old, cries unaccountably. Her father finds that running the vacuum cleaner quiets her down immediately. He also finds it keeps her quiet more or less indefinitely, or at least until he cannot stand the sound of the vacuum any longer.

Daniel, fourteen months old, sometimes gets fussy. His mother finds that playing music quiets him down rapidly. Familiar melodies and vocal singing seem to keep him quiet the longest, although every kind of music works for at least a little while.

Most adults would guess that Daniel perceives some sort of meaning from what he hears, such as the melodic structure of the songs or some of the words being sung. But LaVonne cannot get meaning from what she hears; more likely she quiets because she tunes out, or "averts her ears" from, the noise of the vacuum cleaner.

Localization of Sounds   Research confirms these informal impressions. Under certain conditions infants can indeed organize the sounds they hear, and in this sense they can hear as well as perceive what they hear. For example, infants just two months old can locate sounds, as suggested by the fact that they orient their heads toward certain noises, such as a rattle (Morrongiello, 1994). But they often take much longer to respond than do older children or adults. Instead of needing just a fraction of a second, as adults do, full-term infants require an average of two to three seconds before orienting toward ("looking at") a sound that occurs off to one side. Infants born one month preterm require even more time to respond. These delays may explain why pediatricians and others used to believe newborn infants cannot hear: the sounds they offered to the babies, such as a single hand clap, may not have lasted long enough for the infants to respond.

Although infants can locate sounds, their skill at doing so is somewhat limited. They are better able to locate relatively high-pitched sounds, such as those made by a flute or a small bird, than low-pitched sounds, such as that made by a foghorn (Spetner & Olsho, 1990). This fact has sometimes led some experts to suggest that infants have a "natural" preference for female—that is, high-pitched—human voices. Studies of voice preferences, however, have not confirmed this possibility consistently, probably because newborns' range of special sensitivity lies well above the pitch of even female voices and because male and female voices usually are more similar in overall quality than gender stereotypes suggest. Instead, it is more accurate to say that infants prefer sounds in the middle range of pitches, which is the range most similar to human voices, male or female.

Coordination of Vision and Hearing   The localization of sounds suggests that even very young babies coordinate what they see with what they hear; they seem to use sound to direct their visual gaze. But is this what really happens? As reasonable as this interpretation seems, the evidence suggests a more complicated story (Morrongiello, 1994). In their first efforts to turn their heads, very young babies (one or two months old) act more as though head turning is a reflex than a search for something to see. The behavior does not habituate, meaning a young baby is just as likely to turn toward a sound after many presentations as she was after the first presentation. Also, the behavior occurs even in the dark, when there is no chance to actually see the source of a sound. Only by age five or six months do these reflexive qualities change: by that age, babies habituate quickly to repeated presentations and search only in the light, when there is something to see. In these ways, then, hearing and vision have become coordinated, but it has taken several months of learning for the change to occur.

Culture and Infant Perception   How, if at all, might culture influence the ways infants see and hear? Research on this problem is sketchy; most psychologists, even those with a special interest in culture, usually assume cultural influences require time after birth to develop and, therefore, begin to emerge only toward the end of infancy. Even among older children and adults, however, cultural influences on perception seem to be much smaller than on language, problem solving, styles of thinking, or social relationships. For example, adults from twenty different societies all perceive the same color of blue to be the "best," or truest example of blue regard-less of their culture of origin or the number of color terms in their particular language (Berlin & Kay, 1969). If the adults show such unanimity, then, presumably so, do young infants from these cultures.

What Do You Think?

Might there be a way to help babies coordinate vision and hearing better and sooner? Think of some ways to accomplish this; also, think of any negative side effects of deliberately encouraging this development. Ask a few classmates—or, better yet, a few recent parents—for their opinions of whether your ideas can in fact succeed and have positive impact.

INFANT COGNITION

As perceptual skills develop, children begin to put them to cognitive uses. A one-month-old infant may notice the dark eyes painted on the face of a doll and stare a long time at them out of interest. But an eighteen-month-old can do more than that: he can talk to the doll in babbles that resemble language or cuddle the doll briefly as though it were a real person. All in all, the older infant combines perception with other skills he is developing. In doing so, he shows the first signs of cognition, or methods for thinking or gaining knowledge about the world.

At first, infant cognition has little to do with the symbolic forms that develop in most children and adults. Instead, it emphasizes active experimentation with and manipulation of materials. Only by the end of infancy does truly symbolic thought emerge. Even then it is still interspersed with large amounts of concrete doing, seeing, and hearing. Nevertheless, its mere existence marks a significant new development for the child.

Piaget's Theory of Sensorimotor Intelligence

Piaget's theory of cognitive development, described in Chapter 2, provides one of the most complete outlines of infant intelligence available (Piaget, 1963). According to

During the first year, infants explore objects with their senses, and often through mouthing or chewing. Gradually they shift their attention from these sensorimotor actions to the objects on which they perform the actions—an important sign that they are developing mental representations of objects.

this viewpoint, infants think by way of *sensory* perceptions and *motor* actions: by doing things to and with the objects they see. Piaget called this activity **sensorimotor intelligence.** He identified six stages during infancy that mark significant developments in sensorimotor intelligence; these are summarized in Table 6.1.

In general, these stages show two trends as infants grow older. First, infants show a trend toward symbolic thinking. Instead of needing to handle a toy car to understand it, an infant becomes increasingly able to visualize, or think about, a car without actually touching or seeing one. This ability becomes very strong by the end of the first two years of life; for Piaget, it helps mark the end of infancy. Changes in infants' toys reflect this development trend, as indicated in Table 6.2.

Second, infants form cognitive structures that Piaget called *schemes.* In relation to infants, **schemes** are organized patterns of actions or concepts that help the baby make sense out of and adapt to the environment. Schemes develop well before infants can represent objects or events through language or motor skills. A newborn baby's initial grasping motions constitute an early scheme, as do her earliest sucking motions. Eventually, as described shortly, internal, or mental, concepts and ideas develop out of such patterns of behavior. These too are sometimes called *schemes* (or sometimes *schemas* or *schemata*); but Piaget himself more often called cognitive structures and patterns that develop later by names such as *operations* or *systems,* depending on their exact nature (Miller, 1993).

As we discuss more fully in Chapter 2, Piaget argued that sensorimotor intelligence develops by means of two complementary processes, assimilation and accommodation. **Assimilation** consists of interpreting new experiences in terms of existing schemes. A baby who is used to sucking on a breast or bottle may use the same action on whatever new, unfamiliar objects he encounters, such as rubber balls or his own fist. **Accommodation** consists of modifying existing schemes to fit new experiences. After sucking on a number of new objects, an infant may modify this action to fit the nature of each new object; she may chew on some new objects (her sweater) but not on others (a plastic cup).

The interplay of assimilation and accommodation leads to new schemes and eventually to the infant's ability to symbolize objects and activities. Let's see how Piaget believed this transition occurs.

Stage 1: Early Reflexes—Using What You're Born With (Birth to One Month)
According to Piaget, cognitive development begins with reflexes, those simple, in-

TABLE 6.1   *Some Features of Infant Cognition According to Piaget*

Stage	Age in Months	Characteristics
1: Early reflexes	Birth–1	Reliance on inborn reflexes to "know" the environment; assimilation of all experiences to reflexes
2: Primary circular reactions	1–4	Accommodation (or modification) of reflexes to fit new objects and experiences; repeated actions focusing on infant's own body
3: Secondary circular reactions	4–8	Repeated actions focusing on objects; actions used as means toward ends, but haphazardly; early signs of object permanence
4: Combined secondary circular reactions	8–12	Deliberate combinations of previously acquired actions (or schemes); AnotB error; early signs of sense of time
5: Tertiary circular reactions	12–18	Systematic application of previously acquired actions (or schemes); well-organized investigation of novel objects, but always overt
6: The first symbols	18–24	First symbolic representations of objects; true object permanence; deferred imitation

Source: Piaget (1963).

TABLE 6.2 **Toys That Support Cognitive Development in Infancy**
As infants get older, their toys tend to involve more complex motor skills, as well as language and make-believe. Can you see how these trends are reflected in the lists below?

Birth–2 Months	6–12 Months	12–24 Months
Mobile in crib	Squeeze toys	Dolls, especially large ones
Rattle	Nested plastic cups	Toy telephone
Music box	Boxes with lids	Puzzles (5–10 pieces)
	Soft ball	Vehicles (cars, boats, train)
	Stuffed animals	Sandbox, shovel, and pail
	Pots and pans	Water toys (cups, funnel, etc.)
	Picture books (especially cloth or cardboard)	Picture books with simple words

born behaviors that all normal babies can produce at birth. As it happens, the majority of such reflexes remain just that—reflexes—for the individual's entire life; sneezing patterns and blinking responses, for example, look nearly the same in adults as they do in infants. But a few are notable for their flexibility, chiefly sucking, grasping, and looking. These behaviors resemble reflexes at birth, but they quickly begin to be modified in response to experiences such as sucking on the mother's breast, on toys, and on the child's own hand. They give infants a repertoire from which to develop more complex skills, and their susceptibility to influence makes them especially important to cognitive development during infancy.

Take sucking. Mothers who have breast fed know the first feeding or two can be awkward: the infant noses around inefficiently for the nipple and may fail to connect with it even when the nipple is right under her nose, so to speak. But within a week or two she finds it noticeably faster, usually to the relief of her mother. In the same period, she probably also has begun sucking on other objects: her fist, the corners of her blanket, her daddy's little finger. Sometimes she simply sucks on air. All these sucking motions differ slightly from one another in style or form, and each evolves into a *scheme* in the Piagetian sense.

Stage 2: Primary Circular Reactions—Modifying What You're Born With (One to Four Months)   Soon after the baby begins modifying his early reflexes, he begins to build and differentiate action schemes quite rapidly. In fact, within a month or so he sometimes repeats them endlessly for no apparent reason. Because of its repetitive quality, Piaget calls this behavior a **circular reaction.** The baby seems to be stimulated by the outcome of his own behavior, so he responds for the mere joy of feeling himself act. At this point the circular reactions are called **primary circular reactions,** because they still focus on the baby's own body and movements. Waving an arm repeatedly constitutes a primary circular reaction; so does kicking again and again.

During this period, the young infant practices her developing schemes widely, and the behaviors rapidly become less reflexive. The baby may shape her mouth differently for sucking her fist and for sucking her blanket. In this sense she begins to recognize the objects all around her, and implicitly she also begins to remember previous experiences with each type of object. But this memory has an automatic or object-focused quality, unlike the large variety of more conscious memories children have later in life.

Stage 3: Secondary Circular Reactions—Making Interesting Sights Last (Four to Eight Months)   As they practice their first schemes, young infants broaden their interests substantially. Before long, in fact, they move their attention beyond their own bodily actions to include objects and events immediately around them. Shaking his arm, for example, no longer captivates a baby's attention for its own sake; he has become too skilled at arm shaking for it to do so. Now a behavior like this

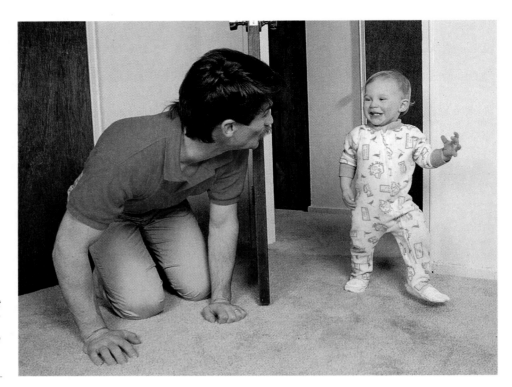

Playing peek-a-boo becomes popular with babies as they approach their first birthday. Even though the father disappears for a moment, the baby seems to believe that he still exists behind the door, as shown by the baby's delight when he reappears.

becomes useful rather than interesting. A baby at this stage may accidentally discover that shaking his arm will make a mobile spin over his head in his crib, or create an interesting noise in a toy he happens to be holding, or make parents smile with joy. In all these cases, shaking an arm becomes a means to other ends. At best it is a primitive means, however, because the usefulness of the behavior originally develops by chance.

Once primitive means are discovered, a baby at this stage will repeat a useful procedure endlessly to sustain and study the interesting results. The repetition is a circular reaction like those in the previous stage, but with an important difference: now the circular reactions orient toward external objects and events rather than to the baby's own body and actions. Now results matter. If arm shaking fails to keep the mobile spinning, the baby will soon stop her effort. If she finally figures out the nature of the mobile, she will also stop. Either way, the repetition is not governed by her earlier motivation simply to move. To differentiate this new orientation from the earlier one, Piaget called such repetitions **secondary circular reactions:** repetitions motivated by external objects and events.

Secondary circular reactions create two parallel changes in the child's motor schemes. On the one hand, the infant uses existing schemes even more widely than before. He tries to suck on more and more of the toys that come his way. On the other hand, he begins to discover that schemes can be combined to produce interesting results. He may happen to reach toward an object (one scheme) and discover that doing so makes it possible to grasp the object (another scheme). At first, the combination occurs accidentally; but once it does occur, the baby at this stage can produce the new combination of schemes deliberately on future occasions.

Secondary circular reactions also implicitly show that the infant is now acquiring at least a hazy notion of **object permanence,** a belief that objects exist separately from her own actions and continue to exist even when she cannot see them. In the first two stages of infant cognition, objects often seem to disappear from the baby's mind as soon as she loses sight of them or no longer touches them. She may stare at or grasp a toy duck, but a parent or an older sibling can sometimes take it from her without causing distress; at most, the baby will simply keep staring blankly where the duck used to be and then turn to other activities. As Piaget might have claimed, out of sight is out of mind in early infancy.

This is not so, however, as babies enter the second half of their first year. By stage 3, they will look for an object briefly if they have been watching it carefully or manipulating it just beforehand. Naturally, their first searching skills leave something to be desired, so it helps if the hidden object is actually partly visible and within easy reach: the toy duck's tail should stick out from under a blanket if that is where the toy is hidden. But the first signs of symbolic thought are there, because the infant must have some idea of the toy duck if she is going to bother searching for it.

Stage 4: Combined Secondary Circular Reactions—Deliberate Combinations of Means and Ends (Eight to Twelve Months)   At this stage, instead of just happening on connections among schemes by accident, the infant intentionally chooses to use a scheme as a means toward an end. In stages 1 and 2, he may have developed separate schemes for opening his mouth and for chewing food. In stage 3, he may have accidentally discovered that the first scheme is a means toward the other: mouth opening is a means toward eating. Now, in stage 4, the baby starts using this means-end connection purposefully. Like a young bird in a nest, he opens his mouth to "produce" food to chew on. Of course, he may eventually discover that the connection does not always work: sitting with his mouth wide open may sometimes produce no food at all or occasionally produce bad-tasting medicine instead of good-tasting food.

At this stage, the infant still lacks alternatives to the single-purpose, fragmented schemes he has developed so far. As he encounters the limitations of these schemes, he gradually modifies and expands (or accommodates, as Piaget would say) his initial schemes that connected means with ends. He may learn to open his mouth at the sight of some foods but not others. He may also add other behaviors to the mouth-opening scheme, such as pointing to favorite foods, thereby turning the original scheme into a more general food-requesting scheme. As these accommodations occur, the infant moves into the next stage of cognition.

The relatively fixed, stereotyped quality of schemes at this stage may derive from the infant's heavy reliance on motor action as a means for understanding objects. One of the most dramatic illustrations of this possibility is the **AnotB error** (read "A, not B, error"), illustrated by the following sequence. Hide a toy under a blanket while the infant carefully watches. Normally she can retrieve the toy easily at this stage. But then make the problem more complicated: hide the toy under blanket A, then transfer it to blanket B. Do this in full view of the infant. Where does the child look first for it? Not under the correct blanket, B, but under blanket A, where she previously retrieved the toy successfully. Figure 6.2 illustrates the procedure.

FIGURE 6.2
The AnotB Error
The AnotB error occurs during sensorimotor stage 4 (about eight to twelve months), when the baby is still learning to combine means (searching behaviors) with ends (finding a hidden object). Even though the baby has watched a toy being moved to a new spot, he will search for it where it was first hidden.

Step 1: Hide toy   **Step 2:** Move the toy   **Step 3:** Baby searches

The infant makes this mistake, Piaget argues, because her knowledge of the toy really amounts to memories of the actions she has taken with it, especially memories of successful actions. Some studies of the AnotB error support this interpretation, but overall, the research suggests that several other factors—the number of locations to search, for example, or delays before the baby can begin searching—also can influence success at the task (Wellman et al., 1987). In one variation of the task, babies watch while the toy is moved among three locations: from blanket A to blanket B to blanket C. Under these conditions the babies tend to reach for blankets A and B about equally, even though Piaget would have predicted that their fixed motor response would lead them to reach primarily for blanket A.

Stage 5: Tertiary Circular Reactions—Active Experimentation with Objects (Twelve to Eighteen Months)   At stage 5, the infant deliberately varies the schemes for producing interesting results, or ends. Previously, at stage 4, he could intentionally combine schemes, but only one pair at a time and only if an appropriate situation for using the combination happened to occur. Now, in dealing with a new object, the baby can run through a repertoire of schemes in a trial-and-error effort to learn about the object's properties. Piaget called the variations **tertiary circular reactions,** meaning third-level circular reactions, to distinguish them from the simpler forms of repetition that dominate the earlier stages.

These variations in behavior, however, are still organized largely by trial and error rather than by systematic plans. Given a rubber ball, for example, some babies may try dropping it from different heights and onto different objects. But no matter how delighted these infants are with the results of these variations, they will not think to vary the dropping conditions carefully or experimentally. Such actions require planning and consequently also require considerably more ability to represent objects and situations than the infant has yet developed.

Meanwhile, babies still cannot solve problems by running through solutions in their heads prior to overt action. Their belief in object permanence at stage 5 shows this limitation. They no longer make the AnotB error, but they still can be fooled if the search problem is made a little harder. A ball shifted from blanket A to blanket B still can baffle infants if they do not actually see it moved. They may not think to look under blanket B if they did not actually see the ball put there. Instead, they simply stare at the situation, perhaps looking surprised and confused. Babies respond this way even if a moment earlier they successfully solved a classic AnotB problem in which they did see the ball get moved. Taken together, these behaviors suggest two things. First, infants are tied less than before to previous successful actions for help in solving problems. Second, they may still fail to mentally form the solutions to problems in the absence of action.

Stage 6: The First Symbols—Representing Objects and Actions (Eighteen to Twenty-Four Months)   At this stage, the motor schemes the child previously explored and practiced overtly begin to occur symbolically. For the first time, the infant can begin to envision, or imagine, actions and their results without actually having to try them out beforehand.

Consider a stage 6 child who wants a favorite toy that is just barely out of reach on a high shelf. Near the shelf sits a small stool that she has played with numerous times. How to get the toy? Earlier in infancy, the baby might simply have stared and fussed and eventually either given up or cried. At this later stage, things are quite different. The baby surveys the situation, observes the stool, and pauses briefly. Then, with a purposeful air, she places the stool under the toy, climbs up, and retrieves the toy. What is important here is the lack of false starts or, conversely, the presence of only a single, correct attempt. The infant may succeed even though she never before used the stool to reach high-up objects. According to Piaget, trial and error is no longer the method of choice; now the infant tries out solutions mentally to envision their results.

Skill with mental representations makes true object permanence possible. A child at the end of infancy will search for a toy even after it has been fully hidden and even if it was hidden without his witnessing the act of hiding. If a ball disappears behind some shelves, he will go around to the other side to look for it. He will search appropriately, even though he cannot know in advance exactly where behind the shelves the ball will turn up. In the ball-and-blanket situation described earlier, the child can now play more complex games of hide-and-seek. She usually looks first under the blanket where the toy disappeared; if she fails to find it there, she will search under any and all other blankets and sometimes even under the table and in the experimenter's pockets. Relatively extensive search is made possible in part by the child's new conviction that toys and other objects have a permanent existence independent of her own activities with them. In other words, they do not just disappear.

Mental representations also make possible deferred imitation, a behavior that will figure prominently in play and learning later in childhood. In *deferred imitation,* the child copies, or duplicates, a behavior—or at least aspects of a behavior—at a significantly later time than when he first witnessed it, sometimes days or even weeks later. Having seen her father brush his teeth, the stage 6 child does so too, but she may also do so twelve hours later, when her father is not even around. Or, having heard his older sibling exclaim, "Yum! Good!" at one night's dinner menu, the child may do so as well. But he makes his exclamation at dinner two days later, even if none of the other family members feel quite so ecstatic about the food.

All these behaviors depend on the child's ability to form and maintain representations (thoughts or memories) of the relevant experiences, which later become available for expression again. As we will see, representational skill proves crucial in early childhood. It contributes to children's play, because much play involves reenactment of previous experiences and roles. It makes possible much language development, because the child must learn to use words and expressions when they are appropriate and not just at the time she hears them uttered. And it makes possible the first real self-concept, because sooner or later the child realizes that he too has a (relatively) permanent existence akin to the permanence of all the things and people in his life, whether toys, pet dogs, or parents.

Baby Jill's Intelligence: An Example

The relationships among the six stages of sensorimotor intelligence become clearer if we look at how an infant might use the same object differently at different ages. Baby Jill acquired a ball when she was born and used it for the next several years. During that time, of course, her ways of using the ball changed dramatically, as shown in the following descriptions (comments are in italics). The ball was about four inches in diameter and was made out of rubber, but had a cloth covering. Mostly it was red, but it had a large black spot on each side, so it looked rather like an eyeball when viewed from the proper angle.

1. *Stage 1: Early reflexes*   When Jill first came home from the hospital, her mother suspended the ball over Jill's diaper-changing table so that the black spot looked down at Jill directly. Day after day, Jill stared hard at the ball and its black spot and followed it whenever her mother made it swing gently.

Here Jill used one of her earliest reflexes, in this case visual tracking of objects.

Jill was modifying, or accommodating, her reflexes—sucking, grasping, tracking—to fit new experiences she was undergoing. Her interest still lay primarily in her own actions rather than in the objects she was encountering.

By now her attention had shifted away from her own body (primary circular reactions) to an object outside herself and to what it could do (secondary circular reactions).

Jill had become interested in combining schemes or actions. Her exploration of the effects of these schemes, however, was still guided primarily by chance discoveries.

Jill's investigations of the ball now had become rather deliberately varied, as though she were purposely trying out a conscious repertoire of actions to see what effect each would have on the ball.

In searching for the lost ball, Jill showed a perception of object permanence—a belief that the ball continued to exist even when out of sight. To hold this belief, she must have formed some sort of symbolic representation of the ball in her mind.

2. *Stage 2: Primary circular reactions* At two months, Jill sucked on the ball a lot and grabbed at it whenever one of her parents put it directly into her hands. The ball was just soft enough for Jill to do these things. She still liked to look at the ball swinging above her changing table, but she was starting to find her parents' faces more interesting.

3. *Stage 3: Secondary circular reactions* At six months, Jill discovered that she could make the ball swing above her changing table simply by waving her hands and feet. Every once in awhile, one of her limbs would accidentally catch the ball and send it spinning and swinging wildly.

4. *Stage 4: Combining secondary circular reactions* When Jill was ten months old, her father took the ball down one day during a diaper change and put it behind a bottle of talcum powder. Jill looked hard at the partially hidden ball, then firmly knocked over the bottle of powder and got hold of the ball. Her father was dismayed at how hard she had hit the bottle but also was somewhat impressed. He did not remember her acting so purposefully before just to get something else.

5. *Stage 5: Tertiary circular reactions* At fifteen months, Jill preferred to have the ball down on the floor where she could get at it. One day she gathered together all the balls in the house—five, to be exact. She tried bouncing each one down the stairs in turn and noticed that some seemed to bounce higher than others. Another time she tried floating the balls in the toilet. They all floated well except for her original red-and-black ball, whose cloth covering got waterlogged. (For some reason, her parents did not enjoy her putting the balls in the toilet.)

6. *Stage 6: Symbolic representation* Just before her second birthday, Jill lost her red-and-black ball. She looked in her usual storage spots: her bottom dresser drawer and her (now little used) changing table. Where was it, anyway? When she could not find it, she asked her parents for help because she knew it had to be around somewhere.

By this point, both Jill and the ball had gone through a lot together. At the end of her infancy, Jill had considerable skill at motor manipulation of objects as well as some beginnings of mental representation of objects. She no longer needed to have an object such as the red-and-black ball literally in hand. The ball had assisted in this development, as had several other toys and numerous sensory and manipulative experiences with them.

Assessment of Piaget's Theory of Infant Cognition

Piaget's theory has stimulated considerable study of infant cognition. A lot of this research has confirmed the main features of the theory, whereas other research has called attention to additional aspects of infancy that at least complicate Piaget's original presentation, if they do not contradict it outright. Here is a sampling of both the confirmations and the complications.

The Integration of Schemes   Do infants begin life with fundamentally separate sensorimotor schemes, as Piaget argued, and only gradually learn to combine them? Some such combining surely must occur, but there is also evidence for the opposite trend: some important schemes may begin as integrated wholes and only later become differentiated into parts (Lewkowicz & Lickliter, 1994). Newborn infants will reach for and grasp a small object placed in front of them at the proper distance, and will do so even if the object is only a projected image of one. Such behavior implies that young babies tend to regard sight and touch as connected rather than separate, or, in Piagetian terms, that they have a single early scheme for seeing and reaching, rather than one scheme for seeing and another, separate scheme for reaching.

Vision and hearing also may have inborn integrated schemes. As pointed out earlier, infants just a few days old will turn, as though by reflex, to look at the source of a sound as long as the direction lies within their physical capacity to turn. In addition, they show signs of connecting their parents' faces and voices within two or three weeks: they will look longer at a photograph of their mothers, for example, if a recording of the mothers' voices is playing. And infants just a few months old prefer looking at sights that match a soundtrack to sights that do not match. Suppose a young infant looks at two films side by side, one with a kangaroo bouncing up and down and the other with a toy donkey doing the same thing but at a different speed. If a soundtrack of bouncing rhythms is made to coincide with one film but not the other, the infant will spend more time watching the soundtrack-coordinated picture.

Such evidence complicates Piaget's assertion that schemes begin primarily as separate, discrete reflexes and do not begin to be integrated until midway through infancy. At the same time, however, the evidence does not really contradict Piaget. Given the complexity of human beings, it is perfectly possible for both trends to occur at once. Some schemes may begin as integrated wholes and develop that way in at least certain situations, and others may begin as relatively specific reflexes and combine later.

Motor Versus Cognitive Limitations   Some infant psychologists question Piaget's six stages because they believe the descriptions of the stages confuse the child's motor abilities with his or her cognitive or thinking abilities (Meltzoff et al., 1991). Object permanence, for example, implicitly depends on a child's capacity to conduct a manual search: to walk around the room, lift and inspect objects, and the like. Perhaps younger infants "lack" classic object permanence, this argument goes, simply because they lack motor skills or at best use them only clumsily.

To test this possibility, psychologists have designed new tests of object permanence that require only visual search rather than motor coordination (Baillargeon, 1993). In one experiment, infants were habituated to (repeatedly shown) the sight of a toy car sliding down an inclined track from the left and then rolling off to the right, as shown

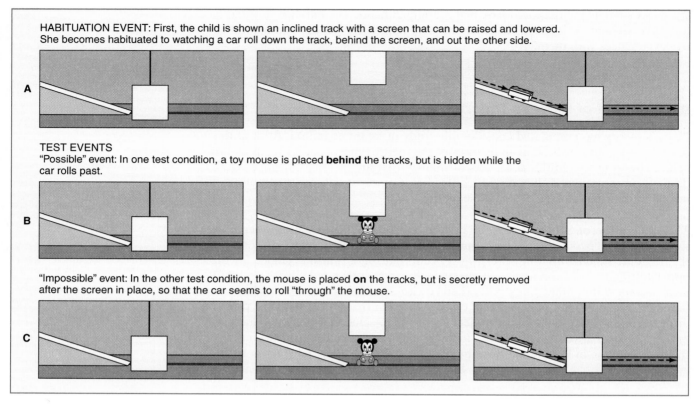

HABITUATION EVENT: First, the child is shown an inclined track with a screen that can be raised and lowered. She becomes habituated to watching a car roll down the track, behind the screen, and out the other side.

A

TEST EVENTS
"Possible" event: In one test condition, a toy mouse is placed **behind** the tracks, but is hidden while the car rolls past.

B

"Impossible" event: In the other test condition, the mouse is placed **on** the tracks, but is secretly removed after the screen in place, so that the car seems to roll "through" the mouse.

C

FIGURE 6.3

Evidence of Object Permanence in Infants

First, the infant becomes habituated to watching a car roll down a track, behind a screen, and out the other side. In one test condition, a toy mouse is placed behind the tracks but is hidden while the car rolls past. In the other test condition, the mouse is placed on the tracks but is secretly removed after the screen is in place so that the car seems to roll "through" the mouse. Infants stare longer at the second impossible event, suggesting that they already "believe in" object permanence.
Source: Baillargeon & DeVos (1991).

in Figure 6.3. In the middle of this track was a small screen concealing the middle portion of the track and obstructing a view of the car for part of its trip along the track. During habituation, the babies watched the car slide down the ramp, behind the screen, and out the other side. Between car trips, the screen was lifted temporarily to show that there was nothing behind it that might affect the car's movements.

After the infants had gotten used to seeing this setup and watching the car disappear and reappear predictably, they were shown one of two test events. In the first event, the screen was lifted and a toy mouse was placed directly behind the tracks. Then the screen was lowered, and the car made its usual run down the ramp and out the right side of the screen. This was called the "possible test event." The second test event was the same, except that the toy mouse was placed directly *on* the tracks. Then the screen was lowered, the car was released, it disappeared behind the screen, and—surprise!—it reappeared out the right side of the screen anyway, even though the mouse had been placed on the tracks. This was called the "impossible test event." In reality, the experimenters secretly removed the toy mouse before the car could hit it, using a hole concealed in the back of the test apparatus.

Under these conditions, infants as young as 3½ months looked significantly longer at the *im*possible test event than at the possible test event. The most plausible interpretation is that the impossible event violated assumptions the infants made about the permanence of objects: they seemed to assume the toy mouse should cause a collision, presumably because they believed it continued to exist behind the screen even when they could not see it. They also seemed to assume objects retain their usual physical properties even when invisible—that the car could not simply pass through the mouse, for example, just because it was hidden.

This evidence of early object permanence, though, does not mean young infants are ready yet to reason about hidden objects in the ways older children or adults might do. If a preschool child experienced the experiment just described, he or she would very likely suspect a trick of some sort and consciously puzzle over what the trick might be. The three- or four-month-old infant still has much developing to do before being able to do this kind of thinking. By requiring manual search skills, Piaget's tasks may have delayed children from displaying their preexisting object permanence until rudimentary reasoning skills had become established. Hence Piaget's assertion that full object permanence (the stage 6 described earlier) involves conscious problem solving: a deliberate search for the object.

The Effects of Memory   Piaget explains most infant thinking in terms of motor schemes: repeated, familiar actions that allow infants to understand their environment. The AnotB error in particular supposedly reflects the child's dependence on overt actions or motor schemes of this type. But does it really? Maybe the error really shows the infant's poor memory, which has not yet developed very far. After all, in the AnotB task, the baby at least has to remember, first, that the toy has been moved recently, and second, that it began by lying under the first blanket. As obvious as these ideas may seem to adults, a young infant may have trouble remembering them.

Considerable evidence suggests that memory does in fact affect infants' performance on many tasks, including, but not limited to, the AnotB task (Baillargeon, 1993). Imposing slight delays—just a few seconds—on the infant's search interferes with appropriately searching for an object much more for younger infants than for older ones. Much of the change may reflect younger infants' difficulties in attending to and retaining relevant cues about the object to be searched for. Younger babies seem to remember less of what they are looking for.

These trends imply that infants may have a notion of object permanence, but find it demanding to remember the relevant facts needed to search: where they last saw the object and when and whether the object was in fact moved. The most complete explanation of the AnotB error, therefore, may involve both motor and memory development: infants probably use memory when they can, but supplement it with Piagetian motor schemes whenever necessary (Case, 1992). If an infant cannot recall where a toy is hidden, at least she can reenact the means she used to find it in the past. This multiple strategy actually resembles the way adults sometimes search for a lost object: if you cannot recall where you left it, you may retrace your steps up to the time you remember seeing it last—in essence, using an action scheme.

Performance Versus Competence   These questions about motivation illustrate a more general problem with Piagetian theory as applied to both children and infants: by emphasizing the nature of competence, it tends to neglect the immediate causes of performance. An infant—or anyone, for that matter—may be *able* to do something but not perform the action for any of a number of reasons. Even if an infant shows his highest competence in one situation, he may fail, for various reasons, to do so in a situation that differs from the first one only slightly. As mentioned earlier, even a few seconds' delay can change some infants' success rates on the AnotB task, creating very different impressions about their underlying competence based on performance. Problems with distinguishing competence from performance crop up throughout psychology and throughout developmental psychology in particular.

What Do You Think?

Between about eight and twelve months of age, many babies show distress at separations from their primary caregiver (usually the mother). Some psychologists suggest that the distress is a partial result of their budding belief in object permanence. Do you think this might be true? How you might explain your position to a new parent who is concerned about her baby's distress?

BEHAVIORAL LEARNING IN INFANCY

One framework for studying the specific performance of infants has come from **behaviorism,** or what psychologists sometimes also call *learning theory*. As described in Chapter 2, learning theory focuses on changes in particular behaviors (sometimes called *responses*) and on the specific, observable causes and consequences (reinforcements, or lack thereof, and punishments) of those behaviors. Typically, learning theorists identify three kinds of behavioral learning: classical conditioning, operant conditioning, and imitation.

Infants show signs of all three types of learning, at least by about age three months. Infant psychologists have not concentrated equally on each type of learning, however; rather, the majority of studies of infant learning concern operant conditioning (Lipsitt, 1990). This fact makes conclusions about operant conditioning in infants more definite than those about the other types.

Classical Conditioning

As described in Chapter 2, classical conditioning consists of transferring control of a reflex response by pairing two stimuli together. One of the stimuli (the unconditioned stimulus, or US) is chosen from among those that automatically produce a particular unconditioned response (UR). The other (the conditioned stimulus, or CS), is chosen from among those that do not. Figure 6.4 shows a simple example of how classical conditioning might occur for an infant.

Although it may matter little whether an infant blinks to music, certain other classically conditioned behaviors may significantly affect an infant's long-term development. One example is the conditioning associated with a parent's face, a stimulus that initially is relatively neutral. Looking at a parent usually occurs together with a variety of emotional and physiological responses. Hunger pangs and hunger satisfaction often *both* occur in the presence of the parent's face, because the parent usually approaches the baby when she is hungry and stays with her until she has finished feeding. The process is shown in Figure 6.5.

Eventually, therefore, the mere sight of the parent can trigger both positive and negative responses in the child. Classical conditioning occurs reliably and clearly from about age six months onward (Lipsitt, 1990). Before that age, however, efforts to demonstrate this kind of conditioning have produced conflicting results. Some infant reflexes prove conditionable to some neutral stimuli, but not all combinations of stimuli and responses can be conditioned. For example, a musical tone can be

FIGURE 6.4

Classical Conditioning in Infancy: A Simple Example

In its most basic form, classical conditioning involves pairing an unconditioned stimulus (puff of air) and an unconditioned response (eye blink) with a neutral stimulus (musical tone) repeatedly until the stimulus becomes conditioned to elicit the response as well.

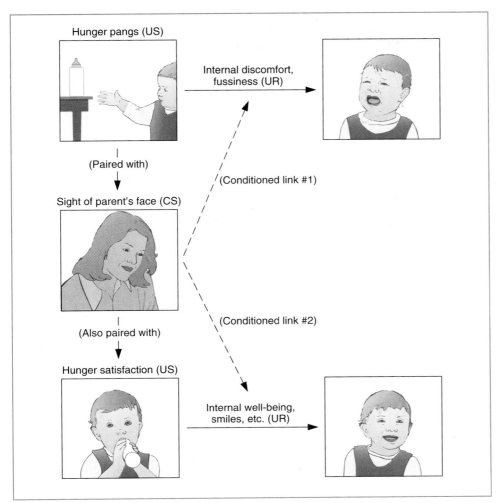

Hunger pangs (US)

(Paired with)

Sight of parent's face (CS)

(Conditioned link #1)

Internal discomfort, fussiness (UR)

(Also paired with)

(Conditioned link #2)

Hunger satisfaction (US)

Internal well-being, smiles, etc. (UR)

FIGURE 6.5
Classical Conditioning in Infancy: A More Complex Example
With infants (as with other human beings), more than one response can sometimes be conditioned to the same stimulus, creating ambivalent, or mixed, responses. In this case, the infant has learned to associate her caregiver with both hunger and hunger satisfaction.

conditioned to an eyeblink response even in three-month-old infants, but it cannot be successfully conditioned to a reflexive change in infants' pupil size. A change in lighting can reliably make infants' pupils shrink, but pairing a tone with the change in lighting does not condition this reflex, no matter how many pairings occur.

These irregularities imply that young infants may be genetically prepared to learn certain kinds of connections from their environment and genetically constrained from or limited in learning others. Perhaps they are especially sensitive to some connections in their world, such as a tone and a puff of air, but not others, such as a tone and a change in brightness. Because such constraints have long been recognized in studies of conditioning among animals, it seems reasonable to expect analogous limitations among human beings (Harper, 1988, Chapter 3). As infants become toddlers, they presumably overcome some of these limitations in classical conditioning, because their ability to think and reason begins to govern their responses to stimuli as well as classical conditioning.

Operant Conditioning

In operant conditioning as most infants experience it, a child gets a reward, or positive reinforcement, if she performs some simple action or set of actions. By turning her head, for example, she may get to see an interesting toy or picture. In this case the reinforcement is viewing the interesting toy, and head turning becomes the learned, or conditioned, behavior. Such actions tend to be performed more often than actions that are not reinforced.

Working with Gillian Luppiwiski, INFANT CARE PROVIDER

Fostering Infants' Thinking

Gillian Luppiwiski has worked as a caregiver in an infant day care center for ten years. She made numerous comments about her work: the changes she sees in the babies as they grow, the responses of mothers and fathers, the interest that even infants and toddlers show in one another. When I asked her to comment on infants' thinking abilities, she began talking about their language and problem-solving behaviors and about how she and other caregivers support it.

Kelvin: What do you notice most about these children when you're working here?

Gillian: They change so much! Like day and night. Last fall Jocelyn could hardly move; she got so frustrated watching the older children walk around! But now she's all over the place, into *everything*—and happy as a lark.

Kelvin: Can you figure out what she thinks about? Does it even make sense to ask about her "thoughts"?

Gillian: Oh, yes. Like when we get out the play doh, and she starts using it—poking it with her fingers, talking about it. She just started naming it, you know; she says "doh" and looks at you with a smile. And "wed" when it's red. That's her favorite color.

Kelvin: So her language is developing?

Gillian: Yes, and the play doh helps with that. It gives her something to talk about. We support her comments, saying things like "That's right! We've got red play doh today."

Kelvin: What about other times? Even when she's not talking, does it seem like Jocelyn's "thinking"?

Gillian: Definitely! Take the climber: she loves to climb up there and sit with Joel. That teaches her about space and depth, but she learns more by *doing* it than by talking about it. Shelley (another caregiver) might talk about it, comment on it verbally when she sees Jocelyn climbing. But Jocelyn mainly learns it by doing it.

Kelvin: Do you ever "teach" them anything directly?

Gillian: We don't so much teach them as make it possible for them to learn. That's how I'd put it. Shelley or I might put out a few puzzles one day, and talk with a child when she chooses to work on one—encourage her to persist in putting it together, maybe give a hint or two, but not do it for her.

Or the other day Danny started getting out *all* the trucks! He lined them all up with the big ones at one end and the smaller ones at the other end. Sorted them! It was great to see. He needed help, though, in finding enough room to do this without tripping over Jocelyn and the others. He commented on the lineup: "All the trucks!" And so did I, by challenging him gently: "Are you sure you have them *all*?"

Kelvin: So he was grouping? Classifying things?

Gillian: Yes. In his own way, his own two-year-old way. "Developmentally appropriate practice"—that's what educators are always talking about. That's what makes us a real *infant* center, and different from a preschool center. We try to provide developmentally appropriate things and support the children for using them.

What Do You Think?

1. Considering what Gillian said, how important is an infant care center for fostering a child's thinking ability? How does it compare to experiences that an infant or toddler might have at home?

2. Gillian says, "We don't so much teach them as make it possible for them to learn." How comfortable are you with this idea? Can it apply to working with older children (preschoolers, school-age, adolescents) or only to infants and toddlers? Consult with a few classmates about this question; what do they think about it?

3. At times Gillian seems to equate language development with cognitive development. Is there some way to distinguish these two processes in an infant center? Brainstorm an example or two of how you might do this if you were a caregiver.

As the examples of research in this chapter show, infants are quite capable of learning through operant conditioning. Newborns will learn to suck on their hands longer if doing so yields a tiny amount of sugar water delivered through a tube in the corners of their mouths. Or they will learn to blink their eyes more often if doing so causes a pleasant voice to speak or a melody to play. One reason infants seem to learn to breast feed so easily is the strong reinforcement the behavior brings in the form of mother's milk and being touched and held closely.

As with classical conditioning, infants are predisposed to learn these particular behaviors. All examples of operant conditioning in infants rely on those few behaviors that young babies already exhibit, which are mainly their inborn reflexes. By nature, reflexes occur easily—in fact, almost *too* easily. As parents often discover, any slight provocation, such as a touch on the baby's cheek, can stimulate sucking movements in young babies. Such readiness to respond creates confusion about when infant responses really constitute learning rather than general excitement. For example, when do sucking movements show true operant learning: a specific behavior performed more often because a particular reinforcement results from it? And when do sucking movements simply amount to a reflex that is itching to occur, so to speak, and would occur in response to almost any stimulus?

The confusion between learning and excitement diminishes as babies grow older, because they acquire behaviors that are more truly voluntary. Even as babies get older, however, they acquire many behaviors, both desirable and regrettable, through what appears to be operant conditioning. A six- or nine-month-old will babble longer and more frequently if parents smile and express praise when he does so. A twelve-month-old will learn to wave good-bye sooner and more frequently if reinforced with praise or encouragement. And a two-year-old may learn to scream at her older sibling when she wants a toy the older child has because her screaming has been inadvertently re-inforced: it causes the older child to simply abandon the toy, or it summons a parent who assumes (not always accurately) the older child somehow caused the screaming.

Of course, these effects refer primarily to immediate, short-term ones, which sometimes differ from long-term effects of reinforcement. An example often impor-tant to parents is crying: will picking up the baby to quiet his crying actually reinforce him for crying in the long term? Conditioning theory would predict that it would, but most research on the impact of crying has found that fast, sensitive response to crying actually leads to *less* crying (St. James-Roberts et al., 1993). However, the quieting is not reliable in the short term, but may take many months to become a definite, obvi-ous response to being picked up. This is a long enough delay to cause parents a lot of worry about whether they are "spoiling" their child by responding to her crying.

Imitation

As make-believe play demonstrates, children obviously learn to imitate at some point in development. But exactly how early, and by what processes? Early research on these questions generally suggested that infants can engage in different kinds of imitation at different points during infancy (Piaget, 1962). It found that infants imitated actions they could literally see themselves perform (for example, in a mirror) sooner than those they could observe only in a model. Much research over the past two decades confirms this hypothesis. Imitating a hand gesture such as waving, for example, proves easier than imitating an unusual face made by an adult (Meltzoff & Kubl, 1994). Also,

Imitation provides a rich source of learning for most children, even during infancy. This toddler appears to be learning how to brush his teeth by copying his mother! To be effective, though, imitation requires both sym-bolic thought and the development of motor skills.

deferred imitation may not appear until close to a child's second birthday; by that time, the child can imitate a gesture an entire day after seeing a model perform it.

Despite their preference for visible actions, infants sometimes imitate actions that are relatively invisible to themselves. One-week-old babies tend to stick out their tongues in imitation of adults and wiggle their fingers after seeing adults model this behavior. Distinguishing voluntary imitation from general, automatic excitement, however, remains a problem, as it does with other studies of very young babies. One research study highlighted this ambiguity especially well. It showed babies pictures of human faces depicting various emotions (Kaitz et al., 1988). Although the babies responded with emotional facial expressions of their own, their expressions did not match those in the pictures. In fact, the emotions on the babies' faces were hard to classify at all; they just looked "wrought up" at the sight of expressive human faces. At present, therefore, we still have more to learn about the origins of imitation during the newborn period.

Perspectives

Extremes in Language Acquisition: What Do They Mean?

As mentioned in this chapter and again in Chapter 9, children vary enormously in the rate at which they acquire language. Figure 6.6 shows just how dramatic the differences are for one aspect of language, vocabulary. The graph compares the top 10 percent of infants with the bottom 10 percent as judged by the number of words each group understands and produces in normal conversation (Fenson et al., 1994). At age ten months, for example, the low group can understand about 10 words and produce none; at the same age, the high group already understands about 150 words and can produce about 10. By sixteen months, the low group still has not caught up: these infants then understand about 90 words, compared to the high group's 350 words. At sixteen months, the low group can also produce about 10 words—similar to the high group eight months earlier—but the high group has begun using about 180 words. Equally dramatic diversity exists for other features of language acquisition, such as the acquisition of syntax and the use of the nonverbal gestures that accompany normal discourse.

Should parents and other caregivers become concerned about such extremes? Are the "slow" infants showing some sort of language disorder and the "fast" infants showing signs of genius? Although it is tempting to think so, the research evidence suggests a more complicated interpretation (Bates et al., 1995). For one thing, children often follow individual pathways toward full language acquisition, pathways that do not necessarily parallel the path taken by children as a group. Whereas children as a group experience a burst in vocabulary learning during the second year of life, for example, individual children actually experience this increase in a variety of ways: some increase their vocabularies slowly and steadily, others increase it in sudden but small steps, and still others delay this learning for several months (Bates & Carnevale, 1993).

Second, different features of language are normally learned at different times and have different rates and patterns of acquisition. Receptive vocabulary (words understood) is generally learned sooner than expressive vocabulary (words produced), though not necessarily. Vocabulary that refers to objects is generally learned quickly before a baby's first birthday, after which vocabulary that refers to feelings undergoes a period of rapid growth (Bates et al., 1994), but again not for every child. In reality, an individual infant or toddler may acquire one feature of language more quickly than another, yet still end up with serviceable language skills in the end.

Extreme delay or acceleration is also ambiguous, because most observations of it are relative only to average trends in English. Do infants in other language communities acquire individual features of language at a pace and sequence similar to those of English-speaking infants? Language researchers have begun to study this question, but will have to do much more work on many languages before they have definitive answers. Part of the problem stems from the differences in structure of the world's languages. Compared to English, for example, some languages have more numerous verb forms (look at the multiple verb conjugations in French!), which may pose special challenges to a one-year-old infant even if her parents or older siblings are quite capable of learning and using them.

What Do You Think?

How do you suppose *mothers* might become conditioned to breast feeding, either positively or negatively? Think about "what's in it" for them, as well as what hassles breast feeding can create. If possible, talk to one or two breast-feeding mothers about their experiences (preferably one who has breast fed more than one baby). Then write an "advice sheet" to help expectant mothers maximize the satisfactions of breast feeding (operant conditioning) as well as associate breast feeding with positive experiences and feelings (classical conditioning).

LANGUAGE ACQUISITION

When Michael, the son of one of the authors, was an infant, he went through several phases in using language:

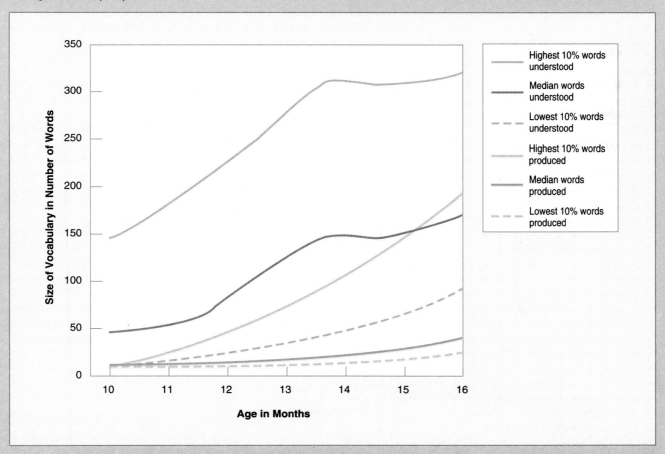

FIGURE 6.6
Extremes in Vocabulary Acquisition
Vocabulary is one of the most variable features of language acquisition. Some infants already produce more words at ten months than other infants produce at sixteen months, and the diversity is almost as dramatic for words understood (but not produced). However, the differences do not necessarily persist into later childhood.
Source: Fenson et al. (1994).

At twelve weeks, Michael made open-mouthed, cooing noises when he was feeling content. Sometimes these sounds were vaguely similar to ordinary vowel sounds, but they seemed to vary unpredictably. Michael cooed a lot in the morning when he first woke up, which pleased his father and mother.

By six months, Michael had added consonant sounds to his vocalizations to produce complicated babbling noises. His most productive time for this activity continued to be the morning, although he "said" quite a lot whenever he was feeling generally content. Certain sounds seemed to be favorites: *da* and *gn*. Sometimes Michael repeated these and other sounds—*da, da, da, da.* His father thought Michael repeated sounds when he was feeling especially happy.

At fifteen months, Michael could produce about six words, but he did not pronounce them as adults would. The family cat was *dat;* his favorite food, yogurt, sounded like *yugun;* and airplanes were simply *der!* (as in "Look there!"). He seemed to understand dozens of words and sentences, although it was hard to be sure because he probably picked up clues about meaning from the behavior of his parents. When Michael was tired one day, he came immediately when his mother said, "Come sit here" in a sympathetic tone of voice. But when she said the same thing in a cross tone of voice the next day, he looked at her with an impish smile and went the other way.

One day close to his second birthday, Michael sat "reading" a children's book to himself. Occasionally real phrases could be heard ("bug ate leaf"), but mostly Michael sounded as though he were mumbling or talking in the next room. When he finished, he walked to the kitchen and phrased a three-word question: "What's for lunch?"

As these examples show, language is a fundamental feature of infant and child development and an equally fundamental concern for parents, teachers, and other professionals who work with children (see the accompanying Perspectives box for a discussion of some of these concerns). A great deal of language develops during infancy; indeed, language is one of the most clearly human of all developments of this age period and perhaps of the entire lifespan.

Language has several aspects, and infants must acquire them all to become verbally competent. When listed separately, the array is an impressive set of achievements for such young people!

- They must learn the sounds of the language (its **phonology**).
- They must learn its words (its **lexicon**).
- They must learn the meanings of words (**semantics**).
- They must learn the purposes and ways in which words and sentences normally get used in conversation (**pragmatics**).
- They must piece together the organization of words into sentences and connected discourse (**syntax**).

Infants must acquire all of these aspects of language to be able to express their feelings, get what they want, and describe their activities to others.

Phonology and semantics develop rapidly during infancy and, therefore, are the focus of this chapter. Syntax begins rapid development only late in infancy, when children begin combining words into phrases and sentences. Pragmatics begins early but continues to undergo important developments throughout childhood. Because of these differences in timing, we discuss syntax along with other aspects of early childhood cognition in Chapter 9. We briefly discuss language use (pragmatics) in this chapter, but also say more about it in Chapter 9. In this section, we emphasize how children acquire phonology and describe their earliest achievements in semantics and the pragmatic uses of language.

Phonology

Every language uses a finite number of **phonemes,** or sounds that speakers of the language consider distinctive and that combine to make the words of the language. English has about forty-one phonemes; other languages have more or fewer than this number. Specific phonemes result from particular physical arrangements of the vocal apparatus: the tongue, mouth, nose, throat, and vocal cords. Often very small physical changes in the apparatus can create distinctly different phonemes. The sounds /th/ and /t/, for example, differ primarily in how tightly the tongue is held against the upper teeth. Other equally small changes may be routinely ignored by native speakers. The /k/ in *key,* for example, actually sounds different than the /k/ in *ski.* The first is made by releasing a puff of air (called *aspiration*) from the roof of the mouth; the second involves little or no puff of air and sounds closer to a clicking noise. What matters is not the objective, auditory features of the sound but whether speakers of the language normally perceive occurrences of the sound as equivalent. If they do, as in the examples of /k/, the sounds are defined as examples of one phoneme. If they do not, as in /t/ and /th/, the sounds are defined as different phonemes.

Perceiving Phonemes   In acquiring language, infants must be sensitive to phonemes and ignore any meaningless variations. Although the task may seem demanding, it actually proves surprisingly easy, even for a baby—so easy, in fact, that some language specialists suspect human beings are genetically and physiologically predisposed toward noticing phonemic differences (Archibald, 1995).

A variety of evidence supports this possibility. As mentioned earlier, infants just one month old can distinguish between vocalizations and nonhuman sounds. They tend to turn toward the source of the vocalizing and to show other physical signs of attending to human voices even in the midst of nonhuman noise. At the very least, such attention should make learning phonemic distinctions possible, although not inevitable.

Infants also seem predisposed to hear certain phonemes categorically, meaning they perceive sounds as belonging completely to one phoneme or another and never as somewhere in between (Jusczyk et al., 1990). Such categorical perception should make language acquisition inherently easier. However, it is not a uniquely human ability. Similar perceptual abilities exist in rhesus monkeys and even in chinchillas (Kuhl & Padden, 1983); yet monkeys and chinchillas do not learn to talk! Presumably they lack other crucial skills, anatomy, and experiences that human infants normally have. So perception of phonemes must be necessary to language acquisition but not sufficient for it.

Babbling   Although skill at producing phonemes takes longer to develop, it too seems biologically influenced. Sometime between four and eight months of age, infants begin babbling in increasingly complex ways. They apparently do so for the sole reward of hearing themselves vocalize, a form of play with sound and an example of a Piagetian primary circular reaction.

What suggests that babbling is motivated intrinsically? The most important evidence is the fact that all physically normal infants begin babbling at about the same age (about six months), regardless of the culture or language to which they are exposed. Furthermore, an observational study of deaf infants found the babies "babbling" with their hands. These infants could not babble orally, but they had been exposed to American Sign Language and were observed to make repetitive hand gestures analogous to the oral babbling of hearing infants (Pettito & Marentette, 1991).

Despite this finding, most research suggests a significant influence on babbling by parents and other members of an infant's language community. Although the study on deaf infants observed a type of babbling in these babies, the fact that the babbling was gestural rather than oral suggests that the infants' language environment influenced the form their babbling took. Other research on deaf infants has confirmed this conclusion. Contrary to a long-held belief, deaf infants do *not* babble orally in the same way hearing infants do; rather, they begin oral babbling some months later, and even then babble only if they hear sound that is amplified, such as through a hearing aid (Marschark, 1993).

Research on hearing infants also shows that the language environment shapes oral babbling significantly (Emmorey & Reilly, 1995). If you ask listeners to guess the language background of a babbling baby from hearing a tape recording of the child, their success rates are not perfect, but success is much better than chance. If the infant belongs to French-speaking parents, for example, she seems to produce sounds characteristic of French speakers rather than sounds of some other language group.

Despite this evidence of bias, babies make many babbling sounds unrelated to their native language. When infants finally limit their sounds to their own language, they apparently do so partly by their own choice and in an effort to produce their first real words. At that point, which occurs around the first birthday, parents' language also starts influencing infants' language more directly, as we explain later in this chapter. Overall, therefore, infants who babble do not use sounds as symbols. In playing with sounds, they show an important prerequisite for later communication with people.

Semantics and First Words

The semantics (or meanings) of a language, and of words in particular, are never mastered fully even by adults. To test this idea on yourself, scan any page of a large, unabridged dictionary and see how far you go before you encounter an unfamiliar word. Most people, it seems, never learn even a majority of the words or terms in their native language. This is because words get much of their meanings from the real world rather than from other words. Most of us simply do not live long enough to learn all of these relationships with the real world.

Learning semantics, therefore, is something children begin in infancy but do not nearly complete (see Table 6.3). Somewhere around their first birthday, most infants will use their first words or at least make sounds that parents take to be words. For a few months after that, new words are comparatively rare; but beginning around eighteen to twenty-one months, additions begin occurring at a dramatic rate. By their second birthday, infants may be using as many as fifty words appropriately, though some may still be acquiring their first words by this date and most still have only a limited command of many words. From ages two to three years vocabulary increases rapidly, thanks partly to the child's newly emerging skill in constructing longer sentences. An average three-year-old may know several hundred words; an average five- or six-year-old can use a few thousand words, or about one-half the vocabulary she or he will ever command, even as an adult (Anglin, 1993). Note, however, that these averages hide large differences among individual children, both in the overall size of their vocabularies and, as explained next, in the types of words they learn.

These figures refer only to children's **expressive language,** their ability to actually use words and sentences appropriately in conversation. Expressive language is complemented by **receptive language,** the ability to understand or comprehend lan-

TABLE 6.3   *Milestones in Language Acquisition During Infancy*

Approximate Age	Vocal Accomplishment
4 weeks	Cries of displeasure
12 weeks	Contented cooing, squealing, gurgling; occasional vowel sounds
20 weeks	First signs of babbling; most vowel sounds, but only occasional consonants
6 months	Babbling well established: full range of vowel sounds and many consonants
12 months	Babbling includes the melody or intonation of the language; utterances signal emotions; first words are produced; the child understands several words and simple commands
18 months	Expressive vocabulary of between 3 and 50 words; intricate babbling interspersed with real words; occasional two- and three-word sentences
24 months	Expressive vocabulary of between 50 and 300 words, although not all used accurately; babbling gone; many two-word sentences or even longer; nonadult grammar; the child understands most simple language intended for him or her

Source: P. DeVilliers & Devilliers (1978)

guage used by others. Generally, receptive language develops sooner than expressive language does; put in plainer terms, babies can understand more than they can say (Bates et al., 1988). The difference in receptive and expressive capacities shows up in many exchanges between parents and their infants. For example, if a father asks his ten-month-old, "Can I have a bite of your cookie?", the baby may offer him one. But the infant may not use any of those words himself for several more months and may not combine them into a sentence for another year or more.

Individual Differences in First Words   What words do children use first? On the whole, they prefer nominals—labels for objects, people, and events—much more than other kinds of words, such as verbs or modifiers (Hart, 1991). Among nominals, they are most likely to name things that are used frequently or that stand out in some way. The child's own mother or father therefore may be named early, but not always as early as the parents expect. *Dog* may appear as an early word more often than *sun* or *diaper* does, even though children probably experience the latter two objects more frequently than they do dogs.

Other research has found that children vary in how much they emphasize different language functions in their first utterances (Bloom, 1993). Most children have a *referential style,* meaning their first words refer to objects and objective events—*car, book,* and so on. Others have an *expressive style,* using words to express feelings and relationships—*hello* and *goody!* During the second year of life, infants with a referential style tend to make more rapid advances in vocabulary, though whether this advantage continues into the preschool years is unclear. Presumably these differences are encouraged partly by differing family environments. Some families may speak of objects more often than they do of feelings, or vice versa. But to some extent, word preferences may also represent a learning strategy adopted by the child; just as she may find a word easier if she already knows the phonemes in it, she may also find an utterance easier if she already has used similar ones on previous occasions.

Influencing Language Acquisition

Although many of these comments may make language acquisition seem beyond human influence, adults do in fact affect this process. The most important influence is

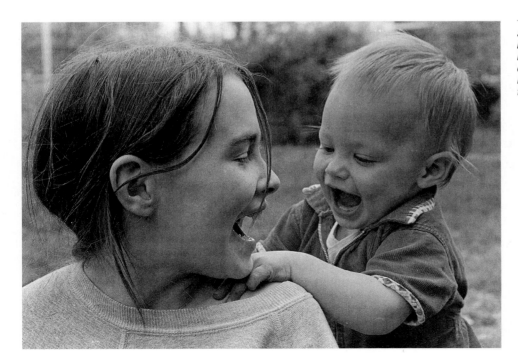

Siblings serve as important models of behavior and language for younger infants as they grow and develop. What do you suppose this girl is saying to her infant sister, and what do you suppose the infant will learn from it?

A Multicultural View

Cognitive Effects of Talking to Infants: A Cross-Cultural Perspective

Although the text implies strong support for mothers' talking with their infants, a different impression of this practice occurs if you view it in a cross-cultural context. Then the frequent one-way "conversations" and direct gazing between mother and baby seem a bit less natural or inevitable, and even a bit strange.

In North America, the practice is widely regarded as a positive experience: talking with and gazing at a nonverbal infant increases in frequency until the child begins producing her own language, around the first birthday, and cuddling and holding close decrease at the same time. Parents are even given professional assistance when these changes in interaction do not occur (Yoder & Warren, 1993)! Mothers themselves believe that talking with and gazing at infants stimulates infants' intellectual competence.

Research evidence seems to support the mothers' belief. Children who have verbally interactive mothers during infancy do show better language comprehension as four-year-olds and do show higher competence at solving simple problems involving both verbal and nonverbal reasoning (Bornstein & Tamis-Lemonda, 1989). But

there is contrary evidence as well. In China, for example, mothers talk to infants relatively little but cuddle and hold them relatively a lot (Ho, 1994). Yet Chinese culture values educational success and Chinese children perform well in school.

The fact is that the effects of maternal talk on infants are not really clear. But it is probably not a matter of stimulating thinking and language development, as many mothers themselves might believe. Maternal talk probably is much too complex for a two- or three-month-old infant to learn by hearing it directly. Instead of providing a language model directly, therefore, early verbal interaction may serve other purposes in infants' development: maybe it simply reflects the mother's general interest in and responsiveness to her child. Parents who enjoy talking to their babies as newborns are likely to still enjoy talking to them several years later, when the babies have become capable of learning and using language more effectively. If so, the relationship between early talk and later competence is a good example of a *correlation* (an association) that is not also a *cause*. In that case, too, North American mothers could (in theory) talk with their

parents, as you might expect. But other adult caregivers can also make a difference for infants and toddlers who have regular contact with them.

Parental Influences   Even when infants are very young, parents often talk to them as though they were full-fledged adult partners in a conversation (though not equally in all cultures; see the accompanying Multicultural View box). Consider this mother speaking to her three-month-old child:

MOTHER: How is Kristi today? *(pause)* How are you? *(pause)* Good, you say? *(pause)* Are you feeling good? *(pause)* I'm glad for that. *(pause)* Yes, I am. *(pause)* What would you like now? *(pause)* Your soother? *(pause)* Um? *(pause)* Is that what you want? *(pause)* Okay, here it is.

By asking questions in this "conversation," the mother implies that Kristi is capable of responding, even though her infant is much too young to do so. Furthermore, the mother leaves pauses for her baby's hypothetical responses. Observations of these kinds of pauses show that they last just about as long as in conversations between adults (Roth, 1987); it is as though the mother is giving her baby a turn to speak before taking another turn herself. When her child remains silent, the mother even replies on her behalf. In all these behaviors, the mother teaches something about turn taking in conversations, and she expresses her faith that the infant eventually will learn these conventions herself.

When infants finally begin speaking, parents continue this strategy. At the same time, however, they also simplify their language significantly. Sentences become

Constant close contact between caregiver and infant, as between this mother and her children, may encourage more nonverbal communication and result in infants who fuss relatively little. Crying and fussing, which we associate with infancy in our society, may actually be a precursor to verbal communication, which parents tend to encourage in North American society.

newborns a good deal less in the earliest months and still expect the babies to end up with good language skills eventually! This would be true, though, only if a mother were responsive and caring throughout the child's infancy, and only if the mother did begin interacting verbally as soon as the infant showed signs of actually understanding and using language. This developmental pattern in fact describes mother-infant relationships in China to a certain extent (though not perfectly).

These ideas remain speculation, though, because mothers' language practices cannot, and probably should not, be manipulated simply to explore their effects on children. In any society, parents need to interact with their babies in ways they consider natural. But comparing cultural beliefs can nonetheless give clues about the deeper, less obvious effects of particular cultural practices (Greenfield, 1994). Mother-infant "conversations" are a good example of a culture-bound practice: virtually all parent advice books urge parents to talk with their babies. Yet in doing so, the books join parents in assuming a particular cultural value: that skillful oral expression is desirable and should be encouraged as much as possible.

shorter, although not as short as the child's, and vocabulary becomes simpler, although less restricted than the child's (Gallaway & Richards, 1994). These extra strategies help teach a new lesson, namely that words and sentences do, in fact, communicate and that language is more than interesting noises and babbling. By keeping just ahead of the infant's own linguistic skills, parents can stimulate the further development of language.

This style is called **infant-directed speech,** or *caregiver speech,* meaning a dialect or a version of language characteristic of parents talking with young children. In addition to shorter sentences and simpler vocabulary, speech in "motherese" has several unique features. It tends to unfold more slowly than speech between adults and to use a higher and more variable, or singsong, pitch; it generally contains unusually strong emphasis on key words ("Give me your *cup*"). Parents speaking motherese also tend to repeat or paraphrase themselves more than usual ("Give me the cup. The cup. Find the cup, and give it."). These features seem to make the speech more understandable to the child. When adults listen to sentences with the words acoustically muffled, they can guess the emotional tone or "message" from the pitch patterns of the muffled words. More important, though, is that they can do so most accurately if the sentences have the exaggerated pitch patterns of infant-directed speech (Fernald, 1989).

Research shows clearly that parents' conversations with babies are extremely important to the infants' development. The Harvard Preschool Project, a longitudinal study conducted at Harvard University, observed the contacts between parents and their infants that occurred naturally in the families' own homes (B. White, 1993). At various intervals, the infants were assessed for both intelligence and social skills. When the assessments were correlated with the results of the home observations, one result stood out clearly: the most intellectually and socially competent infants had parents who directed large amounts of language at them. The most

As its name implies, "infant-directed speech" is a style of talking that happens only between adult and child. It uses simplified grammar and vocabulary, repetitive phrases, and exaggerated intonations that may assist infants to acquire language.

competent babies received about twice as much language as the least competent infants in this study did. But the most competent infants also stimulated interactions with their parents, primarily by procuring various simple kinds of help, such as in pouring a glass of juice or placing the final block on a tower. These "services" probably benefited the infants by offering many opportunities for parents to talk with them ("Shall I put the block on top?").

More recent research shows that certain types of conversation can encourage children's language development (Bloom, 1993). One helpful kind is *contingent dialogue,* or conversation that responds sensitively, specifically, and immediately to children's verbalizations. When an infant says "Teddy?" to his parent, for example, the parent does not ignore the comment but replies or extends it meaningfully, perhaps by saying, "I'm not sure where Teddy is; I haven't seen him this morning" or "Would you like Teddy now?"

Another valuable kind of conversation is "scripted" or *textual dialogue,* routine or ritualized language embedded in a highly familiar situation. The setting itself is so familiar that it assists in interpreting the language. Many everyday routines promote this kind of language: bathing and diapering, for example, encourage the same predictable remarks time after time ("Are you wet?"; "First let's take your shirt off"). So do children's songs and nursery rhymes. Despite their repetitiveness—in fact, precisely because of it—textual dialogues allow children to place language in a larger, more meaningful context.

Paradoxically, however, a bit of parental *insensitivity* or conversational *incompetence* also may help infants develop their language skills. Expressing moderate ignorance about an infant's intended meanings can challenge the infant to speak more fully and explicitly. This sort of "beneficial ignorance" may account for how fathers and siblings assist in the development of infant language. Because fathers and siblings tend to know an infant less well than mothers do (despite today's changing family roles), they speak relatively explicitly and elaborately with one- and two-year-olds and prompt relatively explicit language from the infants in return ("Do you want another drink?" instead of "Another drink?").

Influences of Professional Caregivers   Language acquisition can also be supported by other adults who interact with infants extensively, notably professional caregivers in family child care or infant care centers. Their forms of influence parallel those of parents (Koralek et al., 1993). Contingent dialogue (extending the child's verbal initiatives), for example, can easily take place at an infant care center: a toddler may name objects in the room ("Book!") or pictures displayed on the wall ("Cat!"), and the caregiver can extend those early initiatives into longer dialogues ("Yes, it's a pretty cat. Do you like cats?"). Contextual dialogue (familiar language routines or rituals) can also occur: a caregiver and child may engage in predictable exchanges in preparing to go home each day ("Have you found your coat?"; "Now zipper it up"). To succeed, these dialogues must be simplified; that is, they should rely on infant-directed or "caregiver" speech that takes the infant's early stage of language into account. Table 6.4 lists some additional ways caregivers can assist in language development.

But important differences also exist between caregiver influences and parent influences. One concerns intensity and frequency: caregivers usually do not see a particular infant or toddler for as many hours as a parent does, nor do they develop relationships as emotionally intense as parents'. Another difference concerns cultural expectations: it is common for caregivers (but rare for parents) to come from a cultural or language background that differs from the children's. The gap can create confusion and misunderstanding between caregiver and child or between caregiver and parent. If a caregiver and a child speak different primary languages, one may lack facility with some of the words and expressions needed to communicate with the other.

At a more subtle level, a language gap may contribute to differences in fundamental attitudes or values. In observing parent-teacher conferences for grade-school-age children, Patricia Greenfield found that teachers focused much more on a child's individual achievement, whereas parents focused on the child's social compatibility (Greenfield, 1995). The result was misunderstanding and dissatisfaction with the conference. Presumably a similar problem could occur between parents and caregivers of infants, though research has not yet been done to test this possibility specifically.

All things considered, parents, caregivers, and others constitute a far more positive than negative influence on language development. Given their importance to the process, it should not be surprising that nearly all children acquire high verbal competence in just a few years. Language acquisition is "overdetermined": society supports language learning in so many ways that if a child fails to experience that support in one way, she or he is likely to experience it in some other way. So most of us do learn to talk!

TABLE 6.4   ***Interactions That Support Language Development***

Interaction	Purpose
Sitting on the floor with infant and reading books, telling stories, or singing songs	Builds trust, models interesting activities using language
Holding infant close, looking into infant's face, smiling, and talking to infant	Builds trust, models dialogue or conversation
Responding to infant's first words and gestures using caregiver's own words and gestures	Encourages dialogue and conversation, shows respect for infant's language initiatives
Offering simple choices to infant verbally ("Do you want to paint or to play outside?")	Stimulates infant to attend to language; calls attention to relationship between language and actions
Encouraging infant (especially if a toddler) to express desires and resolve differences using words ("What do you want to do?")	Encourages child to practice language; demonstrates power of verbal expression

What Do You Think?

Work with five or six classmates to discover the first few words each of you spoke. Find out, too, something about the situation in which you spoke your first words. Pool your results. Are there any features common to either the words or the settings? Any ideas about why there was (or was not) common ground? If possible, pool your group's results with those from other groups until you have information from the entire class.

THE END OF INFANCY

The word *infant* comes from a Latin term meaning "not speaking." By this standard, a child approaching his second birthday is no longer an infant. He is now talking and often using more than one word at a time.

Almost from birth, the child communicates nonverbally: she smiles and frowns, gestures and babbles. She uses these skills to both develop and demonstrate her cognitive abilities, but she also uses them to develop social relationships, as described in the next chapter. Both by thinking and by communicating, the two-year-old learns who she is as well as who her parents and siblings are. At the same time, when all goes well, she becomes attached to these people as individuals, and her early, vague emotions turn into feelings with more focus. Pleasure becomes love, rage becomes anger, and anxiety becomes fearfulness. As the next chapter shows, these are not mere changes in labels; they signify real emotional and social growth.

SUMMARY OF MAJOR IDEAS

1. Perception is the immediate organization and interpretation of sensation, whereas cognition refers to all the processes (including perception) by which humans acquire and process knowledge.

Ways of Studying Perception and Cognition in Infants

2. Infants' arousal is reflected by changes in their heart rates (HRs) as long as the stimuli that caused arousal are relatively gentle and persistent.

3. Infants' recognition of the familiar is reflected by their habituation to stimuli—the tendency to attend to novel stimuli and ignore familiar ones.

Infant Perception

4. Studies of visual perception show that infants under six months of age perceive, or at least respond to, a variety of lines and patterns, such as those usually found on a human face.

5. Young infants, including newborns, show size and shape constancy in visual perception, meaning they respond to objects somewhat independently of the objects' distance and orientation.

6. Infants also show sensitivity to depth, as in the visual-cliff experiments, as well as to objects that loom at them.

7. Infants do not orient themselves in space reliably and accurately until they are nearly eighteen months old.

8. Babies can localize sounds to some extent at birth, but do not do this accurately until about six months of age.

9. Cultural background probably plays a small role in infant perception, at least during the first year of life.

Infant Cognition

10. Piaget has proposed six stages of infant cognitive development during which infants' schemes become less egocentric and increasingly symbolic and organized.

11. The most important achievement of these six stages is the use of symbolic representation, as shown by infants' increasingly firm belief in object permanence.

12. Research on Piaget's six stages generally confirms his original observations, but it also raises questions about the integration of early schemes and the effects of motor skills, memory, and motivation on infants' cognitive performance.

Behavioral Learning in Infancy

13. Learning theory offers a framework for understanding immediate, specific changes in infant behavior.

14. Like older children and adults, infants typically experience three kinds of behavioral learning: classical conditioning, operant conditioning, and imitation.

15. Behavioral learning tends to be ambiguous in infants less than three months old because it is difficult to distinguish learning from general, automatic excitement.

Language Acquisition

16. To become verbally competent, babies must learn the phonology (sound), lexicon (words), semantics (meaning), pragmatics (rules of use of language), and syntax (organization of language).
17. Babbling begins around six months of age and becomes increasingly complex until it disappears from use sometime before the infant's second birthday.
18. Infants show important individual differences in their selection of first words, but generally they use words for objects in their environment that are distinctive in some way.
19. Adults influence language acquisition mainly through modeling simplified utterances, recasting their infants' own utterances, and directing considerable language at the child as she or he grows.
20. Professional caregivers influence language acquisition in ways similar to parents, but they must also recognize the potential effects of a cultural gap between caregiver and child.

KEY TERMS

perception *(163)*
cognition *(163)*
habituation *(165)*
visual cliff *(169)*
sensorimotor intelligence *(172)*
scheme *(172)*
assimilation *(172)*
accommodation *(172)*
circular reaction *(173)*
primary circular reaction *(173)*
secondary circular reaction *(174)*
object permanence *(174)*
AnotB error *(175)*
tertiary circular reaction *(176)*
behaviorism *(181)*
phonology *(188)*
lexicon *(188)*
semantics *(188)*
pragmatics *(188)*
syntax *(188)*
phoneme *(188)*
expressive language *(190)*
receptive language *(190)*
infant-directed speech *(194)*

FOR FURTHER READING

Marshack, Marc. *The Psychological Development of Deaf Children.* New York: Oxford University Press, 1993.

This book is organized much like a small developmental psychology textbook, but it focuses completely on the development of children who are deaf or whose hearing is severely impaired. The chapters about language development make especially interesting reading. Deaf children's acquisition of American Sign Language parallels hearing children's acquisition of oral language, though with some interesting twists and differences.

Nelson, Katherine. *Narratives from the Crib.* Cambridge, Mass.: Harvard University Press, 1989.

Professor Nelson describes the earliest emergence of discourse in infants and toddlers. Her focus is not on language structure per se but on language functions or uses in communicative contexts. Skills at using language appropriately, it turns out, develop just as rapidly as grammar and vocabulary do; one realm of language development does not wait for another realm before undergoing its own evolution.

Rogoff, Barbara. *Apprenticeship in Thinking: Cognitive Development in Social Context.* New York: Oxford University Press, 1990.

Rutkowski, Julie. *The Computational Infant.* New York: Harvester Wheatsheaf, 1993.

Here are two books about infancy written from very different perspectives. Barbara Rogoff's book is based on a Vygotskian perspective (see Chapter 2 for more on that) and emphasizes the ways infants as individuals "borrow," or take in, thinking. Julie Rutkowski's book is based on an information-processing perspective (see Chapter 2 again) and shows how much (maybe even most) of infants' thinking is analogous to computerlike processing, especially if you assume the computer is gradually improving its capacities because of earlier experiences.

White, Burton. *The First Three Years of Life.* Rev. ed. New York: Simon and Schuster, 1993.

This is a relatively popular parent advice book with a distinctly cognitive emphasis. Much of the advice is based on the results of an important project about infant education that occurred in the early 1980s and was directed by Burton White. His advice is generally sensible, and he misses few opportunities to encourage parents to stimulate their infants' thinking wherever possible.

7

THE FIRST TWO YEARS

Psychosocial Development

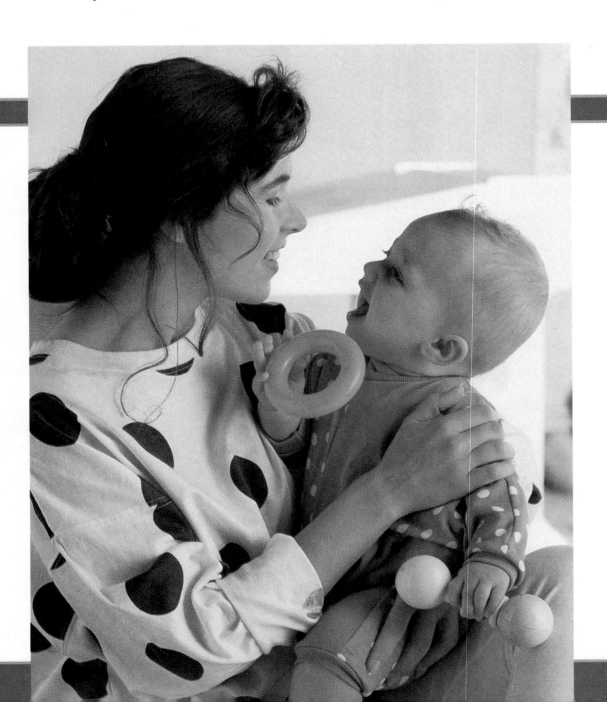

Emotions and Temperament in Infancy

Emotions in Infancy
Temperament

Early Social Relationships

Transition to Parenthood
Caregiver-Infant Synchrony
Social Interactions with Fathers and Siblings
Interactions with Nonparental Caregivers
Interactions with Peers

Attachment Formation

Phases of Attachment Formation
Assessing Attachment: The "Strange Situation"
Consequences of Different Attachment Patterns
Influences on Attachment Formation
Limitations of Attachment Theory

Toddlerhood and the Emergence of Autonomy

Sources of Autonomy
Development of Self-knowledge and Self-awareness
Development of Competence and Self-esteem

The Competent Toddler

Focusing Questions

• In what ways is a newborn infant capable of participating in the social world? How does caregiver-infant synchrony expand an infant's social capabilities?

• What emotional capabilities does an infant have? How do differences in infants' temperaments affect their social development?

• What experiences enable an infant to develop secure emotional attachments with their caregivers? What are the consequences if secure attachments fail to develop?

• How do an infant's interactions with father, siblings, and peers differ from those with his or her mother? What are the effects of day care and maternal employment on infant and toddler development?

• Why is autonomy so central to development during toddlerhood? What qualities of parenting contribute to its successful development?

E ven as a newborn, Alberto was an easy baby to feed and comfort. He was also very active and responsive to the sights and sounds in his environment. Even when tired or overstimulated by the people around him, he seemed able to calm himself with just a little help from his caregiver. When he was five weeks old, Alberto just loved attention. His smiles and excitement were irresistible, and he responded to anyone who paid attention to him—from his parents to his older brother and sisters to Luisa, the family dog. However, a special mutual responsiveness seemed to be present whenever Alberto interacted with his mother, Maria, or his father, José. With either of them, Alberto's smiles, sounds, and movements seemed so highly in tune with theirs that they appeared to be having a real conversation.

By the time Alberto was four months old, he began to show a preference for his mother and his oldest sister, Lydia, who helped Maria care for him. When he saw or heard either of them, he became especially happy, active, and noisy, which caused some jealousy among other family members.

Between ages nine and eleven months, Alberto's preferences for specific people became much stronger and more obvious. He clearly preferred his mother to any other adult and responded to his sister Lydia more than to any of the other children. Now able to crawl, he tried to follow his mother wherever she went, and he cried when she left the room. During this period, he also began to do something he had never done before: he sometimes became upset when unfamiliar people visited, even if they were friendly to him.

By the time he was almost two, Alberto was walking and talking well, had begun toilet training, and could do many things himself. He continued to be an active and happy child, but sometimes he became frustrated and upset if he did not succeed at a task. Fortunately, talking to him and giving him just the right amount of helpful guidance usually worked. Although he still demanded a good deal of attention from his mother and still preferred to play with Lydia, he rarely got upset when other family members cared for him. He also seemed quite happy to socialize with almost all friendly visitors, even those he had never met before.

These changes in Alberto are typical of some of the important psychosocial changes that occur during infancy. Infancy is the time when children learn to walk, think, talk, and, in a very broad sense, become more fully "human." From the moment of birth, infants differ in their characteristic activity levels and stylistic patterns of responding to the people and events in their new environment. And although infants highly depend on their caregivers to meet their needs, they are anything but passive. Infants become active, sophisticated observers and participants in their own psychosocial development.

As an infant grows older, she comes to form close and enduring emotional attachments with the important people in her life and sometimes shows her concerns about them very dramatically. She wails when a strange nurse approaches her in the doctor's office, and she greets her mother or father warmly when one of them

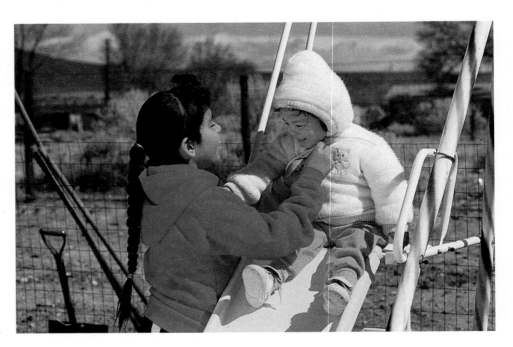

Each member of a family has a unique style of interacting with a new infant.

"rescues" her from the nurse. At other times, the baby may participate in relationships in more subtle ways, such as attending closely to older brothers and sisters while they play—more closely than her siblings attend to her. At still other times, she may express her needs or feelings in ways that confound the people around her; for example, she may refuse particular foods when a parent offers them but take them happily from a baby sitter.

These behaviors convey two major themes of psychosocial development in infancy: trust and autonomy. Infants learn what to expect from the important people in their lives. They develop strong feelings about whom they do (and do not) like to be with and what foods they prefer. The conflicts of trust versus mistrust and autonomy versus shame and doubt intertwine closely during their first two years, although many observers of children believe trust develops earlier than autonomy does (Erikson, 1963; Maccoby, 1980; Stern, 1985a).

In this chapter, we first discuss the important roles emotions and temperament play in infancy. Next, we explore the essential role of early social interactions and attachments in the development of trust and in the achievement of autonomy. We examine the ways in which attachments are formed. Finally, we look at the emergence of self-knowledge and self-awareness during later infancy and toddlerhood.

EMOTIONS AND TEMPERAMENT IN INFANCY

The healthy cries of a newborn infant make it clear that infants are capable of feeling and expressing their emotions even at birth. During the first three months, infants spend about two hours crying during a typical day. Healthy babies produce four types of cries—the basic hunger cry, the angry cry, the pain cry, and the fussy irregular cry—all of which provide their caregivers with useful information about their physiological states of discomfort (Bruner, 1983; St. James-Roberts & Halil, 1991). For most parents, however, the pattern of caregiving behaviors is not highly correlated with the specific causes of the infant's cries, meaning mothers and other caregivers tend to use the same basic routines to respond to the infant's different cries. These include rocking or moving the baby in a rhythmic manner; talking or making soothing sounds; holding the baby upright against their shoulder; touching the baby by patting, rubbing, kissing, and hugging; cradling the baby in their arms; checking the baby's diaper, or feeding the baby; giving a pacifier; or showing the baby a toy or some other feature of the environment. Parents and other caregivers also use context (such as how recently the baby was fed or changed) to determine the meanings of the baby's cries (Gustafson & Harris, 1990). Over time, as infants gain better control over their crying, crying serves to convey a wider range of messages to their caregivers (Zeskind et al., 1985). In the following sections, we discuss the role of early emotions and *temperament*—the infant's characteristic way of feeling and responding.

Emotions in Infancy

While researchers have long recognized changes in infants' crying, smiling, frustrations, and fear of strangers and novel stimuli, there is now a growing appreciation of the range and complexity of infant emotions. This appreciation has taken some time to develop because infants' limited awareness of their emotions and ability to communicate their feelings has made the scientific study of infant emotions difficult. For example, videotape studies reveal that an infant only a few weeks old is able to produce facial expressions corresponding to the range of adult emotional states, even though the infant's expressions of emotion, particularly negative emotions, do not always result from the same events that typically produce them in adults. Similarly, while physiological aspects of emotion, such as changes in heart rate, can be reliably measured, their relationships to specific emotions are not always clear (Camras et al., 1993; Oster et al., 1992). One reason for this lack of specificity is that babies' expectations and understandings appear to play an important role in their emotional reactions. For example, an incongruous stimulus, such as a mother's face covered with a mask, will produce a fear response in some situations but smiling and laughter in others.

While researchers still disagree about the earliest age at which particular emotions are present, they generally agree that most babies can reliably express basic joy and laughter by three or four months, fear by five to eight months, and more complex emotions such as shame, embarrassment, guilt, envy, and pride during toddlerhood (Izard, 1994; Izard & Malatesta, 1987; Lewis, 1992; Lewis et al., 1989; Weinberg & Tronick, 1994). Table 7.1 shows the approximate ages at which certain infant emotions appear.

Expressions of emotion play an important role in development by providing vital information to infants and their caregivers about ongoing experiences and interactions. Caregivers "read" these messages and use them to guide their actions in helping the infant to fulfill his needs (Gianino & Tronick, 1988; Tronick, 1989). Very young infants also appear to be sensitive to the positive and negative emotions of their caregivers; they are quite capable of responding to adult fears and anxieties. These responses are likely based on cues similar to those adults use, such as slight variations in voice quality, smell, and touch, as well as variations in facial expression and body language. As they get older, infants display these feelings with increasing frequency and predictability.

Another important change in the emotional life of an infant is the baby's growing ability to *self-regulate* her own emotional states. During the first year of life, an infant's emotional activities also serve as coping behaviors that allow the baby to regulate her own expressive behaviors and associated emotional states, especially negative ones. These *self-directed regulatory behaviors* include looking away, self-comforting, and self-stimulation. They allow the infant to control her negative feelings by shifting

TABLE 7.1 **Development of Infant Emotions**

Approximate Age (in months)	Emotion
0–1	Social smile
3	Pleasure smile
3–4	Wariness
4–7	Joy, anger
4	Surprise
5–9	Fear
18	Shame

Sources: Izard (1982); Sroufe (1979).

her attention away from a disturbing event or by substituting positive for negative stimuli. This helps the infant adjust her emotional state to a comfortable level at which she can successfully maintain interaction with her surroundings (Gianino & Tronick, 1988; Thompson, 1990; Tronick, 1989). During the second year, increases in the capacity for emotional self-regulation also reflect her growing ability to respond to the feelings and needs of others through helping, sharing, and providing comfort (Zahn-Waxler et al., 1992). Claire Kopp (1982) has proposed that the modulation, or self-regulation, of behavior develops over a series of five successive phases. These phases are described in Table 7.2. Emotional self-regulation in infancy from the viewpoint of development theorists was discussed in Chapter 2.

Temperament

Temperament refers to an individual's consistent pattern or style of reacting to a broad range of environmental events and situations. Most researchers agree that differences in primary reaction tendencies such as sensitivity to visual or verbal stimulation, emotional responsiveness, and sociability appear to be present at birth, prior to any significant interaction with the external environment. However, researchers disagree on how much such differences are due solely to genetic inheritance and how much they reflect prenatal influences and more subtle environmental experiences during and shortly after birth (Kagan & Snidman, 1991; Kagan et al., 1995; Rothbart, 1989). Although studies have found that identical twins are significantly more alike than fraternal twins in smiling behavior and in the tendency to be anxious or curious in response to strangers, they may elicit more similar responses from their parents than fraternal twins do, making it hard to sort out the reasons for these early differences (Freedman, 1976; Plomin & Rowe, 1979).

TABLE 7.2 **Development of Behavioral Self-Regulation (modulation) During Infancy: Phases of Self-Regulation**

Phases	Approximate Ages	Features	Cognitive Requisites
Neurophysiological modulation	Birth to 2–3 months	Modulation of arousal, activation of organized patterns of behavior	
Sensorimotor modulation	3 months–9 months+	Change ongoing behavior in response to events and stimuli in environment	
Control	12 months–18 months+	Awareness of social demands of a situation and initiate, maintain, cease physical acts, communication, etc. accordingly; compliance, self-initiated monitoring	Intentionality, goal-directed behavior, conscious awareness of action, memory of existential self
Self-control	24 months+	As above; delay upon request; behave according to social expectations in the absence of external monitors	Representational thinking and recall memory, symbolic thinking, continuing sense of identity
Self-regulation	36 months+	As above; flexibility of control processes that meet changing situational demands	Strategy production, conscious introspection, etc.

Source: Kopp (1982), p. 202. Table 2.

During phase 1 (neurophysiological modulation), the infant becomes able to regulate its patterns and states of sleep, arousal, and waking activity. During phase 2 (sensorimotor modulation), the sensorimotor schemes described by Piaget are used to regulate behavior. During phase 3 (control), the infant intentionally controls and directs its behavior and is aware of the social demands of others. During phase 4 (self-control), language and representational thinking allow increased behavioral self-control. During phase 5 (self-regulation), self-control becomes more conscious, purposeful, and flexible in response to changing demands of the situation.

A Talk with . . . Jennifer, Age Eight Months, and Her Parents

Infant Temperament

The following is part of an interview conducted with the Granoff family in the living room of their apartment. Members of the family are Jennifer, age eight months; her brother, Thomas, age three; her sister, Loretta, age fifteen; and her parents, Joyce and Michael.

Interviewer: You mentioned earlier that Jennifer has been an easy baby from the time she was born. Please tell me more about that.

Michael: She has always had a very even disposition. The only time she is ever cranky is when she needs to sleep or when she's hungry, but we usually feed her often enough, so that doesn't happen too much.

Joyce: She is an extremely regular baby. She goes to bed every night at about the same time and sleeps all night long. When she wakes up, she is cheerful and waits patiently in her crib until we get there. Sometimes we don't even know that she's awake. Some babies are grumpy. They wake up screaming and crying. Her brother is sometimes that way. People I used to work with have a little girl who's a little younger than Jennifer, and a completely different baby—wiry, squirmy, and difficult to hold and to comfort.

Interviewer: Is it harder or easier to have that kind of baby?

Joyce: I don't know. I think that her parents find her more difficult. She seems to need to interact with her parents all of the time and constantly demands attention. Jennifer is remarkably independent. And although she'll fuss a little if she realizes that you have left her by herself in her room for more than a couple of minutes, once you come back, then she'll be all right. Her brother, Thomas, was very different. It was always a struggle to put him to sleep, and he was much more difficult to comfort.

Interviewer: What calms Jennifer when she's unhappy?

Michael: Singing, food, walking with her, rocking her, sitting with her on the couch.

Interviewer: Do different things work for different children?

Michael: I think that many of the same things work, but there are also differences. One of the things that worked for her brother was patting him on the back, which she doesn't like. It has never worked for her. She could care less. I keep trying to do it, and it's never worked.

Joyce: The astonishing thing about having more than one kid is how unique they are.

Interviewer: How early can you tell that?

Joyce: From the first day.

Michael: I probably can't say the first day, though I'm sure that Joyce can. I would say I definitely noticed it in the first week, though.

Interviewer: Your husband mentioned earlier that Thomas was much more active and communicative from the start.

Joyce: Oh, he was. It was clear very early that he was tuned into exactly what we were doing. His doctor called him a very visual kid. He was always looking, looking, looking at everything. You could always see that he was intensely interested in things around him. Jennifer is also interested and curious. Her brother was more focused. She'll get interested and curious, but without that intensity. She'll get interested in things that come her way or will play by herself. He reaches out. He'll look out at things, for example, when he's riding in a car.

Interviewer: You seem to have a strong feeling that temperamental differences are important.

Joyce: Yes, I do. Often I feel that kids turn out to be the way they are. You really can't do much about it. Their temperaments seem to come with them. You can mold and shape other things, but temperament seems to be pretty much set.

What Do You Think?

1. How can you explain Jennifer's qualities that her parents describe without referring to the concept of temperament?

2. How closely does Joyce and Michael's understanding of temperament fit with the discussion in this chapter? In what ways does it differ?

3. If you could talk with them, what additional questions would you ask the Granoff family?

Parents certainly report differences in their infants' temperaments even shortly after birth. Baby Alberto and his sister Lydia, who were discussed at the beginning of this chapter, are a typical example. Their parents clearly remember that unlike Lydia, who was a fussy and somewhat difficult baby to care for and comfort during her first few months, Alberto was a very easy baby who was no trouble at all.

In a now classic study of temperament, Alexander Thomas and Stella Chess used parents' reports of differences in their babies on the following nine dimensions: (1) activity level, (2) rhythmicity (regularity of eating, sleeping, and elimination), (3)

Infants vary in temperament, from easy-going to difficult; these variations may affect their long-run development significantly.

approach-withdrawal to or from novel stimuli and situations, (4) adaptability to new people and situations, (5) emotional reactivity, (6) responsiveness to stimulation, (7) quality of mood (positive or negative), (8) distractibility, and (9) attention span (Thomas & Chess, 1977, 1981). They found three general patterns of temperament.

Easy babies (40 percent of the sample) showed mostly positive moods, regular bodily functions, and good adaptation to new situations. *Difficult babies* (10 percent) displayed negative moods, irregular bodily functions, and high stress in new situations. *Slow-to-warm-up babies* (15 percent) resembled the difficult ones but were less extreme; they were moody and relatively unadaptable, but did not react vigorously to new stimuli. Finally, *mixed-pattern babies* (35 percent) did not fall neatly into any of the first three groups.

Because the original classification of temperaments was based solely on parents' reports, which tend to be unreliable, more recent studies have used two additional measures of temperament: multiple behavior ratings (by pediatricians, nurses, teachers, and other individuals familiar with the child) and direct observation of the child. These studies have confirmed earlier findings of temperamental differences at birth (Plomin, 1989; Seifer et al., 1994).

Classifying babies by temperamental pattern has been helpful in predicting problems for the minority of children who are difficult or slow to warm up, but not for the majority of children whose temperaments are less extreme. Newborn infants whose biological rhythms are irregular, who experience discomfort during feeding and elimination, and who do not communicate their needs clearly tend to be more difficult for their parents and are more likely to experience problems in developing close relationships with them. For example, mothers of temperamentally easy infants have been found to be more positive in their caregiving, including the amount and quality of visual and physical contact and stimulation, soothing, and responsiveness to their babies' positive signals, than mothers of difficult babies (Kerr et al., 1994; van den Boom & Hoeksma, 1994).

How stable are early differences in temperament? Temperamental differences observed toward the end of the first year, including reactivity to stress, irritability, sociability, shyness, inattentiveness, and activity level, are somewhat predictive of later temperament, although predictions based on temperamental differences among newborns are considerably less reliable (Carlson et al., 1995; Gunnar et al.,

1995; Kagan & Snidman, 1991; Rothbart, 1989). Temperamental characteristics such as lack of control, approachability, and sluggishness in early childhood have been associated with similar characteristics and with behavior problems in adolescence (Caspi et al., 1995). Based on the current evidence, infant temperament alone does not appear to be very predictive of later behavior.

This may in part reflect the influence of experience and context on temperament. Temperamental qualities, much like other characteristics observable at birth (see Chapter 3), do not operate in a vacuum. In most cases, the degree to which an infant's early temperamental style contributes to personality development is likely to be influenced by the reactions the child evokes from parents and other caregivers and by how good a *fit* exists between the child's temperamental style and the attitudes, expectations, and responses of the parents. For example, the fit between an infant who is very active and demanding and parents who expect this of their new baby is likely to be much better than the fit between a similar baby and parents who expect their infant to be more passive and less demanding (Rickman & Davidson, 1995; Thomas & Chess, 1977).

Infant-family fit can also influence the degree to which infant temperament remains constant or changes. Jay Belsky and his colleagues found that changes from high to lower negativity between ages three and nine months were related to the mother's personality, the quality of mother-infant interactions, and the quality of the parents' relationship to each other. Changes from low to very low negativity between ages three and nine months were related to the father's personality, the quality of father-infant interactions, and marital factors (Belsky et al., 1991).

The particular culture a child grows up in may also influence various temperamental characteristics by assigning them different meanings and by responding to them differently. Margot Prior and her colleagues compared parent ratings of temperament in four-to-eight-month-old infants from four cultural groups: American, Chinese, Australian, and Greek (Prior et al., 1987). Table 7.3 presents their results.

Prior suggests that the temperamental differences she found may be as much a product of the mother's behavior as the infant's. For Chinese and Greek infants who are low on rhythmicity, mothers may be more "child centered," placing greater emphasis on immediately fulfilling the infant's needs. For American and Australian

TABLE 7.3 *Comparison of Infant Temperament in Four Cultural Groups*

Dimension	Cultural Group			
	American	Australian	Greek	Chinese
Activity level	H	H	L	L
Rhythmicity	H	H	L	L
Approach-withdrawal	H	H	L	L
Adaptability	H	H	L	L
Emotional reactivity	L	L	H	H
Responsiveness to stimulation	L	L	H	H
Quality of mood	H	H	L	L
Distractibility	H	H	L	L
Attention span	H	H	L	H

Note: H = high level of the temperamental quality; L = low level of the temperamental quality.

American and Australian infants were rated low on emotional reactivity and responsiveness to stimulation and high on all others. Greek infants were rated high on emotional reactivity and responsiveness to stimulation and low on all others. Chinese infants were rated high on emotional reactivity, responsiveness to stimulation, and attention span, and low on all others. Further research is needed to determine the degree to which these differences are due to child care practices and to differences that are present at birth.

Source: Prior et al. (1987).

infants (high rhythmicity), mothers are more likely to set meal and sleep times according to their own adult schedules. Similarly, the lower adaptability and distractibility scores of Greek and Chinese infants may reflect the fact that they have not learned to adapt to varying demands of the social environment as early as Australian and American infants have and may be more persistent and less easily distracted from their attempts at self-gratification. An alternative possibility is that the differences found reflect inherited group differences in temperament, an interpretation that is consistent with recent findings of temperamental differences among four-month-old infants observed in Boston; Dublin, Ireland; and Beijing, China (Kagan et al., 1995).

What conclusions can we draw? Infant temperament is certainly an important influence on early social and emotional development. In most cases, however, its contribution is best understood as a product of the ongoing interactions among an infant's inherited temperamental predispositions, the responses of his or her parents and other caregivers, and the overall developmental environment.

What Do You Think?

What advice would you give to parents about how to respond to differences in their children's temperaments? What role did temperament play in your own family?

EARLY SOCIAL RELATIONSHIPS

Infants seem to have a natural tendency to be social participants. Not only do newborns show preferences for their mothers' voices shortly after birth; some evidence also suggests that their perception of speech can be influenced by prenatal exposure to their mothers' speech (DeCasper & Spence, 1986; DeCasper et al., 1994). Immediately after birth, infants are capable of many social responses. For example, a newborn will turn his head toward the sound of a human voice and actively search for its source, attend to and show preference for a voice with a female pitch, and pause regularly in his sucking pattern for human voices but not for similar nonhuman tones. He will even prefer the smell and taste of human milk over those of formula, water, or sugar water (Brazelton, 1976).

Transition to Parenthood

Parent-child relationships begin even before a child is born. Almost as soon as pregnancy is confirmed, parents form *images* of the child, images of what she or he will be like and of how they as parents will respond and cope with this new human presence (Galinsky, 1987). They often experience both excitement and fear, the precise mix depending on how much support they have for becoming parents as well as the history of support, or lack thereof, that they had for being children themselves years ago. Even after the baby is born, these images can influence the parents' internal experiences and expectations regarding a child, although this "mental portrait" is now subject to ongoing revision based on the parents' ongoing interactions and experiences with their baby (Ferholt, 1991; Stern, 1985a, 1985b).

Having a child, particularly if it is the first, represents a major life transition that is accompanied by personal, familial, social, and, for many people, professional changes. For most parents, having a child leads them to become less concerned about themselves and more concerned with the well-being of others and about the future as embodied in their child. This parental shift away from self-centeredness

With the birth of a new baby, parents must suddenly think about their personal priorities in new ways—ways that take the child's needs into account. Getting to know the child's temperament and habits is a major challenge at first, but one at which most parents succeed.

usually comes at some emotional cost, however. During the first two years of rearing an infant, many mothers find themselves removed from much of their normal contact with other adults to devote themselves to infant care and fathers report working harder at their jobs (Bronstein, 1988; C. Cowan et al., 1991).

To accommodate the additional family tasks involved in caring for a new infant, the division of roles between husband and wife tends to become more traditional, regardless of the wife's employment, educational level, preexisting arrangements, or beliefs about gender roles. Social and emotional patterns between parents also appear to change, as reflected in significant decreases in shared leisure and sexual activities, in fewer positive interactions with each other, and in decreased marital satisfaction and greater marital conflict (C. Cowan et al., 1991; Levy-Shiff, 1995).

To better understand these changes, Rachel Levy-Shiff (1994) studied marital adjustment in 102 couples from diverse sociocultural backgrounds from pregnancy through the first eight months following the birth of their first child. She found that higher levels of *paternal involvement* with the baby, especially in caregiving, was the most important reason for the decline in marital satisfaction for *both* spouses. Levy-Schiff suggests that during the transition to parenthood, men and women must first solve the internal and interpersonal dilemmas of reorganizing their lives to adjust to the new demands and responsibilities of childrearing. In most families, the birth of a first child results in gender roles becoming more differentiated and traditional, with women assuming both the main responsibilities for child care and the majority of housework. The physical and emotional drain that new mothers experience may lead them to feel negative toward their husbands because of "overload" and because of unfulfilled prenatal expectations that caring for the new baby would be more fully shared.

Fathers who are more involved in *coparenting* and sharing housework demonstrate that they are not just husbands but also good friends who are committed to meeting their partners' needs in ways that are caring and fair. It is also likely that shared involvement in child care and the burdens of housework increase a husband's empathy and appreciation for his wife's experience. Self-respecting participation by men is also likely to reduce the guilt they would feel if they failed to take

Working with   **Rachelle Turner,** INFANT DAY CARE COORDINATOR

Understanding Infant Social Development

Rachelle is the infant coordinator in a day care center, where she has taught for the past four years. She began working as a day care teacher during her college years and plans to eventually work as a therapist in a program serving young children and their families. Rachelle was interviewed in my office.

Rob: What do you like most about working with infants?

Rachelle: I find working with infants fascinating because so much is packed into the first year of life. It's amazing to see how rapid the changes are. Because you're with the children eight hours a day, five days a week, you can observe the very small changes in development that happen, even on a week-to-week basis.

Rob: What differences in early infant temperament do you find?

Rachelle: There are differences in napping patterns, for example. If, as an infant, a child needs you to rub his back or rock him gently to go to sleep, often he will want the same kind of thing as a three-year-old when he is going down for a nap on a cot. Or you might see him rocking himself to go to sleep. On the other hand, there's the child you can just put in his crib, and he'll just grab his blanket and go to sleep. When he's older, you can say, "OK, it's nap time," and he'll get on his cot and go to sleep. It often seems like children are their own person from day one.

Rob: Do you have another example?

Rachelle: Some infants aren't happy until they can crawl and go get what they want, while others seem perfectly content with just sitting up and having you plop toys in front of them. Infants can really differ in how active or passive they are in learning to crawl or walk and in their style of exploring their physical and social world. They also differ in their moods and in whether they are irritable or not.

Rob: What about their social relationships?

Rachelle: Their changing interactions with other children are interesting. A five-month-old infant will be attracted to another child, but will not, of course, play with the child. She'll pull the other infant's hair and touch its face and clothes. She'll want to explore it and see what it is, just like a doll. Toward the end of the first year, infants recognize their friends, and smile and laugh when they see them. They now want to go on the climber or play blocks together.

Rob: So their social skills change from exploring each other as objects to interacting with each other as unique individuals?

Rachelle: Yes.

an active role in sharing these new burdens. Interestingly, by freeing up their wives' time and conveying a spirit of cooperativeness, husbands create opportunities for more high-quality time with their wives, the lack of which is a major cause of upset for many new fathers (Belsky et al., 1995; Levy-Schiff, 1995).

Caregiver-Infant Synchrony

Frequently the social interactions between parent (or other caregiver) and infant involve a pattern of close coordination and teamwork in which each waits for the other to finish before beginning to respond. This pattern of closely coordinated interaction is called **caregiver-infant synchrony.** Recall the description of Alberto at the beginning of this chapter. Even infants only a few weeks old are able to maintain and break eye contact with their mothers at regular intervals and to take turns with them in making sounds and body movements, and that videotape studies reveal that mother and baby have "conversations" that resemble adult dialogue in many ways, except for the child's lack of words (Fish et al., 1993; Stern, 1985b, 1992; Tronick, 1989).

How do such exchanges occur? A mother may gaze steadily at her baby, waiting patiently for her to vocalize, move, or at least look. When the action eventually occurs, the mother may respond by imitating the infant's gesture or by smiling or saying something. She times her responses to allow the baby a turn in this game, just as though the child were a fully competent person in a social exchange. As the interaction continues, the baby typically shows increasing tension: her movements and

Rob: What changes do you see during the second year?

Rachelle: Once they can actually say the child's name, they'll call him to come play. Games like hide-and-seek, chasing each other, or knocking blocks over together. They interact because the child makes it fun. It's not the imagination that three-year-old friends have, but it's definitely play and excitement when they see each other. They'll run up to each other, and they'll hug and kiss and be affectionate, and they know the other child isn't a doll. And if one gets hurt, they'll say, "Oh, Anne has a boo-boo," because she's a person in their life.

Rob: What have you observed about infants' ability to form attachment relationships with nonparental adult caregivers?

Rachelle: If you are affectionate and responsive to an infant's unique habits and needs around feeding, changing, and sleeping, and comforting and stimulation, she'll quickly come to know you and form an attachment to you. Particularly if a child is in day care full time, if an unfamiliar parent or delivery person comes into the center, or if a child is upset for some other reason, she will crawl or run to a caregiver or want to be held or to sit in your lap.

Rob: How does it feel from the caregiver's perspective?

Rachelle: Very strong feelings of attachment develop. Remember, unlike a typical household where laundry, cooking, and other tasks compete with child care, we spend almost all of our time observing and interacting with the children. I get very attached. When children leave, it's very hard to have children coming in and out of your life. You think about them constantly.

Rob: Are parents sometimes jealous of your relationship with their baby?

Rachelle: Yes. A parent might give the child excessive gifts, or become critical of the teacher, or make a point of telling the teacher something she didn't know about the child. I try to reassure parents by asking them for information about their child and by being interested in changes they have observed rather than just focusing on changes I have noticed.

What Do You Think?

1. What qualities do you think make a good day care teacher?

2. As a current or prospective parent, how comfortable would you feel putting your child in Rachelle's care? Why?

3. How closely do Rachelle's examples of temperamental differences and attachment fit your own understandings based on reading the chapter?

---

sounds become not only more frequent but more sudden and jerky as well. At some point, the infant becomes overstimulated and breaks the tension by looking away from her mother and spends the next few moments looking at or touching objects instead of the mother. This provides a break from sociability, although, of course, social exchanges may serve equally well as rest periods from nonsocial interactions. In any case, after a suitable interval mother and infant recapture each other's attention, and the cycle of turn taking begins all over again (Stern, 1985b, 1992).

Until an infant is several months old, responsibility for coordinating this activity rests with the caregiver. But after a few months, the baby becomes capable of initiating social interchanges and influencing the content and style of his caregiver's behavior. Not surprisingly, babies who are particularly sociable early in infancy are likely to have mothers who form especially strong emotional attachments, or connectedness, with them later in infancy (Tronick et al., 1982). Some of this continuity is created by the baby rather than the mother. The smiles, gazes, and vocalizing of a friendly infant prove hard for his mother to resist, and after several months of experience with such a baby, the mother becomes especially responsive to his communications. Presumably the mother's increased responsiveness in turn reinforces her infant's sociable nature.

Of course, older babies influence their caregivers in other ways. In a study of mothers' efforts to teach infants less than a year old to search for a hidden object, researchers found that a mother's teaching style depended a lot on how her baby acted during the orientation period that preceded the experiment. Mothers adjusted their teaching approach to the skill levels of their children. If the baby already showed some skill at reaching for objects, the mother tended simply to demonstrate

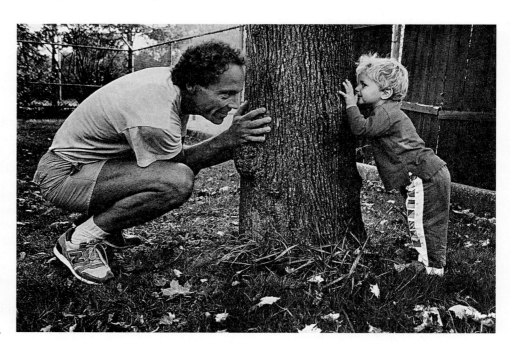

Parents and their toddlers often show a striking synchrony in their movements and gestures. In these exchanges, it is often hard to tell who is leading whom.

or model the task. If not, she was more likely to work up to the task through many steps, first placing the object visibly within easy reach, then hiding it partially, then hiding it still more (Cohn & Tronick, 1987; Dowd & Tronick, 1986). Finally, infants as young as six months are able to actively engage their mothers in helping them to achieve their goals, such as gaining access to a desired toy or helping them make a toy work (Mosier & Rogoff, 1994).

As we will see shortly, the goodness of fit between caregiver-infant temperament and a well-developed capacity for caregiver-infant synchrony are both important aspects of the development of "good enough" caregiver-infant relationships that serve as the basis for healthy development. Caregiver-infant relationships that lack the mutual awareness and responsiveness that makes synchrony possible may reflect childrearing difficulties and can place an infant at risk for developmental problems. Studies of interactions between depressed mothers and their infants, for example, have found that mothers' negative moods influence their babies' moods and can affect their longer-term relationships (Field, 1987; Isabella & Belsky, 1991; Nolen-Hoeksema et al., 1995; Radke-Yarrow et al., 1993).

Social Interactions with Fathers and Siblings

Although infants may interact more with their mothers than with anyone else, they actually live in a network of daily social relationships in which a number of other people make at least minor—and sometimes major—contributions to their social lives. Fathers often belong to this network, and so do siblings. How do a baby's contacts with these people compare to those with his or her mother?

Father-Infant Interactions   In recent years, fathers have become increasingly involved in the care of infants and young children, spending around two or three hours per day compared with nine hours for mothers. In a small but significant number of instances, fathers assume the role of primary caregiver, reversing the traditional expectations that fathers should set personal and professional goals over investing time and care in their children and the paternal role (Belsky et al., 1984b;

Garbarino, 1993; Lamb et al., 1987; Parke, 1981). Infants' social episodes with their fathers follow the same cycle of buildup and withdrawal that characterizes infants' interactions with their mothers. Success at maintaining high levels of caregiver-infant synchrony is related to the goodness of fit between their stress levels, personality characteristics, attitudes and expectations, and the characteristics and needs of the babies (Noppe et al., 1991; Yogman et al., 1977).

Nevertheless, although mothers and fathers play many of the same games, their styles differ. Play episodes with fathers tend to have sharper peaks and valleys: higher states of excitement and more sudden and complete withdrawals by the baby. Fathers tend to jostle more and talk less than mothers do, and they rough-house more and play ritual games such as peek-a-boo less. Fathers also devote more time with their babies to play than mothers do—40 percent versus 25 percent (Kotelchuck, 1976). These differences in style also appear in middle childhood, and such playful interactions may help prepare infants for future play with peers (Parke et al., 1988).

How do we explain these differences? Past experience with infants, the amount of time routinely spent with young children, difficult work schedules, and fathers' expectations about the stresses and responsibilities of parenting may all play a role. When researchers compared fathers who served as primary, full-time caregivers with fathers who took the more traditional secondary-caregiver role, they found differences in how the two groups played with their infants. Primary-caregiver fathers acted very much like mothers, smiling more and imitating their babies' facial expressions and vocalizations more than secondary-caregiver fathers did. However, all the fathers were quite physical when interacting with their infants (Field, 1987; Hwang, 1986; Noppe et al., 1991).

Interactions with Siblings   Approximately 80 percent of children in the United States and Europe grow up with siblings. The time they spend together in their early years frequently is greater than the time spent with their mothers or fathers. In many cultures, children are cared for by siblings. From age one or two they are fed, comforted, disciplined, and played with by a sister or brother who may be only three or four years older (Dunn, 1985; Weisner & Gallimore, 1977). First-born children are likely to monitor the interactions of their mother and the new baby very closely and try to become directly involved themselves. Children as young as eighteen months attempt to help in the bathing, feeding, and dressing of their sibling. At times they also try to tip over the baby's bath, spill things, and turn the kitchen upside down when they feel jealous of their mother's attention to the new baby. Conflict between siblings is most likely to occur when parents are seen as giving preferential treatment to one child (Dunn, 1985, 1988; Stewart et al., 1987).

In talking to their younger siblings, children make many of the same adjustments their parents do, using much shorter sentences, repeating comments, and using lots of action-getting techniques (baby talk, or "parentese"). In turn, infants tend to respond to their siblings in much the same way they do to their parents. But they also quickly learn the ways siblings differ from parents, particularly young siblings. Because younger children lack their parents' maturity and experience, they are less able to focus consistently on meeting the baby's needs rather than their own. For example, a four-year-old who is playing with his eight-month-old sister may not notice that she is becoming overstimulated and tired and needs to stop. On another occasion, he may become jealous of the attention she is getting and "accidentally" fall on her while giving her a hug. If parents (and other caregivers) keep in mind the needs and capabilities of each of their children and provide appropriate supervision, interactions with siblings are likely to benefit the development of both their new infant and his or her brothers and sisters.

Interactions with Nonparental Caregivers

In recent years, caregiving has become increasingly important in the lives of preschool children because many more mothers have started working outside the home, even before their children have begun public school. By 1990, about 55 to 60 percent of all mothers with children less than six years of age worked outside the home, and experts predict the proportion will rise even higher by the end of the century (Children's Defense Fund, 1992; United States Bureau of the Census, 1991). All of these parents require suitable, high-quality care for their children for either all or part of the day. The arrangements they actually make depend on the age of the child, on their own preferences (usually familylike settings), and on the kinds of services available in the community. Among all parents who work at least part time or more, about 45 percent arrange for a relative to come into the home or take the child to the relative's home (United States Bureau of the Census, 1991). Another 40 percent arrange for a nonrelative to care for the child in the child's home or, more commonly, in the caregiver's home. That leaves only about 15 percent of infants, toddlers, and preschoolers to be cared for in formal child care centers. Figure 7.1 summarizes current child care arrangements for children under two years of age.

In addition to good physical facilities and developmentally appropriate programs, high-quality care for infants is best ensured by employing caregivers who are well trained and supervised and responsive to the physical, cognitive, social, and emotional needs of infants and their families.

Grandparents   For the majority of well-functioning families, and in most cultural groups in North America, grandparents become welcome companions for the new child (Werner, 1991), as well as secondary sources of practical advice and child care. This is especially true when the grandparents live geographically close to the parents, they are relatively young and in good health, and the family itself belongs to a cultural group (such as Mexican-Americans) that values the participation of the extended family in raising children (Ramirez, 1989; Slomin, 1991).

Infant and Toddler Center Care   Almost one-half of all mothers with infants work and therefore need care for their babies. One relatively recent solution, though still

Good infant and toddler care, like good preschool care, involves stimulating children to explore their environment. These toddlers are finding much to investigate in this basket of plastic fruit and other objects.

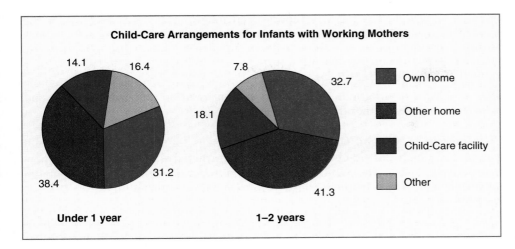

Child-Care Arrangements for Infants with Working Mothers

Under 1 year:
14.1
16.4
38.4
31.2

1–2 years:
7.8
32.7
18.1
41.3

Own home
Other home
Child-Care facility
Other

FIGURE 7.1
Current Child Care Arrangements for Working Mothers with Children under One Year and with Children Between One and Two Years
The majority of infants and toddlers whose mothers work are cared for in their own or another home. Somewhat more toddlers than infants go to child care facilities. Infants are more likely than toddlers to be cared for in "other" situations, such as accompanying their parents to work.

not common, is child care centers that specialize in serving infants and toddlers (Fein & Fox, 1990). These centers usually are regulated more strictly than centers for preschoolers are. Typically child care authorities require a closer ratio of adults to children, such as one adult for every three or four infants, as well as facilities for changing diapers, washing clothes, preparing food, and providing places for children to sleep. Often a licensed infant or toddler center must have a registered nurse on its staff, whereas a preschool center need have only a nurse or a doctor to call at a nearby clinic. Activities involve a mixture of supervised play, projects to stimulate language development, and physical routines such as sleeping, bathing, and eating. Since these requirements are relatively expensive to provide, and because controversy surrounds the very idea of out-of-home care for infants, infant and toddler centers remain much scarcer than centers for preschoolers.

Family Day Care Homes   Family day care homes care for only limited numbers of children—usually fewer than six—in the homes of the caregivers. The hours and activities tend to be similar to those for child care centers, but children's activities usually are organized in ways more similar to families. Children still engage in supervised play or crafts, for example, but they are more likely to do it together as a single group. Because the number of children and adults is smaller, the environment can feel more intimate than at a larger center and transitions between activities often occur more spontaneously and quickly.

Research on the effectiveness of family day care has found that compared to child care center programs, their success depends less on professional training and more on the family caregiver's own pride and motivation in serving children and on her or his "sense of mission" in providing particular kinds of experiences for children (Pence & Goelman, 1991). This may be partly because family caregivers work more autonomously than staff at centers do. By working at home, they are more likely to work alone rather than as part of a team and to have less opportunity to receive and therefore benefit from training. The autonomy of family day care homes is also reflected in the large (in fact, unknown) number of family day care providers who operate with no official license or government regulation. Most are women who take in a few children of friends or neighbors, sometimes simultaneously caring for their own preschool children or infants. Government child care authorities usually deplore the lack of licensing in family day care homes (Kontos, 1992; Leavitt, 1991), but because homes necessarily entail privacy, it is difficult to enforce licensing regulations.

What are the effects of family day care and infant center care? The fact that many family day care homes are unlicensed and unregulated has tended to focus research attention away from evaluating their long-term benefits and toward the more pressing tasks of assessing the qualities of family caregivers (Fischer & Eheart, 1991) and increasing the percentage of licensed family day care programs (Leavitt, 1991; M. Nelson, 1991). Judgments of the relative success of programs have been made (Pence & Goelman, 1991), but they have focused primarily on the daily processes of programs—the quality of conversation between caregiver and child, for example—rather than on long-term outcomes.

Characteristics of Good Child Care　What makes for good child care? Small group size, a high staff-to-child ratio, and a well-trained staff certainly are important (Howes, 1987). The number of children in the group should be small enough to allow caregivers to interact with each child in a stimulating and sensitive fashion. An adult-child ratio of one to four or less for children two years and younger and one to seven or less for children between two and three years are recommended. Caregiver stability and continuity also are important, because they help ensure that each child can form attachments with caregivers. Lack of continuity may make it difficult for an infant to continue to form multiple attachments and adversely affect his or her development. A turnover rate of no more than one or two primary caregivers over a year is recommended.

Finally, caregivers should have formal training in child development. Well-trained caregivers are more likely to plan care based on expectations of developmentally appropriate behaviors and to distinguish such behaviors from maladaptive ones. They are also more likely to be aware of the factors that help foster emotional relationships that are secure and developmentally supportive.

What preparation is needed to become an effective child care teacher? A study of three hundred teachers from randomly selected child care centers in five representative metropolitan areas of the United States found that for preschool teachers, a bachelor's degree in any subject or specialized training at the college level is sufficient, whereas infant and toddler teachers are more likely to need specialized college-level training to be effective (Howes et al., 1992).

Interactions with Peers

Young babies show considerable interest in other infants and in much the same ways they show interest in their parents: by gazing, smiling, and cooing. Sociability of this kind develops with peers at the same time and at the same rate that it does with parents (Field & Roopnarine, 1982; Vandell, 1980). As you might expect, babies become more social with experience. In one study of infants and toddlers in a nursery school class, all the children became friendlier with one another during the four-month semester, vocalizing, smiling, and exchanging toys more frequently. Interestingly, the infants came close to equaling the toddlers (who were fifteen months older) in both types and amounts of social behavior (Hartup, 1989; Roopnarine & Field, 1982). When given the choice, infants often prefer playing with their peers to playing with their mothers. In play situations, infants more frequently look at and follow their peers, and toddlers are more likely to talk with, imitate, and exchange toys with their peers than with their mothers (Rubenstein & Howes, 1976).

Toddlers in day care spend about 25 percent of their time interacting positively with other toddlers. They are more likely to express positive feelings and play competently with peers than with adults or when by themselves. Repeated contact with a peer in a familiar setting with a familiar caregiver and minimal adult interference appears to facilitate the development of peer friendship. Peers also support the autonomy of toddler from mother and offer the toddler an alternative source of stimulation and comfort (Hartup, 1989; Rubenstein & Howes, 1983). So far, there is no evidence that toddlers who have attended day care relate with peers differently than children who have had equal access to peer experiences in their homes.

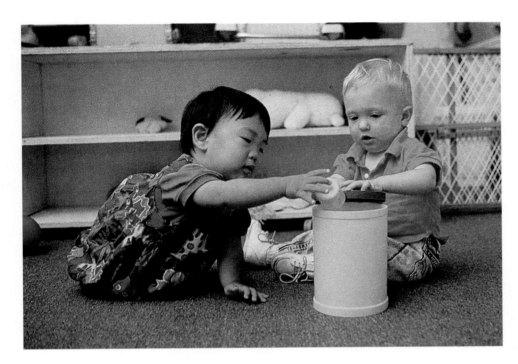

Infants show considerable interest in interacting with other infants and when given the opportunity may prefer playing with their peers than with their parents.

In conclusion, although infants' social interactions with their parents and other adult caregivers generally are their most important early social experiences, interactions with siblings and peers also contribute to their social development. The quality and developmental impact of experiences with siblings and peers will reflect to some extent the degree to which parental supervision of such contacts considers the needs of both the baby and the other children.

What Do You Think?

What advice would you give to prospective parents about maternal employment and child care arrangements for infants?

ATTACHMENT FORMATION

Attachment refers to the strong and enduring emotional bond that develops between infant and caregiver during the infant's first year of life. This relationship is characterized by reciprocal affection and a shared desire to maintain physical closeness (Ainsworth, 1973; Bowlby, 1969).

The concept of attachment has been most strongly influenced by the ethological perspective and, to a lesser extent, by the psychoanalytic approach. In the ethological view, the ties between infant and caregiver develop from the activation of a biologically based motivational system that is an inherited adaptation of human evolution. This system helped ensure survival by protecting infants from environmental dangers (Bowlby, 1969). Because the nature of the child-caregiver relationship is widely viewed as being central to successful child development, studies of attachment have come to play an important role in development theory, research, and application. Another influence has been the work of theorists who emphasize the importance of "working models," internalized social relationships with significant caretakers (Biringen, 1994).

Attachment—the tendency of young infants and their caregivers to seek physical and emotional closeness— provides an important basis for achieving secure and trusting relationships during early childhood.

Although attachment cannot be observed directly, it can be inferred from a number of commonly observed infant behaviors that help establish and maintain physical closeness with caregivers (Bowlby, 1969, 1973, 1980). Three of these behaviors—crying, cooing, and babbling—are *signaling behaviors;* four others— smiling, clinging, nonnutritional sucking, and following—are *approach behaviors.* While researchers do not agree as to whether these *specific* attachment behaviors are biologically inherited, many believe that the tendency to seek proximity is biologically determined and essential to infant survival in much the same way food is.

One important source of support for attachment theory comes from a well-known series of studies of infant rhesus monkeys by Harry Harlow (Harlow, 1959; Harlow & Harlow, 1962). Infant monkeys who were taken away from their mothers at birth and raised with artificial wire and terrycloth substitute mothers displayed many of the attachment behaviors just mentioned. When forced to choose, they preferred physical *contact comfort* with a warm, soft, terrycloth substitute mother that did not provide food to contact with a cold, hard, wire mother that provided milk from a bottle but was not soft and huggable. Harlow also found that infant monkeys that were deprived of physical closeness but were otherwise well cared for exhibited extreme fear and withdrawal, an inability to establish social and sexual relations with peers, and much higher rates of illness and death.

Although we must be cautious about drawing conclusions about human infants from studies of monkeys, Harlow's findings suggest that contact comfort, a key attachment behavior, may be a primary need during infancy that is relatively independent of the need for food and the other sources of oral pleasure that psychodynamic theorists such as Freud thought to be the basis of emotional development. They also suggest that severe deprivation of physical closeness with a caregiver may have major negative consequences for subsequent development. The work of René Spitz (1945, 1946), who studied infants reared in institutional settings, suggests that consistency and reliability of caregiver responsiveness is also important. Spitz found that infants who experienced frequent changes in caregivers and who lacked at least one caregiver who was consistently responsive to their needs found it extremely difficult to establish social and emotional infant-caregiver connections.

Currently most developmental psychologists believe attachment relationships develop over time as a cumulative product of the infant's repeated experiences in interaction with her main caregiver during the first year (Isabella, 1993). They also believe attachment involves a highly mutual and interactive partnership between caregiver and child, who both have strong, although unequal, needs to achieve physical and emotional closeness with each other. This view is influenced by recent discoveries about the interactive nature of social relations between infants and their caregivers.

Once attachment with the mother (or other primary caregiver) is established, the infant uses her as a *secure base* from which to explore the environment. As the infant gradually increases his distance from the mother, the *attachment behavioral system* and accompanying feelings of fear and anxiety are more likely to be activated, and the infant begins to seek proximity (closeness) to the caregiver once again. This pattern is also activated when the infant encounters dangers such as strangers, darkness, or animals approaching. The balance between activation of the attachment system and activation of exploratory behaviors varies with the particular context and developmental level of the child (Biringen, 1994).

Phases of Attachment Formation

According to John Bowlby (1969), attachments develop in a series of phases determined partly by cognitive changes (described in the previous chapter) and partly by interactions that appear to develop quite naturally between infants and their caregivers. Table 7.4 presents these four phases. Note that *separation anxiety,* an infant's disturbance at being separated from her caregiver, and *stranger anxiety,* a wariness and avoidance of strangers, appear near the beginning of phase 3. The achievement of object permanence (see Chapter 2) is thought to be an important basis for separation anxiety and attachment development.

TABLE 7.4   Four Stages of Attachment Formation

Phase 1: Indiscriminate Sociability (birth–2 months)

Responds actively with cries, smiles, coos, and gazes to promote contact and affection from other people; uses limited attachment behaviors less selectively than when older.

Phase 2: Attachments in the Making (2–7 months)

Increasing preference for individuals most familiar and responsive to needs; preferences reinforce parents' affection; accepts certain forms of attention and care from comparative strangers; tolerates temporary separations from parents.

Phase 3: Specific, Clear-cut Attachments (7–24 months)

Preferences for specific people become much stronger due to ability to represent persons mentally (Piaget's fourth stage of sensorimotor development; see Chapter 6); ability to crawl and walk enables toddler to seek proximity to and use caregiver as a safe base for exploration; increasing verbal skills allow greater involvement with parents and others; both *separation anxiety*—an infant's disturbance at being separated from the caregiver—and *stranger anxiety*—a wariness and avoidance of strangers— appear near the beginning of this phase.

Phase 4: Goal-coordinated Partnerships (24 months onward)

By age two, increasing representational and memory skills for objects and events; growing ability to understand parental feelings and points of view and to adjust his or her own accordingly; growing capacity to tolerate short parental absences and delays and interruptions in parents' undivided attention makes possible cooperation with others to meet needs; changing abilities are related to secure attachment relationships grounded in a sense of basic trust.

Source: Bowlby (1969).

A Multicultural View

Cross-cultural Variations in Attachment

Almost all infants become attached to their parents in some way. However, the patterns by which they do so vary around the world. Studies on the Strange Situation report that whereas 60 to 65 percent of children studied appear to be securely attached, rates of insecure attachment are much more variable (van Ijzendoorn & Kroonenberg, 1988). Among infants from northern Germany, for example, anxious-avoidant attachment patterns occur twice as often as they do among North American infants. Among infants from Japan, on the other hand, anxious-resistant responses occur approximately three times as often as they do in the United States, while anxious-resistant attachment is virtually nonexistent (Bretherton & Waters, 1985; Takahashi, 1990).

These variations result partly from differences in cultural values around the world and partly from the childrearing practices these values foster. In northern Germany, people value personal independence especially strongly (Grossmann et al., 1985) and believe children should obey parents more consistently than is usually expected in North America. As a result, infants need to learn not to make excessive demands on parents; they must minimize crying and fussing and do without extra bodily contact. During early infancy, mothers encourage these qualities by remaining relatively unresponsive to their infants' moment-by-moment behavior. Thus, in northern Germany, unresponsiveness may not signify personal rejection of the child as much as a desire to raise a good citizen. The results show up in the Strange Situation as anxious-avoidant attachment: a larger than usual number of young children seem indifferent when reunited with their mothers.

Childrearing practices probably also influence the attachment responses of Japanese children. Separations between Japanese infants and their mothers are quite rare by North American standards. Most Japanese infants have very little experience with strangers. Typically they are left alone or with another adult only two or three times per month on average, usually someone already intimate with the child, such as the father or a grandparent (Mikaye et al., 1985). Their extreme protests to the Strange Situation resemble the anxious-resistant pattern of crying, anger, fear, and clinging when the mother returns. As with the German infants, however, it is more likely that these

Assessing Attachment: The "Strange Situation"

The most widely used method for evaluating the quality of attachment to a caregiver is called the **Strange Situation.** Originally developed by Mary Ainsworth for infants who are old enough to crawl or walk, the procedure consists of eight brief social episodes with different combinations of the infant, the mother, and a strange adult (Ainsworth et al., 1978). It presents the infant with a cumulative series of stressful experiences: being in an unfamiliar place, meeting a stranger, and being separated from her caregiver.

The first episode lasts for thirty seconds and the remaining seven for three minutes each: (1) parent and infant enter the room with the experimenter; (2) parent as a secure base: the baby plays with toys and explores the room while her mother is seated; (3) reaction to an unfamiliar adult: a stranger enters the room, sits down, and talks to the mother; (4) separation anxiety: the parent leaves the infant alone with the stranger, who responds to (and comforts) the infant if necessary; (5) reaction to reunion: the parent returns, greets (comforts) the baby, and the stranger leaves; (6) separation anxiety: the mother leaves and the baby is left alone in the room; (7) comforted by a stranger: the stranger again enters the room and offers comfort to the infant; (8) reunion: the parent again returns, the stranger leaves; the parent greets/comforts the baby and tries to interest her in playing with the toys.

Based on the infants' patterns of behavior in the Strange Situation, Ainsworth and her colleagues identified three main groups. Most of the infants studied (approximately 65 to 70 percent) displayed a **secure attachment** pattern. When first alone with their mothers, they typically played happily. When the stranger entered, they were somewhat wary but continued to play without becoming upset. But when they were left alone with the stranger, they typically stopped playing and searched for or crawled after their mothers; in some cases, they cried. When the mothers returned, the babies were clearly pleased to see them and actively sought contact and behaviors represent the fulfillment of typical cultural practices rather than failures in childrearing.

Some researchers have also noted that distribution of attachment types may vary within as well as across cultures. In a study of infants from southern Germany, the distribution of attachment types did not differ significantly from those reported for infants in the United States (Grossmann & Grossmann, 1990; van Ijzendoorn & Kroonenberg, 1988). Studies of attachment among Israeli infants raised in kibbutz communities provide further evidence of cultural differences in attachment within a particular society. Kibbutz children were raised in communal peer groups by *metapelot* (nurse/educators), spending regular time with their families during evenings, weekends, and holidays. Kibbutz infants successfully formed attachments to both their parents and their communal caregivers, but a larger proportion displayed insecure attachment patterns compared to Israeli infants raised in the city or infants raised in the United States (Aviezer et al., 1994; Sagi et al., 1994).

Cultural values and practices, however, cannot explain all the differences. Even in northern Germany, for example, many babies become securely attached even though their mothers follow culturally approved practices of aloofness. In Japan, some infants become anxious-resistant even though their mothers follow essentially Western childrearing styles, which include considerable experience with baby sitters and other nonparental caregivers. Observations of these babies in their homes suggest that they were born with somewhat irritable or fussy temperaments, which may predispose them to becoming anxious-resistant despite their mothers' practices.

On balance, attachment seems to result from the combination of several influences, including cultural values, inborn temperament, and the childrearing practices of the particular family. The developmental meaning of attachment may vary too. What looks like an attachment failure for one child may be a success for another, depending on the circumstances.

interaction, staying closer to them and cuddling more than before. When left alone with the stranger again, the infants were easily comforted; although signs of distress were stronger, they quickly recovered from the upset by actively seeking contact with their mothers on their return.

The second group of infants (about 10 percent) were classified as displaying an **anxious-resistant attachment** pattern. They showed some signs of anxiety and, even in the periods preceding separation, stuck close to their mothers and explored only minimally. They were intensely upset by separation. When reunited with their mothers, they actively sought close contact with them but at the same time angrily resisted the mothers' efforts to comfort them by hitting them and pushing them away. They refused to be comforted by the stranger as well.

The third group of infants (about 20 percent) displayed an **anxious-avoidant attachment** pattern. They initially showed little involvement with their mothers, treating them and the stranger in much the same way. They rarely cried when separated and, when reunited, showed a mixed response of low-level engagement with their mothers and a tendency to avoid them.

The three attachment patterns have been studied in many other countries. In all cases, around 60 to 65 percent of the children are reported to be securely attached, whereas rates of insecure attachment are much more variable (van Ijzendoorn & Kroonenberg, 1988). The accompanying Multicultural View box discusses cross-cultural variations in attachment.

Consequences of Different Attachment Patterns

Secure attachment early in infancy benefits babies in several ways during their second year of life. For one thing, securely attached toddlers tend to cooperate better with their parents than other babies do (Londerville & Main, 1981). They comply better with rules such as "Don't run in the living room!", and they are also more willing to learn new skills and try new activities their parents show them (such as when a parent says, "Sit with me for a minute and see how I do this"). When faced with problems that are too difficult for them to solve, toddlers who are securely attached are more likely than others to seek and accept help from their parents. At age five, these children tend to adapt better than other children to changes in preschool situations (Arend et al., 1979; Matas et al., 1978; Slade, 1987).

Less securely attached infants may not learn as well from their parents (Matas et al., 1978). Anxious-resistant infants often respond with anger and resistance to their parents' attempts to help or teach them. Such babies may at times invest so much time and energy in conflicts that they are unable to benefit from their parents' experience and to explore their environment. Given a roomful of toys and a mother who has recently returned from an absence, for example, a child may use up a lot of time alternating between being angry at and snuggling with his mother instead of getting on with his play. Anxious-avoidant infants do not have this particular problem, but because of their tendency to avoid interaction with their parents, they also miss out on parental efforts to teach or help them and ultimately may discourage parents from even trying to help.

Such differences in attachment appear to persist even into the preschool years. One study found that children rated as securely attached at age one seemed more likely to seek attention in positive ways in nursery school at age four (Sroufe et al., 1983). When they needed help because of sickness or a hurt, or just wanted to be friendly, they found it easy to secure attention by approaching their teachers fairly directly, and they seemed to enjoy the attention when they received it. Less securely attached infants, whether anxious avoidant or anxious resistant, tended to grow into relatively dependent preschool children. They sought more help more frequently but seemed less satisfied with what they got. However, methods of seeking attention differed between the two groups. Anxious-resistant children showed signs of chronic complaining or whining, whereas anxious-avoidant children tended to approach their teachers very indirectly, literally taking a zigzagging path to reach them. Having done so, they typically waited passively for the teachers to notice them.

These findings do not necessarily imply that secure attachments are set early in infancy once and for all. Instead, attachment is likely to be an extended process, one that in fact takes years to unfold fully, and prediction of future adjustment based on early attachment patterns will depend on the *continuity of caregiving* the child receives (Main et al., 1985). The parental factors that contribute to a baby's insecure relationships at age one are likely to still be operating at age four, and the child's attachment style will continue to reflect the quality of her experiences with her parents. On the other hand, changes in family circumstances and in parent-child relationships can alter the quality of earlier attachments, for better or worse. For example, a reduction in family stress and an increase in social support for parenting can positively affect the way a mother responds to her infant and the quality of the mother-child relationship (Feiring et al., 1987; Thompson et al., 1982).

Although we have emphasized the major role of the parents in parent-child interactions and in the development of the attachment relationship, the process is by no means one-sided. From birth onward, the infant plays an active role in initiating and responding to interactions with his caregivers. How strongly his temperamental predispositions influence this process depends largely on how well they fit and interact with the temperaments, expectations, and capabilities of his parents.

Influences on Attachment Formation

So far we have emphasized the general aspects of attachment. In this section, we discuss some of the factors that appear to influence the quality of attachment between infants and their mothers, as well as other important caregivers.

The Role of the Mother   A major determinant of individual differences in attachment is the quality of the infant-mother relationship during the first year of life. A mother's capacity to respond sensitively and appropriately to her infant and to feel positively about her baby and the baby's strengths and limitations appears to be more important than the amount of contact or caregiving. Mothers of securely attached infants are more responsive to their babies' crying, more careful and tender in holding them, and more responsive to their particular needs and feelings during both feeding and nonfeeding interactions than are mothers of less securely attached infants (Ainsworth et al., 1978; Belsky et al., 1984b; Crockenberg & McCluskey, 1986).

Differences in infant temperament are likely to affect the mother-infant relationship and the quality of attachment. Infants with irritable temperaments tend to receive less maternal involvement, which in turn may negatively influence the quality of attachment. With the right interventions, however, such negative cycles may be interrupted.

In one recent study of the influence of temperament and mothering on attachment, Dymphna van den Boom (1994) helped mothers to respond to their temperamentally difficult six-month-old infants in more sensitive and developmentally appropriate ways by adjusting their behaviors to the infants' unique cues. Mothers gained practice in imitating their infants' behaviors and repeating their own verbal expressions. They also learned to notice when their infants were gazing at them and when they were not, and to coordinate the pace and rhythm of their own behavior with that of their infants. Mothers who received such help were found to be significantly more responsive, stimulating, visually attentive, and controlling of their infants' behavior than a similar group of mothers who did not get assistance. Intervention infants had higher scores on sociability, self-soothing, and exploration and cried less, and at twelve months of age were much more likely to be securely attached.

Being securely attached herself makes the mother more likely to have a child who is securely attached. The quality of the mother-child relationship is influenced by the mother's perceptions, expectations, and assumptions (sometimes called *working models*) about her infant, herself, and their relationship. Past mother-infant interactions, the mother's memories of her own childhood, and similar factors also may play a significant role in mother-child attachment relationships (Biringen, 1990; Stern, 1985b).

While children are most likely to form strong attachment relationships with their mothers, who most often are their primary caregivers, they may form equally strong attachments with their fathers. And because a growing number of families with young children have two working parents or are headed by a single mother who works, maternal employment and day care have come to play an increasing role in the development of attachment. In the following sections, we explore the role of fathers and the contribution of maternal employment and nonmaternal child care to the development of attachments in infancy.

The Role of the Father   Most studies have found no differences in most babies' preferred attachment figures during their first two years. Infants appear to be equally attached to both mother and father, even though the mother typically is the primary caregiver. As we pointed out earlier in the chapter, however, fathers and mothers interact with their infants somewhat differently. Fathers generally are more vigorous and physical in their interactions, and mothers are quieter and more verbal (Belsky, Lerner, & Spanier, 1984; Lamb, 1977a, 1977b).

For infants and fathers, security of attachment at twelve months can be predicted from the qualities of their interactions at three months, the father's attitudes toward and reports about the infant and the paternal role, and the amount of time spent with the infant (Cox et al., 1992). In addition, the security of attachment to one parent also appears to be closely related to the security of attachment to the other parent. Thus, an infant with a secure (or insecure) attachment to her

Good quality day care can play an important role in the lives of working mothers and their children.

Perspectives

Family-Leave Policies in the United States and Europe

In 1993, the United States enacted its first national family-leave policy, guaranteeing up to twelve weeks of unpaid leave per year to any worker who is employed for at least twenty-five hours per week at a company with more than fifty employees. Family leaves are allowed after the birth of a child or an adoption to care for a child, spouse, or parent with a serious health condition, as well as for a health condition that makes it impossible for the worker to perform a job. After the leave, the worker is assured of his or her old job or an equivalent position (*The New York Times*, 1993).

How does U.S. family-leave policy compare with that in other countries? Most industrialized countries have much more generous policies than those in the United States, providing not only more extended leaves of absence so that working parents can take care of their young children but also financial support for part or all of the leave period (Kamerman, 1991; Zigler & Frank, 1988). In Sweden, West Germany, and France, one parent can take a paid infant care leave supported by the employer or a social insurance fund. If both parents choose to continue to work, they are guaranteed access to high-quality day care for their child. In Sweden, either the mother or the father is entitled to a twelve-month paid leave to stay home with a new infant. The parent on leave is reim-

bursed 90 percent of her or his salary for the first nine months following the child's birth, receives $150 per month for the next three months, and then is allowed to continue with an unpaid leave and a job guarantee for six additional months until the child is eighteen months old. An interesting sidelight is that only a very small percentage of fathers actually take advantage of this opportunity, and when they do, the bulk of feeding and nurturance during nonwork hours still appears to be performed by the mother (Kamerman, 1991; Lamb et al., 1982).

In France, a working parent is entitled to 90 percent reimbursement for four months through the social security system and then up to two more years of unpaid leave with a job guarantee, provided she or he works for a company with more than two hundred employees. In West Germany, a parent taking a leave of absence from work is entitled to 100 percent reimbursement for three months and then $285 per month for four more months.

It seems evident that while the twelve weeks of unpaid leave provided by the recent U.S. family-leave policy is a step in the right direction, policies in Europe go much farther in helping parents to directly meet the needs of their babies without undue economic hardship and risk to their jobs.

mother is likely to have the same quality of attachment relationship to her father (Fox et al., 1991).

The Effects of Maternal Employment   As we noted earlier, approximately 50 percent of mothers with infants one year old or under and around 60 percent of mothers with three-to-five-year-olds are in the work force. The number of working mothers with young children is expected to continue to increase (United States Bureau of the Census, 1990b). Family-leave policies in the United States and Europe are discussed in the accompanying Perspectives box.

Most infants of mothers who are employed either full or part time are securely attached, although full-time employed mothers are somewhat more likely than part-time employed and nonemployed mothers to have insecurely attached infants (Belsky, 1988; Clarke-Stewart, 1989; L. Hoffman, 1989). However, these results must be viewed with caution, since the effects of maternal employment on the infant or young child are rarely direct. They are almost always based on a variety of family factors, including economic and cultural differences, the mother's "morale," the father's attitude toward his wife's employment, the type of work and number of hours it demands, the husband-wife relationship, the father's role in the family, the availability and quality of nonmaternal care, and the mother's and feelings about separation (Hoffman, 1989; Silverstein, 1991).

The work of Cynthia Stifter and her colleagues is a good example. They compared mother-child interactions and attachment patterns in families in which mothers returned to full- or part-time employment outside the home before their infants were five months old with those in families in which mothers remained home full time, and found that employment did not directly affect attachment. However, employed mothers were experiencing high levels of separation anxiety as a result of the severe time constraints imposed by work schedules and were more likely to have infants who developed anxious-avoidant attachments. Although they were equally sensitive and responsive to their infants as working mothers who were not anxious, highly anxious mothers were much more likely to be "out of synch" and overcontrolling when interacting with their infants.

The Effects of Day Care and Multiple Caregivers   The growing number of dual-wage and single-parent families and changing views about childrearing and family life have led to increased interest in nonmaternal child care to supplement the care given within families. Increased use of infant center care has also raised questions about its effects on infant and toddler development. The effects of day care and other forms of nonmaternal care on attachment in infants and toddlers are difficult to evaluate for many of the same reasons cited in the discussion of maternal employment. A child's gender, her or his temperament, the mother's (and father's) feelings about both day care and maternal employment, and the mother's reasons for working all play a role. Other factors include the type of child care arrangement (day care center, in-home day care, relative), the stability of the arrangement, the child's age of entry, the quality of day care, and the quality of the child-caregiver relationship (Belsky & Rovine, 1988; Scarr et al., 1989).

While some infant care researchers have found evidence that one-year-olds who attend centers more than twenty hours per week tend to form less secure attachments to their parents (Belsky & Nezworski, 1988; Belsky & Rovine, 1988), others have reported that negative attachment outcomes tend to be associated with little or part-time rather than full-time infant care and that babies in infant care centers show *more* social confidence than do infants reared at home (Anderson, 1989; Roggman et al., 1994).

The majority of infants receiving full-time center care actually appear to be quite securely attached to one or both of their parents (Clarke-Stewart, 1989). For

Day care, even for infants and toddlers, has few negative effects on children, as long as the care is of high quality and parents feel satisfied with it.

the minority who appear to have insecure attachments, it is not yet clear whether the infant center care per se makes them less secure or whether the variety of other factors just mentioned are responsible.

What about attachments to multiple caregivers? While expectations based on infant-mother attachment relationships may help guide an infant in forming new attachments, infants and nonmaternal caregivers are capable of establishing unique and independent relationships based more on their reciprocal exchanges and individual qualities than on a "model" developed from mother-child interactions (Zimmerman & McDonald, 1995). The attachments infants form with their center caregivers, for example, appear to be no less secure than their attachments to their parents, and the two sets of attachments are relatively independent of each other. Thus, even an infant who exhibited an insecure pattern of attachment relationships with his or her family might still form secure attachments with other caregivers (Goosens & van Ijzendoorn, 1990).

There is also evidence that in a variety of other contexts, including extended families and communal childrearing settings such as the Israeli kibbutz and the Efe people of Zaire, secure relationships with multiple professional and nonprofessional caregivers are not only possible but may also contribute to the child's well-being by either adding to a network of secure attachments or compensating for their absence (Aviezer et al., 1994; Tronick et al., 1992). On the Israeli kibbutz, infants and toddlers are raised in same-age peer groups by community child care providers. Among the Efe, infants and toddlers experience a pattern of multiple relationships—with mother, father, other adults, and children. In such cases, the extended family or community childrearing network may be more predictive of attachment relationships than the mother-child relationship alone.

Limitations of Attachment Theory

Attachment research has had mixed success at helping us understand the development of the parent-infant relationship. Atypical infants who differ from normal infants in their everyday parent-infant interactions often cannot be reliably distinguished based on attachment classifications. In addition, it frequently is not possible to reliably predict later attachment from early mother-infant attachment classifications. Tiffany Field (1987) suggests that the problem may lie in overreliance on the Strange Situation as the standard for measuring complex processes involved in the parent-infant and other caregiving relationships. The Strange Situation depends on a single occurrence of a limited number of rather specific mother-infant interactions that take place in a context that does not represent the broad range of situations within which attachment relationships naturally occur. Understanding and prediction of attachment may therefore require a more complex and ecologically meaningful model.

More valid assessments of attachment might be achieved by studying caregiver-infant interactions longitudinally over the entire first year, for longer periods of time, and in contexts that more closely represent those in which caregiver-infant relationships typically occur. There is reason to believe that the same detailed and sophisticated methods that have been helpful in studying caregiver-infant synchrony may also help us to better understand the complex parent-child interactions as well as the cognitive and affective components of the internal working models involved in attachment relationships.

What Do You Think?

What advice would you give new parents about the roles of fathers, maternal employment, and infant day care in supporting secure and responsive attachment relationships and optimal social/emotional development for their infants? What recommendations would you give to your representatives in Congress regarding programs to make infant day care available to families with both working and nonworking mothers?

TODDLERHOOD AND THE EMERGENCE OF AUTONOMY

By the second year of life, the relatively secure base of attachment that most infants have achieved with their parents and other family members allows them to begin to shift their attention outward to the physical and social world. Despite lingering anxieties about separations, the achievement of a basic sense of trust in their relationships with their caregivers enables toddlers to become increasingly interested in new people, places, and experiences. For example, an eighteen-month-old may no longer bother to smile at his mother while he plays near her, and he does not need to return to her for reassurance as often as he used to.

Parents may welcome these changes as a move toward greater independence and at the same time experience a loss of intimacy for which they may not be quite ready. But for various reasons, this shift is both inevitable and developmentally important. For one thing, an older infant can move about rather easily and therefore find much to explore without help from others. The newfound abilities to crawl, climb, and walk make her more interesting as a playmate for other children and

After their first birthday, infants begin to show increasing autonomy in their play and other activities, which sometimes leads them to unsafe situations. This autonomy is fostered by their improving motor skills and cognitive development.

thus less dependent on her parents for her social life. For another, her rapidly developing thinking and communication skills contribute to her increasing autonomy.

These competencies create new challenges for both toddlers and their families as a new developmental crisis emerges: autonomy versus shame and doubt. **Autonomy** is the ability to govern and regulate one's own thoughts, feelings, and actions freely and responsibly while overcoming feelings of shame and doubt. Toddlers must somehow practice making choices—an essential feature of autonomy—in ways that cause no serious harm to themselves or others.

Parents must learn to support their child's efforts to be autonomous, but must do so without overestimating or underestimating the child's capabilities or the external dangers and internal fears he faces. If they are unable to provide such support and instead show their disapproval of failures by shaming their child, a pattern of self-blame and doubt may develop. *Shame* appears to arise out of both the loss of approval by important people and the child's negative thoughts about himself for failing to live up to certain expectations or standards (Lewis, 1992). In such a case, the child is more likely to be either painfully shy and unsure of himself or overly demanding, self-critical, and relatively unable to undertake new activities and experiences freely.

Parents must help their infant master this crisis of autonomy by continually devising situations in which their relatively mature baby can play independently and without undue fear of interference—by putting the pots and pans within reach but hiding the knives, for instance. Children also need social as well as physical safety. Chewing on a sister's drawing or dumping the dirt out of the flowerpots may not have dangerous physical consequences, but it can have negative social effects. Thus, parents must help their infants learn how to avoid social perils by being selective about their activities.

Sources of Autonomy

Why should infants and toddlers voluntarily begin to exert self-control over their own behavior? Developmental psychologists have suggested several possible answers to this question based on the various theories outlined in Chapter 2. Each has some plausibility, although none are complete in themselves.

Identification   According to psychoanalytic theory, **identification** is the process by which children wish to become like their parents and other important attachment figures in their lives. The intensity of a young child's emotional dependence on her parents creates an intense desire to be like them to please them and guarantee their love. This dependence also creates anger because of the helplessness and fear of abandonment the infant inevitably experiences during even brief periods of separation. Because it is so upsetting to be angry at the very person you depend on for love and care, identification can also be motivated by the unconscious desire to protect oneself from the distress by being like the person who is the object of that anger. Both mechanisms, of course, may operate at once, and either may function without the child's awareness.

Operant Conditioning   **Operant conditioning** stresses the importance of reinforcement for desirable behaviors. According to this view, adults will tend to reinforce a child for more grown-up behaviors, such as independent exploration ("What did you find?") and self-restraint ("I'm glad you didn't wet your pants"). Operant conditioning resembles identification in assuming parents can motivate children, but it also assumes their influence occurs in piecemeal ways; that is, the child acquires specific behaviors rather than whole personality patterns, and the behaviors eventually add up to autonomy and self-control.

Observational Learning   According to the theory of **observational learning,** the key to acquiring autonomy and self-control lies in the child's inherent tendency to observe and imitate parents and other caregivers. If parents act gently with the child's baby sister, for example, the child will come to do so too (although his interpretation of *gently* may occasionally be influenced by feelings of sibling rivalry). Similarly, if a young child observes her mother taking pots and pans from the kitchen cabinet, it is a fair bet that she will attempt to do the same. In fact, much home "childproofing" is necessitated by a young child's skill at observational learning. The process of observational learning implies that autonomy and self-control are acquired in units, or behavioral chunks, that are bigger than those described by operant conditioning but smaller than those acquired in identification.

Social Referencing: A Common Denominator   All three explanations of developing autonomy have something in common: they involve **social referencing,** the child's sensitivity to the feelings of his parents and other adults and his ability to use these emotional cues to guide his own emotional responses and actions (Campos & Stenberg, 1981; Tronick, 1989). For example, infants and toddlers exhibit social referencing when they visit a strange place. Should they be afraid of the new objects and people or not? How safe is it to be friendly and to explore? In the absence of past experiences of their own, they evaluate such situations based on their parents' responses: if their parents are relaxed and happy, they are likely to feel that way too; if their parents are made tense or anxious by the situation, the children probably will feel that way also. Even very young infants use their caregivers and even strangers to guide their responses, for example, approaching and playing with unfamiliar toys if a nearby stranger is smiling and avoiding them if the person looks fearful (Klinnert et al., 1986).

Development of Self-knowledge and Self-awareness

The sense of self that develops late in infancy shows up in everyday situations as well as in situations involving self-control. One very interesting series of studies by Michael Lewis and his colleagues explored the development of self-knowledge in infants nine to twenty-four months old by testing their ability to recognize images of themselves in mirrors, on television, and in still photographs (M. Lewis & Brooks-Gunn, 1979a; M. Lewis et al., 1985). Because most of the infants could not verbally indicate whether or not they recognized themselves, the researchers secretly marked each infant's nose with red rouge. When placed in front of a mirror, infants from fifteen to twenty-four months of age touched their bodies or faces more frequently than they did before they were marked. Infants around fifteen to eighteen months also began to imitate their marked images by making faces, sticking out their tongues, or watching themselves disappear and reappear at the side of a mirror. These self-recognition behaviors never occurred in infants younger than fifteen months and increased from 75 percent at eighteen months to 100 percent at twenty-four months. When presented with videotaped images of themselves in which a stranger sneaked up on them, infants as young as nine months displayed self-recognition based on *contingent cues,* that is, connections between their own movements and the movements of the image they were viewing. By approximately fifteen months, infants were increasingly able to distinguish themselves from other infants by using *noncontingent cues* such as facial and other physical features (Lewis & Brooks-Gunn, 1979a).

Aspects of Self-awareness   Developmental researchers have outlined several dimensions, or themes, in the development of self-awareness toward the end of the

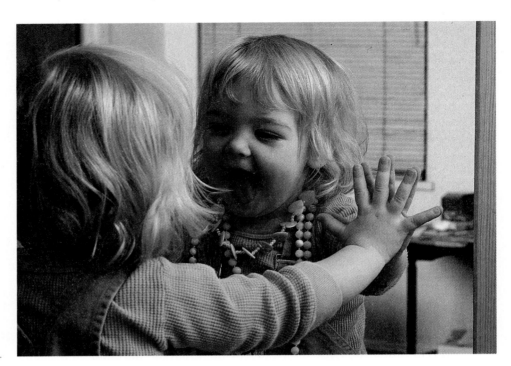

This toddler's responses to her own reflection in the mirror are an important indicator of her developing self-knowledge and self-awareness.

first year of infancy (Kagan, 1991). Although a child often expresses self-awareness in very ordinary situations, this fact does not diminish its importance to the child.

By the end of their second year, most children show an increasing appreciation of the standards and expectations of others regarding their behavior toward both people and things. For example, a broken toy can trouble a child even if he did not break it; he may show it to an adult and verbally express concern and a need for help ("Broken!" or "Daddy fix?"). A crack in the kitchen linoleum may now receive close scrutiny, even though several months earlier it went unnoticed and several months later it may go unnoticed again. Language that implies *knowledge of standards*— evaluative vocabulary such as *bad, good, dirty, nice*—appears as well (Bretherton et al., 1981). Such knowledge combines with other behaviors to suggest that the child is beginning to sense an identity for herself. There is also reason to believe that verbal and nonverbal reactions of toddlers to flawed objects are associated with the early development of a sense of morality. When faced with situations in which they believe they have been responsible for a "mishap" such as breaking a toy, toddlers' responses include acceptance of responsibility, apologies, focus on reparations (repairing the wrong), and distress (Kochanska et al., 1995).

By age two, children show satisfaction in purposely *initiating challenging activities* or behaviors for themselves, and they often smile at the results (see Figure 7.2). A child builds a tower of blocks higher than usual and smiles broadly the moment she completes it. Another makes a strange noise—say, a cat meowing—and then smiles with pride. Still another puts his teddy bear carefully to bed under a blanket and then giggles. In each case, the child confronts a task that is somewhat difficult by her current standards, but attempts it anyway. Her behavior suggests an awareness of what competent performance amounts to and of her own ability to succeed. This knowledge reflects part of her sense of self and contributes to its further development. (We discuss the development of competence more fully later in this chapter.)

Whether or not he can talk much yet, a two-year-old sometimes *directs adults' behavior*. He invites an adult to play, handing her a pretend teacup, or requests help, looking imploringly at a nearby adult after struggling unsuccessfully to open a small box. These behaviors may include language, but they do not need to; a gesture or a well-timed glance often can accomplish the same thing. Whether verbal or not, however, the child apparently believes he can influence adult behavior. In essence, he implies he is now a person living among other people, even if he still lacks many of the skills he sees in older children and adults.

Development of Competence and Self-esteem

From the beginning of infancy through the end of toddlerhood, children achieve a growing sense of basic trust, autonomy, competence, and ultimately self-esteem. In fact, these developments go hand in hand. Autonomy, as we discussed, is made possible by a child's secure and basically trustworthy relationships with her primary caregivers. **Competence** (skill and capability) develops as a result of the child's natural curiosity and desire to explore the world and the pleasure she experiences in successfully mastering and controlling that world (B. White, 1959, 1975). Much like the infant's need for proximity and attachment to her caregivers, her motivation to explore and master the world is thought to be relatively autonomous and independent of basic physiological needs for food, water, sleep, and freedom from pain.

FIGURE 7.2
Typical Daily Experiences of Young Children
This figure describes the social and nonsocial activities of infants in three age groups (twelve to fifteen months, eighteen to twenty-one months, and twenty-four to twenty-seven months) during a typical day at home. Note the higher percentage of cooperative activity for the middle group. Also, note differences in the percentage of time spent in eating, gaining information, nontask activity/passing time, and exploration and mastery among the three age groups.
Source: B. L. White (1993).

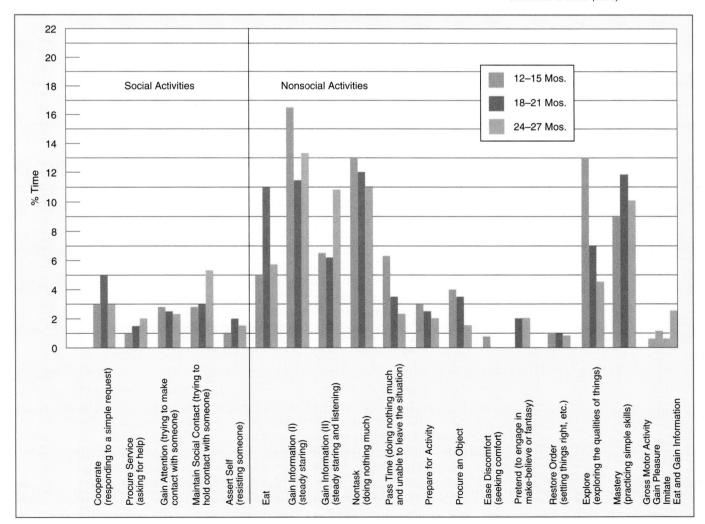

Based on many years of observational study, Burton White (1993) suggests that a socially competent toddler is likely to display capabilities in the following areas:

1. Getting and holding the attention of adults in socially acceptable ways
2. Using adults as resources after first determining that a task is too difficult
3. Expressing affection and mild annoyance to adults
4. Leading and following peers
5. Expressing affection and mild annoyance to peers
6. Competing with peers
7. Showing pride in personal accomplishment
8. Engaging in role play or make-believe activities

What everyday rules for behavior guide parents' efforts to socialize their toddlers and preschool-age children? To answer this question, Heidi Gralinski and Claire Kopp (1993) observed and interviewed mothers and their children in these age groups. They found that for fifteen-month-old toddlers, mothers' rules and requests centered on ensuring the children's safety and, to a lesser extent, protecting the families' possessions from harm; respecting basic social niceties ("Don't bite"; "No kicking"); and learning to delay getting what they wanted (versus getting it immediately). As children's ages and cognitive sophistication increased, the numbers and kinds of prohibitions and requests expanded from the original focus on child protection and interpersonal issues to family routines, self-care, and other concerns regarding the child's independence. By the time children were three, a new quality of rule emerged: "Do not scream in a restaurant, run around naked in front of company, pretend to kill your sister, hang up the phone when someone is using it, fight with children in school, play with guns, or pick your nose."

Not surprisingly, a toddler's social competence is influenced by the nature of the parent-toddler relationship. Even though they do not spend more time interacting with their children than mothers of less competent children, mothers of highly competent children support and encourage their toddlers' curiosity and desire to explore the world around them by providing a rich variety of interesting toys and experiences that are both safe and appropriate to the children's level of competence. They also play with their toddlers in ways that are responsive to the children's interests and needs and use language their infants can clearly understand.

Observations of mothers and their two-year-olds found that toddlers' capacity for both compliance with parental directions and self-assertion was associated with *authoritative parenting* relationships (see Chapter 10) consisting of a combination of control and guidance and an appropriate sharing of power with warmth, sensitivity, responsiveness, and child-centered family management techniques. High levels of defiance and parent-toddler conflict were most likely to be associated with more authoritarian, power-assertive control strategies. In situations where the toddler had said "no" to the mother, maternal negative control was most likely to elicit defiance (B. White, 1975; Crockenberg & Litman, 1990).

Mothers of competent toddlers are also more likely to encourage their children to accomplish the tasks they had initiated themselves by actively guiding them and praising them for achievements rather than actually performing the tasks for them (B. White, 1993, 1975). As you might expect, this approach requires considerable patience, the ability to tolerate the child's frustration when things do not work out the first few times, and a firm belief in the child's need and potential to be an autonomous and competent person. Perhaps the most important quality of these mothers is their ability to interact sensitively and appropriately with their children and to experience pleasure and delight (at least most of the time) in these interactions. The same quality appears to be most important in the development of secure attachment relationships and continues to be important throughout childhood.

Toddlers who grow up in supportive environments are likely to be better adjusted in their development than children whose environments are less supportive. A natural outcome of such parenting is the early emergence of a strong sense of **self-esteem:** a child's feeling that he is an important, competent, powerful, and worthwhile person whose efforts to be autonomous and take initiative are respected and valued by those around him (Erikson, 1960; Harter, 1983). The development of self-esteem during infancy and toddlerhood is closely tied to the achievement of a positive ratio of autonomy versus shame and doubt and initiative versus guilt during the developmental crises that, according to Erikson, occur during this period (Erikson, 1963). As we shall see, the childhood experiences that follow infancy continue to make major contributions to this important aspect of identity.

What Do You Think?

If you were the primary person responsible for the care of a toddler for a week, which toddler needs and behaviors would provide the biggest challenges for you? Which would be the easiest for you? Why? If you have cared for a toddler, answer in terms of your own experience.

THE COMPETENT TODDLER

In a matter of just months, a baby may have tripled in weight and doubled in height. She has learned to move about freely and independently and has formed important relationships with particular people and places. The mature toddler is starting to know that she is a unique individual like everyone else. As we saw in Chapter 6, she has also made a good start in developing her capacities to think, listen, and talk. It generally becomes clear somewhere around her second birthday that she is definitely not a baby anymore!

But what, then, has the child become? For convenience, the next several chapters simply call him a "preschooler," a child who is too young to begin elementary school. Note, however, that a considerable number of children who are not yet school age attend day care centers, family day care, or nursery school on a regular basis. Although a preschool child may be too young for elementary school, he definitely is ready—and eager—to learn more about the physical and social worlds outside his immediate family. If all has gone reasonably well up to now, he can use his family as a secure base from which to explore these larger worlds, which include the children next door, the department store downtown, and the children and teachers at a nursery school or day care setting.

From the two-year-old's point of view, home is still a very important place, but it is no longer the entire world. From her parents' point of view, the daily burden of child care has declined markedly, although it certainly has not disappeared yet. A toddler may not need to have her diapers changed for much longer, but she will still need prepared meals for years to come. She may no longer seek attention several times per hour, but she will continue to seek it many times a day. The child still has a lot of growing and learning to do in the preschool years that follow.

SUMMARY OF MAJOR IDEAS

Emotions and Temperament in Infancy

1. Infants appear to be capable of a complex range of emotional responses and are quite sensitive to the feelings of their caregivers. They probably use cues similar to those adults use, such as variations in voice quality, smell, touch, facial expression, and body language.

2. Even at birth, infants exhibit differences in temperament, their patterns of physical and emotional responsiveness and activity level. These differences both influence and are influenced by the feelings and responses of their caregivers.

Early Social Relationships

3. Newborn infants have a natural tendency to actively participate in their social world.

4. *Caregiver-infant* synchrony refers to the closely orchestrated social and emotional interactions between an infant and his or her caregiver and provides an important basis for the development of attachment relationships.

5. The similarities in the type and quality of an infant's interactions with mother and father are much greater than the differences.

6. The effects of nonmaternal care and maternal employment on infant and toddler development depend on the specific circumstances, but in general do not appear to be negative.

7. When given the opportunity to do so, infants engage in active social interactions with their siblings and peers and often prefer them to their parents as playmates.

Attachment Formation

8. Attachment, the tendency of young infants and their caregivers to seek and maintain physical and emotional closeness with each other, is thought to provide an important basis for achieving secure and trusting relationships during early infancy.

9. Attachment develops in a series of phases from indiscriminate sociability at birth to goal-coordinated partnerships at two years.

10. The Strange Situation, in which the infant is confronted with the stress of being in an unfamiliar place, meeting a stranger, and being separated from his or her parent, has been used to study the development of attachment.

11. Secure attachment is most likely to develop when the caregiver responds sensitively and appropriately to the infant and the infant can use the caregiver as a safe base for exploration.

12. Insecurely attached infants tend to be less able than securely attached infants to get help from parents and teachers when they need it or to accept it when it is offered.

13. Infants are equally capable of forming secure attachments to their mothers and to their fathers, and to other caregivers as well, even though in the majority of families the mother is the primary caregiver.

14. The effects of both maternal employment and day care on attachment depend largely on how the mother feels about herself and her role as a parent and how the situation helps or hinders her ability to care for and enjoy her baby. The quality of her experience and the quality and consistency of the day care are also important.

The Emergence of Autonomy

15. Sources of the growing autonomy that characterizes the second year of infancy include identification, operant conditioning, observational learning, and social referencing.

16. Toddlerhood also brings significant increases in self-knowledge and self-awareness. These changes are reflected in the toddler's increasing awareness of adult standards, distress at behaviors modeled by unknown adults, and tendencies to smile following an accomplishment and give directions to adults.

17. Toddlers are strongly motivated to achieve greater competence through successfully mastering and controlling the physical and social worlds around them. Competence is fostered by parents who encourage their infant's curiosity by providing opportunities that are challenging, safe, and appropriate to the child's capabilities.

18. Increased self-esteem in the infant is the natural outcome of supportive parenting.

KEY TERMS

temperament *(202)*
caregiver-infant synchrony *(208)*
attachment *(215)*
Strange Situation *(218)*
secure attachment *(218)*
anxious-resistant attachment *(219)*
anxious-avoidant attachment *(219)*

autonomy *(226)*
identification *(226)*
operant conditioning *(226)*
observational learning *(227)*
social referencing *(227)*
competence *(229)*
self-esteem *(231)*

FOR FURTHER READING

Belsky, J., R. Lerner, and G. Spanier. *The Child in the Family.* Reading, Mass.: Addison-Wesley, 1984.

This book explores how the contexts of family, work, neighborhood, culture, and society jointly and interactively influence the social and emotional development of children and their caregivers. Its discussions of such complex and timely issues as divorce, maltreatment, and the dual-worker family are particularly interesting.

Leach, P. *Babyhood.* 2nd ed. New York: Knopf, 1987.

This is a straightforward, well-documented, nontechnical, and highly informative discussion of the physical, intellectual, and emotional development of infants, with an emphasis on helping parents.

Lieberman, A. F. *The Emotional Life of the Toddler.* New York: The Free Press, 1993.

This book provides sensitive, practical coverage of the world of the toddler, including the parents' experience, temperamental differences, toddler-parent conflicts, divorce, and child care. It provides many helpful, real-life examples.

Philadelphia Child Guidance Center. *Your Child's Emotional Health: The Early Years.* New York: Macmillan, 1994.

This book explores the important issues parents must deal with during the first six years, including eating, sleeping, sexuality, discipline, shyness, fear, aggression, stress, separation anxiety, and toilet training, and offers guidance on how to effectively respond.

Phillips, D., ed. *Quality in Child Care: What Does Research Tell Us?* Washington, D.C.: National Association for the Education of Young Children, 1987.

This collection of papers reviews what researchers have found about conditions that foster quality child care.

Stern, D. N. *The First Relationship.* 4th ed. Cambridge, Mass.: Harvard University Press, 1985.

This is an updated version of Stern's readable account of the development of infant-parent communication.

White, B. *The First Three Years of Life.* Rev. ed. New York: Simon & Schuster, 1993.

Based on a TV series by the same name, this book provides interesting, detailed observational descriptions of children and their interactions with their families during the first three years of life. A particularly useful feature is its specific recommendations to parents on how to actively support the physical, emotional, and intellectual development of their child.

PART FOUR

Early Childhood

Although most of us remember relatively little of our early childhood years, parents often believe those years are among the most gratifying for their children. Perhaps this is because children begin participating in their families more fully during this time. Now they talk and play with parents and siblings much more—and, of course, they sometimes infuriate everyone more, too. In all these senses they "belong" more fully than ever.

Preschoolers become more social during this period partly because of the more complex motor skills they acquire; riding a trike or climbing a jungle gym can impress parents as well as friends. In addition, their new cognitive skills allow preschool children to engage in extended conversations and try out new social roles in play. The preschooler's world is a rapidly expanding one, and for parents as well as children, the early childhood years are both exhausting and exhilarating.

8

EARLY CHILDHOOD

Physical Development

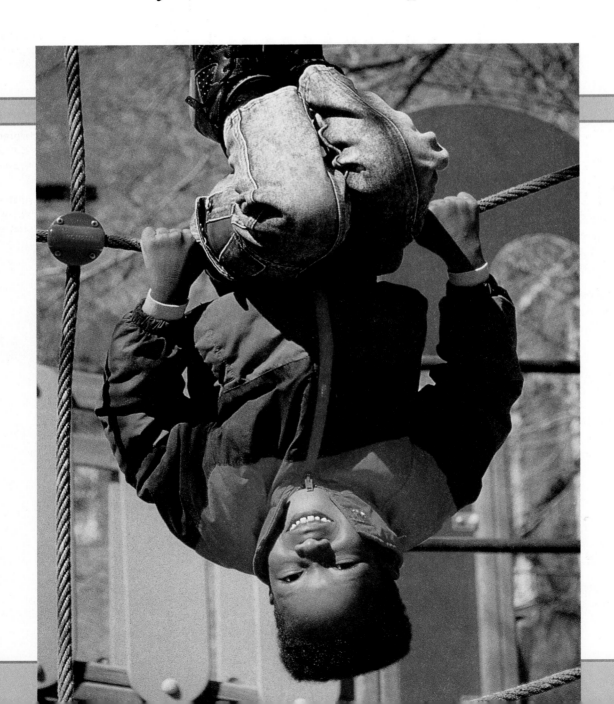

Influences on Normal Physical Development

Genetic Background
Disease
Nutritional Needs During the Preschool
 Years
Social Influences on Growth
Psychological Inhibitors to Growth

The Connection Between Health and Poverty

Poverty as a Health Problem
Responding to Child Poverty

Brain Development

Organization of the Brain
Hemispheric Lateralization
Lateralized Behaviors

Other Bodily Changes

Preschool Sensory Development
Bladder and Bowel Control

Motor Skill Development

Fundamental Motor Skills
Can Motor Skills Be Taught?
Fine Motor Coordination: The Case of
 Drawing Skills
Gender Differences in Physical Development

Effects of Children's Physical Growth

Effects on Adults
Effects on the Child

Focusing Questions

- What influences how rapidly preschool children grow, and why do they develop different bodily proportions?

- How does the brain become organized during early childhood?

- What motor skills do children acquire during the preschool years, and what refinements do they undergo?

- How do children's physical and motor development affect relationships between parents and young children?

During the preschool years, from ages two to five, children grow more slowly than they did during infancy, but growth continues to have a major impact on their lives as a whole. Physical growth not only makes new motor skills possible but also affects children's social, emotional, and cognitive development. To understand something of these relationships, consider two children, Maria and Kimberly, learning to swim. Each enrolls in the same swimming class, but before long Maria is swimming better than Kimberly. Why?

Most of the time such a difference stems from a mixture of physical, social, emotional, and cognitive factors. Maria is larger than Kimberly; even at the beginning of the swimming class, she was able to hold her breath longer and paddle more powerfully. She also gets more social support from home for learning to swim; her parents are devoted swimmers and take her to the pool between lessons. Because of differences such as these, Maria has developed a concept of herself as a good swimmer, one who is strong, holds her breath well, and can count on help at swimming when she needs it.

In this chapter we look closely at such factors, investigating how physical growth and motor skills influence each other and psychological processes during early childhood. First, we examine the overall nature and extent of physical growth. Then we look at some motor skills typically acquired during early childhood. Some of these skills, such as learning to walk, are relatively universal among all children. Other skills, such as ice skating, are rather unique to particular groups of children. Woven into our discussion are implicit notions of what constitutes typical, or "normal," physical development. As we point out repeatedly, however, such norms do not in and of themselves dictate how children *should* develop physically. Evaluating growth is also important, but it differs from describing growth. Throughout the chapter, we keep this distinction in mind.

INFLUENCES ON NORMAL PHYSICAL DEVELOPMENT

Physical growth in the preschool years is relatively easy to measure and gives a clear idea of how children normally develop during this period. Table 8.1 shows the two most familiar measurements of growth, standing height and weight. At age two, an

TABLE 8.1 *Average Height and Weight During Early Childhood*

Age (Years)	Height (Inches)	Weight (Pounds)
2	34.5	27.0
3	37.8	31.5
4	40.9	36.0
5	43.6	40.5

Source: Engels (1993).

average child in North America measures about thirty-three or thirty-four inches tall, or about two feet and ten inches. Three years later, at age five, he measures approximately forty-four inches, or about one-third more than before. The typical child weighs about twenty-seven pounds on his second birthday but about forty-one pounds by his fifth. (See also Figure 8.1.) Meanwhile, other measurements change in less obvious ways. The child's head grows about one inch in circumference during these years, and his body fat decreases as a proportion of his total bodily tissue.

For any preschool child who is reasonably healthy and happy, physical growth is remarkably smooth and predictable, especially compared to many cognitive and social developments. All in all, physical growth contains no discrete stages, plateaus, or qualitative changes such as those Piaget described for cognitive development. At the same time, however, large differences develop among individual children and among groups of children. Sometimes these differences affect the psychological development of young children; at other times they simply create interesting physical variety among human beings.

The overall smoothness of growth means that childhood height and weight can predict adult height and weight to a significant extent, although not perfectly. A four-year-old who is above average in height tends to end up above average as an adult. Nevertheless, correlation between childhood height and adult height is

FIGURE 8.1
Growth and Height from Two to Eighteen Years

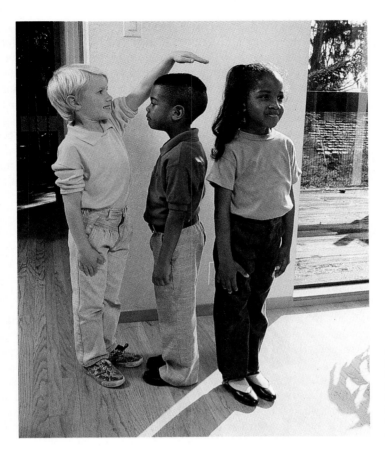

As a result of improvements in nutrition and health care, children in industrialized nations are often taller than in earlier times. But there are important variations among societies—even among industrialized ones—which apparently are genetically influenced.

imperfect because of individual differences in nutrition and health and, most of all, in the timing of puberty. In particular, children who experience puberty later than average tend to grow taller than children who experience it early (Sanfilippo et al., 1994). Variations in the timing of puberty therefore can alter a child's relative size as an adult.

Genetic Background

Most dimensions of growth are influenced substantially by heredity. Tall parents tend to have tall children, and short parents typically have short children. Weight shows similar patterns, although it can be influenced strongly by habits of exercise and diet. Nevertheless, a tendency to be heavy or thin is inherited to a significant extent. Contrary to popular belief, both parents contribute equally to these tendencies. Sons do not necessarily resemble their fathers' growth patterns more than their mothers', nor do daughters resemble their mothers' more than their fathers'. A child with one tall parent and one short parent therefore stands equal chances of being either tall or short. On the average, in fact, such children are middling in height, although they vary widely as individuals.

Races and ethnic groups around the world also differ in growth patterns (Eveleth & Tanner, 1990). Children from Asiatic groups, such as Chinese and Japanese, tend to be shorter than European and North American children. The latter, in turn, are usually shorter than children from African societies. Shape differs among these groups as well, although the differences do not always become obvious until adolescence. Asiatic children develop short legs and arms relative to their torsos, and relatively broad hips. African children do just the opposite: they develop relatively long limbs and narrow hips. Olympic athletes reflect these differences; records consistently show Asiatics performing better in events requiring upper-body strength, such as wrestling, gymnastics, and weightlifting, whereas Africans tend to excel in events requiring a long stride, such as running (Falkner & Tanner, 1986).

Such trends do not result from differences in nutrition or health care. Well-off children from these societies show the same relative differences, even though their diets are comparable in overall quality. And, with a minor exception noted shortly, the same differences exist whether children are living in their native country or have emigrated to another, more affluent one, where medical care may be better. Apparently nutrition and health care affect growth, but they do not override genetic and cultural factors.

Disease

Although serious illnesses interfere with growth, it often is hard to judge exactly how much. The trouble is that children with serious illnesses often have other conditions that retard growth; they may have been small for date or suffered from chronically poor nutrition during infancy. These conditions can lead not only to slow growth but also to various sicknesses, which in turn may contribute to the problem.

To hold back growth, an illness must be fairly major. Preschool-age children in certain impoverished rural parts of Central America tend to be shorter and lighter in weight if they suffered continually from diarrhea during infancy (Pinstrup-Anderson et al., 1995), but similar children are not shorter and lighter if their illnesses consisted mainly of upper-respiratory-tract infections (colds). Children from affluent parts of the same societies usually do not get sick enough to suffer impaired growth, nor do children from societies that are generally well off. Middle-class American children are just as likely to grow large (or small) if they catch colds frequently as they are if they do not.

Certain specific diseases and conditions do retard growth, in many cases by reducing the normal absorption of nutrients over a long period of time. Childhood diabetes can hinder growth, at least partly by interfering with the normal use of sugars in the body. So can any chronic infection of the intestine, such as amoebic dysentery or worms, by preventing the normal digestion of foods. Nutritional deficits can also result from chronic intolerance to certain foods, such as the gluten in wheat products or the lactose in milk products. Children with these conditions suffer in various ways, but to a large extent they simply become malnourished and, like other malnourished children, do not grow as rapidly as usual.

Not all diseases that influence growth do so by affecting nutrition. About one preschool child in ten thousand develops a deficiency in the **endocrine glands,** the glands that produce growth hormones (Sanfilippo et al., 1994). As a result, growth simply slows down considerably; by age five, an afflicted child may measure only about 2½ feet tall (or 85 centimeters), which is about 9 inches (or 15 centimeters) shorter than average. Occasionally doctors can trace such growth deficiencies to an anatomical disorder (such as a tumor) of the glands that control growth. More often, however, they can find no obvious cause. In either case, the condition usually can be treated with injections of whatever hormones the child appears to be missing.

However, injections of hormones are a useful strategy only for children who have a diagnosed hormone deficiency and do not deviate far from normal height or weight. Because growth hormones are powerful medicines full of unknown side effects, doctors tend to prescribe them only in situations where their benefits are certain and their risks are small. Hormones do not make a desirable treatment for children who are merely shorter than average but want to become taller or whose parents want them to grow taller.

Once the causes of slow growth are diagnosed correctly and treated, children often can recover by growing much faster than usual until they have reached the normal range of size for their age. At that point, growth slows down again to comparatively normal rates and becomes relatively immune to short-term and minor changes in the child's health and nutrition. This process often is called **catch-up growth.** It suggests that genetics may influence the rate of physical growth significantly as long as children receive basically good nutrition and physical care. Immunizations during infancy and childhood probably also promote normal growth by preventing major diseases, whether or not a child happens to be slow growing. Table 8.2 lists the most common immunizations and the ages at which children typically receive them.

Nutritional Needs During the Preschool Years

For a time, a young preschooler (such as three years old) may eat less than he or she did as a toddler and become much more selective about foods as well. Michael (the son of one of the authors) ate every meal voraciously as a two-year-old; a year later he rarely finished a meal, even though he was significantly taller and heavier by then. Elizabeth (the daughter of the same author) followed a similar pattern, except more pronounced. As a toddler she ate most foods except ice cream ("Too sweet," she said!), but as a young preschooler she sometimes hardly ate—though she did decide then that she liked ice cream.

Parents may worry about such changes, but in fact they are normal and result from the slowing down of growth after infancy. Preschool children simply do not need as many calories per unit of their body weight as they did immediately after birth. They do need variety in their foods, however, just as adults do, to ensure adequate overall nutrition. Given preschoolers' newfound selectiveness about eating, providing the variety needed for good nutrition can sometimes be a challenge to parents and other caregivers.

How can one ensure healthy variety in a preschool child's diet? Experts generally discourage coercion ("Eat your vegetables because I say so!"), since it teaches children to associate undesired foods with unpleasant social experiences (Endres & Rockwell, 1993). They also discourage using sweet foods as a reward for eating undesired foods ("If you eat your vegetables, then you can have your ice cream"), because it implicitly overvalues the sweets and undervalues the undesired food still further. The best strategy seems to be casual, repeated exposure to the food without insisting that the child eat it (Andrien, 1994). Observations of children's eating habits confirm what parents often suspect as well: children's food preferences are influenced by the adult models around them. In the long term, preschoolers tend to like the same foods their parents and other important adults like.

TABLE 8.2   *Typical Ages Recommended for Immunizations*

0–2 months	Hepatitis
2–6 months	Diphtheria, tetanus, and pertussis (DPT), polio, and haemophilus
6–18 months	Hepatitis booster, haemophilus booster
15–18 months	DPT booster, polio booster
4–6 years	DPT booster, polio booster
10–12 years	Measles, mumps, and rubella (MMR)
14–16 years	Tetanus and diphtheria booster

Source: American Academy of Pediatrics (1992).

A Multicultural View

Cultural Influences on Children's Sleep

The development of children's sleep is a primary worry for American parents. One study found that it is the most commonly discussed single issue during periodic well-child visits to pediatricians and that concern about children's sleep remains high throughout both infancy and early childhood (Harkness et al., 1995a). Parents of three- and four-year-olds worry almost as much as parents of six-month-old infants about whether their children are falling asleep quickly enough, staying asleep long enough, and resting peacefully enough. Bedtime routines evolve to help meet these goals: they are supposed to calm children down and help them sleep better.

Doctors and parenting experts in our society tend to assert that sleep cycles depend on physical maturity and that interruptions and irregularities are something children will eventually "grow out of." Yet the fact that parents continue to worry about sleep even when their children become preschoolers suggests that more than physical maturity is at stake. In some sense, it seems, children must be "learning" to sleep.

Cross-cultural comparisons support this possibility. A comparison of families from the Netherlands with families from Boston, for example, found important differences between children's sleep in the two societies (Harkness et al., 1995b). Dutch infants and preschoolers went to bed more than an hour earlier, on average, than their American counterparts, and they got significantly more sleep throughout infancy and the preschool years. They also experienced less variation in their bed times and waking times. In these ways, children from the Netherlands were sleeping "better" than children from the United States.

Why the difference? In this and another study, interviews with American and Dutch parents offered clues (Harkness et al., 1992). In describing their children's sleep patterns, American mothers referred frequently to the "innateness" pattern: they seemed to believe that regularity in a child's sleep is determined genetically. Children are born more or less regular, and parents can alter the innate regularity only in limited ways. Mostly they must learn to live with the pattern nature has prescribed.

The Dutch parents, on the other hand, often talked about the need for "the three Rs" of parenting: *Rust, Regelmaat,* and *Reinheid* (rest, regularity, and cleanliness). They commented relatively frequently on the child's need to learn how to organize his or her day and, therefore, to become independent eventually. Consistent with this view, the Dutch parents arranged for more regularity in children's daily lives than did the American parents; they more often arranged family errands, for example, so as not to interrupt or alter naps or mealtimes.

American parents certainly talked about establishing regular sleep patterns, but in doing so they focused mostly on the regularity of *nighttime* routines and ignored regularity during the day. Although parents themselves seemed unaware of it, daytime priorities contradicted the belief in regular sleep: parents emphasized responsiveness to the child and provision of stimulating activities filled with novelty. A stimulating day, in this view, fosters the child's cognitive and social development. In addition, American parents had more hectic, varied schedules themselves, making it hard to provide regularity for their children. As a result, compared to

Social Influences on Growth

Variations in growth can result from cultural and psychological factors. (See the accompanying Multicultural View box for a discussion of cultural influences on children's sleep.) Sometimes much stress in a family can keep children from growing normally, a condition called **failure to thrive** (Money, 1992). Children with this condition seem apathetic and weak, and their relationships with parents tend to involve conflict and impaired rapport.

The condition apparently results from situations that interfere with normal positive relationships between parent and child, especially during infancy or the early preschool period. For example, parents suffering from the stresses of unemployment, chronic conflicts, or other painful circumstances may make a scapegoat of a child who needs more attention than other children in the family do. The result is a deprived relationship that may lead the child to eat poorly or be plagued by constant anxiety. This nervousness can interfere with sleep or the production of growth hormones.

Even in situations such as these, however, the causes of failure to thrive are poorly understood. Some mothers of children who fail to thrive show obvious psy-

Dutch parents, American parents developed relatively elaborate bedtime rituals to calm their children down and compensate for the excitement (and relative unpredictability) of the day.

Of course, even some American parenting experts see a connection between regularity during the day and regularity at night. One best-selling book on children's sleep (Ferber, 1986) urges parents to develop regular daytime routines as soon as possible after childbirth if they wish their child to have a regular nighttime sleeping experience. But for now this advice will be hard for many parents to follow, given the competing cultural belief in providing stimulation for the child and the continuing cultural tolerance for hectic daytime schedules for parents.

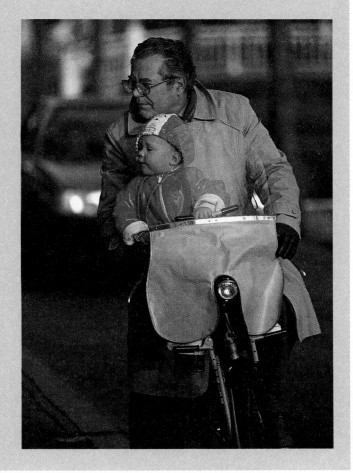

Research has found that Dutch children sleep more soundly at night than American children, apparently because their daytime routines are more regular and predictable. This father, for example, takes his son to school every morning without fail—and perhaps without knowing, contributes to his regular sleep at night.

chological problems, but the majority show little out of the ordinary that might account for the children's condition (Weil, 1992). Instead, most mothers express reasonably normal beliefs about and goals for their children. Most hold fairly moderate standards of discipline, for example, though perhaps inclining a bit toward strictness, and most seem somewhat less affectionate than average. Yet across society as a whole, most children with slightly strict, slightly unaffectionate mothers do *not* develop failure to thrive. What, then, is different about the few who do develop this problem?

One possibility is that failure to thrive results from a poor match between parents' expectations and the child's inherent styles of responding. The lack of synchrony is the result of many factors operating together for quite some time. Conflicts between parents and grandparents can contribute to stress between parents and child; so can unemployment or other economic hardship. A child whose natural response style is slow also is a bit more vulnerable, as is a child with a serious, prolonged illness. In these cases, the child tends not to respond as parents expect, and if the parents take the child's unresponsiveness personally, their relationship with the child can eventually deteriorate. But note that no *one* circumstance "causes" failure to thrive; rather, it grows out of a pattern or sequence of circumstances.

If failure to thrive has not persisted for too long, it usually can be reversed in the short run through special nutritional and medical intervention to help the child regain strength and begin growing normally again. Of course, this strategy will not solve any long-term problems in the relationships between parents and failure-to-thrive children. Such problems require relieving parents of some of their stress through counseling or training workshops in the skills of parenting. Long-term solutions also require psychological help for the child in learning new, less passive responses to people. They also require practical help, such as jobs for unemployed parents or high-quality child care for those who need it.

What Do You Think?

How do you suppose parents evaluate their child's height and weight? Explore this issue by asking parents three questions: (1) "How tall is your child?"; (2) "How much does she or he weigh?"; and (3) "Are that height and weight about right, or too high or too low?" Try involving as many classmates as possible in this survey, and pool your results. Then focus on this question: Do parents' evaluations of height and weight have any relationship to the actual size of their child?

THE CONNECTION BETWEEN HEALTH AND POVERTY

In economically well-off settings, preschool children are among the healthiest human beings alive: they experience comparatively few major illnesses as long as they get enough of the right things to eat and as long as their parents have reasonable access to modern medical care. As parents often note, preschoolers do experience frequent minor illnesses: various respiratory infections, ear infections, and stomach flus. These typically strike a young child several times per year, which is three or four times as often as for adults and about twice as often as for school-age children (Engels, 1993). For well-fed children whose families have access to medical care, however, these illnesses rarely prove serious or life threatening. For their parents, of course, colds and flu cause worry, as well as challenges in arranging child care if a parent works.

Poverty as a Health Problem

But there is a problem with this optimistic picture of preschool health: about 30 percent of all families in the United States, and countless others worldwide, have poor access to medical care, mainly because they live at or near the poverty level. Young children from these families are substantially less healthy than those from middle- and high-income families. Low-income preschoolers contract 25 to 50 percent more minor illnesses than do preschoolers as a whole, and they are more often malnourished, meaning they chronically lack essential vitamins, iron, or protein (American Academy of Pediatrics, 1993; Wadsworth, 1986). Figure 8.2 illustrates the impact of child poverty on some aspects of health.

Whether in North America or around the world, minor illnesses and malnourishment put children's health at risk for additional illnesses, both minor and major. Malnourishment also seems to contribute to delays in social, language, and cognitive development, possibly because of a lack of energy. In one study based in Kenya

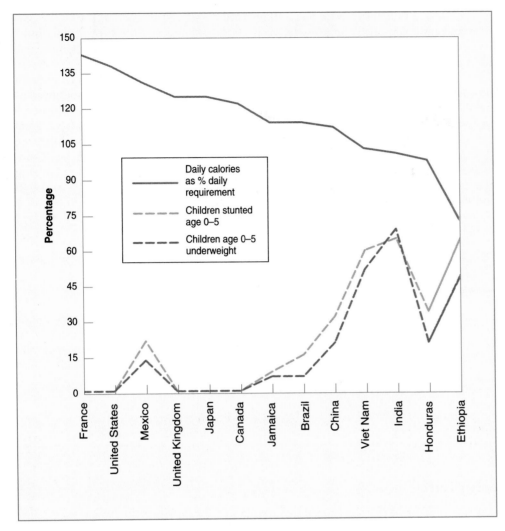

FIGURE 8.2
**Physical Impact of Poverty
on Growth**
The percentage of children who are
underweight and stunted (excessively
short) tends to be smaller in countries
where children receive more food calories, but the relationship is far from
perfect.
Source: United Nations International Children's Emergency Fund (1995).

(Africa), for example, even a temporary food shortage (a few months of drought locally) hurt children's health and school performance two years later (McDonald et al., 1994).

Responding to Child Poverty

How can we counteract these problems? In general, strategies can focus either on individuals and their particular communities or on systematic reorganization of the health care system as a whole. Among individually oriented strategies, an important one is to educate children and families about health and nutrition. For example, pamphlets can be distributed in schools or medical clinics, and public health nurses can make presentations in classrooms, community clubs, or churches.

Educational activities can be effective if they build on the knowledge of health and nutrition low-income parents and their children already have and avoid assuming that the public is completely ignorant about these matters. Mexican-American children as young as four years, for example, have good knowledge about the effects of cleanliness, but often need more information about nutrition (Olvera-Ezzell et al., 1994). A similar pattern exists among their parents (Sanjur, 1995). In this sort of situation, it is helpful to organize intervention programs aimed at providing parents and children with the knowledge they need. However, such programs must respect the culture and economic situations of the families, which usually influence food preferences in major ways.

Another individually oriented intervention is direct aid to families to prevent illnesses. Food distribution centers ("food banks"), for example, give food away to needy families in specific communities. Typically they rely heavily on volunteers from churches or other community agencies and receive their supplies from local grocery stores, restaurants, or farmers with surpluses to give away. Typically, too, they fail to meet the demand for their services (United States Congress Select Committee on Hunger, 1992). Because of this problem, many experts favor reorganizing the health care system in broader, more systematic ways than is possible through individual action (see the accompanying Perspectives box).

BRAIN DEVELOPMENT

By the preschool years, the brain has grown to nearly its final adult size and begins to function physically in adultlike ways (Brierley, 1994). Nerve fibers continue to interconnect among themselves. Therefore, even though no new nerve cells actually are created, a young child's brain looks increasingly dense and complex when viewed under a microscope.

Perspectives

Reforming Children's Health Care

The health care system provides less help to poor families than it does to more well-off ones. The gap begins before birth: low-income mothers are less likely to receive medical attention during pregnancy, causing health problems in themselves or their fetuses to be overlooked. The gap continues after birth: infants of low-income mothers are less likely to receive checkups from a doctor and less likely to be seen by a doctor if they get sick (United States Select Committee on Children, Youth, and Families, 1992).

Why does access to health care depend so heavily on personal income? In the United States, medical services for the poor are paid through Medicaid, a federally sponsored insurance program created in the 1960s. Medicaid pays for basic health services, but only up to a point; it will pay for taking a child with an earache to a general practitioner, for example, but it will reimburse the doctor only up to a certain point. Doctors who wish to charge more are free to do so, but in the process they price themselves out of the market for low-income families. In effect, therefore, low-income parents have significantly fewer doctors and clinics to choose from than higher-income parents do, even though (as pointed out in this chapter) their children experience more illnesses than do children from middle- and upper-income families (Fitzgerald et al., 1995).

For this and other reasons, low-income parents are more likely than others to wait until a child's illness is serious, or even life threatening, before seeking medical help. Instead of getting antibiotics immediately when a preschooler shows signs of a bacterial ear infection, for example, parents may wait until the infection threatens the child with actual hearing loss or until the child has become chronically run down and therefore will require more time to regain strength.

To make matters worse, efforts to limit the soaring costs of medical services have led many states to make the standards for eligibility for Medicaid stricter than they originally were (United States Congressional Budget Office, 1993). In recent years, therefore, a person or a family has had to be "poorer" than before, in some states even living at only *one-half* the income level of the official federal poverty line. Some states have also set limits on services, such as the number of days a person can stay in a hospital or the number of visits permitted to a doctor per year. Still others have required preauthorization from state health authorities for services that exceed a certain cost (say, $500).

What can society and concerned individuals do to reduce these economically based inequalities in health

Organization of the Brain

Given its complexity, how does the brain sort out and perform the diverse functions of being human? Contrary to a widespread belief, it does *not* work like a telephone switchboard; individual stimuli or thoughts do not confine themselves to selected nerve fibers, as though the fibers acted as wires. Instead, a stimulus generates neural activity over wide areas of the brain and sometimes even in the entire brain. Some of this response shows itself when electrodes are placed on a person's head. But the locations of brain activity can be mapped even more accurately by injecting tiny, harmless amounts of radioactive substances into the blood and measuring which parts of the brain then accumulate especially large amounts of the substances. Active brain cells and fibers, which require larger amounts of blood, therefore give off more radiation and can be "photographed" with this technique, a medical procedure called *tomography* (Seeram, 1994).

What does tomography show about brain activity in preschoolers? For one thing, it shows that most stimuli (sights and sounds) cause at least some neural activity throughout the brain; activity is never fully localized. At the same time, though, particular areas do respond more strongly to certain types of stimuli. A visual image, such as the sight of a cat, produces the strongest activity in an area called the **visual cortex,** located near the back of the head in the cerebral cortex. The sounds of speech produce their primary response in the **auditory cortex** and specifically in a place called **Wernicke's area,** located near the left side of the cerebral cortex. Simple voluntary movements, such as lifting an arm, produce their largest neural activity in the **motor cortex,** located just forward of the top of the head. The child's own speech usually produces its primary activity in a region called

care? Numerous reforms have been proposed, most of them centering on one of three ideas: community involvement, prevention, and reorganization of services. Reforms that focus on community involvement seek to reduce the distance, both psychological and geographical, between medical staff and the people they serve. Some hospitals and cities have established small community health clinics in areas of greatest need (the inner city). They hire medical staff who deliberately try to establish rapport with the parents and children who seek help, recruit local community members to serve on their governing and advisory boards, and charge low fees based on families' ability to pay.

Reforms that focus on prevention seek to keep disease from striking in the first place. By their nature these actions may not seem strictly related to "health," because they often deal with relatively healthy children (who have not gotten sick yet) and with the conditions that make illness likely rather than with illness itself. Lead poisoning is a good example: community health experts often cite this substance as the most hazardous health threat to preschool children in modern society (Tesman & Hills, 1994). Lead accumulates in the body and eventually causes damage to the nervous system, sickness, and even death. Children (and adults) pick it up accidentally from many sources, but the most prominent culprit is the interior wall paint used in about 75 percent of all homes and apartments built before 1980. Since there is no real cure for lead poisoning, prevention strategies have dominated the response of the health care profession: educating parents to the dangers, pressing for legislation outlawing lead-based paints (and also lead-based gasoline, incidentally), and even removal of leaded paint in some homes.

Reforms that focus on reorganization generally involve more self-conscious planning of medical services. Basing immunization and health screening programs in schools, for example, often allows the programs to reach a higher percentage of children than basing the same programs in a community health clinic (Behrman, 1993). Also, making better use of "front-line" professionals often can improve access dramatically without compromising quality of care: the majority of childhood illnesses, for example, can be treated effectively by a nurse rather than a medical doctor, as long as the nurse knows when a particular illness deserves referral to the doctor.

Broca's area, located on the left side of the cerebral cortex and somewhat to the front. Figure 8.3 illustrates these and other areas of specialized activity.

Hemispheric Lateralization

During the preschool years, children begin showing definite **hemispheric lateralization,** the tendency for the left and right halves of the brain to perform separate functions. In general, the left hemisphere deals increasingly with information on an item-by-item or linear basis, and the right hemisphere identifies relationships or patterns among the items (Bianci, 1993).

The difference in function is quite noticeable in a task called **dichotic listening.** In this task, a child wears headphones that feed sounds or information to each ear separately. Because of the layout of the nerve cells in the brain, the experimental sounds are conducted to particular hemispheres for processing. The sounds initially go to the hemisphere *opposite* the ear that receives each sound. Under these conditions, if the information given to each ear is provided sequentially, such as a string of random digits, the ear connected to the left hemisphere tends to hear its sounds relatively earlier and with fewer errors. But if the information emphasizes patterns, such as melodies, the right hemisphere functions better.

Observations such as these imply that the hemispheres specialize in certain functions even in young children. However, most everyday tasks probably obscure hemispheric specialization simply because they usually require the activity of both halves of the brain. A child in nursery school, for example, might discover that a shape is a cube, but most likely he will handle it with both hands, look at its overall shape, and count the corners—all at once.

Lateralized Behaviors

In contrast to hemispheric lateralization, lateralized behaviors are quite evident in everyday life, even among preschool-age children. **Lateralized behaviors** are actions individuals prefer to perform with one side of their bodies more than with the other. The best example is handedness: offer a toy to a five-year-old, and most likely she will take it with her right hand rather than her left. But people of all ages show lateral preferences (usually right-sided) for a variety of behaviors. Most of us have a favorite

FIGURE 8.3
Areas of the Brain

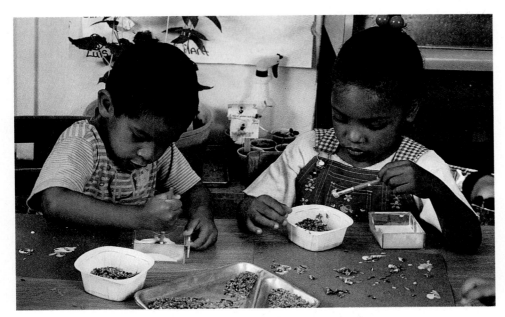

Most children show a number of lateralized behaviors—apparently a genetic trait. One of these boys, for example, prefers gluing with his right hand, and the other prefers gluing with his left hand. In addition to hand preference, most children also have a preferred foot, a preferred eye, and a preferred ear.

eye for looking through a telescope or keyhole, a preferred ear for listening on the telephone, and a preferred foot for squashing a bug on the floor (Gabbard, 1989).

Lateral preferences emerge during the preschool years and become stable about the time children begin school, and must have at least partly biological or genetic origins. It is hard to tell what experiences might cause a majority of three-year-olds to choose to use their right ears for listening to a seashell. Hand preference runs in families: siblings and twins are much more likely than other individuals to prefer the same hand, as are parents and their children. Boys are left-handed significantly more often than girls are, and children with genetically caused mental retardation are much more likely than usual to be left-handed (Coren, 1992). All of these facts imply genetic influences on lateralized behaviors.

But learning probably does affect lateral preferences somewhat. Among preschool children, right-hand bias is strongest for behaviors that are taught explicitly, such as eating with a spoon or using scissors, and weakest for behaviors children usually learn spontaneously, such as digging in a sandbox. Also, right-hand bias increases during the lifespan. About 85 percent of children favor their right hand during the preschool years, but more than 95 percent of adults do so during old age. This shift may not seem like much, but it is too large to occur by chance. Learning must account for it.

What Do You Think?

Is it a problem to be left-handed? Talk with a left-handed classmate about this, or offer your opinions about the problem if you yourself are left-handed. In view of left-handers' complaints, do you think teachers should support left-handedness in young children or encourage left-handers to switch?

OTHER BODILY CHANGES

Preschool Sensory Development

Visual acuity, or sharpness of vision, improves during the preschool years. For toddlers, acuity for distant, stationary objects or shapes, such as the letters on a traditional eye examination chart, is only about 20/60, meaning a two-year-old recognizes shapes at twenty feet that an adult can recognize at sixty feet. Paradoxically, children's near vision often is imperfect as well: many preschoolers have trouble focusing on shapes that are less than about two feet away. By about age five, distant vision improves substantially for most preschoolers, but near vision remains a problem for some during the early school years. About one child in ten needs glasses by age seven, even after vision has matured (Engels, 1993). The proportion continues to rise throughout childhood, especially around puberty.

For most children *auditory acuity,* or sharpness of hearing, is more fully developed by the preschool years than visual acuity. But hearing a specific tone in the midst of other tones can be confusing. Inability to isolate sounds may account for some children's apparent distractibility when they first enter school. In a classroom, even accidental rustling noises can compete strongly with the teacher's voice for the child's attention, especially if a child's native language is not English (Christenson & Delgado, 1993).

Bladder and Bowel Control

Sometime during the preschool years, most children acquire control of their bladder and bowels. As parents will testify, the process includes many false starts and accidents. Most commonly, daytime control comes before nighttime control, sometime before a child's third birthday, although individuals vary widely and somewhat unpredictably. Typically too, daytime control of the bladder and bowels occurs at very nearly the same time. Some pediatricians believe this fact implies that children decide when they wish to begin exercising control, perhaps to begin feeling more grown up. In the early stages of toilet training, therefore, reminders and parent-led visits to the toilet may make little difference to most toddlers. Nonetheless they may help in the long term as a form of behavioral conditioning: a child comes to associate seeing and sitting on the toilet with the relief of emptying a full bladder, as well as with the praise parents confer on the child for successes.

Nighttime bladder control often takes much longer to achieve than daytime control. About one-half of all three-year-olds still wet their beds at least some of the time, and as many as one in five six-year-olds do the same (American Psychiatric Association, 1994). The timing of nighttime control depends on several factors, such as how deeply children sleep and how large their bladders are. It also depends on anxiety level; worried children tend to wet their beds more often than relaxed children do. Unfortunately, parents sometimes contribute to young children's anxieties by becoming overly frustrated about changing wet sheets night after night.

Achieving control over bladder and bowels reflects the large advances children make during these years in controlling their bodies in general. As infants, they could not always be sure of reaching successfully even for a nearby object, and their first efforts to crawl and to walk often ended in falls or moves in the wrong direction. During the preschool years, those problems no longer occur. Instead of concentrating on whether they can simply get their bodies to move, children of this age can begin focusing on what they actually want to do with their bodies.

What Do You Think?

Imagine how you would talk to a parent who was concerned about the child's bet wetting at night. What would you say? If you are not sure, you may first want to read one or two parent advice books (such as Dr. Spock) on this topic. If you or your instructor can arrange it, try acting out a meeting between a concerned parent and a child care center worker or director to discuss bed wetting.

MOTOR SKILL DEVELOPMENT

As young children grow, they become more skilled at performing basic physical actions. Often a two-year-old can walk only with considerable effort; hence the term *toddler.* But a five-year-old can walk comfortably in a variety of ways: forward and

In the long run, successful bladder control depends on both physical growth and the children's own motivation. Forcing a child prematurely to control herself or himself may produce results, but only in the immediate future.

backward, quickly and slowly, skipping and galloping. A five-year-old also can do other vigorous things that were impossible a few years earlier. He can run, jump, and climb, all with increasing smoothness and variety. He can carry out certain actions that require accuracy, such as balancing on one foot, catching a ball reliably, or drawing a picture.

In this section, we examine in more detail how children reach milestones such as these under naturally occurring conditions. Because natural conditions vary a great deal in real life, we must take a certain range of conditions for granted. In particular, we assume children have no significant fears of being active—that they have a reasonably (but not excessively) daring attitude toward trying out new motor skills, they are in good health, and their physical growth has evolved more or less normally. For some children, unfortunately, these conditions are not met. For them, we may need to modify the following descriptions.

After examining motor development, we look at the effects of altering such conditions. Can very young children be taught motor skills? Can they become skillful sooner or more fully by receiving training from adults? Will such training affect physical skill development later on in childhood and adolescence? As you will see, the answers to these questions are not definite, but they do have interesting implications for people who care for young children.

Fundamental Motor Skills

Preschool children obviously have moved well beyond the confines of reflex action, which constituted the first motor skills of infancy. From ages two to about five, they experiment with the simple voluntary actions that adults use extensively for their normal activities, such as walking, running, and jumping (Kalverboer et al., 1993). For older children, these actions usually are the means to other ends. For very young children, they lie very much in the foreground and frequently are goals in themselves. Table 8.3 summarizes some of these activities.

Walking and Running From a child's point of view, walking may seem absurd at first: it requires purposely losing balance, then regaining balance rapidly enough to keep from falling (Rose & Gamble, 1993). As older infants, children still must pay attention to these facts, even after a full year or so of practice. Each step is an effort in itself. Children watch each foot in turn as it launches (or lurches) forward; they may pause after each step before attempting the next. Typically too infants are top-heavy; this requires them to plant their feet far apart, as though straddling a horse, to keep from falling down. Despite these precautions, spills are plentiful in infancy, and walking often is rather slow.

TABLE 8.3 *Milestones in Preschool Motor Development*

Approximate Age	Gross Motor Skill	Fine Motor Skill
2.5–3.5 years	Walks well; runs in straight line; jumps in air with both feet	Copies a circle; scribbles; can use eating utensils; stacks a few small blocks
3.5–4.5 years	Walking stride 80 percent of adult; runs at one-third adult speed; throws and catches large ball, but stiff-armed	Buttons with large buttons; copies simple shapes; makes simple representational drawings
4.5–5.5 years	Balances on one foot; runs far without falling; can "swim" in water for short distance	Uses scissors; draws people; copies simple letters and numbers; builds complex structures with blocks

Note: The ages given above are approximate, and skills vary with the life experiences available to individual children and with the situations in which the skills are displayed.
Source: Kalverboer et al. (1993).

Working with Audrey Reimer, SPEECH-LANGUAGE PATHOLOGIST

The Psychological Impact of Motor Skill Development

Audrey Reimer is a speech-language pathologist who works for an agency that serves infants and preschoolers with multiple disabilities. In most of her work, therefore, she forms part of a team of specialists. Audrey pointed to this fact as one of the major satisfactions of her job.

Audrey: For instance, there's Michael. He has limited oral language. His hearing and visual acuity are good, but he has CP [cerebral palsy], so his motor control is full of challenges.

Kelvin: What do you mean?

Audrey: Well, when he tries to speak orally, it's often difficult to understand him; the muscles he needs for talking are affected as well. I and the OT [occupational therapist] have been working to figure out additional ways to help him communicate. But it's taken some work, since he also lacks control of fine motor skills.

Kelvin: Why should that matter? Why should his motor skills interfere with something cognitive like language?

Audrey: He *can* understand a lot, and has ideas and choices that he wants to express, but his physical capabilities restrict his ability to do so.

Kelvin: How do you know? It must be hard to establish a "channel" of communication.

Audrey: Well, it is. When he was a preschooler here at our day program, we worked with him to use his eye gaze to communicate. We discovered that he had good control of his eyes. So we arranged for Michael to look at an array of pictures. At snack time,

for example, one of us would put a few pictures on a board. Michael would look at the picture indicating his choice of snack—milk or juice—and communicate that way. It's as if he is saying, "I want the juice, not the milk."

Kelvin: So his physical abilities influence how he communicates and shows his cognitive skills?

Audrey: Exactly. And lately his vocabulary has increased to the point where eye gaze isn't enough anymore. He can do it better than ever, but there's only so many pictures you can gaze at conveniently. So lately the OT and I have introduced Michael to an electronic scanning device—really a computer that displays pictures. The screen has a light or cursor that Michael can move from one picture to another, and when it gets to the right picture, he can hit a switch to choose it.

Kelvin: So that lets Michael scan a lot more pictures, and probably more quickly too.

Audrey: That's the idea: to allow him to communicate more fully. But the trouble has been to find the best "access site," as we've been calling it, for Michael. His CP makes it hard to use a hand or arm the way you or I might to trigger a switch or press a computer key. We had to experiment with alternatives. But we did find one: his head. He can move his head easily and reliably. So we've mounted a switch on a metal arm that attaches to his wheelchair—or anywhere. The

arm can be moved to wherever Michael is sitting. When he wants to choose a picture, he moves his head against the switch on the metal arm. It's working well.

Kelvin: I wonder whether to think of your work with Michael as "physical" or "cognitive." How would you describe it yourself?

Audrey: Both at once—and social, too. We've been helping Michael to communicate, which gives him new cognitive skills and helps to develop his relationships with others. But we've had to do it by looking carefully at Michael's motor abilities and needs. They're really all of one piece—all Michael.

What Do You Think?

1. Given how Audrey describes her work with Michael, would you consider that work to be basically related to language or to motor skill development? Explain your view to a classmate.

2. As an experiment, try holding a discussion with one or two classmates using eye gaze *only*. This will probably work best if you choose a topic you are all familiar with, such as "My favorite recreational activity." For pictures, try using a large mail-order catalogue (like Eddie Bauer). Afterward, talk about how well eye gaze works for communication and how you might expect to improve if you practiced it further.

3. Think about the aspects of language (phonetics, semantics, syntax, pragmatics) and the landmarks of motor skill acquisition mentioned in the chapter. How does Audrey's work with Michael deal with these aspects and landmarks?

But after a year or so of experience, children usually can walk without looking at their feet. Around their second or third birthday, their steps become more regular and their feet get closer together. Stride, the distance between feet in a typical step, remains considerably shorter than that of a normal adult. This makes short distances easy to walk but long distances hard for a few more years.

Running appears early in the preschool years, shortly after walking begins to smooth out. At first it looks more like a hurried walk than a true run, and the child may have trouble stopping herself once she has begun. Also, at first the run may not really involve one of its defining features, namely a brief instant of complete separation from the ground. Not until the end of the preschool period, around age five, are these problems corrected. By then the child probably is swinging her arms as she strides to counterbalance the large, twisting motions of her legs. These arm motions also help the child to stop. Without their counterbalancing effect, children go into a sort of uncontrolled spin at the end of the run.

Jumping   At first, a jump is more like a fast stretch: the child reaches for the sky rapidly, but his feet fail to leave the ground. Sometime around his second birthday, one foot, or even both feet, may finally leave the ground. Such early successes may be delayed, however, because the child may put his arms backward to help himself take off, as though trying to push himself off the floor. Later, perhaps around age three, he shifts to a more efficient arm movement—reaching forward and up as he jumps—which creates a useful upward momentum.

Success in these actions depends partly on the type of jump the child is attempting. Jumping down a step is easier than jumping across a flat distance, and a flat or broad jump is easier than a jump up a step. By age five or so, most children can broad-jump across a few feet, although variations among individuals are substantial.

Throwing and Catching   For infants and toddlers, first throws may happen by accident. The child may just be waving an object and happen to release it suddenly, and away it goes. Once intentional throwing begins, however, children actually adopt more stereotyped methods initially than they do later in childhood. At first, they launch all balls in much the same way—usually with a general forward lurch—regardless of the balls' size or weight. As skill develops, children vary their movements according to the balls' characteristics; they give more wrist movement to small balls and more arm movement to large ones. At the same time, children begin to vary among themselves even in how they throw the same type of ball. Some develop a persistent wrist twist over and above the twist needed for particular balls, whereas others develop a special torso turn all their own.

Catching proceeds through similar phases. Early in the preschool period, children may extend their arms passively to receive an oncoming ball. Naturally this method works only if the thrower aims the ball perfectly. By around age four, children introduce flexibility to their methods by moving their hands in last-minute responses to the oncoming ball, and so forth. By school age, some children have become very skillful at catching: their arms and hands remain flexible until the ball actually arrives and therefore can compensate for unexpected angles and speeds as the ball approaches. Not surprisingly, this technique demands far less accuracy by the thrower.

During the preschool period, most motor skills—like running—develop through children's own informal activities, rather than through purposeful teaching. This fact makes free play and exploration especially important for this age group.

Can Motor Skills Be Taught?

In general, caregivers and parents can influence the learning of motor skills by providing opportunities to practice them. But the specific skills adults encourage vary a lot, depending on the needs of the child and the priorities of the adults. A physically normal child is not likely to receive "instruction" in a fundamental skill such as walking, whereas a child with a physical disability is likely to receive help in this very skill. Some children, with or without disabilities, may acquire specialized motor skills, such as ballet or swimming, that cannot be practiced unless opportunities are provided deliberately.

Preschool children respond well to specialized training to the extent that the training respects their current stage of development and takes advantage of their growing abilities to plan and coordinate fundamental motor actions (Poest et al., 1990). The result is unusually early learning of specialized skills before many adults would expect it to be possible. Later, during the school years, specialized skills may acquire social value because they confer status and respect on a child and help to

Skills that require fine motor coordination—like painting this butterfly—develop through identifiable steps or stages. At first children tend to make random marks or scribbles; later they coordinate these into patterns; still later they become increasing recognizable as such.

win friends. A good baseball player usually is in demand, and children who know how to swim are more likely to be invited to swimming parties.

Fine Motor Coordination: The Case of Drawing Skills

Not all motor activities of young children involve the strength, agility, and balance of their whole bodies. Many require the coordination of small movements but not strength. Tying shoelaces calls for such **fine motor coordination;** so do washing hands, buttoning and zipping clothing, eating with a spoon, and turning a doorknob.

One especially widespread fine motor skill among young children is drawing. In North American culture, at least, virtually every young child tries using pens or pencils at some time and often tries other artistic media as well. The scribbles or drawings that result probably serve a number of purposes. At times they may be used mainly for sensory exploration; a child may want to get the feel of paintbrushes or felt-tip pens. At other times, drawings may express thoughts or feelings; a child may suggest this possibility by commenting, "It's a horse, and it's angry." Children's drawings also probably reflect their knowledge of the world, even though they may not yet have the fine motor skills they need to convey their knowledge fully. In other words, children's drawings reveal not only fine motor coordination but also their self-concepts, emotional and social attitudes, and cognitive development.

Drawing shows two overlapping phases of development during the preschool period. From about 2½ to 4 years, children focus on developing nonrepresentational skills, such as scribbling and purposeful drawing of simple shapes and designs. Sometime around age four, they begin attempting to represent objects (Coles, 1992). Yet although representational drawings usually follow nonrepresentational ones, the two types stimulate each other simultaneously. Children often describe their early scribbles as though they referred to real things, and their practice at portraying real objects helps them to further develop their nonrepresentational skills.

Prerepresentational Drawing   Around the end of infancy, children begin to scribble. A two-year-old experiments with whatever pen or pencil is available to him, almost regardless of its color or type. In doing so, he behaves like an infant and like a child. As with an infant, his efforts focus primarily on the activity itself: on the motions and sensations of handling a pen or pencil. But like an older child, a two-year-old often cares about the outcome of these activities: "That's a Mommy," he says, whether it looks much like one or not. Contrary to a popular view of children's art, even very young children are concerned not only with the process of drawing but with the product as well (Dyson, 1990).

A child's interest in the results of her drawing show up in the patterns she imposes on even her earliest scribbles. Sometimes she fills up particular parts of the page quite intentionally—the whole left side, say, or the complete middle third. And she often emphasizes particular categories of strokes: lots of straight diagonals or many counterclockwise loops (Raines, 1990). Different children select different types of motions for emphasis, so the motions are less like universal stages than like elements of a personal style.

Representational Drawing   While preschool children improve their scribbling skills, they also develop an interest in representing people, objects, and events in their drawings. This interest often far precedes their ability to do so. A three-year-old may assign meanings to scribbles or blobs in his drawing; one blob may be "Mama," and another may be "our house." Events may happen to these blobs, too: Mama may be "going to the store" or "looking for me." During the preschool years, and for a long time thereafter, the child's visual representations are limited by his comparatively rudimentary fine motor skills. Apparently he knows more, visually speaking, than his hands can portray with pens or brushes. Figure 8.4 shows this

3 years, 2 months

3 years, 7 months

4 years, 0 months

4 years, 0 months

4 years, 2 months

4 years, 9 months

5 years, 1 month

FIGURE 8.4
**Samples of a Preschooler's
Drawings (Ages Three to Five)**

tendency for one particular child. Only as the child reaches school age do her drawings of people become relatively realistic.

Sex and Gender Differences in Physical Development

As is true during infancy, preschool boys and girls develop at almost exactly the same average rates (Malina & Bouchard, 1991). This applies to practically any motor skill of which young children are capable, and it applies to both gross and fine motor skills. Any nursery classroom therefore is likely to contain children of both sexes who can run very well and children of both sexes who can paint well or tie their shoelaces without help. This is especially true among younger preschool children (age three or four).

By the time children begin kindergarten (usually at age five), slight gender differences in physical development and motor skills appear, with boys tending to be (slightly) bigger, stronger, and faster. Yet these differences are noticeable only as averages and only by basing the averages on very large numbers of children (Tanner, 1990). Despite the slight differences, therefore, more than 95 percent of children are more skillful and bigger than some members of *both* sexes and less skillful and smaller than certain others of both sexes. The small difference in the average makes no practical difference in the everyday lives of most children or in the lives of the teachers and parents who sometimes plan physical activities for them.

Nonetheless, the fact remains that by the time children start school, a few children in any community are bigger, stronger, and faster than *any* other children, and most of them are boys. Furthermore, these few individuals may get much more than their share of attention because of their superior physical skills. This contributes to the (mistaken) impression that boys are larger and more skillful than girls in general. In this way (among others), gender stereotypes are born.

On the average, boys and girls develop motor skills at almost the same rate during the preschool years. But marked differences emerge among individuals within each sex even at this age.

As differences in motor skills emerge, they might be more accurately called *gender* differences than *sex* differences, because they probably derive partly from the social roles boys and girls begin learning early in the preschool years. Part of the role differences includes how preschool children spend their time. Preschool boys do spend more time than girls in active and rough-and-tumble play, and girls spend more time doing quiet activities such as drawing or playing with stuffed animals. Children of both sexes, furthermore, reinforce or support one another more for engaging in gender-typed activities (Davies, 1991). These differences may give the impression that boys are incapable, or at least less capable, of fine motor skills and that girls are physically weaker.

Perhaps such differences develop for some children by the end of the school years simply as a result of differences in practice that have accumulated over a period of years. Perhaps, too, boys choose active play partly for genetic or hormonal reasons. In any event, five-year-olds have only begun to accumulate these differences in motor experience and to make appropriate gender-typed choices in their play. Taken as groups, preschool girls and boys really differ very little.

What Do You Think?

Suppose you are a child care center worker, and one of your four-year-olds seemed especially clumsy at throwing and catching a ball. Should you do something about this, and if so, what should you do? Consult with a few classmates for their opinions about this. Would you feel the same way if the child seemed clumsy or "uninspired" at drawing?

EFFECTS OF CHILDREN'S PHYSICAL GROWTH

Effects on Adults

The new motor skills that preschooler develop bring with them new risks and create new safety concerns for their parents and other caregivers. What hazards may be waiting for these three-year-olds?

The physical and motor developments that affect a child during the preschool years also affect the adults in the child's life, most notably parents or other caregivers. The changes in the child create, or at least encourage, major changes in how these people deal with him (Luster & Okagaki, 1993). This happens in two ways: through changes in the child's facial features and through changes in his or her overall size and motor ability.

Changes in Facial Features   From birth—and despite any biases from their own parents—children vary in how attractive their faces seem to adults and other children. As a rule, some individuals look younger that others of the same age. In general, having a young-looking face depends on having large features and a large forehead; that is, facial features should be wide-set and located relatively low on the front of the skull. Even slight changes in these proportions (just a fraction of an inch) can make an adult seem many years older or younger, an infant seem six months older or younger, or a preschooler seem one or two years older or younger.

In general, younger-looking children are also rated as more attractive than older-looking children by both adults and peers, and adults tend to expect more mature behaviors from older-looking children (Langlois et al., 1990). This coincidence of stereotypes—of youthfulness and attractiveness—may contribute to important differences in how parents and other adults respond to preschoolers as individuals. A three-year-old who looks like a four-year-old therefore may be expected to speak more fluently at nursery school or to behave more confidently in new or strange situations, even if the child is not yet ready to do so. Since the child is also more likely to be considered relatively unattractive, there is some risk that a vicious cycle of social interactions will develop: the less attractive child is disliked more to begin with but

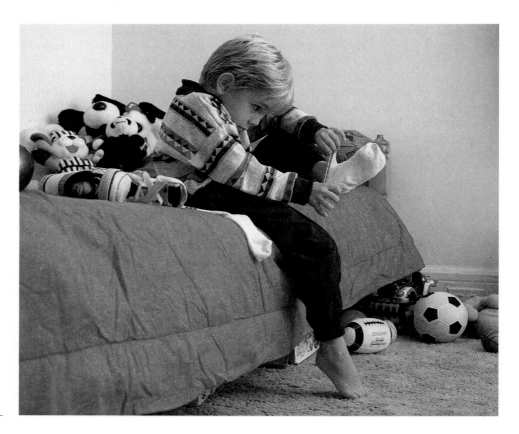

Perfecting new motor skills allows preschoolers to take care of many actions and routines for themselves, when only months earlier they had to be supervised and assisted. But the resulting independence can also challenge parents to make sure that children <u>are</u> doing what they now <u>can</u> do.

disliked even more for failing to do what he supposedly is "able" to do. To overcome this risk, parents and other caregivers need to be made aware of the impact of facial attractiveness (Langlois, 1992). More research is needed, however, to understand how attractiveness influences interpersonal attitudes and expectations, and especially how it affects attitudes and expectations among a preschool child's peers.

Changes in Size and Motor Skill   Consider the changes in size that preschool children experience. A two-year-old often is still small enough to be handled. When necessary, parents can pick her up and move her from one place to another, physically remove her from danger, and carry her (at least partway) if a distance is too far for her to walk. By age five, a child often has outgrown these physical interactions, not only figuratively but literally. Parents or other adults may still lift and cuddle him sometimes in play or in an emergency, but they probably are beginning to avoid doing so on a regular basis. To a significant extent, the child may now simply be too bulky and tall. More and more rarely can parents save a child from danger by picking him up suddenly or speed him along a long hallway by carrying him piggyback. They must somehow get the child to do these things for himself.

Usually, of course, parents succeed at this task. By age five, a child can think and talk about her own actions much more than before, and these improvements help guide her own actions. The handling that used to be literal now becomes mostly figurative: now *handling* means negotiating and discussing with the child rather than lifting her up or carting her around.

Improvements in motor skills also change the agenda for a child's daily activities. A two-year-old may spend a good part of his day experimenting with fundamental skills: walking from one room to another, tearing toilet paper to shreds, or taking pots and pans out of a cupboard. These activities often are embedded in an active social and cognitive life: the child may smile (or frown) at his parents while he works and may "talk" about what he is doing as well. But the motor aspects of his activities absorb a significant part of his attention throughout the day. The child may return repeatedly to a staircase, for instance, as though compelled to get the hang of climbing it; no reward needs to lie at the top step except the satisfaction of a job well done.

A two-year-old's parents therefore must spend a lot of time ensuring that the child comes to no physical harm in her motor explorations. They must make sure the child does not fall down the stairs, tumble into the toilet bowl, or discover a sharp knife among the pots. Their role as safety experts can dominate their contacts with the child, particularly if the child is active.

By the end of the preschool period, minute-to-minute physical surveillance recedes in importance, even though, of course, a concern about safety remains (see Table 8.4 for common accidents and their remedies). Rules about dangers make their appearance ("Don't climb on that fence; it's rickety"), along with the hope that a five-year-old can remember and follow the rules at least some of the time. The shift toward rules also results from increasing confidence in the child's motor skills. Now parents are apt to believe their child can go up and down stairs without stumbling very often—and they are usually right.

During the preschool period, many parents discover a special need for patience in their dealings with their children. Simple actions such as tying shoelaces or putting on socks may take longer than before simply because children now insist on doing many of these things themselves. For similar reasons, walking to the store may now take longer; a three- or four-year-old may prefer to push the stroller rather than ride in it, thus slowing everyone down. And preschoolers may have their own agenda on a walk, such as noticing little rocks on the sidewalk or airplanes in the sky, that differs from parents' goals. On good days these behaviors offer some of the joys of raising children, but on bad days they often irritate even well-meaning parents.

TABLE 8.4   *Common Accidents, Remedies, and Preventions among Preschoolers*

Accidents	What to Do	How to Prevent
Drowning	Unless you are trained in water safety, extend a stick or other device. Use heart massage and mouth-to-mouth breathing when and as long as needed.	Teach children to swim as early in life as possible; supervise children's swim sessions closely; stay in shallow water.
Choking on small objects	If a child is still breathing, do not attempt to remove object; see a doctor instead. If breathing stops, firmly strike child twice on small of back. If this does not help, grab child from behind, put your fist just under his or her ribs, and pull upward sharply several times.	Do not allow children to put small objects in mouth; teach them to eat slowly, taking small bites; forbid vigorous play with objects or food in mouth.
Cuts with serious bleeding	Raise cut above level of heart; apply pressure with cloth or bandage; if necessary, apply pressure to main arteries of limbs.	Remove sharp objects from play areas; insist on shoes wherever ground or floor may contain sharp objects; supervise children's use of knives.
Fractures	Keep injured limb immobile; see a doctor.	Discourage climbing and exploring in dangerous places, such as trees and construction sites; allow bicycles only in safe areas.
Burns	Pour cold water over burned area; keep it clean; then cover with *sterile* bandage. See a doctor if burn is extensive.	Keep matches out of reach of children; keep children well away from fires and hot stoves.
Poisons	On skin or eye, flush with plenty of water; if in stomach, phone poison control center doctor for instructions; induce vomiting only for selected substances.	Keep dangerous substances out of reach of children; throw away poisons when no longer needed. Keep syrup of ipecac in home to induce vomiting, but use *only* if advised by doctor.
Animal bites	Clean and cover with bandage; see a doctor.	Train children when and how to approach family pets; teach them caution in approaching unfamiliar animals.
Insect bites	Remove stinger, if possible; cover with paste of bicarbonate of soda (for bees) or a few drops of vinegar (for wasps and hornets).	Encourage children to recognize and avoid insects that sting, as well as their nests; encourage children to keep calm in presence of stinging insects.
Poisonous plants (e.g., poison ivy)	Remove affected clothing; wash affected skin with strong alkali soap as soon as possible.	Teach children to recognize toxic plants; avoid areas where poisonous plants grow.

Sources: Adapted from Green (1994); Bain (1993).

Physical development changes recreation and play too. At age two, a child probably cannot play baseball; by age five, he may make something of a start at it. At age two, he may enjoy looking at pictures in a book and drawing a few lines of his own; by age five, he may spend long periods making elaborate pictures himself. At age two, he may listen and bounce to music in a general way; by age five, he may swing to it with more refined movements.

These new skills often have teachable elements, and that fact can create new relationships with parents and other caregivers. Now adults can begin showing and encouraging the practice of new skills in a more active, sustained, and focused way than before; in fact, depending on their personal interests and values, they may even feel obligated to do so. Both adult and child may find such teaching and learning easier because they no longer have to monitor the child's every fundamental physical action. A few years before, one false step might have made a young child fall. But now this term has a metaphorical meaning. False steps for a five-year-old usually mean mistakes rather than actual physical stumblings. And while a fall may still mean just a physical tumble to a parent, it is also beginning to be experienced as a failure by the child.

Effects on the Child

As the preceding discussion implies, physical growth gives preschool children many opportunities for increased self-esteem. Now they can walk, skip, and run reliably, whereas before they could only "toddle." Now they can reach for specific objects without fear of breaking, dropping, or crushing them. Now they can write their own names, whereas before they could at most only say them. All these developments, as well as others, give a young child reason to feel proud.

By age five, as long as they have been well supported emotionally, children are firm believers in the value of physical growth. Parents admonish preschoolers to "act like a big boy/girl." Peers emulate older children by showing off their best motor skills to one another—their best ball throws, their best tricks on a swing set at the park, or their best chalk drawings on the sidewalk. "Growing up" becomes a goal, one that more children approach with optimism because the hassles, worries, and limitations of adulthood still seem invisible, incomprehensible, or at least far away. For a number of years longer, many young children concentrate on consolidating their cognitive and social talents because their physical development, for now at least, seems to be both reliable and vigorous.

What Do You Think?

All things considered, is it more relaxing to be the parent of a preschooler or the parent of an infant? Or are the stresses neither greater nor smaller, but just different? This question makes a great topic for a class debate, particularly if you can get a panel of actual parents to judge the success of it afterward!

SUMMARY OF MAJOR IDEAS

Influences on Normal Physical Development

1. Between ages two and five, growth slows down and children take on more adult bodily proportions.

2. Usually growth is rather smooth during the preschool period. Genetic and ethnic background affect its overall rate, as do the quality of nutrition and children's experiences with illness.

3. Children's appetites are often smaller in the preschool years than in infancy, and preschoolers become more selective about their food preferences.

4. If children fall behind in growth because of poor nutrition or hormonal deficiencies, they often can achieve catch-up growth if slow growth has not been too severe or prolonged.

5. A few children suffer from failure to thrive, a condition marked by reduced physical growth, possibly as a result of family stress and conflict.

The Connection Between Health and Poverty

6. A substantial proportion of children, even in well-off countries, live in families with poor access to medical care and therefore experience greater risk of illness and inadequate nutrition.

7. Some of the health risks of poverty can be counteracted by programs aimed at nutrition education and by direct distribution of food to families in need.

Brain Development

8. Although the brain continues to function as a whole, certain areas develop special importance for particular mental and motor functions.

Other Bodily Changes

9. Visual acuity and auditory acuity increase during the preschool period.

10. Children tend to achieve daytime bladder and bowel control early in the preschool period and nighttime bladder control late in this period.

Motor Skill Development

11. Preschoolers acquire and refine many fundamental motor skills, including walking, running, jumping, hopping, climbing, throwing, and catching.

12. Adults can teach some motor skills, but many skills seem to develop simply through young children's natural daily experiences.

13. Fine motor skills such as drawing also emerge during the preschool years.

14. Children's drawings begin with scribbles or prerepresentational drawings and later include representational drawings as well.

15. Boys and girls develop almost identical motor skill competence during the preschool years, but social influences lead each gender to practice and improve separate gender-related skills to some extent.

Effects of Children's Physical Growth

16. Between ages two and five, children's increasing physical competence causes parents to monitor their safety in new ways and to make up and revise rules for their children to follow.

17. Preschoolers' increasing physical independence can challenge parents' patience in a variety of situations.

18. In general, children's growth and motor development help them learn about their world and help parents teach their children as well.

19. Preschoolers' physical accomplishments are a source of pride and self-esteem.

20. Because their physical development now seems assured, five-year-olds can begin turning their attention to consolidating cognitive and social talents.

KEY TERMS

endocrine glands *(240)*
catch-up growth *(241)*
failure to thrive *(242)*
visual cortex *(247)*
auditory cortex *(247)*
Wernicke's area *(247)*
motor cortex *(247)*
Broca's area *(248)*
hemispheric lateralization *(248)*
dichotic listening *(248)*
lateralized behavior *(248)*
fine motor coordination *(254)*

FOR FURTHER READING

Coren, Stanley. *The Left-hander Syndrome.* New York: Free Press, 1992.

Here is a readable introduction to the nature and consequences of lateralization and especially of handedness. The author discusses theories about why handedness occurs, as well as the associations between handedness and cognitive and social skills (e.g., with learning disabilities). The associations are a bit inconclusive, but they make interesting reading.

Grant, James. *The State of the World's Children, 1995.* New York: Oxford University Press, 1995.

This is the annual report by UNICEF (United Nations International Children's Emergency Fund) on the welfare of children around the world. Most of it focuses on two problems: poverty in general and children's physical health in particular. Authoritative tables of statistics (e.g., on mortality rates) are interspersed with concise essays interpreting the figures and proposing actions needed to improve the lives of children.

Jackson, Marni. *The Mother Zone: Love, Sex, and Laundry in the Modern Family.* New York: Holt, 1993.

Marni Jackson writes of her experiences as a new mother of a preschool boy, with ample comments on her worries and growing wisdom as a parent. She focuses strongly on physical concerns (such as her son's illnesses), but ties these to other concerns wherever appropriate (such as the evolution of family relationships).

Paley, Vivian. *Kwamzaa and Me: A Teacher's Story.* Cambridge, Mass.: Harvard University Press, 1995.

Vivian Paley has written numerous books that vividly describe her life in early childhood classrooms from the point of view of both herself as teacher and her children as members of a classroom community. In this book, she focuses on an African American preschooler and how both he and she learn new things about his racial heritage during the school year.

9

EARLY CHILDHOOD

Cognitive Development

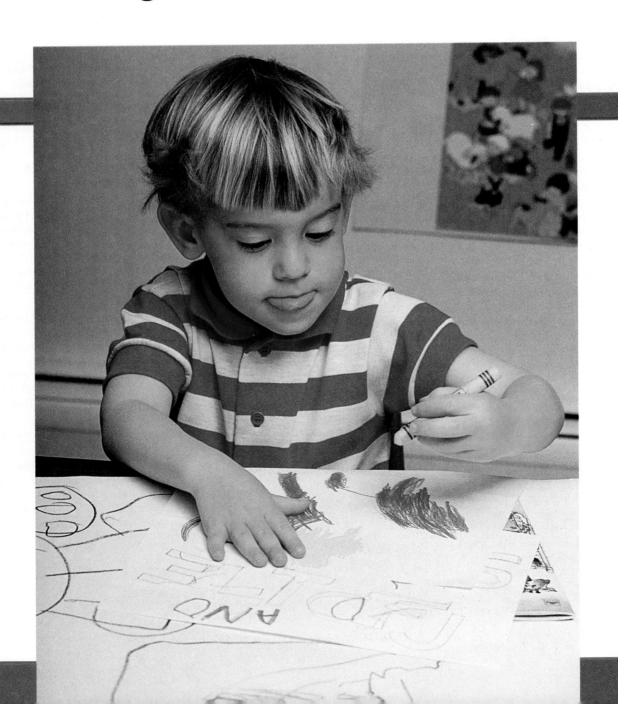

Thinking in Preschoolers

Piaget's Preoperational Stage
Symbolic Thought
Children's Theories of Mind
The Appearance-Reality Distinction
Other Aspects of Children's Conceptual
    Development
Distinguishing Natural Kinds and Artifacts
How Cognitive Development Occurs
Neostructuralist Theories of Cognitive
    Development

**Language Acquisition in the
Preschool Years**

The Nature of Syntax
Beyond First Words: Semantic and
    Syntactic Relations
Mechanisms of Language Acquisition
Innate Predisposition to Acquire Language:
    LAD
Parent-Child Interactions

Language Variations

Gender Differences in Language
Socioeconomic Differences in Language
Language of Deaf and Hearing-Impaired
    Children

**Relationships Between Language
and Thought**

Piaget: Action as the Basis for Both
    Language and Thought
Vygotsky: The Gradual Integration of
    Language and Thought

Early Childhood Education

Early Education and Cognitive Theories
    of Development
Effectiveness of Early Childhood Education
Cultural Diversity and Best Practice in Early
    Education

Focusing Questions

- What are the special strengths and limitations of preschoolers' thinking?

- How does the language of preschool children differ from that of older children and adults?

- What factors influence preschool children's language development?

- What is early childhood education like, and how is it influenced by children's cognitive development and by cultural differences?

W hile a child is growing physically, another miracle unfolds: when he is just about two years old, he begins representing the world to himself and others in ways that were unknown during infancy. For one thing, he can talk and understand much of other people's speech. "Kitty run!" the boy says, pointing to the local cat. "Yes," replies his father. "She's chasing a bird." The young boy nods and says, "Bird gone now. Bad kitty?" and looks to his father for confirmation. "It's okay this time," the father says. "The bird flew away soon enough." Unlike an infant, this child does not really need to handle or manipulate the objects he is thinking about. He can comment on the cat even after it has disappeared.

For another thing, this young preschool child can reenact experiences in new and creative ways through make-believe, a form of pretend play in which he simulates people, objects, animals, and activities in his efforts to understand them. The next day, this child may "become" the cat—crouching down, ready to pounce. If asked what he is doing, he will probably know that it is "just pretend." He is not likely to think he has actually become a cat, no matter how convincing his performance. Through make-believe, he is beginning to create and understand symbols.

Although this child's symbolic, or representational, skills still leave much to be desired, they mark a major achievement. In this chapter and the next, we look at several kinds of symbolic skills and at how young children use them. In this chapter we concentrate on thinking, or problem solving, and on early language acquisition. In Chapter 10 we focus on more social activities, such as play, family relationships, and early relationships outside the family. As we will see, these topics are far more inseparable in real life than they are in textbooks.

THINKING IN PRESCHOOLERS

During the preschool years, young children extend their ability to represent objects and experiences into many new realms of activity and thinking. They begin to notice, for example, that their particular way of viewing the objects across a room differs from the perspective of a family member already sitting on the other side. They begin to distinguish between appearances and reality; that is, when you cover a doll with a costume, it still is "really" the same doll. They even develop implicit theories of how the human mind works: that other minds experience both beliefs and desires and that people's actions are the joint product of both rather than of just one or the other.

Much of the research on these developments owes its intellectual roots to the observations and theorizing of Jean Piaget. During the 1960s and 1970s, considerable effort went toward testing his ideas about cognitive development. On the whole, the research led first to modifications of and, in some cases, challenges to Piaget's major proposals, such as the existence of comprehensive cognitive stages that unfold in a predictable order (Case & Edelstein, 1993). To put these later findings in proper context, however, we must first keep in mind Piaget's key ideas about the changes young children experience during the preschool years.

Piaget's Preoperational Stage

At about age two, according to Piaget, children enter a new stage in their cognitive development (Piaget, 1963). Infancy has left them with several important accomplishments, such as the belief that objects have a permanent existence and the capacity to set and follow simple goals, such as removing all the clothes from every drawer in the house. Infancy has also left them with the knowledge that of all their senses register the same world; now a child knows that hearing her mother in the next room means the child will probably see her soon and that seeing her probably also means she will hear from her.

The preoperational stage, roughly ages two through seven, extends and transforms these skills. During this stage, children become increasingly proficient at using **symbols,** words or actions that stand for other things. During this period, they also extend their belief in object permanence to include **identities,** or constancies,

Preschoolers' play often relies on their growing abilities to represent objects and events symbolically. A carpet becomes a zoo and rows of blocks become fences enclosing zoo animals. A lot of new language skills get stimulated by this sort of activity as well.

of many types: a candle remains the same even as it grows shorter from burning, and a flower growing out of the sidewalk remains the same flower even though its growth changes its appearance from day to day.

Preoperational children also sense many **functional relationships,** or variations in their environments that normally occur together. Preschool children usually know that the hungrier they are, the more they will want to eat; the bigger they are, the stronger they tend to be; and the faster they walk, the sooner they will arrive somewhere. Of course, they still do not know the precise functions or relationships in these examples—exactly how *much* faster they will arrive if they walk a particular distance more quickly—but they do know that a relationship exists.

These are all cognitive strengths of preschool children, and they mark cognitive advances over infancy. But as the *pre-* in the term *preoperational* implies, Piaget's original theorizing actually focused on the limitations of young children's thinking relative to that of older, school-age children. The term *operations* referred to mental actions that allow a child to reason about events he or she experiences. Piaget's observations suggested that from age two to seven, children often confuse their own points of view with those of other people, cannot classify objects and events logically, and often are misled by single features of their experiences. As later sections of this chapter point out, however, more recent research has substantially qualified this perspective; in essence, it has found that children often are more cognitively astute than Piaget realized. Their specific cognitive skills are all based on a key ability that Piaget *did* recognize: the ability to represent experiences symbolically.

Symbolic Thought

As we just noted, *symbols* are words, objects, or behaviors that stand for something else. They take this role not because of their intrinsic properties but because of the intentions of the people who use them. A drinking straw is just a hollow tube and does not become a symbol until a preschooler places it in the middle of a mound of sand and declares it to be a birthday candle. Likewise, the sound /bahks/ lacks symbolic meaning unless we all agree that it refers to a hollow object with corners: *box.*

Probably the most significant cognitive achievement of the preoperational period is the emergence and elaboration of **symbolic thought,** the ability to think by making one object or action stand for another. Throughout their day, two-year-olds use language symbolically, such as when they say "Milk!" to procure a white, drinkable substance from the refrigerator. They also use symbolic thought in make-believe play by pretending to be people or creatures other than themselves. By about age four, children's symbolic play often combines complex actions (getting down on all fours), objects (using a table napkin for a saddle), language (shouting "Neigh!"), and coordination with others (getting a friend to be a rider).

Symbolic thinking helps preschool children organize and process what they know. Objects and experiences can be recalled more easily if they have names and compared more easily if the child has concepts that can describe their features. Symbols also help children communicate what they know to others, even in situations quite different from the experience itself. Having gone to the store, they can convey this experience to others either in words ("I went shopping") or through pretend play ("Let's play store, and I'll be the clerk."). By its nature, communication fosters social relationships among children, but it also fosters cognitive development by allowing individual children to learn from the experiences of others. More precisely, communication allows individuals to learn from the symbolic representations of others' experiences. Not surprisingly, these benefits do not occur all at once. Preschool children need time and practice to hone symbolic skills to high levels of proficiency.

Children's Theories of Mind

As part of their growing symbolic abilities, preschool children develop ideas about how thinking itself occurs and how thinking leads to action in everyday activities. These ideas often are called a **theory of mind,** a stable, though informal framework with which to understand others' beliefs and desires and to predict their actions (Wellman, 1990). Unlike truly scientific theories, a child's theory of mind is not based on systematic experimentation, nor are the terms in it defined as carefully. But a child's theory of mind shares important characteristics with any scientific theory. It contains a core of key ideas that are relatively resistant to change or disproof, as well as other ideas that are more peripheral and more subject to change as a result of experience. For example, a core idea of a child's theory of mind might be that people *have* ideas, beliefs, and desires and these are fundamentally more intangible than everyday objects: the thought of a dog is intangible, even though the dog itself is very tangible. A peripheral idea—one subject to disproof by experience—might be that the thought of a dog necessarily leads a person to seek out a real, live dog to play with.

Considerable evidence exists that preschool children have a simple "theory" of mind in the sense just described. They clearly understand that other people have thoughts and feelings and that these mental entities are distinct from the reality of everyday objects. In one experiment, investigators asked three- and four-year-olds several versions of the following story (Bartsch & Wellman, 1995):

> Sam wants to find his puppy. It might be hiding in the garage or under the porch. Sam thinks his puppy is under the porch. Where will Sam look for his puppy—in the garage or under the porch?

In some versions, the story mentioned only where the puppy was *not* (i.e., not in the garage); in others, it mentioned that Sam changed his mind ("his mother tells Sam that she saw the puppy in the garage"); in still others, the investigators first asked the child where *she* thought the puppy was, and then she described Sam as thinking the puppy was in the opposite place. In all of these versions, children performed extremely well—with 85 to 90 percent accuracy—suggesting that they knew the only relevant consideration in solving the problem is what was in Sam's mind. It was not relevant, for example, whether the child being interviewed believed the puppy was in a particular place.

On the basis of this study and others, Henry Wellman proposed a basic *belief-desire psychology* for young (three-year-old) preschoolers (Wellman, 1990). In this theory of mind, the child distinguishes between beliefs (what you know or think) and desires (what you want) and distinguishes both of these from actions (what you do). As children grow older, they elaborate on this basic, informal psychology by adding other sorts of mental entities—emotions that influence thinking, such as boredom or fear—to their theories of mind. The elaborations allow older preschoolers to solve problems that would be beyond the understanding of three-year-olds.

One such problem is the **false-belief task,** in which the child is expected to know how a person would respond despite having false or incorrect information (Olver & Ratner, 1994). A relatively basic false-belief task would pose the problem of misinformation explicitly: "Jane wants to find her kitten. Jane's kitten is really in the playroom, but Jane thinks her kitten is in the kitchen. Where will Jane look for her kitten? Where is the kitten really?" Another version might only imply that Jane is mistaken, for example, by having her mother move the kitten without Jane's knowledge. In either version, however, this problem proves very hard for three-year-olds: they consistently think Jane will look where the kitten *really* is rather than where she *thinks* it is. Not until age five do children solve the problem with a high degree of accuracy.

Why should children need this extra maturity? One possibility is that false-belief tasks make heavy demands on reasoning: the child must attend not only to where the kitten really is but also to where Jane thinks it is. Another is that preschoolers' theory of mind is not fully elaborated; preschoolers may know that thoughts exist but do not yet appreciate their consequences for behavior (Flavell et al., 1995).

The Appearance-Reality Distinction

One result of developing a theory of mind is that preschoolers gradually realize that things are not always what they seem to be. This realization is the **appearance-reality distinction:** a knowledge of when and why an object looks different than it "really and truly" is. This concept is surprisingly difficult for many three-year-olds but very easy for most six-year-olds.

In one of many experiments to investigate this ability, three-year-olds were shown a cutout of an animal, such as a pink-colored seal; then the investigators slid a green filter over the cutout. They asked the children, "What color does the seal look like now? Is it really and truly green?" More than half of the children answered the second question incorrectly; they knew the seal had changed color but claimed it was "really" green. In another part of the experiment, the investigators showed objects that looked exactly like another object, such as an eraser that was shaped and painted to look like a banana. They asked, "Does it look like an eraser or a banana? Is it really an eraser or a banana?" On this task, three-year-olds overidentified with reality: they knew the object was really an eraser, but they now denied that it looked like a banana.

In general, three-year-olds seem unable to hold *both* the appearance and the reality of an object in mind at the same time. Interestingly, they find it much easier to make distinctions between pretense and reality (Harris & Kavanaugh, 1993). Suppose an investigator asks a child to pretend that a seal is "really" a different color or that a string is "really" a snake. When questioned about these pretenses, the child clearly distinguishes between the real color of the seal and its pretend color and between the real string and the pretend snake. The reason for the greater success in identifying pretense is not clear, but it may be related to engaging in make-believe play, an almost universal activity during early childhood. Distinguishing appearance from reality, on the other hand, requires developing the additional knowledge of the nature of false beliefs.

Other Aspects of Children's Conceptual Development

In addition to the concepts described in the previous sections, preschool children develop specific cognitive skills as a result of their growing symbolic ability. As Piaget originally pointed out, for example, they become able to classify objects, and by the end of the preschool period some can even attend to changes in objects involving more than one feature at a time. They move beyond rote counting to a meaningful understanding of the concept of *number*. They also acquire an intuitive sense of the differences among fundamentally different types of concepts, such as the difference between a living dog and a toy robot made to act like a dog.

Classification Skills   Classification refers to the placement of objects in groups or categories according to some specific standards or criteria. Young preschool children, even those just three years old, can reliably classify objects that differ in just one dimension, or feature, especially if that dimension presents fairly obvious contrasts. Given a collection of pennies and nickels, a preschooler usually can sort them by color, which is their most obvious dimension of difference. Given a boxful of silverware, a young child might sort the items by type: knives, forks, and spoons.

Or she might group dishes by how they are used in real life, putting each cup with one saucer rather than separating all the cups from all the saucers. These simple groupings represent cognitive advances over infancy. Later, during the middle years, children will become able to group objects by more than one dimension at the same time. But that will be later.

Reversibility and Conservation   Some classification problems require **reversibility** in thinking, or the ability to undo a problem mentally and go back to its beginning. If you accidentally drop a pile of papers on the floor, you may be annoyed, but you know that in principle the papers are all there: you believe (correctly) that the papers that have scattered can be "unscattered" if you pick them up and sort them into their correct order again. Reversibility, it turns out, contributes to a major cognitive achievement of middle childhood: **conservation,** or the ability to perceive that certain properties of an object remain the same or constant despite changes in the object's appearance. On average, children do not achieve conservation until about age six.

To understand reversibility and conservation, consider the following task. First, you show a preschool child two tall glasses with exactly the same amount of water in each (see Figure 9.1). Then the child watches you pour the water from one of the glasses into a third, wide glass. Naturally, the water line in the wide glass will be lower than it was in the tall one. Finally, you ask the child, "Is there more water in the wide glass than in the [remaining] tall glass, or less, or just as much?"

Children less than five years old typically say that the tall glass has either less or more water than the wide glass, but not that the two glasses are the same. According to Piaget, this happens because the child forgets the identity of the water levels that she saw only a moment earlier; in this sense, she is a nonreversible thinker and cannot imagine pouring the water back again to prove the glasses' equality. Instead she is limited to current appearances. More often than not, a big difference in appearance leads her to say that the amount of water changes as a result of its being poured. In Piagetian terms, she fails to conserve, or believe in the constancy of the amount of liquid despite its visible changes (Inhelder & Piaget, 1958). Not until the early school years do conservation and reversibility become firmly established.

In the meantime, tasks that require conservation are affected significantly by how they are presented or described to the child. When given a series of conservation tasks, for example, a child tends to alternate conserving with nonconserving responses (Elbers et al., 1991). Why? Perhaps repeating the question makes some children believe the experimenter wants them to change their response; after all, why else would she repeat herself? Because most children begin the conservation task by agreeing that the glasses hold equal amounts of water, obliging children may feel compelled to give nonconserving responses against their own better judgment.

FIGURE 9.1
Conservation of Liquid Quantity
Does a child believe liquid quantity remains constant (is "conserved") despite changes in its shape? The method illustrated here, or some variation of it, is often used to answer this question.

First, you show a preschool child two tall glasses with exactly the same amount of water in each.

Then the child watches you pour the water from one of the glasses into a third, wide glass.

Finally, you ask the child, "Is there more water in the wide glass than in the (remaining) tall glass, or less, or just as much?"

A child who lacks reversibility (is non-conserving) in thinking about liquids says either, "The tall glass has more," or "The wide glass has more." She is fooled by its appearance.

It seems, therefore, that children may take Piagetian tasks as social events as well as cognitive ones.

The Concept of Number   Like many parents, Piaget correctly noted that children do not fully grasp how the conventional number system works during the first few years of life (Piaget, 1952). Preschoolers may, of course, count, such as when a three-year-old says, "One, two, three, blast off!" before tossing a ball high into the air. But such counting, Piaget argued, lacks understanding; it essentially is a rote activity. To fully understand number, a child must comprehend three ideas. The first is that a one-to-one correspondence exists between items in a set and number names; the second is *cardinality,* the idea that the total number of a set corresponds to the last number named when the items are counted; and the third is *ordinality,* the concept that numbers always occur in a particular order (the second item to be counted is always called the "second," for example).

Research stimulated by these ideas about number generally has concluded that Piaget underestimated preschoolers' knowledge of number. Many four-year-olds, and even some three-year-olds, can reliably say the numbers in sequence, at least up to some modest limit such as *five* or *six*. They also know that different sets of items should be counted with the same sequence of numbers, that each item should be counted only once, and that any set can be counted in more than one order. For this and other reasons, some psychologists have argued that children may have an innate conception of number (Gelman & Greeno, 1988), though of course they must also learn the conventional number names from experience.

This evidence is persuasive, but it may not justify concluding that number knowledge is innate. Experiments by Karen Wynn (1992) suggest that children as young as three years understand something of the notion of numerosity—that numbers refer to specific amounts. In one study, a three-year-old was shown pairs of pictures, each portraying a different number of animals. In one pair, one picture showed a single animal and the second showed several (such as five); in the other pair, one picture showed exactly one *more* animal than in the other picture (such as five in one picture and six in the other). The procedure is illustrated in Figure 9.2. For both pairs of pictures, children were asked to point to the picture that showed a particular number ("Can you show me the five animals?").

This procedure produced several interesting results. First, even three-year-olds who could count had trouble choosing between the pictures that were closely matched in numerosity; choosing between five animals and six animals, for example, was difficult, even for children who could count to six or beyond. On the other hand, the same three-year-olds reliably identified which picture had "more" when several animals were paired with just a single animal; choosing between five animals and one animal, for example, was relatively easy. Only older preschoolers (four

FIGURE 9.2
Judging Numerosity Without Counting
Even when they could count, three-year-olds often failed to identify the picture with only one more item in it. But they could identify the picture that contained many more items.

Question for child: "Which picture has the five animals?"

Judgment #1:
Extreme difference in number of objects

Judgment #2:
Small difference in number of objects

years and up) could reliably choose "more" when the numbers were very close, and when they did so, they tended to solve them for *all* possible numbers rather than for only selected numbers. A four-year-old who could point to six animals instead of five, for example, was likely to also point correctly to seven instead of eight or four instead of five.

These results imply that young children first acquire a general notion of numerosity whether or not they can count yet. They also suggest that it takes a relatively long time—about a year—to acquire knowledge of precise numerosities (exactly what *five* really means) and that children seem to acquire knowledge of all of these precise numbers at about the same time.

Distinguishing Natural Kinds and Artifacts

Piaget observed that preschool children often express **animism,** the belief that non-living objects are in fact alive or conscious or both. If asked, "Why do the clouds move?", a child might answer, "Because they want to" or "Because the wind tries to move them." Underlying the charm of these remarks is an implication that the clouds and the wind have desires and goals just as people do.

What leads to this sort of behavior? Research has approached this question by reframing Piaget's original observations as a problem concerning how children learn to distinguish between natural kinds and artifacts. **Natural kinds** are things with an intrinsic essence and with origins in other things of the same kind. A cat, for example, is a natural kind because it has an essential "catness," perhaps related to its genetic structure and genetic origins, that still exists even if the cat is painted to look like a skunk. **Artifacts,** on the other hand, are things created and defined by external causes. A hammer is an artifact because it is manufactured to be a hammer; it is not born from a mother and father hammer as a cat is born from a mother and father cat.

How early do children learn to distinguish between natural kinds and artifacts? Is there an early age at which the two concepts are confused or regarded as the same? If so, the confusion may account for some of the animism Piaget observed: if a child calls a small clock a "baby clock" and a large one a "mother clock," for example, she may be on her way to viewing these artifacts as living creatures. Another child who (unfortunately) pulls the wings off an insect out of sheer curiosity may be showing similar confusion: the insect is considered just a "thing"—an artifact.

Research provides some support for these possibilities, though with qualifications. In one series of studies, preschool children confused the truly defining features of natural kinds with more superficial features but seemed to understand the nature of artifacts clearly (Keil, 1989). Investigators showed children two sets of pictures. One set showed a raccoon and a skunk, and the other showed a coffeepot and a bird feeder that had roughly the same shape as the coffeepot (see Figure 9.3). The investigators showed the raccoon in the first set to children and said, "Some scientists studied this animal very carefully and found that they had

FIGURE 9.3
Children's Understanding of Artifacts and Natural Kinds
Children do not clearly distinguish artifacts and natural kinds until well into the middle years. In the experiment illustrated here, five-year-olds tended to think the animal was still a raccoon, even though its essential features were really those of a skunk. Such confusion may contribute to the animism that Piaget observed in young children's thinking.
Source: Adapted from Keil (1989).

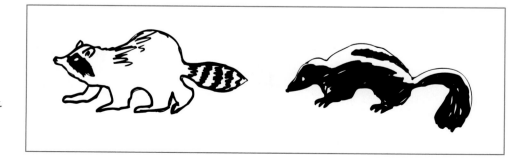

the blood of a skunk and that their insides were like a skunk. They also found out that this animal's mommy and daddy were skunks, and when they have babies, the babies will be skunks. What do you think this animal is, a raccoon or a skunk?" Strictly speaking, therefore, the "raccoon" had the defining features of a skunk. Nevertheless, five-year-olds still tended to regard the animal as a raccoon; not until about age nine or ten did children discount its appearance and believe the information in the verbal description qualified the animal to be a skunk. Confusion about what constituted a truly "natural" kind seemed widespread well into the middle years of childhood.

On the other hand, five-year-olds in the same study were clear about what qualified an object to be an artifact. After being told that scientists discovered that the bird feeder had really been made from a coffeepot, all the children asserted that it was nonetheless "really" a bird feeder, not a coffeepot. They did not need five more years of maturity to develop this certainty as they did for the concept of natural kinds.

It is tempting to conclude, as Piaget did, that five- and six-year-olds indeed show animism and that they do so because they find the nature of natural kinds—and especially living creatures—difficult to understand. Young children seem to develop an informal "theory" of natural kinds as early as their third or fourth year. The informal theory grows out of their knowledge of human bodily behaviors and functions and generalizes to other living creatures: a natural kind is one that (like the child) breathes, eats, sleeps, and the like (Carey, 1988; Hickling & Gelman, 1995). As their knowledge of human functioning and anatomy increases, a theory develops ("animals are physically like people") that guides their thinking about differences among creatures and between natural kinds and artifacts.

How Cognitive Development Occurs

Complexities in cognitive performance such as those just described may occur because preschool children depend on the social context or circumstances to develop new cognitive skills. Children do not simply learn fundamental thinking skills alone, merely interacting with and thinking about objects and experiences. Instead, either

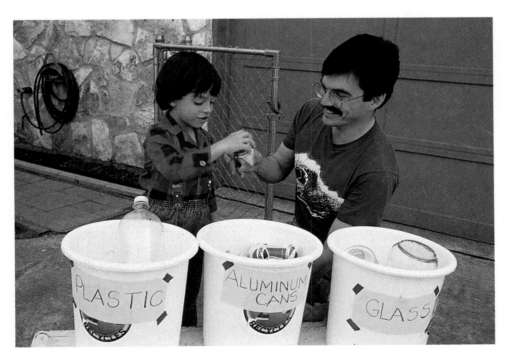

A lot of cognitive change occurs because of the mutual development of meaning that happens in the "zone of proximal development," where two people focus on a common activity. In this case the father stimulates his son to learn about the son's growing knowledge and abilities.

directly or indirectly, they learn from adults or older, more experienced peers (Rogoff et al., 1993). The older children provide models for how to solve problems, and they offer hints and information about how to approach or think about a problem. The help sometimes is deliberate (such as in school) or accidental (such as at home in many cases), but either way it allows a child to handle problems that are just a bit beyond those she or he can deal with alone.

The gap in difficulty between independent thinking and socially supported thinking is called the **zone of proximal development,** the area in which problems are too difficult to solve alone but not too hard to solve with support from adults or more competent peers. The concept originated with Soviet psychologist Lev Vygotsky (Newman & Holzman, 1993) and has created a lot of interest among developmental psychologists because it suggests how stages and skills may emerge and evolve. In learning about number, for example, everyday conversations between parent and child play a significant role:

PARENT: Here are four books for you and the same for your brother.
CHILD: The same? *(He investigates his brother's pile of books.)* No, he has more *(spoken with annoyance)*.
PARENT: No, really, they're the same. Take another look.
CHILD: He does have more.
PARENT: Try laying his out in a row. Then lay yours out, too. Then compare.
CHILD *(does as suggested, then counts each row)*: One, two, three, four. One, two, three, four. The same! *(He looks satisfied.)*

In this example, the parent provides a framework that the child cannot provide for himself and that allows the child to solve the problem for himself. First, the parent states the problem in a helpful way ("They're the same"); then she gives hints about how to solve it. But the final solution remains with the child. The help occurs in the child's personal zone of proximal development. Without it, the child might not have solved the problem, at least at this point in his cognitive development.

Neostructuralist Theories of Cognitive Development

As the studies described so far suggest, preschoolers show considerable new strengths in using symbolic thought. They can take others' perspectives to some extent, they develop a usable theory of how the human mind works, and they can distinguish between appearances and reality at least some of the time. Many of Piaget's classic observations on Swiss children have proven true: preschool children have trouble focusing on two dimensions of an object at once and therefore have difficulty with conservation tasks throughout most of the preschool period. Other Piagetian observations have underestimated children's ability and stimulated research that has led to new ways of thinking about children's capacities. For example, unlike Piaget's claims, preschool children do have a partial understanding of number and can make important distinctions between living and nonliving objects, as shown by the studies about natural kinds.

Strictly speaking, much of the research on children's conceptual development does not really contradict Piaget's general approach; it just complicates our picture of children's cognitive development. Many psychologists have sought to keep Piaget's commitment to stagelike progressions in development and at the same time revise the content or details of those progressions (Case & Edelstein, 1993). Instead of proposing comprehensive, "grand" stages of thinking, as Piaget did, they argue that stages may be much more focused in content. Research based on this premise has in fact identified stages of spatial representation, of mathematical ability, and of interpersonal awareness, among others (Case, 1992). Each of these skills seems to develop through predictable stages, but do so independently of the other domains. As individuals, children therefore show unique patterns and timing of development across many areas of thinking and skills (Wozniak & Fischer, 1993).

This newer view of cognitive stages is sometimes called **neostructuralist** or **neo-Piagetian theory** because of its roots in the ideas of Piaget. As a result of focusing attention on more specific cognitive achievements, it has also paid more attention to *how,* or by what processes, children acquire new cognitive skills. One neostructuralist line of research explored the process of learning to draw by noting how it consists of the successive coordination of simpler skills (Dennis, 1992). An infant begins her second year of life able to visually track objects as well as reach for objects. With practice, by the time she reaches age three, the child has learned to coordinate these two schemes into a single cognitive skill that enables scribbling. As the child continues to practice with this newly consolidated scheme, she begins coordinating it with other, more advanced schemes, such as *comparing* scribbles with the orientation and edges of the paper. When tracking edges of a paper and tracking scribbles eventually become coordinated, the child can finally begin controlling lines and curves. Now the stage is set for her first representational drawings, such as stick-figure people.

From the neostructuralist perspective, then, cognitive development during the preschool years is not all of one piece when it unfolds but has many components— many forms of thinking, as well as perceptual and language developments. As a result, it is important to understand each piece separately from the others and to combine them to get a well-rounded picture of young children. Therefore, in the next section we look at another major piece of the puzzle of children's thinking: language acquisition.

What Do You Think?

What do you think parents of young children believe about preschoolers' cognitive abilities? What if you asked them (1) how much their children know when parents are happy or upset and (2) whether children and adults outside the family know when other children are happy or upset? Would parents' beliefs about these questions coincide with the research described in this section? If possible, interview a few real-life parents to test your predictions.

LANGUAGE ACQUISITION IN EARLY CHILDHOOD

For most children, language expands rapidly after infancy. Dramatic development occurs in *syntax,* or the way the child organizes utterances. But significant changes also occur in semantics and in pragmatics. As we mentioned in Chapter 6, *semantics* refers to what the child means by his utterances. *Pragmatics* is how the child adjusts his utterances to the needs and expectations of different situations and speakers; it might also be called "communicative competence."

Because of the comparative importance of syntactic development during the preschool years, we emphasize this particular topic here, leaving major discussion of semantics and communication for Chapter 12. This approach does not imply, however, that these three aspects of language develop in isolation from one another. Quite the contrary: as the discussion of syntax emphasizes, how a child organizes an utterance (her syntax) depends partly on what she wants to say and the meaning of her words (her semantics) and partly on when she wants to say it and to whom (her pragmatics or communicative competence). Conversely, her meanings and intentions sometimes stimulate her to learn new ways to organize utterances and

"We don't say 'I losed my dime.' We say 'I LOSTED it.' "

As children acquire language, they sometimes overregularize their grammar, as the girl in the cartoon is doing by insisting that -ed be added to make the past tense. Since errors like this are never (or only rarely) spoken by adults, they suggest that children actively—though unconsciously—search for grammatical rules or syntax of language.

stimulate the adults in her life to model them as well. The examples that follow illustrate some of these relationships.

The Nature of Syntax

The **syntax** of a language is a group of rules for ordering and relating its elements. Linguists call the elements of language *morphemes.* **Morphemes** are the smallest meaningful units of language; they include words as well as a number of prefixes and suffixes that carry meaning (the /s/ in *houses* or the /re/ in *redo*) and verb-tense modifiers (the /ing/ in *going*).

Syntactic rules operate on morphemes in several ways. Sometimes they mark important relationships between large classes or groups of words. Consider these two pairs of sentences:

1a. John kissed Barbara. *and* 2a. Frank kisses Joan.
1b. Barbara kissed John.   2b. Frank kissed Joan.

These sentences differ in meaning because of syntactic rules. In the first pair, a rule about the order, or sequence, of words tells us who is giving the kiss and who is receiving it: the name preceding the verb is the agent (the kisser), and the name following the verb is the recipient (the "kissee"). In the second pair, the morphemes /es/ and /ed/ tell something about when the event occurred; adding /es/ to the end of the word signifies that it is happening now, but adding /ed/ means it happened in the past. These rules, and many similar ones, are understood and used by all competent speakers of the language. Unlike textbook authors, however, the speakers may never state them and may be only barely aware of them.

Syntactic rules vary in how regular or general they are. Most apply to large, open-ended groupings or classes of words. This quality makes them **generative;** that is, speakers can create or generate brand-new sentences almost infinitely by applying the rule to brand-new morphemes. The preceding examples are generative in this sense. Replacing *John* with *fish,* for example, and *Barbara* with *water* creates the strange sentence "Fish kissed water." This sentence may sound odd, but it nevertheless conveys some idea of who was doing the kissing and who was receiving it. Even nonsense words can fit into the same syntactic framework: "Gokems kissed splibs." We may have no idea of who (or what) *gokems* and *splibs* are, but the syntax of the sentence still tells us which one was the kisser and which the kissee. To this extent, the syntax conveys meaning independently of the words slotted into the sentence form.

Unfortunately for a child learning to talk, some syntactic rules have only a small range of application, and still others have irregular exceptions. Most words, for example, signal pluralization (the existence of more than one) by having an /s/ or /es/ added at the end; *book* means one volume, and *books* means more than one. But a few words use other methods to signal the plural. *Foot* means one, and *feet,* not *foots,* means more than one; *child* means one and *children* more than one; and *deer* can mean either one animal or several.

Thus, in acquiring syntax, a young child confronts a mixed system of rules. Some apply widely and regularly, and others apply narrowly and exceptionally. Added to these complexities is the fact that the child often hears utterances that are grammatically incomplete or even incorrect. Somehow he or she must sort these out from the grammatically acceptable utterances while at the same time trying to sort out the various syntactic rules and the contexts for using them. On the face of it, the child's task seems daunting; yet somehow most children manage it within a few years' time. Their success makes a powerful argument that human beings are innately predisposed to acquire language. No other cognitive task is achieved with so little deliberate effort or direct teaching in such a short time, either during early childhood or in any other period of life.

Beyond First Words: Semantic and Syntactic Relations

Before age two, children begin linking words when they speak. Initially the words seem to be connected by their *semantic relations,* or the meanings intended for them, rather than by *syntactic relations,* the relations among grammatical classes of words such as nouns, verbs, and adjectives. This is particularly true when the child is still speaking primarily in two-word utterances (sometimes called **duos**). As the mean length of a child's utterances increases to three words and more, syntactic relations become much more noticeable.

Duos and Telegraphic Speech   These ideas were documented in a classic set of three case studies of early language acquisition by Roger Brown (1973). When the children Brown observed were still speaking primarily in two-word utterances, their utterances were organized around eight possible semantic relationships; these are listed in Table 9.1, along with examples. The meanings of the utterances were determined by the intended relationships among the words, and the intentions of the preschool speakers often were discernible only by observing the context in which the utterances were made. "Mommy sandwich" could mean "the type of sandwich Mommy usually eats," or "Mommy is eating the sandwich," or "Mommy, give me a sandwich," all depending on the conversational context.

The reason for the ambiguity is that two-word utterances leave out indicators of syntactic relationships. One syntactic indicator is word order: due to word order, "the boy chased the girl" means something different than "the girl chased the boy." Children who still speak in duos do not use word order randomly, but they do tend to be less predictable about it than more linguistically mature children, whose utterances can be several words long. Another indicator of syntactic relationships is inflections, prepositions, and conjunctions. An older child will add 's to indicate possession (as in "Mommy's sandwich") and use words such as *in* and *on* to indicate location (as in "jump on the stair"). Leaving these indicators out makes the speech sound stilted and ambiguous; therefore, it is also called **telegraphic speech,** presumably because it sounds like a telegram. Telegraphic speech is characteristic of children's first efforts to combine words (around eighteen months to two years), but it can persist well after children begin using longer, more syntactic utterances some of the time.

TABLE 9.1   Semantic Relations in Two-Word Utterances

Relationship	Example
Agent + action	Baby cry
Action + object	Eat cookie
Agent + object	Bobby cookie
Action + locative (location)	Jump stair
Object + locative	Teddy bed
Possessor + possessed	Mommy sandwich
Attribute + object	Big dog
Demonstrative + object	There Daddy

A child's earliest utterances are organized not according to adultlike grammar but according to particular semantic or meaning-oriented relationships such as those listed in this table. Often the intended, underlying relationships are ambiguous and can be discerned only by an attentive, observant adult at the time of the utterance.

Regularities and Overgeneralizations   After highly individual beginnings, certain aspects of syntax develop in universal and predictable patterns. The present progressive form *-ing* occurs quite early in most children's language, the regular plural morphemes *-s* and *-es* somewhat later, and articles such as *the* and *a* still later (Marcus et al., 1992).

At a slightly older age, most children begin using auxiliary verbs to form questions, but they do so without inverting word order, as adults normally do. At first, a child will say, "Why you are cooking?" and only later "Why are you cooking?" This suggests that language acquisition involves more than just copying adult language; after all, adults rarely model incorrect forms. To a certain extent, children's language seems to compromise between the new forms children hear and old forms they already can produce easily.

Sometimes, in fact, early syntax becomes *too* regular, and children make **overgeneralizations.** Around age three, a preschool child may say, "I runned to the store" or "All the childs came." In each case, the child uses the wrong but more regular form as opposed to the correct but irregular forms of an earlier age. Usually, by early school age he shifts back again, although not necessarily because anyone teaches him or forces him to do so. Apparently his overgeneralizations represent efforts to try out new rules of syntax that he has finally noticed.

The Predisposition to Infer Grammar   As these examples suggest, young children seem to infer grammatical relationships rather than simply copy others' speech. Few parents try purposely to teach talking, and those who do usually discover that direct efforts tend to fail. Consider this example:

CHILD: My teacher holded the rabbits, and we patted them.
MOTHER: Did you say your teacher held the baby rabbits?
CHILD: Yes.
MOTHER: What did you say she did?
CHILD: She holded the rabbits, and we patted them.
MOTHER: Did you say she held them tightly?
CHILD: No, she holded them loosely.

Despite her mother's apparently unsuccessful attempt to encourage adult grammar in this situation, the child almost certainly will switch from *holded* to *held* eventually. The child, not the adults around her, seems to control the timing of this change; she, not her mother, must solve the grammatical puzzles posed by language.

"I runned to the store"

"Unpour the water, please"

"All the childs came!"

A classic study of early syntax showed the importance of the child's own inferences about grammatical rules. Instead of asking children about real words, the experimenter showed them pictures of imaginary creatures and actions that had nonsense words as names (Berko, 1958). With one picture, a child was told, "Here is a wug." Then he was shown two pictures and told, "Here are two of them. Here are two ——." Most children, even those as young as 2½, completed the sentences with the grammatically correct word, *wugs*. Because they could not possibly have heard the term before, they must have applied a general rule for forming plurals, one that did not depend on copying any language experiences specifically but came from inferring the underlying structure of many experiences taken together. The rule most likely operated unconsciously, because these children were very young indeed.

The Limits of Learning Rules   Such skill at acquiring syntactic rules, however, obscures a seemingly contradictory fact about the acquisition of syntax: much syntax must be learned by rote. As we have pointed out, most children use irregular forms (such as *foot/feet*) correctly before they shift to incorrect but more regular forms. The most reasonable explanation for the change is that they pick up the very first sentence forms simply by copying, word for word, the sentences they hear spoken. Presumably they copy many regular forms by rote, too, but the very regularity of these forms hides the haphazard, unthinking way in which children acquire them.

Although children eventually rely on rule-governed syntax, they probably still learn a lot of language by rote. Many expressions in a language are *idiomatic*, meaning they bear no logical relation to normal meanings or syntax. The sentence "How do you do?", for example, usually is not a literal inquiry as to how a person performs a certain action; and the sentence "How goes it?", meaning "How is it going?", does not even follow the usual rules of grammar. Because words and phrases such as these violate the rules of syntax and meaning, children must learn them one at a time.

Mechanisms of Language Acquisition

Exactly how do children learn to speak? For most children, several factors may operate at once. In general, current evidence can best be summarized as follows: language seems to grow through the interaction of an active, thinking child with certain key people and linguistic experiences. The preceding sections describe in part this active, thinking child; the following sections describe some possible key interaction experiences.

Reinforcement   A commonsense view, one shared by behaviorally oriented psychologists, is that children learn to speak through reinforcement. According to this idea, a child's caregiver reinforces vocal noises whenever they approximate a genuine word or utterance, and this reinforcement causes the child to vocalize in increasingly correct (or at least adultlike) ways (Skinner, 1957). In the course of babbling, an infant may happen to say "Ma-ma-ma-ma," to which his proud parent smiles and replies cheerfully, "How nice! You said 'Mama'!" The praise reinforces the behavior, so the infant says "Ma-ma-ma-ma" more often after that. After many such experiences, his parents begin to reinforce only closer approximations to *mama*, leading finally to a true version of this word.

Among preschool children, the same process could occur if parents reinforced correct grammatical forms and ignored or criticized errors or relatively immature utterances. Parents might respond more positively to the sentence "I have three feet" than to the sentence "I have two foots." According to the principles of reinforcement (see Chapter 2), the child would tend not only to use the correct version more often but also to generalize the correct elements of this sentence to other, similar utterances.

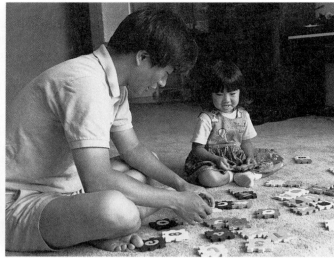

Imitation accounts for a very large part of human learning. This grandmother is modeling both skills in reading to her granddaughter, even before the girl can actually read. The father is modeling skills at solving puzzles, as well as conversational skills. In both cases the skills are "caught," not taught explicitly.

Analysis of conversations between parents and children confirms this possibility, at least in indirect form and for the early stages of language acquisition. One study compared parents' responses to simple but grammatical sentences made by their two- and three-year-old children to their responses to ungrammatical utterances (Penner, 1987). Parents did not correct their children's grammar directly, but they were more likely to elaborate on the child's topic if the utterance was a grammatical one. The tendency was most pronounced, however, when preschoolers were just beginning to use syntactic forms, speaking in sentences that vacillated between two and three words in length rather than in much longer sentences. Other research has documented that these elaborations seem to involve a two-way influence (Moerk, 1992): on the one hand, the child speaks more as a result of the parent's elaborations; on the other, the parent is more likely to fine-tune his or her own utterances to match the child's growing syntactic skills.

Imitation and Practice   In some sense, children obviously must imitate their native language to acquire it. This is an idea borrowed from the social learning variety of behaviorism. In daily life, though, the process of imitation is subtle and often indirect. Children do not imitate everything they hear, but most copy certain selected utterances, often immediately after hearing them. Sometimes the utterances chosen for imitation involve familiar sentence forms that contain new, untried terms, and sometimes they contain familiar terms cast into new, untried forms. The imitated terms and forms return later in the child's spontaneous speech. At first these utterances resemble the rote learning mentioned earlier, and they seem to help the child by emphasizing or calling attention to new morphemes and syntax.

The following four-year-old child had never before heard the form *-ish*, meaning "something similar to":

FATHER: We need to paint the fence soon. Maybe a kind of brownish-red.
CHILD *(Pauses, listening)*: Brownish-red. What's brownish-red?
FATHER: It's what you get when you mix brown and red. Brownish-red, or reddish-brown, or brownish-reddish.
CHILD *(Smiles and pauses again)*: Brownish-red. Brownish-red.

Imitation may also help children acquire language by initiating playful practice with new expressions. The child in essence plays around with the new forms she learns and in doing so consolidates her recently acquired knowledge (see Chapter 10 on play). Because quite a bit of language play remains unobserved by adults, its extent is hard to judge, but a lot obviously does go on even in children as young as two

A Talk with Audrey, Age Four

Cognitive Development in the Preschool Years

Audrey was interviewed shortly after she returned from her day care center. She asked me to come with her to the porch, where her toys were.

Interviewer: Audrey, you were saying that you like to eat chicken. What is chicken?

Audrey: Chicken is animal. And when it's dead it turns into food chicken.

Interviewer: When it's dead it turns into food?

Audrey: Yes.

Interviewer: And then you eat it up?

Audrey: Yes.

Interviewer: Where does the food go after you put it in your mouth?

Audrey: First we put it in the oven.

Interviewer: And then what?

Audrey: And then we eat it all up.

Interviewer: Audrey, you seem to be very big. Are you growing?

Audrey: Yes, I'm four. First I was one, then I was three, and then four. And now I'm almost five.

Interviewer: And what happens when you get to be four? Do you get bigger?

Audrey: Yes. And I get five. You get 1, 2, 3, 4, 5, 6, 7, 8, 9, 10, 11, 12, 13, 14, 15, 16, 17, 18, 19, 20, 21, 22, 23, 24, 25, 26, 27, 28. We die when we get to be thirty.

Interviewer: We die when we get to be thirty? Why?

Audrey: 'Cause we're old. We're too much. We're too much numbers.

Interviewer: Audrey, do you know any stories you can tell me?

Audrey: No, I can't read stories. I'm going to sing "Somewhere over the Rainbow."

Interviewer: Okay.

Audrey (singing): Somewhere, over the rainbow, clouds are blue, and the land that I love, the one thing I love about . . . it's happy little bluebird fly beyond the rainbow, fly away . . . goodbye!

Interviewer: That was a lovely song.

Audrey: When am I going to come on the tape recorder?

Interviewer: You are on the tape recorder. You can see, when the little red light went on, it shows you are on the tape recorder.

Audrey: When is my voice going to come on it?

Interviewer: You want to hear your voice?

Audrey: Yes.

Interviewer: Okay, I'll turn it off and I'll let you hear yourself, and then we can talk some more. Okay?

Audrey: Okay. When we turn it off, we can hear my voice gonna come on the tape recorder.

Interviewer: Now, I'm going to play it back so you can hear your voice. . . . Now I have turned the recorder on again.

Audrey: I curled my hair today.

Interviewer: You did? Why did you do that?

Audrey: Because I wanted a haircut. I got hair in my eye.

Interviewer: Why are you holding your hair up now?

Audrey: So it can't get inside my ear.

Interviewer: Oh, when you put the earphones on to hear yourself on the tape recorder.

Audrey: So I can hear myself sing "Somewhere over the Rainbow."

Interviewer: Okay, I'm going to stop the tape recorder now. . . . Now the tape recorder is back on again.

Audrey: Do you want to see me do letters in Spanish?

Interviewer: You can do letters in Spanish?

Audrey: Yes. Uno, dos, tres, quatros, cinquo . . .

Interviewer: How did you learn to do that?

Audrey: I didn't. Sammy told me because Sammy can do that.

Interviewer: And Sammy is your friend.

Audrey: Yes.

What Do You Think?

1. What specific comments of Audrey are good examples of the characteristics of preschool thinking discussed in this chapter?

2. In what ways are Audrey's comments examples of typical preschooler speech?

3. Why does Audrey seem so unselfconscious about being tape recorded? How would you interpret her behavior differently if she were equally unselfconscious as an adult?

---

years (Messer, 1994). For example, the four-year-old mentioned above was talking to herself a few days later, just before falling asleep at night:

CHILD: You know what you get when you mix blue and red? Bluish-red. Bluish-reddish. Bluish-radish. Reddish, radish. You know what you get when you mix white and red? Whitish-red. Reddish-white. What do you get when you mix white and white? Whitish-white. Whitish-white?

The earlier discussion of colors evidently set the stage for this monologue. At the least, the earlier, imitative encounter helped call the form *-ish* to the child's attention, and at the most it precipitated practice with this form.

Innate Predisposition to Acquire Language: LAD

The ease and speed children show in acquiring language have caused some linguists and psychologists to conclude that children have an innate predisposition, or built-in tendency, to learn language (Chomsky, 1994). For convenience, the innate tendency is sometimes called the *language acquisition device,* or *LAD.* According to this viewpoint, LAD functions as a kind of inborn road map to language. It guides the child to choose appropriate syntactic categories as he tries to figure out the comparatively confusing examples of real speech that he ordinarily hears. It helps him find his way through the mazelike structure of language with relatively few major errors instead of having to explore and construct his own language map, as the Piagetian viewpoint implies.

The most persuasive reason for postulating the LAD is the *poverty of content* in the speech to which most infants and preschoolers are exposed. According to this argument, the language children encounter is too incomplete and full of everyday grammatical errors (too "impoverished") to serve as a satisfactory guide in learning the grammatical structure of the language (Baker, 1995). Parents sometimes speak in incomplete sentences, sometimes make grammatical errors, and sometimes do not speak at all when speaking might prove helpful to a child learning the language.

Despite the poverty of content, children seem remarkably resilient about acquiring language. Children isolated from language through parental neglect, for example, have learned some language later in life, but their language usually is limited in amount and complexity. In a less tragic example, identical twins often create a private language that they speak only with each other. In many cases their private language seems to delay normal language development, though the delay rarely causes serious lasting damage to their development (Mogford, 1993).

A final piece of evidence that a LAD exists is that preschool children do not simply copy their parents' language directly, yet they seem to figure out and use many of its basic syntactic relationships remarkably well. The classic "wug" experiment discussed earlier illustrates this ability dramatically. In forming plurals they had never heard spoken before, children suggest that they have a grammatical skill that is more innate than learned.

The Limits of LAD   Although this evidence suggests that children have a built-in ability to acquire language, it does not show that experience plays no role at all. The evidence from twins and neglected children emphasizes just the opposite: that certain experiences with language may be crucial, especially early in life. Ordinarily practically every preschooler encounters these experiences. They may consist of hearing others talk and of being invited to respond to others verbally. But the fact that they happen to everyone does not mean children do not learn from them; it means only that what children learn is universal.

Furthermore, experiences affect the version of language children acquire, even when they supposedly grow up in the same language community. As pointed out earlier, children vary in the vocabulary they learn and in the grammar they use; even by age three or four, children often do not define grammatical categories as abstractly as adults do or necessarily in the same way other children do. Most preschoolers eventually revise their grammatical categories to coincide with conventional adult grammar, thus obscuring their individuality. But as we will see in Chapter 12, large differences persist in older children's styles of communicating, even after children have mastered the basic structure of language.

All things considered, the fairest conclusion we can draw is a moderate one: that children are both predisposed to acquire language and in need of particular experiences with it. Skill with language is neither given at birth nor divorced entirely from other cognitive development. A special talent for language may be given to all normal children, however, and many crucial experiences for developing that talent may happen to occur rather frequently among infants as they grow up.

It can be hard to estimate children's cognitive abilities from their conversations. More often than not, though, parents are apt to overestimate rather than underestimate their children. This bias may indirectly assist the children's further development by leading parents to provide relatively stimulating conversations and tasks.

Parent-Child Interactions

Certain kinds of verbal interactions apparently help children acquire language sooner and better. Parents can help by speaking in relatively short sentences to their preschoolers and using more concrete nouns than pronouns, though this also depends on whether the task or topic at hand calls for concrete or abstract ideas (Sorsby & Martlew, 1991). In the following pair of comments, the first helps a child learn language more than the second does:

PARENT 1: Take your shoes off. Then put your shoes in the closet. Then come kiss Mama goodnight.

PARENT 2: After you take off your shoes and put them in the closet, come kiss me goodnight.

As we note in Chapter 6, the simplified style of the first set of comments is one aspect of a version of language called **infant-directed speech,** or sometimes "motherese." Another aspect of this version is the use of a high-pitched voice. Infant-directed speech is used intuitively by adults with young children and even by older children with younger children (Messer, 1994).

One of the most helpful kinds of verbal interactions is **recasting** a child's utterances: repeating or reflecting back what the child says, but in slightly altered form. For instance:

CHILD: More milk.

PARENT: You want more milk, do you?

Recasting helps because it highlights slight differences among ways of expressing an idea. In doing so, it may make the child more aware of how she expresses her idea—its form or organization—as well as call attention to the idea itself.

The techniques for stimulating language development have in common the fact that they provide young preschoolers with a framework of language that simultaneously invites them to try new, unfamiliar language forms and simplifies and clarifies other aspects of language. Some psychologists call this framework **scaffolding** (Bruner, 1983): like real scaffolds used in building construction, parents' language scaffolds provide a temporary structure within which young children can build their own language structures. As such, it functions much like Vygotsky's zone of proximal development mentioned earlier: helpful scaffolding changes and grows in response to the child's continuing development, always building a bit beyond the child's current independent abilities but never very far beyond.

These and similar findings have been translated into curricula for education of young children and even of infants (Spodek & Saracho, 1993). Fortunately, the most useful methods of interaction often are those that parents and teachers use intuitively anyway; training for them therefore really consists of emphasizing and refining their use.

What Do You Think?

Suppose you were asked to speak to a parent group, and a parent complained of her four-year-old's use of poor grammar. What advice could you give to this parent? Rehearse your comments with a classmate to determine how appropriate they are.

LANGUAGE VARIATIONS

Not surprisingly, parents vary in how they talk to their children, and these differences may influence the version of language children acquire as they grow up. It is unclear, however, how language variations affect other aspects of children's development, such as thinking ability. Later, in Chapter 12, we discuss variations related to cultural differences—for example, the "Black English" that some African-Americans speak in certain situations. First, though, consider three other sources of language variation: gender, socioeconomic status, and hearing ability.

Gender Differences in Language

Within any one community, girls learn nearly the same syntax boys do, but they acquire very different pragmatics, or discourse patterns. On the whole, the differences reflect society's gender stereotypes. For example, girls phrase requests indirectly more often than boys do; girls more often say, "Could you give that to me?" instead of "Give me that." Also, they more frequently expand on comments made by others rather than initiating their own. These differences appear especially in mixed-gender groups and are noticeable not only in adults but in children as soon as they are old enough to engage in conversation (Coates, 1993). In some Asian societies these differences are even more marked, resulting in separate female and male speech styles.

The sexes reinforce their language differences with certain nonverbal gestures and mannerisms. Girls and women tend to maintain more eye contact than boys and men do; they blink their eyelids at more irregular intervals and tend to nod their heads as they listen (Arliss, 1991). Boys and men use eye contact a good deal less in ordinary conversation, blink at regular intervals, and rarely nod their heads when listening. When these actions accompany the verbal differences, boys and girls (and men and women) run a distinct risk of misunderstanding each other. A boy talking to a girl may find the girl overly agreeable because she nods her head so much and never changes the subject, whereas a girl talking to a boy may find him self-centered because he seems not to acknowledge her comments and tends to change the subject.

Gender differences in discourse patterns may contribute to gender segregation: members of each sex may feel that members of the other sex do not really understand them, that they do not "speak the same language." Boys and girls therefore begin drifting apart during the preschool years almost as soon as they begin using language (Ramsey, 1995) and as a partial result of acquiring language. The emerging segregation, in turn, reinforces gender differences in language patterns (Fagot, 1994). Boys reinforce one another for their assertive discourse style, and girls and their (mostly female) teachers reinforce one another for their "considerate" style. In the end, then, cognitive development supports social development, and social development supports cognitive development.

Socioeconomic Differences in Language

Most research has found children of low socioeconomic status (SES) to be less verbal than middle- or high-SES children (Heath et al., 1991). In practice, this means low-SES children perform less well in verbal test situations, but outside of those situations their language differences are less clear-cut. These facts have created controversy about the importance of socioeconomic differences in language development.

What is the significance of socioeconomic differences in tests of language development? Some psychologists point out that most tests of language skills favor middle-class versions of English in both vocabulary and style of *discourse,* or conversational patterns. This bias is due to the content selected for individual test questions and to the ways tests are normally conducted. A question on one of these tests might ask children to describe a dishwasher, but few low-SES families own this appliance. Other questions might draw on experiences that only middle-SES children usually enjoy, such as trips on airplanes or visits to museums.

Other psychologists point out that conventional methods of testing are inherently more threatening to low-SES children. For one thing, the people who give such tests (teachers, graduate students) usually have more power and status (John-Steiner et al., 1994). The greater inherent threat of test taking makes some low-income children more cautious in their responses and hence less verbal. Moreover, some cultures consider it rude to ask questions if one does not understand what to do.

Perhaps most important, middle-SES families use styles of discourse that include many "test" questions or questions to which parents already and obviously know the answers. At the dinner table, parents may ask their preschooler, "What letter does your name begin with?" even though they already know the answer and their child knows that they know. Exchanges such as these probably prepare young children for similar exchanges on genuine tests by making testing situations seem more natural and homelike.

In contrast, low-SES children more often lack prior experience with "test" question exchanges. They can give relatively elaborate answers to true questions such as "What did you do yesterday morning?" when the adult really does not know the answer. But they tend to fall silent when they suspect the adult already can answer the question (for example, "What are the names of the days of the week?"). Their silence is unfortunate, because rhetorical, or "test," questions become especially common when preschoolers enter school and because active participation in questioning and answering helps preschoolers' learning substantially.

Language of Deaf and Hearing-Impaired Children

Children with hearing impairments often do not develop oral language skills as fully as other children do, but they are quite capable of acquiring a language of gestures called **American Sign Language (ASL).** In fact, language development in ASL children provides much of the reason for considering ASL a true language, one as useful for communication as any verbal language, such as English.

How can this be so? Signing consists of subtle gestures of the fingers and hands made near the face. In general, each gesture functions like a morpheme. For example, holding the fingers together gently (which signers call a "tapered *O*") can mean either *home* or *flower,* depending on whether it is placed near the cheek or under the nose. Other sign-morphemes affect the syntax of expressions: gestural equivalents of *-ing* and *-ed*. Individual signs are linked according to syntactic rules, just as in English. After some practice, signers can "speak" (or gesture) as quickly and effortlessly as people who use English can.

What happens to infants and young children with hearing impairments who grow up learning ASL from their parents as their first language? Studies show they

Carolyn Eaton, PRESCHOOL TEACHER

Introducing Sign Language to Young Children

Carolyn Eaton teaches in a nursery school that serves only children who are deaf or who have moderate or severe hearing impairment. Everyone in the school communicates in American Sign Language (ASL): teachers, the children themselves, and (as much as possible) the parents. When they start the program, the children and parents often know very little ASL. How do they acquire this new language? Carolyn talked about some of the ways.

Carolyn: In a lot of ways the program really looks like any other nursery program, though maybe one with a lot of language emphasis. We always have a theme for the week. That's how we organize the vocabulary, the signs.

Kelvin: Can you give an example of a theme?

Carolyn: Last week's theme was "The Three Little Pigs." I told the story in ASL and read a picture book—one of the children had to hold it because I needed two hands to sign with. I emphasized key signs, like the ones for *pig* and *three* and the signs for *brick* and *straw* and *house.* I invited the children to make those signs with me when I came to them in the story.

Kelvin: Do you do other things related to the week's theme?

Carolyn: We'd have other conversations—in ASL, of course—about pigs and animals. And about trusting strangers, for that matter—that's in that story too! We might act out the story at some point, with signs instead of words. It depends partly on the vocabulary and fluency of the children.

Kelvin: Is it harder to understand preschoolers' signing than adults'?

Carolyn: It varies with the child, just like oral language. Most three- and four-year-olds tend to use less complex sign vocabulary and simpler expressions than adults. I found it hard at first to simplify my signing appropriately, the way you simplify oral language for young hearing children. There's also a signing equivalent of "motherese" that you have to learn, or you won't be understood.

Kelvin: I noticed a parent today in the class signing to the kids. Does that happen a lot?

Carolyn: We have a parent volunteer just about every day. Since not all parents can volunteer, we have the kids take home a page each day that describes what's going on in the class and shows drawings of the signs we're currently emphasizing. We encourage the parents to learn them and use them at home. We also run two signing classes for the families of the preschoolers to help them communicate with their signing child.

Kelvin: Is it hard for them to learn?

Carolyn: Like everything else, people vary a lot. Some start learning immediately as soon as they learn that their child will always be deaf, and they're fluent by the time the child is a toddler. Others still haven't learned by the time the child is in grade school. Personally, I think it has a lot to do with how accepting the parents are of the child's hearing impairment. If they're still grieving over the child's loss, they make less progress at ASL.

Kelvin: Your program does seem language oriented—ASL oriented that is.

Carolyn: It really is, though we also deal with all the other stuff that happens to children—friendships among peers, for example. Did you see that argument between two kids that was going on just as you were arriving today?

Kelvin: It looked fierce, judging by the children's faces. What was it about?

Carolyn: Well, Billy wrecked a roadway that two other kids had made in the sand table. They were upset, signed Billy to get lost, and that got Billy upset. That's when I stepped in.

Kelvin: I noticed how intently you were looking at Billy when you gave him a "talking to."

Carolyn: I sure was—in all ASL conversations, not just scoldings, you have to look to see the signs. You get good at reading people's moods that way too, especially if you learn signing as early as these children did.

What Do You Think?

1. Judging by Carolyn's comments, how does the acquisition of ASL resemble the acquisition of oral language? How does it differ?

2. Among speech-language pathologists and deaf people generally, there has been heated debate about whether to emphasize ASL experiences, even if they sometimes segregate children from the hearing community, or to emphasize oral language experiences, even if the hearing-impaired children have trouble acquiring them. How might you decide between these alternatives? Compare your thoughts on this issue with one or two classmates' thoughts.

experience the same steps in signing development that speaking children do in language development. At about the age when infants babble, signing children begin "babbling" with their hands, making gestures that strongly resemble genuine ASL signs but that signers recognize as gestural "nonsense" (Marschark, 1993). As with verbal babbling, signing infants apparently engage in gestural babbles playfully when waking up in the morning or going to sleep at night.

When signing infants reach ages two and three, they experience a phase of one-word signing similar to the holophrases described in Chapter 6 and often observed

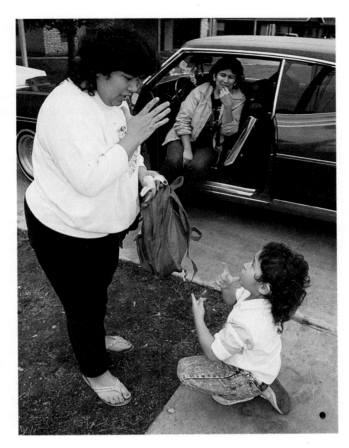

Sign language has the qualities of oral language, including grammar, subtlety, and expressiveness. This mother and child are communicating about the child's day at nursery school. Unfortunately in hearing communities (such as classrooms), it can be hard to appreciate the capacities of sign language.

among speaking children. They also experience two-word, telegraphic signing. As with speech, their signs at this point often omit important syntactic gestures and do not follow the usual conventions of word order (or, in this case, signing order) (Bellugi et al., 1993). Signing vocabulary increases rapidly during the early preschool period, in amounts comparable to the increases speaking children experience. Even the kinds of words acquired parallel those speaking children acquire; signing preschoolers tend to learn signs for dynamic, moving objects first, as is true for speaking children.

Still another reason to consider ASL a true language comes from observations of hearing preschoolers whose parents purposely used both English and ASL during the period when the children normally acquired language (Prinz & Prinz, 1979). During their preschool years, these children became thoroughly bilingual, using ASL and English interchangeably. Especially significant, however, were their patterns of language development, which essentially paralleled those shown by conventionally bilingual children. A clear example concerned vocabulary. Like verbal bilinguals, these children first acquired a single vocabulary that intermingled elements from both ASL and English but included few direct translations. If a child understood and used the sign for "tree," she or he would be unlikely to understand and use the spoken word *tree*. The children eventually acquired translations and thus finally possessed duplicate vocabularies. But acquiring duplicate terms took several years, just as it does with verbally bilingual children.

What Do You Think?

How do you think early childhood teachers should respond to language variety in preschoolers? Should they encourage it, discourage it, or simply accept it? This is an important issue in education and would make for a lively debate in class!

RELATIONSHIPS BETWEEN LANGUAGE AND THOUGHT

The variations observed in language suggest a crucial issue: how are language and thought related? Is language just another type of thought or a skill in itself? The close connection between these two activities makes this question important but at the same time hard to answer. If you are talking, chances are you are also thinking (but see the accompanying Perspectives box for an exception); and if you are thinking, you are probably either talking to others or verbalizing inwardly, at least a little.

Despite the potential confusion between these activities, psychologists have often attempted to explain their relationship (Piatelli-Palmarini, 1994). One explanation, often associated with Piaget, emphasizes the importance and priority of action in creating both language and thought. Another, often associated with the psychologists Jerome Bruner and Lev Vygotsky, proposes more equal roles for language and thought in which they develop independently but eventually become interdependent. Let us look briefly at each of these viewpoints.

Piaget: Action as the Basis for Both Language and Thought

Piaget and his supporters argue that action or activity promotes initial language development. Children need to manipulate objects and to have a rich variety of concrete experiences (Piaget & Inhelder, 1971). This idea makes considerable sense to anyone who works with preschool children; such children, for example, often learn the concepts of *heavier* and *lighter* more easily if they have lots of actual experiences with hefting and observing objects of different weights. If young children are taught the definitions of these words without having such experiences, they often just learn the words by rote—presumably an inferior way to learn them.

According to the Piagetian viewpoint, children's language can achieve no greater sophistication or complexity than their general level of cognitive develop-

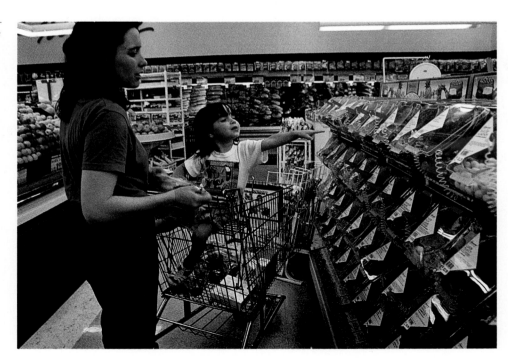

Sometimes it seems as if preschoolers know more than they can say. This girl can show her mother exactly what her family likes to eat even though she may not be able to identify all of the foods by name. She may also know her way around the grocery store, even though she may have trouble stating this knowledge explicitly.

Perspectives

Christopher, the Multilingual Savant: Speaking Without Understanding

Christopher is a striking example of a *savant*, a person with exceptional talent in one area of human functioning but serious limitations in other areas. Christopher's particular talent was languages. He could read English, his first language, by age three (even when printed upside down!) and became able to read and speak two or three foreign languages during elementary school with no explicit tutoring from anyone. As a young adult, Christopher could read, speak, and translate among the following languages with at least some fluency: Danish, Dutch, Finnish, French, German, Greek, Hindi, Italian, Norwegian, Polish, Portugese, Russian, Spanish, Swedish, Turkish, and Welsh.

Yet when observed carefully, Christopher showed many signs that he could not understand most of what he said or read in any language he used (Smith & Tsimpli, 1995). He failed most forms of the false-belief tasks described in this chapter. In one of these tasks, for example, experimenters hid a toy in full view of Christopher and a five-year-old girl. The girl was asked to leave the room and, unbeknown to her, the toy was moved from one location to another, again in full view of Christopher. Where did Christopher think the *girl* would look for the toy afterward? Christopher responded in the same way a three-year-old might, even when he was an adult: he believed the girl would look in the *new* location, even though it was unknown to her. In essence, Christopher seemed not to understand the question being posed: he did not reflect on the girl's thoughts, as requested.

Christopher also seemed unable to reflect on his own thinking. He was incapable of lying, even in fun, and incapable of either making or understanding remarks that were ironic, sarcastic, or otherwise full of double meanings. In general, meaning one thing and thinking another was impossible. His translations among languages lacked attention to linguistic pragmatics, to the subtleties and social context of communication, even though his vocabulary and syntax were good.

Finally, Christopher failed completely to learn artificial languages that were structured in ways that were logically simple but linguistically unnatural. For example, he failed to learn an artificial language in which negation

was indicated by adding a particular word after the *third* word of a sentence, whatever that word happened to be, rather than before or after the verb as in most naturally occurring languages. Even though this language rule is logically simple, and even though Christopher had learned many other languages, he could not learn to use it even haltingly.

Considered together, these observations have important implications for language and cognitive development. First, they provide a partial answer to the relationship between language and thought (see page 000 in this chapter): it may not be true, as Piaget proposed, that thinking ability must develop prior to linguistic ability. Language may sometimes develop much further than thought. Second, these observations suggest that second languages may be learned differently than first languages. With a first language in particular, a child may be predisposed toward, or "hard-wired" for, acquisition; she or he may possess a language acquisition device (LAD) such as the one proposed by Chomsky (1994). With later languages, however, the child may draw on his or her thinking abilities more fully, comparing vocabulary, syntax, and pragmatics in the new language with these features in the original language (Ellis, 1994). The more underlying parallels that exist between the new language and the old one, the less the child will have to think or reason to acquire it. A child who cannot reason easily therefore will have trouble with an artificial language structured in ways that are uncharacteristic of traditional human languages.

More generally, Christopher's story suggests that human intelligence may exist in *modules*, or discrete abilities that function somewhat autonomously. An ability to coordinate cognitive modules (for example, language and reasoning) may itself prove to be a type of cognitive module (Gunnar & Maratsos, 1992). For professionals and parents, this may mean discovering what those modules are for individual children. It may also mean adjusting our expectations of children to fit the realities of their cognitive "architecture": for example, not every child who is good with words should be expected to be good with reasoning, vice versa.

ment permits. Cognitive ability consists of several interrelated symbolic skills, such as those described earlier in this chapter. All symbolic skills supposedly develop together, and their mutual dependence results in the general cognitive stages of development described by Piaget. But their mutual dependence also means that language cannot, in principle, become more complex than a child's other symbolic skills.

Much evidence supports the idea that activity governs initial language acquisition. Two-year-olds do tend to show more advanced language if they have achieved object permanence—the belief, described in Chapter 6, that objects exist even when they are not directly experienced (Smolak, 1982). Older children too show a close correlation between certain language habits and conservation tasks, such as the water-glass task described earlier. Children who are able to conserve use coordinate expressions relatively often; they say the glass is "shorter but wider" or "taller but thinner" (H. Sinclair, 1969). The nonconservers more often express such ideas in two separate statements: "This one is wider. That one is taller."

Piagetians and many language specialists point out that language has no priority in the normal timetable of development; for twelve to eighteen months, in fact, an infant obviously thinks with little help from language (Bloom, 1993). When language does appear, it develops in conjunction with other symbolic activities, most notably make-believe and dramatic play. But it does not necessarily lead to or cause these activities.

Vygotsky: The Gradual Integration of Language and Thought

As plausible as these facts and arguments sound, they ignore important evidence that language can also guide other cognitive developments, including both early sensorimotor development and later symbolic thinking. Three-year-old Paloma seems to talk to herself to improve her sensorimotor skill at making a sand castle:

PALOMA: Now pour this *here.* Now little more. Oops! Too much. No spill. First I clean this up, then start again. Like this. *(Pouring)*

Events such as this led Lev Vygotsky to propose that language and thought develop independently at first but gradually become integrated with each other sometime during childhood (Vygotsky, 1987; Newman & Holzman, 1993). In his view, early speech is learned with little understanding; toddlers imitate words and grammatical constructions, but with only superficial comprehension of what they hear. At this point in development, toddlers' thinking occurs with little help from language, resembling a sort of mental shorthand.

As two- and three-year-old children acquire more verbal skill, they begin using speech overtly to guide their actions. But this self-guiding speech does not show egocentrism, as Piaget argued, as much as it shows preschool children's need for external support in solving problems—as Paloma perhaps needs. Paloma had this conversation with her mother at about the same time she built the sand castle:

PALOMA: What's an eggplant?
MOTHER: A purple thing that people eat.
PALOMA: Does it have eggs on it?
MOTHER: No, but it's long like an egg.
PALOMA: *(pausing)*: When can I see one?
MOTHER: Tomorrow at the store. I'll show you.

In this conversation, Paloma's and her mother's language and thought worked together closely, one guiding the other to benefit Paloma's thinking. As she gains maturity, however, Paloma will more often tend to hold such conversations with herself to guide her own thinking. At first these monologues will be spoken out loud, but gradually they will become internalized into a mental dialogue, a term Vygotsky calls **inner speech.**

Inner speech becomes common late in the preschool period and indicates that the child's language and thought have at last become fused, with each guiding the other (Diaz & Berk, 1992). But some situations still prompt their separation. Even adults sometimes use their verbal knowledge to guide further learning when they are not sure of what they are doing. Following the instructions on an income tax form, for example, may prompt considerable overt self-talk ("Add line 23 to line 24 and enter on line 25") to ensure that you truly understand what you are doing.

Whatever their precise relationship, language and thought remain only partly coordinated during the preschool years and especially during the early part of this

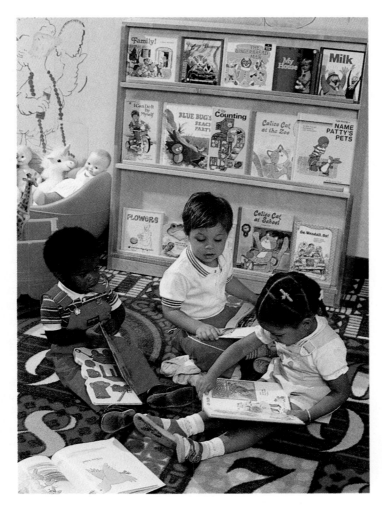

In addition to learning how language is structured, preschoolers acquire skill with communication, or how language is used. In discussing their picture books, for example, these children are practicing not only vocabulary and grammar, but also how to have a conversation.

period. This partial degree of coordination may actually account for some of preschoolers' most delightful qualities: often they can say exactly what they think, even though at other times their verbal comments carry *more* meaning than they realize. "Are you my friend?" asked one four-year-old of a playmate at nursery school. "Yes," replied the other child, "but only until 11:30" (when school ended and she went home). The reply served as a matter-of-fact statement of the extent of the children's friendship. Interpreted from an adult perspective, though, it carries extra meaning, since adult notions of friendship usually assume a continuing relationship, even during absences.

What Do You Think?

Do you ever think without talking or talk without thinking? Collect a list of these incidents from yourself, and friend or classmate. What practical implications do such separations of talking and thinking have for professionals (such as teachers) who rely heavily on verbal communication with children?

EARLY CHILDHOOD EDUCATION

Developing cognitive skills influence an important experience for many preschool children: early childhood education. Programs for three- and four-year-olds take many forms. Look at these experiences:

- Juan goes to *family day care* for three full days each week. His care occurs in his caregiver's home, with only four other children.

- Denzel goes to a *child care center* full time, five days a week. The center consists of two rooms modified from a church basement. About twenty children attend the center and are cared for by four adults.

- Cary goes to a part-time *nursery school* four mornings per week. There are twelve children and two adults.

Early Education and Cognitive Theories of Development

Despite the diversity implied by these examples, high-quality early education programs are usually based on some sort of developmental perspective. Some programs draw heavily on Piaget's ideas about cognitive development (Demetriou & Shayer, 1992). They provide sensorimotor activities, such as sand and water play, as a basis for fostering preoperational activities such as make-believe play.

Other programs organize cognitive activities around structured materials, which teachers guide children to use in particular ways. Nurseries and centers inspired by Maria Montessori (Montessori, 1964; Cuffaro, 1991) give children sets of cylinders graded by size and designed to fit snugly into a set of size-graded holes in a board. A child experiments with the cylinders and holes to discover the best way to fit them.

Still other early education programs borrow from Vygotsky's views of cognition as originating in social and cultural activities. These programs emphasize cooperative problem-solving activities and *emergent literacy,* a way of introducing reading and writing by situating it in everyday, valued experiences (Morrow, 1993). For example, instead of teaching children to recognize letters or familiar words at a special time each day, the early childhood teacher might simply provide a classroom rich in print materials and encourage children to come to him with words or letters that they themselves want to learn.

Effectiveness of Early Childhood Education

Evaluations of early childhood programs suggest that a wide range of approaches, including those just mentioned, are about equally effective in promoting overall cognitive growth, although the choice of curriculum does seem to influence the *pattern* of skills that children acquire (Schweinhart et al., 1993).

Three factors seem to underlie successful early childhood programs, whatever their format and curriculum. First, the staff of successful programs regard themselves as competent observers of children's educational needs and as being capable of making important decisions in tailoring a curriculum to particular children (Hills, 1992). Second, the vast majority of successful programs and teachers view an early childhood curriculum as an integrated whole rather than consisting of independent subject areas or skills (Bredekamp & Rosegrant, 1992). Singing a song, for example, is not just "music"; it also fosters language development, motor skills (if the children dance along), arithmetic (through counting and rhythm), and social studies (if the words are about people and life in the community).

Third, successful early childhood programs involve parents, either directly as volunteers in the classroom or indirectly as advisers on governing boards, in certain school activities, or in additional services that support families. The federally sponsored program of early education called *Head Start,* for example, owes much of its effectiveness to parent involvement (United States Department of Health and Human Services, 1994). To get federal funding, local centers are required to create parent advisory boards to guide policy and practice at the centers. They are also encouraged to provide other family support services, such as parent support groups and dental screening for children.

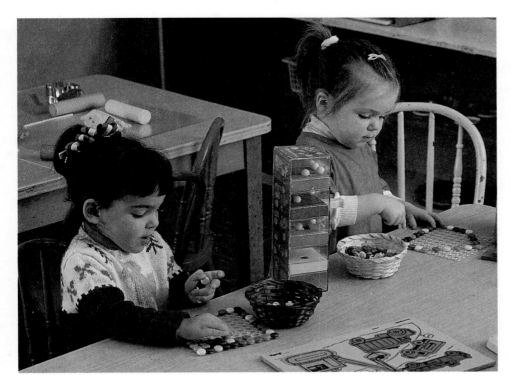

Providers of early childhood programs face the challenge of making activities developmentally appropriate. One way is to include classroom materials that invite exploration by the children. Another is to allow children to choose among activities.

Cultural Diversity and Best Practice in Early Education

A careful look at successful programs for young children raises an important question: are there "best" ways to support children's learning despite the cultural and individual diversity among children? A major professional association for early childhood education, the National Association for the Education of Young Children (NAEYC), argues that there are and has described its recommendations in detail in an influential book called *Developmentally Appropriate Practice: Birth to Age Eight* (Bredekamp, 1987; Kostelnik, 1992). **Developmentally appropriate practices** are ways of assisting children's learning that are consistent with children's developmental needs and abilities. Table 9.2 lists a few of the practices recommended by the NAEYC as they relate to the preschool years.

TABLE 9.2 **Developmentally Appropriate Practices with Preschoolers**

Principle	Examples
Caregivers provide ample space for active play	Program has access to outdoor space or gymnasium with climbing apparatus, tricycles, etc.
Caregivers allow children choices in activities	Classroom has several learning centers: dramatic play (dress-up), block building, books and reading area, art area, etc.
Caregivers provide long periods of uninterrupted time	Group transitions (e.g., from indoor to outdoor activities) are kept to a minimum; activities tend to begin and end individually
Activities and materials are relevant to children's experiences	Books are gender fair and culture fair; relevant cultural holidays are noted and celebrated through appropriate activities in class
Caregivers ensure that the environment is safe and free of hazards	Climbing apparatus has soft mats underneath (if indoors) or soft sand (if outdoors); furniture is sturdy; sharp objects (knives, scissors) are supervised carefully when used

Source: Adapted from Bredekamp (1987).

A Multicultural View

Parents' Beliefs about Intelligence: A Cross-cultural Perspective

In our society, parents mean particular things when they refer to children's *intelligence:* they are usually talking about a child's verbal skills and reasoning abilities, especially as they occur in school or school-like tasks. This view of intelligence is so deeply grounded in our culture that an entire psychological field has developed to measure it, complete with standardized "intelligence" tests and experts to help teachers and parents interpret the tests.

But not all societies think of intelligence in this way. The Kipsigis in East Africa frame the idea of intelligence rather differently, placing it more explicitly in its social context (Harkness & Super, 1992a). They speak of a child being *ng'om,* meaning not only verbally skilled and sociable but also responsible to others. A child who is *ng'om* is quick to learn household tasks, for example, but also reliable about doing them without being reminded. The Kipsigis recognize, in principle, that a child can have verbal skill in the abstract. In practice, however, they regard such an isolated or abstract skill as a unique ability that requires a special term to describe it: *ng'om en sukul,* or "smart in school." Furthermore, *ng'om* is a quality shown only by preschoolers; neither an infant nor an adult can be *ng'om,* since she or he is not expected to be responsible to others in the same way preschoolers are.

Such a socially embedded notion of intelligence differs radically from the usual North American idea. In our society, parents are likely to distinguish clearly between a child's sense of responsibility to others and his or her intelligence (Goodnow, in press). They may consider the former desirable but not an intrinsic part of intelligence as such. When interviewed about the qualities shown by preschoolers, parents of preschoolers tend to name relatively "cognitive" features: an intelligent child is inquisitive, curious, imaginative, self-reliant, and able to play independently (Harkness & Super, 1992b). These features of intelligence take individual autonomy for granted rather than social harmony: being intelligent is something you do by or on behalf of yourself, not with or on behalf of others.

These cultural differences begin to make sense if we consider the settings in which Kipsigis and North American parents and preschoolers live. A Kipsigis preschooler

The NAEYC recommendations seem reasonable in many ways. Who can object, for example, to providing children with choices for their preschool play or to supporting their dialogues and initiatives with comments from the teacher or caregiver? Yet cross-cultural comparisons of early childhood programs complicate the picture somewhat by revealing that some practices in early education in North America are really culture bound rather than universally beneficial to children.

In Japan, for example, preschool programs are more likely to value large-group activities (such as singing or putting on a skit) in the belief that such activities develop commitment to the child's community—in this case, the community of the classroom (Kotloff, 1993). The time given to large-group activities, however, would probably seem excessive to some preschool educators in North America, where the development of individual initiative is more highly valued.

In Italy, preschool programs emphasize involvement of parents much more heavily than do most North American programs. They also place children in permanent groups from their entrance at age three until they leave the program for public school at age six. Unlike in North America, little effort is needed to maintain and justify these practices, because Italian culture already supports them: women (but not men) are expected to avoid paid employment and form extended social networks of support with other relatives, with one another, and (in this case) with their children's teachers (Edwards et al., 1993).

These comparisons suggest that the best practices in early education may need to take account of cultural differences and values regarding children's development (Mallory & New, 1994). For programs in ethnically diverse societies such as the United States, this means more than including songs and brief mentions of the holidays of various cultural groups. The central values and attitudes of cultural groups served by a particular center or nursery school must find their way into the daily typically is part of an extended family. There are likely to be children of all ages close at hand, related to one another in largely complex ways; older children typically care for younger children from an early age; and children's chores are likely to take on "real" economic importance as children get older. Such a setting seems sure to reward children for showing responsibility to others.

In our own society, a preschooler is likely to live with a small family; relatively few or even no immediate relatives may be close at hand; parents expect that school will figure prominently in the preschooler's future; and parents themselves (including mothers) are likely to be working for a living. This sort of setting favors children who can "teach themselves" to a certain extent, that is, play with and learn from materials on their own. It also favors children who orient themselves toward school-like activities—toward number and memory games, for example, and books and letters. An "intelligent" child is one who can do these things, which have much less to do with responsibility to others than is the case for a Kipsigis child (Harkness et al., 1992). Cultural differences such as these can pose problems for many preschoolers in our own society when they finally enter school. Historically, modern schooling has encouraged the culturally conventional definitions of intelligence as individual activity and those of cognitive activity as separate from the daily needs of the community. Students generally "do their own work" and focus on tasks (such as a set of math problems) that are created specially for school settings.

When these assumptions do not fit the cultural expectations of particular children or their families, however, teachers are challenged to modify them. Teachers must then find other ways for children to "be intelligent"— ways that involve greater responsibility to others, for example, and greater concern for the real needs of the child's community. Though it takes effort, there are ways to accomplish these changes in teaching philosophy; some of them are discussed in Chapter 12.

activities of the program. Particular centers will therefore experience cultural diversity in different ways:

- A program serving a rural community of Amish or Hutterite children will need to take seriously the value of learning outdoors from the natural environment, sometimes even in the winter (Wardle, 1995).

- A program serving urban Appalachian children in northern schools will have to recognize and honor the importance of religion in the lives of many Appalachian families, even if these families now live in a much more secular, urban environment (Klein, 1995).

- A program serving Native American children in the Northwest will need to recognize the importance of cooperation to many of these children and their families and their aversion to individual striving to "better" oneself (Soldier, 1993).

In these culturally diverse programs, cognition or thinking itself can take on diverse meanings (see the accompanying Multicultural View box). Educators who work with young children therefore need to do more than understand preschool cognition: they also need to explore how it might be understood and used by particular children and communities with specific social relationships and values. The next chapter turns to these important topics.

What Do You Think?

Is early childhood education a "social" or a "cognitive" activity? After you have formed an opinion about this question, try to discuss it with one or two experienced teachers of young children. Has your opinion changed at all as a result?

Early childhood programs often serve children from differing cultural backgrounds. The diversity can be enriching if caregivers encourage cooperative activities, like the game these two children are playing, and if caregivers include stories, activities, and information that recognizes and respects children's cultural differences.

SUMMARY OF MAJOR IDEAS

Thinking in Preschoolers

1. The preoperational stage of thinking, defined by Piaget, is characterized by increased symbolic thinking and new knowledge of identities and functional relationships.

2. Children's new reliance on symbolic thought helps them recall experiences, solve problems more effectively, and communicate with others about their experiences.

3. Preschool children have developed a simple theory of the human mind by the time they are three years old.

4. Young preschool children have trouble distinguishing between appearances and reality, but by the end of the preschool period they have made substantial improvements in this skill.

5. Preschool children can classify objects accurately as long as the system or criteria used for classifying are relatively simple.

6. Preschoolers often cannot solve problems that require reversible thinking, such as the classic Piagetian tasks of conservation.

7. Preschoolers' distinctions between natural kinds and artifacts suggests that they may hold informal theories about biological functioning.

8. At age three, preschoolers have some knowledge of how the number system works, but they do not achieve full understanding until about age four or five.

9. Neostructuralist theories of cognitive development use Piaget's belief in stages but focus on relatively specific cognitive skills of the child.

Language Acquisition in Early Childhood

10. During the preschool years, children make major strides in acquiring the syntax, or grammar, of their native language.

11. Young children's first word combinations are related by semantics and omit syntactic relationships.

12. One important syntactic error preschool children make is overgeneralization.

13. Although preschoolers learn a great deal of language through the process of inference, they also learn some language by rote.

14. Infants and preschoolers are reinforced, but only indirectly, for using correct syntax in their earliest utterances.

15. Children probably acquire some syntax through imitation and practice of language models.

16. The ease with which children acquire language despite the poverty of the content of speech they hear may mean children possess an innate language acquisition device, or LAD.

17. Parents probably assist children's language acquisition by recasting their children's own utterances, using a special style of talk called *infant-directed speech,* and providing scaffolding that supports their children's language efforts.

Language Variations

18. Language varies among children according to gender in ways that support gender stereotypes.

19. Language varies according to socioeconomic class in ways that prepare middle-class children better than low-SES children for school settings.

20. Children who are deaf or hearing impaired often learn American Sign Language, which has all of the properties of an oral language.

Relationships Between Language and Thought

21. Two major theories have been proposed to explain the relationship between language and thought: Piagetian and Vygotskian.
22. According to Piaget, language develops only as rapidly and as far as other symbolic functions, such as dramatic play, do.
23. According to Vygotsky, language and thought begin as independent functions and gradually become integrated during the preschool years.
24. Piaget's viewpoint implies that language reflects primarily general cognitive development, whereas Vygotsky's suggests that language and thought eventually come to assist each other's development equally.

Early Childhood Education

25. Early childhood education programs come in a variety of forms, many of which have been influenced by theories of cognitive development.
26. Three factors characterize successful programs in early childhood education: a staff that is oriented toward observing the children, an integrated view of the curriculum, and significant involvement of parents in the program.
27. Cultural diversity challenges early childhood educators to identify teaching practices that are not only developmentally appropriate but also culturally appropriate.

KEY TERMS

symbol *(264)*
identity *(264)*
functional relationship *(265)*
symbolic thought *(265)*
theory of mind *(266)*
false-belief task *(266)*
appearance-reality distinction *(267)*
classification *(267)*
reversibility *(268)*
conservation *(268)*
animism *(270)*
natural kind *(270)*
artifact *(270)*
zone of proximal development *(272)*

neostructuralist (neo-Piagetian) theory *(273)*
syntax *(274)*
morphemes *(274)*
generative rules *(274)*
duo *(275)*
telegraphic speech *(275)*
overgeneralization *(276)*
infant-directed speech *(281)*
recasting *(281)*
scaffolding *(281)*
American Sign Language (ASL) *(283)*
inner speech *(288)*
developmentally appropriate practice *(291)*

FOR FURTHER READING

Bishop, Dorothy, and Kay Mogford, eds. *Language Development in Exceptional Circumstances.* Hillsdale, N.J.: Erlbaum, 1993.

This book contains chapters by a number of experts about children whose language acquisition and development are unusual in some way, including children who are deaf, visually impaired, mentally challenged, or extremely neglected. It makes good reading for anyone who is interested in working with such children and therefore needs to understand the limits of "universal" trends in language development.

Case, Robbie, ed. *The Mind's Staircase: Exploring the Conceptual Underpinnings of Children's Thought and Knowledge.* Hillsdale, N.J.: Erlbaum, 1992.

This book is based on a neostructuralist perspective and shows the potential of that approach. Robbie Case and other authors describe more than a dozen different lines of research supporting the notion of a hierarchy of cognitive stages but focusing the stages on specific skills or realms of activity far more than Piaget did. This perspective is a useful one for teachers.

Morrow, Leslie. *Literacy Development in the Early Years.* 2nd ed. Boston: Allyn & Bacon, 1993.

In contrast to the Bishop and Mogford book, this one describes practical approaches to language and literacy that a teacher (or even a parent) can use with normally functioning young children. It presents an excellent discussion of emergent literacy, ways to introduce young children to reading and writing that seem natural and appealing.

Smitheran-Donaldson, Geneva. *Black Talk: Words and Phrases from the Hood to the Amen Corner.* Boston: Houghton Mifflin, 1994.

This is a dictionary of one of the most prominent varieties of English in the United States: Black English, a topic discussed in Chapter 12 of this text. It shows the extent to which vocabulary, syntax, and pragmatics can differ from "standard" English (the kind most often spoken on a TV network newscast). It also shows that variations from the "standard" are rich in meaning when understood and translated.

10

EARLY CHILDHOOD

Psychosocial Development

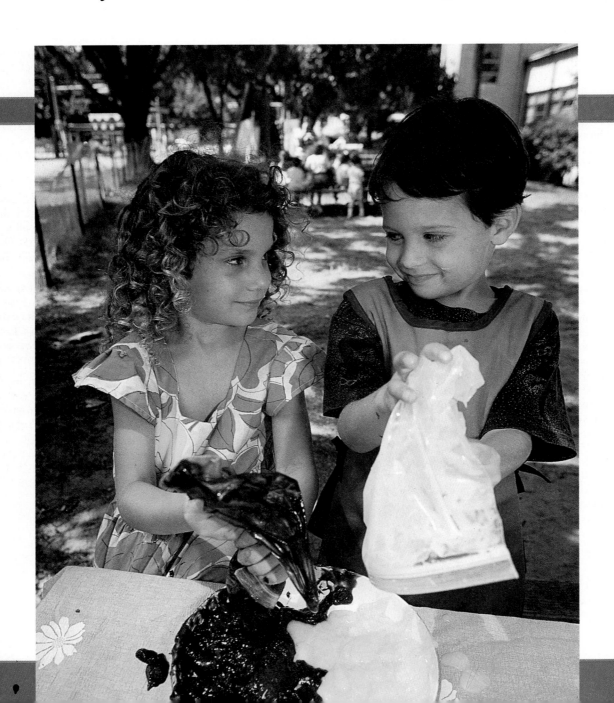

Play in Early Childhood

The Nature of Play
Theories of Play
Cognitive Levels of Play: Developmental
    Trends
Social Levels of Play
Other Influences on Play

Relationships with Others

Relationships with Parents
Relationships with Siblings
Friendships in Early Childhood
Empathy and Prosocial Behavior
Conflict and Aggression
The Effects of Television

Gender Development

Developmental Trends During Early
    Childhood
Influences on Gender Development
Androgyny

Child Abuse and Neglect

Causes
Consequences
Treatment and Prevention

The End of the Preschool Years

W hen Melissa was two, she used to crouch down on the floor with her rear end sticking out in imitation of the prominent haunches of Tigger, the family cat. From time to time, she made a noise sort of like a cat's meow. Keeping her head low, she looked around carefully for acknowledgment from her parents. Occasionally she walked like a cat, although her walk looked more like a rabbit's hopping. Tigger herself was not impressed by all of this.

Melissa's skills as a performer and her active awareness of her audience illustrate an important milestone during the preschool years: the development of psychological and social skills. During the preschool years, many activities and events that occupy a child's waking hours involve social interaction with other people. These others include parents and siblings, as well as friends and acquaintances in the neighborhood and community. The social skills and unique personality a preschool child develops are largely a result of social interactions within and outside his or her family.

In this chapter, we first look at three areas of psychosocial development: play, relationships with others, and gender roles. We conclude by examining the tragic problem of child abuse and neglect.

PLAY IN EARLY CHILDHOOD

In our society and many others, play dominates the preschool years. Every child plays, it seems, and virtually all observers of young children see lots of examples of play. What are the play activities of a preschooler like, and what important contributions does play make to a child's development? Before we tackle these questions, we must first agree on what we mean by *play*.

The Nature of Play

One useful approach to defining *play* focuses on the attitudes and dispositions of children themselves (Rubin et al., 1983). First, play is *intrinsically* (rather than *extrinsically)* motivated. Children engage in play mainly because it is enjoyable and reinforcing for its own sake rather than because it is useful in achieving external goals.

Second, play is *process oriented.* Children generally are more interested and involved in the *process* of doing things than in the *product* of what they do (Schwartzman, 1978; Vandenberg, 1978). At the local playground, for instance, children may care very little about the goal of using the slide, to get from top to bottom, but likely

Focusing Questions

- What important developmental achievements occur during the preschool years?

- What distinguishes play from other activities, and why is play so important in preschoolers' development?

- What types of play occur among preschoolers? What changes are observed as they approach school age?

- How do different styles of parenting influence preschoolers' relationships with their peers?

- How do preschoolers handle conflicts with their peers?

- How does a young child's understanding of gender differences change during the preschool years? What are some of the important factors that influence a child's flexibility about gender role stereotypes?

- What appear to be the main factors that contribute to child abuse and neglect? What are the consequences of maltreatment?

In early childhood, the process of doing things often matters more than the outcome. Even taking a bath can seem like play.

care a lot about their style of sliding—whether they go head first or feet first, or how fast they go.

Third, play is *creative* and *nonliteral.* Although it resembles real-life activities, it differs from them in that it is not bound by reality. For example, a child who is "play fighting" looks different than one who really is fighting (Aldis, 1975), and a child playing Mommy typically acts differently than one who is actually caring for a baby brother or sister. The features that reveal an activity as play rather than the real thing vary with the particular type of play and the situation; a play fight may include smiles and laughter, and a make-believe mother may be overly bossy. Whatever the signs, they communicate the message that "this behavior is *not* what it first may appear to be." Even so, it is common for a preschooler to become so caught up in a round of dramatic play that he forgets for a moment that it is not real and becomes truly frightened when his make-believe mother tells him he has been bad and must sit in the corner.

Fourth, play tends to be governed by *implicit rules,* that is, rules that can be discovered by observing the activity rather than rules that are formally stated and exist independently of the activity. For example, although no rule book exists for playing house, children implicitly understand that there can be only one mother and one father and that these actors must live up to certain expectations. If one player deviates too widely from the expected role, the other children are likely to correct her for it ("Hey, mommies don't suck on baby bottles; only babies do!").

Fifth, play is *spontaneous* and *self-initiated,* meaning it is engaged in only under a child's own free will and is not evoked or controlled by others. Sixth, play is *free from major emotional distress.* Play does not normally occur when a child is in a state of fear, uncertainty, or other kinds of significant stress.

Theories of Play

There are three main theoretical approaches to play: psychoanalytic, learning, and cognitive. Although each theory emphasizes a somewhat different aspect of play, all hold that play activities make a major contribution to the development of important social and emotional skills and understandings during the preschool years.

Psychoanalytic Theory Psychoanalytic theories emphasize the social and emotional importance of play in early childhood. For one thing, play gives a child an opportunity to *gain mastery* over problems by rearranging objects and social situations in ways that allow him to imagine he is in control. Following an especially painful and upsetting experience such as being suddenly separated from a parent who is hospitalized for a serious illness, a child may display *repetition compulsion,* repeating the experience over and over in her symbolic play with dolls or other toys to gain greater control or resolution of her distress.

Play also allows a child to use fantasy to *gain satisfaction for wishes and desires* that are not possible to fulfill in reality due to limitations in the child's abilities and life situation. Another function of play is to provide an opportunity for *catharsis,* the release of upsetting feelings that cannot be expressed otherwise. Finally, play allows a child to *gain increased power* over the environment by rearranging it to suit his own needs and abilities (Lewis, 1993).

A major strength of the psychoanalytic approach is that it helps us appreciate the importance of fantasy and inner life in children's play. A limitation is its vagueness about precisely how developmental changes result from play.

Learning Theory Learning theorists view play as an opportunity for children to safely try out new behaviors and social roles. In their view, play is a major means by which children progressively learn adult social skills, either through successive reinforcement of behaviors that come closer and closer to correct adult behaviors or through the processes of observational learning and imitation described in Chapter 2.

For example, what might a three-year-old who is playing with wooden blocks be learning about the adult world? For one thing, building with blocks gives the child an opportunity to learn about the nature and design of physical structures and space. The child also learns about how hard blocks are, how high they can be piled, and how many small ones equal a larger one. He might also learn about his own capabilities and limitations as a builder: how high he can reach, how many blocks he can carry at once, and so forth.

Playing with blocks also exposes the child to adult expectations and practices, such as when and where blocks can be used, picked up, and stored and how to share blocks, take turns, and cooperate with others. According to learning theory, a child learns in three ways: through her own experience of being praised or encouraged for her own actions (direct reinforcement); through observations of adults and other children being reinforced for their activities (vicarious reinforcement); and through the experience of setting a goal and achieving it (cognitive or self-reinforcement).

Cognitive Theory Cognitive theorists have identified four major kinds of play that they believe develop sequentially in parallel with the major stages of cognitive development (Piaget, 1962; Smilansky, 1968). Table 10.1 describes the different types of cognitive play.

TABLE 10.1 **Types of Cognitive Play**

Type	Description and Examples
Functional play	Simple, repetitive movements, sometimes with objects or own body. Example: shoveling sand; pushing a toy
Constructive play	Manipulation of physical objects to build or construct something. Example: building with blocks
Pretend play	Substitutes make-believe, imaginary, and dramatic situations for real ones. Example: playing house or Superman
Games with rules (age 5 or 6)	Play is more formal and governed by fixed rules. Example: jumping rope; hide-and-seek

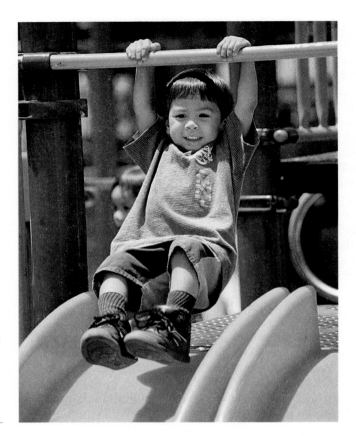

This three-year-old going down a slide is engaged in functional play, which focuses on simple, repeated body movements. Although this kind of play is especially prevalent among infants and toddlers, older children often engage in it, too.

Cognitive Levels of Play: Developmental Trends

Functional Play   **Functional play,** which involves simple, repeated movements such as splashing water or digging in a sandbox, is most common during the sensorimotor period. Because it requires no symbolic activity, functional play makes up an especially large part of the play activity of older infants and toddlers—more than one-half, in fact. By the time a child reaches kindergarten or first grade, however, functional play has decreased to less than one-quarter of her total play (Hetherington et al., 1979; Sponseller & Jaworski, 1979). The shift occurs partly because many symbolic activities incorporate some of the physical activities characteristic of functional play. Functional play does not disappear in later childhood as much as it becomes combined with other playful ends.

Constructive Play   **Constructive play** involves manipulation of physical objects, such as using blocks to build or construct something. This form of play is evident in older infants and preschoolers, although it is not always clear where functional play ends and constructive play begins. For example, a child who at first appears to be building a mountain out of sand may forget about her goal and end up just shoveling the sand for the fun of it. As the child grows older, however, the constructive elements of play become quite clear. Not only does she build a mountain; she builds it in a certain shape and adds a road leading to it and perhaps a car or two to make the trip.

Pretend Play   **Pretend play** (also called *fantasy* or *dramatic play*) substitutes imaginary situations for real ones, as in playing house or Superman, and dominates the preoperational period. Pretend play occurs even among toddlers and probably begins as soon as a child can symbolize, or mentally represent, objects. Family roles (including mother, father, brother, sister, baby, and even family pet) and *character*

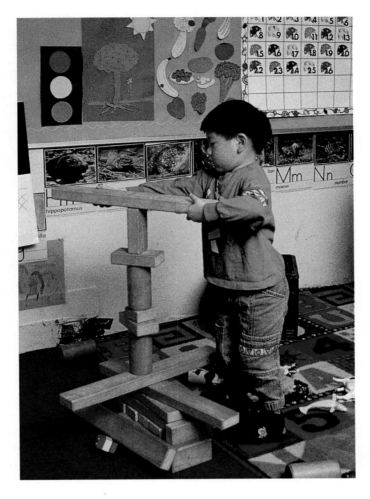

Constructive play, such as block building, is probably the most common form of play in early childhood.

roles based on fictionalized heros such as Batman, Ninja Turtles, and Power Rangers are most likely to be dramatized by preschool children. Pretend play grows in frequency and complexity during the preschool years and eventually decreases again later in childhood, when social pressures to act more "grown-up" reduce it in public settings {Dunn, 1985; Howes & Matheson, 1992; Lytinen, 1991; Rubin & Krasnor, 1980). The complexity, flexibility, and elaborateness of preschoolers' fantasy play also appear to be positively related to both the support and the nurturance preschoolers receive from their parents, as well as to the specific reinforcement parents give them for such play (Ladd & Hart, 1992).

Pretend play is a good example of how new forms of experience are assimilated into existing schemes of cognitive understanding. In addition to allowing the child to practice and expand schemes already acquired, such play contributes to the consolidation and expansion of cognitive skills during the preschool years (Piaget, 1962; Vygotsky, 1967). The alternation between pretense and reality involved in pretend play also gives children an opportunity to practice and more fully understand these distinctions. Through their play with nonrealistic toys and objects, children become better able to internally represent and manipulate objects in the form of symbols and fantasy rather than solely in terms of realistic representations (Flavell et al., 1986; Rubin et al., 1983; Ungerer et al., 1981).

Games with Rules   **Games with rules,** such as Simon Says and hide-and-seek, first appear during the concrete operational period, when children are five or six years old, and peak in frequency toward the end of elementary school (Eifermann, 1971;

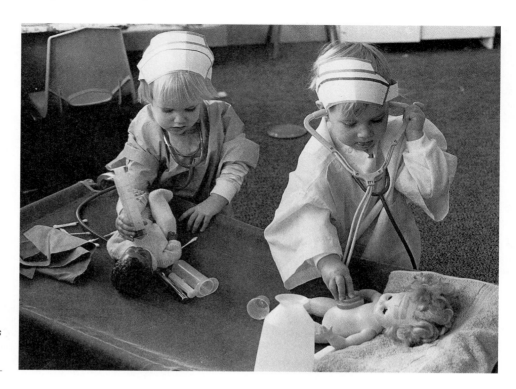

In dramatic play, children take on pretend roles, like the two "nurses" here. Realistic props, such as the uniforms, stethoscopes, and bottles in this photograph, encourage dramatic play, but they are not always necessary.

Rubin & Krasnor, 1980). The rules for many such games apparently develop out of the more flexible, "made-up" rules of pretend play. Instead of continuing to negotiate roles and behaviors as they go along, young children gradually learn to agree on them beforehand and to stand by their agreements throughout a play episode. Due to their greater formality, games with rules can become traditions handed down from one sibling to another, from older to younger playmates, and from generation to generation (Opie & Opie, 1969). Hopscotch, for example, has been around in some form for decades.

By early elementary school, most children can play games with rules. Not only do these games cultivate motor skills, but they also teach social skills, such as learning to take turns and knowing how to be a good winner or loser.

These children are involved in parallel play. They are probably aware of each other's presence, but they are using separate toys and are preoccupied primarily with their own activities.

Social Levels of Play

Play also varies according to how social it is, that is, how much and in what ways children involve others in their play activities. Several decades ago, Mildred Parten studied social participation among children ages two to five and proposed that children's play develops in six stages, or levels, of sociability (Parten, 1932). Although subsequent researchers have questioned whether Parten's categories actually form a developmental sequence, her distinctions continue to be useful to people who study young children (Rubin et al., 1976, 1978). Table 10.2 describes the six types of play Parten identified.

TABLE 10.2 ***Parten's Social Levels of Play***

Type	Description and Examples
Unoccupied play	The child wanders about, watching whatever is of momentary interest, but does not become involved in any activity
Solitary play	The child plays alone with different toys or other objects and with no direct or indirect awareness of or involvement with other children, even if nearby
Onlooker play	The child watches others play without actually entering into the activities; is clearly involved with what is happening and usually is within speaking distance of the participants
Parallel play	Involves two or more children playing with the same toys in a similar way, in close proximity and with an awareness of each other's presence; do not share toys, talk, or interact except in very minimal ways
Associative play	Children engage in a common activity and talk about it with each other, but do not assign tasks or roles to particular individuals and are not very clear about their goals
Cooperative play	Children consciously form into groups to make something, attain a goal, or dramatize a situation; one or two members organize and direct the activity, with children assuming different roles and responsibilities

Source: Parten (1932).

Changes with Age   Social participation in different types of play also varies with age. Even very young infants actively interact with the objects and people in their environment, and by twelve months their play interactions with peers become more frequent, particularly those that involve toys. Access to peers through play groups or day care and parental support tend to increase the likelihood of peer play.

In Mildred Parten's work (see above), parallel play appeared to be the most frequent type of preschool play activity, accounting for almost half of the observed play activities, whereas solitary play accounted for about one-fourth, associative play one-fifth, and cooperative and unoccupied play less than one-tenth of the total. Parten found that parallel and solitary play declined throughout the preschool years. On the other hand, associative play and cooperative play, which involve greater social participation, increased with age (Parten, 1932).

Often a preschooler's play combines several of the types Parten described. For example, observations of free play among three-year-olds reveal that parallel play is frequently followed by associative or cooperative group play, and parallel play serves as a transitional, or warm-up, strategy that enables a child to move into play involving others (Bakeman & Brownlee, 1980). These findings suggest that the ability to cooperate develops sequentially and that this sequence of play styles probably continues to help children successfully cooperate with others in new situations. The ability to cooperate with others in achieving common goals is an important aspect of successful social relationships throughout one's life.

As preschoolers get older, play involving coordinated interactions increases. These interactions include imitation; complementary exchanges in which playmates take different roles, such as driver or passenger in pretend play; and more complex combinations of imitation and complementary exchanges (Eckerman et al., 1989). Preschool children's highest level of peer social play also increases with age, progressing through a sequence of parallel play, simple social play, complementary and reciprocal play, cooperative social pretend play, and finally complex social pretend play. Children who spend more of their play time in complex forms of play appear to have greater overall social competence with their peers (Howes & Matheson, 1992).

Although play involving high degrees of social participation increases during childhood and adolescence and tends to dominate throughout the rest of one's life, all forms of play continue to be important to various degrees. For example, the random, nondirected activity of a shy teenager at a party has much in common with the unoccupied play of a preschooler; devotees of jigsaw or crossword puzzles clearly engage in forms of solitary play; television viewing and involvement in spectator sports are basically onlooker play activities; and aerobics, weightlifting, and in-line skating sometimes have strong parallel-play aspects.

Other Influences on Play

Setting   Although the cognitive and social levels of play are important, the composition of a particular child's play is also likely to be influenced by the range of play opportunities caregivers provide and the types of play they encourage. One hallmark of play is that children have a choice of activities that they find enjoyable and suit their needs and wants at particular times. This is what is meant by providing children with developmentally appropriate play opportunities. For example, a parent or caregiver who insists that the child always be learning something or trying something new may make play a stressful rather than a rewarding experience for the child.

The availability of physical space and play materials and the overall quality of a child care environment can also can make a difference. Studies have found that children in child care centers with qualified staffs, developmentally appropriate programs, and suitable facilities and equipment engage in much less unoccupied and solitary play than do children in centers of lower quality. In addition, preschoolers in the better-quality centers have been found to interact more positively with adults. They also appear to develop complex forms of pretend play at earlier ages and engage in it more frequently than do children in centers that are only minimally adequate (Howes & Matheson, 1992; Vandell & Powers, 1983).

Children's play is also influenced by other economic, cultural, and situational factors. For example, developmentally appropriate play among preschoolers is more likely to occur when they have access to safe, well-designed, and well-equipped play areas than when the play environment is less adequate (Susa & Benedict, 1994). Having adequate time for play is also important. Large amounts of television viewing can reduce the amount of time available for play, and watching programs with high levels of violence has been associated with decreased levels of fantasy play (van-der-Voort & Valkenburg, 1994). Also, although play is a universal activity and occurs in all cultures, its frequency, forms, and functions also vary with cultural values and expectations and with physical, social, and economic contexts (Roopnarine et al., 1994). For example, in countries such as Kenya, India, Ecuador, and Brazil, where many children spend a large part of the day doing household chores and assisting their families in getting food or money, time and opportunity for play are far more limited than for children in Mexico, the Philippines, or the United States (Campos et al., 1994; A. Hoffnung, 1992; Whiting & Whiting, 1975).

Even when free time, space, and toys are limited, however, most children find a way to play. They use common household objects such as pots, pans, and furniture, as well as outdoor items such as trees, sticks, rocks, sand, empty cans, and discarded equipment, as props for their make-believe and sociodramatic play. However, the range and developmental appropriateness of play activities under such circumstances are likely to be more restricted than in the case of children who play in more supportive settings.

What play materials are thought to be appropriate for a preschool child growing up in the United States? Table 10.3 summarizes age-appropriate recommendations for preschool play materials.

Siblings   The presence of siblings also influences play. A series of studies of two-year-olds revealed that their older siblings often (and with some success) tried to engage them in dramatic role playing well before age two. In some of these families

TABLE 10.3   *General Characteristics and Appropriate Play Materials for the Preschool Child*

Age	General Characteristics	Appropriate Play Materials
2	Uses language effectively. Large-muscle skills developing, but limited in the use of small muscle skills. Energetic, vigorous, and enthusiastic, with a strong need to demonstrate independence and self-control.	Large-muscle play materials: Swing sets, outdoor blocks, toys to ride on, pull toys, push toys. Sensory play materials: Clay, fingerpaints, materials for water play, blocks, books, dolls and stuffed animals.
3	Expanded fantasy life, with unrealistic fears. Fascination with adult roles. Still stubborn, negative, but better able to adapt to peers than at age two. Early signs of product orientation in play.	Props for imaginative play (e.g., old clothes). Miniature life toys. Puzzles, simple board games, art materials that allow for a sense of accomplishment (e.g., paintbrushes, easels, marker pens, crayons).
4	Secure, self-confident. Need for adult attention and approval— showing off, clowning around, taking risks. More planful than threes, but products often accidental. Sophisticated small-muscle control allows for cutting, pasting, sewing, imaginative block building with smaller blocks.	Vehicles (e.g., tricycles, Big Wheels). Materials for painting, coloring, drawing, woodworking, sewing, stringing beads. Books with themes that extend well beyond the child's real world.
5	Early signs of logical thinking. Stable, predictable, reliable. Less self-centered than at four. Relaxed, friendly, willing to share and cooperate with peers. Realistic, practical, responsible.	Cut-and-paste and artistic activities with models to work from. Simple card games (e.g., Old Maid), table games (e.g., Bingo), and board games (e.g., Lotto), in which there are few rules and the outcomes are based more on chance than on strategy. Elaborate props for dramatic play.

Source: Fergust Hughes (1991), p. 70.

the children played together constantly, and many of the two-year-olds were able to collaborate in play at surprisingly sophisticated levels (J. Dunn, 1985).

What Do You Think?

Many political leaders (and a significant number of parents who have voted for them) have criticized spending money on preschool programs where children spend their time playing rather than learning important preschool skills. How would you respond to such critics regarding the importance of play for preschool children?

RELATIONSHIPS WITH OTHERS

As our discussion of play shows, young children spend a good deal of time relating to others. Most of the time, these contacts are positive: children share and cooperate, converse with and smile at one another, and in general show at least rudimentary evidence of empathy, or mutual understanding. Such **prosocial behavior** sometimes leads to the development of genuine friendships. But social contacts can be negative, too. Conflict and aggression occur at least as often among young children as they do among older children and adults, and certain forms occur more often. In this section, we first look at preschoolers' relationships with parents, siblings, and other children. Then we examine both the prosocial and aggressive social interactions that typically occur during the preschool years.

Relationships with Parents

During the preschool years, the attachment relationships between children and their parents and other caregivers discussed in Chapter 7 continue to play a central role in their social and emotional development. Preschool children's expanding powers to initiate verbal and physical activity and their exploding powers of imagination can at times be a challenge to their parents. These changes require parents to support their children's efforts to take on the world while also appreciating young children's limitations and need for restraints that protect their physical and emotional safety and self-esteem. Preschoolers often test the limits their parents impose on their behavior and often are inconsistent in their ability to understand and conform to parental wishes. At times they express their strong desire to control their environment by refusing to eat certain foods or wear certain clothing or by insisting on playing the same game or having the same story read to them over and over again. How effectively parents respond to this "limit testing" depends partly on their beliefs and characteristic styles of parenting and partly on the quality of the parent-child relationship.

Understanding the need for family rules poses a challenge to preschoolers, but making them also creates a challenge for parents, at least those living in the individualistic culture of mainstream North America. In this society, unlike most others, parents are expected to devise their own standards for rearing children, largely independently of other families' standards or expectations—a kind of "private enterprise" system of childrearing. For instance, it is up to parents as individuals to decide how much anger their child should be allowed to express, how early and well she should learn manners, or how much candy she can eat. Parents' independence in deciding these standards increases their power in shaping their child's behavior in the short run. But it also increases their dilemmas over which standards to choose, since they observe that other parents often make choices different than their own. Furthermore, as preschoolers grow and learn more about friends' fami-

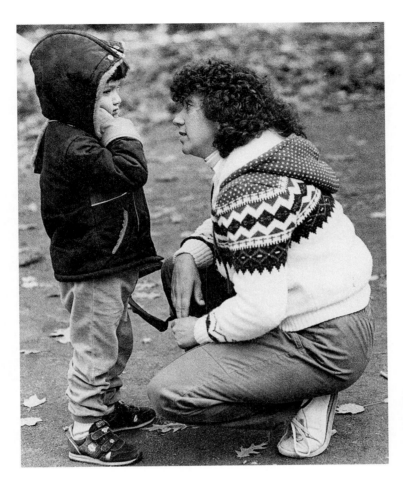

All parents discipline their children sometimes. Their methods make a difference; calling attention to the consequences of misbehavior is generally more effective than spanking, at least in the long run.

lies, they notice variations in family rules fairly quickly and use this information to bargain for more favorable rules at home. If the neighbors always eat ice cream (or watch TV or stay up late), why not do the same here at home?

Enforcing family rules may be less of a problem in cultures and societies that encourage less individualism and stronger, more prolonged interdependence among kin, community, or both. In Chinese-American and Japanese-American families, for example, grandparents and other relatives retain considerable prestige and influence in childrearing matters even after a couple has married and given birth to children (Chao, 1994; Huang & Ying, 1989; Nagata, 1989). Even as preschoolers, children are taught ways to show respect for their elders, such as caution in asking questions and readiness to obey orders. In such a situation, parents lose some decision-making authority to grandparents, in-laws, or "the community." But parents also gain family and community backing for their position: it is not just an adult or two, Mom and (sometimes) Dad, who decide whether talking in a loud voice is rude but an extended array of relatives and friends (Skolnick & Skolnick, 1989). (See the accompanying Perspectives box for a discussion of extended family members' participation in childrearing.)

Patterns of Parental Authority   One of the most important aspects of a parent-child relationship is the parent's style of authority. Observations of North American families of preschoolers suggest that childrearing styles can be classified into four groups: *authoritative, authoritarian, permissive-indulgent,* and *permissive-indifferent* (Baumrind, 1971, 1973; Darling & Steinberg, 1993; Maccoby & Martin, 1983). In most families, however, none of these styles exist in a "pure" form and parenting styles can

Perspectives

Extended Family Supports for Childrearing

In American society in particular, parents are held, and hold themselves, responsible for the physical care of their children. Whether parents are rich or poor, Caucasian or African-American, divorced or married, society expects them to provide food for their children, as well as clothing and a place to sleep. In reality many families share these responsibilities with relatives, friends, and professionals of various kinds. In a typical week, a child may spend significant time not only with his biological parents but also with a grandparent, a neighbor, and (depending on the child's age) a teacher or day care center worker. The mixture of responsibility depends partly on the local circumstances of the particular family. It also reflects cultural and economic differences. Mexican-American families, for example, value the participation of grandparents and other relatives in childrearing. Many nonwhite families report the participation in family life of *fictive kin*, neighbors or friends who develop a relationship with the family that closely resembles that of a blood relative (Ramirez, 1989).

These additional adults supplement what parents provide, often literally by providing alternative persons to cook meals and arrange other daily routines and by bolstering the psychological goals and emotional supports provided by the biological parents. A study of African-American families confirmed this conclusion by investigating the emotional climate in two- and three-generational families (Tolson & Wilson, 1990). Interviews with all members of the families, including the children, found that three-generational families (those with a resident grandparent) saw themselves as organized more informally and spontaneously than two-generational (two-

parent) families, which in turn saw themselves as organized more informally and spontaneously than one-parent families. In other words, the greater the number of parents (including a grandparent), the *fewer* the rules for children to follow and the *more* flexible the daily scheduling of activities, even though larger families had to coordinate the activities of more individuals. While this trend may seem contradictory, the family members themselves suggested the reason when interviewed: more adults in the house meant individual parents had more back-up support in carrying out their functions as parents and therefore needed to rely on preset procedures less heavily.

The benefits of back-up support are psychological as well as physical. The interviews just described also found that African-American families with more than one parent placed significantly greater emphasis on moral and ethical issues and on determining how best to deal with both individual members and people outside the family (Tolson & Wilson, 1990). To achieve this benefit, however, it did not matter whether the second "parent" was a father; it occurred just as frequently when a mother and a grandmother were the resident parents. Other research, in fact, suggests that it may not even matter whether the additional parents live at home, as long as they participate actively in the life of the family. In another interview study, successful minority single parents reported developing and depending on networks of family and personal relationships (Lindblad-Goldberg, 1989). What mattered was not the form or pattern of the networks but their existence and importance in helping the parent carry out the roles of childrearing.

change as children grow older and as other family changes occur. Table 10.4 summarizes the main patterns of parental authority.

Authoritative Parenting   **Authoritative** parents exert a high degree of control over their children and demand a lot of them, but they are also responsive, child centered, and respectful of their children's thoughts, feelings, and participation in decision making. For example, although it may be easier for a parent to respond to her child's request for help in building something or getting dressed by doing it for him, an authoritative parent is likely to provide only the amount of help that will enable him to successfully accomplish the task himself. Such parents tend to be democratic and rational in their decision making and to respond to their children with warmth and empathy. When their children misbehave, these parents attempt to understand why and to explain the reasons for the restrictions or punishments that follow.

Preschoolers of authoritative parents tend to be self-reliant, self-controlled, and able to get along well with their peers (C. Hart et al., 1992; Pettit et al., 1988). Authoritative parenting is also associated with high self-esteem, internalized moral standards, psychosocial maturity, autonomy, and academic success. In addition, it appears to foster relationships with peers and family that display the same qualities

TABLE 10.4   Patterns of Parental Authority

Pattern	Control	Clarity of Communication	Maturity Demands	Nurturance
Authoritative	High	High	High	High
Authoritarian	High	Low	High	Low
Permissive-indulgent	Low	Mixed	Low	High
Permissive-indifferent	Low	Low	Low	Low

Authoritative parents display high levels of control, clarity of communication, demands for mature behavior, and nurturance. Authoritarian parents also show high levels of control and maturity demands but are low on clarity of communication and nurturance. Permissive-indulgent parents are low on control and maturity demands, high on nurturance, and inconsistent in how clearly they communicate with their children. Permissive-indifferent parents display low levels of all four dimensions.

of warmth and respect for others during middle childhood, adolescence, and beyond (Baumrind, 1991; Darling & Steinberg, 1992; Franz et al., 1991). The relationship between authoritative parenting and prosocial behavior is discussed later in this chapter.

Authoritarian Parenting   **Authoritarian** parents also are demanding of their children and exert high control over them. However, they tend to be less warm and responsive than authoritative parents. They also tend to be arbitrary and undemocratic in decision making, imposing their rules or views on their children based on their own greater power and authority, with little sensitivity to their children's thoughts and feelings. Parent-child relationships that depend on arbitrary, "power-assertive" control and ignore children's thoughts, emotions, and need for independence often have a negative effect on children. Children of authoritarian parents tend to be relatively distrustful of others and unhappy with themselves and to have poorer peer relations, poorer school adjustment, and lower school achievement than do children with authoritative parents (C. Hart et al., 1990; Putallaz, 1987). Further discussion of these issues appears in Chapter 16.

In the extreme, the combination of rigid and arbitrary power assertion and insensitivity to a child's thoughts and feelings can increase the likelihood of child maltreatment, which is discussed later in this chapter. By modeling disrespectful and insensitive behavior, such parenting can elicit and reinforce similar behavior in children and lead to escalating cycles of negative reinforcement and coercion (Patterson, 1982).

Authoritarian parenting is more frequent in large families and in working-class families (Greenberger et al., 1994), and fathers are more likely to be authoritarian than mothers. Authoritarian parenting is also more common in cultures in which family relations are hierarchically structured based on age, family role, and gender. Ruth Chao (1994) has questioned the validity of Western European concepts of authoritative and authoritarian parenting for Chinese families. Chinese childrearing is based on Confucian principles that require children to show loyalty to and respect for their elders and require elders to responsibly train, discipline, and otherwise "govern" young children. High degrees of parental authority and control are viewed as positive and essential aspects of the *chiao shun,* or "training," needed to set a standard of acceptable family and community conduct. Chao suggests that cultural differences such as these may explain why authoritarian parenting, which is associated with poor school achievement among European-American children, is linked to high school achievement among Chinese children. Central to such cultural differences are differences in values and assumptions about what kind of people parents want their children to be and what kinds of parenting and other developmental influences will best help them get there.

Permissive Parenting   *Permissive parents* appear to show two patterns. **Permissive-indulgent** parents are warm, sensitive, caring, and generally responsive to their children's thoughts and feelings. However, they exert low levels of control and make relatively few demands, permitting their children to make almost all of their own decisions. Also, while they clearly communicate their warmth, love, and caring, their communication tends to be less clear in situations requiring that they set limits on their children's behavior. **Permissive-indifferent** parents are detached and emotionally uninvolved. They are inconsistent in setting and maintaining age-appropriate standards and expectations for their children and in fulfilling their parental responsibilities (Maccoby & Martin, 1983).

Children with permissive-indulgent parents tend to lack self-reliance and self-control and to have lower self-esteem as they enter their adolescent years. This is also true of children with permissive-indifferent parents, who seem to be emotionally detached and not to care what their children do (Loeb et al., 1980). These children tend to have various degrees of developmental difficulties, including a low ability to tolerate frustration and to control their impulsive and aggressive behavior. They also tend to have difficulty in making life choices and in setting long-term goals. At the extreme, permissive-indifferent parents neglect their children's physical and emotional needs, leaving them with more serious developmental and emotional problems associated with child abuse and neglect (discussed later in this chapter).

Mixed Parenting Styles   Most parents, of course, do not fit neatly into any one of these categories; rather, most show mixtures of all four parenting styles. At one time or another, even the best parents ignore their child's misbehavior and justify themselves on the basis of sheer power—perhaps when they (or their child) are too tired to explain for the tenth time why it is time to go to bed. In addition, the situations in which families live may influence the effectiveness of a particular parenting style. For example, the clear-cut expectations and standards of behavior associated with authoritarian parenting may offer certain advantages to families living in neighborhoods where drug use and violence leave little margin for error (Grusec & Lytton, 1988).

Changes over Time   Patterns of childrearing also tend to change over time. Authoritarian parents, for instance, often ease up and shift to a more permissive or authoritative style as their children grow older. Changes in the family situation, such as the birth of another child, also can make a difference. Because of the experience gained from rearing their first child, parents frequently are more comfortable and flexible in rearing the children who follow. In addition, older siblings often help parents in caring for younger children, which in most cases lessens the stresses of parenting. On the other hand, additional children increase the family's overall child care and economic burdens, so more relaxed parenting is not always the outcome. Other changes within a family, such as in employment, standard of living, and health, also may influence childrearing. Families that are under stress tend to be more rigid, arbitrary, and authoritarian in rearing their children than families that are not. Finally, because they lack confidence and competence in clearly setting or negotiating limits, permissive parents may find it more difficult to move to being authoritative and democratic than authoritarian parents, who in turn must ease up on their unilateral limit setting and learn to be more democratic.

The Child's Influence   The parenting style and disciplinary techniques a parent displays may be influenced to some degree by the particular actions of the child. For example, one study of how mothers responded to their children's misbehavior found that the type of discipline the parents chose was determined more by what the child did than by a general childrearing style. Threats of punishment were widely used for most misdeeds, but reasoning and discussion were frequently used when the child's actions caused psychological harm to others (Grusec & Kuczynski, 1980).

Ultimately it is the parent's responsibility to establish the sort of parent-child relationship that fosters the developmental goals parents value for their children. In North America, these goals include confidence and capacity for self-regulation, independence, and self-esteem, all of which set the stage for a child's future social interactions. The authoritative parenting style seems to be most in tune with these goals and probably is most successful in the long term because it models and encourages qualities that are desirable for all children. Although no parent displays these qualities 100 percent of the time, most parents, given adequate motivation and support, can develop relationships with their children that more fully reflect those qualities.

Relationships with Siblings

As we noted in our discussion of play, brothers and sisters are major participants in the social activities of many preschoolers. Studies of children's behavior toward their siblings have shown that most young children are very interested in babies and their repetitions, explanations, and "language practice" speech are very similar to those of adult caregivers. Older siblings provide important role models for their preschool brothers and sisters, helping them learn social skills and parental expectations. And preschoolers listen carefully to conversations between their parents and older brothers and sisters, as reflected in their efforts to join in family conversations (Dunn & Shatz, 1989). Both the friendly and the aggressive interactions of siblings contribute to the development of preschoolers' understandings of the feelings, intentions, and needs of people other than themselves (J. Brown & Dunn, 1992; J. Dunn, 1985).

Interactions with siblings often differ from those with parents. Conversations between siblings tend to be more reciprocal, with both children freely talking about their personal interests and feelings. In contrast, mother-child conversations typically focus more on the child's feelings. Observations of the interactions between preschool-age siblings and their parents over a fourteen-month period revealed that conversations about feelings increased between siblings and decreased between children and their mothers (J. Brown & Dunn, 1992; Slomkowksi & Dunn, 1992). Preschoolers' awareness of caregiving interactions between parents and younger siblings contributes to their own capacity to respond to their younger siblings' distress with appropriate caregiving behaviors (Garner et al., 1994).

Other factors also help explain why children develop sophisticated perceptions about their siblings. For one thing, siblings know one another very well because they spend so much time together. They also share very similar sources of excitement, pleasure, joy, and fear. In addition, the family setting in which brothers and sisters work, play, and fight is emotionally intense, involving feelings of conflict, jealousy, and affection. It therefore is very important that young children understand what their siblings are feeling or intending to do (J. Dunn, 1985).

Studies of several societies have found that older siblings serve two psychological functions for younger brothers and sisters. First, they help transmit customs and family expectations. Second, they provide challenges that (hopefully) lead the younger children to new learning (Ervin-Tripp, 1989; Weiser, 1989). Both functions may occur unconsciously. In North American society, for example, an older child may demonstrate to a sibling that athletic ability is important simply by choosing to use free time playing softball or hockey with neighborhood friends. But what happens when the younger child attempts to play these same games with the older sibling? The older child may try to assist, but may set tasks that the younger child finds challenging or even impossible at first, such as batting a ball or staying upright on a pair of skates while swinging a hockey stick. Older siblings do make allowances for lesser competence due to a sibling's younger age, but generally not as much as parents do. In explaining a task to a younger sibling, for example, older children simplify their language somewhat, but less so than their parents do (Hoff-Ginsberg & Krueger, 1991).

Given the social opportunities siblings offer, one might expect children growing up with brothers and sisters to develop social skills earlier and more rapidly, and perhaps end up with better skills, than children who lack siblings. But having siblings can have its down side as well. For instance, an older sister can be an excellent teacher and role model for her younger brother, but her relative competence and need to outshine him may make it more difficult for him to develop certain social skills than if he were not in his older sister's shadow. Similarly, caring for a younger sibling is likely to enhance the younger child's social competence, but being burdened with her care may also limit the older child's opportunities to spend time with his peers. How siblings will affect a particular child's social development is likely to depend on the degree to which parents recognize and respond appropriately to the social needs of all of their children.

Friendships in Early Childhood

Preschool children are simultaneously pulled in two directions. On the one hand, they seek the security and intimacy that come from playing continually with a familiar friend; on the other, they want to participate in the variety of activities that many different children make possible. Although preschool friendships often involve shared activities and recognition of similarities, solidarity between two children sometimes results in exclusion of a third. In the following example, which takes place at a sink in a preschool classroom, Yolanda's alliance with Deanne involves exclusion of Shawn:

YOLANDA: I have some gum and candy—not for Shawn.
SHAWN: Why not?

During early childhood, friendships depend heavily on shared activities that children enjoy. Only later do more abstract qualities, such as intimacy and mutual loyalty, become important.

A Talk with Larry, Age Four

Friendship and Play in Early Childhood

Larry, age four, was interviewed in his bedroom after he returned from his daycare center.

Interviewer: Tell me about your friends, Larry. Do you have a best friend?

Larry: No.

Interviewer: Who are some of the friends you play with?

Larry: Kimmy, Judy. Nobody else.

Interviewer: And what do you do with your friends? What do you play?

Larry: Play dough. . . . You make it into things.

Interviewer: Why is someone your friend?

Larry: We play together. With baseball cards.

Interviewer: How?

Larry: We put doubles together.

Interviewer: What do you do with your doubles?

Larry: You pile them together.

Interviewer: What do you do during the day?

Larry: I like to play games and Mouse-trap and Safely Home and Wheel of Fortune and go to that store across the street.

Interviewer: What do you do when you get up in the morning?

Larry: Get dressed. Sometimes I watch TV.

Interviewer: And then what do you do?

Larry: I eat breakfast. I have all kinds of food. What you want. Bubble gum!

Interviewer: I mean for regular breakfast, not silly breakfast. What would you have?

Larry: Cereal.

Interviewer: And then what happens, after you have your breakfast?

Larry: I go to day care.

Interviewer: Tell me about day care. What is day care?

Larry: You play and there's a lot of toys and there's bikes and balls. A lot of bikes. And Big Wheels. Tricycles. A train. And drinks.

Interviewer: And drinks?

Larry: Right. And food. And there's a couch there. And there's a closet.

Interviewer: What about people? Who else is there?

Larry: Kimmy and Judy.

Interviewer: How many other kids are there at day care?

Larry: Ten people. And two new kids. Eric and Jason. And Aaron.

Interviewer: And are there grown-ups at day care too?

Larry: Yes. Lots and lots and lots.

Interviewer: What do the grown-ups do at day care?

Larry: They tell us what to do.

Interviewer: What do they tell you?

Larry: Don't do bad things. Like hit or bite.

Interviewer: No hitting, no biting.

Larry: No throwing pillows, but you can make a hideout.

Interviewer: Do you make a hideout?

Larry: No. But you can if you want to. If you ask them if it's okay, you can make a hideout. And if they say no, we can't. And if they say yes, we can. And we play and go outside.

Follow-up Questions

1. In Larry's view, what is the basis of friendship? How does this fit with the discussion of preschool friendships in this chapter?

2. Which social and cognitive levels of play described in this chapter characterize Larry's play?

3. How typical are the types of aggression that Larry reports of children his age?

YOLANDA: 'Cause you won't help.
SHAWN: I'm rinsing.
DEANNE: These are hardly even clean. I have a whole bunch of lollipops.
YOLANDA: Me too. I'm not giving Shawn any gum.
SHAWN: Yes, you are.
YOLANDA: No, I ain't. I'm going to give Deanne gum 'cause . . .
DEANNE: 'Cause I don't fight with you?
YOLANDA: Yes.
DEANNE: I'll give Shawn a little teeny piece.
YOLANDA: Yes, give him a little teeny piece. . . . See, you're not helping.
SHAWN: I'm rinsing.
DEANNE: I already rinsed it twice.

The Evolution of Friendship   Even infants and toddlers show preferences for particular children of their own age. Given a choice among several peers in a playroom, a one- or two-year-old is likely to smile at and approach his particular friend more often than a nonfriend. He will also be more skillful at taking turns with a friend than with a nonfriend. If two friends are playfully making noises or movements, for example, they will wait longer for each other to finish and generally coordinate their activity better than two children who are not friends might (Furman, 1982; Howes & Mueller, 1984; Vandell, 1980).

John Gottman and Jennifer Parkhurst (1980) made extensive home observations of preschoolers between ages three and six as they played with friends and new acquaintances. Play between younger children and their friends included frequent and extensive fantasy role playing, whereas older children's friendships focused more on the actual activities they were doing than on make-believe roles. Younger children communicated more clearly with their friends than did older children and were more responsive to their friends' requests for information or explanation. They also worked harder to create a "climate of agreement" by avoiding disagreements. They did this by immediately discussing the reasons for a disagreement or explaining them away and by using positive social comparisons with their friends to create a sense of common ground and solidarity. Older children were better able to tolerate differences and disagreements and had less need to use positive social comparisons to manage conflict in their friendships.

Due to the "management" problems just noted and the emphasis on overt, concrete, shared activities—such as whether to build a sand castle, how to draw a dog, how to cook a pretend dinner—early friendships tend to be somewhat unstable and may change on a weekly or even daily basis. A preschool child will drop a friend relatively easily and later make up to her just as easily. Sometimes she will even exchange goods for friendship: "If you give me a piece of candy, I'll be your best friend!"

Nonetheless, preschoolers are also capable of sustaining relationships with playmates that last for a year or more (Howes, 1988). These preferences are an important step toward forming more lasting friendships later in childhood, as well as a basis for learning to get along with others. By age three to four, friendships become more involved and durable. Certain pairs of children develop a liking for each other and purposely try to spend time together. In fact, approximately 80 percent of three-to-four-year-olds spend a substantial amount of time with at least one special "associate" or playmate. Children in nursery school spend at least 30 percent of their time with one other peer. Typically, the pairings develop in situations that encourage physical proximity, such as the children's neighborhood play group, day care center, or preschool classroom (Hinde et al., 1985). Pairs of preschool friends exhibit greater reciprocity and interdependence with each other in their parallel play, requesting and following/imitating activities than they do with mere acquaintances (Goldstein et al., 1989).

By the end of the preschool period, stable friendships do emerge, but they are not necessarily as reciprocal or intimate as adult friendships are. A child may choose a friend because the friendship enhances his status among his peers. Having an especially popular friend may help a child feel more popular himself. Or a child may choose a friend because the friend has a desirable possession or skill, perhaps an especially attractive train set at home or the ability to attract playmates. Because these relationships are somewhat more permanent than earlier ones, they are in a sense more mature or adultlike, but they still tend to focus mainly on fulfilling one-way, or self-centered, needs. Truly mutual and reciprocal relationships do not become common until the school years.

Conceptions of Friendship   During the preschool years, children also develop ideas about the nature of friendship. These notions largely parallel the actual friendship behaviors they reveal. In the minds of younger preschoolers, a friend is someone who does certain things with you; she is someone (anyone, in fact) whom you like to play with, share toys with, or talk with a lot. "A friend," as one preschooler put it, "lets you hold his doll or truck or something."

As children near school age, more permanent, personal qualities enter into their conceptions (Furman, 1982). Now the crucial features of a friend are more often dispositional, that is, related to how the friend is likely to behave in the future. A friend is still very much "someone you like," but she is also someone whom you trust, whom you can depend on, and who likes and admires you. To be friends in this sense, two children must know each other's likes and preferences better than before, and they must also be increasingly aware of thoughts and feelings that the friend may keep hidden. Nevertheless, each child is still likely to focus primarily on his own needs to the exclusion of his friend's. As one child said, "A friend is someone who does what you want"; and as another said, "A friend doesn't get you in trouble." Neither of these children understands that sometimes he or she should return these favors; later, during the school years, they will likely think of this.

Empathy and Prosocial Behavior

Empathy is the ability to vicariously experience the emotions of another person. Empathy is thought to play an important role in the successful development of friendships and other close emotional relationships (Eisenberg et al., 1989). *Prosocial behavior* refers to positive social actions that benefit others, such as sharing, helping, and cooperating. Some prosocial behaviors are *altruistic,* meaning they are voluntarily aimed at helping others with no expectation of rewards for oneself. The development of both empathy and prosocial behavior is related to sound parent-child relationships and secure attachment during infancy and toddlerhood (see Chapter 7).

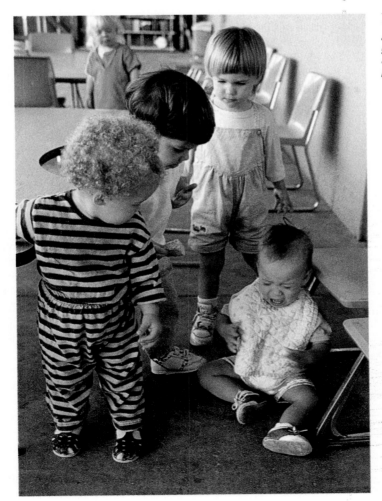

These two toddlers are concerned about the unhappy baby. Important gains in children's capacity for empathy and emotional support occur during the preschool years.

The Extent of Empathy and Helpfulness   In a variety of situations, preschool children will respond helpfully to another person's distress. For example, observational reports by mothers of the prosocial behavior of their four- and seven-year-olds at home indicate that spontaneous helping occurred in both age groups more frequently than did sharing and giving, affection and praise, or reassuring and protecting (Grusec, 1991). Young children show a strong tendency to empathize in other situations as well. One study of children at a day care center playground found that more than 90 percent of the time, a crying child generated concerned and mostly helpful responses from the other children (Sawin, 1979). About half of the children who were near the distressed child looked as though they would cry themselves. Almost 20 percent of the nearby children tried to console the child directly (and their actions did, in fact, help reduce the crying); other children sought out an adult on the playground; still others threatened revenge on the child who caused the upset. In contrast, naturalistic studies by Carolee Howes and her colleagues of young children's responses to crying in day care settings found that somewhat fewer than 20 percent of crying incidents received a response, 70 percent were ignored, and fewer than 40 percent of the children intervened prosocially by mediating, consoling, or offering information to a teacher (Howes & Farver, 1987; Phinney et al., 1986).

Developmental Trends   Prosocial behavior, or helpfulness, is well established by the time a child reaches the preschool years. An early, classic study found that all of the following helping behaviors occurred with significant frequency among four-year-olds (Murphy, 1937): assisting another child; comforting another child; protecting another child; warning another child of danger; giving things to another child; and inquiring of a child in trouble. Fifty years later, these and similar helping behaviors are still quite evident, not only among preschool children but even among children younger than two (Eisenberg & Mussen, 1989; Radke-Yarrow & Zahn-Waxler, 1987).

Between ages two and six, children give increasingly complex reasons for helping and are more strongly influenced by nonaltruistic as well as altruistic motives and concerns (Eisenberg et al., 1989; Yarrow & Waxler, 1978). An older child may justify her helpfulness in terms of gaining approval from peers in general rather than in terms of her concern for the well-being of the child in distress. Or she may justify withholding help because of fear of disapproval from adults, for example, if she has been instructed to let the day care or nursery school teachers handle children in trouble. In fairness to older preschoolers, however, younger children also may have reasons such as these but are not yet able to verbalize them clearly (Fabes et al., 1988).

Sources of Prosocial Behavior   Potential sources of individual differences in prosocial responses include age, gender, temperament, child care experience, social competence with peers, and friendship status (Farver & Branstetter, 1994). Prosocial behaviors increase with age due to gains in cognitive functioning, social skills, and moral reasoning and to more socialization experiences that enhance prosocial responsiveness (Eisenberg & Mussen, 1989). No consistent gender differences in prosocial responses have been found, although some studies have found girls to be more prosocial than boys.

There is some evidence that differences in temperament affect children's prosocial behavior. Young children who display high levels of prosocial behavior tend to be active, outgoing, and emotionally expressive. This pattern is similar to the temperamentally *easy child,* whose high levels of adaptiveness, positive mood, and approachfulness may help him initiate and sustain more peer interaction than *difficult* or *slow-to-warm-up children,* who are more likely to avoid peer contact (Buss & Plomin, 1984; Farver & Branstetter, 1994).

Early exposure to prosocial experiences with peers, parents, and other important individuals may be the best predictor of subsequent prosocial behavior. Jo Ann

Farver and Wendy Branstetter (1994) studied prosocial behavior among preschoolers ages 3 to 4½ in three child care programs. They found that it was the type and quality of peer contact children experienced, rather than the length of time children spent in their prior or current preschool programs, that most influenced their prosocial tendencies. Early peer relationships are most likely to foster prosocial responsiveness when teachers, parents, and other adults create an environment that supports it and provides models for children to observe and imitate.

Prosocial competence among preschoolers may also depend on how often parents initiate informal play activities. Gary Ladd and Craig Hart (1992) found that children whose parents frequently arranged for them to play with peers and actively involved them in arranging play activities displayed higher levels of prosocial behavior. Children who more frequently initiated informal peer contacts were better liked by their classmates.

Overall differences in parenting styles also appear to influence preschoolers' prosocial behavior. Children whose parents are authoritative in their disciplinary styles engage in more prosocial, empathic, and compassionate behavior and less antisocial behavior in day care, playground, and other play settings than children whose parents have authoritarian discipline styles (Hart et al., 1992; Main & George, 1985; Zahn-Waxler et al., 1979).

Cross-cultural studies have provided some additional insights about the significance of parental support and encouragement. In mainly rural societies where mothers worked in the fields and children assumed major child care and household responsibilities, children had greater opportunity to experience prosocial roles and to behave prosocially. Firstborn children, who had the most helping experience, tended to be more prosocial than lastborn or only children. Children raised in close-knit, communal Israeli kibbutz communities, which place high value on cooperation and prosocial behavior, exhibited higher levels of cooperation and prosocial behavior than children from rural or big-city areas (Eisenberg et al., 1990; Whiting & Edwards, 1988).

What practical steps can parents and teachers take to increase altruism and prosocial behavior in the children they care for? Two techniques that have proven successful in increasing such behavior among preschoolers are (1) verbal approval and encouragement and (2) arranging play opportunities that allow children to discover firsthand the benefits of cooperation and helping (Orlick, 1981; Slaby & Crowley, 1977). Preschool children are also more willing to help if adults call attention to other children's distress. For example, when young children who played a game for prizes were told they could share them with less fortunate children who wouldn't win any, a number of children voluntarily donated their winnings after the game and also reported feeling sad for their less fortunate peers. They were more likely to do so if the adults had called attention not only to their peers' lack of winnings but also to the nonwinners' distressed feelings (Howard & Barnett, 1981).

Conflict and Aggression

So far our discussion of social relationships has focused on the ability of preschoolers to get along reasonably well with one another. However, preschoolers also get very angry and express their feelings in aggressive ways: grabbing one another's toys, pushing, hitting, scratching, and calling names. What types of interpersonal conflicts make preschoolers angry, and how do they cope with their angry feelings? Richard Fabes and Nancy Eisenberg (1992) observed the causes of anger and reactions to provocations among preschool children between ages 3 and 6½ while they were at play. Conflict over possessions was the most common cause of anger, and physical assault was the second most frequent cause. In most types of anger conflicts, most children responded by expressing angry feelings (particularly boys) or by actively attempting to defend themselves in nonaggressive ways (particularly

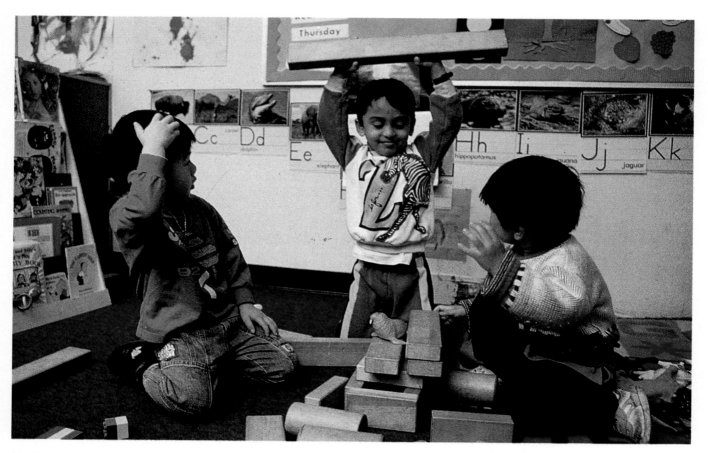

Hostile aggression among preschoolers is frequently associated with frustrations at being unable to solve a conflict over toys and with angry and jealous feelings that may result when excluded from a desired activity with peers.

girls). Active resistance was most likely in conflicts over material things such as toys and least likely in conflicts involving compliance with teachers and other adults. In contrast, venting of angry feelings was least likely for material conflicts and most likely for compliance conflicts with adults, suggesting that the particular coping strategy chosen depends in part on how controllable the child sees the situation to be. Children's use of aggressive revenge (hitting or threatening) and tattling was most frequent when anger was caused by physical assault.

The Nature of Aggression   **Aggression** refers to actions that are intended to harm another person or an object. Aggressive actions frequently are divided into two types. **Instrumental aggression** involves actions in which one person hurts another as a means to achieving a nonaggressive end. Instrumental aggression frequently involves conflicts over objects, territory, and perceived rights or privileges. **Hostile aggression** refers to actions in which hurting another person is the major goal, such as when a child who is teased or taunted by another child retaliates by pushing or hitting. Quite frequently, aggressive behavior is associated with a child's frustration at being unable to solve a conflict; for example, one child hits another because her attempts to get a turn with a favorite toy have all failed. Generally, judgments about whether a child's aggressiveness is instrumental or hostile are based on the child's motivations, his level of knowledge about the effects of his actions, previous patterns of response in similar situations, and whether or not destructive consequences have resulted.

Changes in Aggression During Early Childhood   During the preschool years, the frequency of instrumental aggression declines as children become better able to understand the reasons for their frustration and anger, whereas the frequency of hostile aggression increases (Shantz, 1987). Young preschoolers show aggression in more physical ways than older preschoolers do. As children get older, verbal aggression such as making insulting remarks increases, whereas physical aggression such as pushing, hitting, and grabbing declines (McCabe & Lipscomb, 1988).

Consistent with these changes are changes in the causes of aggressive behavior. Preschool children of all ages respond to assertiveness and instrumental aggression with about the same frequency. In the case of *blocking behaviors*—actions that interfere with a child's current activities, such as keeping her from the toys she wants to use—preschool children of all ages respond with hostile aggression around one-quarter of the time (Hartup, 1974). Personal insults, however, are another story. As preschool children get older, they insult one another more often and respond to insults with increasing frequency—nearly 80 percent of the time by age five (Krasnor & Rubin, 1983). And they respond in kind: insulting remarks and ridicule generate insults and ridicule in retaliation. In part this occurs because children perceive one another's intentions more accurately as they get older, and they are also more vulnerable to these kinds of attacks.

Influences on the Development of Aggression   When expressed in acceptable ways, aggression may be not only tolerable but even desirable. Assertive or instrumental-aggressive actions allow a child to communicate and fulfill legitimate needs, such as when he takes back a toy that is rightfully his or stands up for his integrity against unfair insults. Often, however, hostile motivations complicate matters and create additional distress. The anger and rage children sometimes experience can be quite upsetting to them as well as to their parents and others. For example, a mother who observes her four-year-old attack a playmate, perhaps biting her or pulling her hair, is likely to be upset for multiple reasons, including her own child's unhappiness, the pain and distress of the other child, her belief that biting is "dirty fighting," and concerns about how all of this reflects on her as a parent.

Temperamental Differences   Temperamental differences that are present at birth may make aggressive behavior more likely during early childhood. For example, babies who are low in their ability to regulate their physical and emotional states and high in emotional intensity may be especially prone to overt expressions of anger, frustration, and aggressive behavior, whereas babies with a high ability to regulate these states are more likely to cope more constructively with their anger and frustration. Consistent with this view, Nancy Eisenberg and her colleagues found that babies with especially "difficult" temperaments at six months of age experienced significantly more conflict with their mothers at age three than babies with less difficult temperaments. At six months, temperamentally difficult infants displayed irregular levels of activity, including sudden bursts of arm waving and general restlessness (Eisenberg & Fabes, 1992; Eisenberg et al., 1994).

When they were three years old, these children responded less cooperatively than did children who had easier temperaments as infants. They were also more likely to get into trouble a second time, ignore their parents' disciplinary efforts, and respond in insulting and unpleasant ways. Their parents used a wide variety of methods to attempt to control them, including forbidding certain activities, threatening punishment, and using physical restraint. Thus, the ongoing interactions between these difficult children and their parents seemed likely to be escalating a cycle of aggression (Eisenberg et al., 1994). Of course, many active or difficult babies do not become aggressive three-year-olds, perhaps because the expression of temperament is largely a product of child-caregiver interactions.

Gender   Gender differences appear to affect aggressive behavior. Throughout the preschool years, boys exhibit more overall aggressive behavior than girls do (Maccoby & Jacklin, 1980). This difference holds true across a broad range of social classes, ethnic groups, and cultures. It is also true across a wide range of aggressive behaviors; contrary to common belief, girls do not specialize in verbal aggression (such as name calling) or boys in physical aggression (such as pushing and hitting). Although, there do not appear to be significant differences in the types of anger conflicts boys and girls experience, boys are more likely than girls to vent their feelings when angered, whereas girls are more likely to actively resist by verbally defending themselves (Fabes & Eisenberg, 1992).

One reason for these differences may be that girls and boys have different goals in their coping responses to anger provocations. Boys may be more likely to use coping strategies designed to meet their own needs, whereas girls may select strategies to maximize interpersonal harmony. The childrearing and educational philosophies and practices of parents and teachers may contribute to such differences. For example, parents tend to play more roughly with boys and be more tolerant of their physically assertive and aggressive actions and to be less tolerant of similar behavior in girls, encouraging them instead to use verbal accommodation in such situations (Mills & Rubin, 1990; Ross et al., 1990).

Childrearing Styles   As in the case of prosocial behavior discussed earlier, styles of childrearing and the overall quality of the parent-child relationship are likely to significantly influence children's use of aggression in coping with interpersonal anger. In one study, children who were abrasive and aggressive in interacting with their mothers and whose mothers used control that was negative and unclear were more likely to be aggressive, low in prosocial behavior, and unsuccessful with their peers compared to mothers whose guidance was more respectful (Kochanska, 1992).

All of the following childrearing characteristics have been found to contribute to aggressiveness in preschoolers, especially when they are part of an ongoing pattern (Baumrind, 1971; B. Martin, 1975):

1. Lack of acceptance of the child, dislike of the child, and criticism of the child for being the sort of person she or he currently is or is becoming

2. Excessive permissiveness, particularly if it includes indifference to the child's true needs for reasonable but consistent limits and emotional support

3. Discipline that does not respect the child's ability and need to understand the reasons for the punishment and its meaning to the parent

4. Inconsistent discipline, which fails to provide the child with a reasonable and predictable basis for learning to regulate his or her behavior

5. A "spare the rod and spoil the child" attitude, which often results in impulsive and overly harsh use of discipline

6. Unclear rules and expectations for the child, particularly those regarding interactions with other family members

There is some evidence that both permissive-indifferent and extreme forms of authoritarian parenting styles, discussed earlier in this chapter, are likely to be associated with higher levels of aggression and lower levels of prosocial behavior. As we noted earlier, parent-child relationships that depend on arbitrary, "power-assertive" control and ignore children's thoughts, emotions, and need for independence can have negative effects, including greater distrustfulness of others and unhappiness with themselves, poorer peer relations, poorer adjustment to school, and lower school achievement compared to other children (Hart et al., 1990; Putallaz, 1987).

Perhaps the most important factor influencing the development of aggression in young children is the quality of the parent-child relationship. Children whose parents accept their hostile-aggressive impulses and actions and at the same time provide guidance that is respectful and who actively help them discover nonhostile, or instrumentally aggressive, alternatives for resolving conflicts and asserting their needs are most likely to learn to successfully manage their aggression. The childrearing orientation of such parents closely corresponds to the authoritative parenting style, which is strongly associated with the development of prosocial behavior.

Peer Influences   Peers can also contribute to aggression by acting in ways that provoke aggressive retaliation. Presumably a child surrounded by provocative peers eventually will acquire a similar style herself and, in doing so, will stimulate further aggressive behavior in her peers.

Some preschool children are continually involved in conflicts. They constantly either lose battles and arguments or lose potential friends by depending too much on hostile, aggressive actions to get what they need. Observations of preschool children in the playground indicate that such children are likely to experience declining peer acceptance as the school year progresses (Ladd et al., 1988). Why do some children have such difficulties? Kenneth Dodge and his colleagues have proposed that a combination of low peer status and lack of social competence in the preschool period may contribute to a child's tendency to behave aggressively. When entering a new group, aggressive children have difficulty in accurately processing and evaluating information about what is expected and generating appropriate responses when faced with threat or provocation. Such children may have a social-cognitive bias that leads them to overestimate the harmful intentions of their peers and to respond aggressively in situations that do not warrant it (Dodge, 1986; Dodge & Coie, 1987). The aggressive, hostile behavior of an unpopular preschooler may also be his way of externalizing any anger and distress he is experiencing in his family.

Media Influences   As many concerned parents realize, television, films, and other media exert a strong influence on children, and much of that influence centers on physical violence. Researchers estimate that three-to-four-year-olds watch two or more hours of television each day and that viewing TV violence increases children's aggressive behavior, at least in the short run (Huston et al., 1989). Numerous well-documented studies indicate that watching violence *disinhibits*, or releases, violent behavior in children who are already prone to anger and aggression. Most children, however, react by becoming desensitized to the pain and hurt that result from aggression.

Preschool children have a special problem in coping with violence in the media: their lack of skill in figuring out the motives of characters portrayed and the subtleties of plots. A heinous murder on television may look the same to a preschooler as one committed in self-defense or to protect innocent people (Collins et al., 1981). Also, some of the most violent TV programs are those produced for children; Saturday morning cartoons average more than twenty violent acts per hour (Gerbner et al., 1986). Adult supervision and help in understanding television programs therefore are especially important for very young children. Unfortunately, one of television's main attractions for some parents is that it makes adult supervision unnecessary by keeping children passively occupied. The broader developmental role of television in the lives of preschool-age children is discussed later in this chapter.

Responding to Aggressive Behavior   Children who have difficulty controlling their aggression experience considerable problems. Often they become aggressive at inappropriate times and in self-defeating ways, getting into fights with children and adults who are stronger than they are. Peers and parents alike find it difficult not to attribute malicious motives to children who seem out of control and appear unresponsive to generally agreed-upon standards of behavior (Kutner, 1989). Children who are overly aggressive can stimulate strong feelings of inadequacy, guilt, anger, and loss of control in their parents, leading to an increased risk that parents will respond in angry, punitive ways.

Spanking and Other Forms of Punishment   In general, preschoolers conform to parental expectations, especially if those expectations are communicated in a clear, understandable way that conveys warmth and respect for the child. Even when preschoolers resist, patient explanation and responsiveness to the child's feelings and perceptions generally resolve the problem. In instances when a preschooler "loses it" and throws a tantrum or refuses to comply with a parent's reasonable and necessary demands, firm but respectful physical restraint and guidance may also be needed until the child has regained self-control. In dangerous situations requiring immediate action, such as when a child runs into the street or is about to touch something hot, parents may use strong reprimands or spanking to stop the risky behavior and prevent it from happening again.

Some parents, however, rely on spanking and punishment as a regular part of their childrearing discipline. James Comer and Alvin Poussaint, two prominent child psychiatrists, point out that children who were spanked by thoughtful, loving parents rarely have problems as a result of the spanking. They also note that while many well-behaved and well-adjusted adults were never or rarely spanked as children, many others were spanked fairly often (Comer & Poussaint, 1992). Nevertheless, Comer and Poussaint caution that punishment is not the best way to provide discipline, especially in cases where parents are having difficulty with their preschoolers.

What problems are associated with spanking and punishment in general? While verbal or physical punishment can suppress misbehavior in the short run, it is not an effective or desirable long-run strategy, particularly if it is harsh or frequent. One obvious problem is that preschoolers are very likely to imitate the behavior of the adult models who punish them (Bandura, 1991; Emery, 1989). Using aggressive behavior such as verbal threats or spanking to reduce a child's unacceptable behavior is likely to increase the very behavior it seeks to control. A child who is hit by an angry parent learns to act on her own anger in similar ways, which is surely not the lesson her parents intend. A second problem with spanking and other forms of punishment is that a child quickly learns to fear and avoid the punishing adult, thus reducing opportunities for adult supervision and constructive adult-child interactions. Third, because punishment quickly suppresses the child's undesirable behavior in the short run, it serves to reinforce adult reliance on punishment and reduce the likelihood of exploring other ways to respond to the child's unacceptable behavior. Fourth, to the extent that punishment reduces the guilt a child feels for misbehaving, it reinforces the child's reliance on external (parental) control rather than internal, self-control of his behavior (Comer & Poussaint, 1992). Excessive reliance on spanking and other forms of punishment is strongly associated with child maltreatment, a topic discussed later in this chapter.

Helping Aggressive Children and Their Parents   Several principles have emerged from work with aggressive children and their families (Kutner, 1989; Patterson, 1982; Patterson et al., 1989). The most successful approaches frequently involve working with the entire family. The first step is to carefully observe the child's interactions with peers and adults to discover consistent patterns in what triggers the aggression and how each family member may unintentionally reinforce the patterns of problem behavior.

Structure, predictability, and consistency of routine are important for all preschoolers, especially for children who have difficulty controlling their aggressive behavior. For such children, aggressive outbursts are most likely to occur in unstructured and ambiguous situations. Such circumstances aggravate their tendency to distort information about potential harm and to perceive themselves as being at risk. Thus, neutral behavior, such as the approach of another child, is misinterpreted as an aggressive act (Dodge, 1986).

Once the patterns of aggression are discovered, parents can learn to recognize the early signs and intervene by either changing the situation or removing their preschooler before things escalate. The most successful methods involve reinforcement of positive behaviors through warmth, affection, and parental approval, assertiveness training to help the child meet her needs for attention in less self-destructive ways, and increasing predictability and consistency in the child's everyday life. (Kutner, 1989; Patterson, 1982).

Another successful approach to modifying destructive family processes and problems with childhood aggression uses social learning theory methods such as coaching, modeling, and reinforcing alternative patterns of parent-child interaction. After carefully observing the parent-child interaction, the therapist describes and then demonstrates alternative ways to deal with the child's hostile, aggressive, or disobedient behaviors. As parents gain more confidence in their competence, they become more effective parents; as children learn to resolve conflicts in more appropriate ways, their problematic behavior decreases (Patterson, 1976, 1985).

The Effects of Television

Ninety-eight percent of American homes have at least one television set, and a TV set is on for a total of 7.1 hours per day in a typical household (Huston et al., 1989). Most children are exposed to television from the time they are born, and American children spend more time, on average, watching TV than in any other waking activity, including play. A typical six-month-old is in front of a TV set almost 1.5 hours per day, and by three years most children avidly watch their favorite shows (Liebert & Sprafkin, 1988).

Viewing time increases during the preschool years and peaks at about 2.5 hours per day just before a child enters elementary school. Viewing then decreases slightly with the beginning of school, but at about age eight it increases steadily, reaching an average of about four hours per day during adolescence (Liebert & Sprafkin, 1988). (See Figure 10.1.) The same basic developmental pattern has been found in a number of European countries, Canada, and Australia, although the amount of viewing time varies with program availability and the number of broadcast hours (Liebert & Sprafkin, 1988). Not surprisingly, the types of programs children prefer to watch change with age. Until they are three or four, children prefer programs such as "Sesame Street" and "Mister Rogers' Neighborhood," which are designed for children and feature language, characters, and events at a level children can readily understand. Children ages three to five tend to watch more cartoons, and children ages five to seven increasingly watch comedies, action shows, and special-interest programs that are more cognitively demanding and aimed at general audiences (Huston et al., 1990). Boys and girls appear to watch equal amounts of television.

Television viewing has been found to influence children's social development in a number of areas, including aggression, prosocial behavior, consumer behavior, and gender stereotypes. The relationships between viewing aggression on TV and children's aggressive behavior were already discussed. In addition, longitudinal studies have found that the amount of TV violence viewed at age eight may be predictive of the seriousness of boys' aggressiveness at age nineteen and of the average severity of criminal behavior at age thirty for both males and females (Eron, 1987; Huesmann et al., 1984).

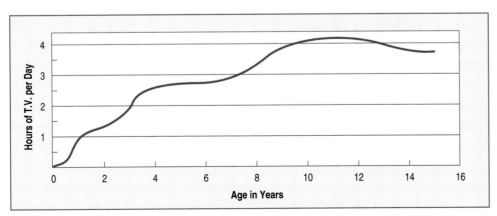

FIGURE 10.1
Changes in the Amount of TV Viewing with Age
Daily TV viewing time increases during the preschool and school years, with children viewing 1.5 hours daily at age two, 2.5 hours at age four, 3.5 hours at age eight, and a peak of 4.0 hours at age eleven.
Adapted from Bukatko & Daehler (1995, p. 626).

Television programs designed for children and for adults often convey a highly stereotyped and distorted social world that values being male, youthful, beautiful, and white are valued over being female, old, handicapped, dark-skinned, or foreign born (Greenberg, 1986; Huston et al., 1989; Liebert & Sprafkin, 1988). Despite recent efforts to broaden the portrayals of gender roles, women continue to be cast in strongly sex-typed roles: teachers, secretaries, nurses, or (most commonly) home-makers. On television, women solve problems less frequently, need help more often, listen better and talk less than men do, and behave in other gender-stereotypical ways (Huston & Alvarez, 1990; United States Commission on Civil Rights, 1977). These patterns also prevail for children's television despite widespread concern about the ways gender stereotypes limit girls' expectations. One reason for this may be that boys, who are reinforced largely by their peers, show much greater interest in shows with action heroes than in programs that present less stereotypic male activities. The significance of these patterns is not lost on advertisers, who are interested in buying time on programs that most effectively sell their products.

However, television is also a very useful educational tool for supporting children's intellectual and social development. Studies have found, for example, that programs that model cooperative, prosocial behavior are likely to increase children's prosocial behavior and that children who are exposed to non-gender- and non–racially stereotyped programs are more likely than other children to behave in less stereotypic ways (Liebert & Sprafkin, 1988).

Differences in family circumstances significantly affect young children's TV viewing. Children from lower socioeconomic levels watch more television than those from families that are better off (Greenberg, 1986). Having a mother who works outside the home and attending day care or preschool, however, may decrease the amount of TV viewing. And while having an older brother or sister to play with may decrease TV watching, having younger siblings may increase it (Pinon et al., 1989).

The types of programs TV networks provide and the choices parents make about what their children may or may not view appear to be the most important factors affecting young children's viewing patterns (Huston et al., 1990). Families vary considerably in their attitudes toward television and the amount and type of guidance they provide for their children. While nearly 40 percent of parents of preschoolers sometimes use TV to keep their children occupied, almost 40 percent regularly limit the number of hours their children can watch, and close to 50 percent have consistent rules regarding which types or which specific programs their children are allowed to view (Comstock, 1991).

To better understand how parents regulate their children's TV viewing, Michelle St. Peters and her associates conducted a two-year longitudinal study of television-viewing patterns of families with five-year olds (St. Peters et al., 1991). Whereas the majority of children's programs were viewed without parents, most adult programs were watched with parents, although watching programs together declined with age. Based on the degree to which parents regulated their children's TV viewing (high versus low regulation) and to which they encouraged TV watching (high versus low), the investigators classified families into four types. *Laissez-faire* parents provided low levels of regulation or encouragement; *restrictive* parents provided high regulation and low encouragement; *promotive* parents had few regulations and high levels of encouragement; and *selective* parents highly regulated their children's TV watching and encouraged specific types of viewing (see Table 10.5).

How did parents' supervisory styles influence their children's television viewing? As Table 10.5 indicates, the number of hours of TV children viewed per week was highest for the promotive style (21.2) and lowest for the restrictive style (11.9), with selective (19.2) and laissez-faire (17.6) supervisory styles falling in between. The same pattern was evident for the types of programs children watched. For example, children whose parents encouraged TV watched more educational programs, such as "Sesame Street" and "Mister Rogers' Neighborhood," and more adult programs,

TABLE 10.5   *Styles of Parental Regulation and Number of Hours of Television Their Children Watch Each Week*

Style of Supervision	Degree of Regulation	Degree of Encouragement	Hours of TV Viewed per Week
Laissez-faire	Low	Low	17.6
Restrictive	High	Low	11.9
Promotive	Low	High	21.2
Selective	High	High	19.2

Source: Adapted from St. Peters et al. (1991), p. 1419.

Children whose parents do not encourage TV viewing (laissez-faire and restrictive) watch the fewest hours of TV; children whose parents encourage viewing (promotive and selective) watch the most hours.

including comedy, game shows, and action-adventure shows, than children who were not encouraged. Children whose TV viewing was regulated watched similar amounts of educational programs but significantly fewer adult programs. These findings suggest that parents can substantially influence their children's TV viewing by providing appropriate supervision and guidance.

Many older preschoolers, especially those with school-age brothers and sisters, also spend a lot of time watching prerecorded videos and playing video and computer games. Here too it is important that parents ensure that such activities are appropriate in content and do not interfere with their children's involvement in other important play and related activities.

What Do You Think?

What style of parental authority best describes what you experienced as a child? How did it change as you grew older? Which pattern of parenting do you currently provide or plan to provide for your children? Why?

GENDER DEVELOPMENT

Gender influences important aspects of social development in early childhood. As used here, the term **gender** refers to the behaviors and attitudes associated with being male or female. Most children go through at least three steps in gender development (Shepherd-Look, 1982). First, they develop beliefs about **gender identity,** that is, which sex *they* are. Second, they develop **gender preferences,** attitudes about which sex they wish to be; gender preference does not always coincide with gender identity. Third, they acquire **gender constancy,** a belief that the sex of a person is biologically determined, permanent, and unchanging, no matter what else about the person changes. All three aspects of gender contribute to a child's general knowledge of society's expectations about **gender role stereotypes** (also called *sex roles*), or the culturally "appropriate" patterns of gender-related behaviors.

Developmental Trends During Early Childhood

From age two onward, preschoolers use gender role stereotypes to guide their behaviors. Children's gender preferences and knowledge of stereotypes increase significantly with age: whereas twenty-four-month-old infants typically do not show consistent gender preferences in toys and activities, thirty-month-olds consistently

Gender role stereotyping starts early.

prefer "same-gender" over "opposite-gender" objects. In contrast to gender-based preferences for toys and activities, preschool children develop gender stereotypes about personal qualities relatively slowly. Only by age five or so do children begin to know which gender is "supposed" to be aggressive, loud, and strong and which is "supposed" to be gentle, quiet, and weak. This kind of knowledge continues to develop throughout childhood and adolescence, but during the preschool years it has only begun to emerge (Huston, 1983; Thompson, 1975).

Most children acquire gender identity, the ability to label themselves correctly as boys or girls, between ages two and three and are able to correctly label other children and adults as well (Huston, 1983). Some children develop gender identity early, before age of twenty-eight months, and others not until later. Early identifiers exhibit significantly more gender-stereotyped play, such as building and car play for boys and doll play for girls, than later identifiers do (Fagot & Leinbach, 1989; Fagot et al., 1992).

Gender constancy, the understanding that one's sex is permanent and will never change, first appears by age four or five. A young preschool child may say she can switch gender just by wanting to or say that even though she is a girl now, she was a boy as an infant or may grow up to become a man as an adult. And a two-year-old may have only a hazy notion of what defines gender, believing perhaps that certain hairstyles, clothing, and toys make the crucial difference. Most children, however, achieve a reliable sense of gender constancy between ages seven and nine (Emmerich & Sheppard, 1982).

Gender Schema Theory   *Gender schema theory* proposes that children actively socialize themselves in their gender roles through a process of social learning and cognitive development (Bem, 1983; Martin et al., 1990; Ruble, 1988). A *schema* is a pattern of beliefs and stereotypes about gender that children use to organize information about gender-related characteristics, experiences, and expectations. A child's *gender schema* is thought to develop through a series of stages. First, a child learns through social experiences what kinds of things are directly associated with each sex, such as "boys play with cars" and "girls play with dolls." Around age four to six, the child moves to the second stage and begins to develop more indirect and complex associations for information relevant to her own sex but not for the opposite sex. By age eight or so, the child moves to the third stage, where she has also learned the associations relevant to the opposite sex and has mastered the gender concepts of masculinity and femininity that link information within and among various content areas (Martin et al., 1990).

Influences on Gender Development

Parents   Many theorists hold parents responsible for the development of gender differences, either blaming or congratulating them depending on the theorist's point of view. A close look suggests that parents do deserve some credit, but perhaps not as much as is commonly thought. When asked about their childrearing philosophies, parents tend to express belief in gender equality, but their actions often differ from their statements (Fagot, 1982). Observations of parents playing with their preschool children reveal that parents support their children for gender-stereotyped activities more than for cross-gender activities; a boy gets praised more for playing with blocks than for playing with dolls. Parents generally support physical activity in boys more than in girls, by both praising it and participating in it. Possibly as a by-product of these differences, boys get punished more often and more physically than girls do. Also, as children approach school age, parents begin assigning household chores according to gender: girls more often fold the laundry, and boys more often take out the trash. Parents are also more likely to reward sons for being assertive, independent, active, and emotionally unexpressive and to reward daughters for being accommodating, dependent, more passive, and emotionally expressive (Fagot & Hagan, 1991; Lytton & Romney, 1991).

Nancy Chodorow (1978) has proposed that the gender differences between girls and boys are related to differences in their experiences of identity formation during their early years, when women are usually their exclusive caregivers. In this view, girls' identities and personality development are based on similarity and attachment to their mothers, who provide models for nurturing, caregiving, and closeness. Boys' identities and personality development are based on difference, separateness, and independence from these qualities, for to be a male in our society means possessing qualities that are incompatible with those traditionally associated with being a woman. Thus, Chodorow believes, women's capacity to nurture, raise children, and develop close relationships and men's capacity to separate themselves from their feelings and participate in the isolating and alienating world of work are rooted in these early experiences.

According to this view, the task of identity formation for a boy may be more difficult in that it requires a certain degree of rejection of essential qualities of his primary female caregiver. At the same time, the higher degree of similarity and continuity of experience between daughter and mother may make it more difficult for a girl to separate from her mother and establish an independent and separate identity. After discussing the influence of peers and the media on gender differences, we will return to the question of how we define gender difference and what its consequences are.

Peers   In some ways, peers may shape gender differences more strongly than parents do. Early in the preschool years, even before age three, children respond differently to partners of the opposite sex than to those of the same sex (Maccoby, 1990). In play situations, girls tend to withdraw from a boy partner more often than from a girl partner, and boys heed prohibitions made by another boy more often than they do those that come from a girl. Even when preschoolers are not playing actively, they watch peers of the same sex more often than they do peers of the opposite sex.

Children of this age also respond to a reinforcement more reliably if it comes from a child of their own sex. If a boy compliments another boy's block building, the second boy is much more likely to continue building than he is if a girl compliments it. Conversely, if a boy criticizes the building, the other boy is more likely to stop than if a girl criticizes it. Parallel patterns occur for girls, who tend to persist in whatever other girls compliment or praise and stop whatever they criticize or ignore. For both sexes, teachers' reinforcements have less influence than peers' in determining children's persistence at activities (Fagot, 1982). What makes these patterns important is that children tend to reinforce play activities that are considered appropriate for their own sex. Children who deviate from expected gender-stereotyped activities, such as boys playing with dolls, often find themselves largely ignored, even after they return to expected activities (Lamb & Roopnarine, 1979). Thus, peer pressures to practice conventional gender roles are both strong and continuous, and they occur even if teachers and other adults try to minimize gender-typed play.

Television   As we noted earlier, television and other media are also significant influences on gender development.

Androgyny

Androgyny refers to a situation in which gender roles are flexible, allowing all individuals, male and female, to behave in ways that freely integrate behaviors traditionally thought to belong exclusively to one or the other sex (Kaplan & Bean, 1976). In this view, both girls and boys can be assertive *and* yielding, independent *and* dependent, instrumental (task oriented) *and* expressive (feelings oriented). Sandra Bem (1974, 1976) and others (e.g., Lamke, 1982a, 1982b) have found that adolescent and young adult males and females use both masculine and feminine characteristics to describe their own personalities. Bem believes androgynous individuals are less concerned about which activities are appropriate or inappropriate and therefore are more flexible in their responses to various situations (Bem, 1981).

How we choose to define *gender* also can affect our understanding of what it means to be male or female. On the one hand, definitions that tend to exaggerate positive gender differences run the risk of perpetuating gender role stereotyping and inequality; on the other hand, definitions that minimize real differences may be used to deny boys and girls the physical, cognitive, and social developmental opportunities appropriate to their different gender-related needs. One positive consequence of focusing on differences associated with gender is that it increases our awareness and appreciation of feminine (and masculine) qualities. A positive consequence of efforts to minimize gender differences is to help equalize treatment under the law and access to equal opportunity for males and females (Hare-Mustin & Marecek, 1988).

What are the implications of androgyny? Because the notion of androgyny challenges certain fundamental beliefs that individuals have about gender, it holds the potential to reduce gender role stereotyping and its detrimental developmental effects in early childhood and beyond. The idea of androgyny also contributes to our

The ease with which this preschool girl includes in her play both the traditional male role of bus driver and the traditional female role of her mother vividly illustrates the flexible qualities associated with androgyny.

understanding of sexual orientations that are not traditionally heterosexual, a topic discussed in Chapter 16.

What Do You Think?

In what ways have you been personally influenced by gender role stereotyping? What advice might you give to parents and teachers for reducing such stereotyping? Should they encourage children to be more androgynous?

CHILD ABUSE AND NEGLECT

Child abuse and neglect by parents and other caregivers are a serious social problem, with more than 1 million new cases reported each year. A significant number of these cases involve infants, toddlers, and preschool-age children, who are particularly vulnerable because of their immaturity and dependence. *Child abuse* may be physical, sexual, or emotional; *neglect* may be physical or emotional (Finkelhor, 1995; Krugman & Davidson, 1990; Rosenberg, 1989).

Causes

The causes of physical child abuse and neglect are best understood within the developmental-ecological contexts within which they occur. These include parent and child characteristics, parenting and parent-child interactions, and the broader context of family, community, and culture (Belsky, 1993).

Preschoolers are particularly vulnerable to child abuse because of their immaturity and dependence. The destructive impact of abuse is often serious and long term.

Parent and Child Characteristics   One explanation for the transmission of maltreatment from one generation to the next is that the aggressive and antisocial behavior involved in abuse was previously learned through modeling and direct reinforcement by the parent during her or his own childhood. The risk of maltreatment is much higher when parenting is extremely authoritarian (overly harsh and lacking in empathy) or when it is permissive-indifferent and neglectful of a child's needs. This explanation, however, fails to explain why two-thirds of parents who were abused themselves do not abuse their own children.

A second, more promising explanation of the causes of abuse is based on the idea of *internal working models,* the mental representations that organize and guide a parent's experiences, relationship, and interactions with the child (Bowlby, 1988; Farrangy et al., 1991; Stern, 1985b). The internal working models of an abusive parent are based on past experiences with the child, the parent's own childhood experiences, and the beliefs and expectations held by his or her own abusive parents. The working models of an abusing parent are often characterized by a distorted, unbalanced view of the child (overly negative or overly positive) and are associated with pervasive failures in parental empathy, parent-infant synchrony, and attachment (Belsky, 1993; Ferholt, 1991; Main & Goldwyn, 1989; A. Miller, 1990; van Izendoorn, 1992).

Mothers who are "at risk" for being abusive because they themselves were abused as children are much less likely to abuse their own children if they experienced one nonabusive, supportive, and close relationship while growing up. These mothers are also likely to display greater self-awareness regarding their own abuse, to be involved in a satisfying social relationship, and to have more extensive social supports than mothers who do abuse (Belsky, 1993; Caliso & Milner, 1992).

Personality characteristics that significantly undermine the ability to provide good parenting may also increase the risk of abuse, particularly if they interfere with getting social and emotional support from others. Difficulty with impulse control, emotional instability, high levels of depression, anxiety, or hostility, and alcohol

A Multicultural View

The Cultural Context of Child Abuse and Neglect

Can the ideas one culture holds about child abuse and neglect be validly applied to others? According to Jill Korbin, who has extensively studied child abuse and neglect in many different cultural and societal contexts, culturally appropriate definitions of child abuse and neglect require an awareness of both the viewpoint of an "insider" to a particular culture, termed the *emic* perspective, and the viewpoint of an "outsider" to that culture, or the *etic* perspective (Korbin, 1991, 1987, 1981). Such definitions must include three dimensions: (1) cultural differences in childrearing practices, (2) treatment of children that deviates from cultural norms, and (3) societal abuse and neglect.

Cultural differences in childrearing include practices considered acceptable in the culture in which they occur but abusive or neglectful by outsiders. For example, most middle-class American parents believe it is developmentally important for young children to sleep separately from their parents, but traditional Japanese and Hawaiian-Polynesian cultures, which highly value interdependence among family members, view isolating chil-

dren at night as potentially dangerous to healthy child development. Another example concerns a woman in London who cut the faces of her two young sons with a razor blade and rubbed charcoal into the cuts. She was arrested for child abuse, but officials soon learned that she and her children belonged to an East African tribal group that traditionally practiced facial scarification. When viewed from within her culture, her actions were an attempt to protect her children's cultural identity, for without such markings they would be unable to participate as adults in the culture of their birth (Korbin, 1987).

Many cultures have practiced such initiation rights as a normal part of childrearing before and during adolescence. Where, for example, is the line drawn between circumcision during adolescence and circumcision at birth? How would a European or an American convince traditional people in highland New Guinea that circumcision is more painful for an adolescent than for an infant? How would traditional highland New Guinea people convince Europeans or Americans that (1) circumcision has no meaning for an infant, who cannot understand its

and drug abuse can all impair a parent's capacity to respond to a child in empathic and responsible ways.

What characteristics of children may put them at risk for abuse? Although a young child is never to blame for his or her own abuse, in some circumstances certain characteristics, such as a difficult temperament, prematurity, a physical disability, hyperactivity, or other developmental problems, may contribute to an increased risk of abuse (Belsky, 1980).

Parenting and Parent-Child Interactions   Parenting and parent-child interactions also play a role. Abusive parents are more likely than nonabusive parents to rely on physical punishment and negative control strategies such as hitting, grabbing, and pushing, or threats and disapproval, rather than on reasoning to guide or discipline their children. They are also less likely to appropriately adjust their disciplinary techniques to different kinds of misbehavior (Belsky, 1993). During an abusive episode, the *instrumentally aggressive* behavior (physical punishment) on which an abusive parent relies is transformed into an act of interpersonal violence. A parent with a strong predisposition toward anxiety, depression, and hostility may become so irritated with the child that she or he loses control and physical or verbal punishment escalates into abuse.

Family, Community, and Cultural Factors   Poverty, unemployment, marital conflict, social isolation, and family pathology can increase the risk of abuse; so can shorter-term stressors such as emotional distress, economic or legal problems, or the birth of a new baby (Belsky, 1988; Cicchetti & Olson, 1990; Garbarino, 1992). Economic conditions, child and family social welfare policies, and cultural values and expectations regarding the care and protection of children can indirectly contribute to the risk of abuse and neglect. For example, societies that condone the use of violence against women (who are the primary caregivers of children) are likely to have higher rates of child abuse than societies that treat women with respect. The deep cultural significance, and (2) infancy is a time when the child should be spared all discomfort? How is the line drawn between facial scarification and orthodontia (braces), both of which cause pain and discomfort but are intended to enhance the child's attractiveness?

Idiosyncratic child abuse and neglect involves treatment of children that deviates from established standards of acceptable treatment within a particular culture. Although they may differ, all societies have such standards. For example, in one Polynesian culture known for its indulgence of children, a child can be pinched lightly on the mouth for misbehavior, but more severe punishments are prohibited. When one man left a scratch on the lip of his grandchild, he was severely criticized by his cultural group. By their *emic* standards his behavior was abusive, although from the *etic* perspective of American parents it is unlikely that such behavior would be of great concern.

Societal abuse and neglect refers to harm caused to children by societal conditions such as poverty and inadequate housing, health care, and nutrition, all of which either contribute significantly to abuse or neglect or are considered abusive or neglectful in themselves. For example, the widespread famine in Ethiopia and Somalia and the inadequate nutrition in India and Chile have had devastating effects on the physical, cognitive, and socioemotional development of millions of children. In many countries physical, sexual, and emotional exploitation and abuse of children are very common. Even in affluent countries such as our own, social policy regarding aid to parents with dependent children, early childhood health care and nutrition, child care, and employment can significantly harm (or help) the development of young children. Where does responsibility lie, and what should be done about this?

It seems likely that neither a single, universal standard nor a completely relativistic, "anything goes" standard for determining abuse and neglect is acceptable. The challenge, then, is to develop an approach that incorporates developmental values and standards for "good enough" care and treatment of children that should be universal and values standards that afford more room for cultural and societal diversity.

role of differing cultural values and expectations regarding child maltreatment is discussed in the accompanying Multicultural View box.

Consequences

Neglected infants, toddlers, and preschoolers often are deprived of sufficient food, clothing, shelter, sanitation, and medical care, which may interfere with their physical, intellectual, social, and emotional development and place them at risk of serious illness and even death (Egeland, 1988). Abused or neglected preschoolers often develop emotional problems that include insecure attachment relationships, lack of empathy, and emotional detachment. They are also more likely to exhibit behavioral problems, such as aggressiveness and withdrawal, toward peers than other children are (Cicchetti & Olson, 1990; Dodge et al., 1990; Klimes-Dougan & Kistner, 1990; Pianta et al., 1989). Physical abuse in early childhood is linked to aggressive and violent behaviors in adolescents and adults, including violence toward nonfamily members, children, dating partners, and spouses (Kendall-Tackett et al., 1993; Malinosky-Rummell & Hansen, 1993).

The most common symptoms reported for preschoolers who have been sexually abused include nightmares, general posttraumatic stress disorder, depression and emotional withdrawal, regressive and immature behavior, anxiety disorders, and problems with aggression and inappropriate sexual behavior (Kendall-Tackett et al., 1993). The developmental stage at which sexual abuse occurs is particularly significant in determining longer term outcomes. For example, incest (sexual abuse by a parent or other family member) disrupts the development of social functioning and self-esteem and increases risk for borderline and multiple personality, eating disorders, and substance abuse in adolescence and adulthood (Finkelhor, 1995; Spaccarelli, 1994). (See Chapter 16 for a discussion of special problems of adolescence.)

Working with   Javier Hernandez, PRESCHOOL PROGRAM COORDINATOR

Play and Friendships Among Preschoolers

Javier coordinates a privately run preschool program that serves a middle- and working-class community. A parent himself, he has a degree in early childhood education and has worked in preschool and daycare programs for almost six years. Javier was interviewed during nap time in the daycare center office and talked about ways in which children's playing styles evolve over time.

Rob: Your program serves a wide age range. Do you see the kids' play change as they grow older?

Javier: Yes, I do. Most of the two-year-olds' play involves sharing toys and turn-taking: "It's my turn, it's your turn." They might share building blocks or crayons. They also can follow simple directions, like meeting for circle time at the beginning and end of the day.

Rob: And how do three-year-olds play differently?

Javier: Between three and three and a half, we see an amazing increase in dramatic and fantasy play. The games become more complex and are rarely what they appear to be. The two-year-olds see the climber as just a climber, but the three-year-olds see it as a car, a spaceship, a house, or anything else they may decide. The kids all make up different names and are deeply into imaginative role-playing, and they're always trying to involve you in their fantasy play.

Rob: What about rules?

Javier: They're very interested in rules—setting them and following them. They'll tell each other, "Oh, we can't do that now" or "We can't go that way" or "That's not the way we do it" or "You have to sit down." They like structure and delight in pointing out the right and wrong way to do things. There's a lot of tattling. I frequently overhear, "You're going to get in trouble if you do that" or "You can't walk up the slide."

Rob: This is quite different behavior than the two-year-olds.

Javier: The two-year-olds are more apt to hit or push another kid, who cries until the teacher comes over. For three-year-olds, the one who is hit or pushed cries but then tells the teacher, "He hit me," and watches to see what you're going to do about it.

Rob: So this also reflects the superior verbal and cognitive abilities of three-year-olds?

Javier: Yes. The two-year-olds do a lot of copy-catting and parrot talking. What one wants, the other one wants, and they want everything to be the same. Their attention spans are much shorter, and they change their minds quickly. They often forget what they want, and you can never be sure just what they're after.

Treatment and Prevention

Treatment of child abuse and neglect involves working directly with the abused infant, toddler, or preschooler, the parents, and the family after abuse (or the threat of abuse) has been discovered. One goal is to protect the child from further mistreatment and help her recover from the physical and psychological consequences. Another is to assist the abusing parent(s) in establishing a parent-child relationship and family environment that adequately ensures the preschooler's safety and supports his developmental needs.

Intensive professional help, including family counseling and psychotherapy, often are used to help parents and child understand the causes, consequences, and personal meanings of their destructive feelings and behaviors so they will be able to live together in less destructive ways. A key aspect of treatment is to help parents improve their parenting skills. Self-help groups such as Parents Anonymous, parent aides who assist abusive and neglectful families in their homes, crisis nurseries, foster care for the abused child, and short-term residential treatment for family members or the entire family unit are among the treatment alternatives that have met with some success (Helfer & Kempe, 1987; Starr, 1979; Willis et al., 1992).

Early intervention programs that target "high-risk" families, including those headed by disadvantaged teenage mothers and minorities, have focused on helping parents improve their parenting skills, the family climate, and their ability to better cope with the stressful life events and conditions. Such programs include early and extended contact between parents and their newborn infants to improve the early parent-child relationship, parent education about child development and everyday child care problems, and home visitors and parent aides who assist parents with young children. They also offer training and support in home safety, money man-

Rob: And the three-year-olds?

Javier: They have much longer attention spans. They'll get so involved in a story that they won't move a muscle. And you have to explain every detail of every picture in the book.

Rob: To satisfy their desire to fully understand exactly what is going on?

Javier: Exactly. Two-year-olds will keep on saying *why* just for the sake of it. Three- and four-year-olds really want a solid answer and are generally satisfied once they hear one they like. They're really listening to what you're saying, whereas the two-year-olds are mainly practicing their verbal skills.

Rob: What about friendships and prosocial behavior among preschoolers?

Javier: If a two-year-old is aggressive toward another and you say, "That wasn't very nice. You hurt his feelings, and I think you need to say you are sorry," she may go over to the child and say, "Sorry" but five minutes later might do the same thing again. Three- and four-year-olds tend to be more aware of other children's feelings and of their own. They base their friendships on who is nice to them and are better able to appreciate how it feels to be hurt. If you say, "Well, would you like it if she did that to you?" they are likely to say, "No, I wouldn't like it."

Rob: Are they better able to take care of each other?

Javier: Yes. We have two children who started in the infant room and went all the way up to kindergarten together. By the last few months that they were here, if Larry said anything to Jenelle that she was sensitive about, she would just fall apart because "He's my best friend." She would get very sad and look to us to help them make up and mend their friendship. Then Larry would apologize, and they would hug. Older preschoolers seem to know a lot about each other's personalities. They know what to expect of each other and are very aware of what other children are doing.

What Do You Think?

1. In what ways do Javier's descriptions of preschool friendships parallel the discussion of preschool friendship and its management in the chapter?

2. In what ways do Javier's examples of preschool play and peer interactions demonstrate the interplay of cognitive and social development?

3. How do Javier's observations of preschooler's play compare with those of Pamela Mitchell, the primary school teacher whose interview appeared in Chapter 1?

agement, job finding, health maintenance and nutrition, leisure time counseling, and help in developing stronger social support networks (Rosenberg & Reppucci, 1985; Willis et al., 1992).

Other prevention efforts attempt to reduce or eliminate the causes of abuse by changing more general conditions that affect *all* children and families. These *social policy* efforts include education for parenthood programs, elimination of corporal punishment, the development of a bill of rights for children, and various social policy supports for parents and their children, including more and better jobs, funding for preschools and day care centers, affordable health care, and so forth.

What Do You Think?

If you were a preschool teacher, what behaviors in a child might lead you to suspect child maltreatment? What advice might you give to parents who may be at risk for abusing or neglecting their children?

THE END OF EARLY CHILDHOOD

Although the early childhood period, considered as a whole, may not bring about physical changes as dramatic as those of infancy, the cognitive, social, and emotional changes that occur may be even more striking. By age five or six, a child has both worked and played with symbolic skills quite a lot, and sometimes is beginning to do so according to prearranged rules. He can form friendships that last at least a bit beyond the here and now and that both foster and draw on genuine understanding of others. His increasing social sophistication may also allow him to use less aggressive means of asserting his needs and dealing with conflict. All these new skills, both positive and negative, are strongly guided by the child's gender role: a concept to which the child himself makes important contributions during the preschool years.

But human development is far from over at this point. The child's social world broadens widely in the years ahead, most obviously through her entry into school and the development of important social relationships outside her family. Major changes also occur in the child's cognitive abilities and in her physical growth and ability to use her body. The following chapters explore these and other important features of the child's development as she progresses through middle childhood.

SUMMARY OF MAJOR IDEAS

1. Even the physical and cognitive activities of preschool children are highly social.

Play in Early Childhood

2. Play is the major waking activity of preschoolers.
3. Play involves intrinsic motivation, process rather than product, pretense, and implicit and flexible rules.
4. Psychoanalytic theory emphasizes the mastery and wish fulfillment functions of play, whereas learning theory stresses the acquisition of social skills through imitation and observation.
5. Cognitive theory emphasizes that play develops in a sequence that generally parallels the major stages of cognitive development.
6. Functional play involves simple, repeated movements or manipulation of the body or inanimate objects. In constructive play, a child manipulates objects to build or construct something. Pretend, or make-believe, play allows the child to practice motor skills and rehearse social roles. Play involving games with rules focuses more heavily on the rules themselves.
7. Parten has identified six social levels of play: unoccupied, solitary, onlooker, parallel, associative, and cooperative play.
8. Unoccupied and solitary play are fairly unsocial. Onlooker and parallel play indicate increasing social awareness but minimal social interaction. Associative play involves mutual interaction in a common activity. In cooperative play, children develop common goals.
9. Although the preferred forms of social play change with age, all forms are observable throughout life.
10. The type of setting and the presence of siblings facilitate the development of social play.

Relationships with Others

11. Authoritative parents show a high level of control, strong demand for maturity, and high sensitivity and responsiveness to their children's needs and feelings. Their children tend to show greater self-reliance, self-control, and achievement.
12. Authoritarian parents exhibit a high degree of control and demand for maturity but low sensitivity and responsiveness

to their children's thoughts and feelings. Their children tend to be more distrustful, be unhappy with themselves, and show lower school achievement than other children.
13. Permissive-indulgent parents are warm, caring, and responsive to their children's feelings, but exert little control and make few maturity demands. Their children tend to lack self-reliance and self-control.
14. Permissive-indifferent parents are detached, uninvolved, and inconsistent in their parenting. Their children tend to lack self-reliance and self-control and may be at risk for more severe social and emotional problems.
15. Parents often use mixtures of parenting styles and may change their preferred style as their children grow older.
16. Both siblings and friends contribute to social development during the preschool years. Ultimately, however, it is the parent's responsibility to establish the sort of parent-child interactions that foster positive social relationships.
17. Whereas early friendships are unstable and depend on specific shared activities, friendships among older preschoolers involve expectations about future behavior and popularity considerations.
18. Preschoolers' friendships become more durable and involve a greater degree of shared activity with age. As they near school age, the more permanent and personal qualities of friendship become increasingly important.
19. As children grow older, the support and judgments of parents and other adults contribute increasingly to children's feelings of empathy and prosocial activities.
20. Preschoolers commonly exhibit both hostile aggression and instrumental (nonhostile) aggression to assert their needs and resolve conflicts. As they grow older, verbal methods replace physical ones and overall aggression declines.
21. Temperamental differences, gender, family childrearing practices, peers, and the media all influence the form and frequency of aggressive behavior.
22. Children who cannot control their aggression can be helped to do so with methods such as assertiveness training and social learning theory strategies. Parents can learn to spot the triggers of their children's aggression and respond effectively.

23. Television viewing significantly influences preschoolers' social development in such areas as aggression, prosocial behavior, and gender stereotyping.

Gender Development

24. During early childhood, children acquire an understanding of gender-typed behaviors and gender identity. A sense of gender constancy, the belief that being male or female is biologically determined and permanent, typically is not achieved until ages seven to nine.

25. Because the development of stereotypes about personal qualities appears to depend on the ability to think abstractly, children do not gain a clear and stable concept of gender until the school years.

26. Influences on gender development include differential expectations and treatment of boys and girls by parents, peers, and the media.

27. A more flexible approach to gender roles enables children to adopt more androgynous behaviors and attitudes.

Child Abuse and Neglect

28. More than 1 million cases of child abuse are reported annually. Types of abuse include physical, psychological, and sexual abuse. Neglect can be physical or emotional.

29. Causes of child abuse and neglect occur at the levels of the individual parent, the family, the community, and the culture.

30. Consequences of child abuse and neglect include a range of developmental, adjustment, and emotional problems, although no single set of symptoms results from abuse.

31. Responses to abuse frequently focus on treating the victims and their families. Prevention efforts include early intervention programs targeting "high-risk" families and attempts to change more general conditions that affect all children and families.

KEY TERMS

functional play *(300)*
constructive play *(300)*
pretend play *(300)*
games with rules *(301)*
prosocial behavior *(306)*
authoritative
  parenting *(308)*
authoritarian
  parenting *(309)*
permissive-indulgent
  parenting *(310)*
permissive-indifferent
  parenting *(310)*

empathy *(315)*
aggression *(318)*
instrumental
  aggression *(318)*
hostile aggression *(318)*
gender *(325)*
gender identity *(325)*
gender preference *(325)*
gender constancy *(325)*
gender role
  stereotypes *(325)*
androgyny *(328)*

FOR FURTHER READING

Adcock, D., and M. Segal. *Making Friends: Ways of Encouraging Social Development in Young Children.* Englewood Cliffs, N.J.: Prentice-Hall, 1983.

This book describes the development of friendships among preschool children in preschool and day care settings. It provides many examples, illustrations, and useful suggestions for parents, teachers, and other caregiving adults.

Erikson, E. *Childhood and Society.* New York: Norton, 1950.

Of particular interest in this classic book are Erikson's cross-cultural observations of childhood among the Sioux Indians, who were hunters, and among the Yuroks, who were fishers. Also interesting are his discussions of play and his presentation of the psychosocial theory of development.

Galinsky, E., and J. David. *The Preschool Years: Family Strategies That Work—From Experts and Parents.* New York: Ballantine Books, 1988.

This book provides a broad range of practical advice for parents who face the challenges of raising preschool children. It includes many illustrations from parents themselves.

Garbarino, J. *Children and Families in the Social Environment.* 2nd ed. New York: Aldine de Gruyter, 1992.

This book gives an up-to-date and readable application of the ecological approach to understanding the contributions of social environmental contexts to developmental change.

Louv, R. *Childhood's Future.* Boston: Houghton Mifflin, 1990.

The author is a journalist who immersed himself thoroughly in all issues related to children's welfare to write this book. The primary theme is the interrelatedness of family, economic, and children's needs. The author describes how child care, the development of talent, women's rights, and economic development all affect one another in other important ways.

Roopnarine, J. L., J. E. Johnson, and F. H. Hooper, eds. *Children's Play in Diverse Cultures.* Albany, N.Y.: State University of New York Press, 1994.

This book explores play as both a universal and a culture-specific activity in a wide range of cultural settings. Fascinating descriptions of children's play in India, Taiwan, Japan, Polynesia, Puerto Rico, Italy, Africa, and Canada are included.

Tobin, J., D. Wu, and D. Davidson. *Preschool in Three Cultures: Japan, China, and the United States.* New Haven, Conn.: Yale University Press, 1989.

This book presents a thorough and colorful description of caregiving in three world-power societies. The authors identify a number of universal issues underlying preschool and child care. For example, how much should children be encouraged to be independent, and how much should they be encouraged to conform and cooperate?

Zigler, E., and S. J. Styfco, eds. *Head Start and Beyond: A National Plan for Extended Childhood Intervention.* New Haven, Conn.: Yale University Press, 1993.

Edward Zigler is one of the creators of Head Start. This book describes the history of Head Start, describes and evaluates three existing programs, and proposes a new plan to achieve a comprehensive and effective policy for meeting the developmental needs of American children who live in poverty.

PART FIVE

Middle Childhood

Because growth slows after the preschool years, children in middle childhood have more time and energy to develop skills of all sorts, from riding a skateboard to making friends. All their years of language practice and symbolic play finally pay off: School-age children often can think rather logically, even if only about concrete matters. Partly because of these new competencies and partly due to school life, peers take on more importance than ever before.

Perhaps because children are now old enough to be aware of these changes, as adults they often remember middle childhood as the best years of their childhood. For most children of this age, the world seems secure, their health is excellent, and their abilities improve visibly and steadily year by year.

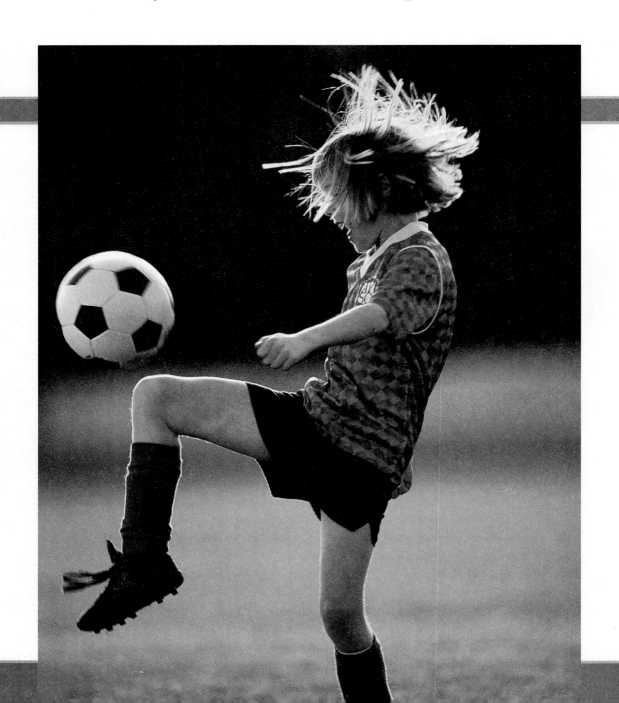

11

MIDDLE CHILDHOOD

Physical Development

Trends and Variations in Height
and Weight

Height Variations Due to Puberty
Excess Weight and Obesity

Motor Development and Athletics
in the Middle Years

Physical Effects of Early Athletics
Psychological Effects of Early Athletics
Gender and Early Athletics

Health and Illness in Middle
Childhood

Death Rates and Accidents among
    Schoolchildren
Illnesses
AIDS and the School-age Child
Attention Deficit Hyperactivity Disorder

Effects of Growth on Thinking
and Feeling

Focusing Questions

- What trends in height and weight occur among school-age children?

- How do differences in growth affect children's feelings about one another and about themselves?

- What improvements in motor skills do children usually experience during the school years, and how do they affect children's involvement in athletic activity?

- What kinds of illnesses, accidents, and physical conditions tend to occur among schoolchildren? How do children's family and community circumstances affect them?

- What is the relationship between physical growth and psychological development during the middle years?

armen and Mercedes were sisters. When Carmen was four and Mercedes eight, they found an old pair of roller skates in a trash can behind their apartment building. The skates were too small for Mercedes, so Carmen got to keep them. Carmen could not believe her good fortune; their mother had always said they could not afford "extras" like skates.

But Carmen's pride was short-lived. To Carmen's dismay, their mother bought Mercedes a brand-new pair of skates. "It's more practical," their mother tried to explain to Carmen, "because Mercedes won't grow out of them as fast as you will. And anyway, she'll work at them, use them a lot." Carmen thought *she* would use skates a lot too. But time proved her mother was right: Carmen used her skates only occasionally, but Mercedes was outside on hers almost every day. One time she even took lessons for a week when the city offered them as part of its summer recreation program. In these ways, Mercedes eventually acquired quite a talent for roller-skating.

In general, as Carmen and Mercedes' mother observed, children's physical growth slows down during middle childhood (ages six to twelve) even more than it does during early childhood. But as with Mercedes' skating talents, the results of growth begin to show more than ever before. Specific physical skills are easier to teach than they used to be because children now find them easier to learn. For a school-age child, instruction and practice in baseball make a more obvious difference in skill development than they did when he was still a preschooler. This means the child can now acquire physical and athletic skills that may give him a lifetime of satisfaction. But children *can* get hurt during physical activity, and athletic games can emphasize competition that is unrealistic or unpleasant.

Children are relatively healthy during the school years, but they do sometimes have accidents or get sick. A few children also develop problems that have ambiguous physical causes, and such children may show excessive motor activity even in quiet situations or difficulties in learning specific academic skills. Such problems may originate from subtle differences in how the nervous system operates in these children, although this is far from certain.

In this chapter, we review these ideas in more detail. We begin by looking at normal trends and variations in overall growth during the middle years. Then we examine specific motor skill and athletic development and their psychological effects on children. Finally, we discuss health in the school years, with special reference to children who are overly active.

TRENDS AND VARIATIONS
IN HEIGHT AND WEIGHT

As Figure 11.1 shows, children grow steadily during middle childhood, from about forty-six inches and forty-five pounds at age six to almost sixty inches and eighty

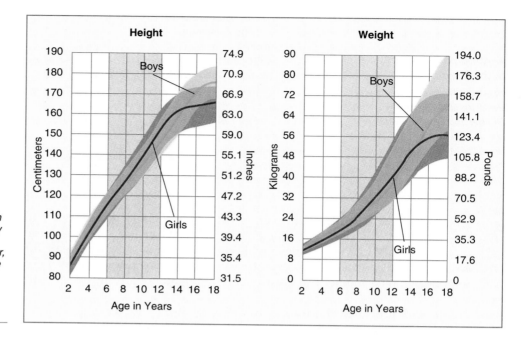

FIGURE 11.1
Growth in Height and Weight from Two to Eighteen Years
During the early middle childhood, children continue to grow at a smooth rate, though more slowly than in early childhood and infancy. By the middle and later parts of this period, however, weight and height begin to accelerate as children move into puberty. The growth spurts usually begin sooner for weight than for height and sooner for girls than for boys.

Late in childhood, girls often grow taller and faster than boys of the same age. The disparity can create awkward moments for members of both sexes, though many children do not seem to be concerned about it at all.

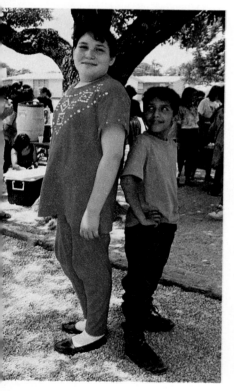

pounds at age twelve (Engels, 1993). At the same time, variations among children are often significant. Figure 11.2 shows, for example, that the average height of eight-year-old girls varies from forty-five inches in South Korea to almost fifty-one inches in Russia. And at any one age within any one society, individual variations are even more dramatic. The shortest and tallest six-year-olds in North America differ by only two or three inches, but the shortest and tallest twelve-year-olds differ by more than one foot. The changes are a source of both pride and dismay to individual children.

Growth gives children the potential to participate in activities with new skillfulness: whether playing softball or hiking in the woods, they can do it better than ever before. But growth can also create problems for them, and the difficulties typically have both physical and psychological aspects. Stereotypes about size and shape exist among school-age children as well as among adults. Wearing glasses may typecast some children as "geeks," and big ears may typecast others as "clowns." The most prominent physical stereotypes, however, concern overall size and weight. Very small children may seem younger than they really are, and as a result their teachers and friends may treat them with less respect than they deserve. An overweight child may be regarded as unattractive, so friends and teachers may not respond to her as warmly as they otherwise would. Such reactions may occur unconsciously. And even though physical appearance may really stem largely from biological influences, children with the "wrong" looks may blame themselves.

Height Variations Due to Puberty

As we have noted, toward the end of the elementary school years, girls tend to become significantly taller than boys of the same age. The difference results partly from girls' earlier puberty and partly from the timing of the growth spurt associated with puberty for each gender. For boys, a spurt in height tends to follow the other physical changes of adolescence, such as the growth of pubic hair and the deepening of the voice. For girls, a spurt in height usually occurs before the growth of breasts and pubic hair.

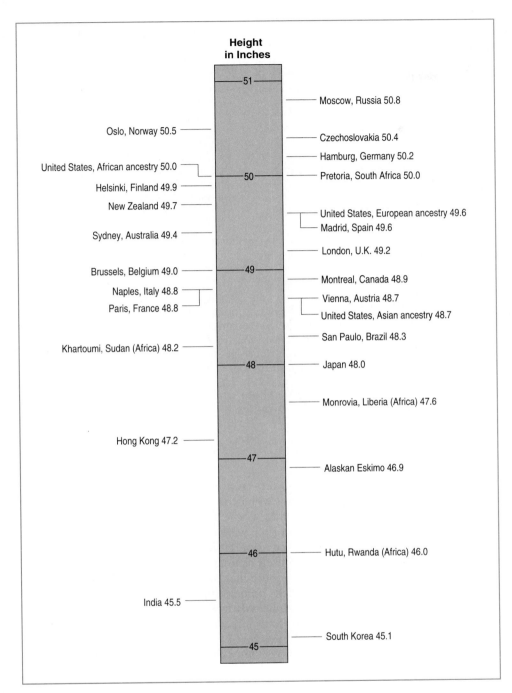

Height in Inches

Moscow, Russia 50.8

Oslo, Norway 50.5

Czechoslovakia 50.4

Hamburg, Germany 50.2

United States, African ancestry 50.0

Pretoria, South Africa 50.0

Helsinki, Finland 49.9

New Zealand 49.7

United States, European ancestry 49.6

Madrid, Spain 49.6

Sydney, Australia 49.4

London, U.K. 49.2

Brussels, Belgium 49.0

Montreal, Canada 48.9

Naples, Italy 48.8

Vienna, Austria 48.7

Paris, France 48.8

United States, Asian ancestry 48.7

San Paulo, Brazil 48.3

Khartoumi, Sudan (Africa) 48.2

Japan 48.0

Monrovia, Liberia (Africa) 47.6

Hong Kong 47.2

Alaskan Eskimo 46.9

Hutu, Rwanda (Africa) 46.0

India 45.5

South Korea 45.1

FIGURE 11.2
Ethnic and Cultural Differences in Growth
Differences in height are associated strongly with cultural and ethnic background. This chart summarizes the heights of eight-year-old girls from a number of nations and regions of the world. Girls from eastern and northern Europe are nearly six inches taller than girls of the same age from India and South Korea. Similar trends occur for boys.
Source: Adapted from Meredith (1978).

Inevitably these changes create temporary embarrassment for at least some girls and boys. Late in childhood, most children become aware of social expectations or stereotypes about attractiveness, such as the idea that men "should" be taller than women. But this awareness dawns precisely when many children exhibit the opposite pattern. This discrepancy undoubtedly is felt more acutely by some children than by others; it may feel worse for children who seek the attentions of the opposite sex most strongly, yet find they are the "wrong" height. The exact amount by which a child deviates from height standards may matter little, except at the extremes. Very tall girls and very short boys are most likely to feel out of place (Scraton, 1992), though numerous exceptions exist.

A Multicultural View

Dieting in Cross-Cultural Perspective

In our society, self-administered dieting and exercise has become a major industry. Countless books have been published to help individuals lose weight and gain muscle, and many of them are intended for children (see, for example, Schwarzenegger & Gaines, 1994). Attaining a culturally valued bodily "look" can become a major personal project, one that for many children begins in late childhood and continues well into adulthood.

At the heart of North Americans' preoccupation with body image is not only a concern with nutrition and health but also a commitment to crucial cultural values. One of these values is *individualism,* a belief that people are fundamentally autonomous and responsible for themselves. From this notion comes the belief that your body indeed belongs to you and that you personally are responsible for how it looks. How it compares to social ideals of physical beauty therefore indicates your success as a member of society as well as your ongoing commitment to participation in society. A lean, thin body (supposedly) shows self-discipline and restraint, two socially admired qualities, because it implies that you have been eating and exercising responsibly. To achieve these

things, numerous individuals embark on exercise and diet programs for varying periods of time. Girls and women are especially likely to do so, since they are almost certain to be judged by their physical appearance repeatedly, even during childhood (Bordo, 1993).

Yet a preoccupation with diet and exercise is not universal. The Fiji islanders in the South Pacific, for example, seem generally indifferent to the size or weight (Becker, 1994). At the same time, they have definite ideals about physical appearance: a person should have sturdy calf muscles, for example, and generally look "well fed" (a bit plump by our standards). Furthermore, despite their indifference to size and weight, the Fijians comment on one another's physical looks constantly and directly. Everyday greetings often include teasing about whether a person looks fatter (or thinner) than in the past. Daily conversations about persons not present ("gossip") also refer frequently to a person's size, particularly if his or her size seems to have changed.

The paradox of personal indifference combined with public frankness is accounted for by the Fijians' fundamental orientation to their *community* rather than to

Excess Weight and Obesity

At least one American child in ten suffers from **obesity,** meaning the child weighs more than 130 percent of the normal weight for his or her height and bone size (Cassell, 1994). This means that a child who is fifty-four inches tall weighs more than eighty-five pounds instead of a normal weight of about sixty-five pounds. How does such a child feel about his or her size? Accepting social stereotypes about weight means regarding herself or himself as unattractive. But rejecting those standards means disagreeing with peers about what makes a person good looking. The dilemma is particularly acute for girls, since cultural norms emphasize physical appearance, especially thinness, more heavily in females than in males. (But note: in some other cultures, physical size is not important to individuals' social success. See the accompanying Multicultural View box.)

In the long run, obesity causes physical problems as well. Children who continue to be obese into adulthood run more risk of a variety of minor illnesses, as well as of a few major ones such as heart disease and diabetes (Rotatori & Fox, 1989). Partly as a result, they also tend to live shorter lives. Overweight people tend to be significantly less active than people of normal weight, even by the standards of our relatively sedentary society, and their lack of exercise can further aggravate their weight problem and the risks connected with it. For all these reasons, obese children deserve help, even if their problem cannot be resolved easily.

Unfortunately, as most people who have tried it know, losing weight permanently is difficult to do. It is even more difficult for children than for adults, for both physical and psychological reasons. Unlike people who become overweight as adults, children sometimes gain weight by growing more fat cells, and once these cells have formed, they prove very difficult to lose or destroy (Poissonet et al., 1988). In contrast, individuals who begin gaining weight later in life do not grow new fat cells; rather, the volume, or size, of existing ones expands. Compared to themselves as individuals. What is important to an individual Fijian is not personal achievement or standing out from the average but showing a nurturing and caring attitude toward friends, family, and children. A primary vehicle for attaining these goals is food: serving food is a major way to show interest and attention to others' needs, both physical and emotional. According to custom, Fijians open their windows and doors during mealtimes so that the event becomes more truly public, and anyone passing by is cordially (and sincerely) invited in to share the food. Extra food is routinely prepared for each meal to allow for this possibility, because it is considered a social disgrace to be unable to share food generously with whoever happens to come by.

The Fiji islanders, therefore, consider dieting to be self-centered and irresponsible because it prevents a person from either giving or receiving nurturance from the community. In a sense, a person's body "belongs" to the community rather than to the individual. Secret eating is a serious social mistake, as is secret noneating (dieting). Parents observe their children carefully for changes in appetite, as well as for changes in weight (either up or down) that may imply fluctuations in appetite. They do so not because they want their children to achieve a certain size but because they want them to participate fully in both the giving and receiving of community care, and an important way of participating is through food.

In Fiji, it is not the cultivation of a certain body image that confers prestige, as in North American society. Instead, it is the cultivation of social relationships, particularly those that make nurturance possible. Is this orientation preferable to our own? The focus on caregiving spares most Fijian children from worries about their physical appearance, as well as from discouragement caused by unsuccessful dieting or exercise programs to improve physical looks (Sault, 1994). But a negative effect also is possible: the focus on community can create problems for children who *must* limit their eating for health reasons, such as diabetes or intestinal flu. In a strongly communal society, these situations can prove especially worrisome to both child and family, since they require deliberately limiting participation in a central social practice: the daily abundant sharing of food.

childhood obesity, therefore, "middle-aged spread" is a relatively correctable problem, although still far from easy to cope with.

For a child, losing weight can be difficult for other reasons as well. Any dieting or exercise scheme must have the full support of the child's parents and siblings, because they usually have a substantial influence on meal preparation and on the child's daily lifestyle (Pittman & Kaufman, 1994). Yet family members may find support is difficult to sustain over the long periods of time most weight control programs require. The collective will power may just not be there, especially because overweight children tend to have siblings and parents who are overweight themselves. Table 11.1 lists some additional guidelines for treating a childhood weight problem successfully.

TABLE 11.1 *Guidelines for Responding to a Child's Weight Problem*

1. *Make sure the child really needs to lose weight.* Weighing only a little (10 percent) more than average poses no medical risk and may cause a child few social problems in the long term. If a child is teased for his or her weight, learning ways to cope with the teasing may be more effective than trying to lose weight.

2. *Consult with a doctor or a trained nutritionist before starting the child on a diet program.* A diet should aim at stabilizing weight or causing a loss of only about one pound per week at most. It should be balanced nutritionally and include snacks. Crash diets or food fads should be avoided at all costs; they are not effective and can seriously jeopardize a child's health.

3. *Develop a program of exercise appropriate for the child.* Start slowly and build up gradually. Try to incorporate activities that the child enjoys and that can fit into his or her daily routines conveniently.

4. *Seek support from the child's whole family, as well as from teachers or others whom the child sees regularly.* These people must show respect for the child's efforts, offer encouragement, and avoid tempting the child to break a diet or give up on exercise. Most of all, participate *with* the child in programs of activity or programs to control eating.

What Do You Think?

Do you think concern about height and weight is really a gender issue? Why or why not? Check your perceptions by polling ten male and ten female acquaintances (it's easier if you collaborate in doing this task) about whether they weigh more than the ideal, less than the ideal, or close to it. Then ask them how they think members of the opposite sex would rate themselves, on average.

MOTOR DEVELOPMENT AND ATHLETICS IN MIDDLE CHILDHOOD

Fundamental motor skills continue to improve during the school years and gradually become specialized in response to each child's particular interests, physical aptitudes, life experiences, and the expectations of others. Unlike a preschooler, an older child no longer is content simply to run, jump, and throw things; now she puts these skills to use in complex, active play. Sometimes this consists of informal, child-organized games, such as hide-and-seek, in which the child uses her motor skills. At other times, as described next, active play involves formal sports such as gymnastics, swimming, or hockey.

During the school years, children develop the ability to play games with rules. Some of these games are informal, such as after-school hopscotch, and some are formal and adult sponsored, such as Little League softball. In any case, traditional team sports now begin to have meaning for children because they can understand

Working with   Katherine Paterson, PEDIATRIC OCCUPATIONAL THERAPIST

Diagnosing Children's Coordination Difficulties

Katherine Paterson is a pediatric occupational therapist. She works with children who have difficulties carrying out age-appropriate activities. Typically the problems have a physical basis, but they also affect everyday responsibilities (like schoolwork) or social relationships (like making friends) significantly. The challenge, as Katherine points out, is to pinpoint the nature of these links as clearly as possible and then devise a program that will help the child overcome his or her difficulties. Here is how she described this process.

Katherine: When the kids first come to you, they might present just one or two "simple" problems. Take Paul, who's nine. A few months ago, his teacher referred him to me because he had trouble following directions and couldn't print words. But he had great people skills! He tried to get along and didn't act up in class. I suspect that's why he was nine years old

by the time I saw him. He probably faded into the woodwork.

Kelvin: What did you do once you started seeing him?

Katherine: It's like detective work. You've got to figure out what's behind the "official" problem that you first hear about. I started out by talking at length with Paul's classroom teacher and the school's special ed consultant. And I talked with his parents; you've got to involve them a lot from the first, because they know so much about their kids and potentially can help them so much in the future.

Kelvin: Were Paul's parents at all defensive about Paul's being sent to an occupational therapist?

Katherine: Well, they were sure worried. But they also wanted the best for Paul. We'd work out a plan together that helps Paul use his strengths to address his needs.

Kelvin: Could you give some specifics?

Katherine: Well, for instance, when I did my standardized assessments I discovered that Paul did really well at perceiving shapes. He could pick them out easily even when they were imbedded in a complicated drawing, rotated, or oriented in unusual ways. That skill will eventually help him with his reading at school.

Kelvin: Is standardized testing always part of your initial assessment?

Katherine: Usually. I use tests that look at underlying physical and cognitive processes—visual perception, for example, and motor coordination. I also test for auditory perception, but only enough to figure out whether a child needs to see a speech-language pathologist as well as see me.

Kelvin: Don't kids get pretty impatient and restless with being tested?

Katherine: Well, it does take time. Sometimes I break the testing into and abide by a game's rules. At the same time, children's improvements in co-ordination and timing enhance their performance in all kinds of sports, whether individual or group. Swimming, for instance, reveals the benefits of increasing coordination: some preschoolers can swim quite well, but usually only school-age children achieve adultlike coordination, speed, and grace in their strokes and breathing. The same holds for other informal, individual activities, such as riding a bicycle, roller blading, and jumping rope.

What lasting physical and psychological effects do early athletics have on children? This question has not been studied as thoroughly for children as it has for adolescents and adults, but a few tentative answers are possible. On balance, athletic activity probably helps children much more than it hurts them. However, it does carry a few significant risks.

Physical Effects of Early Athletics

The most obvious physical risks in athletics are sports-related injuries: bruises of various kinds and severity, damage to muscles (sprains), and broken or dislocated bones (Kibler & Chandler, 1993). Do such injuries actually pose a problem for child development? Some researchers point out that a substantial number of athletes incur injuries, even in childhood (Duff, 1992). The injuries usually receive only short-term medical attention: once bones or muscles appear to be healed, they are promptly ignored, and the athlete is encouraged to return to play. Given the special stresses of athletic activity, this short-run approach may allow minor but long-term disabilities to develop.

several sessions, especially if the child is very young or impulsive—has trouble sitting still. But it's worth it! The test results give clues about what might be wrong. Paul's tests revealed that he had some trouble remembering sequences of information; recalling several shapes in series, for example, often mixed him up. I suspect that may relate to his reading and writing problems at school. Maybe he can't keep letter or word sequences in mind reliably.

Kelvin: What else do you do when a child first comes to you?

Katherine: Observe him—you know, I keep saying "him," not "her," but they do tend to be boys!—when he's drawing or playing with the toys we have here. I interact during these times, too, to see how he responds to my directions and suggestions. Sometimes a child behaves differently dur-

ing these informal times compared to the more formal testing times.

Kelvin: Once the initial assessments are done, what happens?

Katherine: It depends on the child, of course. I recommended that Paul visit an occupational therapist regularly—me, in this case—and some further consultations with the school staff. The visits with me will actually serve two purposes: helping Paul with his visual sequencing and motor coordination and providing a good time to talk with Paul's parents about his needs and progress. I invite parents to the sessions so I can show them what we're doing. I try to give parents one or two activities to do with the child between visits, some sense of a goal that's realistic. That's so important, both for the child's self-esteem and for the parents.

With the school staff, I discuss what my assessment turned up and

we brainstorm ideas that might help Paul in class. For instance, we considered if it might help Paul to get some practice writing on a computer. That way, he doesn't have to perfect his penmanship before he can begin writing longer pieces.

What Do You Think?

1. Think about the major domains of development (physical, cognitive, and social). Chapter 1 pointed out that these are not necessarily separate. How does Paul's case seem to support this idea?

2. Katherine noted that the children she sees tend to be boys, and research indeed confirms this gender imbalance among children with school-related learning difficulties. Consult with several classmates about this fact, and generate some possibilities about why it may be true.

3. How might a family's income level influence a child's chances of success with an occupational therapist?

Other researchers point out that most children who are injured during sports have relatively minor injuries, and the benefits of participation therefore considerably outweigh the risks. They cite the physical benefits of athletics. For example, children involved in regular athletics may develop better physical endurance than nonathletic children; this means their hearts and large muscles may function more efficiently (Rowland, 1993). As a result, they may be better able to undertake ordinary daily activities with less effort.

Psychological Effects of Early Athletics

The immense popularity of early athletics probably stems at least in part from the psychological benefits attributed to participation. Sports, it is hoped, develop achievement motivation, teamwork, and a tolerance for or even enjoyment of competition. How well do early athletics in fact realize these goals?

Training in Achievement Motivation   Most sports provide standards against which children can assess their performances. Goals can be scored, distances measured, and times clocked. Children's performances can then be compared with the youngsters' own previous scores, with those of their peers, or with those of top-scoring individuals or teams.

Whether this information really encourages higher athletic achievement depends on how a child uses it. A kindergarten child tends to remember her sports history poorly. She therefore approaches each performance as a unique event. For example, she may find each swim meet enjoyable in its own right, but think little about bettering a past performance or correcting previous mistakes. During the school years, however, comparing oneself to standards becomes a prominent concern (Weiss, 1993). This concern does motivate some children to better their performances, but it also undermines motivation for children who believe athletic standards are arbitrary, externally imposed, or unreasonably difficult to meet.

In middle childhood, children continue to refine fundamental motor skills, such as running, walking, or throwing. They show the biggest improvements in activities—like this game involving jumping and leaping—that require both coordination and timing simultaneously.

Teamwork and Competition   Many sports promote teamwork, that is, cooperation with a selected group of individuals. This goal certainly is a positive one, but it comes only if a child's team wins. What happens to losers? Among schoolchildren,

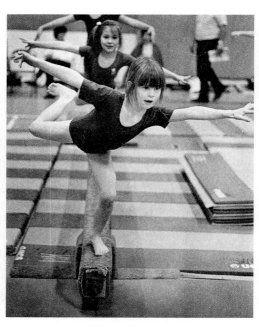

A Talk with John, Age Eleven

Growing Older

John was interviewed after school in his bedroom, which contained three fish tanks, plants, a cat, and a number of models and other construction projects he had worked on.

Interviewer: John, how old are you now?

John: I was eleven in August.

Interviewer: What is it like to be eleven? Have you noticed yourself getting bigger?

John: I don't know. You do grow more.

Interviewer: How do you know?

John: I just have. My parents tell me, too. They say I've grown a lot.

Interviewer: Can you notice some things about your body compared with the way you were at nine or ten?

John: I don't know. I can reach things better. And I can run better, faster, and for a longer time if I go for a jog with my mom and dad.

Interviewer: What other things can you do better?

John: It's easier to play my guitar with bigger hands. It used to be harder to reach my fingers around the neck to make chords, and now it's getting easier. It's still not that easy, though.

Interviewer: What about sports?

John: I like to play baseball, soccer, and basketball. Getting bigger and stronger helps there. You can hit the ball farther and throw better. In soccer, being able to run and kick hard

are important, and I can play much better than I did a couple of years ago. Of course, I also have more experience at playing.

Interviewer: What other things can you do that you couldn't do a couple of years ago?

John: I'm a better bike rider than I used to be. It's easier for me to ride. My legs are longer, and my seat is as high as it can go. Some of my clothing is also too small for me.

Interviewer: How is your size compared with other kids your age?

John: I think about the same size. Some kids are smaller and some are bigger . . . taller and heavier.

Interviewer: What does an eleven-year-old do to stay healthy and strong?

John: They don't want to get too fat.

Interviewer: Do you think about that?

John: Yes.

Interviewer: What would make you too fat?

John: Not getting any exercise and maybe eating too much candy and things like that. I don't think that will happen to me, but some kids are overweight, and that's not healthy.

Interviewer: What other changes have you noticed in yourself?

John: My parents used to have to tell me to clean up my room, but I just keep it clean now. And I do my work and my parents don't have to tell me to do it.

Interviewer: Do you think differently about your work now? Does it feel different?

John: I still don't like it—I never have, and I probably never will. I just do it before my parents tell me, and then I'm done. And that way I don't get nagged.

Interviewer: Do people treat you differently now that you're older?

John: Yes. They treat me more like an adult than a little kid. Instead of just telling me to do something, now they sometimes talk about it. They discuss it with me. I also have more responsibilities. I have to take care of my sister when I get home from school and sometimes till five o'clock, when my parents get home.

Interviewer: Any other changes?

John: I can go to my friend's house by myself. And I can stay home alone. And I can have my own room, too.

What Do You Think?

1. What physical changes seem most important to John?

2. What effects have athletics had on John's development?

3. In what ways has John's physical development affected his psychosocial development?

even the most gracious loser shows significant stress. Research has found that losers become less sociable, refuse to talk about the game, and miss game practices more often than winners do (Gould, 1993). Losing teams also show a marked tendency to pinpoint blame by scapegoating individual members or events during a sporting season. If one "big play" seemingly lost a crucial basketball game, the players may dwell on that event more than it deserves, and they may stew about one or two players who seemed most responsible for that play.

For some children, the path away from being a loser consists of training harder to win. For substantial numbers of others, however, it consists of learning not to take a sport too seriously—to treat it as "just a game" played for social and health reasons rather than for competitive success. Unfortunately the historical association of athletics with competition, glory, and "manliness" (for boys) can make this

Athletic activity can support the development of achievement motivation. This girl is proud, for example, of the yellow belt that she has earned in judo. But it can also foster competitiveness among peers: what are the children in the background thinking who did not receive an award?

transition difficult for certain sports in some communities (Messner & Sabo, 1994). When a truly recreational approach to sports proves impossible, some children may adopt new interests and activities (such as watching television) that have fewer health benefits than sports do.

Gender and Early Athletics

In North America, girls are especially likely to drop out of athletic activity late in their middle years. On the whole, they do so for cultural rather than physiological reasons (Scraton, 1992). Throughout childhood, they compare favorably with boys in strength, endurance, and motor skill, and late in childhood girls also tend to be physically more mature than boys. But beginning at about age twelve, they begin to perform less well than boys on tests of physical skills: they run slower, jump less far, and lift less weight (see Figure 11.3). Because physical training can eliminate these differences (Hunter-Griffin, 1990), their relatively poor performance most likely results from social expectations about gender. At the time of puberty, some girls begin to emphasize nonathletic pursuits such as listening to rock music or reading or talking with friends. (Some boys, of course, do the same.) Fortunately, gender role standards may be shifting, and athletic activity may be getting more attractive for both sexes, as well as more accessible for girls than in the past (Ontario Ministry of Culture, Tourism, and Recreation, 1994).

What Do You Think?

Do childhood athletics by nature foster a competitive spirit among players? Or does competitiveness simply depend on stimulation by coaches and parents? This issue can spark a good in-class debate, particularly if individuals have to advocate the position *opposing* their usual point of view!

HEALTH AND ILLNESS IN MIDDLE CHILDHOOD

In middle childhood, children usually are relatively healthy in the sense that they rarely experience serious illnesses or accidents with medical consequences (but see also the accompanying Perspectives box). They also have colds and minor viral illnesses less often than preschool children and infants do. But illnesses and accidents still occur in this age group, which partly accounts for why medical professionals and parents sometimes disagree about whether or not schoolchildren are really healthy. From a doctor's perspective, schoolchildren do not need advanced medical services as much as most other age groups do. From a parent's perspective, though, the illnesses schoolchildren do get can still be very disruptive.

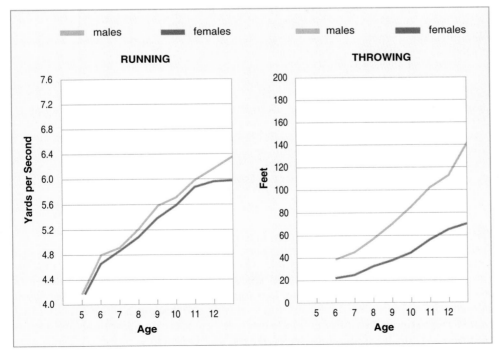

FIGURE 11.3
Running Speed and Throwing Distance for Boys and Girls at Different Ages
As the data indicate, despite changing gender roles in society, boys still tend to run faster and throw farther than girls during middle childhood. The data summarize a number of studies carried out since 1960. The gender gap increases as children enter adolescence.
Source: Gallahue (1989), adapted from Haubenstricker & Seefeldt (1986).

How Children Understand Death

In modern society, death has become rare in childhood and common in old age. This seemingly natural state of affairs actually is quite unusual: throughout history and around the world, the majority of deaths have occurred in infants and children. Today's reversal of this trend has had benefits, of course, but it may also leave children unprepared to understand and cope with death when they do experience it at close hand. Instead of seeming natural, inevitable, and universal, death may seem a rare and arbitrary event, a catastrophe that befalls only a few people. Such a view may create confusion about the nature and meaning of death.

Studies confirm that children have only a hazy understanding of death, even well into middle childhood. Early in this period, around age six, they describe death with analogies that are often reversible: "Death is when you go to sleep," said one six-year-old, as though death ended in waking up again. Often the analogies refer not to universal events but to special ones: "Death is going on a trip," for example, implying that not everyone will die since not everyone goes on trips (Webb, 1993). Perhaps for these reasons, young children do not seem to fear death as much as older children and adults do. They reveal concern and distress about the general idea of death, but unless they experience the death of a close relative (such as a parent) directly, their concerns tend to be comparatively limited. Not until around age ten do the majority of children realize that death is irreversible, permanent, and universal. But even their concern is rather abstract and emphasizes physical inevitability rather than psychological repercussions: "Dying is when your heart stops beating forever."

All of these developments occur more rapidly and vividly, though, if a child has had a life-threatening illness (such as leukemia) or lost a close relative, especially a parent (Bertoia, 1993). These children face challenges that develop their understanding of death very quickly. First, they must *understand* the death as realistically as possible: it indeed has occurred, cannot be ignored, and will never be undone. Unfortunately, younger children may have trouble grasping this reality because their general cognitive understanding is limited. Second, children must have chances to *grieve,* or mourn their loss, and work through the feelings they still have about the

person who died. The extent and nature of their grieving will depend on how emotionally attached they were to the deceased person, their overall cognitive maturity, and the support they receive for expressing their sadness. As one nine-year-old girl put it, "What bothered me most about my mother's death was that no one gave me a chance to talk about it; they were too busy with their own problems." Another child said, "My little brother didn't seem to react when my sister died [of meningitis]—but I can't tell if it's because he wasn't very close to her emotionally, or because he was only four at the time, or because Mom and Dad kept telling him how 'strong' he was not to cry."

Either despite or because of their cognitive limitations, children react strongly to the death of the most important people in their lives—usually their parents. Research shows that the effects can be quite long-lived (Silverman & Worden, 1993). Even ten years after losing a parent, bereaved children tend to be more submissive and introverted and less aggressive than other children, even children who have lost a parent through divorce. As you might expect, though, the extent and nature of a child's reactions depend heavily on the circumstances: losing a mother can be harder for a child than losing a father, on average, because the remaining parent (the father) more often has had less practice in expressing his own grief and has fewer social relationships to offer emotional support. The reactions of the surviving parent and other relatives also affect the child's ability to come to terms with the death. A parent absorbed in his or her own grief is less able than usual to comfort a school-age child.

What can professionals do to help children come to terms with death in general and a specific person's death in particular? The answer depends partly on the extent of their own involvement. Social workers and nurses who assist families following particular deaths can encourage children to talk about the death, say what they think and feel, and ask about what perplexes them. Teachers and school counselors can do this too when a classmate has died. In addition, they can explore the issues and feelings about death in more general ways by incorporating the topic into the overall school curriculum (United States Department of Health and Human Services, 1993).

Death Rates and Accidents among Schoolchildren

One sign of good health in schoolchildren is their very low **mortality,** or the proportion who die at a given age. In recent years, only about three or four children in every ten thousand between ages six and thirteen die, compared to twice this number among preschoolers and four times this figure among adolescents (United States Department of Commerce, 1995). The low rate for school-age children is part of a long decline extending back over the past century.

The decline in mortality has changed the relative importance of various causes of death. Infectious diseases, such as pneumonia and chronic diarrhea, have become very infrequent among children from middle-income families in North America. As a result, accidents have become relatively more important as a cause of death among children. The largest number of childhood deaths in recent years have resulted from motor vehicle accidents (National Safety Council, 1995). A majority of those deaths were children who were not wearing seat belts while riding with their parents or other relatives.

But school-age children do sometimes die from other kinds of accidents (see Figure 11.4). Some children face much greater risk for certain accidents than others do, either because their environments pose more risks or because their parents and other adults responsible for them do not recognize the risks and, therefore, fail to teach the children proper safety precautions.

What are the reasons for the greater number of accidents? During the school years, children begin playing in and exploring larger territories. In particular, they

FIGURE 11.4

Selected Causes of Death in Childhood and Youth

For both children and youth, deaths by accidents outnumber deaths by life-threatening illness, as these figures on mortality rates show. Both causes of death occur more frequently during adolescents, reflecting typical changes in lifestyle that lead to risks (e.g., driving an automobile).
Sources: Adapted from United States Department of Commerce (1995) and World Health Organization (1995).

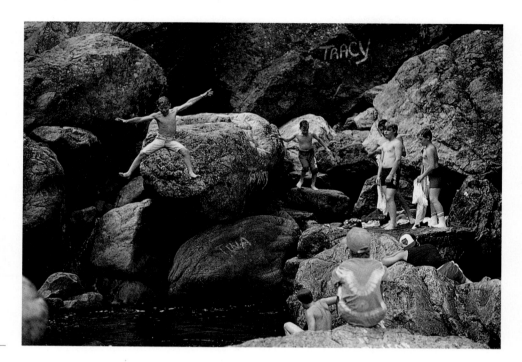

As children get older, their everyday activities make them more likely to experience accidents. The risks are greatest, as with these boys swimming, when activities take them to unfamiliar places and when peers challenge each other to attempt risky behaviors.

investigate the neighborhood around their homes and schools, despite its unknown dangers. Because the improvised games (usually sports) children play at this age require more space than the play of preschoolers does, children in urban and some suburban areas often play in the street. They may do their best to avoid traffic, but games such as baseball may require sudden sprints and allow no time to check for cars.

When not playing at formal and informal games, school-age children are deeply curious about the wider world that has become available since their preschool years. Poking around neighbors' backyards, they may find old equipment or machinery that looks too interesting not to investigate. Or they may find flammable or toxic substances, such as gasoline or paint thinner, that supposedly have been stored away safely. Construction sites are especially inviting: they contain pieces of debris and partially completed nooks and crannies that make good hiding places. Unfortunately, these interesting spaces often lack structural strength; children can slip and fall in them, and pieces of steel or wood can land on their heads.

Most of the time, accidents from such sources are relatively minor. But a significant number cause fractures, poisoning, or open wounds that require medical attention. Somewhere between 5 and 10 percent of all visits to doctors by schoolchildren, in fact, are for treatment of accidents such as these (Wright & Leahey, 1994).

Illnesses

On the average, schoolchildren get sick only about one-half as often as preschoolers do. From their parents' point of view, however, illnesses probably still seem rather frequent; nearly one-quarter of the parents in one survey reported that during the preceding two weeks their children were "too sick to carry on as normal" (Coiro, 1994), meaning the children stayed home from school for at least one day. As parents often point out, a sick child has a substantial impact on the work and leisure schedules of the rest of the family, especially parents.

Acute Illness   Most common childhood diseases are **acute illnesses,** meaning they have a definite beginning, middle, and end. Most childhood acute illnesses, such as colds, gastrointestinal flu, chicken pox, and measles, develop from *viruses,* complex protein molecules that come alive only when they infect a host tissue (such as a child's nose). Despite popular belief, no drugs can combat viral infections. (This is not the case with bacteria that invade the body; they can be effectively fought off with antibiotic drugs.) Instead, viral illnesses must run their course, and the child's natural immunities must work the real cure.

For such diseases, doctors usually prescribe simple bed rest. Sometimes they also prescribe medications, more to prevent complications than to cure the illness. Many ear infections, for example, arise from viral infections, but doctors sometimes prescribe antibiotic drugs to prevent a more serious bacterial ear infection from developing.

Chronic Illness   By the school years, about 5 to 10 percent of children develop **chronic illnesses,** or conditions that persist for many months without significant improvement. In the United States and other developed countries, the most common chronic conditions occur in the lungs and affect breathing (United Nations International Children's Emergency Fund, 1995). Some children develop *asthma,* or persistent congestion in the lungs; others develop chronic coughs or allergies. Still other chronic complaints concern specific sensory organs. About one child in one hundred, for example, experiences problems in hearing or seeing.

Social Influences on Illness   The seriousness and frequency of illnesses vary a lot according to children's social and economic circumstances. Consider income differences among families. In general, parents in higher-income families report that their school-age children get sick just about as often as parents from lower-income families do for their children. But the higher-income parents also report keeping their children at home for shorter periods of time. In the highest 25 percent of families, children stay at home for an average of only 1½ days per illness, whereas in the lowest 25 percent, they stay at home for nearly 5 days per illness (Fitzgerald et al., 1994).

What accounts for this difference? Low-income families probably lack money for doctors' visits, access to special child care when a child is sick, and permission to take time off from work to tend to a sick child. Therefore, to merit staying home from school or visiting a doctor, a child must have a relatively major illness, such as a seriously high fever or severe diarrhea. The result of these circumstances shows in the longer average stay at home when illness finally receives special attention.

Race and gender appear to matter too. African-American families report fewer illnesses per child than do white families of similar income, and all families of both races report more illnesses for girls than for boys of the same age (Johnson, 1995). In fact, school-age girls appear to get sick almost as often as preschool children of both sexes do; boys, however, get sick less frequently as they get older.

Note, however, that these trends result partly from families' beliefs about illness as well as from real differences. Girls may not necessarily get sick more often than boys do; rather, training in gender roles may lead them to talk about their ailments and request medical treatment more often. For similar reasons, parents may be more apt to consider girls physically delicate and therefore to keep them home for minor illnesses they would not consider serious in boys. These facts may mean that girls exaggerate the extent of their illnesses, that boys hide the extent of theirs, or both.

AIDS and the School-age Child

Acquired immunodeficiency syndrome (AIDS) is a viral illness that gradually destroys the body's ability to combat other diseases. In all officially recorded cases so far the disease has proven fatal, although often not for several years. Its frequency

As the problem of AIDS has reached public awareness, some schools have begun AIDS education programs even in elementary schools, like these children. Questions remain, however, about this practice: how much should be taught at this age? How explicit about sexuality should it be?

has increased dramatically since the 1980s. In 1981–1982 only 838 cases of AIDS were reported in the entire United States, but by the 1990s the number had grown to about 30,000 new cases per year (United States Department of Commerce, 1995). Approximately ten times these numbers of people become infected every year with **human immunodeficiency virus (HIV),** the virus that eventually triggers the actual symptoms of AIDS.

So far only about 1 to 2 percent of AIDS victims have been schoolchildren, but concerns about the disease have spread throughout society and filtered down into the elementary schools and homes of this age group. Without doubt, some fears come from prejudice against the populations in which AIDS first appeared in North America, namely male homosexuals and heavy users of addictive drugs that are injected intravenously. (In some other parts of the world, such as Africa, AIDS first appeared among heterosexuals.) Fear of catching the disease from casual contact at school has become common, even though current medical evidence shows that AIDS is not spread in this way (Cohen & Durham, 1993). Some parents therefore have demanded the immediate, complete removal from school of any child known to have contracted the disease.

Such demands raise difficult issues about civil rights and fairness in education. Should school leaders respect parents' wishes, even if the wishes are based on clearly mistaken notions about AIDS? Or should they keep a child with AIDS in school out of respect for the child's right to an education, even at the risk of alienating significant numbers of parents? In the short term, these questions have no easy answers.

But longer-term solutions may be possible. One is to offer education at school and other community agencies about sexuality in general and AIDS in particular. Curricula concerning AIDS already have been written and published (Sepulveda et al., 1992), and some school districts have begun using them. It is hoped that an AIDS curriculum can help correct students' misinformation about the disease and therefore help them avoid contracting AIDS and encourage them to respond sensibly when and if they learn of classmates who have the disease.

Another long-term solution lies with school staff, whose own attitudes and actions can make a major difference in a community's reactions to news of a child with AIDS. For teachers and principals, the key responses seem to be a calm attitude about the child, accurate knowledge about AIDS, and active efforts to communicate its lack of contagiousness through casual contact (see Table 11.2).

Attention Deficit Hyperactivity Disorder

A small number of school-age children seem extremely active and have considerable trouble concentrating on any one activity for long (American Psychiatric Association, 1994). Their problem is called **hyperactivity,** or **attention deficit hyperactivity disorder (ADHD).** A second-grade teacher described one student with ADHD like this:

> Joey was friendly when you greeted him; "Hi!" he would say brightly, and smile. But he would never settle down. First he dumped the class's main supply of pencils out on a table; he sort of lunged at one of the pencils, but before he began writing, he left the table, looking for something new. During a reading lesson, I asked Joey to read silently until I finished helping another child; but Joey found this hard to do. He glanced in my direction; tapped a neighboring child on the shoulder; giggled; and kept scanning the room for "more." A child happened to drop a book; Joey laughed at this harder than the others, and jumped up quickly to pick the book up. He was probably trying to help, but in doing so he knocked his own papers all over the floor. Instead of picking up the papers, he only picked up his pencil, and headed off to sharpen it. And the morning was still only half over!

In the long run, behavior such as this both results from and contributes to emotional problems, conflicts with teachers and other adults, and poor relationships with peers. Such social problems eventually aggravate the child's troubles with concentrating. Joey, for example, may become wrought up over conflicts with teachers and self-conscious about what peers think of his behavior. He may become so upset, in fact, that he gets even more fidgety than before.

Reactions to Children with ADHD   Overly active children cause parents and teachers a lot of worry, and excessive activity is one of the most common reasons for referring children to psychiatrists and other health professionals (Weiss & Hechtman, 1993). How many children really have ADHD, however, depends somewhat on who is doing the estimating. Professional school psychologists usually estimate that around 5 to 10 percent of school-age children are seriously overactive. Teachers give a somewhat higher figure. Parents give the highest figure of all; in one survey, fully one-half of all parents of preschool and school-age boys considered their child's activity level a major source of concern (C. Smith et al., 1987). All of the estimates agree that the majority of highly active children—about 85 percent—are boys.

Excessive activity presents more problems in some situations than in others. During outdoor play, very active children hardly stand out at all and seem to make and be

---

TABLE 11.2   Important Facts about AIDS

1. AIDS can be, and has been, contracted by heterosexuals as well as homosexuals.
2. Quarantining (isolating) people with AIDS is both impractical and unethical.
3. AIDS does not spread by casual contact, such as a handshake or exposure to a sneeze by an infected person.
4. Uninfected people can protect themselves from AIDS by avoiding contact with other people's blood for any purpose (sharing drugs, piercing ears, becoming "blood brothers"), avoiding specific sexual practices, and using latex condoms during all forms of sexual intercourse.
5. There is no known cure for AIDS, and it takes many years for a person infected with the AIDS virus (HIV) to begin experiencing symptoms.

friends about as well as any other children do. The structured atmosphere of most school classrooms poses more problems. During class, children with ADHD often get out of their seats, respond aggressively to teachers and peers, and run the risk of losing not only opportunities to learn but also the affection and respect of friends.

Note that *most* children show excessive activity *some* of the time. This fact may not make dealing with ADHD any easier, but it does make the disorder seem more understandable and manageable. Only a few children really exhibit extremely high activity levels consistently enough to warrant professional attention. Experts suggest five criteria for deciding when activity poses a truly serious problem (Ingersoll & Goldstein, 1993):

1. The overactivity occurs even when it is clearly inappropriate, such as when the child is riding in a car or sitting at a meal.

2. Seriously overactive children consistently fail to respond to pressures to inhibit their activity.

3. Seriously overactive children seem to always respond at the same rapid pace, even when they are trying to respond more slowly, such as when drawing a picture.

4. Seriously overactive children show other, related problems, such as high distractibility and difficulties in making friends.

5. Seriously overactive children exhibit poor academic achievement without evidence of sensory, physical, or cognitive disability.

Only children who meet all or most of these criteria warrant the often misused label *hyperactive;* all others probably should be considered simply *very active* or *overactive.*

Causes of ADHD   Most psychologists and medical researchers agree that ADHD has biological roots, but they do not know for sure what those are (Rutter, 1995). It seems likely that ADHD in individual children has different causes: one child may have suffered oxygen deprivation during birth, for example, whereas another child may have been exposed to toxic substances such as lead (found in the paint in many older houses). Certain foods, especially those with artificial additives, may contribute to hyperactivity in some children, but probably only to a minority of ADHD children and possibly only to those who already are predisposed to ADHD for other reasons. Head injuries are more common among children with ADHD than among other children, but it is not clear whether the injuries caused high activity or whether hyperactivity made children prone to the injuries (by bumping into things at high speed, for example).

In addition to biological explanations, it is tempting to believe that a child's parents or social environment may accidentally precipitate hyperactivity in some way, such as by setting rules for behavior that are too precise or rigid. For example, forbidding children to wiggle in their seats in class actually makes many children more rather than less restless. Riding in a car for a long time may make a child restless. Children with naturally active temperaments may comply with these restrictions only with great difficulty, especially if they are imposed repeatedly over a long period.

However, research evidence is ambiguous about whether certain parents or teachers are so strict in their treatment of children that they singlehandedly cause or lead to hyperactivity in individual children. It is true that parents of ADHD children tend to impose strict behavioral requirements on their children, but this style may be as much a response to the child's behavior as a cause of ADHD in the first place. In one study, ADHD children were given medication to reduce their activity levels; subsequent observations revealed that the parents became less strict than before the medication was given (Barkley, 1985). It is also true that many parents are strict without their children becoming hyperactive. The most reasonable conclusion, then, is that parents or teachers probably do not cause hyperactivity directly, but they may accidentally aggravate it in some cases by responding to very active children inappropriately. What adults need are not new personalities but specific techniques and advice for dealing with such children.

Helping Children with ADHD and Their Families   Because no one is sure what makes some children overactive, and because ADHD usually persists throughout an individual's childhood and beyond, no single strategy for treating or dealing with the condition exists. However, a group of strategies have proven helpful for the majority of children with this problem.

To reduce immediate symptoms, the most effective treatment is a stimulant medication. One common and effective stimulant has been *Ritalin* (also called *methylphenidate*), which, paradoxically, quiets the child's behavior by "waking up" the central nervous system, that is, making it more alert. When used properly, Ritalin has no short-term, negative side effects; contrary to popular belief, it does not make the child lethargic, depressed, drowsy, or lacking in spontaneity (Johnston, 1991). Instead, it makes the child less bossy, argumentative, and noisy and better able to focus on tasks. As you might suppose, these changes allow more positive relationships to develop with both adults and peers, especially when combined with a diet that reduces the child's mood changes.

In addition to medication, behavior modification often helps to alter some of the most undesirable or counterproductive behaviors of an ADHD child. As the term implies, **behavior modification** is a psychotherapeutic technique that identifies specific behaviors that need changing, as well as straightforward techniques for eliminating or reducing them (Kazdin, 1994). In classrooms, one behavior modification technique consists of using high-status peers to model or demonstrate appropriate behaviors. The active child simply watches a classmate complete an assignment slowly instead of at lightning speed; then the child tries to copy the same slow style in doing the assignment himself. The teacher, of course, reinforces (usually with praise) the modulated behavior when it occurs.

One key quality of behavior modification is its consistency and predictability, and parents and teachers can help significantly by striving to provide these qualities in the child's everyday environment. At home this means meals, play times, and bedtimes should come at about the same times every day and follow roughly the same pattern. At school, lessons should have a regular, predictable format. In either setting, rules of acceptable and unacceptable behavior should be clear, simple, and relatively consistent. All of these strategies help the ADHD child by temporarily reducing the demands on her attention-directing capacities and allowing these abilities to develop at the child's own pace.

What Do You Think?

Some experts argue that children with ADHD are not so much "disturbed" as "disturbing." What do you suppose they mean by this comment? Speculate about ways that home and school could be made less "disturbing" for a hyperactive child. Try out your ideas on a teacher or some other person with experience with children's behavior problems.

EFFECTS OF GROWTH ON THINKING AND FEELING

This chapter has shown us some ways in which physical growth can influence the other aspects of a child's development during the elementary school years. Growth may seem slower or less eventful than either before or after this period, but this is true only in a strictly physical sense. Psychologically, a child's growth makes new

The new physical skills of middle childhood allow new social activities, whether they are formal athletics or spontaneously running a line, like these girls. When all goes well, new physical skills also promote a child's belief in himself or herself, as an increasingly competent person who can make independent decisions.

social opportunities possible, such as participation in sports. When growth problems such as childhood obesity do develop, they often cause serious psychological side effects during the school years. Also, some abnormal physical developments, such as brain damage, have effects that closely resemble purely psychological developments—so closely, in fact, that distinguishing between the physical and mental aspects may confuse our understanding of the child as much as help it. Real children consist of minds, bodies, and feelings combined; only textbooks separate these three elements. Keeping this idea in mind may help clarify the next two chapters, which concern school-age children's thinking and social relationships.

SUMMARY OF MAJOR IDEAS

Trends and Variations in Height and Weight

1. Although growth slows during middle childhood, children of any single age still show significant differences in height and weight.

2. Differences in size and body build contribute to the stereotypes and impressions children form about one another.

3. Toward the end of the elementary school years, girls tend to grow taller than boys, and this difference can create embarrassment for some children.

4. A few children weigh significantly more than average, and they sometimes experience social rejection and risk medical problems if their condition persists.

5. Obesity can be treated, but it takes the support of parents and siblings over a period of time to ensure success.

Motor Development and Athletics in the Middle Years

6. Improvements are especially marked for skills that emphasize coordination and timing rather than strength and size.

7. Many children become involved in athletics, whether formal and organized or informal and spontaneous.

8. Certain popular sports carry definite physical risks, but these may be outweighed by the physical benefits of regular activity.

9. Athletics may encourage achievement motivation in children and, in some sports, teamwork as well.

10. Team sports encourage both cooperation and competition, but the latter can have harmful psychological effects on some children.

Health and Illness in Middle Childhood

11. Overall, schoolchildren are among the healthiest people in society, as shown by their low mortality.

12. Because children today die much less often from infectious illnesses, accidental injuries (especially motor vehicle accidents) have become comparatively more serious problems.

13. Compared to preschoolers, school-age children catch fewer minor acute illnesses, but a small percentage do suffer from significant chronic medical problems.

14. Parents' income levels and beliefs about illness affect how much children actually stay at home as a result of getting sick.

15. AIDS has not yet infected large numbers of school-age children, but it poses a serious psychological threat in some communities.
16. Attention deficit hyperactivity disorder (ADHD) affects a small percentage of school-age children.
17. Because parents and teachers find ADHD very difficult to deal with, they may be inclined to overestimate its prevalence.
18. ADHD may result from a combination of genetic, physical, and social causes.
19. Treatment of ADHD sometimes includes medications, special diets, and behavior modification techniques.

KEY TERMS

obesity *(342)*
mortality *(350)*
acute illness *(352)*
chronic illness *(353)*
acquired immunodeficiency
  syndrome (AIDS) *(353)*

human immunodeficiency
  virus (HIV) *(354)*
hyperactivity *(355)*
attention deficit hyperactivity
  disorder (ADHD) *(355)*
behavior modification *(357)*

FOR FURTHER READING

Ingersoll, B., and S. Goldstein. *Attention Deficit Disorder and Learning Disabilities: Realities, Myths and Controversial Treatments.* New York: Doubleday, 1993.

Pittman, T., and M. Kaufman. *All Shapes and Sizes: Promoting Fitness and Self-esteem in Your Overweight Child.* Toronto: Harper Perennial Books, 1994.

These two books recognize the fact that a child with special needs affects parents and family life substantially. The first book speaks to parents and professionals about responding helpfully to a child who is overly active. The second one offers advice to parents about raising a child who is overweight. Both are full of practical advice as well as general discussion about the social and psychological impact of the child's problem.

Cahill, B., and A. Pearl, eds. *Intensive Participation in Children's Sports.* Champaign, Ill.: Human Kinetics Press, 1993.

Messner, M., and D. Sabo. *Sex, Violence, and Power in Sports.* Freedom, Cal.: Crossing Press, 1994.

These two books consider the psychological effects of athletic activity. The first contains reviews of research on this issue and conveys a hopeful but cautious viewpoint about children's involvement. The second pays special attention to gender issues: does athletics promote power-oriented, "macho" relationships in boys and men? The authors believe it does.

Cohen, F., and J. Durham, eds. *Women, Children, and HIV/AIDS.* New York: Springer, 1993.

Sepulveda, J., H. Fineberg, and J. Mann. *AIDS: Prevention Through Education.* New York: Oxford University Press, 1992.

The authors of the first book focus on the newest aspect of the AIDS problem: children and women who are contracting the disease. The authors of the second book describe specific ways both children and adults can be educated about AIDS. Both books are helpful to nurses, teachers, or others responsible for educating the public about AIDS.

12

MIDDLE CHILDHOOD

Cognitive Development

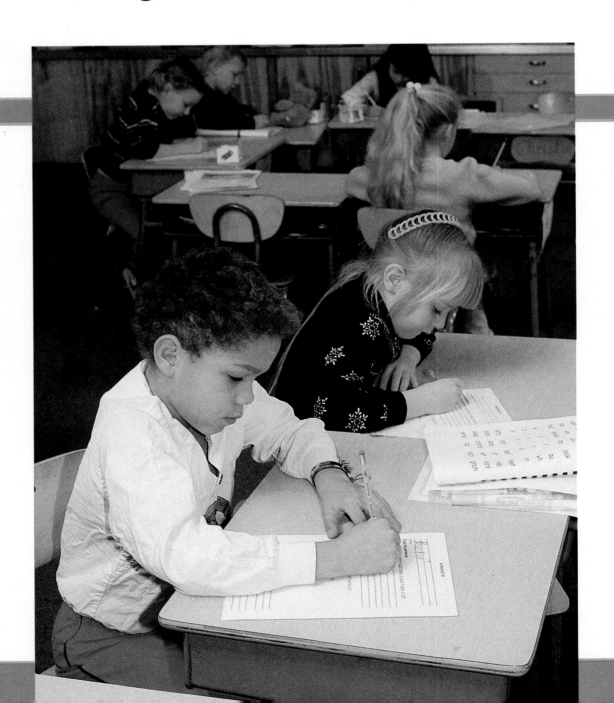

Piaget's Theory: Concrete Operational Skills

Conservation in Middle Childhood
Conservation Training
Other Concrete Operational Skills
Piaget's Influence on Education

Information-Processing Skills

Memory Capacity
Influences on Memory Development
Metacognition and Learning Strategies
Difficulties with Information Processing:
    Learning Disabilities

Language Development in the Middle Years

Understanding Metaphor
Bilingualism and Its Effects
Black English

Defining and Measuring Intelligence

Issues Regarding Intelligence
Psychometric Approaches to Intelligence
Information-Processing Approaches to
    Intelligence
Sociocultural Approaches to Intelligence

Cognition and Social Development

One day two brothers, ages seven and nine, constructed a "science museum" in their living room. They systematically selected all the best chairs and blankets as building materials. Then they found all their stuffed animals and put them on display in the museum, grouping them both by color and by size. They finished the museum by hanging a sign reading "ANIMAL MUSEUM. TIKETS $1." Not many people bought tickets, but this did not stop the boys from having a lively conversation about their project.

This activity drew on the kinds of cognitive skills school-age children have in greater abundance than preschool children do. It required the boys to make the building and to remember where to find particular stuffed animals. Making the sign took a rudimentary knowledge of reading and writing. The project also required the knowledge that museums store interesting objects in systematic ways and often cost money to visit.

In this chapter, we examine the development of cognitive skills such as these. We pay special attention to how parents and teachers influence their development, both unconsciously and deliberately. First, we look at Piaget's now classic research on thinking during children's middle childhood years and at how and why this research has influenced education even though newer research has not fully supported Piaget's ideas. Then we discuss an alternative to Piagetian theory called *information-processing theory,* a viewpoint that focuses on how children use memory and learning strategies during the school years—and sometimes fail to use them. Next, we look at how children differ in their thinking and learning styles and how these styles influence their success in school. Finally, we examine two topics that have implications for children's social relationships and therefore provide a bridge to Chapter 13. The first topic is language: how children differ in their styles of speaking and how these variations can affect children's educational and social success. The second is the nature of intelligence: what developmental psychologists mean by the concept, how they measure it as a result of their interpretations, and how their measurement practices have influenced school-age children and their families, both for better and for worse.

Focusing Questions

- What new cognitive skills do children acquire during the school years? What are the psychological and practical effects of these new skills?

- How does memory change during the middle years? How do these changes affect thinking and learning?

- What new changes in language emerge during the middle years?

- What is general intelligence, and how can it be measured?

- How does acquiring two languages affect a child's cognitive development?

PIAGET'S THEORY: CONCRETE OPERATIONAL SKILLS

As we discussed in Chapter 2, Jean Piaget developed a comprehensive theory of cognitive development from birth through adolescence. During middle childhood, according to this theory, children become skilled at **concrete operations,** mental activities focused on real, tangible objects and events. Concrete operations have three interrelated qualities, none of which is reliably present among preschool children:

decentration, sensitivity to transformations, and reversibility (Piaget, 1965). *Decentration* means attending to more than one feature of a problem at a time. For example, in estimating the number of pennies spread out on a table, a school-age child probably will take into account not only how large the array is but also how far apart individual pennies seem to be. *Sensitivity to transformations* means having different perceptions of the same object and combining them in logical ways. For example, when judging whether the amount of liquid in a glass stays the same after being poured into a new container, a school-age child concentrates on the actual process of change in appearance—the transformation—rather than on how the liquid looks either before or after pouring. *Reversibility* of thought means understanding that certain logical operations (for example, addition) can be reversed by others (subtraction). All in all, the concrete operational child constructs a view of the world that emphasizes quantitative relationships for the first time. Now many facts seem logically necessary that earlier appeared arbitrary or even incomprehensible. In judging whether the amount of liquid stays the same when transferred to a new container, the child now reasons that the amount *must* be the same if nothing was added or taken away when the liquid was poured.

To understand these features of concrete operations, let's compare how preschool and concrete operational children solve the same problem. Consider how Ken and Maria each got started making a batch of muffins:

> Ken, age four, needed guidance from his day care teacher to cook, but even with her help he kept coming dangerously close to ruining the recipe. The teacher set out the ingredients Ken needed—flour, sugar, salt, baking powder—and some containers. Ken liked the bag of flour (it was bright red), so he picked it up and happily began pouring flour into a large bowl. His teacher stopped him from overdoing it: "We need only one cup," she said. "But there isn't as much in the bowl," said Ken, meaning the flour had spread out in the bowl and therefore looked like less. "Okay," said the teacher, "but we still need to measure one cup. How can we do that?" Ken took a *two*-cup measuring cup, filled it to overflowing, and dumped the contents into the bowl. Now there was far too much flour! Apparently the teacher's comment about the amount and her implied advice to measure the flour had meant nothing to Ken.
>
> Maria, age ten, worked much more independently than Ken had and had a better sense of what she was doing. After setting out all the ingredients and containers she needed, Maria poured exactly one cup of flour into the bowl. Just then her teacher came by. "Hmm," she said, "that doesn't look like very much flour." (It was a big bowl, so the flour had spread out pretty far.) "It's what the recipe said," replied Maria. "Are you sure?" the teacher asked. "Yep," insisted Maria. To prove it, she poured the flour back into the one-cup measuring cup she had first used. "See? Nothing added, nothing taken away. So it's *got* to be right."

There are many reasons why these two children differed in their cooking performances, including different prior experiences with cooking, measuring, and even reading. But for Maria, part of the difference was likely the development of concrete operations. She was less distracted by immediate sensory cues, such as the color of the flour bag and the exhilaration of pouring out large amounts of flour. Most important, though, Maria felt a certainty about the quantity of flour that was based on an explicit logical principle. "Nothing added, nothing taken away" implied that the amount had not changed even though it looked smaller at the bottom of a big bowl.

Concrete operations cause important transformations in the cognitive skills children develop in the preoperational period. In classifying objects, children can group things in more than one way at a time by about age seven. They know that a person can be *both* a parent and a teacher at the same time, for example, rather than just one or the other. They also understand that some classifications are inclusive of others—for example, that a particular animal can be both a dog and a pet. As a result, they usually can answer correctly a question such as "Are there more boys in your class or more children?" Preschool children, in contrast, often fail to answer such a question correctly unless it is further simplified or clarified.

Conservation in Middle Childhood

Some cognitive skills make their first real appearance during middle childhood. Probably the best known of these skills is **conservation,** a realization that certain properties of an object necessarily remain constant despite changes in the object's appearance. An example of conservation of quantity is the one described in Chapter 9 involving two tall, narrow glasses containing exactly the same amount of water. If you empty one glass into a wide, low tray, you create a substantial perceptual change in the water; it looks quite different than before and quite different than the water in the remaining tall glass (see Figure 12.1). Will a child know that the wide tray has the same amount of water the tall glass does? If he does, he conserves, meaning he shows a belief in the water's underlying constancy despite a perceptual change.

Piaget (1965) found that after about age seven, most children did indeed conserve quantity in the water glass experiment. In fact, he found that by a year or two later, children conserved on a lot of other tasks as well, including the following (also illustrated in Figure 12.1):

FIGURE 12.1
Conservation Experiments
As Piaget demonstrated, conservation (or the perception of invariance) emerges on a wide scale in middle childhood. In some cases, the child realizes that amounts of liquid or of solid mass remain constant; in other cases, he or she realizes that length or number remain constant. Early in middle childhood, however, the child often holds one of these beliefs without necessarily holding another, or holds one belief only on some occasions and not on others.

	Original Setup	Alter as Shown	Ask Child	Usual Answer
Conservation of liquid			Which has more liquid?	Has more
Conservation of mass			Do they both weigh the same, or does one weigh more than the other?	Weighs more
Conservation of number			Are there still as many pennies as nickels, or more of one than the other?	More
Conservation of length			Are they the same length, or is one longer?	Is longer
Conservation of length			Is one pencil as long as the other, or is one longer?	Is longer

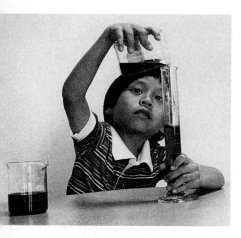

In one of the most widely known Piagetian tasks, children evaluate whether the amount of liquid stays the same when poured into a beaker of a different shape. Most children over the age of six believe that the amount does stay the same, a dramatic change from the preschool years.

1. *Pennies and nickels* Lay out two matching rows of coins, one row of pennies and the other of nickels. The rows should have the same number of coins, and each penny should be set next to one of the nickels. Then bunch up the coins in one row, but not those in the other. Ask, "Are there still as many pennies as nickels, or are there more of one than the other?"

2. *Bent wires* Start with two identical wires or pipe cleaners. Then bend one of them in an arc or circle. Ask, "Is one wire just as long as the other, or is one of them longer?"

3. *Overlapping pencils* Set two identical pencils parallel to each other. Then shift one pencil up or down by an inch or so. Ask, "Is one pencil just as long as the other, or is one of them longer?"

4. *Clay balls* Start with two identical clay balls. Flatten one so that it looks like a pancake. Ask, "Do these two pieces of clay weigh the same, or does one weigh more than the other?"

Each of these tasks requires some form of conservation. The clay balls, like the water glasses, require conservation of mass, the bent wires and the pencils conservation of distance or length, and the coins conservation of number. Children in the middle years tend to conserve on all of these properties.

Typically a child does not acquire all of these conservation concepts at exactly the same time, a phenomenon Piaget called **décallage,** which is a French term meaning "gap." Piaget believed such gaps occur because children do not yet grasp the general principles underlying conservation and therefore do not apply them to tasks that are logically similar. Critics have argued, however, that *décallage* may prove that concrete operational skills do not really form a coherent, universal stage in the sense Piaget proposed (Demetriou et al., 1992). This skepticism has led some psychologists to investigate whether skills such as conservation can be learned through explicit teaching.

Conservation Training

Specialists agree that children do not begin life conserving but instead acquire this skill somehow. How do they do it? Piaget argued that biological maturation and countless experiences with physical objects that show conservation properties enable children to mentally construct conservation. These experiences are numerous and diverse, and although they can be taught explicitly, Piaget believed they have a fuller, more general influence on development if allowed to emerge naturally.

But many psychologists have tried to teach conservation anyway. In recent studies, investigators tried to prevent children from being distracted by coaching them to talk about what was happening ("Nothing is being added or taken away") or to compare the important dimensions closely ("Watch the height *and* the width"). Such efforts do produce greater conserving in a large number of children, though not in all (Bijstra et al., 1991; Field, 1987). Conservation has even been taught successfully to children with mental retardation (Hendler & Weisberg, 1992).

However, trained children often do not maintain conservation concepts the same way "natural" conservers tend to do; they are more likely to give up their belief at even a slight provocation. When experimenters surreptitiously remove a bit of clay in the clay balls experiment, for example, most children easily accept the change. "Natural" conservers are more steadfast in their commitment to conservation, although even they frequently give up their belief. All in all, it seems conservation may not unfold during childhood as inevitably as Piaget first believed.

School-age children can often use their spatial relations skills to make accurate maps of familiar places, such as their own neighborhoods. But like some adults, they often have trouble using a map as a guide to an <u>un</u>familiar place.

Other Concrete Operational Skills

Piaget described many other forms of knowledge that emerge during middle childhood (Piaget, 1983). For one thing, children become able to *seriate,* or arrange objects in sequence according to some dimension such as length or size. For another, they understand *temporal relations,* or the nature of time, better than they did as preschoolers; an eight-year-old knows that time unfolds in a single, constant flow marked by calendars, clocks, and landmark events. Children at this age can also represent the *spatial relations* of their surroundings. They can make maps and models of familiar places, such as their homes, their classrooms, or the local shopping mall.

Piaget's Influence on Education

Although Piaget commented on educational issues (Piaget, 1970), he never intended his research to serve as a theory of education. At no time, in particular, did he offer advice about problems that normally concern teachers, such as how to teach reading or other conventional school subjects, how to motivate students, or how to evaluate students' learning. Nonetheless, his ideas and approach have significantly influenced educators, particularly those in early childhood education (Elkind, 1994). At the heart of this influence is Piaget's *constructivist philosophy:* the assumption that children develop their own concepts through active engagement with the environment. Also at the heart is Piaget's emphasis on stages of cognition. These two ideas have jointly influenced teaching methods, curriculum content, and methods for assessing student progress.

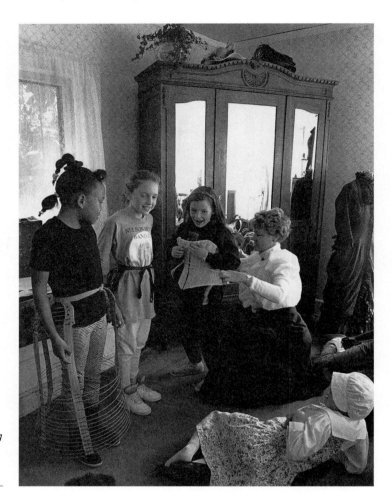

Piaget's idea that thinking begins with manipulation and activity has supported many elementary education programs to emphasize active learning as a teaching strategy. Here, fifth-grade girls try on nineteenth-century undergarments at a historic house.

Teaching Methods   Educators have borrowed Piaget's idea that true knowledge originates from active manipulation of materials (Seifert, 1993). Children learn about weights, for instance, by actually weighing various objects on a scale rather than by reading about weights in a book or hearing their teacher talk about them. A commitment to active learning, in turn, encourages teachers and curriculum planners to put more tangible activities into educational programs wherever possible, as well as to sequence activities from the tangible to the abstract. Reading about insects still has a place in learning about those creatures, but collecting (and handling) some real bugs probably should come first.

Curriculum Content   Piagetian theory has influenced specific curriculum content by providing many specific ideas about what cognitive competencies to expect from children of particular ages or levels of development. The conservation skills described earlier imply that elementary school children should develop a greater ability to solve problems no matter *how* the problems are presented. Compared to preschoolers, older children should be less distracted by seemingly small changes in drawings in their books or seemingly insignificant changes in how a teacher phrases assignments. In Piagetian terms, the children have become more "decentered."

Likewise, acquisition of concrete operations should help school-age children in a number of other ways. For instance, many academic tasks require multiple classification, which preschoolers often do not understand reliably. A written assignment may ask children to "list all the machines you can think of that begin with *c*." This task requires classifying objects in two ways at once: first, by whether or not something is in fact a machine, and second, by whether or not it begins with the letter *c*.

Traditional methods of assessment create complex responses in students. As with Calvin in this cartoon, responses are not always constructive. Piaget has inspired some educators to shift to modes of assessment that emphasize the process of thinking rather than the outcomes—for example, by interviewing students or by examining portfolios of their work, rather than single polished products.

Piaget's cognitive theory has guided many curriculum planners and teachers to select and evaluate academic tasks such as these. The theory itself does not, of course, lead to accurate selections for all children, because not all children move through Piagetian stages at the same rate. In addition, most children are capable of abstract thinking to a certain extent, even if they are not as skilled as adolescents or adults are (Metz, 1995). Despite these limitations, though, Piagetian theory gives us valuable guidance about how children gradually adapt and reorganize their thinking as they grow older.

Assessment of Students' Progress　Throughout his work, Piaget emphasized the importance of children's actual thought processes and what those processes actually allow children to accomplish. This approach is evident in Piaget's heavy use of partially structured interviews and problem-solving tasks. Many educators believe such dialogues and tasks offer a much better way to assess students' progress than do traditional classroom tests and assignments, which tend to emphasize knowledge that is rote and taken out of context (Hill & Ruptic, 1994). Recent revisions to Piaget's approach, sometimes called "neo-Piagetian" theory, have made the approach even more attractive to educators by focusing more closely on *how* children learn and proposing cognitive stages that are more specific, and therefore more accurate, than Piaget's original proposals (Case & Edelstein, 1994).

What Do You Think?

Given Piaget's ideas about how thinking develops in middle childhood, what would be a good way to evaluate students' academic work in elementary school? Work with a classmate or two to devise an evaluation plan for a favorite grade level and subject. Then see how your plan compares to plans devised by classmates and (if possible) to those composed by an experienced teacher.

INFORMATION-PROCESSING SKILLS

During middle childhood, children show important changes in how they organize and remember information. Their short-term memories already are well developed, even at age five. In most other respects, their ways of processing information show significant limitations compared to those of adults, but the limitations diminish during this period.

Memory Capacity

According to popular wisdom, children remember better as they get older. But how true is this idea really? In everyday life, children obviously do not perform as well as adults do on some tasks, such as remembering to put away their clothes at the end of the day. But in other ways they seem to perform as well; they will remember their grandparents when they see them again after months or even years of absence.

Short-Term Memory   Some of these differences in memory may depend on which parts of the information-processing model the children happen to be using. Some tasks rely primarily on *short-term memory (STM),* a feature of thinking that holds information only for a short period, perhaps up to twenty seconds (see Chapter 2). On tasks that emphasize short-term recognition memory, school-age children perform less well than adults do. Experimenters have demonstrated this tendency by showing subjects a set of digits briefly and then immediately asking them whether the set included a particular digit (Cowan, 1995; Dempster, 1981). Under these conditions, recognition of a test digit improved steadily, with eight-year-olds remembering only about three digits and adults remembering about seven. Not surprisingly, too, the time it took a subject to recognize a test digit *did* depend on how many digits were shown in the original set, regardless of the person's age. Showing six digits made the task take longer than showing just three, no doubt because the subject evaluated the test digit against a larger number of alternatives.

This study assessed a variation of **recognition memory,** in which a person merely compares an external stimulus or cue with preexisting experiences or knowledge. Recognition memory is involved when children look at snapshots of a holiday celebration months in the past: their faces light up, and they may describe aspects of the celebration they had apparently forgotten. **Recall memory,** in contrast, involves remembering information in the absence of external cues, such as when trying to remember a friend's telephone number without looking it up. Recall generally is more difficult than recognition, but it shows the same developmental trend recognition does: middle-childhood children can recall better than preschoolers, but not as well as adults (see Figure 12.2).

Long-Term Memory   *Long-term memory (LTM)* is the feature of thinking that holds information for very long periods, perhaps even indefinitely. It is not clear how much long-term memory changes during childhood, or even whether it changes at all, because LTM relies increasingly on complex strategies of informa-

FIGURE 12.2
Developmental Changes in Recall Memory
In the study represented here, children were asked to recall a series of digits shortly after hearing them. The points on the graph represent the average number of digits subjects were able to recall, and the bars represent the ranges of typical performance at each age. Recall of digits improves during middle childhood and almost reaches adult levels by age twelve, though not quite.

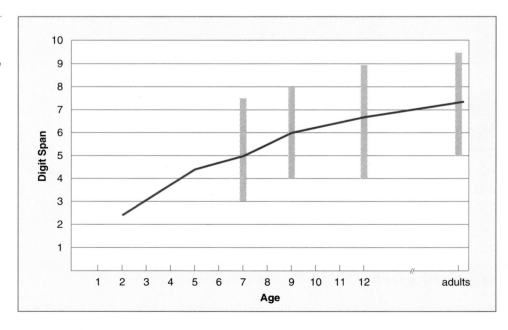

tion storage and retrieval. Younger children may remember less because they have experienced fewer memorable events or because they use fewer methods of deliberately remembering information and experiences.

To understand how LTM changes during childhood, consider how children and adults recall short stories they have heard (Wolf, 1993). By age six, children already understand the basic narrative structure of stories—that such stories contain characters, situations, and plots with a beginning, a middle, and an end. Not surprisingly, therefore, children show many similarities to adults in recalling stories. Like adults, they recall important features of a story ("Goldilocks was not supposed to enter the bears' house") and ignore or forget trivial details ("Goldilocks was wearing brown shoes"). They also recall the essences of sentences rather than their exact wording.

But compared to adults, the recollections of school-age children include fewer inferences based on the sentences they actually hear (McNamara et al., 1991). If adults hear the two sentences "Red Riding Hood's grandmother was baking" and "Grandmother set the cookies out on the table," they automatically infer that (1) grandmother had an oven and (2) she was the one who took the cookies out of the oven. Because of these inferences, adults are relatively likely to think they actually heard this information and to remember a sentence that actually was not used, such as "Grandmother finished her baking in the oven before she put the cookies out." Schoolchildren are far less likely to include such inferred sentences, although they are more likely to do so than preschool children are. As children get older, they seem to read between the lines more frequently, at least when recalling stories. This tendency lends color and detail to their retellings as they get older, although they sometimes risk misstating the "facts" of a story.

Implications for Elementary Education   The "architecture" of memory may affect how children can learn during the school years. A younger student who can remember only three bits of information needs to have information organized in smaller chunks than an older student who can remember six bits at a time. The younger child may have trouble remembering a phone number long enough to dial it, for example, unless the teacher can offer some learning strategies for doing this task (see the next section for some suggested strategies). More significant for learning, research shows that elementary students' ability to solve arithmetic problems is correlated with the extent of their short-term memories: in one study, "larger" short-term memory meant greater accuracy in solving problems (Swanson et al., 1993). Children's limitations on long-term memory, on the other hand, pose a different challenge: school-age children *can* remember ideas and facts for long periods, but their teachers may need to help them to see connections among the stories, ideas, and other material that they learn in school.

Influences on Memory Development

As many of the preceding examples imply, LTM develops partly because other, related cognitive changes occur during childhood. One of these changes is an improvement in logical reasoning, such as that described by Piaget. Another is an increase in specific knowledge or facts. Still another is an improvement in the learning strategies used in solving problems, including problems that depend on long-term memory.

The Effects of Logical Reasoning on Memory   Reasoning skills affect children's memory, and because reasoning often improves with age, memories of specific experiences sometimes actually improve gradually rather than deteriorate. In a classic Piagetian study that illustrates this fact, experimenters showed children a series of

FIGURE 12.3
Seriation of Sticks
Concrete operational children can arrange a series of sticks by length much more accurately than younger, preoperational children can. Piaget found, however, that performance by preoperational children improved spontaneously over a period of several months: later seriations were more accurate than earlier ones, even when no practice occurred between trials.

(a) Correct seriation

(b) Alignment of only one end

(c) Seriation of only part of the sequence

sticks of various lengths (see Figure 12.3); then they asked the children to reproduce the series from memory by drawing pictures of it (Piaget & Inhelder, 1973). Several months later, they asked the children to draw the series from memory again.

As you might expect, on both occasions preschool children reproduced the series with considerably less accuracy than older, school-age children did; the younger ones simply drew a random group of sticks or perhaps correctly sequenced only part of the series. The later drawings, however, showed a surprising result: nearly three-quarters of the children's drawings actually improved in accuracy over the first ones. Although some of the change probably reflected improvements in motor skills, the drawings were too simple to have depended on motor development entirely. Some of the improvement probably also reflected the children's increasing understanding of the underlying concept of seriation. Development of this concept apparently aided their later drawings, at least in part.

Other research suggests that children's ability to make inferences affects what they remember. Consider this task, which calls for recognition of sentences. Ask children to listen to a set of sentences that express simple relationships, such as "Carlos is older than Bill," "Bill is older than Nicole," and so on. Later, ask them to recognize whether certain sentences were in fact part of the original list. Some of the test sentences should indeed be identical to the originals ("Bill is older than Nicole"); some should be logically true but worded differently ("Bill is younger than Carlos"); and some should be logically false but worded similarly ("Nicole is older than Carlos"). On a task such as this, people of all ages will falsely "recognize" some sentences that were not in the first list. As it turns out, their mistakes suggest how memory and reasoning may affect each other.

What determines which sentences they falsely recognize? The sophistication of their reasoning skills is partly responsible (Howe et al., 1992). Among young children (around age five), the similarity of wording seems to matter the most; in the preceding examples, a kindergartner is comparatively likely to think she heard "Bill is older than Carlos. By the middle elementary school years, logical consistency matters more; a third- or fourth-grade child will think he heard "Carlos is older than Nicole." Apparently his more developed reasoning skills color his memory. In reality, he may have heard only "Carlos is older than Bill" and "Bill is older than Nicole." From these he reasons immediately that Carlos must be older than Nicole, but he apparently forgets that a sentence about Carlos and Nicole was not given.

Studies of both false recognition and spontaneous improvements in recall suggest that memory is not passive but active; it is not inert and unchanging (a memory "bank") but growing, developing, and changing. This fact can help children as they grow older: in school, for example, material learned five years earlier can seem more meaningful than it did when it was recalled immediately after it was learned. But it can also pose serious problems in situations where accuracy is at a premium. Children who have been sexually abused, for example, sometimes must testify in court about abusive events they experienced or witnessed in the distant past. How much can their testimony be trusted as accurate? There is no simple answer to this question, but research suggests that the overall theme, or "message," of children's memories remains accurate over the long term even though their recollection of details may change significantly (Zaragoza, 1995). In other words, a child may be accurate in recalling being abused during a period of childhood even though but not be accurate about all of the specific times and places the abuse occurred.

Familiarity and Richness of Knowledge   Common sense suggests that prior knowledge influences what a child can learn and remember. A child who knows a lot about animals will have an easier time learning the concepts of *mammal* and *reptile* than will a child who knows little about animals, even if neither child has dealt with these concepts before. In this sense, knowledge leads to more knowledge—an obvious advantage in school learning, in particular.

Familiarity matters not only during learning but during recall. One widely cited study showed this to be true by observing a young child who had expert knowledge about dinosaurs (Chi & Ceci, 1987). The child could name and describe forty-six different dinosaurs, telling about their size, appearance, eating habits, and behavior. He could do so, however, only if given ample time (literally hours) and encouragement from adults. In a short, straightforward test of his recall, he named familiar dinosaurs far more often than he named less familiar ones. Being "familiar" in this case meant the child had had more prior experience with reading about a particular species in books, playing with toy models of it, and viewing its skeleton in a museum (although *not*, presumably, more experience with seeing it on the hoof).

More often than not, older children show greater familiarity with, or richness of knowledge about, a variety of topics simply because they have lived longer and therefore have accumulated more facts. But this is not always true. Like the dinosaur expert, many young children have special areas of knowledge or experience that outstrip those of older children and therefore promote unusually good

Expertise includes a rich knowledge base in a specific area, as with this young expert in raising chickens. Her elaborate knowledge of this activity fosters better organized, longer-lasting memory and probably allows her to remember many details about these chicks and their behavior.

A Multicultural View

Cultural Differences in Learning Mathematics

Research consistently shows that children from China and Japan learn mathematics sooner and more thoroughly than children from North America do. The advantage occurs not only in basic written computation (problems such as "How much is 34 × 26?") but in a range of other mathematical skills, such as knowledge of concepts, graphing, estimating amounts, and mental calculations. The differences favoring Chinese and Japanese children emerge as early as first grade, widen considerably by the end of the elementary school years, and persist throughout high school (Stevenson et al., 1993). Furthermore, international differences in mathematics achievement are wide and substantial: the highest-achieving percentage of American students perform mathematics only about as well as the lowest-achieving percentage of Chinese or Japanese students.

The clearest explanations for these differences center on cultural influences, especially on educational practices and attitudes toward achievement. One obvious cultural difference is the priority given to mathematics. Observations of Chinese and Japanese classrooms reveal that Asian teachers devote double or triple the amount of time to mathematics instruction each week that their U.S. counterparts do. Most of this extra time involves the class as a whole group: the teacher gives verbal explanations of mathematical procedures and ideas and illustrates them using simple, concrete materials such as blocks and sticks of fixed, known sizes.

In American classrooms, in contrast, teachers spend more time with children individually or in small groups and simultaneously assign tasks or seatwork to occupy the remainder of the class. These practices reflect American teachers' strong belief in individualizing instruction. But they also encourage students to concentrate on getting paperwork done to the exclusion of interacting with the best-educated person in the classroom, the teacher.

Differences in mathematics achievement may also stem from broader cultural beliefs about the sources of educational success. Comparisons of parents in Japan and the United States, for example, show that Japanese parents tend to attribute success to students' effort and motivation and failure to lack of motivation or family problems (White, 1993). In the United States, parents tend to attribute success to ability and failure to lack of ability. They are also more likely to believe a failing child has a physical impairment, such as minimal brain damage or some other condition that is strictly "within" the child. The differences in attitudes can be seen in parental responses to homework: apparently because Asian parents believe more strongly that effort pays off, they tend to involve themselves in helping their children with homework more heavily than American parents do (Stevenson & Stigler, 1992).

All in all, international differences in mathematics learning challenge a widely held belief in North American society that mathematical knowledge is inherently more formal, difficult, and inaccessible than other kinds of knowledge and that success in math therefore depends on an innate, unchanging ability held by only a select number of individuals (Restivo et al., 1993). This belief may reduce the effectiveness of many American teachers in teaching math compared to many other subjects and cause many American parents to give up relatively easily on supporting their children's efforts to learn mathematics.

memory. There are child experts in baseball and chess and among music lovers and performers (see the Multicultural View box on cultural differences in learning Mathematics).

Metacognition and Learning Strategies

As children grow older, they pick up more knowledge about thinking itself, about how learning and memory operate in everyday situations and how a person can improve his or her cognitive performance. Psychologists sometimes call this type of knowledge **metacognition,** meaning "knowledge about cognition" (Volk, 1995).

Compared to older children, young children are notably oblivious of factors that can affect their problem-solving performance. For example, ask two children of different ages which set of numbers will be harder to remember:

8 1 5   or   3 9 2 6 8 1 4 7

Both preschool and school-age children will tell you that the first set is easier to remember than the second set. They will differ, though, in how accurately they predict their chances of actually remembering each set. In general, the younger the

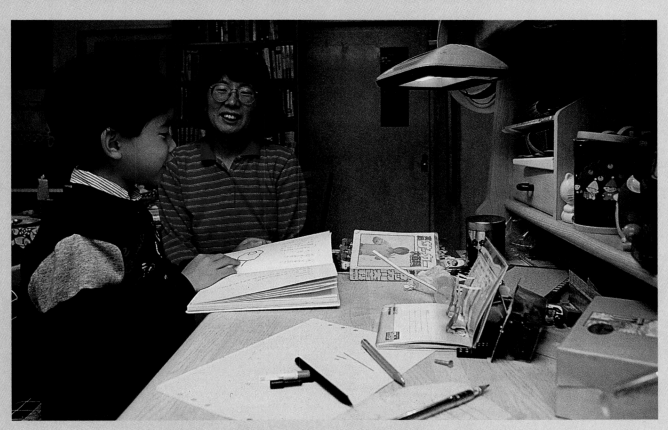

Japanese students have some of the highest scores on mathematics tests of any students in the world. Japanese teachers spend much more time at mathematics than do American teachers, and parents are more likely than their American counterparts to treat nightly tutoring and assistance as a high priority.

child, the less accurate the prediction: a six-year-old might tell you she can remember the eight-digit set but in fact be unable to do so.

By age ten or so, a child's predictions are much more accurate. He might tell you he can remember the eight digits, but also qualify the prediction: he might remember it only for awhile or only if he can use some supplementary strategy such as writing the numbers down. These ideas are metacognitive in that they imply increasingly accurate knowledge of how thinking and memory operate.

Types of Learning Strategies   Improvements in metacognitive knowledge are correlated with, but do not necessarily bring about, improvements in broad **learning strategies,** or general methods or techniques that help in solving a variety of problems. Typically such strategies draw not only on preexisting skills, such as the language skills developed during early childhood, but on brand-new ones, such as the emerging conservation abilities described by Piaget and neo-Piagetian theorists. Learning strategies give school-age children major advantages over younger children in solving certain types of problems (Rafoth, 1993).

Attention to Detail   During the school years, children notice details much more frequently. For example, try showing children several similar pictures, only

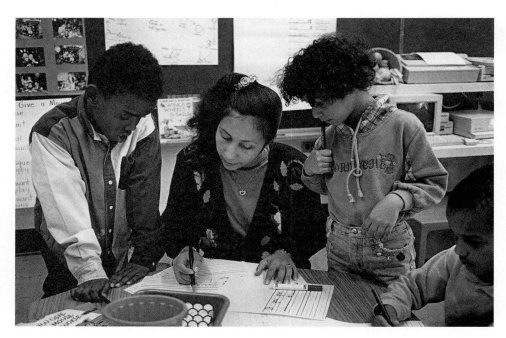

As children gain educational experience, they acquire new strategies for learning, such as attending to important details and knowing how much attention to give to specific subtasks. Teachers and parents can help by modeling these strategies and encouraging children to use them, particularly if they explain the advantages of strategic thinking.

two of which are exactly the same. On the whole, younger children will make relatively more errors in finding the identical pictures. Observing their eye movements carefully shows they get sidetracked more often by the most noticeable aspects of the drawings. As a result, they sometimes forget to check all the details systematically, even when the details are crucial to solving the problem.

Rehearsal   The term *rehearsal*, which literally means "hearing again," refers to a purposeful repetition of information, either silently or aloud. Older children engage in rehearsal more often and with less prompting than younger children do (Bjorkland, 1990). To see this difference, ask children of different ages to remember a set of numbers (1, 2, 3, 5, 8, 13, . . .), and take note of how they do so. Older children are more likely to review the digits to themselves somehow, perhaps by whispering them, looking at them, or pointing to each one repeatedly. If younger children use any of these strategies at all, they are likely to apply them haphazardly.

Organizing Tactics   Older children more often notice the structure, or organization, of new information and exploit that structure more effectively. For example, older children are more likely to notice that each number in the preceding list is the sum of the two numbers preceding it, and may simply use this relationship to remember the entire series.

Elaboration   Older children more often relate new information to their prior knowledge, as well as embellish it and add complexities to it. This strategy is really the outcome of the other three: elaboration inevitably results from attention to detail, rehearsal, and organization of new information.

Strategies such as these explain much of the advantage older children have over younger ones in learning new material. Not only do older children know more strategies; they also use them more widely, spontaneously, and appropriately. The developmental difference is especially obvious when they are learning arbitrary information, the kind that takes deliberate effort to remember.

However, young children do not completely lack learning strategies; often they merely use overly simple or unreliable ones (Miller, 1990). For example, a three- or four-year-old often will point at and label the objects and words in a book, but will not do so consistently. Also, preschool children can be trained to use strategies such as rehearsal, even if they never do so as effectively as older children do. Simply reminding them to say each name on a list makes a big difference in later recall. So does recasting a problem in more familiar terms; school-age children, especially younger ones, can learn a list of "things to buy at the store much more effectively than they would if the same list were presented as an arbitrary memory task.

Much of the difference between younger and older children concerns how reliably and automatically they invoke learning strategies. Older children are less likely to need special coaching or specially designed problems to remember successfully. They can extract organization from material that is not already well organized, and they can do so more often even when not explicitly asked for such behavior. In this sense, they are more able learners than younger children are.

Mechanisms for Acquiring Learning Strategies   Children acquire these strategies in at least three ways: trial and error, logical construction, and observational learning (Siegler, 1995). Each strategy can be seen in children's own naturally occurring activities, sometimes in combinations, and each can be assisted by parents and teachers.

Trial and Error   Sometimes children encounter effective strategies more or less by accident, or through trial and error. Often this process occurs in the midst of pre-existing, more logical learning strategies. Some schoolchildren write many essays and follow all the advice of their teachers before they discover, by accident, the methods that work best for them. Even though their teachers advise them to make an outline first, and even though they do so repeatedly, they eventually may discover that simply writing a first draft produces better results.

Logical Construction   A lot of so-called random learning of strategies may really reflect logical construction of knowledge instead. *Logically constructed* knowledge refers to one form of children's active efforts to understand the world—the type of learning Piaget emphasized and sometimes also called *schemas*. Such thinking may especially help children extend learning strategies to brand-new situations. For example, children sometimes demonstrate knowledge of certain social relationships even though they rarely see people acting out such relationships. They can dramatize the behavior of firefighters even though they have not seen actual fires or observed firefighting behaviors. Even what they see of fires in the media tends to lack the detail they put into their reenactments. Instead, they seem to follow mental scripts, or inferences constructed from knowledge of what fighting a fire *must* be like.

Observational Learning   These examples may also involve observational learning, as described in Chapter 2. In many situations, children watch others talking and acting and witness the consequences of those activities as well. Such observations provide models for children's learning strategies at other times and places, even those far from the original demonstrations.

Siblings often learn by observation. A younger sister may watch her older sibling plead with their parents for an extra cookie. If the pleading proves successful, the younger child is likely to use the same method herself later; but if the pleading does not work, she is relatively unlikely to imitate this particular behavior.

Helping Children to Acquire Learning Strategies   All of the processes just described can, and often are, assisted by adults. Parents may purposely demonstrate effective ways to remember the time of an appointment by writing it down as soon as they hear it and pointing out the fact that they have done so to their child. Teachers may help children solve a problem in long division by encouraging them to whisper each step in the process to themselves as they do it.

When interventions such as these are carried out systematically, they constitute various forms of *strategy training,* or coaching in when and how to apply learning strategies to new and difficult problems. Evaluations of strategy training have concluded that it improves learning substantially (Rosenshine & Meister, 1994), although the amount of improvement depends on exactly how much a child understands the purposes and potential benefits of the training. The simplest forms—what might be called **blind training**—lead children to use particular learning strategies but do not give them any reasons for doing so or even explain that they are actually using strategies. More complex forms not only lead children to use strategies but also emphasize the advantages of using them. Sometimes they also teach children ways to monitor the progress of their own learning. These more complex forms might be called **informed training.**

In any case, learning strategies do seem to help children organize and process information, at least for problems similar to those for which they first learn the strategies. In and of themselves, however, learning strategies do not ensure metacognition. In fact, children do not show metacognition or learning strategies in a wide variety of situations until adolescence or even adulthood, and such strategies do not enhance problem-solving performance reliably until then either. Given the rather abstract quality of knowledge *about* thinking, we should not be surprised at this. After all, a child cannot judge a math problem's difficulty or select strategies for solving it—that is, use metacognitive skills—before she has accumulated some basic experience with math problems, and accumulating that experience may simply take more time than most children have had by age ten or twelve.

Difficulties with Information Processing: Learning Disabilities

During the middle years, about 5 percent of children develop **learning disabilities,** disorders in basic information processing that interfere with understanding or using language, either written or spoken (Lerner, 1993). Usually a learning disability causes poor academic achievement, although low achievement is not in and of itself evidence of a learning disability. Learning disabilities have no obvious physical cause, as blindness or hearing impairment do, and do not result from a general slowness of thinking, as mental retardation does.

Learning disabilities take many forms. One of the more common forms is called *dyslexia,* literally an inability to read. The diversity of symptoms among children with dyslexia reflects the diversity among learning disabilities in general. For some children, dyslexia consists of "word blindness:" they can read letters singly (such as *c, a,* or *t*) but not in combinations that make words, such as *cat.* In other forms of dyslexia, children can read words but fail to comprehend them. They can copy words accurately or transcribe them from oral dictation, but they cannot explain what they have written afterward, no matter how simple the vocabulary. Some children with dyslexia can read combinations of digits that make large numbers; for example, they can read *123* as "one hundred and twenty-three" but not as "one, two, three," even when they try. Most children with dyslexia have these problems in combination. Yet they seem normal in every other respect; their everyday conversations seem perfectly intelligent and their motor skills just as developed as other children's.

Causes of Learning Disabilities   What causes some children to have a learning disability such as dyslexia? The symptoms sometimes resemble what happens to individuals who suffer injuries to their brains (Rourke & Del Dotto, 1994). For this reason, some professionals have suggested that many learning disabilities, including dyslexia, may reflect undetected minimal brain damage that occurred during the birth process or even before birth. This hypothesis is extremely hard to prove, however. It also discourages some parents and professionals from helping children with learning disabilities on the grounds (probably mistaken) that organically based problems are beyond control.

Working with   Terry Wharton, SPECIAL EDUCATION TEACHER

Giving Children a Second Chance to Learn

Terry Wharton has a wide range of experience in classroom teaching and special education. He currently teaches a class of 2nd to 4th graders who have shown significant behavioral and emotional problems in regular classrooms. There are only eight students in his class, all of them boys, and two teacher assistants—definitely not the typical teacher-to-student ratio. Terry spoke about the philosophy guiding his program and about how he and his assistants reconcile it with conventional academic expectations for the primary grades.

Terry: We emphasize making the class nonpunitive and nonaversive. For these kids, school has been a disaster socially—lots of fights with classmates, conflicts with teachers and other adults. We have to provide successes and confidence to counteract the downward spiral of their self-esteem.

Kelvin: How do you do that without leading to further fights and conflicts? Eight of these kids in one room could be explosive!

Terry: Well, we do have to plan activities carefully and guide their choices more than usual. At the start of the year, the children only come for half a day, and I plan a series of activities they are sure to enjoy and to be able to do, like setting up a personal date-book or calendar to use later in the year. By the end of that first day, they really feel successful.

Kelvin: Given your students, how much is it like ordinary school?

Terry: Oh lots, actually! Academics is a priority. We have a "news" time where everyone relates some interesting personal experience. Then I read to them for a few minutes. Then they write in journals, either about the story or about something else that concerns them.

Kelvin: Do the kids like the journals?

Terry: I must admit, at first they resisted. They seemed very self-conscious about their writing skills and about revealing their thoughts and feelings. But lately it's been amazing; you should read them! Their growth with the journals is impressive. They talk about the story, or about their fears and hopes for their family.

Kelvin: What about math?

Terry: They don't seem as uncomfortable about math as they do about writing and reading; I'm not sure why. We work on basic arithmetic skills using some of the latest manipulatives.

Kelvin: Manipulatives?

Terry: Like sets of unit blocks that you can combine to illustrate addition problems. They seem to like that. But you know what surprised me the most? Workbooks! When I taught a regular primary-grade class, I tried to avoid those because I felt they were too structured, but these students love them; they even ask to do them! I think it gives them a feeling of clear progress and a sense of control over their own efforts. They can *see* clearly that they are getting work done.

Kelvin: So your program is indeed academic? You do work on cognitive skills?

Terry: Absolutely. The cognitive skills develop only because we're also supporting these students socially, though. The two go hand in hand. I think that's true for all children, but working with these kids with behavior problems has really brought that idea home to me.

Kelvin: Where else do you see academic and social connections?

Terry: With the parents, certainly. We make a big effort to involve the parents in our program. Several times a year we have "family celebrations," lunches where the child's whole family is invited. The parents have responded enthusiastically. Some parents work as volunteers in the school. They've been a real help, and even if they are not in the same classroom, it's reassuring to be in the same building as their child.

Kelvin: These sound like good ideas for *all* classrooms and parents. Do you agree?

Terry: Yes, I do. But they're especially valuable for these particular parents because they've had so many bad experiences with schools, either because of their child's problems or when they were students themselves. It builds their confidence as parents.

What Do You Think?

1. Do you think that Terry would define the word *cognitive* the same way this chapter does?

2. Terry did not comment on the fact that his class is all boys. Do you think gender is important to consider in teaching a class like this? Why or why not?

3. Terry mentions that his students enjoy workbooks for mathematics, even though he personally did not consider them a good idea initially. How do you feel about this issue? What do you suppose Piaget or an information-processing theorist would say about using workbooks?

A more helpful explanation for learning disabilities focuses on cognitive functions rather than on brain anatomy. In this view, disabilities may result from subtle differences in how the mind of a child normally organizes and processes information. To see what this idea means, consider what children must do to read an ordinary page of print. First, they must perceive the letters and words as visual patterns. Then they must combine those patterns into larger strings that constitute phrases and sentences. Finally, they must connect those strings with meanings to form ideas.

While all of these steps are going on, they must also scan ahead to recognize the up-coming visual patterns on the page. If any of these steps fails to occur or occurs in the wrong sequence or at the wrong speed, a child may appear dyslexic.

Such problems in processing information may lie at the heart of many learning disabilities. Some children with dyslexia may, for example, find visual recognition especially difficult or time consuming. Several researchers have reached this conclusion after studying a phenomenon called *perceptual masking,* in which some letters are hard to read because of the presence of other letters nearby. To understand this problem, consider the following arrangement of letters:

w e k

q w e k l

a q w e k l m

s a q w e k l m n

d s a q w e k l m n p

g f d s a q w e k l m n p y b

c v g f d s a q w e k l m n p y b h t

If you look at the *e* in the top line, you probably will still be able to see the letters *w* and *k* clearly using your peripheral vision (the corner of your eye). If you look at the *e* in a line farther down, you can still see the end letters relatively clearly, but the middle letters become almost impossible to pick out clearly. Trying to notice the middle letters does help you to perceive them, but when you make this effort, the end letters become hard to discern. Perceiving one set of features in this display masks others; hence the term *perceptual masking.* Without a lot of practice, few people, adults or children, can see very many letters at once.

Some (though not all) children with dyslexia show especially strong perceptual masking (Vellutino, 1991). Compared to normal readers, they must stare at words for rather long periods, consciously shifting attention from one subset of letters to another in a way similar to the staring required to "see" the letters displayed on this page. Once they figure out the letters in a word, however, they can connect meanings with them fairly quickly and accurately. For these children, verbal association may occur much sooner than visual perception.

The gap in speed between perceiving and associating may account for many errors made by children with dyslexia. A ten-year-old may look at the word *conceal* and say something like "concol," or look at *alternate* and say "alfoonite." In making these mistakes, children may literally be reading what they see and guessing about the rest. Unfortunately, they may see fewer letters than normal readers usually discern. To put it differently, trying to see all letters clearly may simply take too much time and effort, and overall reading comprehension breaks down as a result.

Helping Children with Learning Disabilities   Because learning disabilities become a problem primarily in school settings, school professionals have taken increasing responsibility in recent years for helping children who develop these problems. Most commonly, help consists of careful diagnosis of which steps of thinking cause difficulty for a child, followed by individual instructional plans to strengthen those particular steps (Lyon, 1993). Children with problems in perceptual masking can be given exercises in which they purposely work to improve this skill. Often such special work can be done in a regular class during a normal school day, but at least some of it requires individual tutoring so that the professional can monitor and give precise assistance to the child's thinking as it actually occurs. Depending on the child's needs and the school's circumstances, regular classroom teachers, parents, or trained special educators can act as tutors, as well as additional sources of encouragement and support for the child.

Note that children with learning disabilities usually are old enough to have feelings and opinions about their problems. Eventually, in fact, the major problem in some learning disabilities may become *self-consciousness* about failing to learn,

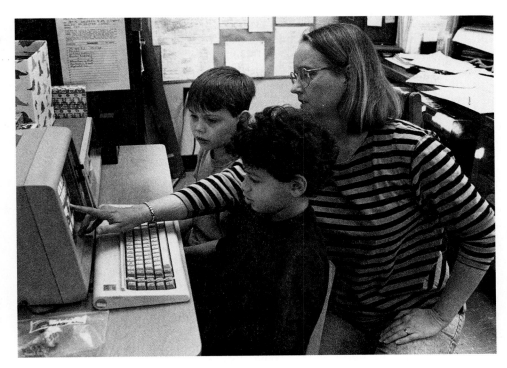

There are numerous ways of helping children with learning disabilities, but no single way is guaranteed to be effective. This teacher, for example, is helping two boys with their reading by using a computer which deliberately slows down the presentation of words, "reads" the text out loud if the boys request it, and offers hints if the boys do not answer its reading related questions correctly.

in addition to any cognitive or perceptual problems as such. A child who cannot read well usually becomes painfully aware of this fact sooner or later and worries about what teachers, parents, and peers may think of her as a result. Adults can help with this problem by being optimistic about the child's eventual capacity to learn academic skills and encouraging tolerance of differences among classmates and other peers.

What Do You Think?

Think about the methods you yourself have used to remember new information. What are they, and how are they consistent with the discussion in this chapter about how memory develops during the middle years? Compare your own memory strategies with those of classmates. Are they similar or different?

LANGUAGE DEVELOPMENT IN MIDDLE CHILDHOOD

Language continues to develop during middle childhood. Vocabulary keeps growing, of course, and the ways children use words and sentences become more subtle and complex and more like adults' (Anglin, 1993). Contrary to the impressions young school-age children sometimes give, they have not necessarily mastered syntax. They often are confused by a number of common sentence forms until well into the elementary school years. To six-year-olds, for example, the sentence *The baby is not easy to see* means "The baby cannot see very well"; the sentence *I don't think it will rain tomorrow* is likely to mean "I know for a fact that it won't rain."

Understanding Metaphor

One of the most interesting language developments in middle childhood concerns understanding metaphor. A **metaphor** is a figure of speech in which a word or an expression ordinarily used for one thing is used for another ("the perfume is bright sunshine"). Children can understand a variety of metaphors even in the preschool years, comparing color and personality ("He is blue") and objects and personality ("It was a friendly house"), among other things (Broderick, 1991). At first, however, they often assume a metaphor refers to a physical similarity rather than to an underlying conceptual relationship. The sentence *My brother is a rock,* for example, is taken to mean "My brother sits very still, like a rock" or "My brother is very hard when you touch or punch him, like a rock." Even the types of physical similarities are restricted at this age. In one study comparing preschoolers and school-age children, youngsters listened to tones of various pitches—some very low and some very high—and were asked which pitch was brighter or dimmer and bigger or smaller (Marks et al., 1987). Four-year-olds readily described the low pitches as "dim" and the high pitches as "bright." But not until age eleven did children also reliably describe low pitches as "big" and high ones as "small," as adults tend to do.

Children do not reliably interpret a metaphor in conceptual or relational terms until about age ten (Winner, 1988). By that age, the sentence *My brother is a rock* is taken psychologically rather than physically: now the term *rock* is assumed to refer to a personality trait, so the sentence might mean "My brother is unfeeling or reserved." The sentence *Your words are music to my ears* no longer means literally that you are singing, as some preschoolers assume, but that "Your ideas produce a pleasurable feeling in me, like the feeling I get listening to music."

At least two factors explain the developmental changes in children's understanding of metaphor. One is the child's growing sensitivity to the context of communications: calling a person a *butterfly* means one thing when the person is beautifully dressed but another when the person is behaving restlessly. Children take enough time to note such variations in the context of a metaphor to be able to interpret it correctly (Anderson, 1992). The other factor is the significant information-processing demands of metaphor: to understand it, the child must grasp not only the literal meaning of the sentence and its terms but also the speaker's intended meaning. This is basically an example of metacognition, discussed earlier, since the child must treat the metaphor itself as an object of thought in trying to discern its nonliteral, intended meaning. It is not surprising, therefore, that children do not become proficient in understanding metaphors until well into middle childhood. It is also not surprising that research has found that school-age children who fail to comprehend metaphorical language tend also to experience language and learning disabilities (Smith & Tsimpli, 1995). Their failure probably is not a cause of their disabilities, but it may be a symptom of a more general difficulty with metacognitive thinking and the learning strategies that metacognition makes possible.

Bilingualism and Its Effects

Although most monolinguals may not realize it, a majority of children around the world are able to speak two languages and therefore are bilingual (Paulston, 1988). Bilingualism is common in the United States even though the nation is officially monolingual; somewhere between 30 million and 35 million individuals (about 10 to 15 percent) regularly use another language in addition to English (United States Bureau of the Census, 1993) (see Figure 12.4). Does this skill benefit their cognitive development? Research suggests that it does, but primarily when they acquire both languages equally well and when both languages are treated with respect by teachers and other representatives of the community (Bialystok & Hakuta, 1994). Language specialists call such children **balanced bilinguals.**

Cognitive Effects of Bilingualism   For one thing, balanced bilingual children show greater cognitive flexibility—skill at detecting multiple meanings of words and alternative orientations of objects—than monolingual children do. Bilingual chil-

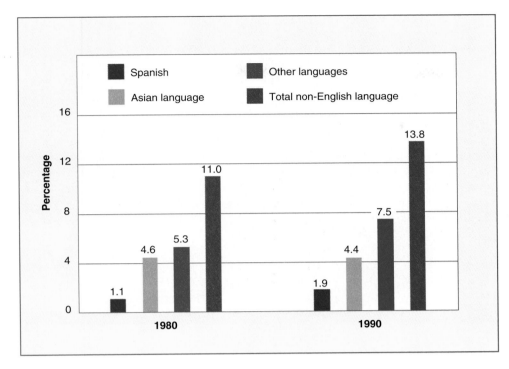

FIGURE 12.4
Children Five Years and Older from Homes Where a Language Other Than English Is Spoken, 1980 and 1990 •
The percentage of homes in which a non-English language is spoken has been growing. The single most common non-English language is Spanish. In some cities and regions, the proportion of non-English speakers is far higher than shown in this graph. Source: United States Bureau of the Census, 1993.

dren can substitute arbitrary words for normally occurring words relatively easily without changing any other features of the sentence. If asked to substitute *spaghetti* for *I* in the sentence "I am cold," bilingual children more often produce the exact substitution "Spaghetti am cold" and resist the temptation to correct the grammar ("Spaghetti is cold"), thereby violating the instructions for the task. Presumably such a skill stems from bilinguals' special experience with the arbitrary, conventional nature of words and language.

In part, such flexibility shows **metalinguistic awareness,** the knowledge that language can be an object of thought. Metalinguistic awareness develops because bilingual experiences often challenge children to think consciously about what to say and how to say it (Jimenez et al., 1995). A question such as "What if a dog were called a cat?" therefore poses fewer conceptual problems for bilinguals. So do follow-up questions such as "Would this 'cat' meow?" or "Would it purr?"

However, all of these cognitive advantages apply primarily to balanced bilingual children, those with equal skill in both languages. What about the unbalanced bilinguals, those with more skill in one language than in the other? Does knowledge of a second language help, even if it is limited? Evidence is scarce, but what there is suggests that unbalanced bilingualism has mixed effects on children's thinking skills, largely because of the interplay of social attitudes surrounding language differences in society (Pease-Alvarez, 1993).

Social Effects of Bilingualism   When children acquire two languages, one language usually has more prestige than the other. In the United States, the "best," or most important, language almost always is English. Its prestige results not only from its widespread use but also from its association with success and power: all the important people in American society, it seems, speak English fluently. These circumstances create negative attitudes or stereotypes about people who speak other languages and challenge educators to overcome social prejudices at the same time they facilitate learning new grammar, vocabulary, and usage.

The influence of language on attitudes has been well documented through experiments using the *matched guise technique* (Giles & Coupland, 1991). In this type of experiment, perfectly balanced and fluent bilinguals tape record standard

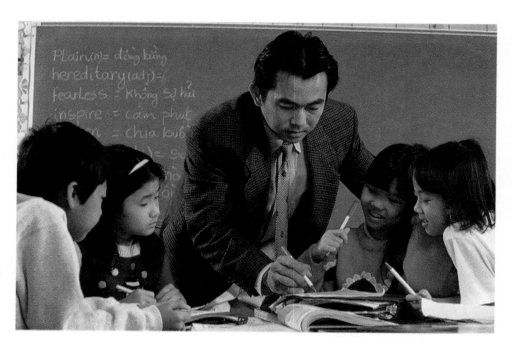

Fully bilingual children have cognitive advantages over monolinguals, but only as long as both languages and their related cultures are treated with respect by teachers and society. These Vietnamese children are well on their ways to becoming bilingual; what attitudes will they encounter about their language and heritage?

messages in each of their two languages, and the messages are interspersed among other tape-recorded messages to disguise the identities of the bilingual speakers. Then listeners evaluate the competence and social attractiveness of each speaker. Time after time, two consistent trends occur in studies of this type. First, speakers of English are rated more highly than speakers of other languages. Second, listeners from non-English-speaking cultural groups rate the English speakers more highly than they do speakers of their own language. The prestige of English, in other words, comes from sources in addition to English speakers themselves.

Negative attitudes toward non-English languages reduce children's school performance by making them less willing to use their primary, or first, language in public and reducing their self-confidence about linguistic skills in general. Fortunately, however, educational programs exist that can counteract these effects by treating children's first language as an educational resource rather than a liability. Overall, research favors *additive bilingual education,* programs that develop language skills in *both* of a child's languages rather than attempting to replace a first language with English (Perez & Torres-Guzman, 1992). As a practical matter, such programs usually are conducted partly in each language, depending on children's current language skills, but they do not confine either language to isolated "lessons" lasting only short periods each day. The challenge is a double one: to foster new language skills while also promoting respect for a child's original language and culture. In countries where language is less strongly associated with economic or social status (for example, Canada, where about 25 percent of the population speaks French as a first language), bilingual education often does not include this double agenda. Therefore, successful bilingual programs more often emphasize simple immersion in a second language and tend to ignore a child's first language without negative educational effects (Lambert et al., 1993).

Black English

In the United States, some African-Americans use a dialect, or version of English, called **Black English,** that differs from the middle-class dialect that linguists call *Standard English.* The two versions differ in three ways (Sutcliffe, 1992). First, certain sounds occur differently: for example the sound /th/ becomes /d/, making the word *this* sound like *dis.* Second, certain grammatical forms differ. The verb *to be* is used to indicate a continuing situation or condition. The sentence "The coffee be cold" means approximately "Every day the coffee is always cold"; but the sentence "The coffee cold" is closer to meaning "The coffee is cold this time." Third, Black English contains many words and expressions that have meanings very different than those in Standard English. The word *bad* can mean something undesirable ("I have a bad cold") but also something highly desirable ("She look bad" usually means "She looks very good").

Studies of Black English have found it to be as complex as any other language, including Standard English, and equally capable of expressing the full range of human thought and emotion (Smitherman-Donaldson, 1994). Unfortunately, society's attitudes toward it remain rather negative, which has created dilemmas for teachers of students who use Black English. Should students be allowed to speak this dialect in class, or even be encouraged to do so, because they know it best? Or should they always be expected to use Standard English to prepare them to function better in mainstream (white) society? Educators typically recommend a compromise: teachers should respect Black English, appreciate its richness, and allow students to use it in class some of the time. But they should also show students how Black English has influenced and enriched Standard English (Holloway & Vass, 1993)—where, for example, did the term *cool,* meaning "terrific," come from? Teachers should also encourage students to practice Standard English because it probably will help them in situations where they must communicate more formally.

What Do You Think?

Think about a language you wish you could speak fluently. Why would you like to be able to use this language? In forming your opinion, what assumptions are you making about the culture or people who use this language?

DEFINING AND MEASURING INTELLIGENCE

Intelligence refers to adaptability, or, put differently, to a general ability to learn from experience. Usually intelligence also refers to the ability to reason abstractly, sometimes using language to do so, and it includes the ability to integrate old and new knowledge. In recent years, some psychologists have also used the term *intelligence* to refer to social skills, talents of various kinds (such as a talent for music), or bodily skills. The traditional orientation toward reasoning and problem solving, however, still dominates discussions of intelligence, and partly as a result, many standardized tests have been developed to measure these forms of intelligence.

Issues Regarding Intelligence

Because so many definitions of intelligence exist, it is not surprising that psychologists continually debate a number of issues related to it. Here is a sampling.

How Many Abilities?   Both common sense and research suggest that abilities come in many forms. But do these forms add up to one truly general intelligence or to an assortment of "intelligences"? Some theories of intelligence emphasize relatively specific skills; others stress one rather general ability, sometimes called *g* (Spearman, 1927). In practice most psychologists acknowledge the presence of both general and specific factors, although they differ in emphasis and in the number of specific factors proposed.

As Calvin's scribbling implies, there are obviously many forms of intelligence, but not all are recognized in academic settings! Often in everyday thinking, intelligence is equated with the school-related abilities of reading and mathematics, which is one reason why students may worry if they think that they lack it.

How Are Abilities Related?   Assuming specific skills contribute to intelligence in some way, how do they do it? Are they a loose conglomeration, even a hodgepodge, of diverse skills? The contents of some psychometric tests of intelligence, which often contain a wide range of discrete problems, seem to imply a diverse conglomeration. Are they a discrete number of moderately general but unrelated abilities? That idea is implied by some information-processing views of intelligence, as well as other views. Or do the elements of intelligence bear logical, structured relationships to one another in which each requires the others for its full expression? The most widely known version of this view is Piaget's theory of cognitive stages, explained in Chapter 2.

What Role Does Experience Play in Developing Intelligence?   Most psychologists argue that certain experiences can modify intelligence, that is, give a person more of one ability or less of another. But since they disagree about the nature of abilities, they also differ over the influence of experience on intelligence. Attending a cognitively enriching preschool program, one designed to stimulate problem-solving and verbal skills, has been shown to raise children's scores on traditional, standardized tests of intelligence (or IQ) in the short term and sometimes even in the long term (Schweinhart et al., 1993). At the same time, though, children's IQ scores correlate with, or tend to parallel, the IQ scores of close relatives, such as parents and siblings, even when children do not live in the same household as the relatives. Thus, heredity also influences intelligence, at least in the specific form expressed on IQ tests.

In answering the major questions about intelligence, psychologists have worked from a number of perspectives. The oldest and therefore best developed is the **psychometric approach,** which is based on standardized, quantitative measurement of abilities and achievement. More recently, researchers oriented toward *information processing* and toward *sociocultural* issues also have developed theories of intelligence, although these approaches have not been tied to standardized testing to any significant extent.

Psychometric Approaches to Intelligence

Psychometric definitions of intelligence have developed out of *standardized tests,* all of which share three important features. First, they always contain clearly stated questions that have relatively specific answers. The questions usually draw on logical reasoning and verbal skills, which schools typically require. Second, standardized tests always include clear, standard procedures for administration and scoring. Often they provide a script for the person giving the test, as well as specific printed advice about when and how to credit particular answers. Third, such tests present information about how large groups of comparable individuals perform to allow evaluation of the performances of particular groups or individual children (Scarr, 1991).

Kinds of Standardized Test   Standardized tests serve many purposes, but for convenience we can classify them into two major groups: achievement tests and aptitude, or ability, tests. **Achievement tests** measure individuals' existing skills or knowledge; they try to assess current attainment in a particular realm of human behavior. Children often encounter such tests in the form of scholastic achievement tests, such as tests of reading achievement or of arithmetic achievement. By nature, such tests usually draw heavily on the typical curriculum content of the subject area being tested.

Aptitude tests measure ability or try to estimate future performance in some realm of behavior. A test of scholastic aptitude, for instance, tries to estimate a child's potential for success in school. Because of their goal, aptitude tests contain a broader range of questions than achievement tests do. A scholastic aptitude test probably would include questions from several major school subjects and draw on basic academic skills such as reading and mathematical reasoning.

In practice, aptitude and achievement tests are less distinct than these definitions make them sound. Often achievement tests are very effective predictors of future performance; children's current skills in arithmetic, for instance, predict their future mathematical performance about as well as any aptitude test can do. Also, aptitude tests can successfully predict future progress only by sampling skills and knowledge children have already attained. Nonetheless, the distinction remains useful for those who develop and use tests. In general, measuring aptitude means looking to the future, whereas measuring achievement means assessing the past.

Once norms have been calculated, standardized tests, and especially achievement tests, can serve two purposes. On the one hand, they can help educators know how well particular schools or classrooms are functioning in general. For example, all classrooms using a particular curriculum can be compared with classrooms using another curriculum, or all classrooms in one school can be compared with all classrooms in the city or even with a national cross-section.

On the other hand, standardized tests sometimes can aid individual children. The most common approach involves screening students who need special educational help. If teachers find that a certain student is learning the curriculum very slowly, they may ask a school psychologist to test her general scholastic ability in the hope of diagnosing or clarifying her learning problems. Although the results of such a test cannot stand alone, they often contribute to the complex process of assessing the learning needs of a particular child.

As you may suspect, standardized tests do not serve either of these purposes perfectly. Factors other than ability, such as a child's health or motivation to succeed, affect performance. So do physical disabilities, such as visual impairment. More indirectly, cultural and language differences among children affect performance on standardized tests. These additional influences deserve special discussion because they affect all children throughout society.

Biases of Intelligence and General Ability Tests   Although they attempt to measure general qualities, tests of ability and intelligence contain various biases. For example, many intelligence tests rely heavily on language in all of its forms—listening, speaking, and reading. Many also emphasize problems that have specific answers and that play down divergent or creative thinking. Also, although they do not focus on speed, intelligence tests tend to favor children who answer fairly rapidly and take little time to mull over their solutions.

Because schools also emphasize all of these features, intelligence tests measure academic ability better than they do any other skill. Some psychologists, in fact, have suggested calling them measures of *academic intelligence* or of school ability to make this limitation clear (Anastasi, 1989).

The biggest problem with intelligence tests, however, comes from their cultural assumptions, which have originated entirely from white, middle-class experiences in Western Europe and North America. The tests show their assumptions or biases in at least two ways. First, individual questions often demand knowledge that children can gain only by thorough immersion in white, middle-class society. One question might ask children to describe the purpose of a garden hose, thereby assuming previous contact with a garden in their backyards. Another question might ask children to define the word *drama* or *concerto,* thereby assuming the sort of education that provides this information.

Even when tests avoid this type of bias, they suffer from other, more subtle cultural assumptions. Some ethnic groups and cultures do not value conversations that emphasize abstract or general propositions, as is common in classrooms or intellectual discussions; using this style may seem rude or at least boring (Heath, 1993). Children from these groups therefore cannot be expected to take tests that rely heavily on this form of dialogue. Also, in some cultural groups contact with strange adults is extremely rare, so children from such groups may find sitting alone in a room with an unfamiliar test administrator rather perplexing or even frightening. For such children, any questions the administrator asks may seem much less important than figuring out this adult's real motives.

Common Misinterpretations of Intelligence Tests   Because of these problems, intelligence tests sometimes have been strongly criticized. Some school districts and states have even banned the less reliable group tests altogether. Individual intelligence tests generally have remained in use, however, because they are especially helpful in diagnosing children with special learning needs and are always administered by relatively well-trained psychologists.

A lot of criticism has stemmed from misinterpretations of the results of intelligence tests. In one way or another, all of the following mistakes have turned out to be all too easy to make:

1. *Equating test scores with all forms of ability* As we already pointed out, intelligence tests primarily measure academic talent. Yet life abounds with many other kinds of talent, from cooking or playing the piano to always saying the tactful thing. The further removed these talents are from academics, the less accurately intelligence tests can measure or predict them.

2. *Confusing intellectual differences with levels of intelligence* Most intelligence test scores reflect how much a child differs from other, comparable children. They usually do *not* report how much a child actually knows at any given point in time. Yet in many situations, actual knowledge may matter more than differences in knowledge, such as when a child tries to fix a bicycle or find his way home along an unfamiliar street.

3. *Assuming too much validity* Because intelligence tests give numerical scores, adults are tempted to think they are more precise than they really are. In reality, small differences in scores among children often reflect random variations rather than true differences in intelligence. Test manuals usually point out this fact, but unfortunately the information does not always reach parents, and even teachers or school psychologists may forget it.

4. *Assuming too much reliability and stability* Likewise, because intelligence tests give numerical scores, it is tempting to assume that the numbers are fixed and stable and that one administration of a test will yield the same score that a subsequent administration does. In reality, intelligence test scores are not perfectly reliable or stable, and in fact may vary significantly among test occasions. Administrations separated by long periods (several years) are particularly likely to produce different scores for the same individual.

Information-Processing Approaches to Intelligence

Psychologists have responded to these criticisms by developing other definitions and theories of intelligence. One way or another, all of the newer approaches broaden the nature and sources of intelligence. From these perspectives, more children seem to qualify as "intelligent" than is the case when children are assessed psychometrically.

The Triarchic Theory of Intelligence   An approach that draws explicitly on principles of information-processing theory is the **triarchic theory of intelligence** proposed by Robert Sternberg (Sternberg, 1994). This theory broadens the psychometric approach by incorporating recent ideas from research on *how* thinking occurs. To do this, Sternberg proposed three realms of cognition or, in his words, "subtheories" (hence the name *triarchic*), each of which contributes to general intelligence.

The first realm of intelligence concerns the *components* of thinking. These resemble the basic elements of the information-processing model described in Chapter 2. Components include skills at coding, representing, and combining information, as well as higher-order skills such as planning and evaluating one's own success in solving a problem or performing a cognitive task.

The second realm of intelligence concerns how individuals cope with their *experiences*. How effectively do they respond to novelty in solving new problems? For example, a person may follow a dinner recipe accurately when it is written in imperial measurements (ounces, teaspoons) but fail miserably when the same recipe is presented in metric units (milliliters, grams). How quickly can that person adjust to the new form of the task and solve it as automatically as was possible with the old form?

The third realm of intelligence concerns the *context* of thinking. A person shows this form of intelligence to the extent to which he or she can adapt to, alter, or select environments relevant to and supportive of the person's abilities (Sternberg & Wagner, 1994). In taking a university course, for example, a student may try diligently to complete the course assignments as given, in essence adapting herself to the environment of the course. If this strategy does not work satisfactorily, the student may complain about the assignments to the professor in an effort to alter them. If the altered assignments do not work for her, the student may drop the course and select another. All of these behaviors show contextual intelligence (though not necessarily of a kind that may please professors!).

Table 12.1 summarizes the three realms of thinking or cognition. These realms describe the processes of intelligence in more detail than classic psychometric approaches to intelligence have done. They also suggest an explanation for why individuals sometimes seem intelligent in different ways: perhaps one person has an advantage at internal processing of information, another adjusts to new experiences especially well, and a third has a knack for adapting, altering, or selecting appropriate environments in which to work. Given these possibilities, it would not be surprising if psychometric tests favored certain children and cultural groups more than others, since the environments of some families and cultures foster the learning of testlike behaviors more than others do.

TABLE 12.1   **The Triarchic Theory of Intelligence**

Realm of Intelligence	Examples
Componential	Coding and representing information; planning and executing solutions to problems
Experiential	Skill with novel problems and familiar problems in novel settings; skill at solving problems automatically as they become familiar
Contextual	Deliberate adaptation, alteration, and selection of learning environments to facilitate problem solving

The triarchic theory of intelligence, developed by Robert Sternberg, identifies three different realms of thinking: componential, experiential, and contextual. Philosophically, the theory is rooted in information-processing theory.

Musical intelligence is not well assessed on most classical tests of general ability, even though some psychologists (for example, Howard Gardner) believe that it constitutes a unique form of talent or intelligence. Children who play an instrument may—or may not—be particularly studious at school.

Gardner's Theory of Multiple Intelligences   Like Sternberg, Howard Gardner (1993a) has proposed that general ability consists of several elements or factors. However, Gardner has defined these factors in ways that reflect the influence of culture and society even more explicitly than the triarchic theory does. He argues that not one but **multiple intelligences** exist and take the following forms:

1. *Language skill* A child with this talent speaks comfortably and fluently and learns new words and expressions easily. She also memorizes verbal materials, such as poems, much more easily than other children do.

2. *Musical skill* This child not only plays one or more musical instruments but also sings and discerns subtle musical effects. Usually musical talent also includes a good sense of timing, or rhythm.

3. *Logical skill* A child with this skill organizes objects and concepts well. Using a microcomputer, for example, comes easily, as does mathematics.

4. *Spatial skill* This child literally can find his way around. He knows the streets of the neighborhood better than most children his age do; if he lives in the country, he can find his way across large stretches of terrain without getting lost.

5. *Kinesthetic, or body balance, skill* This child is sensitive to the internal sensations created by body movement. As a result, she finds dancing, gymnastics, and other activities requiring balance easy to learn.

6. *Interpersonal and intrapersonal skills* A child with interpersonal skill shows excellent understanding of others' feelings, thoughts, and motives. A child with intrapersonal skill has a good understanding of his own. For children with either or both of these skills, handling social encounters comes relatively easily.

(Interpersonal and intrapersonal skills may really amount to two distinct forms of intelligence, but the research evidence has made Gardner unsure about this.)

Gardner argues that the six intelligences are distinct, for several reasons. First, some of them can be physically located within the brain. Certain language functions occur within particular, identifiable parts of the brain, as do kinesthetic or balance functions. Second, the intelligences sometimes occur in pure form; some individuals with mental retardation play a musical instrument extremely well, even though their language ability may be limited and they cannot reason abstractly. Third, each intelligence involves particular, core skills that clearly set it off from the others. Being musical requires a good sense of pitch, but this skill contributes little to the other intelligences.

Like Sternberg's ideas, the theory of multiple intelligences implies criticisms of psychometric definitions of intelligence and of the standardized intelligence testing associated with psychometric definitions. Strictly speaking, however, the notion of multiple intelligences may really criticize the *use* of conventional tests beyond their intended purposes. As we pointed out earlier, such tests are designed to predict academic skills and therefore heavily emphasize verbal and logical activities. But school is not everything in life, despite its prominence in children's lives. Perhaps, as Gardner himself argues, the fact that school attendance is compulsory has actually interfered with understanding intelligence because it may have made us all value verbal and mathematical skills more highly than we should (Gardner, 1993b)(see the Perspectives box on gifted students).

Sociocultural Approaches to Intelligence

Sociocultural definitions of intelligence give even more importance than information-processing theories do to the social setting. In the **sociocultural perspective,** intelligence is not actually "in" individual persons but instead is to be found in the interactions and activities that occur *among* individuals (Wertsch et al., 1995). In this view, it is not the individual who adapts to, learns, and modifies knowledge but the person and his or her environment in combination. For example, a child may make many mistakes on a test of arithmetic computation but be able to locate the

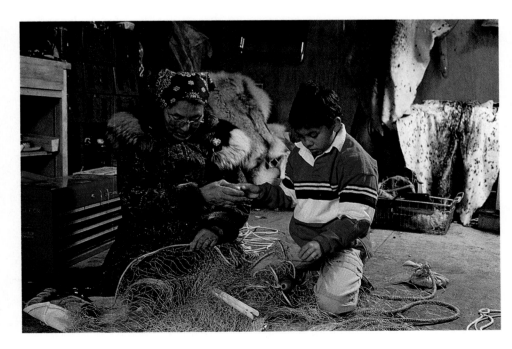

Even though repairing a fishnet may be too difficult for this boy to do alone, he is able to make repairs successfully when assisted by a more experienced adult. Changes in performance because of such assistance is part of what Vygotsky meant by the zone of proximal development.

Perspectives

Gifted Students: Victims or Elite?

For years certain educators have expressed concern about *gifted students,* those capable of high performance in some or all academic areas, in social leadership, or in the performing arts (see Table 12.2 for a summary of their characteristics). Because of their talent, some educators feared that these students are especially likely to become bored with the normal curriculum, become isolated from their peers socially, and, in some cases, become permanently unproductive in school and career as a result (Ross, 1993). Even though their "problem" was too much talent, some educators believed gifted students were potential victims of conventional schooling in much the same way students with learning disabilities or physical challenges are.

In response to these concerns, some schools have created programs of gifted education. Typically these include a "pull-out" program: for an hour or two each week, students designated as gifted work in a separate classroom on activities designed to meet their needs. Often students work independently on projects of their own choosing, such as learning all about local butterflies, designing their own computer program, or creating a portfolio of paintings. Sometimes they are also linked with experts from the community (called *mentors*) to assist them in developing these interests. Their regular classroom teachers are encouraged to recognize the gifted students' interests and abilities by allowing extra time to pursue the projects and periodically grouping the more gifted children together for tasks related to the regular curriculum (Gallagher & Gallagher, 1994).

This portrait of gifted education is attractive, but it has proven highly controversial. A number of educators, parents, and political leaders argue that gifted education creates an elite, overprivileged group of students (Margolin, 1994). Particularly in the pull-out part of gifted programs, students receive much more time and attention from a teacher than in a typical classroom, and they enjoy much more freedom in using their time. Ironically, it is argued, the curriculum for gifted students is much *less* rigorous than that for regular students; even though they are capable of it, gifted children do not necessarily read more books, write more essays, or learn more mathematics than others do. Furthermore, the gifted programs tend to treat students as if they were broadly talented in all areas, even though research and professional teachers' experiences suggest that almost all students have selected talents—math but not English, for example, or music but not athletics (Gardner, 1993b). This circumstance makes gifted programs more compatible with the preexisting strengths of well-to-do families and of white, English-speaking families, which may constitute a subtle form of racism.

How has gifted education responded to these criticisms? One strategy has been to make entrance into gifted programs more flexible: rely less on standardized test scores and more on students' own interest in volunteering for the program. Another is to arrange more activities for gifted students in the regular classroom and fewer in pull-out situations (Maker, 1993). A third is to redefine gifted education as *enrichment:* activities that tie

---

most economical items at the local candy store almost infallibly, even if the items come in odd sizes ($1\frac{7}{8}$ versus $2\frac{1}{4}$ ounces) or odd prices (34 cents versus 49 cents) (Chaiklin & Lave, 1993). That is because the knowledge needed for comparison shopping is contained not only in the shopper's mind but also in the overall structure of shopping in the candy store's environment. With practice, a child learns how to sort out pricing clues that depend very little on the computational procedures learned in grade school. Some of the clues involve rough estimations, such as when the prices of two items differ widely but their sizes differ only a little. Others involve nonarithmetic knowledge, such as recommendations from other shoppers or memories of where the store kept the bargains on previous visits. The intelligence needed for comparison shopping thus is only partly "in" the child; the rest is more accurately said to be distributed among the store shelves, the conversations with other shoppers, and the history of events at the store.

A key concept in understanding the sociocultural view of knowledge is the *zone of proximal development (ZPD),* originated by the Russian psychologist Lev Vygotsky and discussed in Chapter 9 (Vygotsky, 1978; Wertsch, 1985). The ZPD refers to the level of problem solving at which a child cannot solve a problem alone but can do so when assisted by an adult or a more competent peer. For example, a six-year-old may find the telephone directory too difficult to use alone but may be quite able to look up a phone number when given a bit of help from a parent. Implicit in conventional curriculum goals (reading, arithmetic, and the like) to students' own prior interests and talents. When pull-out activities are offered, therefore, all students may be invited, and the activities focus only on particular areas of the normal curriculum.

Integrating gifted and regular education in these ways is more equitable or fair, but it does not eliminate the basic educational controversy underlying gifted education: the tension between fostering excellence and fostering equality of education. Some researchers argue, for example, that having highly talented students work with less talented ones may actually accentuate elitism rather than reduce it. Differences between higher and lower performers become obvious to all students, day in and day out, and may create tensions within the classroom (Gallagher, 1993). Students may still prefer classmates with similar levels of academic motivation, both to work with and to be friends with; so informal social segregation may develop even in a room that is officially integrated. In addition, enrichment activities are harder to schedule if they invite volunteers and focus on specific school subjects; they cannot overlap with regular class times since some students, although ahead and motivated in the enrichment subject, may need extra help in the "regular" subject that they happen to be missing. That leaves lunch periods and before and after school for enrichment periods, times that teachers may already need for class preparations and for "refueling." Given these problems, it is to their credit that many excellent enrichment programs exist in the schools and that they have succeeded reasonably well in creating flexible yet challenging learning opportunities.

TABLE 12.2 *Some Characteristics of Gifted Students*

Characteristic	Examples
Well-above-average ability	Can think abstractly; skilled at verbal and numerical reasoning; adapts well to novel situations; rapid and accurate memory
Task commitment	Shows high level of interest, enthusiasm, perseverance, and self-confidence; sets high standards for success
Creativity	Shows original thoughts; open to new experiences and information; curious, speculative, sensitive to detail and to aesthetic characteristics of ideas and things

Source: Renzulli (1986).

the ZPD is the idea of shared knowledge, or shared cognition. Knowledge of how to use the directory exists at first in the interaction or relationship between two people—parent and child—and only gradually becomes located fully within the developing child. Likewise, knowledge of academic skills such as reading and mathematics also begins in the interactions between adults and children and only later becomes internalized by individual children. In fact, as the internalization progresses, children tend to perform better on tests of reasoning and language and therefore seem more "intelligent" in the psychometric sense.

Note that in emphasizing the social context of intellectual development, the sociocultural approach turns the issue of cultural bias on psychometric tests into an outcome to be expected and explored rather than a problem to be overcome or minimized. From the sociocultural perspective, cultural influences are the source or foundation of thinking rather than a mere backdrop or secondary factor that modifies individuals' cognitive performances. What becomes puzzling instead is why individual families and cultures vary so much in the social settings and interactions—the zones of proximal development—that they arrange for their children (Goodnow et al., 1995). Why does one culture promote skills in verbal dialogue more heavily than another culture does? And why do some families in a particular culture nonetheless adopt their culture's priorities more completely than others do?

What Do You Think?

Should standardized tests of ability be used in schools? If so, when and with whom, and for what purpose? Consult with several classmates about this issue. Then, if possible, compare the opinions of several professionals, such as a special education teacher and an occupational therapist. How do you think their work affects their opinions?

COGNITION AND SOCIAL DEVELOPMENT

Among all the ideas discussed in this chapter, one especially stands out: cognition rarely develops in isolation from social and emotional experiences. To use memory strategies successfully, for example, children must want to use them, must believe that others value their use, and must enjoy the effort involved in solving memory-related problems. These requirements encompass social and emotional issues, and they influence cognition significantly. Partly for this reason, the next chapter looks more closely at social and emotional influences on development during the middle years. To do so effectively, the chapter temporarily places cognitive development in the background. We return to issues in cognition when we discuss adolescence later in the book.

SUMMARY OF MAJOR IDEAS

Piaget's Theory: Concrete Operational Skills

1. School-age children develop concrete operational thinking, or reasoning that focuses on real, tangible objects.

2. A very important new skill is conservation, the belief that certain properties, such as size and length, remain constant despite perceptual changes in the object.

3. Efforts to train children in conservation have had moderate success, although when applied in a variety of circumstances training does not persist as strongly as naturally developed conservation does.

4. Concrete operational children also acquire new skills in seriation, temporal relations, and spatial relations.

5. Considered as a whole, Piagetian ideas about cognitive development have influenced many educators' styles of teaching, the content of their curricula, and their methods of assessing students' progress.

Information-Processing Skills

6. Information-processing models divide thinking into several components, including short-term memory, long-term memory, recognition memory, and recall memory.

7. Both short-term and long-term memory improve with age, partly as a result of other cognitive developments such as growing skills in using learning strategies.

8. Improvements in logical reasoning sometimes assist the development of long-term memory, as does increasing richness or familiarity of knowledge as schoolchildren grow older.

9. Learning strategies are acquired in a variety of ways, and sometimes they can be taught to children explicitly.

10. Learning disabilities can be understood in part as the result of problems in information processing, and providing learning assistance based on this perspective can sometimes benefit students.

Language Development in Middle Childhood

11. Although school-age children already are quite skillful with language, they continue to have difficulties with certain subtle features of syntax.

12. During middle childhood, children become much better able to understand metaphorical uses of language.

13. Bilingual children develop certain cognitive advantages over monolingual children, at least if their bilingualism is relatively balanced; these advantages include cognitive flexibility and metalinguistic awareness.

14. Often, however, bilinguals must cope with prejudices against one of their languages and against the culture that language represents.

15. Black English is an example of an important dialect of English spoken by some African-Americans in some situations (but not by all or in all circumstances).

Defining and Measuring Intelligence

16. Intelligence is a general ability to learn from experience. However, psychologists do not agree on many of the specific implications of this definition.

17. Traditionally intelligence has been studied from the perspective of psychometric testing, but newer perspectives based on information-processing theory and on sociocultural principles have challenged this perspective.

18. A view of intelligence based on information-processing theory is the triarchic theory of Robert Sternberg, which divides intelligence into components, experiences, and the context of thinking.

19. Howard Gardner's theory of multiple intelligences identifies six distinct cognitive capacities: language skill, musical skill, logical skill, spatial skill, kinesthetic skill, and interpersonal and intrapersonal skills.

20. The sociocultural view of intelligence regards thinking as being distributed among individuals who interact and communicate, and it locates cognitive development in the zone of proximal development.

KEY TERMS

concrete operation *(361)*
conservation *(363)*
décallage (364)
recognition memory *(368)*
recall memory *(368)*
metacognition *(372)*
learning strategy *(373)*
blind training *(376)*
informed training *(376)*
learning disability *(376)*
metaphor *(379)*
balanced bilingual *(380)*
metalinguistic
   awareness *(381)*

Black English *(382)*
intelligence *(383)*
psychometric approach
   to intelligence *(384)*
achievement test *(385)*
aptitude test *(385)*
triarchic theory of
   intelligence *(387)*
multiple intelligences *(388)*
sociocultural perspective
   on intelligence *(389)*

FOR FURTHER READING

Arias, Beatriz, and Ursula Casanova, eds. *Bilingual Education: Politics, Practice, and Research. 92nd Yearbook of the National Society for the Study of Education, Part 2.* Chicago: University of Chicago Press, 1993.

Here is a good introduction to current issues in bilingual education, as well as emerging directions in this field. An assortment of researchers and practitioners contribute to the volume. Note, though, that the book is heavily slanted toward the situation in the United States and that issues surrounding bilingual education depend heavily on the society in which they occur.

Feldman, David, Mikail Csikszentmihalyi, and Robert Sternberg, eds. *Changing the World: A Framework for Studying Creativity.* Westport, Conn.: Praeger, 1994.

Sternberg, Robert, and Todd Lubart. *Defying the Crowd: Cultivating Creativity in a Culture of Conformity.* New York: Free Press, 1995.

These two books focus on creativity—what it means and what it needs to flourish. The first book looks at the social nature of creativity as well as its cognitive nature. If you are interested in this topic, you might also consult a work by Howard Gardner called *Creative Minds* (New York: Basic Books, 1993). The second book discusses the influence of Sternberg's triarchic theory of intelligence.

Gardner, Howard. *Frames of Mind: The Theory of Multiple Intelligences.* 2nd ed. New York: Basic Books, 1993.

Gardner, Howard. *The Unschooled Mind: How Children Think and How Schools Should Teach.* New York: Basic Books, 1991.

The first book explains Gardner's theory of multiple intelligences: the distinctions among linguistic, musical, logical, spatial, kinesthetic (body balance), interpersonal, and intrapersonal intelligence. The second book discusses the implications of this view for modern education, especially the fact that schools currently favor some forms of intelligence much more than others.

Perkins, David. *Software Goes to School: Teaching for Understanding with the New Technologies.* New York: Oxford University Press, 1995.

Perkins, David. *Smart schools: From Training Memories to Educating Minds.* New York: Free Press, 1992.

This author is a philosopher with an interest in the psychology of education, especially from the perspective of information processing. In these two books, he applies this perspective on cognition to major new issues in reforming schools, such as the use of computer technologies and ways to encourage cooperative learning. The books are especially useful for those interested in teaching.

13

MIDDLE CHILDHOOD

Psychosocial Development

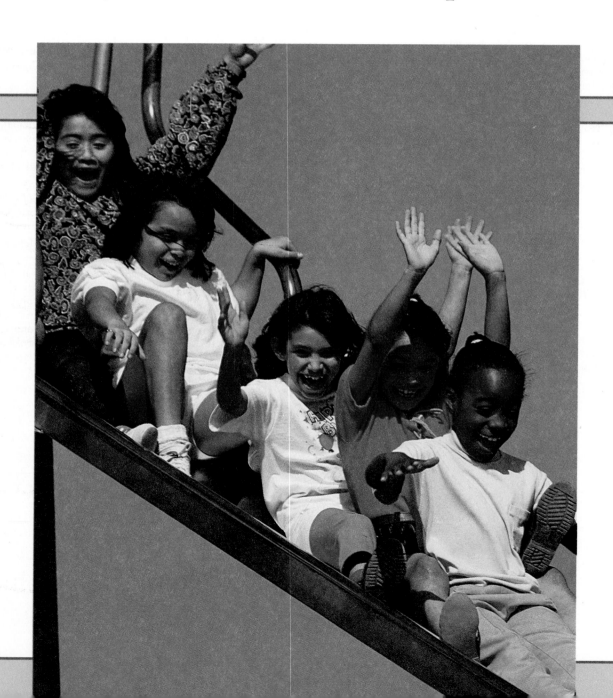

Psychosocial Challenges of Middle Childhood

The Sense of Self

The Development of Self in Childhood
Processes in Constructing a Self

The Age of Industry and Achievement

Latency and the Crisis of Industry
Achievement Motivation

Peer Relationships

What Theorists Say about Peer
  Relationships
The Functions of Peers
Influences on Peer Group Membership
Popularity, Social Acceptance, and
  Rejection
Conformity to Peers

Family Relationships

The Quality of Parent-Child Relationships
  in Middle Childhood
The Changing Nature of Modern Families
Divorce and Its Effects on Children
The Effects of Work on Families
Other Sources of Social Support

School Influences

School Culture
The Informal Curriculum
Teacher Influences
The Student's Experience

Beyond Childhood

N ickie is nine years old and in second grade. Between practicing soccer, baseball, and basketball and playing with his friends, playing video games or watching TV with his older brother Alex, doing his homework, walking the dog, and carving a model race car for his Cub Scout den with his father, he is always on the go. Until recently, if asked about his popularity or how he was doing at school or sports, Nickie would answer with a noncommittal "OK" or "I don't know." Lately, however, he has begun to talk more about himself: who he is and how well he is (or is not) doing as a ballplayer, a friend, a student, a brother, and a son.

Middle childhood is a time when the developmental changes of infancy and the preschool years are rapidly consolidated and children ready themselves for adolescence and the movement to full adulthood. By the time they start school, most children have learned something about human nature and are beginning to pick up various practical skills. During middle childhood, society fosters these developments further by requiring children to attend school to learn socially valued skills such as reading and writing.

School also provides children with more contacts with **peers,** other children of similar age and maturity. Peers offer certain benefits, such as freedom from the watchful eyes of parents and teachers. But they also demand loyalty and conformity. "Be nice to everyone except Rachel" may be a rule in one circle of friends; "Do the assignment, but don't work too hard on it" may be a rule in another. Middle-childhood children must learn to coordinate these expectations with those of parents, who sometimes disagree with peers.

To meet all of these demands simultaneously, children must learn to regulate their behavior from within. Somehow they must find ways to control their expressions of aggression, impatience, grief, and other strong impulses and emotions. Doing so becomes easier as they develop concepts of themselves as individuals, knowledge of their own needs and values, and a sense of how these needs and values compare with those of other people. In this chapter, we discuss these developments as they occur from approximately age six to about age twelve.

Focusing Questions

- What major developmental challenges do children face during middle childhood?

- What important changes occur in a child's sense of self during middle childhood?

- What is meant by *achievement motivation,* and what forms does it take?

- How do peers contribute to development during middle childhood?

- How have changes in the nature of the family, such as increases in the proportion of single-parent and dual-wage-earner families, affected children's development?

- In what important ways do schools influence development during middle childhood?

PSYCHOSOCIAL CHALLENGES OF MIDDLE CHILDHOOD

During the middle years, children's psychosocial development includes five major challenges: the challenge of knowing who you are, the challenge to achieve, the challenge of peers, the challenge of family relationships, and the challenge of school. We will first summarize the nature of those challenges and then discuss them in greater detail in the sections that follow.

The Challenge of Knowing Who You Are   Throughout middle childhood, children develop a deeper understanding of the kinds of people they are and what makes them unique. They also acquire a more fully developed sense of self as a framework for organizing and understanding their experiences. These notions do not yet constitute a final, stable identity, such as that developed during adolescence and adulthood, but they do lay the groundwork for later development. During the middle years, a child at least can ask, "Am I a popular sort of person?" or "Am I a good athlete?" The answers may still be rather simplistic, but they are beginning to take on meaning nonetheless.

The Challenge to Achieve   Some psychologists consider the major crisis of this age period to be the development of competence, self-confidence, and willingness to achieve to the best of one's ability. Of course, children care about their competence even in infancy. But during middle childhood, this motive is complicated by children's growing awareness of others' opinions about their efforts.

The older of two siblings showed this awareness one afternoon when talking with his sister about their paintings. Michael, age seven, said, "That's a nice painting, Elizabeth, but not as nice as usual." Elizabeth, age three, seemed unaware of insult; she simply smiled and continued to discuss her picture. Then she tried to be friendly by reciprocating: "That's a nice picture too, Michael, but not as nice as yesterday's." Michael looked pained and insisted, "It is *so* a good one!"

Both Elizabeth and Michael revealed some understanding of achievement in this interchange. They seemed to know that paintings vary in quality and that painters need encouragement for their work. But Michael seemed more concerned about meeting certain standards of achievement. He worried about Elizabeth's implication that he might have fallen below these standards, and he also worried about whether Elizabeth had noticed this fact.

The Challenge of Peers   The third major challenge of middle childhood is relationships with other children, or peers. As we point out later in this chapter, peers serve even more important purposes for schoolchildren than they do for preschoolers, and most middle-years children choose to spend a great deal of their time in peer-related activities.

The Challenge of Family Relationships   Despite the strong influence of peers, family relationships have far from disappeared from the lives of schoolchildren. Later in this chapter we discuss several important aspects of family life, including recent changes in family roles and family membership due to changing employment patterns and divorce rates. These changes in the traditional family structure have raised the questions of who is responsible for doing what within a family and what constitutes a family in the first place. Furthermore, all too often school-age children must share the challenge of holding the family together. We will examine several current perspectives on these issues from parents and psychologists and see how these and other changes in the family affect school-age children.

The Challenge of School   During middle childhood, school is second only to the family in influence on children's social and emotional development. Observing and interacting with a large number of diverse children and adults other than their parents give children an opportunity to learn new social skills, values, and beliefs and to develop a fuller sense of identity. In this chapter we explore how school culture, the informal or "hidden" curriculum, teacher influences, and the student's own experiences contribute to development during the middle years.

During the middle years, children develop preliminary notions of their personal qualities and psychological identity. What do you suppose this girl's sense of herself might be?

THE SENSE OF SELF

Throughout infancy, childhood, and adolescence, children actively construct a **sense of self,** a structured way of thinking about themselves that helps them organize and understand who they are based on the views of others, on their own experiences, and on cultural categories such as gender and race. This structure rapidly evolves during the middle years and becomes increasingly organized and complex. In fact, although a sense of self often is called a *self-concept,* it functions more as a theory that organizes a pattern of related ideas than as a single concept. A child actively constructs and continually revises his or her sense of self based on increasing age and experience (Wylie, 1974/1979).

For example, at age six, Mina loved playing with dolls and also loved holding and caring for babies. She noticed that her parents and others commented on this preference, so nurturance became part of Mina's idea of herself: "I'm someone who likes babies," she sometimes thought. But later experiences modified this idea. Toward the end of elementary school, Mina discovered that she often preferred playing softball to playing house. Somehow, at age ten or eleven, she had to incorporate this reality into her sense of self: "I'm a good ballplayer," she realized. By the start of adolescence, she still was not sure how to reconcile these two concepts of herself: her interest in child care and her interest in sports. Someday she may succeed in doing so, but not at age twelve.

To a large extent, a child's notion of self grows out of social experiences with other selves or, put more plainly, out of contacts with other children and adults. Learning what it means to be female, for example, occurs as girls meet other individuals who also are female. Learning what it means to be happy occurs as children see other people express happiness. As personal and individual as a sense of self is, then, it reflects generalizations about others, and it cannot develop without considerable social contact (Lewis & Brooks-Gunn, 1979b).

The Development of Self in Childhood

How do children acquire a sense of self? The first step involves basic social labels or categories. By the end of the second year of life, most children can correctly label their gender ("I'm a boy" or "I'm a girl"), their age ("I'm two"), and their species ("I'm a person"). Labels such as these pave the way for later, more complete knowledge of self.

Self-constancy   At first, however, most such labels lack permanence. At age two or three, a boy may claim he can become a girl under certain circumstances—"when I grow up" or "if I grow my hair long" (Marcus & Overton, 1978). Or a very young child may say she can become a different individual "if I change my name" (Guardo & Bohan, 1971). **Self-constancy,** a belief that identity remains permanently fixed, does not become firm until the early school years, sometime after age six. At this time, a child becomes convinced he will stay the same person indefinitely into the future, will remain human in all circumstances, and will keep his gender forever. Beliefs such as these are what a sense of self means.

At the same time the child is developing a sense of personal constancy, her reasons for believing in constancy are shifting. Younger children, up to age five or six, tend to define themselves in terms of observable features and behaviors such as hairstyles or how fast they can run (Bannister & Agnew, 1971; Rosenberg, 1979). These qualities have the advantage of being easily seen and comprehended, but as features of self-identity they have certain disadvantages. For one thing, they often are rather unstable; a child's running speed usually improves as the weeks and months go by. For another, they often are relative to particular people or situations; being big defines a child in one way among her nursery school peers but in another way among members of her family.

The First Beliefs in Psychological Traits   Around age eight, some children form a more stable sense of self by including psychological traits in their self-descriptions. At first, the traits are feelings and qualities that have no apparent reference to other human beings; "I am brave," says the child, or "I am cheerful." By implication these traits describe him as an entire personality and in all possible situations, with little recognition of people's usual variations in moods. At first, too, the child describes the traits in bold, global terms that ignore the possibility that opposing feelings or qualities sometimes exist within the same person. The child may vacillate in describing his own qualities without realizing it. Sometimes he will say, "I am dumb," meaning *completely* dumb, and other times he will say, "I am smart," meaning *completely* smart (Harter, 1977). Neither statement suggests the child recognizes that both descriptions contain an element of truth.

By the end of the middle years, fuller integration of contradictory traits occurs. Around age ten or twelve, children begin to recognize that they can feel more than one way about any particular situation or person; they can both like and hate their teachers or enjoy and dislike school more or less at the same time (Selman, 1980). As they do so, they also begin using trait labels in less global ways and more often to express qualities in particular situations. When an older child says, "I am smart," she no longer means "I am always smart in every possible way and in every activity." Now she more likely means "I am smart in a number of significant situations, but not in all." During the middle years, children become increasingly able to interrelate the different categories of traits and develop more patterned and integrated self-descriptions (Damon & Hart, 1988; Fischer et al., 1990).

These changes contribute to the development of a more flexible sense of self, in which the same individual can be characterized in a variety of ways depending on the circumstances. The situation-bound qualities middle-years children express usually describe them more accurately than the global traits and observable features younger children rely on. But a middle-childhood child's consciousness of inner traits still lacks the subtlety and flexibility found in adolescents and adults, who recognize that the stability of self involves multiple dimensions and ongoing change.

However, significant cultural differences exist in how the concept of self is constructed, and the idea of self is probably not a discrete psychological entity in all cultures (Hoare, 1994). In Asian countries such as India, Japan, and Nepal, for example, three distinct senses of self appear to exist simultaneously even in adulthood: a familial self, in which one's sense of self is defined almost exclusively in relationship to one's family; a spiritual self, which is defined and organized in terms of religious beliefs; and an individualized self, which is closer to the European-American sense of self just described (Roland, 1988).

Processes in Constructing a Self

To a large degree, the process of developing an identity and a sense of self during middle childhood reflects a growing awareness of relationships with other people (Damon & Hart, 1988). Children construct their identities by distinguishing their thoughts and feelings from those expressed by others. When children of various ages are asked how they would feel if their parents expressed certain emotions, such as sadness, anger, or happiness, preschoolers are likely to say they would feel the same emotions: they would be angry if their parents were angry, sad if they were sad, and so on. Older children, however, are more likely to name complementary rather than identical emotions; if their parents felt angry, for example, they would feel fearful (Harter & Barnes, 1983).

Additional evidence comes from studies of how children gradually acquire a fuller understanding of shame and pride. By the early middle years (age six or seven), children begin explicitly mentioning an external audience in defining these two terms (Seidner et al., 1988). For example, one seven-year-old's definition was "My teacher was proud when I earned 100 percent on the test"; another's was "My mother was ashamed when I lost my temper at the neighbor." Such attention to others implies awareness that others sometimes observe the child's self. More important, it suggests that school-age children distinguish between their own emotions and those of others—something they must do to develop a mature sense of self.

A child's emerging sense of self during middle childhood is part of a broader process of personality development. In the following section, we briefly discuss how two major developmental theorists, Sigmund Freud and Erik Erikson, view this process.

What Do You Think?

What do you remember about changes in your sense of self during your school years? What conflicting traits do you recall, and how did those traits get integrated?

THE AGE OF INDUSTRY AND ACHIEVEMENT

When viewed as part of the overall life span, the years from six to twelve seem especially important to the achievement of competence. Children spend countless hours in school acquiring skills in reading, writing, and mathematics. Many of these hours also contribute to learning of the unofficial curriculum of school: how to get

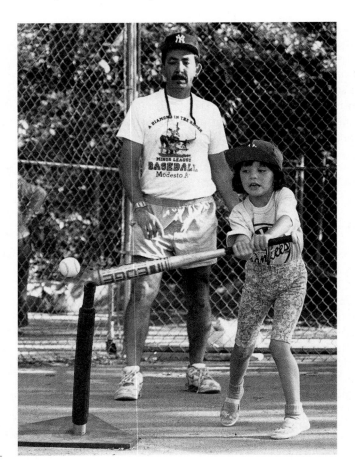

School-aged children often devote themselves to the long, slow mastery of complicated skills, such as learning to hit a ball.

along with teachers and with other children. Outside of school, children often devote themselves to the long, slow mastery of particular skills. One child may spend years learning to play baseball; another may devote the same amount of time to learning how to care for a zoo of pet hamsters, dogs, and birds.

Latency and the Crisis of Industry

Psychodynamic theories such as those proposed by Freud and Erikson explain such behavior in terms of the emotional relationships that precede it in early childhood. As we describe in Chapter 10, preschool children feel envy, awe, and competitiveness with respect to their parents. At first, these feelings have a magical quality: children simply want to be like their parents. Inevitably they are disappointed to learn that merely wanting such things does not make them come true.

In this regard, Freud emphasized the emotional hardship of preschoolers' disappointment and their consequent repression of their magical wishes toward their parents (Freud, 1983). A five-year-old, he argued, cannot continue indefinitely to wish for intimacy with his opposite-sex parent and for success in competition with his same-sex parent. These feelings (which Freud termed the *Oedipus* and *Electra conflicts*) disrupt life if they persist too long. Thus, the child eventually represses the feelings, meaning he pushes them completely out of awareness. As it happens, this repression occurs at about the time most children begin school—around age six or seven—and continues until adolescence. Freud called this the **latency** period, meaning a child's earlier unresolved feelings have gone underground and are waiting to resurface in the future (at the beginning of adolescence). During this period, the schoolchild focuses on building competencies and skills as a defense—an unconscious, self-protective behavior—against her earlier romantic feelings toward her parent. Developing talents, whether in sports, art, academics, or whatever, also helps to keep the child's mind off her earlier disappointment, which lingers on unconsciously.

Erikson agreed with Freud's account up to this point, but he went beyond it to stress not only the defensive, negative functions of skill building but its positive functions as well (E. Erikson, 1963, 1968). According to Erikson, children respond to their romantic feelings toward their parents not only by repressing them but also by trying consciously to become more like their parents and more like adults in general. Becoming competent helps children reach this goal in two ways. First, it helps them through *identification,* a process by which they experience themselves as being like their parents and thus capable of becoming genuine adults; second, it helps them to gain similar recognition from others.

Erikson called this process the crisis of **industry versus inferiority,** meaning children of this age concern themselves with their capacity for *industry,* or the ability to do good work. Children who convince themselves and others of this capacity develop relatively confident, positive concepts of themselves. Those who do not tend to suffer from feelings of poor self-esteem and *inferiority,* a sense of inadequacy or general lack of competence. According to Erikson, most children end up with a mixture of self-confidence and fear of inferiority, but self-confidence predominates in most cases (we hope).

In addition, the crisis of industry versus inferiority gives healthy school-age children a more or less permanent motivation to achieve particular, definable standards of excellence. A child's continuing sense that she can achieve and that her industry will pay off is shaped by her earlier successes and failures in school. No longer is she happy just to draw pictures, for example; now she must draw *well.* With persistence and support, children often do reach higher standards of excellence in many activities than they did as preschoolers, and most of the time they are happy about doing so.

Partly because of the connection between industry and increasing competence, psychologists have devoted a lot of attention to the development of achievement motivation in middle-childhood children. The next section describes some of this work.

Achievement Motivation

Achievement motivation is the tendency to show initiative and persistence in attaining certain goals and increasing competence by successfully meeting standards of excellence (Atkinson & Feather, 1966; Beck, 1978). What matters most is the approach to a task rather than the importance of the task itself. An individual can reveal achievement motivation as either a student or a college professor, for example, and as either an amateur checkers player or a world-class chess grand master. As long as the individual strives toward a standard of excellence that is reasonable for her, she possesses achievement motivation. Usually, too, her motivation leads to increased competence compared to her previous level.

Differences in Achievement Motivation   There appear to be two distinct kinds of achievement motivation: one that focuses on competence as such and one that emphasizes the judgments people make about competence (Chapman & Skinner, 1989; Dweck & Leggett, 1988; Ginsburg & Bronstein, 1993). The first type of motivation, called **learning orientation,** relies on *intrinsic motivation,* that is, motivation that comes from within the learner and relates directly to the task and its accomplishment. A learning orientation leads children to concentrate on learning as an end in itself; they will practice jumping rope just to see whether they can do it. The second type of motivation, called **performance orientation,** involves *extrinsic motivation,* meaning motivation comes not from the learner but from other individuals who see and evaluate him. In this instance, the person the child is trying to please or satisfy is not himself but others.

The differences between the two orientations can be seen in children who are learning to swim. To the extent that they adopt a learning orientation, they enjoy the actual activity: practicing new strokes, working up to higher speeds, and so on. They also feel relatively free to invite criticisms from coaches or fellow swimmers because these comments often can help them improve.

But for children who adopt a performance orientation, swimming is less enjoyable in itself and more a means of winning approval from others. Such children are more concerned about receiving compliments from coaches and swimming friends or performing well in competitive swim meets. If others criticize aspects of their swimming, the comments are not welcome. Ironically, too much concern with pleasing others may indirectly limit these children's ability to learn.

Motivational orientations play an important role in children's development. For example, higher levels of intrinsic motivation have been found to be related to an internal sense of control, feelings of enjoyment, and various mastery-related characteristics such as curiosity, creativity, exploration, and persistence in completing tasks and a preference for taking on challenges. They are also associated with higher academic performance and learning, feelings of academic competence, and perceptions of what contributes to academic success or failure (Ginsburg & Bronstein, 1993).

Observations of children, especially in academic situations, reveal two other distinctive styles of achievement motivation. Some children display a more adaptive and self-confident "mastery orientation" pattern of achievement behavior characterized by a quest for challenge, persistence in the face of obstacles, and an ability to take failure in stride. Other children display a less confident pattern of learned helplessness. *Learned helplessness* refers to the tendency to prematurely give up efforts to achieve a goal and assume a certain problem cannot be solved without even trying. This pattern usually is related to repeated past failures to solve a problem or escape from an uncomfortable or painful situation (Seligman, 1975).

Thus, failure experiences with math in first and second grade may result in a self-defeating pattern of avoiding challenges, low persistence in the face of difficulty, and high levels of anxiety and confusion when failure does occur. This pattern of learned helplessness is more likely to be found in girls, particularly those who are bright (Dweck, 1986).

One promising approach to helping children increase their performance motivation is *attribution retraining,* which helps children learn to replace their learned helplessness with mastery-oriented views of themselves (Dweck & Leggett, 1988; Licht & Dweck, 1984). Children are presented with learning experiences that allow for some failures. They are assisted by their teacher or other adult to reinterpret their failures in terms of factors they can learn to control rather than as the result of their lack of intellectual ability, over which they have no control (Dweck & Leggett, 1988). In one series of studies, Carol Dweck found that children who were doing poorly at math improved their performance when they were encouraged to believe their failures were under their own control and helped to understand the reasons for their failures, which included sloppy papers, careless errors, too little time spent on the task, failure to follow directions, and inadequate practice with similar math problems (Dweck et al., 1978a, 1978b). Success has also been reported using *cooperative learning,* a method in which children of different ability levels are assigned to learning teams (for example, math) and reinforced for good performance as a team. Each student is given learning tasks that are appropriate to his or her level, and students on the team are encouraged to help one another and monitor one another's performances (Slavin, 1987).

Achievement Motivation in Middle Childhood   During the middle years, children become more performance oriented than they were at earlier ages. At the beginning of this period, children express considerable optimism about their abilities. Kindergartners tend to rank themselves at the top of their class in scholastic ability, even though they rank other children relatively accurately (Stipek & Hoffman, 1980). This implies a learning orientation; for young children, achievement is something they do without either the involvement or the evaluations of others (Frieze et al., 1981).

During the next several years, however, children begin to believe that having an ability depends partly on whether other people give them credit for having it. This belief lies at the core of the performance orientation. It does not replace a learning orientation; rather, it takes a place alongside it. Now being "smart" means partly that a child's teachers, parents, and friends *say* she is smart and partly that she possesses certain skills in reading, mathematics, and the like regardless of what others say (Feld et al., 1979).

Successful achievement becomes more complicated in the middle years. Consider swimming. Late in infancy and during the preschool years, a child may be motivated to learn to swim simply by being given chances to experiment in the water. In middle childhood, however, he may ask himself what other people, especially parents and friends, will think about his learning to swim. Will they consider this skill a true achievement? Most people will value swimming to some extent, of course. But even very respectable progress in swimming may not look like much of an achievement if the child's family and friends hold very high athletic standards or place little value on athletics in the first place.

Environmental factors can also influence motivational orientation. Environments that provide optimal challenge, provide feedback that promotes competence, and support children's autonomous and independent behaviors are likely to facilitate the development of intrinsic motivation, whereas environments that strongly emphasize extrinsic rewards, deadlines, and adult control tend to undermine intrinsic motivation and foster an extrinsic motivational orientation (Deci & Ryan, 1987).

Family factors are also important. Golda Ginsburg and Phyllis Bronstein examined how parental monitoring of homework, parental reactions to grades, and general family style influenced achievement motivation orientation among fifth-grade children (Ginsburg & Bronstein, 1993). When parents heavily supervised their children's homework (by helping, checking, reminding, insisting), reacted to grades with punishment, criticism, uninvolvement, or extrinsic rewards, and displayed overcontrolling (authoritarian) or undercontrolling (permissive) styles of parenting, children were more likely to have extrinsic (performance) motivational orientations and lower academic performance. On the other hand, children whose parents responded to grades with encouragement and were supportive of their children's autonomy (authoritative parenting style) were more likely to have intrinsic motivational orientation and higher academic performance. The contributions of socioeconomic level and social class to these differences will be discussed shortly.

Differences in cultural backgrounds also can influence children's achievement orientations. For example, Chinese and Japanese mothers believe more strongly than American mothers do that academic success depends on one's own efforts rather than on factors beyond one's control, such as inborn ability or external conditions. This intrinsically motivated, achievement-oriented view is likely shared by their children and may help account for the higher academic achievement of Asian

A Multicultural View

Parental Expectations and Academic Achievement

Differences in academic achievement among African-American, white, and Hispanic children appear early during the elementary school years and continue throughout elementary, junior, and senior high school. One study found that at second grade, about 5 percent of white children and more than 15 percent of African-American and Hispanic children were performing below grade level in mathematics, and by sixth grade 20 percent of white children, more than 40 percent of Hispanic children, and 50 percent of African-American children were performing below grade level (Norman, 1988).

One popular explanation is that lower achievement of minority children is due to low levels of achievement motivation resulting from poverty, family disruption, inadequate academic support, and low parental expectations for children's academic success. This view has been challenged by a large-scale study of African-American, Hispanic, and white urban elementary school children and their mothers (Stevenson et al., 1990). In that study, Harold Stevenson and his colleagues examined the role parents played in their children's education and parents' and children's beliefs about children's current school performance and their educational future. Mothers and teachers were also asked how the children's performances might be improved.

What did the researchers find? First, when only families from similar economic and educational backgrounds were compared, the achievement levels of the African-American and Hispanic children were *not* substantially lower than those of the white children. Second, beliefs about the children's educational achievement held by both the Hispanic and African-American children and their mothers were very similar to those typically associated with higher rather than lower levels of achievement.

When the entire sample was looked at, the following findings emerged. All mothers agreed that parents should work closely with their children on schoolwork. African-American mothers expressed the greatest interest in helping their children, followed by Hispanic and then white mothers. Hispanic mothers were less confident about their knowledge of English and of the American school system, but were still eager to help their children with schoolwork, stressed the importance of school, and had high regard for their children's intellectual abilities and academic achievement. They also shared with the African-American mothers (and their children's teachers) a strong belief in the importance of homework, the necessity of competency examinations, and the potential value of a longer school day. They held high expectations for their children's futures, though not as high as those of the African-American and white mothers.

Most of the African-American mothers were familiar with what teachers expected of their children. They reported spending more time teaching their children academic skills than the other parents and evaluated their children's skills, abilities, and academic achievement in reading and math very highly. Their children rated their own performances very highly as well and believed they were working hard. Surprisingly, though, African-American students' evaluations of their school performances were unrelated to their actual levels of achievement in reading and math, which suggests they had not received or internalized realistic feedback about their academic performances from either their parents, their teachers, or both (Alexander & Entwisle, 1988; Bock & Moore, 1986).

These findings challenge the view that the low performances of African-American and Hispanic elementary

students over American students (Stevenson & Lee, 1990). The accompanying Multicultural View box discusses ethnic differences in parental expectations for academic achievement.

As children grow older, they shift toward a performance orientation and become more similar to adults in their achievement motivation. This in part reflects the increasing importance of peers and children's changing perceptions of social comparisons (Pomerantz et al., 1995). At this stage, children take others' opinions more and more seriously and often seek out those opinions on a variety of matters. Achievement motivation, it turns out, is just one peer-related concern among many.

What Do You Think?

Survey several classmates about their current learning orientations and the extent to which those orientations grew out of middle childhood experiences. What advantages and disadvantages do you see in each of these orientations?

As discussed in the multicutural view, active encouragement and support from parents plays an important role in fostering academic achievement during the middle years.

school children are due to low levels of achievement motivation, parental expectations, or parental support. What, then, accounts for the decreasing academic achievement of minority elementary school children and increasing rates of academic failure and dropping out in junior and senior high school? One possibility is that teachers and staff may have lower academic expectations for minorities, who are overrepresented in the low academic tracks compared with other student groups, leaving these students with both inadequate preparation and unrealistic expectations about the academic demands of junior and senior high school (Reed, 1988). As these children approach adolescence, the schools they attend and the families in which they live fail to adequately meet their emerging needs for intellectual challenge and academic support, for adult supervision and independence, and for relationships with teachers and parents that enable them to believe a relationship exists between their academic efforts and the rewards available to them in American society (Eccles, 1993; Stevenson et al., 1990).

PEER RELATIONSHIPS

Throughout childhood, some of children's most important relationships involve peers. The peer group is second only to the family as a context within which developmental changes occur (Hartup, 1989). As early as age two, children enjoy playing with or next to one another, and by age three or four they often prefer the company of peers, even when adults are available. Time spent with peers increases steadily during middle childhood. By the late elementary school years, about one-half of children's social interactions are with peers (Ellis et al., 1981).

What Theorists Say about Peer Relationships

Piaget According to Jean Piaget, one important function of peers is to help school-age children overcome their *egocentrism,* or their tendency to assume everyone views the world in the same way they do (Piaget, 1963). In the course of playing together, children inevitably run into conflicts over toys and priorities, arguing over who should use a new set of felt pens or over what and where they should draw. In settling such disagreements, children gradually come to understand and value different points of view, a capacity that is central to living successfully in a pluralistic, democratic society.

In Piaget's view, the ability of parents and other authority figures to foster these cognitive developments is limited because they cannot behave as true equals with children. Often adults give orders to children, and although they may give them pleasantly ("Please clean up your room before dinner"), they expect compliance, not discussion or negotiation. Even parents who treat their children with greater respect and equality cannot really function as equals with children. For one thing, they often lack the same leisure interests and tastes. For another, parents' skill levels often do not match their children's; a mother and daughter may both enjoy cooking, but the child cannot do it as well as her mother can. The mother can become "equal" with her child only by pretending to be less experienced than she really is.

Sullivan   The most comprehesive theory about peers was proposed by Harry Stack Sullivan (Sullivan, 1953; Youniss, 1980). Like Piaget, Sullivan argued that relationships with peers have fundamentally different qualities than those with adults. In particular, peers foster skills in compromise, cooperation, and competition. But unlike Piaget, Sullivan emphasized the value of peers in promoting emotional health. Peers create a life for children outside their families, and in doing so they help correct the emotional biases families inevitably give their children, biases that Sullivan called emotional **warps**. For instance, an eight-year-old with shy, reserved parents may learn from peers that not all people are shy and reserved. Or a ten-year-old whose parents care little about competitive athletics may discover from peers that athletic competition matters quite a lot to some people.

According to Sullivan, this form of learning occurs during the **juvenile period,** which begins around age five and continues until nine or ten. In this period, children show increasing interest in playmates of similar age and status. As they near the end of the elementary school years, they supposedly focus this interest on just a few select friends of the same sex, whom Sullivan called *chums.* These relationships provide children with models for later intimate relationships.

Support for Theories about Peer Relationships   Research on peer relationships supports Piaget's and Sullivan's ideas in broad outline, but not in certain specifics. Conflict with peers does stimulate children's progress in solving cognitive problems, as Piaget proposed. Two seven-year-olds do learn from a discussion with each other about whether "the oldest people are always the tallest," but they learn only if they are already thinking at about the same level of maturity (N. Bell et al., 1985). Otherwise, such discussions easily turn into confrontation and browbeating as the more advanced child forces the other to comply with her point of view.

Research also supports Sullivan's claim that playmates and peers matter a lot to school-age children. Some relationships become closer and more important than others, of course, but few actually become intimate in the sense Sullivan proposed. Children's comments about intimacy in friendship do increase greatly between childhood and adolescence, although friendships in which children share their most private or personal thoughts and feelings probably are relatively rare (Berndt, 1988; Youniss, 1980).

Peer relationships acquire a special intensity during late childhood and the transition to adolescence that typically occurs between fifth and seventh grades. During this period, children have increased unsupervised contact with peers and begin to place greater importance on peers' approval, views, and advice. At the same time, they spend less time with their parents and display greater emotional distance and psychological independence from them (Brown, 1990; Larson & Richards, 1991).

The Functions of Peers

All things considered, peers probably serve a variety of purposes, including some that duplicate the functions of parents. Like parents, peers can give a child a secure emotional base during anxiety-provoking experiences. Sometimes the mere presence of a friend increases a child's confidence in such situations; observing another child being examined by the dentist, for example, tends to calm the observing child when her turn comes (Melamed et al., 1975). Like parents, peers help define ethical norms for a child. Peers also help define friendship in particular, although, contrary to widespread belief, standards of likability parallel those of adults more often than not (Hartup, 1983, 1989). Also like parents, peers do a lot of teaching: they show a child how to paint or how to throw a ball. Sometimes schools take advantage of this process by arranging for children to tutor one another in academic skills (Allen, 1976). The accompanying Perspectives Box discusses the nature and function of peer activities.

Children's reliance on peers versus parents for help appears to increase with age. According to fourth-graders, friends provide support less frequently than do mothers and fathers, the most frequent providers. Seventh-graders, however, believe same-sex friends and parents are equally supportive, whereas tenth-graders view same-sex friends as the most frequent source of support (Furman & Buhrmester, 1992). Peer activities appear to serve several main functions. First, they provide a context for sociability, enhancement of relationships, and a sense of belonging. Second, they promote concern for achievements and a reliable and integrated sense of who one is. Finally, they provide opportunities for instruction and learning (Zarbatany et al., 1990).

Although the functions of children's relationships with peers show considerable similarity to those with adults, several features are unique to peer relationships. Attachments with parents and other adults or older children are "vertical and complementary," meaning they involve individuals who have greater knowledge, competence, and social power. Peer relationships, in contrast, are "horizontal and symmetrical" in that they involve individuals of approximately equal knowledge, competence, and social power (Hartup, 1989). They are by nature voluntary and involve reciprocal relationships among comparative equals. These facts mean a child must act in a way that explicitly supports the relationship—be friendly, that is—if he expects the relationship to survive. And he must do so with another individual whose social skills may be little better or even a bit worse than his own. Children apparently understand these differences intuitively, because they typically attribute an obedience orientation to relationships between adults and children but attribute play and recreation orientations to relationships among children (Berndt, 1988; Youniss, 1980).

Influences on Peer Group Membership

Most of children's peer interactions occur in groups. In defining a peer group, elementary school children emphasize the importance of shared activities such as talking, hanging out, walking to school, talking on the telephone, listening to music, playing games, and just acting silly; however, sharing attitudes becomes most important as children approach adolescence (O'Brien & Bierman, 1988; Zarbatany et al., 1990). Living in the same neighborhood, attending the same school, and participating in the same community organizations all contribute to the likelihood that peer groups will form.

The Psychological Functions of Preadolescent Peer Activities

Peer activity is a central feature of middle childhood. It plays an important role in acquiring skills and knowledge and developing the personal and interpersonal goals that guide and give meaning to children's behavior and values. To learn more about the psychological functions of pre-adolescent peer activities, Lynne Zarbatany, Donald Hartmann, and Bruce Rankin asked fifth- and sixth grad-ers from middle-class neighborhoods in Canada to keep weeklong diaries of important types of peer activities (Zarbatany et al., 1990). Children also kept track of the specific behaviors their peers exhibited during each activ-ity and which behaviors they liked and disliked. A second group of fifth- and sixth-grade children then rated the fre-quency of each activity, its importance, and which positive and negative behaviors they would most (or least) like to occur during the ten most frequently reported activities.

Table 13.1 lists the twenty most common activities re-ported and how girls and boys ranked the importance of each. As expected, some gender differences were found. Boys preferred contact and noncontact sports more and played more contact sports than girls did, whereas girls tended to rate talking about hairstyles, clothing, shop-ping, attending church, and baby sitting higher than boys did and spent more time in these activities.

Such peer activities appear to serve three major func-tions. First, they provide a context for sociability, en-hancement of relationships, and a sense of belonging. Second, they promote concern for achievement and self-worth. Third, they provide opportunities for instruction and learning. Peers also provide validation from others of emerging aspects of the self, such as attitudes, interests, and worthiness, and serve as a comparison group against which children can gauge their skills and abilities. Accep-tance and inclusion by peers and opportunities for assess-ing the unique capabilities of self are important functions served by preadolescent peer activities.

Different peer activities appeared to support different psychosocial achievements. For instance, noncompetitive activities such as TV watching and "hanging out" provide opportunities for socializing and enhancing relationships but less opportunity to identify unique aspects of the self. In contrast, competitive activities such as noncontact sports are less relationship oriented but enable young-sters to evaluate their own unique skills and abilities.

These researchers see several implications in their findings. First, children may require exposure to a variety of activities to benefit from the full range of psychosocial experiences. For example, cultural norms that limit a girl's exposure to team sports may deprive her of oppor-tunities to learn skills important to the world of work, such as negotiation and conflict resolution. Likewise, a boy's strong investment in team sports and lower interest in relationship-oriented activities such as baby sitting or talking on the telephone may inhibit the development of skills for establishing intimacy.

The results also suggest that peer behavior is best un-derstood in terms of the activity in which it occurs. For example, behaviors that are supportive may promote re-lationships while watching TV or listening to music, but may support skill achievement or a greater sense of self-worth in noncontact sports activities.

Finally, the effectiveness of a behavior may depend on the nature of the activity in which it appears. For exam-ple, while humor tended to be a highly desired behavior, indiscriminate use of humor was not particularly valued while playing team sports, where it could be misinter-preted as criticism. Similarly, criticism and "nagging" were not much of a problem while traveling to and from school with friends, but could create difficulty if they oc-curred while eating in the cafeteria, where chances for public embarrassment were much greater.

TABLE 13.1 Peer Activities of Fifth- and Sixth-Graders

Activity	All	Boys	Girls
*Noncontact sports	1	1	4
*TV/music	2	2	1
*Conversing	3	4	2.5
*Telephone	4	6.5	2.5
*Physical games	5	3.5	5.5
Parties	6	3.5	7
Hanging out	7	6.5	8.5
Acting silly	8	8	10
*Shopping	9	13.5	5.5
Cards/board games	10	7	15.5
*Contact sports	11	5	22
Baby sitting	12	15	8.5
Secrets	13	13.5	11
Clubs (e.g., scouts)	14	10	13
Play with pets	15	9	17
*Academic	16	13	15.5
Arts and crafts	17	15	14
*Travel/school	18	10.5	17.5
Walking to school	19	13.5	18
*Eating	20	12	21.5

Importance columns: All, Boys, Girls

* = ten most frequently reported activities.
Source: Adapted from Zarbatany et al. (1990).

Listed above are the twenty most important peer activities reported, ranked in order of importance for fifth- and sixth-grade boys and girls combined and separately for girls and boys. With the exception of shopping and contact sports, two highly gender-stereotyped activities, boys and girls are quite similar on which of the ten most frequently reported activities are most important.

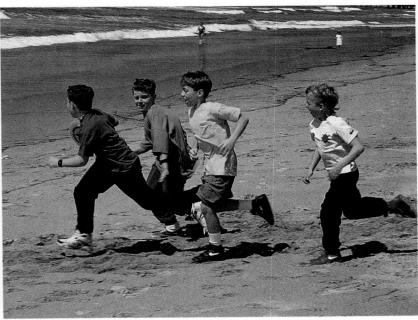

During the middle years, children tend to associate with peers of the same sex. Girls' friendships tend to be more intimate, whereas boys' friendships often reflect male stereotypes.

Children's peer groups are not simply random assortments of individuals but are influenced by many factors. Three of the most important factors are age, gender, and race or ethnic background. Let us look briefly at each of these in turn.

Age Children play mostly with others of approximately the same age and, when asked, say they prefer to be friends with their agemates. But contrary to a common impression, schoolchildren may spend anywhere from one-quarter to one-half of their time with companions who are more than two years older or younger and say they prefer to seek help and comfort from older children (Ellis et al., 1981; French, 1984). School imposes an upper limit on these cross-age contacts, however, because classrooms usually group children according to age.

Groups with mixed ages have certain special qualities. Older children show more nurturant behavior, such as tying the shoelaces of a younger child or buttoning the child's sweater. Younger children show greater dependence by asking for help with schoolwork or agreeing to older peers' preferences for play activities. However, mixed-age groups also tend to be less "sociable" than same-age groups; they chat or have friendly conversations less often, for example. Same-age groups encourage the opposites of all of these qualities: children give and receive less practical help, show more friendliness to one another, and get into conflicts more often (Brody et al., 1983; Furman & Buhrmester, 1992).

Gender Although mixed-gender play occurs during the elementary school years, first-graders generally name children of their own gender as best friends. Observations of younger schoolchildren during free play show that during cooperative play periods, they interact about four times as often with children of their own gender as they do with those of the opposite gender (Maccoby & Jacklin, 1987). This ratio actually increases as children approach adolescence; by third grade most peer groups contain only one gender, and by fifth grade virtually all do. As children move into middle school and adolescence, however, the trend reverses (Shrum et al., 1988).

How do we interpret this tendency toward gender-based separation during middle childhood? Eleanor Maccoby argues that gender differences emerge primarily in social situations and vary with the gender composition of the dyads (two-person relationships) and groups involved (Maccoby, 1990). She suggests that children spontaneously choose same-gender playmates even in situations where they are not

Working with   Lisa Truong, FOURTH-GRADE TEACHER

Reducing Gender Role Stereotyping in Play

Lisa Truong is a fourth-grade teacher at a "follow-through" elementary school that serves students from citywide head-start preschool and kindergarten programs as well as children from the local neighborhood. Her classroom is a well-organized, friendly, cheerful place filled with children's drawings and other projects. Lisa provides richly detailed observations of gender differences in peer group and play activities among fourth-graders.

Rob: How would you describe peer relations among fourth-graders?

Lisa: Often children's academic ability sets the tone and pace for their friendships. Children who do well academically tend to be friends with other kids who are bright.

Rob: Why do you think this is so?

Lisa: In part because of parent pressure. Parents are interested in their children having good friends. Another reason

may be that much of the teaching here occurs in small skill groups. These group children with the same academic needs together. They also focus on group dynamics, teaching the children to work with other people. When we go outside for recess, the children do tend to stay in those same groups.

Rob: What other factors seem to influence peer groups?

Lisa: Boy-girl differences are very important. As much as I've tried to encourage girls to play football or soccer and boys to do things like four-square and jump-rope, it really does break down by gender as to how they play outside. Girls tend to play jump-rope, and boys tend to play soccer on the field—it's almost automatic. Girls also tend to go to the swings and slide much more than the boys.

Rob: Why do you think this happens?

Lisa: At this age, girls are getting more

social and interactive. Often I see girls walking slowly and talking. Even their jump-rope is more consistently interactive and coordinated—with turn taking and things like that—than the boys' play. You should see the girls play four-square! It involves a lot of verbal interaction and social coordination.

Rob: How so?

Lisa: Four people stand in a 10-foot-by-10-foot square drawn in chalk and divided into four smaller squares. The person in the fourth square is in control of whatever the category will be. So, for example, that person will say "Colors" and then bounce the ball into any of the other players' squares. They will have to name a color and catch the ball, or they're out.

Rob: There's a rhythm to it?

Lisa: You have to keep the rhythm, and you can't name the same color

under pressure from adults to do so because they find same-gender play partners more compatible.

During the preschool years, two factors seem to be important. First, the rough-and-tumble style and emphasis on competition and dominance that is characteristic of boys appear to be unappealing to most girls, who in general prefer play that is more cooperative and less aggressive. Second, girls discover that boys are becoming increasingly unresponsive to their influence and, therefore, avoid playing with them. At a time when children are actively involved in learning how to influence their play partners and integrate and coordinate activities with those of others, girls discover that their growing reliance on polite suggestion to influence others is increasingly ineffective with boys and, therefore, avoid choosing boys as playmates (Maccoby, 1990).

The idea that playmate selection may be more heavily influenced by sharing gender-based play activities than by merely being of the same gender is supported by a recent laboratory study of choice of playmates among six-to-eight-year-olds reported by Gerianne Alexander and Melissa Hines (Alexander & Hines, 1994). When given the choice of selecting a playmate based on gender versus preferred style of play, style of play appeared to be more important for both boys and girls. Boys chose female playmates who had masculine play styles (including toys, rough-and-tumble play, and activity level), whereas girls chose male playmates with more feminine play styles.

Girls' long-term friendships more often tend toward exclusive intimacy than boys' do. One study tested this idea by using a questionnaire that invited children to name their best friends (Eder & Hallinan, 1978; Hallinan, 1981). The differences they found in friendship patterns between boys and girls are illustrated in Figure twice—or animal, country, movie star, or whatever the category is. The categories get more complex as the year goes on. The kids almost always start the year with colors, and by the end of the year it will be something much more specific, like Madonna's songs or names of rock stars. This group of girls also made up a great hand-clapping game about music groups; the way they thought it through and the rules they made up were fascinating.

Rob: What are the boys doing?

Lisa: They're playing soccer and kickball, building forts, or skateboards, if they can. Or they'll collect things and investigate the environment. At the beginning of the year, we studied insects and their natural habitats in science. Once the boys got outside, they tried to find every single little bug they could, and they would come in and show it.

Rob: It seems fourth-grade boys are less interested in make-up games than girls.

Lisa: Yes, that's true. Boys tend to play games that emphasize physical rather than social interaction and where they follow rules that are already made up for them.

Rob: How permanent are these peer group patterns?

Lisa: They seem long-lasting. The group I described was made up of five girls who are very, very close. They're all good students, and all happen to be white. I've been trying to encourage them to be less of a clique and interact with other people more.

Rob: How else might teachers encourage greater interaction?

Lisa: Our school is committed to helping children interact in a way that doesn't break down along sex role or racial lines. I talk to them about it

very up-front, and I say I think there should be more interaction between boys and girls and blacks and whites. When we have social studies activities, the rule is that groups will be mixed. The children understand this and help make it work.

What Do You Think?

1. Lisa's observations of her students illustrate how closely play and social development are interrelated. What examples in the interview demonstrate this?

2. How has Lisa attempted to reduce gender role stereotyping in her fourth-graders' peer group and play activities? Based on this chapter, what additional things might she consider trying?

3. Discuss how Lisa's observations demonstrate the interaction of physical, cognitive, and social domains in her fourth-graders' development. How are the three domains reflected in gender differences in peer groups and play activities?

13.1. The girls more often made mutually exclusive choices (dyads, or two-person relationships). Triads, in which a third girl's choice was not reciprocated, also occurred more often. Boys more often formed patterns in which no choice was reciprocated. Several boys might have picked one another as friends, even though no one was picked in return. Judging by these choices, boys spread their social attention widely, whereas girls tend to focus it on just a few individuals. Stated differently, boys' friendships tend to be extensive, and girls' friendships tend to be intensive.

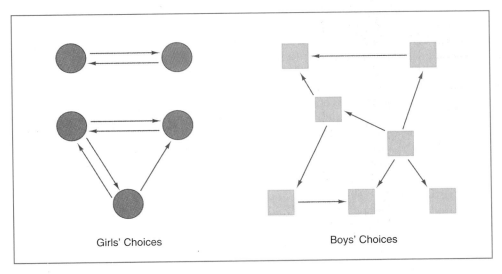

Girls' Choices   Boys' Choices

FIGURE 13.1

Typical Patterns of Peer Friendships among Girls and Boys
Girls' friendships tend to involve reciprocal, two-person relationships and three-person relationships in which a third girl's choice is not reciprocated. Boys more often form patterns in which no choice is reciprocated.

Differences between school age girls and boys sometimes reflect culturally supported gender stereotypes.

Over time, children find same-gender play partners more compatible and segregate themselves into same-gender groups. As children enter adolescence, childhood patterns carry over into cross-gender interactions in which girls' styles may put them at a disadvantage. While patterns of mutual influence may be more symmetrical in intimate male-female couples, the distinctive styles of the two genders are still present and subsequently manifest themselves in the roles and relationships of parenthood (Maccoby, 1990).

Gender Boundaries   Alan Sroufe and his colleagues have used the concept of gender boundaries to help explain the influence of gender on peer relationships during middle childhood and preadolescence. *Gender boundaries* refer to the elaborate system of rules and rituals that surround cross-gender interactions between boys and girls. The cycle of teasing and retaliation that a ten-year-old boy endures from his peers at summer camp when he is seen leaving a girls' tent (where he went only to get his radio) reflects the seriousness of the boundaries and of the consequences if they are crossed. The boy is obligated to retaliate by chasing and hitting his tormenters to reestablish his place in the group (Sroufe et al., 1993).

Based on extensive videotaped observations of ten-to-eleven-year-old children participating in summer day camps, Sroufe and his colleagues found that preadolescents face a complex developmental task of maintaining a clear gender boundary while simultaneously finding opportunities to express interest in and learn about members of the other gender. Same-gender friendships promote the learning of skills for group functioning and prevent premature heterosexual intimacy, while the taunting, name calling, and chase games that occur between groups of boys and girls allow them a safe, protected way to explore cross-gender relationships. Table 13.2 lists some of the "rules" that appear to regulate middle childhood gender boundaries in a day camp setting.

Adult norms and expectations regarding gender stereotyping can also make a significant difference. For example, children growing up in families that downplay gender typing in their childrearing values and practices are less stereotyped in their activities, interests, and gender-typed beliefs. Such children seem able to understand and use *both* gender-typed and non-gender-typed beliefs and behaviors related to gender. However, gender flexibility in children's play behavior or friendship preferences is more likely to be evident in situations where it is supported, or at least not actively discouraged, by parents, teachers, and other adults (Hoffman, 1989; Maccoby, 1990; Moorehouse, 1991; Weisner & Wilson-Mitchell, 1990).

For interesting firsthand observations and discussion of the role of gender in peer group play, see the Working With interview on page 410.

Race and Ethnic Background   Patterns of segregation and preferences based on racial and ethnic differences are a fact of life in much of our society (Asher et al., 1982; Shrum et al., 1988). Racial and ethnic awareness are especially important during middle childhood, because children of this age are in the process of committing themselves to society and to the values and standards of the majority culture. They are also developing their own self-concepts.

TABLE 13.2 *Gender Boundary Rules of Middle Childhood: Under What Circumstances Is Contact with the Other Gender Permissible?*

Rule:	The contact is accidental.
Example:	You're not looking where you are going and you bump into someone.
Rule:	The contact is incidental.
Example:	You go to get some lemonade and wait while two children of the other gender get some. (There should be no conversation.)
Rule:	The contact is in the guise of some clear and necessary purpose.
Example:	You may say, "Pass the lemonade," to persons of the other gender at the next table. No interest in them is expressed.
Rule:	An adult compels you to have contact.
Example:	"Go get that map from X and Y and bring it to me."
Rule:	You are accompanied by someone of your own gender.
Example:	Two girls may talk to two boys, though physical closeness with your own partner must be maintained and intimacy with the others is disallowed.
Rule:	The interaction or contact is accompanied by disavowal.
Example:	You say someone is ugly or hurl some other insult or (more commonly for boys) push or throw something at them as they pass by.

Source: Sroufe et al. (1993), Table 1, p. 456.

Racial segregation and racial preference often reflect certain types of prejudice. *Prejudice* is a positive or negative attitude toward an individual based solely on the person's membership in a particular group. Prejudices are frequently based on *stereotypes,* patterns of rigid, overly simplified, and generally inaccurate ideas about the characteristics of another group of people. Stereotypes often involve negative ideas associated with race, ethnic or cultural background, religion, social class, age, gender, and sexual orientation. While prejudices based on stereotypes do not necessarily determine a person's overt behavior, they often do. Frequently prejudice is associated with *discrimination*—actions toward members of the targeted group, such as exclusion or mistreatment, that reflect prejudicial attitudes toward that group.

Studies that asked children to name their friends have found that children are more likely to name peers of their own race, particularly if that race is the majority one. This trend begins in the preschool years and increases over middle childhood until children reach junior high school (Asher et al., 1982; Shrum et al., 1988; Singleton & Asher, 1979). Additional research is needed to explore how factors such as residential patterns, neighborhood, and school characteristics influence children's cross-race peer preferences (DuBois & Hirsch, 1990).

Can racial and ethnic prejudice be reduced? A school setting that is ethnically diverse may foster peer interactions and friendships among different ethnic groups. A study of kindergartners and third-graders in a school that was extremely ethnically diverse found that children of European-, Hispanic-, African-, and Asian-American backgrounds interacted and formed friendships with cross-ethnic as well as same-ethnic peers (Howes & Wu, 1990). But although close cross-race friendships are more likely to develop in integrated schools, they are difficult to maintain outside of school unless the children live in interracial neighborhoods or participate in team sports or other integrated activities (DuBois & Hirsch, 1990; Howes & Wu, 1990).

Cooperative learning experiences that allow mixed groups of children to work as a team to achieve common academic goals also have had some success in fostering cross-race acceptance and enhancing children's self-esteem (Johnson et al., 1984; Katz & Zalk, 1978; Slavin, 1986). In one program based on this "jigsaw" technique, children from different racial and ethnic backgrounds were assigned to different parts of a single project. They quickly learned to work together to complete the task and developed more positive feelings about both themselves and one another (Aronson & Bridgeman, 1979).

A school setting that is ethnically diverse may foster peer interactions and friendships among children from different ethnic groups.

Elementary school programs that emphasize multicultural competence and awareness by integrating multicultural activities in both academic and extracurricular activities and actively involve children's families and other community members in school activities can successfully foster friendship and peer acceptance among students from different racial, ethnic, and cultural backgrounds (Bojko, 1995). *Magnet schools* that use specialized programs in science, language, or the arts to attract students from school districts representing a variety of ethnic and cultural backgrounds have also succeeded in increasing diversity on a long-term basis (Rossell, 1988).

Popularity, Social Acceptance, and Rejection

Early in middle childhood, children begin to evaluate one another in various ways. By second and third grades, children already hold cultural stereotypes about body build; for example, they judge boys who are muscular more favorably than boys who are fat or thin (Staffieri, 1972). Easily noticed characteristics, such as having the "right" hairstyle or an attractive-sounding name, are quite important to acceptance in the early grades. As children get older, they increasingly choose their friends on the basis of personal qualities such as honesty, kindness, humor, and creativity (Furman & Bierman, 1983; Reaves & Roberts, 1983). However, they still evaluate one another and confer more popularity on some children than on others.

The Popular Child   When peers are asked to evaluate one another's popularity, or likability, by "nominating" whom they like most or would choose to play with, children generally are classified as "popular" or as occupying one of three unpopular statuses: "rejected," "controversial," or "neglected." Popular children receive many positive and very few negative votes from their peers; rejected children receive many negative and few positive peer nominations; controversial children receive many positive and negative peer nominations; and neglected children receive few positive or negative nominations (Coie et al., 1982).

Popular children are viewed by their peers as being confident, good-natured, kind, outgoing, and energetic (Dodge, 1986; Hartup, 1983). Highly visible abilities and achievements help, especially in athletics, but also in academics or social activities. Stylish clothing and special material possessions, such as an expensive fashion watch, also influence status with peers.

Popular children are well liked; they easily initiate and maintain social interactions and understand social situations. They possess a high degree of interpersonal skills and tend to behave in ways that are prosocial, cooperative, and in tune with group norms (Asher et al., 1982). In studies of play groups of seven- and eight-year-olds who did not previously know one another, successful, popular children demonstrated their social skills by first observing how the group functioned, then conforming to the behaviors that were expected, and finally commenting positively on the group's activities (Dodge et al., 1983; Dodge et al., 1986). Some of these assets, such as peer competence and athletic ability, remain valuable to children as they move into adolescence, and others (such as the fashion watch) may not. But during childhood, such advantages create prestige for individual children within particular peer groups and also make membership in the "best," or highest-status, groups possible. Because of the importance of peer relationships during the school years, the interpersonal competencies associated with peer acceptance and popularity are likely to have a positive impact not only on a child's current adjustment but also on her or his longer-term psychological well-being.

The Unpopular Child   Peers describe unpopular children, particularly those classified as "rejected," as unpleasant, disruptive, selfish, and having few positive characteristics. Such children are likely to exhibit socially inappropriate aggression, hyperactivity, inattention or immaturity, and, not surprisingly, behavioral and academic problems in school (Bierman et al., 1993). Because they lack the social skills needed to successfully join and participate in peer groups, they are blamed by peers for their own deviance and are often actively disliked and excluded from activities (Coie et al., 1991; Dodge et al., 1990; Juvonen, 1991; Pope et al., 1991).

Unpopular children may behave aggressively or selfishly without realizing it. Ironically, since they tend to be excluded from groups, they find few chances to learn new ways of relating.

Among both boys and girls, the highest levels of aggression are displayed by children who are classified as unpopular-rejected. However, girls and boys appear to differ in the form their aggressive behavior most typically takes. Boys are more likely to attack peers through *overt aggression* (such as hitting, pushing, or verbally threatening to hurt others), whereas girls are more likely to display *relational aggression* involving harming others through purposeful manipulation and damage of their peer relationships (Crick & Grotpeter, 1995).

The likelihood of aggressive behavior is also influenced by social context. For example, one study of seven-to-nine-year-old African-American boys found that aggressive behavior between two children was more likely in group situations characterized by a tense, negative atmosphere; high levels of aversive verbal and nonverbal behavior, such as criticizing, teasing, grabbing, and pushing; high levels of competitiveness; and low levels of cooperation and group cohesion (DeRosier et al., 1994).

Family and neighborhood contexts also are important. In a large-scale study of second-through-fifth-graders, Janis Kupersmidt and her colleagues found that problems with aggression and peer rejection are most likely for low-income African-American children from single-parent homes and least likely for middle-class white children (Kupersmidt et al., 1995). Living in middle-class neighborhoods had a strong protective effect on aggressive behavior and peer rejection, particularly among those African-American children from low-income, single-parent homes who also lived in such neighborhoods.

For children living in war zones or in other violence-plagued communities where gang and drug activity and the wounding and killing of friends and relatives are everyday occurrences, the developmental toll is immense. Youngsters who are exposed to ongoing violence suffer from chronic emotional distress, learning problems, sleep disturbances, and preoccupation with their own safety and the safety of those they depend on and care about. They are also more likely to have problems with aggression, impulse control, and conflict resolution in both school and non-school settings, although how successfully they cope with their circumstances depends also on the support and guidance they get from family members and school personnel (DeAngelis, 1991; Garbarino, 1992; Kozol, 1995).

Considerable success in reducing aggression and fostering prosocial behavior has been reported for school-based intervention programs designed to teach older elementary and junior high school children assertiveness and interpersonal cognitive problem-solving skills (Hudley & Graham, 1993; O'Donnell et al., 1995; Shure & Spivak, 1988). While there is good reason to believe that peer rejection and childhood aggression can be reduced by improving social support and overall neighborhood life, no studies of such interventions have been reported so far.

Friends   During the early middle years, friendships provide an arena for "activity and opportunity"; children base friendships on shared interests and activities, exchanges of possessions, and concrete supportive behaviors (Rawlins, 1992; Selman, 1981). "A friend," according to one six-year-old, "is someone who plays what *you* want to play." Another says, "A friend lets you use his painting set." These comments emphasize the child's own needs rather than the friend's. But even when all parties are considered, friendships among younger school-age children tend to focus on practical behaviors rather than on psychological qualities:

TONY *(age eight)*: Benjy, if you share your Galactica rocket with me, I'll be your friend.
BENJY *(also age eight)*: Give me another piece of candy, will you? Then we'll see.
TONY: But I already gave you three pieces. Come on, can't I play with your rocket?
BENJY: It's really *my* rocket.
TONY: I'm your friend, so you should give me a turn.
BENJY: Not now. Maybe later. Where's the candy?

As children move into later childhood and preadolescence, *equality* and *reciprocity* become key elements of friendship interactions. Exchanging favors and sharing activities continue to matter as children get older, but by the time they enter fifth and sixth grades, they place greater emphasis on psychological qualities such as intimacy, trust, mutual support, and loyalty (Keller & Wood, 1989; Rawlins, 1992). Friendship begins to involve a concept of a relationship based on a reciprocity between equals, each with distinct but compatible personalities. Sharing between friends shifts from an unreflective, symmetrical reciprocity based on "tit-for-tat" to a cooperative reciprocity involving a more mutual and deliberate sharing of assistance and resources that are intended to serve as tokens of friendship (Rawlins, 1992; Youniss & Volpe, 1978). Actually doing the same things or sharing the same objects becomes correspondingly less important.

To some extent, this change reflects children's increasing ability to coordinate social perspectives, meaning they increasingly see themselves as others view them. Younger children realize that in many situations two people see things differently, but they nonetheless have trouble coordinating their own perspectives with those of friends. As a result, they often alternate between trying to change their friends' viewpoints to fit their own and trying to make themselves feel the same way their friends do.

By second or third grade, children become better able to live with differing perspectives within their friendships and feel less pressure to choose between one or the other. By fifth or sixth grade, children can even adopt an independent, or third-party, perspective, comparing their own point of view with their friends' (Berndt, 1988; Furman & Bierman, 1984; Selman, 1980). As one eleven-year-old put it about a good friend, "He thinks that I don't study enough, and that he studies just about the right amount for schoolwork. But you know what *I* think? I think that I'm just trying to keep schoolwork from bothering me too much, and that *he* works too hard. I wonder what the teachers think." Judging by statements such as this, friendship at this stage appears to be an intimate collaboration between two people who are mutually committed to building the relationship, which has acquired an importance beyond the particular needs of either friend.

The quality of middle childhood friendships is also important. While children with low, medium, and high peer group acceptance report having friends, better-accepted children are more likely to be involved in friendships that include higher levels of validation and caring, help and guidance, conflict resolution, and intimate exchange and lower levels of conflict and betrayal. The friendships of children with low levels of peer acceptance are more problematic in these areas. Low levels of friendship quality and low peer acceptance both contribute to children's feelings of loneliness and social dissatisfaction and together can seriously undermine children's feelings of well-being (Parker & Asher, 1993).

Conformity to Peers

Because peer groups involve social equals, they give children unique opportunities to develop their own beliefs without having parents or older siblings dominate or dismiss them. But in doing so, peer groups also present challenges. Acceptance and support by groups matter intensely to children, who are still learning what kind of people they are and acquiring the skills they need to interact with others. As a result, peer groups often influence their members very strongly indeed: they demand conformity to group expectations in return for continued acceptance and prestige.

Pressures to conform sometimes lead children to violate personal values or needs or those of parents and other adult authorities (Fine, 1982). One child might feel pressured into paying dues she cannot afford, joining fights she does not want to participate in, or shunning children who do not belong to her own group. Another might feel pressured to wear clothes that his parents consider outrageous or to perform poorly at school. In return for these behaviors and attitudes, the children remain in good standing with their peers. Despite these differences, however, there tends to be high agreement between peer group and parents on important issues such as moral and ethical standards, standards of appropriate behavior, schooling, and future goals (Damon, 1988).

Peer groups can exert positive pressures as well. For example, they can encourage athletic achievement above and beyond what physical education teachers can generate in their students, and they can create commitments to fairness and reciprocity, at least within an immediate circle of peers: "When someone buys a candy bar at the drugstore, she shares it with the rest of us. Then we do the same thing the next time if *we* get something nice." Whether the pressures are positive or negative, however, peer groups offer a key setting for acquiring social skills, evaluating and managing personal relationships, and handling competition and cooperation.

A study of the natural, self-selected peer groups of fourth- and fifth-graders conducted by Thomas Kinderman (1993) found that children tend to associate with peers who share similar norms regarding involvement in school. Children who were academically oriented and highly engaged in school tended to affiliate with classmates who had similar motivational orientations; the same was true for children who were disengaged from school and lacked academic motivation. Although their memberships changed somewhat during the year, peer groups remained quite stable with regard to their norms regarding academic orientation.

What Do You Think?

Children's growing exposure to peer group influences during middle childhood is a source of concern for both parents and teachers. What advice might you give to parents and teachers regarding the best ways to deal with this challenge?

FAMILY RELATIONSHIPS

Despite the growing importance of peers, families continue to influence children's development strongly during middle childhood. However, parental influence differs from that of peers due both to their greater experience and psychological maturity and to the greater material resources and power they possess. In this section, we discuss how the particular circumstances and characteristics of families affect family relationships and psychosocial development during middle childhood.

The Quality of Parent-Child Relationships in Middle Childhood

During middle childhood, as children gradually learn more about their parents' attitudes and motivations and the reasons for family rules, they become better able to control their behavior. This change has a major impact on the quality of relations between school-age children and their parents (Galinsky, 1987). Parents find themselves monitoring the moment-to-moment behavior of their children less closely than in earlier years. They need not always watch carefully as their child pours a glass of milk, and they do not always have to remind him to use the toilet before getting in the car.

Nevertheless, parents do continue to monitor children's efforts to take care of themselves, but in more indirect ways (Maccoby, 1984). Instead of simply arranging for a child's friend to visit, parents increasingly use comments such as "If you want to have Lin sleep over next week, you'd better call by tomorrow." Instead of helping their child put on each item of clothing in the morning, they will more likely

This mother's willingness to help her son pursue his interests—in this case, build a wooden truck from a model kit—illustrates an important aspect of effective parent-child relationships during the middle years.

confine themselves to some simple reminder ("It's time to get dressed") on the assumption that the child can take care of the details of dressing.

These changes contribute to one stereotype of parenting during the middle years: the notion that parenting consists only of fixing meals, providing taxi service, and enforcing a few rules. In reality, this stereotype does not take into account the activities parents and children often still do together, from shopping to watching television to holiday celebrations. It also fails to consider the emotional ties that underlie these activities. If children have become securely attached during the preschool years, they and their parents often enjoy each other's company more than ever during middle childhood.

By this period, parents and children have accumulated a history of experiences together that makes family relations increasingly unique and meaningful. One study documented this idea by analyzing letters school-age children wrote to a local newspaper about "What Makes Mom Great" (Weisz, 1980). Many of the children said they valued their mothers' enduring presence in their lives: "She is always there to listen," said one child. They also valued the empathy or sensitivity their mothers provided: "She always seems to know how I feel." These comments imply that the bonds between parents and children typically are very strong during middle childhood.

The Changing Nature of Modern Families

The stereotype of a typical family—a father who works, a mother who cares for the family full time—shows little similarity to families of today. In 1955, 60 percent of families in North America fit this popular stereotype. By the early 1990s, only 7 percent of North American families conformed to this model (Children's Defense Fund, 1993; Hodgkinson, 1985).

Today an increasing number of mothers work outside the home. Currently two out of three married women with children under eighteen are employed, more than double the rate in 1960 (Statistical Abstracts of the United States, 1995a). When both single and married women with children under eighteen are considered, more than half are employed outside the home, a trend that is expected to increase

During middle childhood, the quality of parent-child relationships may vary with changing developmental needs and family circumstances.

"*During the next stage of my development, Dad, I'll be drawing closer to my mother—I'll get back to you in my teens.*"

through the year 2000 (United States Department of Labor, 1992). Figure 13.2 summarizes this trend.

Divorce also has become much more common (see Figure 13.3). Between 1960 and 1993, the U.S. divorce rate tripled, with half of all marriages in the United States ending in divorce. Approximately 25 percent of children younger than eighteen live in single-parent households, 88 percent with their mothers and 12 percent with their fathers. It is estimated that children of divorce spend an average of six of their first eighteen years in a single-parent home (Children's Defense Fund, 1993; Statistical Abstracts of the United States, 1995b). Because approximately two-thirds of divorced parents remarry, most children of divorce will live in a *reconstituted family* consisting of parent, stepparent, siblings, and stepsiblings. And in almost half of these cases, the second marriage will end in divorce as well (Glick & Lin, 1987; Hetherington et al., 1989).

Divorce and Its Effects on Children

Most parents who divorce must make major adjustments in their lives, and these adjustments often affect their children deeply. First, many divorcing parents face sudden economic pressures. Some find themselves financially responsible for two households, that of their former spouse and children and that of the new spouse and children. Many divorced mothers must take on new or additional employment to meet their household responsibilities, and even so their standard of living frequently declines. For many of these women, a reduction of economic resources often is accompanied by dependence on welfare; poorer-quality housing, neighborhoods, schools, and child care; and the need to move to a neighborhood they can afford, which often leads to loss of social support for the child from familiar friends, neighbors, and teachers. In contrast, both noncustodial and custodial fa-

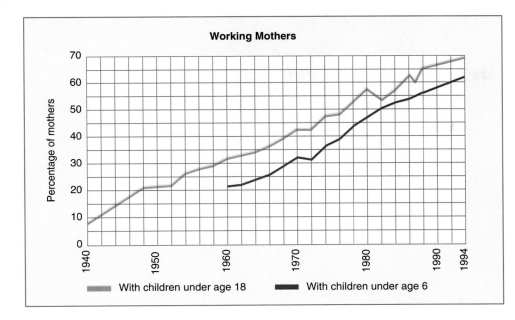

FIGURE 13.2
Percentage of Working Mothers, 1940-1990
The long-term trend for working mothers with children is expected to increase through the year 2000.
Source: Statistical Abstracts of the U.S. (1995a)

thers are more likely to maintain or improve their standard of living following divorce (Hetherington et al., 1989).

Divorce involves many psychological pressures as well. The parent who takes primary custody of the children must learn to manage a household alone, which is a major physical and psychological burden. Some parents may feel deeply isolated from relatives or friends to whom they used to feel close. If relatives do live nearby, divorcing parents often must rely on them for the first time, simply to procure help with child care and household work. Yet these helpers may disapprove of the divorce.

Even before actual separation and divorce, many such families go through long periods of distress, tension, and discord. For most, these pressures continue to create stress for two or three years following separation (Hetherington et al., 1982; Hetherington et al., 1989).

Divorce is especially hard for children during middle childhood. Having outgrown the self-centeredness of the preschool years, school-age children increasingly identify with and rely on their parents as role models to help them establish their own sense of who they are and how they should behave. At a time when children are just learning to be independent from home life, divorce threatens the safe base

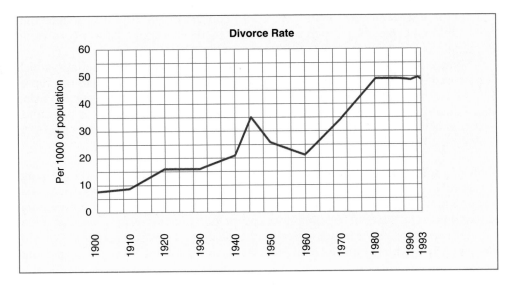

FIGURE 13.3
Percentage of U.S. Marriages Ending in Divorce, 1900–1990
Since the middle 1980s, approximately half of all marriages in the United States have ended in divorce.
Source: Statistical Abstracts of the U.S. (1995b)

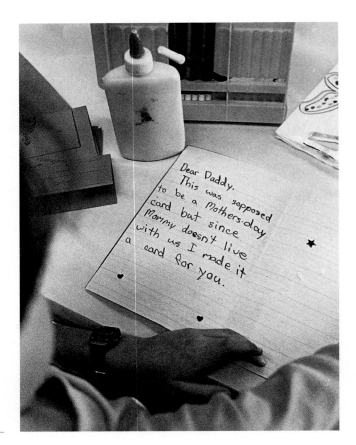

For children of divorce, Mother's Day and other family holidays serve as painful reminders of the changes and losses that have occurred. Children often respond to such challenges in creative ways.

they have come to rely on to help make increasing independence possible. The loyalty conflicts frequently created by parents who are competing for their children's allegiance can make children fearful that they will lose one of their parents in the process.

Judith Wallerstein conducted a long-term follow-up study of middle-class children who were between six and eight years old at the time of their parents' divorce. She found that even ten years later, these children were burdened by fear of disappointment in love relationships, lowered expectations, and a sense of powerlessness. When compared to children who were older or younger at the time of the breakup, middle-childhood children fared far worse in their emotional adjustment and overall competence, including school and social relationships. The profound unhappiness with current relationships and concerns regarding future ones that these children experienced often were masked by their overall conformity to social expectations (Wallerstein, 1987, 1989). (See Table 13.3.)

Some critics have questioned the degree to which Wallerstein's findings, which were based on naturalistic, case study techniques with a middle-class sample, represent the entire population of parents and children of divorce. Future research using more quantitative approaches and families from a broader range of backgrounds will help determine the validity of her findings (Hetherington & Furstenberg, 1989; R. Weiss, 1989).

Differing Effects on Boys and Girls   On the whole, girls and boys tend to respond differently to divorce. Boys often express their distress in *externalizing* ways, becoming more aggressive, willful, and disobedient during the period surrounding separation and divorce. They often lose access to the parent with whom they identify most strongly—their father—because the majority of divorced children live with their mothers and are more frequently victims of parental power struggles and inconsistencies in matters of discipline (Santrock & Warshak, 1979). In a study of children six years after divorce, Mavris Hetherington (1988, 1991) found that whereas mothers and daughters had reestablished close and positive relationships, problems between mothers and sons persisted. Whereas the most common parenting style for divorced mothers with daughters was authoritative, the most common style with sons was authoritarian and the next most common permissive, suggesting that mothers either tried to control their sons' behavior with power assertiveness or gave up trying. In addition, girls may encounter increased risk of sexual abuse from stepparents and parents' dating partners in the period following divorce (Spacarelli, 1994).

Girls appear to become less aggressive as a result of divorce, tend to worry more about schoolwork, and often take on more household responsibilities. This suggests they are *internalizing,* or holding inside, their distress by trying to act more helpful and responsible than usual (Block et al., 1981). Daughters of divorced parents may also become overly preoccupied with their relationships with males. They are more likely to become involved in dating and sexual activities at an early age, sometimes before the end of elementary school, and more likely to get pregnant and have conflict-ridden relationships with males during their teen years (Wallerstein, 1987; Wallerstein & Blakeslee, 1989; Wallerstein & Kelly, 1980).

Certain factors can help reduce the negative effects of divorce during the school years. Perhaps the most important are parents' efforts to reduce their own conflicts and cooperate in providing the best parenting possible for their children (Kline et al., 1989). Also important is the appropriate use of professional help to successfully work out postdivorce arrangements, resolve emotional conflicts more effectively, and develop the skills needed to sustain strong and supportive parent-child relationships (Stolberg & Walsh, 1988).

Custody Arrangements   Relationships between parents and children frequently deteriorate during and immediately after a divorce. The parent with physical custody of the children (usually the mother) finds herself dealing not only with her

TABLE 13.3   *The Psychological Tasks of Children of Divorce*

Task 1: Understanding the divorce	Children must first learn to accurately perceive the immediate changes that divorce brings. Later they learn to distinguish between fantasized fears of being abandoned or losing their parents and reality so that they can evaluate their parents' actions and draw useful lessons for their own lives.
Task 2: Strategic withdrawal	Children and adolescents need to get on with their own lives as quickly as possible and get back, physically and emotionally, to the normal tasks of growing up. This poses a dual challenge to children, who must actively remove themselves emotionally from parental distress and conflict to safeguard their individual identities and separate life course.
Task 3: Dealing with loss	Children must overcome two profound losses: the loss of the intact family, together with the symbolic and real protection it provided, and the loss of the presence of one parent, usually the father, from their lives. They must overcome the powerful sense of rejection, humiliation, unlovableness, and powerlessness they feel and feelings of self-blame for causing the divorce.
Task 4: Dealing with anger	The major task for children is to resolve their anger at being hurt by the very people they depend on for protection and love. They must recognize their parents as human beings capable of making mistakes and respect them for their efforts and courage.
Task 5: Working out guilt	Young children often feel responsible for divorce, thinking their misbehavior may have caused one parent to leave. They need to separate from guilty "ties that bind" them too closely to a troubled parent and go on with their lives.
Task 6: Accepting the permanence of the divorce	At first, children's strong need to deny the divorce can help them cope with the powerful realities they face. Over time, they must accept the divorce as a permanent state of affairs.
Task 7: Taking a chance on love	Achieving realistic hope regarding relationships may be the most important task for both the child and society. Children must create and sustain a realistic vision of their own capacity to love and be loved, knowing that separation and divorce are always possible. Mastering this last task—which depends on successfully negotiating all of the others—leads to psychological freedom from the past and to a second chance.

Source: Adapted from Wallerstein & Blakeslee (1989).

children but also with major new responsibilities for earning a living and making peace—at least in her mind—with the reality of divorce (Hetherington et al., 1989).

Parents without physical custody of the children (usually fathers) do not face these daily hassles, but they do report feeling rootless, dissatisfied, and unjustly cut off from their children. Seeing his children every other week or on school vacations may prevent a father from knowing them intimately and being part of their everyday lives, and lead him to become increasingly reliant on special events (such as going to Disney World), when contacts do occur. Noncustodial parents may also believe their financial and emotional support for their children go unappreciated. Perhaps for these reasons, although fathers often increase the amount of time they spend with their children immediately after divorce, they soon decrease such time well below what it was before the divorce (Furstenberg et al., 1982; Hetherington et al., 1989).

Sometimes parents are able to establish *joint custody,* a legal arrangement in which parental rights and responsibilities continue to be shared in a relatively equal manner. The mechanics of the arrangement vary with the child's age and the family's circumstances. The children may live with each parent during alternate weeks, parts of weeks, or even parts of the year. Or, when the children are older, one or more children may live with one parent and the rest with the other parent. Joint custody tends to promote greater contact with both parents after divorce, facilitate fathers' involvement, and make mothers' parenting responsibilities less burdensome. Its success, however, depends on parents' willingness and ability to rearrange their lives and maintain the levels of mutual respect and cooperation required to make this arrangement work (Arditti, 1992).

Remarriage and Blended Families   Most divorced parents remarry within a few years, creating **blended families** consisting of the remarried parents and their children. The most common type of blended family occurs when a mother marries a man who does not have custody of his children by a previous marriage. In these situations, the stepfather and stepchildren must somehow acknowledge the previous attachments they bring to the new family. Children must recognize and accept the fact that their new stepfather has other children, about whom he cares a great deal, living somewhere else. Also, the new stepfather must accept the fact that his stepchildren have another, "real" father somewhere and strong attachments to their mother.

Younger children appear able to eventually form an attachment with a competent stepparent and to accept the stepparent in a parenting role. Older children and young adolescents are more vulnerable and less able to adapt to the transition of remarriage due to the developmental tasks they face. Stepfathers who establish parent-child relationships based on warmth, friendly involvement, and mutual respect rather than on assertion of parental authority are more likely to be accepted by boys. The same qualities apply to girls as well, although daughters, especially those approaching adolescence, appear to have a more intense and sustained negative psychological reaction to their mothers' remarriage and more difficulty accepting and interacting with their new stepfathers (Giles-Sims & Crosbie-Burnett, 1989; Hetherington, 1989; Vuchinich et al., 1991). Stepmothers generally are more emotionally involved and take a more active role in discipline than stepfathers do, but gaining acceptance from the stepchildren is not easy for them either (Ganong & Coleman, 1987; Hetherington et al., 1989).

More difficult challenges arise when both parents bring children from previous marriages to live in the same household. The children must learn to get along not only with the parents but also with one another despite the prolonged distress of previous divorces. Parents in this type of blended family report especially high rates of stress and daily conflict, at least during the first year or two of the new marriage (Hetherington et al., 1989; Hobart, 1987; Santrock & Sitterle, 1987).

Table 13.4 presents suggestions for parenting during or following divorce.

TABLE 13.4   *Suggestions for Divorcing Parents with School-Age Children*

1. Don't pretend that the divorce is "good," and don't expect your child to appreciate your reasons for the divorce.
2. Avoid assigning blame for the divorce or criticizing the other party in your child's presence.
3. Reassure your child that she or he did not cause the divorce and will continue to be loved and cared for by both parents.
4. Don't put your child on the spot by involving him or her in divorce-related decisions.
5. Keep your child informed about divorce-related events and decisions in a timely and frank manner.
6. Avoid making changes in your child's normal routines as much as possible.
7. Allow your child full freedom to express his or her feelings both to you and to other trusted adults.

Here are some suggestions for helping children handle parental dating and remarriage:

1. Wait until you know your new romantic interest fairly well before arranging for your friend and your child to spend time together.
2. Allow your child to get used to this person gradually, at the child's own pace.
3. Keep your child informed about your relationship, but don't force your child to make decisions about it.
4. Involve your child in plans regarding living arrangements, marriage, and other important changes in an appropriate manner.
5. Seek agreement with your new partner or spouse on childrearing philosophy and practices.

Source: Adapted from Philadelphia Child Guidance Center (1994), pp. 85–90.

The Effects of Work on Families

Work affects family life profoundly, although not always in simple or straightforward ways. Jobs determine daily schedules, of course, which in turn affect how much time parents have for their children. Job schedules also influence which parent or child does particular household chores. At a more subtle level, work affects parents' self-esteem and thus their happiness as human beings and as parents. Jobs also determine income and therefore affect many aspects of family life (Greenberger et al., 1994; Kohn et al., 1986). All of these effects are magnified by the fact that an increasing number of families are headed by two working parents or by a single parent who works.

Effects of Maternal Employment   Despite the once popular view that mothers should stay at home to care for their children, research suggests that maternal employment as such usually does children no developmental harm (Hoffman, 1984). What does matter is whether a woman chooses to work or not to work. Mothers who can make this choice and who live in relatively supportive families apparently suffer no setbacks in their relations with their children. Mothers who feel forced either to work or not to work are less fortunate; they report more stressful relations with their children.

However, maternal employment often does influence children's development in some ways. Most of these influences are positive, or at least not negative. For example, families with working mothers divide housework and child care more evenly than do families without employed mothers (Hoffman, 1983). In dual-worker families, fathers do some household chores relatively more often and spend more time alone with their children (although mothers still do the majority of housework and child care). In families with working mothers, children often are expected to help with household chores and caring for younger brothers and sisters. It is quite common for a parent to instruct her ten-year-old to pick up several things from the grocery store, set the table, and put the casserole in the oven.

The blend of housework and breadwinning seems to create less stereotyped attitudes in the children of working mothers regarding the "proper" roles of mothers and fathers. Both sons and daughters witness nurturant behavior in their fathers

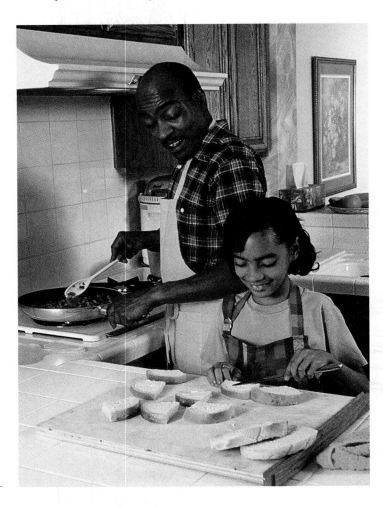

In families where mothers work, other family members often share household responsibilities. Sometimes this results in less stereotypic role models of male and female behavior.

and occupational competence in their mothers. Especially as they approach adolescence, children are likely to support women's employment in general (Hoffman, 1989; Scarr, 1984), and daughters usually expect to work outside the home when they get older. Studies of school-age children of employed women indicate that they are as well or better adjusted and hold less rigid views of gender roles than do children of women who do not work outside the home (L. Hoffman, 1980, 1984a, 1984b; Moorehouse, 1991).

Many working mothers compensate for possible negative effects of their employment through more frequent shared activities or "quality time" with their children. A high level of shared mother-child activities serves as a buffer against the long hours and other disruptive demands of full-time jobs. Also, children are likely to match or exceed their peers in school achievement and adjustment when shared mother-child activities are more frequent (Moorehouse, 1991).

Effects of Paternal Unemployment   Involuntary paternal unemployment can create significant economic, social, and psychological disruption for children and their families. Loss of income can require parents and their children to make major sacrifices in their lifestyles. In many cases, the search for a new job or for affordable housing may cause a family to uproot itself, forcing children and parents to leave their friends and social support network behind. Leaving their existing school and neighborhood peers and gaining acceptance in a new neighborhood and school is particularly difficult during middle childhood (Liem & Liem, 1988; McLoyd, 1989; Price, 1992).

Children who experience family economic hardship are vulnerable to a broad range of difficulties, including peer relations, academic performance, and psychological adjustment. However, the impact of such hardships is significantly influenced by how severe they are, how long they last, and how well parents can mobilize their material and psychological resources to deal with adversity while continuing to provide good parenting for their children (Bolger et al., 1995).

After-School Care   Dividing energies between home and work can be challenging. One common challenge working parents face is finding after-school supervision for their children. In cases where after-school programs do not exist and siblings, friends, and other relatives are not available, older (and sometimes younger) elementary-school-age children are left at home by themselves. Many parents in this situation carefully work out after-school procedures, including strict limits on what a child may do and a checkup phone call from work to ensure that everything is okay; others leave their children to their own resources.

How different after-school care arrangements affect children appears to depend on the quality of the programs, family economic resources, and neighborhood safety. Jill Posner and Deborah Vandell (1994) recently compared the effects of formal after-school programs with three other arrangements (mother care, informal adult supervision, and self-care) for a sample of low-income third-graders from nine urban schools. They found that attending after-school programs was associated with better grades and conduct in school as well as better peer relations and emotional adjustment.

Children who attended such programs were exposed to more learning opportunities, spent more time in enrichment lessons (such as music and dance), and spent less time watching TV and in unstructured neighborhood activities than children in other forms of care. For many low-income children, enrichment lessons and team sports typically were unavailable unless the children participated in an after-school program.

Formal after-school programs provided more structured activities with adults and peers, such as regular periods of intensive, one-on-one academic work with teachers and involvement with adults and peers in plays, musical programs, and cooperative art projects. They also positively influenced children's academic performance and conduct in school, work habits, and emotional adjustment. In contrast, unsupervised activities in their urban neighborhoods presented opportunities to engage in undesirable behaviors with deviant peers.

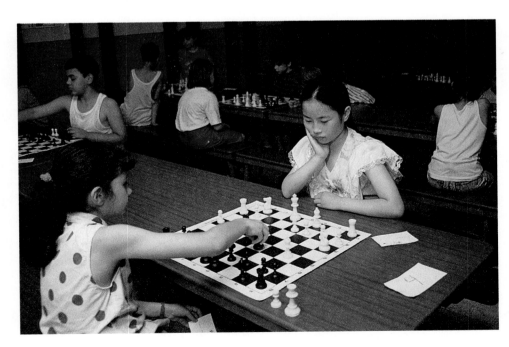

Well run after school-programs such as the one in the picture provide a safe, supervised environment and interesting activities for children whose parents work schedules prevent them from being at home after the school day.

Formal after-school programs may be less important for children who live in communities that provide safe and constructive after-school opportunities. Nevertheless, even for these children, close parental monitoring of their after-school plans and activities and authoritative parenting (respectful acceptance and firm control) tend to promote academic performance and social adjustment as well as keep them out of trouble. Lower levels of such parental involvement and stressful, unsupportive family circumstances are associated with poorer academic and social adjustment and more problem behaviors (Galambos & Maggs, 1991; Steinberg, 1986; Vandell & Ramanan, 1991).

Other Sources of Social Support

So far we have emphasized two major sources of social experiences for children: peers and parents. Most middle-childhood children establish other sources of social support as well. One study documented this fact by interviewing schoolchildren about people, places, and activities that they found satisfying and helpful in conducting their lives (Bryant, 1985). To stimulate the children's thinking, the interviewers took them on long walks around their neighborhoods. From time to time, the interviewers asked questions about what they saw ("Do you know who lives there?"; "Is this where you go to relax?").

This approach revealed a large number of social supports for school-age children (see Table 13.5). Many children reported seeking out adults other than their parents, especially grandparents, to talk with and confide in. Family pets, and sometimes even neighbors' pets, also served as confidants. Children reported using hobbies to unwind and feel better about themselves (although some of the hobbies, such as collecting stamps or playing a musical instrument, were relatively nonsocial). Other children reported having special hideaways where they went to be alone for awhile. Many children sought out peers for activities when they needed an emotional lift or felt confused; but this was not the case on every occasion, and not all of the children did so.

In general, as children moved through middle childhood, their sources of support increasingly broadened. This made them better able to manage particular stresses, whether inside or outside their families. At all ages during the elementary school years, children seemed happiest when they reported the widest range of social supports and when that range emphasized informal rather than formal supports.

TABLE 13.5 **Sources of Support Reported by School-Age Children**

Support	Average Number Mentioned in Interviews
Homes and informal meeting places where child feels free to visit	5.5
Peers and siblings named among ten most important individuals	4.5
Formally sponsored activities (public library, community pool, church or temple)	4.5
Adults (including parents) named among ten most important individuals	3.0
Hobbies that child attributes to self	2.3
Special places to go to be alone	2.1
Pets (including neighbors') considered as a special friend	1.7
Make-believe friends and make-believe identities	1.6
Grandparents and others of grandparents' generation named among ten most important individuals	1.3

Source: Bryant (1985).

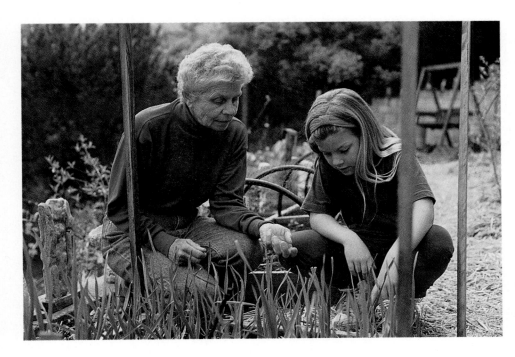

During the school years, grandparents and other adults and older children within and outside the immediate and extended family provide invaluable sources of social support for children.

What Do You Think?

What are your views about the impact of maternal employment on child development? In what ways do your views reflect your own experiences as a child?

SCHOOL INFLUENCES

Next to the family, school probably is the single most important developmental influence during middle childhood. Each year children spend more than eleven hundred hours at school and often many additional hours in school-related activities. According to Erik Erikson (1963), school is one of the main arenas in which children resolve the crisis of industry versus inferiority. Interactions with teachers and peers give children important opportunities to develop cognitive and social skills, gain knowledge about the world, and cultivate peer relationships (see the discussion of peers earlier in this chapter) that are central to the development of self-concept during the middle years.

School Culture

Each school has its own culture, which includes the values, beliefs, traditions, and customary ways of thinking and behaving that make it unique and distinguish it from other schools and institutions. One school may especially value its innovative academic programs and the high achievement levels of its students, another the degree of student involvement in school-sponsored activities, and a third the active involvement of parents in providing special resources. The closer the fit between the school culture and the values and expectations of the children (and families) it serves, the more likely it is that the school's developmental impact will be positive. Students both learn and feel better in classrooms in which the instructional approach, pattern and rhythm of verbal interaction and student participation, and strategies for motivating students are in tune with their family and cultural expectations (Minuchin & Shapiro, 1983; Tharp, 1989).

The Informal Curriculum

Schools influence children through two curricula. The **formal curriculum** helps children acquire the academic knowledge and skills thought to be necessary for successful participation in society. The **informal curriculum**—the implicit norms, expectations, and rewards for certain ways of thinking and acting that are conveyed by a school's social and authority relationships—teaches students the social roles and behaviors society expects. The left side of the report card, which evaluates a child's academic performance, reflects the formal, more explicit curriculum; the right side, which includes such areas as attendance, work habits, social skills, cooperation, competition, friendship, gender roles, sexuality, and relationships to other racial and ethnic groups, reflects the informal, or "hidden," curriculum (Ruble, 1983; Thorne, 1986).

Teacher Influences

With the exception of their parents, most elementary school children spend more time with their teachers than with any other adults. Teachers therefore play a very significant role in the lives of middle-years children. Observational studies of daily classroom life reveal that the elementary school teacher engages in as many as one thousand interpersonal exchanges with pupils each day (Cazden, 1988). Many of these interactions involve communicating academic material, regulating students' verbal and nonverbal activity, evaluating student participation and providing feedback, dispensing supplies, and keeping track of time so things go as scheduled.

Teachers' styles of classroom management vary considerably. However, all effective teachers establish learning environments that are calm, predictable, and engaging and provide smooth transitions from one activity to the next. Effective teachers also stay on top of the classroom situation by keeping in tune with their students, in both their communication of academic content and their responses to the constantly changing social and emotional needs of thirty or more children (Linney & Seidman, 1989).

Teachers' beliefs and expectations regarding their students' potential also can affect students' performance and overall school adjustment by changing students' behavior in the anticipated direction and thereby serving as a *self-fulfilling prophecy.* Early research by Robert Rosenthal and Lenore Jacobson found that when elementary school teachers were given information that falsely identified randomly selected students as potential academic "bloomers," those gains actually did occur for first- and second-graders but not for students in grades three through six (R. Rosenthal & Jacobson, 1968). Although they were generally unaware of doing so, the teachers treated students for whom they had high expectations differently, giving them more challenging materials and demanding (and more frequently rewarding) better performance (Brophy, 1983; M. Harris & Rosenthal, 1985).

Teachers may also unintentionally communicate negative expectations of students who don't conform to their own. Ray Rist closely observed a single classroom of African-American students in an urban elementary school on a daily basis, from the first day of kindergarten through the last day of third grade. He found that by the eighth day of kindergarten, the teacher had assigned students to permanent "slow-learner," "average," and "fast-learner" groups. Because she had no knowledge of the children's academic ability or cognitive development, her evaluation was based primarily on students' economic status. Children who were assigned to the slow-learner table turned out to be those who were poorly dressed and whose families were on welfare; students who were middle class in their dress and behavior were seated together in the average or fast-learner groups. A similar pattern of classroom organization was repeated by their first- and second-grade teachers, the only difference being that these teachers based their decisions on children's test scores and readiness material from the prior year rather than on their subjective judgments. The result of this "objective" placement was to reinforce the social class divisions initiated by the kindergarten teacher (Rist, 1973).

Rist and other investigators have found that these different groups within the same classroom receive different treatment. The fast-learner group is much more likely to receive academic assignments and the slow learners busywork. In most grades, the teacher directs two to five times as much control-oriented and somewhat less supportive behavior toward the slow-learner group than toward the fast-learner group. Controlling behavior includes verbal and nonverbal reprimands, time-out, and physical restraint; supportive behavior includes verbal praise, smiles, and hugs (Dusek, 1985).

The Student's Experience

What do students experience in the classroom? According to Philip Jackson (1968, 1986), delay, denial, interruption, and social distraction are among the most prominent aspects of children's classroom experiences. Particularly in traditional, teacher-centered classrooms, students spend a great deal of time waiting for the teacher or other students, denying fulfillment of their needs until given permission to do so by the teacher, and contending with distractions and social disruption. Students must wait to ask a question, wait to get permission to leave their seats, wait to have a question answered, wait for the next assignment, or wait for their chance to use the stapler (Jackson, 1968).

Research by Karen Duffy (1996), who asked college students to recall their most memorable school experiences, supports the idea that for many students school is not a positive experience. Out of forty students, thirty-four reported nonacademic experiences that were negative, including being belittled and mistreated by teachers and being exposed to physical violence among classmates.

Although these observations are cause for concern, many classrooms are conscientiously organized to minimize these difficulties and provide a learning environment that is academically stimulating and supportive of children's developmental needs (Lightfoot, 1983). For example, small class size and teachers' aides can increase the quality of classroom life for both students and teachers (Finn & Achilles, 1990). The *open classroom* approach, which encourages children to take an active role in the learning process, and *cooperative learning* techniques, which support children of varying abilities in working together to achieve both individual and shared learning goals, also have proven to enhance the quality of classroom life and students' psychological and academic performances (Horwitz, 1979; Slavin 1990a, 1990b).

Effective schools provide an environment with clear rules and expectations, effective controls, open communication, high nurturance, and respectful relationships that encourage students to participate as fully as possible in school and classroom life. Not surprisingly, effective teacher-student relationships tend to be authoritative in that their qualities parallel those of the authoritative parenting style discussed earlier in the chapter.

Finally, effective school environments provide children with opportunities to freely interact with and form developmentally beneficial relationships with children of different ages, developmental levels, and backgrounds. Many of the peer-related developments discussed earlier in this chapter occur in school-related settings. Further discussion of schooling appears in Chapter 16.

The preceding discussion has by no means exhausted what is known about the impact of schools on middle-years children. However, it is clear that school experiences play a major role in how children experience and interact with others, how they perceive and feel about themselves, and how they generally develop psychosocially.

Waiting to be called on in class can sometimes seem to take forever. Unfortunately, in many classrooms, waiting to get the teacher's attention constitutes a major aspect of a student's experience.

What Do You Think?

How did teacher expectations influence your own elementary school performance?

BEYOND CHILDHOOD

In a variety of ways, middle childhood is the time when a child becomes a person in a more adult sense than ever before. This happens partly because the child has begun accumulating considerable experience with other people of roughly the same age and maturity and partly because of cognitive developments. Children begin setting goals and working toward them in more adult ways by taking into account others' opinions about their achievements as well as their own interest in learning.

As we point out several times in this chapter, the developments of the middle years do not always result in happy feelings and experiences. With their newly developed maturity, children are able to hurt and snub some of their peers as well as make new friends, and they are now able to worry about peer evaluations as well as be commendably open-minded. Life has not gotten happier just because the child has gotten older, but it is not necessarily unhappier either.

Taken together, these experiences create a new, more mature sense of self within children of this age, one that has more inward or psychological properties than that of early childhood. In the years ahead, during adolescence, this psychological self becomes still more elaborate. Contrary to widespread belief, the adolescent years do not necessarily prove any more or less difficult than the middle childhood or early childhood years do, although some individuals, for special reasons, encounter unique challenges.

SUMMARY OF MAJOR IDEAS

Psychosocial Challenges of Middle Childhood

1. During middle childhood, children face challenges concerning the development of an identity or a sense of self, achievement, peer relationships, family relationships, and school.

The Sense of Self

2. During middle childhood, children develop a sense of self, acquire a belief in self-constancy and in relatively permanent psychological traits, and learn to distinguish their thoughts and feelings from those of others.

The Age of Industry and Achievement

3. According to some psychodynamic theorists, schoolchildren repress their earlier romantic attachments to their parents and focus instead on developing a sense of industry and achievement.

4. During middle childhood, children shift their achievement orientation from an exclusive focus on learning, or task orientation, to a performance orientation that includes others' responses to their achievements.

Peer Relationships

5. Piaget believes that peers help children overcome their egocentrism by challenging them to deal with perspectives other than their own.

6. According to Sullivan, peers help children develop democratic ways of interacting and also offer the first opportunities to form close or intimate relationships with others.

7. In general, peers seem to serve unique functions by creating voluntary relationships of equality among children.

8. Groups of peers vary in membership and behavior in terms of age, gender, and race or ethnic group. Peer groups tend to segregate themselves by both gender and race.

9. Popular children possess a number of socially desirable qualities, including well-developed social skills and confidence in themselves. Unpopular children exhibit less desirable qualities, such as aggression, selfishness, and bossiness.

10. Early in middle childhood, a friend is someone with whom a child shares activities and toys, but later in this period a friend becomes someone whom the child can count on and with whom she or he can share intimacies.

11. Peers exert pressure to conform on individual children, and this pressure can have either positive or negative effects.

Family Relationships

12. In recent years, divorce has become more common in North American families and usually creates stress for all members of the family, although girls and boys react differently to divorce.

13. Blended families, which result from remarriage, pose considerable challenges; however, younger children form attachments with stepparents more easily than adolescents do.

14. Many mothers now work at least part time, and their employment generally does not seem to have any negative effects on their children. Nevertheless, maternal employment influences the division of household labor and children's attitudes about gender roles.

15. When fathers are unemployed, both they and their families experience significant stress.

16. Providing good after-school supervision is a challenge for working parents. For children in unsupportive environments, formal after-school programs offer considerable benefits.

17. Schoolchildren often find emotional support from adults other than parents, as well as from friends, pets, and hobbies.

School Influences

18. Children are influenced by their school's culture. This influence is more likely to be positive if the school's culture and the child's familial culture are compatible.

19. The informal, or hidden, curriculum—the school's implicit values, norms, and expectations—has a subtle but powerful effect on children.

20. The environment a teacher creates and his or her expectations of students shape children's school experiences.

21. From the students' perspective, school is often a place where they may encounter denial of needs, interruptions, delays, and social distractions. Cooperative learning and open classrooms, however, can contribute to greater student involvement and learning.

KEY TERMS

peers *(395)*
sense of self *(397)*
self-constancy *(398)*
latency *(400)*
industry versus
 inferiority *(401)*
achievement
 motivation *(401)*

learning orientation *(401)*
performance
 orientation *(402)*
warp *(406)*
juvenile period *(406)*
blended family *(424)*
formal curriculum *(430)*
informal curriculum *(430)*

FOR FURTHER READING

Axline, V. *Dibs: In Search of Self.* New York: Ballantine, 1964.

This classic tells the true story of how a boy with an emotional disturbance eventually overcame his disability with the help of therapists and others. The story reveals several ways a disability can interfere with the usual challenges of childhood, especially the challenge of identity development.

Dunn, J. *Brothers and Sisters.* Cambridge, Mass.: Harvard University Press, 1985.

This book describes how siblings' relationships evolve during childhood, especially middle childhood. The author cites many vivid examples of brothers and sisters getting along and failing to get along. The examples challenge many common assumptions about siblings, such as the belief that siblings' fighting shows that siblings do not care about one another. On the contrary, in some situations siblings seem to understand one another better than their parents do.

Kidder, T. *Among Schoolchildren.* Boston: Houghton Mifflin, 1989.

Based on teaching and observational experience, this book vividly and sensitively describes the ups and downs of life in school from both the teacher's and the students' perspectives.

Klagsbrun, F. *Married People: Staying Together in the Age of Divorce.* New York: Bantam Books, 1985.

This book explores the reasons some marriages improve and flourish the longer they last, whereas others dissolve quickly and still others persist under considerable tension. The author describes interviews with numerous couples and uses their comments to suggest why some marriages survive longer than others do.

Kotlowitz, A. *There Are No Children Here.* New York: Anchor Books, 1989.

Kozol, J. *Amazing Grace: The Lives of Children, the Conscience of the Nation.* New York: Crown Publishers, 1995.

Here are two vivid and moving firsthand accounts of what community and family life are like for minority children growing up in a large, poor, inner-city neighborhood.

Philadelphia Child Guidance Center. *Your Child's Emotional Health: The Middle Years.* New York: Macmillan, 1994.

This is a clearly written guide for parents about emotional development during the middle years. It offers practical advice about how to deal with such issues as sexuality, fear, discipline, sibling rivalry, and depression and how to distinguish between normal and troubled behavior.

Wallerstein, J., and S. Blakeslee. *Second Chances: Men, Women and Children a Decade After Divorce.* New York: Ticknor & Fields, 1989.

This rich, readable book describes the results of a long-term study of the lives of families that have undergone divorce. The use of case studies brings the experiences of the children and their parents to life.

PART SIX

Adolescence

The adolescent years present new and unique challenges for children. They must come to terms with their bodies as they suddenly grow taller and become sexually mature. They must establish more equal relationships with their parents. And they must come to grips with the need to leave home eventually and become independent individuals.

How stressful these challenges prove to be depends on a variety of circumstances. For some teens, the timing of puberty can make these years especially hard (or easy). For others, their newly forming ability to reason abstractly can make life seem suddenly confusing at the same time it reveals exciting new possibilities for the future. For most young people, dating, or even just talking to, the opposite sex proves both intriguing and frustrating as they slowly overcome childhood tendencies to relate only to members of their own sex. All in all, the changes of adolescence can be difficult, but on average they are neither more nor less challenging than those children face during other periods of life.

14

ADOLESCENCE

Physical Development

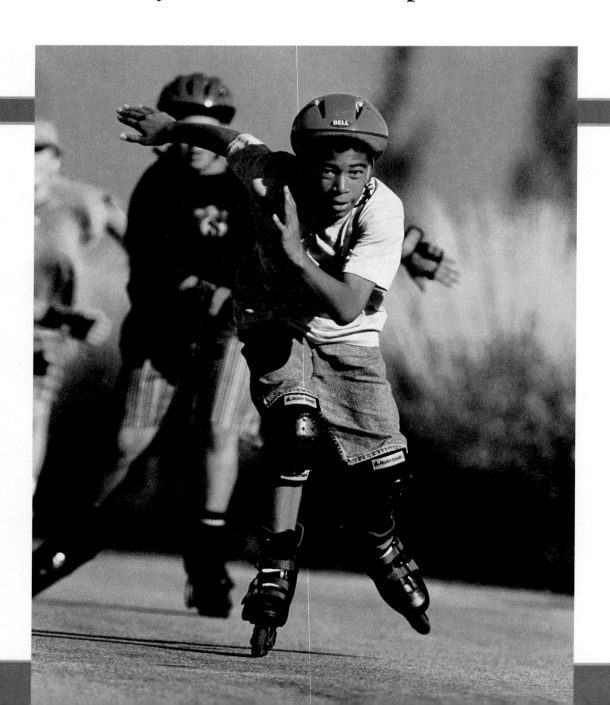

The Concept of Adolescence

Adolescence: From Idea to Social Fact
Theoretical Views of Adolescence

Growth in Height and Weight

The Secular Trend

Puberty

Primary Sexual Maturation
Maturation of Secondary Sex Characteristics
Hormonal Changes and Their Physical
   Consequences
The Extent of Physical Sex Differences

**Psychological Effects of Physical
Growth in Adolescence**

Body Image and Self-esteem
Early- Versus Late-Maturing Adolescents

Health in Adolescence

Continuity with Health in Childhood
Causes of Death among Adolescents
Adolescent Health Problems

Finally Young Adults?

Focusing Questions

- What is meant by *adolescence,* and what changes in society contributed to its gaining recognition as a developmental stage?

- What changes in height and weight can be expected during adolescence, and how do they differ for girls and boys?

- What is puberty, and what important physical changes occur for girls and boys during this process?

- What are the social and emotional effects an early, "on-time," and late pubertal development, and how do they differ for girls and boys?

- What major health problems do adolescents face, and why are adolescents more at risk than other age groups?

D avid is fourteen. Ever since the beginning of last summer, there have been some very noticeable changes in the way he looks and acts. He has grown nearly two inches in the last six months, and his mom jokes that his pants and sleeves will have to be reintroduced to his ankles and wrists before too long. But this rapid growth is no joking matter to David. Although he was well coordinated and athletic in junior high school, he is now clumsy, constantly tripping over himself and bumping into things. Rather than being an advantage, his increased height seems to be limiting his ability to play baseball, his favorite sport.

David's voice is changing too. Sometimes it sounds the way it always has; at other times it is deeper, like his father's. But often it seems to bounce around out of control, cracking and breaking as it fluctuates between the two. David has definite signs of a mustache on his upper lip and the fuzzy beginnings of a beard on his cheeks. Although David has become very shy and modest about his body lately, his dad has noticed that he has hair under his arms and around his pubic area.

David's personality also has changed. Usually a pretty easygoing and responsible person who is a pleasure to be around, he now seems very moody and self-centered. He blows up or sulks at unpredictable times and often fails to do what is expected of him around the house or at school.

David's sister, Miriam, is twelve. In the past year, she too has been undergoing some striking physical changes. Not only has she gained three inches and thirteen pounds, but it is obvious to everyone that her body is rapidly changing. Her bust and hips have filled out, and she has considerable curves where just a year ago she had none at all. Miriam has begun to menstruate and, like David, has grown hair under her arms and in her pubic area. Like her brother, she has become much shier and more uncomfortable about her body. Although she seems proud of becoming a woman, she easily blushes when someone mentions how grown-up she has become, and she worries that she is too fat.

Except for her increased shyness and embarrassment about the changes in her body, Miriam has shown no striking changes in personality. She is much less willing to wrestle with her brother than she was just a few months ago, but she continues to be quietly responsible around the house and to do well at school. She lives up to her childhood reputation of being emotionally "steady as a rock."

As you certainly have guessed, both David and Miriam are undergoing many of the changes of adolescence. In this chapter and the two that follow, we explore the major physical, cognitive, social, and emotional developments that occur during adolescence. First, let us take a brief look at the concept of adolescence itself.

THE CONCEPT OF ADOLESCENCE

Adolescence is the stage of development that leads a person from childhood to adulthood. Marked by the major physical changes of puberty and important cognitive and social developments, it is generally considered to begin around age ten and end sometime around age twenty-two. *Early adolescence* lasts roughly from ages ten to fourteen, including the middle school (or junior high school) years. *Middle adolescence,* ages fifteen through seventeen, includes the high school years. *Late adolescence* occurs between ages eighteen and twenty-two.

Every society uses ceremonies and rituals such as confirmation, bar mitzvah, graduation, and marriage to signify important changes in a person's life stage status, and the transition to adulthood is one of the most important and widely recognized changes that all people experience. In societies that still have relatively simple, agricultural economies and traditional cultural and social practices, this transition is fairly smooth and predictable and grows out of a long period of preparation. For example, when a teenage Australian aborigine goes on his year-long walkabout through the desert with only a few simple weapons to protect him, his chances of returning safely are high because he has spent much of his childhood learning skills to help him meet this challenge. Similarly, in many tribal cultures, a girl's initiation into womanhood is preceded by years of instruction in and imitation of the adult roles and activities she is now expected to perform.

In modern industrial societies such as ours, however, the roles and responsibilities a person is expected to assume when reaching sexual maturity are much less predictable, largely because our technology and values are changing so rapidly. Our rites of passage tend to be more symbolic than real, and the transition from childhood to adulthood can be rather difficult and prolonged. For example, a girl in a hunting-and-gathering society such as the Innuit of Alaska or the Bushman of Africa has a good idea of what her adult work will be: bearing and caring for children, gathering and preparing food, and the like. But a girl in computer-age North America has little idea of what kind of work she will do, what kind of family she will have, or even where she will live.

Adolescence: From Idea to Social Fact

Most of us take the idea of adolescence for granted, but in fact it is a relatively modern concept. Its discovery, or recognition, in technological societies was largely a response to the social changes that accompanied industrial development in the nineteenth century in Europe and the United States (see Chapter 1 for a discussion of this development).

In fact, some researchers have proposed that adolescence was defined as a separate stage of development primarily to prolong the years of childhood so that the aims of the new urban-industrial society that rapidly developed after the Civil War could be fulfilled (Bakan, 1975). According to this view, the spread of railroads and the telegraph, accompanied by a general shift in population from the country to the industrial cities and the addition of a huge number of immigrants, threatened the American way of life. Because so much was changing so fast, people felt a growing fear that society would get out of control—that the country would be overrun by foreigners and the crowded, dirty cities would breed crime and immorality. There were three major legal responses to this national "identity crisis": compulsory education, requiring children to attend school; child labor laws, regulating the age and hours children and adolescents could work; and special legal status and procedures for juveniles, including those who were "delinquent." Together these developments played a major role in making adolescence a social reality (Bakan, 1975).

Although some teenagers experience periods of turmoil during adolescence, for most, adolescence is neither more nor less difficult than earlier periods of life.

Theoretical Views of Adolescence

Since the "discovery" of adolescence in the United States, two somewhat conflicting views about its basic nature have emerged. One view sees adolescence is a time of "storm and stress," a period when major physical, intellectual, and emotional changes create tremendous upset and crisis within the individual and conflict between the person and society. As you may recall, Sigmund Freud believed development is full of conflict, especially in adolescence. Erik Erikson and others have suggested that a lack of stable and predictable role expectations due to rapid changes in society may make the transition from childhood to adulthood more difficult (Erikson, 1963, 1968; Elkind, 1984).

Current research, however, suggests that adolescence is not intrinsically a time of severe "storm and stress" in personality development or in relationships with parents. Most adolescents in the United States adapt to the changes in themselves quite well and adjust to the changing demands and expectations of parents and society in a relatively smooth and peaceful way. The same appears to be generally true in a number of other cultures, including Australia, Bangladesh, Hungary, Israel, Turkey, and Germany, where approximately 75 percent of teenagers have been found to have positive self-images and good emotional adjustment (Offer et al., 1988).

While adolescence is not an unusually problematic period for most youngsters, in the United States and Great Britain the onset of adolescence is associated with more frequent negative feelings among many adolescents and increased rates of behavioral and psychological problems for some (Brooks-Gunn & Warren, 1989; Hamburg, 1994; Larson & Ham, 1993). In certain ethnic groups, for example, between 15 and 20 percent of adolescents in the United States drop out of school before completing high school; adolescents have the highest arrest rate of any age group; and a growing number of adolescents use alcohol and drugs on a regular basis (Eccles et al., 1993). How negative or positive the changes associated with adolescence are likely to be will depend on the degree of fit between adolescents' developing needs and the opportunities offered them by their social environments, school and home perhaps being two of the most important. And the increased stress some adolescents experience may not be due simply to the external environment but may also result from developmental changes in adolescents' subjective construction of their environments (Larson & Ham, 1993).

We discuss these and other social aspects of adolescence in greater detail in the next two chapters. In the following sections, we look more closely at the physical changes of adolescence and their effects on development.

What Do You Think?

In what ways has the "discovery" of adolescence as a developmental stage been helpful for teenagers and their families? In what ways has it been a problem? What has your personal experience with adolescence been?

GROWTH IN HEIGHT AND WEIGHT

Compared to childhood, the years of adolescence include less overall growth in height and weight but significantly greater irregularity and unevenness in the pattern and pace of growth. As Figure 14.1 shows, the average height for both boys and girls at twelve years is about fifty-nine or sixty inches. By age eighteen, the average height for boys is sixty-nine inches, whereas the average for girls is only sixty-four inches.

Much of this rapid change in height and weight is due to a dramatic **growth spurt,** which is preceded and followed by years of comparatively little increase. The change in height is particularly striking, as Figure 14.2 shows. The maximum rate of growth occurs around age eleven or twelve for girls and about two years later for boys. In those years, many girls grow three inches in a single year and many boys grow more than four inches (Marshall, 1978).

The reason for males' greater average height is that boys start their growth spurt two years later than girls do and thus undergo two additional years of childhood growing. The average girl is around fifty-four or fifty-five inches tall when she begins her growth spurt, whereas the average boy is fifty-nine or sixty inches tall when he begins his. Because both boys and girls add around nine or ten inches during adolescence and grow relatively little afterward, women end up being shorter than men on average (Tanner, 1981; Thissen et al., 1976).

FIGURE 14.1
Growth in Height and Weight from Two to Eighteen Years

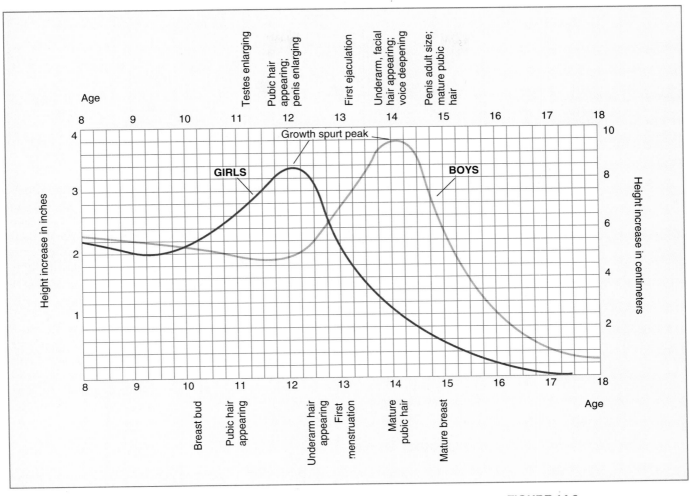

Age

Testes enlarging
Pubic hair appearing; penis enlarging
First ejaculation
Underarm, facial hair appearing; voice deepening
Penis adult size; mature pubic hair

GIRLS

Growth spurt peak

BOYS

Height increase in inches

Height increase in centimeters

Breast bud
Pubic hair appearing
Underarm hair appearing
First menstruation
Mature pubic hair
Mature breast

Age

FIGURE 14.2
Physical Development During Adolescence

Interestingly, growth patterns and height during childhood are better predictors of adult height than growth patterns and height during adolescence are. That is, a tall ten-year-old is more likely to become a tall adult than is a tall thirteen-year-old who was short as a ten-year-old (Faust, 1977). Although weight also increases during adolescence (see Figure 14.1), it is more easily influenced than height by diet, exercise, and general lifestyle, and therefore changes in weight are less predictable. Girls begin puberty with slightly more total body fat than boys do. During puberty, total body fat declines for boys from an average of 18 or 19 percent to 11 percent of body weight, whereas for girls it increases from about 21 percent to around 26 or 27 percent (D. Sinclair, 1990). The average weight gain during the growth spurt is about thirty-eight pounds for girls and forty-two pounds for boys, although how it is distributed varies considerably among individuals.

Adolescents differ greatly in their rates and patterns of growth and its impact on their lives. David, the fourteen-year-old we described at the beginning of the chapter, is a good example. Although he is somewhat below average in height and weight for his age group, he currently wears a size 12½ shoe—five shoe sizes larger than he wore two years ago! His family teases him about this, and David secretly fears he will always have very oversize feet because his arms, legs, and other assorted body parts have not yet caught up.

On the other hand, Miriam is concerned that she is too fat, her chest is too big, and her legs are too short for the rest of her body, that is, for boys to find her attractive. Because Miriam's parents and friends, both male and female, think she is

The considerable growth in height and weight during adolescence is generally accompanied by significant increases in the amount of food that is consumed.

very attractive and not fat at all, we might ask why Miriam has such different perceptions of herself. One answer might be **adolescent egocentrism,** the tendency of adolescents (both girls and boys) to find it difficult to perceive the world (and themselves) through anyone's eyes but their own. This is particularly true of their perceptions of how they look and of how others perceive them. An adolescent's view of her own irregularities and regularities, her personal ideals regarding how she should look, and current social ideals of attractiveness all contribute to a very complicated and confusing state of affairs.

Much of the unevenness in growth typical of this period smooths out over time. But not everyone ends up with the height, weight, and other physical characteristics that match society's ideals or, for that matter, the individual's own. Later in this chapter, we discuss how the increase in body fat in adolescent girls and rigid cultural norms regarding body shape and size may contribute to fairly widespread problems with diet and nutrition and, in some cases, to eating disorders such as anorexia and bulimia.

The Secular Trend

The **secular trend** refers to the tendency of succeeding generations to achieve physical maturation at an earlier age and to end up heavier and taller than their parents. These generational differences include body weight, height, body build, body fat, strength, age of growth spurt onset, and age of menarche (first menstrual period). For example, today's boys generally reach their full height between eighteen and twenty and girls between thirteen and fourteen, whereas in 1880 the average male did not reach full height until between twenty-three and twenty-five and the average female between nineteen and twenty (Tanner, 1989).

Perhaps even more significant, the average age at which girls have their first menstrual period has dropped from between fifteen and seventeen a hundred years ago to between twelve and fourteen today in both the United States and Western Europe. This is of considerable concern, since no evidence exists that earlier onset of puberty is accompanied by earlier gains in social and emotional development that would equip children to successfully manage their sexuality. Also, the first ovulation can occur before the first menstrual period, and some girls as young as eight years (third grade) are becoming fertile. The secular trend also helps to explain why adolescence in industrial societies occurs over a longer period of time than in less developed countries, where puberty may begin much closer to the beginning of adulthood (Chumlea, 1983).

How can the secular trend be explained? Improvements in health care, diet, and overall living conditions are thought to be the major reasons for earlier maturation. Because the onset of puberty usually depends on reaching a certain body weight, improvements in diet have led to achievement of that weight at earlier ages than in previous generations. In addition, early childhood diseases that limit growth have been largely eliminated, and nutrition and medical care have greatly improved

A Talk with Jason, Age Fourteen

Physical Development at Age Fourteen

Jason agreed to be interviewed if I would give him a ride to soccer practice afterward. The interview was conducted in the kitchen of his home over an after-school snack.

Interviewer: What physical changes have you noticed in kids your age?

Jason: When we were in fifth grade, all the guys were taller than the girls, or at least the same height. And then, in sixth grade, the girls shot up and all got much taller than us.

Interviewer: How did that feel?

Jason: We didn't grow in seventh grade. We had sex education, so we started to understand it. So in sixth grade, seventh, and part of eighth grade, all the guys were much less developed than the girls and much less tall and less heavy and everything. And then the later part of eighth grade we all shot up.

Interviewer: I noticed. How tall are you now?

Jason: Five-eleven.

Interviewer: Almost as tall as me.

Jason: We all shot up. I'm as tall as my older brother.

Interviewer: Are there other differences besides height that you've noticed in kids your age?

Jason: Weight, for example, because some people were heavy before. The weight was not really part of them. It was excess. Now people have become heavier but more solid. I'm gaining weight, not a lot of weight. I've gained weight and it's in my bones, in my muscle, and in my skin and just a little bit of fat. I'm gaining it all over as opposed to gaining it in just fat. I'm gaining it in muscle.

I think that as you get older, guys become less ashamed of their bodies and more likely to expose them. Not necessarily all the way, but just to take off your shirt. It's easier for them to do that because now they're bigger . . . now they feel that they can expose their chest and they don't have to be embarrassed about it.

Interviewer: Have you noticed differences in how rapidly people develop?

Jason: Different parts of people develop at different times. Some people stay shorter but get a full beard sooner. But they're not gonna shoot up as far. And some people shoot up and grow a beard at about the same time, but people in all four years of high school are getting interested in shaving and stuff like that. And usually it would seem ridiculous to an outsider to shave the little hair that you grow on your mustache, but it's a big thing to someone to have to shave, or at this age it's important to look the best you can even if it's just a few hairs to get off.

Interviewer: How do kids your age deal with staying healthy?

Jason: They know what is healthy, but they don't necessarily follow what is always healthy.

Interviewer: Why do you think that is?

Jason: 'Cause, you know, there's the simple fact that junk food tastes good. And the other thing is that it is overemphasized that kids shouldn't eat that much junk food. I don't eat that much junk food. I eat a little bit, but I also eat really good food, too. I eat plenty of it to survive. So anything above that really doesn't matter.

Interviewer: Do you think that most kids basically eat a good diet and that junk food is on top of it?

Jason: A lot of girls don't need to eat as much, because they have stopped growing. But they still need to eat more than they do eat. They starve themselves to a certain extent when they are hungry because they think, "Oh, God, I have to lose weight!" I think it's just a fad just to be able to say it. It makes people feel better about themselves to say, "I'm fat, look at me, I'm fat," because they really want other people to say, "No, you're not." I think a lot of girls in the teenage years eat a crummy breakfast and then don't eat lunch and then go all day without eating. They eat at night. And then they go to sleep. Which is the wrong method. If you're only going to eat one meal a day, you should eat breakfast.

Interviewer: Why is that?

Jason: Because you need the nutrition more during the day when you are active. At night you don't really need that much.

What Do You Think?

1. How does Jason feel about the effects of physical maturation? How consistent are his views with those presented in the chapter?

2. What nutritional problems might be related to the eating habits of Jason's peers?

3. How typical of adolescents his age are his views about health?

for children in developed countries. We can expect that a similar trend will occur wherever adequate nutrition and living conditions are available to all children and their families (Malina, 1979).

What Do You Think?

What pattern (timing, rate) did changes in your own height and weight follow during adolescence? What do you remember thinking and feeling about those changes?

PUBERTY

Rapid increases in height and weight are only one part of a large pattern of changes, called **puberty,** that lead to the completion of sexual development or *reproductive maturity.* For females, the completion of reproductive maturity is signaled by the beginning of *menstruation;* for males, it is heralded by the *ejaculation of mobile sperm.* Puberty is marked by striking changes in both primary and secondary sex characteristics. **Primary sex characteristics** make sexual reproduction possible. For girls, these include complex changes in the vagina, uterus, fallopian tubes, and ovaries; the most obvious sign of these changes is the beginning of menstrual periods. For boys, changes in primary sex characteristics include development of the penis, scrotum, testes, prostate gland, and seminal vesicles, which lead to the production of enough sperm to enable successful reproduction. Changes in **secondary sex characteristics** include enlargement of the breasts, growth of body hair, and deepening of the voice. Associated with these developments are important changes in the levels of hormones present in the blood stream. These powerful chemicals play a major part in initiating and regulating all of the changes associated with puberty.

Primary Sexual Maturation

For boys, the most significant sign of sexual maturation is rapid growth of the penis and scrotum (the sack of skin underneath the penis that contains the testicles), which begins at around age twelve and continues for about five years for the penis and seven years for the scrotum (Meredith, 1967). The penis typically doubles or triples in length, so locker room comparisons are almost inevitable as boys become increasingly aware of obvious changes in themselves and their friends. Although penis size has almost nothing to do with eventual success at overall sexual functioning, for adolescent boys it sometimes seems to be an all-important sign of their new status as men (Malina, 1990; Marshall & Tanner, 1974).

During adolescence, enough live sperm are produced in the testes to make reproduction a real possibility for the first time. Sometime around age twelve, boys are likely to experience their first ejaculation of **semen,** a sticky fluid produced by the prostate gland, which is located near the penis just inside the body cavity. Semen carries the sperm to the penis and provides it with a medium in which to live after ejaculation. Most boys have their first ejaculation during masturbation; as **nocturnal emissions,** or "wet dreams," during sleep; or, less frequently, as emissions that occur spontaneously upon waking. Most males report experiencing nocturnal emissions about one or two years before puberty; the accompanying dreams are frequently but not always erotic in nature. The sexual changes just discussed and the unexpected erections and uncomfortable sexual fantasies and sensations that boys sometimes experience are common sources of embarrassment. Less frequently, they are a source of more serious discomfort and conflict.

For girls, the appearance of the first menstrual period, called **menarche,** signals sexual maturity. In most societies, menarche also symbolizes the shift from girlhood to womanhood (Logan, 1980). Nevertheless, menarche occurs rather late in a girl's sexual maturation and is preceded by a number of other changes, including enlargement of the breasts, the appearance of pubic hair, and broadening of the hips and shoulders. Next, as the growth spurt peaks, the uterus, vagina, labia, and clitoris develop, as do the ovaries.

For most girls, menstruation involves a certain degree of inconvenience and discomfort, but also feelings of happiness about the specialness of their reproductive capacity and their womanhood. Adequate information about menstruation, including practical details about the purchase and use of sanitary napkins and tampons, personal hygiene, and birth control, is important. The same holds for knowledge about *dysmenorrhea* (menstrual cramps) and *premenstrual syndrome (PMS),* a pattern of behavioral, emotional, and physical symptoms that may occur approximately a week before menstruation (Wilson & Keye, 1989). In addition, contact with women who have positive feelings about their monthly cycles will help make menarche a positive experience and allay fears and negative attitudes about it (Brooks-Gunn & Ruble, 1982; Brooks-Gunn & Warren, 1989). As we will see, the same informative and supportive climate can also help girls deal with the other physical changes of puberty. Later in this chapter, we will look at the various psychological effects of physical growth in adolescence.

Maturation of Secondary Sex Characteristics

Breasts   Girls first develop breast "buds," or slightly raised nipples, at the beginning of puberty. During the following several years, the nipples grow darker, the areolas (the pigmented areas surrounding the nipples) increase in size, and the breasts continue to grow until they reach their full size.

Given the attention our culture devotes to breasts, it is not surprising that breast development is a potential source of concern for many adolescent girls. Breasts that are "too big," "too small," or the "wrong" shape may cause embarrassment, and in many cases girls experience outright harassment due to these physical developments.

Boys too undergo a small amount of breast development, and their areolas become larger and darker much as they do in girls. A few boys experience enough

For girls, breast development is one of the major occurrences of puberty, and getting a first bra can be an important event. Likewise, the growth of facial hair—and thus the need to shave—is a significant milestone for adolescent boys.

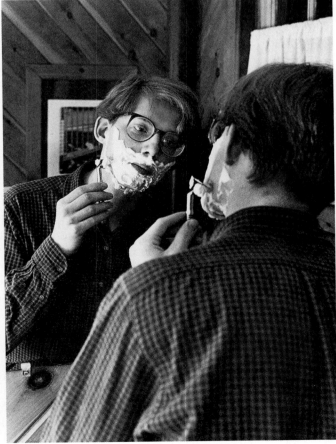

tissue growth to cause them some embarrassment, but these "breasts" usually return to typical male size in a year or two.

Hair   When their genital development is relatively advanced, both boys and girls acquire more body hair, although boys generally grow more of it than girls do. The first growth is simply a fine fuzz around the genitals called **pubic hair,** which then darkens and becomes coarser. At the same time, underarm or **axillary hair** begins to appear; this eventually becomes dark and coarse as well.

Although considerable differences exist among individuals, in girls pubic hair and axillary hair begin to appear around age eleven and are fully grown by about age fourteen; in boys they begin around age twelve and continue until about age eighteen. At age fifteen or so, many boys begin growing facial hair, which usually appears first as a mere suggestion of a mustache that begins on the outer corners of the lips and gradually grows inward toward the nose. For both girls and boys, however, there are inherited ethnic and individual differences in the amount of facial and body hair that develops. For example, some boys have little or no facial hair, or hair growth is limited to their upper lips or chins. Eventually boys may grow real whiskers on the chin and cheeks, as well as hair on the chest and back, although these later developments usually do not become obvious until around age seventeen or older (Tanner, 1990). Cultural attitudes and expectations influence women's feelings about axillary hair during puberty. For example, whereas many women in our culture spend considerable time and money to rid themselves of "unsightly" underarm, leg, and facial hair, women in a number of European countries believe this hair is attractive and do not attempt to remove it.

Voice   In both sexes, the voice deepens near the end of puberty and becomes richer in overtones so that it sounds less like a flute or whistle and more like a violin or clarinet. These changes make the adolescent's voice sound more truly adult, but the fluctuations in voice qualities that some adolescents experience can be a cause of considerable (although usually temporary) embarrassment.

Like many of the other changes of puberty, the deepening of the voice is not limited to one sex. Boys' voices do deepen somewhat more than girls' do, but social expectations encourage many girls to talk in voices that are higher than is comfortable, necessary, or natural for them (Henley, 1977; Sachs et al., 1973).

Hormonal Changes and Their Physical Consequences

For both boys and girls, the onset of puberty brings increases in the levels of all sex hormones in the blood, but the pattern by which it does so differs for each sex. **Testosterone** (also called *male sex hormone*), a particular type of androgen, and **estrogen** (or *female sex hormone*) are two of the most important sex hormones. Although both hormones are present in males and females, the high concentration of testosterone in boys stimulates the growth of the penis and related male reproductive organs, and the high concentration of estrogen in girls stimulates the growth of the ovaries and vagina. Androgens are thought to influence the strength of the sex drive in both genders.

Hormones affect more than just sexual characteristics. For example, they are responsible for the typical differences between girls' and boys' overall body builds. In general, the sex that has shorter bones and more rounded curves (female) also has higher estrogen levels, and the sex that has longer bones and larger muscles (male) also has higher levels of testosterone (Tanner, 1990).

Testosterone stimulates muscle and bone growth in both sexes. Throughout childhood, boys and girls are about equally muscular. They have roughly the same number and sizes of muscle fibers, and they can exert about the same amount of strength with their muscles. Although individual children vary around the averages, as groups the two sexes differ very little.

Puberty significantly changes this equality. During puberty, boys typically become more muscular looking than girls, even though girls too become more muscular as they grow. Boys experience close to a fourteenfold increase in the size of the largest muscle fibers between early childhood and adolescence, with most of the increase occurring during adolescence. Girls, in contrast, experience only a tenfold increase (Brasel & Gruen, 1978; Malina, 1990).

Some of this difference may result from life experiences more specific to boys than to girls. For example, teenage boys receive greater encouragement and opportunity to participate in sports and more responsibilities that involve physical work and other heavy muscular activity. Differences in hormone levels may also be influenced by differences in behavior and life experiences. Sustained exercise, for example, tends to increase a person's level of testosterone (L. Rogers & Walsh, 1982).

Estrogen stimulates increased deposits of subcutaneous fat (fat under the skin). It also stimulates the final maturation of bones, a process in which the growing areas within individual bones finally become hard and fixed in size. Throughout childhood, boys and girls tend to possess almost identical amounts of fat (or adipose) tissue (F. Johnston et al., 1974).

During adolescence, however, the two sexes begin to differ noticeably in their proportions of fat tissue. Boys tend to keep most of their fat deposits, which are simply stretched over their increasingly larger bodies. Because boys' muscles and bones tend to grow particularly rapidly during puberty, boys' fat tissue decreases as a proportion of their total body weight. The overall result is a relatively muscular, bony-looking person, at least compared to a typical girl. Girls, on the other hand, develop significant new deposits of subcutaneous fat during adolescence while maintaining those produced during childhood. The new fat develops in all the locations that make girls look typically female: in their breasts, hips, buttocks, thighs, and upper arms. The new fat tissues combine with girls' smaller muscles and bones to make young females significantly more rounded than young males. By the end of adolescence, fat accounts for more than one-fourth of their body weight compared to about one-eighth in males (Chumlea et al., 1983).

The Extent of Physical Sex Differences

As the preceding discussion reveals, the sex differences that develop during puberty are matters of emphasis or degree. Except for eggs, sperm, and form of genitals, every physical structure and every characteristic exists in both sexes, sometimes in surprisingly similar amounts or levels. Both sexes grow new hair as a result of puberty, and both develop substantially larger muscles and bones. The physical differences between males and females are triggered by the same set of hormones, which are produced in much the same ways in both sexes.

Even differences in the timing of puberty are less significant than they first appear to be. The two-year gap between the sexes occurs mainly in the most visible physical change of puberty, the growth spurt. As it happens, the spurt in growth is one of the first changes girls undergo and one of the last boys experience. Changes that are less visible, such as the development of adult genitalia and shifts in hormonal balances, occur at almost the same average ages. On the whole, puberty begins and ends at nearly the same age for both sexes (Tanner, 1990).

From a biological standpoint, then, the sexes do not represent physical opposites as much as they do related but distinct patterns of similar physical elements and processes. The physical similarity between the sexes has not, of course, prevented society from constructing different roles and expectations for males and females. Indeed, society tends to focus a great deal on gender differences and to exaggerate their significance. As we will see, the physical changes of puberty are associated with intensified gender-related role expectations: the social and cultural expectations about differences in female and male roles and behaviors (Huston & Alvarez, 1990; Unger & Crawford, 1992).

What Do You Think?

What surprised you about the discussion of similarities and differences in physical development in males and females? Do you think puberty is easier or more difficult for the other gender? In what ways?

PSYCHOLOGICAL EFFECTS OF PHYSICAL GROWTH IN ADOLESCENCE

Given how rapid the physical changes of puberty are, it is not surprising that adolescents often are preoccupied and dissatisfied with the way they look. Although dissatisfaction is most noticeable during the early adolescent years, it is also very common during the later teen years (Harter, 1990a; Heilbrun & Friedberg, 1990).

Body Image and Self-esteem

For many adolescents, and especially for females, judgments about their physical appearance may be the most important factor in their self-esteem (Harter, 1990b). Even the most attractive teenager worries about her hair, her nose, or a pimple on her chin. What determines how much discomfort a particular adolescent feels about her own body?

For one thing, conventional standards of attractiveness have considerable influence. In our culture, people of all ages find certain body builds more attractive than others. Although individuals obviously differ, most children and adolescents clearly consider the muscular, athletic, *mesomorphic* body type most attractive for males and a more slender, *ectomorphic* body type most attractive for females, and view a rounder, more padded *endomorphic* body type as less than ideal for either. (Figure 14.3 depicts each of these body types.) The majority of males and females do not have body types that fit these ideals, and many are concerned that they are too fat. This is truer for girls than for boys. An adolescent girl's body is becoming rounder and fuller due to the normal increases in fat associated with puberty; yet our society

FIGURE 14.3
Three Body Types
Conventional standards of attractiveness, which favor a mesomorphic body type for men and a slender, ectomorphic body type for women, influence adolescents' body image and self-esteem.

Endomorph   **Mesomorph**   **Ectomorph**

Working with   Barbara Donohue, NUTRITIONIST

Treating Nutritional Problems and Eating Disorders During Adolescence

Barbara Donohue is a nutritionist in private practice. She works with children, teenagers, and adults, both individually and in small groups, and is a school consultant. Barbara was interviewed in the waiting room of her office. Her interest in kids is revealed by the books, toys, and computer games and the informal atmosphere. Our discussion focused on Barbara's approach to helping adolescents overcome eating disorders.

Rob: What kind of training is required to become a nutritionist?

Barbara: You need four years of college, with a major in nutrition and food service. You then do an eighteen-month internship, after which you must pass certification exams. A major focus of my internship was working with the nutritional problems of children and adolescents.

Rob: What general problems do you see in adolescents' nutritional habits?

Barbara: Since schools allow only twenty minutes for lunch, most teens skip lunch or eat very little so they have more time to socialize with their friends. More and more adolescent girls are cutting back on protein intake and eating just vegetables and fruits to lose weight and be thin enough to feel they will be accepted. This pressure to diet causes many overweight teens to eat a lot of high-fat foods secretively. Sometimes it's only when parents find candy and other food wrappers that they discover why their child is overweight.

Rob: How are teenagers referred to your practice for help?

Barbara: Sometimes they're referred at their own request. An overweight youngster who's experiencing problems at school may finally bring it up with a parent, and then they decide together to get help. Or a parent may contact me and say, "My child has a weight problem; can you help us solve it?" and bring the child in. Referrals also come from pediatricians, therapists, or other professionals who are concerned about a child's nutrition and weight.

Rob: What happens next?

Barbara: Generally I'll start by meeting with the child and parents together. Then I'll meet with the teen and the parents separately to evaluate whether I'll need to make a referral for psychological help too. If you have a teen who's emaciated or severely obese, and nobody listens to her when she's talking—or if she tries to say something and someone answers for her—there's a good chance that the teen or the family may need additional help.

Rob: What techniques do you use to help teens change their nutritional habits?

Barbara: Usually I use a behavioral approach. We set weekly goals, such as eating more fruit and less high-fat foods, and keep careful food records. If a teen has problems successfully meeting the goals, I say, "If that didn't work, what do you think would work?" Then we revise the goals together.

Rob: How do you work with more severe problems such as anorexia?

Barbara: For starters, I'll take a thorough medical and social history. For example, I might find out that my client's compulsion to avoid eating fat started after her aunt died of heart disease; the disorder was an attempt to protect herself from dying. My job is to help teenagers learn about good nutrition and how to be more flexible about their eating. I'll often use issues the teen raises as support. For example, I might tell this girl that vitamin E may help prevent heart disease, that fats contain vitamins A, D, E, and K, and that some fats are necessary for a healthy diet.

Rob: Are the issues always so straightforward?

Barbara: Well, no. I saw one fourteen-year-old girl who refused to get psychological help. My work focused on helping her increase her food intake enough so that she could think more clearly and come to see that food was not the main issue. I helped her realize that her confused thinking and mood swings were related to her starvation diet and that her constant obsession with food made it difficult to think about anything else. I asked her, "How often during the day do you think about food?" "All the time," she said. "Well, that's because you're starving. If you can eat just a little more, that will help."

Rob: This must be difficult, given how afraid anorectics are of gaining weight.

Barbara: My approach is to help them to eat just a little more each time and understand what is actually happening if the scale moves. For a starving person, a small increase in food intake may cause a temporary weight gain of three or four pounds due to fluid shifting. They take one look and can't eat again. So I have to help them understand that this doesn't reflect a real weight gain. The anorectic teen may have a hard time accepting that, so to help I'll say something like "Let's figure out what you ate and how much of the weight gain could be due to your additional food intake and how much to fluid retention." Careful food records and clear, logical explanations are both important here.

Rob: This must be a very slow process.

Barbara: Usually the best you can count on is an average gain of about four ounces per week, with many ups and downs. Anorectics aren't really safe until fats are part of their regular diet and they're comfortable with it. Generally it's a two-to-three-year process to get back to a healthy weight and develop a healthy approach to food that they can rely on.

What Do You Think?

1. In what ways do Barb Donohue's observations of adolescents' eating behaviors coincide with your own behaviors or observations?

2. What other concepts from behavioral theory discussed in Chapter 2 may be useful in understanding Barb Donohue's approach?

3. In what ways do Barb's experiences as a nutritionist parallel the discussion of eating disorders in this chapter's Perspectives box?

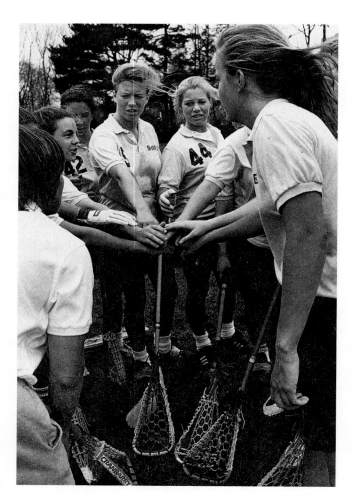

For these girls, participating in after-school activities such as lacrosse can make an important contribution to their developing a comfortable body image and sense of self-esteem.

holds a slender, ectomorphic standard for female beauty and still values physical attractiveness as a woman's most important asset (Allgood-Merten et al., 1990; Heilbrun & Friedberg, 1990; Koff et al., 1990).

Adolescents evaluate themselves and their peers according to such stereotypes. Teenage males with mesomorphic body builds and females with ectomorphic builds tend to be judged as more attractive than those with other body types. They also tend to have more friends and to be rated relatively highly in status or prestige among their peers (Clausen, 1975; Sigelman et al., 1986). Conventionally attractive youngsters may develop greater self-esteem than others because of the appreciation they receive. Under the wrong conditions, however, a youngster who receives approval for something that is a matter of genetic chance may come to believe he is not appreciated for other important qualities and cannot influence the opinions of his friends by his conduct (Livson & Peskin, 1981a). Teenagers who are physically "unattractive" may compensate by developing other desirable qualities, such as being energetic and outgoing, having a good sense of humor, and being a good listener.

Whether or not an adolescent considers himself truly attractive depends on more than what he thinks his peers think (Lerner et al., 1989). Social contexts such as family, school, and community also can play a role. For example, in a recent study of pubertal girls and boys from two different communities, girls from one community were less satisfied with their bodies and weight than girls from the other community (Richards et al., 1990). Greater involvement and satisfaction in after-school activities, including sports, and perceptions that their school environments provided opportunities for peer acceptance were related to higher satisfaction with body weight and appearance.

As we have noted, perceptions about attractiveness are strongly influenced by the existing cultural stereotypes for feminine and masculine beauty. (See the accompanying Multicultural View box for a discussion of the effects of ethnic differences in physical appearance on adolescents' social development.) Role models from fashion magazines, movies, and television help to create and cultivate these stereotypes. Although there may be more than one "ideal" type for men and women—which may reflect trends such as our society's growing appreciation for physical fitness—only a very small percentage of teenagers have bodies that come even reasonably close. In recent years, the benchmark of feminine beauty has been the "prepubertal look": lean, long-legged, and lithe (Faust, 1983). But puberty and the associated increases in fat deposits and redistribution of fat make this ideal impossible to maintain for the majority of girls (Richards et al., 1990).

One consequence is that successive generations of teenagers have attempted to modify their bodies to fit the prevailing ideals, sometimes with tragic results. Obsessive concern with being slender has led many teenage girls to adopt diets that are seriously deficient in nutrition (Fowler, 1989). Anorexia nervosa and bulimia are eating disorders that involve distorted relationships between eating and body image; they appear to be connected, at least in part, to cultural stereotypes. We discuss these conditions more fully in the Perspectives box that appears later in this chapter.

Compulsive efforts to increase muscle mass may combine body building, unsafe dieting, and use of steroids and other drugs. Such a regimen poses serious health hazards to an increasing number of male and, more recently, female athletes. Steroids have been banned in most athletic programs because they have been shown to cause liver damage, testicular shrinking, increased cholesterol levels, and elevated blood pressure. Use of steroids has also been linked to emotional problems, including depressive and psychotic symptoms (Pope & Katz, 1988).

Adolescents who have atypical physical characteristics because of inherited or acquired abnormalities sometimes face more serious psychological problems regarding their bodies. For example, children who are badly scarred or whose movements are spasmodic must learn to cope with these added burdens. As suggested by the film *Mask,* which portrays an adolescent whose face and head are grossly disfigured, strong, loving, support from parents and friends help a child with a disability to feel good about himself and his body. Although physical appearance certainly is important, beauty and positive self-concept really *are* more than skin deep.

Early- Versus Late-Maturing Adolescents

The timing of puberty can make a lasting difference to the psychological development of an adolescent, particularly if physical maturation is very early or very late. The positive and negative effects of early, on-time, and late maturation, however, depend partly on gender and partly on whether they are short term or longer term.

Early-maturing boys seem to experience certain initial advantages. Their more muscular and mesomorphic appearance appears to gain them favorable responses from peers, teachers, and other important people sooner and for longer than their agemates. Early-maturing boys seem to respond to these changes and the favorable attitudes they elicit in very positive ways: they appear to be more self-confident and generally strike others as being more mature and competent than their peers, and are more likely to be chosen as leaders in high school (Livson & Peskin, 1981a, 1981b; Tobin-Richards et al., 1983). There are also some disadvantages, however. Early-maturing boys are found to be more somber, less spontaneous and creative, more submissive, and less flexible than their peers. They tend to be less open to new experiences and more conforming to adult values and expectations, perhaps due to pressures they feel to live up to the expectations that accompany their adult, masculine body image (Brooks-Gunn, 1987).

A Multicultural View

How Do Ethnic Differences in Physical Appearance Affect Social Development During Adolescence?

Physical appearance plays a very important role in adolescent development, especially during the junior and senior high school years, when attitudes about physical differences can significantly affect social acceptance and popularity. How ethnic differences in physical appearance affect social development was one of the questions addressed by Jeannie Kang in her recent study of identity development in eighteen Korean-American female college students, ages eighteen to twenty-one, from a variety of regional backgrounds (Kang, 1990).

For the majority of these young women, junior high was the hardest and most confusing time. They reported being very concerned with how they looked and whether they could fit in, but having little awareness or understanding of conflicts regarding their ethnic identity during that period. Very few remembered feeling socially successful or accepted as part of the "popular crowd" during their high school years. For many, it was not until they were sophomores or juniors in college that they experienced mainstream social acceptance and more fully explored the meaning of bicultural identity.

Regional differences played an important role in how differences in physical appearance affected their social and emotional experiences. For girls who grew up as part of a small and isolated ethnic minority in all-white communities in the Midwest, the "blue-eyed, blond hair, cheerleader" type was the sole standard of beauty and popularity—a standard they could never hope to achieve. Girls from these communities were more likely to feel ostracized and less likely to succeed in their social adjustment during their high school years than girls who grew up in more heterogeneous communities that provided alternative models of beauty and popularity and greater social acceptance of ethnic differences.

The majority of the adolescents reported a period of withdrawal from the coed social scene during high school. During this period, they rechanneled their energies into other activities. Academic achievement, extracurricular activities, work, and friendships rather than group social life became their major sources of self-esteem. Even so, many found that ethnic differences were still important because their choices of activities reinforced the stereotypic notion that Korean-Americans (and other Asian-Americans) are "naturally" adept in math, science, and music.

These women also experienced considerable conflict between the cultural values, traditions, and expectations of their immigrant parents (who spoke little English) and

What about the long-term effects? Adult males who were early maturers were found to be relatively responsible, sociable, and self-controlled, but they also continued to be more rigid, moralistic, and conforming than their peers. This may be partly because although their muscular, mesomorphic physiques enabled them to excel early in athletics and to physically resemble culturally desirable stereotypes, they became overdependent on these early advantages and experienced a loss of self-esteem when their on-time and later-developing peers eventually caught up (Petersen & Taylor, 1980).

Late-maturing boys still resemble children, at least physically, as late as age sixteen. Teachers, parents, and other observers tend to judge them unfavorably, viewing them as impulsive, immature, and lacking in self-confidence. In school, late-maturing boys tend to be regarded as socially inferior to earlier-maturing peers and often regard themselves this way as well. Boys who are late developers may be perceived as childish and socially immature, in part because their self-consciousness about their delayed physical development limits their opportunities to become involved in sports and social activities. On the other hand, their physical immaturity may, to some degree, protect them from the increasing pressures to become sexually and socially active—which their on-time and early-developing peers find hard to resist—and allow them greater freedom to develop their own unique identities.

Early-maturing girls often feel less attractive and more concerned about their physical appearance, are more awkward and ill at ease in social situations, experience less support from their peers, and have poorer self-concepts (Peskin, 1973; Tobin-Richards et al., 1983). Unlike with early-maturing boys, who frequently experience athletic achievement and expectations for leadership and success, early maturation those of mainstream American culture as represented by schools, peer groups, and the media. This conflict of cultures was particularly difficult for many of the girls, whose limited knowledge of Korean language and traditions made it difficult to communicate with their parents and other relatives. Even something as simple as getting a suntan, a major leisure time activity for many American adolescents, proved a source of cultural conflict. A beautiful, golden tan has long been highly valued in mainstream American culture, but most Korean-American parents forbid tanning because in Korea being tan is associated with being uneducated and lower class. In fact, one of the most rebellious things a Korean girl can do is get a really deep tan.

Most of the women reported that they did not really begin to come to terms with the meanings of these ethnic differences until their college years. Often it was not until their second or third year of college that they were able to more actively explore personal issues of bicultural identity and acceptance (or lack of it) by both minority and mainstream cultures. College was the first time many of these women found themselves with a sizable peer group of Korean-Americans among whom they could explore issues of identity and cultural difference.

The task of forging a coherent bicultural identity out of these two conflicting cultural experiences was a challenging one that potentially influenced every aspect of a Korean-American adolescent's experience. Even during the college years, physical difference remained a metaphor for the women's efforts to achieve a comfortable resolution of the dilemma of bicultural identity. Several girls recalled how they were reminded of this by being called a "banana" and a "twinkie," derogatory terms occasionally used by Korean-Americans to criticize a person who they believe has embraced a mainstream, white American identity to the exclusion of her or his identity as a Korean.

By the end of this decade, the majority of children in the United States will be from non-European backgrounds (Carnegie Council on Adolescent Development, 1992). Hopefully this increasing cultural pluralism will bring greater acceptance of bicultural identity among Koreans as well as other cultural groups.

often puts a girl out of step with common standards for female beauty. Because of the hormonal changes of puberty, she becomes relatively tall, muscular, and sometimes heavyset for her age, whereas her later-developing agemates remain relatively slender and short. And because she also becomes more shapely and sexually mature, she may find herself in dating and sexual encounters for which she is not psychologically ready. Although a girl who has achieved puberty may have mature physical characteristics, there is no reason to assume she is emotionally ready to make decisions about birth control or about sexual relationships. Nor should she be assumed to be developmentally ready to take on greater responsibility for adult work in or outside the home.

Recent studies in the United States, Sweden, and Finland found that early-maturing girls have more problem behaviors, including truancy, academic problems, and drug and alcohol use (Aro & Taipale, 1987; A. Peterson, 1987; Simmons et al., 1987; Statton & Magnusson, 1990). However, once early-maturing girls successfully navigate the next several years, they are likely to enjoy increased status and popularity and be better able to cope with the challenges of adolescence than their peers. This may partly be a result of the skills they learned in dealing with earlier problems or because life may have become easier for these early maturers as their later-blooming peers caught up.

Late-maturing girls exhibit a less clear-cut pattern. In contrast to their early-maturing peers, they appear to experience social advantages throughout adolescence. In one study, teachers and other observers rated late-maturing girls as more attractive and as better leaders, and they did in fact become school leaders relatively often (Livson & Peskin, 1981b). As with boys, the long-term effects of maturation differed from the immediate or short-term effects. At age thirty, women who were early maturers were found to be more poised and self-directed than late maturers, especially those who had encountered difficult circumstances in adulthood, such as divorce or serious illness.

What about adolescents who mature "on time"? *On-time-maturing boys* tend to feel less attractive than do early-maturing boys but more attractive than do later maturers. This suggests that their perceptions of attractiveness are related to how close they are to physical adulthood. *On-time-maturing girls* typically have more positive body images and greater feelings of social attractiveness than do early- or late-maturing girls (Tobin-Richards et al., 1983).

Table 14.1 summarizes the reactions to puberty of early-, on-time-, and late-maturing adolescents.

What conclusions can we draw? Early-maturing boys experience positive effects initially and mixed effects later, whereas early maturation for girls is initially a distressing experience but in the longer run generally has a more positive impact. On-time maturation is experienced positively by both boys and girls. Late-maturing boys initially experience some difficulties, but in the longer run benefit from these experiences. Late-maturing girls appear to have an easier time during adolescence, but it is not clear whether they experience significant longer-range benefits.

The timing of puberty may also influence how much freedom and opportunity a child has to develop a strong sense of self and prepare for the eventual challenges of adolescence. If puberty comes when society "prefers" it to come—early for boys and late for girls—an adolescent may have little reason to develop a strong inner sense of self because he is too busy attempting to live up to societal expectations: that he be sexually active and involved in structured extracurricular activities, for example, rather than spend more time on informal activities and on his own. On the other hand, if puberty comes at the "wrong" time, an adolescent may feel much more pressed to understand herself. Indeed, she may feel forced to do a lot of reflecting to understand and overcome the feelings of anger and social inferiority that arise from failing to fulfill society's timetable for physical maturation. As with all developmental conflict, however, the experience of mastering the challenge may actually be beneficial rather than detrimental to future personality development.

Most adolescents, of course, mature at more or less the average age rather than at extremely early or late ages. Thus, the typical adolescent experiences a mixture of pressure to conform to social standards and the need to reflect on her or his true identity.

What Do You Think?

Get together with several classmates to discuss how body type (mesomorphic, ectomorphic, or endomorphic) and the timing of maturation affected your adolescent development. How

TABLE 14.1   Adolescents' Reactions to the Onset of Puberty

Time of Onset	Reaction	Male	Female
Early	Initial	Positive	Negative
	Later	Negative	Positive
On time	Initial	Positive	Positive
	Later	Positive	Positive
Late	Initial	Negative	Positive
	Later	Positive	Mixed

For adolescents who begin puberty on time, initial and later reactions are positive for both males and females. For early-maturing males, initial reactions are positive and later reactions are negative, while the reverse is true for early-maturing females. Late-maturing males first react negatively and later react positively. Late-maturing females first react positively, and later reactions are mixed.

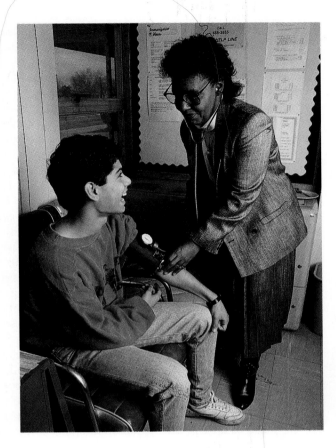

School-based health care programs that are responsive to the special needs and vulnerabilities of adolescents can make an important contribution to helping teenagers to take responsibility for their own health care.

closely did these experiences fit the patterns discussed in the text? What might teachers and parents do to help early- and late-maturing adolescents deal with the physical changes they are undergoing?

HEALTH IN ADOLESCENCE

In some ways, adolescents are among the healthiest of all people. They tend to have fewer colds and ear infections than young children or adults do. And compared with adults, they suffer fewer of the illnesses and physical damage associated with prolonged exposure to physical and emotional stress and with aging.

Nevertheless, adolescents actually experience *greater* health risks than either younger children or adults do. Compared to either age group, they are much more likely to be injured in motor vehicle accidents, misuse alcohol and other substances, experience unwanted pregnancy, and have inadequate diet and health and mental health care (Dougherty, 1993; Jessor, 1993; Takanishi, 1993).

Continuity with Health in Childhood

The health and health care patterns of most children show considerable consistency and continuity from early childhood through adolescence. This is true of common, recurring illnesses, patterns of use of medical services, and children's overall levels of health as judged by doctors and other health care professionals. Children who visit the doctor frequently when young continue to do so as adolescents, whereas those who visit less frequently early in life tend to maintain this pattern (Starfield & Pless, 1980).

Factors such as social class and the quality and accessibility of services play a major role in adolescent patterns of use (and underuse) of health and mental health services and health-related behaviors (Hamburg, 1994; Taylor et al., 1991; Terre et al., 1992). Because health care and health insurance are extremely expensive, many families cannot afford to pay for care that adequately meets their needs. If such families receive inferior medical care and are treated in belittling ways (as is often the case), their children are more likely to develop negative attitudes toward doctors and hospitals. In contrast, children and adolescents from families whose financial resources allow them more regular and positive contacts with the health care system are likely to have more favorable attitudes and better health habits.

Inadequate understanding of the relationship between their behavior and their health may also affect how much responsibility adolescents assume for their own health. As noted in Chapter 11, not until adolescence are children able to understand health in terms of multiple causes and cures and to realize that interrelationships among thoughts, feelings, and changes in physical health are important (Hergenrather & Rabinowitz, 1991; Millstein, 1989; Sigelman et al., 1993). But although adolescents may be similar to their parents in their estimates of risks to their health and in their cognitive decision-making processes regarding health care, they (and their parents) still frequently display significant gaps in their knowledge about what does and does not cause illness and how to safeguard their health (Quadrel et al., 1993).

For many teenagers, health care that is affordable, accessible, and responsive to their particular developmental needs and level of understanding appears to be the most important factor in determining whether they receive adequate care. Consider Genelle Wallace, a teenager from a poor family who recently discovered she was pregnant. It is very likely that her family's lack of health insurance and a regular doctor, along with the difficult psychological issues involved, will substantially reduce her chances of seeking or receiving adequate prenatal care. There is growing evidence, however, that under the right circumstances, adolescents (and even younger children) from a broad range of backgrounds can become very competent managers of their own health. Programs to encourage self-care have had significant success, especially when they are based in junior and senior high schools and offer comprehensive health care and family planning to teenagers. The success of such programs is due not only to the quality and appropriateness of the health services provided but also to their accessibility, assurances of confidentiality, and the reduction or elimination of financial barriers (Hamburg, 1994; Millstein, 1989).

Causes of Death among Adolescents

Although adolescents are less affected by the health problems that lead to death in younger children and adults, the death rate during adolescence is one of the highest for all age groups. Both the risky environments in which teenagers live and the risk-taking behavior associated with adolescence undoubtedly contribute to this statistic (Eccles et al., 1993).

Because of their lifestyles, males are significantly more at risk than females are. Middle- and working-class males are likely to believe that risk taking and experimentation with cars and motorcycles, alcohol, and drugs are signs of masculinity. Poor and minority males are at still greater risk for accidental death and homicide, because the dangerous inner-city environments in which many of them live and the lifestyles they often lead are likely to involve the use and sale of drugs, participation in gangs, and exposure to various forms of physical violence, including the use of lethal weapons (Takanishi, 1993). Leading causes of adolescent deaths are motor vehicle accidents (more than fifteen thousand per year), homicide and other forms of intentional violence (more than six thousand per year), and self-inflicted harm or suicide (more than five thousand yearly) (Garland & Zigler, 1993; Hammond & Yung, 1993; Millstein, 1989; Spivak et al., 1988).

Adolescent Health Problems

Although adolescents are not prone to the infectious diseases of childhood, they often adopt habits that are damaging to their health. Poor diet, lack of sleep, use of alcohol or drugs, and unsafe sexual practices can all lead to a number of serious diseases. Infectious mononucleosis, hepatitis, and a variety of *sexually transmitted diseases (STDs)* constitute major health risks during adolescence (see Table 14.2).

Sexually Transmitted Diseases   Teenagers and young adults under twenty-five account for more than 50 percent of the 20 million STD cases reported annually. It

TABLE 14.2   *Common Infectious Diseases During Adolescence*

Disease	Cause	Symptoms	Incidence	Treatment
Non–Sexually Transmitted Diseases				
Infectious mononucleosis	Virus	Sore throat, fever, swollen glands, extreme fatigue, enlarged spleen		Rest and good nutrition
Hepatitis	Virus transmitted through blood transfusions, injections, or sexual activity; transmission; also, inadequate sanitation	Acute infection of liver		Antiviral drugs
Sexually Transmitted Diseases				
Syphilis	Bacteria; transmitted by direct sexual contact with infected individual	Sores and lesions on genitals and mucous membranes; if untreated, CNS damage	134,000 new cases per year	Antibiotics
Gonorrhea	Bacteria; transmitted by direct sexual contact with infected individual	Infection of mucous membrane of urethra and genital areas; pain in urinating, vaginal discharge; if untreated, may cause pelvic inflammatory disease and sterility in women	1.9 million new cases per year	Antibiotics
Genital warts	Virus; transmitted by direct sexual contact	Small, painless growths on penis, urethra, rectal areas in males, genitals and anus in females; if untreated, increased risk of cervical cancer	1 million new cases per year	Removal
Genital herpes	Virus; transmitted by direct sexual contact with infected individual	Chronic, painful inflammation and lesions on genitals and other areas of sexual contact	200,000 to 500,000 new cases per year	Antiviral drugs; no cure as yet
Chlamydia	Bacteria; transmitted by direct sexual contact	Pain in urination, discharge from penis; vaginal discharge, abdominal discomfort; if untreated, may cause pelvic inflammatory disease, sterility	4 million new cases per year; most common STD	Antiviral drugs
Acquired immunodeficiency syndrome (AIDS)	Virus transmitted by body fluids from infected person		As of 1992, 671 males and 275 females age thirteen to nineteen, and 7,820 males and 1,762 females ages twenty to twenty-four	New antiviral drugs such as AZT may slow replication of the virus. No effected treatment has been developed so far.

Sources: Centers for Disease Control (1993a, 1993b); Shafer & Moscicki (1991); Amschler (1991).

Danger and opportunity. Automobiles give teenagers a great deal of independence. But they also have drawbacks: auto collisions are the leading cause of death in adolescence.

is estimated that 25 percent of adolescents will become infected with an STD before graduating from high school (Shafer & Moscicki, 1991). With the exception of prostitutes and homosexual men, adolescent females have the highest rates of gonorrhea, cytomegalovirus, chlamydia, and pelvic inflammatory disease of any age group (Cates & Rauh, 1985). STDs can cause pelvic inflammatory disease, which places young women at risk for subsequent development of ectopic pregnancy and infertility (Shafer & Moscicki, 1991).

Risk factors for STDs include the increased acceptability of early sexual activity throughout our culture and inadequate use of contraceptives. Use of the birth control pill has replaced condoms as the favored method for birth control among teenagers. But condoms provide significant protection against venereal diseases, whereas the pill provides none. Inadequate health and sex education at home and in the schools must also be held accountable (Brooks-Gunn & Furstenberg, 1989; *Statistical Abstract of the United States,* 1992). As we discuss next, sexual experimentation and unprotected sex, particularly in the case of poor and minority adolescents who participate in the sex-for-drugs exchanges common in the drug subculture, place adolescents at great risk for all STDs, including AIDS.

First diagnosed in the United States in the early 1980s, *AIDS (acquired immunodeficiency syndrome)* is perhaps the best-known and most feared sexually transmitted disease in the 1990s. Without treatment, about 50 percent of individuals infected with human immunodeficiency virus (HIV) develop AIDS within ten years of becoming infected, and another 40 percent or more develop other clinical illnesses associated with HIV infection. Although new antiviral drugs such as AZT (zidovudine, formerly known as azidothymidine) have been shown to slow replication of the virus and improve survival prospects, as yet no definitive data exist on how long an adolescent diagnosed as having AIDS can survive (United States Department of Health and Human Services, 1990).

As of 1992, 671 males and 275 females between thirteen and nineteen years old and 7,820 males and 1,762 females between ages twenty and twenty-four were diagnosed with AIDS. Males ages thirteen to twenty-four accounted for 3.8 percent of all male AIDS cases, and females in this age group accounted for 39 percent of all female AIDS cases (Centers for Disease Control, 1993b). To date, more than 440,000 cases of AIDS and 250,000 deaths from AIDS and AIDS-related causes have been reported in the United States, making it the leading killer of Americans from twenty-five to forty-four years old (Altman, 1995).

Experts are alarmed at the speed with which AIDS is spreading among teenagers. The number of adolescents who are infected with the HIV virus but have not yet developed AIDS is not known at present. But given that young adults in their twenties currently represent almost 20 percent of all reported cases of AIDS and the virus has up to a ten-year incubation period, it is likely that many of these cases were transmitted during the teenage years (Centers for Disease Control, 1993b).

AIDS destroys the body's ability to maintain its normal immunity to diseases; death often results from pneumonia or related complications. The disease is transmitted through introduction of the HIV virus through body fluids from an infected person. The most common methods of transmission are sexual intercourse with an infected person, contact with the blood of an infected person (through sharing of needles or through a blood transfusion), and contact of a child with an infected mother during pregnancy, birth, and (possibly) breast feeding (Shafer & Moscicki, 1991). Because the AIDS virus cannot survive in air, water, or things people touch, it does not spread through casual, day-to-day contact. AIDS has *never* been transmitted by sharing food; shaking hands; hugging; using the same dishes and utensils; being spit, drooled, or cried on; or having any form of casual contact.

The risk of contracting AIDS is extremely high for the large number of poor and minority adolescents and young adults who engage in intravenous drug use (Shafer & Moscicki, 1991). One group of particular concern is the 1.5 million homeless adolescents in the United States whose sexual and substance abuse behaviors place them at an especially high risk for AIDS. Four percent of homeless teenagers—roughly sixty thousand—are estimated to be infected with HIV, a rate two to ten times higher than that for other adolescent samples in the United States, including teenage mothers (Rotheram-Borus et al., 1991).

AIDS Education and Prevention   A growing number of teenagers now receive formal instruction about AIDS in school. Most know that sexual intercourse and sharing needles are the main routes to getting AIDS and that condoms reduce the risk of transmission. However, for a variety of social and psychological reasons, the

The growing danger of AIDS and other sexually transmitted diseases during adolescence has led to many new educational programs designed to reduce these risks. As part of the national AIDS Quilt Project, students are adding to the quilt the names of people they have known who have died of AIDS.

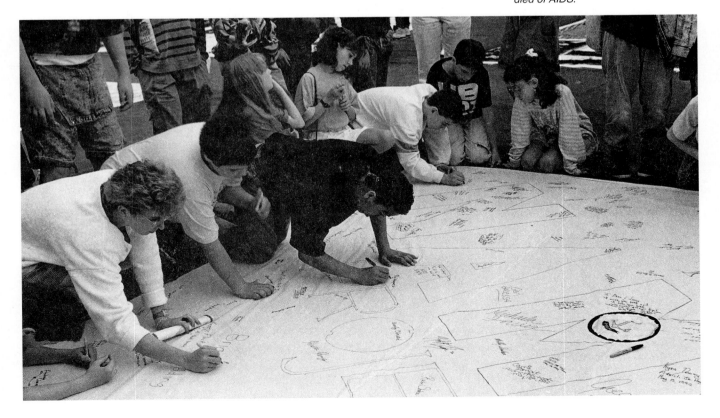

use of condoms has not increased as rapidly as youngsters' knowledge of why they are important. Sexually active adolescents need to know ways to protect themselves against AIDS. Perhaps most important is practicing safe sex, including massage, petting, masturbation, and kissing (provided there is no chance of direct contact between the body fluids of the partners). Kissing on the lips also is safe. No cases of AIDS have been traced to deep-tongue, "French" kissing, but because small amounts of HIV have been found in saliva, people who have open sores in their mouths or wear braces on their teeth are better off avoiding this practice. There is no such thing as "100 percent safe" sexual intercourse, but some sexual practices and behaviors are *safer* than others in that they very significantly reduce (but do not eliminate) the risk of contracting AIDS. One such practice is to correctly use latex condoms along with a spermicide and water-based lubricant. A second is to be monogamous—to have sexual intercourse with only one person—and that person should have no history of intravenous drug use or sexual contact with high-risk individuals. A third alternative is to screen and limit the number of one's sexual partners. A fourth is abstinence, that is, not engaging in sexual intercourse at all (Hein & DiGeronimo, 1989).

Drug and Alcohol Abuse   High rates of experimentation with drugs and of drug abuse are typical of adolescence. In our society, as in many others, drinking alcoholic beverages represents a rite of passage associated with the adolescent's transition to adulthood. Although drugs differ in many ways, experimentation with psychedelics and other "mind-altering" drugs, such as LSD, psilocybin, and mescaline in the 1960s and traditional use of peyote among Native American cultures in the southwestern United States, can also be thought of as serving a rite of passage function. Choices of drugs and patterns of use may, of course, change over time. More important, drug use has great potential for harm, particularly for adolescents.

Use of alcohol and drugs is associated with motor vehicle accidents, homicides, and suicides, the leading causes of death and injury among teenagers and young adults. Close to half of all deaths from motor vehicle crashes in this age group involve alcohol use. As of 1991, 88 percent of high school seniors had used alcohol, 36.7 percent had tried marijuana, and 7.8 percent had used cocaine at least once. These figures indicate a decline in the use of marijuana, stimulants, and sedatives by high school students (as well as college students and young adults) over the last five years (L. Johnston et al., 1992). (See Figure 14.4.)

Developmental Effects of Drug Abuse   For several reasons, the effects of drug abuse on development are extremely destructive, particularly if the use is prolonged or chronic. First, even short-term use of illegal drugs such as heroin, cocaine, crack, and Quaaludes exposes the user to considerable physical risk of injury or death due to overdose, contamination of the drug, or both. Second, even moderate use of certain drugs may have destructive physical and psychological effects; they may disrupt normal patterns of eating, sleeping, and physical activity and mask psychological problems that require attention. Third, a number of these drugs cause physical addiction and psychological dependence. Physical addiction involves a biological dependence on the drug; withdrawal can be painful and sometimes life threatening. In most cases, tolerance to the drug increases with prolonged use, requiring higher doses to maintain the same level of effect and thus increasing the user's exposure to the drug's negative effects.

Finally, even if a proper medicinal dose of the drug itself is not physically dangerous, as is true with heroin, the physical, social, and psychological risks involved in supporting a habit are enormous. Teenagers addicted to heroin are, with few exceptions, forced to sell drugs and steal to support their habit. They are at great risk for using unreliable and contaminated drugs and for contracting hepatitis or even AIDS from dirty and infected needles. They are exposed to situations that are both physically and psychologically violent. And the time and energy needed to support a habit often force them to abandon normal social, emotional, and intellectual

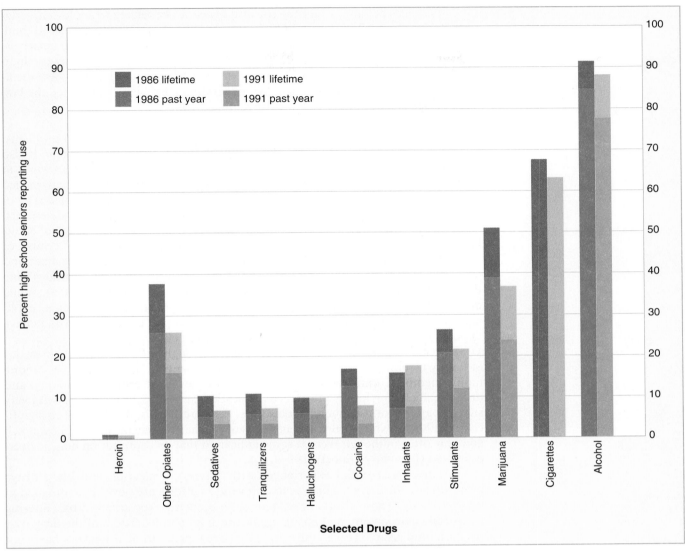

FIGURE 14.4
Use of Selected Drugs among High School Seniors, 1986 and 1991
Between 1986 and 1991, the percentage of high school seniors who reported using the drugs listed in the figure declined for all drugs except hallucinogens and inhalants. The largest decreases occurred for marijuana, cocaine, and other opiates.
Source: Johnston et al. (1992).

endeavors and threaten to halt their identity development prematurely. Teenagers living in poverty-stricken, crime-ridden areas and homeless teens are vulnerable to involvement in the drug trade, which to them may appear to be the only route to survival or success (Price, 1992; Rotheram-Borus et al., 1991).

Causes of Drug Abuse   Problem drug use is often both a symptom and a cause of personal and social maladjustment and is best understood in the context of an individual's personality and developmental history. For example, a longitudinal study of marijuana and related drug use among eighteen-year-olds who were first recruited at age three found three different drug use groups: frequent users, experimenters, and abstainers (Shedler & Block, 1990). *Frequent users,* who used marijuana once a week or more and had tried at least one other drug, were more alienated, impulsive, and anxious than *experimenters* were. *Abstainers,* who had never tried marijuana or any other drug, were more anxious, emotionally constricted, and lacking in social skills than were drug experimenters. In addition, both frequent users and abstainers were judged to have experienced poorer maternal parenting as young children compared to drug "experimenters," who had used marijuana a few times. These findings should not be interpreted as advocating drug experimentation; they are simply consistent with the fact that the majority of adolescents who experiment with marijuana do not subsequently become drug abusers.

Differences in patterns of drug use also appear to be related to adolescent judgments about drugs. Both low- and high-drug-use high school students tend to think of drug use primarily as a personal issue, involving potential harm to themselves, rather than in terms of morality or social convention. However, high-drug-use individuals seem more likely to minimize the personal risks involved and to view themselves as the only authority on drug use, undermining the views of parents, the law, and other sources of authority (Shedler & Block, 1990).

Alcohol and Tobacco　Chronic alcohol abuse can lead to severe health problems, including destruction of the liver and damage to the central nervous system. It also seriously disrupts the drinker's ability to function effectively in school, at work, at home, and in other settings. Because alcohol is heavily advertised and socially valued as a sign of adulthood and independence, is readily available at low cost, and is a potent short-term reducer of anxiety, it continues to be very popular among adolescents.

The use of tobacco products also has been widely advertised as a sign of adulthood. Early adolescents are particularly susceptible to this "ready-made" symbol of maturity. Although most adolescents are aware that smoking causes cancer and heart disease, more than one-third (36.0 percent) of all students in grades nine through twelve report using tobacco (Centers for Disease Control, 1991a). While overall smoking rates for teenagers have decreased over the last fifteen years, smoking among females and minorities has risen, at least in part because advertisers have targeted them as a highly lucrative market (Johnston et al., 1992).

Patterns of both drinking and smoking are strongly influenced by the lifestyles of family members and peers and by the environments in which they live. Among family members, minimal, moderate, and heavy levels of drinking, smoking, and drug use, including legally prescribed medications, are strongly associated with very similar patterns of use among adolescents. Peer pressure is also thought to significantly influence which drugs a teenager uses, in what circumstances, and how much and how often, although there is some indication that its contribution may be overestimated (Bauman & Ennett, 1994).

Because most initial experiences with cigarettes, alcohol, and illicit drugs occur during the early teenage years, prevention efforts are now being directed at this age group. These efforts have focused on reducing exposure to drugs, altering the social environment, and changing the attitudes and behaviors of the drug user (or potential user). In general, however, drug prevention programs have not

Drinking and cigarette-smoking make some teenagers feel more grown-up and more sociable and accepted by their friends. As a result, alcohol and cigarettes are used by more teenagers than any other drug.

Whereas most teenagers suffer no shortage of calories their diets often lack balance and rely heavily on "fast foods" which are high in fats.

proven very effective. Those that show promise are peer programs and school-based prevention efforts involving life skills training designed to increase knowledge and build confidence and overall social competence in areas such as risk assessment, decision making, self-directed behavior change, capacity to cope with anxiety, and conflict resolution (Botvin & Tortu, 1988; Hamburg, 1994; Newcomb & Bentler, 1989).

Nutritional Problems   Adolescents have the highest "unsatisfactory" nutritional status of any age group. The average teenage girl requires approximately 2,200 calories per day, and the average adolescent boy needs about 2,800. Boys' nutrient intakes come closer to recommended daily allowance levels than girls' do, because boys eat relatively larger amounts of food for their body weight; also, girls diet more frequently.

The food habits of adolescents, which include an increased tendency to skip meals (especially breakfast and lunch), snacking (particularly on "junk" foods), consumption of fast foods, and dieting, place them at dietary risk. Surprisingly, iron-deficiency anemia, one of the most common nutritional disorders in this age group, is found more frequently in boys than in girls (American Academy of Pediatrics, 1985). Inadequate nutrition can interfere with a teenager's ability to concentrate at school and work and to actively engage in activities with peers. Poor nutritional habits established during adolescence can have more serious health consequences if continued on a long-term basis.

Like dependence on drugs, food dependence and the obesity that frequently results are problems that affect a significant portion of the teenage population. Currently it is estimated that 15 percent of today's teenagers are significantly overweight. Major causes of obesity include a biologically inherited tendency to be overweight, childhood diet and family attitudes and habits regarding food, and lack of exercise (Epstein & Wing, 1987; Maloney & Klykylo, 1983). Adolescents and young adults who are overweight suffer increased health risks, including hypertension, respiratory disease, orthopedic disorders, and diabetes.

Obesity is particularly difficult for adolescents who already are struggling to develop a comfortable and realistic view of their changing bodies. It can significantly impair teenagers' sense of themselves as physically attractive people and their overall identity development. In some cases, obesity can severely limit social opportunities due to both exclusion by peers and self-isolation. Because overweight adolescents do not conform to the social ideal of thinness, they also suffer from discrimination that limits their access to education, employment, marriage, housing, and health care (De-Jong, 1993; Gortmaker et al., 1993).

Excessive thinness is also a problem. Despite a growing appreciation of physical strength and fitness in women, a lean body is still the dominant cultural standard for feminine beauty. Many adolescent girls try to lose weight to achieve a degree of slenderness that may not be possible for them. Inadequate knowledge about dietary requirements and poor judgment lead to inadequate nutrition for many teenage girls.

An extreme form of this quest for thinness is **anorexia nervosa,** a physical and psychological disturbance in which the afflicted teenager starves herself, exercises compulsively, and develops an increasingly unrealistic view of her body. Ninety-five percent of anorexics are females. Many anorexics also suffer from **bulimia,** a disorder that compels them to eat huge amounts of food and then make themselves vomit to avoid gaining weight. The causes, symptoms, and treatment of these disorders are discussed in the accompanying Perspectives box and in the "Working With" interview on page 449.

"Working With" interview on page 449.

Perspectives

Two Serious Eating Disorders: Anorexia Nervosa and Bulimia

Anorexia nervosa and bulimia are two emotional disorders characterized by severely abnormal eating patterns, an obsession with food and weight, and the "relentless pursuit of excessive thinness" (Bruch, 1979). *Anorexia nervosa* affects approximately 0.2 percent, or one in five hundred, adolescent girls and young women, and bulimia affects between 1.0 and 2.8 percent. Also, it is estimated that approximately 20 percent of adolescent girls (2.5 million) exhibit less extreme bulimic behaviors and an additional 20 percent engage in less extreme but still unhealthy dieting behaviors (Graber et al., 1994).

The major symptom of anorexia is extreme weight loss (approximately 20 to 25 percent of body weight) through self-starvation that is tied to an obsessive fear of becoming fat. Anorexic youngsters experience severe disturbances in three areas of psychological functioning. First is a *disturbance in body image.* A girl (we'll call her Jill) is five feet, six inches tall and weighs eighty-seven pounds. Jill looks like a walking skeleton, but when she views herself in the mirror, she sees someone who is too fat and needs to continue dieting. The second disturbance is *misinterpretation of internal and external stimuli:* although she is literally starving to death, Jill enjoys the feeling of hunger and her flat, empty stomach, both of which make her feel thinner. The third disturbance is a *pervasive sense of ineffectiveness and helplessness* about her ability to direct her life (Attie & Brooks-Gunn, 1989; Bruch, 1979, 1988). Other symptoms of anorexia include excessive, compulsive exercise; amenorrhea (the cessation of menstruation); hyperactivity; social isolation; and feelings of insecurity, loneliness, inadequacy, shame, and guilt (Attie et al., 1990; Frank, 1991; Solnit et al., 1986).

Bulimia is a related eating disorder that frequently involves a recurrent "binge-purge" syndrome in which as many as 4,800 calories are eaten at a time, mostly in the form of sweets and other "forbidden" and fattening foods, and then immediately "purged" by forced vomiting, laxatives, and other cathartics. Approximately half of all anorectics also have bulimic eating patterns (Attie et al., 1990; Leon & Dinklage, 1989; Solnit et al., 1986).

Causes

Women at greatest risk for bulimia likely are those who have accepted and internalized most deeply the social and cultural norms that equate fat with bad, thinness with beauty, and beauty with good (Streigel-Moore et al., 1986). Most anorectics are girls from financially and socially successful upper-middle-class and upper-class families. Many feel burdened by their parents' success and an overwhelming obligation to be at least as special and successful as their parents were. Their eating behaviors serve as a means of forestalling and/or avoiding the physical, sexual, and psychosocial changes and challenges of puberty and adolescence, which they do not feel ready to face. The behaviors also give them a means of asserting control over their own bodies and daily activities and of resisting the intense pressure to conform to the parental expectations they experienced throughout their childhood (Bruch, 1979; Leon & Dinklage, 1989; Romeo, 1984).

Anorexia and bulimia are frequently associated with a serious family disturbance, and in particular with a mother-daughter relationship that is overprotective, rigid, and rejecting or hostile and with mothers who themselves are preoccupied with thinness and have dis-

What Do You Think?

Why do you think adolescents are at such high risk for injury, death, and health problems? What recommendations regarding these issues might you make to a group of high school students and their parents?

FINALLY YOUNG ADULTS?

After all the bodily changes adolescents experience, they certainly look like adults. But as we have pointed out, they do not consistently *feel* like adults yet. Especially early in adolescence, teenagers are often uncomfortable with their new physical features, which take up the foreground of their thinking, feeling, and acting. Young people often are self-conscious, meaning (among other things) they are highly conscious of their bodies. The nature and strength of that self-consciousness depend in part on the nature, strength, and timing of puberty in all of its facets.

turbed eating patterns (Attie et al., 1990). There is also evidence that sexual abuse may be involved in some cases (Shapiro & Rosenfeld, 1987).

Treatment

Successful treatment generally requires a multiple focus. First, it must deal with the starvation problem in a way that addresses both the anorectic's need for control and the distortions in her thinking. This typically requires a highly restricted hospital environment that allows careful observation and the use of behavior modification to strictly reduce or eliminate rewards for behaviors leading to weight loss and reinforce more appropriate eating behaviors. Antidepressant medications have also proven helpful in reducing the depression and risk of suicide that are present in many cases (McDaniel, 1986). Second, the treatment must address the underlying family problems and abnormal interactions among family members that are invariably related to anorexia. Finally, individual therapy with the anorectic adolescent must focus on helping her to uncover her own abilities and resources for independent thinking, judging, and feeling. It must help her to achieve autonomy and self-directed identity by helping her to become aware of, express, and act on her own impulses, feelings, and needs (Bruch, 1979, 1980; Leon & Dinklage, 1989; Shapiro & Rosenfeld, 1987).

Individuals with anorexia, like this teenage girl, suffer from serious confusion about their body image. Their compulsive dieting and exercise are attempts to attain culturally imposed standards of female beauty and gain control over their lives. No matter how thin they become, they are likely to view themselves as "too fat."

Given the newness of their physical changes, it is not surprising that adolescents lack awareness of or concern for their health. So far in life, they have had little reason to be aware or concerned. Soon, however, this perspective changes. Just as their bodies develop during the teen years, so do their thoughts, feelings, and social relationships. These developments eventually help them become truly adult in the physical sense as well as other realms.

SUMMARY OF MAJOR IDEAS

The Concept of Adolescence

1. Adolescence, which begins around age ten and lasts until about age twenty-two, is a developmental period of transition between childhood and adulthood.

2. Adolescence was "discovered" in the early part of this century as a way of prolonging childhood in a period of rapid social and economic change.

3. Compulsory education, child labor laws, and special laws to combat "juvenile delinquency" helped solidify the idea of adolescence.

4. Some theories of adolescence emphasize the "storm and stress" of this period, but current research finds it no more conflict ridden than earlier periods of development. For most youngsters, the experience of adolescence depends on the goodness of fit between developmental needs and the opportunities that are available.

Growth in Height and Weight

5. Adolescents make significant increases in height and weight, but the unevenness of the adolescent "growth spurt" is even more striking.

6. Increases in height can be predicted fairly accurately. Predicting weight increases is more difficult, in part because they are influenced by differences in diet, exercise, and lifestyle.

7. During the last century, children have tended to begin physical maturation and puberty earlier and to grow taller and heavier than their parents. This secular trend is thought to reflect improvements in diet, health, and overall living conditions.

Puberty

8. In addition to increases in height and weight, a larger pattern of changes occurs that leads to full physical and sexual maturity, or puberty.

9. Primary sexual maturation among boys includes rapid growth of the penis and scrotum and the production of fertile semen.

10. Menarche, or the beginning of menstrual cycles, is a complex biological process that signals the beginning of sexual maturity for girls.

11. In many cultures, including our own, the onset of menarche can be stressful, in part due to the strong personal and cultural expectations associated with it.

12. Maturation of secondary sex characteristics includes enlargement and development of the breasts, growth of body hair, deepening of the voice, and increased production of sex-related hormones.

13. Male and female hormones affect both sexes, although in differing degrees and with different effects.

14. Although girls and boys are equally muscular prior to adolescence, during puberty boys experience significantly greater increases in muscle tissue than girls do. Girls experience a somewhat greater increase in body fat than boys do.

15. Differences in how muscle and body fat are distributed rather than in their absolute amounts account for many of the differences in the physical appearances of male and female adolescents.

Psychological Effects of Physical Growth in Adolescence

16. Most adolescents are preoccupied with their physical appearance; a teenager's body image is influenced by conventional standards of attractiveness.

17. An adolescent's feelings of attractiveness depend on the evaluations of peers, parents, and self and affect self-esteem.

18. For boys, the effects of early maturation are positive in the short run but somewhat negative in the long run. Late maturation appears to have the reverse effects.

19. For girls, early maturation is more stressful in the short term but positive in the long run. Late maturers tend to experience benefits during adolescence and no serious long-run negative effects.

Health in Adolescence

20. There is considerable continuity between childhood and adolescent patterns of illness and health care. Both are influenced by individual and family attitudes and resources.

21. Adolescents are a high-risk group for injury and death due to risky lifestyles and their myth of invulnerability.

22. Growth in a child's ability to understand concepts of illness and health appears to follow stages of cognitive development.

23. Major health problems during adolescence include sexually transmitted diseases; alcohol, tobacco, and drug abuse; and inadequate diet.

KEY TERMS

adolescence *(438)*
growth spurt *(440)*
adolescent
  egocentrism *(442)*
secular trend *(442)*
puberty *(444)*
primary sex
  characteristics *(444)*
secondary sex
  characteristics *(444)*

semen *(444)*
nocturnal emission *(444)*
menarche *(444)*
pubic hair *(446)*
axillary hair *(446)*
testosterone *(446)*
estrogen *(446)*
anorexia nervosa *(464)*
bulimia *(464)*

FOR FURTHER READING

Bell, R., et al. *Changing Bodies, Changing Lives: A Book for Teens on Sex and Relationships.* New York: Random House, 1988.

This unusual book is based on interviews with hundreds of teenagers throughout the country as well as with parents, sex educators, and junior and senior high school teachers. Relying on direct quotes from the teenagers themselves for much of its material, the book provides thorough, practical, and readable information about the physical, sexual, and emotional changes of puberty and adolescence.

Bruch, H. *Conversations with Anorexics.* New York: Basic Books, 1988.

Bruch, H. *The Golden Cage: The Enigma of Anorexia Nervosa.* New York: Vintage Books, 1979.

These two very readable books about the causes, effects, and treatment of this life-threatening eating disorder are based on the author's own clinical experience as a researcher, therapist, and consultant.

Elkind, D. *All Grown Up and No Place to Go: Teenagers in Crisis.* Reading, Mass.: Addison-Wesley, 1984.

This intense and stimulating book deals with the pressures toward premature adulthood experienced by teenagers in a rapidly changing society. It is based on case studies, research, and clinical experiences of one of the best-known experts on adolescence.

Hamburg, D. A. *Today's Children: Creating a Future for a Generation in Crisis.* New York: Times Books, 1994.

This is an interesting and readable review of how changes in family structure and in social norms regarding marriage, divorce, work, nutrition, and violence have placed adolescents at greater developmental risk. It describes social policy alternatives and innovative programs to improve the lives of children and adolescents.

Hein, K., and T. DiGeronimo. *AIDS: Trading Fears for Facts. A Guide for Teens.* Mount Vernon, N.Y.: Consumers Union, 1989.

This up-to-date, well-researched guide for adolescents answers a wide range of questions about AIDS in clear and nontechnical language.

McCoy, K., and C. Wibbelsman. *The New Teenage Body Book.* New York: The Body Press/Perigree Books, 1992.

This book focuses on the physical changes of adolescence and the feelings teenagers experience. It addresses common concerns about appearance, health care, diet and eating problems, teen sexuality, sexually transmitted diseases, birth control, and teen pregnancy and parenthood.

15

ADOLESCENCE

Cognitive Development

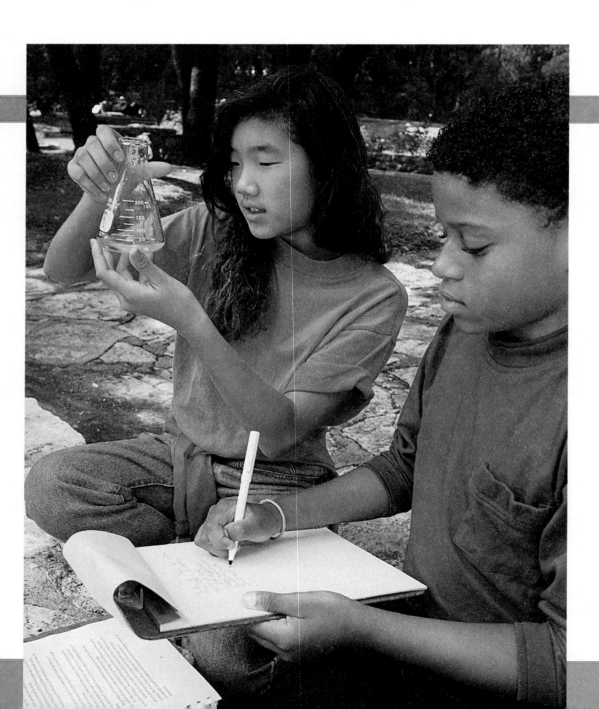

General Features of
Adolescent Thought

The Cognitive Developmental
Viewpoint: Formal Thought

Possibilities Versus Realities
Scientific Reasoning
Logical Combination of Ideas
Concrete Versus Formal Thought:
   Reasoning about Bending Rods
Cognitive Development Beyond Formal
   Thought
Implications of the Cognitive Developmental
   Viewpoint

Information-Processing Features
of Adolescent Thought

Improved Capacity to Process Information
Expertise in Specific Domains of
   Knowledge
Implications of the Information-Processing
   Viewpoint

Supporting Adolescents'
Cognitive Development

The Nature of Critical Thinking
Programs to Foster Critical Thinking

The Development of
Social Cognition

Egocentrism During Adolescence
The Development of Political Ideas
Religious Beliefs and Orientation

Moral Development:
Beliefs about Justice and Care

Kohlberg's Six Stages of Moral Judgment
Enduring Issues about the Development
   of Moral Judgment
Gilligan's Ethics of Care
The Ethics of Care During Adolescence

Focusing Questions

- To what extent and in what situations are adolescents capable of abstract reasoning?

- How do adolescents show their improved information-processing skills in everyday activities?

- How can one support or foster skillful and critical thinking in adolescents?

- How does cognitive development affect adolescents' knowledge and beliefs about political processes, religion, and morality?

J acob and Maria, both twelfth-graders, were discussing abortion.

"What's the big deal about abortion, anyway?" asked Jacob. "Why not just let anybody get one who wants one? It's a personal choice, like deciding which college to go to."

"You sound like you don't care about the people involved," said Maria. "How would you feel if *you* needed an abortion?"

"But I won't ever need one," Jacob replied smugly. "Only girls get pregnant, you know."

"That's why you don't understand," said Maria. "What if it's *your* body that can grow babies, and everybody expects *you* to grow one at the right time, like when you get married? And everybody expects you *not* to grow one at the wrong time, like during high school. How do you deal with all those people—your parents and friends, and the baby's father too?"

Jacob looked thoughtful at this comment. Then he said, "You're getting bogged down in what other people think. Try to imagine what you yourself would want to do with your life if you found out you were pregnant."

"I do that," said Maria, "and I also try to think about what the baby would want to do with *his* or *her* life if I allowed it to live."

This example reveals a number of new cognitive competencies that adolescents acquire. Jacob and Maria reason about possibilities rather than about actual events; neither of them has ever experienced an abortion. They also make generalizations as a basis for specific conclusions; for Jacob, abortion is generally "a personal choice" and should always be treated as such. These are cognitive abilities that middle-years children also show in some situations, but not as often or as reliably. Thinking in the middle years is more tied to the concrete than it is in adolescence.

In this chapter, we look at thinking in the adolescent years. We do so from two general viewpoints. The first is the *cognitive developmental viewpoint,* often associated with the work of Piaget. The second is the more recent approach of *information-processing theory,* which analyzes human thinking as a complex storage, retrieval, and organizing system for information, much like a computer. Because each of these theories is discussed elsewhere in this book, we focus here on their relevance to adolescence.

In real life, of course, thinking is always "about" something in particular. In recognition of that fact, we also discuss adolescents' ideas about themselves and about morality, politics, and religion. The two general theories about adolescent cognition help us understand how adolescents (and others) make decisions about right and wrong, about the consequences of political actions, and about the nature of God.

469

GENERAL FEATURES OF ADOLESCENT THOUGHT

Teenagers' new cognitive competencies broaden the horizons of their world substantially. For example, the question "What if a nuclear war broke out?" is more meaningful to an adolescent than to a child, even though both are equally inexperienced with actual nuclear war. So is the question "What if I had been born really poor or fabulously rich?" Adolescents can imagine what these situations might be like even though they have not experienced them in a concrete way. In general, thinking about the possible creates a new skill for speculating about important events and guessing about daily experiences (Kahlbaugh & Haviland, 1991). It also stimulates adolescents to daydream or fantasize about their actions and feelings. And it helps them make more astute inferences about human motivations ("Perhaps she did that because . . . ").

Tied to this ability is a greater capacity to plan ahead. Contrary to what frustrated parents sometimes claim, adolescents can set and plan goals for themselves, and they can do so much more competently than children can. Sometimes such goals are socially approved ones, such as making sure to take the best courses to get into a desirable college. Just as often, however, goals seem to lack redeeming value by conventional adult standards, such as when an adolescent carefully plans and finances an expensive trip to a rock concert in a faraway city.

Another way to state these competencies is to say that during adolescence, young people develop an ability to think about thoughts and to do so in a logical way. Most of the time such thinking serves some purpose, such as developing a better understanding of human nature or figuring out the best way to have fun. But sometimes thinking about thoughts has no concrete content at all. Many adolescents are quite capable of thinking simply about the forms of statements or propositions, even when the statements lack content entirely:

Some wugs are glibs.
All glibs are bots.

Compared to children, teenagers think more often about possibilities and about the future; they also daydream and fantasize more. What do you suppose this adolescent is thinking about?

From these two statements, some adolescents can decide, and even enjoy deciding, whether or not any "wugs" are in fact "bots." (The answer, incidentally, is that some "wugs" are indeed "bots," though not necessarily all of them.)

What Do You Think?

How did your thinking change when you became a teenager compared to when you were in elementary school? Consider both *what* you thought about and *how* you thought, and compare your experiences with those of a few friends or classmates.

THE COGNITIVE DEVELOPMENTAL VIEWPOINT: FORMAL THOUGHT

The cognitive developmental viewpoint (the one discussed in Chapter 2) interprets adolescents' cognitive changes as a stage of cognitive development, one in which a person acquires **formal operational thought.** This sort of thinking differs from *concrete operational thought* (discussed in Chapters 9 and 12) in three important ways: emphasizing the possible versus the real, using scientific reasoning, and skillfully combining ideas (Keating, 1991).

Possibilities Versus Realities

Formal thought involves attention to possibilities rather than merely to actual realities. A parent discovered this feature when he tried to get his two children to make suggestions about how to improve the humdrum weekly chicken dinner. "Fried is fine," said his nine-year-old. "I like it the way we always have it." But the fourteen-year-old insisted on a more complicated response: "Let me think about that," she said. Later she remarked, "Can we make some brand-new sauce for it? Maybe one of the cookbooks has some ideas." Even though the older child had never eaten chicken cooked this way, she thought about trying it.

Scientific Reasoning

Formal thought also involves scientific reasoning, the same kind psychologists use in designing many of their studies of human development. This quality reveals itself when adolescent students must solve some problem systematically. For example, how do youngsters in an art class figure out methods for mixing basic colors of paint to produce various intermediate shades and other colors? Those capable of formal operations in effect design an experiment to test all the available combinations of colors. They form hypotheses, or hunches, about how certain colors affect each other when mixed. Then they try out their hypotheses by mixing each basic color with every other basic color, being careful to try every possibility. By carefully observing the results of this procedure, they can draw logical conclusions about how to mix colors. This procedure in effect uses the scientific method.

In contrast, concrete operational children rarely act so systematically. Like the formal operational thinkers, they probably would mix colors, but they would do so haphazardly and might not take careful note of the results of their experiments. As a result, they may not learn to mix colors as rapidly as older, formal operational thinkers do. When confronted with this problem, of course, some younger children might draw on previous experience with art materials to solve it; but then their performance would reflect memory about how to mix colors rather than true scientific reasoning.

Many teenagers become able to solve problems scientifically. But like these students in a biology laboratory class, and like most adults, they still need ample concrete experiences to support their abstract thinking. Commonly, too, they may have trouble using scientific thought outside a structured school situation.

Logical Combination of Ideas

The third feature of formal operational thought involves combining ideas logically. Unlike less cognitively mature children, formal thinkers can hold several ideas in mind at once and combine or integrate them in logical ways. When asked to explain why some students perform better in school than others do, concrete operational thinkers are likely to latch on to one reason or another: "Some kids are smarter" or "Some kids work harder." In contrast, formal operational thinkers often give combinations of reasons, as this first-year university student did:

> Well, I think it depends. Sometimes it pays just to be smart. But it also helps to work hard—except when the teacher doesn't notice. Some kids do better too because they have taken courses before in the same area. Your first class in literature is likely to be harder than your fifth class in that subject.

As this example shows, the ability to combine ideas sometimes makes formal operational thinkers qualify their opinions more than pre–formal operational thinkers do.

Concrete Versus Formal Thought: Reasoning about Bending Rods

To understand the features of formal thought, consider how children at different stages of cognitive maturity approach a problem that Piaget designed (Inhelder & Piaget, 1958). A set of flexible rods is attached to the side of a basin of water. The rods differ in length, thickness, and material (metal or wood). In addition, a number of small weights are attached to the ends of the rods (see Figure 15.1). A friendly experimenter, perhaps a teacher, asks the child to determine what factor or factors control how far the rods bend toward the water. Does the amount of bending depend on the rods' length, on their thickness, on what they are made of, or on the weight attached to them?

Imagine you are a middle-years child asked to solve this problem. Your attention would be captured primarily by the apparatus itself. You would enjoy varying anything that seemed to vary—in this case, the length of the rods and the attached weights. You would also enjoy comparing one rod with another—wooden rods with metal ones and thick rods with thin ones. But your observations and comparisons would lack a system. You might vary more than one factor at a time (length *and* thickness) or forget to vary one of the factors at all. This haphazardness would likely prevent you from solving the problem fully, although you nevertheless might make a number of useful observations about the apparatus. The haphazard quality would also mark your efforts as concrete operational. At this age and stage, you would still be closely tied to the real or concrete.

As a formal operational thinker, however, you would approach the problem much more systematically. First, you would make some good guesses (or hypotheses) about the solution to the problem. You would take mental note of several factors that looked as though they might affect how far the rods bend: length, thickness, and weight, as well as whether the rods were made of wood or metal. Having noticed these possibilities, you would go on to the next step: devising and carrying out an informal experiment for testing each hypothesis in turn while holding all of the other factors constant. If you began by varying the weights on the rods, you would make sure to use only rods of the same thickness, length, and material. Otherwise you could not be sure whether any variations in bending came from differences in weight or from differences in one of the other factors. Having checked for the effects of weight in this way, you would go on to test the effects of each remaining factor, keeping the other three factors constant in every case.

The formal operational approach contrasts sharply with the less systematic efforts of younger children. It guarantees that, given enough time, you will find a

FIGURE 15.1

Experiment Requiring Formal Operational Thought

In this experiment, originally conducted by Piaget, the subject is asked to discover the factors that influence how far various rods bend toward the surface of a table, as shown here. Individuals who have developed formal operational thinking are able to test several factors (e.g., thickness of rods, length of rods, weights on rods) systematically and describe the bases for their explanation in a logical manner.

Rods of different thicknesses and lengths mounted on side of table

Washers of different weights

1. Invite student to vary angles of rods by hanging various washers on them and by changing the rods' lengths by pushing and pulling them through the holes where they are mounted.

2. Ask student: "What causes the rods to bend until they just barely touch the table?" And then ask: "How can you prove your theory?"

solution to the problem if a solution actually exists. It also makes more cognitive demands on you: you must devise hypotheses, plan a way to test them, and draw reasonable conclusions from your observations. Using concrete operations, in contrast, simply requires careful observation of events as they unfold; in thinking concretely, the child in essence asks from moment to moment, "Is what I am looking at a solution?"

Cognitive Development Beyond Formal Thought

Piaget and other psychologists have identified formal, or abstract, thought as a major achievement of the adolescent years. But for most human beings, it may not be the final or highest cognitive achievement. One clue to this possibility comes from adolescents themselves: some teenagers overuse logical thinking when they first achieve facility with it (Leadbetter, 1991). They may believe all problems, including ambiguous ones such as achieving world peace, can be solved by the proper application of rational principles and careful reasoning. Teenagers may fail to notice that some problems by nature resist the application of general logic and may inherently have multiple, partial solutions.

Consider Ana, a twelfth-grader who recently has begun sleeping with her boyfriend. Ana gets along well with her parents, and she knows they will worry and feel hurt if they learn of her sexual involvement. She also believes that in general, friends and family should have no secrets. By continuing her sexual activities, she seems to be violating this principle. On the other hand, she and her boyfriend regard their intimacy as a private matter, and she worries that telling her parents would violate this privacy, which she also considers her right. Telling her parents might also create a lot of bad feelings among Ana, her boyfriend, and her parents. In this case, her principles do not seem to point her toward a good solution: Ana believes that no matter what she does, somebody will get hurt, some ethical principle will be violated, or both.

Ana's situation suggests the importance of nonrational choices or judgments in solving real-life problems. Like Ana, many people may wish to be reasonable; that is, they may wish to rely on formal logic and may even believe they use it a lot. But in practice, most people use formal logic consistently only when solving academic problems posed by teachers, especially when the problems are deliberately scientific in nature (Bartsch, 1993). Less systematic reasoning serves as well or better for solving daily problems.

For older adolescents, the cognitive challenge consists of converting formal reasoning from a goal in itself to a *tool* used for broader purposes and tailored to the problems at hand (Myers, 1993). Ana cannot reach a sound decision about informing her parents of her sexual activities if she focuses on formal principles about truthfulness and privacy to the exclusion of more personal facts, which in this case include her knowledge of her boyfriend's and her own parents' probable responses and feelings. Taking these circumstances into account leads to the "best," or most mature, solution, but it may not lead to a solution that is fully logical in Piaget's sense.

Implications of the Cognitive Developmental Viewpoint

According to Piaget, formal operations begin developing early in adolescence and are fully formed by the end of the high school years. All teenagers supposedly develop wide-ranging thinking abilities that have a formal, abstract nature and apply to many specific experiences and daily problems. In reality, however, the actual cognitive performances of adolescents fail to conform to this picture in several ways. First, a majority of adolescents (and even adults) use formal thinking inconsistently or even fail to use it at all (Lakoff, 1994). In explaining why a car is not working properly, for example, many adolescents and adults merely describe the car's symptoms: "The brakes are making a weird noise" or "It won't shift into third gear." By focusing only on visible symptoms, such comments are in effect concrete operational; even a school-age child could make them. They cast doubt on whether formal thinking really develops as universally as concrete operational thinking does.

Most experimental studies of formal operational thinking have confirmed that cognitive performance depends a lot on how it is observed or measured (Overton, 1994). In a typical study, adolescents solve a Piagetian task, such as why a pendulum swings faster or slower. Is it affected by the length of the cord holding it, by the amount of weight on the end, or by the angle from which it starts? (The actual solution is length: shorter pendulums swing faster and longer ones swing slower, with the other variables having no effect.) In a task such as this, adolescents do best at demonstrating and drawing a solution and worst at describing a solution verbally, although many exceptions occur. For example, more individuals can show the importance of length by actually displaying swinging pendulums of different lengths, but fewer people can explain the ideas underlying the demonstration verbally and coherently.

The result is that formal operational thought does describe adolescents' thinking, but only partially or intermittently. Formal thought helps teenagers to argue with their parents more skillfully than they could as children, thereby contributing to the stereotype of teenagers as being relatively "rebellious." Formal thought also makes teenagers more skillful at cultivating friendships, potential dates, and social contacts; now they can imagine and anticipate the consequences of various friendly (and unfriendly) strategies. And formal thought means teenagers are more ready than children are to grapple with philosophical and abstract topics at school: literary analysis can now begin to make sense, for example, and so can at least some theoretical concepts in science.

At other times, however, especially when not using formal thought, adolescents can seem much younger than their years. They may argue with parents skillfully, but sometimes their goal may be petty, such as permission to stay out just a few minutes longer than usual. Social encounters may be planned to facilitate meeting a potential date, but the new date himself or herself may be a dubious choice of acquaintance. And broad concepts and principles learned in school can be treated as irrelevant to teenagers' everyday concerns (Forlizzi, 1993).

What Do You Think?

Outside of school- or job-related tasks, most people actually use formal operational thinking rather little in their everyday lives. How much do *you* actually use it? Think of a situation other than school (shopping, visiting a friend, cooking) in which you need to use abstract thinking to function effectively. What does your answer imply about the place of formal thought in adolescents' overall development?

INFORMATION-PROCESSING FEATURES OF ADOLESCENT THOUGHT

As we saw in Chapter 2, information-processing theory sees human cognition as a complex storage and retrieval system, governed largely by an "executive" control system that transfers information between short- and long-term memory and organizes information for more efficient and meaningful handling and retrieval. When cognition is viewed this way, development consists largely of overcoming the bottlenecks in processing information, especially those caused by the limited capacities of the executive and short-term memory. As children mature into adolescents, they develop strategies for taking in, organizing, and remembering larger amounts of information more quickly and with less effort. The most important of these strategies are included in Figure 15.2 and explained more fully next.

Improved Capacity to Process Information

Typically an adolescent can deal with, or process, more information than a child can. A first-grader may remember three or four random digits (3 9 5 1), but a teenager usually can remember six or seven. And when a first-grader asks an adult how to spell a word, he can hold only two or three letters in his mind at a time; the adult has to dole them out singly or in very small groups (*LO . . . CO . . . MO . . . TI . . . VE*). A teenager can more often encounter much longer groupings of letters and still reconstruct the word accurately.

These differences may result from either of two sources. The first source is what information-processing psychologists sometimes call *structural capacity*, meaning a person's basic "mental power," or cognitive ability (Case, 1991). Differences in structural capacity are like the differences in physical strength between adolescents and children: because teenagers have bigger and more powerful muscles, they naturally can accomplish more physically. The same is true for performance on cognitive tasks: adolescents may be able to handle longer-term projects than children can, partly because their brains can handle more information at any one time.

The second source of differences between children and adolescents is sometimes called *functional capacity,* the ability to make efficient use of existing mental abilities. Differences in functional capacity are more like the improvements in physical performance that come to a gymnast who already is perfectly conditioned: at a certain point in her training, her performance improves mainly because she learns to coordinate her movements more precisely, rest her muscles when she does not really need them, and take into account the unique features of the gymnasium in which she is performing. Similarly, functional capacity on cognitive tasks requires

FIGURE 15.2
Developmental Changes in Information Processing
Although the basic nature of information processing remains constant from childhood to adolescence, important changes occur in several features, as the figure indicates. Short-term memory may increase in capacity, control processes become more efficient, and long-term memory contains more specific knowledge as well as knowledge about problem solving, or "how to think."

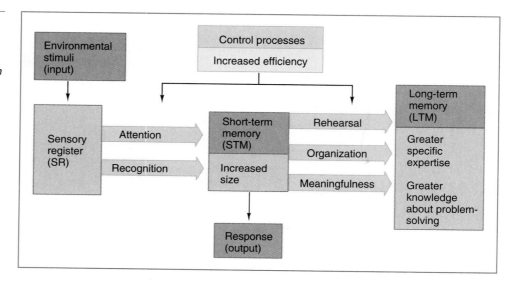

A Talk with Joan, Age Fifteen

Thinking in Adolescence

Joan is a slender, poised young woman of fifteen with a friendly but serious manner. She was interviewed on the back porch of her home after school.

Interviewer: How have your thinking and intellectual activity changed over the past several years?

Joan: For some kids it looks like they haven't changed very much, but for me they have. You read and think about different things—like *1984*—more than you did before, and the discussions you have are a lot different . . . about bigger things.

Interviewer: Why does a book like *1984* appeal to you now?

Joan: Well, you can understand it now. I mean, you can start thinking about all the different . . . the big questions . . .

Interviewer: What would be an example?

Joan: Like . . . the type of government. Serious things. Now if I read a fairy tale it's fun, but I'm not so into it. It's not quite as interesting, while before it was exciting.

Interviewer: Have there been changes in the way you use your mind to figure out problems at school?

Joan: I don't think so. I mean, it's like I do more advanced math and stuff, but it doesn't seem to me that I couldn't have understood it before if someone had taught it to me. Of course, now you don't just deal with facts. You sort of write essays and things and read. You have to think about the connections. Which I'm not sure I couldn't have done before.

Interviewer: How has your thinking about problems changed?

Joan: It's hard to remember. I mean, I talked about problems before, but I suppose that I didn't think about so many realistic things. I remember thinking about "what if" after I read something or saw something, but it was generally about fantasy rather than something like world war or the nuclear threat. I think I could have learned what I am learning now in sixth grade. When we get into more interesting things like in history and English, I end up talking about it out of school more. Like with my parents and with some friends. When it's not just facts. I mean, you never talk about math and French out of school, but you may talk about a book you read in history or something connected with other things.

Interviewer: Do you feel more like an intellectual equal with adults?

Joan: I don't ever remember feeling like I was not an equal. I always thought that if I didn't know it now, I'd learn it in a few months, and then I would definitely be as smart or smarter.

Interviewer: Are all kids able to think the same way you do?

Joan: Well, it sort of divides up more. I mean, before there were lots of different levels, and it was basically who could learn faster. And it's not like some kids just never get that far and some kids, even if they don't get that far fast, are able to think about things. . . . So I think it does divide up more into two separate groups instead of many levels.

Interviewer: Have you thought about the reasons for this?

Joan: Well, sometimes I think it might be just like who spends time thinking about things. And sometimes I think the upper group are just extremely smart. I mean, I think a lot of it's how much energy you're putting into it and how much interest you have in thinking about it.

Interviewer: So the lower group may spend less time thinking . . .

Joan: Or at that time in their lives, they're not bothering to think so much about these things; they're worrying about other things. And some people look like they're thinking about things, and when you talk to them, . . . they're not, really.

Interviewer: Do you get fooled the other way too?

Joan: Yes. And then you talk to them and they say something really smart that they thought of, and you say, "Hmmm!"

What Do You Think?

1. What signs of adolescent egocentrism do you see in Joan?

2. Which of Piaget's stages of cognitive development best describes Joan's thinking? How typical do you think she is of children her age?

3. Joan mentions her increasing interest in what she calls the "big questions." What might this interest signify about her cognitive approach to moral and political issues?

coordinating existing skills to best advantage—recalling facts about World War II by grouping them according to theme or topic, for instance.

In terms of cognitive development, it usually is hard to discriminate between the relative influences of structural and functional capacity, that is, between how much of an adolescent's improved thinking comes from greater ability to hold information in mind and how much comes from greater efficiency in processing information (King & Kitchener, 1994). Almost any cognitive task allows an individual to perform it more efficiently with practice; yet the person himself may not be aware that he is trying to do so. For example, many adolescents can write term papers much more easily than they could when they attended elementary school, but try as they may, they may be unable to explain *why* they can do so. Did their extra years of practice make them smarter than before, or simply more efficient at using skills they have always had? Research on information processing suggests that cognitive development consists of a bit of both.

Expertise in Specific Domains of Knowledge

By adolescence, many individuals have become comparative experts in specific domains of knowledge or skill. These domains may or may not have much to do with school learning. One teenager excels in knowledge of mathematics, whereas another excels in knowledge of baseball and still another excels in getting along with people.

Much of such expertise may depend not on generalized development of cognitive structures, as Piagetian theorists would claim, but on the long, slow acquisition of large amounts of specific knowledge, along with better organization of that knowledge. Studies of experts and novices among adults suggest this possibility. Experts in physics know many more concepts about physics than beginners do, but they do not necessarily know more about geography, English grammar, or other areas of knowledge (Gregg & Leinhardt, 1995). Experts also know more about problem solving in their particular field of expertise. A mathematician remembers countless formulas, equations, and solution methods, thanks to years of experience in memorizing them. Her memories naturally help her to solve new problems as they come up; she may realize that a new equation is similar to one she has worked with before and simply recall how she responded to the earlier formula.

Ironically, then, expertise often makes creative problem solving unnecessary. Instead of using valuable energy in thinking through a solution, the expert can simply recall *heuristics,* or general strategies for solving classes or types of problems. (Table 15.1 illustrates the use of heuristics for solving problems in two different

Compared to younger girls who like to make pottery, these teenagers are more planful and more able to carry out complicated projects. These changes in their potting skills probably happen both because they are able to hold more ideas and plans in mind at one time, and because they can coordinate their activities—and even their hand movements—more skillfully than before.

TABLE 15.1 *Examples of Problem-Solving Strategies (Heuristics) in Two Academic Subjects*

Problem in Social Studies	*What have the media been saying about the impact of computers on society?*
	Novice-level strategy: Search all of the headlines in the newspaper for the past year.
	Expert-level strategy: Search the headlines for the past week or two; look for references to and dates of references further back in the past; check only those dates.
Problem in Algebra	*How to factor the equation $12x^2 - xy - 6y^2$?*
	Novice-level strategy: Try multiplying every possible set of linear combinations—$(x + y)$, $(x - y)$, $(2x + y)$, $2x - y)$, $(x + 2y)$, $(x - 2y)$, etc.—until you find one that gives the correct answer.
	Expert-level strategy: Search for clues that eliminate the need to try every possible linear combination; e.g., try only combinations in which the final terms multiply to −6.

academic areas.) This advantage, however, is confined to specific domains or types of problems. An expert's performance therefore contradicts a widespread (but not entirely justified) impression of Piaget's theory: that it proposes powerful, abstract strategies that develop across many domains at once. Outside of his field, an expert must struggle for solutions just like the rest of us. Within his field, on the other hand, he often may only look as though he is reasoning at a high level, when in reality much of his performance amounts to a simple recall—the kind we all engage in when we remember the letters of the alphabet or a phone number.

This conclusion does not mean, however, that experts work only by simple recall. On the contrary, their larger number of memories may free them to focus on more difficult aspects of a problem or on aspects they have never encountered before. If you have to make an oral presentation on a topic that you already know well, for example, you may spend *more* time planning its overall design and purpose and relatively *less* time on the details of final preparation. To a large extent, the final preparations take care of themselves because you can draw on a rich array of ideas and concepts about your topic.

Implications of the Information-Processing Viewpoint

By focusing on the detailed features of problem solving, the information-processing viewpoint provides a valuable complement to the broader approach of cognitive developmental theory. By focusing on the fine details of thinking, information-processing theory offers more insights into why individuals vary in their thinking performances from one occasion to the next. Some psychologists have also tried to identify developmental trends in information processing (Case & Edelstein, 1993). Their research has emphasized specific sequences within particular domains of thinking rather than the more global stages of the cognitive developmental approach. In this way, the information-processing viewpoint resembles research on adolescents' cognition about interpersonal and social knowledge.

What Do You Think?

Think of an activity or area of knowledge in which you consider yourself a relative expert. How much of your expertise has resulted from knowing a lot of specific facts about the

Working with | **Carole Castleton, PSYCHIATRIC GROUP WORKER**

Cognitive Strategies for Social Problems

Carole Castleton has worked for seven years as a group therapist at an adolescent psychiatric treatment center. Most of the teenagers who come to the center have emotional difficulties; often they are depressed, withdrawn, or even suicidal. When I began the interview, I expected Carole to describe numerous social problems among the teens at the center. What I learned, though, is that it's more accurate to think of their problems as social and cognitive simultaneously.

Kelvin: What exactly do you do at the treatment center?

Carole: I'm a group therapist. I coordinate several dozen groups, both for outpatients and inpatients. We try to find out what sort of group will best help each teenager on arrival.

Kelvin: So the groups differ, not just the teens?

Carole: For sure. We create groups in all sorts of modalities—psychoeduca-tional, expressive, supportive, insight oriented. Each kid thinks and feels in a unique way, so each needs a unique style of group.

Kelvin: I'm not familiar with many of the terms you just used—for instance, what's a psychoeducational group like?

Carole: Well, that group would have some structure and a theme or goal—"communication," for instance. All group activities would focus on how kids talk and listen, on nonverbal "messages," on differences between assertive and aggressive, and so on. If I needed to talk about managing personal stress with these kids, I would do it in a way that also dealt with issues of communication.

Kelvin: Wouldn't you do this sort of thing with *all* of the groups?

Carole: Not in the same way. An expressive group, for instance, would revolve around art work, art explo-rations—clay, free drawing, that sort of thing. Sometimes the leader might suggest a task, like "try drawing your family," but the emphasis is always on the artistic activity itself: the kids communicate through their art, not with words.

Kelvin: How do you decide which group might be the "best fit" for a particular teen?

Carole: That's the big challenge of my job! When teenagers first arrive, I meet with them to learn something about their background and why they came to the center. Even that initial meeting reveals something about their communication styles—do they use words, do they like to work with their hands? Do they like—even *need*—to move around a lot? We also have whole-staff meetings to assess each youngster's strengths and to fig-ure out what sort of experiences she's likely to respond to positively. Very few actually seem suited to insight

area? How much has resulted from organizing your knowledge better than other people do? Compare your opinions with those of a classmate or friend who is an expert in an area other than yours.

SUPPORTING ADOLESCENTS' COGNITIVE DEVELOPMENT

Adolescents' cognitive changes result partly from informal everyday experiences, such as discussions with friends or family members about ideas and points of view that are new or with which the teenager does not agree. But they can also be influenced deliberately, as sometimes happens in school curricula or other educational programs intended to stimulate young people to think in new ways and adopt new perspectives. What do such interventions involve?

The Nature of Critical Thinking

Programs to encourage adolescents' thinking vary somewhat among themselves, of course, and go by a variety of names, including *problem solving, reflective* therapy—explicity talking about their problems. They do seem to function well in other ways.

Kelvin: So the *way* a teenager thinks makes quite a difference for treatment! It's not just "pure emotion" that's the challenge?

Carole: It's everything—emotion, social life, thinking. You can really see it when you look at their school experiences. Usually these have been wrecked by terrible home experiences—by abuse, by a nasty divorce between the parents, by family "secrets" that make it hard for a kid to think straight.

Kelvin: An example?

Carole: This boy who came last spring, just thirteen or fourteen years old, "young" compared to most others here. He had been hyperactive when he was in elementary school, on Ritalin [a drug to control hyperactivity]. His parents were divorced. When he came, his stepdad kept saying, "The boy doesn't listen, he's not disciplined"—as if it were the boy's choice, the boy's fault. He wasn't reading or writing in school, got in fights with teachers.

Well, our observations confirmed some of this—he *was* restless, he *would* fidget during groups and seem like he wasn't listening, he *did* get really mad sometimes. But we also found that he *could* read, though at a pretty basic level.

One day he came to group late. We were building Lego models, copying from photos. The other kids had been taking a long time, but he got his done much faster than everybody else!

Kelvin: What did that tell you about him?

Carole: That he was visual and tactile—sight and touch oriented. He was not verbally oriented, yet his stepdad and his teachers had been "talking at" him for years, trying to get through to him and to make him function verbally. It just didn't work. He didn't think that way. His strengths had been missed, and all sorts of emotional conflict had been the result.

What Do You Think?

1. The different groups Carole describes seem consistent with Gardner's notion of "multiple intelligences" (see page 00). How, then, do you account for her comment that "very few [teens] actually seem suited for insight therapy"? What might prevent these teenagers from fully developing this sort of thinking?

2. How could the center prepare a teen who prefers to communicate nonverbally (e.g., via art work) to return to school, where most academic activities depend on verbal give-and-take?

3. Suppose most of the teenagers at the treatment center had criminal records instead of histories of depression and withdrawal. How might that change the center's treatment priorities? Would that influence the emphases of the groups?

thinking, or *creativity.* For our purposes here, we will use the term **critical thinking,** meaning reflection or thought about complex issues, usually to make decisions or take actions. Despite its name, critical thinking refers not to thinking that is negative or complaint ridden but to thinking that is thoughtful, yields new insights, and gives a basis for intelligent choice. Critical thinking is a broad, practical skill: it can help a person figure out why an unfamiliar appliance broke down, compose a term paper, resolve a conflict with a friend, or decide what kind of career to pursue.

What does critical thinking involve? Educators and psychologists have analyzed it in various ways, but usually point out the following elements (King & Kitchener, 1994):

1. *Basic operations of reasoning* To think critically, a person must be able to classify, generalize, deduce conclusions, and perform other logical steps mentally.

2. *Domain-specific knowledge* To deal with a problem, a person must know something about its topic or content. To evaluate a proposal for a new, fairer tax system, a person must know something about the existing tax system. To resolve a personal conflict, a person has to know something about the person with whom he is having the conflict.

3. *Metacognitive knowledge* (knowledge about how human thinking works, including one's own). Effective critical thinking requires a person to monitor

when she really understands an idea, know when she needs new information, and predict how easily she can gather and learn that information.

4. *Values, beliefs, and dispositions* Thinking critically means valuing fairness and objectivity. It means having confidence that thinking does in fact lead to solutions. It also means having a persistent and reflective disposition when thinking.

Interestingly, research has found that students themselves understand these elements of critical thinking (Nichols et al., 1995). Furthermore, compared to grade-school children, adolescents regard critical thinking as a fairer and more appropriate purpose of schooling (see Figure 15.3).

Programs to Foster Critical Thinking

Educators have devised a number of programs intended to foster the qualities needed for critical thinking (French & Rhodes, 1992), many of which serve adolescents. The programs differ in their particulars: they last for various lengths of time, emphasize different thinking skills, and draw on content from different areas of the standard school curriculum. Some programs are integrated into the curriculum, meaning they replace a traditional course in some subject area; others are taught separately and draw content from several areas at once.

FIGURE 15.3
Students' Ratings of Fairness of Critical Thinking as a Goal of School
As students get older, they perceive critical thinking to be a fairer or more appropriate goal of schooling. In other parts of this particular study, students also increasingly rated critical thinking as more likely to get students excited about learning and to get them to help one another more.
Source: Adapted from Nichols et al. (1995).

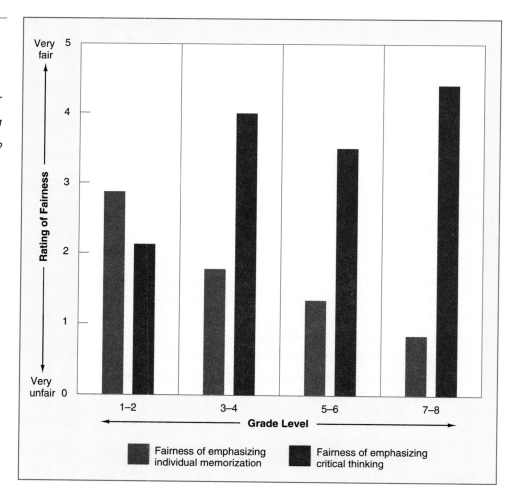

But experts do agree on several general principles that enhance the quality of programs that teach critical thinking. First, teaching thinking is best done directly and explicitly. Critical thinking does not develop on its own by unconscious osmosis, so to speak (Keefe & Walberg, 1992). Watching the teacher or a classmate think critically does not guarantee that a student will become a better thinker. Neither does giving a student a lot of practice in simple mental operations, such as basic addition or simple logical puzzles.

Second, good programs for teaching thinking offer lots of practice at solving actual problems. Merely describing the elements of critical thinking (as this text is doing) does not turn students into skillful thinkers. To accommodate the need for practice, the most successful educational programs last as least a full academic year and sometimes also weave the thinking skills into other, related courses to extend the effects of the program still further.

Third, successful programs try to create an environment explicitly conducive to critical thinking. Typically they expect teachers to model important critical thinking skills themselves, such as thinking out loud while they explain a solution to a problem. The programs also expect teachers to convey confidence in students' ability to think while providing constructive, explicit criticism of ideas, whether their own or the students'. For example, one technique is to invite individual students to temporarily act as teacher or constructive critic (Slavin, 1995). To make time for these activities, most critical thinking programs tend to minimize individual seatwork, a time-consuming activity that is found in much traditional classroom instruction but gives students little on-the-spot feedback about the quality of their thinking processes.

Whatever their differences, programs that teach critical thinking draw on the spirit, if not the literal research findings, of several strands of cognitive theory concerning the adolescent years. One strand is Piagetian, with its concern for how logic and reasoning gradually develop. Another is information-processing theory, with its focus on specific ways of organizing ideas and coordinating new ideas with pre-existing ones. A third strand is the concern with the human context of cognitive development in adolescence: how people and settings affect a young person's thinking. We describe this third strand of cognitive development next.

What Do You Think?

Some educators argue that you cannot teach thinking skills in *general,* since a person always thinks about something in *particular.* Why do you think they take this position? This issue makes for a useful debate in class. Try adopting a position contrary to the one you truly embrace!

THE DEVELOPMENT OF SOCIAL COGNITION

No matter which approach they take, most developmental psychologists agree that the new cognitive skills of adolescents have important effects on their **social cognition,** that is, their knowledge and beliefs about interpersonal and social matters. In this section, we look at the most important forms of social cognition. We begin with a description of the special form of self-centeredness, or **adolescent egocentrism,** that affects teenagers' reactions to others and their beliefs about themselves. We consider what causes this form of egocentrism and how those causes affect three other important kinds of social cognition: moral beliefs, political attitudes, and religious orientation.

The teenagers shown here illustrate two aspects of adolescent egocentrism: a preoccupation with the reactions of others and a belief that serious catastrophes may happen to others but never to them.

Egocentrism During Adolescence

When adolescents first begin reasoning abstractly, they often become overly impressed with this skill; it seems to them that anything can be solved "if only people would be reasonable" (that is, logical). This attitude can make teenagers idealistic and keep them from appreciating the practical limits of logic (Bowers, 1995). They may wonder why no one has ever "realized" that world war might be abolished simply by explaining to all the world powers the obvious dangers of war. Or they may wonder why their parents have not noticed the many "errors" they have made in raising children.

The development of formal thought also leads to a new kind of confusion between an adolescent's own thoughts and those of others. This confusion of viewpoints amounts to a form of egocentrism. Unlike the egocentrism of preschoolers, which is based on concrete problems, adolescent egocentrism concerns more abstract thoughts and problems. Consider what happened to Neira. When she was fourteen, she had to perform at a figure-skating recital. For weeks beforehand, she practiced daily to prepare. As the performance date drew near, she naturally began to worry about how well she would do. In fact, she became convinced that "everyone" was talking about her particular performance and wondering how good it would be. Her parents encouraged her not to worry and assured her that "people always like what you do on your skates." To Neira, however, these comments suggested that her parents did not appreciate the unique importance of *her* performance. Even after the recital, Neira fretted about others' reactions to it: Had they liked it? What were they saying about it?

The Imaginary Audience   Adolescent egocentrism like Neira's sometimes shows itself in teenagers' preoccupation with the reactions of others. Thirteen-year-olds often fail to differentiate between how they feel about themselves and how others feel about them. Instead, they act as though they are performing for an **imaginary audience,** one that is as concerned with their appearance and behavior as they themselves are (Elkind, 1985).

Teenagers also reveal concern with an imaginary audience through *strategic interactions* with their peers, encounters that aim to either reveal or conceal personal information indirectly. Telephoning often serves as a strategic interaction, especially for younger teenagers. Frequent phone calls help sustain a belief in personal popularity with an imaginary audience, so a teenager may subtly encourage others to phone by casually promising to share special gossip or secrets "if you call me tonight." An adolescent can also create the appearance of popularity by talking on the phone for very long periods of time so that potential callers get a "busy" signal, implying that the youngster is too popular to reach easily by telephone. This message can also be conveyed to the person on the line with an offhand comment such as "Gotta go; I'm expecting some other calls."

The Personal Fable   As a result of their egocentrism, teenagers often believe in a **personal fable,** or the notion that their own lives embody a special story that is heroic and completely unique. For example, one high school student may be convinced that no love affair has ever reached the heights of romance of his involvement with a classmate. Another may believe she is destined for great fame and fortune by virtue of (what she considers to be) her unparalleled combination of charm and academic talent. Still another may "know" that even though serious catastrophes happen to others, they will never happen to him; he will never get seriously ill, or have trouble finding a job, or die.

In experiencing these feelings and ideas, adolescents fail to realize how other individuals feel about them as well. Early in adolescence, they still have only limited empathy, or the ability to understand reliably the abstract thoughts and feelings of others and compare those thoughts and feelings with their own. In fact, much of adolescence consists of developing these social skills. So does most of adulthood, for that matter; we never really finish learning how to understand others or comparing our own experiences with those of others. But adolescence serves as the time when most people begin learning to consider other viewpoints in relation to their own and developing complex ideas about moral, political, and religious questions, among others, in response.

However, not all teenagers seem equally egocentric, and even those who do show this quality only when compared to adults, not to younger children. Investigations of adolescents' belief in an imaginary audience show that teenagers are just as likely to develop greater empathy or interpersonal sensitivity during this developmental period as they are to develop greater self-centeredness (Lapsley, 1991). Accurate awareness of others' opinions about oneself apparently develops alongside, and sometimes even instead of, self-conscious preoccupation with others' opinions. The relative balance between these two developments depends, among other things, on the quality of relationships between parents and the adolescent: closer and more supportive relationships lead to greater realism and less self-consciousness.

The Development of Political Ideas

Perhaps not surprisingly, political thinking develops in ways that parallel other forms of cognition and continually reveals both progress and limitations. Teenagers often hold more sophisticated political ideas than children do; they handle political ideas and opinions more abstractly and see more relationships among them. They view the formation of laws and legal regulations more democratically, seeing them as something that applies equally to everybody in society rather than to isolated

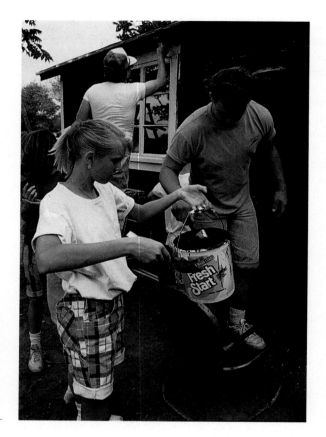

Participation in social causes—like these two youths painting a house for a charitable cause—both reflects and builds adolescents' involvement in the community and society. It also builds more sophisticated thinking about societal needs. Chances are, though, that participation also serves personal needs, like making new friends.

individuals or selected groups (Adelson, 1991; Torney-Purta, 1990a). In these ways, adolescent political thinking draws on elements of formal operational thought and the relatively advanced forms of moral thinking. At the same time, however, adolescents reveal substantial gaps and inconsistencies in their political thinking. These suggest that political thinking is not acquired in an all-or-nothing, stagelike way but involves acquiring large amounts of specific political knowledge—an idea consistent with the information-processing viewpoint.

To understand these developments, consider a common political issue: poverty. What must be done to eliminate it? Can it really ever be eliminated? The answers given by two (imaginary) children, one in sixth grade and one in twelfth grade, differ in significant ways that reflect the children's cognitive development. The answers also have some common limitations despite the six years of living and learning that separate the two youngsters. First, the sixth-grader:

INTERVIEWER: Do you know what I mean by *poverty*?

SIXTH-GRADER: No.

INTERVIEWER: It means being poor—not having any money. Could you make it so no one was poor?

SIXTH-GRADER: Um . . . if they got people to really work hard, then maybe. But if you were retired or just lazy, I don't know. You've already put in lots of years working.

INTERVIEWER: Do you think we could make it so that there wouldn't be poor people any more?

SIXTH-GRADER: Maybe, in the future, if they could enforce the law that all lazy people should work.

The twelfth-grader answered in this way:

INTERVIEWER: Do you think we could ever eliminate poverty?

TWELFTH-GRADER: Yes, because this country is highly advanced and rich. I mean, we give away money for all kinds of things—roads, starving nations, and such. Why not spend some money at home here? Buy fewer bombs, make more jobs—even for young kids like me!

Aside from obvious differences in content, how do these two responses differ in cognitive form? First, the adolescent seems to better understand that a political problem may concern many aspects of society at once (Torney-Purta, 1990b). Unlike the younger child, he points out how poverty may be related to or aggravated by activities beyond the borders of his own particular country, the United States, by implying that poverty abroad may worsen poverty at home by stimulating foreign aid and thereby draining away dollars. In contrast, the younger child implies that poverty is simply the fault of the individuals who experience it (Leahy, 1990). If only they would work harder, they might escape their problem with little or no help from the rest of society and with little impact on society.

The two children also have different views of how governments can help ordinary people. The sixth-grader implies that the most helpful thing government can do about poverty is to act like the police: the government should make poor people work harder ("enforce the law that all lazy people should work"). The twelfth-grader, on the other hand, suggests that government and citizens can genuinely cooperate with each other. In his view, the government should identify the people or groups who need money the most and give it to them; after all, these are the domestic poor, not the foreign poor.

Although the twelfth-grader's ideas are more abstract and less personal than the sixth-grader's, neither youngster expresses a true *ideology,* or coherent philosophy, about poverty. Admittedly, neither has a chance to do so in the short interviews quoted earlier; longer talks might allow them to show their political knowledge and sensitivities more completely. But probably not; studies show that most adolescents lack a consistent, conscious system of beliefs about politics (Haste & Torney-Purta, 1992). Instead, they tend to approximate consistency, frequently contradict themselves, and often base political ideas on values that are unconscious to some extent. The twelfth-grader in this example may freely contradict himself when the topic shifts to the problems of strategic planning for national defense by deciding that foreign economic aid does serve a useful, if indirect, purpose by gaining allies abroad.

Of course, in a highly individualistic society such as the United States, lack of a coherent ideology may also represent a final or true maturity rather than a failure to attain one. Like most adolescents, very few adults really have explicit, complex political philosophies, and many tend to hold rather personalized beliefs on specific issues. The attitudes of the sixth-grader have been stated publicly in the U.S. Congress, as well as in many other adult forums. Yet sophisticated ideas about aspects of the political process often are expressed by young people as well, as long as they are speaking from experiences they have actually had (Coles, 1993).

Religious Beliefs and Orientation

During adolescence, cognitive development also affects both specific religious beliefs and overall religious orientation. In general, specific beliefs become more sophisticated or complex than they were during childhood. The concept of religion, for example, evolves from relatively superficial notions to subtler and more abstract ones. A child of ten is more likely to identify a religion by observable behaviors (a Catholic is "someone who goes to mass every Sunday"), whereas a teenager is more likely to identify it according to beliefs (a Jew is "someone who believes in one God and doesn't believe in the New Testament"). These changes occur partly due to young people's developing cognitive skills and partly because they are accumulating greater general knowledge of the world and of religion in particular (Coles, 1990).

For those involved in religious education and development, children's acquisition of specific beliefs such as these often matters less than their development of an overall view of the world, or of a *faith*—a coherent orientation to religious experiences that guides their responses to life. Faith is much more general than "mere" beliefs are: it usually involves feelings as well as thoughts. Due to its breadth, faith often touches on topics and problems that are not explicitly religious in content, such as the meaning of birth and death or the best ways to handle personal relationships (Noddings, 1993).

In childhood, religious orientation amounts largely to loose groupings of concrete religious beliefs and images, often with relatively little coordination and seemingly little relevance to daily experiences (J. Fowler, 1991). A ten-year-old might describe God like this, for example:

INTERVIEWER: Can you tell me what God is?

MILLIE: God is a like a saint. He's good and he like—he like rules the world, but in a good way. And . . .

INTERVIEWER: How does he rule the world?

MILLIE: Well, he—not really rule the world, but um—let's see, he like—he lives on top of the world, and he's always watching over everybody. At least he tries to. And he does what he thinks is right. He does what he thinks is right and tries to do the best and—he lives up in heaven and . . .

INTERVIEWER: What does God look like?

MILLIE: I imagine that he's an old man with a white beard and white hair wearing a long robe and that the clouds are his floor and he has a throne. And he has all these people, and there's angels around him. (J. Fowler, 1981, pp. 138–140)

Millie describes God in concrete terms that have little relevance to daily life. In contrast, a fifteen-year-old offers fewer visual images; for her, God is more of a universal presence that she believes permeates her life and helps her:

INTERVIEWER: What do you think God is?

LINDA: God is different to a lot of people . . . I just feel . . . he's there. There might not be any material proof, but I *know*. I can bet my life on it. Really. I know because he *has* talked to me. . . . [Once when I had trouble with my friends,] I remembered that, you know, there was *God,* and I just asked him to tell me something, tell me what I could do, because why can't I be good friends with everybody? Go places with her one time, and then with her and him, and you know, with everybody? (J. Fowler, 1981, pp. 155–156)

For this adolescent, God is not so much a person living in a specific place as an abstraction. God is a relationship that transcends specific situations and experiences and that helps to give those specifics fuller meaning.

Religious orientation need not come out of an organized religion, of course, and for many adolescents and adults it does not. Many teenagers prefer to develop a personal faith without reference to other groups' or individuals' beliefs. Take this sixteen-year-old, who grew up attending an unusually liberal Protestant church and whose ideas resemble those of many people who never attend church at all:

INTERVIEWER: What means the most to you?

BRIAN: Just life. It fascinates me. I don't know what goes on before or after birth or death. And some things scare me. The unknown is really a factor in my life because I like to think about it a lot and the reason why everything got here. It really bothers me a lot because I don't know the answers and no one knows the answers, and I can't turn to anyone to get the answers—except to God, if there is a God. Maybe someday I'll get a vision from the Almighty! *(spoken sarcastically)* (J. Fowler, 1981, p. 159)

These ideas have much of the scope of Linda's comments. Despite appearances, however, they may partly reflect social conformity rather than true, spontaneous conviction. Paradoxically, Brian may be conforming to an ideal of nonconformity or independent thinking. He implies this possibility elsewhere in the interview by stating that the worst thing that could happen to him would be to agree with conventional, majority opinions. But although Brian and Linda differ dramatically in the source of their religious orientation—Brian comes from a relatively secular, humanist social environment and Linda from a more traditional Christian denomination—they are not entirely opposite in their thinking. Compared to Millie, they share a quality of comprehensiveness; their specific beliefs range relatively widely over life's issues and fit together at least some of the time.

These developments may result from changes both in general cognitive structures and in knowledge and information-processing strategies. As Piaget predicted for other realms of knowledge, Brian and Linda have developed the capacity to think abstractly, and as a result they may have reconstructed their childhood beliefs and faith to use their new abilities. At the same time, they have had several years in which to acquire new knowledge about religion, God, and the meaning and dilemmas of life (Heller, 1994). Along with this knowledge may have come new, broad strategies for dealing with and organizing this knowledge, strategies similar in scope to Piaget's formal operations but with greater application to religious problems. Therefore, in their own ways, Brian and Linda may have become modest experts about faith, although not about the same kind of faith.

As these comments suggest, cognition significantly influences many areas of adolescent life that are essentially social in nature. And vice versa: a motivation to have many friends, for example, can foster the strong development of empathy, which is in part a cognitive skill. Similarly, deep involvement with a religion can promote relatively sophisticated knowledge and thinking about religious beliefs, at least as they exist in that particular religion. In real life, cognitive and social development do not divide up neatly as they are made to do in textbooks such as this one. (See, for example, the Multicultural View box on lives of moral commitment.) Their blending shows up again in the next chapter, in which we discuss adolescents' psychosocial development. As we will see there, most psychosocial developments assume the types of cognitive accomplishments discussed in this chapter. Some, such as identity development, do so rather explicitly, but all at least imply an awareness of teenagers' growing ability to think.

What Do You Think?

A young person once said, "My parents get smarter every year." In what sense is this probably true? In what sense is it probably the young person who is getting smarter? If possible, after articulating your ideas about these questions, consult with a parent to get her or his own views about them.

MORAL DEVELOPMENT: BELIEFS ABOUT JUSTICE AND CARE

As adolescents gradually overcome egocentrism in their personal relationships, they develop a personal **morality,** or sensitivity to and knowledge of what is right and wrong. Moral thinking develops in two ways: in the form of increasingly logical and

A Multicultural View

Cross-cultural Misunderstandings in the Classroom

Consider these classroom situations and their impact:

☐ Student 1 is quiet when his teacher speaks to him, but he generally looks down at the floor or away from her when she speaks. Even when the teacher encourages him to express his own ideas, the Student pauses and looks away for what feels like an eternity to the teacher.

☐ Student 2 writes an essay for a social studies class entitled "Jobs in the Coming Global Economy." To the teacher, the essay seems to meander all over the place and does not state its theme until the final paragraph. "It's as if you were telling me what you were thinking," the teacher wrote on the essay afterward, "instead of stating and then justifying a position."

☐ Student 3 rarely answers questions completely when the teacher calls on her in class; she just mumbles an answer or remains silent. But when collaborating with a small group on a project or an activity, she is lively, talkative, and focused on the task.

There are many possible reasons for these situations. One common explanation is *cross-cultural miscommuni-*cation, culturally based differences in how individuals interpret comments and behaviors. Observations of conversations show that cultures vary in communication styles and that children acquire the styles in the course of learning their native language (Scollon & Scollon, 1994).

Cultural communication styles can vary in the following ways, among others:

1. *Timing:* speakers expect different lengths of pauses between conversational turns, from many seconds to only a fraction of a second or even to a "negative" pause (overlapping comments).

2. *Deductiveness/inductiveness:* in some cultures, speakers are expected to state their point immediately (use a "topic sentence") and then justify their position; in others, speakers more often lead up to the main point indirectly, describing their thought processes along the way.

3. *Politeness indicators:* in some cultures, it is especially important to indicate respect for those in authority, chiefly by listening quietly and allowing an authority to determine the topic and length of a conversation.

abstract principles related to fairness and justice and in the form of increasingly sophisticated ways of caring about the welfare of friends, family, and self (Noam & Wren, 1993). (See the accompanying Perspectives box.) Each of these trends is somewhat related to gender, with boys emphasizing ethical thinking about justice rather abstractly and girls emphasizing ethics of care. But the gender difference is not large; most individuals develop both kinds of ethical thinking to a significant extent. A major theory of the development of justice was originated by Lawrence Kohlberg, and a major theory of the development of care was conceived by Carol Gilligan. Both are stage theories in the cognitive developmental tradition, reminiscent of Piaget's approach to cognitive development.

Kohlberg's Six Stages of Moral Judgment

Lawrence Kohlberg proposed six stages of moral judgment that develop slowly, well into middle age (Schrader, 1990). The stages were derived from interviews conducted in much the same style as Piaget's classic interviews about cognitive development: children and adults of various ages responded individually to hypothetical stories that contained moral dilemmas. The original interviewees were all males, but in later studies Kohlberg and his associates extended the research to include females.

Table 15.2 summarizes the six proposed stages. The stages form a progression in two ways. First, earlier stages represent more egocentric thinking than later stages do. Second, earlier stages by their nature require more specific or concrete thinking than later stages do. For instance, in stage 1 (called *heteronomous morality*), a child makes no distinction between what he believes is right and what the world tells him is right; he simply accepts the perspectives of the authorities as his own. By stage 4 (social system orientation), when the child is an adolescent, he

These cultural differences can pose problems whenever members of more than one culture come together to interact. For children and adolescents, therefore, cultural mismatch is especially likely in classrooms, particularly in contacts between teachers and students. If the teacher "speaks the culture" of white, mainstream English, she or he will tend to use and expect relatively short pauses between conversational turns in classroom discussions. The teacher will also tend to use and expect a deductive style of turn taking, with the topic stated immediately by whoever initiates a conversational exchange. And although the teacher may expect moderate indications of respect for his or her right to initiate topics of conversation, she or he may also expect students to initiate ideas and concerns of their own.

When a student's culture supports other communication styles, the teacher can easily get the impression that the student is either unintelligent, lacking in confidence, or deliberately resistant to learning (Lustig & Koester, 1993). Yet these sorts of mismatches are precisely what occur, and always to the disadvantage of the student. What the teacher sees and hears are pauses that are too

long, eye contact that is poor, comments that stray from the topic, and silence in response to invitations to speak. What the student experiences, though, may be quite different: he or she may see and hear a teacher who is too talkative, stares at individuals too much, and seems insincere in issuing invitations to ask questions.

But such misunderstandings can be overcome. Training in intercultural communication exists and is effective when focused on the key cultural misunderstandings of particular conversational partners. In the teaching profession, some of the most elaborate training occurs for teachers of English as a Second Language (Paulston, 1992), but programs are also developing in many business communities (Brislin & Yoshida, 1994; O'Hara-Devereaux & Johansen, 1994), where economic activity increasingly spans more than one country, language, and cultural community. The programs vary in detail, of course, but share a common assumption: that awkwardness between culturally different speakers is likely the result of legitimate differences in communication styles rather than of inferiority of one style or the other.

realizes that individuals vary in their points of view, but he still takes for granted the existing overall conventions of society as a whole. He cannot yet imagine a society in which those conventions might be purposely modified, for example, by passing laws or agreeing on new rules. Only by stages 5 and 6 (ethics) can he do so fully.

In the middle years, children most commonly show ethical reasoning at stage 2, but some may begin showing stage 3 or 4 reasoning toward the end of this period

TABLE 15.2   *Kohlberg's Stages of Moral Judgment*

Stage	Nature of Stage
Preconventional Level *(emphasis on avoiding punishments and getting awards)*	
Stage 1 Heteronomous morality; ethics of punishment and obedience	Good is what follows externally imposed rules and rewards and is whatever avoids punishment
Stage 2 Instrumental purpose; ethics of market exchange	Good is whatever is agreeable to the individual and to anyone who gives or receives favors; no long-term loyalty
Conventional Level *(emphasis on social rules)*	
Stage 3 Interpersonal conformity; ethics of peer opinion	Good is whatever brings approval from friends as a peer group
Stage 4 Social system orientation: conformity to social system; ethics of law and order	Good is whatever conforms to existing laws, customs, and authorities
Postconventional Level *(emphasis on moral principles)*	
Stage 5 Social contract orientation; ethics of social contract and individual rights	Good is whatever conforms to existing procedures for settling disagreements in society; the actual outcome is neither good nor bad
Stage 6 Ethics of self-chosen universal principles	Good is whatever is consistent with personal, general moral principles

Perspectives

What Creates a Life of Moral Commitment?

Both Kohlberg's and Gilligan's theories concern moral beliefs rather than moral actions: they describe what people know and believe about right and wrong, without predicting whether in fact they will actually do what they believe. In everyday life, of course, we often do *not* choose what we believe is the most moral course of action. The gap between actions and beliefs exists even though we gradually come to be very consistent in our beliefs and even in knowing what actions we should take, whether or not we take them (Keller & Edelstein, 1993).

Yet some individuals do seem to act according to their beliefs relatively consistently—so consistently, in fact, that they make a way of life out of their moral commitments. Take Suzie Valadez, a resident of the border city of El Paso, Texas. Every morning for the past thirty years, Suzie has packed sandwiches and other supplies and driven to Cuidad Juarez, the neighboring town on the Mexican side of the border. Along with friends and members of her family, she distributes the food to the poor and homeless at the town dump; later she often visits a

school and a medical clinic that she helped to organize for the area. Naturally, she has become a valued part of the community, and residents have affectionately nicknamed her "Queen of the Dump" to honor her efforts.

What motivates someone like Suzie Valadez to work so untiringly on behalf of the poor? Anne Colby and William Damon have studied this question at length and suggested several explanations in a book called *Some Do Care: Contemporary Lives of Moral Commitment* (1992). After interviewing Suzie and other highly committed individuals at length, they concluded that developing sophisticated moral *beliefs* has little to do with leading a committed life. When asked to solve hypothetical moral problems (such as "Should a husband steal a drug to save his dying wife?"), Suzie and others like her reasoned about the problems in a range of ways, but ways that were typical of the population as a whole. When analyzed according to Kohlberg's six-stage framework of moral judgment, for example, the morally committed individuals stated beliefs that clustered around the "conventional" levels of development.

(Colby & Kohlberg, 1987). For the majority of youth and adults, stage 3 (interpersonal orientation) and stage 4 (social system orientation) characterize their most advanced moral thinking. In stage 3, a person's chief concern is with the opinions of her peers: an action is morally right if her immediate circle of friends says it is right. Often this way of thinking leads to helpful actions, such as taking turns and sharing toys or materials. But often it does not, such as when a group of friends decide to let the air out of the tires of someone's car. In stage 4, the person shifts from concern with peers to concern with the opinions of community or society in the abstract: now something is right if the institutions approve. This broader source of moral judgment spares stage 4 children from the occasional tyranny of friends' opinions; now they will no longer steal hubcaps just because their friends urge them to do so. This change makes teenagers less *opportunistic* than children are, less inclined to judge based on immediate rewards or punishments they experience personally. Instead they evaluate actions on the basis of principles of some sort. For the time being, the principles are rather conventional; they are borrowed either from ideas expressed by immediate peers and relatives or from socially accepted rules and principles, whatever they may be. If friends agree that premarital sex is permissible, many teenagers are likely to adopt this idea as their own, at least as a general principle. But if friends or family believe premarital sex is morally wrong, teenagers may adopt this alternative belief as a principle. (Note, however, that whether a teenager actually acts according to these principles is another matter. Moral action does not always follow from moral belief.)

A few older teenagers develop **postconventional moral judgment,** meaning that for the first time ethical reasoning goes beyond the judgments society convention-

Rather than finding predictable stages of development, a number of authors (including Colby and Damon) have found that moral commitment is a lifelong evolution, one that merely begins during childhood and adolescence (Wilson, 1993). Suzie Valadez's childhood, for example, was consistent with her later commitment to the poor and to children, but her childhood would also have been consistent with some other form of adult life. As a child and youth, for example, Suzie showed great liking for others and an outgoing personality. She also received tremendous support for this quality from her parents, friends, and other relatives. But many other young people have these experiences in childhood without becoming particularly committed to serving the poor as adults.

What factors propelled Suzie's movement toward moral commitment? One factor was her interest in listening to others' concerns, even when their lives and perspectives differed from her own. By listening to the needs of the poor in particular, she could respond more appropriately, and eventually—and paradoxically—she became a better leader and independent advocate in the long term. Other factors were more accidental: one of her sisters died as a young adult, for example, and this event deepened Suzie's religious commitments and led her to affiliate with a new church community that supported its members more actively.

Although the details of her life were unique, Suzie Valadez shared important underlying qualities with other people leading morally committed lives. Colby and Damon (1992) identified several of these qualities. For example, in addition to a desire to listen closely to others, these people seem to enjoy collaborating with others even when their goals or values differ, and they actively seek new knowledge and skills from others who differ from them. These involvements stimulate the person to rethink his or her own values at increasingly profound and permanent levels and eventually to transform them into lasting moral commitments and lifestyles. But the process of transformation takes more than the seventeen-odd years or so of childhood and adolescence; it requires a lifetime.

"Ben is in his first year of high school, and he's questioning all the right things."

A youth's level of moral judgment depends on the reasoning that leads to the judgments, not on the judgments as such. In this cartoon, Ben may express judgments that seem principled, but if they were adopted simply to conform, as his mother implies, then his level of moral thinking is closer to Kohlberg's middling, conventional level.

ally makes about right and wrong (Colby & Kohlberg, 1987). Adolescents' growing ability to use abstract formal thought makes this possible; unlike schoolchildren, they can evaluate ethical ideas that *might* be right or wrong, given certain circumstances that can only be imagined.

Enduring Issues about the Development of Moral Judgment

Kohlberg's six stages of moral judgment have held up well when tested on a wide variety of children, adolescents, and adults (see Figure 15.4). The stages of moral thinking shown in Table 15.2 do seem to describe how moral judgment develops, at least when individuals focus on hypothetical dilemmas posed in stories. When presented with stories about risky but fictional sexual behaviors, adolescents of both sexes evaluated the actions of the stories' characters in line with Kohlberg's stages (Jadack et al., 1995).

Even so, Kohlberg's theory of moral judgment leaves a number of important questions unanswered. One is whether the theory really recognizes the impact of prior knowledge on beliefs; another is whether the theory distinguishes clearly enough between conventions and morality. The most important lingering question has to do with gender differences: does Kohlberg's theory really describe the moral development of girls as well as that of boys?

Issue 1: Form Versus Content of Moral Beliefs   Despite the theory's plausibility, a number of developmental psychologists have questioned important aspects of it. Can the form of ethical thinking really be separated from content to the degree Kohlberg proposes? Perhaps not. Some studies have found that when people reason about familiar situations, they tend to have more mature (that is, higher-stage) ethical responses (Lickona, 1991). For instance, children have a better sense of fair-

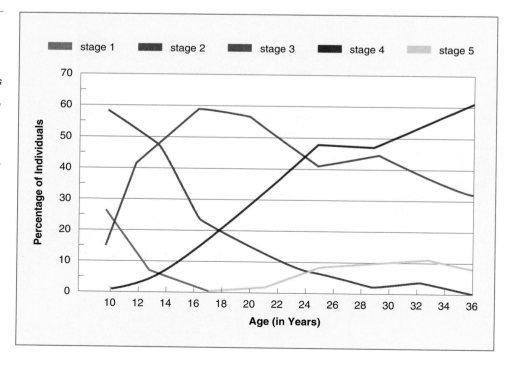

FIGURE 15.4
The Development of Moral Reasoning
In a longitudinal follow-up study of Kohlberg's original sample, Colby and her colleagues confirmed that subjects showed consistent upward advances in moral reasoning with age. The graph shows the extent to which subjects gave responses characteristic of each of Kohlberg's six stages from age ten through adulthood. With development, responses associated with the preconventional level (stages 1 and 2) declined, whereas responses associated with the conventional level (stages 3 and 4) increased. Few young adults moved to the postconventional level of moral reasoning.
Source: Adapted from Colby et al. (1983).

ness about playing four-square on the playground than about whether to steal a drug for a spouse who is dying (one of Kohlberg's fictional dilemmas). In addition, young women think in more mature (more "developed") ways about ethical problems of special concern and familiarity to women, such as whether to engage in pre-marital sex or whether to have an abortion (Bollerud et al., 1990). To some extent, therefore, what someone thinks about affects the ethics she applies.

Issue 2: Conventions Versus Morality   According to some psychologists, some inconsistencies in moral beliefs may arise because the theory does not fully distinguish between social conventions and morality (Nucci & Turiel, 1993). **Social conventions** refer to the arbitrary customs and agreements about behavior that members of society use, such as table manners and forms of greeting and of dressing. *Morality,* as we already pointed out, refers to the weightier matters of justice and right and wrong. By nature, social conventions inevitably generate widespread agreement throughout society, whereas morality does not necessarily do so. Yet Kohlberg's six-stage theory glosses over these differences by defining some of its stages in terms of social conventions and others in terms of morality. Stage 4 (social system orientation), for example, seems to refer to social conventions as well as to moral matters, but stage 5 (social contract orientation) refers only to moral judgment.

Studies that have in fact distinguished between convention and morality have produced a less stagelike picture of moral development. Suppose children are asked questions such as these:

Is it wrong to steal? *(morality related)*

Is it wrong to hit another person? *(morality related)*

Is it wrong for a group to change the rules of a game? *(convention related)*

Is it okay for a country to make the traffic lights blue and purple instead of red and
    green? *(convention related)*

Throughout the middle years and beyond, most children believe hitting and stealing are wrong but changing the rules of a game or changing the color of traffic lights is acceptable (Smetana et al., 1991). If true morality develops at all, then, it seems to begin doing so even before the school years. By kindergarten, children already clearly distinguish between moral and conventional behavior.

Issue 3: Gender Differences in Morality?   One especially important criticism of Kohlberg's theory of moral justice has to do with possible gender bias. Do Kohlberg's stages describe both sexes equally well? And does his theory undervalue ethical attitudes that may develop more fully in girls and women than in boys and men? The best-known investigations of these questions have been pursued by Carol Gilligan and her associates, described next.

Gilligan's Ethics of Care

According to Gilligan, boys and girls tend to view moral problems differently (Gilligan, 1982, 1990). As they grow up, boys learn to think more often in terms of general ethical principles that they can apply to specific moral situations. They might learn that deceiving is always bad in principle and evaluate a specific instance of deception of a friend against this generalization. The principles boys learn also tend to emphasize independence, autonomy, and the rights of others. This orientation biases boys to ignore or minimize others' possible needs: if a friend is at home sick with a cold, it may seem better to leave the friend alone until he gets better rather than check on how well he is recovering.

Girls tend to develop a different sort of morality as they grow up. Instead of seeing moral judgment as a set of abstract principles to apply to specific situations, girls tend to develop an ethics of care, a view that integrates principles with the contexts in which judgments must be made (see Table 15.3). A girl therefore may think deception is usually bad but also believe deception is ethical in certain circumstances, such as when a friend needs reassurance about the quality of a term paper that is actually mediocre but took a lot of time and effort. Viewing ethics in context grows out of a general concern for the needs of others more than for one's independence. A friend who is depressed therefore deserves a visit or a phone call; leaving her alone seems more like neglect than like respect for her autonomy.

These differences are only tendencies, not dramatic or sharply drawn gender differences. But they are enough, argues Gilligan, to make Kohlberg's theory seem to underrate the moral development of girls and women. Concern with context and with others' needs causes girls to score closer to the middling, conventional levels of moral judgment, where peers' opinions matter most. Asked if a child should inform authorities about a friend who often shoplifts small items from a local department store, a girl is likely to give priority to one part of the problem in particular: that of balancing each person's views and needs in the particular situation. Doing so means wondering, among other things, whether informing will alienate peers not only from the shoplifter but also from the informer. On the other hand, it also means wondering whether keeping silent will make her risk losing the trust and respect of important adults, such as parents and teachers. It also means considering the amount of emotional pain that will befall the shoplifting friend at the hands of either angry parents or the police. Taking all of these considerations into account can make the final decision seem hesitant, tentative, and apparently lacking in principle, whichever way the decision goes.

Reviews of moral judgment have qualified Gilligan's ideas somewhat but have also lent them support. When faced with hypothetical dilemmas, females show as much capacity as males to reason in terms of abstract ethical principles (Gilligan & Wiggins, 1987). When faced with real-life dilemmas, however, girls make different choices (Bollerud et al., 1990; J. Brown, 1990). For example, adolescent girls who personally confront the decision of whether to engage in premarital intercourse often show more concern than do boys for the context in which they make their decisions and for the impact of their decisions on the emotional needs of others. As with Kohlberg's justice-oriented stages, however, a needs-oriented ethics of care takes time—years, in fact—to develop.

The Ethics of Care During Adolescence

As with the morality of justice, young people develop an ethics of care during adolescence, but like ethical justice, it remains somewhat conventional during the teenage years. As middle-years children, they develop significant concern about

TABLE 15.3   *Gilligan's Stages of Moral Development*

Stage	Features
Stage 1 *Survival orientation*	Egocentric concern for self, lack of awareness of others' needs; "right" action is what promotes emotional or physical survival
Stage 2 *Conventional care*	Lack of distinction between what others want and what is right; "right" action is whatever pleases others best
Stage 3 *Integrated care*	Coordination or integration of needs of self and of others; "right" action takes account of self as well as others

Source: Gilligan (1982).

Moral development involves more than learning to reason about moral principles. It also involves learning to care about others, and to reconcile their needs for care with your own. These youths seem to be on their way to learning to care—the one by tutoring younger children who need learning assistance, and the other by providing companionship for the elderly in a retirement home.

others' needs and welfare and begin viewing actions as good if the actions take others' needs and welfare into account (Larrabee, 1993). However, egocentrism persists in that teenagers often fail to distinguish between actions that merely *please* others and actions that are "right" in a deeper, ethical sense. For example, if parents will be pleased if their adolescent enrolls in complex science and mathematics courses in high school, doing so may seem "right" to the youngster, even if he has little interest or aptitude in those areas.

As with the ethics of justice, a few individuals move beyond conventional pleasing of others toward *integrated care,* in which the young person realizes that pleasing everyone is not always possible but it is important to balance everyone's needs, including her own (Larrabee, 1993). Deciding whether or not to take a part-time job, for example, now becomes a matter of reconciling the impact of the job on family, friends, and self. Some individuals may gain (the teenager herself may earn more money and make new friends), but others may lose (parents and friends may see less of her). The gains and losses must be balanced rather than viewed completely as gains.

Overall, then, the moralities of justice and care begin taking into account a broader array of both interpersonal circumstances and general principles than was true during the school years. Teenagers more often refer to principles in evaluating actions, although they still do not always act on their principles. Often they also regard pleasing others as ethically good or right, even though they are learning to deal with the impossibility of pleasing everyone perfectly. Like many other cognitive developments, these changes result from adolescents' growing capacities to reason abstractly.

What Do You Think?

Suppose you are starting your first job in a helping profession, such as nursing or teaching. How much would you want your work to be guided by an ethics of justice and how much by an ethics of care? Exchange your views on this question with a classmate or a friend.

SUMMARY OF MAJOR IDEAS

General Features of Adolescent Thought

1. During adolescence, teenagers become better able than before to consider hypothetical possibilities and plan ahead.

The Cognitive Developmental Viewpoint: Formal Thought

2. During adolescence, teenagers develop formal operational thought, or the ability to reason with ideas regardless of their content.

3. Formal thought is characterized by an ability to think about possibilities, by scientific reasoning, and by an ability to combine ideas logically.

4. In general, formal thought fosters systematic solutions to many cognitive problems.

5. In daily life, however, adolescents (and adults) often do not use formal thinking, even when it would be appropriate to do so.

6. Some research suggests that formal operations are not the final point of cognitive development.

Information-Processing Features of Adolescent Thought

7. During adolescence, information-processing skills continue to improve.

8. Teenagers acquire greater expertise in particular areas of knowledge or skill, and they come to allocate their attention to tasks more efficiently.

9. Both structural and functional capacities improve as a result of development, and both probably contribute to improved cognitive performance.

Supporting Adolescents' Cognitive Development

10. Teachers and other adults can intervene to encourage critical thinking, or reflection about complex issues to make decisions or take actions.

11. Programs to foster critical thinking usually do so explicitly and directly, offer lots of practice in solving problems, and create an environment conducive to critical thinking.

The Development of Social Cognition

12. Despite their improved cognitive skills, adolescents still sometimes show egocentrism by believing in an "imaginary audience" and in a "personal fable," or a biography of their lives.

13. Teenagers also begin seeing more relationships among political problems and developing a greater sense of society as a community.

14. During adolescence, youngsters develop relatively abstract understandings of God and begin forming a personal faith, or a coherent, guiding orientation to religious experiences.

Moral Development: Beliefs about Justice and Care

15. Adolescents develop two forms of morality at the same time, one oriented toward justice and one oriented toward caring.

16. Kohlberg proposes six stages in the development of moral judgments oriented toward justice.

17. A number of issues have not been resolved about Kohlberg's theory, including the role of form versus content of beliefs, the difference between conventions and morality, and the possibility of gender differences in morality.

18. Carol Gilligan proposes a theory of moral development oriented toward interpersonal caring; on average, it may be slightly more characteristic of females than males, though many exceptions exist.

KEY TERMS

formal operational thought *(471)*
critical thinking *(481)*
social cognition *(483)*
adolescent egocentrism *(483)*

imaginary audience *(485)*
personal fable *(485)*
morality *(489)*
postconventional moral judgment *(492)*
social conventions *(495)*

FOR FURTHER READING

Belenky, M., B. Clincy, N. Goldberger, and J. Tarule. *Women's Ways of Knowing: The Development of Self, Voice, and Mind.* New York: Basic Books, 1988.

These authors present phases, or types, of thinking and learning that they believe characterize women as they develop from adolescents to adults. They base their ideas on extensive interviews with women of all ages and socioeconomic levels. This book is about cognition, but cognition viewed in the context of gender differences.

Colby, Anne, and William Damon. *Some Do Care: Contemporary Lives of Moral Commitment.* New York: The Free Press, 1992.

The authors describe dramatic examples of individuals whose lives seem to be guided by moral imperatives to care for those less fortunate. Most of the people are "just plain folks," though one or two are moderately well known in their own fields of work. The authors also comment on the factors that created such strong moral commitments, leading individuals well beyond talking about what is right to actually doing something to achieve a better world.

Noddings, Nel. *The Challenge to Care in Schools: An Alternative Approach to Education.* New York: Teachers' College Press, 1992.

Nel Noddings is a philosopher concerned with what an ethics of care implies for teaching and learning in schools. In this book she discusses this problem thoughtfully, looking at some of the problems that an ethics of care presents, such as how to care about students with whom one feels rather distant. Despite these challenges, Noddings believes an ethics of care provides a better basis for teachers than an ethics of justice.

Sternberg, Robert, and Thomas Lubart. *Defying the Crowd: Cultivating Creativity in a Culture of Conformity.* New York: The Free Press, 1995.

The authors describe the nature of creativity, likening it to an economic investment with both high risk and high potential payoffs. They also talk about the conditions a person needs to develop his or her own creativity. Their perspective implies that creativity is within the reach of most individuals, though the conditions supporting personal creative development may not always be easily arranged for everyone.

16

ADOLESCENCE

Psychosocial Development

Individuation and Identity Development
Theories of Identity Development

Social Relationships During Adolescence
Relationships with Parents
Divorce, Remarriage, and Single Parenthood
Friendship
Peer Groups
The Influence of School and Work

Sexuality During Adolescence
Sexual Fantasies and Masturbation
Heterosexuality
Nonheterosexual Orientations
Sex and Everyday Life

Special Problems of Adolescence
Adolescent Pregnancy and Parenthood
Teenage Depression and Suicide
Juvenile Delinquency

The Emerging Adult

Focusing Questions

- What conflicts do adolescents typically experience in their search for identity? What factors support or hinder successful identity development?

- What special challenges does adolescence pose for parents? How do differences in parenting style affect parent-teenager relationships?

- In what ways do adolescent friendships and peer groups play a constructive role, and how are concerns about their negative influence justified?

- What changes in sexual activities and attitudes occur among teenagers, and how are they related to other aspects of adolescent development?

- Why are adolescents at risk for problems such as pregnancy, depression, and delinquency?

As we have discovered, a number of dramatic physical and cognitive changes occur during puberty and adolescence. Although the rate at which these changes occur varies greatly, by the end of this period most adolescents look like adults and are physically and intellectually capable of most adult activities. But as important as these physical changes are, the changes that occur in the psychosocial domain may be even more significant. Perhaps the most important change is the progress adolescents make in achieving a full-fledged and integrated psychological identity that is mature, adult, unique, and separate from those of parents, friends, and other important childhood figures. An identity gives teenagers a more integrated and more permanent sense of who they really are, what they really need, what they believe in, and what they are and are not capable of doing. Barbara, who has just begun her senior year of high school, put it this way:

> It's not just that I'm all grown up now—physically, I mean. It's that I have grown up inside, too. I feel different, more like a grownup than a child. Although there are still many things I'm unsure of, I finally have a much clearer sense of who I am and what is important to me and what I believe in. And this may sound strange, but the sense of independence and separateness that I now feel means I can often be close to my parents and friends without losing a sense of who I am and my confidence in my ability to succeed at achieving the things I really want. In a way, it feels like I'm at the end of a long journey and ready to start off on a new one.

As Barbara's thoughts suggest, an enhanced capacity for psychological autonomy, intimacy, and relatedness to parents, family, and friends and significant strides in achievement and self-esteem are also important accomplishments of adolescence (Allen et al., 1994).

In this chapter, we explore the process of adolescent identity development as well as the related processes by which adolescents develop a healthy sense of autonomy, industry and achievement, intimacy, and sexuality. We explore several important aspects of the teenager's social world, including relationships with parents and peers, the development of friendships, and the impact of school and work. We also look at adolescent sexuality and how it is influenced by current social trends and personal beliefs. Finally, we explore the special problems adolescents face today and some strategies for preventing them.

INDIVIDUATION AND IDENTITY DEVELOPMENT

Individuation is the process by which an adolescent develops a unique personal identity or sense of self, one distinct and separate from all others. Individuation is thought to consist of four separate but overlapping subphases: differentiation,

For each of these adolescents, it is likely that their willingness to engage in activities that diverge from cultural expectations reflects a strong sense of individual identity and self-direction.

practice and experimentation, rapprochement, and consolidation of self (Josselson, 1980). During the *differentiation* subphase, which occurs early in adolescence, the teenager recognizes that he is psychologically different from his parents. This discovery often leads him to question and reject his parents' values and advice, even if they are reasonable. For example, although as a twelve-year-old Barbara enjoyed and did well in her music lessons, she refused to continue them because they were her parents' idea rather than her own. During this period, the realization that parents are not as wise, powerful, and all-knowing as she earlier thought sometimes leads a youngster to overreact and reject *all* of their advice (Josselson, 1980).

While the transition to adolescence is not without its stresses, parental fears of losing their influence are sometimes greatly exaggerated.

"Soon you will be entering a phase, son, in which you will no longer pay attention to anything I have to say. Please let me know when that changeover occurs."

In the *practice and experimentation* subphase, the fourteen- or fifteen-year-old believes he knows it all and can do no wrong. He may deny any need for caution or advice and actively challenge his parents at every opportunity. He also increases his commitment to friends, who provide the support and approval he previously sought from adults. In a discussion of plans to go to a heavy-metal rock concert, for example, Alonzo will completely dismiss his parents' concerns about the dangers in attending, insisting that his friends, who went to last year's concert, have assured him that it was perfectly safe.

During the *rapprochement* subphase, which occurs toward the middle of adolescence, a teenager has achieved a fair degree of separateness from her parents and is able to *conditionally* reaccept their authority. Often she alternates between experimentation and rapprochement, at times challenging her parents and at other times being conciliatory and cooperative. Although Maria, who has just turned fifteen, goes to great lengths to accept responsibility around the house, she often becomes highly indignant when her parents still insist on a curfew and on knowing where she is going when she leaves the house in the evening.

During the final, *consolidation-of-self* subphase, which lasts until the end of adolescence, youngsters develop a sense of personal identity, which provides the basis for understanding self and others and for maintaining a sense of autonomy, independence, and individuality. Parents often are surprised at how much careful thought an eighteen- or nineteen-year-old has given to who he is and how strong his sense of personal direction can be. For example, in a two-hour discussion with his mother that occurred quite by chance, Jorge, a high school senior, revealed that first and foremost he thought of himself as an artist and worked very hard to develop a special way of seeing and translating what he saw into creative works. He also considered himself a person who was good at helping others. He said that he planned on first attending art school and becoming an artist, but thought he would eventually earn his living as a social worker or some other type of mental health professional.

The process of individuation continues throughout the teenage years and often into young adulthood. As we will see shortly, it dovetails with Erikson's theory, which holds that the major task of adolescence is to resolve the crisis of identity successfully.

Theories of Identity Development

The Crisis of Identity Versus Role Confusion   According to Erik Erikson (see Chapter 2), the key developmental challenge of adolescence is to resolve the crisis of **identity versus role confusion** (E. Erikson, 1963). In forming an identity, an adolescent selectively accepts or rejects the many different aspects of herself that she acquired as a child and forms a more coherent and integrated sense of unique identity (Damon & Hart, 1988; Harter, 1989; Harter & Monsour, 1992). During the middle years, she may have simply formed disconnected, relatively separate impressions about herself: on one occasion she noticed that she excelled at hockey and on another that she excelled at swimming. In adolescence, however, she mulls over the significance of all of these impressions taken together: Do they mean that I am generally athletic? That I am popular? Or that I am merely a conformist, just devoting myself to whatever others value—in this case, sports?

An adolescent's increasing capacity for abstract thought and self-understanding (see Chapter 15) plays a central role here. It is important that society and its representatives also recognize and appreciate his uniqueness. The ways a teenager's family, community, and society in general respond can be more or less in tune with his own feelings about himself.

During the final stage of adolescent identity formation, a youngster may experience a confusion of roles more deeply than she ever did before or will again. At times, she can be vulnerable, aloof, and lacking in commitment, as well as demanding and opinionated. Nevertheless, Erikson believes all these traits are important elements of the normal "I dare you" and "I dare myself" *role experimentation* that is important to identity formation. The risk taking and psychological instability of adolescence should not be hastily interpreted as signs of serious problems, an insight we will return to later in this chapter. A number of identity outcomes are possible, each varying in its particular qualities and in how successfully it has resolved conflicts among its various aspects (E. Erikson, 1975).

Psychosocial Moratorium   According to Erikson, adolescence provides a **psychosocial moratorium,** a period during which the young adult is free to suspend or delay taking on adult commitments and to explore new social roles. The goal of role experimentation is to find a place, or niche, that is clearly defined and yet seems uniquely made for him. He may devote this time to academics, to trying out different jobs, to travel, to social causes, or even to delinquency, depending on prevailing social, cultural, and economic conditions as well as on his individual capacities and needs.

The type of psychosocial moratorium an adolescent encounters (or whether she encounters one at all) will largely depend on the opportunities for exploring a variety of roles that are provided by her family, culture, society, and the particular historical period in which she lives. For example, children growing up under conditions of poverty and deprivation or during periods of war and social upheaval are likely to experience more limited and less supportive moratorium opportunities than children living under more optimal circumstances.

Identity Diffusion   **Identity diffusion,** or the failure to achieve a relatively coherent, integrated, and stable identity, may take a number of forms. The first is *avoidance of closeness* with others. A second form, *diffusion of time perspective,* involves the belief that one is out of step with others, that important opportunities may be lost forever. It is sometimes accompanied by feelings of depression and despair over whether the pain and confusion surrounding identity will ever end and a comfortable sense of identity will finally be achieved. The third form, *diffusion of industry,* may involve an inability to concentrate on school- or work-related tasks or an excessive preoccupation with a single activity, such as reading or dating, that interferes with accomplishing other things. A final form of identity diffusion is the choice of a negative identity. A **negative identity** involves the disparagement and rejection of the roles and opportunities that are valued and made available by one's family and community and an acceptance of socially undesirable roles, such as that of a juvenile delinquent. Problems of identity confusion are more likely to occur and are more difficult to resolve in families experiencing serious problems such as alcoholism or drug abuse, physical or sexual abuse, marital conflict, and parental separation or divorce.

Various historical, cultural, and personal events and experiences may affect how one resolves one's identity. For example, many people who grew up during the Great Depression developed identities that were preoccupied with work, economic survival, and self-sacrifice. Some people who grew up in the 1960s, when many challenged or rejected traditional social roles, developed identities based on alternative roles. Similarly, individuals who are deprived of adequate opportunities and resources because they are poor or belong to a disadvantaged minority group may face special challenges in their identity development (Phinney, 1989; Spencer & Markstrom-Adams, 1990).

The Relationship Between Identity and Intimacy   Successful resolution of the crisis of identity versus role confusion prepares the adolescent for the crisis of intimacy versus isolation, which occurs in early adulthood. A clear and coherent sense of identity provides a basis for achieving intimacy in friendships and love relationships and for tolerating the fear of losing one's sense of self when intimacy becomes very intense and of experiencing loneliness and isolation if a relationship ends. The tendency for teenage couples to break up suddenly and then unexpectedly reconcile may in part reflect a level of identity resolution that is not yet up to the task of sustaining intimacy. It is much more difficult to work out conflicting needs and expectations with someone who lacks a clear picture of who she is and what she needs. It is also harder to meet someone else's needs if one is unclear about one's own needs and identity. Thus, the development of identity provides an important basis for intimacy.

Identity Status   Guided by Erikson's ideas, researchers such as James Marcia have been able to empirically study identity development during adolescence. Marcia interviewed students ages eighteen to twenty-two about their occupational choices and religious and political beliefs and values, all central aspects of identity (Marcia, 1967, 1980). He classified students into four categories of **identity status** based on judgments about (1) whether or not they had gone through an "identity crisis" as described by Erikson and (2) the degree to which they were now committed to an occupational choice and to a set of religious and political values and beliefs (see Table 16.1):

TABLE 16.1   *Crisis and Commitment in Marcia's Theory of Identity Status*

Identity Status	Crisis	Commitment
Achieved	Present	Present
Diffused	Present/absent	Absent
Moratorium	In process	In process
Foreclosed	Absent	Present

Source: Marcia, (1980).

According to James Marcia, students can be classified into four categories of identity status based on the presence or absence of an identity crisis and whether or not they are committed to an occupational choice and a set of religious values and beliefs.

1. *Identity-achieved* individuals had experienced and successfully resolved a period of crisis concerning their values and life choices and were now able to feel commitment to an occupation and to a religious and political ideology. Their occupational choices and their religious and political beliefs were based on serious consideration of alternatives and were relatively independent of those of their parents.

2. *Identity-diffused* individuals may or may not have experienced a crisis, but showed little concern or sustained commitment regarding occupational choice and religious and political beliefs.

3. *Moratorium* individuals were presently *in* crisis, actively struggling to make commitments and preoccupied with achieving successful compromises among their parents' wishes, the demands of society, and their own capabilities.

4. *Foreclosed* individuals had "prematurely" committed themselves to important aspects of identity without having experienced any significant conflict or crisis. Consequently, it was difficult for them to tell where their parents' goals for them ended and where their own goals began. Their college experiences served mainly to confirm the childhood beliefs to which they rigidly held rather than provide challenging alternatives.

Most adolescents seem to progress toward a status of identity achieved. Researchers using Marcia's categories have found that for both males and females, identity achievement is rarest among early adolescents and most frequent among older high school students, college students, and young adults. During junior and senior high school, identity diffusion and identity foreclosure are the most common identity statuses. Although diffused and foreclosed statuses significantly decrease during the later high school and college years, only about one-third of college juniors and seniors and one-quarter of adults studied are found to be identity achieved (Archer & Waterman, 1988; Meilman, 1979).

The proportion of individuals at each identity status appears vary with the specific identity area involved. Identity achievement was the most frequent status in the area of *religious beliefs;* identity achievement and moratorium were the most frequent statuses where *vocational choice* was concerned; identity foreclosure was the most common status in the area of *sex role preferences;* and identity diffusion was the most frequent status in the area of *political philosophies* (Archer, 1982; Meilman, 1979; Pomerantz, 1979; Waterman, 1982, 1985).

Few differences between males and females have been found on measures of identity. Both genders are equally represented among the four identity statuses and seem to develop in similar ways. Although early studies suggested that the identity statuses may have different psychological meanings and consequences for males and females, more recent research indicates that the meanings and implications appear to be quite similar for both sexes (Archer & Waterman, 1988; Gilligan, 1987).

Whereas high school students often begin as foreclosed due to their lack of autonomy and dependence on others for direction, or diffused because they still are not thinking in a long-term manner about careers and future plans, many students engage in active role experimentation (moratorium) throughout high school and college, as reflected in the increased frequency of casual dating, changes in majors and shifts in career plans, and the like. Movement toward identity achievement increases during early adulthood.

During late adolescence and early adulthood, both identity achievement and moratorium statuses are generally viewed as healthy outcomes, whereas foreclosed and diffused identities are seen as more problematic. Being identity achieved in today's society is probably rarer among teens than in previous eras. First, today's adolescents have far more options than ever before. Second, technological and social changes are becoming so rapid and complex that identity resolution takes a longer time to achieve.

A Talk with Don, Age Eighteen

Social Relationships among Adolescents

Don took time out between homework and football practice to be interviewed. He is athletically built and of average height.

Interviewer: In general, what do kids your age look for in friends?

Don: Right now, a friend to me can be anybody. I don't care if they have a drinking problem. That's up to them, although I wouldn't like a person to drink too much. I have a lot of friends who are college freshmen already, I have friends who are my own age, and I have friends who are sophomores and juniors in high school.

Interviewer: What are relationships with parents like for kids your age?

Don: I think they give you a lot more freedom when you're a freshman or sophomore and come down on you when you're a junior or senior. They tell you that once you get your license, you can drive me around and you can do this or that once you start dating; they won't be as strict. But it tends to be somewhat the opposite. Like I didn't get my license until I was almost eighteen years old.

Interviewer: How come?

Don: My father, who I am living with right now, my only parent, kind of uses a two-way street. He tends to say, "Don't bring up the past when you're trying to prove your point," but when he's trying to prove his point, he always brings up the past. He'll say something like "You're almost grown, but while you're living under my roof, you'll play by my rules." So you're in a no-win situation. It's plain and simple.

Interviewer: How did this affect your getting a license?

Don: My father would not let me go for my license test until he thought that I drove at a level that he was proud of. He said, "I don't want you to be like all those other kids who can barely drive." I wouldn't say I'm a pro or specialist, but I was at a higher level and my skills were more refined when I got my license. That's how my father wanted it to be, and I'm happy now because of it. And I say, "Hey, well, he was right." I can drive better. I can drive on the highway and in the city and take control of certain situations where another person might freeze.

Interviewer: What other hassles do older teenagers have with their parents?

Don: Being a senior now, I find that I never really know what my father is going to say. I mean, I'll come in and he'll say, "Ah, it's one-thirty," and you start to say, "The movie didn't get out until this time, we had a flat tire, we ran out of gas . . ." and he goes, "It's okay, just be in a little bit earlier next time." And you go upstairs and you sit there and go, "Huh?" And then another time, you come in and he says, "It's two-thirty—where have you been?", and you're saying, "We were just all over Freddie's house, we rented a couple of movies, we watched them on the VCR, and after that we sat and talked about our teachers. Nothing really big; it was a boring night." And he says, "It's two-thirty, you should have been in here a long time ago," and this time he really gets on me. So you say, "I really don't understand this." And it gets a lot trickier, too. They start saying things like "You're going to be in college next year. You should work on this because when you go to college, your roommate won't want you to have a messy room."

Interviewer: Is your father worried about your leaving?

Don: Maybe not worried too much, but worried to a point of thinking, "Have I taught him the right way, or have I taught him enough to make his own way?"

What Do You Think?

1. Which parenting style best characterizes the relationship between Don and his father?

2. What indications of a generation gap between Don and his father do you see?

3. Which of Josselon's four subphases of individuation does Don's description of his social relationships reflect.

What Do You Think?

To what degree have you experienced the developmental crisis of identity versus role confusion proposed by Erikson? Which of Marcia's four identity statuses best describes your own at the present time?

SOCIAL RELATIONSHIPS DURING ADOLESCENCE

The search for identity and the achievement of a mature psychological sense of autonomy and relatedness affect all of an adolescent's relationships. Ties with parents must make room for an increasing interest in peers and a new commitment to the life among comparative equals that peers provide. A young teenager's efforts to become more physically and emotionally separate from his parents and closer to his friends may be stressful, but more often than not the problems and conflicts of this period are relatively minor. Full-blown upheavals and more serious problems of adolescence are most likely to occur in families and communities in which a poor fit exists between the developmental needs of adolescents and the opportunities and supports that are available (Eccles et al., 1993; Offer & Schonert-Reichl, 1992).

Before we discuss social relationships during adolescence, let's take a brief look at how adolescents spend their time and whom they spend it with. Mihaly Csikszentmihalyi and Reed Larson (1984) asked seventy-five ninth-through-twelfth-grade girls and boys from different ethnic and social class backgrounds to carry electronic pagers for a week. Each teenager was "beeped" eight times during waking hours each day and, after each beep, completed a self-report form describing the activity, where it occurred, and who else was involved at the time. Figures 16.1 and 16.2 show the results of the study. The teenagers spent 41 percent of their waking hours at home, 32 percent at school, and 27 percent in public places, including work, friends' homes, yard or garage, cars, and stores or restaurants. Almost three-quarters of their reported activities occurred at home or in school, settings that generally have a great deal of adult supervision.

As Figure 16.1 shows, 29 percent of their activities (about 4.6 hours per day) involved classwork, studying, or other "productive" activities; 31 percent (5.0 hours per day) involved maintenance; and 40 percent (6.4 hours per day) consisted of leisure pursuits, socializing being the most frequent. Figure 16.2 shows that about one-fifth (19 percent) of their waking hours were spent alone and more than half were spent with peers, 27 percent in class and 29 percent outside the classroom.

Relationships with Parents

Even though the majority of teens get along well with their parents on a daily basis, parent-teenager relationships are likely to feel slightly unstable or "out of joint" some of the time (Csikszentmihalyi & Larson, 1984). In part, this is because teenagers are likely to perceive discrepancies between themselves and their parents in how their families function—whether individuals really get along with one

FIGURE 16.1
How Adolescents Spend Their Time
Source: Csikszentmihalyi & Larson (1984).

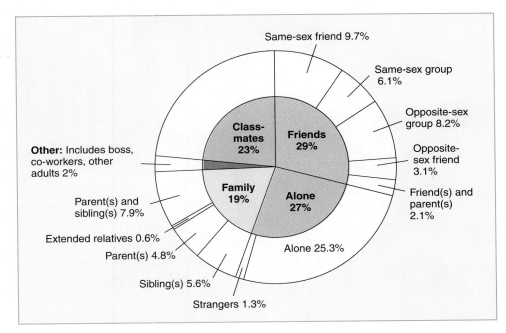

Same-sex friend 9.7%

Same-sex group 6.1%

Opposite-sex group 8.2%

Opposite-sex friend 3.1%

Friend(s) and parent(s) 2.1%

Alone 25.3%

Strangers 1.3%

Sibling(s) 5.6%

Parent(s) 4.8%

Extended relatives 0.6%

Parent(s) and sibling(s) 7.9%

Other: Includes boss, co-workers, other adults 2%

Class-mates 23%

Friends 29%

Family 19%

Alone 27%

FIGURE 16.2
With Whom Adolescents Spend Their Time
Source: Csikszentmihalyi & Larson (1984).

another, for example, and who really makes decisions around the house (Carlson et al., 1991). Parents may think they listen to their teenager's opinions about what household chores she should do, but she herself may regard the "listening" as shallow or meaningless, since parents evidently decide who does what chores anyway. When and if discrepancies such as these come into the open, conflicts usually arise ("You always say X, but you really mean Y!"). That is the bad news. The good news is that the conflicts frequently serve as catalysts for further growth in teenagers' social maturity and to reconcile gaps between parents and their nearly grown children (Holmbeck & O'Donnell, 1991). An important task of adolescence is to achieve adequate psychological separation, or independence, from one's parents.

Achieving psychological separation entails four important accomplishments: *functional independence,* the ability to manage one's own personal and practical affairs with minimal help from one's parents; *attitudinal independence,* a view of oneself as unique and separate from one's parents and having a personal set of values and beliefs; *emotional independence,* freedom from being overly dependent on parents for approval, intimacy, and emotional support; and *conflictual independence,* freedom from excessive anxiety, guilt, resentment, anger, or responsibility to one's parents (Moore, 1984, 1987; Sullivan & Sullivan, 1980).

From the perspectives of adolescents themselves, the most significant indicators of successful separation from parents are gaining economic independence, living on their own, graduating from school, and being free to make their own life choices without being overly concerned about what their parents may think (Moore, 1987).

In our culture, leaving home is a powerful metaphor for achieving psychological separation, and differences in how parents and adolescents understand and react to this experience are fairly common. For example, parents generally expect their children to leave home at an older age and and for a specific purpose, such as marriage. Their adolescent children, on the other hand, often expect to live on their own before they get married (Goldscheider & Goldscheider, 1987, 1989). Many of the everyday conflicts between adolescents and their parents over chores, curfews, school, and social activities reflect different perspectives about the approaching separation. Adolescents' tendency to view themselves as increasingly emancipated from their parents' conventional perspectives and control may create conflict

Although leaving home is often accompanied by mixed feelings, the overall quality of adolescent-parent relationships often improves after teenagers have left.

between a parent's need to maintain the usual family norms while allowing the child increasing independence (Smetana, 1988).

The changes and conflicts teenagers experience often stimulate similar unresolved feelings in their parents. As one parent put it, "Sometimes I'm not sure which is more upsetting to me, my teenage daughter's pain and confusion about who she is or similar feelings that are stirred up from my own difficult adolescence." Higher levels of parent-adolescent conflict are more likely to occur in families experiencing divorce, economic hardship, or other serious stressors (Flanagan, 1990; Smetana, Yau, Restrepo, & Braeges, 1991).

The overall quality of adolescent-parent relationships often improves for adolescents who have successfully left home and are living on their own. In one study, students who no longer lived at home during their first year of college showed greater affection toward their parents, improved communication, and a greater sense of independence than students who remained living at home (Sullivan & Sullivan, 1980). Reasons for leaving home are, of course, quite important. Separating is often much more difficult for adolescents who leave home because of stressful family relationships. They are more likely to experience feelings of emotional detachment, broken ties, irregular communication, and visits home that are uncomfortable and infrequent (Moore, 1984).

Despite the many changes taking place, however, the majority of adolescents and parents continue to get along rather well together. They also tend to share similar attitudes and values about important issues and decisions such as ideas of right and wrong, what makes a marriage good, or the long-run value of education (Collins, 1991; Csikszentmihalyi & Larson, 1984; Larson & Richards, 1994; Youniss & Smollar, 1985).

Where adolescents and parents do differ is in the emphasis, or strength, of those attitudes and values. Most disagreements between teens and parents are about matters affecting the teenager's current social life and behavior, such as styles of dress, hair length, choices of friends, dating, curfews, telephone use, participation in household chores and family activities, and choice of music. For preferences such as these, teenagers agree more with their peers than with their parents. Yet when it comes to the basic attitudes and values that guide long-term life choices, adolescents have consistently rated their parents' advice more highly than their friends' (Carlson et al., 1991; Curtis, 1975).

Parenting Styles   During adolescence, a fine line exists between sensitive, respectful parental involvement and intrusive overinvolvement that does not adequately respect adolescents' need for separateness and independence. A parent-adolescent relationship that establishes a secure emotional base provides a context within which a mutually satisfactory exploration of autonomy and relatedness is most likely to occur (Allen et al., 1994). Adolescents whose families displayed an *authoritative parenting style* (high levels of acceptance, supervision, and respect for children's autonomy) and a high degree of parental involvement in schooling experienced better relationships at home and better performance and social adjustment at school (Smetana, 1995; Steinberg et al., 1992b).

Of course, not all families provide this type of relationship. While warm, caring, and supportive parenting appears to be associated with constructive and effective solutions to family problems, parent-child relationships that are hostile and uncooperative frequently result in conflict and failure (Rueter & Conger, 1995). Teresa Fuhrman and Grayson Hombeck (1995) found that, depending on family circumstances, different levels of autonomy and intimacy may be associated with positive adolescent adjustment. In families with parent-adolescent relationships that were warm, positive, and low in conflict, *lower* levels of emotional autonomy and *higher* levels of relatedness were associated with positive adjustment. In more stressful, less supportive family environments, however, *higher* levels of autonomy and emotional detachment and *lower* levels of relatedness contributed to positive adolescent adjustment.

Parenting style and the quality of the parent-child relationship can exert influence far beyond the boundaries of the family. This is important, since during adolescence youngsters spend increasing amounts of time outside the home. Contact among parents in a community and between adolescents and nonfamilial adults can benefit (or harm) children by creating and supporting shared community expectations regarding adolescent behavior (Coleman, 1988). Anne Fletcher and her colleagues surveyed approximately forty-five hundred fourteen-to-eighteen-year-olds concerning their families' parenting practices and their own academic achievement, psychosocial competence, behavior problems, and internalized distress (Fletcher et al., 1995). Adolescents whose friends described their parents as authoritative earned higher grades in school, spent more time on homework, felt more academically competent, and reported lower levels of delinquency and substance abuse.

Most parents and teenagers have plenty of disagreements and conflicts, but they tend to share long-run interests, goals, attitudes, and values.

Children's perceptions of their relationships with their parents may also influence their relationships with peers, particularly during early adolescence (Fuligni & Eccles, 1993). As children enter early adolescence, they desire relationships with parents that are more mutual, less restrictive, and provide increased opportunities to participate in making decisions that affect their own lives. Children who do not perceive these qualities in their relationships with their parents may come to believe that their parents will never acknowledge that they are maturing and deserve to be treated more like adults. These teenagers may sacrifice other developmentally important experiences with adults for the sake of peer relationships that appear to offer greater opportunity for mutually respectful and supportive interactions. They are less likely to seek advice from their parents and more likely to consult with friends about important issues. In some cases, they may orient toward peers so strongly that they are willing to forgo their parents' rules, their schoolwork, and even their own talents to ensure peer acceptance (Fuligni & Eccles, 1993).

While continued parent-adolescent alienation and excessive orientation toward peers can have serious negative long-term implications, this is the exception rather than the rule. More commonly, the parent-child relationship undergoes positive changes during middle and later adolescence, frequently aided by constructive relationships that teenagers develop with other adults, including relatives, teachers, coaches, camp counselors, and other community members.

In summary, parents and adolescents get along best when decision making is consistent and collaborative, decisions are perceived as being fair and reasonable rather than arbitrary, and the developmental needs and sensitivities of all family members, both parents and children, are respected. Self-reliance and self-control and the successful academic and social achievement associated with authoritative parenting during childhood are also fostered by these qualities during the adolescent years (Baumrind, 1989, 1991; Hart et al., 1990).

Social Class Differences   As noted earlier, adolescents are significantly influenced by the type of family in which they grow up. One useful way to describe families is by **social class,** which is determined by parents' level of education, income, and type of work, as well as by their lifestyle and cultural values. Studies of social class and conformity among families in the United States, Great Britain, and Italy have found that differences between the values, childrearing practices, and expectations of middle-class parents and those of working- and lower-class parents closely parallel differences in the amount of autonomy, independence, and satisfaction experienced in their day-to-day work experiences (Greenberger et al., 1994; Kohn, 1969; Kohn et al., 1986).

Adolescents in middle-class families were encouraged to be independent and to regulate or control their own behavior rather than rely on the rewards or punishments of others to determine how they would act. The parents' childrearing styles tended to be democratic or authoritative rather than authoritarian. Working-class parents were much more authoritarian than middle-class parents in their childrearing patterns and were less likely to support their children's attempts to be independent and participate in family decision making until their children were ready to leave home (Kohn, 1969; Kohn et al., 1986).

Recent research supports these findings (Greenberger et al, 1994; Steinberg et al., 1991). For example, Laurence Steinberg and his colleagues found similar relationships among parenting styles, social class, ethnicity, and family structure in a sample of ten thousand ninth-through-twelfth-grade students from white, African-American, Hispanic, and Asian backgrounds. Authoritative parenting (based on student reports of high levels of parental acceptance, control, and autonomy) was generally more common in middle-class than in working-class families, although ethnic differences and differences in family structure were also important. Table 16.2 presents the percentages of authoritative families for each social class and ethnic group. In addition, for all ethnic groups and family types, adolescents from authoritative families had better school grades, were more self-reliant, and exhibited less delinquent behavior than those from nonauthoritative families (Steinberg et al., 1991).

Divorce, Remarriage, and Single Parenthood

The impact of separation and divorce on adolescent development depends on a variety of factors, including when the divorce occurs, the nature and duration of family conflict before and after the divorce, the quality of the child's relationship with both the absent parent (usually the father) and the parent with primary physical custody, and the family's economic circumstances following the divorce. Separation from the father early in life seems to have a greater effect on both girls and boys than later separation does (Frost & Pakiz, 1990; Hetherington & Clingempeel, 1992; Wallerstein, 1984, 1987; Wallerstein & Corbin, 1989). (See Chapter 13 for a detailed discussion.) Adolescents who experience multiple parenting transitions are most severely affected and are much more likely to experience unhealthy family climates, display more disruptive behavior, and have poorer school achievement than children who have not experienced a parenting transition due to divorce (Kurdek et al., 1995).

Divorce and its aftermath are particularly hard for teenagers, who tend to be sensitive about being "normal" and insecure about their identities. Even ten years after the divorce, many adolescent children continue to have feelings of anger and self-blame and difficulty accepting the permanence of the divorce (Wallerstein & Blakeslee, 1989; Wallerstein & Corbin, 1989). Similar long-term consequences of divorce for adolescents and young adults have been reported for Switzerland, England, and Finland (Aro & Palosaari, 1992; Binder et al., 1981; Wadsworth et al., 1990).

Divorce often makes it more difficult for teenagers to achieve realistic hopes about their own love relationships. Jay, who is fourteen, said, "Dad left because Mom bored him. I do that all the time." Pamela, also fourteen, said, "I'm afraid to use the word *love*. I tell my boyfriend that I love him, but I can't really think about it without fear" (Wallerstein, 1983, p. 241). Nevertheless, most adolescents of divorce do make their way, although it usually isn't easy. Barbara, a seventeen-year-old whose parents separated when she was ten, reported the following: "My mom

TABLE 16.2:   *Percentages of Families with Authoritative Parenting Styles in Different Social Classes, Ethnic Groups, and Parenting Situations*

Ethnic Group	Working-Class Family Structure		Middle-Class Family Structure	
	Biological Parents	Other[*]	Biological Parents	Other
White	17.2	11.5	15.0	17.6
African-American	13.4	12.2	14.0	16.0
Hispanic	10.7	9.8	15.8	12.9
Asian	7.5	6.1	15.6	10.8

Adapted from Steinberg et al. (1991), Table 1, p. 25.

[*]Includes single parent, stepfamilies, and other family arrangements.

Social class differences: Middle-class parents were more likely to be authoritative than working-class parents in all ethnic groups, with the exception of white biological parents.

Ethnic differences: The highest percentage of authoritative parenting occurred for whites, followed by African-Americans, Hispanics, and Asians.

Differences in family structure: In both working-class and middle-class Hispanic and Asian families and for working-class white and African-American families, authoritative parenting occurred more frequently with biological parents than with other parenting arrangements. For both middle-class white and African American families, however, authoritative parenting was less frequent with biological parents than with other parenting arrangements.

and I are real close now. I stopped being angry at her when I was fifteen, when I suddenly realized that all of the kids who lived in tract houses with picket fences were not any happier than I was. It took me a long, long time to stop blaming her for not being in one of those houses" (Wallerstein, 1983, p. 239).

As in middle childhood (see Chapter 13), adjustment to divorce during adolescence is strongly influenced by parents' ability to resolve their own angry feelings and allow their child to do the same. If denied this opportunity, the child will continue to be burdened with a loyalty conflict and with less than satisfactory role models for his or her own future relationships. The quality of relationships with divorced parents and with current family members also appears to play a key role in how successfully these youngsters negotiate the tasks of later adolescence and young adulthood (Portes et al., 1992; Wallerstein, 1987; Wallerstein & Blakeslee, 1989).

Although a single-parent family is the most likely outcome of divorce, several other possibilities exist. The single parent may remarry and bring a stepparent into the family or may not remarry but bring a new partner into the family who serves as a "stepparent." In some cases, divorced parents continue to share parenting with or without sharing legal custody. Living with a stepparent can be particularly hard for an adolescent because of the lack of commonly accepted roles for stepparents and stepchildren and the teenager's intense need to be independent of adult control and authority. Both teenagers and their parents may also find it difficult to switch to a new set of rules and expectations (Hetherington, 1989a; Lutz, 1983).

Although relationships with parents are very important in shaping an adolescent's development, another set of social influences are extremely important as well. In the following sections, we discuss the roles of friendship and peer relationships in adolescent development.

Friendship

Friends matter a lot during adolescence. Unlike most adults, who often try to "improve" many of a teenager's behaviors and skills, friends offer easier and more immediate acceptance and thus ease the uncertainty and insecurity of the adolescent years. They also offer reassurance, understanding and advice, and emotional and social support in stressful situations. The opportunity to share inner feelings of disappointment as well as happiness with close friends enables the adolescent to better deal with her emotional ups and downs. Furthermore, a capacity to form close, intimate friendships during adolescence is related to overall social and emotional adjustment and competence (Buhrmester, 1990; Reid et al., 1989).

Sam, age thirteen, describes a best friend this way:

> A best friend to me is someone you can have fun with and you can also be serious with about personal things, about girls or what you're going to do with your life or whatever. My best friend, Jeff, and I can talk about things. His parents are divorced too, and he understands when I feel bummed out about the fights between my mom and dad. A best friend is someone who's not going to make fun of you just because you do something stupid or put you down if you make a mistake. If you're afraid of something or someone, they'll give you confidence. (R. Bell, 1980, p. 62)

Especially during early and middle adolescence, youngsters' unquestioning appreciation of friends helps them to become more independent of parents and other representatives of authority and to resist the seemingly arbitrary demands of family living. Friends also promote independence simply by providing knowledge of a world beyond the family. Teenagers learn through their friends that not every young person is required to be home by the same hour every night, that some parents expect their children to do more household chores than other parents do, and that other families hold different religious or political views. The processes of sharing feelings and

Sharing interests with friends is important to teenagers, as it is to children. At the same time, though, less tangible qualities such as loyalty, mutual respect, and intimacy become increasingly important in friends, especially among older adolescents.

beliefs and exploring new ideas and opinions with friends play an important role in helping adolescents define their sense of self (Rawlins, 1992).

Qualities of Adolescent Friendships   Friends strongly influence an adolescent's development by virtue of their positive and negative characteristics, attitudes, values, and behaviors and through the quality of the friendship. A friendship based on mutual respect and trust, intimacy, and prosocial behavior is likely to help the adolescent cope with stressful situations in the family and in school. Friendships that lack these qualities are likely to be less helpful or even destructive (Dusek, 1991).

During the teenage years, the basis of what makes a close friendship changes. When asked to define close friendships and how they are initiated, maintained, and ended, adolescents report that *mutual understanding* and *intimacy* are most important, whereas school-age children emphasize shared activities. Unlike cooperation between younger children, adolescent mutuality depends on the understanding that other people share some of one's own abilities, interests, and inner experiences and on an appreciation of each person's uniqueness. In fact, early adolescents share a fascination with the particular interests, life histories, and personalities of their friends; young teenagers want to understand friends as unique individuals and be understood by them in the same way. The ability of adolescents to recognize the advantages of complementary relationships—relationships in which two people with different strengths and abilities cooperate for mutual benefit—makes possible friendships that involve greater commitment, permanence, and loyalty (Damon, 1983; Youniss, 1980).

Intimacy in adolescent friendships includes self-revelation, confidence (in keeping secrets), and a sense of exclusivity. Here is how Taisha, who is fifteen, and Cherell, age sixteen, describe a friend:

> A friend is a person you can talk to, you know, show your feelings and she'll talk to you. You can talk more freely to a friend. Someone you can tell your problems to and she'll tell you her problems. They are open. . . . A friend is a person you can really tell your feelings to. . . . You can be yourself with them.
>
> Friends can keep secrets together. They can trust that you won't tell anybody. You won't expect them to tell anybody else. You know she won't tell anybody anything. If you tell somebody something, they won't use it to get revenge on you when you get into a fight. You talk about things you wouldn't tell other people. (Youniss, 1980, p. 181)

Gender Differences   Friendships formed by boys generally involve lower levels of intimacy than those of girls, who are better able to express feelings and more comfortable with giving emotional support to one another. During the junior high and early high school years, girls appear to develop greater intimacy with the opposite sex than boys do. They also tend to have one or two close friends, whereas adolescent boys often have many friends with whom they are less intimate. These differences are likely influenced by traditional gender role stereotyping, which defines and values intimacy much more strongly as a feminine than a masculine quality. Adolescent boys may be more likely to equate intense intimacy exclusively with heterosexual friendships, whereas girls at this age can be comfortably close with both male and female friends. Toward the end of the eleventh grade, however, differences between same-sex and opposite-sex friends decrease (Buhrmester & Furman, 1987; Furman & Buhrmester, 1992; Sharabany et al., 1981). We explore these and related issues more fully later in this chapter.

Interethnic Friendships   Friendships between adolescents from different ethnic groups tend to be the exception. One national study of students enrolled in more than one thousand public and private high schools in the United States found that fewer than 3.5 percent of the eighteen thousand friendships identified by students involved African-American and white friends (Hallinan & Williams, 1989). However, the social contexts in which potential friendship interactions occur seem to make an important difference. In a recent study of school and neighborhood friendship patterns of African-American and white students who attended an integrated junior high school, most students reported having a close other-race school friend, but only about one-quarter saw such a friend frequently outside school (DuBois & Hirsch, 1990). Interracial school friendships that extended to nonschool settings were significantly more common among youngsters who lived in integrated rather than segregated neighborhoods and among African-American than among white students. African-American adolescents have also been found to be less peer oriented and to place less importance on having friends who are similar to themselves compared to white adolescents. They also appear to have more extensive neighborhood friendship networks but fewer interactions with friends during the school day than white students do (DuBois & Hirsch, 1990; Giordano et al., 1993).

Peer Groups

Peer groups play an even greater role in the everyday lives of adolescents than they do for younger children. They also tend to be more structured and organized, frequently include individuals from a relatively wide age range, and are much less likely to be all male or all female (Dusek, 1991; Furman, 1989). Adolescent peer groups are an important component of the network of social relationships that follow a person over his or her lifetime, changing in structure but providing continuity in the exchange of support. Who is included in this *convoy of support* is determined by the adolescent's

Peer group cliques such as the one pictured here help young teenagers to achieve a degree of intimacy and security and to share important interests, activities, and experiences with a few close friends.

emotional attachment to the person and by the person's role in the adolescent's life (Levitt et al., 1993).

Peers provide a teenager with critical information about who he is, how he should act, what he is like, and so forth. They offer him an environment for making social comparisons between his own actions, attitudes, and feelings and those of others. These are important ingredients in an adolescent's development of self-concept and identity (Connolly et al., 1987). Most important, peer groups provide a support base outside of the family from which the teenager can more freely try on the different identity roles that ultimately will contribute to her adult personality: popular, jock, brain, normal, druggie, outcast, partyer, punk, grind, clown, banger, druggie, nerd, lover, and so forth (Brown et al., 1993; Durbin et al., 1993; Gavin & Furman, 1989). Peer groups can also exert powerful pressures to conform. Especially when the family fails to serve as a constructive corrective force, such pressures may contribute to a prolonged period of identity diffusion or to premature identity foreclosure, for example, as a teenage parent, drug addict, or gang member (Dishion et al., 1988; Patterson & Dishion, 1985).

Peer Group Structure   Adolescent peer groups generally are of two types, the clique and the crowd. The **clique** is a small, closely knit group of two or more members (with an average of six members) who are intimately involved in a number of shared purposes and activities and exclude those who are not. The **crowd** is a larger, less cohesive group of between fifteen and thirty members (with an average of twenty members) and generally consists of from two to four cliques (Dunphy, 1963).

Clique membership allows a teenager to have a few select friends whom she or he knows well and who share important interests and activities, whereas membership in a crowd provides contact with a much broader group of peers on a more casual basis. The small size and intimacy of a clique make it like a family in which the adolescent can feel comfortable and secure. The major clique activity seems to

It is probably no coincidence that all these teenagers wear similar clothing. Adolescent peer groups do encourage conformity, although they also allow for a certain amount of diversity and role distinctions among their members.

be talking, and cliques generally meet during the school week. Advantages of clique membership include security, a feeling of importance, and acquisition of socially acceptable behaviors (such as academic, social, or athletic competence) that are part of conforming to the clique's norms. However, conformity can also suppress individuality and may promote "in-group" snobbishness, intolerance, and other negative values and behaviors. Involvement with a clique of antisocial peers is associated with various adolescent adjustment problems, including substance abuse, dropping out of school, delinquency, and gang membership, although which is cause and which is effect is uncertain (Dishion et al., 1988; Patterson & Dishion, 1985). Clique membership peaks in early adolescence and then declines; the percentage of adolescents who are connected with several cliques but are not themselves clique members increases (Shrum & Cheek, 1987).

Crowds usually gather at parties and other organized social functions, which typically take place on weekends. They tend to include both males and females, thereby providing opportunities for mixed-gender interactions and promoting transition from same-gender to mixed-gender cliques. Crowd membership also provides opportunities to interact with individuals from a broad range of backgrounds and experiences, but can also promote snobbishness and can pose real or imagined threats to parental and teacher authority.

How are cliques, crowds, and friendship related? Kathryn Urberg and her associates (1995) studied the school-based peer networks of more than three thousand sixth-to-twelfth-graders from three school systems serving working- and lower-middle-class families of varying ethnic backgrounds. Peer networks became more exclusive with increasing age. Female students were more connected to the peer network than were male students, and ethnic groups that were in a numeric minority were less integrated into school peer networks than the majority group. Best friends were in the same clique about 90 percent of the time but in the same crowd only about 50 percent of the time, and the average clique or loose group had members with two to four different crowd affiliations.

Parental Influence   Parents of adolescents are frequently concerned that their children will be excessively influenced by peer pressure and that peer influence will replace their own guidance. Laurence Steinberg and Anne Levine (1990) suggest

TABLE 16.3   Guidelines for Parents Concerning Their Adolescents' Friends

Helping Adolescents to Deal with Peer Pressure

- Build self-esteem by helping your adolescent discover her or his strengths and special talents.
- Encourage independence and decision making within the family.
- Talk about situations in which people have to choose among competing pressures and demands.
- Encourage your adolescent to anticipate difficult situations and plan ahead.
- Encourage your adolescent to form alliances with peers who share his or her values and your family's values.
- Know your adolescent's friends.
- Don't jump to hasty conclusions based on peers' appearance, dress, language, or interests.
- Allow time for peer activities.
- Remain close to your adolescent.

When to Be Concerned

- If your adolescent has no friends at all.
- If your adolescent is secretive about her or his social life.
- If your adolescent suddenly loses all interest in friends.
- If all of your adolescent's friends are much older than him or her.

Source: Adapted from Steinberg & Levine (1990), pp. 183–187.

that parents can help their adolescents with their friendships and relationships with peers in a number of ways (see Table 16.3). The accompanying Perspectives box discusses recent research findings on parental influence.

Popularity and Social Acceptance   Popularity is very important to teenagers. Often it is linked with membership in a particular clique or crowd and, in ethnically diverse schools, to peer groups that are identified by ethnic categories such as Asian, Puerto Rican, Mexican-American, and African-American (Brown, 1990; Clark & Ayers, 1988). Personal qualities also influence popularity. In general, both boys and girls who are popular are perceived as being tolerant, flexible, lively, cheerful, energetic, self-confident, and physically attractive. They are also described as sympathetic, helpful to others, and committed to their friends. Adolescents who are ill at ease and lacking in self-confidence and who respond to uncomfortable situations by acting timid, nervous, or withdrawn are more likely to be neglected and socially ignored by peers, whereas teens who appear to be conceited and demanding are apt to be more actively disliked and rejected (Clark & Ayers, 1988; Conger, 1977).

Residential instability also can reduce chances of being popular. Adolescents who began the academic year in a new school due to a change in family residence were found to have fewer friends and less intimacy with their best friends than those who were residentially stable. Boys who had moved encountered more instances of peer rejection than did those who had not (Vernberg, 1990). Unpopular children are most likely to face peer rejection when their overaggressiveness or oversubmissiveness is accompanied by unresponsiveness to the needs of others. Unpopular students generally report higher levels of loneliness and concern about their relationships with others (Parkhurst & Asher, 1992).

The Influence of School and Work

In the United States and other modern, industrialized countries, school plays a central role in adolescents' development. American teenagers spend most of their days attending school, engaging in extracurricular activities, and doing homework. Laws that require them to attend school until age sixteen, social expectations, parental pressures, and vocational requirements help keep most adolescents in high school through graduation and, increasingly, in post–high school education of some kind.

Can Parents Influence Their Adolescent's Choice of Peer Group?

It has been a long accepted view that parental influence sharply declines during adolescence due to the increasing counterinfluence of peer groups over which parents have little control. However, recent large-scale studies of high school students have challenged this view.

Bradford Brown and his colleagues studied parenting practices and peer affiliation in a sample of more than thirty-seven hundred high school students ages drawn from a variety of socioeconomic brackets, ethnic backgrounds, family structures (e.g., first-time two-parent, divorced, remarried), and types of communities (urban, suburban, and rural) (B. Brown et al., 1993). To determine peer group affiliation, they asked school administrators to identify a set of boys and girls in each grade, within each ethnic group in multiethnic schools, who represented a good cross-section of the student body. They then interviewed these students in small groups composed of individuals of the same gender, grade level, and ethnic background. Each group then developed a list of the school's major crowds and identified two boys and two girls in the same grade who were the leaders or most prominent members of each crowd.

A sample of the identified leaders, each accompanied by a friend of her or his own choosing, were then individually interviewed and asked to place each student in the same grade level in one of the crowds that had been named. In addition, the entire sample of students were surveyed about family characteristics, parenting practices, and adolescent behaviors related to academics, drug use, and self-reliance.

Brown and his colleagues found that differences in levels of authoritative parenting as reflected by parental monitoring, encouragement of achievement, and support for joint decision making were significantly associated with teenagers' levels of academic achievement, drug use, and self-reliance. These factors, in turn, were closely related to

the type of crowd an adolescent belonged to (popular, jock, brain, normal, druggie, and outcast). Figure 16.3 diagrams the relationships among parenting practices, adolescent behaviors, and peer group membership.

The authors concluded that parents have the capacity to indirectly influence the behaviors by which teenagers become associated with a particular crowd and that peer group norms serve to reinforce behaviors and predispositions to which parents have already contributed through their parenting strategies and/or family background characteristics. Although parenting practices and family background cannot *determine* a teenager's crowd affiliation, their influence should be taken seriously.

How might this parental influence work? In a survey of approximately forty-five hundred fourteen-to-eighteen-year-olds from the same schools we have just described, Anne Fletcher and her colleagues attempted to answer this question (Fletcher et al., 1995). They asked students about parenting practices in their families and about their academic achievement, psychosocial competence, behavior problems, and personal distress. The researchers also asked each student's friends to independently evaluate the degree to which authoritative parenting was present in the peer network, as indicated by parental acceptance and involvement, behavioral supervision and strictness, and granting of psychological autonomy.

What did they find? Adolescents whose friends described their parents as authoritative earned higher grades in school, spent more time on homework, had more positive perceptions of their academic competence, and reported lower levels of delinquency and substance abuse. Fletcher and her colleagues suggest that authoritative parenting is associated with adolescent competence; that competent, well-adjusted adolescents with authoritative parents select (and are selected by) peers who are similar in competence and background; and that

---

Schools serve two primary functions: they provide students with an opportunity to grow socially and emotionally, and they offer them the skills and knowledge they need to become economically independent and productive members of society (Dusek, 1991). As noted in Chapter 13, schools influence identity development through the academic demands of the *formal curriculum,* which includes basic knowledge and skills in such areas as reading, writing, mathematics, and science, and through an *informal curriculum,* which exposes students to teachers (and peers) who serve as role models for academic achievement, motivation to learn, skill mastery, self-improvement, and assumption of responsibility, leadership, and respect for authority.

For early adolescents, the transition to middle school or junior high school may be a period of increased social and emotional stress. Compared to students who remain in elementary school through eighth grade, students entering junior high school appear to have less positive attitudes toward school, poorer academic achievement, less adequate leadership skills, and lower levels of participation in extracurricular activities following school entry. Girls display a drop in self-esteem,

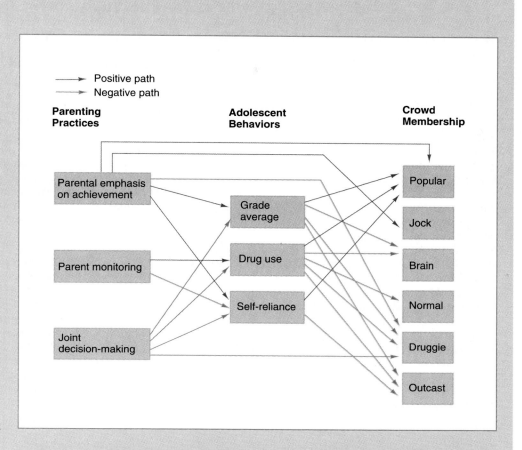

FIGURE 16.3
Parenting Practices, Adolescent Behaviors, and Crowd Membership
Parenting practices such as emphasis on achievement, monitoring of teenagers' behaviors, and joint decision making positively influence adolescents' grade averages, drug use, and self-reliance. These adolescent behaviors, in turn, are associated with the type(s) of crowd(s) a teen belongs to, as indicated by the arrows.
Source: Brown et al. (1993), Figure 3, p. 476.

experiences within their peer group maintain and strengthen their higher level of adjustment. Less competent adolescents with nonauthoritative parents are more likely to select peers who are similar to themselves, thus maintaining and amplifying their limitations. The presence of authoritativeness among one's friend's parents may decrease the likelihood that an adolescent will engage in delinquent activities due to the higher level of shared social control provided by a network of authoritative parents.

and boys are more likely to be bullied than boys who remain in elementary school for seventh and eighth grades (Eccles et al., 1993; Simmons & Blyth, 1987).

School transition is particularly difficult for poor urban youth. One study found negative effects such as a decline in self-esteem, inadequate preparation for class, and lower grades. Daily hassles with the school increased while social support and extracurricular involvement decreased, and peer values were perceived as more antisocial. These changes were common across races/ethnic groups and genders (Seidman et al., 1994).

Critics have questioned whether the structure, curriculum, and overall climate of the middle school fits the developmental needs of early adolescents. They suggest that young adolescents still require a protective school environment that provides levels of supervision and support from teachers, administrators, and parents that will allow them to safely develop autonomy and independence. In these critics' view, middle or junior high school settings should be more like elementary schools, and transitions between settings should be more gradual (Eccles et al., 1993; Eccles & Harold, 1993; Simmons, 1987).

A Multicultural View

Adaptive Strategies of Families of Minority Youth

Nearly one-third of all adolescents in the United States are from non-European-American family backgrounds (see Figure 16.4), and by the year 2000 the majority of children in our school systems will belong to ethnic minority groups from diverse cultural backgrounds (Carnegie Council on Adolescent Development, 1992). Ethnic minority families face many challenges. These include mastering a new language and set of cultural norms; coping with the economic, social, and emotional stresses of relocation; and dealing with the negative stereotypes, ethnic and racial prejudice, and economic and social discrimination they frequently encounter. *Adaptive strategies* are the unique cultural patterns ethnic minorities use to promote the survival and well-being of the community, families, and individual members of the group. Adaptive strategies help them gain access to educational, medical, political, and legal services, employment, housing, and other important resources and services. These strategies are reflected in the childrearing goals and practices found in these groups (Harrison et al., 1990). Three of the most important adaptive strategies are (1) the extended family, (2) biculturalism, and (3) ancestral world views.

The *extended family* includes parents, children, and other relatives such as aunts, uncles, grandparents, and cousins, as well as some individuals not biologically related. In African-American extended families, for example, the high degree of interdependence among three or more generations of kin (child, parent, grandparent), as well as nonbiological family members, helps to provide the material aid such as food, shelter, clothing, money, child care, household maintenance, and social and emotional support that are critical for effective family functioning (Harrison et al., 1990; Stack, 1981). Hispanic-American families also show high degrees of connectedness, loyalty, and solidarity with parents and other relatives and of interdependence and mutual support (McGoldrick et al., 1982).

Biculturalism involves the ability to function optimally in more than one cultural context and to flexibly switch patterns of thinking and behaving in ways that are appropriate and adaptive to what the particular situation demands. Benefits of bicultural (and multicultural) competence include greater cognitive flexibility and the ability to appreciate differing cultural values and perspectives (Harrison et al., 1990).

Ancestral world views refer to the basic beliefs and assumptions held by a given culture regarding human beings and the world in which they live. For example, the dominant European-American world view emphasizes an *individual self* that places motivations, rights, and responsibilities primarily within the individual. In Asian cultures, two additional senses of self also are present: a "familial self," based on a person's relationships, roles, responsibilities, and expectations as an inseparable part of the extended family, and a "spiritual self," which reflects one's relationship to religious beliefs, practices, and philosophical orientations (Roland, 1988). In many Native American tribal cultures, for example, adolescents commonly undertake a quest for a guardian spirit. Once attained, the person's relationship with that spirit plays a major role in guiding future life choices and development (Harrison et al., 1990). Ancestral world views emphasize *collectivism,* or loyalty to the family and group, and a more fluid, flexible, and multidimensional sense of self than is the case in the majority European-American culture, both of which may help ethnic minorities deal with the challenges they face.

Adaptive strategies appear to be related to two important aspects of childrearing among ethnic minority families. The first is a *positive orientation toward ethnic groups* (their own and others), which helps to promote biculturalism and acceptance of ancestral world views by teaching children to view their role within the family and society in terms of relationships and obligations to the

School Failure and Dropping Out   Approximately 25 percent of all students drop out of high school, and dropout rates approach 60 and 70 percent in some urban high schools. Michele Fine (1991, 1986), who has extensively studied this problem, reports that 22 percent of the poorest students drop out; dropout rates are 22.7 percent for Native Americans, 18.7 percent for Hispanics, 16.8 percent for African-Americans, 12.2 percent for whites, and 4.8 percent for Asians (Fine, 1991). Fine conducted interviews with high school students who dropped out or were forced to leave before graduating. Students left school for different reasons. Some left because they did not believe a high school diploma is worth working for, since people they knew who did finish school remained unemployed due to an inavailability of jobs. A second group left school to provide economic and other support for their families. A third group left because their impoverished life circumstances made it too difficult for them to fit in either academically or socially. A final group dropped out because they had difficulty adjusting to the demands of teachers and school administrators and felt too alienated to continue (Fine, 1986).

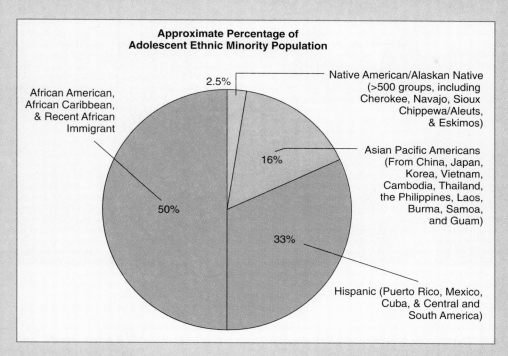

Approximate Percentage of Adolescent Ethnic Minority Population

African American, African Caribbean, & Recent African Immigrant — 50%

2.5% — Native American/Alaskan Native (>500 groups, including Cherokee, Navajo, Sioux Chippewa/Aleuts, & Eskimos)

16% — Asian Pacific Americans (From China, Japan, Korea, Vietnam, Cambodia, Thailand, the Philippines, Laos, Burma, Samoa, and Guam)

33% — Hispanic (Puerto Rico, Mexico, Cuba, & Central and South America)

FIGURE 16.4

Ethnic Minority Youth in the United States
Adolescents with African origins make up the largest percentage of ethnic minority youth in the United States, followed by adolescents from Hispanic, Asian Pacific, and Native American/ Alaskan Native backgrounds.
Source: Adapted from Harrison et al. (1990), p. 350.

family and to maintain solidarity with their ethnic group. The second, a stress on *socialization for interdependence,* is a logical extension of an emphasis on interdependence within extended families and of the ancestral world view of collectivism. Given the formidable barriers to achieve- ment confronting ethnic minorities in American society, the pathway frequently has been through collective actions that create opportunities for individual achieve- ment (Harrison et al., 1990).

Adolescents who have recently immigrated, particularly those from impover- ished or war-torn countries, are also at risk for dropping out. Not only must they adjust to the economic and social stresses of a new country, language, and culture; frequently they must also deal with a profound sense of cultural exclusion and lack of social acceptance in schools whose standards for academic performance and social behavior fall far below those of their own culture. Many of these students report that the disillusionment and sense of *cultural vertigo* they experienced, rather than the other challenges they faced, caused them to lose their sense of purpose for going to school and therefore to drop out (Salett & Koslow, 1994). It is unlikely that a single set of educational standards and strategies can effectively serve the diverse needs of the many ethnic groups that attend our schools. (The adaptive strategies used by families of ethnic minority youth are discussed in the accompany- ing Multicultural View box.)

How can schools for adolescents be improved? The Carnegie Council on Ado- lescent Development established a Task Force on Education of Young Adolescents

For many high school students, working a moderate number of hours provides an opportunity outside of the home for gaining experience and the material rewards needed to have an independent life with peers.

to help answer this question for middle schools (Carnegie Council on Adolescent Development, 1989; Hamburg, 1992). The task force commissioned papers, interviewed experts, and met with teachers and principals, health professionals, and leaders of youth-serving organizations. Their main recommendations, called "Turning Points," are summarized in Table 16.4.

Many of these same recommendations apply to good high schools. Ted Sizer (1992) has suggested that good schools do the following: (1) allow students and teachers to work and learn in their own appropriate ways; (2) insist that students clearly exhibit mastery of their schoolwork; (3) provide appropriate and effective incentives for students and teachers; (4) focus students' work on using their minds; and (5) keep the structure simple and therefore flexible. Ernest Boyer (1983), who conducted an influential study of secondary (high school) education in the United States, found that successful, high-quality high schools emphasized high academic standards; a common, core curriculum; flexible electives; and a humanistic approach to education that considered the developmental needs of the students and communities they served.

Despite the shortcomings just discussed, the majority of high schools still do a fairly good job. Studies of a variety of successful traditional and *alternative high schools,* both private and public, indicate that high school education that is responsive to the educational and developmental needs of adolescents from the broadest range of backgrounds and life situations is possible, provided the motivation and resources are available (Lightfoot, 1983; Trickett, 1991).

Employment   The majority of teenagers report participating in "formal" paid work outside the home, and many others engage in "informal" paid work such as babysitting and yardwork within their own homes (Fine et al., 1990; Mortimer et al., 1992a). Informal work is likely to be a first paid job. Because it is fairly continuous with the chores and responsibilities of childhood, it provides a more gradual transition to the demands of adult work. Formal adult work typically takes place in commercial or other organizational settings. It represents a greater departure from childhood work and involves more impersonal relationships with adults, closer supervision, and more systematic monitoring of job performance (Mortimer et al., 1992b). The types of jobs frequently reported by teenagers include supermarket,

TABLE 16.4: *Turning Points: Recommendations for Transforming Middle School Education*

1. Create communities for learning by dividing large middle-grade schools into smaller ones.
2. Teach a core curriculum of substantive knowledge to all students in ways that foster curiosity, problem solving, and critical thinking.
3. Organize schools in ways that maximize opportunities for success for *all* students through cooperative learning, flexible scheduling, and expanded opportunities for learning within and outside of the school.
4. Provide teacher training that specifically prepares teachers to meet the unique academic and developmental needs of young adolescents.
5. Shift primary responsibility and authority for middle schools to teachers and principals, and establish community-school governance committees composed of teachers, parents, administrators, support staff, and community representatives.
6. Create school environments that promote physical and mental health.
7. Establish respectful, working alliances between school staff and parents of middle school students.
8. Establish cooperative partnerships between the school and community organizations.

Sources: Carnegie Council on Adolescent Development (1989); Hamburg (1992).

restaurant, or retail store worker; bus driver; office worker; and semiskilled worker (Green, 1990).

Work during adolescence serves three important functions. First, it facilitates the transition from school to work. Second, it provides structure for involvement in family- and school-related activities. Finally, it provides an arena outside of home and school for gaining social experience and the material rewards needed to have an independent life with peers (Green, 1990). How work influences adolescent mental health and adjustment depends upon the type and level of workplace stress, the relevance job related skills to future careers, and particularly for girls, the compatibility between the demands and experiences of work and school (Mortimer et al., 1992a).

The intensity of formal work as measured by the number of hours worked per month is also important. Students who work more than ten hours per week do more poorly academically, report more psychological problems (depression, anxiety, fatigue, sleeping difficulty), and physical problems (headaches, stomachaches, colds) than other students (Mortimer et al., 1992a, 1992b; Steinberg et al., 1993; Steinberg & Dornbusch, 1991). They are also more likely to use drugs, smoke cigarettes, and engage in delinquent activities, regardless of ethnicity, socioeconomic level, or age. In contrast, working fewer than ten hours per week generally appears to have no negative effects.

For most high school students, working more than a moderate number of hours per week may be developmentally unwise, because it interferes with academic activities, exposes them to negative environments and role models, and limits the amount of monitoring and supervision they receive from parents, teachers, and other positive role models. Many students, particularly those receiving appropriate levels of adult monitoring and support, make sensible decisions about the role of work in their lives. For example, Green (1990) found that students who saw work as interfering with other interests or who were skeptical of overcommitment to "material" things appeared to adjust accordingly by working either seasonally or less regularly. Students working part-time jobs also seemed well aware of the difference between dead-end jobs and careers, regardless of their family, educational, and occupational situations (Green, 1990).

What Do You Think?

Think about your own separation and individuation with regard to your parents. How similar were your concerns to those described in the chapter?

In what ways are your own experiences similar to the text's description of the development of friendship and peer groups? In what ways do they differ?

SEXUALITY DURING ADOLESCENCE

The popular idea that adolescence is a highly sexual period of life is correct. However, people tend to focus on sexual intercourse and the risks of pregnancy rather than consider the broader pattern of interrelated changes involved. During adolescence, the expression of sexual urges interacts closely with the need to establish a secure sexual identity that is reasonably free from anxiety and helps to fulfill the need for intimacy through close, collaborative relationships with others. Teenagers intensely and passionately engage in establishing intimate relationships independent of their families, developing social skills, experimenting with new social roles, and establishing a unique personal identity. Sexual maturity is a central aspect of acting and feeling like a mature, adult person and being recognized as one.

Sexual Fantasies and Masturbation

Sexual fantasies about real or imaginary situations often accompany masturbation, although adolescents of all ages report having sexual fantasies throughout their waking hours. Both sexes have reported that they most commonly fantasize about "petting or having intercourse with someone [they] are fond of or in love with" (Miller & Simon, 1980). Regarding the second most common fantasy, however, males reported imagining anonymous sex ("petting or having intercourse with someone you don't know"), whereas females reported imagining intimate but not explicitly sexual activity ("doing nonsexual things with someone you are fond of or in love with").

Approximately 70 percent of boys and 45 percent of girls surveyed have reported having masturbated by age fifteen, and about 65 percent of boys and 50 percent of girls ages sixteen to nineteen have reported masturbating once a week or more. Sexually experienced adolescents tended to masturbate more than those who

Reasons for dating vary widely, from a desire to "be seen" and thus gain status or to have a good time, to intrinsic interest in friendship with a particular member of the opposite sex.

were less experienced, but boys tended to give up masturbation when they were involved in an ongoing sexual relationship, whereas girls tended to masturbate more often (Coles & Stokes, 1985; Dreyer, 1982). Feelings of discomfort and guilt resulting from cultural and religious beliefs about masturbation have decreased in recent years. However, many teenagers still find the subject embarrassing; fewer than a third of teenagers questioned in one study reported that they felt no guilt at all (Coles & Stokes, 1985). It is likely that current efforts to encourage safe sexual practices in the face of the AIDS epidemic will lead to increased acceptance of and decreased guilt about masturbation.

Heterosexuality

Sexual Experience   During the last thirty years, sexual activity among college-age adolescents has significantly increased, particularly among females. In the mid-1960s, only 29 percent of college-age females and 65 percent of males reported having had premarital intercourse; in 1980, roughly 63 percent of college females and 77 percent of college males reported having had premarital intercourse at least once; and by 1988, 74 percent of college females and 82 percent of college males reported having had premarital intercourse (Murstein et al., 1989; Robinson & Jedlicka, 1982). (See Figure 16.5.) The percentage of college-age men and women who report having had

FIGURE 16.5
Sexual Activity among Older Adolescents, 1965–1988
Sources: Murstein et al. (1989); Robinson & Jedlicka (1982).

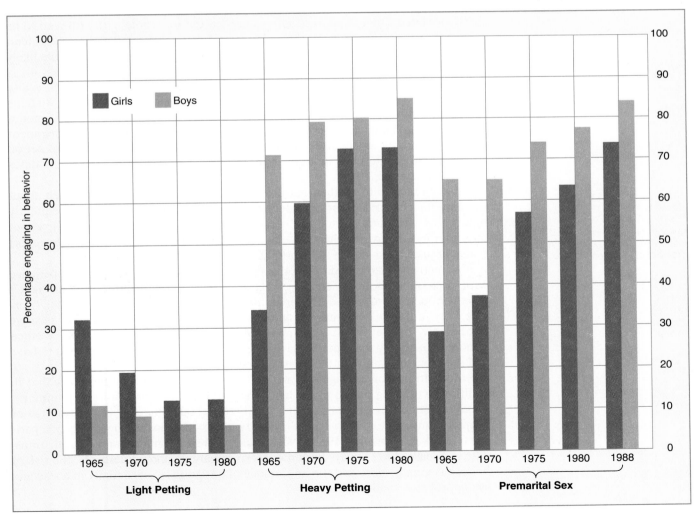

sex with only one person and believing in having sex only with someone they are deeply involved with emotionally has also increased (Abler & Sedlacek, 1989).

The timing of first sexual intercourse is related to several factors. First intercourse at an early age is more likely with early puberty, a personality style that is risk taking and impulsive, a history of substance abuse, fewer years of education, a single-parent family, a disadvantaged socioeconomic status, and nonwhite ethnicity. First intercourse at a later age is more likely with late timing of puberty, a personality style that includes a religious orientation and traditional values, absence of substance use, higher levels of education, a two-parent family, an advantaged socioeconomic status, and white or Hispanic ethnicity (Miller & Moore, 1990; Sonenstein et al., 1991).

Sexual Attitudes   The "sexual revolution" of the 1960s and 1970s resulted in greater acceptance of premarital intercourse, masturbation, and homosexuality and a decline in the double standard holding that sexual activity outside of marriage is less acceptable for females than for males. In the 1980s and 1990s, however, teenagers appear to have had more cautious attitudes concerning sexual activity. Some studies have found that the double standard seems to have made a comeback, with both girls and boys viewing males as being responsible for initiating and pursuing sexual activity and females as being responsible for setting the limits on how far to go. Other reports, however, have found that the double standard has declined and that both male and female adolescents reject sexual relationships that exploit women (Darling et al., 1984; Dreyer, 1982; Morrison, 1985).

Although types of sexual activity may now be fairly similar for boys and girls, differences in attitudes and expectations persist. On the whole, girls still tend to be more conservative than boys in their sexual attitudes, values, and actions. Boys tend to be more sexually active and to have more sexual encounters. Girls are more likely to emphasize intimacy and love as a necessary part of sexual activity and less likely to engage in sex merely as a physically pleasurable activity (Leigh, 1989; S. White & DeBlassie, 1992). One study of thirty-six hundred Canadian high school students found that although there was fairly high agreement between males and females about holding hands and kissing on the first date and a fair degree of agreement regarding necking, males were much more likely to think it was all right to pet on the first date and to have intercourse either on the first date or after a few dates (Bibby & Posterski, 1985).

When asked to recall their reasons for first intercourse and how they felt about the experience, female and male college students differ. While both frequently report that "we both wanted to," were curious, and loved or cared deeply about their partners, many more women cite partner pressure and many more men report sexual arousal and a desire to "score" as reasons (Koch, 1988).

Women and men also differ in their emotional reactions to their first experience with intercourse. Both are equally likely to say it was "okay," "fine," or "all right"; however, men more frequently report that it was "pleasant," "pleasurable," "terrific," or "fantastic," whereas women are more likely to say it was neither positive nor negative or that it was a disappointment or a disaster (Koch, 1988). Women also are more likely than men to have been in a committed relationship and to have had intercourse again with their first partner (Darling et al., 1992).

Motivations for teenage sex are not only sexual. Adolescents report that in addition to offering pleasure, sex helps them to confirm masculinity or femininity, get affection, rebel against parents, feel better about themselves, get revenge or degrade someone, express anger, alleviate boredom, and ensure the loyalty of a partner (Hajcak & Garwood, 1989). Nevertheless, while pregnancy and sexually transmitted diseases have always been a concern to parents and adolescents, the risk of AIDS has greatly increased the importance of initiating sexual activity in a safe and age-appropriate manner.

For these teenage couples, the junior/senior prom is an opportunity to experiment with intimacy, sexuality, commitment, as well as other complex activities and roles associated with adulthood.

Dating   Dating is a major activity during adolescence and serves a variety of purposes. It can be a form of recreation involving both entertainment and sexual stimulation; it can be a way to gain status by enhancing a teenager's reputation and popularity; and it can be a means of asserting independence and separating from one's family. Teenagers also date to learn social skills and thus increase their interpersonal competence, and to experiment with sexual activity. Courtship, or searching for a husband or a wife, is another reason to date (Damon & Hart, 1982).

Since the beginning of this century, dating has tended to begin earlier, thus increasing the time span over which teenage dating takes place. Currently many adolescent girls begin dating at age twelve and boys at age thirteen, with almost one-half of boys and more than one-half of girls reporting dating at least once a week and approximately one-third dating two or three times per week. Only 10 percent of male and female seniors report never having dated (Savin-Williams & Berndt, 1990).

Dating is a major avenue for exploring sexual activity. In recent years, there has been a growing awareness that dating situations may lead to sexual activity that is coerced. *Date rape* refers to a situation in which a person, usually a female, is forced to have sex with a person she is dating. It is estimated that as many as 25 percent of sixteen-to-nineteen-year-old females are victims of date rape (Sorenson & Bowie, 1994). In one large-scale study of college men and women, more than three-quarters of the women reported having been treated in a sexually aggressive way (being forced to engage in sexual acts ranging from kissing to petting to sexual intercourse) and more than one-half of the men reported acting in a sexually aggressive manner on a date, either in high school or in college (Muehlenhard & Linton, 1987).

Another study reported that date rape and other forms of sexual aggression were most likely to occur between two partners who knew each other fairly well, often for almost a year prior to the incident (Muehlenhard & Linton, 1987). Sexual aggression was most likely when a man initiated the date, provided transportation, and paid for the date, and was also more likely if both people got drunk and ended up in the man's dorm room or apartment. It is likely that the cultural expectation that the boy initiate and the girl limit sex, discussed earlier, and the persistent tendency in our culture to blame the victim continue to be contributing factors to this problem (Blumberg & Lester, 1991).

Nonheterosexual Orientations

Due largely to the political and educational efforts of the "equal rights" and "gay rights" movements, public acceptance of nonheterosexual orientations has increased significantly during the past several decades. This acceptance acknowledges the right of individuals to freely practice their own sexual orientations and lifestyles and to receive protection from discrimination. In one interview study, approximately two-thirds of the adolescent respondents said that in principle they approved of same-sex petting and kissing in its various forms (Dryer, 1982). However, other researchers have found that **homophobia** (dislike and fear of homosexuals) remains strong among adolescents. In another study of American adolescents, 75 percent of females and 84 percent of males expressed disgust for homosexual acts; however, females seemed to be more tolerant of homosexuality and less fearful about being identified as homosexual than males were (Stokes, 1985). Another survey found that most heterosexual college students, both male and female, would not want to marry someone who had had even a single homosexual experience (Williams & Jacoby, 1989).

Reliable statistics on sexual orientation are difficult to obtain. A study of thirty-eight thousand adolescents in grades seven through twelve found that 88.2 percent described themselves as predominantly heterosexual (exclusively interested in the other sex), 1.1 percent as predominantly homosexual or bisexual (interested in members of both sexes), and 10.7 percent as uncertain about their sexual orientation (Remafedi et al., 1992).

Because the widespread homophobia in their environments makes communication seem dangerous, gay, lesbian, and bisexual adolescents are likely to experience feelings of attraction for members of the same gender for several years before *coming out,* or publicly acknowledging their sexual orientation (Patterson, 1995). A study by Ritch Savin Williams found that for gay males initiation of sexual behavior with same-sex partners appeared to be closely associated with biological changes of puberty (early maturers initiated same-sex encounters earlier than did late maturers), whereas sexual behavior with opposite-sex partners began according to a youngster's age and level of social and emotional development (Savin-Williams, 1995).

As yet no agreement exists on the specific pattern of factors that lead to the development of nonheterosexual orientations. Experiences within the family have long been considered an important contributor. Richard Green (1980, 1987) studied the development of a group of boys referred to a clinic because of gender-atypical behavior during childhood and found they were more likely to identify themselves as gay or bisexual later in life than a group of same-age boys who did not show gender-atypical behavior in childhood. A recent review of past research on this issue by Michael Bailey and Kenneth Zucker found that cross-gender behavior in childhood was strongly associated with nonheterosexual orientations in adolescence and adulthood for both males and females (Bailey & Zucker, 1995). A number of researchers are also exploring the possibility that biological and genetic predispositions play a role in the development of nonheterosexual orientations (Patterson, 1995).

The challenging task of achieving a secure sexual identity is considerably more difficult for nonheterosexual adolescents, who have the added burdens of grappling with their difference and the anxieties and dangers involved. Homosexual and bisexual teenagers often experience rejection by their families, peer groups, schools, places of worship, and other community institutions—the very groups that adolescents depend on for support. The verbal abuse, the AIDS-related stigmatization, the threat of physical attack, and other forms of victimization they experience put them at greater risk for mental health problems. Strong family support and self-acceptance, however, can serve as buffers against these negative outcomes (Hershberger & D'Augelli, 1995).

Sex and Everyday Life

Although sexuality plays an important role in adolescents' feelings, fantasies, and social relationships, it does not necessarily dominate their lives. Sexual experience involving intercourse is the exception for most junior high school students. And although sexual activity increases during high school, most adolescents have intercourse on a rather sporadic, unpredictable basis, if at all. Masturbation and various forms of petting appear to be the mainstay of many adolescents' sexual activity.

As we noted earlier, changes in sexuality during adolescence involve not only physical maturation and the development of new social skills; they also play a major role in the development of intimacy and personal identity. Sometimes identity development is complicated by sexual issues. It can also be affected by social problems specific to teenagers, as we will see in the next section.

What Do You Think?

When you were an adolescent, what were your attitudes toward premarital sex, dating, and nonheterosexual orientations? In what ways, if any, have your attitudes changed since then?

SPECIAL PROBLEMS OF ADOLESCENCE

In Chapter 14, we looked at the special physical and health risks adolescents face as a group. Their lack of experience, their need to experiment with new and sometimes risky social roles, and the lack of educational and economic opportunities and social support they frequently encounter can place adolescents at high risk for developing certain psychosocial problems. In the following section, we discuss three special problems of adolescence: teenage pregnancy and parenthood, adolescent depression and suicide, and juvenile delinquency.

Adolescent Pregnancy and Parenthood

Each year more than 1.1 million American teenagers between ages fifteen through nineteen become pregnant; most of those pregnancies were not intended (United States Department of Health and Human Services, 1990). It is estimated that 19 percent of white females and 41 percent of African-American females become pregnant by age eighteen and that close to 66 percent of all white and 97 percent of all African-American teenage first-time mothers were unmarried when they became pregnant (Earle, 1990; Furstenberg et al., 1989).

Unsound Contraceptive Practices   The great majority of teenage pregnancies are the result of inadequate or no contraception. Many teenagers are startlingly uninformed about the basics of reproduction, believing they are "immune" to pregnancy or at least at very low risk. Approximately one-half of all teenagers do not use contraceptives the first time they have sex, and many, particularly younger adolescents, delay for a year or more after the first intercourse before using contraception (Hofferth & Hayes, 1987; United States Bureau of the Census, 1992b).

Although birth control pills are popular, they are not reliable during the first month of use. Only foam and condoms or a diaphragm and contraceptive jelly are

Working with

Working with   Janet Whallen, NURSE PRACTITIONER

Helping Pregnant Teenagers

Janet Whallen was interviewed in her office, which is located in a neighborhood health care center serving disadvantaged Hispanic and African-American individuals and families. Janet's warm, low-key style made it easy to see why teenagers would find her easy to talk with. Our interview focused on the experiences of pregnant teens.

Rob: What special problems do pregnant teenagers face?

Janet: Most of the sexual relationships these teenagers are involved in are fairly short-lived. A young woman or man might have three or four partners in a year. When a young woman becomes pregnant, the chances that she'll still be with the same boyfriend when she delivers nine months later are fairly slim.

Rob: Nine months would be a long relationship?

Janet: For someone who is only fourteen or fifteen, it is. Very few of these girls have the baby's father with them in any way, shape, or form at the time of delivery.

Rob: Why is this so?

Janet: Sometimes the guy gets scared or loses interest because the girl is starting to get fat. Or the girl or guy was already losing interest even before the pregnancy occurred. Whatever the reason, I think shorter relationships are fairly typical of early adolescent behavior.

Rob: In what other ways are the experiences of pregnant teenagers typical of adolescents in general?

Janet: They have very little sense of the implications of the decisions they make. They make most choices based on short-term consequences, and those choices are tightly connected to peer approval. There are also lots of rebellion issues against important adults, whether parents or teachers.

Rob: How does this rebelliousness affect pregnancy?

Janet: Teenagers are very sensitive about many things, from small issues to big ones: being told to eat certain things or to wear certain clothes—you know, "you're going to look fat if you wear that"—about smoking or not smoking, getting home on time after school or staying out late on Friday night, about how their parent will feel about their being sexually active or getting pregnant. I have to be very careful to give advice in a way that they don't find threatening.

Rob: Sounds like typical adolescent behavior.

Janet: I have kids who will come in for an appointment with four or five giggling teenage friends, who'll sit outside the office and heckle and laugh. They'll all be talking about who is going out with whom, who passed notes to whom in class, who cut class for what reasons, where they bought their clothes. You would never know you were in the middle of an inner-city clinic for pregnant teenagers.

really effective for first intercourse. But adolescents do not like to use these contraceptives because they imply a preparedness for sex, are expensive or unavailable when needed, can be messy, reduce pleasure, and increase anxiety due to inexperience in their use. Irregular use of contraception is associated with low economic status, poor communication with parents, lack of knowledge about contraceptives, having teenage friends who became parents, low educational achievement and aspirations, high levels of anxiety, low self-esteem, and feelings of fatalism, powerlessness, and alienation (Brooks-Gunn & Furstenberg, 1989).

Choosing Between Abortion and Parenthood   Although most teenage mothers report that they did not plan to become pregnant and would not choose to do so if they had a choice, the more than 50 percent who decide to have their babies become increasingly committed to motherhood during the course of the pregnancy. A teenager's reactions to unplanned pregnancy are influenced by a variety of factors, including her feelings about school, her relationship with the baby's father, her relationship with her parents, perceived family support for keeping the child, how many of her peers have become parents, and her sense of self-esteem (Furstenberg et al., 1989; Faber, 1991).

Approximately 44 percent of all teenage pregnancies end in abortion, which is roughly 25 percent of all abortions performed in the United States (United States Bureau of the Census, 1992; Hayes, 1987). The experience of an abortion may be psychologically stressful for teenagers. How an abortion will affect a particular teenager depends on her feelings and attitudes about pregnancy and abortion; the

Rob: Are these pregnant teenagers in danger of losing connection with their peer culture?

Janet: Not as much as you might think. Unlike in middle-class communities, where teenagers are expected to complete high school and go to college, there is relatively little stigma attached to becoming pregnant during high school—although there may be a little bit more if pregnancy occurs in junior high.

Rob: Why do teenagers become pregnant in the first place?

Janet: I wish I knew the answer to that one! Failure to use effective birth control is, of course, the immediate factor. And some teenagers want to have a little baby to care for and be close to and to feel important and needed, or they see pregnancy as a way to gain adult status. Another reason is that sex is a big deal and getting pregnant isn't.

Rob: What do you mean?

Janet: Many of these kids become sexually active at age twelve or thirteen, and some even before they start having their periods. Most of them have little extra money, so they don't go shopping, or buy CDs, or collect this or that. A lot of them are involved in Pentecostal or Baptist churches, so they don't do drugs and they don't drink. But they do sex.

Rob: It's an enjoyable activity, and it's inexpensive.

Janet: Well . . . intimacy is involved too, but for many young teens, sex is mainly a way to have immediate fun. Getting pregnant simply happens, with little thought about its deeper social, emotional, or philosophical significance.

Rob: What social supports are available to these youngsters?

Janet: Family or extended family members often will babysit and share other child care responsibilities. Sometimes the boyfriend's family will also become involved, even when he's out of the picture. Many teen moms are back to being teenagers fairly soon after having their babies. Some graduate from high school and get a job, and a few go on to college. A significant number do not finish school. Unfortunately, we are finding that an increasing number get pregnant again soon after the first baby.

What Do You Think?

1. If Janet Whallen were working with pregnant teens in the community in which you spent your adolescence, in what ways might her observations be different? In what ways might they be the same? Why?

2. What are your views about the causes of teenage pregnancy?

3. What strategies might you recommend for preventing teen pregnancy among poor, inner-city youth?

attitudes of and support available from parents, other adults, peers, and her sexual partner; and her overall personal adjustment and life circumstances (Franz & Reardon, 1992; Hardy, 1991).

Consequences of Teenage Parenthood   Many teenage mothers may see having a baby as a way to prematurely crystallize their identity, because motherhood and marriage promise to establish them in a secure adult role and help them escape role confusion. For some, teenage parenthood and marriage also promise an intense, intimate, and lasting relationship with another person, a relationship that they themselves may have been deprived of and may figure heavily in their search for identity (Furstenberg et al., 1989).

Such fantasies are generally not realized, however. Teenage mothers are less likely to finish high school, find a stable paying job, enter secure marriages, or achieve equal job status or income in their lifetimes. Teenage fathers are less negatively affected, largely because they generally do not assume responsibility for raising their children (Furstenberg et al., 1989).

Teenage mothers are more likely than older women to experience complications such as anemia and toxemia during pregnancy, as well as prolonged labor. Their babies are more likely to be premature, have low birth weight, and have neurological defects, and are also more likely to die during their first year (see Chapter 4). The children of teen mothers also are more likely to suffer developmentally, displaying poorer cognitive and social functioning in preschool and elementary school and a higher rate of learning and social adjustment problems as adolescents, than are

For expectant teen couples such as this one, a good high school pregnancy and parenting program and support from family, friends, and each other can have a major impact on how well they cope with the challenges of early parenthood.

children born to older mothers. They are also more likely to become teenage parents themselves. Because they are still children themselves and focused on their own developmental needs, teenage mothers may be less emotionally equipped to be competent parents (Furstenberg et al., 1989). To learn more about this problem, read the "Working With" interview on page 532.

Prevention and Support Programs   Prevention of teenage pregnancy requires a delay of early sexual activity as well as improved use of contraceptives among sexually active teenagers. Prevention programs have taken four approaches: (1) educating teens about sexuality and contraception, (2) changing their attitudes about early

Teenage pregnancy is no joke. Pregnant teenagers, especially those as young as Cindy, face increased risks of complications during pregnancy and childbirth and of delivering premature and low birthweight babies compared to older mothers. Their children are more likely to experience developmental problems. Teen mothers often encounter difficulties in becoming competent parents while they are still in need of parenting themselves.

sexual involvement, (3) providing contraceptive and family-planning services, and (4) increasing girls' self-esteem to give them higher aspirations for education and career. Currently contraception and family-planning services appear to have the highest chance of success. The increased awareness of the need for contraception due to the AIDS epidemic may contribute to the prevention of teen pregnancy.

Most services aimed at providing medical, educational, financial, and parental support have had only moderate success. Prenatal care programs have been the most successful of these services, because teens who obtain adequate prenatal care are more likely to have healthy babies than those who do not. School-based medical clinics that provide easy access to contraceptives and support for teenagers and their problems also have been very effective.

There is also a growing awareness that different prevention approaches may be needed for different types of at-risk teenagers. Teens who are at risk for pregnancy because they are problem prone in general may need different help than teens who are depressed or teens whose alternative lifestyles place them at risk for pregnancy (Lancaster & Hamburg, 1986; McCullough & Scherman, 1991).

Teenage Depression and Suicide

Between 20 and 25 percent of adolescents report having experienced depressed moods during the last six months. A depressed *mood* involves periods of sadness, unhappiness, or blue feelings for an unspecified period of time and is usually experienced with other negative emotions, such as fear, guilt, or anger, and with other problems, such as anxiety and social withdrawal (Petersen et al., 1993). Approximately 5 percent of all adolescents display a *depressive syndrome,* a pattern of depressive symptoms that include feeling lonely, unloved, mistreated, worthless, nervous, fearful, guilty, self-conscious, suspicious, sad, or worried (Peterson et al., 1993).

Finally, at any given point in time, approximately 7 percent of adolescents suffer from a **clinical depression,** meaning their depression is severe enough to be diagnosed as an emotional disorder that requires treatment by a mental health professional. The symptoms of clinical depression include (1) a depressed or irritable mood for most of the day, (2) decreased interest in pleasurable activities, (3) abnormal weight gain or loss, (4) sleep problems, (5) psychomotor agitation or retardation (being physically tense and overactive or slowed and underactive), (6) fatigue or loss of energy, (7) feelings of worthlessness and excessive guilt, (8) impaired concentration and decision-making ability, and (9) repeated thoughts about suicide, plans of suicide, or actual suicide attempts (Petersen et al., 1993).

Suicide is the third leading cause of death among children ages fifteen to nineteen. Between 6 and 13 percent of adolescents have reported attempting suicide at least once in their lives, and the ratio of attempted to successful suicides is estimated to be as high as fifty to one (Garland & Zigler, 1993; Meehan et al., 1992). Suicide attempts are estimated to be three to nine times more common among girls, but boys succeed three times as often, in part because they use more effective methods such as knives and guns (Holden, 1986).

The majority of teenagers who attempt suicide have experienced serious family difficulties, including parent-child conflict, divorce, neglect, and abuse. Depression often is a factor. Suicide attempts almost always represent cries for help with the personal turmoil and feelings of intense loneliness, isolation, and hopelessness that such youngsters experience (Blumenthal & Kupfer, 1988; Rubenstein et al., 1989; Spirito et al., 1989; Trautman & Shaffer, 1989). Although most teenagers who are not depressed still experience moments of unhappiness, and most who are depressed do not attempt suicide, signs of unhappiness and depression should not be dismissed, particularly if they persist. Also, because a large percentage of those who attempt suicide have threatened or attempted it before, such threats should be taken very seriously.

Attempts to prevent suicide include early detection and intervention in family and personal crises, school-based education about depression and suicide risk factors, training in problem-solving and coping skills, crisis counseling, and emergency hot lines. Treatment for teens who attempt suicide generally involves therapy with both the adolescent and his or her family (Garland & Zigler, 1993; Rubenstein et al., 1989). The film *Ordinary People* provides an excellent portrayal of a teenager's suicide attempt, the events and family circumstances involved, and the treatment received.

Juvenile Delinquency

Juvenile delinquency refers to a pattern of destructive or antisocial activities and law-breaking offenses committed by adolescents. In 1990, more than 1.75 million juveniles were arrested for less serious *status offenses* such as vandalism, joy-riding, drug abuse, or running away and almost 650,000 for more serious crimes such as larceny or theft, robbery, or forcible rape. (Federal Bureau of Investigation, 1991; Patterson et al., 1989).

There is some evidence that the route to chronic delinquency may follow a predictable developmental sequence of experiences. The first step involves ineffective parenting and problematic family interaction processes, both of which frequently contribute to childhood conduct disorders. In the second step, the conduct-disordered behaviors lead to academic failure and peer rejection. During later childhood and early adolescence, continuing failure at school and peer rejection lead to a third step: increased risk for depressed mood and involvement in a deviant peer group. Children who follow this developmental sequence are assumed to be at high risk for engaging in chronic delinquent behavior (Patterson et al., 1989).

Factors associated with delinquency include a caregiver-child relationship characterized by hostility, lack of affection, underinvolvement, and lack of supervision; overly harsh and authoritarian methods of discipline; a high degree of family conflict and disorganization; a parent with a personality disturbance and a delinquent history of her or his own; impoverished living conditions; lack of attachment to any prosocial institution such as school, job, or church; lack of positive adult role models; and exposure to neighborhood environments in which violence, crime, and delinquent behavior are prevalent (Dishion et al., 1995; Romig et al., 1989; Sarafino & Armstrong, 1986).

Gangs   Many delinquent youngsters belong to gangs. A *gang* is a relatively permanent group of individuals with a clearly identified leadership and organizational structure and clear role expectations for its members. Gangs identify with or claim control over "territory" in the community and engage in violence and other forms of illegal behavior on an individual or group basis (Miller, 1990). A gang is likely to have a group name, an initiation rite, nicknames for members, and gang symbols such as colors, tattoos, hand signs, or jewelry. Gangs often engage in illegal activities such as fighting, vandalism, theft, and dealing drugs (Winfree et al., 1994). The rising incidence of gang-related homicides, drive-by shootings, home invasions, and related violent and illegal activities in schools and communities is a growing national concern (Burke, 1990; Pryor & McGarell, 1993; Takata & Zevitz, 1990).

Typically gangs are formed by individuals from poor and racial or ethnic minority and immigrant backgrounds (Burke, 1990). Traditionally gang members have mainly been adolescent males, but the growth of gangs in prisons and increased gang involvement in the drug trade have expanded the age range to include children as young as nine as well as adults, and also increased female involvement to some degree (Goldstein & Soriano, 1994; Lasley, 1992).

Gangs are thought to provide alternative economic opportunities and social supports for disadvantaged and alienated youths who face high levels of uncertainty, instability, and danger in their families and neighborhoods. For such adolescents, gang membership offers—a surrogate "family," a sense of identity and belonging, and status, power, and protection, as well as the material benefits of criminal activity (Curry & Spergel, 1988; Knox, 1991).

A gang typically reinforces its members for associating exclusively with other members, conforming to pro-gang attitudes and behaviors, and rejecting the values of parents, teachers, and mainstream peers (Winfree et al., 1994). Many of the individual, family, and social factors associated with gang membership, gang activity, and its prevention are similar to those associated with juvenile delinquency.

Reducing and Preventing Delinquency   Most adolescents, of course, do not become delinquents or join gangs. Adolescents who are at risk for delinquency can sometimes be helped by programs that make available the support and opportunities that will allow successful experimentation with other roles and identities. These include community houses, YMCAs, police athletic leagues, summer camps, crisis drop-in centers, and telephone hot lines, as well as outpatient and residential treatment programs to assist more disturbed teenagers and their families. Unfortunately, such interventions have been found to produce mostly short-term effects and lose their impact unless continued on a long term basis (Patterson et al., 1989).

Intensive early childhood intervention programs for at-risk preschool children and their families have achieved significant success at reducing delinquency and related problems later in life (Zigler et al., 1992). The High/Scope Perry Preschool Program, for example, provided a high-quality preschool, weekly home visits by teachers, and extensive parent involvement for three- and four-year-olds from low-income families. Long-term longitudinal follow-up studies of these children at age nineteen found significantly lower rates of school dropout, illiteracy, unemployment, welfare dependence, and arrests for delinquent or criminal behavior than for a comparable group of children who did not participate in the program (Hamburg, 1992; Schweinhart & Weikart, 1988). Parent training programs designed to improve family management practices with at-risk preadolescents have also yielded promising results (Kazdin, 1987).

What Do You Think?

What advice might you give to concerned parents regarding how they can protect their children from teenage pregnancy and delinquency? What advice might you give to the governor of your state regarding programs to prevent these problems?

THE EMERGING ADULT

We have reached the end of our discussion of adolescence. We saw how relationships with parents, friendships, and activities with groups of peers contribute to the development of identity during this stage. We also discussed the important contribution of sexuality and sexual experiences to identity formation and explored several special problems that can interfere with identity achievement. Just as the growth spurt and physical changes of puberty and the development of formal cognitive thinking at the beginning of adolescence culminate the long series of maturational and cognitive changes that begin with conception and birth, the achievement of identity culminates the psychosocial developments that precede it.

Although adolescence marks both the end of childhood and the last developmental stage covered in this book, it by no means marks the end of development. As we note at the beginning of this section of the text, adolescence is a period of transition to adulthood, and many other important developmental changes are yet to come.

By the end of adolescence, most young people have achieved a much more coherent sense of who they are and are ready to face the challenges of early adulthood.

The social changes of adolescence show vividly one of the major themes of this book: individuals change dramatically as they grow up. As we have seen, in a matter of months an infant who smiles at everyone becomes devoted to particular adults and siblings, and in just a few years more people well outside the family compete seriously with these attachments. The other domains of development show equally dramatic changes. In just a few years, a child grows physically from diapers to climbing trees and riding a bicycle; in just a few years more, she or he starts looking (almost) like an adult. Cognitive changes are equally sweeping: individuals change from infants who think by looking and touching to children who can reason out concrete problems to teenagers who can imagine possibilities they have never personally experienced.

Yet no matter how dramatic they are, developmental changes remain whole, continuous, and human. For convenience, this book has divided human change into topics and discussed the topics one at a time. But real children and youths do not come so divided. As this book has tried to show, children and adolescents not only grow, think, and feel; they also do all of these things at once and in a pattern that makes each person truly unique.

SUMMARY OF MAJOR IDEAS

Individuation and Identity Development

1. A key task of adolescence is successful resolution of the psychosocial crisis of identity versus role confusion.

2. The process of individuation, or becoming a separate and independent person, appears to follow a fairly predictable pattern: differentiation, practice, and experimentation; rapprochement; and consolidation of self.

3. Identity formation involves selectively keeping and integrating certain aspects of one's earlier childhood identity and discarding others.

4. Successful resolution of the identity conflicts typical of adolescence depends in part on having adequate opportunities to experiment with different identities and roles.

5. Erikson calls the period of experimentation and uncertainty that precedes the achievement of a stable adult identity the *psychosocial moratorium.*

6. Marcia has identified four identity statuses among older adolescents: identity achievement, identity diffusion, moratorium, and foreclosure.

Social Relationships During Adolescence

7. While they are not conflict free, relationships between adolescents and their parents are for the most part mutually rewarding.

8. Teenagers appear to feel most positive about authoritative parenting styles and more negative about parents who are authoritarian.

9. Although adolescents and their parents may differ on some of the details of everyday life, they generally agree on the more important questions involving basic values.

10. Social class differences influence the educational and career expectations parents have for their adolescent children and adolescents have for themselves.

11. In recent years, an increasing number of adolescents have encountered the stresses of growing up in a family that has experienced divorce, remarriage, or single parenthood.

12. During adolescence, friendships become increasingly stable, intimate, and mutual.

13. Both small, cohesive cliques and larger, less intimate crowds appear to be important aspects of peer group participation.

14. Teenagers participate in peer groups to please parents and teachers, gain peer acceptance and popularity, and conform.

15. The difficulties many young adolescents experience during the transition to junior high school have raised questions about redesigning schools to better meet young teenagers' developmental needs.

16. The quality of a school's curriculum and its social relationships within and outside the classroom affect students' academic performance, personal development, and the likelihood of dropping out.

17. Work can be a constructive experience for adolescents if it is kept to moderate levels and is appropriate to their educational and other developmental needs.

Sexuality During Adolescence

18. Adolescents' sexual needs are closely tied to their need to establish a secure identity and to achieve both intimacy and independence.

19. Masturbation and sexual fantasies play a significant role in adolescents' sexual development.

20. Girls and boys differ in their reasons for their first experience of sexual intercourse and in their attitudes toward sexual activities.

21. In the United States, dating is the major pathway to adolescents' sexual activity. Unfortunately, sexual aggression and date rape continue to be serious problems.

22. Although acceptance of youngsters with nonheterosexual orientations has increased, the prejudice and discrimination that still exist make identity development more difficult for these adolescents.

Special Problems of Adolescence

23. Although a great deal is known about the causes, pregnancy and parenthood continue to be a major problem faced by a growing number of adolescents.

24. Two other problems common during adolescence are juvenile delinquency and depression.

KEY TERMS

individuation *(501)*
identity versus role
  confusion *(504)*
psychosocial
  moratorium *(504)*
identity diffusion *(504)*
negative identity *(505)*
identity status *(505)*
social class *(512)*
clique *(517)*
crowd *(517)*
homophobia *(530)*
clinical depression *(535)*
juvenile delinquency *(536)*

FOR FURTHER READING

Bell, R., et al. *Changing Bodies, Changing Lives: A Book for Teens on Sex and Relationships.* New York: Vintage, 1988.

This book provides accurate and up-to-date information on a variety of issues affecting the lives of teenagers, including sexuality, relationships with friends and parents, and typical adolescent problems.

Dryfoos, J. G. *Adolescents at Risk: Prevalence and Prevention.* New York: Oxford University Press, 1990.

This book provides a synthesis of the current research on delinquency, substance abuse, teen pregnancy, and school failure, with a focus on prevention strategies and programs.

Garrod, A., L. Smulyan, S. I. Powers, and R. Kilkennly. *Adolescent Portraits: Identity, Relationships and Challenges.* Boston: Allyn & Bacon, 1992.

This book provides firsthand accounts by college-age adolescents of their experiences with gender, work, values, ethnicity, sexuality, and peer and family relationships. Each section gives brief theoretical overviews.

Larson, R., and M. H. Richards. *Divergent Realities: The Emotional Lives of Mothers, Fathers, and Adolescents.* New York: Basic Books, 1994.

This book reports a fascinating study in which fathers, mothers, and adolescents carried electronic pagers for a week and reported on their activities and emotions at random times when signaled by the researchers.

Philadelphia Child Guidance Center. *Your Child's Emotional Health: Adolescence.* New York: Macmillan, 1994.

Written by the staff of one of the best-known child guidance centers, this book provides practical information and concrete recommendations for parents regarding the emotional development and mental health needs of their adolescent children.

Steinberg, L. D., and A. Levine. *You and Your Adolescent: A Parent's Guide to Development from 10 to 20.* New York: Harper & Row, 1990.

This book provides useful suggestions for parents of adolescents based on research and observation by a leading expert in the field.

Glossary

accommodation   According to Piaget, the process of modifying existing ideas or action-skills to fit new experiences.

achievement motivation   Behavior that enhances competence or enhances judgments of competence.

achievement test   A test designed to evaluate a person's current state of knowledge.

acquired immunodeficiency syndrome (AIDS)   A viral illness that gradually destroys the body's ability to combat other diseases.

acute illness   A disease with a definite time of onset and lasting for a fixed and relatively short period of time.

adaptation   Piaget's term for the process by which development occurs; concepts are deepened or broadened by assimilation and stretched or modified by accommodation.

adolescence   The stage of development between childhood and adulthood, around ages ten to twenty-two.

adolescent egocentrism   The tendency of adolescents to perceive the world (and themselves) from their own perspective.

adoption study   A research method for studying the relative contributions of heredity and environment in which genetically related children reared apart are compared with genetically unrelated children reared together.

aggression   A bold, assertive action that is intended to hurt another person or to procure an object.

allele   One of several alternative forms of a gene.

American Sign Language (ASL)   A system of gestures used in place of oral language by individuals with hearing impairments.

amniocentesis   A prenatal diagnostic method in which a sample of amniotic fluid is withdrawn and tested to detect chromosomal abnormalities.

amniotic sac   A tough, spongy bag filled with salty fluid that surrounds the embryo, protects it from sudden jolts, and helps to maintain a fairly stable temperature.

androgyny   A tendency to integrate both masculine and feminine behaviors into the personality.

animism   A belief that nonliving objects are alive and human.

anorexia nervosa   A physical and psychological disturbance that causes a person to refuse to eat sufficient food and to develop an increasingly unrealistic view of his or her body; most individuals with anorexia are teenage girls.

AnotB error   The tendency of infants to look for a hidden object in the first place it disappears (at "A") rather than where they have seen it most recently (at "B").

anxious-avoidant attachment   An insecure bond between infant and caregiver in which the child rarely cries when separated from the caregiver and tends to avoid or ignore the caregiver when reunited.

anxious-resistant attachment   An insecure bond between infant and caregiver in which the child shows signs of anxiety preceding separation, is intensely upset by separation, and seeks close contact when reunited while at the same time resisting the caregiver's efforts to comfort.

Apgar Scale   A system of rating newborns' health immediately following birth based on heart rate, strength of breathing, muscle tone, color, and reflex irritability.

appearance-reality distinctions   The ability to distinguish apparent perceptions from real qualities of objects; acquired during the preschool period.

aptitude test   A measurement of ability that estimates future performance in some realm of behavior.

artifact   A manufactured or humanly crafted object; often distinguished from a "natural kind."

assimilation   According to Piaget, a method by which a child responds to new experiences by using existing concepts to interpret new ideas and experiences.

attachment   An intimate and enduring emotional relationship between two people, such as infant and caregiver, characterized by reciprocal affection and a periodic desire to maintain physical closeness.

attention deficit hyperactivity disorder (ADHD)   See *hyperactivity*.

auditory cortex   An area of the brain, located near the left side of the cerebral cortex, where the sounds of speech produce their primary response.

authoritarian parenting   A style of childrearing characterized by a high degree of control and demands on children's maturity and a low degree of clarity of communication and nurturance.

authoritative parenting   A style of childrearing characterized by a high degree of control, clarity of communication, maturity demands, and nurturance.

autonomy   In Erikson's theory, a child's ability to govern and regulate her or his own thoughts, feelings, and actions freely and responsibly while at the same time overcoming feelings of shame and doubt.

autonomy versus shame and doubt   According to Erikson, the psychosocial crisis of children ages one to three involving the struggle to control their own thoughts, feelings, and actions; the second of Erikson's developmental stages.

balanced bilingual   A person who is equally fluent in two languages rather than more fluent in one language than in the other.

behavior genetics   The scientific study of the relationship between genotype and phenotype, especially with regard to intelligence, personality, and mental health.

behaviorism   A learning theory that focuses on changes in specific observable behaviors and their causes.

behavior modification   A body of techniques based on behaviorism for changing or eliminating specific behaviors.

Black English   A dialect or version of English spoken by many African Americans.

blended family   A family created from a combination of stepchildren, stepparents, and stepsiblings.

blind training   The teaching of learned strategies without informing the learner of the benefits of the strategies.

brainstem   A relatively primitive, or "lower," area of the brain; along with the midbrain, this area regulates relatively automatic functions such as breathing, digestion, and consciousness.

Broca's area   An area of the brain located on the left side of the cerebral cortex; vital to the production of language. See also *Wernicke's area*.

bulimia A disorder in which a person, usually a teenage girl, eats huge amounts of food and then vomits it to avoid gaining weight.

caesarean section A childbirth procedure in which the baby is removed surgically from the mother's abdomen.

canalization The tendency of many developmental processes to unfold in highly predictable ways under a wide range of conditions.

caregiver-infant synchrony Patterns of closely coordinated social and emotional interaction between caregiver and infant.

case study A research study of a single individual or small group of individuals considered as a unit.

catch-up growth The process by which children recover from slow growth by growing faster than usual until they reach the normal size for their age.

central nervous system The brain and nerve cells of the spinal cord.

cephalocaudal principle The tendency for organs, reflexes, and skills to develop sooner at the top (or head) of the body and later in areas farther down the body.

cerebellum The part of the brain that coordinates muscles and maintains physical balance.

cerebral cortex The "higher" part of the brain; along with the cerebrum, it controls vision, hearing, and touch, as well as motor actions such as lifting an arm.

chorionic villus sampling (CVS) A medical procedure for detecting genetic abnormalities before birth in which a small bit of tissue surrounding the embryo is removed and examined microscopically.

chromosome A threadlike, rod-shaped structure containing genetic information that is transmitted from parents to children; each human sperm or egg cell contains twenty-three chromosomes, and these determine a person's inherited characteristics.

chronic illness A disease lasting a long period of time (such as several months or more) and changing only very slowly.

circular reaction Piaget's term for an action often repeated, apparently because it is self-reinforcing.

classical conditioning According to Pavlov, learning in which a neutral stimulus gains the power to bring about a certain response by repeated association with another stimulus that already elicits the same response.

classification Putting objects in groups or categories according to some set of standards or criteria.

clinical depression A pattern of depressive symptoms that is severe enough to require treatment by mental health professionals. Symptoms include depressed or irritable mood, decreased interest in pleasurable activities, abnormal weight gain or loss, sleep problems, over- or underactivity, fatigue or loss of energy, excessive feelings of worthlessness and guilt, impaired concentration and decision making, and thoughts, plans or attempts at suicide.

clique A small, closely knit peer group of two or more members (average of six members) who are intimately involved in a number of shared purposes and activities and exclude those who are not.

cognition All processes by which humans acquire knowledge; methods for thinking or gaining knowledge about the world.

cognitive development The area of human development concerned with cognition; involves all psychological processes by which individuals learn and think about their environment.

competence According to Robert White, children's increased skill and capability in successfully exploring, mastering, and controlling the world around them.

conception The moment at which the male's sperm cell penetrates the female's egg cell (ovum), forming a zygote.

concordance rate The percentage of instances in which both members of a genetically similar pair of individuals (e.g., identical twins) display a particular all-or-none trait such as cystic fibrosis, Huntington's disease, or schizophrenia.

concrete operations Logical thinking about concrete or tangible objects and processes; especially characteristic of children in the middle years.

conservation A belief that certain properties (such as quantity) remain constant despite changes in perceived features such as dimensions, position, and shape.

constructive play A type of play that involves manipulation of physical objects to build or construct something.

control group In an experimental research study, the group of subjects who experience conditions similar or identical to the experimental group, but without experiencing the experimental treatment.

correlation An association between two variables in which changes in one variable tend to occur with changes in the other. The association does not necessarily imply a causal link between the variables.

critical period Any period during which development is particularly susceptible to an event or influence, either negative or positive.

critical thinking Reflection or thinking about complex issues, usually to make decisions or take actions.

cross-sectional study A study that compares individuals of different ages at the same point in time.

crowd A large, loosely knit peer group of between fifteen and thirty members (average of twenty members) that generally consists of from two to four cliques.

décallage Literally "gap"; Piaget's term for the differences in when a child acquires the skills of a particular cognitive stage.

deoxyribonucleic acid (DNA) A molecule containing hereditary information; has a chemical structure of two chains of polynucleotides arranged in a double helix or spiral.

dependent variable A factor that is measured in an experiment and that *depends on,* or is controlled by, one or more independent variables.

development Long-term changes in a person's growth, feelings, patterns of thinking, social relationships, and motor skills.

developmentally appropriate practice Methods and goals of teaching considered optimal for young children given current knowledge of child development.

dichotic listening A task in which an individual is fed information or sounds to each ear separately; demonstrates hemispheric lateralization.

domain A realm of psychological functioning.

dominant gene In any paired set of genes, the gene with greater influence in determining physical characteristics that are physically visible or manifest.

dramatic play A cognitive level of play involving pretense; begins as soon as a child can symbolize or mentally represent objects. Also called *make-believe.*

duo   A two-word utterance.

ego   According to Freud, the rational, realistic part of the personality; coordinates impulses from the id with demands imposed by the superego and by society.

ego integrity versus despair   According to Erikson, the final psychosocial crisis, reached during late adulthood and old age, in which one looks back on one's life with dignity, optimism, and wisdom while facing the despair resulting from the negative aspects of old age.

embryo   The fully implanted blastocyst; refers specifically to the developing human from the second to eighth week after conception.

embryonic stage   Stage in prenatal development that lasts from week 2 through week 8.

empathy   A sensitive awareness of the thoughts and feelings of another person.

endocrine glands   Glands that produce growth hormones.

estrogen   A sex hormone, sometimes called the *female sex hormone* because its high concentration in girls stimulates the growth of the ovaries and vagina during puberty.

experimental group   In an experimental research study, the group of subjects who experience the experimental treatment while in other respects experiencing conditions similar or identical to the those of the control group.

experimental study   A study in which circumstances are arranged so that just one or two factors or influences vary at a time.

expressive language   Language that a child can actually use appropriately in conversation.

failure to thrive   A condition in which an infant seems seriously delayed in physical growth and is noticeably apathetic in behavior.

false-belief task   A type of research design that tests children's awareness of the difference between what they know and what other persons might believe.

fetal alcohol syndrome (FAS)   A congenital condition exhibited by babies born to mothers who consumed too much alcohol during pregnancy. They do not arouse easily and tend to behave sluggishly in general; they also have distinctive facial characteristics.

fetal presentation   Refers to the body part of the fetus that is closest to the mother's cervix; may be head first (cephalic), feet and rump first (breech), or shoulders first (transverse).

fetal stage   The stage in prenatal development that lasts from the eighth week of pregnancy until birth.

fetus   An embryo that has developed its first bone cells, after about eight weeks of gestation.

fine motor coordination   The ability to carry out smoothly small movements that involve precise timing but not strength.

fine motor skills   Voluntary movements of the body that involve the small muscles located throughout the body.

first stage of labor   In childbirth, the stage that begins with relatively mild and irregular contractions of the uterus. As contractions grow stronger, the cervix dilates enough for the baby's head to begin fitting through. May take from eight to twenty-four hours for a first-time mother.

formal curriculum   The traditional academic curriculum that helps students acquire the knowledge and skills thought to be necessary for successful participation in society.

formal operational thought   Thinking based on previously acquired concrete mental operations and involving hypothetical reasoning and attention to the structure or form of ideas.

freestanding birth clinic (FBC)   Nonhospital facilities organized to provide family-centered maternity care for women who are at low risk for obstetrical complications.

functional play   A cognitive level of play that involves simple, repeated movements and a focus on one's own body.

functional relationships   Variations in an environment that normally occur together.

games with rules   A cognitive level of play involving relatively formal activities with fixed rules.

gamete   A reproductive cell (sperm or ovum).

gender   The thoughts, feelings, and behaviors associated with being male or female.

gender constancy   A belief that a person's sex is biologically determined, permanent, and unchanging, no matter what else about that person changes.

gender identity   One's beliefs about what sex one is.

gender preference   Attitudes about the sex one prefers to be.

gender role stereotypes   The culturally "appropriate" patterns of gender-related behaviors expected by society. Also called sex roles.

gene-environment relationship   May be passive, active, or evocative, depending on whether an infant or child passively accepts, stimulates (evokes), or actively seeks and creates situations and experiences that support or increase genetically influenced behavioral traits such as shyness or intelligence.

gene   A molecular structure, carried on chromosomes, containing genetic information; the basic unit of heredity.

generative rules   Syntactic rules that allow speakers to generate new sentences almost infinitely by applying them to new morphemes.

generativity versus stagnation   The seventh of Erikson's psychosocial crises, reached in middle adulthood, in which one must balance the feeling that one's life is personally satisfying and socially meaningful with feelings of purposelessness.

genotype   The set of genetic traits inherited by an individual. See also *phenotype*.

germinal stage   The stage in prenatal development that occurs during the first two weeks of pregnancy; characterized by rapid cell division. Also called the *period of the ovum*.

glia   Brain cells that emit a sheathing that encases neurons and their fibers; helps to transmit impulses more quickly and reliably.

gross motor skills   Voluntary movements of the body that involve the large muscles of the arms, legs, and torso.

growth spurt   A rapid change in height and weight that occurs in puberty and is preceded and followed by years of comparatively little increase.

habituation   The tendency to attend to novel stimuli and ignore familiar ones.

hemispheric lateralization   A tendency for the left and right halves of the brain to perform separate functions.

hemophilia   A disease in which the blood fails to clot properly and therefore is characterized by excessive bleeding; example of a sex-linked recessive trait.

heritability estimate   The degree to which variation among an individual's phenotypic behaviors can be attributed to genetic influences.

heterozygous   Describes a genotype consisting of distinct forms of chromosomes for the same gene.

homozygous A genetic condition in which an individual inherits two identical genes at a particular location on a particular chromosome.

hormones Chemicals produced by the endocrine glands and secreted directly into the bloodstream.

hostile aggression Aggressive behavior in which harm is a primary intent.

human immunodeficiency virus (HIV) The virus known to cause the disease AIDS. See *acquired immunodeficiency syndrome*.

hyperactivity Excessive levels of activity and an inability to concentrate for normal periods of time. See *attention deficit hyperactivity disorder*.

hypothesis A precise prediction based on a scientific theory; often capable of being tested in a scientific research study.

id In Freud's theory, the part of an individual's personality that is present at birth, unconscious, impulsive, and unrealistic, and that attempts to satisfy a person's biological and emotional needs and desires by maximizing pleasure and avoiding pain.

identification In psychoanalytic theory, the conscious and unconscious ways in which children experience themselves as being like their parents and other important role models and strive to be like them.

identity (1) Piagetian term for the constancy of an object. (2) A unique and relatively stable set of personal characteristics.

identity diffusion A failure to achieve a relatively coherent, integrated, and stable identity.

identity status Marcia's four categories of identity development: identity achievement, identity diffusion, moratorium, and foreclosure.

identity versus role confusion The fifth of Erikson's psychosocial crises, in which one must integrate one's many childhood skills and beliefs and gain recognition for them from society.

imaginary audience A characteristic of young adolescents in which they act as though they are performing for an audience and believe that others are as concerned with their appearance and behavior as they themselves are.

implantation The attachment of the blastocyst to the wall of the uterus.

independent variable A factor that an experimenter manipulates (varies) to determine its influence on the population being studied.

individuation The process by which an adolescent develops a unique and separate personal identity. Consists of four subphases: differentiation, practice and experimentation, rapprochement, and consolidation.

industry versus inferiority Erikson's fourth crisis, during which children concern themselves with their capacity to do good work and thereby develop confident, positive self-concepts or else face feelings of inferiority.

infant-directed speech The style or register of speech used by adults and older children when talking with a one- or two-year-old infant.

infant mortality rate The frequency with which infants die compared to the frequency with which they live.

informal curriculum The implicit norms, expectations, and rewards for certain ways of thinking and acting that are conveyed by a school's social and authority relationships; teaches students the social roles and behaviors society expects.

information-processing theory Explanations of cognition that focus on the precise, detailed features or steps of mental activities. These theories often use computers as a model for human thinking.

informed consent An agreement to participate in a research study based on understanding the nature of the research, protection of human rights, and freedom to decline to participate at any time.

informed training The teaching of learning strategies that includes telling and showing the learner the reasons for using the strategies.

initiative versus guilt Erikson's third crisis, during which a child's increasing ability to initiate verbal and physical activity and expanding imaginative powers lead to fantasies of large and sometimes frightening proportions.

in loco parentis In developmental research, the principle that investigators should act in the best interests of the child at all times.

inner speech Toddlers' "mental shorthand"; thinking that occurs with little help from language.

instrumental aggression Assertive behavior with a goal in mind; the action ends when the goal is achieved and sometimes may unintentionally hurt others.

integrated care In Gilligan's theory, a form of moral development that combines care for others with care for oneself.

intelligence A general ability to learn from experience; also refers to ability to reason abstractly.

interview A face-to-face, directed conversation used in a research study to gather in-depth information.

intimacy versus isolation The sixth of Erikson's psychosocial crises, in which young adults must be able to develop intimate relationships with others while dealing with the fear of loss of identity that such intimacy entails.

juvenile delinquency A pattern of destructive or antisocial activities and lawbreaking offenses committed by adolescents.

juvenile period Proposed by Sullivan, it is a period between ages five and ten when children show increasing interest in developing intense friendships or "chum relationships" with peers of the same gender.

latency According to Freud, the stage of development between the phallic and genital stages. Sexual feelings and activities are on hold as the child struggles to resolve the oedipal conflict.

lateralized behavior An action that individuals prefer to perform with one side of their bodies more than the other.

learning disability Difficulty in learning a specific academic skill such as reading or arithmetic.

learning orientation Achievement motivation that comes from the learner and the task.

learning strategies General methods or techniques that help to solve a variety of problems.

lexicon The words or units of meaning of a language.

longitudinal study A study of the same subjects over a relatively long period, often months or years.

low birth weight A birth weight of less than 2,500 grams (about 5½ pounds).

make-believe See *dramatic play*.

meiosis A complex process by which gametes form; involves duplication and division of reproductive cells and their chromosomes.

menarche The first menstrual period.

metacognition Knowledge and thinking about cognition, how learning and memory operate in everyday situations, and how one can improve cognitive performance.

metalinguistic awareness The ability to attend to language as an object of thought rather than attending only to the content or ideas of a language.

midbrain The area of the brain that, together with the brainstem, regulates relatively automatic functions such as breathing, digestion, and consciousness.

midwife A woman experienced in pregnancy and childbirth who traditionally served as the primary caregiver during pregnancy, childbirth, and the month or two following delivery.

mitosis The creation of new cells through duplication of chromosomes and division of cells.

morality Sensitivity to and knowledge about what is right and wrong.

Moro reflex The reflexive startle response of newborns. Healthy infants fling their arms out suddenly and sometimes shake all over or cry in response to a sudden loud noise or sudden loss of support.

morphemes The smallest meaningful units of language; include words as well as a number of prefixes and suffixes that carry meaning.

mortality The proportion of persons who die at a given age; the rate of death.

motor cortex The area of the brain, located just forward of the top of the head, where simple voluntary movements produce their largest neural activity.

motor skills Physical skills using the body or limbs, such as walking and drawing.

multifactorial disorder Disorders resulting from a combination of genetic and environmental factors.

multiple intelligences According to Howard Gardner's theory of intelligence, alternative forms of intelligence or adaptability to the environment.

myelin The sheathing, emitted by glia, that encases neurons and their fibers.

natural kind An object that is born from another of the same kind and cannot be constructed artificially from other materials.

naturalistic research A study in which the researcher purposely observes behavior as it normally occurs in its natural setting.

nature (1) The essence or basic character of a person or thing. (2) The inborn qualities of a person.

negative identity A form of identity diffusion involving rejection of the roles preferred by one's family or community in favor of socially undesirable roles.

neonate A newborn infant.

neostructuralist (neo-Piagetian) theories Theories of cognitive development that are based on the general notion of stagelike development but focus on more precise areas of thinking and mechanisms of development than Piaget's original theory proposed.

neurons Nerve cell bodies and their extensions or fibers.

nocturnal emission Ejaculation of semen during sleep.

non-REM sleep A relatively quiet, deep period of sleep. See also *REM sleep*.

norms Behaviors typical at certain ages and of certain groups; standards of normal development.

nurture Environmental influences and experiences that affect a person's development.

obesity The state of being extremely overweight, specifically more than 130 percent of normal weight for height and bone size; affects one American child in ten.

object permanence According to Piaget, the belief that people and things continue to exist even when one cannot experience them directly; emerges around age two.

object relations The child's relationships with the important people (called objects) in his environment and the process by which their qualities become part of his personality and mental life.

observational learning The tendency of a child to imitate or model behavior and attitudes of parents and other nurturant individuals.

operant conditioning According to Skinner, a process of learning in which a person or an animal increases the frequency of a behavior in response to repeated reinforcement of that behavior.

overgeneralizations Utterances in which a child shifts from using correct but irregular forms to using wrong but more regular forms; represent efforts to try out newly noticed rules of syntax.

ovum The reproductive cell, or gamete, of the female; the egg cell.

peers Individuals who are of approximately the same age and developmental level and who share common attitudes and interests.

perception The neural activity of combining sensations into meaningful patterns.

performance orientation Achievement motivation stimulated by other individuals who may see and evaluate the learner rather than by the intrinsic nature of the task itself.

period of transition A very brief period between the first and second stages of labor during which the cervix approaches full dilation, contractions become more rapid and intense, and the baby's head moves into the birth canal.

permissive-indifferent parenting A style of parenting in which parents' permissiveness reflects an avoidance of childrearing responsibilities, sometimes with detrimental results.

permissive-indulgent parenting A style of parenting in which parents make relatively few demands on their children but clearly communicate their warmth and interest and provide considerable care and nurturance.

personal fable Adolescents' belief that their own lives embody a special story that is heroic and completely unique.

phenotype The set of traits an individual actually displays during development; reflects the evolving product of genotype and experience. See also *genotype*.

phoneme A sound that combines with other sounds to form words.

phonology The individual vocal sounds of a language.

physical development The area of human development concerned primarily with physical changes such as growth, motor skill development, and basic aspects of perception.

placenta An organ that delivers oxygen and nutrients from the mother to the fetus and carries away the fetus's waste products, which the mother will excrete.

postconventional moral judgment In Kohlberg's theory, an orientation to moral justice that develops beyond conventional rules and beliefs.

premature baby A baby born prior to the thirty-seventh week of pregnancy; also called a *preterm baby*.

prepared childbirth   A method of childbirth in which parents have rehearsed or simulated the actual sensations of labor and delivery well before the actual delivery date.

pretend play   Play that substitutes imaginary situations for real ones. Also called fantasy or dramatic play.

preterm baby   See *premature baby*.

primary circular reaction   According to Piaget, a behavior that is repeated and focuses on the baby's own body and movements; occurs during the second stage of infant cognition (usually at about one to four months of age).

primary sex characteristics   Characteristics that make sexual reproduction possible. For girls, consist of the vagina, uterus, fallopian tubes, and ovaries; for boys, consist of the penis, scrotum, testes, prostate gland, and seminal vesicles.

primitive reflex   An inborn behavioral response of newborn infants that serves no obvious physical purpose; contrasted to a survival reflex.

prosocial behavior   Positive social contacts; actions that benefit others.

proximodistal pattern   Growth that exhibits a near-to-far pattern of development, from the center of the body outward.

psychometric approach to intelligence   A view of intelligence based on identifying individual differences in ability through standardized test scores.

psychosocial development   The area of human development concerned primarily with personality, social knowledge and skills, and emotions.

psychosocial moratorium   According to Erikson, the latency period that precedes puberty and provides a temporary suspension of psychosexual development.

puberty   The period of early adolescence characterized by the development of full physical and sexual maturity.

pubic hair   Hair that grows around the genital area as a result of puberty.

punishment   According to Skinner, any stimulus that temporarily suppresses the response that it follows.

random sample   In research studies, a group of subjects from a population chosen such that each member of the population has an equal chance of being selected.

range of reaction   The range of possible phenotypes that an individual with a particular genotype might exhibit in response to the particular sequence of environmental influences he or she experiences.

recall memory   Retrieval of information by using relatively few external cues.

recasting   Rephrasing or restating an utterance expressed by a child; a process thought to encourage language acquisition and development.

receptive language   Language that is understood or comprehended when used by others.

recessive gene   In any paired set of genes, the gene that influences or determines physical characteristics only when no dominant gene is present.

recognition memory   Retrieval of information by comparing an external stimulus or cue with preexisting experiences or knowledge.

reflex   An involuntary, automatic response to a stimulus. The very first movements or motions of an infant are reflexes.

reinforcement   According to Skinner, any stimulus that increases the likelihood that a behavior will be repeated in similar circumstances.

REM sleep   A relatively active period of sleep, named after the rapid eye movements that usually accompany it. See also *non-REM sleep*.

reversibility   Piaget's term for the ability to undo a problem mentally and go back to its beginning.

rooting   A reflexive searching behavior that orients an infant to the mother's breast or to a bottle.

scaffolding   Providing a framework or cognitive support for a child's learning and thinking.

scheme   According to Piaget, a behavior or thought that represents a group of ideas and events in a child's experience.

scientific method   General procedures of study involving (1) formulating research questions, (2) stating questions as a hypothesis, (3) testing the hypothesis, and (4) interpreting and publicizing the results.

second stage of labor   The period of labor that starts with "crowning," the first moment the baby's head can be seen, and ends with the baby's birth; usually lasts between sixty and ninety minutes.

secondary circular reaction   According to Piaget, the third stage of infant cognition, which occurs at age four to eight months; repeated behaviors that are motivated by external objects and events.

secondary sex characteristics   Sex characteristics other than the sex organs, such as extra layers of fat and pubic hair.

secular trend   (1) In general, any long-term historical trend. (2) In human development, the tendency of each new generation in industrialized countries to grow larger and heavier and to experience puberty earlier than their parents did.

secure attachment   A healthy bond between infant and caregiver. The child is happy when the caregiver is present, somewhat upset during the caregiver's absence, and easily comforted upon the caregiver's return.

self-constancy   The belief that one's identity remains permanently fixed; established sometime after age six.

self-esteem   An individual's belief that he or she is an important, competent, powerful, and worthwhile person who is valued and appreciated.

semantics   The purposes and meanings of a language.

semen   A sticky fluid produced by the prostate gland; carries sperm to the penis and provides it with a medium in which to live after ejaculation.

sense of self   A structured way children have of thinking about themselves that helps to organize and understand who they are based on the views of others, their own experiences, and cultural categories such as gender and race.

sensorimotor intelligence   According to Piaget, thinking that occurs by way of sensory perceptions and motor actions; characteristic of infants.

sex-linked recessive traits   Recessive traits resulting from genes on the X chromosome.

sickle-cell disease   A genetically transmitted condition in which a person's red blood cells intermittently acquire a curved, sickle shape. The condition sometimes can clog circulation in the small blood vessels.

sleep apnea   Temporary stoppage of breathing during sleep.

small-for-date infant   An infant who develops more slowly than normal during pregnancy; can be born full term or preterm.

social class   The social stratum of an individual or family that is determined by parents' level of education, income, and type of work, as well as by their lifestyle and cultural values.

social cognition   Knowledge and beliefs about interpersonal and social matters.

social conventions   Arbitrary customs and agreements about behavior that members of a society use.

social referencing   The child's sensitive awareness of how parents and other adults are feeling and ability to use these emotional cues as a basis for guiding his or her own emotional responses and actions. Social referencing is important for the development of autonomy.

sociocultural perspective on intelligence   A view of intelligence that emphasizes the social and cultural influences on ability rather than the influence of inherent or learned individual differences.

sperm   Male gametes, or reproductive cells; produced in the testicles.

Strange Situation   A widely used method for studying attachment; confronts the infant with a series of controlled separations and reunions with a parent and a stranger.

sucking   One of the neonate's first and most powerful reflexes, triggered by any object intruding into the mouth.

sudden infant death syndrome (SIDS)   "Crib death" syndrome in which apparently healthy infants stop breathing unaccountably and die in their sleep; most frequently strikes infants between ages two and four months.

superego   In Freud's theory, the part of personality that acts as an all-knowing, internalized parent. It has two parts: the conscience, which enforces moral and social conventions by punishing violations with guilt, and the ego-ideal, which provides an idealized, internal set of standards for regulating and evaluating one's thoughts, feelings, and actions.

survey   A research study that samples specific knowledge or opinions of large numbers of individuals.

survival reflex   An inborn behavioral response of newborn infants that serves a clear physical purpose, such as breathing.

symbol   A word, object, or behavior that stands for something else.

symbolic thought   Cognition that makes one object or action stand for another.

syntax   The organizational rules of words and phrases in a language; its grammar.

telegraphic speech   Early utterances that leave out most articles, prepositions, and conjunctions.

temperament   Individual differences in quality and intensity of emotional responding and self-regulation that are present at birth, are relatively stable and enduring over time and across situations, and are influenced by the interaction of heredity, maturation, and experience.

teratogen   Any substance a pregnant woman is exposed to that can harm the developing embryo or fetus.

tertiary circular reaction   According to Piaget, repeated variations of action schemes, organized by trial and error; the fifth stage in infant cognition, occurring between ages twelve and eighteen months.

testosterone   A sex hormone; sometimes called the *male sex hormone* because its high concentration in boys stimulates the growth of the penis and related male reproductive organs.

theory of mind   Coherent, theorylike beliefs about how human thinking occurs that develop during the first few years of life.

third stage of labor   The final stage of labor, in which the afterbirth (placenta and umbilical cord) is expelled; normally lasts only a few minutes.

triarchic theory of intelligence   A view of intelligence as consisting of three components: (1) adaptability, (2) information-processing skills, and (3) the ability to deal with novelty.

trust versus mistrust   In Erikson's theory, the psychosocial crisis of children from birth to one year involving whether they can rely on their parents to reliably meet their physical and emotional needs.

twin study   A research method for studying the relative contributions of heredity and environment in which the degree of similarity between genetically identical twins (developed from a single egg) is compared with the similarity between fraternal twins (developed from two eggs).

ultrasound   A prenatal diagnostic method that allows medical personnel and others to view the fetus by projecting high-frequency sound waves through the mother's womb.

umbilical cord   Three large blood vessels that connect the embryo to the placenta, one to provide nutrients and two to remove waste products.

validity   The degree to which research findings measure or observe what is intended.

visual cliff   The classic laboratory setup of a ledge covered by a sheet of glass; used to test the acquisition of depth perception. Young babies crawling on the glass discriminate between the two sides of the "cliff."

visual cortex   The area of the brain located near the back of the head in the cerebral cortex, where visual images produce the strongest activity.

warp   Sullivan's term for describing the emotional biases families frequently give their children, such as a tendency to be shy and reserved or to be outgoing and sociable.

Wernicke's area   The part of the auditory cortex in which the sounds of speech produce their primary response.

zone of proximal development   According to Vygotsky, the level of difficulty at which problems are too hard for children to solve alone but not too hard when given support from adults or more competent peers.

zygote   The single new cell formed when a sperm cell attaches itself to the surface of an ovum (egg).

References

Abler, R. M., & Sedlacek, W. E. (1989). Freshman sexual attitudes and behaviors over a 15-year period. *Journal of College Student Development, 30,* 201–209.

Adams, G. R., & Gullotta, T. P. (Eds.). *From childhood to adolescence: A transitional period?* Newbury Park, Cal.: Sage.

Adelson, J. (1991). Political development. In R. Lerner, A. Petersen, & J. Brooks-Gunn (Eds.), *Encyclopedia of adolescence: Vol. 1* (pp. 792–793). New York: Garland.

Ainsworth, M. (1973). The development of infant mother attachment. In B. M. Caldwell & H. N. Ricciuti (Eds.), *Review of child development research: Vol. 3.* Chicago: University of Chicago Press.

Ainsworth, M. (1975). *Infancy in Uganda.* Baltimore: Johns Hopkins University Press.

Ainsworth, M. (1979). Infant-mother attachment. *American Psychologist, 34,* 932–937.

Ainsworth, M., Blehar, M., Waters, E., & Wall, S. (1978). *Strange-situation behavior of one-year-olds. Its relation to mother-infant interaction in the first year and to qualitative differences in the infant-mother attachment relationship.* Hillsdale, N.J.: Erlbaum.

Aldis, O. (1975). *Play fighting.* New York: Academic Press.

Alexander, G. M., & Hines, M. (1994). Gender labels and play styles: Their relative contribution to children's selection of playmates. *Child Development, 65,* 869–879.

Alexander, K. L., & Entwisle, D. R. (1988). Achievement in the first 2 years of school: Patterns and processes. *Monographs of the Society for Research in Child Development, 53*(2, Serial No. 218).

Allen, J. P., Hauser, S. T., Bell, K. L., & O'Conner, T. G. (1994). Longitudinal assessment of autonomy and relatedness in adolescent-family interactions as predictors of adolescent ego development and self esteem. *Child Development, 65,* 179–194.

Allen, V. (1976). *Children as teachers: Theory and research on tutoring.* New York: Academic Press.

Allgood-Merten, B., Lewinsohn, P., & Hops, H. (1990). Sex differences in adolescent depression. *Journal of Abnormal Psychology, 99,* 55–63.

Altman, L. K. (1995, January 31). AIDS is now the leading killer of Americans from 25 to 44. *The New York Times,* p. C7.

American Academy of Pediatrics. (1989). *The facts on breastfeeding.* Elk Grove Village, Ill.: Author.

American Academy of Pediatrics. (1991). *Facts about children with AIDS.* Elk Grove Village, Ill.: Author.

American Academy of Pediatrics. (1992). *Immunization protects children.* Brochure.

American Academy of Pediatrics. (1993). *Pediatric nutrition handbook* (3rd ed.). Elk Grove Village, Ill.: Author.

American College of Obstetricians and Gynecologists (ACOG). (1990). *Planning for Pregnancy, Birth, and Beyond.* New York: Dutton.

American Psychiatric Association. (1994). *Diagnostic and statistical manual of mental disorders* (4th ed.). Washington, D.C.: Author.

American Psychological Association. (1992). Ethical principles of psychologists and code of conduct. *American Psychologist, 47*(12), 1992.

American Red Cross. (1992). *American Red Cross community first aid and safety.* St. Louis: Mosby Yearbooks.

Ames, L. B. (1983). *Your one-year-old.* New York: Dell.

Anastasi, A. (1989). *Psychological testing* (6th ed.). New York: Macmillan.

Anderson, B. (1989). Effects of public day care: A longitudinal study. *Child Development, 60,* 857–866.

Anderson, E. (1992). *Speaking with style: Sociolinguistic skills of children.* New York: Routledge.

Andrien, M. (1994). *Social communication in nutrition: A methodology for intervention.* Rome: Food and Agricultural Organization of the United Nations.

Anglin, J. (1993). Vocabulary development: A morphological analysis. *Monographs of the Society for Research on Child Development, 58*(10, Serial No. 238). Chicago: University of Chicago Press.

Apgar, V. (1953). A proposal for a new method of evaluation in the newborn infant. *Current Research in Anesthesia and Analgesia, 32,* 260.

Apgar, V., & Beck, J. (1973). *Is my baby all right?* New York: Trident.

Archer, S. L. (1982). The lower age boundaries of identity development. *Child Development, 53,* 1551–1556.

Archer, S. L., & Waterman, A. S. (1988). Psychological individualism: Gender differences or gender identity? *Human Development, 31,* 65–81.

Archibald, J. (Ed.). (1995). *Phonological acquisition and phonological theory.* Hillsdale, N.J.: Erlbaum.

Arditti, J. A. (1992). Differences between fathers with joint custody and noncustodial fathers. *American Journal of Orthopsychiatry, 62,* 186–195.

Arehart-Treichel, J. (1981). Down's syndrome: The father's role. *Science News, 116*(22), 381–382.

Arend, R., Gove, F., & Sroufe, L. (1979). Continuity of individual adaptation from infancy to kindergarten: A predictive study of ego-resiliency and curiosity in preschoolers. *Child Development, 50,* 950–959.

Ariès, P. (1962). *Centuries of childhood: A social history of family life* (R. Baldick, trans.). New York: Vintage.

Arliss, L. (1991). *Gender communication.* Englewood Cliffs, N.J.: Prentice-Hall.

Aro, H. M., & Palosaari, U. K. (1992). Parental divorce, adolescence, and transition to young adulthood: A follow-up study. *American Journal of Orthopsychiatry, 62,* 421–429.

Aro, H. M., & Taipale, V. (1987). The impact of timing of puberty on psychosomatic symptoms among fourteen- to sixteen-year-old Finnish girls. *Child Development, 58,* 261–268.

Aronson, E., & Bridgeman, D. (1979). Jigsaw groups and the desegregated classroom: In pursuit of common goals. *Personality and Social Psychology Bulletin, 5,* 438–446.

Asher, S., Renshaw, P., & Hymel, S. (1982). Peer relations and the development of social skills. In S. Moore & C. Cooper (Eds.), *The young child: Reviews of research: Vol. 3.* Washington, D.C.: National Association for the Education of Young Children.

Aslin, R. (1987). Visual and auditory development in infancy. In J. Osofsky (Ed.), *Handbook of infant development* (2nd ed.) (pp. 5–97). New York: Wiley.

Aslin, R. (1993). Perception of visual direction in human infants. In C. Granrud (Ed.), *Visual perception and cognition in infants,* pp. 91–120. Hillsdale, N.J.: Erlbaum.

Atkinson, J., & Feather, N. (Eds.). (1966). *A theory of achievement motivation.* New York: Wiley.

Attie, I., & Brooks-Gunn, J. (1989). Development of eating problems in adolescent girls: Response or cause of stress? In R. Barrett, L. Biener, & G. Baruch (Eds.), *Gender and stress* (pp. 218–254). New York: The Free Press.

Attie, I., Brooks-Gunn, J., & Petersen, A. (1990). A developmental perspective on eating disorders and eating problems. In M. Lewis & S. M. Miller (Eds.), *Handbook of developmental psychopathology* (pp. 409–420). New York: Plenum Press.

Aviezer, O., van Ijzendoorn, M. H., Sagi, A., & Schuengel, C. (1994). "Children of the Dream" revisited: 70 years of collective early child care in Israeli kibbutzim. *Psychological Bullletin, 116,* 99–116.

Bailey, J. M., & Zucker, K. J. (1995). Childhood sex-typed behavior and sexual orientation: A conceptual analysis and quantitative review. *Developmental Psychology, 31,* 43–55.

Baillargeon, R. (1991). Object permanence in infants: Further evidence. *Child Development, 62,* 1227–1246.

Baillargeon, R. (1993). The object concept revisited: New directions in the investigation of infants' physical knowledge. In C. Granrud (Ed.), *Visual perception and cognition in infants,* pp. 265–316. Hillsdale, N.J.: Erlbaum.

Bain, L. (1993). *Parents' guide to childhood emergencies.* New York: Delta.

Baird, P., & Sadovnick, A. D. (1987). Life expectancy in Down syndrome. *Journal of Pediatrics, 110,* 849–854.

Bakan, D. (1975). Adolescence in America: From idea to social fact. In R. E. Grinder (Ed.), *Studies in adolescence* (3rd ed.). New York: Macmillan.

Bakeman, R., & Brownlee, J. (1980). The strategic use of parallel play: A sequential analysis. *Child Development, 51,* 873–878.

Baker, C. (1995). *English syntax* (2nd ed.). Cambridge, Mass.: MIT Press.

Bamford, F., Bannister, R., Benjamin, C., Hillier, V., Ward, B., & Moore, W. (1990). Sleep in the first year of life. *Developmental Medicine and Child Neurology, 32,* 718–724.

Bandura, A. (1989). Social cognitive theory. In R. Vasta (Ed.), *Annals of Child Development. Theories of child development: Revised formulations and current issues.* Greenwich, Conn.: JAI Press.

Bandura, A. (1991). Social cognitive theory of moral thought and action. In W. Kurtines & J. Gewirtz (Eds.), *Handbook of moral behavior and development: Vol. 1* (pp. 45–104). Hillsdale, N.J.: Erlbaum.

Banks, M., & Dannemiller, J. (1987). Infant visual psychophysics. In P. Salapatek & L. Cohen (Eds.), *Handbook of infant perception: Vol. 1.* Orlando, Fla.: Academic Press.

Banks, M., & Sharman, E. (1993). Spatial and chromatic visual efficiency in human neonates. In C. Granrud (Ed.), *Visual perception and cognition in infants,* pp. 1–46. Hillsdale, N.J.: Erlbaum.

Bannister, D., & Agnew, J. (1971). The child's construing of self. In J. Cole (Ed.), *Nebraska symposium on motivation.* Lincoln: University of Nebraska Press.

Barkley, R. (1985). Developmental changes in the mother-child interactions of hyperactive boys: Effects of two dose levels of Ritalin. *Journal of Child Psychology and Psychiatry, 26*(5), 705–715.

Barkley, R. (1990). *Attention deficit hyperactivity disorder: Handbook for diagnosis and treatment.* New York: Guilford Press.

Barlow, D. H., & Durand, V. M. (1995). *Abnormal psychology: An integrative approach.* Pacific Grove, Cal.: Brooks/Cole.

Barr, H. M., Streissguth, A. P., Darby, B. L., & Sampson, P. D. (1990). Prenatal exposure to alcohol, caffeine, tobacco, and aspirin: Effects on fine and gross motor performance in 4-year-old children. *Developmental Psychology, 26,* 339–348.

Bartol, B. (1986, July 28). Cocaine babies: Hooked at birth. *Newsweek,* pp. 56–57.

Bartsch, K. (1993). Adolescents' theoretical thinking. In R. Lerner (Ed.), *Early adolescence: Perspectives on research, policy, and intervention,* pp. 143–159. Hillsdale, N.J.: Erlbaum.

Bartsch, K., & Wellman, H. (1995). *Children talk about the mind.* New York: Oxford.

Bates, E., Bretherton, I., & Snyder, L. (1988). *From first words to grammar.* Cambridge, U.K.: Cambridge University Press.

Bates, E., & Carnevale, G. (1993). New directions in research on language development. *Developmental Review, 13,* 436–470.

Bates, E., Dale, P., & Thal, D. (1995). Individual differences and their implications for theories of language development. In P. Fletcher & B. MacWhinney (Eds.), *Handbook of child language.* Oxford, U.K.: Blackwell.

Bates, E., Marchman, V., Thal, D., Fenson, L., Dale, P., Reznick, J., Reilly, J., & Hartung, J. (1994). Developmental and stylistic variation in the composition of early vocabulary. *Journal of Child Language, 21*(1), 85–124.

Bates, J. (1979). A naturalistic study of sex differences in children's aggression. *Merrill-Palmer Quarterly, 25,* 193–203.

Bauman, K. E., & Ennett, S. T. (1994). Peer influence on adolescent drug use. *American Psychologist, 49,* 820–822.

Baumrind, D. (1971). Current patterns of parental authority. *Developmental Psychology, 4,* 1–103.

Baumrind, D. (1973). The development of instrumental competence through socialization. In A. Pick (Ed.), *Minnesota symposium on child psychology: Vol. 7.* Minneapolis: University of Minnesota Press.

Baumrind D. (1989). Raising competent children. In W. Damon (Ed.), *Child development today and tomorrow* (pp. 349–378). San Francisco: Jossey-Bass.

Baumrind, D. (1991). Effective parenting during the early adolescent transition. In P. Cowan & M. Hetherington (Eds.), *Family transitions.* Hillsdale, N.J.: Erlbaum.

Baumrind, D. (1991). Parenting styles and adolescent development. In R. M. Lerner, A. C. Petersen, & J. Brooks-Gunn (Eds.), *The encyclopedia of adolescence.* New York: Garland.

Beck, R. (1978). *Motivation: Theories and principles.* Englewood Cliffs, N.J.: Prentice-Hall.

Becker, A. (1994). Nurturing and negligence: Working on others' bodies in Fiji. In T. Csordas (Ed.), *Embodiment and experience: The existential ground of culture and self* (pp. 100–115). New York: Cambridge University Press.

Behrman, R. (Ed.). (1993). *The future of children: School-linked services.* Los Altos, Cal.: Center for the Future of Children, The David and Lucille Packard Foundation.

Belka, D. (1994). *Teaching children games.* Champaign, Ill.: Human Kinetics Press.

Bell, N., Grossen, M., & Perret-Clermont, A.-N. (1985). Sociocognitive conflict and intellectual growth. In M. Berkowitz (Ed.), *Peer conflict and psychological growth.* New Directions for Child Development, No. 29. San Francisco: Jossey-Bass.

Bell, R. (1980). *Changing bodies, changing lives: A book for teens on sex and relationships.* New York: Random House.

Bellugi, U., Van Hoek, K., Lillo-Martin, D., & O'Grady, L. (1993). The acquisition of syntax and space in young deaf signers. In D. Bishop & K. Mogford (Eds.), *Language development in exceptional circumstances* (pp. 132–149). Hillsdale, N.J.: Erlbaum.

Belsky, J. (1980). Child maltreatment: An ecological integration. *American Psychologist, 35,* 320–335.

Belsky, J. (1988). The "effects" of infant day care reconsidered. *Early Childhood Research Quarterly, 3,* 235–272.

Belsky, J. (1988). Child maltreatment and the emergent family system. In K. Browne, C. Davies, & P. Strattan (Eds.), *Early prediction and prevention of child abuse* (pp. 291–302). New York: Wiley.

Belsky, J. (1993). Etiology of child maltreatment: A developmental-ecological analysis. *Psychological Bulletin, 114,* 413–434.

Belsky, J., Crnic, K., & Gable, S. (1995). The determinants of coparenting in families with toddler boys: Spousal differences and daily hassles. *Child Development, 66,* 629–642.

Belsky, J., Fish, M., & Isabella, R. (1991). Continuity and discontinuity in infant negative and positive emotionality: Family antecedents and attachment consequences. *Developmental Psychology, 27,* 421–431.

Belsky, J., Gilstrap, B., & Rovine, M. (1984a). Stability and change in mother-infant and father-infant interaction in a family setting: One-to-three-to-nine months. *Child Development, 5,* 706–717.

Belsky, J., Gilstrap, B., & Rovine, M. (1984b). The Pennsylvania Infant and Family Development Project, I: Stability and change in mother-infant and father-infant interaction in a family setting. *Child Development, 59,* 692–705.

Belsky, J., Lerner, R., & Spanier, G. (1984). *The child in the family.* Reading, Mass.: Addison-Wesley.

Belsky, J., & Nezworski, T. (Eds.). (1988). *Clinical implications of attachment.* Hillsdale, N.J.: Erlbaum.

Belsky, J., & Rovine, M. (1988). Nonmaternal care in the first year of life and the security of infant-parent attachment. *Child Development, 59,* 157–176.

Bem, S. L. (1974). The measurement of psychological androgyny. *Journal of Consulting and Clinical Psychology, 42,* 155–162.

Bem, S. L. (1976). Probing the promise of androgyny. In A. Kaplan & J. Bean (Eds.), *Beyond sex-role stereotypes: Readings toward a psychology of androgyny.* Boston: Little, Brown.

Bem, S. L. (1981). Gender scheme theory: A cognitive account of sex typing. *Psychological Review, 88,* 354–364.

Bem, S. L. (1983). Gender schema theory and its implications for child development: Raising gender-aschematic children in a gender-schematic society. *Signs, 8,* 598–616.

Berg, W. K., & Berg, K. (1987). Psychophysiological development in infancy: State, startle, and attention. In J. Osofsky (Ed.), *Handbook of infant development* (2nd ed.). New York: Wiley.

Berk, L. E. (1994, November). Why children talk to themselves. *Scientific American,* 78–83.

Berko, J. (1958). The child's learning of English morphology. *Word, 14,* 150–177.

Berlin, B., & Kay, P. (1969). *Basic color terms: Their universality and evolution.* Columbus, Ohio: Merrill.

Berndt, T. J. (1988). The nature and significance of children's friendships. In R. Vasta (Ed.), *Annals of child development: Vol. 5* (pp. 155–186). Greenwich, Conn.: JAI Press.

Bernhardt, J. S. (1990). Potential workplace hazards to reproductive health. *Journal of Obstetrical and Gynecological Nursing, 19,* 53–62.

Bertoia, J. (1993). *Drawings from a dying child: Insights into death from a Jungian perspective.* London: Routledge.

Bialystok, E., & Hakuta, K. (1994). *The science and psychology of second language acquisition.* New York: Basic Books.

Bianci, V. (1993). *Mechanisms of brain lateralization.* Philadelphia: Gordon and Beach.

Bibby, R. W., & Posterski, D. C. (1985). The emerging generation: An inside look at Canada's teenagers. Toronto: Irwin.

Bierman, K. L., Smoot, D. L., & Aumiller, K. (1993). Characteristics of aggressive-rejected, aggressive (nonrejected), and rejected (nonaggressive) boys. *Child Development, 64,* 139–151.

Bijstra, J., Jackson, S., & Van Geert, P. (1991). Progress to conservation: Conflict or correct answer? *European Journal of Psychology of Education, 3,* 291–301.

Binder, J., Dobler-Mikola, A., & Angst, J. (1981). An epidemiological study of minor psychiatric disturbances. A field study among 20-year-old females and males in Zurich. *Social Psychiatry, 16,* 31–41.

Biringen, Z. (1990). Direct observation of maternal sensitivity and dyadic interaction in the home: Relations to maternal thinking. *Developmental Psychology, 26,* 278–284.

Biringen, Z. (1994). Attachment theory and research: Application to clinical practice. *American Journal of Orthopsychiatry, 64,* 404–420.

Bjorklund, D. (Ed.). (1990). *Children's strategies.* Hillsdale, N.J.: Erlbaum.

Blackman, J. A. (1990). *Medical aspects of developmental disabilities in children birth to three* (2nd ed). Rockville, Md.: Aspen Publishers, Inc.

Blanck, G. (1990). The man and his cause. In L. C. Moll (Ed.), *Vygotsky and education: Instructional implications and applications of sociohistorical psychology.* Cambridge, U.K.: Cambridge University Press.

Blatt, R. J. R. (1988). *Prenatal tests.* New York: Vintage.

Block, J. H., Block, J., & Morrison, A. (1981). Parental agreement-disagreement on child-rearing orientations and gender-related personality correlates in children. *Child Development, 52,* 965–974.

Bloom, L. (1993). *The transition from infancy to language: Acquiring the power of expression.* New York: Cambridge University Press.

Blumberg, M. L., & Lester, D. (1991). High school and college students' attitudes toward rape. *Adolescence, 26,* 727–729.

Blumenthal, S. J., & Kupfer, D. G. (1988). Overview of early detection and treatment strategies for suicidal behavior in young people. *Journal of Youth and Adolescence, 17,* 1–23.

Bock, R. D., & Moore, E. G. J. (1986). *Advantage and disadvantage: A profile of American youth.* Hillsdale, N.J.: Erlbaum.

Bogdon, J. C. (1993). Childbirth practices in American history. In B. K. Rothman (Ed.), *The encyclopedia of childbearing.* New York: Henry Holt, 1993.

Bojko, M. (1995). The multi-cultural program at O'Brien Elementary School. Personal communication.

Bolger, K. E., Patterson, C. J., Thompson, W. W., & Kupersmidt, J. B. (1995). Psychosocial adjustment among children experiencing persistent and intermittent family economic hardship. *Child Development, 66,* 1107–1129.

Bollerud, K., Christopherson, S., & Frank, E. (1990). Girls' sexual choices: Looking for what is right: The intersection of sexual and moral development. In C. Gilligan, N. Lyons, & T. Hanmer (Eds.), *Making connections: The relational worlds of adolescent girls at Emma Willard School* (pp. 274–285). Cambridge, Mass.: Harvard University Press.

Bordo, S. (1993). *Unbearable weight: Feminism, Western culture, and the body.* Berkeley, Cal.: University of California Press.

Bornstein, M. (1989). Information processing (habituation) and stability in cognitive development. *Human Development, 32,* 129–136.

Bornstein, M., & Tamis-Lemonda, C. (1989). Maternal responsiveness and cognitive development in children. In M. Bornstein (Ed.), *Maternal responsiveness: Characteristics and consequences.* San Francisco: Jossey-Bass.

Botvin, G. J., & Tortu, S. (1988). Preventing adolescent substance abuse through life skills training. In R. H. Price, E. L. Cowen, R. P. Lorion, & J. Ramos-McKay (Eds.), *Fourteen ounces of prevention: A casebook for practitioners.* Washington, D.C.: American Psychological Association.

Bowers, R. (1995). Early adolescent social and emotional development: A constructivist perspective. In M. Wavering (Ed.), *Educating young adolescents,* pp. 79–110. New York: Garland.

Bowlby, J. (1969). *Attachment and loss: Vol. 1. Attachment.* New York: Basic Books.

Bowlby, J. (1973). *Attachment and loss: Vol. 2. Separation, anxiety, and anger.* New York: Basic Books.

Bowlby, J. (1980). *Attachment and loss: Vol. 3. Loss, sadness, and depression.* New York: Basic Books.

Bowlby, J. (1988). *A secure base: Clinical applications of attachment theory.* London: Routledge.

Boyer, E. L. (1983). *High school: A report on secondary education.* New York: Harper & Row.

Brasel, J., & Gruen, R. (1978). Cellular growth: Brain, liver, muscle and lung. In F. Falkner & J. Tanner (Eds.), *Human growth: Vol. 2.* New York: Plenum Press.

Brazelton, T. B. (1976). Early mother-infant reciprocity. In V. C. Vaughn III & T. B. Brazelton (Eds.), *The family: Can it be saved?* Chicago: Yearbook Medical Publishers.

Bredekamp, S. (Ed.). (1987). *Developmentally appropriate practice in early childhood programs serving children from birth through age 8* (expanded ed.). Washington, D.C.: National Association for the Education of Young Children.

Bredekamp, S., & Rosegrant, T. (Eds.). (1992). *Reaching potentials: Appropriate curriculum and assessment for young children.* Washington, D.C.: National Association for the Education of Young Children.

Bretherton, I., McNew, S., & Beeghly-Smith, M. (1981). Early person knowledge as expressed in gestural and verbal communications. In M. Lamb & L. Sherrod (Eds.), *Infant social cognition.* Hillsdale, N.J.: Erlbaum.

Bretherton, I., & Waters, E. (1985). Growing points in attachment theory. *Monographs of the Society for Research in Child Development, 50*(12, Serial No. 209).

Brierly, J. (1994). *Give me a child until he is seven: Brain studies and early childhood education.* Washington, D.C.: Falmer Press.

Brislin, R., & Yoshida, T. (1994). *Intercultural communication training: An introduction.* Thousand Oaks, Cal.: Sage.

Broderick, V. (1991). Young children's comprehension of similarities underlying metaphor. *Journal of Psycholinguistic Research, 20,* 65–81.

Brody, G. H., Graziano, W. G., & Musser, L. M. (1983). Familiarity and children's behavior in same-age and mixed-age peer groups. *Developmental Psychology, 19,* 569–576.

Brody, J. E. (1993, February 10). Adult years bring new afflictions for DES "babies." *The New York Times,* p. C–12.

Brody, J. E. (1995). The use of alcohol linked to rise in fetal illness. *New York Times,* April 7, A-27, col. 1.

Bronfenbrenner, U. (1989). Ecological systems theory. In R. Vasta (Ed.), *Annals of child development: Vol. 6. Six theories of child development: Revised formulations and current issues.* Greenwich, Conn.: JAI Press.

Bronstein, P. (1988). Marital and parenting roles in transition. In P. Bronstein & C. Cowan (Eds.), *Fatherhood today: Men's changing role in the family* (pp. 3–12). New York: Wiley.

Brooks-Gunn, J. (1987). Pubertal pressures: Their relevance for developmental research. In V. B. Van Hasselt & M. Hersen (Eds.), *Handbook of adolescent psychology* (pp. 111–130). New York: Pergamen Press.

Brooks-Gunn, J., & Furstenberg, F. (1989). Adolescent sexual behavior. *American Psychologist, 44,* 249–257.

Brooks-Gunn, J., & Ruble, D. (1982). The development of menstrual-related beliefs and behaviors during early adolescence. *Child Development, 53,* 1567–1577.

Brooks-Gunn, J., & Warren, M. (1989). Biological and social contributions to negative affect in young adolescent girls. *Child Development, 60,* 40–55.

Brooten, D. (Ed.). (1992). *Low-birth-weight neonates.* Philadelphia: Lippincott.

Brophy, J. (1983). Research on the self-fulfilling prophecy and teacher expectations. *Journal of Educational Psychology, 75,* 631–666.

Brown, B. B. (1990). Peer groups and peer cultures. In S. S. Feldman & G. R. Elliot (Eds.), *At the threshold: The developing adolescent* (pp. 171–196). Cambridge, Mass.: Harvard University Press.

Brown, B. B., Mocents, N., Lamborn, S. D., & Steinberg, L. (1994). Parenting practices and peer group affiliation in adolescence. *Child Development, 64,* 467–482.

Brown, J. R. (Ed.). (1990). *Plant population genetics, breeding, and genetic resources.* Sunderland, Mass.: Sinaeur Associates.

Brown, J. R., & Dunn, J. (1992). Talk with your mother or your sibling? Developmental changes in early family conversations about feelings. *Child Development, 63,* 336–349.

Brown, L., & Gilligan, C. (1992). *Meeting at the crossroads: Women's psychology and girls' development.* Cambridge, Mass.: Harvard University Press.

Brown, R. (1973). *A first language: The early stages.* Cambridge, Mass.: Harvard University Press.

Browne, J. C. M., & Dixon, G. (1978). *Antenatal care.* Edinburgh: Churchill Livingstone.

Bruch, H. (1979). *The golden cage: The enigma of anorexia nervosa.* New York: Vintage.

Bruch, H. (1988). *Conversations with anorexics.* New York: Basic Books.

Bruner, J. (1983). *Child's talk: Learning to use language.* New York: Norton.

Bruner, J. (1990). *Acts of meaning.* Cambridge, Mass.: Harvard University Press.

Bryant, B. (1985). The neighborhood walk: Sources of support in middle childhood. *Monographs of the Society for Research on Child Development, 50* (3, No. 210).

Buckley, K., & Kulb, N. (Eds.). (1983). *Handbook of maternal-newborn nursing.* New York: Wiley.

Buhrmester, D. (1990). Intimacy of friendship, interpersonal competence, and adjustment during preadolescence and adolescence. *Child Development, 61,* 1101–1111.

Buhrmester, D., & Furman, W. (1987). The development of companionship and intimacy. *Child Development, 58,* 1101–1113.

Burke, T. (1990). Home invaders: Gangs of the future. *The Police Chief, 57,* 23.

Buss, A. H., & Plomin, R.(1984). *Temperament: Early developing personality traits.* Hillsdale, N.J.: Erlbaum.

Byard, R., & Cohle, S. (1994). *Sudden death in infants, children, and adolescents.* New York: Cambridge University Press.

Byne, W. (1994, May). The biological evidence challenged. *Scientific American,* 50–55.

Cahan, E. (1994). John Dewey and human development. In R. Parke, P. Ornstein, J. Rieser, & C. Zahn-Waxler (Eds.), *A century of developmental psychology* (pp. 145–170). Washington, D.C.: American Psychological Association.

Cairns, R. B., Leung, M., Buchanan, L., & Cairns, B. D. (1995). Friendships and social networks in childhood and adolescence: Fluidity, reliability and interrelations. *Child Development, 66,* 1330–1345.

Caliso, J., & Milner, J. (1992). Childhood history of abuse and child abuse screening. *Child Abuse and Neglect, 16,* 647–659.

Campos, J., & Stenberg, C. (1981). Perception, appraisal, and emotion: The onset of social referencing. In M. Lamband & L. Sherrod (Eds.), *Infant social cognition.* Hillsdale, N.J.: Erlbaum.

Campos, R., Antunes, C. M., Raffaelli, M., Halsey, N., Ude, W., Greco, M., Greco, D., Ruff, A., & Rolf, J. (1994). Social networks and daily activities of street youth in Belo Horizonte, Brazil. *Child Development, 65,* 319–330.

Campos, R., Raffaelli, M., Greco, W., Ruff, A., Rolf, J., Antunes, C., Halsey, N., & Greco, D. (1994). Social networks and daily activities of street youth in Belo Horizonte, Brazil. *Child Development, 65,* 319–330.

Camras, L. A., Sullivan, J., & Michel, G. (1993). Do infants express discrete emotions? Adult judgments of facial, vocal, and body actions. *Journal of Nonverbal Behavior, 17,* 171–186.

Carey, S. (1988). Reorganization of knowledge in the course of acquisition. In S. Strauss (Ed.), *Ontogeny, phylogeny, and historical development.* New York: Ablex.

Carey, S., & Gelman, R. (1991). *The epigenesis of mind: Essays on biology and cognition.* Hillsdale, N.J.: Erlbaum.

Carlson, C. I., Cooper, C. R., & Spradling, V. Y. (1991). Developmental implications of shared versus distinct perceptions of the family in early adolescence. *New Directions for Child Development, 51,* 13–32.

Carlson, E. A., Jacobvitz, D., & Sroufe, A. L. (1995). A developmental investigation of inattentiveness and hyperactivity. *Child Development, 66,* 37–54.

Carnegie Council on Adolescent Development. (1989). *Turning points: Preparing American youth for the 21st century.* Washington, D.C.: Task Force on Education of Young Adolescents.

Carnegie Council on Adolescent Development. (1992). A matter of time: Risk and opportunity in the nonschool hours. Report of the task force on youth development and community programs. New York: Carnegie Corporation of New York.

Case, R. (1991a). *The mind's staircase: Exploring the conceptual underpinnings of children's thought and knowledge.* Hillsdale, N.J.: Erlbaum.

Case, R. (1991b). General and specific views of the mind, its structure, and its function. In R. Case (Ed.), *The mind's staircase* (pp. 3–16). Hillsdale, N.J.: Erlbaum.

Case, R. (1991c). A neo-Piagetian approach to the issue of cognitive generality and specificity. In R. Case (Ed.), *The mind's staircase* (pp. 17–36). Hillsdale, N.J.: Erlbaum.

Case, R. (1991d). Advantages and limitations of the neo-Piagetian position. In R. Case (Ed.), *The mind's staircase* (pp. 37–51). Hillsdale, N.J.: Erlbaum.

Case, R. (1992). Neo-Piagetian theories of intellectual development. In H. Beilin & P. Pufall (Eds.), *Piaget's theory: Prospects and possibilities.* Hillsdale, N.J.: Erlbaum.

Case, R., & Edelstein, W. (1994). *The new structuralism in cognitive development: Theory and research on individual pathways.* New York: Kargar.

Caspi, A., Henri, B., McGee, R. O., Moffitt, T. E., & Silva, P. A. (1995). Temperamental origins of child and adolescent behavior problems: From age three to age fifteen. *Child Development, 66,* 55–68.

Cassell, D. (1994). *Encyclopedia of obesity and eating disorders.* New York: Facts on File Press.

Cates, W., Jr., & Rauh, J. L. (1985). Adolescents and sexually transmitted diseases: An expanding problem. *Journal of Adolescent Health Care, 6,* 1–5.

Cazden, C. (1988). *Classroom discourse.* Portsmouth, N.H.: Heinemann.

Centers for Disease Control. (1993a). *National overview of sexually transmitted diseases: STD/HIV problem assessment.* Washington, D.C.: Author.

Centers for Disease Control. (1993b, February). *HIV/AIDS surveillance report* (year-end edition). Washington, D.C.: Author.

Cepecchi, M. R. (1994, March). Targeted gene replacement. *Scientific American,* 52–59.

Cernoch, J., & Porter, R. (1985). Recognition of maternal axillary odors by infants. *Child Development, 56,* 1593–1598.

Chafel, J. (1993). *Child poverty and public policy.* Washington, D.C.: The Urban Institute.

Chaiklin, S., & Lave, J. (Eds.). (1993). *Understanding practice: Perspectives on activity and context.* New York: Cambridge University Press.

Chan, S. (1991) *Asian Americans: An interpretive history.* Boston: Twayne Publishers.

Chang, H., & Trehub, S. (1977a). Auditory processing of relational information by young infants. *Journal of Experimental Child Psychology, 24,* 324–331.

Chang, H., & Trehub, S. (1977b). Infants' perception of temporal grouping in auditory patterns. *Child Development, 48,* 1666–1670.

Chao, R. K. (1994). Beyond parental control and authoritarian parenting style: Understanding Chinese parenting through the cultural notion of training. *Child Development, 65,* 1111–1119.

Chapman, M., & Skinner, E. A. (1989). Children's agency beliefs, cognitive performance, and conceptions of effort and ability: Individual and developmental differences. *Child Development, 60,* 1229–1238.

Chasnoff, I. J., Griffith, D. R., MacGregor, S., Dirkes, K., & Burns, K. A. (1989). Temporal patterns of cocaine use in pregnancy: Perinatal outcome. *Journal of the American Medical Association, 262,* 1741–1744.

Cheek, D. (1974). Body composition, hormones, nutrition and growth. In M. Grumbach, G. Grave, & F. Mayer (Eds.), *Control of the onset of puberty.* New York: Wiley.

Cherry, F. (1995). *"Stubborn particulars" of social psychology: Essays on the research process.* New York: Routledge.

Chi, M. (1985). Interactive roles of knowledge and strategies in the development of organized sorting and recall. In S. Chipman, J. Segal, & R. Glaser (Eds.), *Thinking and learning skills: Vol. 2. Research and open questions* (pp. 457–483). Hillsdale, N.J.: Erlbaum.

Chi, M., & Ceci, S. (1987). Content knowledge: Its role, representation, and restructuring in memory. In H. Reese (Ed.), *Advances in child development and behavior: Vol. 20.* New York: Academic Press.

Chi, M., Glaser, R., & Farr, M. (1989). *The nature of expertise.* Hillsdale, N.J.: Erlbaum.

Children's Defense Fund. (1990). Women, children get squeezed out of food program. *CDF Reports, 12,* 1,6.

Children's Defense Fund. (1993). *Progress and peril: Black children in America: A fact book and action primer.* Washington, D.C.: Author.

Children's Defense Fund. (1995). *The state of America's children.* Washington, D.C.: Author.

Chodorow, N. (1978). *The reproduction of mothering.* Berkeley: University of California Press.

Chomsky, N. (1994). *Language and thought.* Wakefield, R.I.: Moyer Bell Publishers.

Christensen, K., & Delgado, G. (Eds.). (1993). *Multicultural issues in deafness.* White Plains, N.Y.: Longman.

Chumlea, W., Knittle, J., Roche, A., Siervogel, R., & Webb, P. (1983). Size and number of adipocytes and measures of body fat in boys and girls 10 to 18 years of age. *American Journal of Clinical Nutrition, 37.*

Cicchetti, D., & Olson, K. (1990). The developmental psychopathology of child maltreatment. In M. Lewis & S. Miller (Eds.), *Handbook of development psychopathology.* New York: Plenum Press.

Clark, M. L., & Ayers, M. (1988). The role of reciprocity and proximity in junior high school friendships. *Journal of Youth and Adolescence, 17,* 403–411.

Clarke-Stewart, K. A. (1989). Day care: Maligned or malignant? *American Psychologist, 44,* 266–273.

Clausen, J. (1975). The social meaning of differential physical and sexual maturation. In S. Dragastin & G. Elder (Eds.), *Adolescence and the life cycle.* New York: Halsted.

Coates, J. (1993). *Women, men, and communication* (2nd ed.). New York: Longman.

Cogan, R. (1980). Effects of childbirth preparation. *Clinical Obstetrics and Gynecology, 23,* 1–14.

Cohen, F., & Durham, J. (Eds.). (1993). *Women, children, and HIV/AIDS.* New York: Springer.

Cohn, J. F., & Tronick, E. Z. (1987). Mother-infant face-to-face interaction: The sequence of dyadic states at 3, 6 and 9 months. *Developmental Psychology, 23,* 68–77.

Coie, J. D., Dodge, K. A., & Coppotelli, H. (1982). Dimensions and types of social status: A cross-age perspective. *Developmental Psychology, 18,* 557–570.

Coie, J. D., Dodge, K. A., Terry, R., & Wright, V. (1991). The role of aggression in peer relations: An analysis of aggression episodes in boys' play groups. *Child Development, 62,* 812–826.

Coiro, M. (1994). *Health of our nation's children.* Hyattsville, M.B.: United States Department of Health and Human Services.

Colby, A., & Damon, W. (1992). *Some do care: Contemporary lives of moral commitment.* New York: The Free Press.

Colby, A., & Kohlberg, L. (1987). *The measurement of moral judgment.* New York: Cambridge University Press.

Colby, A., Kohlberg, L., Gibbs, J., & Lieberman, M. (1983). A longitudinal study of moral development. *Monographs of the Society for Research on Child Development, 48*(1–2, Serial No. 200).

Cole, M. (1990). Cultural psychology. In J. Berman (Ed.), *Nebraska symposium on motivation, 1989: Cross-cultural psychology* (pp. 279–336). Lincoln, Neb.: University of Nebraska Press.

Cole, P. M., & Putnam, F. W. (1992). Effect of incest on self and social functioning: A developmental psychopathology perspective. *Journal of Consulting and Clinical Psychology, 60,* 174–184.

Coleman, J. (1988). Social capital in the creation of human capital. *American Journal of Sociology, 94,* 95–120.

Coles, R. (1990). *The spiritual life of children.* Boston: Houghton Mifflin.

Coles, R. (1992). *Their eyes meeting the world: Drawings and paintings of children.* Boston: Houghton Mifflin.

Coles, R. (1993). *The call of service: A witness to idealism.* Boston: Houghton Mifflin.

Coles, R., & Stokes, G. (1985). *Sex and the American teenager.* New York: Harper & Row.

Collins, W. A. (1991). Shared views and parent-adolescent relationships. *New Directions for Child Development, 51,* 103–110.

Collins, W., Sobol, B., & Westby, S. (1981). Effects of adult commentary on children's comprehension and inferences about a televised aggressive portrayal. *Child Development, 52,* 158–163.

Columbo, J. (1993). Infant cognition: Predicting intellec-

tual functioning (pp. 30–81). Newbury Park, Cal.: Sage Publications.

Comer, J. P., & Poussaint, A. F. (1992). *Raising black children.* New York: Plume.

Comstock, F. (1991). *Television and the American child.* San Diego: Academic Press.

Conger, J. (1977). *Adolescence and youth: Psychological development in a changing world* (2nd ed.). New York: Harper and Row.

Connolly, J., White, D., Stevens, R., & Burstein, S. (1987). Adolescent self-reports of social activity: Assessment of stability and relations to social adjustment. *Journal of Adolescence, 10,* 83–95.

Coren, S. (1992). *The left-hander syndrome.* New York: Free Press.

Cowan, C., Cowan, P., Heming, G., & Miller, N. (1991). Becoming a family: Marriage, parenting, and child development. In P. Cowan & M. Hetherington (Eds.), *Family transitions* (pp. 79–110). Hillsdale, N.J.: Erlbaum.

Cowan, N. (1995). *Attention and memory.* New York: Oxford University Press.

Cox, M. J., Owen, M. T., Henderson, V. K., & Margand, N. A. (1992). Prediction of infant-father and infant-mother attachment. *Developmental Psychology, 28,* 474–483.

Crick, N. R., & Grotpeter, J. K. (1995). Relational aggression, gender, and social-psychological adjustment. *Child Development, 66,* 710–722.

Crockenberg, S. B., & Litman, C. (1990). Autonomy and competence in 1-year-olds: Maternal correlates of child defiance, compliance, and self-assertion. *Developmental Psychology, 26,* 961–971.

Crockenberg, S. B., & McCluskey, K. (1986). Change in maternal behavior during the baby's first year of life. *Child Development, 57,* 746–753.

Csikszentmihalyi, M., & Larson, R. (1984). *Being adolescent: Conflict and growth in the teenage years.* New York: Basic Books.

Cuffaro, H. (1991). A view of materials as the texts of the early childhood curriculum. In B. Spodek & O. Saracho (Eds.), *Issues in early childhood curriculum* (pp. 64–85). New York: Teachers College Press.

Curry, G. D. & Spergel, I. (1988). Gang homicide, delinquency, and community. *Criminology, 26,* 381–405.

Curtis, R. (1975). Adolescent orientations toward parents and peers: Variations by sex, age, and socioeconomic status. *Adolescence, 10,* 483–494.

Cushman, P. (1991). Ideology obscured: Political uses of the self in Daniel Stern's infant. *American Psychologist, 46,* 206–219.

D'Alton, M. E., & DeCherney, A. H. (1993). Prenatal diagnosis. *New England Journal of Medicine, 32,* 114–120.

Damon, W. (1983). *Social and personality development: Infancy through adolescence.* New York: Norton.

Damon, W. (1988). *The moral child.* New York: Cambridge University Press.

Damon, W., & Hart, D. (1982). The development of self-understanding from infancy through adolescence. *Child Development, 53,* 831–857.

Damon, W., & Hart, D. (1988). *Self-understanding in childhood and adolescence.* New York: Cambridge University Press.

Darling, C. A., Kallen, D. J., & Van Dusen, J. E. (1984). Sex in transition, 1900–1984. *Journal of Youth and Adolescence, 13,* 385–399.

Darling, N., & Steinberg, L. (1993). Parenting style as context: An integrative model. *Psychological Bulletin, 113,* 487–496.

Darwin, C. (1977). A biographical sketch of an infant. *Mind, 2,* 286–294.

Davies, B. (1991). Accomplishment of genderedness in preschool children. In L. Weis, P. Altbach, G. Kelly, & H. Petrie (Eds.), *Critical perspectives in early childhood education.* Albany, N.Y.: State University of New York Press.

Davis, E. (1993). Common complaints of pregnancy. In B. K. Rothman (Ed.), *The encyclopedia of childbearing.* New York: Henry Holt.

Davis-Floyd, R. E. (1986). Birth as an American rite of passage. In K. L. Michaelson (Ed.), *Childbirth in America: Anthropological perspectives.* South Hadley, Mass.: Bergin & Garvey.

DeAngelis, T. (1991, January). Living with violence: Children suffer, cope. *APA Monitor, 22,* 26–27.

DeCasper, A. J., Lecanuet, J. P., Busnel, M. C., & Granier-Deferre, C. (1994). Fetal reactions to recurrent maternal speech. *Infant Behavior and Development, 17,* 159–164.

DeCasper, A. J., & Spence, M. J. (1986). Prenatal maternal speech influences newborns' perception of speech sounds. *Infant Behavior and Development, 9,* 133–150.

Deci, E. L., & Ryan, R. M. (1987). The support of autonomy and the control of behavior. *Journal of Personality and Social Psychology, 56,* 1024–1037.

de Cubas, M. M., & Field, T. (1995). Children of methadone-dependent women: Developmental outcomes. *American Journal of Orthopsychiatry, 63,* 266–276.

DeJong, W. (1993). Obesity as a characterological stigma: The issue of responsibility and judgments of task performance. *Psychological Reports, 73,* 963–970.

Demetriou, A., & Shayer, M. (1992). Neo-Piagetian theories of cognitive development: Implications and applications for education. New York: Routledge.

Demetriou, A., Shayer, M., & Efklides, A. (Eds.). (1992). *Neo-Piagetian theories of cognitive development.* London: Routledge.

Dempster, F. (1981). Memory span: Sources of individual and developmental differences. *Psychological Bulletin, 89,* 63–100.

Dennis, S. (1992). Stage and structure in the development of children's spatial reasoning. In R. Case (Ed.), *The mind's staircase* (pp. 229–245). Hillsdale, N.J.: Erlbaum.

DeRegt, R. H., Minkoff, H. L., Feldman, J., & Schwartz, R. H. (1986). Relation of private or clinic care to the Cesarean birth rate. *New England Journal of Medicine, 315,* 619–624.

DeRosier, M. E., Cillessen, A. H. N., Coie, J. D., & Dodge, K. A. (1994). Group social context and children's aggressive behavior. *Child Development, 65,* 1068–1079.

DeVilliers, P., & DeVilliers, J. (1978). *Language development.* Cambridge, Mass.: Harvard University Press.

De Vries, L. B., Halley, D. J., Oostra, B. A., & Niermeijer, M. F. (1994). The fragile-X syndrome: A growing gene causing familial intellectual disability. *Journal of Intellectual Disability Research, 38,* 1–8.

DeVries, R. (1994). *Moral classrooms, moral children: Creating a constructivist atmosphere in early education.* New York: Teachers' College Press.

Diamond, A. (1993, July). Science meets practice on PKU studies' findings. *APA Monitor,* 16–17.

Diamond, J. (1989, February). Blood, genes, and malaria. *Natural History,* 8–18.

Diaz, R., & Berk, L. (1992). *Private speech: From social interaction to self-regulation.* Hillsdale, N.J.: Erlbaum.

Dishion, T. J., Andrews, D. W., & Crosby, L. (1995). Antisocial boys and their friends in early adolescence: Relationship characteristics, quality, and interactional process. *Child Development, 66,* 139–151.

Dishion, T. J., Reid, J. B., & Patterson, G. R. (1988). Empirical guidelines for a family intervention for adolescent drug use. *Journal of Chemical Dependency Treatment, 1,* 181–216.

Dodge, K. A. (1986). A social information processing model of social competence in children. In M. Perlmutter (Ed.), *Minnesota symposia on child psychology: Vol. 18.* Hillsdale, N.J.: Erlbaum.

Dodge, K. A., & Coie, J. D. (1987). Social-information-processing factors in reactive and proactive aggression in children's peer groups. *Journal of Personality and Social Psychology, 53,* 1146–1158.

Dodge, K. A., Coie, J. D., Pettit, G. S., & Price, J. M. (1990). Peer status and aggression in boys' groups: Developmental and contextual analysis. *Child Development, 61,* 1289–1309.

Dodge, K. A., Pettit, G. S., McClaskey, C. L., and Brown, M. M. (1986). Social competence in children.

Monographs of the Society for Research in Child Development, 51(2, Serial No. 213).

Dodge, K. A., Schlundt, D. C., Schoken, I., & Delugach, J. D. (1983). Social competence and children's sociometric status: The role of peer group entry strategies. *Merrill-Palmer Quarterly, 29,* 309–336.

Dougherty, D. M. (1993). Adolescent health: Reflections on a report to the U.S. Congress. *American Psychologist, 48,* 193–201.

Dowd, J., & Tronick, E. Z. (1986). Temporal coordination of arm movements in early infancy: Do infants move in synchrony with adult speech? *Child Development, 57,* 762–776.

Dreyer, P. H. (1982). Sexuality during adolescence. In B. B. Wolman (Ed.), *Handbook of developmental psychology.* Englewood Cliffs, N.J.: Prentice-Hall.

Dubois, D. L., & Hirsch, B. J. (1990). School and neighborhood friendship patterns of blacks and whites in early adolescence. *Child Development, 61,* 524–536.

Duff, J. (1992). *Youth sports injuries: Medical guide for parents and coaches.* New York: Collier Books.

Duffy, K. G. (1996). *Community Psychology.* Boston: Allyn & Bacon.

Dunn, J. (1985). *Sisters and brothers.* Cambridge, Mass.: Harvard University Press.

Dunn, J. (1987). The beginnings of moral understanding. In J. Kagan & S. Lamb (Eds.), *The emergence of morality in young children* (pp. 91–111). Chicago: University of Chicago Press.

Dunn,, J., & Shatz, M. (1989). Becoming a conversationalist despite (or because of) having an older sibling. *Child Development, 60,* 399–410.

Dunphy, D. C. (1963). The social structure of urban adolescent peer groups. *Sociometry, 26,* 230–246.

Durbin, D. L., Darling, N., Steinberg, L., & Brown, B. B. (1993). Parenting style and peer group membership among European-American adolescents. *Journal of Research on Adolescence, 3,* 87–100.

Dusek, J. B. (Ed.). (1985). *Teacher expectancies.* Hillsdale, N.J.: Erlbaum.

Dusek, J. B. (1991). *Adolescent development and behavior* (2nd ed.). Englewood Cliffs, N.J.: Prentice-Hall.

Dweck, C. S. (1986). Motivational processes affecting learning. *American Psychologist, 41,* 1040–1048.

Dweck, C. S., Davidson, W., Nelson, S., & Bradley, E. (1978). Sex differences in learned helplessness: II: The contingencies of evaluative feedback in the classroom. III: An experimental analysis. *Developmental Psychology, 14,* 268–276.

Dweck, C. S., & Leggett, E. L. (1988). A social-cognitive approach to motivation and personality. *Psychological Review, 95,* 256–273.

Dyson, A. (1990). Symbol makers, symbol weavers: How children link play, pictures and print. *Young Children, 45*(2), 50–57.

Eagle, M. (1984). *Recent developments in psychoanalysis: A critical evaluation.* New York: McGraw-Hill.

Eakins, P. S. (1989, September). Obstetric outcomes at the birth place in Menlo Park: The first seven years. *Birth, 16,* 123–129.

Earle, J. (1990). *Keeping pregnant and parenting teens in school.* Alexandria, Va.: National Association of State Boards of Education.

East, M. C., & Steele, P. R. M. (1987). Inhaling heroin during pregnancy: Effects on the baby. *British Medical Journal, 296,* 754.

East, P. L., & Rook, K. S. (1992). Compensatory patterns of support among children's peer relationships: A test using school friends, nonschool friends, and siblings. *Developmental Psychology, 28,* 163–172.

Easterbrooks, M. A. (1989). Quality of attachment to mother and to father: Effects of perinatal risk status. *Child Development, 60,* 825–830.

Eccles, J. S. (1993). Development during adolescence: The impact of stage-environment fit on young adolescents' experiences in schools and families. *American Psychologist, 48,* 90–101.

Eccles, J. S., & Harold, R. D. (1993). Parent-school involvement during the early adolescent years. *Teachers College Record, 94,* 568–587.

Eccles, J. S., Midgley, C., Wigfeld, A., Buchanan, C. M., Reuman, D., Flanagan, C., & MacIver, D. (1993). Development during adolescence: The impact of stage-environment fit on young adolescents' experiences in schools and families. *American Psychologist, 48,* 90–101.

Eckerman, C. O., Davis, C. C., & Didow, S. M. (1989). Toddlers' emerging ways of achieving social coordinations with a peer. *Child Development, 60,* 440–453.

Eder, D., & Hallinan, M. (1978). Sex differences in children's friendships. *American Sociological Review, 43,* 237–250.

Edwards, C., Gandini, L., & Furman, G. (Eds.). (1993). *The hundred languages of children.* Norwood, N.J.: Ablex.

Egeland, B. (1988). The consequences of physical and emotional neglect on the development of young children. In A. Cowan (Ed.), *Child neglect.* Washington, D.C.: National Center on Child Abuse and Neglect.

Eifermann, R. (1971). Social play in childhood. In R. Heffon & B. Sutton-Smith (Eds.), *Child's play.* New York: Wiley.

Eisenberg, N., & Fabes, R. A. (1992). Emotion, self-regulation, and social competence. In M. Clark (Ed.), *Review of personality and social psychology. Vol. 14: Emotion and social behavior* (pp. 119–150). Newbury Park, Cal.: Sage.

Eisenberg, N., Fabes, R. A., Nyman, M., Bernzweig, J., & Pinuelas, A. (1994). The relations of emotionality and regulation to children's anger-related reactions. *Child Development, 65,* 109–128.

Eisenberg, N., Fabes, R. A., Schaller, M., & Miller, P. (1989). Sympathy and personal distress: Development, gender differences, and interrelations of indices. In N. Eisenberg (Ed.), *Empathy and related emotional responses: New directions for child development* (pp. 107–126). San Francisco: Jossey-Bass.

Eisenberg, N., Hertz-Lazarowitz, R., & Fuchs, I. (1990). Prosocial moral judgment in Israeli kibbutz and city children: A longitudinal study. *Merrill Palmer Quarterly, 36,* 273–285.

Ekstrom, R., Goertz, M. E., Pollack, J. M., & Rock, D. A. (1986). Who drops out of high school and why? Findings from a national study. *Teachers College Record, 87,* 356–373.

Elbers, E., Wiegersma, S., Brand, N., & Vroon, P. (1991). Response alternation as an artifact in conservation research. *Journal of Genetic Psychology, 152,* 47–56.

Elkind, D. (1984). *All grown up and no place to go: Teenagers in crisis.* Reading, Mass.: Addison-Wesley.

Elkind, D. (1985). Egocentrism redux. *Developmental Review, 5,* 218–226.

Elkind, D. (1994a). *A sympathetic understanding of the child* (3rd ed.). Boston: Allyn & Bacon.

Elkind, D. (1994b). *Ties that stress: The new family imbalance.* Cambridge, Mass.: Harvard University Press.

Ellis, R. (1994). *The study of second language acquisition.* New York: Oxford University Press.

Ellis, S., Rogoff, B., & Cromer, C. (1981). Age segregation in children's social interactions. *Developmental Psychology, 17,* 399–407.

Emery, R. E. (1989). Family violence. *American Psychologist, 44,* 321–328.

Emmerich, W., & Sheppard, K. (1982). Development of sex-differentiated preferences during late childhood and adolescence. *Developmental Psychology, 18,* 407–417.

Emmorey, K., & Reilly, J. (Eds.). (1995). *Language, gesture, and space.* Hillsdale, N.J.: Erlbaum.

Endres, J., & Rockwell, R. (1993). *Food, nutrition, and the young child* (4th ed.). Columbus, Ohio: Merrill.

Engels, J. (1993). *Pocket guide to pediatric assessment* (2nd ed.). St. Louis: Mosby.

Epstein, C. J. (1989). Down syndrome (trisomy 21). In C. R. Scriver, A. L. Beaudet, W. S. Sly, & D. Valle (Eds.), *The Metabolic Basis of Inherited Disease* (6th ed., Vol. I). New York: McGraw-Hill.

Epstein, L. H., & Wing, R. R. (1987). Behavioral treatment of childhood obesity. *Psychological Bulletin, 101,* 331–342.

Erikson, E. (1963). *Childhood and society* (2nd ed.). New York: Norton.

Erikson, E. (1968). *Identity, youth and crisis.* New York: Norton.

Erikson, E. (1975). "Identity Crisis" in autobiographical perspective. In E. Erikson, *Life history and the historical moment.* New York: Norton.

Eron, L. D. (1987). The development of aggressive behavior from the perspective of a developing behaviorism. *American Psychologist, 42,* 435–442.

Ervin-Tripp, S. (1989). Sisters and brothers. In P. Zukow (Ed.), *Sibling interaction across cultures: Theoretical and methodological issues* (pp. 184–196). New York: Springer-Verlag.

Eveleth, P., & Tanner, J. (1990). *Worldwide variation in human growth* (2nd ed.). New York: Cambridge University Press.

Faber, N. B. (1991). The process of pregnancy resolution among adolescent mothers. *Adolescence, 26,* 697–716.

Fabes, R. A., & Eisenberg, N. (1992). Young children's coping with interpersonal anger. *Child Development, 63,* 116–128.

Fabes, R. A., Eisenberg, N., McCormick, S. E., & Wilson, M. S. (1988). Preschoolers' attributions of the situational determinants of others' naturally occurring emotions. *Developmental Psychology, 24,* 376–385.

Fagot, B. I. (1982). Adults as socializing agents. In T. Field, A. Huston, H. Quay, L. Troll, & G. Finley (Eds.), *Review of human development.* New York: Wiley.

Fagot, B. I. (1994). Peer relations and the development of competence in boys and girls. In C. Leaper (Ed.), *Childhood gender segregation: Causes and consequences: New directions for child development* (pp. 53–66). San Francisco: Jossey-Bass.

Fagot, B. I., & Hagan, R. (1991). Observations of parent reactions to sex-stereotyped behaviors: Age and sex effects. *Child Development, 62,* 617–628.

Fagot, B. I., & Leinbach, M. D. (1989). The young child's gender schema: Environmental input, internal organization. *Child Development, 60,* 663–672.

Fagot, B. I., Leinbach, M. D., & O'Boyle, C. (1992). Gender labeling, gender stereotyping, and parenting behaviors. *Developmental Psychology, 28,* 225–230.

Falkner, F., & Tanner, J. (Eds.). (1986). *Human growth: Vol. 3. Methodological, ecological, genetic and nutritional effects on growth.* New York: Plenum Press.

Fantz, R. (1963). Pattern vision in newborn infants. *Science, 140,* 296–297.

Farrangy, P., Steele, H., & Steele, M. (1991). Maternal representations of attachment during pregnancy predict the organization of infant-mother attachment at one year of age. *Child Development, 62,* 891–905.

Farver, J. M., & Branstetter, W. H. (1994). Preschoolers' prosocial responses to their peers' distress. *Developmental Psychology, 30,* 334–341.

Faust, M. S. (1977). Somatic development in adolescent girls. *Monographs of the Society for Research on Child Development,* No. 169.

Faust, M. S. (1983). Alternative constructions of adolescent growth. In J. Brooks-Gunn & A. C. Petersen (Eds.), *Girls at puberty: Biological and psychosocial perspectives* (pp. 105–125). New York: Plenum Press.

Fausto-Sterling, A. (1985). *Myths of gender: Biological theories about women and men.* New York: Basic Books.

Federal Bureau of Investigation. (1991, August). *Uniform crime reports for the United States.* Washington, D.C.: U.S. Department of Justice.

Fein, G., & Fox N. (1990). *Infant day care.* Norwood, N.J.: Ablex.

Feinbloom, R. I., & Forman, B. Y. (1987). *Pregnancy, birth and the early months: A complete guide.* Reading, Mass.: Addison-Wesley.

Feiring, C., Fox, N. A., Jaskir, J., & Lewis, M. (1987). The relation between social support, infant risk status, and mother-infant interactions. *Developmental Psychology, 23,* 400–405.

Feld, S., Ruhland, D., & Gold, M. (1979). Developmental changes in achievement motivation. *Merrill-Palmer Quarterly, 25,* 43–60.

Fenson, L., Dale, P., Reznick, J., Bates, E., Thal, D., & Pethick, S. (1994). Variability in early communicative development. *Monographs of the Society for Research on Child Development, 59*(5, Serial No. 242).

Ferber, R. (1986). *Solve your child's sleep problem.* New York: Simon & Schuster.

Ferholt, J. B. (1991). Psychodynamic parent psychotherapy: Treating the parent-child relationship. In M. Lewis (Ed.), *Comprehensive textbook of child psychiatry.* New York: Saunders.

Fernald, A. (1989). Intonation and communicative intent in mothers' speech to infants. *Child Development, 60,* 1497–1510.

Field, D. (1987). A review of preschool conservation training. *Developmental Review, 7,* 210–251.

Field, J. (1987). Development of auditory-visual localization in infants. In B. McKenzie & R. Day (Eds.), *Perceptual development in early infancy* (pp. 175–198). Hillsdale, N.J.: Erlbaum.

Field, T. M. (1978). Interaction and attachment in normal and atypical infants. *Journal of Consulting and Clinical Psychology, 55,* 853–859.

Field, T., & Roopnarine, J. (1982) Infant-peer interactions. In T. Field (Ed.), *Review of human development.* New York: Wiley.

Fine, G. A. (1982). Friends, impression management, and preadolescent behavior. In S. Asher & J. Gottman (Eds.), *The development of children's friendships.* New York: Cambridge University Press.

Fine, G. A., Mortimer, J. T., & Roberts, D. F. (1990). Leisure, work, and the mass media. In S. Feldman & G. Elliott (Eds.), *At the threshold: The developing adolescent* (pp. 225–252). Cambridge, Mass.: Harvard University Press.

Fine, M. (1986).Why urban adolescents drop into and out of high school: The ideology of school and work. *Teachers College Record, 87,* 393–409.

Fine, M. (1991). *Framing dropouts: Notes on the politics of 84 urban public high schools.* New York: State University of New York Press.

Finkelhor, D. (1995). The victimization of children: A developmental perspective. *American Journal of Orthopsychiatry, 65,* 177–193.

Finn, J. D., & Achilles, C. M. (1990). Answers and questions about class size: A statewide experiment. *American Educational Research Journal, 27,* 557–577.

Fischer, K. (1980). A theory of cognitive development: The control and construction of hierarchies of skills. *Psychological Review, 87,* 477–531.

Fischer, K., & Pipp, S. L. (1984a). The process of stage transition: A neo-Piagetian view. In R. Sternberg (Ed.), *Mechanisms of cognitive development.* San Francisco: Freeman.

Fischer, K., & Pipp, S. L. (1984b). Processes of cognitive development: Optimal level and skill acquisition. In R. J. Sternberg (Ed.), *Mechanisms of cognitive development* (pp. 45–90). New York: Freeman.

Fischer, J., & Eheart, B. (1991). Family day care: A theoretical basis for improving quality. *Early Childhood Research Quarterly, 6,* 549–563.

Fischer, K., Shaver, P., & Carnochan, P. (1990). How emotions develop and how they organize development. *Cognition and Emotion, 4,* 81–127.

Fish, M., Stifter, C. A., & Belsky, J. (1991). Conditions of continuity and discontinuity in infant negative emotionality: Newborn to five months. *Child Development, 62,* 1525–1537.

Fish, M., Stifter, C. A., & Belsky, J. (1993). Early patterns of mother-infant dyadic integrations: Infant, mother, and family demographic antecedents. *Infant Behavior and Development, 16,* 1–18.

Fitzgerald, H., Lester, B., & Zuckerman, B. (1994).

Children of poverty: Research, health, and policy issues. New York: Garland.

Flanagan, C. A. (1990). Change in family work status: Effects on parent-adolescent decision making. *Child Development, 61,* 163–177.

Flavell, J. (1992). Perspectives on perspective taking. In H. Beilin & P. Pufall (Eds.), *Piaget's theory: Prospects and possibilities.* Hillsdale, N.J.: Erlbaum.

Flavell, J., Green, F., & Flavell, E. (1986). Development of knowledge about the appearance-reality distinction. With commentaries by M. Watson & J. Campione. *Monographs of the Society for Research on Child Development, 51*(1, Serial No. 212).

Flavell, J., Green, F., & Flavell, E. (1995). Young children's knowledge about thinking. *Monographs of the Society for Research on Child Development 60* (1, Serial No. 243).

Fletcher, A. C., Darling, N. E., Steinberg, L., & Dornbusch, S. M. (1995). The company they keep: Relation of adolescents' adjustment and behavior to their friends' perceptions of authoritative parenting in the social network. *Developmental Psychology, 31,* 300–310.

Forlizzi, L. (1993). Transferring literacy between the classroom and life: Metacognition, personal goals, and interests. In R. Lerner (Ed.), *Early adolescence: Perspectives on research, policy, and intervention* (pp. 201–220). Hillsdale, N.J.: Erlbaum.

Forrest-Pressley, D., Mackinnon, G., and Waller, T. (1985). *Metacognition, cognition and human performance.* Orlando, Fla.: Academic Press.

Fowler, B. (1989). Relationship of body-image perception and weight status to recent change in weight status of the adolescent female. *Adolescence, 24,* 557–568.

Fowler, J. (1981). *Stages of faith: The psychology of human development and the quest for meaning.* San Francisco: Harper & Row.

Fowler, J. (1991). *Stages of faith and religious development.* New York: Crossroads Press.

Fox, N. A., Kimmerly, N. L., & Schafer, W. D. (1991). Attachment to mother/attachment to father: A meta-analysis. *Child Development, 62,* 210–225.

Frank, E. S. (1991). Shame and guilt in eating disorders. *American Journal of Orthopsychiatry, 61,* 303–306.

Franz, C. E., McClelland, D. C., & Weinberger, J. (1991). Childhood antecedents of conventional social accomplishment in midlife adults: A 36-year prospective study. *Journal of Personality and Social Psychology, 60,* 586–595.

Franz, W., & Reardon, D. (1992). Differential impact of abortion on adolescents and adults. *Adolescence, 27,* 161–172.

Frazer, A. M., Brockert, J. E., & Ward, R. H. (1995). Association of young maternal age with adverse reproductive outcomes. *New England Journal of Medicine, 332,* 113.

Freedman, D. (1976). Infancy, biology, and culture. In L. P. Lipsitt (Ed.), *Developmental psychobiology: The significance of infancy.* New York: Wiley.

French, D. C. (1984). Children's knowledge of the social functions of younger, older, and same-aged peers. *Child Development, 55,* 1429–1433.

French, J., & Rhodes, C. (1992). *Teaching thinking skills: Theory and practice* (2nd ed.). New York: Garland.

Freud, S. (1983). *A general introduction to psychoanalysis* (rev. ed.). New York: Washington Square Press.

Frieze, I., Francis, W., & Hanusa, B. (1981). Defining success in classroom settings. In J. Levine & M. Wang (Eds.), *Teacher and student perceptions.* Hillsdale, N.J.: Erlbaum.

Frisch, R. (1983). Fatness, puberty, and fertility: The effects of nutrition and athletic training on menarche and ovulation. In J. Brooks-Gunn & A. Peterson (Eds.), *Puberty in girls: Biological and psychological perspectives.* New York: Plenum Press.

Frost, A. K., & Pakiz, B. (1990). The effects of marital disruption on adolescents: Time as a dynamic. *American Journal of Orthopsychiatry, 60,* 544–555.

Fry, J. (1974). *Common diseases: Their nature, incidence, and care.* Philadelphia: Lippincott.

Fuhrman, T., & Holmbeck, G. N. (1995). A contextual-moderator analysis of emotional autonomy and adjustment in adolescence. *Child Development, 66,* 793–811.

Fuligni, A. J. & Eccles, J. S. (1993). Perceived parent-child relationships and early adolescent's orientation toward peers. *Developmental Psychology, 29,* 622–632.

Furman, W. (1982). Children's friendships. In T. Field (Ed.), *Review of human development.* New York: Wiley.

Furman, W. (1989). The development of children's social networks. In D. Belle (Ed.), *Children's social networks and social supports.* New York: Wiley.

Furman, W., & Bierman, K. L. (1983). Developmental changes in young children's conceptions of friendship. *Child Development, 54,* 549–556.

Furman, W., & Bierman, K. L. (1984). Children's conceptions of friendship: A multidimensional study of developmental changes. *Developmental Psychology, 20,* 925–931.

Furman, W., & Buhrmester, D. (1992). Age and sex differences in perceptions of networks of personal friendships. *Child Development, 63,* 103–115.

Furstenberg, F. F., Brooks-Gunn, J., & Chase-Lansdale, L. (1989). Teenaged pregnancy and childbearing. *American Psychologist, 44,* 313–320.

Furstenberg, F. F., Spanier, G., & Rothschild, N. (1982). Patterns of parenting in the transition from divorce to remarriage. In P. Berman & E. Ramey (Eds.), *Women: A developmental perspective.* Washington, D.C.: National Institutes of Health.

Gabbard, C. (1989). Foot lateralization and psychomotor control in four-year-olds. *Perceptual and Motor Skills, 68,* 712–715.

Galambos, N. L., & Maggs, J. L. (1991). Out-of-school care of young adolescents and self-reported behavior. *Developmental Psychology, 27,* 644–655.

Galinsky, E. (1987). *The six stages of parenthood.* Reading, Mass.: Addison-Wesley.

Gallagher, J. (1993). Comments on McDaniel's "Education of the Gifted and the Excellence-Equity Debate." In J. Maker (Ed.), *Programs for the gifted in regular classrooms* (pp. 19–22). Austin, Tex.: Pro-Ed Publishers.

Gallagher, J., & Gallagher, S. (1994). *Teaching the gifted child* (4th ed) Boston: Allyn & Bacon.

Gallaway, C., & Richards, B. (1994). *Input and interaction in language acquisition.* New York: Cambridge University Press.

Gandelman, R. (1992). *Psychobiology of behavioral development.* New York: Oxford University Press.

Ganong, L. H., & Coleman, M. (1987). Effects of parental remarriage on children: An updated comparison of theories, methods, and findings from clinical and empirical research. In K. Pasley & M. Ihinger-Tallman (Eds.), *Remarriage and stepparenting: Current research and theory* (pp. 94–140). New York: Guilford Press.

Garbarino, J. (1982). Sociocultural risk: Dangers to competence. In C. Kopp & J. Krakow (Eds.), *Child development in a social context.* Reading, Mass.: Addison-Wesley.

Garbarino, J. (1992). *Children and families in the social environment* (2nd ed.). New York: Aldine de Gruyter.

Garbarino, J. (1992). *Children in Danger.* New York: Jossey-Bass.

Garbarino, J. (1993). Reinventing fatherhood. *Families in Society, 74,* 52–54.

Gardner, H. (1993a). *Frames of mind: The theory of multiple intelligences* (2nd rev. ed.). New York: Basic Books.

Gardner, H. (1993b). *Multiple intelligences: Theory in practice.* New York: Basic Books.

Garland, A. F., & Zigler, E. (1993). Adolescent suicide prevention: Current research and social policy. *American Psychologist, 48,* 169–182.

Garner, P. W., Jones, D. C., & Palmer, D. J. (1994). Social cognitive correlates of preschool children's sibling caregiving behavior. *Developmental Psychology, 30,* 906–911.

Garver, K. L., & Garver, B. (1994). The human genome project and eugenic concerns. *American Journal of Human Genetics, 54,* 148–158.

Gavin, L., & Furman, W. (1989). Age differences in adolescents' perceptions of their peer groups. *Developmental Psychology, 25,* 827–834.

Gelman, R., & Greeno, J. (1988). On the nature of competence: Principles for understanding in a domain. In L. Resnick (Ed.), *Knowing and learning: Issues for a cognitive science of instruction* (pp. 125–186). Hillsdale, N.J.: Erlbaum.

Gerbner, G., Gross, L., Signorielli, N., & Morgan, M. (1986). *Television's world: Violence profile No. 14–15.* University of Pennsylvania, Annenberg School of Communications, Philadelphia.

Gesell, A. (1926). *The mental growth of the preschool child* (2nd ed.). New York: Macmillan.

Gesell, A., & Thompson, H. (1929). Learning and growth in identical infant twins. *Genetic Psychology Monographs, 6,* 1–125.

Gianino, A., & Tronick, E. Z. (1988). The mutual regulation model: The infant's self and interactive regulation coping and defense. In T. Field, P. McCabe, & N. Schneiderman (Eds.), *Stress and coping* (pp. 47–68). Hillsdale, N.J.: Erlbaum.

Gibson, E., & Walk, R. (1960). The visual cliff. *Scientific American, 202,* 64–71.

Giles, H., & Coupland, N. (1991). Language attitudes: Discursive, contextual, and gerontological considerations. In A. Reynolds (Ed.), *Bilingualism, multiculturalism, and second language learning* (pp. 21–42). Hillsdale, N.J.: Erlbaum.

Giles-Sims, J., & Crosbie-Burnett, M. (1989). Adolescent power in stepfather families. *Journal of Marriage and the Family, 51,* 1065–1078.

Gilligan, C. (1982). *In a different voice: Psychological theory and women's development.* Cambridge, Mass.: Harvard University Press.

Gilligan, C. (1987). Adolescent development reconsidered. In C. Irwin (Ed.), *Adolescent social behavior and health.* San Francisco: Jossey-Bass.

Gilligan, C. (1990). Teaching Shakespeare's sister: Notes from the underground of female adolescence. In C. Gilligan, N. Lyons, & T. Hanmer, *Making connections: The relational worlds of adolescent girls at Emma Willard School* (pp. 6–29). Cambridge, Mass.: Harvard University Press.

Gilligan, C., & Wiggins, G. (1987). The origins of morality in early childhood relationships. In J. Kagan & S. Lamb (Eds.), *The emergence of morality in young children* (pp. 277–305). Chicago: University of Chicago Press.

Ginsburg, G. S., & Bronstein, P. (1993). Family factors related to children's intrinsic/extrinsic motivational orientation in academic performance. *Child Development, 64,* 1461–1474.

Giordano, P. C., Cernkovich, S. A., & Demaris, A. (1993). The family and peer relations of black adolescents. *Journal of Marriage and the Family, 55,* 277–287.

Glasser, W. (1967). *Reality Therapy.* New York: Harper & Row.

Glick, P. C., & Lin, S. (1987). Remarriage after divorce: Recent changes and demographic variations. *Sociological Perspectives, 30,* 162–179.

Goldscheider, C., & Goldscheider, F. (1987). Moving out and marriage: What do adults expect? *American Sociological Review, 52,* 278–285.

Goldscheider, C., & Goldscheider, F. (1989). Family structure and conflict: Nest leaving expectations of young adults and their parents. *Journal of Marriage and the Family, 51,* 87–97.

Goldson, E. (1992). The longitudinal study of very low birthweight infants and its implications for interdisciplinary research and public policy. In C. Greenbaum & J. Auerbach (Eds.), *Longitudinal studies of children at psychological risk: Cross-national perspectives* (pp. 43–64). Norwood, N.J.: Ablex.

Goldstein, A. P., & Soriano, F. I. (1994). Delinquent gangs. In L. Eron & J. Gentry (Eds.), *Violence and youth: Psychology's response: Vol. II. Papers of the American Psychological Association on Violence and Youth.* Washington, DC: American Psychological Association.

Goldstein, S., Field, T., & Healy, B. T. (1989). Concordance of play behavior and physiology in preschool friends. *Journal of Applied Developmental Psychology, 10,* 3337–3351.

Golombok, S., Cook, R., Bish, A., & Clare, M. (1995). Families created by the new reproductive technologies: Quality of parenting and social and emotional development of the children. *Child Development, 66,* 285–298.

Goodnow, J. J. (1976). The nature of intelligent behavior: Questions raised by cross-cultural studies. In L. B. Resnick (Ed.), *The nature of intelligence.* Hillsdale, N.J. Erlbaum.

Goodnow, J. J. (1995). From household practices to parents' ideas about work and interpersonal relationships. In S. Harkness & C. Super (Eds.), *Parents' cultural belief systems: Their origins, expressions, and consequences.* New York: Guildford Press.

Goodnow, J. J., Miller, P., & Kessel, F. (Eds.). (1995). *Cultural practices as contexts for development.* San Francisco: Jossey-Bass.

Goosens, F. A., & van Ijzendoorn, M. H. (1990). Quality of infants' attachments to professional caregivers: Relation to infant-parent attachment and day-care characteristics. *Child Development, 61,* 832–837.

Gordon, E. W. (1995). Putting them in their place. *Readings: A Journal of Reviews and Commentary in Mental Health, 10,* 8–14.

Gorman, C. (1993, June 13). Thalidomide's return. *Time,* June 13, p. 67.

Gortmaker, S. L., Must, A., Perrin, J. M., Sobol, A. M., & Dietz, W. H. (1993). Social and economic consequences of overweight in adolescence and young adulthood. *New England Journal of Medicine, 329,* 1008–1012.

Gottesman, I. I. (1963). Heritability of personality: A demonstration. *Psychological Monographs, 77* (Whole No. 572).

Gottlieb, G. (1991). Experiential canalization of behavioral development: Theory. *Developmental Psychology, 27,* 4–13.

Gottman, J., & Parkhurst, J. (1980). A developmental theory of friendship and acquaintanceship. In A. Collins (Ed.), *Minnesota symposia on child psychology: Vol. 13.* Hillsdale, N.J.: Erlbaum.

Gould, D. (1993). Intensive sport participation and the prepubescent athlete: Competitive stress and burnout. In B. Cahill & A. Pearl (Eds.), *Intensive participation in children's sports* (pp. 19–38). Champaign, Ill.: Human Kinetics Press.

Graber, J. A., Brooks-Gunn, J., Paikoff, R. L., & Warren, M. P. (1994). Prediction of eating problems: An 8-year study of adolescent girls. *Developmental Psychology, 30,* 823–834.

Gralinski, J. H., & Kopp, C. (1993). Everyday rules for behavior: Mothers' requests to young children. *Developmental Psychology, 29,* 573–584.

Grant, J. (1986). *The state of the world's children.* Oxford, U.K.: Oxford University Press.

Green, D. L. (1990). High school student employment in social context: Adolescents' perceptions of the role of part-time work. *Adolescence, 25,* (425–434).

Green, M. (1994). *Sigh of relief: A first-aid handbook for childhood emergencies.* New York: Bantam Books.

Green, R. (1980). Homosexuality. In H. Kaplan, A. Freedman, & B. Sadock (Eds.), *Comprehensive textbook of psychiatry: Vol. 2* (3rd ed.). Baltimore: Williams & Wilkins.

Green, R. (1987). *The "sissy boy" syndrome and the development of homosexuality.* New Haven, Conn.: Yale University Press.

Greenberg, B. S. (1986). Minorities and the mass media. In J. Bryant & D. Zillman (Eds.), *Perspectives on mass media effects.* Hillsdale, N.J.: Erlbaum.

Greenberger, E., O'Neill, R., & Nagel, S. K. (1994). Linking workplace and homeplace: Relations between the nature of adults' work and their parenting behaviors. *Developmental Psychology, 30,* 990–1002.

Greenfield, P. (1994). Independence and interdependence as developmental scripts: Implications for theory, research, and practice. In P. Greenfield & R. Cocking

(Eds.), *Cross-cultural roots of minority child development* (pp. 1–40). Hillsdale, N.J.: Erlbaum.

Greenfield, P. (1995, March 30). *Independence and interdependence in school conferences between Anglo teachers and Hispanic parents.* Paper presented at the biennial meeting of the Society for Research on Child Development, Indianapolis.

Gregg, M., & Leinhardt, C. (1995). Mapping out geography: An example of epistemology and education. In *Review of Educational Research, 64*(2), 311–361.

Gregg, R. (1993). "Choice" as a double-edged sword: Information guilt and mother-blaming in a high-tech age. *Women and Health, 20,* 53–73.

Greil, A. L. (1993a). Infertility: Overview. In B. K. Rothman (Ed.), *The encyclopedia of childbearing.* New York: Henry Holt .

Greil, A. L. (1993b). Infertility: Cross-cultural and historical aspects. In B. K. Rothman (Ed.), *The encyclopedia of childbearing.* New York: Henry Holt.

Grimes, D., & Gross, G. (1981). Pregnancy outcomes in black women aged 35 and older. *Obstetrics and Gynecology, 58,* 614–620.

Grossmann, K. E., & Grossmann, K. (1990). The wider concept of attachment in cross-cultural research. *Human Development, 33,* 31–47.

Grossmann, K., Grossmann, K., Spangler, G., Suess, G., & Unzner, L. (1985). Maternal sensitivity and newborns' orientation responses as related to quality of attachment in northern Germany. In I. Bretherton & E. Waters (Eds.), Growing points of attachment theory and research. *Monographs of the Society for Research on Child Development, 50,* 233–256.

Grusec, J. E. (1991). Socializing concern for others in the home. *Developmental Psychology, 27,* 338–342.

Grusec, J. E., & Kuczynski, L. (1980). Direction of effect in socialization: A comparison of the parent's versus the child's behavior as determinants of disciplinary technique. *Developmental Psychology, 16,* 1–9.

Grusec, J. E., & Lytton, H. (1988). *Social development.* New York: Springer-Verlag.

Guardo, C., & Bohan, J. (1971). Development of a sense of self-identity in children. *Child Development, 42,* 1909–1921.

Gunnar, M. R., & Maratsos, M. (Eds.). (1992). *Modularity and constraints in language and cognition: The Minnesota symposia on child psychology: Vol. 25.* Hillsdale, N.J.: Erlbaum.

Gunnar, M. R., Proter, F. L., Wolf, C. M., Rigatuso, J., & Larson, M. C. (1995). Neonatal stress reactivity: Predictions of later emotional temperament. *Child Development, 66,* 1–13.

Gustafson, G. E., & Harris, K. L. (1990). Women's responses to young infants' cries. *Developmental Psychology, 26,* 144–152.

Guttmacher, A., & Kaiser, I. (1984). *Pregnancy, birth, and family planning.* New York: Signet.

Hajcak, F., & Garwood, P. (1989). Quick-fix sex: Pseudosexuality in adolescents. *Adolescence, 23,* 75–76.

Hall, C. S., & Lindzey, G. (1978). *Theories of personality* (3rd ed.) New York: Wiley.

Hallinan, M. T. (1981). Recent advances in sociometry. In S. Asher & J. Gottman (Eds.), *The development of children's friendships.* New York: Cambridge University Press.

Hallinan, M. T., & Williams, R. A. (1989). Interracial friendship choices in secondary schools. *American Sociological Review, 54,* 67–78.

Hamburg, D. A. (1994). *Today's children: Creating a future for a generation of crisis.* New York: Times Books.

Hamill, P., Drizd, T., Johnson, C., Reed, R., Roche, A., & Moore, W. (1979). Physical growth: National Center for Health Statistics percentiles. *Clinical Nutrition, 32,* 607–629.

Hamilton, N. G. (1989). *Self and others: Object relations in theory and practice.* Northvale, N.J.: Jason Aronson.

Hamilton, P. M. (1984). *Basic maternity nursing* (5th ed.). St. Louis: Mosby.

Hanshaw, J. B., Dudgeon, J. A., & Marshall, W. C. (1985). *Viral diseases of the fetus and newborn* (2nd ed.). Philadelphia: Saunders.

Hardy, J. B. (1991). Pregnancy and its outcome. In W. R. Hendee (Ed.), *The health of adolescents: Understanding and facilitating biological, behavioral, and social development* (pp. 250–281). San Francisco: Jossey-Bass.

Hare-Mustin, R. T., & Marecek, J. (1988). The meaning of difference: Gender theory, postmodernism, and psychology. *American Psychologist, 43,* 455–464.

Hareven, T. (1986). Historical changes in the family and the life course: Implications for child development. In A. Smuts & H. Hagen (Eds.), *History and research in child development. Monographs of the Society for Research in Child Development, 50* (4–5, Serial No. 211).

Harkness, S., & Keefer, C. (1995, February). *Cultural influences on sleep patterns in infancy and early childhood.* Paper presented at the annual meeting of the American Association for the Advancement of Science, Atlanta.

Harkness, S., & Super, C. (1992). Parental ethnotheories in action. In I. Sigel, A. McGillicuddy-DeLisi, & J. Goodnow (Eds.), *Parent belief systems: The psychological consequences for children* (2nd ed., pp. 373–392). Hillsdale, N.J.: Erlbaum.

Harkness, S., Super, C., & Keefer, C. (1992). Learning to be an American parent: How cultural models gain directive force. In R. D'Andrade & C. Strauss (Eds.), *Human motives and cultural models* (pp. 163–178). New York: Cambridge University Press.

Harkness, S., Super, C., Keefer, C., Raghavan, C., & Kipp, E. (1995). Ask the doctor: The negotiation of cultural models in American parent-patient discourse. In S. Harkness & C. Super (Eds.), *Parents' cultural belief systems: Their origins, expressions, and consequences.* New York: Guilford Press.

Harkness, S., Super, C., Keefer, C., van Tijen, N., & van der Vlugt, E. (1995, February). *Cultural influences on sleep patterns in infancy and early childhood.* Paper presented at the annual meeting of the American Association for the Advancement of Science, Atlanta.

Harlow, H. (1959). Love in infant monkeys. *Scientific American, 200,* 68–74.

Harlow, H., & Harlow, M. (1962). Social deprivation in monkeys. *Scientific American, 207,* 136–144.

Harper, L. (1988). *The nurture of human behavior.* Norwood, N.J.: Ablex.

Harris, M., & Rosenthal, R. (1985). Mediation of interpersonal expectancy effects: 31 meta-analyses. *Psychological Bulletin, 97,* 363–386.

Harris, P. (1983). Infant cognition. In Paul Mussen (Ed.), *Handbook of child psychology: Vol. 4.* New York: Wiley.

Harris, P., & Kavanaugh, R. (1993). *Young children's understanding of pretense.* Chicago: University of Chicago Press.

Harrison, A. O., Wilson, M. N., Pine, C. J., Chan, S. Q., & Buriel, R. (1990). Family ecologies of ethnic minority children. *Child Development, 61,* 347–362.

Hart, B. (1991). Input frequency and children's first words. *First Language, 11,* 289–300.

Hart, C. H., DeWolf, D. M., Wozniak, P., & Burts, D. C. (1992). Maternal and paternal disciplinary styles: Relations with preschoolers' playground behavioral orientations and peer status. *Child Development, 63,* 879–892.

Hart, C. H., Ladd, G. W., & Burleson, B. R. (1990). Children's expectations of the outcomes of social strategies: Relations with socioeconomic status and maternal disciplinary styles. *Child Development, 61,* 127–137.

Harter, S. (1977). A cognitive-developmental approach to children's expression of conflicting feelings and a technique to facilitate such expression in play therapy. *Journal of Consulting and Clinical Psychology, 45,* 417–432.

Harter, S. (1983). Developmental perspectives on self-system. In E. M. Hetherington (Ed.), *Handbook of child psychology: Vol. 4. Socialization, personality, and social development* (4th ed., pp. 275–285). New York: Wiley.

Harter, S. (1989). Processes underlying adolescent self-concept formation. In R. Montemayor (Ed.), *Advances in adolescent development: Vol 2. Transition from childhood to adolescence.* New York: Russell Sage Foundation.

Harter, S. (1990a). Self and identity development. In S. Feldman & G. Elliot (Eds.), *At the threshold: The developing adolescent.* Cambridge, Mass.: Harvard University Press.

Harter, S. (1990b). Processes underlying adolescent self-concept formation. In R. Montemayor, G. R. Adams, & T. P. Gullotta (Eds.), *From childhood to adolescence: A transitional period?* Newbury Park, Cal.: Sage.

Harter, S., & Barnes, R. (1983). *Children's understanding of parental emotions: A developmental study.* Unpublished paper, 1981. Cited in S. Harter, *Developmental perspectives on the self-system.* In P. Mussen (Ed.), *Handbook of child psychology: Vol. 4.* New York: Wiley.

Harter, S., & Monsour, A. (1992). Developmental analysis of conflict caused by opposing attributes in the adolescent self-portrait. *Developmental Psychology, 28,* 251–260.

Hartup, W. (1974). Aggression in childhood: Developmental perspectives. *American Psychologist, 29,* 336–341.

Hartup, W. (1983). Peer relations. In P. Mussen (Ed.), *Handbook of child psychology: Vol. 4.* New York: Wiley.

Hartup, W. (1989). Social relationships and their developmental significance. *American Psychologist, 44,* 120–126.

Haste, H., & Torney-Purta, J. (Eds.). (1992). *The development of political understanding.* San Francisco: Jossey-Bass.

Hayne, H., Rovee-Collier, C., & Borza, M. (1991). Infant memory for place information. *Memory and Cognition, 19,* 378–386.

Heath, S. (1993). *Identity and inner-city youth: Beyond ethnicity and gender.* New York: Teachers' College Press.

Heath, S., Mangolia, L., Schlecter, S., & Hull, G. (Eds.). (1991). *Children of promise: Literate activity in linguistically and culturally diverse classrooms.* Washington, D.C.: National Education Association.

Heilbrun, A., & Friedberg, L. (1990). Distorted body image in normal college women: Possible implications for anorexia nervosa. *Journal of Clinical Psychology, 46,* 398–401.

Hein, K. D., & DiGeronimo, T. F. (1989). *AIDS: Trading fears for facts. A guide for teens.* Mount Vernon, N.Y.: Consumers Union.

Helfer, R. E., & Kempe, R. S. (Eds.) (1987). *The battered child* (4th ed.). Chicago: University of Chicago Press.

Heller, D. (1994). *Talking to your child about God.* New York: Berkley Publishers.

Hellige, J. (1993). *Hemispheric asymmetry: What's right and what's left.* Cambridge, Mass.: Harvard University Press.

Helton, A., McFarlane, J., & Anderson, E. T. (1987). Battered and pregnant: A prevalence study. *American Journal of Public Health, 77,* 1337–1339.

Hendler, M., & Weisberg, P. (1992). Conservation acquisition, maintenance, and generalization by mentally retarded children using equality-rule training. *Journal of Experimental Child Psychology, 53,* 258–276.

Henley, N. (1977). *Body politics: Power, sex, and nonverbal communication.* Englewood Cliffs, N.J.: Prentice-Hall.

Hergenrather, J. R., & Rabinowitz, M. (1991). Age-related differences in the organization of children's knowledge of illness. *Developmental Psychology, 27,* 952–959.

Hernstein, R. J., & Murray, C. (1994). *The Bell Curve: Intelligence and Class Structure in the American Life.* New York: The Free Press.

Hershberger, S. L., & D'Augelli, A. R. (1995). The impact of victimization on the mental health and suicidality of lesbian, gay, and bisexual youths. *Developmental Psychology, 31,* 65–74.

Hetherington, E. M. (1988). Family relations six years after divorce. In K. Pasley & M. Ihinger-Tallman (Eds.), *Remarriage and stepparenting: Current research and theory* (pp. 185–205). New York: Guilford Press.

Hetherington, E. M. (1989a). Coping with family transitions: Winners, losers, and survivors. *Child Development, 60,* 1–18.

Hetherington, E. M. (1989b). Divorce: A child's perspective. *American Psychologist, 44,* 303–312.

Hetherington, E. M. (1991). The role of individual differences and family relationships in children's coping with divorce and remarriage. In P. A. Cowan & M. Hetherington (Eds.), *Family transitions* (pp. 165–194). Hillsdale, N.J.: Erlbaum.

Hetherington, E. M. (1995, March 30). *The changing American family and the well-being of children.* Paper presented at the biennial meeting of the Society for Research on Child Development, Indianapolis.

Hetherington, E. M., & Clingempeel, W. (1992). Coping with marital transitions: A family systems perspective. *Monographs of the Society for Research in Child Development, 57* (2–3, Serial No. 227).

Hetherington, E. M., Cox, M., & Cox, R. (1979). Play and social interaction in children following divorce. *Journal of Social Issues, 35,* 26–49.

Hetherington, E. M., Cox, M., & Cox, R. (1982). Effects of divorce on parents and children. In M. Lamb (Ed.), *Nontraditional families: Parenting and child development.* Hillsdale, N.J.: Erlbaum.

Hetherington, E. M., Cox, M., & Cox, R. (1985). Long-term effects of divorce and remarriage on the adjustment of children. *Journal of the American Academy of Psychiatry, 24,* 518–530.

Hetherington, E. M., & Furstenberg, F. (1989). Follow-up. Letter to the editor. *Readings: A Journal of Reviews and Commentary in Mental Health,* 22–23.

Hetherington, E. M., Stanley-Hagen, M., & Anderson, E. (1989). Marital transitions: A child's perspective. *American Psychologist, 44,* 303–312.

Hickling, A., & Gelman, S. (1995). How does your garden grow? Early conceptualization of seeds and their place in the plant growth cycle. *Child Development, 66,* 856–876.

Hill, B., & Ruptic, C. (1994). *Practical aspects of authentic assessment.* Norwood, Mass.: Christopher-Gordon Publishers.

Hills, T. (1992). Reach potentials through appropriate assessment. In S. Bredekamp & T. Rosegrant (Eds.), *Reaching potentials: Appropriate curriculum and assessment and for young children: Vol. 1* (pp. 43–65). Washington, D.C.: National Association for the Education of Young Children.

Hinde, R. A. (1989). Ethological relationships and approaches. In R. Vasta (Ed.), *Annals of Child Development: Six theories of child development—Revised formulations and current issues.* Greenwich, Conn.: JAI Press.

Hinde, R. A., Titmus, G., Easton, D., & Tamplin, A. (1985). Incidence of "friendship" and behavior to strong associates versus non-associates in preschoolers. *Child Development, 56,* 234–245.

Hirsch, M. B., & Mosher, W. D. (1987). Characteristics of infertile women in the United States and their use of fertility services. *Fertility and Sterility, 47,* 618–625.

Ho, D. (1994). Cognitive socialization in confucian heritage cultures. In P. Greenfield & R. Cocking (Eds.), *Cross-cultural roots of minority child development* (pp. 285–314). Hillsdale, N.J.: Erlbaum.

Hoare, C. H. (1994). Psychosocial identity development in United States society: Its role in fostering exclusion of cultural others. In E. P. Salett & D. R. Koslow (Eds.), *Race, ethnicity and self: Identity in multicultural perspective.* Washington, D.C.: National Multicultural Institute, 1994.

Hobart, C. (1987). Parent-child relations in remarried families. *Journal of Family Issues, 8,* 259–277.

Hodapp, R., & Mueller, E. (1982). Early social development. In B. Wolman (Ed.), *Handbook of developmental psychology.* New York: Wiley.

Hodgkinson, H. L. (1985). *All one system: Demographics of education, kindergarten through graduate school.* Washington, D.C.: Institute of Educational Leadership.

Hoff-Ginsberg, E., & Krueger, W. (1991). Older siblings as conversational partners. *Merrill-Palmer Quarterly, 37,* 465–482.

Hofferth, S., & Hayes, C. (Eds.). (1987). *Risking the future: Adolescent sexuality, pregnancy and childbearing: Vol. 2. Working papers and statistical reports.* Washington, D.C.: National Academy Press.

Hoffman, L. W. (1980). The effects of maternal employment on the academic attitudes and performance of school-aged children. *School Psychology Review, 9,* 319–336.

Hoffman, L. W. (1983). Increased fathering: Effects on the mother. In M. Lamb & A. Sagi (Eds.), *Fatherhood and family policy.* Hillsdale, N.J.: Erlbaum.

Hoffman, L. W. (1984a). Maternal employment and the young child. In M. Perlmutter (Ed.), *The Minnesota symposium on child psychology: Vol. 17.* Hillsdale, N.J.: Erlbaum.

Hoffman, L. W. (1984b). Work, family, and the socialization of the child. In R. Parke (Ed.), *Review of child development research: Vol. 7.* Chicago: University of Chicago Press.

Hoffman, L. W. (1988). Cross-cultural differences in childrearing goals. In R. A. LeVine, P. M. Miller, & M. M. West (Eds.), *Parental behavior in diverse societies: New directions for child development.* San Francisco: Jossey-Bass.

Hoffman, L. W. (1989). Effects of maternal employment in the two-parent family. *American Psychologist, 44,* 283–292.

Hoffman, L., & Hoffman, M. (1973). The value of children to parents. In J. T. Fawcett (Ed.), *Psychological perspectives on population.* New York: Basic Books.

Hoffnung, A. (1992). *Shoeshine boys of Cuenca, Ecuador.* Unpublished paper, Reed College, Portland.

Holden, C. (1986). Youth suicide: New research focuses on growing social problem. *Science, 233,* 839–841.

Holloway, J., & Vass, W. (1993). *African heritage of American English.* Bloomington, Ind.: Indiana University Press.

Holmbeck, G., & O'Donnell, K. (1991). Discrepancies between perceptions of decision making and behavioral autonomy. In R. Paikoff (Ed.), *Shared views of the family during adolescence* (pp. 51–70). San Francisco: Jossey-Bass.

Horgan, J. (1993, June). Eugenics revisited. *Scientific American,* 120–128.

Horwitz, R. A. (1979). Psychological effects of the "open classroom." *Review of Educational Research, 49,* 71–86.

Howard, J., & Barnett, M. (1981). Arousal of empathy and subsequent generosity in young children. *Journal of Genetic Psychology, 138,* 307–308.

Howe, M., Brainerd, C., & Reyna, V. (Eds.). (1992). *The development of long-term memory.* New York: Springer-Verlag.

Howes, C. (1987). Quality indicators in infant and toddler child care: The Los Angeles Study. In D. Phillips (Ed.), *Quality in child care: What does research tell us? Research Monographs of the National Association for the Education of Young Children: Vol. 1* (pp. 81–88). Washington, D.C.: National Association for the Education of Young Children.

Howes, C. (1988). Peer interaction of young children. *Monographs of the Society for Research in Child Development, 53*(Serial No. 2170), 1–78.

Howes, C., & Farver, J. M. (1987). Toddlers' responses to the distress of their peers. *Journal of Applied Developmental Psychology, 8,* 441–452.

Howes, C., & Matheson, C. C. (1992). Sequences in the development of competent play with peers: Social and social pretend play. *Developmental Psychology, 28,* 961–972.

Howes, C., & Mueller, E. (1984). Early peer friendships: Their significance for development. In W. Spiel (Ed.), *The psychology of the twentieth century.* Zurich: Kindler.

Howes, C., Whitebrook, M., & Phillips, D. (1992). Teacher characteristics and effective teaching in child care: Findings from the National Child Care Staffing Study. Special issue: Meeting child care needs of the 1990s: Perspectives on day care: II. *Child and Youth Care Forum, 21,* 399–414.

Howes, C., & Wu, F. (1990). Peer interactions and friendships in an ethnically diverse school setting. *Child Development, 61,* 537–541.

Huang, L., & Ying, Y. (1989). Chinese-American children and adolescents. In J. Gibbs & L. Huang (Eds.), *Children of color* (pp. 30–66). San Francisco: Jossey-Bass.

Hudley, C., & Graham, S. (1993). An attributional intervention to reduce peer-directed aggression among African-American boys. *Child Development, 64,* 124–138.

Huesmann, L. R., Eron, L. D., Lefkowitz, M. M., & Walder, L. O. (1984). Stability of aggression over time

and generations. *Developmental Psychology, 20,* 1120–1134.

Hunt, C. (Ed.). (1992). *Apnea and SIDS.* Philadelphia: Saunders.

Hunter-Griffin, L. (1990). The young female athlete. In J. Sullivan & W. Grana (Eds.), *The pediatric athlete* (pp. 69–78). Park Ridge, Ill.: American Academy of Orthopedic Surgeons.

Huston, A. C. (1983). Sex-typing. In P. Mussen (Ed.), *Handbook of child psychology: Vol. 4.* New York: Wiley.

Huston, A. C. (1994). *Children in poverty: Designing research to affect policy.* Social policy report, vol. 8(2). Ann Arbor, Mich.: Society for Research on Child Development.

Huston, A. C., & Alvarez, M. M. (1990). The socialization context of gender role development in early adolescence. In R. Montemayor, G. R. Adams, & T. P. Gullota (Eds.), *From childhood to adolescence: A transitional period?* Newbury Park, Calif.: Sage.

Huston, A. C., Watkins, B., & Kunkel, D. (1989). Public policy and children's television. *American Psychologist, 44,* 424–433.

Huston, A. C., Wright, J. C., Rice, M. L., Kerkman, D., & St. Peters, M. (1990). Development of television viewing patterns in early childhood: A longitudinal investigation. *Developmental Psychology, 26,* 409–420.

Hutt, C. (1979). Exploration and play. In B. Sutton-Smith (Ed.), *Play and learning.* New York: Gardner.

Hwang, C. P. (1986). Behavior of Swedish primary and secondary caretaking fathers in relation to mother's presence. *Developmental Psychology, 22,* 749–751.

Ingersoll, B., & Goldstein, S. (1993). *Attention deficit disorder and learning disabilities: Realities, myths and controversial treatments.* New York: Doubleday.

Inhelder, B., & Piaget, J. (1958). *The growth of logical thinking from birth to adolescence.* New York: Basic Books.

Institute of Medicine, Committee to Study Prevention of Low Birth Weight. (1985). *Preventing low birth weight.* Washington, D.C.: National Academy Press.

International Food Information Council. (1993). *Starting solids.* (On-line) Located at http://ificinfo.health.org.

Isabella, R. A. (1993). Origins of attachment: Maternal interactive behavior across the first year. *Child Development, 64,* 605–621.

Isabella, R. A., & Belsky, J. (1991). Interactional synchrony and the origins of infant-mother attachment: A replication study. *Child Development, 62,* 373–384.

Izard, C. E. (1994). Innate and universal facial expressions: Evidence from developmental and cross-cultural research. *Psychological Bulletin, 115,* 288–299.

Izard, C. E., Hembree, E. A., & Huebner, R. R. (1987). Infant's emotion expressions to acute pain. *Developmental Psychology, 23,* 105–113.

Izard, C. E., & Malatesta, C. (1987). Perspectives on emotional development: I. Differential emotions theory of early emotional development. In J. Osofsky (Ed.), *Handbook of infant development* (2nd ed., pp. 494–554). New York: Wiley.

Jackson, P. (1968). *Life in classrooms.* New York: Holt, 1968.

Jackson, P. (1986). *The practice of teaching.* Chicago: University of Chicago Press.

Jadack, R., Hyde, J., Moore, C., & Keller, M. (1995). Moral reasoning about sexually transmitted diseases. *Child Development, 66,* 167–177.

Jensen, A. R. (1969a, Winter). How much can we boost I.Q. and scholastic achievement? *Harvard Educational Review,* 1–123.

Jensen, A. R. (1969b). Reducing the heredity-environment uncertainty: A reply. *Harvard Educational Review, 39,* 449–483.

Jessor, R. (1993). Successful adolescent development among high-risk settings. *American Psychologist, 48,* 117–126.

Jimenez, R., Garcia, G., & Pearson, D. (1995). Three children, two languages, and strategic reading: Case studies in bilingual/monolingual reading. *American Educational Research Journal, 32*(1), 67–97.

John-Steiner, V., Panofsky, C., & Smith, L. (Eds.). (1994). *Sociocultural approaches to language and literacy.* New York: Cambridge University Press.

Johnson, R. (Ed.). (1995). *African-American voices: African-American health educators speak out.* New York: National League for Nursing.

Johnson, D. W., Johnson, R. T., & Maruyama, G. (1984). Goal interdependence and interpersonal attraction in heterogeneous classrooms: A meta-analysis. In N. Miller & M. B. Brewer (Eds.), *Groups in contact: The psychology of desegregation.* New York: Academic Press.

Johnston, F., Hamill, P., & Lemshow, S. (1974). *Skinfold thickness of youths 12–17 years.* U.S. Public Health Service Publication No. 132. Washington, D.C.: U.S. Government Printing Office.

Johnston, L., O'Malley, P., & Bachman, J. (1992). *Drug use among American high school students, college students and other young adults: National trends through 1991.* Rockville, Md.: National Institute on Drug Abuse.

Johnston, R. (1991). *Attention deficits, learning disabilities, and ritalin: A practical guide.* San Diego: Singular Publications.

Joshi, M., & MacLean, M. (1994). Indian and English children's understanding of the distinction between real and apparent emotion. *Child Development, 65,* 1372–1384.

Josselson, R. (1980). Ego development in adolescence. In J. Adelson (Ed.), *Handbook of adolescent psychology.* New York: Wiley.

Jusczyk, P., Bertancini, J., Bijeljac-Babac, R., Kennedy, L., & Mehler, J. (1990). The role of attention in speech perception by young infants. *Cognitive Development, 5,* 265–286.

Juvonen, J. (1991). Deviance, perceived responsibility, and negative peer reactions. *Developmental Psychology, 27,* 672–681.

Kagan, J. (1984). *The nature of the child.* New York: Basic Books.

Kagan, J. (1991). The theoretical utility of constructs for self. Special issue: The development of self: The first three years. *Developmental Review, 11,* 244–250.

Kagan, J., Arcus, D., Snidman, N., Feng, W. Y., Handler, J., & Greene, S. (1995). Reactivity in infants: A cross-national comparison. *Developmental Psychology, 30,* 342–345.

Kagan, J., & Snidman, N. (1991). Temperamental factors in human development. *American Psychologist, 46,* 856–862.

Kahlbaugh, P., & Haviland, J. (1991). Formal operational thinking and identity. In R. Lerner, A. Petersen, & J. Brooks-Gunn (Eds.), *Encyclopedia of adolescence: Vol. 1* (pp. 369–372). New York: Garland.

Kaitz, M., Meschulach-Sarfaty, O., Auerbach, J., & Eidelman, A. (1988). A re-examination of newborns' ability to imitate facial expressions. *Developmental Psychology, 24,* 3–7.

Kakar, S. (1982). *The inner world: A psychoanalytic study of childhood and society in India.* Delhi: Oxford University Press.

Kalverboer, A., Hopkins, B., & Geuze, R. (1993). *Motor development in early infancy and late childhood.* New York: Cambridge University Press.

Kamerman, S. B. (1991). Child care policies and programs: An international overview. *Journal of Social Issues, 47,* 179–196.

Kamin, L. M. (1995, February). Behind the curve. *Scientific American,* 99–103.

Kang, J. (1990). *Identity development in Korean-American college women.* Unpublished manuscript, Yale University.

Kao, G. (1995). Asian-Americans as model minorities? A look at their academic performance. *American Journal of Education, 103,* 121–159.

Kaplan, A., & Bean, J. (Eds.). (1976). *Beyond sex-role stereotypes: Readings toward a psychology of androgyny.* Boston: Little, Brown.

Kaplan, L. (1995). *No voice is ever wholly lost.* New York: Simon & Schuster.

Katz, P., & Zalk, S. (1978). Modification of children's racial attitudes. *Developmental Psychology, 14,* 447–461.

Kazdin, A. E. (1987). Treatment of antisocial behavior in children: Current status and future directions. *Psychological Bulletin, 102,* 187–203.

Kazdin, A. E. (1993). Adolescent mental health: Prevention, treatment and programs. *American Psychologist, 48,* 127–141.

Kazdin, A. E. (1994). *Behavior modification in applied settings* (5th ed.). Pacific Grove, Cal. Brooks/Cole.

Keating, D. (1991). Adolescent cognition. In R. Lerner, A. Peterson, & J. Brooks-Gunn (Eds.), *Encyclopedia of adolescence: Vol. 1* (pp. 119–129). New York: Garland.

Keefe, J., & Walberg, H. (Eds.). (1992). *Teaching for thinking.* Reston, Va.: National Association of Secondary School Principals.

Keefer, C., & Brazelton, T. (1994). *Child care and culture: Lessons from Africa.* New York: Cambridge University Press.

Keil, F. (1989). *Concepts, kinds, and cognitive development.* Cambridge, Mass.: MIT Press.

Keller, M., & Edelstein, W. (1993). The development of the moral self from childhood to adolescence. In G. Noam & T. Wren (Eds.), *The moral self* (pp. 310–336). Cambridge, Mass.: MIT Press.

Keller, M., & Wood, P. (1989). Development of friendship reasoning: A study of interindividual differences and intraindividual change. *Developmental Psychology, 25,* 820–826.

Kendall, D. B., Davies, M., Warus, D., & Yamaguchi, K. (1986). The consequences in young adulthood of adolescent drug involvement. *Archives of General Psychiatry, 43,* 746–754.

Kendall-Tackett, K. A., Williams, L. M., & Finkelhor, D. (1993). Impact of sexual abuse on children: A review and synthesis of recent empirical studies. *Psychological Bulletin, 113,* 164–180.

Kermoian, R., & Campos, J. (1988). Locomotor experience: A facilitator of spatial cognitive development. *Child Development, 59,* 908–917.

Kerr, M., Lambert, W. W., Stattin, H., & Klackenberg-Larsson, I. (1994). Stability of inhibition in a Swedish longitudinal sample. *Child Development, 65,* 138–146.

Kibler, W., & Chandler, T. (1993). Musculoskeletal adaptations and injuries associated with intense participation in youth sports. In B. Cahill & A. Pearl (Eds.), *Intensive participation in children's sports* (pp. 203–216). Champaign, Ill.: Human Kinetics Press.

Kinderman, T. A. (1993). Natural peer groups as contexts for individual development: The case of children's motivation in school. *Child Development, 29,* 970–977.

King, P., & Kitchener, K. (1994). *Developing reflective judgment.* San Francisco: Jossey-Bass.

Kisilevsky, B. S., & Muir, D. W. (1984). Neonatal habituation and dishabituation to tactile stimulation during sleep. *Developmental Psychology, 20,* 367–373.

Kisilevsky, B. S., Muir, D. W., & Low, J. A. (1992). Maturation of human fetal responses to vibroacoustic stimulation. *Child Development, 63,* 1497–1508.

Klahr, D. (1989). Information processing approaches. In R. Vasta (Ed.), *Annals of child development: Vol. 6. Six theories of child development* (pp. 133–187). Greenwich, Conn.: JAI Press.

Klein, H. (1995). Urban Appalachian children in northern schools: A study in diversity. *Young Children, 50(3),* 10–16.

Klimes-Dougan, B., & Kistner, J. (1990). Physically abused preschoolers' responses to peers' distress. *Developmental Psychology, 26,* 599–602.

Kline, M., Tschann, J. M., Johnston, J. R., & Wallerstein, J. S. (1989). Children's adjustment to joint and sole physical custody families. *Developmental Psychology, 25,* 430–438.

Klinnert, M. D., Emde, R. N., Butterfield, P., & Campos, J. J. (1986). Social referencing: The infant's use of emotional signals from a friendly adult with mother present. *Developmental Psychology, 22,* 427–432.

Knox, G. W. (1991). *An introduction to gangs.* Berrien Springs, Mich.: Vande Vere.

Koch, P. B. (1988). The relationship of first intercourse to later sexual functioning concerns of adolescents. *Journal of Adolescent Research, 3,* 345–362.

Kochanska, C., Casey, R. J., & Fukumoto, A. (1995). Toddlers' sensitivity to standard violations. *Child Development, 66,* 643–656.

Kochanska, G. (1992). Children's interpersonal influence with mothers and peers. *Developmental Psychology, 28,* 491–499.

Koff, E., Rierdan, J., & Stubbs, M. (1990). Gender, body image and self-concept in early adolescence. *Journal of Early Adolescence, 10,* 56–68.

Kohlberg, L. (1966). A cognitive-developmental view of sex-role development. In E. Maccoby (Ed.), *The development of sex differences.* Stanford, Cal.: Stanford University Press.

Kohlberg, L. (1976). Moral stages and moralization: The cognitive-developmental approach. In T. Lickona (Ed.), *Moral development and behavior.* New York: Holt, Rinehart and Winston.

Kohn, M. L. (1969). *Class and conformity: A study in values.* Homewood, Ill.: Dorsey Press.

Kohn, M. L., Slomczynski, K. M., & Schoenbach, C. (1986). Social stratification and the transmission of values in the family: A cross-national assessment. *Sociological Forum, 1,* 73–102.

Kontos, S. (1992). *Family day care: Out of the shadows and into the limelight.* Washington, D.C.: National Association for the Education of Young Children.

Kopp, C. (1982). Antecedents of self-regulation: A developmental perspective. *Developmental Psychology, 18,* 199–214.

Kopp, C., & Parmalee, A. (1979). Prenatal and perinatal influences on infant behavior. In J. Osofsky (Ed.), *Handbook of infant development.* New York: Wiley.

Koralek, D., Colker, L., & Dodge, D. (1993). *The what, why, and how of high-quality early childhood education: A guide for on-site supervision.* Washington, D.C.: National Association for the Education of Young Children.

Korbin, J. E. (1987). Child abuse and neglect: The cultural context. In R. E. Helfer & R. S. Kemp (Eds.), *The battered child* (4th ed.). Chicago: University of Chicago Press.

Korbin, J. E. (1991). Cross-cultural perspectives and research directions for the 21st century. *Child Abuse and Neglect, 15,* 67–77

Korner, A. (1987). Preventive intervention with high-risk newborns: Theoretical, conceptual, and methodological perspectives. In J. Osofsky (Ed.), *Handbook of infant development* (pp. 1006–1036). New York: Wiley.

Kostelnik, M. (1992). Myths associated with developmentally appropriate practice. *Young Children, 47(4),* 17–25.

Kotelchuck, M. (1976). The infant's relationship to the father: Experimental evidence. In M. E. Lamb (Ed.), *The role of the father in child development.* New York: Wiley.

Kotloff, L. (1993). Fostering cooperative group spirit and individuality: Examples from a Japanese preschool. *Young Children, 48(3),* 17–24.

Kozol, J. (1995). *Amazing Grace: The Lives of Children and the Conscience of the Nation.* New York: Crown Publishers.

Krasnor, L., & Rubin, K. (1983). Preschool social problem solving: Attempts and outcomes in naturalistic interaction. *Child Development, 54,* 1545–1558.

Krugman, R., & Davidson, H. (1990). *Child abuse and neglect: Critical first steps in response to a national emergency.* Washington, D.C.: Department of Health and Human Services, U.S. Advisory Board on Child Abuse and Neglect.

Kuhl, P., & Padden, D. (1983). Enhanced discriminability at the phonetic boundary for the place feature in macaques. *Journal of the Acoustical Society of America, 73,* 1003–1010.

Kupersmidt, J. B., Griesler, P. C., DeRosier, M. E., Patterson, C. J., & Davis, P. W. (1995). Childhood aggression and peer relations in the context of family and neighborhood factors. *Child Development, 66,* 360–375.

Kurdek, L. A., Fine, M. A., & Sinclair , R. J. (1995). School adjustment in sixth graders: Parenting transitions, family climate, and peer norm effects. *Child Development, 66,* 430–445.

Kurtz, S. (1992). *All the mothers are one: Hindu India and the cultural reshaping of psychoanalysis.* New York: Columbia University Press.

Kutner, L. (1989, March 16). Parent and child: Responding to aggressive behavior. *New York Times,* p. C–1.

Ladd, G. W., & Hart, C. H. (1992). Creating informal play opportunities: Are parents' and preschoolers' initiations related to children's competence with peers? *Developmental Psychology, 28,* 1179–1187.

Ladd, G. W., Price, J. M., & Hart, C. H. (1988). Predicting preschoolers' peer status from their playground behaviors. *Child Development, 59,* 986–992.

Lakoff, G. (1994). What is a conceptual system? In W. Overton & D. Palermo (Eds.), *The nature and ontogenesis of meaning* (pp. 41–90). Hillsdale, N.J.: Erlbaum.

La Leche League International. (1991). *The womanly art of breastfeeding* (5th ed.). New York: Plume Books.

Lamaze, F. (1970). *Painless childbirth: Psychoprophylactic method.* Chicago: Henry Regnery.

Lamb, M. (1977a). The development of mother-infant and father-infant attachments in the second year of life. *Developmental Psychology, 13,* 637–648.

Lamb, M. (1977b). Father-infant and mother-infant interactions in the first year of life. *Child Development, 48,* 167–181.

Lamb, M., Frodi, A., Hwang, C., & Steinberg, J. (1982). Mother- and father-infant interactions involving play and holding in traditional and nontraditional Swedish families. *Developmental Psychology, 18,* 215–221.

Lamb, M., Pleck, J. H., Charnov, E. L., & Levine, J. A. (1987). A biosocial perspective on paternal behavior and involvement. In J. B. Lancaster, J. Altmann, A. S. Rossi, & L. R. Sherrod (Eds.), *Parenting across the life span: Biosocial dimensions.* New York: Aldine de Gruyter.

Lamb, M., & Roopnarine, J. (1979). Peer influences on sex-role development in preschoolers. *Child Development, 50,* 1219–1222.

Lambert, W., Genesee, F., Holobow, N., & Chartrand, L. (1993). Bilingual education for majority English-speaking children. *European Journal of Psychology of Education, 8,* 3–22.

Lamke, L. K. (1982a) Adjustment and sex-role orientation. *Journal of Youth and Adolescence, 11,* 247–259.

Lamke, L. K. (1982b). The impact of sex-role orientation on self-esteem in early adolescence. *Child Development, 53,* 1530–1535.

Lancaster, J., & Hamburg, B. (1986). *School-age pregnancy and parenthood.* New York: DeGruyter.

Lane, C. (1994, December). The tainted sources of "The Bell Curve." *The New York Review of Books,* 14–19.

Langlois, J. (1992). The origins and functions of appearance-based stereotypes: Theoretical and applied implications. In R. Eder (Ed.), *Developmental perspectives in craniofacial problems.* New York: Springer-Verlag.

Langlois, J., Roggman, L., Casey, R., & Rieser-Danner, L. (1990). Infants' differential social responses to attractive and unattractive faces. *Developmental Psychology, 26,* 153–159.

Langlois, J., & Stephan, C. (1981). Beauty and the beast: The role of physical attractiveness in the development of peer relations and social behavior. In S. Brehm, S. Kassin, & F. Gibbons (Eds.), *Violence and the mass media.* New York: Harper and Row.

Lapsley, D. (1991). Egocentrism theory and the "new look" at the imaginary audience and personal fable. In R. Lerner, A. Petersen, & J. Brooks-Gunn (Eds.), *Encyclopedia of adolescence: Vol. 1* (pp. 281–286). New York: Garland.

Larrabee, M. (1993). *An ethic of care: Feminist and interdisciplinary perspectives.* New York: Routledge.

Larson, R., & Ham, M. (1993). Stress and "storm and stress" in early adolescence: The relationship of negative events with dysphoric affect. *Developmental Psychology, 29,* 130–140.

Larson, R., & Richards, M. H. (1991). Daily companionship in late childhood and early adolescence: Changing developmental contexts. *Child Development, 62,* 284–300.

Larson, R., & Richards, M. H. (1994). *Divergent realities: The emotional lives of mothers, fathers and adolescents.* New York: Basic Books.

Lasley, J. R. (1992). Age, social context, and street gang membership. *Youth and Society, 23,* 434–451.

Lawson, A., & Rhode, D. L. (1993). *The Politics of Pregnancy: Adolescent Sexuality and Public Policy.* New Haven, Conn.: Yale University Press.

Leadbetter, B. (1991). Relativistic thinking in adolescence. In R. Lerner, A. Petersen, & J. Brooks-Gunn (Eds.), *Encyclopedia of adolescence: Vol. 1* (pp. 921–925). New York: Garland.

Leahy, R. (1990). Development of concepts of economic and social inequality. In V. McLoyd & C. Flanagan (Eds.), *Economic stress: Effects on family life and child development.* San Francisco: Jossey-Bass.

Leary, W. E. (1995, January 31). Sickle cell trial called success, halted early. *The New York Times,* p. C–1.

Leavitt, R. (1991). Family day care licensing: Issues and recommendations. *Child Care and Youth Forum, 20,* 243–254.

Leboyer, F. (1975). *Birth without violence.* New York: Knopf.

Lee, F. R. (1995, May 9). For women with AIDS, anguish of having babies. *The New York Times,* pp. A1, B6.

Leifer, M. (1977). Psychological changes accompanying pregnancy and motherhood. *Genetic Psychology Monographs, 95,* 68.

Leigh, B. C. (1989). Reasons for having sex: Gender, sexual orientation, and relationship to sexual behavior. *Journal of Sex Research, 26,* 199–209.

Leon, G. R., & Dinklage, D. (1989). Obesity and anorexia nervosa. In T. H. Ollendick & M. Hersen (Eds.), *Handbook of child psychopathology* (2nd ed., pp. 247–263). New York: Plenum Press.

Lerner, J. (1993). *Learning disabilities* (6th ed.). Boston: Houghton Mifflin.

Lerner, R., Jovanovic, J., & Lerner, J. (1989). Objective and subjective attractiveness and early adolescent adjustment. *Journal of Adolescence, 12,* 225–229.

LeVay, S., & Hamer, D. H. (1994, May). Evidence for a biological influence in male homosexuality. *Scientific American,* 44–49.

Levine, G., & Parkinson, S. (1994). *Experimental methods in psychology.* Hillsdale, N.J.: Erlbaum.

Levine, R., Dixon, S., Levine, S., Richman, A., Leiderman, P., Levy, M., & *Schwartz* (Eds.). (1994). *Vagal control of the heart: Experimental basis and clinical implications.* Armonk, N.Y.: Futura Publishing Company.

Levitt, M. J., Guacci-Franco, N., & Levitt, J. L. (1993). Convoys of social support in childhood and early adolescence: Structure and function. *Developmental Psychology, 29,* 811–818.

Levy-Shiff, R. (1994). Individual and contextual correlates of marital change across the transition to parenthood. *Developmental Psychology, 30,* 591–601.

Lewis, C. T. (1993). Prenatal care in the United States. In B. K. Rothman (Ed.), *The encyclopedia of childbearing.* New York: Henry Holt.

Lewis, J. M. (1993). Childhood play in normality, pathology and therapy. *American Journal of Orthopsychiatry, 63,* 6–15.

Lewis, M. (1992). *Shame: The Exposed Self.* New York: The Free Press.

Lewis, M., & Brooks-Gunn, J. (1979a). *Social cognition and the acquisition of self.* New York: Plenum Press.

Lewis, M., & Brooks-Gunn, J. (1979b). Toward a theory of social cognition: The development of the self. In I. Uzgiris (Ed.), *Social interaction and communication during infancy.* San Francisco: Jossey-Bass.

Lewis, M., Brooks-Gunn, J., & Jaskir, J. (1985). Individual differences in visual self-recognition as a function of mother-infant attachment relationship. *Developmental Psychology, 21,* 1181–1187.

Lewis, M., Sullivan, M. W., Stanger, C., & Weiss, M. (1989). Self-development and self-conscious emotions. *Child Development, 60,* 146–156.

Lewkowicz, D., & Lickliter, R. (1994). *The development of intersensory perception.* Hillsdale, N.J.: Erlbaum.

Liebmann-Smith, J. (1993). Infertility: Overview. In B. K. Rothman (Ed.), *The encyclopedia of childbearing.* New York: Henry Holt.

Licht, B., & Dweck, C. (1984). Determinants of academic achievement: The interaction of children's achievement orientations with skill area. *Developmental Psychology, 20,* 628–632.

Lickona, T. (1991). Moral development in the elementary school classroom. In W. Kurtines & J. Gewirtz (Eds.), *Handbook of moral behavior and development: Vol. 3* (pp. 143–162). Hillsdale, N.J.: Erlbaum.

Liebert, R. M., & Sprafkin, J. (1988). *The early window: Effects of television on children and youth* (3rd ed.).New York: Pergamon Press.

Liem, R., & Liem, J. H. (1988). Psychological effects of unemployment on workers and their families. *Journal of Social Issues, 44,* 87–105.

Lightfoot, S. L. (1983). *The good high school: Portraits of character and culture.* New York: Basic Books.

Lindblad-Goldberg, M. (1989). Successful minority single-parent families. In L. Combrinck-Graham (Ed.), *Children in family contexts* (pp. 116–134). New York: Guilford.

Lindell, S. G. (1988). Education for childbirth: A time for change. *Journal of Obstetrics, Gynecology, and Neonatal Nursing, 17,* 108–112.

Linn, S., Lieverman, E., Schoenbaum, S. C., Monson, R. R., Stubblefield, P. G., & Ryan, K. (1988). Adverse outcomes of pregnancy in women exposed to diethylstilbestrol in utero. *Journal of Reproductive Medicine, 33,* 3–7.

Linney, J. A., & Seidman, E. (1989). The future of schooling. *American Psychologist, 44,* 336–340.

Lipsitt, L. (1990). Learning and memory in infants. *Merrill-Palmer Quarterly, 35,* 53–66.

Lipsitt, L., & Kaye, H. (1964). Conditioned sucking in the newborn. *Psychonomic Science, 1,* 29–30.

Livson, N., & Peskin, H. (1981a). Perspectives on adolescence from longitudinal research. In J. Adelson (Ed.), *Handbook of adolescent psychology.* New York: Wiley.

Livson, N., & Peskin, H. (1981b). Psychological health at 40: Predictions from adolescent personality. In D. Eichorn, J. Clausen, N. Haan, M. Honzik, & P. Mussen (Eds.), *Present and past in middle life.* New York: Academic Press.

Loeb, R. C., Horst, L., & Horton, P. J. (1980). Family interaction patterns associated with self-esteem in preadolescent girls and boys. *Merrill-Palmer Quarterly, 26,* 203–217.

Logan, D. D. (1980). The menarche experience in twenty-three foreign countries. *Adolescence, 58,* 247–257.

Londerville, S., & Main, M. (1981). Security of attachment, compliance, and maternal training methods. *Developmental Psychology, 17,* 289–299.

Lorenz, K. (Ed.). (1970). *Studies in animal and human behavior: Vol. 1.* Cambridge, Mass.: Harvard University Press.

Lozoff, B. (1989). Nutrition and behavior. *American Psychologist, 44,* 231–236.

Ludington, S., Hadeed, A., & Anderson, G. (1990). Physiological response to skin-to-skin contact in hospitalized premature infants. *Journal of Perinatology, 11,* 19.

Luria, A. R. (1976). *Cognitive development: Its cultural and social foundations.* Cambridge, Mass.: Harvard University Press.

Luster, T., & Okagaki, L. (1993). *Parenting: An ecological perspective.* Hillsdale, N.J.: Erlbaum.

Lustig, M., & Koester, J. (1993). *Intercultural competence: Interpersonal communication across cultures.* New York: HarperCollins.

Lutz, P. (1983). The stepfamily: An adolescent perspective. *Family Relations, 32,* 367–376.

Lyon, G. (1993). *Better understanding learning disabilities: New views for research and their implications for education and public policy.* Baltimore: Paul Brookes.

Lytinen, P. (1991). Developmental trends in children's pretend play. *Child Care, Health and Development, 17,* 9–25.

Lytton, H., & Romney, D. M. (1991). Parents' sex-related differential socialization of boys and girls: A meta-analysis. *Psychological Bulletin, 109,* 267–296.

Maccoby, E. E. (1980). *Social development, psychological growth, and parent-child relations.* New York: Harcourt Brace Jovanovich.

Maccoby, E. E. (1984). Socialization and developmental change. *Child Development, 55,* 317–328.

Maccoby, E. E. (1990). Gender and relationships: A developmental account. *American Psychologist, 45,* 513–520.

Maccoby, E. E., & Jacklin, C. (1974). *The psychology of sex differences.* Stanford, Cal.: Stanford University Press.

Maccoby, E. E., & Jacklin, C. (1980). Sex differences in aggression: A rejoinder and reprise. *Child Development, 48,* 964–980.

Maccoby, E. E., & Jacklin, C. (1987). Gender segregation in childhood. In H. Reese (Ed.), *Advances in child development and behavior: Vol. 20.* New York: Academic Press.

Maccoby, E. E., & Martin, J. A. (1983). Socialization in the context of the family: Parent-child interaction. In E. M. Hetherington (Ed.), *Handbook of child psychology: Vol. 4. Socialization, personality, and social development* (4th ed., pp. 1–101). New York: Wiley.

MacGregor, S. N., Keith, L. G., Chasnoff, I. J., Rosner, M. A., Chisum, G. M., Shaw, P., & Minogue, J. P. (1987). Cocaine use during pregnancy: Adverse perinatal outcome. *American Journal of Obstetrics and Gynecology, 1,* 66–90.

Mahler, M., Pine, F., & Bergman, A. (1975). *The psychological birth of the human infant: Symbiosis and individuation.* New York: Basic Books.

Main, M., & George, C. (1985). Responses of abused and disadvantaged toddlers to distress in agemates: A study in the day care setting. *Developmental Psychology, 21,* 407–412.

Main, M., & Goldwyn, R. (1989). Predicting rejection of her infant from mother's representation of her own experience: Implications for the abused-abusing intergenerational cycle. *Child Abuse and Neglect, 8,* 203–217.

Main, M., Kaplan, N., & Cassidy, J. (1985). Security in infancy, childhood, and adulthood: A move to the level of representation. In I. Bretherton & E. Waters (Eds.), *Growing points of attachment theory and research. Monographs of the Society for Research on Child Development, 50*(209).

Maker, J. (Ed.). (1993). *Programs for the gifted in regular classrooms.* Austin, Tex.: Pro-Ed Publishers.

Makin, J., & Porter, R. (1989). Attractiveness of lactating females' breast odors to neonates. *Child Development, 60,* 803–810.

Malatesta, C. A., Culver, C., Tesman, J. R., & Shepard, B. (1989). The development of emotion expression during the first two years of life. *Monographs of the Society for Research in Child Development, 54,* 1–140.

Malina, R. M. (1979). Secular changes in size and maturity: Causes and effects. In A. F. Roche (Ed.), Secular trends in human growth, maturation, and development. *Monographs of the Society for Research in Child Development, 44*(Whole No. 3–4).

Malina, R. M. (1990). Physical growth and performance during the transition years (9–16). In R. Montemayor, G. R. Adams, & T. P. Gullotta (Eds.), *From childhood to adolescence: A transitional period?* (pp. 41–62). Newbury Park, Cal.: Sage.

Malina,, R. M., & Bouchard, C. (1991). *Growth, maturation, and physical activity.* Champaign, Ill.: Human Kinetics Books.

Malinosky-Rummell, R., & Hansen, D. J. (1993). Long-term consequences of childhood physical abuse. *Psychological Bulletin, 114,* 68–79.

Mallory, G., & New, R. (Eds.). (1994). *Diversity and developmentally appropriate practice: Challenges for early childhood education.* New York: Teachers' College Press.

Maloney, M. J., & Klykylo, W. M. (1983). An overview of anorexia nervosa, bulimia and obesity in children and adolescents. *Journal of the American Academy of Child Psychiatry, 22,* 99–107.

Mandel, J. L., Monaco, A. P., Nelso, D. L., Schlessinger, D., & Willard, H. (1992). Genome analysis and the human X chromosome. *Science, 258,* 103–109.

Mandler, J. (1988). How to build a baby: On the development of an accessible representational system. *Cognitive Development, 3,* 113–136.

Marcia, J. (1967). Ego identity status: Relationship to change in self-esteem, "general maladjustment," and authoritarianism. *Journal of Personality, 35,* 119–133.

Marcia, J. (1980). Identity in adolescence. In J. Adelson (Ed.), *Handbook of adolescent psychology.* New York: Wiley.

Marcus, D., & Overton, W. (1978). The development of cognitive gender constancy and sex role preferences. *Child Development, 49,* 434–444.

Marcus, G., Pinker, S., Ullman, M., Hollander, M., Rosen, T., & Xu, F. (1992). Overregularization in language acquisition. *Monographs of the Society for Research on Child Development, 57*(4, Serial No. 228).

Margolin, L. (1994). *Goodness personified: The emergence of gifted children.* New York: Aldine de Gruyter.

Markman, H. J., & Kadushin, F. S. (1986). Preventive effects of Lamaze training for first-time parents: A short-term longitudinal study. *Journal of Consulting and Clinical Psychology, 54,* 872–874.

Marks, L., Hammeal, R., & Bornstein, M. (1987). Similarity and comprehending metaphor. *Monographs of the Society for Research in Child Development, 52*(1, Serial No. 215).

Marschark, M. (1993). *Psychological development of deaf children.* New York: Oxford.

Marshall, W. (1978). Puberty. In F. Falkner & J. Tanner (Eds.), *Human growth: Vol. 2.* New York: Plenum Press.

Marshall, W., & Tanner, J. (1974). Puberty. In J. Davis & J. Dobbing (Eds.), *Scientific foundations of pediatrics.* London: Heinemann Publishers.

Martin, B. (1975). Parent-child relations. In F. Horowitz (Ed.), *Review of child development research: Vol. 4.* Chicago: University of Chicago Press.

Martin, C. L., Wood, C. H., & Little, J. K. (1990). The development of gender stereotype components. *Child Development, 61,* 1891–1904.

Matas, L., Arend, R. A., & Sroufe, L. A. (1978). Continuity of adaptation in the second year: The relationship between quality of attachment and later competence. *Child Development, 49,* 547–555.

Maziade, M., Boudreault, M., Copte, R., & Thivierge, J. (1986). Influence of gentle birth delivery procedures and other perinatal circumstances on infant temperament: Developmental and social implications. *Journal of Pediatrics, 108,* 134–136.

Mazzocco, M. M., Nord, A. M., Van-Doorninck, W., Greene, C. L., et al. (1994). Cognitive development among children with early-treated phenylketonuria. *Developmental Neuropsychology, 10,* 133–151.

McCabe, A., & Lipscomb, T. J. (1988). Sex differences in children's verbal aggression. *Merrill-Palmer Quarterly, 34,* 389–401.

McCall, R. (1981). Nature-nurture and the two realms of development: A proposed integration with respect to mental development. *Child Development, 52,* 1–12.

McCall, R., & Kagan, J. (1967). Stimulus schema discrepancy and attention in the infant. *Journal of Experimental Child Psychology, 5,* 381–390.

McCauley, E., Kay, T., Ito, J., & Treder, R. (1987). The Turner syndrome: Cognitive deficits, affective discrimination, and behavior problems. *Child Development, 58,* 464–473.

McCullough, M., & Scherman, A. (1991). Adolescent pregnancy: Contributing factors and strategies for prevention. *Adolescence, 26,* 809–816.

McDaniel, K. D. (1986). Pharmacological treatment of psychiatric and neuro-developmental disorders in children and adolescents (Parts 1, 2, & 3). *Clinical Pediatrics, 25,* 65–71, 198–224.

McDonald, A. D., Armstrong, B. G., & Sloan, M. (1992a). Cigarette, alcohol, and coffee consumption and congenital defects. *American Journal of Public Health, 82,* 91.

McDonald, M., Sigman, M., Espinosa, M., & Neumann, C. (1994). Impact of a temporary food shortage on children and their mothers. *Child Development, 65,* 404–415.

McGoldrick, M., Pearce, J. K., & Giordano, J. (Eds.). (1982). *Ethnicity and family therapy.* New York: Guilford.

McGrath, P. (1990). *Pain in childhood: Nature, assessment and treatment.* New York: Guildford Press.

McKay, S. (1993). Labor: Overview. In B. K. Rothman, (Ed.)., *The encyclopedia of childbearing.* New York: Henry Holt.

McKenzie, C. (1983). Risk factors in perinatology. In C. McKenzie & K. Vestal (Eds.), *High-risk perinatal nursing.* Philadelphia: Saunders.

McKussick, V. A. (1988). *Mendelian inheritance in man: Catalogues of autosomal dominant, autosomal recessive, and X-linked phenotypes* (7th ed.). Baltimore: Johns Hopkins University Press.

McLoyd, V. C. (1989). Socialization and development in a changing economy: The effects of paternal job and income loss on children. *American Psychologist, 44,* 243–252.

McNamara, T., Miller, D., & Bransford, J. (1991). Mental models and the construction of meaning. In P. Pearson (Ed.), *Handbook of reading research: Vol. 2* (pp. 490–511). New York: Longman.

McTigue, J. (1993). Endometriosis. In B. K. Rothman (Ed.), *The encyclopedia of childbearing.* New York: Henry Holt.

Meehan, P. J., Lamb, J. A., Saltzman, L. E., & O'Carroll, P. W. (1992). Attempted suicide among young adults: Progress toward a meaningful estimate of prevalence. *American Journal of Psychiatry, 149,* 41–44.

Meilman, P. (1979). Cross-sectional age changes in ego identity status during adolescence. *Developmental Psychology, 15,* 230–231.

Melamed, B., Hawes, R., Heiby, E., & Glick, J. (1975). Use of filmed modeling to reduce uncooperative behavior of children during dental treatment. *Journal of Dental Research, 54,* 797–801.

Meltzoff, A., & Kuhl, P. (1994). Faces and speech: Inter-model processing of biologically relevant signals in infants and adults. In D. Lewkowicz & R. Lickliter (Eds.), *The development of intersensory perception* (pp. 335–370). Hillsdale, N.J.: Erlbaum.

Meltzoff, A., Kuhl, P., & Moore, M. K. (1991). Perception, representation, and control of action in newborns and young infants. In M. Weiss & P. Zelazo (Eds.), *Newborn attention: Biological constraints and the influence of experience* (pp. 377–411). Norwood, N.J.: Ablex.

Menkes, J. (1994). *Textbook of child neurology* (5th ed.). Philadelphia: Williams and Wilkins.

Meredith, H. (1967). A synopsis of pubertal changes in youth. *Journal of School Health, 37,* 171–176.

Mervis, C., Johnson, K., & Scott, P. (1993). Perceptual knowledge, conceptual knowledge, and expertise. *Cognitive Development, 8,* 194–156.

Messer, D. (1994). *The development of communication: From social interaction to language.* New York: Wiley.

Messner, M., & Sabo, D. (1994). *Sex, violence, and power in sports.* Freedom, Cal.: Crossing Press.

Metz, K. (1995). Reassessment of developmental constraints on children's science instruction. *Review of Educational Research, 65*(2), 93–128.

Michelsson, K., Rinne, A., & Paajanen, S. (1990). Crying, feeding and sleeping patterns in 1 to 12-month-old infants. *Child: Care, health and development, 116,* 99–111.

Miller, A. (1990). *For your own good: Hidden cruelty in child-rearing and the roots of violence.* New York: Noonday Press.

Miller, B. C., & Moore, K. A. (1990). Adolescent sexual behavior, pregnancy, and parenting: Research through the 1980's. *Journal of Marriage and the Family, 52,* 1025–1044.

Miller, M. A. (1993). Smoking in pregnancy. In B. K. Rothman (Ed.), *The encyclopedia of childbearing.* New York: Henry Holt.

Miller, P. (1990). The development of strategies of selective attention. In D. Bjorklund (Ed.), *Children's strategies* (pp. 157–184). Hillsdale, N.J.: Erlbaum.

Miller, P., & Simon, W. (1980). The development of sexuality in adolescence. In J. Adelson (Ed.), *Handbook of adolescent psychology.* New York: Wiley.

Miller, P. H. (1993). *Theories of developmental psychology* (3rd ed.). New York: W. H. Freeman.

Miller, W. B. (1990). Why the United States has failed to solve its youth gang problem. In C. R. Huff (Ed.), *Gangs in America* (pp. 263–287). Newbury Park, Cal.: Sage.

Mills, R. S. L., & Rubin, K. H. (1990). Parental beliefs about problematic behavior in early childhood. *Child Development, 61,* 138–151.

Millstein, S. G. (1989). Adolescent health: Challenges for behavioral scientists. *American Psychologist, 44,* 837–842.

Minuchin, P., & Shapiro, E. (1983). The school as a context for social development. In E. M. Hetherington (Ed.), *Handbook of child psychology: Vol. 4. Socialization, personality and social development* (4th ed.). New York: Wiley.

Mistretta, C., & Bradley, R. (1985). Development of the sense of taste. In E. Blass (Ed.), *Handbook of behavioral neurobiology* (pp. 205–236). New York: Plenum Press.

Moerk, E. (1992). *A first language taught and learned.* Baltimore: Paul Brookes.

Mogford, K. (1993). Language development in twins. In D. Bishop & K. Mogford (Eds.), *Language development in exceptional circumstances* (pp. 80–95). Hillsdale, N.J.: Erlbaum.

Molfese, D., Burger-Judisch, L., & Hans, L. (1991). Consonant discrimination by newborn infants: Electrophysical differences. *Developmental Neuropsychology, 7,* 177–195.

Moll, L. C. (Ed.). (1990). *Vygotsky and education: Instructional implications and applications of sociohistorical psychology.* Cambridge, U.K.: Cambridge University Press.

Money, J. (1992). *The Kasper Hauser syndrome of "psychosocial dwarfism": Deficient statural, intellectual and social growth induced by child abuse.* Buffalo, N.Y.: Prometheus Books.

Montagu, A. (Ed.) (1975). *Race and IQ.* New York: Oxford University Press.

Montessori, M. (1964). *The Montessori method.* New York: Schocken Books.

Moore, D. (1984). Parent-adolescent separation: Intrafamilial perceptions and difficulty separating from parents. *Personality and Social Psychology Bulletin, 10,* 611–619.

Moore, D. (1987). Parent-adolescent separation: The construction of adulthood by late adolescents. *Developmental Psychology, 23,* 298–307.

Moore, K. L. (1983). *Before We Are Born: Basic Embryology and Birth Defects* (2nd ed.). New York: Saunders.

Moorehouse, M. J. (1991). Linking maternal employment patterns to mother-child activities and children's school competence. *Developmental Psychology, 27,* 295–303.

Moran, E. G. (1993). Domestic violence and pregnancy. In B. K. Rothman (Ed.), *The encyclopedia of childbearing.* New York: Henry Holt.

Morrison, D. M. (1985). Adolescent contraceptive behavior: A review. *Psychological Bulletin, 98,* 538–568.

Morrongiello, B. (1994). Effects of colocation on auditory-visual interactions and cross-modality perception in infants. In D. Lewkowicz & R. Lickliter (Eds.), *The development of intersensory perception* (pp. 235–264). Hillsdale, N.J.: Erlbaum.

Morrow, L. (1993). *Literacy development in the early years* (2nd ed.). Boston: Allyn & Bacon.

Morse, J. M., & Park, C. (1988). Differences in cultural expectations of the perceived painfulness of childbirth. In K. L. Michaelson (Ed.), *Childbirth in America: Anthropological perspectives.* South Hadley, Mass.: Bergin & Garvey.

Mortimer, J. T., Finch, M., Shanahan, M., & Ryu, S. (1992a). Work experience, mental health, and behavioral adjustment in adolescence. *Journal of Research in Adolescence, 2,* 25–57.

Mortimer, J. T., Finch, M., Shanahan, M., & Ryu, S. (1992b). Adolescent work history and behavioral adjustment. *Journal of Research in Adolescence, 2,* 59–80.

Mosier, C. E., & Rogoff, B. (1994). Infants' instrumental use of their mothers to achieve their goals. *Child Development, 65,* 70–79.

Muehlenhard, C., & Linton, M. (1987). Date rape. *Journal of Counseling Psychology, 34,* 186–196.

Muir, B. (1983). *Essentials of genetics for nurses.* New York: Wiley.

Munroe, R., Munroe, R., & Whiting, J. (1981). Male sex-role resolutions. In *Handbook of cross-cultural human development.* New York: Garland.

Murphy, L. (1937). *Social behavior and child personality.* New York: Columbia University Press.

Murstein, B. L., Chalpin, M. J., Heard, K. V., & Vyse, S. A. (1989). Sexual behavior, drug, and relationship patterns on a college campus over thirteen years. *Adolescence, 24,* 125–139.

Myers, J. (1993). Curricular designs that resonate with adolescents' ways of knowing. In R. Lerner (Ed.), *Early adolescence: Perspectives on research, policy, and intervention* (pp. 191–206). Hillsdale, N.J.: Erlbaum.

Nagata, D. (1989). Japanese-American children and adolescents. In J. Gibbs & L. Huang (Eds.), *Children of color* (pp. 67–113). San Francisco: Jossey-Bass.

National Safety Council. (1995). *Accident facts: 1994.* Chicago: Author.

Nelson, M. (1991). A study of family day care providers: Attitudes toward regulation. *Child Care and Youth Quarterly, 20,* 225–242.

Nelson, N. M., Murray, W. E., Saroj, S., Bennet, K. J., Milner, R., & Sackett, D. L. (1980). A randomized clinical trial of the Leboyer approach to childbirth. *New England Journal of Medicine, 303,* 655–660.

Newcomb, M., & Bentler, P. (1989). Substance use and abuse among children and teenagers. *American Psychologist, 44,* 242–248.

Newman, F., & Holzman, L. (1993). *Lev Vygotsky: Revolutionary scientist.* New York: Routledge.

New York Times. (1993, Feb. 5). Family leave, p. A8.

New York Times (1995a, April 7). Use of alcohol linked to rise in fetal illness, p. A27.

New York Times (1995b, April 13). 5,600 infant deaths tied to mothers' smoking, p. A–23.

Neyzi, O., Alp, H., & Orhon, A. (1975). Sexual maturation in Turkish boys and girls. *Annals of Human Biology, 2,* 249–251.

Nichols, J., Nelson, J., & Gleaves, K. (1995). Learning "facts" versus learning that most questions have many answers: Student evaluations of contrasting curricula. *Journal of Educational Psychology, 87*(2), 253–260.

Noam, G., & Wren, T. (1993). *The moral self.* Cambridge, Mass.: MIT Press.

Noddings, N. (1992). *The challenge to care in schools.* New York: Teachers' College Press.

Noddings, N. (1993). *Educating for intelligent belief or unbelief.* New York: Teachers' College Press.

Nolen-Hoeksema, S., Wolfson, A., Mumme, D., & Guskin, K. (1995). Helplessness in children of depressed and nondepressed mothers. *Developmental Psychology, 31,* 377–387.

Noppe, I. C., Noppe, L. D., & Hughes, F. P. (1991). Stress as a predictor of the quality of parent-infant interactions. *Journal of Genetic Psychology, 152,* 17–28.

Norbeck, J. S., & Tilden, V. P. (1983). Life stress, social support and emotional disequilibrium in complications of pregnancy: A prospective multivariate study. *Journal of Health and Social Behavior, 24,* 30–46.

Norman, C. (1988). Math education: A mixed picture. *Science, 241,* 408–409.

Nucci, L., & Turiel, E. (1993). God's word, religious rules, and their relation to Christian and Jewish children's concepts of morality. *Child Development, 64,* 1475–1491.

O'Brien, S. F., & Bierman, K. L. (1988). Conceptions and perceived influence of peer groups: Interviews with preadolescents and adolescents. *Child Development, 59,* 1360–1365.

O'Donnell, J., Hawkins, J. D., Catalano, R. F., Abbott, R. D., & Day, L. E. (1995). Preventing school failure, drug use and delinquency among low-income children: Long-term intervention in elementary schools. *American Journal of Orthopsychiatry, 65,* 87–100.

Offer, D., Ostrov, E., Howard, K. I., & Atkinson, R. (1988). *The teenage world: Adolescent's self-image in ten countries.* New York: Plenum Press.

Offer, D., & Schonert-Reichl, K. A. (1992). Debunking the myths of adolescence: Findings from recent research. *Journal of the American Academy of Child and Adolescent Psychiatry, 31,* 1003–1014.

O'Hara-Devereaux, M., & Johansen, R. (1994). *Globalwork: Bridging distance, culture, and time.* San Francisco: Jossey-Bass.

Olds, D. (1988). The prenatal/early infancy project. In R. H. Price, E. L. Cowen, R. P. Lorion, & J. Ramos-McKay (Eds.), *14 Ounces of Prevention.* Washington, D.C.: American Psychological Association.

Olsho, L., Koch, E., & Carter, E. (1988). Nonsensory factors in infant frequency discrimination. *Infant behavior and development, 11,* 205–222.

Olver, R., & Ratner, N. (1994). Children's understanding of false beliefs in two contexts. *Psychological Reports, 75,* 1136–1138.

Olvera-Ezzell, N., Power, T., Cousins, J., Guerra, A., & Trujillo, M. (1994). The development of health knowledge in low-income Mexican-American children. *Child Development, 65,* 416–427.

Omer, H., & Everly, G. S. (1988). Psychological factors in preterm labor: Critical review and theoretical synthesis. *American Journal of Psychiatry, 145,* 1507–1513.

Ontario Ministry of Culture, Tourism, and Recreation. (1994). *Policy on full and fair access for women and girls in sport and physical activity.* Toronto: Author.

Opie, I., & Opie, P. (1969). *Children's games in streets and playgrounds.* London: Clarendon Press.

Orenstein, P. (1995, June 18). Looking for a donor to call dad. *The New York Times,* pp. 28–35, 42, 50, 58.

Orlick, T. D. (1981). Positive socialization via cooperative games. *Developmental Psychology, 17,* 426–429.

Oster, H., Hegley, D., & Nagel, L. (1992). Adult judgments and fine-grained analysis of infant facial expressions: Testing the validity of a priori coding formulas. *Developmental Psychology, 28,* 1115–1131.

Overton, W. (1994). Contexts of meaning: The computational and the embodied mind. In W. Overton & D. Palermo (Eds.), *The nature and ontogenesis of meaning* (pp. 1–18). Hillsdale, N.J.: Erlbaum.

Page, D. C., Mosher, R., Simpson, E. M., Fisher, E. M., Mardon, G., Pillack, J., McGillivray, B., de la Chapelle, A., & Brown, L. G. (1987). The sex-determining region of the human Y chromosome encodes a finer protein. *Cell, 51,* 1091–1104.

Parke, R. D. (1981). *Fathers.* Cambridge, Mass.: Harvard University Press.

Parke, R. D., MacDonald, K. B., Beitel, A., & Bhavnagri, N. (1988). The role of the family in the development of peer relationships. In R. DeV. Peters & R. J. McMahan (Eds.), *Marriages and families: Behavioral treatment and processes.* New York: Brunner/Mazel.

Parke, R. D., Ornstein, P., Rieser, J., & Zahn-Waxler, C. (1994). The past as prologue: An overview of a century of developmental psychology. In R. Parke, P. Ornstein, J. Rieser, & C. Zahn-Waxler (Eds.), *A century of developmental psychology* (pp. 1–70). Washington, D.C.: American Psychological Association.

Parker, J. G. & Asher, S. R. (1993). Friendship and friendship quality in middle childhood: Links with peer group acceptance and feelings of loneliness and social dissatisfaction. *Developmental Psychology, 29,* 611–621.

Parkhurst, J. T., & Asher, S. R. (1992). Peer rejection in middle school: Subgroup differences in behavior, loneliness, and interpersonal concerns. *Developmental Psychology, 28,* 231–242.

Parkins, E. (1990). *Equilibration, mind and brain: Toward an integrated psychology.* New York: Praeger.

Parten, M. (1932). Social play among preschool children. *Journal of Abnormal and Social Psychology, 27,* 243–269.

Patterson, C. J. (1995). Sexual orientation and human development: An overview. *Developmental Psychology, 31,* 3–11.

Patterson, G. R. (1976). The aggressive child: Victim and architect of a coercive system. In L. Hammerlyck, E. Marsh, & L. Handy (Eds.), *Behavior modification and families.* New York: Brunner/Mazel.

Patterson, G. R. (1982). *Coercive family processes.* Eugene, Ore.: Castilia Press.

Patterson, G. R., DeBaryshe, B. D., & Ramsey, E. (1989). A developmental perspective on antisocial behavior. *American Psychologist, 44,* 329–340.

Patterson, G. R., & Dishion, T. J. (1985). Contributions of families and peers to delinquency. *Criminology, 23,* 63–79.

Paulston, C. (Ed.). (1988). *International handbook of bilingualism and bilingual education.* New York: Greenwood Press.

Paulston, C. (1992). *Linguistic and communicative competence: Topics in ESL.* Philadelphia: Multilingual Matters Ltd.

Pease-Alvarez, L. (1993). *Moving in and out of bilingualism: Investigating native language maintenance and shift in Mexican-descent children.* Santa Cruz, Cal.: National Center for Research on Cultural Diversity, University of California.

Pence, A., & Goelman, H. (1991). The relationship of regulation, training, and motivation to quality of care in family day care. *Child Care and Youth Forum, 20*(2), 83–101.

Penner, S. (1987). Parental responses to grammatical and ungrammatical child utterances. *Child Development, 58,* 376–384.

Perez, B., & Torres-Guzman, M. (1992). *Learning in two worlds: An integrated Spanish/English biliteracy approach.* New York: Longman.

Perkins, D. (1992). *Smart schools.* New York: The Free Press.

Peskin, H. (1973). Influence of the developmental schedule of puberty on learning and ego functioning. *Journal of Youth and Adolescence, 2,* 273–290.

Peterson, A. C. (1987). The nature of biological-psychosocial interactions: The sample case of early adolescence. In R. M. Lerner & T. T. Foch (Eds.), *Biological-psychosocial interactions in early adolescence* (pp. 35–61). Hillsdale, N.J.: Erlbaum.

Petersen, A. C., Compas, B. E., Brooks-Gunn, J., Stemmler, M. E., & Grant, K. E. (1993). Depression in adolescence. *American Psychologist, 48,* 155–168.

Petersen, A. C., & Taylor, B. (1980). The biological approach to adolescence. In J. Adelson (Ed.), *Handbook of adolescent psychology.* New York: Wiley.

Peterson, G. H., Mehl, L. E., & Leiderman, P. T. (1979). The role of some birth related variables in father attachment. *American Journal of Orthopsychiatry, 49,* 330–339.

Pettit, G., Dodge, K., & Brown, N. (1988). Early family experience, social problem solving patterns, and children's social competence. *Child Development, 59,* 107–120.

Pettito, L., & Marentette, P. (1991). Babbling in the manual code: Evidence for the ontogeny of language. *Science, 251,* 1493–1496.

Phelan, J. (Ed.). (1992). *Prevention of prematurity.* Philadelphia: Saunders.

Philadelphia Child Guidance Center. (1994). *Your child's emotional health: The middle years.* New York: Macmillan.

Phinney, J. S. (1989). Stages of ethnic identity development in minority group adolescents. *Journal of Early Adolescence, 9,* 34–49.

Phinney, J. S., Feshbach, N. D., & Farer, J. (1986). Preschool children's response to peer crying. *Early Childhood Research Quarterly, 1,* 207–219.

Piaget, J. (1952). *The child's conception of number.* New York: Norton.

Piaget, J. (1959). *The language and thought of the child* (M. Gabain, trans.). London: Routledge & Kegan Paul.

Piaget, J. (1962). *Play, dreams, and imitation in childhood.* New York: Norton.

Piaget, J. (1963). *The origins of intelligence in children.* New York: Norton.

Piaget, J. (1964). *The moral judgment of the child.* New York: The Free Press.

Piaget, J. (1965). *The child's conception of the world.* Totowa, N.J.: Littlefield, Adams.

Piaget, J. (1970). Piaget's theory. In P. Mussen (Ed.), *Carmichael's manual of child psychology* (3rd ed., vol. 1). New York: Wiley.

Piaget, J. (1970). *The science of education and the psychology of the child.* New York: Viking.

Piaget, J. (1983). Piaget's theory. In P. Mussen (Ed.), *Handbook of child psychology: Vol. 1.* New York: Wiley.

Piaget, J., & Inhelder, B. (1971). *Science of education and the psychology of the child.* New York: Viking.

Piaget, J., & Inhelder, B. (1973). *Memory and intelligence.* New York: Basic Books.

Pianta, R., Egeland, B., & Erikson, M. (1989). The effects of maltreatment on the development of young children. In D. Cicchetti & V. Carlson (Eds.), *Child Maltreatment.* New York: Cambridge University Press.

Piatelli-Palmarini, L. (1994). Ever since language and learning: Afterthoughts on the Piaget-Chomsky debate. *Cognition, 50,* 315–346.

Pinon, M. F., Huston, A. C., & Wright, J. C. (1989). Family ecology and child characteristics that predict young children's educational television viewing. *Child Development, 60,* 846–856.

Pinstrup-Anderson, P., Pelletier, D., & Alderman, H. (Eds.). (1995). *Children's growth and nutrition in developing countries.* Ithaca, N.Y.: Cornell University Press.

Pittman, T., & Kaufman, M. (1994). *All shapes and sizes: Promoting fitness and self-esteem in your overweight child.* Toronto: Harper Perennial Books.

Plomin, R. (1989). Environment and genes: Determinants of behavior. *American Psychologist, 44,* 105–111.

Plomin, R. (1990). *Nature and nurture: An introduction to human behavioral genetics.* Pacific Grove, Cal.: Brooks/Cole.

Plomin, R., Emde, R., Braungart, J., Campos, J., Corley, R., Fulker, D., Kagan, J., Resnick, J., Robinson, J., Zahn-Waxler, C., & DeFries, J. (1993). Genetic change and continuity from 14 to 20 months. *Child Development, 64,* 1354–1376.

Plomin, R., McClearn, G. E., Pederson, N. L., Nesselroade, J. R., & Bereman, C. S. (1988). Genetic influence on childhood family environment perceived retrospectively from the last half of the life span. *Developmental Psychology, 24,* 738–745.

Plomin, R., & Rowe, D. (1979). Genetic and environmental etiology of social behavior in infancy. *Developmental Psychology, 15,* 62–72.

Poest, C., Williams, J., Witt, D., & Atwood, M. (1990). Challenge me to move: Large muscle development in young children. *Young Children, 45*(5), 4–10.

Poissonet, C., LaValle, M., & Burdi, A. (1988). Growth and development of adipose tissue. *Journal of Pediatrics, 113,* 1–9.

Pollitt, E. (1987). Effects of iron deficiency on mental development. In F. Johnston (Ed.), *Nutritional anthropology.* New York: Alan R. Liss.

Pollitt, E., Garza, C., & Leibel, R. (1984). Nutrition and public policy. In H. Stevenson & A. Siegel (Eds.), *Child development research and social policy.* Chicago: University of Chicago Press.

Pomerantz, E. M., Ruble, D. N., Frey, K. S., & Greulich, F. (1995). Meeting goals and confronting conflict: Children's changing perceptions of social comparison. *Child Development, 66,* 723–738.

Pomerantz, S. (1979). Sex differences in the relative importance of self-esteem, physical self-satisfaction, and identity in predicting adolescent satisfaction. *Journal of Youth and Adolescence, 8,* 51–61.

Pope, A. W., Bierman, K. L., & Mumma, G. H. (1991). Aggression, hyperactivity, and inattention-immaturity: Behavior dimensions associated with peer rejection in elementary school boys. *Developmental Psychology, 27,* 663–671.

Pope, H., & Katz, D. (1988). Affective and psychotic symptoms associated with anabolic steroid use. *American Journal of Psychiatry, 145,* 487–490.

Portes, P. R., Howell, S. C., Brown, J. H., Eichenberger, S., & Mas, C. A. (1992). Family functions and children's postdivorce adjustment. *American Journal of Orthopsychiatry, 62,* 613–617.

Posner, J. K., & Vandell, D. L. (1994). Low-income children's after-school care: Are there beneficial effects of after-school programs? *Child Development, 65,* 440–456.

Pownall, T., & Kingerlee, S. (1993). *Seeing, reaching, and touching: Relationships between vision and touching in infants.* New York: Harvester and Wheatsheaf.

Price, R. (1992). *Clockers.* Boston: Houghton Mifflin.

Price, R. H. (1992). Psychosocial impact of joblessness on individuals and families. *Current Directions in Psychological Science, 1,* 9–11.

Priel, B., & Zeidman, O. (1990). Infant social behavior in front of a mirror in and in front of a familiar and unfamiliar peer. *Journal of Genetic Psychology, 151,* 483–493.

Primeau, M. R. (1993). Fetal movement. In B. K. Rothman (Ed.), *The encyclopedia of childbearing.* New York: Henry Holt.

Prinz, P., & Prinz, E. (1979). Simultaneous acquisition of ASL and spoken English. *Sign Language Studies, 25,* 283–296.

Prior, M., Kyrios, M., & Oberklaid, F. (1987). Temperament in Australian, American, Chinese, and Greek infants: Some issues and directions for future research. *Journal of Cross-Cultural Psychology, 17,* 455–474.

Pritchett, L. (1993). *Wealthier is healthier.* Washington, D.C.: The World Bank.

Pryor, D. W., & McGarell, E. F. (1993). Public perceptions of youth gang crime: An exploratory analysis. *Youth and Society, 24,* 399–418.

Putallaz, M. (1987). Maternal behavior and children's sociometric status. *Child Development, 58,* 324–340.

Quadrel, M. J., Fischoff, B., & Davis, W. (1993). Adolescent (in)vulnerability. *American Psychologist, 48,* 102–116.

Queen, P., & Lang, C. (1993). *Handbook of pediatric nutrition.* Gaithersburg, Md.: Aspen Publishers.

Radke-Yarrow, M., Nottelmann, E., Belmont, B., & Welsh, J. D. (1993). *Journal of Abnormal Child Psychology, 21,* 683–695.

Radke-Yarrow, M., & Zahn-Waxler, C. (1987). Roots, motives, and patterns in children's prosocial behavior. In J. Reykowski, J. Karylowski, D. Bar-Tal, & E. Staub (Eds.), *Origins and maintenance of prosocial behaviors.* New York: Plenum Press.

Rafoth, M. (1993). *Strategies for learning and remembering: Study skills across the curriculum.* Washington, D.C.: National Education Association.

Raines, S. (1990). Representational competence: (Re)presenting experiences through words, actions, and images. *Childhood Education, 66*(3), 133–139.

Ramey, C. T., Bryant, D. M., Campbell, F. A., Sprling, J. J., & Wasik, B. H. (1988). Early intervention for high-risk children: The Carolina early intervention program. In R. H. Price, E. L. Cowen, R. P. Lorion, & J. Ramos-McKay (Eds.), *Fourteen ounces of prevention* (pp. 32–43). Washington, D.C.: American Psychological Association.

Ramey, C. T., & Ramey, S. L. (1993, Winter). Home visiting programs and the health and development of young children. *The Future of Children, 3,* 129–139.

Ramirez, O. (1989). Mexican-American children and adolescents. In J. Gibbs & L. Huang (Eds.), *Children of color* (pp. 224–250). San Francisco: Jossey-Bass.

Ramsey, P. (1995). Changing social dynamics in early childhood classrooms. *Child Development, 66,* 764–773.

Rapp, R. (1993). Amniocentesis in sociocultural perspective. *Journal of Genetic Counseling, 2,* 183–196.

Rawlins, W. K. (1992). *Friendship matters: Communication, dialectics, and the life course.* New York: Aldine DeGruyter.

Reaves, J., & Roberts, A. (1983). The effect of type of information on children's attraction to peers. *Child Development, 54,* 1024–1031.

Redl, F., & Wineman, D. (1951). *Children Who Hate.* New York: The Free Press.

Reed, R. J. (1988). Education and achievement of young black males. In J. T. Gibbs (Ed.), *Young, black and male in America: An endangered species* (pp. 37–93). Dover, Mass.: Auburn House.

Reid, M., Landesman, S., Treider, R., & Jaccard, J. (1989). "My family and friends": Six- to twelve-year-old perceptions of social support. *Child Development, 60,* 896–910.

Remafedi, G., Resnick, M., Blum, R., & Harris, L. (1992). Demography of sexual orientation in adolescents. *Pediatrics, 89,* 714–721.

Rennie, J. (1994, June). Grading the gene tests. *Scientific American,* 89–97.

Renzulli, J. (1986). The three-ring conception of giftedness: A developmental model for creative productivity. In R. Sternberg & J. Davidson (Eds.), *Conceptions of giftedness* (pp. 53–92). New York: Cambridge University Press.

Restivo, S., VanBendegem, J., & Fischer, R. (1993). *Math worlds: Philosophical and social studies of mathematics and math education.* New York: State University of New York Press.

Richards, M. H., Boxer, A. M., Petersen, A. C., & Albrecht, R. (1990). Relation of weight to body image in pubertal girls and boys from two communities. *Developmental Psychology, 26,* 313–321.

Richter, P. (1993). HIV and pregnancy. In B. K. Rothman (Ed.), *The encyclopedia of childbearing.* New York: Henry Holt.

Rickman, M. D., & Davidson, R. J. (1995). Personality and behavior in parents of temperamentally inhibited and uninhibited children. *Developmental Psychology, 30,* 346–354.

Rist, R. (1973). *The urban school: A factory for failure.* Cambridge, Mass.: MIT Press.

Robinson, I. E., & Jedlicka, D. (1982). Change in sexual attitudes and behavior of college students from 1965 to 1980: A research note. *Journal of Marriage and the Family, 44,* 237–240.

Rogers, L., & Walsh, J. (1982). Shortcomings of the psychomedical research of John Money and co-workers into sex differences in behavior. *Sex Roles, 8,* 269–281.

Roggman, L. A., Langlois, J. H., Hubbs-Tait, L., & Rieser-Danner, L. A. (1994). Infant day-care, attachment, and the "file drawer problem." *Child Development, 65,* 1429–1443.

Rogoff, B. (1990). *Apprenticeship in thinking.* New York: Oxford University Press.

Rogoff, B., & Chavajay, P. (1995). What's become of research on the cultural basis of cognitive development? *American Psychologist, 50,* 859–877.

Rogoff, B., Mistry, J., Goncu, A., & Mosler, C. (1993). Guided participation in cultural activity by toddlers and caregivers. *Monographs of the Society for Research in Child Development, 58*(8, Serial No. 236).

Roland, A. (1988). *In search of self in India and Japan: Toward a cross-cultural psychology.* Princeton, N.J.: Princeton University Press.

Romeo, F. F. (1984). Adolescence, sexual conflict, and anorexia. *Adolescence, 19,* 551–555.

Romig, D. A., Cleland, C., & Romig, J. (1989). *Juvenile delinquency: Visionary approaches.* Columbus, Ohio: Merrill.

Rooks, J. P., et al. (1989, December). Outcomes of care in birth centers. *New England Journal of Medicine, 321,* 1801–1822.

Roopnarine, J. L., & Field, T. (1982). Peer-directed behaviors of infants and toddlers during nursery school play. In T. Field (Ed.), *Review of human development.* New York: Wiley.

Roopnarine, J. L., Johnson, J. E., & Hooper, F. H. (Eds.). (1994) *Children's play in diverse cultures.* Albany, N.Y.: State University of New York Press.

Rose, J., & Gamble, J. (1993). *Human walking* (2nd ed.). Baltimore: Williams and Williams.

Rosenberg, M. S. (1979). *Conceiving the self.* New York: Basic Books.

Rosenberg, M. S. (1989). New directions for research on the psychological maltreatment of children. *American Psychologist, 42,* 166–171.

Rosenberg, M. S., & Repucci, N. D. (1985). Primary prevention of child abuse. *Journal of Consulting and Clinical Psychology, 53,* 576–585.

Rosenhan, D. L. & Seligman, M. E. (1995). *Abnormal psychology.* New York: W. W. Norton.

Rosenshine, B., & Meister, C. (1994). Reciprocal teaching: A review of the research. *Review of Educational Research, 64*(4), 479–530.

Leigh, B. C., 528
Leinbach, M. D., 326
Leinhardt, C., 478
Lemshow, S., 447
Leon, G. R., 464-465
Lerner, J., 376, 450
Lerner, R., 221, 450
Lester, B., 246, 353
Lester, D., 530
Levine, A. D., 518-519
Levine, G., 17
Levine, J. A., 211
Levine, R., 156
Levine, S., 156
Levitt, J. L., 517
Levitt, M. J., 517
Levy, H., 140
Levy, M., 156
Levy-Shiff, R., 207
Lewinsohn, P., 450
Lewis, C. T., 113
Lewis, J. M., 299
Lewis, M., 36, 201, 220, 226, 227, 397
Lewkowicz, D., 179
Lickliter, R., 179
Lickona, T., 494
Lieberman, M., 16, 494
Liebert, R. M., 323, 324
Liebmann-Smith, J., 97, 98
Liem, J. H., 426
Liem, R., 426
Lieverman, E., 108
Lightfoot, S. L., 431, 524
Lillo-Martin, D., 285
Lin, S., 420
Lindblad-Goldberg, M., 308
Lindell, S. G., 121
Lindsey, D., 167
Lindzey, G., 31, 36
Linn, S., 108
Linney, J. A., 430
Linton, M., 529
Lipscomb, T. J., 319
Lipsitt, L., 40, 182
Litman, C., 230
Little, J. K., 326
Livson, N., 450, 451, 453
Loeb, R. C., 310
Logan, D. D., 444
Lollis, S., 320
Londerville, S., 219
Lorenz, K., 137
Low, J. A., 97
Lozoff, B., 111
Ludington, S., 153
Luppiwiski, G., 184
Luria, A. R., 49
Luster, T., 257
Lustig, M., 491
Lutz, P., 514
Lyon, G., 378
Lytinen, P., 301
Lytton, H., 310, 327

Maccoby, E. E., 200, 307, 310, 319, 327, 409, 410, 412, 418
MacDonald, K. B., 211
MacFarlane, J., 111
MacGregor, S., 109
MacGregor, S. N., 109
MacIver, D., 456, 508, 521
Mackinnon, G., 47
MacLean, M., 18
Maddox, A., 456
Maggs, J. L., 428
Magnolia, L., 283
Magnusson, D., 453
Mahler, M., 37, 38, 39
Main, M., 219, 220, 317, 329
Maio, M. L., 201
Maioni, T., 303
Maker, J., 390
Makin, J., 145
Malatesta, C., 201

Malina, R. M., 256, 443, 444, 447
Malinosky-Rummell, R., 332
Mallory, G., 292
Maloney, M. J., 463
Mandel, J. L., 68
Mandler, J., 163
Mann, J., 354
Maratsos, M., 287
Marchman, V., 186
Marcia, J., 505-506
Marcus, D., 398
Marcus, G., 276
Mardon, G., 67
Marecek, J., 329
Marentette, P., 189
Margand, N. A., 221
Margolin, L., 390
Markman, H. J., 121
Marks, L., 380
Markstrom-Adams, C., 505
Marolla, F., 111
Marschark, M., 189, 284
Marsh, F. H., 74, 75
Marshall, W., 440, 444
Martin, B., 320
Martin, C. L., 326
Martin, D. C., 109
Martin, J. A., 307, 310
Martlew, M., 281
Maruyama, G., 413
Mas, C. A., 513
Matas, L., 220
Matheson, C. C., 301
Mays, G. L., 536, 537
Mayseless, O., 219
Mazaide, M., 121
Mazzocco, M. M., 72
McCabe, A., 319
McCall, R., 101, 165
McCarthy, J., 35
McCartney, K., 82, 223
McCauley, E., 70
McClaskey, C. L., 415
McClearn, G. E., 86
McClelland, D. C., 309
McCluskey, K., 221
McCormick, S. E., 316
McCullough, M., 535
McDaniel, K. D., 465
McDonald, A. D., 110
McDonald, L., 224
McGarell, E. F., 536
McGee, R. O., 205
McGillivray, B., 67
McGoldrick, M., 522
McGrath, P., 145
McKay, S., 17
McKenzie, C., 104
McKinlay, S., 109
McKussick, V. A., 64
Mclean, M., 513
McLoyd, V. C., 426
McNamara, T., 369
McNew, S., 228
McTigue, J., 97
Medigue, C., 142
Meehan, P. J., 535
Mehl, L. E., 121
Mehler, J., 189
Meilman, P., 506
Meister, C., 376
Melamed, B., 407
Meltzoff, A., 179, 185
Menkes, J., 146
Meredith, H., 341, 444
Meschulach-Sarfaty, O., 186
Messer, D., 185, 279, 281
Messner, M., 348
Metz, K., 367
Michel, G., 201
Michelsson, K., 139
Midgley, C., 456, 508, 521
Miller, A., 329
Miller, B. C., 528

Miller, D., 369
Miller, M. A., 110
Miller, N., 207
Miller, P., 315, 316, 374, 391, 526
Miller, P. H., 31, 34, 41, 172
Miller, S. S., 462
Miller, T. E., 450
Miller, W. B., 536
Mills, R. S. L., 320
Millstein, S. G., 456
Milner, J., 330
Milner, R., 121
Minogue, J. P., 109
Minuchin, P., 429
Mistry, J., 272
Mitchell, C., 521
Mobley, L. A., 211
Moerk, E., 278
Moffitt, T. E., 205
Mogford, K., 280
Molfese, D., 143
Mollnow, E., 108
Moltz, K. A., 456
Monaco, A. P., 68
Money, J., 242
Monson, R. R., 108
Monsour, A., 504
Montagu, A., 85
Montessori, M., 290
Moore, C., 494
Moore, D., 509, 510
Moore, E. G. J., 404
Moore, K. A., 528
Moore, K. L., 103
Moore, M. K., 179
Moore, W., 141
Moorehouse, M. J., 412, 426
Moran, E. G., 111
Morelli, G. A., 224
Morgan, M., 321
Morrison, D. M., 528
Morrison, V., 164
Morrongiello, B., 170
Morrow, L., 290
Morse, J. M., 122-123
Mortimer, J. T., 524, 525
Moscicki, A., 457, 458, 459
Mosher, R., 67
Mosier, C. E., 210
Mosler, C., 272
Mounts, N. S., 513
Muehlenhard, C., 529
Mueller, E., 210, 314
Muir, B., 72
Muir, D. W., 97, 165
Mumma, G. H., 415
Mumme, D., 210
Munroe, R., 150
Munroe, R., 150
Murphy, L., 316
Murray, C., 84
Murray, W. E., 121
Murstein, B. L., 527
Must, A., 464
Myers, J., 474

Nagata, D., 307
Nagel, L., 201
Nagel, S. K., 309, 425, 512
Nelso, D. L., 68
Nelson, J., 482
Nelson, M., 214
Nelson, N. M., 121
Nelson, S., 402
Nesselroade, J. R., 86
New, R., 292
Newcomb, M., 463
Newell, J. D., 26
Newman, F., 272, 288
Nezworski, T., 223
Nichols, J., 482
Noam, G., 490
Noddings, N., 488
Nolen-Hoeksema, S., 210

Noppe, I. C., 211
Noppe, L. D., 211
Norbeck, J. S., 114
Nord, A. M., 72
Norman, C., 404
Nottelmann, E., 210
Nucci, L., 495
Nyman, M., 319

Oberklaid, F., 205
O'Boyle, C., 326
O'Brien, S. F., 407
O'Carroll, P. W., 535
O'Conner, T. G., 501, 511
O'Donnell, J., 416
O'Donnell, K., 509
Offer, D., 439, 508
O'Grady, L., 285
O'Hara-Devereaux, M., 491
Okagaki, L., 257
Olds, D., 112
O'Leary, K., 301
Olsho, L., 144, 170
Olson, K., 331
Olver, R., 266
Olvera-Ezzell, N., 245
O'Malley, P., 460, 461, 462
Omer, H., 114
O'Neill, R., 309, 425, 512
Opie, I., 302
Opie, P., 302
Orlick, T. D., 317
Oster, H., 201
Ostrov, E., 439
Overton, W., 398, 475
Owen, M. T., 221
Owens-Stively, J., 535

Paajanen, S., 139
Padden, D., 189
Page, D. C., 67
Paikoff, R. L., 465
Pakiz, B., 513
Palmer, D. J., 311
Palosaari, U. K., 513
Pancake, V., 220
Panofsky, C., 283
Park, C., 122-123
Parke, R. D., 211
Parker, J. G., 417
Parkhurst, J. T., 314, 519
Parkins, E., 138
Parkinson, S., 17
Parmalee, A., 126
Parten, M., 303, 304
Paterson, K., 344-345
Patterson, C. J., 416, 427, 530
Patterson, G. R., 309, 322, 323, 517, 518, 536, 537
Paulston, C., 380, 491
Pavlov, I., 39, 40, 42
Payne, A., 22
Pearce, J. K., 522
Pearson, D., 23, 381
Pease-Alvarez, L., 381
Pederson, N. L., 86
Peirano, P., 142
Pelletier, D., 240
Pena, I. C., 126
Pence, A., 213, 214
Penner, S., 278
Perez, B., 382
Perret-Clermont, A. N., 406
Perrin, J. M., 464
Peskin, H., 450, 451, 452, 453
Petersen, A., 453, 464, 465
Petersen, A. C., 450, 451, 452, 454, 535
Peterson, G. H., 121
Pethick, S., 186, 187
Pettit, G., 308
Pettit, G. S., 331, 415
Pettito, L., 189
Phelan, J., 152
Phillips, D., 214, 223

Phinney, J. S., 316, 505
Piaget, J., 12, 30, 31, 43-45, 47-48, 51, 171-177, 179, 181, 185, 189, 264, 265, 268, 269, 271, 286-287, 299, 301, 362, 363-367, 369, 370, 373, 377, 405-406, 472-473, 474, 477, 490
Pianta, R., 331
Piatelli-Palmarini, L., 285
Pillack, J., 67
Pine, C. J., 522, 523
Pine, F., 38
Pinker, S., 276
Pinon, M. F., 324
Pinstrup-Anderson, P., 240
Pinuelas, A., 319
Pipp, S. L., 45
Pittman, T., 343
Pleck, J. H., 211, 528
Pless, I., 455
Plomin, R., 13, 66, 80, 83, 86, 202, 204, 316
Poest, C., 253
Poissonet, C., 342
Pollitt, E., 156
Pomerantz, E. M., 404
Pomerantz, S., 506
Pope, A. W., 415
Pope, H., 451
Porter, R., 144, 145
Portes, P. R., 513
Posner, J. 427
Posterski, D. C., 528
Poussaint, A., 322
Power, T., 245
Powers, C., 305
Pownall, T., 149
Price, J. M., 321, 331
Price, R., 461
Price, R. H., 426
Priel, B., 137
Primeau, M. R., 96
Prinz, E., 285
Prinz, P., 285
Prior, M., 205
Pritchett, L., 159
Proter, F. L., 204
Pryor, D. W., 536
Putallaz, M., 309, 320

Quadrel, M. J., 456
Queen, P., 154

Rabinowitz, M., 456
Radke-Yarrow, M., 202, 210, 316, 317
Rafoth, M., 373
Raines, S., 254
Ramanan, J., 428
Ramey, C. T., 51, 126
Ramey, S. L., 126
Ramirez, O., 212, 308
Ramsey, E., 322, 536, 537
Ramsey, P., 282
Rankin, D. B., 407, 408
Ratner, N., 266
Rauh, J. L., 458
Rawlins, W. K., 416, 417, 515
Reardon, D., 533
Reaves, J., 414
Redl, F., 51, 53
Reed, R. J., 405
Reid, J. B., 517, 518
Reid, M., 514
Reilly, J., 186, 189
Remafedi, G., 530
Rennie, J., 73, 79
Renshaw, P., 412, 413, 415
Renzulli, J., 391
Repucci, N. D., 332
Resnick, J., 13
Resnick, M., 530
Restivo, S., 372
Restrepo, A., 510
Reuman, D., 456, 508, 521
Reyna, V., 370

Reznick, J., 186, 187
Rhode, D. L., 111
Rhodes, C., 482
Rice, M. L., 323, 324
Richards, B., 194
Richards, M., 19-20
Richards, M. H., 407, 450, 451, 510
Richman, A. 156
Richter, P., 106
Rickman, M. D., 205
Ricks, M., 209
Rierdan, J., 450
Rieser-Danner, L., 257
Rieser-Danner, L. A., 223
Rigatuso, J., 204
Rinne, A., 139
Rist, R., 431
Roberts, A., 414
Roberts, D. F., 524
Robinson, I. E., 527
Robinson, J., 13
Roche, A., 440, 442, 447
Rockwell, R., 241
Rodgers, B., 513
Rodin, J., 464
Rogers, L., 447
Roggman, L., 257
Roggman, L. A., 223
Rogoff, B., 45, 48, 49, 210, 272, 405, 409
Roland, A., 74, 399, 522
Romeo, F. F., 464
Romig, D. A., 536
Romig, J., 536
Romney, D. M., 327
Rooks, J. P., 119, 120
Roopnarine, J. L., 214, 305, 327
Rose, J., 251
Rosegrant, T., 290
Rosen, T., 276
Rosenberg, M. S., 329, 332, 398
Rosenfeld, A., 465
Rosenshine, B., 376
Rosenthal, R., 430
Rosett, H., 109
Rosner, M. A., 109
Ross, H., 320
Ross, P., 390
Rossell, C. H., 414
Rotatori, A., 342
Roth, P., 192
Rothbart, M., 202, 205
Rotheram-Borus, M. J., 459, 461
Rothschild, N., 424
Rourke, B., 376
Rovee-Collier, C., 165
Rovet, J. F., 70
Rovine, M., 211, 221, 223
Rowe, D., 202
Rowland, T., 346
Rubenstein, J. L., 214, 535, 536
Rubin, C., 535, 536
Rubin, K., 301, 302, 303, 319
Rubin, K. H., 297, 301, 320
Ruble, D., 445
Ruble, D. N., 326, 404, 430
Rueter, M. A., 511
Ruhland, D., 403
Ruptic, C., 367
Rutter, M., 356
Ryan, K., 108
Ryu, S., 524, 525

Sabo, D., 348
Sachs, J., 446
Sackett, D. L., 121
Sadovnick, A. D., 69
Saenger, G., 111
Sagi, A., 219, 224
St. James-Roberts, I., 185, 200
St. Peters, M., 323, 324, 325
Sale, J., 201
Salett, E., 522
Saltzman, L. E., 535
Salvador, M. A., 211

Sameroff, A. J., 114, 204
Sampson, P. D., 109
Sanfilippo, J., 239, 240
Sanjur, D., 245
Santrock, J., 423, 424
Saracho, O., 281
Sarafino, E., 536
Saroj, S., 121
Sato, D., 108
Sault, N., 343
Savelsbergh, G., 148
Savin-Williams, R. C., 529, 530
Sawin, D., 316
Scarr, S., 82, 223, 384, 426
Schafer, W. D., 222
Schaller, M., 315, 316
Scherman, A., 535
Schlecter, S., 283
Schlessinger, D., 68
Schlundt, D. C., 415
Schoenbach, C., 425, 512
Schoenbaum, S. C., 108
Schoken, I., 415
Schonert-Reichl, K. A., 508
Schowalter, J. E., 464
Schrader, D., 490
Schuengel, C., 219, 224
Schwartzman, H. B., 297
Schwarzenegger, A., 342
Schweinhart, L., 18, 290, 384, 537
Scollon, R., 490
Scollon, S., 490
Scraton, S., 341, 348
Sedlacek, W. E., 528
Seeram, E., 247
Seidman, E., 430, 521
Seifer, R., 204
Seifert, K., 46, 366
Seitz, V., 9
Selekman, J., 71
Seligman, M. E. P., 402
Selman, R., 51, 416, 417
Sen, A., 126
Sepulveda, J., 354
Shafer, M. B., 457, 458, 459
Shaffer, D., 535
Shanahan, M., 524, 525
Shantz, C. U., 319
Shapiro, E., 429
Shapiro, E. G., 465
Sharabany, R., 516
Sharman, E., 168
Shatz, M., 311
Shaver, P., 398
Shaw, P., 109
Shayer, M., 290, 364
Shedler, J., 461, 462
Sheldon, S., 140
Shepherd-Look, D., 325
Sheppard, K., 326
Shrum, W., 409, 412, 413, 518
Shulman, S., 412-413
Shure, M. B., 416
Siefer, R., 114
Siegler, R., 375
Siervogel, R., 442, 447
Sigelman, C., 456
Sigelman, C. K., 450
Signorielli, N., 321
Silber, S. J., 91, 92, 98
Silberstein, L. R., 464
Silva, P. A., 205
Silverman, P., 350
Silverstein, L. B., 222
Simmons, R. G., 453, 521
Simon, W., 526
Simpson, E. M., 67
Sinclair, D., 441
Sinclair, H., 288
Sinclair, R. J., 513
Singleton, L., 413
Sitterle, K., 424
Sizer, T. R., 524
Skinner, B. F., 39, 40, 42, 277

Skinner, E. A., 401
Skolnick, A., 307
Skolnick, J., 307
Slaby, R. G., 317
Slade, A., 220
Slater, A., 164
Slavin, R., 483
Slavin, R. E., 403, 431
Sloan, M., 110
Slomczynski, K. M., 425, 512
Slomin, M., 212
Slomkowski, C. L., 311
Sloper, P., 68
Smetana, J. G., 495, 510, 511
Smilansky, S., 299
Smith, C., 355
Smith, L., 283
Smith, N., 287, 380
Smitherman-Donaldson, G., 383
Smolak, L., 287
Smollar, J., 510
Smoot, D. L., 415
Snidman, N., 202, 205, 206
Snyder, L., 191
Sobol, A. M., 464
Sobol, B., 321
Soldier, L., 293
Solnit, A. J., 464
Sommerville, J., 10
Sonenstein, F. L., 528
Sorenson, S., 529
Soriano, F. I., 536
Sorsby, A., 281
Spaccarelli, S., 332, 423
Spangler, G., 218
Spanier, G., 221, 424
Spassov, L., 142
Spearman, C., 383
Spence, M. J., 206
Spencer, M. B., 505
Spergel, I., 537
Spetner, N., 170
Spire, J., 140
Spirito, A., 535
Spitz, R., 216-217
Spivak, G., 416
Spodek, B., 281
Sponseller, D., 300
Spradling, V. Y., 509, 510
Sprafkin, J., 323, 324
Sprling, J. J., 51
Sroufe, A. L., 204
Sroufe, L., 220
Sroufe, L. A., 201, 204, 220, 412-413
Stack, C., 522
Staffieri, J. R., 414
Stanger, C., 201
Stanley-Hagen, M., 420, 421, 424
Starfield, B., 455
Stark, L., 535
Starr, R., 332
Stattin, H., 204
Statton, H., 453
Stechler, G., 535, 536
Steele, H., 329
Steele, M., 329
Steele, P. R. M., 108
Steiger, C., 118, 119
Stein, A., 104
Stein, Z., 111
Steinberg, J., 222
Steinberg, L., 307, 309
Steinberg, L. D., 428, 511, 513, 517, 518-519, 520, 525
Steininger, M., 26
Stemmler, M. E., 535
Stenberg, C., 227
Stern, D., 37, 38, 39
Stern, D. N., 200, 206, 208, 209, 221, 329
Sternberg, R., 387
Stevens, R., 517
Stevenson, H. W., 372, 404, 405
Stewart, R. B., 211
Stifter, C. A., 208, 223

Stigler, J., 372
Stipek, D., 403
Stokes, G., 527, 530
Stolberg, A. L., 423
Stout, B. C., 108
Stratford, B., 68
Streigel-Moore, R., 464
Streissguth, A. P., 109
Stubblefield, P. G., 108
Stubbs, M., 450
Styne, D., 239, 240
Subramanian, S., 66
Sue, S., 75
Suess, G., 218
Sullivan, A., 509, 510
Sullivan, H. S., 406
Sullivan, J., 201
Sullivan, K., 509, 510
Sullivan, M. W., 201
Super, C., 156, 292, 293
Susa, A. M., 305
Susser, M., 111
Sutcliffe, D., 382
Swanson, H., 369

Taffel, S. M., 125
Taipale, V., 453
Takahashi, K., 218
Takanishi, R., 455, 456
Takata, S., 536
Taloney, L., 456
Tamis-Lemonda, C., 192
Tamplin, A., 314
Tanner, J., 239, 240, 444
Tanner, J. M., 256, 440, 442, 446, 447
Taub, H., 126
Taussig, C., 537
Taylor, B., 452
Taylor, D. K., 456
Teberg, A. J., 126
Teller, J., 167
Terre, L., 456
Terry, R., 415
Tesla, C., 320
Tesman, J., 247
Thal, D., 186, 187
Tharp, R. G., 429
Thelan, E., 82
Thissen, D., 440
Thivierge, J., 121
Thomas, A., 203-204, 205
Thompson, H., 150
Thompson, R. A., 25, 202, 220
Thompson, S., 326
Thompson, W. W., 427
Thorne, B., 430
Tilden, V. P., 114
Titmus, G., 314
Tobin-Richards, M. H., 451, 452, 454
Tolson, J. M., 518

Tolson, T., 308
Torney-Purta, J., 486, 487
Torres-Guzman, M., 382
Tortu, S., 463
Trautman, P. D., 535
Treder, R., 70
Trehub, S., 165
Treider, R., 514
Trickett, E., 524
Tronick, E. Z., 201, 202, 208, 209, 210, 211, 224, 227
Trujillo, M., 245
Truong, L., 410-411
Tschann, J. M., 423
Tsimpli, I., 287, 380
Turiel, E., 495
Turkheimer, E., 81
Turman, H., 144-145
Turner, R., 208
Turner, S., 68

Ullman, M., 276
Unger, R. K., 448
Ungerer, J. A., 301
Unzner, L., 218
Urban, J., 412-413
Urberg, K. A., 518
Uttal, D. H., 404, 405

Valkenburg, P. M., 305
VanBendegem, J., 372
Vandell, D., 427
Vandell, D. L., 214, 305, 314, 428
Vandenberg, B., 297, 301
van den Boom, D., 221
van den Boom, D. C., 204
van-der-voort, T. H. A., 305
Van-Doorninck, W., 72
Van Dusen, J. E., 528
Van Geert, P., 364
Van Hoek, K., 285
van Ijzendoorn, M. H., 218, 219, 224, 329
Van Tuyl, S. S., 211
Vass, W., 383
Vaughn, B. E., 114
Vellutino, F., 378
Vernberg, E. M., 519
Volk, T., 372
Volpe, J., 417
Vorhees, C. W., 108
Vroon, P., 268
Vuchinich, R. A., 424
Vuchinich, S., 424
Vygotsky, L., 45, 48, 49, 50, 288, 301, 390
Vyse, S. A., 527

Waddington, C. H., 81
Wadsworth, M., 244, 513
Wagner, E., 202

Wagner, R., 387
Wainer, H., 440
Walberg, H., 483
Walder, L. O., 323
Walk, R., 169
Wall, S., 218, 221
Waller, T., 47
Wallerstein, J. S., 422, 423, 513, 514
Walsh, J., 447
Walsh, P., 423
Walther, F. J., 126
Wang, V., 74, 75
Ward, B., 141
Wardle, F., 293
Warren, M., 439, 445
Warren, M. P., 465
Warren, S., 192
Warshak, R., 423
Wasik, B. H., 51
Waterman, A. S., 506
Waters, E., 218, 221
Watkins, B., 321, 323, 324
Watson, K., 303
Waxler, C., 316
Webb, N., 350
Webb, P., 442, 447
Weikart, D., 18, 290, 384, 537
Weil, J., 243
Weinberg, M. K., 201
Weinberger, J., 309
Weiner, L., 109
Weisberg, P., 364
Weiser, T., 311
Weisman, J. R., 201
Weisner, T. S., 211, 412
Weiss, M., 201, 346
Weiss, R., 422
Weisz, J., 419
Wellman, H., 20-21, 176, 266
Welsh, J. D., 210
Werner, E., 212
Wertsch, J. V., 48, 49, 389, 390
Westby, S., 321
Wharton, T., 377
White, B., 194, 230
White, B. L., 229
White, D., 517
White, M., 372
White, R., 230
White, S. D., 528
Whitebrook, M., 214
Whitehurst, G., 22
Whiteworth, L. A., 450
Whiting, B. B., 305, 317
Whiting, J., 150, 151, 305
Wigfeld, A., 456, 508, 521
Wiggins, G., 490, 492, 495-496
Willard, H., 68
Williams, C., 157
Williams, J., 253

Williams, J. D., 530
Williams, L. M., 332
Williams, R. A., 516
Willis, D. J., 332
Wilson, C., 445
Wilson, J., 493
Wilson, M., 308
Wilson, M. N., 522, 523
Wilson, M. S., 316
Wilson-Mitchell, J. E., 412
Wineman, D., 51
Winfree, L. T., 536, 537
Wing, R. R., 463
Winner, E., 380
Witt, D., 253
Wolf, C. M., 204
Wolf, D., 369
Wolfson, A., 210
Wood, C. H., 326
Wood, F., 355
Wood, P., 417
Woolston, J., 158
Worden, J., 350
Wozniak, P., 308, 317
Wozniak, R., 273
Wren, T., 490
Wright, J. C., 323, 324, 325
Wright, L., 352
Wright, V., 415
Wu, F., 413
Wylie, R., 397
Wynn, K., 269

Xu, F., 276

Yarrow, M., 316
Yau, J., 510
Ying, Y., 307
Yoder, P., 192
Yogman, M., 211
Yonas, A., 167
Yoshida, T., 491
Youniss, J., 406, 407, 417, 510, 515, 516

Zahn-Waxler, C., 13, 202, 316, 317
Zalk, S., 413
Zane, N., 75
Zaragoza, M., 371
Zarbatany, L., 407, 408
Zeidman, O., 137
Zelazo, P. R., 301
Zeskind, P. S., 201
Zevitz, R., 536
Zigler, E. F., 222, 537
Zigler, E., 456, 535, 536
Zimmerman, L., 224
Zucker, K. J., 530

Subject Index

Abandonment, fear of, 226
Abilities
    adapting to context, 387
    aptitude tests measuring, 385, 386
    popular children and, 415
Abortion
    prenatal screening and, 75, 77
    spontaneous, 104
    teenage, 532–533
Abruptio placenta, 124
Abstainers, 461
Abstract reasoning, 383
    adolescence, 471–474, 484
    egocentrism and, 484
    gifted students, 391
    identity development and, 504
    intelligence tests and, 386
    logical tasks and, 48–49
    middle childhood, 367
    moral, 16
    neo-Piagetian theories, 45
    religious beliefs and, 489
    academic achievement
    after-school programs and, 427
    Asian youth, 23
    contraceptive use, 532
    cultural influences, 372
    divorce and, 513
    learning disabilities, 376
    mathematics, 372
    overactive children, 356
    parental expectations, 404–405
    parenting style and, 309–310, 511, 520
    teacher's expectations about, 430
Academic competence, 402
Academic failure, delinquency and, 536
Academic standards, 524
Accidents
    adolescents, 455, 456
    middle childhood, 351–352
    preschoolers, 259(tab)
Accommodation, 44, 172, 175
Achievement
    academic, see Academic achievement
    individual, 15
    middle childhood, 396, 399–405
    parental expectations, 404–405
    popular children, 415
    standards of, 396
Achievement motivation
    athletics and, 346
    differences in, 401
    peers, 418
    psychodynamic theories, 400–401
Achievement tests, 385
Acquired immunodeficiency syndrome,
        see AIDS
Action(s)
    imitating, 185–186
    language development and, 286
    moral, 492–493, 497
    operant conditioning, 183–185
    Piaget's theory of cognitive develop-
        ment, 181
    predicting, 266
    reinforced, 183–185
    representing, 176–177, 178
    rewards for, 183–185
    schemes, 43–44
    self–guidance, 258
Action schemes, Piaget's theory of cogni-
    tive development and, 173
Active learning, 366
Active play, in middle childhood,
    344–349
Active role of child, in development,
    30–31, 39

cognitive approaches, 47
contextual approaches, 50
psychodynamic theories, 39
social cognitive learning approach, 42
Activities
    initiating challenging, 228
    self-directed, 31, 36
Acute illnesses, 352–353
Adaptation, 44
Adaptive strategies, families of minority
    youth and, 522–523
Additive bilingual education, 382
ADHD (attention deficit hyperactivity
    disorder), 355–357
Adolescence
    adult roles in, 10
    aggressive and violent behavior in,
        332, 529
    cognitive development in, 468–498
    concept of, 438–440
    domains of development, 5(fig)
    early, 438
    late, 438
    methods of studying, 16–24
    middle, 438
    physical development in, 436–466
    political beliefs, 506
    predicting behavior problems in, 205
    psychosocial development in,
        500–538
    psychosocial theory and, 37
    realistic expectations, 8
    religious beliefs, 506
    theoretical views of, 439–440
Adolescent egocentrism, 442, 483–485,
    497
Adolescent parents, 533
    difficulties of, 104, 111, 126
    poverty and, 104
    preventing abuse and, 332
Adolescent pregnancy, 455, 531–533
    daughters of divorced parents, 423
    prenatal care and, 104
    preterm births, 152
    prevention of, 534–535
    United States, 111
Adolescent special problems, 52–53,
    531–537
    delinquency, see Delinquency
    drug use, 456, 458, 459, 460–462, 525
    health, 455, 456
    homeless, 459, 461
    parenthood, see Adolescent parents
    pregnancy, see Adolescent pregnancy
    sexually transmitted diseases, 458
    suicide, 456, 460, 535–536
Adoption, 73, 79
Adoption studies, 83–84
Adult(s), effects of children's physical
    growth on, 257–260
Adult behavior, children directing,
    228–229
Adult height, 238–239
Adulthood, transition to, 438
Adult roles, teenagers assuming, 10
Advocacy, 9
African-American children
    AIDS and, 106
    extended families, 522
    illnesses, 353
    intellectual development, 84
    parental achievement expectations,
        404–405
    white friends, 516
African-American mothers, prenatal
    care and, 112, 113(fig)
African children, physical development
    and, 239–240

African cultures
    facial scarification and, 330
    motor skill development, 150–151
After-school care, 427–428
Age, maternal, see Mother's age
Age of viability, fetus and, 96
Aggression
    changes during early childhood,
        318–319
    child abuse and, 329, 331–332
    date rape and, 529
    divorce and, 422
    hostile, 318–319
    influences on development of, 319–321
    instrumental, 318–319
    nature of, 318
    permissive parenting and, 310
    preschool years, 317–323
    psychosocial theory and, 36
    relational, 416
    responding to, 321–323
    social cognitive learning approach
        and, 42
AIDS (acquired immunodeficiency syn-
        drome), 353–355
    adolescence, 458–460, 527, 528
    blood transfusions and, 68
    facts, 355(tab)
    homophobia and, 530
    perinatal transmission of, 105, 106–107
Alcohol use
    adolescence, 439, 456, 460–462, 529
    early-maturing girls, 453
    maternal, 105, 109, 152
Alleles, 65–66, 85
Allergies, 353
Alpha-fetoprotein, 76, 77
Alternative high schools, 524
Altruism, 315, 317
American children
    achievement orientation, 403–404
    chronic illness, 353
    ethnic minorities, 523(fig)
    infant mortality, 159
    infant temperament, 205–206
    parents' reasons for having, 100–101
    sleep and, 242–243
American Sign Language (ASL),
    283–285
Amniocentesis, 76, 93, 94(fig), 95
Amphetamines, used during delivery,
    122(tab)
Ancestral world views, 522
Androgens, 446
Androgyny, 328–329
Anger
    aggressive behavior and, 317–320
    coping responses, 320
    divorce and, 513, 514
    modeling parent's behavior and, 322
Animal studies, gene-environment inter-
    actions and, 83
Animism, 270
Anorexia nervosa, 451, 464–465
AnotB error, 175–176, 181
Antisocial behavior, 536
    child abuse and, 329
    peers, 518
Anxious-avoidant attachment, 218, 219,
    220
Anxious-resistant attachment, 219, 220
Apgar Scale, 134
Appearance
    adolescence, 441–442, 448–451
    body image and, 342
    effects of changes in, 257–258
    ethnic differences, 452–453
    genetics and, 63

infant responding to, 142
newborns, 133–137
popularity and, 519
psychosocial development and, 5
self-esteem and, 448–451
stereotypes about, 340, 341, 342, 414,
    451, 452–453, 464
Appearance-reality distinction, 267
Approach behaviors, 216
Aptitude tests, 385
Arithmetic problems
    short-term memory and, 369
    See also Mathematics
Arousal states, 142, 164
Artifacts, 270–271
Artificial (donor) insemination (DI), 79, 98
Asian children/youth
    achievement orientation, 403–404
    mathematics learning, 372–373
    physical development and, 239–240
    stereotype of, 23
Asian cultures
    genetic counseling and, 74–75
    parenting style, 309
Aspiration, 189
Assertiveness, 416
Assimilation, 44, 172
Association studies, 86
Associative play, 303(tab), 304
Asthma, 3535
Athletics
    early-maturing boys, 452
    gender and, 34–349
    middle childhood, 344–349
    muscle growth and, 447
    physical effects of early, 345
    popular children and, 415
    psychological effects of early, 346–348
    skill in playing, 30
    steroid use and, 451
At-risk babies
    Apgar Scale, 134–135
    sudden infant death syndrome,
        140–141
At-risk children, 9
    accidents, 351–352
    delinquency, 536
At-risk families, 51
    child abuse and, 330, 332
    genetic counseling and, 74–75, 78–79
At-risk mothers, prenatal care and, 112
Attachment formation
    abused children, 329, 331
    blended families, 424
    cross-cultural variations in, 218–219
    infants, 50, 136–137, 209, 215–224
    influences on, 220
    object relations theory and, 37–38
    phases of, 217
    prosocial behavior and, 315
    secure, 218–224
Attention
    cognition and, 163
    to detail, 374
    heart rate and, 164
    object constancy and, 168
    Piaget's theory of cognitive develop-
        ment and, 173
    self–regulating emotions and, 202
    temperament and, 204
    unpopular children and, 415
Attention deficit hyperactivity disorder
    (ADHD), 355–357
Attitudes
    adolescent independence and, 509
    language gap and, 195
Attribution retraining, 402
Audience, imaginary, 484–485

Auditory acuity
    infants and, 143–144
    preschool years, 250
Auditory cortex, 247, 248
Auditory perception in infants, 169–170
Australian infants, temperament and, 205–206
Authoritarian parents, 309–310
    aggressive behavior and, 320
    child abuse and, 329
    divorce and, 423
    socioeconomic status, 512
Authoritative parents, 308–309
    adolescent psychosocial development and, 511, 512
    divorce and, 423
    peer group choice and, 520
    prosocial behavior and, 320
    socioeconomic status, 512, 513(tab)
    toddler's psychosocial development and, 230
Authority, 75, 307–311, 503
Autonomy
    adolescent, 513, 511
    collective versus personal, 74
    defined, 226
    emergence of, 225–231
    shame and doubt versus, 31, 36, 231
Averages, "typical" child and, 8
Axillary hair, 446
AZT (zidovudine), 106, 458

Babbling, 188, 189–190, 284
Baby biography, 10
Balanced bilinguals, 380
Behavior(s)
    adult standards of, 14
    aggressive, see Aggression
    altruistic, 315, 317
    antisocial, 329, 518, 536
    approach, 216
    attachment, 216
    autonomous, 226
    blocking, 319
    changes in, 5
    circular reaction, 173
    classical conditioning and, 40, 41(fig), 182–183
    correlations between, 22
    deferred imitation and, 177
    directing adult's, 228–229
    effects of prenatal stimulation on, 97
    emic standards, 331
    environment and, 64, 80–87
    etic perspective on, 331
    everyday rules for, 230
    evolution and, 50
    expectations of others and, 228
    exploratory, 217
    genetics and, 63–64, 80–87
    health and, 456
    hyperactive, 355–357
    imitation, 185–186
    infant, 144–145
    initiating challenging activities, 228
    instrumentally aggressive, 330–331
    lateralized, 248–249
    learning theory and, 181–187
    modeling, 209–210
    naturalistic research, 19
    norms, 12
    observational learning and, 41
    operant conditioning and, 40, 183–185, 226
    prosocial, see Prosocial behavior
    responding appropriately to, 8
    self-control and, 418
    self-directed regulatory, 201–202
    signaling, 216
    social, 515
    "typical" child acquiring, 8

Behavioral learning, 30, 39, 42, 52(fig)
    classical conditioning, 40, 41(fig), 182–183
    imitation, 185–186
    infants and, 181–187
    language acquisition and, 277–278
    operant conditioning, 40, 183–185
Behavior genetics, 80–87
Behavior problems
    abused children, 331
    predicting, 205
    unpopular children, 415
Belief(s)
    critical thinking and, 482
    justice and care, 489–498
    political, 506
    religious, 487–489, 506
    sharing with friends, 515
Belief-desire psychology, 266
Belonging, sense of, 408
Biased sample, 21
Biculturalism, 453, 522
Bilingualism, 23, 380–382
Biography, baby, 10
Biological changes, 30, 44
Biological drives, Freudian theory and, 32
Biological growth, see Physical development
Biological processes, human reproduction and, 59–63
Biosocial human evolution, 85
Birth, 114–127
    brain damage during, 376
    family and, 126–127
    fetal monitoring during, 125
    at home, 119,120
    in hospital, 118–119
    labor stages, 115–117
    maternal perceptions of pain during, 122–123
    medicinal methods during, 121–122
    nonhospital settings, 119–120
    preparation for, 118–119
    problems during, 123–125
    process of, 115–117
    settings and methods, 117–123
    nonhospital settings, 119–120
    See also Labor
Birth control, 111, 458, 531
Birth control pills, 531
Birthing rooms, 118–119
Birth weight
    low, 113(tab), 125–126, 141, 151–154, 533
    prenatal care and, 113(tab)
    teenage pregnancy and, 533
Bisexuality, 530
Black English, 382–383
Bladder control, preschool years, 250
Blastocyst, 92–93
Blended families, 424
Blocking behaviors, 319
Blood, AIDS transmitted in, 459
Blood transfusions, hemophilia and, 68
Blood type, inheritance of, 65–66
Bodily proportions, newborns, 136–137
Bodily skills, intelligence and, 383, 388
Body
    changes in use of, 4
    See also Appearance
Body balance skill, 388
Body fat
    fat cells, 158
    gender differences in, 441, 447
Body hair, puberty and, 446
Body image
    disturbance in , 464
    obesity and, 463–464
    self-esteem and, 448–451
Body shape, racial differences in, 240
Body types, 448
Bone growth, testosterone and, 446–447
Borderline personality, sexual abuse and, 332

Bowel control, preschool years, 250
Boys
    activity level, 355
    adolescent deaths and, 456
    adolescent friendships, 516
    adolescent nutrition, 463
    aggressive behavior, 319–320
    body hair, 446
    body image, 448–451
    divorce and, 422–423
    early athletics, 348–349
    early-maturing, 451–452
    ethics of care, 495
    growth spurt, 440
    handedness and, 249
    Hindu families, 14
    identity formation, 327
    illnesses, 353
    language differences, 282
    late-maturing, 452
    on-time-maturing, 454
    peer activities, 408, 409–412
    physical development in preschool years, 256–257
    primary sexual maturation, 444
    running speed and throwing distance, 349(fig)
    secondary sex characteristics, 445–446
    sudden infant death syndrome, 141
    voice changes, 446
Brain, organization of, 247–248
Brain damage, 376
Brain development
    infants, 138–139
    preschool years, 246–249
Brainstem, 138
Braxton-Hicks contractions, 115
Brazil, low-income children in, 23
Breadth of focus
    behavioral learning approaches and, 42
    cognitive approaches and, 48
    contextual approaches and, 50
    psychodynamic theories and, 39
    social cognitive learning approach and, 42
Breast development, 445
Breast feeding
    formula versus, 154–156
    Hindu sects, 14
    multicultural view, 156–157
    sense of smell and, 144–145
Breathing
    low birth weight and, 152(fig), 153
    newborns, 133, 135
    See also Respiratory problems
Breech presentation, 114, 124
Broca's area, 248
Bronfenbrenner's ecological settings for developmental change, 7–8
Bulimia, 451, 464–465

Caesarean section, 120, 124–125
Calcium, pregnancy and, 112
Canalization, 81–82, 101–102
Care
    beliefs about, 489–498
    ethics of, see Ethics of care
Caregivers
    attachment to, 215–224
    continuity of care, 220
    effects of children's physical growth on, 257–260
    frequent changes, 217
    infant synchrony, 208–210, 211
    multiple, 223–224
    See also Professional caregivers
Caregiver speech, 194
Case study, 23–24
Catch-up growth, 241
Catharsis, 299
Cause, correlations and, 22
Cells, 60(fig)
    division of, 62

Central nervous system
    alcohol abuse and, 462
    infant development, 137–139
    skill development and, 45
Cephalic presentation, 114
Cephalocaudal growth pattern, 93
Cephalocaudal principal, skill development and, 148
Cephalopelvic disproportion, 124
Cerebellum, 138
Cerebral cortex, 138, 139
Cervix, 91, 116, 117
Change
    context for, 31–32
    desirable, 16
    information processing and, 46–47
    longitudinal studies and, 19
    nature of, 3–8
    Piaget's cognitive theory and, 44
    undesirable, 16
Character roles, 300–301
Characteristics, correlations between, 22
Child/children
    active versus passive role in development, 30–31, 39
    advocates for, 9
    effects of physical growth on, 260
    history of, in Western society, 10
    influence on parenting style, 310–311
    informed consent and, 25
    methods of studying, 16–24
    popular, 414–415, 519
    prenatal influences on, 101
    realistic expectations for, 8
    reasons for having, 100–101
    unpopular, 415–416, 519
Child abuse and neglect, 310, 329–332
    physical punishment and, 322, 330–331
    sexual abuse, 6, 332, 371, 465
    suicide attempts and, 535
Child and family policy, 9
Childbirth, see Birth
Child care
    attachment formation and, 223–224
    coparenting, 207–208, 210–211
    good, 214
    grandparents and, 212
    language acquisition influences, 195
    maternal employment and, 425
    sick children and, 353
Child care centers, serving infants and toddlers, 212–214
Child care teacher, preparation for, 214
Child characteristics, child abuse and neglect and, 329–330
Children, see Child/children
Children's welfare
    researcher and, 26
    family policy, 9
Chinese children
    infant temperament, 205–206
    mathematics learning, 372
    parenting style and, 309–310
    talking with, 192, 193
Chlamydia, 97
Choices
    autonomy and, 226
    capacity to freely make, 36
    giving children, 11
Chorion, 77
Chorionic villi, 77
Chorionic villus sampling (CVS), 76–77
Chromosomal disorders,prenatal screening for, 76
Chromosomes, 59, 60(fig), 61–62
    abnormal, 68–70
    gender determination and, 66–67
    inheriting extra, 70
    karyotypes of, 59, 60
    meiosis and, 62
    mitosis and, 62–63
Chronic illness, 353
Chums, 406

Cigarette smoking, see Smoking
Circular reactionprimary, 173
Circular reactions
    secondary, 173–176, 178
    tertiary, 176–178
Civil rights, AIDS and, 354
Class differences, see Socioeconomic
    status
Classical conditioning, 40, 41(fig),
    182–183
Classification
    middle childhood, 362
    preschool years, 267–268
Cleft palate/lip, 73
Climate, allelic adaptations to, 85
Clique, 517–518
Clitoris, 444
Cocaine, maternal use of, 105, 108–109
Codominance, 65
Cognition
    defined, 163
    meta-, 46, 47, 372–376
    realms of, 387
    shared, 391
    social development and, 392
Cognitive ability, basic, 476
Cognitive control processes, 46–47
Cognitive development, 5
    cultural context and, 48–49
    drawing revealing, 254
    early education and, 290
    first two years, 162–196
    gender roles and, 326
    information processing theory, 46–48
    language acquisition and, 187–195
    malnutrition and, 156, 244
    neo-Piagetian theories, 45, 47–48,
        53(fig)
    observational learning and, 41
    physical growth and, 358
    Piaget's theory, see Piaget's theories
    play and, 11, 299
Cognitive development in adolescence,
    468–498
    critical thinking, 480–4833
    egocentrism, 483, 484–485
    formal thought, 471–475
    general features of, 470–471
    information–processing features,
        475–479
    moral development and, 489–498
    political ideas, 485–487
    religious beliefs, 487–489
    social cognition, 483–98
    supporting, 480–483
Cognitive development in first two
    years, 162–196
    arousal, 164
    auditory perception, 169–170
    behavioral learning, 181–187
    classical conditioning, 182–183
    habituation, 164–165
    heart rate, 164
    imitation, 185–186
    language acquisition, 186, 187–195
    memory, 164–165
    operant conditioning, 183–185
    perception, 163, 154–171
    phonology, 188–190
    Piaget's theory of sensorimotor intelli-
        gence, 171–181
    semantics, 188, 190–191
    toys supporting, 173(tab)
    visual perception, 166–169
    ways of studying, 164–165
Cognitive development in middle child-
    hood, 361–392
    concrete operational skills, 361–365
    conservation, 364–365
    information–processing skills,
        367–379
    intelligence, 383–392
    language development, 379–383
    learning disabilities, 376–379

    learning strategies, 372–376
    memory, 367–372
    peers and, 406, 408
    Piaget's theory, 361–365
Cognitive development in preschool
    years, 262–294
    appearance-reality distinction, 267
    children's theories of mind, 266–267
    classification skills, 263
    conservation, 268
    distinguishing natural kinds and arti-
        facts, 270–271
    early childhood education and,
        289–294
    language acquisition and develop-
        ment, 263, 273–289
    language/thought relationships,
        286–289
    learning strategies, 374–375
    memory, 368, 369
    neostructuralist theories of, 272–273
    numbers concepts, 269–270
    Piaget's preoperational stage, 264–265
    recall, 368
    reversibility, 268
    symbiotic thought, 265
    zone of proximal development,
        271(fig), 272
Cognitive flexibility, bilingualism and,
    380–381
Cognitive functioning, children of teen
    mothers, 533
Cognitive module, 287
Cognitive reinforcement, 299
Cognitive skills
    concrete operations, 362
    conservation, 363–364
    pretend play and, 301
    preterm infants, 153
Cognitive strategies, solving social prob-
    lems and, 480–481
Cognitive structures, 45
Cognitive tasks
    functional capacity, 476
    structural capacity, 476–478
Collective autonomy, genetic counseling
    and, 74
Collectivism, 522
Colors, infant perception of, 167
Coming out, 530
Communal childrearing, attachment for-
    mation and, 224
Communication
    competence in, 273
    context of, 380
    cultural styles, 490–491
Communication skills, autonomy and,
    226
Community
    adolescent behavior expectations, 511
    child abuse and, 331
    involvement in health care reform, 247
    orientation to, 342–343
    violence-plagued, 416
Competence
    achievement motivation and, 401–402
    authoritative parenting and, 520
    cliques and, 518
    communicative, 273
    dating and, 529
    development of, 229, 396, 399–405
    feeling lack of, 401
    multicultural, 414
    performance versus, 181
    Piaget's theory of cognitive develop-
        ment, 181
    psychosocial theory, 37
Competition
    athletics and, 346–348
    peers and, 406
Competitiveness, aggressive behavior
    and, 416
Compliance, toddler's capacity for, 230
Compromise, peers and, 406

Conception, 60, 61(fig), 91–92
    technological alternatives to normal,
        98–99
Conceptual thinking, 163
    logical skill and, 388
    metaphors and, 380
Concordance rates, 83
Concrete operational thought, 471
    formal thought versus, 472–474
    games with rules and, 301–302
    memory and, 370
    Piaget's theory, 43(tab), 48, 361–367,
        370, 472–474
Conditioned response, 40
Conditioned stimulus, 182–183
Conditioning theories
    classical conditioning, 40, 41(fig),
        182–183
    operant conditioning, 40, 183–185, 226
Condoms, 459, 460, 531
Conduct disorders, delinquency and, 536
Confidentiality, research and, 24
Conflicts
    adolescent-parent, 509–510, 511
    with peers, 406
    preschool years, 317–323
    psychosexual development and, 33
    psychosocial, 34–37
Conflictual independence, 509
Conform, pressures to, 417–418, 517,
    518–519
Congenital heart disease, 73
Connectedness, sociable infants and, 209
Conscience, 33
Conscious, Freudian theory and, 32
Conservation
    language habits and, 288
    middle childhood, 363–364
    preschool children, 268
    training, 364
Consistency
    ADHD children and, 357
    changing aggressive behavior and,
        322
Consolidation-of-self subphase, adoles-
    cent identity and, 503
Constancy, longitudinal studies and, 18
Constructive play, 299, 300
Constructivist philosophy, 365
Contact comfort, 216
Context
    adapting abilities to, 387
    aggressive behavior, 416
    attractiveness and, 450
    cognitive development, 48–49
    communication, 380
    development and, 7–8, 14–15, 31–32,
        48–50, 53
    temperament and, 205
Contextual developmental theories,
    48–50, 51, 53
Contextual dialogue, 195
Contingent cues, self-recognition based
    on, 227
Contingent dialogue, 194, 195
Continuity
    caregiving, 220
    in development, 13
Contraceptives, 111, 458, 531–532
Control, variances in, 19–22
Control, sense of, intrinsic motivation
    and, 402
Control group, 21–22
Control processes, cognitive, 46–47
Convoy of support, 516–517
Cooperation
    peers and, 406
    prosocial behavior and, 315, 317
    television teaching, 324
Cooperative learning, 402–403, 413, 431
Cooperative play, 303(tab), 304
Coordinated interactions, in play, 304
Coordination, difficulties with, 344–345
Coparenting, 207–208, 210–211

Coping skills
    preventing abuse and, 332
    triarchic theory of intelligence and,
        387
Core self, 38
Correlation coefficient, 22
Correlations, 22
Counseling, genetic, 73–79
Counting skills, 269–270
Crack cocaine, 108
Crawling, 148
Creative play, 298
Creative thinking, intelligence tests and,
    385
Creativity, gifted students and, 391
Creeping, 148
Crib death, 140, 141
Criminal behavior, television violence
    and, 323
Critical period in prenatal growth, 102,
    103(fig)
Critical thinking, 480–483
Cross-cultural miscommunication,
    490–491
Cross-sectional study, 17–18
Crowd, 517, 518, 520
Crying
    responding to, 185, 221
    types of, 200–201
Cultural assumptions, intelligence tests
    and, 385–386, 391
Cultural differences
    achievement orientations, 403–404
    breast feeding and, 156–157
    children's sleep, 242–243
    communication, 490–491
    genetic counseling, 74–75
    height, 341(fig)
    infant temperament and, 205–206
    learning mathematics, 372–373
    motor development, 150–151
    parental achievement expectations,
        404–405
    perceptions of pain during childbirth
        and, 122–123
    prosocial behavior, 317
    self-concept and, 399
    See also Multicultural view
Cultural factors, play and, 305
Cultural vertigo, 523
Culture
    alcohol use and, 109
    authoritarian parenting and, 309
    bilingualism and, 382
    child abuse context, 330–331
    cognitive development and, 48–49
    practicesearly childhood education
        and, 292–293
    food preferences and, 246
    infant perception and, 170–171
    professional caregiver's background,
        195
    race and, 84
    school, 429
    stereotypes for attractiveness,
        448–451, 453, 464
    temperament and, 84
    women's axillary hair and, 446
    world view and, 522
    zones of proximal development and,
        391
Curriculum
    formal, 430
    gifted students and, 390
    informal, 430
    middle school, 521
    Piaget's influence on, 366–367
    quality high schools, 524
    unofficial, 399–400
Custody, divorce and, 423–424
Customs, siblings transmitting,
    311
Cystic fibrosis, 71, 78
Cytomegalovirus, 105, 106

Dangers, autonomy and, 226
Date rape, 529
Dating
    adolescence, 529
    daughters of divorced parents and, 423
    early-maturing girls, 453
Day care
    attachment formation and, 223–224
    See also Child care
Daydreams, in adolescence, 470
Deafchildren, 189, 283, 284–285
Death
    adolescent, 456, 460, 535–536
    AIDS and, 458
    alcohol and drug use, 460
    infant, 126, 140, 141, 159, 533
    newborns, 126, 140, 141
    schoolchildren, 350–351
    sudden infant death syndrome, 140, 141
    suicide, 535–536
    understanding, 350
Décallage, 364
Decentration, 362
Defense mechanisms, 33
Deferred imitation, 177
Delinquency, 505, 536
    antisocial peers and, 518
    parenting style and, 511
    preventing, 537
    working adolescents, 525
Delivery, see Birth
Democratic parents, 512
Dependence, 226
Dependent variable, 21
Depression, adolescent, 535–536
Depressive syndrome, 535
Depth perception, 168–169
Descriptive observation, Piaget and, 12
Desires, gaining satisfaction for, 299
Despair, psychosocial theory and, 37
Detail, attention to, 373–374
Developed countries, chronic illness in, 353
Development
    birth weight and, 126
    Bronfenbrenner's four ecological settings for, 7–8
    cognitive, see Cognitive development
    context and, 7–8, 14–15, 31–32, 48–50, 53
    continuity and discontinuity and, 13
    continuous, 31, 39, 50
    deficit and, 15–16
    defined, 3
    difference and, 15–16
    domains of, 4–5, 6
    ecological systems and, 7–8
    example of (Jodi), 6–7
    informal theories of, 29
    landmarks of, 5(fig)
    Mahler's phases of, 38
    milestones, 15–16
    nature of, 3–8
    nature and nurture, 13
    personal experiences and, 6–7
    physical, 4, 5
    physical, see Physical development
    Piaget's theories of, see Piaget's theories
    prenatal influences on, 101–114
    psychosocial, see Psychosocial development
    shape of, 31(fig)
    stages of, see Stages of development
    standards of normal, 12
    studying, 3–26
    theories of, 28–54
    trends, 16
    universal, 7, 14–15
Developmental disability, children of teen mothers and, 533
Developmentally appropriate play opportunities, 304

Developmentally appropriate practices, in early childhood education, 291–293
Developmental problems
    permissive parenting and, 310
    risk of abuse and, 330
Developmental psychology
    genetics and, 87
    uses of, 8–10
Developmental study, 3–26
    basic issues in, 12–16
    confidentiality and, 24
    correlations and, 22
    descriptive observations in, 12
    early precursors to, 10
    emergence of modern, 10–12
    ethical constraints on, 24–26
    experimental studies, 20–22
    full disclosure of purposes, 24–25
    history of, 10–12
    individual's freedom to participate, 25
    informed consent and, 25
    in loco parentis and, 25–26
    methods of, 16–24
    naturalistic studies, 19–20
    reasons for, 8–10
    sampling strategies, 22–24
    scientific method, 16–17
    variations in control, 19–22
    variations in time frame, 17–19
Developmental themes, 30–32
    behavioral learning approaches, 42
    cognitive approaches, 47–48
    contextual approaches, 50
    psychodynamic approaches, 39
Developmental theories, 28–54
    active versus passive role of child and, 30–31, 39
    behavioral learning, 39–41, 52(fig)
    cognitive, 43–48, 53(fig)
    comparison of, 51–54
    contextual, 48–50, 53
    developmental themes and, 30–32
    Erikson's, see Erikson's theories
    ethological approach, 50
    Freudian, 32–33, 39, 52(fig)
    nature of, 29–32
    Piaget's, see Piaget's theories
    psychodynamic, 32–39, 51, 52(fig)
    social cognitive learning, 41–42, 53(fig)
Diabetes, 240, 342, 463
Dialogue
    contingent, 194, 195
    textual, 194, 195
Diaphragm, 531
Dichotic listening, 248
Diet
    birth weight and, 152
    earlier maturation and, 442
    hyperactivity and, 356
    infants, 154–158
    influencing weight through, 239
    pregnancy and, 100, 111–112
Diethylstilbestrol (DES), 105, 108
Dieting, 342–343, 463
Differentiation subphase, adolescent identity and, 502
Difficult babies, 204
Difficult children, 316, 319
Diffusion of industry, 504–505
Diffusion of time perspective, 504
Dilated cervix, 116
Directive approach to authority, 75
Direct learning, 43
Disabilities
    developmental, see Developmental disability
    learning, see Learning disabilities
    risk of abuse and, 330
    sports-related injuries and, 345
Disadvantaged circumstances, failure to thrive and, 158

Discipline, 243, 307(fig)
    aggression and, 319, 320, 321–322
    divorce and, 423
Discrimination, 413
Diseases
    breast-fed infants, 154–155
    genetic, 70–73
    inherited, 68
    physical growth effects, 240–241
    prenatal influences, 104–107
    See also Illnesses
Divorce
    adolescent development and, 513–514
    effects of, 420–425, 535
    percentage of US marriages ending in, 421(fig)
    poverty and, 9
    psychological tasks of children of, 423(tab)
    suicide attempts and, 535
DNA (deoxyribonucleic acid), 59–61
Domains of development, 4–5, 6
Domestic violence, during pregnancy, 111
Dominant gene, 64–65
Dominant gene disorders, 70–71
Doubt, autonomy versus, 31, 36, 231
Down syndrome, 68–69, 76(tab), 78, 103
Dramatic play, 300
Drawing
    representational, 254
    samples, 255
    skills, 254
Dropouts 518, 522–523, 533
Drugs
    medicinal, 105, 107–108
    nonmedicinal, 108–110
    See also Medications
Drug use, 439
    adolescence, 456, 458, 459, 460–462, 525
    AIDS and, 106
    birth weight and, 152
    early-maturing girls, 453
    maternal, 105, 107–110, 152
    sexually transmitted diseases and, 458, 459
    types of drugs, 461(fig)
    working adolescents, 525
Duos, 273
Dyslexia, 376, 378
Dysmenorrhea, 445

Early adolescence, 438
Early childhood, domains of development, 5(fig)
Early childhood education, 289–293
Early-maturing boys, 451–452
Early-maturing girls, 452–453
Easy babies, 204
Easy child, peer contact and, 316
Eating disorders, 332, 449, 451, 464–465
Ecological systems, contexts of development and, 7–8
Ecological systems theory, 31–32, 49
Economic factors
    dropping out and, 522
    gang membership and, 536
    play and, 305
    prenatal care and, 112, 113(fig)
    See also Socioeconomic status
Economic hardship, 126
    divorce and, 420
    failure to thrive and, 243
    paternal unemployment and, 426
    preterm births and, 152
Economic independence, 509
Ectoderm, of blastocyst, 93
Ectomorphic body type, 448–450
Education
    addressing child poverty and, 245
    AIDS, 354, 459–460
    bilingual, 382
    child care teachers, 214
    cognitive development and, 48–49

critical thinking, 482–483
early childhood, 289–293
equality of, 391
gifted students and, 390–391
improving, 524, 525(tab)
individualizing, 372
learning disabilities and, 378
memory capacity and, 369
middle childhood, 396, 429–431
multicultural activities, 414
parental involvement in, 511
Piaget's influence on, 365
television used for, 324
See also School
Educationally disadvantaged parents, 126
Effacement of cervix, 116
Egg cell, see Ovum
Ego, 32, 35(tab)
Egocentrism
    adolescent, 442, 483–485, 497
    middle childhood, 405–406
    moral action and, 497
Ego integrity, 37
Ego-ideal, 33
Ejaculation of mobile sperm, 444
Elaboration, 374
Elders, respect for, 307, 309
Electra conflict, 400
Electronic fetal monitoring, 125
Embryo, 93–95
    gender determination and, 66–67
Embryonic stage of prenatal development, 91, 93–95
Emergent literacy, 290
Emotion(s), 5
    aggressive behavior and, 317, 319
    boys and, 327
    depression and, 535
    drawings revealing, 254
    effects of growth, 357–358
    expressions of, 201
    grief, 350
    infant, 50, 200–202, 206
    menstruation and, 445
    naturalistic study of, 19–20
    play and, 11, 299
    self-regulation of, 201–202
    twin studies and, 13
    "typical" child acquiring, 8
    unresolved, 400–401
Emotional autonomy, 511
Emotional cues, social referencing and, 227
Emotional growth, school function, 520
Emotional health, peers and, 406
Emotional independence, 509
Emotional problems
    abused children, 331
    divorce and, 422
Emotional support
    adolescent friendships and, 514
    birth and, 126
Emotional warps, 406
Empathic mirroring, 38
Empathy
    abused children and, 331
    adolescence, 485
    authoritative parents and, 308
    parental, 308, 329, 330
    preschool years, 315–316
Employment
    adolescence, 524–525
    divorce and, 420
    effects on families, 425
    genetic disorders and, 73
    maternal, see Mothers, working
    meaningful, 37
    teenage pregnancy and, 533
    workplace hazards, 110
Endocrine glands, deficiency in, 240
Endoderm, of blastocyst, 93
Endomorphic body type, 448–450

English
  Black, 382–383
  Standard, 382–383
Enrichments, gifted education and, 390
Environment
  accidents, 351–352
  adapting abilities to, 387
  critical thinking and, 483
  alcohol and drug use, 462
  effective schools, 431
  exploring from secure base, 217
  failure to thrive and, 158
  genetics and, 64, 66, 80–87
  hyperactivity and, 356
  intellectual development and, 84–85,
    86, 483
  motivational orientation, 403
  motor skill development and, 149–150
  multifactorial disorders and, 72
  play, 304–305
  polygenic phenotypes and, 66
  reaction to, 202
  sociocultural definitions of intelligence
    and, 389
  supportive, 231
Environmental hazards, prenatal devel-
    opment and, 110
Epidural, 121, 122(tab)
Equilibrium, Piaget's cognitive theory
    and, 44
Erikson's theories, 34–37, 39
  adolescence and, 439
  developmental crises, 231, 401
  crises of industry versus inferiority,
    401
  identity development, 504
  psychosocial theory, 30–31, 34–37, 39,
    51, 52(fig)
  summary of, 52(fig)
Estrogen, 446, 447
Ethics
  study methods and, 24–26
  superego and, 33
Ethics of care, 16, 495–498
Ethnicity
  appearance and, 239, 341, 452–453
  friendships with persons of another,
    516
  height and, 341(fig)
  intelligence tests and, 386
  parenting style and, 512–513
  peer group membership and, 412–414
  positive orientation, 522–523
  temperament and, 84
Ethological view, infant-caregiver ties
    and, 215
European children
  infant mortality, 159
  physical development, 239–240
Evocative gene–environment relation-
    ship, 82
Evolutionary biology, development and,
    50
Exercise, 342–343
  influencing weight through, 239, 463
  pregnancy and, 100
  testosterone and, 447
  See also Athletics
Exosystem, 7, 8, 49
Expectations
  effective schools, 431
  informal curriculum and, 430
  minority students, 405
  preschooler behavior, 321
  siblings transmitting, 311
  student achievement, 430
Experiences, 13
  accommodation and, 172
  assimilation of, 44, 172, 301
  attachment formation, 217
  behavioral learning approaches, 42
  cognitive approaches, 47
  comparing with others, 485
  conceptualizing, 163

contextual approaches, 50
development and, 6–7
family history of, 419
Freudian theory, 32
gene–environment relationship and,
    82
habituation and, 165
learning reading and writing through,
    290
making sense out of, 9
organizing and understanding, 396,
    397
perceptions and, 163
Piaget's cognitive theory, 44
psychodynamic approaches, 39
psychodynamic theories, 39
recognition memory and, 368
sense of self, 397, 399
role of maturation versus, 30, 39
social cognitive learning approach
    and, 42
symbolic thought and, 265
temperament and, 205
triarchic theory of intelligence, 387
Experimental group, 21–22
Experimental studies, 20–22
Experimentation
  drug use, 461
  infant, 171
Expertise
  adolescent, 478–479
  genetic counselor and, 75
  middle childhood, 371(fig)
  specialized developments of, 47
Explanations, meaningful, 30
Exploration, 217
  competence and, 229
  safety and, 259
Expressive language, 190–191
Extended families, 74, 293, 522
  attachment formation and, 224
  Hindu sects, 14
  supports for childrearing, 308
Externalizing distress, divorce and, 422
Extinction, 40
Extrinsic motivation, 402
Eye color, genetic transmission of, 64,
    65(fig)

Facial expressions, infant emotions and,
    201
Facial features
  changes in children's, 257–258
  infant, 136–137
Factory towns, 10
Failure
  attribution for, 402
  psychosocial theory and, 37
Failure to thrive, 109, 158–159, 242–244
Fairness
  critical thinking and, 482
  moral thinking and, 490
  principles of, 16
Faith, 488
False labor, 115
False-belief task, 266–267, 287
False recognition task, 370
Familial self, 522
Familiarity, memory and, 371–372
Families
  aggressive behavior and, 416
  alcohol and drug use, 462
  Asian cultures and, 74–75
  at-risk, see At-risk families
  birth effects on, 126–127
  blended, 424
  changing nature of modern, 419–420
  dynamics, 54
  employment effects on, 425
  extended, see Extended families
  interdependence in, 14
  middle childhood relationships, 396,
    418–429
  social class differences, 512

delinquency and, 536
  eating disorders and, 464
  fictive kin, 308
  motivational orientation, 403, 404–405
  reconstituted, 420, 424
Family conversations, 311
Family day care homes, 213–214
Family-leave policies, 222
Family policy, 9, 222
Fantasies
  adolescence, 470
  play, 314
  sexual, 444
Fat, see Body fat
Father(s)
  attachment formation and, 221–222
  authoritarian parenting and, 309
  collective autonomy families and, 74
  coparenting, 207–208, 210–211
  death of, 350
  household chores, 425
  infant interactions with, 205, 210–211
  infant temperament and, 205
  involvement after divorce, 424
  Lamaze method and, 120–124
  play with, 211
  primary caregiver, 210–211
  separation from, 513
  teenage, 111, 533
  transition to parenthood and, 207
  unemployed, 426–427
Father's age, Down syndrome and, 69
Faulty passageway, delivery and, 123,
    124
Faulty passenger, delivery and, 123, 124
Faulty power, delivery and, 123–124
Fears, autonomy and, 226
Feelings, see Emotion(s)
Females
  chromosomes, 60, 66–67
  households headed by, 9
  infertility and, 97
  pregnancy experience, 98–100
  reproductive cells, 91
  sex chromosomes and, 66–67
  See also Girls; Mother(s)
Female sex hormone, 446
Fertilization, 61(fig)
Fetal alcohol effects, 109
Fetal alcohol syndrome (FAS), 109
Fetal stage of development, 91, 95–97
  canalization and, 101–102
  critical period, 102, 103(fig)
  environmental hazards, 110
  risk factors, 102–114
Fetal monitoring, 125
Fetal presentation, 114
Fetoscopy, 76(tab), 77
Fetus, 91, 95–97
  exposure to speech, 206
  full term, 114
  genetic screening and, 75–79
  influences on, 101–114
Fictive kin, 308
Fidelity, psychosocial theory and, 37
Fine motor skills
  drawing and, 254–256
  gender development, 151
  infants, 147, 148–149, 151
First stage of labor, 116
Fit, infant-family, 205
Fixation, Freud's psychosexual stages
    and, 33
Folic acid, 112
Fontanelles, 134
Food, solid, 156, 157, 158
Food banks, 246
Food dependence, adolescent, 463
Food preferences, preschooler, 241
Forceps, 124
Formal curriculum, 430
Formal operational, 48
  adolescence, 469, 471–475
  experiment, 473(fig)

Formal thought, confusion of viewpoints
    and, 484
Formula, breast milk versus, 154–158
Fraternal twins
  IQ score correlations, 82
  studies of, 84
Freestanding birth centers, 119–120
Freud's theories
  adolescence and, 439
  latency period and, 400–401
  personality structure, 32–33
  psychosexual development, 339
  summary of, 52(fig)
Friendships
  adolescence, 514–516, 518
  conceptions of, 314–315
  early childhood, 312–315
  evolution of, 313–314
  interethnic, 516
  middle childhood, 407–414
  very active children, 355–356
  See also Peers
Frustration, aggressive behavior and,
    318, 319
Functional capacity, 476–478
Functional independence, 509
Functional play, 299, 300
Functional relationships, 265
Future, thinking about, 470

Games with rules, 301, 344–349
Gamete intrafallopian tube transfer
    (GIFT), 98–99
Gametes, 59, 61(fig), 91–92
Gang membership, 518, 536–537
Gardner's theory of multiple intelli-
    gences, 388–389
Gazing, 155, 192, 208, 221
Gender, 325
  boundaries, 412, 413(tab)
  genetic determination of, 66–67
  peer group membership and, 409
  prenatal tests for, 76(tab), 78
Gender constancy, 325, 326
Gender development
  influences on, 326–328
  social cognitive learning approach
    and, 42
  social development in early childhood
    and, 325–329
Gender differences
  activity level, 355
  adolescent friendships, 516
  aggressive behavior, 319–320
  body fat, 441, 447
  coping strategies, 320
  divorce effects, 422
  early athletics and, 348–349
  growth spurt, 440
  height changes, 340
  homophobia, 530
  illnesses, 353
  masturbation, 526–527
  in morality, 495–496
  motor development, 151
  peer groups, 327–328, 518
  physical development in preschool
    years, 256–257
  play and, 327
  in punishment, 327
  sexual activity, 527
  sexual fantasies, 526
  suicide attempts, 535
  See also Boys; Girls
Gender equality, 327
Gender identity, 325, 326
Gender preferences, 325
Gender roles, 7, 8
  adolescent identity and, 506
  androgyny and, 328–329
  fathers and, 210–211
  illnesses and, 353
  motor skills and, 151, 257
  peer pressure and, 327–328

play and, 51, 412
television portrayal of , 324, 328
working mothers and, 425
Gender role stereotypes, 325–326, 327
athletic activity, 349
body image, 448–451
height, 341
peer activities, 408, 410–411
sexuality, 528
Gender schema theory, 326
General ability tests, biases of, 385–386, 391
General anesthesia, delivery and, 121–122
Generative syntactic rules, 274
Generativity, psychosocial theory and, 37
Genes, 59, 60(fig)
abnormal, 70–73
canalization and, 81–82, 101–102
DNA and, 59–61
dominant, 64–65
environment relationship, 82
inherited, 63–64
recessive, 64–65, 71–72
Genetic counseling, 73–79
Genetic disorders
counseling for, 73–79
medical treatments, 79
prenatal screening, 75–79
risk of, 70(tab)
Genetic expression, individual, 63–68
Genetics, 13, 58–87
abnormalities, 68–73
behavior and, 63, 80–87
developmental psychology and, 87
diseases, 70–73
DNA and, 59–61
dominant and recessive genes and, 64–65
environment and, 80–87
gender determination and, 66–67
lateral preferences and, 249
measures of influence, 82–83
meiosis and, 62
mitosis and, 62–63
motor skill development and, 149–150
physical growth effects, 239–240
polygenic transmission, 66
race and, 84–85
sex-linked transmission and, 67–68
transmission of multiple variations, 65–66
Genetic screening, 73
Genetic structures, 59, 60(fig)
Genetic testing, preimplantation, 78–79
Genetic transmission
mechanisms of, 59–63
of multiple variations, 65–66
Genital focus
Freudian theory and, 33
psychosocial theory and, 36
Genital herpes, 105
Genotype, 63–64
phenotype influence and, 80–87
range of reaction and, 81
German infants, attachment patterns, 218
German measles, 104
Germinal stage of prenatal development, 91, 92–93
Gifted students, 390–391
Gilligan's ethics of care, 495–496
Girls
adolescent deaths and, 456
adolescent friendships, 516
adolescent nutrition, 463
aggressive behavior and, 319–320
body hair, 446
body image, 448
divorce and, 422–423
early athletics, 348–349
early maturing, 452
eating disorders, 464
ethics of care, 496

growth spurt, 440
handedness and, 249
Hindu families, 14
identity formation, 327
illnesses, 353
language differences, 282
late-maturing, 453
learned helplessness, 402
motor development, 151
on-time-maturing, 454
peers and, 408, 409–412
physical appearance, 449, 451, 452, 453
physical development in preschool years, 256–257
primary sexual maturation, 444–445
running speed and throwing distance, 349(fig)
secondary sex characteristics, 445–446
smoking, 462
sudden infant death syndrome and, 141
voice changes, 446
Glasses, need for, 250
Glia, 138
Gluten intolerance, 240
Goals, adolescent, 470
Gonorrhea, 104, 105
Grammar
Black English, 383
predisposition to infer, 276–277
rules, 276–277, 280
Grandparents, infant interaction with, 212
Grasping, 147, 148–149, 173, 179
Greek infants, temperament and, 205–206
Grieving, 350
Gross motor skills, 147–148, 151
Growth
adolescence, 440–443
catch-up, 241
preschool years, 237–244
undesirable directions of, 16
Growth hormones, 240–241, 242
Growth spurt, 440
Guilt, initiative versus, 36, 231

Habituation, 142, 164–165
Hair, growth in puberty, 446
Handedness, 248, 249
Happiness, 397
Head injuries, hyperactivity and, 356
Head Start, 290
Health
adolescence, 455–464
middle childhood, 349–355
obesity and, 342
poverty and, 244–247
Health care
access to, 244, 246–247
adolescents and, 455–456
child abuse and neglect and, 331
earlier maturation and, 442
failure to thrive and, 244
genetic disorders and, 73
income level and, 246–247, 353
physical growth effects, 240, 241
poverty and, 246–247
prenatal, 112–114
health of preschool children and, 244
Health care system, reforming, 246–247
Health insurance, 456
Health maintenance organizations, genetic disorders and, 73
Health problems in adolescents, 455, 456
Hearing
auditory perception and, 169–170
coordination of vision with, 170
hemispheric lateralization of brain and, 248
inborn integrated schemes and, 179
infants, 143–144
problems in, 353

Hearing-impaired children, language acquisition and development and, 283–285
Heart disease, 73, 342
Heart rates, infant cognition and, 164
Height
adolescence, 440–443
genetic influences on, 83, 239
growth over childhood, 440(fig)
heritability estimate for, 83
maturation and, 30
middle childhood, 339–341
newborns, 135(fig), 137
poverty and, 245(fig)
preschool years, 237–239
puberty and, 340–341
Hemispheric lateralization, 248
Hemophilia, 68
Heredity, see Genetics
Heritability estimates, 82–83
Heroin, maternal use of, 105, 108
Herpes, delivery and, 125
Heteronomous morality, 490
Heterosexuality, 527–530
Heterozygous, 65, 71
Heuristics, 478, 479(tab)
High schools, improving, 524
Hispanic-American families, 522
Hispanic children, 15
AIDS and, 106
parental achievement expectations, 404–405
Historical context development and, 49
HIV (human immunodeficiency virus), 354, 458
Hobbies, as social supports, 428
Holophrases, 284
Home
adolescent leaving, 509, 510
changing locations, 519
childproofing, 148
Home birth, 119, 120
Homeless adolescents, 459, 461
Home visits, social workers and, 9
Homework, parental responses to, 372
Homicides, 9, 456, 460
Homophobia, 530
Homosexuality, 528, 530
Homozygous, 65
Hope, psychosocial theory and, 36
Hormones
growth, 240–241, 242
in pregnancy, 98–99
in puberty, 446–447
Hospitals, childbirth in, 118–119
Hostile aggression, 318–319
Housework, maternal employment and, 425
Human evolution, biosocial, 85
Human face, infant preference for, 166–167
Human genome project, 68, 84–85
Human immunodeficiency virus (HIV), 354, 458
Human mind, children's understanding of, 20–21
Hunches, 471
Huntington disease, 71, 86
Hyperactivity
ADHD and, 355–357
risk of abuse and, 330
unpopular children and, 415
Hypertension, overweight and, 463
Hypotheses, 17, 471

Id, 32
Ideas, formal operational thinkers and, 472
Identical twins, adoption studies, 84
Identification, autonomy and, 226
Identity, 5
adolescent development of, 501–507, 517
adolescent's peers and, 517

alcohol and drug use and, 461
bicultural, 453
divorce and, 513
Erikson's theory of development, 30–31, 34–37
gangs and, 537
gender, 325, 326
gender differences in formation of, 327
intimacy and, 505
middle childhood, 396, 397–399
negative, 505
preschooler's belief in, 264–265, 268
psychosocial theory and, 34–37
role confusion versus, 37, 504
Identity development theories, 30–31, 34–37, 504–506
Identity crises, 34–35, 504–506
Identity diffusion, 504–505, 506, 517
Identity foreclosure, 506, 517
Identity status, 505–506
Ideology, 487
Idiomatic expressions, 277
Idiosyncratic child abuse and neglect, 331
Illnesses
acute, 352–353
adolescence, 457–460
AIDS, 353–355
chronic, 352
death from, 351
interventions to prevent, 246
low-income preschoolers, 244
middle childhood, 352–355
obesity and, 342
social influences on, 353
Imaginary audience, 485
Imagination, object representation and, 176–177
Imitation, 41
deferred, 177
language acquisition and, 278–279
learning through, 185–186
play and, 299
Immunizations, 9, 241
Implantation, 93
Impulse control, permissive parenting and, 310
Inborn qualities, 13
Incest, 332
Independence
adolescence, 503, 509–510, 514, 529
Asian families and, 74
capacity for, 31, 36
dating and, 529
psychosocial theory and, 36
Independent thinking, 272
Independent variable, 21
India, growing up in, 14–15
Individual achievements, white culture and, 15
Individual genetic expression, 63–68
Individualism, 342
adolescence, 501–504
Individuality
adolescence, 503
Asian families and, 74
Individual self, European-American world view and, 522
Induced labor, 124
Industrialization, 10
Industry, inferiority versus, 36–37, 401
Infant(s)
appearance of young, 133
attachment formation, 215–224
auditory perception, 169–170
behavioral changes, 144–145
behavioral learning, 181–187
behavioral self-regulation, 202
boy, 67
canalized development, 81
caregiver synchrony, 208–210, 211
child care centers for, 212–213
cognitive development, 162–196
cognitive effects of talking to, 192–193
competence and, 229–231

Infant(s) *continued*
daily experiences of, 229(fig)
deaths, 10, 149, 533
domains of development, 5(fig)
emergence of autonomy and, 225–231
emotions, 50, 200–202
experience of birth and, 121
facial features of, 136–137
family fit, 205
father's involvement with, 207,
210–211
functional play and, 300
gene-environment relationship and, 82
girl, 67
grandparent interaction with, 212
growth variations, 151–154
id and, 32
language acquisition, 187–195
low-birth-weight, *see* Low birth weight
motor development, 146–151
nervous system development, 137–142
nutrition, 111, 154–158, 240
object relations, 38
peer interaction, 214
perception, 163, 164–169
preterm, 152–154
professional caregivers and, 212–214
psychosocial development, 198–232
reflexes, 145, 146–147
self-esteem and, 231
sense of self and, 227–229
sensory development, 143–146
sibling interaction with, 2111
sleep and, 139–142
small-for-date, 152
social relationships, 206–215
states of arousal, 142
temperament, 50, 200–201, 205
visual perception, 166–169
working models and, 221
Infant day care, attachment formation
and, 223–224
Infant-directed speech, 193, 194, 281
Infectious diseases, adolescence and,
457(tab)
Inferiority, industry versus, 36–37, 401
Infertility, 97–98
Informal curriculum, 430
Information-processing skills
adolescence, 469, 475–479
critical thinking and, 483
intelligence and, 386–389
learning disabilities and, 376–379
learning strategies, 372–376
memory, 367–372
metacognition, 372–376
metaphors and, 380
middle childhood, 367–379
Information-processing theories, 46–47,
361
adolescence and, 469, 475–476
intelligence and, 386–389
learning strategies, 372–376
teaching critical thinking and, 483
Informed consent, 25
Informed training, 376
Inheritance, *see* Genetics
Initiative, guilt versus, 36, 231
Injuries
sports-related, 345–346
See also Accidents
In loco parentis, 25–26
Innate schemes, 43
Inner speech, 288
Instrumental aggression, 318–319,
330–331
Insults, aggression and, 319
Integrated care, 497
Intellectual development
environment and, 81
psychosocial theory and, 37
Intelligence(s)
bodily skills and, 383, 389
cultural differences in defining, 49

defining, 49, 383, 386–389
environment and, 81, 84–85, 86
genetics and, 82, 83, 84, 86
information-processing approaches to,
386–389
intellectual differences versus levels
of, 386
issues regarding, 383–384
measuring, 383–386, 389, 391
modules, 287
multiple, 388–389
parental beliefs about, 292–293
Piaget's theory of sensorimotor,
171–181
psychometric approached to, 384–386
race and, 84–85
range of reaction for, 81
social skills and, 383, 388–389
sociocultural approached to, 389–391
triarchic theory of, 387
See also IQ
Intelligence tests, 384–386
biases of, 385–386, 391
common misinterpretations, 386
multiple intelligences, 389
Interactions
contextual theories and, 49, 50
popular children and, 415
sense of self and, 397, 399
shared cognition and, 391
strategic, 485
with teachers, 430
See also Parent-child interactions
Interdependence, socialization for, 523
Internal consistency, theories and, 30
Internalizing distressdivorce and, 423
Internal working models, child abuse
and, 329
Interpersonal skill, 388–389
Interventions
aggressive behavior, 416
divorce and, 423
failure to thrive and, 244
Interviews, 23
Intimacy
adolescent friendships and, 514,
515–516
adolescent–parent relationship, 511
clique and, 517
identity and, 505
isolation versus, 37, 505
sexuality in adolescence and, 526–531
Intrapersonal skill, 388–389
Intrinsic motivation, 401–402, 403
In vitro fertilization (IVF), 79, 98
IQ
environment and, 81
genetics and, 81, 82
race controversy, 84–85
Iron-deficiency anemia, 463
Isolation
child abuse and, 331
divorce and, 421
intimacy versus, 37, 505
suicide attempts and, 535
Isotreitinoin (accutane), 108
Israeli infants, attachment and, 219
Israeli kibbutz, 224

Japanese children
attachment patterns, 218–219
mathematics learning, 372–373
Joint custody, 424
Jumping skills, 253
Junior high school, 521
Justice
beliefs about, 489–498
sense of, 16
Juvenile delinquency, *see* Delinquency
Juvenile period, 406

Karyotypes, 59, 60
Kinesthetic skill, 388
Klinefelter syndrome, 70

Knowledge
achievement tests measuring, 385
actual versus differences in, 386
expertise in specific domains of,
478–479, 481
integrating old and new roles, 383
logically constructed, 375
metacognitive, 372–376, 481–482
organization of, 13
peer activity, 408
recall and, 5
richness of, 371–372
shared, 391
storing, 5
Knowledge base, 47
Kohlberg's six stages of moral judgment,
490–495

Labia, development of, 444
Labor
contractions, 121
induced, 124
problems during, 123–125
stages of, 115–117
teenage pregnancy and, 533
See also Birth
Lactose intolerance, 240
LAD, *see* Language acquisition device
Laissez-faire parents, television viewing
and, 324
Lamaze method, 120–121
Language
Black English, 383
brain development and, 139
expressive, 190–191
intelligence and, 383
knowledge of standards and, 228
metalinguistic awareness and, 381
metaphorical, 380
play and, 11
receptive, 190–191
Language acquisition and development
action as basis for, 286–288
auditory perception and, 169
bilingualism and, 23, 380–382
Black English, 382–383
changes in, 5
deaf and hearing-impaired children,
283–285
differences in, 16
extremes in, 186, 187
first words and, 191
gender differences and, 282
grammatical rules and, 276–277
infants, 187–195
influencing, 191–195
LAD (language acquisition device), 280
malnourishment and, 244
mechanisms, 277–279
middle childhood, 379–383
motor skills and, 252
parental influences on, 192–194, 278,
281–282
phonology and, 188–190
play and, 264(fig)
pragmatics and, 273, 282
preschool years, 263, 273–289
professional caregiver influences, 195
semantics, 188, 190–191, 273, 275–277
socioeconomic differences and, 283
syntax, 273, 274–277
thought and, 286–289
Language skill, theory of multiple intelligences and, 388
Language acquisition device(LAD), 280,
287
Language use, 385
duos, 275
gender differences in, 282
pragmatics and, 273, 282
recasting, 281
Lanugo, 134, 152
Late adolescence, 438
Latency period, 400–401

Lateralized behaviors, 248–249
Law-breaking offenses, 536
Lead poisoning, 247
Learned helplessness, 402
Learning, 13
active, 366
assessment of, 367
attachment formation and, 220
behavioral approach, 39–41
behavioral, in infancy, 181–187
children of teen mothers, 533
confidence in, 402
conservation, 364
cooperative, 402–403, 413, 431
critical thinking, 482–483
cultural differences in, 372–373
deferred imitation and, 177
defined, 5
direct, 43
familiarity and, 371
grammatical rules, 277, 280
imitation, 185–186
information-processing theory and,
46–47
intrinsic motivation and, 402
language acquisition and, 286
lateral preferences and, 249
motor skills, 149–150, 253–254
neostructuralist theory of, 273
observational, 41, 227, 299, 375
open classroom, 431
operant conditioning and, 183–185
orientation, 401–402, 403
peers and, 406. 408
Piaget's cognitive theory and, 43–44
play and, 11
self-talk and, 288
semantics, 190
social cognitive approach, 41–42, 43
social learning theories and, 32
strategies for, 373–376
Learning difficulties, school programs to
assist with, 9
Learning disabilities
causes of, 376–378
failure to thrive and, 158
helping children with, 378–379
middle childhood, 376–379
preterm infants and, 153
screening for, 385, 386
understanding metaphors and, 380
Learning mathematics, cultural differences in, 372–373
Learning theories, 181
development process and, 31
play and, 299
Less developed countries, infant mortality in, 159
Lexicon, 188
Linkage studies, 85–86
Listening, dichotic, 248
Literacy skills, 22
Literal understanding, 20–21
Liver, alcohol abuse and, 462
Living conditions, earlier maturation
and, 442
Limit testing, in preschool years, 306
Locating sounds, 170
Locomotion, infant, 148, 149
Logical construction, acquiring learning
strategies through, 375
Logical reasoning, 388
adolescence, 470–474
cultural context and, 48–49
standardized tests, 384
Loneliness, 417, 505, 535
Longitudinal study, 18–19, 86
Long-term memory (LTM), 46, 47,
368–369
Looking, 173
Love relationships, divorce effects on
adolescents and, 513
Low birth weight, 125–126, 151
causes of, 152

consequences of, 152–153
help for infants, 153–154
prenatal care and, 113(tab), 152
preterm birth and, 152–153
sudden infant death syndrome and, 141
teenage pregnancy and, 152, 533

Macrosystem, 8, 49
Magnet schools, 414
Mahler's phases of development, 38
Male(s)
  chromosomes, 60, 66–67
  infertile, 97
  reproductive cells, 91–92
  sex chromosomes, 66–67
  sex hormone, 446
  See also Boys, Fathers
Male fetus, inherited diseases and, 68
Malnourishment, 240, 244–245
Manipulation of objects, 366
Marital conflict, birth of child and, 207
Marital factors, infant temperament and, 205
Marital satisfaction, birth of child and, 207
Marriage
  spouse's age correlation, 22
  teenage, 533
Mastery
  cognitive structures and, 45
  competence and, 229
  intrinsic motivation and, 402
  middle childhood, 400
  play and, 299
  psychosocial theory and, 36–37
Masturbation, 526–527, 528
Matched guise technique, 381–382
Maternal, see Mother(s)
Maternal serum alpha-fetoprotein (MSAFP), 76(tab), 78
Mathematics, cultural differences in learning, 372–373
Maturation
  behavioral learning approaches, 42
  cognitive approaches, 47
  contextual approaches, 50
  Piaget's cognitive theory, 44
  psychodynamic approaches, 39
  role of experience versus, 30, 39
  social cognitive learning approach, 42
Meanings
  Black English, 383
  speaker's intended, 380
Media, aggressive behavior and, 321, 323–325
Medicaid, 246
Medical care, see Health care
Medications
  acute illness and, 353
  ADHD, 357
  during delivery, 121–122
  maternal use of, 107–108
Meiosis, 62
Memory
  capacity, 367–369
  cognition and, 163
  continuity versus discontinuity in development of, 13
  familiarity and, 371
  gifted students, 391
  heart rate and, 164
  infant, 164–165
  influences on development, 369–372
  information–processing theory and, 46–47
  logical reasoning and, 369–372
  long-term, 46, 47, 368–369
  Piaget's theory of cognitive development and, 181
  preschool years, 368, 370
  recall, 368, 371
  recognition memory, 368
  short-term, 46, 47, 368, 369
Menarche, 442, 444

Menstrual cycle, fertility during, 92
Menstruation, 442, 444–445
Mental disorders
  hereditary influence on, 83
  See also Depression; Suicide
Mental health care, adolescents and, 455–456
Mental representations, see Representations
Mental retardation, handedness and, 249
Mental scripts, 375
Mental space, 45
Mentors, 390
Mesoderm, of blastocyst, 93
Mesomorphic body type, 448–450
Mesosystem, 7, 8, 49
Metacognition, 46, 47, 372–376
Metalinguistic awareness, 381
Metaphors, middle childhood and, 379–380
Metaphors of mind, children's understanding of, 20–21
Mexican-American children, nutritional knowledge and, 245
Mice, genetic studies and, 83
Micromanipulation (microfertilization), 99
Microsystem, 7, 8, 49
Midbrain, 138
Middle adolescence, 438
Middle childhood
  cognitive development in, 361–392
  domains of development, 5(fig)
  physical development in, 338–358
  psychosocial development in, 394–432
Middle schools, 521
  improving, 524, 525(tab)
Midwife, 118
Milk, see Mother's milk
Minorities
  achievement and, 404–405
  family adaptive strategies, 522–523
  intravenous drug use and, 459
  smoking and, 462
Mirror, 38
Miscarriages, 104
  domestic violence and, 111
Mistrust, trust versus, 31, 36
Mitosis, 62–63
Mixed-pattern babies, 204
Modeling, 41
  ADHD and, 357
  child abuse and, 329
  food preferences, 241
  punishment behaviors, 322
  tasks for infants, 209–210
  television and, 324
Modular intelligence, 287
Mood, depressed, 535
Moral actions, 492–493, 497
Morality, 16, 489
  adolescence, 489–498
  ethics of care and, 495–498
  gender differences, 495–496
  stages of moral judgment, 490–495
  superego and, 33
Moral judgment, Kohlberg's six stages of, 490–495
Moratorium individuals, 506
Moro reflex, 143, 146
Morphemes, 274
Mortality, see Deaths
Mother(s)
  abusive, 330
  anxious, 223
  death of, 350
  drug use by, 105, 107–110
  education level and prenatal care, 113(tab)
  pregnancy experience, 98–100
  prenatal health care and, see Prenatal care
  prenatal exposure to speech of, 206
  psychological problems, 242–243
  separating from, 327

social competence and, 230
transition to parenthood and, 207
weight gain during pregnancy, 99
Motherese, 194, 281
Mother-infant relationship
  attachment formation and, 221
  breast feeding and, 155
  talking with infants, 192, 194, 281
  temperament and, 205
  working mothers and, 221, 222–223
Mothers, working, 293, 419
  attachment formation and, 221, 222–223
  day care arrangements, 212–214
  effects of, 425
  relationship with child and, 222–223
  trends, 421(fig)
  working during pregnancy, 110
Mother's age
  childbearing risks and, 103–104
  Down syndrome and, 69
  prenatal counseling and, 74
Mother's milk
formula versus, 154–158
preference for, 144–145, 206
Motivation
  achievement, see Achievement motivation
  athletics and, 346
Motivations, inferences about, 470
Motor cortex, 247, 248
Motor development
  cultural differences, 150–151
  gender and, 151, 256–257
  infants, 146–151
  middle childhood, 344–349
  Piaget's theory of sensorimotor intelligence and, 172, 175–177
  preschool years, 250–257
  psychological impact of, 252
Motor schemes, Piaget's theory of cognitive development and, 181
Motor skills
  catching, 253
  drawing, 254–256
  effects of changes in, 258
  fine, 147, 148–149, 151, 254–256
  fundamental, 251–253
  gross, 147–148
  jumping, 253
  malnutrition and, 156
  object permanence and, 179–181
  play and, 11
  preterm infants and, 153
  running, 252–253
  teaching, 253
  throwing, 253
  variations in development, 149
  walking, 251–252
Motor vehicle accidents, 456, 460
Mouthing, 146
Moving, paternal unemployment and, 426
Multicultural competence, 414, 522
Multicultural view
  academic achievement and, 404–405
  attachment formation and, 218–219
  breast feeding, 156–157
  child abuse, 330–331
  children's sleep, 242–243
  cognitive development and, 48–49
  cross-cultural misunderstanding in classroom, 40–491
  dieting and, 342–343
  genetic counseling, 74–75
  growing up in India, 14–15
  learning mathematics, 372–373
  parent's beliefs about intelligence and, 292–293
  reasons for having children, 100–101
  talking to infants and, 192–193
  See also Cultural differences
Multifactorial disorders, 72–73
Multiple personality, sexual abuse and, 332

Muscle coordination, 30
Muscle growth, testosterone and, 446–447
Musical skill, 388
Myelin, 138

Native Americans
  infant swaddling, 150(fig)
  motor development in Navaho Indians, 150–151
  peyote use, 460
Naturalistic studies, 19–20, 22
Natural kinds, 270–271
Nature, 13
  motor skill development and, 149–150
Needs, caregiver's ability to meet infant's, 36
Needs of children, advocates for, 9
Negative correlation, 22
Negative identity, 505
Negative reinforcement, 40
Neglect, 310, 329–332
Neighborhood
  aggressive behavior and, 416
  delinquency and, 536
  See also Community
Neonates, see Newborns
Neo-Piagetian theories, 45, 53(fig), 273
Neostructuralist theories, 272–273
Nervous system development, in infants, 137–142
Netherlands, children's sleep patterns and, 242–243
Neural activity, brain and, 247
Neural disorganization infants and, 142
Neural tube defects, 72, 78
Neurological defects, teenage pregnancy and, 533
Neurological limitations, preterm infants and, 153
Neurons, 138
Newborns, 133
  Apgar Scale and, 134–135
  appearance of, 133–137
  bodily proportions, 136–137
  deaths, 126
  height, 135(fig), 137
  maternal diseases and, 104–107
  Moro reflex and, 143, 146
  reflexes 145, 146–147
  sleep and 139–142
  weight, 135–136
Niche picking, 82
Nocturnal emissions, 444
Noises, see Sounds
Nominals, first words, 191
Noncontingent cues, self-recognition based on, 227
Nonreductionist view, environment and genetic influence and, 87
Non-REM sleep, 140
Normal, significance of departures from, 9
Norms, 12
North American children
  drawing and, 254
  failure to thrive and, 158–159
  height of, 238, 239
  infant attachment patterns, 218
  infant motor skill development, 150–151
  infant nutrition, 154, 156
  infant mortality, 159
  malnutrition in, 156
  mathematics learning, 372
  mothers talking to infants, 192
North American culture, body image and, 342
North American families
  childrearing standards and, 306–308
  developmental goals, 311
  stereotype of, 419
Nuclear family, 74
Nucleus, cell, 60(fig)

Number concepts, preschool children and, 269–270
Numerical reasoning, gifted students and, 391
Nurse, home visits by, 9
Nurturance, Hindu families and, 14–15
Nurture, 13
   motor skill development and, 149–150
Nurturing responses, babyish features and, 137
Nutrition
   adolescent, 449, 451, 455, 463–464
   birth weight and, 152
   child abuse and neglect and, 331
   earlier maturation and, 442
   failure to thrive, 244
   first two years, 154–158
   infants, 240
   obesity and 157–158
   physical growth effects, 240, 241
   pregnancy and, 111–112
   preschool years, 241, 244
   sudden infant death syndrome and, 141

Obesity, 340, 342–343
   adolescence, 463
   overnutrition and, 157–158
Object(s), 37, 38
   appearance-reality distinction, 267
   artifacts, 270–271
   concrete operations and, 361–367
   depth perception, 168–169
   logical skill and, 388
   manipulation of, 300
   manipulation of, 366
   natural kinds, 270–271
   referential style and, 191
   seriating, 365
   symbolic thought and, 265
Object constancy, 38, 167–168, 363
Object perception, 167
Object permanence, 174–175, 176, 177, 179–181
   attachment development and, 217
   preschooler's belief in, 264–265, 268
Object relations theories, 32, 37–38, 39, 51
Object representation, 176–177, 178
Objectivity, critical thinking and, 482
Observable features, defining self in terms of, 398
Observation
   descriptive, 12
   naturalistic studies and, 19–20
   scientific method and, 16–17
Observational learning, 41, 375
   autonomy and, 227
   play and, 299
Oedipus conflict, 400
Onlooker play, 303(tab), 304
On-time maturity, 454
Open classroom, 431
Operant conditioning, 40, 183–185, 226
Operations, Piaget's theory of, 265
Opinions of others
   accurate awareness of, 485
   achievement motivation and, 401–403
   growing awareness of, 396
   sense of self and, 397, 399
Organizing tactics, 374
Orthopedic disorders, overweight and, 463
Osmosis, 94
Ovaries, 91
   development of, 444
   environmental hazards and, 69
Overgeneralizations, 276
Overt aggression, 416
Overweight
   adolescence, 463
   prenatal risk and, 104
   teenage obsession with, 449, 451
Overweight. See also Obesity

Ovum, 59, 60–61, 91
   life span, 92
   older women and, 69
   sex chromosomes and, 67
Oxytocin, 115, 117, 123

Pain
   labor and, 121, 122–123
   infant response to, 145
Parallel play, 303(tab)
Parent(s)
   adolescent, see Adolescent parents
   age of, and Down syndrome, 69
   age of, and sudden infant death syndrome, 141
   authority of, 307–311, 503
   death of, 350
   early childhood programs and, 290
   effects of children's physical growth on, 257–260
   gender development influences, 326–327
   independence from one's, 509–510
   infant synchrony, 208–210, 211
   informed consent and, 25
   language acquisition influences, 192–194
   peer group choice and, 518, 520–521
   power struggles, 422
   promotive, 324
   regulation of television viewing by, 324–325
   rejecting values and advice of, 502
   restrictive, 324
   as role models, 421
   romantic feelings toward, 400–401
   selective, 324
   trust in, 31, 36
Parental characteristics, child abuse and neglect and, 329–330
Parental expectations, failure to fulfill, 36
Parent-child relationships
   adolescence, 508–514
   aggression and, 320, 323
   child abuse and, 329, 330–331
   delinquency and, 536
   divorce and, 424
   failure to thrive, 242–243, 244
   language acquisition and, 278, 281–282
   maternal employment and, 425–426
   middle childhood and, 418–419
   preschool years, 306–311
   prosocial behavior and, 315
   social competence and, 230
   stepparents, 424
   transition to parenthood and, 206–208
Parenting
   adolescence and, 511–512
   aggression and, 320
   authoritarian, 309–310, 320, 423, 512
   authoritative, see Authoritative parents
   child abuse and, 330–331, 332
   cultural differences, 330–331
   democratic, 512
   divorce and, 423
   Dutch versus American views, 242
   laissez-faire, 324
   permissive, 310, 423
   permissive-indifferent, 320
   responses to babyish features, 137
Parent-teacher conferences, Anglo-teachers and Hispanic mothers, 15
Passive gene-environment relationship, 82
Passive role, in development, 30–31, 39
Passive smoke, 110
Patterns, infant perception and, 167
Pediatric care, 9
Peer group
   adolescence, 485, 516–519
   adolescent strategic interactions with, 485
   aggression and, 321

alcohol and drug use, 462
antisocial, 518
attractiveness to, 258, 450
cliques, 517–518
cognitive development and, 406, 408
conformity to, 417–418
crowd, 517, 518
delinquency and, 536
functions of, 407
gender development influences, 327–328
gifted students, 390
influences on group membership, 407–414
middle childhood, 395, 396, 405–418
pressure from, 517, 518–519
rejection by, 536
social support from, 428
Peer relationships
   authoritarian parenting and, 309
   authoritative parenting and, 308
   friendships and, 312–315
   infant interaction with, 214
   paternal unemployment and, 426
   Piaget's theory, 405–406
   play interactions, 301–302, 304
   prosocial, 316–317
   psychological functions of, 408
   relationships with parents affecting, 512
   Stack's theory, 406
Pelvic inflammatory disease, 97
Penis, sexual maturation and, 444
Perception
   auditory, 169–170
   culture and, 170–171
   defined, 163
   infant, 163, 164–171
   object, 167–168
   of phonemes, 189
   Piaget's theory and, 172
   ways of studying in infants, 164–165
Perceptual masking, 378
Perceptual skills, cognitive uses, 171
Perceptual-motor development, canalization and, 81
Percutaneous umbilical blood sampling (PUBS), 76(tab), 78
Performance
   behavioral learning and, 181–187
   competence versus, 181
Performance orientation, 402, 403
Perinatal infection, 106
Period of transition, labor, 116–117
Permissive parents, 310
   divorce and, 423
Permissive-indifferent parents, 310, 320
   child abuse and, 329
Permissive-indulgent parents, 310
Personal autonomy, genetic counseling and, 74
Personal experiences, see Experiences
Personal fable, 485
Personality development
   drug abuse and, 461
   Erikson's theory, 30–31, 34–37, 39
   Freudian theory, 32–33, 39
   gender differences in, 327
   sense of self and, 399
   object relations theory, 37–38
   observational learning and, 41
   superego and, 33
   temperamental style and, 205
   timing of puberty and, 454
Personality virtue, 34
Pets, as social supports, 428
Phenotype, 63–64
   canalization and, 81–82
   genotype influence and, 80–87
   range of reaction and, 81
Phenylketonuria, 72, 79
Phonemes, 188, 189
Phonology, 188–190
Physical appearance, see Appearance

Physical closeness, attachment and, 215, 216
Physical development, 4, 5
   evolution and, 50
   gender differences, 256–257
Physical development in adolescence, 436–466
   alcohol and drug abuse, 460–463
   body image and, 448–451
   deaths, 437
   early versus late maturation, 451–454
   growth, 440–443
   health, 455–465
   health problems, 457–465
   nutrition, 463–464
   psychological effects of, 448–454
   puberty, 444–448
   secular trend, 442–443
   self-esteem, 448–451
   sex differences, 447–448
   sexual maturation, 444–446
   sexually transmitted diseases, 457–460
Physical development in first two years, 132–160
   Apgar scale, 134–135
   appearance, 133–137
   arousal, 142
   auditory acuity, 143–144
   bodily proportions, 136–137
   brain growth, 138–139
   breast milk versus formula
   failure to thrive, 158–159
   first few hours, 133–134
   growth, 151–154
   low birth weight, 151–154
   mortality, 159
   motor development, 146–151
   nervous system, 137–142
   nervous system, 137–142
   nutrition, 154–158
   reflexes, 146–147
   sensory development, 143–146
   size, 136–137
   sleep, 139–142
   smell, 144
   taste, 144
   touch, 159
   visual acuity, 143
Physical development in middle childhood, 338–358
   accidents, 350–352
   AIDS and, 353–355
   attention deficit hyperactivity disorder and, 355–357
   death rates, 350–352
   effects on thinking and feeling, 357–358
   health, 349–357
   height, 339–341
   illness and, 352–355
   motor development, 344–349
   weight, 342–243
Physical development in preschool years, 236–260
   auditory acuity, 250
   bladder and bowel control, 250
   brain development, 246–249
   effects on adults, 257–260
   effects on child, 260
   failure to thrive, 242–244
   gender differences, 256–257
   influences on normal, 237–244
   motor skills, 250–257
   nutrition and, 241
   poverty and, 244–246
   sensory development, 249–250
   social influences on, 242–244
   visual acuity, 249–250
Physical disorders, hereditary influence on, 83
Physical problems, working adolescents and, 525
Physical punishment, abusive, 330–331

Physical stereotypes, 340, 341, 342
Physical traits
  genetic transmission of, 63–65
  polygenic transmission, 66
  race and, 85
  sex-linked recessive, 67–68
Piaget's theories
  cognitive development, 43–45, 47–48,
    53(fig), 171–181, 290, 469
  concrete operations 43(tab), 48,
    361–367, 370, 472–474
  conservation tasks, 268, 363–364
  constructivist philosophy, 365
  formal operational thought, 43(tab),
    472–474
  influence of, 12, 365–367
  language/thought relationships,
    286–288
  memory and, 370
  number concepts, 269
  peer relationships, 405
  preoperational stage, 264–265
  schemes, 375
  sensorimotor intelligence, 171–181
  stages of development, 272
  teaching critical thinking and, 483
Placenta, 93, 94
Placenta previa, 124
Planning, adolescent thought and, 470
Play
  accidents and, 351–352
  appropriate materials, 305(tab)
  cognitive development and, 11, 299
  cognitive levels of, 300–302
  constructive, 299, 300
  deferred imitation and, 177
  early childhood, 297–306
  with fathers versus mothers, 211
  functional, 299, 300
  gender differences in, 257, 327
  gender group membership and,
    409–412
  gender roles and, 51, 327, 410
  implicit rules, 298
  infant, 225(fig)
  language skills and, 264(fig)
  middle childhood, 344–349, 409–412
  motor skill development through, 253
  nature of, 297–298
  peers and, 214
  preschool years, 264(fig), 313–314
  pretend, 299, 300–301
  prosocial competence and, 317
  psychosocial theory, 36
  purposes of, 11
  settings, 304–305
  with siblings, 305–306, 311–312
  social levels of, 303–304
  symbolic thought and, 265
  theories of, 298–299
  very active children, 355–356
Policies
  child and family, 9, 222
  preventing abuse, 332
  race and intelligence controversy,
    84–85
Political thinking, adolescence and,
    485–487
Pollutants, 110
Polygenic trait transmission, 66
Polymorphisms, linked, 85–86
Popularity, 414–415
  dating and, 529
  teenagers, 519
Population, sample of, 21
Positive correlation, 22
Positive reinforcement, 40
Possessions, conflict over, 317, 318
Possibilities, adolescents thinking about,
    471
Postconventional moral judgment, 492
Poverty
  adolescent deaths and, 456
  adolescent pregnancy and, 104

child abuse and neglect and, 331
delinquency and, 536
divorce and, 9
dropping out to work and, 522, 523
health care and, 246
health of preschool children and,
    244–247
impact on physical growth, 245(fig)
intravenous drug use and, 459
malnutrition and, 154
prenatal care and, 246
school transition and, 521
US rate of, 9
Poverty of speech content, 280
Power
  authoritarian parenting and, 309
  gaining through play, 299
  gangs and, 537
  gender and, 7–8
  parenting styles and, 320
Powerlessness, divorce and, 422
Practice, language acquisition and,
    278–279
Practice and experimentation subphase,
    adolescent identity and, 503
Pragmatics, 188
Praise, competence and, 230
Predictability
  ADHD, 357
  changing aggressive behavior and, 322
Predictions, accuracy of, 373
Preexisting condition, health care cover-
    age and, 73
Pregnancy
  adolescent, see Adolescent pregnancy
  diseases during, 104–107
  domestic violence during, 111
  experience of, 98–100
  fetal development, 91, 95–97
  Hindu families, 14
  nutrition, 111–112
  prenatal development during, 91–97
  stress and, 114
  trimesters, 102
  weight gain during, 99
  working during, 111
Preimplantation genetic testing, 78–79
Prejudice, 413
Prematurity, 126
  adolescent pregnancy and, 532
  consequences of, 152–153
  help for infants, 153
  risk of abuse and, 330
Premenstrual syndrome (PMS), 445
Prenatal care, 112–114, 152
  low birth weight and, 113(tab)
  poverty and, 246
  teenagers and, 104, 111
Prenatal development
  environmental hazards, 110
  nutrients during, 111–112
  preterm babies, 126
  stages of, 91–100
Prenatal diagnosis, of genetic disorders,
    75–79
Prenatal genetic counseling, 74
Prenatal health care, 112–114
Prenatal influences on child, 101–114
Preoperational stage, 264–265
Prepared childbirth, 120–121
Preschool center, 213
Preschool years
  attachment formation and, 220
  cognitive development in, 262–294
  end of, 333
  physical development in, 236–260
  psychosocial development in, 296–
    333
Pretend play, 299, 300–301
Preterm birth, see Prematurity
Prevention
  AIDS programs, 354, 459–460
  alcohol and drug use, 462–463
  child abuse and neglect, 332

delinquency, 537
  teenage pregnancy, 534–535
Primary circular reactions, 173, 178
Primary sex characteristics, 444–445
Privacy, genetic disorders and, 73
Private speech, 49
Problem solving, 45, 272
  achievement orientation and, 402
  classification skills, 267–268
  cognition and, 163
  concrete operations, 361–367
  critical thinking and, 480–483
  expertise and, 478–479
  formal thought, 471–474
  heuristics, 478–479
  learning strategies, 372–376
  metacognition and, 372
  nonrational choices in, 474
  number concepts, 269–270
  peer conflicts and, 406
  Piaget's theory and, 43, 176–177, 178
  scientific reasoning, 471
  secure attachment, 220
  short-term memory and, 369
  teaching, 375–376, 416
  triarchic theory of intelligence, 387
  zone of proximal development and,
    390–391
Process-oriented play, 297–298
Professional caregivers, 208–209
  attachment formation, 223–224
  infant interaction with, 212–214
  language acquisition influences, 195
Projection, defense mechanism of, 33
Promotive parents, television viewing
    and, 324
Prosocial behavior, 306, 320
  adolescent friendships and, 515
  preschool years, 315, 316–317
  television teaching, 324
Proximodistal growth pattern, 93
Proximodistal principal, 148
Psychedelics, 460
Psychiatrist, genetic counseling and, 78
Psychoanalysis, 32–33
Psychoanalytic theory
  identification and, 226
  play and, 299
Psychodynamic theories, 32–39, 51
  achievement motivation and, 400–
    401
  developmental themes in, 39
  emotional development and, 216
  Freudian theory, 32–33, 39, 52(fig)
  object relations, 32, 37–38
  summary of, 52(fig)
Psychological development
  physical growth and, 238, 357–358
  understanding self and, 9
Psychological effects
  divorce and, 421
  of early athletics, 346–348
  economic hardship and, 426–427
Psychological effects of adolescence
  employment and, 525
  physical growth, 448–454
  separation from parents, 509
Psychological factors, growth in
    preschool years, 242–244
Psychological functions, of preadolescent
    peer activities, 408
Psychological traits, first beliefs in,
    398–399
Psychologist, genetic counseling and, 78
Psychometric approach, to intelligence,
    384–386
Psychosexual development, stages of, 33,
    39
Psychosocial crisis, 34–35
Psychosocial development, 5
  Erikson's theory, 30–31, 34–37, 39,
    52(fig)

Psychosocial development in adoles-
    cence, 500–538
  emerging adult and, 537–538
  friendships, 514–416, 518
  identity development, 501–507
  individuation, 501–504
  parental relationships, 508–514
  peer groups and, 516–519
  school influence, 519–524
  sexuality, 526–531
  social relationships, 507–525
  special problems, 531–537
  work influence, 524–525
Psychosocial development in first two
    years, 198–232
  attachment formation, 215–224
  autonomy emergence, 225–231
  competency, 229–231
  emotions, 200–202
  father-infant interactions, 210–211
  mother-infant interactions, 208–210
  nonparent–infant interactions, 212–214
  peer-infant interactions, 214
  self-awareness, 227–229
  siblings-infant interactions, 211
  social relationships, 206–215
  temperament, 200–201, 202–206
  toddler autonomy, 225–231
Psychosocial development in middle
    childhood, 394–432
  achievement, 401–405
  challenges, 395–396
  family relationships, 418–428
  industry, 399–401
  peer relationships, 395, 405–418
  school influences, 429–432
  sense of self, 397–399
Psychosocial development in preschool
    years, 296–333
  aggression, 317–323
  child abuse and neglect, 329–332
  friendships, 312–315
  gender development, 325–329
  parental relations, 306–311
  play and, 297–306, 313–314
  relationships with others, 306–323
  sibling relations, 311–312
  television effects on, 323–325
Psychosocial moratorium, 504, 506
Puberty, 442, 444–448
  adolescents' reactions to onset of,
    454(tab)
  height variations due to, 340–341
  psychosocial theory, 37
  secular trend, 442
  timing of, and height, 239
Pubic hair, 446
Punishment, 182
  abusive, 330–331
  aggression and, 319, 320, 321–322
  authoritative parents, 308
  gender differences in, 327
  operant conditioning, 40
  school and, 9
  spanking, 321–322
  studying parental methods of, 24–25
  superego and, 33
Purpose, psychosocial theory and, 36

Quantitative relationships, 362
Quickening, 95–96

Race
  friendships with persons of another,
    516
  intelligence and, 84–85
  peer group membership, 412–414
  physical growth and, 239
  prenatal care and, 112, 113(fig)
  as social and cultural category, 84
Racism, gifted programs and, 390
Radiation, 102, 110
Random sample, 21
Range of reaction, 81

Rape, date, 529
Rapprochement subphase, adolescent identity and, 503
Rats, genetic studies and, 83
Reaching, 148–149, 179
Reaction tendencies, temperament and, 202
Reading comprehension, dyslexia and, 378
Reading knowledge, bilingual students and, 23
Reality
    adolescents thinking about, 471
    preschool children distinguishing, 267
Reality principle, 32
Reasoning
    abstract, see Abstract reasoning
    changes in, 5
    cognition and, 163
    critical thinking, 481
    false-belief task, 266
    logical, see Logical reasoning
    memory and, 369–371
    moral, 16
    numerical, 391
    psychosocial development and, 5
    scientific reasoning, 471
Recall memory, 368, 371
Recasting utterances, 281
Receptive language, 190–191
Recessive gene, 64–65
Recessive gene disorders, 71–72
Recessive traits, sex-linked, 67–68
Reciprocally determined learning, 41
Recognition, infant, 164–165
Recognition memory, 368
Reconstituted family, 420, 424
Reductionism, genetic, 86
Referential style, 191
Reflection, critical thinking and, 481
Reflexes
    classical conditioning and, 40, 182
    fetus, 95
    inborn, 146–147
    newborns, 145, 146–147
    Piaget's theory of cognitive development and, 43, 172–173, 177, 179
    primitive, 147
    survival, 147
Rehearsal, 374–375
Reinforced actions, 183–185
Reinforcement, 40, 182
    cooperative learning, 402–403
    in language acquisition, 277–278
    play and, 299
    positive, 183–185
    punishment and, 322
    from same versus opposite sex, 327
Relational aggression, 416
Relationships
    adolescent social, 507–525
    divorce effects on, 513
    empathy and, 315–316
    functional, 265
    infant's social, 206–215
    intimate, see Intimacy
    learning to get along with others in, 399–400
    middle childhood, 396, 418–425
    with mother, see Mother-infant relationship
    object relations theory, 37–38
    with parents, see Parent-child relationships
    peer, see Peer relationships
    preschool years, 306–323
    prosocial behavior and, 315, 316–317
    psychosocial development and, 5
    sense of self and, 399
    siblings, 311–312
Religious beliefs and orientation, adolescence and, 487–489
REM sleep, 140
Remarriage, 424, 514

Repetition compulsion, 299
Repetitive behaviors
    functional play and, 300
    Piaget's theory of cognitive development and, 174
Representational drawing, 254–256
Representations
    object permanence and, 177
    pretend play and, 300–301
Repression, defense mechanism of, 33
Reproductive cells, division of, 62
Reproductive processes, 59–63
Research
    formulating questions, 17
    full disclosure of purposes, 24–25
    interpreting and publicizing results, 17
    stimulating new, 30
    See also Developmental study
Residential instability, popularity and, 519
Residential treatment, adolescents and, 52–53
Respect
    authoritative parenting and, 309
    for women, 331
Respiratory disease
    asthma, 353
    overweight and, 463
Respiratory distress syndrome, 126
Response(s)
    conditioned, 182
    correlations between, 22
    unconditioned, 182–183
Response style, failure to thrive and, 243
Restrictive parents, television viewing and, 324
Rewards, 183–185
    informal curriculum and, 430
    superego and, 33
Rh disease, 79
Rights of children, advocates for, 9
Risk, see At-risk children; At-risk families; At-risk mothers
Risk factors, fetal development and, 102–114
Ritalin, 357
Role confusion, identity versus, 37, 504
Role experimentation, 504
Role models
    attractiveness stereotypes, 451
    lack of positive, 536
    parents as, 421
Role playing, preschool years, 313–314
Rooming in, hospital deliveries and, 119
Rooting, 146
Rubella, 104, 105
Rules
    effective schools and, 431
    for everyday behavior, 230
    family, 306–307, 418
    games with, 299, 301–302
    generative syntactic, 274
    grammatical, 276–277, 280
    hyperactivity and, 356
    play, 298, 299, 301–302
    television viewing, 324
Running skills, 252–253

Safe sex, 460
Safety
    after-school activities and, 428
    autonomous behavior and, 226
    explorations and, 259
    physical restraint and, 322
    play and, 351–352
    rules and, 230
Sample, 21, 22–24
Savant, 287
Scaffolding, language acquisition and, 281
Schema, gender, 326
Schemes, 43–44, 45, 172, 375
Scholastic achievement tests, 385

School
    achievement motivation and, 399–400, 402–405
    failure in, 522–523
    improving, 523–524, 525(tab)
    influences in adolescence, 519–524
    influences in middle childhood, 396, 429–431
    physical punishment in, 9
    student's experience of, 431
    See also Education
School achievement, see Academic achievement
School culture, 429
Scientific evaluation, theories and, 30
Scientific method, 16–17
Scientific reasoning, 471
Scrotum, 91–92, 444
Secondary circular reactions, 173–175, 178
    combined, 175–176, 178
Secondary sex characteristics, 444, 445–446
Second stage of labor, 117
Secular trend, 442–443
Secure attachment, 218–219
Secure base, exploring environment from, 217
Selective parents, television viewing and, 324
Self
    care, 38
    sense of, see Sense of self
    subjective, 38
    understanding, 9
    verbal, 38
Self-assertion, toddlers capacity for, 230
Self-awareness, 227–229
Self-blame, 226
Self-concept, 397
    adolescent peers and, 517
    cultural differences in constructing, 399
    drawings revealing, 254
    early-maturing girls, 452
    industry and, 401
Self-confidence
    bilingualism and, 382
    mastery orientation, 402
    middle childhood, 396
    popularity and, 519
Self-consciousness, learning disabilities and, 378–379
Self-constancy, 398
Self-control, 418
    authoritative parenting and, 308
    adolescence, 512
    autonomy and, 226–227
    physical restraint and, 322
Self-criticism, 36
Self-direction
    psychosocial theory and, 36
    regulating behaviors, 201–202
Self-esteem
    adolescent girls, 520
    authoritative parenting and, 308
    body image and, 448–451
    contraceptive use, 532
    development of, 231
    inferiority and, 401
    permissive parenting and, 310
Self-fulfilling prophecy, 430
Self-inflicted harm, 456
Self-initiated play, 298
Self-knowledge, development and, 227–229
Self-regulation
    aggressive behavior, 319
    infant emotional states, 201–202
Self-reinforcement, 299
Self-reliance
    adolescence, 512
    authoritative parenting and, 308
    permissive parenting and, 310

Self-talk, 288
Self-understanding, 396, 397, 503, 504
Self-worth, peer activities and, 408
Semantics, 188, 190–191, 273, 275–277
Semen, 444
Sensations, perception and, 163, 166
Sense of self
    adolescence, 501–507
    adolescent peers and, 517
    Asian cultures and, 74
    constancy of, 3
    ego and, 32–33
    infants, 227–229
    middle childhood, 396, 397–399
    object relations theories and, 38
    psychosocial development and, 5
    timing of puberty and, 454
Sensitive period, 102, 103(fig)
Sensorimotor activities
    early education and, 290
    functional play, 300
Sensorimotor intelligence, Piaget's theory of, 171–181
Sensory development
    infants 143–146
    preschoolers, 249–250
Sensory register, 46
Sensory stimulation, preterm infants and, 153
Separation anxiety, 217, 218, 226
Separation-individuation phase, 38
Seriation, 365, 370
Sex characteristics
    primary, 444–445
    secondary, 444, 445–446
Sex chromosomes, 60
    inheriting extra, 70
Sex differences, puberty and, 444–448
Sex drive, 446
Sex-linked recessive traits, 67–68
Sex-linked transmission, 67–68
Sexual abuse, 6, 332
    eating disorders and, 465
    memories of, 371
Sexual activitiesdaughters of divorced parents, 423
Sexual activity
    adolescence, 458, 527–531
    unprotected sex and, 458
Sexual aggression, 529
Sexual attitudes, 528
Sexual development, puberty, 442, 444–448
Sexual encounters, early-maturing girls and, 453
Sexual experimentation, 458
Sexual fantasies, during adolescence, 526–527
Sexual feelings, psychosocial theory and, 36
Sexual intercourse
    adolescence, 526, 527–531
    AIDS and, 459
    deciding to engage in, 496
    fantasies about, 526
Sexuality
    adolescence, 526–531
    heterosexuality, 527–530
    homosexuality, 530
Sexually transmitted diseases (STDs), 457
Shame, 226
    Asian cultures, 75
    autonomy versus, 31, 36, 231
    understanding, 399
Shape constancy, 168
Shaping, 40
Shared knowledge, 391
Short-term memory (STM), 46, 47, 368, 369
Shyness, 204, 226
Siblings
    blended families, 424
    hand preference, 249

infant interactions with, 211
modeling behavior and language of, 191(fig)
observational learning, 191(fig), 375
playing with, 305–306, 311–312
relationships with, 311–312
Sickle-cell disease, 71–72, 78
Signaling behaviors, 216
Single parents, 126, 420–424
adolescent development and, 514
employment effects on, 425–426
poverty in, 9
teenage, 111
Size constancy, 167–168
Skills
achievement tests measuring, 385
breadth of, 45
intelligence and, 383–384
peer activity, 408
"typical" child acquiring, 8
Sleep
bedtime routines, 242
bladder control and, 250
infants, 139–142
multicultural view, 242–243
non-REM, 140
preterm infants, 153
REM, 140
Sleep apnea, 141, 153
Slow-to-warm-up children, 204, 316
Small-for-date infants, 126, 152, 240
Smell, in infants, 144
Smoking
adolescent, 462
birth weight and, 152
maternal, 105, 109–110
sudden infant death syndrome and, 141
working adolescents, 525
Social acceptance, teenagers and, 519
Social activity, talking as, 11
Social attitudes
drawings revealing, 254
language differences and, 381–382
Social attractiveness, English speakers and, 382
Social category, race and, 84
Social class, see Socioeconomic status
Social cognition, adolescent, 483–498
Social cognitive learning theory, 41–43, 53(fig)
Social competence, 229–231
aggressive behavior and, 321
cliques, 518
English speakers, 382
popular children, 415
Social context
aggressive behavior and, 416
attractiveness and, 450
Social conventions, 495
Social development
cognition and, 392
infant temperament and, 206
malnourishment and, 244
schools and, 520
See also Psychosocial development
Social dissatisfaction, 417
Social experiences, sense of self and, 397, 399
Social functioning
children of teen mothers, 533
sexual abuse and, 332
Social interactions
development growing through, 49, 50
with fathers, 210–211
with peers, see Peers
Social isolation, see Isolation
Socialization, gender roles, 326
Social labels, sense of self and, 398
Social learning
aggression and, 323
gender roles and, 326
Social learning theories, 32, 323
Social levels of play, 303–304
Socially supported thinking, 272

Social maladjustment, drug abuse and, 461
Social policies
preventing abuse, 332
race and intelligence controversy, 84–85
Social problems, 480–481
policies for addressing, 9
Social referencing, 227
Social relationships, see Relationships
Social roles
adolescent peers, 517
exploring, 504, 506
Social setting, intelligence and, 389–391
Social skills
adolescence, 485, 529
dating and, 529
intelligence and, 383, 388–389
play and, 11, 299
psychosocial theory and, 37
Social support
adolescent friendships, 514
birth and, 126
divorce and, 420
gangs and, 536
paternal unemployment and, 426
peer groups, 516–517
pets and, 428
sources of, 428
Social transmission, 44
Social worker, home visits by, 9
Societal abuse and neglect, 331
Societal attitudes, Black English and, 383
Sociocultural perspective, on intelligence, 389–391
Socioeconomic status
adolescent–parent relationship and, 512
child abuse and neglect, 331
contraceptive use, 532
eating disorders, 464
gifted programs, 390
health care and, 244, 246, 456
health of preschool children, 244–247
illness and, 353
language acquisition and development, 283
peer rejection and, 416
physical growth, 240
teacher expectations, 430–431
television viewing and, 324
Solitary play, 303(tab), 304
Sounds
auditory perception and, 169–170
babbling, 188, 189–190
hemispheric lateralization of brain and, 248
localization, 170
Moro reflex and, 143
phonemes, 188–189
Spatial relations, 365
Spatial skill, 365(fig), 388
Spanking, 307(fig), 321–323
Special education, 377
Speech
brain activity and, 247
infant directed, 193, 194, 281
inner, 288
poverty of content in, 280
prenatal exposure to, 206
telegraphic speech, 275
Sperm
ejaculation of mobile, 444
environmental hazards and, 69
infertility and, 97
Spermatozoa, 59, 60–61, 91–92
life span, 92
meiosis and, 62(fig)
sex chromosomes and, 67
Sperm cells, see Spermatozoa
Spina bifida, 78, 112
Spinal, 121, 122(tab)
Spinal cord, infants and, 137
Spiritual self, 522

Spontaneous play, 298
Sports, see Athletics
Stages of cognition, Piaget's theory, 365
Stages of development, 31, 32, 39
behavioral learning approaches, 42
canalized, 81
cognitive approaches, 48
contextual approaches, 50
Erikson's psychosocial theory, 34–37, 39, 52(fig)
Freudian theory, 32, 33, 39
Mahler's theory, 38
Piaget's theory, 43–44, 265, 272
prenatal, 91–100
psychodynamic theories, 39
psychosexual, 33, 39
social cognitive learning approach, 42
Stern's theory, 38
Stagnation, psychosocial theory and, 37
Standard English, 382–383
Standardized tests, intelligence and, 384–386
Standards
of achievement, 396
achievement motivation and, 401–402
athletics, 346
crisis of industry versus inferiority, 401
knowledge of, 228
Standing, infants and, 148, 149
Startle reaction, 135, 143, 146
Status offenses, 536
Stepping reflex, 82
Stereotypes, 413
appearance, 257, 414
Asian youth, 23
attractiveness, 257
gender role, see Gender role stereotypes
North American families, 419
physical skills, 256
shape, 340
size, 340, 341, 342
television portrayal of, 324, 328
weight, 342
Stern's stages of development, 38
Steroid use, 451
Stigma, Asian cultures and, 75
Stillbirths, 104
Stimulation, sleep patterns and, 242–243
Stimulus
classical conditioning and, 40, 182–183
conditioned, 182–183
habituation to, 165
heart rate and, 164
neural activity and, 247
operant conditioning, 40
unconditioned, 182–183
Stranger anxiety, 217
Strange Situation, attachment and, 218–219, 224
Strategic interactions, 485
Streptomycin, 108
Stresses
adolescence, 439–440
birth and family and, 126
blended families, 424
child abuse and, 331, 332
conception, 92
divorce, 420
failure to thrive and, 242, 243, 244
losing in athletics, 347
maternal employment, 425
parenting styles and, 310
pregnancy, 114
preterm infants, 153
Structural capacity, 476–478
Students
experience of classroom, 431
gifted, 390–391
progress assessment, 367
Studies case, 23–24

Studies
cross-sectional, 17–18
experimental, 20–22
longitudinal, 18–19
naturalistic, 19–20
See also Developmental study
Subjective self, 38
Substance abuse
antisocial peers, 518
parenting style and, 511
sexual abuse and, 332
Sucking, 146, 155, 173
Sudden infant death syndrome, 110, 140, 141
Suicide, teenage, 456, 460, 535–536
Superego, 33
Supportive environments, 231
Surrogate mothering, 98
Surveys, 23
Survival reflexes, 147
Symbiotic representation, 38, 176–177, 178
Symbol(s), preschool use of, 264, 265
Symbolic skills
language and, 287–288
pretend play and, 300–301
Symbolic thought, 265
Synchrony, failure to thrive and, 243
Syntax, 188, 273, 274–277, 379
Syphilis, 104, 105

Talking, private speech, 49
Targeted gene replacement, 83
Taste, infant, 144
Tay-Sachs disease, 72, 78, 79
Teachers
day care, 208–209
influences of, 430–431
Teaching methods, Piaget's influence on, 366
Teamwork, athletics and, 346–348
Telegraphic speech, 275
Television
changes in amount viewed and age, 323(fig)
effects of, 305, 321, 323–325, 328
social cognitive learning approach and, 42
Temperament
aggressive behavior and, 319
attachment formation and, 221
culture and, 84
ethnicity and, 84
infant, 50, 200–201, 202–206
prosocial behavior, 316
risk of abuse, 330
Temporal relations, 365
Teratogen, 102–114
Tertiary circular reactions, 176, 178
Testes, 92
Testing the hypothesis, 17
Testis-determining factor, 67
Testosterone, 446, 447
Tests
achievement, 385
aptitude, 385
standardized, 384–386
Tetracycline, 108
Textual dialogue, 194–195
Thalidomide, 105, 107–108
Theory of mind, preschool children developing, 266–267
Thinking
abstract, see Abstract reasoning
autonomy and, 226
changes in, 5
components of, 387
conceptual, 163
context and, 387
critical, 480–483
information-processing theory, 46–47
language relationships, 286–289
logical, see Logical reasoning

Thinking *continued*
  Piaget's theory, 43
  reversibility of, 362
  schemes, 43–44
  social transmission and, 44
  symbolic, 265
Third stage of labor, 117
Throwing skills, 253
Tobacco
  adolescent use of, 462
  maternal use of, 105, 109–110
  See also Smoking
Toddlers
  child care centers for, 212–213
  competence, 229–231
  emergence of autonomy, 225–231
  functional play, 300
  interactions with peers, 214
  securely attached, 219–220
  self-esteem, 231
  visual acuity, 249
Toilet training, 250
Tomography, 247
Touch, infants and, 145
Toxoplasmosis, 105, 107
Toys, cognitive development in infancy
  and, 173(tab)
Training
  achievement orientation and, 402
  blind, 376
  informed, 376
  learning strategy, 375–376
Traits
  adoption studies, 83–84
  animal studies, 83
  beliefs in psychology, 398–399
  environmental and genetic influence
    on, 80–87
  linkage studies, 85–86
Transformations, sensitivity to, 362
Transverse presentation, 114
Treatment
  ADHD, 357
  child abuse and neglect, 332
  eating disorders, 465
  learning disabilities, 378–379
  obesity, 343
  understanding death, 350
Trends, cross-sectional studies and, 18

Trial and error, acquiring learning
  strategies through, 375
Triarchic theory of intelligence, 387
Trimesters, pregnancy, 102
Trust, mistrust versus, 31, 36
Turner syndrome, 70
Twin studies, 84
  criticism of, 86
  emotional reactions, 13
  hand preference, 249
  motor skill development, 150–151
  temperament, 202
Twins private language of, 280

Ultrasound, 76, 125
Umbilical cord, 93, 94, 95(fig)
  prolapsed, 125
Unconditioned reflex, 40
Unconditioned response, 40
Unconditioned stimulus, 40, 182–183
Unconscious, Freudian theory and, 32
Unemployment, paternal, 426–427
United States
  family-leave policies, 222
  teenage pregnancy in, 111
  See also American children; North
    American children
Universality of development, 14–15
Unoccupied play, 303(tab), 304
Unpopular child, 415–416, 519
Uterus, 91
  delivery and, 114–115
  development of, 444
  rupture of, 124
Utterances, *see* Language use

Validity, 21
Values
  critical thinking and, 482
  language gap and, 195
  life choices, 510
  social class and, 512
Variable(s), 20(fig), 21, 22
Verbal aggression, 319
Verbal self, 38
Verbal skills
  gifted students, 391
  standardized tests, 384

Vernix, 134, 152
Vicarious reinforcement, 299
Viewpoints, 417
  confusion of, 484
  considering others', 485
Violence
  abused children, 332
  adolescent deaths, 456
  child abuse, 330
  on television, 321, 323
  against women, 331
Violent communities, effects on children,
  416
Viruses, 353
Vision
  coordination with learning, 170
  inborn integrated schemes, 179
Vision problems, 353
Visual acuity
  infants, 143
  preschool years, 249–250
Visual cliff, 169
Visual cortex, 247, 248
Visual perception
  dyslexia and, 376, 378
  infant, 166–169
Visual search, object permanence and,
  179–181
Vitamins, pregnancy and, 112
Vocabulary, 190
  expressive, 186
  extremes in learning, 186, 187
  infant-directed speech, 194
  middle childhood, 379
  receptive, 186
  verbally bilingual children, 285
Vocalizations, infants, 188, 189–191
Vocational choice, 506
Voice, changes in puberty, 446
Vygotsky's theories
  cognition and, 290
  integration of language and thought,
    288
  zone of proximal development, 45, 49,
    271(fig), 272, 389, 390–391

Wakefulness, infant, 139–142
Walking, 149, 251–252
Warps, emotional, 406

Weight
  adolescence, 440–443
  excess, 340, 342–343
  genetic influences on, 239
  growth over childhood, 440(fig)
  maturation and, 30
  middle childhood, 342–343
  newborn, 135–136
  overnutrition and, 157–158
  poverty and, 245(fig)
  pregnancy, 99
  preschool years, 237–238
  self-esteem and, 448–450
  See also Overweight; Underweight
Welfarestudying interventions to
  improve, 22
Wernicke's area, 247, 248
Western families
  Hindu families versus, 14
  transition away from intimacy, 15
Western societies, cognitive development
  and, 48–49
White children
  African-American friends, 516
  gifted, 390
  illnesses in, 353
  intellectual development, 84
  prenatal care and, 112, 113(fig)
Will, psychosocial theory and, 36
Wisdom, 37
Wishes, gaining satisfaction and, 299
Withdrawal, abused children and, 331
Women
  age of childbearing, 103–104
  violence against, 331
  See also Females; Mother(s)
Words, first, 191
Work, *see* Employment
Working mothers, *see* Mothers, working
Working parents, routines for infants
  and, 142
Workplace, environmental hazards in,
  110
World view, ancestral, 522

Zone of proximal development, 45, 49,
  271(fig), 272, 389, 390–391
Zygote, 61–62, 67, 92, 93(fig)
Zygote intrafallopian transfer (ZIFT), 99